THE
FACTS ON FILE
ENCYCLOPEDIA OF
WORLD MYTHOLOGY AND LEGEND

THE
FACTS ON FILE
ENCYCLOPEDIA OF
WORLD MYTHOLOGY AND LEGEND

Anthony S. Mercatante

Facts On File®
New York · Oxford

The Facts On File Encyclopedia of World Mythology and Legend

Library of Congress Cataloging in Publication Data

Mercatante, Anthony S.
    The Facts on File encyclopedia of world mythology and legend.
    Includes index.
    1. Mythology—Dictionaries. 2. Folklore—Dictionaries.
I. Title. II. Title: Encyclopedia of world mythology and legend
BL303.M45   1985   291.1'3'0321   84-21218
ISBN 0-8160-1049-8

British CIP data available on request

Printed in the United States of America

10 9 8 7 6 5 4

Dedicated to
John Spina
A loving and devoted friend
of many years

CONTENTS

Foreword

by Robert S. Bianchi, Ph.D., Associate Curator of Egyptian, Classical and Ancient Middle Eastern Art, The Brooklyn Museum, Brooklyn, New York

The world in which we live is a paradox. Astronomers and physicists subscribe to the theory that our universe, the physical space occupied by our planet and its environment, is expanding. In parallel fashion the pool of human knowledge grows ever larger; the number of academic journals published each year in any one scholarly discipline has increased almost ten-fold beyond that published less than a quarter-century ago. Knowledge, like the universe, is expanding at exponential rates. And scholars, overwhelmed by this deluge of data, have retreated into the shelter of specialization, which in almost every academic discipline requires such specific training and focus that these scholars can no longer keep abreast of each and every new development within their own discipline. The Renaissance Man who could once aspire to know all about everything is extinct.

This avalanche of knowledge impacts particularly on any individual interested in the cultural expressions of the world's varied and disparate civilizations, especially since the infrastructure of global communications is capable of making them available to a wider audience than ever before.

Who has not heard about or, indeed, attended any number of blockbuster exhibitions mounted by museums in almost every urban center of the Western World? Wonderful, but specialized, such pursuits. Then consider the frustration that may await he who browses in a favorite bookstore hungering for more only to find there's not a hint of information—in translation or otherwise. And if it's a masterpiece of a non-Western culture, a long and painful search may lie ahead. Such is the intellectual paradox of our times. We are confronted with the varied menus of cultural events virtually daily, and yet which of us truly has the resources—or the time—necessary for a meaningful appreciation of the disparate masterpieces of world civilization. Ironical, this expanding of cultural horizons, predicated upon the degree of specialization in one's own orientation and the existence of precious leisure time. For most of us, the latter dictates our investigatory pursuits and almost certainly predetermines the extent to which we are to succeed in our search.

And so this is where Mr. Mercatante and his book come in. He has recognized this paradox and taken up the challenge. For those individuals who have a deep and abiding interest in the cultures of the world, which can be gathered together under the banner of the "Humanities," and for those of us also possessed of an intellectual curiosity to discovery more about the thematic content of the world's masterpieces in art, music, and literature, this reference work is a must. *The Facts On File Encyclopedia of World Mythology and Legend* is an accurate, easy to read, readily available compendium chock-full of the kind of information that one needs in order to understand the themes encountered in the Humanities. One can look up not only the mythological and legendary figures of the more well known civilizations of Egypt, Greece, and Rome, but also discover a wealth of informative, but little known, data about the civilizations of the Eskimo, the Finns and Slavs, as well as the rich cultures of the Orient, the myths and legends of North America and Australia, even present-day voodoo. Since there is no universally applied system of spelling for the welter of names encountered in the world's many cultures, Mr. Mercatante has included the common variant spellings in an alphabetically arranged Key to Variant Spellings index; this feature in itself will save the reader time and effort when using the encyclopedia.

In my estimation, however, the real value of this book, and the one characteristic that sets it apart from other world mythological reference works is the depth of the entries. If one were to consult any of the more than three-thousand entries that fill this volume with intelligently written, informative data, one would discover that the basic information is supplemented by references to art, music, and literature when appropriate. It is this comprehensive treatment that is most rewarding, because the reader can begin to appreciate just how rich much of the world's great art works really are. The Introduction and various indexes only add to the wealth of information readily available to the reader. The specialized information that led the reader to consult a specific entry in the first place has been expanded to include other areas of consideration. The reader moves from the limited to the expanded, from the appetizer to a splendid full-course meal. And in the process he has thereby come to terms with the intellectual paradox of our times.

Author's Preface

With over three-thousand entries, *The Facts On File Encyclopedia of World Mythology and Legend*, is written to provide an ever-increasing number of readers with a full, comprehensive, ready-reference work on the entire range of world mythology and legend from the ancient Near East to present-day voodoo.

Arranged from A–to–Z, each entry is listed under its most common English spelling as encountered in books and museum publications. For example, the Egyptian god who personified the sky is listed as Geb, not Keb, Qeb, or Seb, because Geb is the most frequently found English transcription of the name. But, as an additional reference tool for the reader, a Key to Variant Spellings at the back of the book lists alphabetically the variant spellings and the entry name they reference. Thus, if the reader knows a name only by one of its variant spellings, he or she can still locate the correct entry by consulting the key. Variant spellings for specific names may also be found at the end of the entry for that name. Though I had hoped to give pronunciations, this was found to be impractical in a work that encompasses so many words from various languages. Many of the names are from dead languages whose pronunciations are no longer known. Even Greek and Roman names, which are familiar to some of us from the Classics, are pronounced differently in various sections of the United States and Great Britain.

After the entry listing, a translation of the name is given when known. The reader, however, must bear in mind that many translations of ancient names are merely scholarly conjectures or folk etymologies. I have given the most commonly accepted meaning of a name when available.

Following the translation of the entry name is a concise definition, usually followed by a longer encyclopedic detailed discussion. As an additional reference aid, citations of relevant art, music, films, and literature are also provided.

Aside from the Key to Variant Spellings, the encyclopedia also provides a Cultural and Ethnic Index, which helps locate as well as list all those entries that apply to one culture, country, or belief system; a complete General Index of over 60 pages; an Annotated Bibliography, listing works in English that the reader may wish to pursue; and an Introduction that explains the various definitions and explanations of myth, legend, folktale, fairytale, and fable.

The numerous illustrations have been chosen from a variety of sources. Some are wonderful art works, others merely helpful in visualizing a particular entry.

All biblical quotations are from the King James or Authorized Version (1611) unless another translation is cited. Often, in entries referring to the Old Testament (Hebrew Scriptures), the ancient Hebrew cult name of God, transcribed as Yahweh, is given. The King James, Revised Standard Version, New English Bible and most other English versions substitute LORD for Yahweh, though the New Jerusalem Bible uses Yahweh in its translation.

Many of the dates given are only approximate. Dates are listed as B.C.E. (Before the Common Era) and C.E. (Common Era) in keeping with the world view of the encyclopedia. For those readers not familiar with this universal dating system, 1989 C.E. corresponds to 1989 A.D. (anno Domini or Year of the Lord) and 300 B.C.E. corresponds to 300 B.C. (Before Christ). When no letters appear after a date it is assumed that it is the Common Era.

As the title indicates, this volume is about world mythology and legend, not religion and theology, but the line between them is often very thin. When entries or comments about theology or religion appear, they are there as a cultural framework to the myths and legends. Some professing Jews, Christians, Moslems, Hindus, and Buddhists, to name the major living religions whose myths and legends are included in the present work, may object to my presentation. If I have misunderstood some point of a particular belief, I apologize in advance. Understanding and charity, professed by all these religions, will clearly see that I had to put aside any sectarian bias when writing the encyclopedia.

I wish to thank especially the following, who read and commented on various entries when in manuscript form: Robert S. Bianchi, Ph.D., Associate Curator of Egyptian, Classical and Ancient Middle Eastern Art, The Brooklyn Museum, Brooklyn, New York; Alexander Carlson (deceased), Late Art Curator, Nicholas H. Morely Collection, Florida; John Charlot, Ph.D., Curator, John Charlot Collection, Hamilton Library, University of Hawaii at Monoa; Roger Corless, Ph.D., Associate Professor of Religion, Duke University, Durham, North Carolina; Daniel Davila, M.A., Chief Librarian and Professor, Queensborough Community College, New York, Ms. Rachel M. Gallagher, Assistant to the Director, Department of Film, The Museum of Modern Art, New York; Edgar Gregersen, Ph.D., Professor of Anthropology, Queens College and Graduate Center, CUNY; Gary Gisondi, Rogers and Hammerstein Archives of Recorded Sound, New York Public Library, Lincoln Center, New York; James J. Greene, Ph.D., Professor of English, The City College of New York, CUNY; John A. Grim, Ph.D., Assistant Professor, Elizabeth Seton College, Yonkers, New York; Ms. Linda Hobson, music; Salvatore J. Iacone, Ph.D., St. John's University, New York; The Rev. James Proud, Priest, Episcopal Diocese of New York; Ronald Suter (deceased), M.A., Fairleigh Dickinson University, Rutherford, New Jersey.

And I also want to thank my family and friends who have given me encouragement on this immense project.

Anthony S. Mercatante

May 14, 1988

Introduction

MYTH, LEGEND, FOLKTALE, FAIRYTALE, AND FABLE

What is a myth, legend, folktale, fairytale, fable? Is each just a different word to describe the same thing, or is there a difference?

Let's begin with the word *myth*, which derives from the Greek word *mythos*, "that which is spoken," or a story. But as soon as we say a myth is a story, we are quick to add that it is an "untrue" story—about gods and goddesses, for example, that never existed. This common definition of myth—as a false or untrue story—is incorrect, however, because it fails to take into account that myths are believed to be literally true by the cultures or societies that produced them. For example, the ancient Egyptians believed Osiris, their god of the dead, was killed by his evil brother Set and later brought back to life to rule over the kingdom of the dead. Just as Osiris died and was resurrected in the story, so each faithful Egyptian believed he or she would also be resurrected in the land of Osiris. For the ancient Egyptians, Osiris was a real human being who existed, and the story about him was literally true. We, of course, do not believe in Osiris and say the stories are not "true." But Christians today believe that Jesus Christ was crucified and rose from the dead, offering to his devoted followers everlasting life in the world to come, just as Osiris's followers believed about their god.

The major difference between Osiris and Jesus for us is that the Egyptian god is no longer believed in, his cult ended, while that of Jesus is still flourishing and practiced in many parts of the world. So we call the ancient Egyptian stories about Osiris and other defunct gods "myths," but we call stories about Jesus and his Apostles "gospel," that is, the good news, or true stories.

But if we examine the matter with objective eyes, we can only conclude that our categories are very ethnocentric. We are obviously prejudiced in favor of our own beliefs. We must therefore keep in mind that one person's theology may be another person's mythology. Thousands of years from now, with our civilization long dead, someone might say that at one time the people of Europe and the Americas worshiped a Semite who was crucified and rose again from the dead, but that god is no longer believed in. I point this to the reader before he or she enters the rich store of myth and legend, because many readers will have been brought up in Judeo-Christian beliefs, which have often labeled other religious beliefs as false.

So far in our quest to define myth we have established two major points: one is that myths are narratives, and the second is that they are believed to be literally true by the cultures or societies that tell the stories.

But who created these myths?

All we can answer is that the stories are of anonymous authorship, orally passed on from one generation to another, stemming from the folk, or people.

How? We don't really known, though numerous theories have been suggested, none of which has unanimous scholarly support. In the 19th century, India was believed by some scholars to be the original source of most of the world's myths. Later the emphasis shifted to Africa. Present-day scholars see this "single source" theory as too simplistic. Numerous cultural, historical and psychological factors contribute to the birth of a myth. If one myth is similar to another myth in a different culture, it doesn't necessarily mean that it was directly borrowed from another culture. But it also doesn't mean that it may not have been influenced by it. Each case has to be studied on an individual basis. No one-source theory can account for the diversity and similarity of myths. For example, the motif of the Hero's Descent to the Underworld is found in ancient Near Eastern (Gilgamesh), Greek (Odysseus), Roman (Aeneas), and Christian (Christ) mythologies. In some cases we know of direct borrowings. Vergil's account of Aeneas' descent in the *Aeneid* is influenced by Homer's account of Odysseus' descent in the *Odyssey*. But what of other similarities? What happens when the same motif is found in very dissimilar places such as Africa, Asia, and Europe? We may ask, Is it from one single place and disseminated, or is it from the same psychological source in the human psyche? No one theory suffices for every myth. It is important to remember also that no matter how similar some myths are, there are also some basic differences in myths from one culture to another. Eskimo mythology doesn't tell us of gardens rich in foliage, nor do Greek myths tell us of ice and snow. Each myth reflects the real world in which it originates.

What kinds of characters inhabit myths?

The main actors and actresses are often deities—such as Zeus, Thor, Venus, and Yahweh—whose deeds, heroic and otherwise, form the basis of the tale. But the gods and goddesses are often joined by mortals, heroes, and heroines, who are in turn joined by semi-divine beings, as well as a host of real and fantastic beings—such as winged horses, dragons, talking animals and plants.

Time is never exact in a myth. Often it takes place in the remote past, the beginning of time, or primeval ages. Many of the incidents do not follow logic, but have an almost dreamlike quality, juxtaposed with extremely realistic happenings; gods and goddesses fly across the sky, or transform themselves into other shapes and forms to have sexual intercourse with mortals; while Adam and Eve seem real enough to us as people, a talking snake does not. Thus, real and unreal elements are combined in a myth, forming a synthesis.

Generally, myths are serious, sacred stories: Adam and Eve in the Garden of Eden or Gilgamesh and his quest for eternal life. But myths are also less than serious, as in the case of Zeus and his amours with boys and women, and the many ways he tries to seduce various creatures while avoiding the ever- watchful eyes of his jealous wife, Hera.

Myths combine realistic scenes from the culture in which they originate with fantastic elements; Zeus and Hera behave very much as a Greek couple did, and in fact, as many married people still do. It is a traditional patriarchal household, with the wife seeing that her husband doesn't stray, and when he does, to make sure his is at least condemned for it. But, no mortal man can transform himself into animals and objects, as Zeus often does to escape his wife's anger.

Thus far in our discussion, we have found myth to be a story orally passed on from one generation to another. But, what happens when the myth is put into literary form, as in Homer, Vergil, and Ovid, to cite three well-known Classical poets? The oral myth now becomes frozen in form in a particular work of art. The reader, however, must bear in mind that the core myth was not invented by the creative writer, but recast to suit his own philosophical and artistic purposes. One has only to compare Homer, Vergil, and Ovid to see the vast differences in temperament among these three poets when narrating a myth. Homer is basically objective; Vergil, subjective; and Ovid, often playful.

When an oral myth is put into written form, it may also be influenced by the particular beliefs of the transcriber. For example, when the Spanish missionaries transcribed South American mythology into Spanish, how much of the native Indian myths were altered to suit their own purposes? How much was left out? Christian missionaries in Africa, when writing down native myths, often distorted them to reflect Christian bias. Sometimes, however, because of the sacred nature of the myth, the native narrators would alter the myth in telling it to protect it from foreigners. Many native narrators were not as naive as the Christian missionaries wished to believe. Often the missionary was told exactly what he wanted to hear.

Let's now see it we can come up with a concise definition of myth that takes into account all that we have said so far. I suggest the following definition:

> MYTH: An anonymous traditional story, orally passed on from one generation to the next, believed to be literally true by the culture that produced it, about gods and goddesses, heroes, heroines, and other real and fantastic creatures, taking place in primeval or remote times.

As long as a myth is believed to be literally true by a culture, the question of its "meaning" does not arise. The myth exists as a living part of the community which produces it. For instance, there are Christians today who take the Bible literally, believing the earth was created in six days, Elijah was taken up to heaven in a fiery chariot, Jonah was swallowed by a whale, and Jesus's physical body arose from the tomb. For these believers, Christian myths are true stories not to be questioned, but to be taken as literal fact.

But the vast majority of thinking people are not so easily satisfied with this simplistic approach. For them, myth contains much that goes against common everyday experience, science, and reason. (We know the earth was not created in six days, people do not fly to heaven in a fiery chariot, whales do not swallow people and later dislodge them, and the dead do not come out of their tombs alive.)

The first people known in history to question the meaning of myths were the ancient Greeks, that race that has given civilization so much that is enduring and worthwhile. They asked themselves such questions as: Did Zeus really castrate his father Cronus? Did Zeus engage in all types of immoral sexual behavior forbidden to mortals? Did Apollo's chariot race across the heavens and bring the day? These and similar questions troubled the intellectual Greeks, many of whom even questioned the very existence of the gods. Xenophanes, who lived some time between the 6th and 5th centuries Before the Common Era, concluded that humans pictured their gods in human form (we call it anthropomorphism) merely as a form of self-flattery. He wrote: "But if cattle and horses or lions had hands, or were able to draw with their hands and do the works that man can do, horses would draw the form of gods like horses, and cattle like cattle, and they would make their bodies such as they each had themselves."

Xenophanes' skeptical, but realistic, approach to the gods was echoed by many educated Greeks, particularly the Stoic philosophers. One way these educated Greeks thought to resolve the logic dilemma was not to accept the myths as literal truth, but to search them for hidden meanings or symbolic content. This approach was best summed up by the Greek historian, Plutarch, who lived at the beginning of the Common Era. In his work, *Isis and Osiris*, a long essay in which he explored Egyptian religious beliefs of his day, he wrote: "whenever you hear the traditional tales which the Egyptians tell about their gods, their wanderings, dismemberments, and many experiences of this sort . . . you must not think any of these tales actually happened in the manner in which they are related." He continues that the tales are to be interpreted "reverently and philosophically," that is, either symbolically or allegorically.

Both words—allegory, from the Greek "to speak figuratively," and symbol, from the Greek for "token, sign"— are used interchangeably. Seeing an allegorical or symbolic meaning behind each myth saved the rational Greeks from having to face the fact that so much of their mythology made no rational sense at all. This approach to interpretation of mythology has been adopted by some schools of Christian thought that see everything in the real world as well as in the Bible in allegorical or symbolic terms. For the medieval Christian, for example, the entire Old Testament was seen as pre-figuring the New Testament. Jonah's three days in the belly of the whale was viewed as symbolic of Christ's three-day entombment. But for medieval Christians there was also no question but that Jonah was swallowed by a whale, literally!

Even during the Renaissance, when so many old and useless ideas were cast aside, the allegorical–symbolic approach to myth was continued. Francis Bacon, writing in his *Wisdom of the Ancients*, says that each myth contains "a concealed instruction and allegory." He then goes on to find the hidden meanings in various classical myths.

Alongside the allegorical–symbolic interpretation, another theory, called Euhermerism, held sway with some thinkers. Euhermerus, a native of Messene, who lived at the beginning of the third century Before the Common Era, wrote a romance in the form of a philosophical journey, called "Sacred Scripture," in which he said that the ancient gods—Zeus, Hera, and the entire pantheon of the Greeks—were nothing but deified mortals. For example, Zeus, he writes, was once a Cretan king; and Zeus and Hera, his wife, were made into deities at their deaths because of their heroic deeds. This approach may account for some deified mortals, such as Christian saints, but it in no way accounts for the origin of all myths.

Symbolic and allegorical approaches to mythology continued well into the 19th century and still find some support in popular contemporary books on mythology. No serious scholar, however, uses this method today. Nevertheless, the symbolic approach to mythology finds an offshoot in the work of Sigmund Freud, the founder of psychoanalysis, and in his one-time disciple Carl G. Jung. He gave various symbolic meanings to well-known myths, coining the term "Oedipus complex," based on the Greek myth, to explain the love of a son for his mother and his hatred of the father. Freud found myths to be "distorted vestiges of the wishful fantasies of whole nations, the secular dreams of youthful humanity." Freud, however, was not the first European thinker to see a psychological basis in mythology. Euripides, for example, often gives psychological motivations to his characters, where the original myths supply none.

While Freudian interpretations of myths have never gained wide acceptance by anthropologists or historians, Freud's influence of the arts, in relationship to mythology, has been tremendous. It is almost impossible to consider such major writers of the present century as James Joyce, T.S. Eliot, Franz Kafka, Thomas Mann, and William Faulkner, without seeing their great debt to Freud's theories regarding mythology and personality.

Ironically, Carl G. Jung, Freud's one-time disciple, has found a much wider popular audience than Freud for his various theories on the meanings of mythology. Jung's theories, which are propagated by his followers with an almost religious zeal, have great appeal to those who seek mystical explanations of myths. The major Jungian concept is that of the "collective unconsciousness." Jung believed that each person had a "second psychic system of a collective, universal and impersonal nature which is identical in all individuals. This collective unconsciousness does not develop individually but is inherited. It consists of pre-existent forms, the archetypes, which can only become consciousness secondarily, and which give definite form to certain psychic contents."

None of this is actually too clear, but Jung believed these universal symbols were found in dreams and myths. For example, mother earth and father sky, which are familiar to us from Greek mythology, where Zeus is the sky god and Gaea the earth goddess. But, world mythology shows us that this concept is not a universal symbol. In ancient Egypt, the sky was a female deity, Hathor, while the earth was a male deity, Shu. This gender reversal may simply stem from the way the Greeks and Egyptians engaged in sexual intercourse. The Greeks preferred what we call the "missionary position," with the man on top and in control, while the ancient Egyptians preferred the woman on top.

Jung's concept of the "collective unconsciousness" stems in part from Freud's statement of "archaic remnants," which Freud believed he found in some patients whose beliefs and actions could not be explained by reference to the individual's own life. Another source for Jung's concept was the 19th-century Swiss author, J.J. Bachofen, who believed there was a continuity in the psychic development of each nation, expressed in the symbolism both of the individual and the group.

So far no evidence has come forward that would support Jung's "collective unconsciousness" and anthropologists have their own explanations for mythology. But even the anthropologists haven't come up with any theory that explains all myths. One of the first was Edward B. Taylor (1832–1917), who saw myths as "sham history" invented by "barbarians." While it is true that some myths are "distorted" history, told to explain a particular natural phenomenon or cultic practice, Taylor's theory does not fit all categories of myths. And certainly the ancient Egyptians and Greeks were not barbarians.

Taylor's major disciple was James George Frazer (1851– 1941), author of the massive *The Golden Bough*, a work which not only has influenced all subsequent studies of religion, but has had a great impact on literature. Frazer believed that myths were closely connected with magic and "used to be acted as a means of producing in fact the events which they describe in figurative language. Ceremonies often die out, while myths survive, and thus we are left to infer the dead ceremony from the living myth."

It is not far from Frazer's belief in magic and its connection with myth to the theory of the close relationship between myth and ritual. Lewis Spence, a popular writer early in this century, summed up the belief that "myth . . . in the strict sense of the term, is the description of a rite, its story, the narrative linked with it. . . . Myth does not seek to 'explain' anything at all in rite or custom . . . but merely to recount or describe the same."

This definition of mythology may fit into some myths— e.g., creation myths, which were recited in some cultures at New Year's festivals—but what happens to myths of the loves of Zeus, or the Oedipus cycle of myths? Are these connected with some lost rite?

Perhaps the most bizarre interpretation of mythology was promulgated by F. Max Müller (1823–1900), a German who taught Sanskrit at Oxford and edited the multi-volume *Sacred Books of the East* series, who coined the phrase "disease of language" to account for the strange and fantastic elements in myths. Müller believed that Aryan was the mother tongue of humankind, spoken in Asia by a small group. This language, according to Müller, lacked the ability to make abstractions, so that the Aryans had to name things as best they could. Thus he explains:

> When we speak of the sun following the dawn, the ancient poets could only speak and think of the
> Sun loving and embracing the Dawn. What is with us a sunset, was to them the Sun growing old,
> decaying or dying. Our sunrise was to them the Night giving birth to a brilliant child.

This first phase of language was the mythopoic era. In time, Müller says, these Aryan people split into various groups and different languages evolved. The old words describing the dawn and sunset remained, but were no longer understood. So the "absurd, strange, or miraculous" elements came into myths.

We have only given very brief summaries of some of the many ways myths have been interpreted through the ages. As can be readily seen, no one theory fits or explains all types of myths. Myths are much more complex and compelling than any theory that attempts to explain them. Myths continue to live on while theories die out. When we use the term *mythology* we mean a collection of myths. Thus, we speak of Greek mythology or Finnish mythology, meaning a cluster of myths from a certain culture, religion, or ethnic group. But when the word *mythology* is used synonymously for fable or legend, it is incorrect, because legends and fables are not myths though they too are anonymous traditional tales.

Legend, derived from the Latin word for "to gather, select, read," and similar to the Greek word for "to gather," is often confused with myth. As with a myth, a legend is an anonymous traditional story passed on from one generation to another. But, whereas a myth has gods and goddesses as its main characters, a legend has historical personages, such as Charlemagne, El Cid, Muhammad, St. Francis of Assisi, or Billy the Kid. But alongside the historical characters are non- historical personages, as well as fantastic beings such as dragons, angels, and demons. In addition, though a legend takes place in historical times as opposed to primeval times, it contains fantastic events. For example, we know for a fact that Muhammad actually lived but that he rode to heaven on the fantastic animal, Al Borak, is certainly open to question!

Of course we may ask, if Achilles or Odysseus actually lived, does that mean that the stories told about them, which we generally call myths, are actually legends? Here, the answer is both yes and no, because the resultant story is a mixture of myth and legend, we would have gods and goddesses as well as historical personages. All this can become quite confusing when scholars question whether Buddha, Jesus, or King Arthur ever actually lived.

While a myth is believed to be absolutely true by the people who tell it, a legend is not necessarily believed to be true. Often, in fact, when we say something is legendary, we generally mean there is no actual historical basis that it ever happened or existed, even though some of the characters in the tale are historical figures. For example, numerous legends cluster around El Cid, but all the events attributed to him did not necessarily occur—and, of course, the fantastic elements remove the stories from actual history. Cervantes has Don Quixote say, "That there is a Cid, there is no doubt," but he goes on to add, "but of the deeds ascribed to him, there is doubt aplenty."

If we then attempt to come up with a concise definition of a legend, we can use the following:

> LEGEND: An anonymous traditional tale, sometimes believed to be true, but not necessarily; orally
> passed on from one generation to another; having as its main characters some historical personages,
> but also fantastic elements such as dragons; taking place in historical times.

However, some legends are actually literary inventions. Thus, the story of George Washington and the cherry tree is not from oral tradition, but was invented by the author of an early biography of the President to instill morality in his young readers. We can call such an example a *literary legend*, in that it uses the stuff of legends but is traceable to one written source. A Saga, from the Old Norse word meaning "story", is a legend from Iceland and Norway written in the Middle Ages.

We now come to the word *folktale*, which denotes an oral narrative, anonymously composed, passed on from one generation to another that is not believed to be literally true; but invented. Folktales are told for entertainment or to instill a sense of community values. They take place "Once upon a time . . .," which means they never actually happened at all. They have generalized characters, such as King, Queen, John, Witch, and are dominated by schematic features: triple groupings, repetition, and suspense. They also include fantastic elements. When a folktale is written down, it becomes part of literature, as in the case of the Grimm's collection of folktales, often inaccurately called *Grimm's Fairy Tales*. The Germans call these stories *Märchen*, which is often translated as *fairytales* into English, even though very few of the tales have any fairies in them! When folktale techniques are used by creative writers, such as Hans Christian Andersen, we have what is generally called a *fairytale*. As you can see, the two terms are often used interchangeably.

If we attempt to come up with a concise definition of *folktale*, we can use the following:

> FOLKTALE: A traditional anonymous tale, dominated by schematic features, orally passed on from one generation to another, whose main characters are generalized beings, such as King, Queen, John, Witch. A folktale takes place 'Once upon a time . . . ," which means the tale has been invented and is not literally true. It is told for entertainment or to instill community values. Other characters in folktales, aside from humans, often are good or demonic beings, spirits, or talking animals.

Moving from our definition of the folktale to that of fable, we find that a *fable*, from the Latin for "to speak, conversation, story," is a very short traditional narrative, again springing from an anonymous source and passed on from one generation to another. There is no indication of time. But, while a folktale often has human characters, most fables have a moral and feature talking animals as the main characters. Often attached to the fable is a "moral" tag. The most famous collection of fables is ascribed to Aesop. Many other collections have evolved over the centuries. Often the traditional fable is used by a creative writer, such as La Fontaine, and turned into a work of great art.

To conclude our collection of definitions, we can use the following for *fable*.

> FABLE: A very short, traditional, anonymous tale, not believed to be literally true, passed on from one generation to another, often having talking animals as the main characters. Often a moral is attached.

As can be gleaned from our short discussion of these familiar words, there are many similarities as well as differences between myth, legend, folktale, fairytale, and fable. No one, for example, would think of Aesop's fable *The Frogs Desiring a King* as being on the same plane as the Oedipus cycle of myths. Yet, both works have a universal appeal—they still speak to us of the human condition. When a creative artist, whether painter, writer, or composer, delves into these rich folk narrative sources, he or she may combine some of the forms, or the forms may exist side by side. Homer's *Odyssey* and Vergil's *Aeneid*, for example, combine myth, legend, and folktale. Scholars debate and study these creative works, attempting to disentangle their complex webs, and we, as readers, can and do benefit from their immense labors. But we can also always enjoy the various creative works, no matter in what particular category we place the traditional narratives. All of these narratives form one section of *folklore*, which includes popular beliefs, customs, proverbs, traditional folk music, rites, arts, crafts, games, and the like.

And we enjoy these works because they hold our attention—they are about us, our hopes, fears, joys and tragedies. Even in our scientific age, when we supposedly have cast aside so many relics from the past, we find these works still vibrant and vital, because they are about us.

What more can we ask?

THE
FACTS ON FILE
ENCYCLOPEDIA OF
WORLD MYTHOLOGY AND LEGEND

Aa. In Near Eastern mythology (Babylonian-Assyrian), consort of the sun god Shamash, sometimes called Makkatu (mistress; queen). Originally Aa may have been a local male sun god whose gender was changed when the worship of the major sun god, Shamash, took precedence, the minor god becoming the female consort of Shamash.

Variant spellings: A, Anunit, Aya.

Aaron

0002

Aaron. In the Bible, O.T., son of Amram and Jochebed and elder brother of Moses and Miriam; married Elisheba; father of four sons. He was a leader of the Exodus.

Aaron, a Levite, is first mentioned in the book of Exodus (4:14). He was appointed by Yahweh (a cult name of the Hebrew god) to be the interpreter of his brother Moses who was "slow of speech" (Exod. 4:16). Aaron is the instrument of many of the miracles associated with the Exodus from Egypt, such as when he caused the rivers of Egypt to turn to blood (Exod. 7:20) and when he brought on Egypt a plague of frogs (Exod. 8:5). But, Aaron was not as strong a personality as Moses. When his brother went up to the mountain to converse with Yahweh, Aaron gave in to the demands of the people and fashioned a golden calf for them to worship (Exod. 32). When Moses descended from Mount Sinai, he found the people worshiping their new god (based on Egyptian deities) and in anger destroyed the tables of stone containing the Ten Commandments

that Yahweh had given him on the sacred mountain. Then he burned the golden calf, ground it to powder, mixed it with water, and forced the worshipers to drink it. Yahweh intended to destroy Aaron for his sin, but Moses intervened and prayed for his brother (Deut. 9:20).

Aaron was then consecrated High Priest of Yahweh by Moses. From that time the legend of Aaron turns almost entirely to his priestly functions. One tells of the rebellion of the sons of Korah (Num. 16:1–35). Korah, a Levite, with Dathan and Abiram, questioned Aaron's right to the priesthood. Moses then challenged them to offer incense to Yahweh (a rite only to be done by the priests). As a punishment Yahweh had the earth open up and swallow Korah and his men.

Aaron was the keeper of the tribal rod, an official talisman that each of the Twelve Tribes possessed. At Yahweh's command Moses ordered each of the 12 to bring its rod to the Tabernacle. When the rods were left in front of the Ark, Aaron's rod miraculously budded, bearing almonds (Num. 17:5–11) and was seen as Yahweh's approval of Aaron's role as priest. Aaron died on Mount Hor at 123 years of age after transference of his priestly robes and office to Eleazar (Num. 20:28). Jewish folk tradition not included in the Bible says that at Aaron's death the cave on the mountain was obliterated by God, but the people claimed that Moses had killed his brother out of jealousy for his popularity. To prove the people wrong, God produced a vision of Aaron on a couch, floating in midair. In Islamic legend Aaron is called Harun. In the Koran (sura 19) Moses and Aaron went up to the mountain together, knowing that one was about to die but not knowing which. They found a coffin that did not fit Moses but fit Aaron. Moses then told Aaron to rest in it, and Aaron was taken up to heaven. Jewish folk tradition records that Aaron is in Paradise seated beneath the Tree of Life, where he instructs priests in their duty. Christian writers during the Middle Ages looked on Aaron as a prefiguration of Christ; thus, just as Aaron was a high priest of the Old Testament, so Jesus was the high priest of the New Testament. Some of the cult objects associated with Aaron in the Old Testament were viewed as prefigurations of the vestments worn by Christian priests and bishops. This, however, is not the actual case; the vestments were based on secular Roman dress of the early Christian era.

Western art frequently pictures Aaron in paintings of Moses. Often Aaron holds a censer and a flowing wand or rod. Sometimes he appears in full priestly vestments, which are described in detail in Exodus (chap. 28). He may wear a turban or a crown that resembles the papal crown of later Christian art. His robe may have bells, which he used to frighten off demons. Tintoretto painted *Worship of the Golden Calf*, and Felix Chretien painted *Moses before the Pharaoh*; the latter portrays Aaron and his magic rod and the transformation of the snakes, as told in the Bible. In music, Rossini's opera *Mosè in Egitto* (Moses in Egypt) and Arnold Schoenberg's opera *Moses und Aron* (Moses and Aaron) both contain roles for Aaron.

In Christian folklore the name "Aaron's beard" is applied to several wild plants, such as St. John's wort, the ivy-leaved toadflax, and meadowsweet. The name is derived from the mention of Aaron's beard in Psalm 133, which also inspired a poem by the 17th-century English poet George Herbert.

"Aaron's rod" is a name given to various plants, including the great mullein and the goldenrod. It is also a name for the divining rod or magic wand used by magicians. The expression "Aaron's serpent" refers to the biblical legend that his rod turned into a serpent and swallowed up the serpents of the Egyptian priests (Exod. 8:10–12).

0003
Aba (above). In North American Indian mythology (Choctaw of Bayou Lacomb, St. Tammany Parish, Louisiana), good spirit, creator, heaven. At first there was a mountain, Nane Chaha (high hills), that had a passage from the top to caverns under the earth. From these caverns emerged the first Choctaws, along with ants. The Choctaws killed the ants' mother, and they called on Aba, who closed the mountain exit, locking in the remaining people and later transforming them into ants.

0004
Abaris. In Greek mythology, a sage who traveled with a magic arrow given him by the god Apollo. Abaris also used the arrow to invoke oracles and later gave it to Pythagoras in exchange for lessons in the latter's philosophy. It was believed that Abaris never ate.

Korah

Abderus (son of battle). In Greek mythology, a son of Hermes and Opus. A male lover of Heracles, the hero sent Abderus to guard the man-eating mares of the Bistonian king Diomedes. When Heracles discovered the lad had been eaten by the mares, he built the city of Abdera in his lover's memory.

Abdiel (servant of God). In medieval Jewish folklore, an angel appearing in *The Book of the Angel Raziel*. Milton's *Paradise Lost* (book 5:805–808) makes Abdiel the angel who opposes Satan's plans to overthrow God's rule. Milton may have borrowed the name Abdiel from 1 Chronicles (5:15) where it is given as the name of the son of Guni and the father of Ahi in the genealogy of Gad. Or Milton may have known the medieval Jewish work since he was well read in rabbinical writings.

Abel (meadow? breath?). In the Bible, O.T., a shepherd, the second son of Adam and Eve. Abel was killed by his brother Cain (Gen. 4:2–8). Yahweh (a cult name for the Hebrew god) favored Abel's offering over Cain's, though the reason is not stated exactly in the Bible. In the New Testament Jesus speaks of Abel as the first martyr (Matt. 23:35), and he was considered so by the writers in the Early Church. In the Koran (sura 5) Abel is called Habil. Albrecht Dürer and William Blake are among the artists who have portrayed Abel's death.

Abenamar and King Don Juan. Late medieval Spanish-Moorish historical ballad.

In 1431 King Juan II of Castile besieged the Moorish stronghold of Granada. After defeating the Moors the king placed the Moorish Infante Abenalmao on the throne. The ballad tells in part how the king questions a Moorish slave, Abenamar, on the condition of the city. The Moorish lad replies with a description of its beauties. The king then says:

> If thou art willing, O Granada
> I will woo thee for my bride,
> Cordova shall be thy dowry,
> And Sevilla by its side.

The answer, however, is

> I'm no widow, good King John,
> I am still a wedded wife;
> And the Moor, who is my husband,
> Loves me better than his life.
>
> (James Young Gibson translation)

Arabic poets, from whom this ballad stems, often used the term *husband* or *spouse* to refer to the lord of a region or city; the city is often spoken of as a bride.

Abe no Seimei. In Japanese mythology, hero-magician, son of the poet Abe no Yasuna and Kuzunoha, a white fox. Abe no Seimei was the court astrologer and is sometimes portrayed with his fox mother, Kuzunoha, who holds a writing brush in her mouth. Abe no Seimei once cured the Emperor Toba of a grave illness when he showed that the emperor's favorite mistress, Tamamo no Maye, was actually a nine-tailed fox who had bewitched him. Sometimes he is portrayed in a wizard's competition, conjuring white mice from an empty box.

Variant spellings: Kamo Yasunari, Kamo Hogon, Abe no Yasunari.

Abe no Yasuna. In Japanese mythology, poet-hero who married a beautiful woman, Kuzunoha, who originally was a white fox.

One day as Abe no Yasuna was walking in the gardens of the temple of the rice god, Inari, reciting his poems aloud, a party of nobles passed by in pursuit of a fox. They were after the fox for its liver, which was used in medicine. The fox ran into the temple gardens, stopping near Abe, who caught the animal and hid it in the folds of his kimono. The pursuers gave up the chase and left the area, and Abe freed the fox. A year later Abe fell in love with a beautiful woman, Kuzunoha, who gave birth to a boy, Abe no Seimei, noted in Japanese tales as a magician. Soon after his birth she died of a fever. Three days later she appeared to her husband in a dream, telling him not to weep, as she was the fox he had saved earlier.

Abere. In Melanesian mythology, a wild woman, seducer and often slayer of men.

Abezi-thibod (the father who is devoid of counsel). In Jewish mythology, an evil spirit who fought against Moses but was finally drowned with the Egyptians in the Red Sea, where he is kept a prisoner under a pillar. He does not appear in the Bible, but in other Jewish writings.

Abgar. In Christian legend, a king of Edessa who corresponded with Jesus. Jesus left no written records, but Christian legend has supplied them in the form of a correspondence with Abgar. In one letter Abgar asks "Jesus the good Savior" to come to heal him because "it is reported that you cause the blind to see, the lame to walk, do both cleanse lepers, and cast out unclean spirits and devils." Abgar's letter is answered by Jesus saying he must "fulfill all the ends" of his mission but will send after his Ascension to heaven one of his disciples "who will cure" the king's disease.

These unhistorical letters are reproduced in Eusebius' *Ecclesiastical History*, written in the fourth century. In a later addition to the letters there is one in which Jesus sends a portrait of himself on a cloth used to wipe his face. Upon touching the portrait, Abgar is cured of his illness. As fantastic as the letters are, some clergymen, both Catholic and Protestant, have defended them as genuine. Up to the middle of the 19th century it was common in some English homes to have the letters framed with a portrait of Christ.

0014

Abhinna. In Buddhism, supernatural knowledge or insight, possessed by the Buddha and those who have been enlightened. One Buddhist text tells of the Buddha and a disciple discussing Abhinna. The disciple asked: "Can an humble monk, by sanctifying himself, acquire the talents of supernatural wisdom called Abhinna and the supernatural powers called Iddhi?"

The Buddha then asked: "Which are the Abhinnas?" The disciple replied: "There are six Abhinnas: (1) the celestial eye; (2) the celestial ear; (3) the body at will or the power of transformation; (4) the knowledge of the destiny of former dwellings; so as to know former states of existence; (5) the faculty of reading the thoughts of others; and (6) the knowledge of comprehending the finality of the stream of life." The sixth Abhinna is possessed only by enlightened beings. Spiritually advanced beings may possess the other five.

0015

Abigail (a father's joy). In the Bible, O.T., a beautiful woman; wife of Nabal (the fool), a wealthy sheep owner. She supported David with food and drink during his exile from King Saul, when her husband refused him help. When Nabal died, David married Abigail (1 Sam. 25:2–42). The name Abigail is used in Elizabethan writings to signify a lady's maid and is found in works of Christopher Marlowe and Beaumont and Fletcher. In the neoclassic age, Pope, Swift, and Fielding also used the name, but their use may partly derive from Abigail Hill (Mrs. Masham), waiting woman to Queen Anne. Rubens painted an *Abigail*.

0016

Ab Kin Xoc. In Mayan mythology, god of poetry, also known as Ppiz Hiu Tec.

0017

Abomination of Desolation. In the Bible, a phrase used by Jesus (Matt. 24:15) as a sign of the approaching destruction of Jerusalem. It refers to the Book of Daniel (9:27, 11:31, 12:11) in the Old Testament. The term is now used for something that is destructive or hateful.

0018

Abore. In the mythology of the Warau Indians of the Guianas of South America, a culture hero. The evil frog woman Wowta made Abore her slave when he was a young boy, but when he grew up, she wished to marry him. Abore lured Wowta toward a hollow tree that he had filled with honey, Wowta's favorite food. When she saw the honey, she became so excited that she got stuck in the hollow tree. Abore then fled in a canoe, reaching the land of the white man, to whom he taught the arts of civilization. Wowta eventually escaped from the tree by turning herself into a small frog.

0019

Abracadabra. A medieval kabalistic charm said to be made up of the Hebrew words *ab* (father), *ben* (son), and *ruach acadsch* (holy spirit). The charm was first used in the second century as a powerful antidote against ague, flux, toothache, and numerous other ailments. The word was written on parchment and suspended from the neck by a linen thread.

Abraham

0020

Abraham (father of a multitude?). In the Bible, O.T. (Gen. 11:26–17:4), the first Patriarch, the founder of the Hebrew people, who was at first called Abram; son of Terah; father of Isaac. Abraham was brought up worshiping many gods; then Yahweh, the Hebrew cult god, revealed himself to Abraham. As a young man Abraham married his half-sister Sara, later called Sarah, and then, under the direction of Yahweh, moved from Ur to Haran. He was driven by famine to Egypt and was accompanied by his nephew Lot. In Egypt he told Sarah to pretend she was his full sister and not his wife, for he feared he would be killed. Pharaoh took Sarah into his harem, and Yahweh sent a plague on Egypt. When Pharaoh discovered he had taken Abraham's wife, he sent Abraham and his wife back to Canaan (Genesis repeats this tale at the court of King Abimelech). Abraham settled in Mamre, and Lot moved to Sodom. Sarah, who had been barren, gave her maid Hagar to Abraham for childbearing, so she could claim the child as her own. When Hagar bore Ishmael to Abraham, the child became a source of contention between Sarah and Hagar. At one point Hagar and Ishmael were sent into the desert to die, but they were saved by an angel of Yahweh. The Lord blessed Abraham, appearing to him one day with two companions (often portrayed in art as three angels). One of the men told him that Sarah would bear a child. She laughed at that because she was too old to bear children; However, a child was born and named Isaac. To test Abraham's faith, Yahweh commanded him to sacrifice his son Isaac, but an angel of Yahweh stopped him at the last moment. When Sarah died at 127 years of age, Abraham bought a cave for her resting place at Machpelah. At the end of his life Abraham gave all of his possessions to Isaac. Then Abraham "died in a good old age, an old man, and full of years; and was gathered to his people" (Gen. 25:8). Nonbiblical works that deal with Abraham are *The Apocalypse of Abraham*, which tells of his youth and his journey to heaven escorted by the angel Jaoel, and *The Testament of Abraham*, which tells of Abraham's death. In the latter the archangel Michael is sent to fetch Abraham to heaven. Abraham, who does not want to die, is shown heaven and the judgment of the dead and then returned to earth. There he is tricked into giving his hand to the Angel of Death.

In medieval Christian belief Abraham was looked on as a prefiguration of Christ. His meeting with the high priest Melchizedek (Gen. 14:18–24), who blessed bread and wine, was seen as a prefiguration of the Last Supper of Jesus and the institution of the Holy Eucharist. Abraham's meeting with the three young men (Gen. 18:1–19) was seen as a symbol of the Christian Trinity and the sacrifice of Isaac as a symbol of the Crucifixion of Jesus, God the Father sacrificing his only Son. In Islamic tradition Abraham's sacrifice took place on the site of the Mosque of Omar at Jerusalem. In Islam, Abraham is called Khalilu'illah (the friend of Allah). In Christian art, Abraham is portrayed as a patriarch with a full beard, and sometimes carrying a knife, alluding to the sacrifice of Isaac. Dierick Bouts's *Abraham Being Blessed by Melchizedek* portrays the patriarch in rich medieval garb.

0021

Abraxas. Name of a god or demon found on Gnostic gems and amulets from the second century C.E. Abraxas' name was used in various magical rites. It was believed to have special power because it contained seven letters with the numeral value of 365, the number of spiritual powers ruling the universe, according to the Gnostics. The god appears on amulets with the head of a cock or a lion and the body of a man with legs that terminate in scorpions, holding in his right hand a club or flail and in his left a round or oval shield. The word *abracadabra*, according to some scholars, is derived from Abraxas. He appears in *The Book of the Angel Raziel*, a mystical work.

Absalom

0022

Absalom (father is peace, prosperity). In the Bible, O.T., King David's third son, known for his physical beauty. He plotted against his father and "stole the hearts of the men of Israel" (2 Sam. 15:6). Riding on a mule in the decisive battle at Ephraim, Absalom was caught by his long hair in an oak tree. He was found by one of David's men, who killed him even though David did not want him killed. David lamented his death: "O my son Absalom, O Absalom, my son, my son!" (2 Sam. 19:4). William Faulkner picked up the lament for the title of his novel *Absalom, Absalom!* The English poet Dryden gave the name Absalom to the Duke of Monmouth, Charles II's natural son, in his satire *Absalom and Achitopel*, which attacks Puritan attempts to exclude the Duke of York from the throne of England because, although the legitimate heir, he was a Roman Catholic.

Absyrtus. In Greek mythology, son of King Aeetes of Colchis; brother of Medea. In her flight from Colchis with her lover Jason, Medea cut Absyrtus into pieces and threw them one by one into the sea, so that Aeetes, stopping to pick them up, would be delayed in his pursuit of the lovers. Some variant accounts say Medea killed Absyrtus in Colchis; others, near Istria. Still other accounts say Absyrtus was not killed by Medea but arrived safely in Illyrium. Ovid's *Tristia* (3.9) tells the tale of Medea and Absyrtus, which is alluded to in Shakespeare's *Henry VI, Part II* (5.2.59). Other works dealing with the tale include Apollonius Rhodius' *Argonautica* (4.3303– 482) and Apollordorus' *Bibliotheca* (Library) (1.9.24).

0024

Abuk and Garang. In African mythology (Dinka of Eastern Sudan), the first woman and man; they were tiny and made of clay. When a pot in which they were placed was opened, they grew larger. The Great Being allotted them one grain of corn each day, but Abuk became selfish and pounded (ground) more. As a result of her greed the sky was offended, though the Dinka associate Abuk with produce, gardens, grain, and waters. She is also the patron of all women. Her symbol is a snake.

0025

Acamas (unwearing). In Greek mythology, son of Theseus and Phaedra; brought up with his brother Demophon by Elephenor, king of Euboea. He was sent with Diomedes as ambassador to Troy to persuade King Priam to send Helen back in peace. After the destruction of Troy, he and his brother restored Theseus to the Attica throne. They then led a colony from Athens to Cyprus, where Acamas died. Acamas was one of the Greeks inside the wooden horse during the siege of Troy. Acamas also is the name of a son of Antenor mentioned in Homer's *Iliad* (book 11), as well as the name of a captain of the Thracians, Trojan allies who were killed by Ajax, according to Homer's *Iliad* (book 11).

0026

Acantha. In Greek mythology, a nymph who was loved by Apollo and was transformed into the acanthus flower.

0027

Acanthus. A large-leaf plant common in the Mediterranean region. In Greek legend the Athenian architect and sculptor Callimachus one day happened to pass a tomb, near which he saw an acanthus plant enfolding both a tile and a basket. He was inspired by the sight to design a capital for a column, since known as the Corinthian order. According to an earlier Greek legend, a young girl died, and her devoted nurse collected her trinkets and ornaments and placed them in a basket near her tomb and covered them with a tile. The nurse set the basket down on an acanthus root, whose stalks and leaves grew up enfolding the basket. It was this tomb that Callimachus saw. In medieval Christian symbolism, the acanthus signified "the awareness and the pain of sin" as well as heaven.

0028

Acarnan and Amphoterus (thistle). In Greek mythology, sons of Alcmaeon and Callirrhoë. When their mother heard of their father's murder by Phegeus and his sons, she prayed to Zeus (who was her lover) to let her sons grow up at once into men to avenge his death. Her prayer was granted, and her two sons killed Phegeus and his sons. Acarnan and Amphoterus then took the jewels of Harmonia and offered them at the shrine at Delphi. Later the two founded a kingdom called Acarnania, named after the elder brother, Acarnan.

0029

Acastus (unstable). In Greek mythology, king of Iolcus, a son of Pelias and Anaxibia; Acastus was one of the Argonauts and a member of the Calydonian boar hunt. His sisters were persuaded by Medea, who was a witch, to cut up their father, Pelias, and boil him to make him young again. They followed Medea's advice, which was a trick to murder Pelias. When Acastus discovered this, he drove Medea and her lover, Jason, from the land and instituted funeral games in honor of his murdered father. During these games Hippolyte (or Astydameia), wife of Acastus, fell in love with her husband's friend, Peleus. When Peleus ignored her sexual advances, she accused him of attempting to rape her. Soon afterward, while Acastus and Peleus were hunting on Mount Pelion, Acastus took Peleus' sword after he had fallen asleep. As a result, Peleus, unable to defend himself, was nearly killed by the centaurs. He was saved by either Chiron or Hermes (ancient accounts differ). Peleus later returned and killed Acastus and his wife. Acastus is the father of Laodameia and is mentioned in Ovid's *Metamorphoses* (book 8).

0030

Acca Larentia (mother of the Lares). In Roman mythology, an ancient Italian earth goddess whose feast was celebrated on 23 December; mother of the Lares. Roman accounts vary. In some she is said to have been the nurse of Romulus and Remus; in others, the mistress of Heracles and the wife of a rich

Etruscan called Tarutius. She was believed to have left great possessions either to Romulus or to the Roman people. Acca Larentia also is said to have had 12 sons, called the Arval Brothers, one of whom was sacrificed each year. She may be connected with Larunda, a Sabine goddess whose feast and sacrifices also were made on 23 December. Acca Larentia is also the name of a companion of Camilla in Vergil's *Aeneid*.

Accolon of Gaul. 0031
In Arthurian legend, a knight loved by Morgan le Fay, sister and enemy of King Arthur. Morgan le Fay gave Accolon the scabbard of King Arthur's sword, which protected its owner from bleeding, no matter how severely wounded. Despite this, however, King Arthur eventually killed Accolon.

Acestes. 0032
In Greek and Roman mythology, a king of Eryx; son of the Sicilian river god Crimisus and a Trojan woman, Egesta (or Segesta), who was sent by her father to Sicily to escape from monsters menacing the area around Troy. Acestes founded the town of Segesta. There he hospitably received the Trojan hero Aeneas after he fled from Troy. Acestes helped Aeneas bury his father on Mount Eryx, and in commemoration of this deed Aeneas built a city there called Acesta. The story of Acestes is told in Vergil's *Aeneid* (book 5).

Achates (agate). 0033
In Roman mythology, the faithful friend of the hero Aeneas in Vergil's *Aeneid*. His devotion to Aeneas was so great that the term *fidus Achates* (faithful Achates) became synonymous with loyalty.

Acheflour. 0034
In some Arthurian legends, mother of Perceval and sister of King Arthur. She was married to Bliocadrans, one of the 12 knights of Wales, who was killed in a tournament. Not wishing their son Perceval to follow in his father's footsteps, after his death, Acheflour pretended to go on a pilgrimage to St. Brandan in Scotland, but left instead for the Waste Forest. There she brought up her son without any knowledge of fighting. She warned Perceval that men in armor were devils and must be avoided.

Achelous (he who drives away grief?). 0035
In Greek mythology, the oldest of the river gods, son of Oceanus and Tethys; also the name of the river in northwestern Greece that forms part of the boundary between Aetolia and Acarnania. Achelous was the eldest of the 3,000 sons of Oceanus and Tethys and was the father of the Sirens. As a water god, Achelous was capable of metamorphosis and could turn himself into a serpent or an ox. In the form of an ox, when fighting with Heracles for the possession of Deianira, he lost one horn, which was later returned

The embassy to Achilles (John Flaxman)

in exchange for the horn of Amalthea. Achelous was worshiped all over Greece and her colonies, especially Rhodes, Italy, and Sicily. At Dodona the oracle's answers always contained an injunction to sacrifice to Achelous. Ovid's *Metamorphoses* (book 8) tells of the god. Milton refers to the horn of Achelous in his *Animadversions Upon the Remonstrant's Defence*, in which he writes: "Repair the Acheloian horn of your dilemma how you can." Rubens portrays the god in his painting *The Feast of Achelous*.

0036

Acheron (woeful). In Greek mythology, river believed to lead to the underworld. Homer, Vergil, and other ancient poets made Acheron the principal river of Hades. The rivers Cocytus, Phlegethon, and Styx were believed to be its tributaries. In Dante's *Divine Comedy*, Acheron forms the boundary of hell, and on its shore all of those who have died in the wrath of God wait to be ferried across by Charon. The origin of the river is explained to Dante by the poet Vergil. Shakespeare's *Macbeth* (3.5.15) alludes to "the pit of Acheron," in *Titus Andronicus* (4.3.44), it is a "burning lake," and in *A Midsummer Night's Dream* (3.2.357) the heaven is carved "with drooping fog as black as Acheron."

Milton's *Paradise Lost* (2.578) makes Acheron one of the four infernal rivers, calling it "sad Acheron of sorrow, black and deep." Acheron, according to some European poets, stands for hell itself.

0037

Achilles (lipless). In Greek mythology, hero, demigod, son of Peleus and the Nereid Thetis; married to Deidamia; father of Neoptolemus (Pyrrhus); father of Caistrus by Penthesilea; originally called Ligyron.

According to Homer, Achilles was brought up by his mother, Thetis, together with his older cousin, Patroclus. Achilles was taught both war and eloquence by Phoenix and the art of healing by the centaur Chiron, his mother's grandfather.

Accounts written after Homer added numerous details to Achilles' youth. According to one ancient account, Thetis, in an effort to make Achilles immortal, anointed him with ambrosia by day and held him in a fire at night to destroy whatever mortal element he had derived from his father, Peleus. One night Peleus saw the boy over the fire and made an outcry. Thetis, angry at the intrusion, left her son and husband and returned to the Nereids. Peleus then took the motherless boy to Chiron on Mount Pelion. There the boy was fed on the entrails of wild animals. At the age of six, he was so strong and swift that he killed wild boars and lions and caught stags without a net or hounds. In a later variation of the myth, Thetis dipped the child Achilles into the river

Thetis entreating Zeus to honor Achilles (John Flaxman)

Styx, making him invulnerable except for the heel by which she held him, the spot in which he later receives his death blow—thus, the expression "Achilles heel."

In another version, Thetis, alarmed by the prophecy of Calchas that Troy could not be taken without the help of Achilles and knowing that he would die in the effort, took the nine-year-old boy to the island of Scyros where, in female dress, he grew up among the daughters of King Lycomedes. Calchas betrayed his whereabouts, and Odysseus, and Diomedes unmasked the hero. Disguised as a merchant, Odysseus spread out female ornaments before the maidens, as well as a shield and a spear. Suddenly, a trumpet sounded the call to battle. The girls fled, but Achilles clutched the arms and said he was ready to fight.

During the first nine years of the Trojan War Achilles led the Greeks on plundering excursions around Troy, destroying 11 inland and 12 seacoast towns.

Angered when Agamemnon took the young girl Briseis, Achilles' mistress, Achilles drew back from the fight, and as a result the Trojans took the Greeks' camp and set their ships on fire. Achilles then relented to the extent of allowing Patroclus, wearing the armor of Peleus, to lead the Myrmidons into battle. Although Patroclus drove the Trojans back, he was killed by Hector, who took Peleus' arms from Patroclus' dead body. Grief for his male lover Patroclus and thirst for vengeance at last overcame Achilles' hatred for Agamemnon, and he reentered the the Trojan War. Furnished with new arms by the smith god Hephaestus, Achilles went out against Hector, the Trojan hero, and eventually killed him. Homer's *Iliad* ends with the burial of Hector and leaves the ultimate fate of Achilles untold.

According to some accounts, Achilles' fate was one he had chosen himself: an early death with undying fame rather than a long but inglorious life. Near the Seasean Gate he was struck by the shaft of Paris, which was guided by Apollo. In a variant account the shaft struck Achilles in his one vulnerable heel. After Achilles' death the Greeks and Trojans fought over his body until Zeus sent down a storm to end the fight. In Homer's *Odyssey*, Achilles' spirit descended to the underworld, where he later met Odysseus, who was journeying to the land of the dead. In non-Homeric variant accounts, Thetis snatched her son's body out of its burning pyre and carried it to the island of Leuke at the mouth of the Danube, where the transfigured hero lives on, sovereign of the Pontus and husband of Iphigenia.

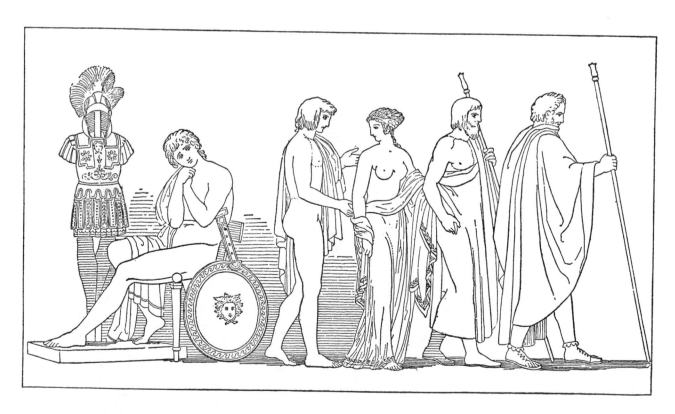

Briseis leaving Achilles' tent (John Flaxman)

Other myths place Achilles in Elysium with Medea or Helen as his wife. Greeks worshiped Achilles at his tomb on the Hellespont, where, according to another account, he appeared to Homer in the full blaze of his armor, and struck the poet blind.

Dante's *Divine Comedy* places Achilles in the Second Circle of Hell, among those who met their death through love. The Italian poet says of him, alluding to popular medieval myth, that "he fought with love at the last." This refers to the widespread medieval legend that Achilles was killed by the treachery of Paris in the temple of Apollo Thymbraeus in Troy. Achilles had been lured there by the promise of a meeting with Polyxena, with whom he was in love and whom the Trojans offered to him if he would desert to their cause. Instead of meeting Polyxena he was killed by Paris. Lully's opera *Achille et Polyxène* (1687) is based on this medieval variation of the Achilles myth.

In addition to *Troilus and Cressida*, where Achilles is a main character, Shakespeare mentions him three times. In *Love's Labour's Lost* (5.2.635) and the narrative poem, *The Rape of Lucrece* (1424), Achilles is one of the figures in the painting of Troy. In the play *Henry VI, Part II* (5.1.100), Achilles' spear is mentioned:

> That gold must round engirt these brows of mine,
> Whose smile and frown, like to Achilles' spear,
> Is able with the change to kill and cure.

This magic spear had wounded King Telephus, who learned from the oracle that only Achilles, who had inflicted the wound, could cure him. Shakespeare's source was probably Arthur Golding's translation of Ovid's *Metamorphoses* (book 12) which says: "I did wound King Teleph with his speare, and when he lay upon the ground,/ I was intreated with the speare to heale him safe and sound." Chaucer, in *The Squire's Tale*, part of *The Canterbury Tales*, also refers to the power of the spear of Achilles, both to kill and to cure. The plant Achillea (milfoil), named after the hero, is supposed to have the power to heal.

The Greek philosopher Zeno told a paradox, titled *Achilles and the Tortoise*, in which Achilles and a tortoise have a race. The hero runs ten times as fast as the tortoise, which has a 100-yard start. Achilles, however, can never overtake the tortoise because in the time it takes him to cover the 100 yards to where the tortoise started, the tortoise has covered 10 yards; while Achilles is covering those 10 yards, the tortoise has gained another yard, and so on.

Achilles contending with the rivers (John Flaxman)

More then 50 operas have been written of the subject Achilles. Notable among them are Pietro Mestastasio's libretto *Achilles in Scyros* (1736) and Hugo von Hofmannsthal's libretto *Achilles auf Skyros*, which was set to music by E. Wellesz in 1929.

Paintings depicting Achilles include *Achilles at the Court of Scyros* by Nicolas Poussin and Peter Paul Rubens's *Thetis Dips Achilles in the Styx* and *Achilles Kills Hector*.

0038

Acidalia. In Greek and Roman mythology, name given to Aphrodite (Venus), goddess of love, after she had washed in the same fountain as the Graces in Boeotia, a district in central Greece bordering on Attica. Both Vergil's *Aeneid* (book 1) and Ovid's *Fasti* (book 5) mention Acidalia.

0039

Acontius of Cea. In Greek mythology, a poor young man who fell in love with Cydippe, daughter of a rich Athenian nobleman. Acontius carved an oath on an apple (or orange or quince). He gave the fruit to Cydippe, and she read out the oath, which said, "I swear by Artemis' Temple that I will marry no one but Acontius." Alarmed at the prospect of a poor match for their daughter, her parents went to the Delphic oracle for guidance and were told to let the lovers marry. Acontius' story is in one of Ovid's *Heroides* (21), verse letters from women of both myth and history to their absent lovers and husbands.

0040

Acrisius (ill judgment). In Greek mythology, king of Argos, son of Abas and Aglaia; great-grandson of Danaus; and brother of Proetus. After an oracle told Acrisius that a son of his daughter Danaë would kill him, Acrisius shut her up in a tower, but Zeus came to her as a shower of gold (urine), and she bore a son named Perseus. When Perseus grew up, he went with his mother to seek Acrisius, who had fled from Argos, fearing the truth of the oracle. Perseus found Acrisius at Larissa in Thessaly and killed him unawares with a discus. His tale is told in Ovid's *Metamorphoses* (book 4).

0041

Actaeus (coast). In Greek mythology, first king of Attica and father of Agraulos. Agraulos married Cecrops, whom the Athenians called their first king, though Actaeus ruled before him.

0042

Actis (beam of light). In Greek mythology, son of Helios and Rhode; brother of Candalus, Cercaphus, Macar, Ochimus, Tenages, and Triopas. Actis and his brothers were the first to sacrifice to Athena. He founded Heliopolis in Egypt. The Colossus of Rhodes was erected in his honor.

0043

Adachigahara. In Japanese legend, a cannibalistic woman spirit, portrayed with a kitchen knife, sometimes preparing to kill a child.

According to one legend, she was a woman of high rank attached to the court of a prince who suffered from a strange disease. The remedy required obtaining the blood of a child born during a certain month. Adachigahara, a faithful servant, killed various children in order to cure her master. When the cure was successful she confessed her guilt but was pardoned.

Another legend tells how one winter evening a pilgrim came to the door of her hut and asked permission to spend the night in her kitchen. Adachigahara at first refused but finally consented. After a few minutes she went out, forbidding her guest to look in a certain room. However, the pilgrim was inquisitive, opened the door, and found the room full of human bones and spattered with blood. Taking his hat and staff, he fled while Adachigahara was returning to her goblin shape.

0044

Adam and Eve (earth man and woman, wife, or the mother of all living?). In Jewish, Christian and Islamic mythology, the first man and woman.

In Genesis (2:4–4:26) Yahweh Elohim, one of the names of God, forms Adam (man) from the earth and gives him life by breathing into him the breath of life. Yahweh forms Eve from the rib of the sleeping Adam. Both are placed in the Garden of Eden and told not to eat fruit from the Forbidden Tree. The couple do so and are cast out of the Garden of Eden. Suffering and death enter the world as a result of their sin. Medieval Christian belief held Adam to be a prefiguration of Christ, Jesus being the first spiritual man as Adam had been the first physical man. According to medieval Christian belief, Eve, the first mother, foreshadowed the Virgin Mary or the Church. The Temptation and Fall was seen by Christians as the foreshadowing of the Annunciation to the Virgin Mary that she would be the mother of Jesus.

In Islamic mythology Allah sent the angels Gabriel, Michael, and Israfel, one after the other, to fetch seven handfuls of earth from different depths and of different colors for the creation of Adam. The angels returned empty-handed because Earth foresaw that the new creature would rebel against Allah and draw down a curse on Earth. Allah then sent a fourth angel, Azrael, who accomplished the mission. Thereafter Azrael was appointed to separate the souls of men from their bodies at death. The earth taken by Azrael was carried to Arabia to a place between Mecca and Tayef, where it was kneaded by the angels and fashioned into human form by Allah. The clay was left to dry for either 40 days or 40 years; then Adam was born. (Forty is a mystical number in Jewish, Christian, and Islamic belief.) Adam's Apple is a folk name for the laryngeal cartilage because, according to folk tradition, the Forbidden Fruit got stuck in Adam's throat. Adam's Ale is water, and Old Adam means man in sin without redemption, according to Christian belief. Adam and Eve, with the serpent who tempted them, frequently appear in Western art. Dürer's *Adam and Eve* is one of the best-known works.

0045
Adamanthaea. In Greek mythology, a Cretan nurse of Zeus who suspended his cradle from a tree so that he was neither on earth nor heaven nor the sea. She had drums and cymbals sounded around the tree to

Adam and Eve

drown out his cries. All of this was done to protect Zeus from the anger of his father, Cronus, who wished to swallow his son to prevent Zeus from replacing him as ruler.

0046

Adam Bell (redness). In medieval British legend, hero who appears in a ballad of the same name. He lived in Englewood Forest, near Carlisle. Clymn of Clouth and William of Cloudesly were his companions. When William was captured and being taken to his execution for robbery, Adam and Clymn saved him. All three then went to London to ask the king's pardon, which was granted at the queen's request. To show their appreciation they all demonstrated their skill in archery. The king was so impressed that he named William a "gentleman of fe" and the other two, yeomen of the bedchamber.

0047

Adapa (man). In Near Eastern mythology, Babylonian hero who lost the gift of immortality for mankind through a trick of the gods.

The myth of Adapa is found in various texts, all incomplete, the earliest dating from the 14th century B.C.E. and found at El- Amarna, Egypt. Adapa was "wise like one of the gods," being under the special protection of his father, the god Ea. Ea gave Adapa "intelligence enough to comprehend the design of the world: but he made him a dying man." One day Adapa went fishing. While he was in the middle of the sea, a storm caused by the south wind capsized Adapa's boat. In a fit of rage Adapa cursed the south wind.

"O south wind," he cried out, "you have overwhelmed me with your cruelty. I will break your wings." (The south wind is often pictured as a winged bird or monster in Babylonian art.)

As Adapa finished his curse, the wings of the south wind were destroyed. For seven days (a number to indicate a rather long though indefinite period) the wind did not blow over the sea or earth. When Anu, the god of heaven, discovered this, he called his god Illabrat to see why the south wind did not blow.

"Why has the south wind not blown for seven days across the land?" the god asked Illabrat.

"My lord, Adapa, the son of Ea, has broken the wings of the south wind," Illabrat replied.

Anu commanded Adapa to appear before him, and Ea prepared his son Adapa for the questioning from the god.

"When you come before Anu, you will be offered the food of death," he said. "Do not eat it. You will also be offered the waters of death. Do not drink. You will be offered a garment. Put it on. You will be offered oil. Anoint yourself. Do not forget now what I have told you."

When Adapa appeared before Anu, he did as his father had told him and refused the food and drink offered, even though Anu said to him it was the food of life and the water of life.

Anu looked at Adapa after he refused and said, "Why did you not eat and not drink? Now you cannot live forever, for you refused the food and water of everlasting life."

"Ea, my lord," replied Adapa, "commanded me not to eat and not to drink."

Then Anu laughed, for Ea had tricked his own son, Adapa, keeping for the gods the gift of immortality.

0048

Adaro. In Melanesian mythology, sun spirits who move about in waterspouts, cross from place to place using rainbows as bridges, or come to earth during sun showers. They are part fish, part human. Their chief is Nyorieru. An Adaro spirit may shoot a man with a flying fish, causing him to become unconscious. Only if a special offering is made in time will the victim recover.

0049

Addanc of the Lake. In the medieval Welsh *Mabinogion*, a monster slain by Peredur, who uses a magic stone that makes him invisible to the monster.

0050

Adder. A common European viper, often said to be deaf in world mythology and folklore. Psalm 58:4–5 reads: "Their poison is like the poison of a serpent: they are like the deaf adder that stoppeth her ear." For medieval Christianity this signified those people who would not listen to the gospel. A 12th-century bestiary by Phillippe de Thaon says that the adder is "sly and aware of evil: when it perceives people who want to enchant it and capture it, it will stop up its ears." St. Augustine equated the adder with the devil.

0051

Adharma (unrighteousness). In Hindu mythology, a son of the god Brahma. He personified unrighteousness or vice, being called "the destroyer of all things."

0052

Adi. In Hindu mythology, a demon slain by the god Shiva. In some texts Adi is a form of the great goddess Devi, the wife of Shiva, who, when angry with her husband, took on the demonic form.

Adi-Buddha (first enlightened one). In Mahayana Buddhism, the primordial Buddha who "was before all," infinite, omniscient, self-existing, without beginning and without end. He is not, however, a creator god, nor equivalent to the Western concept of God. One myth tells how all was void when the mystic sound *Om* became manifest, from which at his own will Adi-Buddha was produced. When the world was created, he revealed himself as a flame issuing from a lotus flower. In Buddhist art of Nepal he is often portrayed in this form. From Adi-Buddha came five Dhyani-Buddhas (Buddhas of Meditation) who are Vairocana, Askhobhya, Amitabha, Amogh asiddhi, and Ratnasambhava.

Adiri. In Melanesian mythology, the land of the dead, located in the west.

Aditi (free; unbounded?). In Hindu mythology, a goddess, the "mother of the world," who, according to some Hindu texts, is the mother of both Indra and Vishnu. Aditi's descendants, the Adityas, are listed as 12, corresponding to the months of the year. In the Rig-Veda, Aditya is one of the names of the sun.

Admetus (untamed). In Greek mythology, an Argonaut, son of Pheres and Periclymene (or Clymene) and husband of Alcestis; father of Eumelus and Perimele. Admetus took part in the Calydonian boar hunt and the voyage of the Argo. Apollo served Admetus for a time as a shepherd, either from love as a reward for his piety or to expiate a capital crime. Admetus wooed Alcestis, the daughter of Pelias, but her father would give her only to one who could yoke lions and boars to a chariot. Admetus accomplished the task with Apollo's aid. Apollo then prevailed on the Moirai (Fates) to release Admetus from death, provided that someone would volunteer to die in his place. When Admetus was about to die after being seized by a sickness, his parents refused to die in his place. Finally, his wife, Alcestis, died for her husband. Alcestis was, however, sent back to the upper world by Persephone, goddess of death; or, according to a variant myth, was rescued out of Hades by Heracles. Euripides' *Alcestis* deals with the tale. The time that Apollo spent with Admetus is the subject George Meredith's poem *Phoebus with Admetus*.

Adno-artina. In Australian mythology, the gecko lizard that challenged Marindi, a dog, to a fight. Marindi was killed and his blood dyed the rocks red.

Altar of the god Moloch

Adrammelech (the lordship of Melech). In Near Eastern mythology, a god worshiped by the people of Sepharvaim.

According to 2 Kings (17:31), the "Sepharvites burnt their children in fire to Adrammelech and Anammelech, the gods of Sepharvaim." In later Jewish legend Adrammelech was turned into one of the ten archdemons, who often appeared in animal forms such as that of a peacock, mule, horse, or lion. In Milton's *Paradise Lost* (book 6:365) the good angels Uriel and Raphael vanquish Adrammelech. The German poet Klopstock, in his epic poem *The Messiah*, calls Adrammelech "the enemy of God, greater in malice, ambition, and mischief than Satan, a fiend more curst, a deeper hypocrite." Adrammelech may be derived from the Babylonian god Anu and the Ammonite god Moloch, to whom children were sacrificed.

The name is also used for a son of Sennacherib in 2 Kings (19:37), who with Sharezer, his brother, murdered his father in the temple of the god Nisroch after they learned their father planned to sacrifice them to the god. The name appears in Josephus's *Antiquities of the Jews* (book 16, chapter 8) as Andromachos and in Greek sources as Adramelos and Ardumuzan.

Variant spellings: Adramelech; Adramelek.

Adrasteia (inescapable). In Greek mythology, a Cretan nymph who was a nursemaid of Zeus; daughter of Melisseus; sister of Ida. Also a country near Troy named for Adrastus, who built a temple to Nemesis. The name also is given to a daughter of Zeus and Necessity, who is identified in some accounts as Nemesis.

0060

Adrastus (he who stands his ground). In Greek mythology, a king of Argos; son of Talaus and Lysimache (or Eurynome or Lysianassa); married to Amphithea; father of Argeia, Aegialeia, Aegialeus, Cyanippus, Deipyle, and Hippodameia. Adrastus led the "Seven against Thebes" in an ill-fated expedition to restore Polynices, son of Oedipus, to the throne of Thebes. In a fight between the three ruling houses in Argos—the Biantidae, Melampodidae, and Proetidae—Adrastus was driven out by Amphiaraus. Adrastus fled to his maternal grandfather, King Polybus of Cicyoun, and later inherited his kingdom. Adrastus was reconciled to Amphiaraus, to whom he gave his sister Eriphyle. He later returned and ruled over Argos, where one stormy night a great scuffle was heard outside the palace. Two fugitives, Polynices and Tydeus (one wrapped in a lion's skin, the other in a boar's skin) had sought refuge in the front court and were fighting for a night's lodging. Adrastus recognized this as the fulfillment of an oracle that had told him to marry his daughters to a lion and a boar. Adrastus gave his daughter Argeia to Polynices and Deipyle to Tydeus. He promised to conduct the two exiles to Thebes and install Polynices on the throne. This is the subject of Aeschylus' play, *Seven Against Thebes*. In the ensuing war only Adrastus escaped destruction by fleeing on his winged horse Arion. Ten years later, with the sons (called the Epigoni) of the slain warriors of this ill-fated expedition and his son Aegialeus, Adrastus marched on Thebes. He took the city but lost his son and died of grief on his way home.

0061

Adrian, St. (the man from Adria). Fourth century. In Christian legend, a military saint in northern Europe during the Middle Ages. Patron of Flemish brewers. Feast, 8 September.

The life of St. Adrian is found in *The Golden Legend*, a collection of saints' lives written in the 13th century by Jacobus de Voragine. Adrian was a pagan officer at the imperial Roman court at Nicomedia. When some Christians were arrested he witnessed their strength and was converted, saying he was to be accounted with them. When the emperor heard this he had Adrian thrown into prison. His wife Natalie, who secretly was a Christian, ran to prison and "kissed the chains that her husband was bound with," according to *The Golden Legend*. She often visited her husband in prison, urging him on to martyrdom. When the emperor heard that women were entering the prison, he ordered the practice stopped. But "when Natalie heard that, she shaved her head and took the habit of a man, and served the saints in prison and made the other women do so."

This state of affairs, however, could not continue. The saint was eventually martyred in the most gruesome way. The prison guards "hewed off his legs and thighs, and Natalie prayed them that they would smite off his hands, and that he should be like to the other saints that had suffered more than he, and when they had hewn them off he gave up his spirit to God." Natalie took her husband's remains and fled the city, settling in Argyropolis, where she died in peace, though she is included among Christian martyrs in the Roman church calendar of saints.

In Christian art St. Adrian is portrayed with an anvil in his hand or at his feet. Sometimes a sword or ax is beside him. His sword was kept as a relic at Walbeck in Saxony, Germany. Emperor Henry II used it when preparing to go against the Turks and Hungarians.

0062

Adu Ogyinae. In African mythology (Ashanti of Ghana), the first man. The Ashanti tell several myths concerning the origin of man. One states that on Monday night the first man, Adu Ogyinae, came to the surface of the earth through holes bored in the ground by a worm. Adu Ogyinae was the leader of a small group of seven men and a few women, as well as a leopard and a dog. Of the entire group, only Adu Ogyinae was not frightened by the new things he saw on the surface of the earth. By Tuesday he managed to calm the others, but they did not begin to build homes until Wednesday. Adu was killed when a tree fell on him. Then the dog was sent in search of fire. Meat was cooked with the flame he brought back and was fed to him to test whether it was safe. When the dog showed no signs of illness, all of the others began to eat. The god of creation then came upon one of the members of the group and made him his assistant. Each year the Ashanti hold ceremonies in the woods to commemorate the first human beings.

0063

Advent (coming). In Christian ritual, first season of liturgical or church year. Its development over the centuries in the Western church was gradual, but by the 13th century it had come to encompass the four Sundays before Christmas. Advent was retained in *The Book of Common Prayer* (1549) of the Church of England but was rejected by the Calvinists and some other Reformers. Two basic motifs or themes developed over the centuries. The first is that of joyous preparation for the Feast of the Nativity, or Christmas. But parallel to this joyous note is the second motif of Advent: preparation for the Second Coming of Christ when He will judge the world. Thus, the traditional color for Advent is purple, stressing the penitential character of the season. During the Middle Ages a fast was observed, with weddings, amusements, and conjugal relations forbidden. The Advent wreath is the principal symbol of the season. It originated in Lutheran Germany a few hundred years ago and has been adopted by many other Christian churches. It consists of a wreath, an ancient symbol of glory and victory, and four candles, one for each Sunday in Advent. Three of the candles are purple; the fourth is rose for *Gaudete* Sunday. Sometimes the center of the wreath has a Christ candle. On the first Sunday of Advent the first candle is lit; on the second Sunday, the second is lit, and so on until all four are lit. The wreath is removed at the feast of Christmas.

0064

Aeacus (bewailing). In Greek mythology, first king of Aegina; son of Zeus by Aegina, a daughter of the river god Asopus in Philius. Zeus, in the form of an eagle, had taken Aegina and carried her off to the island named after her, where Aeacus was born. As king of Aegina, Aeacus ruled the Myrmidons, people whom Zeus had transformed from ants to populate the island. Aeacus was loved by the gods for his piety, and when a drought desolated Greece, his intercession obtained rain from Zeus. The Greeks built Aeacus a temple enclosed with a marble wall. The poet Pindar says that Aeacus helped Poseidon and Apollo construct the walls of Troy.

Because Aeacus was noted for his justice, he was made one of the judges over the dead, along with Minos and Rhadamanthys. At Aegina and Athens he was worshiped as a demigod. His sons by Chiron's daughter Endeis were Telamon and Peleus, the fathers of Ajax and Achilles. Another son, Phocus, by the Nereid Psamathe was killed by his half-brothers, who were then banished by their father for the crime. Ovid's *Metamorphoses* (book 7) and Hesiod's *Theogony* (1003–5) tell of Aeacus.

0065

Aeaea. In Greek mythology, a female hunter who was changed by the gods into an island of the same name to help her escape the pursuit of Phasis, a river god. Odysseus stayed on Aeaea with Circe for a year according to Homer's *Odyssey*. The poet, however, does not identify the location of the island. Later writers have placed it off the western coast of Italy. Cape Cicero, which is south of Rome and was once an island, has also been cited as the original Aeaea.

0066

Aëdon (nightingale). In Greek mythology, daughter of Pandareos, wife of the Theban king, Zethus; and mother of Itylus, whom she killed and fed to her husband.

Envious of her sister-in-law Niobe for having six sons, Aëdon tried to kill the oldest but by mistake killed one of her own. She was changed into a nightingale by Zeus and forever bewailed her fate.

In a later variant myth Aëdon is the wife of Polytechnus at Colophon in Lydia. She angered the goddess Hera by boasting that she lived more happily with her husband than Hera with Zeus. Hera sent Eris (strife) to set a wager between Aëdon and Polytechnus that whoever finished first the piece of work they had in hand (he a chair, she a garment) should be given, by the other, the present of a slave girl as a prize. With Hera's aid Aëdon won. In anger Polytechnus fetched Aëdon's sister Chelidonis on a false pretext from her father's house and subdued her. He then presented her to his wife as her slave. Aëdon did not recognize her sister dressed in slave garments. One day Aëdon overheard Chelidonis lamenting her fate and helped her plot to kill Aëdon's son Itylus, cook him and feed him to his father, Polytechnus. Learning the fate of his son, Polytechnus pursued Chelidonis to her home. But the gods, wishing to prevent more bloodshed, turned them all into birds. Pandareos became an osprey; his wife, a kingfisher; Polytechnus, a pelican; Chelidonis, a swallow; and Aëdon, a nightingale.

0067

Aegeus (goatish?). In Greek mythology, king of Athens; father of the hero Theseus, son of Pandion and Pylia; brother of Lycus, Nisus, and Pallas. With the help of his brothers Aegeus took Attica from the sons of his uncle Metion, who had earlier driven out their father, Pandion. Then, dethroned by Pallas and his sons, Aegeus was rescued and restored to power by his son Theseus. Aegeus then slew Androgeos, son of Minos, and to punish Aegeus, Minos forced him to send seven boys and seven girls to Crete every nine years as victims of the Minotaur. When Theseus set out to free his country from this tribute, he told his father he would change the black sail of his ship to a white sail if he succeeded. But he forgot to switch the sail, and seeing the black sail on the returning vessel, Aegeus believed Theseus had been killed. He threw himself into the Aegean sea, which, according to some accounts, is named after him.

Aegeus had a shrine at Athens where he introduced the worship of Aphrodite, who had left him childless until he honored her. Plutarch's *Life of Theseus* and Mary Renault's novels *The King Must Die* and *The Bull from the Sea* have Aegeus as part of the narrative. Ovid's *Metamorphoses* (book 7) also tells the tale.

Aegialeia. 0068 In Greek mythology, daughter of Adrastus of Argos and Amphithea; wife of Diomedes, sister of Argeia, Aegialeus, Cyanippus, Deipyle, and Hippodameia. In her husband's absence during the Trojan War, Aegialeia prostituted herself to her servants, chiefly Cometes, whom the king had left master of the house. When Diomedes learned of Aegialeia's unfaithfulness, he settled in Daunia.

Aeginetan Sculptures. 0069 The marble pediments of Athena's temple at Aegina, portraying combat between the Greeks and Trojans. They were rediscovered by the modern world in 1811 and removed to Munich. Athena is seen in the center as the protector of the Greeks. Of the figures in the sculpture, ten in the west pediment, representing the contest for the body of Patroclus, are complete.

Aegir (the sea). 0070 In Norse mythology, the sea god, brother of Kari, the air, and Loki, the fire-trickster god; married to Ran, his sister, father of nine daughters, the waves, or wave maidens. Like his brothers Kari and Loki, Aegir belonged to a primeval order of gods, older than the Aesir, the Vanir giants, dwarfs, or elves. Aegir was portrayed as a gaunt old man with long white hair and beard and ever-clutching, clawlike fingers. Whenever he appeared above the waters, it was to destroy ships and take the men and cargo to his underground kingdom. Aegir's servants were Elde and Funfeng, who waited on guests in his banquet hall under the sea. In Anglo-Saxon mythology Aegir was called Eagor. Whenever an unusually large wave came thundering toward a ship, its sailors would cry, "Look out, Eagor is coming!" In ancient Saxon times one of every ten prisoners was sacrificed to Aegir to ensure that the raiders would return safely.

Aegir also was known as Hlér or Ler (the shelterer) and Gymir (the concealer). In the *Prose Edda* he is said to be "well skilled in magic." Aegir and Ran appear in William Morris's *Sigurd the Volsung and the Fall of the Niblungs.*

Aegis (goatskin). 0071 In Greek mythology, the shield forged by Hephaestus that had on it the Gorgon Medusa's head. When Zeus shook the aegis, thunder ripped through the heavens. It was used not only by Zeus but also by Athena and Apollo. Since the word means goatskin, the aegis was said in later myth to be the skin of the goat that had suckled Zeus in his infancy. When the aegis became part of the iconography of Athena, it was portrayed as a shaggy or scaly skin with a fringe of snakes and the Gorgon's head in the middle. Vergil's *Aeneid* (book 8), Ovid's *Fasti* (book 3), and Milton's *Comus* (447) are among the literary works that refer to the shield.

Aegisthus (goat strength). 0072 In Greek mythology, lover of Clytemnestra and murderer of Agamemnon; the son of Thyestes by his daughter, Pelopia. He was suckled by a goat (thus his name) and brought up by Atreus, who had married Pelopia. When Atreus' son Agamemnon left for Troy, Aegisthus became the lover of Clytemnestra, wife of Agamemnon. The two later killed Agamemnon and in turn were killed by Orestes, Agamemnon's son. Aegisthus is one the the main characters in Aeschylus' *Oresteia*, three plays dealing with the myth. He also appears in Sophocles' *Electra* and Seneca's *Agamemnon.*

Aegle (dazzling light). 0073 In Greek mythology, one of the Hesperides, who guarded the golden apples. The name is also that of the youngest daughter of Asclepius and Epine (or Lampetia); a sister of Phaethon, who was transformed into a poplar; and beloved by Theseus when he abandoned Ariadne.

Aegyptus (supine he-goat?). 0074 In Greek mythology, son of Belus and Anchinoë; twin brother of Danaus. Aegyptus conquered the land of Melampodes (black-feet) and named it after himself (Egypt). He fathered 50 sons and compelled Danaus' 50 daughters, against their will, to marry them. He went to Argos, where his sons had pursued their brides, and died there of grief on learning of their deaths at the hands of their wives on their wedding night. A variant of the myth says Aegyptus' only surviving son reconciled him to his brother Danaus, who was the father of the 50 wives. Apollodorus' *Bibliotheca* (Library) tells his tale.

Aeneas (praiseworthy). 0075 In Greek and Roman mythology, Trojan hero appearing in the Latin epic poem the *Aeneid*.

Aeneas was the son of Anchises and the goddess Aphrodite, the brother of Lyrus. He was born on the mountains of Ida and brought up until his fifth year by his brother-in-law Alcathous or, according to a variant myth, by the nymphs of Ida. Though he was a close relative of King Priam of Troy, Aeneas did not enter the war until his cattle had been stolen by the Greek hero Achilles. Priam did not love Aeneas because he knew that Aeneas and his descendants would be the future rulers of the Trojans. At Troy he was highly esteemed for his piety ("pious Aeneas" he is called in *The Aeneid*), prudence, and valor. Often the gods came to his assistance. Thus, Aphrodite and Apollo shielded him when his life was threatened by Diomedes, and Poseidon snatched him out of combat with Achilles.

His escape from Troy is told in several variations. In one he makes his way through the enemy to Ida. In another Aeneas was spared by the Greeks because he had always sought peace and the return of Helen to Greece. A third variation tells how he made his escape during the confusion following the fall of the city. In yet another he is said to have formed a new kingdom out of the wreck of the people and handed it down to his progeny. Several cities on Ida claimed Aeneas as their founder. The myth of Aeneas' emigrating and founding a new kingdom beyond the seas is post-Homeric. His tale, as it is known in Western art and literature, is told in Vergil's *Aeneid* Dante, in *The Divine Comedy*, regards Aeneas as the founder of the Roman Empire. Aeneas is placed by Dante in limbo in company with his ancestress Electra, as well as Hector and Julius Caesar. In British mythology Brutus, the first king of Britain, is the great-grandson of Aeneas. In Shakespeare's *Troilus and Cressida*, the character of Aeneas is not developed, but in *Julius Caesar* (1.2.112) and *Henry VI, Part II* (5.2.62) reference is made to Aeneas' bearing his father, Anchises, on his shoulders. In *Cymbeline* (3.4.60) the hero is "false Aeneas," referring to his desertion of Dido.

0076

Aeneid, The. The Latin epic poem by the Roman poet Vergil (70– 19 B.C.E.) in dactylic hexameters, telling of Aeneas and the founding of a new home for the Trojans.

The poem was left unfinished at Vergil's death. In his will he asked that the work be destroyed, but the Emperor Augustus intervened, and so the poem survived. It is the most influential work of Latin literature and is one of the cornerstones of world literature.

The Aeneid is written in 12 books, or sections. The translation by John Dryden opens with the well-known lines from book 1:

> Arms and the man I sing, who forc'd by fate,
> And haughty Juno's unrelenting hate,
> Expell'd and exil'd, left the Trojan shore.
> Long labors, both by sea and land, he bore,
> And in the doubtful war, before he won
> The Latian realm, and built the destin'd town'
> His banish'd gods restor'd to rites divine,
> And settled sure succession in his line,

> From whence the race of Alban fathers come,
> And the long glories of majestic Rome.
> O Muse! the causes and the crimes relate;
> What goddess was provok'd, and whence her hate;
> For what offense the Queen of Heav'n began
> To persecute so brave, so just a man;
> Involv'd his anxious life in endless cares,
> Expos'd to wants, and hurried into wars!
> Can heav'nly minds such high resentment show,
> Or exercise the spite in human woe?

Book 1: Fate sends Aeneas to Latium to found Rome, but the goddess Juno's hostility delays his success. Juno, seeing him and his Trojans in sight of Italy, bribes Aeolus to raise a storm for their destruction. One Trojan ship is already lost when Neptune learns of the plot and calms the storm. Aeneas escapes, lands in Libya, and rallies his men. Venus appeals to Jupiter, who tells her that Aeneas will be great in Italy. Aeneas' son will found Alba, and his son's sons will found Rome. Juno will eventually relent, and Rome under Augustus will rule the world.

Mercury is sent to secure from Dido, Queen of Libya, a welcome for Aeneas. Meanwhile Aeneas and Achates meet Venus in the forest, where she is disguised as a nymph. Venus tells them Dido's story. Aeneas in reply bewails his own troubles, but Venus interrupts him with promises for success. She then changes before their eyes from nymph into goddess and vanishes. Hidden in a magic mist, Aeneas and Achates approach Carthage. They reach the citadel unobserved and are encouraged when they see scenes from the Trojan War depicted on the city walls. Dido appears and takes her throne. Trojan leaders who Aeneas believed to have died in a storm come to her as supplicants. Ilioneus, their spokesman, tells the story of the storm and asks for help. "If only Aeneas were here!" he says.

Dido echoes his words. The mist scatters and Aeneas appears. He thanks Dido and greets Ilioneus. Dido welcomes Aeneas to Carthage and prepares a festival in his honor. Aeneas sends Achates to summon his son Ascanius and to bring gifts for Dido. Cupid, persuaded by Venus to impersonate Ascanius and inspire Dido with love for Aeneas, arrives with the gifts while the real Ascanius is carried away to Idalia. The night is passed in feasting. After the feast Iopas sings the wonders of the firmament. Dido, bewitched by Cupid, begs Aeneas to tell her his tale of adventure.

Book 2: Aeneas tells his tale. The Greeks, baffled in battle, built a huge wooden horse in which their leaders hide. Pretending to abandon the wooden horse, their fleet sails for Tenedos. The Trojans take the horse into Troy as a trophy, believing the Greeks have given up the war. Sinon, a Greek, brought before King Priam, feigns righteous recriminations against the Greeks. The Trojans sympathize and believe his lies of the wrongs done him by Ulysses (Odysseus in Greek).

Sinon says, "When Greek plans of flight had often been foiled by storms, oracles foretold that only a human sacrifice could purchase their escape."

Chosen for the victim, Sinon had fled. He swears before the Trojans that the wooden horse is an offering to the goddess Pallas (Athena).

"Destroy it and you are lost," he says. "Preserve it in your citadel and your revenge is assured."

Poseidon's serpents strangling Laocoön

Most of the Trojans believe the lying Sinon. Laocoön, a priest, does not, however, and is destroyed when a monster rises from the sea, killing him and his sons. This is taken as a sign by the Trojans that they should take the wooden horse into the city. Cassandra warns them against doing so, but though she was gifted with prophecy, she was also cursed with never being believed.

While Troy sleeps the Greek fleet returns, and Sinon releases the Greeks from the wooden horse. The spirit of the dead Hector warns Aeneas in a dream to flee with the sacred vessels and images of the gods. Panthus then brings news of Sinon's treachery. The city is set aflame by the Greeks. Aeneas heads a group who wish to escape. He and

his followers exchange armor with Greeks slain in the night. The ruse succeeds until they are taken for enemies by their friends. The Greeks rally and the Trojans scatter. At Priam's palace a last stand is made, but Pyrrhus forces the great gates and the defenders are massacred. When Aeneas sees the headless body of Priam, he thinks of his father. Aeneas hastens home but his father, Anchises, refuses to flee. Anchises, seeing a halo about the head of Aeneas' son Ascanius, takes it as an omen and relents. During the escape Creusa, the wife of Aeneas, is lost. He seeks her. Her dead spirit appears to him and tells him to flee.

Book 3. In obedience to oracles the Trojans build a fleet and sail to Thrace. Seeking to found a city, they are warned away by the ghost of Polydorus and visit Anius in Ortygia. Apollo promises Aeneas and his descendants worldwide empire if they return to "the ancient motherland" of Troy, which Anchises says is Crete. The Trojans reach Crete, only to be thwarted again. Drought and plague interrupt this second attempt to found a city. On the point of returning to ask Apollo for a clearer sign, Aeneas is told by the gods of Troy in a dream that the true home of the

Venus (after Titian)

Trojans is Italy. Landing in the Strophades, the Trojans unwittingly wrong the Harpies, whose queen, Celaeno, threatens them with a famine. Panic-stricken, the Trojans coast along to Actium, where they celebrate their national games. They go to Buthrotum, and on a voyage from Dyrrhachium they get their first glimpse of Italy. They land and make offering to Juno, then travel along the coast until they see Mount Aetna. The book ends with the death of Anchises at Drepanum.

Book 4: Dido has fallen in love with Aeneas. She opens her heart to her sister Anna. Dido would yield except for her promised loyalty to her dead husband, Sychaeus. Anna pleads for Aeneas, and Dido, half yielding, sacrifices to the marriage gods. Venus reappears and lies to Juno (goddess of marriage) that she will let Aeneas marry Dido and he will be made king of Carthage. At a hunt Juno sends a storm, and the lovers shelter in a cave where they make love and exchange vows. Jupiter sends Mercury to remind Aeneas of his mission to found a new home for the Trojans in Italy. Aeneas, terrified by the message, prepares to leave. Dido pleads with him, but he says he must obey the gods. In utter misery Dido, on pretext of burning all of Aeneas' love gifts, prepares a pyre and summons a sorceress. Her preparations complete, she utters a lament. Mercury repeats his warning to Aeneas, who sets sail. Daybreak reveals his flight, and Dido, cursing her betrayer, stabs herself.

Book 5: Aeneas, unaware of Dido's suicide, sails away to Acestes in Sicily. He prepares funeral games to mark Anchises' death. Offerings are paid to the spirit of his dead father. Sicilians and Trojans assemble for the first contest, a boat race. Juno schemes to destroy the Trojan fleet while the games are being held. She inflicts madness on the Trojan matrons, who are not allowed to be present at the games, and they set the ships aflame. Jupiter sends rain and saves all but four of the ships, and the Trojans depart. Venus prevails on Neptune, god of the sea, to grant the Trojans a safe journey in return for the death of the helmsman, Palinurus, who is drowned.

Book 6: The Trojans arrive at Cumae. Aeneas visits the Sibyl's shrine. After prayer and sacrifice to Apollo, he asks permission to enter the underworld to visit his father. He must first pluck the Golden Bough. Vergil writes (MacKay's translation):

O sprung of gods' blood, child of Anchises of Troy, easy is the descent into hell; all night and day the gate of dark Dis stands open; but to recall thy steps and issue to upper air, this is the task, this the burden. Some few of gods' lineage have availed, such as Jupiter's gracious favor or virtue's ardor had up-

borne to heaven. Midway all is muffled in forest, and the black sliding coils of Cocytus circle it round. Yet if thy soul is so passionate and so desirous twice to float across the Stygian lake, twice to see dark Tartarus, and thy pleasure is to plunge into the mad task, learn what must first be accomplished. Hidden in a shady tree is a bough with leafage and pliant shoot all of gold, consecrate to nether Juno, wrapped in the depth of woodland and shut in by dim dusky vales. But to him only who first has plucked the golden-tressed fruitage from the tree is it given to enter the hidden places of the earth. This has beautiful Proserpine ordained to be borne to her for her proper gift. The first torn away, a second fills the place with gold, and the spray burgeons with even such ore again. So let thine eyes trace it home, and thine hand pluck it duly when found; for lightly and unreluctant will it follow if thine is fate's summons; else will no strength of thine avail to conquer it nor hard steel to cut it away.

Aeneas sees all of the sights of the underworld and visits his father, Anchises, who explains to him the mystery of the Transmigration of Souls; and the book closes with the revelation to Aeneas of the future greatness of Rome. Aeneas then leaves through the Ivory Gate and sails to Caieta.

Book 7: Passing Caieta and Circeii, Aeneas sails up the Tiber. An embassy is sent to the Latin capital by the Trojans. Latinus offers peace to the Trojans, and to Aeneas his daughter's hand. (All of this was to fulfill the oracles.) Juno again intervenes and summons the demon Alecto, who first excites Amata then Turnus against the peace. War begins. On the side of the Latins are the hero Turnus and the heroine Camilla.

Book 8: The war now started, Turnus sends to Diomedes for help, while Aeneas goes to ask aid of Evander and the Tuscans. Evander receives him kindly, furnishes him with men and sends his son Pallas with him. Vulcan, at the request of Venus, makes arms for her son Aeneas that portray the future greatness of Rome.

Book 9: Turnus takes advantage of Aeneas' absence to set some ships on fire, but they turn into sea nymphs. Turnus then attacks the Trojan camp. Nisus and Euryalus are sent to recall Aeneas.

Book 10: Jupiter calls a council of the gods and forbids them to enter into the battle. Aeneas returns, and the fighting becomes bitter. Turnus kills Pallas; Aeneas kills Lausus and Mezentius.

Book 11: Aeneas erects a trophy of the spoils of Mezentius. A truce is granted for the burying of the dead. The body of Pallas is sent home. Latinus then calls a council to offer peace to Aeneas. Turnus says he will meet Aeneas in single combat. Camilla is killed. The Latins are defeated, and Turnus, learning of the news, hurries to the city, closely followed by Aeneas.

Book 12: Turnus realizes that he must now redeem his promise to meet Aeneas in single combat. The challenge is sent, and the two make ready. Juno tells the nymph Juturna to aid her brother Turnus in the battle. The truce is broken; Aeneas is wounded but is healed by Venus. In the ensuing combat Aeneas kills Turnus:

> He rais'd his arm aloft, and, at the word,
> Deep in his bosom drove the shining sword.
> The streaming blood distained his arms around,
> And the disdainful soul came rushing thro' the wound.

Vergil's great poem was read during the Middle Ages and was consulted as a book of magic, because the poet had the reputation of being a magician. Dante chose Vergil as his guide through hell and purgatory in *The Divine Comedy*. *The Aeneid* influenced Spenser, Tasso, and Milton. The translation by John Dryden was published in 1697 and has become an English classic. The first translation of *The Aeneid* into English verse was by Gavin Douglas, Bishop of Dunkeld in Scotland, published in 1553. Henry, earl of Surrey, published his version in 1557, and William Morris's version appeared in 1876.

In musical settings of *The Aeneid*, the English composer Henry Purcell wrote *Dido and Aeneas* (1689/90) for performance in a girls' school. In 1782 German composer Joseph Martin Kraus (1756–1792) wrote *Aeneaus i Carthago*, which was performed in 1799, some years after the composer's death. The most important operatic version is that of the French Romantic composer Hector Berlioz, which was completed in 1858 in two parts and called *The Trojans*.

Though the *Aeneid* has generally been respected, the English Romantics disliked the work. Samuel Taylor Coleridge wrote: "If you take from Vergil his diction and metre, what do you leave him?" Percy Bysshe Shelley preferred Lucan, and Lord Byron hated Vergil's work intensely.

Aengus. 0077 In Celtic mythology, son of Dagda, god of love and beauty, who had a golden harp. His kisses became birds that hovered invisibly over young men and women, whispering thoughts of love in their ears. In James Joyce's novel *Ulysses* the god is called Aengus of the Birds.

Variant spellings: Angus, Oengus.

Aeolus 0078 (earth destroyer?). In Greek mythology, the god of the winds; son of Hellen and the nymph Ortheis; married to Enarete; father of seven sons, Athamas, Cretheus, Deion, Macareus, Perieres, Salmoneus, and Sisyphus, and seven daughters, Alcyone, Arne, Calyce, Canale, Peisidice, Perimele, and Tanagra, brother of Xuthus and Dorus. In Homer's *Odyssey* (book 10) Aeolus gives Odysseus the contrary winds tied up in a bag, but the sailors let them out, and the ship is blown off course. On his Aeolian island, floating in the far west, its steep cliff encircled by a brazen wall, Aeolus lived in unbroken bliss with his wife and his sons and daughters, whom he wedded to one another. Aeolus also appears in Vergil's *Aeneid* (book 1) and Ovid's *Metamorphoses* (book 11). Aeolus is called Hippotades in some accounts.

Aequalitas 0079 (justly). In Roman mythology, the personification of equity or fairness, as opposed to justice by the letter of the law. Aequalitas was often portrayed as a young woman holding a pair of scales in her left hand.

Aerope 0080 (sky-face). In Greek mythology, wife of Atreus; daughter of Catreus of Crete. She was given by her father to Nauplius to be sold abroad. She married Atreus and bore him Agamemnon and Menelaus, and possibly Anaxibia and Pleisthenes. Aerope was thrown into the sea by Atreus for her adultery with his brother Thyestes.

Aesacus 0081 (myrtle branch). In Greek mythology, son of King Priam of Troy and Arisbe (or Alexiroe); he learned the art of interpreting dreams from his maternal grandfather, Merops. Priam consulted Aesacus about Hecuba's bad dreams prior to the birth of Paris. Aesacus' advice was to have the child killed because he would bring about the destruction of Troy. Aesacus married the nymph Asterope (or Hesperia). When he pursued her, she threw herself into the sea and was changed into a bird. In despair Aesacus also threw himself into the sea and was changed into a diver bird (cormorant). Ovid's *Metamorphoses* (book 11) and Apollodorus' *Bibliotheca* (Library) (3.12.5) tell the story.

Aeshma. 0082 In Persian mythology, archdemon who is the spirit of anger, violence, and devastation, "occasioning trouble by contests, and causing an increase in slaughter." He is the same as the demon Asmodeus who appears in the Book of Tobit (3:8) in the Old Testament Apocrypha.

Variant spelling: Aeshm.

0083

Aesir (god). In Norse mythology, a race of gods and goddesses under the leadership of Odin. They were Balder, Baugi, Bragi, Forsetl, Frey, Heimdal, Hodur, Hoeni, Loki, Njord, Thor, Vilur, Vali, and Vidar. Another group of deities, called Vanir, predated the Aesir. The Vanir group included Boda, Bil, Eir, Fimila, Fjorgyn, Freya, Frigga, Frimla, Fulla, Gefjon, Gerda, Gna, Hnossa, Horn, Jord, Nanna, Saga, Sit, Siguna, Skadi, and Vanadis. The two groups fought but settled their disagreements, all creating the dwarf Kvasir, from whose blood mead was made.

The Frogs Desiring a King

0084

Aesopic fables. Short didactic tales, often with animal characters, ascribed to Aesop, a Phrygian slave who lived in the sixth century B.C.E.

Whether Aesop actually lived is still debated by some scholars, though he is mentioned in the works of Herodotus, Aristophanes, and Plato. He is believed to have been the slave of a man named Iadmon. Tradition says he was a hunchback, born dumb but given the gift of speech by the goddess Isis for his great devotion to her cult. His ability to tell tales or fables won him his freedom, and according to various accounts, he became counselor to Solon and Croesus. His good fortune, however, was short-lived. He was falsely accused and convicted of theft by the citizens of Delphi, who as punishment threw him over a cliff to his death. A plague immediately swept over the city. The citizens, realizing their guilt, offered "blood money" to atone for the murder. Herodotus, in his *History of the Persian Wars* (book 2), says that Iadmon, grandson of the former Iadmon, "received the compensation. Aesop therefore must certainly have been the former Iadmon's slave."

However, the fame of Aesop continued. Tradition says he returned to life to fight at the battle of Thermopylae. A statue was erected to him in Athens some two hundred years after his death. It was placed before the statues of the Seven Sages. One Attic vase from about 450 B.C.E. portrays the fabulist listening to a fox.

One of the most interesting legends in the life of Aesop concerns his telling of the fable *The Frogs Desiring a King* to a mob that was threatening to kill the tyrant Pisistratus, the moral of the fable being "Let well enough alone!" The populace knew the evils of Pisistratus but did not know how evil his successor would be. The fable is typical in that one of the main ingredients of many fables is their conservative nature. Often the moral is one of leaving well enough alone or supporting the status quo. This is somewhat ironic because in early times the fable was used to castigate ruling authorities.

About 300 B.C.E. Demetrius Phalereus collected all of the fables he could find under the title of *Assemblies of Aesopic Tales*. This collection, running to about 200 fables, was used as the basis for a version in Latin verse by Phaedrus or Phaeder in the first century C.E. Like Aesop, Phaedrus also was a slave, freed during the reign of Augustus or Tiberius. Under Tiberius he published two books of his fables. His style was ironic, ridiculing the emperor and his minister, Sejanus. After the death of Sejanus, Phaedrus published a third book of fables, and a fourth and fifth were added in his later years. Phaedrus added many fables of his own to the Aesopic collection, as well as others collected from various sources.

Babrius, believed to have lived in the second century C.E., wrote ten books in Greek called *Aesop's Fables in Verse*. They were lost, however, until 1842, when 123 of the fables were discovered in the monastery at Mount Athos. An additional 95 were added in 1857, though scholars have debated how genuine the fables actually were. The Latin version of Phaedrus, therefore, was the one that was popular during the Middle Ages, although it was not credited to Phaedrus, but to a fictional person named Romulus. By the time *Romulus' Aesop* was in circulation, many tales from various sources, such as those from the East, had come to be credited to Aesop.

The power of the fables to hold the attention of audiences throughout the ages attests to their universal appeal. They are simple, direct, and well told. These characteristics have made them particularly popular with illustrators. The first English edition of Aesop, translated by Caxton from a French version, was published in 1484. By the end of the 15th century there were more than 20 different illustrated editions in Europe. Among the most famous are those of Mondovi, Ulm, and Verona, all published between 1476 and 1479. Among the best known later illustrators are Thomas Bewick (1784), Gustave Doré (1868), Walter Crane (1886), Richard Heighway (1894), Arthur Rackham (1916), Alexander Calder (1931), Antonio Frasconi (1953), and Joseph Low (1963).

Although the fables would seem to be ideal for dramatic musical settings, very few composers have attempted to deal with them. John Whitaker wrote music for English versions of Aesop's fables, and another English composer, W. H. Reed, wrote an orchestral work, *Aesop's Fables*. In 1931 the German composer Werner Egk composed *Der Löwe und die Maus* (*The Lion and the Mouse*) for narrator, chorus, and orchestra. It was written especially for radio. Egk also wrote *Moralities*, using three Aesop fables, with a text by W. H. Auden.

Aethra and Theseus

0085

Aethra (bright sky). In Greek mythology, mother of Theseus by Aegeus or, according to another account, by Poseidon. Homer mentions her as a servant to Helen at Troy, but later Greek myth adds that when the Dioscuri took Aphidnae and set free their sister, whom Theseus had carried off, they brought Aethra to Sparta as a slave. She then accompanied Helen to Troy. When the city fell, she brought her grandsons Acamas and Demophon back to Athens. Hyginus' *Fabulae* (myths, 37) tells her story.

0086

Afanasiev, Alexander Nikolaievitch. 1826–1871. Russian folklorist, compiler of *Russian Folktales* (1855–1863), published in eight parts. Afanasiev's work, which has achieved the status of a Russian classic, was influenced by the Grimms' collection of German folktales. Based partly on oral sources, Afanasiev's work also depended on published sources, so many present-day scholars dismiss his work as being "too literary" and lacking research from primary sources. Aside from this major collection, Afanasiev also published *Russian Popular Legends* (1860), which was banned by the Russian Orthodox church as well as the government because it used "vulgar" words and was critical of both church and state.

Variant spellings: Afanasyeu, Afanasyeff.

0087

Af and Hemah (anger and wrath). In Jewish folklore, two angels created at the beginning of the world to execute God's will.

0088

Afra, St. (dust). Fourth century? In Christian legend, martyr, patron saint of Augsburg, Germany. Invoked by penitent women. Feast, 5 August.

Afra was a common whore who ran a house of pleasure, even though she was the daughter of St. Hilaria. She was assisted in her work by three girls, Digna, Eunomia, and Eutropia. One day Narcissus, a Christian priest fleeing from the pagan authorities, came to her house for protection. He talked with the girls and converted them to Christianity. When the police came, all of them were arrested. Afra, who was brought before a judge who had once bought her favors, was sentenced to death by burning. As she prayed, angels bore her soul to heaven.

Medieval Christian art portrays St. Afra in a boiling caldron or surrounded by flames. Sometimes she is suspended from a tree and beaten or bound to a tree and burned.

0089

Agama. In Mahayana Buddhism, a term used for the collection of sacred writings, roughly equivalent to the Nikaya collection of Theravada Buddhism, containing the discourses of Buddha on general topics.

Agamemnon (very resolute). In Greek mythology, king of Mycenae and Argos; son of Atreus and Aerope; married to Clytemnestra; father of Chrysothemis, Electra, Iphigeneia, Iphianassa, and Orestes, father of Chryses by his slave Chryseis, and father of Pelops and Teledamas by Cassandra; and brother of Menelaus. Agamemnon was commander of the Greek forces in the Trojan War. Driven from Mycenae after the murder of Atreus by Atreus' brother Thyestes, Agamemnon and Menelaus fled to Sparta, where King Tynadaeos gave them his daughters: Clytemnestra to Agamemnon and Helen to Menelaus. Menelaus inherited Tynadaeos' kingdom, and Agamemnon drove out his uncle Thyestes from Mycenae; and as king he extended the country's boundaries. According to Homer's *Iliad*, Agamemnon, though vain and arrogant, was chosen to lead the Greek expedition to rescue his sister-in-law Helen, who had been abducted by Paris. The expedition was stalled at Aulis because Agamemnon had offended Artemis. Calchas, a soothsayer, told Agamemnon that the goddess could be appeased only by the sacrifice of Agamemnon's daughter Iphigenia (or Iphianassa). Agamemnon tricked his wife, Clytemnestra, into sending Iphigenia to Aulis by telling her that Iphigenia was to be married to Achilles. But at Aulis Iphigenia was sacrificed despite the protest of Clytemnestra. Some accounts say that Artemis spared Iphigenia when the goddess beheld the girl's innocence.

Agamemnon displayed further arrogance and invited another plague on the expedition when he refused to accept a ransom from a priest of Apollo, Chryses, who wanted to redeem his daughter Chryseis, who had been given to Agamemnon as a war prize. Agamemnon then took Briseis, Achilles' mistress. In response Achilles laid down his arms and withdrew from the war, though he eventually relented and became the major hero of the Trojan War.

After the Greek victory at Troy, Agamemnon brought home his spoils, including the captive princess Cassandra, who had warned him that he would be killed by his wife. True to the curse of Cassandra (to be always right and never believed), he ignored her warning. His wife, Clytemnestra, prepared a welcoming bath of purification. When he stepped from the bath, she wrapped him in a binding garment, and her lover, Aegisthus, stabbed Agamemnon while Clytemnestra killed Cassandra.

Agamemnon was worshiped by the Greeks as a hero. He appears in Homer's *Iliad* and *Odyssey* (book 4); Aeschylus' *Agamemnon* and *Choephoroe*, Euripides *Electra*, *Iphigenia in Aulis*, *Iphigenia in Tauris*, and *Orestes*; Sophocles *Electra* and *Ajax*; Vergil's *Aeneid* (book 6); Ovid's *Metamorphoses* (book 12); Seneca's *Agamemnon*; and a host of modern works such as T. S. Eliot's *The Family Reunion*, based on the Greek plays; Eugene O'Neill's *Mourning Becomes Electra*; Sartre's *Les Mouches* (The Flies); and works by Giraudoux, Robinson Jeffers, Hofmannsthal, Racine, Shakespeare, and Tennyson.

Agaran. In Arthurian legend, nephew of a hermit encountered by Lancelot in his quest for the Holy Grail.

Agastya (mountain thrower). Legendary Indian sage, author of several hymns in the *Rig-Veda*, the sacred collection of hymns.

In the Hindu epic poem *The Ramayana*, Agastya lived in a hermitage on Mount Kunjara, situated in a most beautiful country to the south of the Vindhya Mountains. He was the chief of the hermits of the South, keeping the Rakshasas, demonic beings who infested the region, under control. Once he was challenged by a Rakshasa named Vatapi, who had taken the form of a ram. Agastya attacked him and ate him up. When Vatapi's brother Ilvala tried to avenge the death, he too was killed by Agastya.

Rama, the hero of *The Ramayana*, visited Agastya with his wife, Sita. The sage received them with great kindness, becoming Rama's friend, adviser, and protector. He gave Rama the bow of the god Vishnu, which the hero used in regaining his kingdom. When Rama was restored, Agastya accompanied him to his capital, Ayodhya.

The longer Hindu epic poem, *The Mahabharata*, relates the legend of the creation of Agastya's wife, Lopamudra. Once Agastya saw a vision of his ancestors suspended by their heels in a pit. He was told by them that they could only be rescued if he had a son. The problem was that Agastya was not married and had no mistress. He then formed a girl out of the most graceful parts of various animals. He took her secretly into the palace of the king of Vidarbha, where she grew up as the daughter of the king. When she came of age, Agastya asked for her in marriage. The king granted the wish even though he disliked Agastya.

Agastya is sometimes called "Ocean Drinker" in reference to the legend that he once drank an entire ocean after it offended him. Another explanation for the title is that he offered his aid to the gods in their battle with the Daityas (giants), who had taken refuge in the ocean.

Agatha, St. (good woman). Third century? In Christian legend, martyr, patron saint of bell founders, girdlers, jewelers, malsters, wet nurses, weavers, and shepherdesses. Invoked against earthquake, fire, lightning, storm, sterility, wolves, and diseases of the breast. Feast, 5 February.

There are many accounts of the saint's life in both Latin and Greek; these influenced the version in *The Golden Legend*, a collection of saints' lives written in the 13th century by Jacobus de Voragine.

Agatha was loved by the Roman consul Quintian, but she wanted to remain a virgin. When Quintian found out she was a Christian, he brought her up on charges. She was handed over to a courtesan, Aphrodisia (or Frondisia), who ran a brothel with her six daughters. All of Aphrodisia's attempts to turn Agatha into a whore failed. When she reported her failure to Quintian, he became so angry that he had Agatha tortured. Her breasts were crushed and then cut off. At night, however, St. Peter and an angel visited her in prison and healed her wounds with "celestial ointment" and then "vanished from her sight."

The next day, when Quintian saw that Agatha's wounds were healed, he ordered that the girl be rolled over hot coals. When this was done, an earthquake shook the city, and the people blamed it on Quintian for mistreating Agatha. Finally, after more gruesome torture the saint asked God to free her spirit, and God answered her plea.

The cult of St. Agatha goes back to the first centuries of Christianity. Her name occurs on a calendar of saints in Carthage written about the sixth century, and she is named in the old Latin Mass. Venantius Fortunatus, the early Christian poet, has a hymn in her honor. In Christian art she is shown in the procession of saints at Sant' Apollinare Nuovo in Ravenna, Italy. One of her attributes, her breasts (during the Middle Ages there were at least six breasts claimed as relics by various churches), were mistaken for loaves of bread in some art works, resulting in the blessing of bread on her feast day. In Sicily she is invoked against the outbreak of fire because, according to her legend, she saved Catania from destruction when Mount Etna erupted. The people took the veil that covered her body and carried it on a spear in procession. As a result of the rite the flames from the eruption stopped spreading.

Sebastiano del Piombo, the 16th-century Italian artist, painted *The Martyrdom of St. Agatha*, taking the removal of her breasts by pincers for his subject. However, the artist seems to be more concerned with the erotic connotations of the exposed breasts than with the saint's martyrdom.

0094

Agathodaemon (good demon). In Greek mythology, a good spirit of the cornfields and vineyards. Liba-

tions of unmixed wine were made to the spirit at meals. In Greek art Agathodaemon was portrayed as a youth holding a horn of plenty and a bowl in one hand, and in the other a poppy and ears of corn.

0095

Agenor. In Greek mythology, a hero, son of Antenor by Theano, a priestess of Athena; brother of Acamas, Achelous, Coon, Crino, Demolem, Glaucus, Helicaon, Iphidamas, Laocoön, Laodamas, Lycam, Polybus, and Polydamas; half-brother of Pedaeus; father of Echeclus. Agenor was one of the bravest heroes of Troy. In Homer's *Iliad* (book 11) he leads the Trojans in storming the Greek entrenchments, and rescues Hector when he is thrown down by Ajax. When he enters into battle with Achilles, he is saved by Apollo. In post-Homeric myth Agenor is killed by Neoptolemus, the son of Achilles. Agenor is also the name of a son of the sea god Poseidon and Libya; king of Phoenicia; twin brother of Belus; married to Telephassa (or Argiore); and father of Cadmus, Cilix, Demodoce, Electra, Europa, Phineus, Phoenix, and Thasus.

0096

Aglaia (bright). In Greek mythology, daughter of Zeus and Eurynome; one of the three Graces. The others were Euphrosyne (joy) and Thalia (blood of life). In some accounts Aglaia is said to be the wife of Hephaestus.

0097

Aglookik. In Eskimo mythology, beneficent spirit who lives under the ice and helps hunters find game.

0098

Agnes of Montepulciano, St. (pure, chaste). 1268–1317. In Christian legend, Dominican abbess. Feast, 20 April.

Agnes was placed in a nunnery at the age of 9 and was made abbess of a new convent at Procino when she was 15 years old. For 15 years she slept on the ground, using a stone pillow, and lived on bread and water until she nearly died and had to "diminish her austerities on account of her health," according to one account. The citizens of her town, Montepulciano, promised to build a convent for Agnes if she would return to them. They tore down some brothels and constructed the convent. When Agnes arrived, she was made the prioress, a position she held until her death. Numerous miracles are recorded in her later life. One tells of how she had a vision in which an angel held her under an olive tree and offered her a cup, saying, "Drink this chalice, spouse of Christ: the Lord Jesus drank it for you." At 49 she died, after telling her nuns she was going to her "spouse," Jesus Christ.

Another saint, Catherine of Siena, visited her tomb, as did Emperor Charles IV. When St. Catherine visited the shrine she stooped to kiss the feet of the "incorrupt body," and the foot "lifted itself to meet her lips," according to legend.

In Christian art the scene of the foot rising is often portrayed. When St. Agnes is shown alone, she is dressed as a Dominican abbess, with white habit and black mantle and with a lamb (for her purity), a lily and a book. Often she is shown gazing on the cross, since she was devoted to the Passion of Christ.

0099

Agnes, St. (pure, chaste). Fourth century C.E. In Christian legend, martyr. One of the Four Great Virgin Martyrs of the Latin, or Western, church; patron saint of betrothed couples, gardeners, and virgins. Invoked to preserve chastity. Feast, 21 January.

Agnes is one of the most popular saints in Christian legend. Her life is discussed by St. Ambrose, who wrote a hymn in her honor, and by St. Augustine, who wrote that she died a virgin martyr at the age of 13. The main source of her legend, however, comes from the early Christian poet Prudentius. *The Golden Legend*, a collection of saints' lives written in the 13th century by Jacobus de Voragine used Prudentius, among others, as a source.

Agnes was loved by a pagan Roman, whose advances she blocked by telling him she was in love with another (Christ) who was better than he. Out of jealousy the young man denounced Agnes as a Christian, and she was sent to a brothel as punishment. When she arrived, her clothes were removed, but God "gave her such grace that the hairs of her head became so long that they covered her body to the feet, so that her body was not seen," according to *The Golden Legend*. God sent an angel who defended her chastity against all assaults from customers of the house. When one man tried to rape her, the devil "took him by the throat and strangled him" and he fell dead.

In the end Agnes was raped and finally martyred, but the various accounts do not agree on how she met her death. *The Golden Legend* says a "sword was put in her body." St. Ambrose, however, says she "bent her neck," meaning she was decapitated. Pope Damascus says she was burned alive. In Rome on her feast two white lambs are offered at the sanctuary rails in her church while a hymn is sung in her honor. The wool from the lambs is used to weave the pallium, part of the vestments worn by archbishops in the Latin Church. The custom may have been derived from the pun on her name; lamb in Latin is *agnus*.

Taking the folk belief that on the saint's eve a young girl could see her future husband, John Keats wrote a magnificent poem, *The Eve of St. Agnes* (1819), a work rich in romantic celebration of erotic love and fantasy. Alfred Lord Tennyson also used the saint in his poem *St. Agnes Eve*, though he attempted to treat the subject in a different manner. José de Ribera, the 17th-century Spanish artist, painted his *St. Agnes*, showing a young girl on her knees, crossing her breasts in modesty, while her long hair and drapery, held by an angel, cover the rest of her body.

0100

Agneyastra. In Hindu mythology, a fire weapon given to Agnivesa, the son of Agni, the fire god.

Agni

0101

Agni (fire). In Hindu mythology, the fire god. In the sacred Indian collection of hymns, the *Rig-Veda*, Agni has more hymns addressed to him than has any other god except the storm god, Indra. Agni is called the messenger and mediator between heaven and earth, announcing to the gods the hymns sung to them and conveying offerings of their worshipers. He invited the worshipers by his crackling flames, bringing fire down on the sacrifice.

The Hindu epic poem *The Mahabharata* tells how Agni, having devoured too many offerings, lost his power. To regain his strength he wanted to consume a whole forest. At first Indra prevented him, but eventually Agni tricked Indra and accomplished his task. In another Hindu epic, *The Ramayama*, Agni is the father of Nila, who aids the hero Rama.

Agni is portrayed as a red man with three legs, seven arms, and dark eyes, eyebrows, and hair. He rides a ram, wears a *yajñopavita* (a Brahmanical thread) and a garland of fruit. Fire issues from his mouth and seven streams of glory radiate from his body.

Gustav Holst wrote *Hymn to Agni*, based on one hymn in the *Rig-Veda*. The work is scored for male chorus and orchestra.

Agni is also called Vahni (he who receives the burnt offerings); Brihaspati (lord of sacred speech) in his role as creative force; Vitihotra (he who sanctifies the worshiper); Dhananjaya (he who destroys riches); Kivalana (he who burns); Dhumektu (he whose sign is smoke); Chagaratha (he who rides on a ram), referring to his mount; Saptajihva (he who has seven tongues); Pavaka (the purifier); and Grihapati, when referring to household fire.

Associated with Agni are the Bhrigus (roasters or consumers), spirits who nourish a fire and are the makers of chariots. Also associated with Agni is Kravyad, the fire that consumes bodies on a funeral pyre. In Hindu folklore today a *kravyad* is a flesh-eating goblin or any carnivorous animal.

0102
Agove Minoire. In Haitian voodoo, a female loa (deified spirit of the dead) who guards groves; symbolized by a phallus carved from wood. Sometimes her symbol is a mirror.

0103
Agramante. In the Charlemagne cycle of legends, a king of Africa who invaded France to avenge the death of his father Troyano. He besieged Paris but was defeated and later killed by Roland (Orlando). He appears in Bolardo's *Orlando Innamorato* and Ariosto's *Orlando Furioso*.

0104
Agrat bat Mahalath. In Jewish mythology, demoness queen who travels about in a chariot causing harm. Her evil actions are confined to the eve of the Sabbath and Wednesdays. Medieval Jewish legend held that she would be destroyed when the era of the Messiah arrived.

0105
Agretes. In Arthurian legend associated with the Holy Grail, a king of Camelot who pretended to be a Christian but persecuted his people when they were converted to Christianity. As punishment he went insane and died.

0106
Agwé. In Haitian voodoo, sea god, married to Erzulie, who as his wife is called La Sirène and is portrayed as a mermaid. Agwé's *vévé*, or symbol, is a large sailboat, and his sacred colors are blue and white. With the blending of voodoo and Christian mythologies in Haiti, Agwé is often identified with St. Ulrich, a 10th century bishop whose symbol is a fish. The Barque d'Agwé is a specially constructed raft on which offerings to Agwé are placed and then sent out to sea. Agwé's home, Zilet en bas de l'eau (island below the sea), is where the souls of the dead live.

Variant spellings: **Agoué, Agoueh R Oyo, Aguet.**

0107
Aharaigichi. In the mythology of the Abipone Indians of South America, principal god, identified with the Pleiades.

Martin Dobrizhoffer, a Jesuit priest in the 18th century, spent 18 years as a missionary in Paraguay. He wrote of the beliefs of the Abipone in his book *History of the Abipones*, which both praises and condemns the Indians:

> I said that the Abipones were commendable for their wit and strength of mind, but ashamed of my too hasty praise, I retract my words and pronounce them fools, idiots, and madmen. Lo! this is the proof of their insanity! They are unacquainted with God, and with the very name of God, yet they affectionately salute the evil spirit, whom they call *Aharaigichi*, or *Queevet*, with the title of grandfather, *Groaperikie*. Him they declare to be their grandfather, and that of the Spaniards, but with this difference, that to the latter he gives gold and silver and fine clothes, but to them he transmits valour.

Dobrizhoffer then goes on to inform his readers that the constellation Pleiades is believed to be closely connected with Aharaigichi, and when it "disappears at certain periods from the sky of South America . . . they [the Indians] suppose that their grandfather is sick" and is going to die. When the stars return again in May, the Indians "with joyful shouts, and the festive sound of pipes and trumpets," congratulate him on the "recovery of his health."

0108
Ahasuerus. In medieval Christian legend, one of the names given to the Wandering Jew. The name is derived from the king of the Medes and Persians mentioned in the Old Testament book of Esther, who in turn is derived from Xerxes I (485–464 B.C.E.).

0109
Ahl-at-tral. In Arabic and Islamic mythology, demons who live beneath the Sahara Desert and appear

as whirling sandstorms, drying up the wells before caravans arrive.

Ahmad. In Islamic legend, the name Jesus Christ called Muhammad when he foretold the Prophet's coming. The Koran (sura 61) says: "And remember when Jesus the son of Mary said, 'O children of Israel! of a truth I am God's Apostle to you to confirm the law which was given before me, and to announce an apostle that shall come after me, whoso name shall be Ahmad.'"

0110

Ahoeitu (day god). In Polynesian mythology, Tongan culture hero, son of the sky god Eitumatupua and his wife, the worm Ilaheva. Born on the the earth, Ahoeitu decided to ascend to the sky to visit his father. However, his heavenly brothers murdered him, cutting him into pieces and eating them. When his father, Eitumatupua, learned what had happened, he ordered his sons to vomit up Ahoeitu. They obeyed, and Eitumatupua restored his son to life with some magic herbs and sent him to rule Tonga.

0111

Ah Puch (to melt, to dissolve, to spoil). In Mayan mythology, god of death, the destroyer, ruler of the lowest of the nine underworlds (Hunhau), where he is chief demon. Ah Puch was the patron god of the number 10. He was associated with three Mayan symbols of death: the dog, the Moan bird, and the owl.

0112

In ancient Mayan mythology Ah Puch was associated with the god of war. Sometimes Ah Puch is identified by scholars with God A of the Mayan letter gods. Today Ah Puch is known in the folklore of the Mayans as Yum Cimil (lord of death). He is believed to prowl about, causing sickness and death. In Mayan art Ah Puch is portrayed with a skull-like head and often a bloated body with decaying flesh. He holds in his hands a skull, symbol of death.

Variant spellings: Ahpuch, Ahal Puh, Ah-Puchah.

Ah Raxá Lac (the lord of the green plate). In Mayan mythology, an earth god, mentioned in the *Popol Vuh*, sacred book of the ancient Quiché Maya of Guatemala.

0113

Ah Raxa Tzel (the lord of the green gourd or blue bowl). In Mayan mythology, a sky god or personification of the sky, mentioned in the sacred book of the ancient Quiché Maya of Guatemala. The name

0114

of the god reflects the belief that the sky was an inverted bowl or gourd.

Ahriman

Ahriman. In Persian mythology, the evil spirit, opposed to the good creator god, Ahura Mazda; in the end Ahriman will be destroyed by the forces of good.

0115

Though the prophet Zarathustra raised Ahura Mazda to the major rank of god and made Ahriman a lesser deity, in earlier Persian mythology both gods were equals and brothers, sons of the great god of time-space, Zurvan. When the two were conceived, Zurvan decided that whichever came to him first would be made king. When the evil Ahriman heard this in his mother's womb, he ripped it open, emerged, and approached his father.

"Who are you?" Zurvan asked.

"I am your son, Ahura Mazda," the evil Ahriman replied.

"Ahura Mazda is light, and you are black and stinking," Zurvan declared.

While they were speaking, Ahura Mazda came out of his mother's womb. Zurvan immediately recognized him and made him king.

"Did you not vow that to whichever of your sons should come first you would give the kingdom?" Ahriman complained.

"You false and wicked one," Zurvan replied, "the kingdom shall be given to you for nine thousand years, but Ahura Mazda is nevertheless king over you and will triumph after that time."

Ahura Mazda then created the heavens and the earth and all beautiful things, but Ahriman created demons, snakes, and all evil.

Ahriman is identified with Iblis, the devil in Islamic mythology. In some works Ahriman, rather than the snake of biblical lore, is pictured as an old man offering Adam and Eve the fatal fruit. One early Persian sculpture portrays Ahura Mazda riding on horseback trampling on Ahriman's snake-covered head.

Variant spellings: Angra Mainyu, Anra Mainyu, Aharman.

0116

Ahtoltecat. In Mayan mythology, silversmith god of the Quiché Maya of Guatemala, patron of the Toltecs, skilled silversmiths.

0117

Ahulane. In Mayan mythology, archer god, portrayed holding an arrow. Ahulane was worshiped on the island of Cozumel, where his cult was connected with warfare, as were those of Ah Chuy Kay, the fire destroyer; Hun Pic Tok, who carried 8,000 spears; Kac-u-Pacat, who carried a shield of fire; and Ah Cun Can, the serpent charmer. Many of these names may have a purely symbolic connection with war and may not be the names of separate deities.

0118

Ahura Mazda. In Persian mythology, good creator god, the wise lord, later called Ohrmazd (Ormuzd). Ahura Mazda is continually battling the evil spirit Ahriman; in the end Ahura Mazda and the forces of goodness will prevail over Ahriman.

According to the prophet Zarathustra, Ahura Mazda created cosmic order. He created both the moral and material worlds and is the sovereign, omniscient god of order. Creator of all things, Ahura Mazda is himself uncreated and eternal. One of the hymns ascribed to Zarathustra says:

O Ahura Mazda, this I ask of thee: speak to me truly!
How should I pray, when I wish to pray to one like you?
May one like you, O Mazda, who is friendly, teach one like me?
And may you give us supporting aids through friendly Justice,
And tell how you may come to us with Good Disposition?

A rock inscription placed by King Darius I has these lines to the god:

There is one God, omnipotent Ahura Mazda,
It is He who has created the earth here;
It is He who has created the heaven there;
It is He who has created mortal man.

In Persian art Ahura Mazda is sometimes portrayed as a bearded man emerging from a winged creature. He is often described as wearing a star-decked robe, and the "swift-horsed sun" is said to be his eye. His throne is in the highest heaven, where he holds court as his angels minister to him.

Variant spellings: Ahura Mazdah; Auhar Mazd.

0119

Ahurani. In Persian mythology, water goddess who watches over rainfall as well as standing water; invoked for health and healing, for prosperity and growth.

0120

Aido Quedo. In Haitian voodoo, a female loa (deified spirit of the dead) who determines man's fate. She is often compared to the Virgin Mary in Christian symbolism.

0121

Aijeke. In Lapland mythology, a wooden god worshiped as late as the 17th century, even though the country was nominally Lutheran. John Scheffer, a professor at the University of Uppsala, in his book *Lapponia*, says the image of Aijeke was always made of birch wood. "Of this wood," he writes, "they make so many idols as they have sacrifices and, when they have done, they keep them in a cave by some hillside. The shape of them is very rude; at the top they are made to represent a man's head." Aijeke's rude shape had two spikes in its head to strike fire with. He was often identified with the Norse god Thor. Aijeke was also called Murona Jubmel (wooden god).

0122

Aino (peerless, splendid). In the Finnish epic poem *The Kalevala* (runes 3–5), a Lapp maiden who was to marry the culture hero Vainamoinen but was drowned instead.

To ransom his life, her brother, the evil Joukahainen, offered Aino to Vainamoinen as a wife. The parents of the girl were happy about the match, but she was not because Vainamoinen was an old man. After Aino met Vainamoinen in the forest while gathering birch shoots for brooms, she was even more determined not to marry. Her mother, however, bribed her with gifts. Aino, dressed in her wedding garments, then wandered out into the fields, wishing she were dead. Stealing down to the river bank, she laid aside her garments and ornaments and swam to a neighboring rock. No sooner did she sit on the rock than it toppled, drowning her. The animals sent a message of Aino's death, by way of the hare, to her mother, who lamented her daughter's death, saying that mothers should not force their "unwilling daughters" to take bridegrooms "that they love not."

Vainamoinen then went fishing for Aino in the rivers. He caught a fish, which he was about to kill when he discovered it was Aino. Not giving up his quest, he asked her to become his wife, but she refused.

The sad fate of Aino inspired the Finnish composer and conductor Robert Kajanus to compose his *Aino* Symphony for chorus and orchestra. The Finnish painter Akseli Gallen-Kallela portrayed the fate of Aino in a triptych.

Aiomun Kondi. 0123 In the mythology of the Arawak Indians of the Guianas, the dweller-on-high. Aiomun Kondi destroyed the earth twice because of the disobedience of humankind. Once he used fire; the

second time, water. He saved one good man, Marerewana, and his family from destruction.

Aipalookvik. 0124 In Eskimo mythology, evil spirit who lives in the sea and attempts to destroy boatmen.

Airyaman. 0125 In Persian mythology, god of healing, invoked against disease, sorcerers, and demons. The good god, Ahura Mazda, called on Airyaman to help expel disease. The god was so successful that he caused 99,999 diseases to cease. In the *Bundahishn*, a sacred Persian book of the Zoroastrians, Airyaman is called he "who gives the world healing of all pains."

Aiwel. 0126 In African mythology (Dinka of Eastern Sudan), hero, founder of a group of men who perform political and religious functions as members of hereditary priesthood, the spear masters. Aiwel was born to a woman whose husband had been killed when a lion, desiring the man's bracelet, bit off his thumb to get it. The stubborn man had refused to give it up. The woman had wanted a son and was able to bear one through the aid of a water spirit. Aiwel was born with a full set of teeth and was able to drink a full gourd of milk at a time. When his

Ajax

mother discovered that it was Aiwel, not his older sister, who was drinking all of the milk, she became very upset. Aiwel told her not to tell anyone or else she would die. Nevertheless, she spoke and died.

Aiwel then joined his father, the water spirit. Returning from the river, he took the form of a man and a multicolored ox, named Longar. As it is the Dinka custom to name a person after the characteristics of his ox, Aiwel was called Aiwel Longar. A drought came and only Aiwel's cattle remained fat. Aiwel then left for a promised land of plenty, asking the people to follow him. At first they refused and when they later tried to follow, he grew angry and killed some of them with his fishing spear. A man called Agothyathik saved some of the people by fighting with Aiwel, and in time Aiwel surrendered.

Aiwel gave fishing spears to the first group of people to cross the river and thus founded the spearmaster clans. Those who came later were given war spears, and they founded the warrior clans. Aiwel left his people, saying that he would return only in time of need.

0127

Ajax (of the earth). In Greek and Latin mythology, Latin form of the Greek Aias, a great hero of the Trojan War. Ajax was the son of Telamon of Salamis and Periboea (or Erioboea), and half-brother of Teucer. He was called Great Ajax because he was taller than the other Greek heroes. Ajax brought 12 ships to Troy, where he proved himself second only to Achilles in strength and bravery, though he is portrayed as rather stupid by Homer in the *Iliad*.

In later mythology Ajax goes mad when the armor of the dead Achilles is offered as a prize to Odysseus for his cunning and not to Ajax for his bravery. Ajax, according to this version, killed himself by falling on the sword given him by Hector. Out of his blood sprang the purple lily, and on its petals could be traced the first letters of his name, *Ai*. His death is the subject of Sophocles' play *Ajax*, he is described in detail in Ovid's *Metamorphoses* (book 13), and he appears in Horace's *Odes* (II, IV, 5)

A statue and temple to Ajax were erected at Salamis, and a yearly festival, the *Aianteia*, was held in his honor. He was also worshiped at Athens, where the tribe Aiantis was named after him. In later Greek mythology he was supposed to linger with Achilles in the island of Leuce.

Another Ajax in Greek mythology was the son of the Locrian king Oileus and was called Locrian or Lesser Ajax to avoid confusion with the Great Ajax. He took 40 ships to Troy. Though he was small, he distinguished himself beside his larger namesake. He was renowned for hurling the spear and was the swiftest runner next to Achilles. On his voyage home, to appease the anger of Athena, he suffered shipwreck on the Gyraean Rocks off the island of Myconos or, according to a variant myth, on the southernmost point of Euboea. Poseidon rescued him, but when Ajax boasted that he had escaped against the will of the gods, Poseidon took his trident and struck off the rock on which Ajax sat, and he sank into the sea.

Other accounts say that Athena's anger fell upon Ajax because when Cassandra had sought refuge at Athena's altar during the taking of Troy. Ajax tore her away by force, causing the sacred image of Athena, which Cassandra was holding, to fall. Though Agamemnon took Cassandra from Ajax, the Greeks left the crime of sacrilege unpunished, and the goddess vented her anger on the whole fleet with shipwrecks and high winds on the way home.

Along with other heroes of the Trojan War, Ajax was believed to live with Achilles in the island of Leuce. The Locrians worshiped him as a hero. A vacant place was left for him in the line when their troops formed for battle.

0128

Ajy. In Siberian mythology, a term meaning creator, birth-giving, life-giving, or nourishing. It is often used in conjunction with the names of various gods and goddesses.

0129

Ajyset (birth giver). In Siberian mythology, mother goddess worshiped by the Yakut; she presided over birth and brought souls from heaven to the newly born. In prayers she was often addressed as Ajy-Khotun (birth-giving mistress) and Ajysyt-Ijaksit-Khotun (birth-giving nourishing mother). Ajyset is similar to another Siberian goddess, Yakut-Kubai-Khotun, worshiped by the Buriat, who lived in the Tree of Life or under its roots. She was considered the mother of men and animals.

0130

Akhenaton (glory of Aten) (1372–1355 B.C.E.). In Egyptian history, the name chosen by Amenhotep IV when he adopted the worship of Aten. The son of Amenhotep III and his commoner wife, Tiye, Amenhotep IV was raised in a court of luxury and peace. Debate still rages as to whether or not he was a co-ruler with his father. In any event, when he ruled as pharaoh in his own right, he changed his name to Akhenaton and moved the capital of Egypt from Thebes to Amarna, a virtually virgin tract of land in middle Egypt. There he dedicated himself to the worship of the sun disk, or Aten, at the expense of the priesthood of Amun at Thebes. Aten was divorced from all anthropological associations and was regarded as a kindly creative force. Akhenaton's own hymn to Aten is close to certain hymns in the Old Testament, although we know that other deities continued to be worshiped alongside Aten. So pervasive was the influence of this new religion that the art of the period underwent a transformation that stressed naturalism in a way unparalleled in earlier periods of Egyptian art. Akhenaton forms the main character in Agatha Christie's play *Akhenaton*, Mika Waltari's novel *The Egyptian* and Philip Glass's opera *Akhenaton*.

Variant spelling: Ikhnaton.

0131

Akhtar. In Persian mythology, zodiacal constellation that makes up the army of the good god, Ahura Mazda.

0132

Akkruva. In Finno-Ugric mythology, fish goddess worshiped in Lapland. Akkruva appeared as a mermaid, the upper part of her body human, her head covered with long hair, and her lower portion that of a fish. She was believed to rise from the sea, combing her hair. When the goddess was in a beneficent mood she helped men catch fish, but she could also be destructive.

Variant spellings: Avfruvva, Havfru.

0133

Akshobhya. In Mahayana Buddhism, one of the five Dhyani-Buddhas. Called the Immovable, his symbol is the thunderbolt and his mount an elephant.

0134

Akubo. In Japanese No plays, the character of a wicked priest, who wears a coarse beard and carries a halberd.

0135

Akuma. In Japanese legend, an evil spirit who carries a sword and a huge head with flaming eyes.

One day a nobleman saw an akuma with a naked sword floating toward him in the sky. Frightened by the hideous sight, the nobleman hid himself under a mat and looking out, saw the akuma enter the house next door. Hearing a terrible uproar, he went to see what had happened and found that his neighbor, in trying to kill the akuma, had accidentally killed his wife, children, and servants.

Variant terms: ma, toori akuma.

0136

Akupera (tortoise, turtle). In Hindu mythology, the name of the tortoise on which the earth is sometimes said to be supported.

0137

Ala. In African mythology (Ibo of Eastern Nigeria), daughter of Chuku (the great god), mother earth, goddess of the underworld, ruler of men, guardian of the harvest, and dispenser of fertility to people and animals. Ala is worshiped all over Ibo country with shrines and special houses, called Mbari, which are square and contain vividly colored mud figures. Ala is portrayed in the center of the house with a wide variety of animals, men, and other gods surrounding her. As ruler of the underworld, Ala receives the dead into her womb or pocket.

0138

Ala. In Russian mythology, daughter of Volos, god of beasts and flocks. Serge Prokofiev's ballet *Ala and Lolli* deals with the myth. In the ballet Ala is taken prisoner by the enemy god and freed by the hero, Lolli, with the help of Volos. Prokofiev used the ballet score for his orchestral *Scythian Suite*.

0139

Al Aaraaf (the partition). In Islamic mythology, the region between paradise and Djahannam or hell, presided over by the beautiful maiden Nesace.

Al Aaraaf is the place for those persons who are morally neither good nor bad, such as infants, lunatics, and idiots, as well as those whose life is a balance of good and evil.

Edgar Allan Poe was fascinated by the idea and wrote in a letter to Isaac Lea that Al Aaraaf "is a medium between Heaven and Hell where men suffer no punishment but yet do not attain that tranquil or even happiness which they suppose to be characteristic of heavenly enjoyment." In Poe's poem *Al Aaraaf* it is a wondrous star surrounded by four suns. A youth, Angelo, is brought there with the hope of entering heaven, but an earthly love prevents him from hearing the call of Nesace.

Variant spelling: Al Arg.

0140

Aladdin. Hero in the tale "Aladdin and the Enchanted Lamp" from *The Thousand and One Nights*. The tale is not included in any manuscript copy of the work. It first appeared in the French translation of the *Nights* by Galland, who heard the tale from a Christian Syrian, Youhenna Diab.

Aladdin is a good-for-nothing son of a poor tailor in China. After his father's death he takes to the streets and turns up at his mother's house only for meals. One day a man pretending to be his uncle gains Aladdin's confidence and takes him to a high and barren mountain. The man then builds a fire and pours on it some perfumes, muttering incantations at the same time. Suddenly the earth quakes and opens, revealing an alabaster slab. Prodded by the sorcerer disguised as his uncle, Aladdin removes the slab and descends into a vault below. It is filled with silver and gold.

"Above the dais," the sorcerer tells Aladdin, "thou wilt find a lamp hung up; take it and pour out the oil that is therein and put it in thy sleeve; and fear not for thy clothes therefrom, for it is not oil. And as thou returnest, thou mayest pluck from the trees what thou wilt, for that is thine as long as the lamp is in thy hand." The sorcerer then gives Aladdin a ring that will protect him from all evil.

Then, as Aladdin is trying to climb out of the vault, the sorcerer closes the marble slab over him. Aladdin calls upon Allah for help and at the same time accidentally rubs the lamp, whereupon one of the marids, the most powerful of the djinn, appears. "Here am I, thy slave," announces the marid. "Ask what thou wilt, for I am his slave who hath the ring in hand, the ring of my lord." Aladdin asks to be freed and the marid obeys his wish. By means of the magic lamp Aladdin obtains wealth, has a palace built and marries Bardroulboudour. When the sorcerer finds that Aladdin has escaped, he sets out to recover the magic lamp. After buying a number of lamps from a coppersmith, the sorcerer goes about the streets, crying: "Who will barter an old lamp for a new?" All the town thinks he is crazy, but Bardroulboudour exchanges the magic lamp for a new copper one. Immediately the sorcerer rubs the lamp, conjures the marid, and orders Aladdin's palace and all his goods transported to Africa, the sorcerer's home.

Aladdin is out hunting while this happens and, rubbing his ring to return to the palace, he is transported to Africa. Later, with the aid of his wife, Aladdin drugs the sorcerer and cuts off his head. After some more adventures (for the sorcerer has an evil brother) Aladdin and his wife live happily until death, the destroyer of delights, separates them.

Aladdin's story has been set to music by many composers (although none of the operas is still performed), and it has been a favorite movie subject.

The palace built by the marid of the lamp had a room with 24 windows, all but one set with precious stones. The last was left for the sultan to finish, but his monetary resources were unequal to the task; thus the phrase, "to finish Aladdin's window," which means to attempt to complete something begun by a master hand or genius. Longfellow's poem on Hawthorne's death concludes:

Ah! who shall lift that wand of magic power
And the lost clue regain?
The unfinished window in Aladdin's tower
Unfinished must remain!

Variant spelling: Alaeddin.

0141
Alains le Gros (rock, noble?). In medieval legend connected with the Holy Grail, the first fisher king. Alains was told by Josephus, keeper of the Holy Grail, to take a net from the table on which the Grail stood and cast it into a lake. One fish was caught, and Alains's men laughed at him for believing the single fish could feed all of them. But Alains prayed over the fish, and it multiplied enough for all of the men to eat. He was then called the "fisher king" or "rich fisher." Afterward all keepers of the Holy Grail were called fisher kings.

0142
Alastor (avenger). In Greek mythology, the name for an avenging demon who follows the footsteps of criminals according to Aeschylus' *Agamemnon*. Shelley used the name for *Alastor, or The Spirit of Solitude* (1816); his first important work, the poem is a condemnation of self-centered idealism. The name Alastor is also borne by a son of Neleus and brother of Nestor, married to Harpalyce.

0143
Albania. In medieval British legend, name for Scotland, derived from Albanact, son of Brute, the first king of Britain. At the death of Brute, Britain was divided by his sons: Locrin got England; Albanact got Albania (Scotland); and Kambler got Cambria (Wales). Albania later became Albany, as in Shakespeare's *King Lear*, in which the Duke of Albany is a Scotsman, although not specifically mentioned in the play.

0144
Alban, St. (man from Alba). Fourth century C.E. In Christian legend, proto-martyr of England. Feast, 22 June.

St. Bede records the life of the saint in his *Ecclesiastical History of the English People*. When the persecution of the Christians in England was ordered by the Emperor Diocletian, Alban, though a pagan, hid a Christian priest. For his crime he was condemned to death. He was first tortured and then led to the place of execution. On the way it was necessary to cross the river Coln. A great crowd had gathered, and the bridge was too narrow for the many people to pass. When St. Alban "drew near the stream," it "was immediately dried up, and he perceived that the water had departed and made way for him to pass," according to Bede's account. When they reached the hill of execution, Alban prayed for water to quench his thirst. A spring suddenly gushed out at his feet. Finally, the saint was beheaded, and the executioner's eyes "dropped to the ground together with the blessed martyr's head."

St. Alban's burial place was forgotten and then rediscovered by King Offic in 793 after the king had seen in a vision where the remains of the saint could be found. A church was built over the spot, and nearby the great Benedictine monastery and the town of St. Alban's in Hertfordshire, England, were built.

The saint is variously portrayed: as a warrior with a cross and sword; crowned with a laurel, with a peer's coronet and cross, with his head cut off, with his head in a holly bush, spreading his cloak with the sun above, and in a scene with the executioner's eyes dropping out.

0145

Albertus Magnus, St. (Albert the Great). 1193–1280 C.E. In Christian legend, bishop and Doctor of the Church, responsible for the introduction of Aristotelian methods and principles to the study of Christian theology. Feast, 15 November. Albert was considered one of the greatest Christian thinkers of the Middle Ages. He was a Dominican friar and later bishop of Ratisbon. The saint is often portrayed with his student St. Thomas Aquinas in works by the Dominican painter Fra Angelico.

0146

Albion (white). In medieval British legend, name for England, possibly based on the white cliffs that face France. Albion is also the name of a giant who conquered the island and named it after himself.

0147

Albiorix. In Celtic mythology, a war god worshiped by the continental Celts at Avignon, France. Ancient Roman writers identified Albiorix with their war god, Mars.

0148

Alcathous (impetuous might). In Greek mythology, king of Megara, the son of Pelops and Hippodameia; brother of Astydameia, Atreus, Chrysippus, Copreus, Lysidice, Nicippe, Piltheus, Troezen, and Thyestes; husband of Evaechme. He slew the Cithaeron lion that had torn Euippus, the son of Megareus, to pieces. As a reward he was given Euaechma, the daughter of Megareus, as well as the throne. With Apollo as his friend and helper, he rebuilt the city walls and one of two fortresses, Alcathoe, that had temples to Apollo and Artemis. A singing stone in the fortress was said to be the one on which Apollo laid down his lyre when at work. Alcathous' eldest son, Ischepolis, was killed in the Calydonian boar hunt. His second son, Callipolis, running with the news to his father when Alcathous was sacrificing to Apollo, scattered the altar fire. Alcathous then struck his son dead, believing the boy had committed sacrilege. By his daughters Automedusa and Periboea, the wives of Iphicles and Telamon, Alcathous was the grandfather of Iolaus and Ajax.

0149

Alcestis (might of the home). In Greek mythology, daughter of Pelias and Anaxibia (or Phylomache); wife of Admetus, king of Pherae in Thessaly. When Admetus, in order to achieve immortality, had to find someone to die in his place, all refused, including his parents; only Alcestis volunteered and gave her life for his. She was later brought back from the underworld by Heracles. She appears in Euripides's play *Alcestis*, in which Admetus is portrayed as being a selfish husband. Many later writers have based their characterizations of Alcestis on Euripides. William Morris wrote *The Love of Alcestis* in 1868, and Robert Browning in *Balaustion's Adventure* (1871) has a translation of Euripides' play in the poem. In medieval tradition Alcestis was the model wife, appearing in Chaucer's *Legend of Good Women*. She is called Celia in T. S. Eliot's play *The Cocktail Party*. In the play Celia prefers to return to the land of the dead because for her it is a greater reality. Milton cites Alcestis in his *Sonnet 23*, and Rilke wrote a poem *Alcestis*. The best known operatic setting is *Alceste* (1767) by Gluck, based on Euripides' play. In the opera Apollo, not Heracles, brings back Alcestis. A modern operatic version is *Alkestis* (1922) by Rutland Boughton in Gilbert Murray's English translation of Euripides' play. There is also *Alkestis* (1924) by Egon Wellesz with a libretto by Hugo von Hofmannsthal.

0150

Alcina (sea maiden). In the Charlemagne cycle of legends, a powerful enchantress, the embodiment of carnal pleasure. Alcina was the sister of Logistilla (reason) and Morgana (lasciviousness). When she grew tired of her sexual conquests, she changed her lovers into trees, fountains, and rocks. The hero Astolpho fell in love with Alcina, and she changed him into a myrtle tree. He was later disenchanted by Melissa, who by means of a magic ring made Alcina's real senility and ugliness appear. Alcina appears in Boiardo's *Orlando Innamorato* and Ariosto's *Orlando Furioso*, as well as in Handel's opera *Alcina*.

0151

Alcinous (mighty mind). In Greek mythology, king of the Phaeacians; husband of Arete; father of Nausicaa; the king with whom Odysseus finds shelter and aid. Alcinous appears in Homer's *Odyssey* (books 6, 7, 8).

Alcithoe (impetuous might). In Greek mythology, daughter of Minyas; sister of Arsippe and Leucippe. She and her sisters were changed into bats for refusing to join the other women of Boeotia in the worship of Dionysus. Ovid's *Metamorphoses* (book 4) tells her tale.

0152

Alcmaeon (mighty endeavor). In Greek mythology, son of Amphiaraus and Eriphyle and brother of Amphilochus. Alcmaeon took part in the expedition of the Epigoni against Thebes. On his return home he killed his mother at the instigation of his father, and as punishment he was driven mad and haunted by the Erinyes. Alcmaeon went to Phegeus, in Psophis, to be purified by Phegeus and was then given Phegeus' daughter Arsinoe (or Alphesiboea). He gave her the jewels of Harmonia, which he had brought from Argos. In a short time the crops failed, and he again went mad. Wandering, he eventually arrived at the mouth of the Achelous River. There he found an island that had not been there when his mother cursed him, and he was cured of his madness. He then married Achelous' daughter Callirrhoë and had two sons, Acarnan and Amphoterus. Unable to resist his wife's entreaties that she have Harmonia's necklace and robe, he went to Phegeus in Arcadia and took them, pretending they would be dedicated at Delphi for the healing of his madness. When Phegeus learned he had been deceived, Alcmaeon was killed. His death was avenged by his two sons. He was worshiped at a sanctuary at Thebes that was said to contain his tomb. Alcmaeon is cited in Dante's *Divine Comedy* (Purgatory, canto 12; Paradise, canto 4).

0153

Alcmene (might of the moon, mighty in wrath). In Greek mythology, daughter of King Electryon of Argos and Anaxo; wife of Amphitryon; mother of Heracles by Zeus. When she died at a great age, Zeus sent Hermes to take her body from its coffin and bring Alcmene to the Elysian Fields. In this heaven Alcmene married Rhadamanthys. When Hermes stole the body of Alcmene, he substituted a large stone, which was placed in a sacred grove in Thebes and worshiped. Alcmene also had an altar in the temple of Heracles at Athens. Ovid's *Metamorphoses* (book 9) tells her tale.

0154

Alcyone (queen who wards off storms). In Greek mythology, wife of Ceyx; daughter of Aeolus and Enarete. When she learned that her husband, Ceyx, had been drowned on his way to consult an oracle, Alcyone threw herself into the sea, and she and Ceyx

0155

both were changed into birds. As long as they built and tended their nest, the Aegean was calm. The term "halcyon days" comes from her name, also rendered Halcyone. Her tale is told in Ovid's *Metamorphoses* (book 11) and in Chaucer's *Book of the Duchess*.

Alcyoneus (mighty ass). In Greek mythology, son of Uranus, whose blood touched Gaea, the earth; eldest and mightiest of the Titans. Alcyoneus could not be overtaken by death in his own country. In the war with the Titans, Heracles had to drag Alcyoneus away from Pallene before he could kill him. The hero lifted him from the earth, his mother, and killed him. Alcyoneus also is the name of a giant who stole the oxen of Helios from the island of Erytheia. As Heracles was crossing the Thracian isthmus of Pallene, Alcyoneus crushed 12 of his wagons and 25 of his men with a huge piece of rock. When the giant hurled it at Heracles, the hero struck it back with his club and killed Alcyoneus with the same blow.

0156

Aldinger, Sir. In medieval British legend, a knight who appears in a ballad. Aldinger is steward to Queen Eleanor, wife of King Henry II. He impeaches her fidelity and submits to a combat to substantiate his charge. However, an angel in the shape of a child establishes the queen's innocence.

0157

A Fury

Alecto (she who rests not). In Greek and Roman mythology, one of the three Furies or Erinyes. The others were Megaera and Tisiphone. Alecto is cited in Vergil's *Aeneid* (book 7), in Dante's *Divine Comedy* (Inferno, canto 9) as "she who wails," and in Shakespeare's *Henry IV, Part II* (5.5.39)

0158

Alectryon. In Greek mythology, a youth who was to watch for the approach of the sun when Ares was making love to Aphrodite so that they would not be discovered by her husband, Hephaestus. Alectryon fell asleep, and the two lovers were discovered. In anger Ares turned Alectryon into a cock, which still heralds the dawn.

Aleine. In Arthurian legend, the niece of Gwaine. She persuaded Perceval to enter the Easter tournament at King Arthur's court, giving him a suit of red armor. He entered the lists unknown and won a vacant seat at the Round Table.

Alexander Nevsky. 1220–1263. In Russian legend, prince- saint who defended Russia against foreign invaders.

The heroic personality Alexander Nevsky, the first prince of Novgorod and (after 1252) great prince of Vladimir and all Russia, is one of the heroes of both Imperial and Soviet Russia. His most famous exploit was the Russian defense of Novgorod in 1242 against the invading Knights of the Teutonic Order. Called to save his country, Prince Alexander through the power of his personality alone, gathered together an enormous army and met the enemy on a frozen lake. There he and his army dealt them a humiliating defeat.

When the prince was laid out for burial, the Metropolitan Archbishop Cyril wanted to place in the prince's hand a "charter with prayers asking for the remission of sins." Alexander, "as if he were alive, extended his hand and took the charter from the hand of the Metropolitan Archbishop," according to one Russian legend.

The famous Russian movie director Sergei Eisenstein used the legend of Alexander for his first sound film, *Alexander Nevsky*. Made one year before the Soviet-Nazi pact, the movie portrays the Germans as complete barbarians. Prokofiev's music for the film was later adapted by the composer for his cantata *Alexander Nevsky* for mezzo-soprano, chorus, and orchestra.

Alexander the Great (he who wards off men). 356–323 B.C.E. In Greek history and legend, king of Macedonia, son of Philip II and Olympias. He was educated by Aristotle. The story of Alexander is a combination of history and legend. His life appears in Greek, medieval Christian, Jewish, and Islamic legends. One legend illustrating his early life and his relationship with his father is told in Plutarch's *Parallel Lives*. Philip had a beautiful white horse, Bucephalus, which could not be tamed. When Alexander succeeded in breaking the horse, Philip is said to have told him that he, Alexander, must seek a larger kingdom because Macedonia was not large enough to reflect his greatness. Alexander's compassion is the subject of another legend in Plutarch's work. It tells of a matron of Thebes who had been raped by one of Alexander's captains after Alexander had sacked that city. She told her captor that she kept her jewels at the bottom of a well. When the officer went to fetch them, she pushed him in. Alexander did not punish the woman because he said she did the right thing. Plutarch also tells the tale of the Gordian knot. During his war against the Persian king Darius, Alexander entered the Phrygian city of Gordium. Here there was a chariot bound with cords in a knot so complex that whoever could untie it would be the ruler of the world. Alexander cut the knot with his sword and took the city. When Alexander became ill, no one would treat him for fear of the consequences if they failed. His friend Philip, however, agreed to procure him medicine. Alexander had just received a letter from one of his generals, Parmenio, that said Philip would murder him. To show his trust in Philip, he showed him the letter while he took the medicine.

Other legends portray Alexander's generosity. After his victory over Darius he treated Darius' family kindly. When Darius was killed by his own men, he gave his last message to Alexander and asked him to care for his family, which Alexander did.

Painters, especially those of the 17th century, frequently portrayed Alexander's marriage to Roxana. She was the daughter of a chieftain of Sogdiana, one of the conquered territories of Asia. There are also stories of her cruelty after his death. Cassander is said to have put her to death.

Alexander reached Egypt in the autumn of 332 B.C.E. According to one legend, he consulted the oracle of Zeus-Amen (a composite god made up of the Greek god Zeus and the Egyptian god Amen) in the Siwa oasis. Amen recognized Alexander as his son and promised him control over the entire world. A short time later Alexander was crowned king of Egypt in the temple of Ptah at Memphis. On his way to the shrine of Zeus-Amen, Alexander made a stop at Rhacotia, a small fishing village and former frontier post of the Pharaohs. Realizing the advantages of the site, Alexander decided to build a new city, to be called Alexandria. The layout of the city was geometric, with wide streets on a rectangular grid. The plan was drawn up by Deinocrates, an architect from Rhodes, and by Cleomenes of Naucratis, who was in charge of the project. According to one legend, the city was in the shape of a Greek garment. The perimeter was laid out by dropping seeds, which birds promptly ate. This seemingly bad omen was interpreted as a good sign by Alexander. Later he left Alexandria and died in Asia. Ptolemy, one of Alexander's generals, was responsible for returning his body to Egypt, and he erected a magnificent tomb for his leader in Alexandria. When Julius Caesar was in Egypt, he asked to see the tomb of Alexander. The Emperor Caracalla is reported to have stolen Alexander's sword from his body. Despite these persistent legends, the burial places of Alexander and the Ptolemies have not been discovered.

The *Alexander Romance* (second century B.C.E.) added numerous mythical episodes to the life of Alexander, such as a trip to the heavens. Most medieval legends of Alexander were influenced by this work. Alexander appears among the Nine Worthies, or Men of Worth, a grouping popular during the Middle Ages. The Latin poem *Alexandreis* (12th century) was very popular, as well as the long French *Roman d'Alexandre*. Alexander appears in one of Racine's early plays, as well as in Dryden's poem *Alexander's Feast*, and he is the subject of a novel, *Fire from Heaven*, by Mary Renault. In art there is Pinturicchio's *Triumph of Alexander*, Jordaens' tapestries, Aldorfer's *Alexander's Victory* (one of Napoleon's favorite art works), and Veronese's *The Family of Darius Before Alexander*. There are more than 100 opera episodes from Alexander's life, though none is currently popular.

Alf (elf). In Norse mythology, a dwarf mentioned in the *Voluspa*, a poem in the *Poetic Edda* that tells of the creation and destruction of the world. The name Alf is used also for a number of other dwarfs and other characters. From it comes, through Old English, the word elf.

Alfadir (all-father). In Norse mythology, a title for Odin, chief of the gods, and often used in Christian times for God. In the *Prose Edda* the Alfadir is said to have existed "from all ages." He formed "heaven and earth, and the air, and all things thereunto belonging." He is credited with the creation of man and is said to have "given him a soul which shall live and never perish though the body shall have moldered away, or have been burnt to ashes. And all that are righteous shall dwell with him in a place called Gimli, or Vingolf; but the wicked shall go to Hel, and thence to Niflheim, which is below, in the ninth world." *Variant spelling*: Alfadur.

0165

Alfar (elves or dwarfs). In Norse mythology, the elves or dwarfs ruled over by the god Frey. The *Prose Edda* gives an account of their origin:

> Then the gods, seating themselves upon their thrones, distributed justice, and bethought them how the dwarfs had been bred in the mould of the earth, just as worms are in a dead body. It was, in fact, in Ymir's flesh that the dwarfs were engendered, and began to move and live. At first they were only maggots, but by the will of the gods they at length partook both of human shape and understanding, although they always dwell in rocks and caverns. Modsognir and Durin are the principal ones.

From Alfar are derived all small creatures, such as alvors, elves, brownies, found in Northern myths and legends. Two groups of Alfar are cited, the *liosalfar* (light elves) who live in Alfheim, and the *dockalfar* (dark elves) who live underground and are mostly of an evil nature. Other names used are *huldu folk* (hidden folk) and *liufliger* (darlings).

The dark dwarfs were so ugly, with their dark skin, green eyes, large heads, short legs, and crow's feet, the gods forced them, under penalty of being turned to stone, to live underground and never show themselves during the daytime. Although less powerful than the gods, the dwarfs were far more powerful than men.

In Northern folklore and legends, dwarfs transport themselves easily from one place to another. They wear red capes that can make them invisible. They like to hide behind rocks and mischievously repeat the last words of every conversation they overhear. Echoes are therefore called "dwarfs' talk." In various countries of Northern Europe their ruler is called Andvari, Alberich, Elbegast, Gondemar, Laurin, or Oberon.

Generally, dwarfs in Northern legends and tales are kind and helpful. Sometimes they knead bread, grind flour, brew beer, and perform countless other tasks. If ill-treated, however, or laughed at, they will leave a house. When Christianity replaced the Northern gods, the dwarfs, in anger, left forever to punish the people for their lack of belief in the old gods.

According to some Northern legends, dwarfs envied man's taller stature and often tried to increase their race's height by marrying human wives or stealing unbaptized children and substituting their own offspring for the human mother to nurse. These dwarf babies were known as changelings. To recover the true child and rid herself of the changeling, a woman had either to brew beer in eggshells or to grease the soles of the changeling's feet and hold them so near the flames that, attracted by their babies' cries, the dwarf parents would come to claim their own child and bring back the human child.

Female dwarfs were believed able to change themselves into maras (or nightmares). If a victim succeeded in plugging the hole through which a mara made her entrance into his room, she wasthen

Ali Baba (Aubrey Beardsley)

at his mercy—he could even marry her. She would be his faithful wife as long as the hole by which she had entered was plugged. If it was open, she would escape.

The *Prose Edda* gives an account of the origin of the Alfar. Offerings of milk, honey, or a small animal were made to the Alfar.

0166

Alfasem. In Arthurian legend, the king of Terre Foraine, converted and baptized by Alains, keeper of the Holy Grail. Alfasem was wounded in both thighs by an angel for sleeping where the Grail had rested. He later died of the wounds.

0167

Alfheim (elf home). In Norse mythology, home of the elves or dwarfs, as well as of the god Frey. It was located in the air between heaven and earth. Sir Walter Scott, in his poem *Thomas the Rhymer*, in *Contributions to the Minstrelsy of the Scottish Border: Imitations of the Ancient Ballad*, uses the words *Elfland* and *Elflyn land*.

0168

Ali. 600?–661 C.E. In Islamic history and legend, husband of Fatima, one of Muhammad's daughters; fourth caliph (656–661).

Numerous legends collected around Ali, as both saint and warrior. He is credited with many miracles, such as raising a man from the dead. Persian Muslims speak of more than 1,000 miracles, although only 60 are recorded. Some Muslim sects believe that Allah became incarnate in the person of Ali by "indwelling." The Nusairi sects regard Ali as the first of the three persons of the Trinity.

As a warrior Ali is said to have killed 523 men in one day. His sword cut them from their horses with such speed that half of each body remained on the horse while the other half fell to the ground. Ali is famous in Persian poetry for his beautiful eyes. The expression *Ayn Hali* (the eyes of Ali) is a term of praise for a person's beauty. Ali was assassinated in 661 by being struck on the forehead with a poisoned saber.

0169

Ali Baba. Hero of the tale "Ali Baba and the Forty Thieves" included in *The Thousand and One Nights* but not in any manuscript copy of the work. It first appeared in the French translation of the *Nights* by Galland, who heard the tale from a Christian Syrian, Youhenna Diab.

Ali Baba and his brother Kassim live in Persia. One day Ali Baba, while collecting wood in the forest, sees 40 thieves enter a cave after saying: "Open, Sesame!" At the first opportunity Ali goes to the cave and says the magic words. It opens, and he discovers that the cave is filled with gold and treasure. He takes some of it home, and in a short time his brother also discovers the secret. Kassim enters the cave but forgets the magic words needed to get out. The thieves return, kill Kassim, cut him into quarters and hang him in the cave.

Ali goes in search of his brother and, finding the body, takes it to a cobbler who can sew it back together so that Kassim's death will appear natural. Through the cobbler, the thieves come in search of Ali in order to kill him too. The head thief poses as an oil merchant and enters Ali's house. He asks Ali if he may store his oil jars in the shed, and Ali agrees. A thief is hiding in each of the jars except one, waiting to kill Ali. The maid Morgiana, needing some oil, goes to the jars. One of the men hears her approach and asks if it is time to come out. She replies, "Not yet." Deciding that they must be robbers, she fills a caldron from the single jar that contains oil and pours the oil over the thieves, killing all of them. Ali, in gratitude, then marries Morgiana.

The tale of Ali Baba is perhaps one of the most popular in the entire collection. It was made into an opera seven times and was filmed in 1902, 1919, 1943, 1952, and 1962. Comic variations, with Eddie Cantor in *Ali Baba Goes to Town* (1937) and Fernandel in 1954, also have been filmed.

0170

Aliosha Popovich. 11th century C.E. In Russian legend, *bogatyr* (epic hero) who appears in the *byliny* (epic songs) and in folktales.

Aliosha, the son of a priest, was a "mighty hero," who grew as much in one day as other babies did in a week, and he achieved a year's growth in one week. When he was fully grown, he asked his father if he could "try his luck in the field of battle." His father agreed if he would take along Maryshko Parnov's son to be his servant. Both set out and journeyed to the realm of Prince Vladimir, who welcomed them.

At the same time the evil Turgarin Zmeevich, "a mighty champion, invaded and scourged Prince Vladimir's kingdom," entering the palace and eating everything in sight. Aliosha challenged him to a duel. The next day, when the two were to fight, Aliosha saw Turgarin Zmeevich flying through the air on his horse. Aliosha called on the Holy Mother of God to send a black cloud to "wet Turgarin's paper wings." The prayer was answered, and the evil one fell to earth. In the ensuing battle Turgarin's head was cut off and carried on a spear to Prince Vladimir.

Variant spelling: Aljosa Popovic.

Alisaunder. In Arthurian legend, son of Prince Boudwin and Anglides. His father was killed by King Mark; and when Alisaunder grew up, his mother handed him his father's doublet, covered with blood. "Avenge your father!" she told the youth. King Mark, however, had Alisaunder slain instead.

Al Jassasa (the spy). In Islamic mythology, the name of the beast or monster in the Koran (sura 27) that will appear at the Last Judgment. According to folklore, he or she (accounts vary) will have a bull head, hog eyes, elephant ears, stag horns, ostrich neck, lion breasts, tiger color, a back like a cat, camel legs, the voice of an ass, and the tail of a ram. The beast will mark those who are saved and those who are damned.

Variant spelling: Al Jassaca.

Alkha. In Siberian mythology, a dragonlike monster who causes eclipses of the sun and moon. In one Buriat myth Alkha swallowed the sun and moon, plunging the earth into utter darkness. The gods became angry and cut his body into two pieces, one part falling to the earth and the forepart remaining in heaven. As a result, although the monster continually tries to swallow the moon and sun, each time they fall out of his back.

In some myths Alkha is called Arakho. In one of these, told by the Buriat, Arakho lived on the earth eating the hairs off people's bodies. This made God angry because hair was needed for man's protection. As a result God cut Arakho into two parts. Yet the monster still tried to swallow the sun and moon.

In a variant myth Arakho drank from a cup prepared by the sun and moon that contained the Water of Life. By drinking from the cup Arakho dirtied it and God cut him in two as a punishment. But Arakho's forepart became immortal. Arakho still chases the moon, leaving his monstrous marks, which are called moon spots.

Al-Khadir (the green one). In Islamic legend, a saint who found the Waters of Immortality or Fountain of Life. He is believed to appear clad in green robes to Muslims in distress. The green symbolizes his unfading youth.

The legend of Al-Khadir appears in various Islamic works, such as *The Thousand and One Nights*, and is partly told in the Koran (sura 18). When Moses, or Musa to use his Arabic name, was preaching to the people, they admired his knowledge and eloquence so much that they asked him if there was any man in the world wiser than he. Musa answered no. Allah was not satisfied with Musa's answer and told the prophet that there was a man who was wiser than he, and the man's name was Al-Khadir. Musa was told to go in search of Al-Khadir and to take along his servant (who was Joshua) and a fish. When they arrived at a certain rock where "two seas" met, the fish disappeared. There are different explanations for this: that the fish, being roasted, jumped out of the basket into the sea; or that Joshua accidentally sprinkled on it some water from the Fountain of Life (for though they did not know it, they had arrived at their destination). The Koran says the "fish took its way in the sea at will."

Suddenly a stranger appeared. It was Al-Khadir, but neither Musa nor Joshua was aware of his identity. Musa said he would like to follow the stranger but the man replied that Musa would complain about what he was going to do. Musa promised not to complain and they all set out. When the stranger scuttled a boat and Musa complained, the stranger reminded Musa of his promise. As they continued on their way and the stranger murdered a boy, Musa was horrified. They then reached a city that refused them hospitality. In it was a wall ready to crumble, but the stranger fixed it. Musa said he should be paid for such services.

The stranger told Musa he would at last explain his actions. "As to the vessel," he said, "it belonged to a poor man who toiled upon the sea. I was minded to damage it, for in their rear was a king who seized every ship by force. As to the youth, his parents were believers and we feared lest he should trouble them by error and infidelity. And we desired that their Lord might give them in his place a child better than he in virtue and nearer in filial piety. And as to the wall, it belonged to two orphan youths in the city, and beneath it was their treasure; and their father was a righteous man; and the Lord desired that they should reach the age of strength, and take forth their treasure the mercy of thy Lord. And not of mine own will have I done this. This is the interpretation of that which thou couldst not bear with patience."

According to some Islamic traditions, Al-Khadir is thought to be Phineas, Elias, and St. George in one because his soul passed by metempsychosis successively through all three.

Al-Khadir is sometimes identified with Khwadja Khidr, who presides over the Fountain of Immortality in Indian Islamic belief. Khwadja Khidr, however, is identified in many parts of India with a river god or with the fish avatar of the god Vishnu. Some Indian Muslims offer prayers to Khwadja Khidr at the first shaving of a boy. Part of the ceremony also consists of launching a small boat.

Along the Indus, Khwadja Khidr is often identified with the river and is seen as an old man clothed in green. When a man escapes drowning, he is said to have evaded Khwadja's domain.
Variant spellings: Al-Khidr, El Khizr.

0175

Allah. In Islam, the proper name of God. The origin of the name Allah goes back before Muhammad, who found that the Meccans worshiped a supreme deity whom they called Allah. Along with Allah, however, they also worshiped a host of lesser gods and "daughters of Allah." When Muhammad set down the first article of Islam (submission), "There is no God save Allah," he attacked belief in any other gods the Meccans worshiped besides Allah, who was the true God. The best summation of the Islamic concept of Allah is found in part of the opening sura of the Koran, called Al-fataih:

In the Name of Allah, the Compassionate, the Merciful.
Praise be to Allah, Lord of the worlds;
The Compassionate, the Merciful!
Thee only do we worship, and to Thee do we cry for help.
Guide Thou us on the straight path;
The path of those to whom thou hast been gracious.

The Al-fataih is recited several times in each of the five daily prayers, and on many other occasions, such as when concluding a bargain. The *Basmala*, "In the Name of Allah, the Compassionate, the Merciful," has become part of the rubric at the head of every sura except the ninth in the Koran. Allah is also addressed as Al-Hayn (the living), Al-Alim (the knowing), Al-Murid (the purposer), As-Sam (the hearer), Al-Basir (the seer), and Al-Mutakallim (the speaker).

0176

Allallu. In the Near Eastern epic poem *Gilgamesh*, a fantastic bird destroyed by the goddess Ishtar. The goddess at one time loved the bird, but she destroyed him as she did all of her lovers. The bird then lamented his fate, saying, "O my pinions!"

0177

Allan-a-Dale (rock, noble). In British legend, a minstrel in the Robin Hood ballads. Robin Hood aided Allan-a-Dale when the minstrel carried off his sweetheart before she could be forced to marry a rich old knight. Allan-a-Dale also appears in Walter Scott's novel *Ivanhoe*.
Variant spellings: Allin-a-Dale, Allen-a-Dale.

0178

Allen, Ethan. 1738–1789. In American history and legend, hero of Vermont during the American Revolution who organized the Green Mountain Boys against the British. Legend says that when he demanded from the British the surrender of Fort Ticonderoga he asked it "in the name of the Great Jehovah and the Continental Congress." In actuality, he is believed to have said, "Come out of there, you damned old rat!" Allen told his own story in his *Narrative of Ethan Allen's Captivity* and appears in Daniel Pierce Thompson's novel *The Greene Mountain Boys* and Van de Water's novel *Reluctant Rebel*.

0179

Allison, Clay. c. 1835–1875. In American history and legend, a gunfighter who was kind when sober and a devil when drunk. Born in Tennessee, he left his father's farm to join the Confederate Army. When the war was lost, Allison went West. One account describes him as over six feet tall, with blue eyes, a long mustache, and hair down to his shoulders. He had a melancholy look and was slightly crippled from having accidentally shot himself in the instep. His changing moods were described by a contemporary: "He was a whale of a fellow, and considerate of his companions; but throw a drink into him, and he was hell turned loose, rearin' for a chance to shoot—in self defense." Another account tells how he challenged a man to fight in an open grave; the winner to bury the loser. Another tale tells how Bill Chunk met his death in 1873 when he tried to draw a gun from under a dinner table. The barrel of his revolver struck the edge of the table, and Allison fired at Chunk. Chunk's head fell on the table and into a plate. Clay coolly replaced his gun and went on with his meal, demanding that the other guests at the table do likewise. Allison died when he fell from a wagon and one of its rear wheels passed over his back.

0180

All Saints' Day. Christian feast celebrated on 1 November to commemorate all of the saints. Sometime in the early part of the seventh century, C.E., Pope Boniface IV obtained permission from the Emperor Phocas to turn the Pantheon in Rome, an old pagan temple to all of the gods and unused since the fifth century, into a place of Christian worship. On 13 May the pope dedicated the pagan temple to St. Mary and All Martyrs. Pope Gregory III (731–741) dedicated a chapel to All Saints in St. Peter's in Rome on 1 November, thus changing the date of commemorating all saints. Some scholars say the date was changed to coincide with a pagan Germanic festival that honored all of the gods, though some Christian scholars (such as Francis X. Weiser in his

Handbook of Christian Feasts and Customs) say the date was changed because the "many pilgrims who came to Rome for the Feast of the Pantheon could be fed more easily after the harvest than in the spring."

In the 15th century Pope Sixtus made All Saints a holy day of obligation for the entire Western, or Latin, church. The feast was retained in *The Book of Common Prayer* of the Church of England. All Hallows' Eve, or Halloween, is celebrated the night before All Saints' Day and is now a secular celebration.

0181

All Souls' Day. Christian feast celebrated on 2 November to commemorate all of the dead. In the tenth century C.E. St. Odilo, Abbot of Cluny—who, according to Christian legend, had heard from a pilgrim to the Holy Land that there was an island where the groans of the souls in Purgatory could be heard asking for prayers to release them—issued a decree that all monasteries of the congregation of Cluny were to keep 2 November as a "day of all the departed ones." On 1 November, All Saints' Day, after vespers or evening prayer the bell was to be tolled and the office of the dead recited. On the next day three masses were to be said for the souls in Purgatory. By the 13th century the feast was established in the Latin, or Western, church.

The Christian feast of All Souls is an adaptation of the custom of setting aside part of the year to remember the dead, found in numerous cultures, from ancient Babylonia and China to the Romans. The Buddhist feast of the dead takes place on the anniversary of the death of Buddha, 15 April; the Romans celebrated their feast of the dead during the *Parentalia*, 13 to 21 February, the end of the Roman year. In some Roman Catholic countries food is left at grave sites for the dead, recalling old pagan rites. In the Philippines tomb niches and crosses are repainted, hedges trimmed, flowers planted, and all weeds removed from the graves. In Poland paper sheets with black borders, called *Wypominki* (naming), with the names of the family dead written on them, are used in religious devotions during the month of November. In the Polish custom it is said that the souls of the departed appear on All Souls' Day as a great light from the parish church. When the light is seen, the parishioners know they are to pray for the dead. In Austria the souls of the dead are said to wander about through the forests, sighing and praying for their release from Purgatory. Children are told to pray aloud when they walk through forests and cemeteries so that the dead know they are praying for their release.

The mixture of Christian and ancient religious rites (mainly from the Druids) is found in Halloween, or as it was earlier called, All Hallows'

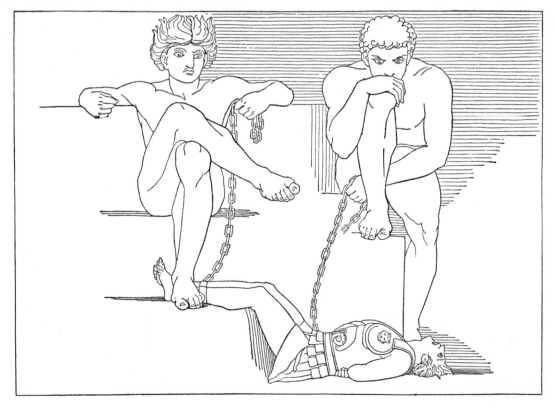

Otus and Ephialtes holding Ares captive (John Flaxman)

Eve or All Saints' Eve. During this time it is believed that demons, witches, and evil spirits roam about the earth and must be appeased by offerings such as sweet cakes. This recalls the belief that the dead must be placated so as not to disturb the living. The demons today, however, have become the popular jack-o'-lanterns—pumpkins with candles or electric lights inside—and mass-produced costumes of witches and demons.

0182

Almond. A nut tree found in warm, temperate countries. In world mythology and folklore the almond is often a symbol of the womb. In Christian art the *mandorla* (Italian for almond) often surrounds figures of Christ, representing the womb of the Virgin enclosing her son. In Genesis (43:11) the almond is among the "best fruits in the land." When Aaron's rod blossomed, it bore almonds overnight. His staff, which in folklore became the magician's wand, plays an important part in the Exodus narrative. After the Exodus from Egypt, Aaron's rod was placed with the rods of the other tribes in the tabernacle; it then "budded, and brought forth buds, and bloomed blossoms, and yielded almonds" (Num. 17:8). This was a sign that Yahweh gave Aaron and his tribe of Levi the exclusive right to the Hebrew priesthood. In Chinese symbolism the almond signifies feminine beauty, fortitude in sorrow and watchfulness.

0183

Aloadae (children of the threshing floor). In Greek mythology, sons of Poseidon by Iphimedia, the wife of Aloeus. Aloeus was the son of Canace and Poseidon. The Aloadae's names were Ephialtes and Otus, and they grew every year an ell in breadth and a fathom in length. In nine years time they were 36 feet high. Their strength was such that they chained up the god Ares and kept him in a brazen cask for 13 months, until their stepmother, Erioboea, told Hermes, who came and freed his brother. The Aloadae threatened to storm heaven by piling Mount Ossa on Olympus and Mount Pelion on Ossa. Homer's *Odyssey* (book 11) says they would have accomplished this feat if Apollo had not slain them with his arrows before their beards had grown, symbols of their strength. A later myth tells of Ephialtes' love for Hera, the wife of Zeus, and Otus's love for Artemis. Still another variation says they were slain by Artemis on the island of Naxos when she appeared as a hind, which they attempted to kill. Instead their spears killed one another by mistake. According to another myth they were bound with snakes to a pillar, back to back, while tormented by the screeching of an owl in the underworld. The two were worshiped as heroes on Naxos and in the Boeotian Ascra, where they were regarded as founders of the

city. Both Homer's *Iliad* (books 5 and 11) and *Odyssey* (book 11) and Vergil's *Aeneid* (book 6) allude to them.

0184

Alonzo de Aguilar, Don. 15th century. Spanish hero in the reconquest of Spain from the Moors and the subject of various ballads.

One ballad, *The Death of Don Alonzo de Aguilar*, tells of his last mission. King Ferdinand of Aragon, husband of Isabella, desires to rid the Sierra of Alpuxarra, mountains not far from Granada, of Moors who refuse to accept the Christian faith. He chooses Don Alonzo to lead his forces. With a thousand men Alonzo reaches Nevada, but before he can reach the ravine, he and his men are detected by the Moors, who hurl rocks at them.

Alonzo escapes into the field. The ballad continues:

> There, like a lion, stands at bay, in
> vain besought to yield;
> A thousand foes around are seen, but
> none draws near to fight;
> Afar, with bolt and javelin, they
> pierce the steadfast knight.
> (John Gibson Lockhart translation)

The Moors then come down from their hiding place and take the body. Washington Irving's *The Conquest of Granada* includes "The Legend of the Death of Don Alonzo de Aguilar" at the end of the book.

0185

Alope (shy as a vixen). In Greek mythology, daughter of Cercyon of Eleusis and, by Poseidon, mother of Hippothoon. After Hippothoon's birth she exposed him in the woods to die. When Alope's father learned of this, he planned to kill her, but Poseidon saved her by changing her into a fountain. Hippothoon was saved by some shepherds and was placed by Theseus on his grandfather's throne.

0186

Alpha and Omega (A Ω). In the Bible, N.T., the first and last letters of the Greek alphabet, used in the Book of Revelation (22:13) as a symbol of God: "I am Alpha and Omega , the beginning and the end, the first and the last." Earlier in the same book (1:3) is the verse "I am Alpha and Omega, the beginning and the ending, saith the Lord," symbolizing the beginning of a new era.

The use of the first and last letters of an alphabet to signify totality was used by many cultures, including the Hebraic. The idea is expressed in a passage in Isaiah (44:6): "Thus saith the Lord the King of Israel, And his Redeemer the Lord of hosts; I am the first, and I am the last; And beside me there is no God."

The early Christians naturally applied the Greek letters to Christ in his role as God-Redeemer. The symbol appears on frescoes, monuments, lamps, etc., as early as the third century C.E. in Rome and was known throughout most of Europe by the early Middle Ages.

Often the Greek letters were combined with other symbolic devices. As a symbol of Christ, they were sometimes used with the cross. Other times they were combined with a wreath (Christian symbol of victory over death), a triangle (symbol of the Christian Trinity) or a circle (symbol of eternity). In some symbolism alpha resembles a compass and omega, a torch, with God both creator (the compass) and destroyer (fire).

0187
Alphege, St. (successor). 11th century C.E. In Christian legend, archbishop of Canterbury. Feast, 19 April. He was made archbishop in 1006; six years later the Danes took the city and the cathedral of Canterbury, killing the people and burning the city. Alphege was kept in prison for seven months; then he was stoned to death because he refused to pay a large ransom for his life. Ten years after his death his body was found "entire and incorrupt," according to medieval Christian legend.

0188
Alphesiboea (bringing many oxen). In Greek mythology, daughter of Phegeus and first wife of Alcmaeon as Arsinoe. Though Alcmaeon was unfaithful to her, she continued to love him and was angry when her brothers killed him. Her brothers shut her up in a box and brought her to Agapenor, king of Tegea, pretending that she had killed her husband. Eventually she died but not before she had her brothers killed by the son of Alcmaeon.

0189
Als. In Persian mythology, demonic beings, found also in later Persian-Islamic, Christian, and Armenian myths and legends. Als are half human, half animal, of both sexes, who live in watery and sandy places. One Christian Armenian legend tells of an encounter St. Peter and St. Paul had with an Al.

One day SS. Peter and Paul were traveling and came to a roadside where a man was sitting in the sand. His hair was made of snakes, his eyebrows of brass, his eyes of glass and his teeth of iron; his face was as white as snow, and he had a tusk like a wild boar.

"What are you, you ugly, unclean beast?" the saints asked him.

"I am the wicked Al. I sit upon the childbearing mother, I scorch her ears and pull out her liver. I strangle both mother and child. Our food is the flesh of little children. We steal unborn infants of eight months and bring them to our demon king. The abyss, the corners of houses, and stables are our abode."

To prevent the Al from doing its evil work, sabers and other weapons are placed under a woman's pillow. After the child's birth the mother is kept awake so that the Als do not have the opportunity to catch her off guard.

0190
Al-Safa and Al-Marwa. Two mounds at Mecca that lie opposite each other. Muslims perform a rite called *sa'y* between the two mounds. The rite is in memory of Hagar (in Arabic, Hadjar) who, according to Islamic legend, ran seven times between al-Safa and al-Marwa to find water for her thirsty son Ishmael.

In another legend Isaf and Na'ila were guilty of indecent conduct in the Kaaba, which is located near al-Safa and al-Marwa. As a result of their sin they were turned into stone statues. Isaf was placed on al-Safa and Na'ila on al-Marwa. In time pagan Arabs began to worship the two as gods.

In another tradition the hills were once the home of night-shrieking demons. They were removed when Muhammad took Mecca from the pagans.

0191
Altis. In Greek cult, a grove sacred to Zeus near Olympia in which the Olympic Games were celebrated. Statues of the champions were placed in the grove.

0192
Altjira (him none made). In Australian mythology, self-existent creator god of the Arunta, conceived of as a man with the feet of an emu. After creation Altjira grew bored with the world and its people and returned to the sky, where he displays little concern for the affairs of humankind.

0193
Aluluei. In Micronesian mythology, god of seafaring. He was killed by his jealous brothers but restored to life by his father, who set numerous eyes in his head to protect him from further harm. His eyes became the stars in heaven and are used by sailors to navigate.

0194
Al-Uzza (the strong, the powerful). In Arabian mythology, goddess whose shrine was destroyed by order of Muhammad.

Al-Uzza, along with Manat, or Manah, the goddess of fate and death, and al-Lat, or Allat, the sun, formed a trinity. Al-Uzza's shrine was located in the valley of Nakhla on the road from Taif to

Mecca. It consisted of three *samura* or acacia trees. There was also a cave where animals were sacrificed to her. The three goddesses, al-Uzza, Manat, and al-Lat, were held in such high regard by the Arabs that Allah once consented to recognize them as intercessors with him. He changed his mind, however, and ordered them wiped out (Koran, suras 53, 22).

The pagan Arabs also worshiped another trinity: Shamshu, the sun (a female divinity), and two male divinities, Athtar (the planet Venus) and Shahar (the moon).

0195
Amadis of Gaul (love-god). In late medieval Spanish legend, hero who appears in an anonymous prose romance, *Amadis of Gaul*, first published in 1508 in four books. Numerous additional books by various authors were added later. Amadis, also called the Lion Knight, from the device on his shield, and Beltenbros (darkly beautiful), from his physical appearance, was the illegitimate son of Perion, king of Gaula (Wales) and Elizena, princess of Brittany. At his birth his mother, anxious to conceal the boy, placed him in an ark and launched him in a stream, which carried him to the Scottish coast. He was then found by the knight Gandales and called "child of the sea." A parchment roll, which Gandales found around the child's neck, declared the boy to be the son of a king and eventually helped to identify him. Amadis loved Oriana (Oriane), and in one episode in the legend the lovers came to Firm Island, once ruled by King Apolidon, whose fantastic palace contained the Arch of True Lovers and the Forbidden Chamber, both used to test Amadis's love for Oriana. Eventually, the two were married and had a son, Esplandian. Numerous operas have been written about Amadis of Gaul; among them Jean Baptiste Lully's *Amadis de Gaule*; Johann Christian Bach's *Amadis de Gaule*; Handel's *Amadigi di Gaula*, sometimes called *Oriana*; and Jules Massenet's *Amadis*. The English poet Robert Southey published an abridged English version of the first four books of Amadis of Gaul in 1803.

0196
Amaethon (laborer, ploughman). In Celtic mythology, culture hero, a god of agriculture, worshiped in Britain; son of Don; brother of Gwydion. He stole a dog, lapwing, and roebuck from Arawn, god of the dead, causing a war called the Battle of Cath Godeau, or Battle of the Trees, in which Gwydion transformed trees into fighting men. Amaethon and Gwydion, along with Llaw, defeated the underworld deities.

0197
Amalthea (tender). In Greek mythology, a goat nymph or goat who suckled the newborn Zeus. According to one account, Amalthea was the daughter of the Cretan king Melisseus, and she brought up the infant Zeus on the milk of a goat, while her sister Melissa (a bee) offered him honey. The horn of the goat was given to her by Zeus, with the promise that she would always find in it whatever she wished. From Amalthea the cornucopia passed to the river god Achelous, who was happy to exchange for it his own horn, which Heracles had broken off. The cornucopia is a common attribute of Dionysus, Plutus, and other deities associated with the earth. In a variant myth, Amalthea was later transformed into the star Capella. Amalthea was the patron of shepherds and frequently appears in 18th-century grottoes, such as the Queen's Dairy at Versailles. She appears as a goat in an early work of the Italian sculptor Bernini and in two paintings by the French painter Poussin. Milton's *Paradise Regained* (book 2.355) refers to her horn, and Keats' *Endymion* (II.448) refers to her role as nurse to Zeus.

0198
Amangons. In Arthurian legend, the king of Logres. In the wells and springs of Logres lived damsels who fed the wayfarers with meat and bread. One day, Amangons wronged a damsel, carrying off her golden cup. Later, subjects of the king followed his example; the damsels never again appeared, and the land became desolate.

0199
Ama-no-hashidate (heavenly stairs). In Japanese Shinto mythology, bridge or stairway between heaven and earth. On it the primeval creator couple, Izanagi and Izanami, stood while forming the earth. One day the bridge collapsed into the sea, forming an elongated isthmus situated to the west of Kyoto in the province of Tamba.

Variants: Ama-no-uki-hasi (floating bridge of heaven), Ame- no-iha-fune (heavenly rocking boat).

0200
Ama-no-Kawa. In Japanese Shinto mythology, the river of heaven, identified with the Milky Way or the rainbow.

Variant spellings: Ama-no-yase-kawa, Ame-no-yasu-no-kawa, Yasu.

0201
Ama-no-Minaka-Nushi. In Japanese Shinto mythology, primeval god, mentioned in the *Kojiki* (records of ancient matters), who stood motionless in the center of the cosmos. In the *Nihongi* (chronicles of Japan), written later than the *Kojiki*, he is called Kuni-

Toko-Tachi-No-Mikoto. He is the ancestor of the primeval creator couple, Izanagi and Izanami.

Amant, Sir. 0202
In Arthurian legend, a knight at the court of King Arthur, slain by King Mark of Cornwall. Amant is mentioned in Malory's *Morte d'Arthur*.

Amareswara (lord of the immortals). 0203
Title often applied to the Hindu gods Vishnu, Shiva, and Indra. The term is also used for the 12 great *lingas* (phalluses) worshiped as forms of the god Shiva.

Amario. 0204
In Japanese mythology, the rain dragon. *Variant spelling*: Amaryu.

Amaterasu Omikami (heaven-shining great goddess). 0205
In Japanese Shinto mythology, sun goddess, born from the left eye of Izanagi, the great primeval creator god. She taught her people to plant rice and weave cloth.

One of the main myths contained in the *Kojiki* (records of ancient matters) tells of the conflict between Amaterasu and her brother Susano, the storm god. One day Susano asked his father, Izanagi, for permission to visit his sister Amaterasu. But as the text says, Susano

> . . . so greatly mortified his august sister Amaterasu Omikami, that she hid herself in a cave, whereupon both heaven and earth became dark; and to entice her forth, the eight million spirits of the Plain of Heaven assembled trees before the cave, bedecked with jewels, lighted bonfires, and laughed aloud with such uproar an obscene dance performed by a spirit- female named Uzume that the goddess in her cave, becoming curious, opened the door to peek out. They held a mirror before her, the first she had ever seen: she was drawn out, and the world again was light. (Based on Basil H. Chamberlain translation)

After the world was restored to light, Susano was exiled and fled to the earth, to Izumo (Japan). His descendants gradually took possession of the land that had given them hospitality. However, Amaterasu later regained possession of her domains. It was then that her grandson Ninigi no Mikoto came in person to rule the land and married the goddess of Mount Fuji. Ninigi was the great grandfather of Jimmu Tenno, the first historical emperor of Japan; thus, the royal house claimed Amaterasu as its first ancestor. The sakaki tree, identified as *Eura ochnacea* and *Cleyera japonica*, is sacred to the goddess. Combs are made from it for the deity. The tree grows around shrines of the goddess, and sprigs of it are used as offerings.

The goddess is worshiped at her great shrine at Ise. She is sometimes called Ohirume, Shimmei, Tenshoko Daijin.

Ama-tsu-kami and Kuni-tsu-kami. 0206
In Japanese Shinto mythology, terms for "heavenly gods" and "earthly gods." However, the distinction between the Ama-tsu-kami, who inhabit the vast region called the Milky Way, and the Kuni-tsu-kami, who inhabit mountains, rivers, and trees of the earth, is not absolute: some of the heavenly gods descend to earth, and some of the earthly gods ascend to the heavens.

Amazon

Amazons (without breast). 0207
In Greek mythology, tribe of female warriors who lived in Cappadocia in Asia Minor. They had only one breast, one having

been removed in youth so that they could more freely shoot their bows. No men were allowed in the tribe. Mating took place at certain seasons with men of another race, and only girl babies were kept. If boys were born, they were killed, maimed, or given to their fathers. The Amazons appear in myths relating to Bellerophon, Heracles, Perseus, and Theseus, all of whom fought against them. Theseus kidnapped the Amazon queen Hippolyta (Antiope). Another Amazon queen, Penthesilea, aided the Trojans and was killed by Achilles during the Trojan War. In Greek art the Amazons are portrayed as manly women with two breasts. Usually they are portrayed on horseback, sometimes in Scythian dress—a tight fur tunic, with a cloak and a kind of Phrygian cap—though sometimes they are portrayed wearing a Dorian tunic tucked up, the right shoulder bare. The most famous statues of Amazons were by Phidias, Polyclitus, and Cresilas. The Greeks often cited the conquest of the Amazons as a triumph of civilization over barbarism. When the Spanish came to the New World, they reported that there was a race of Amazons in Brazil. One Spanish clergyman described them as "very tall, robust, fair, with long hair twisted over their heads, skins around their loins and bows and arrows in their hands, with which they killed seven or eight Spaniards." Amazons are mentioned or cited in Vergil's *Aeneid* (book 5), Apollodorus' *Bibliotheca* (Library, book 2), Herodotus' *Histories* (book 4), and Pausanias' *Description of Greece* (book 7).

0208

Ambapali. Fifth century B.C.E. In Buddhist legend, a courtesan of the city of Vaishaili who offered her house to the Buddha for his use as a meeting place. Buddha said of her, "This woman moves in worldly circles and is a favorite of kings and princes; yet is her heart composed and quieted. Young in years, rich, surrounded by pleasures, she is thoughtful and steadfast. This, indeed, is rare in the world."

0209

Ambrose, St. (immortal). 339–397 C.E. In Christian legend, Doctor of the Church, patron saint of beekeepers, bakers of honey-bread, domestic animals, geese, and wax refiners. Feast, 4 April.

Theseus capturing Hippolyta

Born in Gaul and trained as a lawyer, Ambrose was elected bishop of Milan when he was 35 years old, although at the time he was not even baptized. When this was remedied, he took office and became noted for his strict discipline. He was a close friend of St. Augustine, whose conversion he was partly responsible for, with the help of Augustine's mother, Monica.

As recorded in numerous sources—such as *The Golden Legend*, a series of saints' lives written in the 13th century by Jacobus de Voragine—the most famous episode in the life of St. Ambrose concerns his treatment of the Roman Emperor Theodosius. The emperor had killed some 7,000 men, women, and children as punishment for a small uprising in Thessalonica, where some of his soldiers were injured. St. Ambrose refused to let the ruler enter his church and excommunicated him. After eight months Ambrose consented to relent, on two conditions: first, that the emperor should publish an edict by which no capital punishment could be executed until 30 days after conviction of a crime, and second, that the emperor should perform public penance. Theodosius consented to the arrangement and did public penance in the bishop's church. The scene was sometimes painted to symbolize the authority of the church over secular powers, one of the key issues during the Middle Ages.

According to another legend, when Ambrose was an infant, a swarm of bees alighted on his mouth without harming him. This was taken as a sign that he would be noted for his eloquence. The same tale is told of Plato and numerous Christian saints. Another legend tells how a prefect, Macedonius, closed his doors to the pleas of a poor criminal. When he heard of it, St. Ambrose said to Macedonius, "Thou, even thou, shalt fly to the church for refuge, and shalt not enter." A short time afterward, Macedonius was pursued by some of his enemies and fled for sanctuary to the church. Even though the doors were wide open, he could not find the entrance but walked around as a blind man until he was slain.

In Christian art St. Ambrose is often portrayed as a bishop with miter and crosier. He sometimes holds a book or a pen with the inscription *In carne vivere preter carnem angelicam et non humanam* (to be nourished by food, but rather the food of angels, not of mortals).

0210

Ambrosia (immortal). In Greek mythology, the honey-flavored food of the gods, as nectar was their drink. Doves daily brought ambrosia from the far west to Zeus and the other gods. Ambrosia was also the name given to anointing oil, which was believed to preserve the dead from decay. Homer's *Iliad*

(books 1, 14, 16, 24), Vergil's *Aeneid* (book 1), and Ovid's *Metamorphoses* (book 2) all cite the magic food.

0211

Amburbium (to walk around). In Roman cult, the name for a solemn procession of the people, led by the pontifex and various orders of priests, three times around the boundaries of Rome. It was performed at times of national distress. A hog, a ram and a bull were sacrificed, with special prayers. The rite was adopted by the Christian church as Rogation Days, which are set aside for the harvest and generally are observed on the three days before Ascension Day.

0212

Amenhotep, Son of Hapu. In Egyptian history and legend, sage and minister of Amenhotep III (1379 – 1417 B.C.E.), invoked as an intercessor by the people in times of trouble or need. He was known for his wisdom and for the beautiful temples he had built. In Egyptian art Amenhotep is usually portrayed as a scribe with a roll of papyrus on his knees.

0213

Amesha Spentas. In Persian mythology, seven "immortal bounteous ones," or archangels, created by the good god, Ahura Mazda, and manifestations of himself. They are:

Vohu Manah—the firstborn of Ahura Mazda, who sits at his right hand. He protects animals and appeared to the prophet Zarathustra. Vohu Manah keeps a record of men's thoughts, words, and deeds and acts as a recording angel. Vohu Manah is also known as Bahman.

Asha—truth, the most beautiful of Ahura Mazda's creations. She represents divine law, moral order. Asha is also known as Asha-Vahista or Ardabhisht. The faithful in Zoroastrian belief are called Ashavans, followers of the truth of Ahura Mazda.

Kshathra Vairya—a personification of god's might, majesty, dominion, and power. He helps the poor and weak overcome all evil, protects metals, and is the enemy of the demon Savar, who is responsible for misgovernment. Kshathra Vairya is also known as Shahrevar.

Armaiti—devotion, the daughter of Ahura Mazda who sits at his left hand, presiding over the earth and giving pasture to cattle. She is the personification of faithful obedience, harmony, and religious worship.

Haurvatat—integrity, a personification of salvation, the spirit of health, and protector of water and vegetation. Haurvatat is also known as Khurdad.

Ameretat—immortality or deathlessness. Ameretat, like Haurvatat, is associated with water and vegetation.

Sraosha—obedience, the guardian of the world, who feeds the poor and will later help judge the world.

The Amesha Spentas are the cause of considerable debate among scholars in the Persian mythology. Some scholars believe them to be based on the ancient gods of the Indo-Iranian hierarchy, some of which are also found in Hindu mythology. Others see the seven as manifestations of the one god, Ahura Mazda, similar to the archangels in Christian mythology. Some scholars, in fact, believe the concept of angels in Jewish-Christian mythology is derived in part from the Amesha Spentas.

Variant spellings: Ameshospends, Amshaspands.

0214

Amfortas. In Arthurian legend, the most famous fisher king, keeper of the Holy Grail. In early medieval French works his title is rich fisher, and eventually it became fisher king. In one legend he meets Perceval while he is fishing and invites him to his castle. Perceval is afterward informed that because Amfortas is wounded he is unable to mount his horse; therefore, his only solace is fishing. Amfortas is also called the Maimed King, referring to his condition.

He appears in T. S. Eliot's poem *The Waste Land* as well as in Wagner's last stage work *Parsifal*. In Wagner's opera Amfortas's wound is caused when the king had been enticed into the garden of Klingsor, the evil magician. Klingsor had determined to secure the Holy Grail, the cup used by Jesus at the Last Supper, as well as the spear that had pierced Jesus' side. Wrestling the spear from Amfortas, Klingsor wounded the king in the process. The wound then could only be healed by a guileless fool, who in Wagner's music drama is Parsifal.

0215

Amitabha (Buddha of Infinite Light). In Buddhism, one of the five Dhyani-Buddhas issuing from the Adi-Buddha, the primordial Buddha. In Pure Land Buddhism he is the Supreme Buddha, and Vairocana is not mentioned. In China and Japan he is also known as Amitayus. In Tibet, Amitayus is a subsidiary emanation of Amitabha.

0216

Amnon of Mainz. Tenth century. In Jewish legend, a martyr who refused to be converted to Christianity by force under the archbishop of Mainz. When Amnon refused, his limbs were cut off and he was taken to the synagogue, reciting a fragment of a prayer. After he died he appeared in a dream to another Jew and taught him the complete prayer.

Amitabha

0217

Amoghasiddhi. In Mahayana Buddhism, one of the five Dhyani-Buddhas. He is the Buddha of Infallible Magic, whose symbol is the double-thunderbolt and whose mount is a dwarf.

0218

Amor (love). In Roman mythology, a name given to Cupid, the god of love, son of Venus and Mars; called Eros in Greek mythology.

0219

Amphiaraus (doubly cursed). In Greek mythology, a hero, son of Oicleus and Hypermnestra; married Eriphyle; father of Alcmeon, Amphilocus, Demonassa, and Eurydice; great-grandson of the seer Melampus. Homer says Amphiaraus was a favorite of Zeus and Apollo and was both a hero and a seer, taking part in the Calydonian boar hunt, the voyage of the Argonauts, and the expedition of the Seven against Thebes. Amphiaraus fought with Adrastus, but the quarrel was settled when he married Adrastus' sister Eriphyle. He agreed that any future difference between Adrastus and himself would be settled by Eriphyle. But Eriphyle, bribed by Polynices with the fatal necklace of Polynices' ancestress Harmonia, insisted that her husband, Amphiaraus, join in the war against Thebes. Amphiaraus knew that he would die, and he told his youthful sons Alcmaeon and Amphilochus to avenge his coming death. He warned the other chiefs of the coming disaster but was forced into a final battle with Tydeus. In the fight, just as Amphiaraus was about to die, Zeus opened the earth with his thunderbolt and swallowed up Amphiaraus and Baton, his charioteer.

Amphiaraus was worshiped at Oropus on the frontier of Attica and Boeotis, where he had a temple and an oracle for the interpretation of dreams. Games were also celebrated in his honor.

Variant spelling: Amphiorax.

0220

Amphilochus (double ambush). In Greek mythology, son of the Argive seer Amphiaraus and Eriphyle; Alcmaeon's brother. Amphilochus also was a seer and according to some accounts took part in the war of the Epigoni, or Seven against Thebes, and the murder of his mother. Amphilochus was believed to have founded the Amphilochian Argos near Neckhori in Acarnania. Later myths say he took part in the Trojan War. After the fall of Troy he went with Mopsus and founded the oracle at Mallus. However, the two fought and killed one another for the possession of the shrine. After the funeral pyre had consumed their bodies, their spirits, or ghosts, became close friends. As a result, an oracle was established in their honor. The supplicants would write their questions on wax tablets, and the spirits would answer them in a dream.

0221

Amphion and Zethus (with the moon on either side of him and seeker). In Greek mythology, the Boeotian Dioscuri, twin sons of Antiope by Zeus. A variant account says Zethus was the son of Epopeus. The two infants were exposed to die on Mount Cithaeron and were rescued and reared by a shepherd. When they grew up, they found their mother, who had fled from imprisonment at Thebes, where she had been mistreated by Dirce, the wife of Lycus, who governed Thebes as guardian to Laius. They avenged their mother by tying Dirce to the horns of a bull that dragged her to her death. They then threw Dirce's corpse into a spring near Thebes, which was later renamed after her. They killed Lycus and assumed his throne, or according to a variant account, it was given to them by Lycus when the god Hermes told him to abdicate. They fortified Thebes with walls and towers. Zethus brought up the stones, while Amphion, a harper, fit them together by the music of his lyre. Zethus married Thebe, the daughter of Asopus or, according to a variant account, Aëdon, daughter of Pandareos. Amphion married Niobe. After the destruction of his family by Apollo and Artemis as punishment for a boast by Niobe,

Amphion and Zethus

Amphion killed himself. In a variant myth, Amphion was killed by Apollo for attacking Apollo's priests in revenge for the god's murder of his children. Both brothers were said to be buried in one grave.

0222

Amphisbaena (both ways, to go). Fantastic two-headed poisonous serpent with legs. It could stick one of its heads into the mouth of the other, forming a loop, which enabled it to roll down a road. Aeschylus' play *Agamemnon* compares Clytemnestra, the wife and murderess of Agamemnon, to the animal. During the Christian Middle Ages the bestiaries portrayed the animal as a symbol of the devil. In Milton's *Paradise Lost* (book 10) Satan's followers are turned into scorpions, asps, and "Amphisbaena dire."

Amphitrite (the third one who encircles, i.e., the sea). In Greek mythology, a sea goddess, daughter of Nereus and Doris (or Oceanus and Tethys); wife of Poseidon; mother of Albion, Benthesicyme, Charybdis, Rhode, and Triton. Poseidon saw Amphitrite dancing with the Nereids on the island of Naxos and carried her off. According to a variant account, she fled from Poseidon to Atlas, but Poseidon's dolphin saw her and brought her to the god. Homer does not call her Poseidon's wife but a sea goddess who beats the billows against the rocks. Amphitrite had no separate worship or cult. She was often portrayed with a net confining her hair, with crabs' claws on the crown of her head, being carried by Tritons or by dolphins and other marine animals, or drawn by them in a chariot of shells. The Romans identified her with Salacia, their goddess of the salt waves. Amphitrite appears in Ovid's *Metamorphoses* (book 1) and Keats's *Endymion* (II.108). She appears in Poussin's painting, *The Triumph of Neptune and Amphitrite*.

Amphitryon (harassing on either side). In Greek mythology, king of Tiryns, son of Alcaeus and Astydameia, Hipponome, or Laonome; first husband of Alcmena; father of Iphicles; grandson of Perseus. His father's brother, Electryon, king of Mycenae, went to war against Pterelaus, king of the Taphians and Teleboans, because their sons had carried off his cattle and slain Electryon's eight sons except Licymnius. Electryon left Amphitryon in charge of his kingdom and gave him his daughter Alcmena to be his wife. On Electryon's return Amphitryon killed him in a quarrel (or by accident). Amphitryon fled with his future wife and her brother Licymnius to Creon, king of Thebes. Creon was a brother of Amphitryon's mother. Creon purged Amphitryon of his blood guilt for slaying Electryon and offered him aid against Pterelaus if Amphitryon first would render harmless the Taumessian fox. Alcmena would not wed Amphitryon unless her brothers' deaths were avenged. Having rendered the fox harmless with the help of Cephalus, Amphitryon marched against the Taphians, accompanied by Creon, Cephalus, and other heroes, and conquered their country. While Amphitryon was away at war, Zeus assumed his likeness for the purpose of seducing Alcmena. Later the same night, Amphitryon himself slept with Alcmena. Two children were conceived that night, Heracles and Iphicles. Amphitryon was told by a seer what Zeus had done, and he accepted both children as his sons. According to a variant myth, he put two harmless snakes in their crib to see which son was his and which belonged to Zeus. Heracles seized both snakes and killed them. Amphitryon knew then that Iphicles was his son and Heracles belonged to the god. In a variant account, it was Hera, the wife of Zeus, who placed the snakes in the crib, and they were poisonous and meant to kill Heracles. Amphitryon was killed in a war with Erginus, the Minyan king of Orchomenus.

The seduction of Alcmena by Zeus has had special appeal to playwrights, such as the Roman Plautus, the Frenchman Molière, and the Englishman John Dryden, with music of Henry Purcell. Jean Giraudoux wrote *Amphitryon 38*, saying it was the thirty-eighth version of the story.

Amrita (immortal). Water of life in Hindu mythology, often identified with Soma juice. The Amrita was produced at the churning of the ocean, when the gods and demons, at odds with one another, brought it forth. In some texts Amrita is called Nir-jara and Piyusha.

Amun (the invisible one). In Egyptian mythology, a god whose presence could be sensed in temples when pennants attached to the flagstaves in front of the pylons fluttered. Sometimes Amun and the sun god Ra were combined to form the composite god Amun-Ra. At first Amun was merely a god of local importance. However, after the princes of Thebes gained sovereignty over Egypt, making their city the new capital of the country, Amun became a prominent god in Upper Egypt and was looked upon as "King of the Gods." At that time Amun's sanctuary at Karnak was a comparatively small building, consisting of a shrine surrounded by a few small chambers and a forecourt with a colonnade on two sides. When the Theban princes became kings of Egypt, their priests declared their god Amun not only another form of the great creator sun god who was worshiped under such names as Ra and Khepera, but they gave him all the attributes that were ascribed to the sun gods and proclaimed him the greatest of them all. When Amun was coupled with Ra, forming the composite god Amun-Ra in the Eighteenth Dynasty, he became the mysterious creative power that was the Amun-Ra source of all life in heaven, earth, and the underworld. Eventually the priests of Amun claimed that there was no other god like Amun, who was the "one one" and had "no second."

In Egyptian art Amun-Ra is usually portrayed as a bearded man with a headdress of double plumes, various sections of which are colored alternately red and green or red and blue. Around his neck he wears a broad collar or necklace, and his close-fitting kilt or tunic is supported by elaborately worked shoulder straps. His arms and wrists are decked with armlets and bracelets. In his right hand is the ankh, symbol of life, and in his left the scepter. The tail of a lion or bull hangs from his tunic. Sometimes Amun-Ra is given a hawk's head surmounted by the solar disk encircled by a serpent. When Amun appears with his wife, Amunet, he is often portrayed as a frog-headed man and she as a uraeus- headed woman. When Amun is shown with the uraeus, Amunet is depicted with the head of a cat.

Variant spellings: Amen, Aman, Ammon, Amon, Hammon.

0227

Amycus (loudly bellowing). In Greek mythology, a giant son of Poseidon and Melië, a nymph. Amycus would force everyone who landed on the Bithynian coast to box with him. When the Argonauts wished to draw water from a spring in his country, he forbade them. He was killed in a match with Polydeuces. Ovid's *Metamorphoses* (book 12) and Apollonius Rhodius' *Argonautica* (book 2) tell the tale.

0228

Anael. In Jewish and Christian legend, angel. In Henry Wadsworth Longfellow's dramatic poem *The Golden Legend* (not to be confused with the thirteenth century book of saints' lives) Anael is one of the seven angels that bear the star of Bethlehem. In the Old Testament Apocrypha Book of Tobit (1:22) Anael is the name of Tobit's brother. His son Ahikar served as Sennacherib's cupbearer, accountant, and chief administrator. Ahikar appears in many Oriental tales as an ancient wise man.

Variant spellings: Haniel, Hamiel, Onoel.

0229

Anahita. In Persian mythology, water and fertility goddess who cleaned the seed of the male, blessed the womb of the female, and purified the milk in a mother's breast. According to the Greek historian Strabo, writing in the early part of the first century C.E., the daughters of noble families had to serve in the temple of the goddess at Anatolia as prostitutes before their marriage. The cult of Anahita was found in Armenia, under the name of Anahit, the "great queen," the "one born of gold," the golden mother," who, though a fertility goddess, was not connected with water, as in Persia. In Greece, Anahita often was equated with the goddesses Artemis and Aphrodite.

In Persian art Anahita is portrayed as a beautiful, strong woman, wearing a golden crown with eight rays and surrounded by a hundred stars. She also wears a golden necklace and a dress.

Variant spellings: Anaitis, Aredvi Sura Anahita.

0230

Anakims (long-necked). In the Bible, O.T., race of pre-Israelites in the Holy Land. The term was originally an appellative, "people of the neck" or "necklace."

In the Old Testament the Anakims are described as a tall people, whose gigantic size terrified the Hebrews (Num. 13:28). In Jewish folklore they are considered the offspring of fallen angels and mortal women, alluding to a belief in Genesis (6:2): "That the sons of God [angels] saw the daughters of men that they were fair; and they took them wives of all which they chose." The mystical *Zohar* says the "Hebrews were like grasshoppers in comparison with the Anakims." Erich Von Däniken's *Chariots of the Gods* argues that the Genesis text illustrates that intelligent space travelers visited earth during man's early years on the planet, becoming prototypes of "gods" in many ancient mythologies.

Variant spelling: Rephaim.

0231

Ananda (bliss). Fifth century B.C.E. In Buddhist history and legend, cousin of the Buddha, one of the foremost disciples of the Buddha; noted for his ability to remember all of the sutras, or spoken words, of the Buddha. According to some accounts he compiled the Buddhist writings. In Buddhist art Ananda is portrayed as a monk. In Chinese Buddhist art works he is often shown with Kasyapa, another disciple of the Buddha.

0232

Anansi. In African mythology, trickster who can transform himself into a spider. Known by such names as Gizo, Kwaku Ananse, Nansi, and Miss Nancy, Anansi appears in West African folktales and is also known in the West Indies. One of the most famous tales connected with Anansi was the source for the black American folktale of Brer Rabbit and the Tar Baby. Anansi's son is called Ntikuma or Taçuma.

Anatapindaka (one who gives alms to the unprotected). Fifth century B.C.E. In Buddhist legend, a wealthy layman friend of the Buddha. When Anatapindaka asked the Buddha if he should give up his wealth, the Buddha replied: "I say unto thee, remain in thy station of life and apply thyself with diligence to thy enterprises. It is not life and wealth and power that enslave men but the cleaving to life and wealth and power." 0233

Anath. In Near Eastern mythology (Canaanite), war goddess, queen of heaven, mistress of the gods. In one myth Anath obtained the help of the great god Baal to conquer the mountains of Lebanon and build a temple in his and her honor. She did this by making a feast and destroying all of Baal's enemies when they attended. Part of her cult consisted in sacrifices of young men. One myth reveals the goddess's demonic nature. Aqhat was the son of King Danel (or Daniel) and had a magnificent bow that the goddess wished to possess. She tried every ploy in an unsuccessful effort to trick Aqhat into giving her the bow and finally had him killed. At his death, however, the earth became sterile. Eventually, he was restored to life (though this part is missing from the myth), but the bow and arrows were lost or broken. Anath was portrayed with a helmet, shield, and spear in her right hand, a battle ax or club in her left. The lion was her sacred animal. 0234

Variant spellings: Anat, Anata, Hanata.

Anchises (living with Isis). In Greek and Roman mythology, father of Aeneas; king of the Dardania; loved by Aphrodite; son of Capys and Themiste. Aphrodite loved him for his beauty and bore him Aeneas. When Anchises boasted of her favor, he was either paralyzed, killed, or struck blind by the lightning of Zeus; accounts differ. Vergil's *Aeneid* (book 2) portrays Anchises as being borne out of the burning city of Troy on Aeneas' shoulders and sharing in his wanderings over the sea until they reached Drepanum in Sicily, where Anchises died at age 80 and was buried on Mount Eryx. Aeneas carrying his father is the subject of an early work of the Italian sculptor Bernini, as well as the subject of a painting by Raphael. 0235

Ancient of Days. In the Bible, O.T., title applied to Yahweh, the Hebrew god, in the Book of Daniel (7:9) in the King James Version of the Bible. 0236

Daniel describes a vision: the "Ancient of Days did sit, whose garment was white as snow, and the hair on his head like the pure wool; his throne was like the fiery flame, and his wheels as burning fire" (Dan. 7:9). William Blake, the English poet, used the term "Ancient of Days" for Urizen, his poetical creation who filled the role of Yahweh in his personal mythology. There is a well-known watercolor by the poet depicting the figure. A popular hymn begins with:

Ancient of Days, who sittest throned in
glory;
To thee all knees are bent.

Other translations of Ancient of Days are "a primeval Being" (Moffatt), "a Venerable One" (American Translation), "One . . . crowned with age" (Knox).

Some medieval Jewish commentators found the application of the term to God as too anthropomorphic and explained the title as referring to the angel of Yahweh. Other commentators see the concept going back to the figure of the Persian good god Ahura-Mazda. The popular Christian image of God the Father as an old man wearing white is derived from Daniel's image of the Ancient of Days.

Ancile. In ancient Roman ritual, a small, oval sacred shield, curved inward on either side, believed to have fallen from heaven during the reign of Numa. There was a prophecy that the stability of Rome depended on the ancile; Numa had 11 others made exactly like it so that the right one could not be stolen. The set was sacred to the god Mars and was entrusted to the Salii, Roman priests who had to carry them through the city of Rome once a year. 0237

Andersen, Hans Christian. 1805–1875. Danish author of literary folktales, often based on European folk sources; best remembered for his *Eventyr*. Andersen was noted for his sensitive portrayal of people, which sometimes has been attributed to his being homosexual. He wrote in his autobiography, "I had experienced what it was to be poor and lonely, and to move in luxurious surroundings; I had experienced being scorned and honored." Some of the many operas based on his fairy tales are Alfred Bruneau's *Le Jardin du paradis*, August Enna's *The Princess and the Pea*, Niels-Erich Fougstedt's opera for radio *The Tinderbox*, Ebke Hamerik's *The Traveling Companion*, Douglas Moore's *The Emperor's New Clothes*, and Stravinsky's *The Emperor's Nightingale*. *The Red Shoes* was made into a British film of the same title in 1948. 0238

Andhaka (blind). In Hindu mythology, a demon killed by the god Shiva. Andhaka had 1,000 arms and heads and 2,000 eyes and feet. Despite all of this physical equipment, or because of it, Andhaka walked as if he were a blind man. When he tried to steal the Parijata Tree, which perfumed the whole world with its blossoms, he was killed by Shiva. From this feat Shiva earned the title *Andhaka-ripu* (foe of Andhaka).

Andrew, St. (manly). First century C.E. In the Bible, N.T., one of the Twelve Apostles of Jesus; patron saint of Russia and Scotland; protector of fishermen, fishmongers and sailors. Invoked against gout and stiff neck. Feast, 30 November.

In the New Testament Andrew was the brother of St. Peter. He was one of the first two disciples of Jesus and is considered in Christian tradition to be the first missionary because he brought his brother Peter to meet Jesus. In Mark's Gospel (1:16) both Andrew and Peter immediately "forsook their nets" and followed Jesus when he called them to give up their trade as fishermen. We know nothing further of Andrew after the Resurrection of Jesus. An *Acts of St. Andrew*, which no longer survives complete, was written in the early part of the third century C.E. It depicts St. Andrew as imprisoned at Patras and describes his death by crucifixion, though the type of cross is not mentioned, and scholars have debated as to its form. The one that appears most frequently in Christian art is the X-shape cross, called the *crux decussata*. The cross of St. Andrew appears on the British Union Jack, along with the crosses of St. George and St. Patrick, representing, respectively, Scotland, England and Ireland.

According to legend, Achaius, king of the Scots, and Hungus, king of the Pics, saw St. Andrew's cross in the sky before their battle with Athelstane, which they won. They therefore adopted the cross of the saint as the national emblem.

Andreas, a narrative poem in Old English, formerly attributed to the poet Cynewulf, is based on an early Greek work, *Acts of Andrew and Matthias*. The poem tells of St. Andrew's mission to the Mermedonians, Ethiopian savages who had imprisoned Matthias.

According to *The Golden Legend*, a series of saints' lives written in the 13th century in which numerous earlier sources were combined, Andrew made missionary journeys to Scythian Russia, Asia Minor, and Greece, preaching the gospel. At Nicaea he saved the inhabitants from seven demons that plagued them in the shape of dogs. Later, on another journey, a dead boy was brought to the saint. Andrew asked what had happened and was told

"seven dogs came and strangled him." Andrew said these were the seven he had driven out in Nicaea.

"What wilt thou give to me if I raise him?" he said to the father.

"I have nothing so dear as him; I shall give him to thee," the father replied.

Andrew then raised the boy to life, and he became a disciple of the saint.

Other episodes tell how St. Andrew, dressed as a pilgrim, saved a bishop from yielding to the charms of a courtesan, who in actuality was the devil. Another episode tells how he cured Maximilla, wife of the Roman governor Egeas. When she became a Christian, Maximilla discontinued sexual relations with her husband. This was too much for the man to bear, and St. Andrew was imprisoned and finally crucified as a result.

Luther, in his *Table Talk*, tells of the custom of young girls stripping themselves naked and reciting prayers to St. Andrew on the eve of his feast day, to see "what manner of man it is that shall lead" them to the altar.

In Christian art St. Andrew is usually portrayed as an old man with a white beard, holding his cross or on his knees gazing at it. Perhaps the greatest tribute to the saint is Bernini's magnificent church of Sant' Andrea al Quirinale in Rome (1658–1670). It took the artist 12 years to complete the oval building. Behind the altar is a painting of St. Andrew's martyrdom on the cross. Above the altar is a statue of the saint gesturing toward heaven, which is symbolized by the skylighted opening in the gold dome.

Androcles and the Lion. Medieval European legend of a runaway slave who was saved by a lion. Androcles fled from his evil master and hid in a cave, where he encountered a lion that had a thorn in its paw. Androcles removed it. Later he was recaptured and thrown to the lions in the arena. The lion he had helped was among them and protected Androcles from the other beasts. When the crowd saw this, they demanded Androcles' freedom. The legend is told in *Noctes Atticae* (Attic nights) by Aulus Gellius and inspired George Bernard Shaw's play *Androcles and the Lion*.

Androgeos (man of the earth). In Greek mythology, son of Pasiphae and Minos, king of Crete. He visited Athens at the first celebration of the Panathenaea and won victories over all of the champions. Out of jealousy, King Aegeus sent him to fight the bull of Marathon, which killed him. According to a variant account, Androgeos was killed in an ambush. Minos avenged his son's death by making the Athenians send seven young men and seven young girls every nine years as victims to his Minotaur. Funeral games were held in the Ceramicus at Athens in honor of Androgeus, who was then named Eurygyes. The cult is mentioned in Vergil's *Aeneid* (book 6), Apollodorus' *Bibliotheca* (3.15.7), and Pausanias' *Description of Greece* (1.27.9–10)

0243

Andromache (battle of men). In Greek mythology, wife of Hector and daughter of King Eetion of Cilician Thebes. In Homer's *Iliad* she is considered one of the most moving characters, especially in her parting scene from Hector and when she mourns his death. In later, non-Homeric myth Achilles kills Andromache's father and seven brothers. When Troy is taken, her one son, Astyanax (or Scamander), is hurled from the walls to his death. As part of the spoils after the Trojan War, Andromache was given as the prize to Greek hero Neoptolemus, who first took her to Epirus, then surrendered her to Hector's brother Helenus. After Helenus' death Andromache returned to Asia with Pergamus, her son by Neoptolemus, and there she died. In the myth as told by Euripides in his play *Andromache* and by Vergil in *The Aeneid* (book 3), Hermione, the wife of Neoptolemus, hated Andromache because she knew her husband cared for the woman. The theme of Racine's play *Andromaque* is the jealousy of Hermione. The neoclassical French painter David painted *Andromache Mourning Hector*. There are more than 20 operas based on Andromache's tale, among them one by Martin y Soler (1754–1806) and one by Paisiello (1741–1816), both called *Andromaca*.

0244

Andromeda (ruler of men). In Greek mythology, heroine saved by Perseus; daughter of the Ethiopian king Cepheus, a son of Belus by Cassiopeia; wife of Perseus; mother of Alcaeus, Electryon, Heleus, Nestor, Perses, Sthemelus, and Gorgophone. Cassiopeia had boasted of being more beautiful than any of the Nereids, and Poseidon, to punish her arrogance, sent a flood and a sea monster. An oracle promised an end to the plague that resulted only if Andromeda were to be exposed to the monster, so Cepheus chained his daughter to a rock in the sea. Andromeda was saved by the hero Perseus and promised to him in marriage. At the wedding a violent quarrel arose between the king's brother Phineus (who previously had been betrothed to Andromeda) and Perseus. The hero turned his rival into stone by showing him the Gorgon's head. Andromeda followed Perseus to Argos and became the ancestress of the Perseidae. Athena set Andromeda among the stars at her death. Milton makes reference to this in *Paradise Lost* (book 3.559). There are numerous paintings of the rescue

Andromache fainting after her son is hurled from the wall (John Flaxman)

scene, among the most famous being *Perseus and Andromeda* by Peter Paul Rubens. Other works are by Titian, Piero di Cosimo, and Ingres, as well as an earlier fresco at Pompeii. There are some 20 operas about Andromeda, one by the brother of Franz Joseph Haydn, J. M. Haydn (1737–1806) called *Andromeda e Perseo.*

0245

Andvaranaut (Andvari's ring). In Norse mythology, a magic ring belonging to the dwarf Andvari, stolen by the fire-trickster god, Loki. The ring was given to Hreidmar, king of the dwarfs, in part restitution for the murder by Loki of Hreidmar's son Otter. Andvari, however, cursed the ring so that it would destroy all who came in contact with it. In Germanic mythology and in Richard Wagner's works, the ring belongs to Alberich, another name for Andvari. Alberich appears in Wagner's music dramas *Der Ring des Nibelungen*, which have to do with the magic ring and the tragedy it brings on all who possess it. He also is portrayed by Arthur Rackham in his illustrations for Wagner's Ring Cycle.

0246

Andvari. In Norse mythology, a dwarf who is robbed of his wealth by Loki, the fire-trickster god. He is called Alberich (elf rule) by Wagner in *Der Ring des Nibelungen*. Once the gods Odin, Hoenir, and Loki came down to earth in human guise to test the hearts of various people. They came to the land where Hreidmar, the king of the dwarfs (or elves), lived. The gods had not gone far when Loki saw an otter basking in the sun. Up to his evil tricks, Loki killed the otter, which happened to be Hreidmar's son Otter. He flung the lifeless body over his shoulder, thinking it would make a good meal.

Following his companions, Loki came at last to Hreidmar's house with the dead otter, which he flung on the floor. When Hreidmar saw his dead son, he flew into a rage. Before the gods could act, they were bound and told they could not be freed unless they paid for Otter's death with gold enough to cover his skin–inside and out. The otter skin had the magical property of stretching itself to any size, so no ordinary treasure would suffice. Loki was appointed to find enough gold. He ran to a waterfall where the dwarf Andvari lived.

Loki did not find Andvari but instead saw a salmon in the water, which he knew to be Andvari in disguise. Loki caught the salmon in a net and said he would not free him unless he gave Loki his treasures, including the Helmet of Dread and his hoard of gold. Only his magic ring, Andvaranaut, was Andvari to be allowed to keep. The ring worked like magic, collecting rich ore. But then Loki, greedy as usual,

also took the ring. Andvari cursed it, saying anyone who possessed the ring would be destroyed. In the *Poetic Edda* Andvari says:

> That gold which the dwarf possessed shall to two brothers be cause of death, and to eight princes, of dissension. From my wealth no one shall good derive.

Loki nevertheless took the ring. It was given in the payment to Hreidmar, who gloated over his new treasure. One night his son Fafnir killed him and took the treasure.

The myth, which is the basis of Richard Wagner's *Der Ring des Nibelungen*, is found in the *Poetic Edda* and the *Volsunga Saga*, which also influenced William Morris's epic poem, *Sigurd the Volsung and the Fall of the Niblungs*. Andvari (Alberich) is portrayed by Arthur Rackham in his illustrations for Wagner's Ring Cycle.

0247

Angarad of the Golden Hand. In Arthurian legend, a lady at the court of King Arthur who is loved by Sir Peredur, a knight of the Round Table. She, however, scorns Peredur, and he vows never to speak until she loves him above all men. After a series of adventures, in which he is called the "Dumb Youth" or the "Young Mute," he appears at court but is so changed by his ordeals that he goes unrecognized. Angarad, not knowing it is Peredur, is so moved that she says she loves him above all men. Peredur is then released from his vow.

0248

Angel (messenger). In Jewish, Christian, and Islamic mythology, supernatural being who acts as an intermediary between God and man.

The Old Testament contains numerous references to angels. Sometimes, however, when the expression "angel of the Lord" or "angel of Yahweh" is used, it refers to God himself, particularly in the earlier books of the Bible (for example Gen. 22:11–12). In later books, such as the Book of Daniel, angels are separate from God. The angel Michael is called a "prince" of Israel. By New Testament times belief in good and evil angels was accepted in both Christian and Jewish belief.

Angels multiplied at such a rate in the writings of both Jews and Christians that it was felt necessary to put them into some order. Various Early Church writers attempted this. Dionysius the Areopagite, a mystical theologian of the fifth century, divided the heavenly host into nine orders: seraphim, cherubim, and thrones in the first circle; dominions, virtues, and powers in the second circle; and principalities, archangels, and angels in the third circle. Other writers, both Christian and Jewish—such as St. Ambrose, St. Gregory the Great, and St. Jerome—also made up different lists, some with nine orders, some with seven. Dante's list contains nine orders of angels, whereas Moses Maimonides' list contains ten.

The Koran based its angelology in part on Jewish and Christian writings. It frequently mentions angels, or *malaika*, who bear witness to Allah (sura 3). The righteous must also believe in angels (sura 2). A succinct account of belief in angels is given in sura 13, subtitled "Thunder": "Each hath a succession of angels before him, who watch over him by God's behest."

The Koranic statement reflects the belief, held also in Judaism and Christianity, that individuals and also countries have guardian angels. St. Basil of Caesarea believed each nation had a guardian angel, and in Jewish belief each nation has either a demon or an angel watching over it. The English writer Robert Burton, in his *The Anatomy of Melancholy*, written in the 17th century, says, "Every man has a good and bad angel attending him in particular, all his life long." His statement reflects the Roman Catholic belief found in the Feast of the Holy Guardian Angels, observed on 2 October, which has as its collect: "God, who in thy transcendent providence deignest to send thy holy angels to watch over us, grant our humble petition that we may ever be safe under their protection, and may rejoice in their companionship through all eternity." Popular prints portray an angel guiding a child are still sold today with an appropriate prayer:

> Guardian angel, my guardian dear
> To whom God's love commits me here,
> Ever this day be at my side,
> To rule and guide,
> To guide and rule,
> Amen.

In Christian art angels first appeared as young men without wings. By the fourth century winged angels with long hair and flowing robes, derived from copies of Greek and Roman victory statues, occur in some works. During the fifth century, winged angels with halos, robed in white, appear in scenes taken from the New Testament, as in the mosaic of the *Annunciation* in Santa Maria Maggiore in Rome. Yet when angels appeared in Old Testament scenes, they were usually wingless. By the ninth century the winged angels had finally taken the field. Rembrandt, in his painting *Manoah's Sacrifice*, returned to the old usage and omitted wings on his angel, though he often painted winged angels. Dante Gabriel Rossetti, in his painting the *Annunciation*, has a wingless angel confront a rather

Angels taking soul to heaven

frightened Virgin Mary. Islamic art does not allow the depiction of human beings nor of angels; but Persian art, when it treats Islamic themes, shows angels as delicate creatures with multicolored wings, as in *The Angel Gabriel Appearing to Muhammed* in a manuscript of Jai'al-Tawarikh.

Angels are not confined to canvases and books but also appear in numerous movies, such as the early silent film *Intolerance*. In 1936 *Green Pastures* featured an angel, and in 1941 *Here Comes Mr. Jordan* told the story of a boxer in a plane crash who died before his time was up, so an angel, played by Claude Rains, was assigned the task of finding him a new body. In *Heaven Only Knows* an angel comes to earth to reform a Western badman, and in *The Bishop's Wife* Cary Grant played an angel who comes to earth to aid in the lives of various people.

0249

Angelica (angel, messenger). In the Charlemagne cycle of legends, the heroine who appears in Italian versions of the tale of Orlando (Roland). Angelica was "the fairest of her sex." Daughter of Galafhron, king of Cathay (China), she was sent to Paris to sow discord among the Christians. Orlando fell in love with her, but Angelica did not return his love. Instead, she was passionately in love with Rinaldo. He, however, hated her. But when Angelica and Rinaldo drank from a magic fountain, he fell in love with her, and she began to despise him. In Ariosto's *Orlando Furioso*, Charlemagne sends Angelica to the duke of Bavaria, but she escapes from the castle, only to be seized and bound naked to a rock guarded by a sea monster. Later she is freed by Rogero. Eventually, Angelica marries Medoro, a young Moor, and returns to Cathay, where Medoro succeeds to the throne of her father.

Angel of Hadley. In American history and folklore, popular name given to General William Goffe (died c. 1679), an English Puritan who hid from Royalist forces in the American colonies. Having signed the death warrant of King Charles I, Goffe fled England when the Royalists returned to power. He disappeared from sight, then reappeared in Hadley, Massachusetts, when the village was being attacked by a band of Indians. According to legend, a tall man, of stern look, wearing elkskin garments and carrying a sword and gun, appeared. "Men and brethren," he said to the people, "why sink your hearts? and why are you thus disquieted? Fear ye that the God we serve will give ye up to yonder heathen dogs? Follow me; and ye shall see that this day there is a captain in Israel." Spurred on by these heroic words, the people fought off the Indians. When they wished to thank the stranger who had saved them, he replied: "Not unto me be the glory. I am but the implement frail as yourselves in the hand of Him who is strong to deliver." Then as suddenly as he appeared, he disappeared. In Sir Walter Scott's novel *Peveril of the Peak* one of the characters, Bridgenorth, narrates the incident. It also appears in James Fenimore Cooper's novel *Wept of Wish-ton-Wish*, but its most striking use is made by Hawthorne in his short story "The Gray Champion," part of *Twice Told Tales*, in which the name and locale are changed but the basic legend maintained.

Angry Acrobat, The. Moral fable by the Persian poet Sadi, in his *The Gulistan* (chapter 2, story 43).

A holy man saw an acrobat in a great dudgeon, full of wrath and foaming at the mouth.

"What is the matter with this fellow?" the holy man asked.

"Someone has insulted him," a bystander replied.

"This poor fellow is able to lift hundreds of pounds and hasn't the power to bear one word," the holy man said.

Angurboda (one who bodes danger or sorrow). In Norse mythology, a hideous giantess, wife of the fire-trickster god, Loki; mother of the wolf Fenrir, the goddess of death (Hel), and the gigantic Midgard serpent. Angurboda appears in the *Prose Edda*.

Variant spelling: Angrbotha.

Anhanga. In the mythology of the Amazonian Indians of Brazil, a name for the devil, used along with Korupira, who was the demon of the forest and also was equated with the devil.

Anhanga is formless, living in a person's dream life. He loves to play pranks, often stealing children. In a short tale, "The Yara," by the Brazilian journalist and historian Alfonso Arinhos de Melo Franco, he is described as having a "fearful voice" and scattering "upon the grass and the leaves of the bushes the seeds of the sorrows that kill."

Animisha. In Hindu mythology, epithet often applied to various gods, such as Vishnu, Shiva, and Indra, meaning "who does not wink." All of the gods are said to have non-blinking eyes as one of their characteristics. That is how they can be spotted as gods when they assume human form.

Anius (troublous). In Greek mythology, son of Apollo by Rhoeo (or Creusa). Rhoeo's father, Staphylus of Naxos, a son of Dionysus and Ariadne, put Rhoeo to sea in a box. Rhoeo was carried to Delos and there gave birth to her son Anius. Apollo taught Anius divination and made him priest-king over Delos. Because they were descendants of Dionysus, the daughters of Anius by the nymph Dorippe—called Oeno, Spermo, and Elais—had the gift of turning anything they pleased into wine, corn, or oil. When Agamemnon set sail for the Trojan War, he wished to take the three women to help supply his troops with food. They complained to Dionysus, who transformed them into doves. Vergil's *Aeneid* (book 3) and Ovid's *Metamorphoses* (book 13) tell the story.

Ankh

0256

Ankh. Egyptian hieroglyph for "life," a stylization of a sandal strap, later identified with the Greek tau cross and the Christian *crux ansata*. The tau cross is often identified with the Egyptian hermit St. Anthony the Abbot and was worn by the Knights of St. Anthony, established in 1352.

The Annunciation (Dürer)

0257

Anna (grace, favor) and **Joachim** (the Lord will establish), SS. First century C.E. In Christian legend, parents of the Virgin Mary. Feasts, 26 July for Anna and 20 March for Joachim. Neither Anna nor Joachim is mentioned in the New Testament. Their legend is found in various early apocryphal writings that circulated within the Early Church. One of the major sources is *The Gospel of the Birth of Mary*, once ascribed to St. Matthew and translated from Greek into Latin in the fourth century by St. Jerome.

Joachim was from Nazareth and Anna from Bethlehem; both were of the royal house of King David. The couple was rich but also childless. One day, when Joachim brought his offering to the temple, it was refused by the high priest, Issachar, because Joachim had no children. Joachim was afraid to return home, but an angel appeared to him telling him he would be a father. Afterward the angel appeared to Anna, his wife, saying: "Fear not, neither think that which you see is a spirit. For I am that angel who hath offered up your prayers and alms before God, and now sent to you, that, I may inform you, a daughter will be born unto you, who shall be called Mary, and shall be blessed above all women."

As foretold by the angel, the two met at the Golden Gate. Anna embraced her husband, "hanging about his neck," according to another apocryphal account, *The Protevangelion*. She said, "Now I know that the Lord had greatly blessed me. For behold, I who was a widow am no longer a widow, and I who was barren shall conceive." Then they returned home together. Anna gave birth to a girl, who was called Mary, which in Hebrew is Miriam.

The Franciscans were not satisfied with the apocryphal accounts of Mary's birth and added to the legend. They believed that Mary was conceived when Anna and Joachim kissed at the Golden Gate in Jerusalem. This part of the legend is one of the most popular subjects in Christian art. The whole legend forms part of a series of frescoes done by Giotto.

St. Anna is one of the most popular saints in the Roman Catholic church. About 550 C.E. the Emperor Justinian I built a church in her honor at Constantinople, and her relics were removed there from Palestine in 710.

0258

Anna Perenna. In Roman mythology, an ancient Italian goddess believed to be associated with the revolving year. Every month she renewed her youth and was therefore regarded as a goddess who bestowed long life. On the Ides (15th) of March (then the first month of the year) the Romans held a feast in her honor at the first milestone on the Flaminian Way. In Vergil's *Aeneid* (book 2) Anna Perenna is identified as Dido's sister. According to a later account, she fled to Aeneas in Italy after the death of her sister Dido. Lavinia, Aeneas' wife, was jealous of her, however, and plotted her ruin. In despair Anna Perenna threw herself into the Numicius, becoming a nymph or goddess of the river. Ovid's *Fasti* (3) tells of the goddess and her feast.

Annie Christmas. In American folklore, black heroine, six feet eight inches tall, who could outdrink any man. Annie ran a floating brothel aboard a ship. She dressed in red satin with scarlet plumes and had a 30-foot necklace draped around her neck. Mother of 12 sons, each seven feet tall, she killed herself when she fell in love with a man who did not return her love.

Anpetu wi and Hanhepi wi. In North American Indian mythology (Sioux), the sun and the moon.

Anshar (the totality of what is above). In Near Eastern mythology (Sumero-Akkadian), a primeval sky god who sent out the god Ea, and later his son Anu, to conquer the primeval monster of chaos, Tiamat. In some ancient texts Anshar was regarded as the father of the gods, though his role was later assumed by his son Anu. In some myths he is credited with being the father of Tiamat and is also connected with the primeval god Kishar.

Variant spellings: Assors; Shar.

Ant. A small, wingless insect, often a symbol of industry in world folklore. Both the biblical Book of Proverbs (6:6–7) and the Aesop fable "The Ant and the Grasshopper" use the ant as a symbol of industry. The Japanese represent "ant" in their writing by using the word *insect* combined with the characters that represent unselfishness, justice, and courtesy. In contrast, the Pueblo Indians of North America consider the ant to be vindictive and the cause of disease. In West African belief ant nests are looked upon as homes for demons and evil spirits. In Hindu folklore the ant symbolizes the pettiness of all things.

Antaeus (besought with prayers). In Greek mythology, a Libyan giant son of Poseidon and Gaea (the earth); brother of Charybdis and Ogyges. Antaeus grew stronger every time he touched his mother, the earth. He forced all strangers who ventured into his country to wrestle with him, and being powerfully strong, he killed them. Heracles, on his journey to fetch the apples of the Hesperides, was challenged to wrestle with Antaeus. Heracles lifted him off the ground and held him aloft— away from his mother— —until he died. Antaeus' tomb was near Tingis in Mauretania. One of the most striking representations of Heracles wrestling Antaeus is the statue by Pollaiuolo, *Hercules and Antaeus*, an Italian Renaissance work. There is also a painting by Hans Baldung

Grien (1484/85–1545) titled *Hercules and Antaeus*. Antaeus is also the name given to a friend of Turnus, killed by Aeneas, in Vergil's *Aeneid* (book 10).

Ant and the Grasshopper, The. Aesopic fable, derived from the medieval prose version by Phaedrus.

One frosty autumn day an ant was busily storing away some of the kernels of wheat he had gathered during the summer to eat throughout the coming winter.

A grasshopper, half perishing from hunger, came limping by. Seeing what the industrious ant was doing, he asked for a morsel from the ant's store to save his life.

"What were you doing all during the summer while I was busy harvesting?" inquired the ant.

"Oh," replied the grasshopper, "I was not idle. I was singing and chirping all day long."

"Well," said the ant, smiling grimly as he locked his granary door, "it looks as though you will have to dance all winter."

Moral: It is thrifty to prepare today for the wants of tomorrow.

The ant is nearly always used as an example of hard work. La Fontaine's first fable deals with this subject. It forms the basis for three French operas, all called *La Cigale et la Fourmi*, written in the 19th century. The fable also influenced some North American Indian fables, which derived the story from European versions.

Antar. fl. 600. C.E. In Arabian legend, warrior and poet; subject of *The Romance of Antar*, a popular narrative that developed over the centuries.

At the time *The Romance* opens, the most powerful and best governed of the Bedouin tribes are those of the Absians and the Adnamians. King Zoheir, chief of the Absians, is firmly established on the throne, and the kings of other tribes pay him tribute. The whole of Arabia is subject to the Absians, and all of the inhabitants of the desert dread their power and depredations.

Several chieftains (among whom is Shedad, son of Zoheir) secede from the Absian tribe and set out to seek adventures, to attack other tribes, and to carry off cattle and treasure. These chieftains fight against a tribe called the Djezila, whom they defeat and whose city they pillage. Among the booty is a black woman of extraordinary beauty, the mother of two children. Her name is Zebiba; her eldest son is Djaris, and her youngest Shidoub. Shedad is so taken by the beauty of Zebiba that he gives up all of his booty just to possess her. They live together and she bears him a son, Antar, who is born tawny as an elephant. His eyes are bleared, his head thick with hair, his features hard and fixed. Antar grows up strong and becomes a protector of women, falling in love with one named Ibla.

Antar becomes known as a brave warrior who possesses a fabulous horse, Abjer, and a fantastic sword, Djamy. Every time he goes into battle or returns from combat, he intones: "I am the lover of Ibla." After many adventures, in which he fights for the woman he loves, Antar finally marries her. At one point in his heroic life he is given the title of Alboufauris (the father of horsemen) because of his skill with the animal.

Rimsky-Korsakov's second symphony, *Antar*, depicts a rather melancholy hero who is dissatisfied with women and love. The composer revised the score in 1875 and in 1897, when it was termed a symphonic suite.

Variant spelling: Antarah.

0266

Antelope. Plant-eating, cud-chewing mammal resembling a deer; it has permanent hollow horns that molt annually. In Egyptian mythology the antelope is associated with Anubis, Set, Osiris and Horus; in Roman mythology, Minerva, goddess of wisdom, has the antelope as one of her animals because it was believed to have very sharp eyes. In Hindu mythology the animal is associated with Shiva, Soma, and Chandra. In the *Rig-Veda* antelope-like animals are the steeds of the Maruts, the wind gods. In medieval Christianity the antelope was symbolic of man armed with two horns, one representing the Old Testament and the other the New Testament.

0267

Antenor (instead of a man). In Greek and Roman mythology, a Trojan, counselor to King Priam of Troy; son of Aesyetes and Cleomestra; husband of Athena's priestess Theano, who was the sister of Hecuba; father of 14 sons—Coon, Demoleon, Iphidamas, Polydamas, Laodamas, Polybus, Acamas, Agenor, Archelous, Glaucus, Helicaon, Laocoön, Lycaon, Pedaeus (by a different mother), and one daughter, Crino. When Menelaus and Odysseus came to demand the surrender of Helen from the Trojans, Antenor received them hospitably, protected them from Paris, and then advised them to seek peace. Because of this, later Greek mythology said he betrayed the Trojans by opening the gates to the Greeks, and as a result, when the Greeks took the city, they spared his house and his friends. Some accounts say he told the Greeks to steal the Palladium, a sacred statue that protected Troy, and that he ad-

vised making the Trojan horse. One myth says his ship sailed with Menelaus but was driven off course to Cyrene. He settled there, and his descendants, the Antenoridae, were worshiped as heroes. Another myth tells of his leading the Veneti, driven out of Paphlagonia, taking them by way of Thrace, and Illyria to the Adriatic and then on to the mouth of the Paudus (Po), where he founded Patavium (Padua), the city of the Veneti. Antenor appears in Homer's *Iliad* (book 3), Vergil's *Aeneid* (book 1) and Ovid's *Metamorphoses* (book 13).

0268

Anteros. In Greek mythology, god of passion, mutual love, and tenderness; son of Aphrodite and Ares; brother of Eros, Delmos, Enyo, Harmmia, Pallor, and Phobos. Aphrodite was told by Themis that her son Eros would grow only if he had another brother. As soon as Anteros was born, Eros began to grow, and his strength increased; but whenever Eros found himself at a distance from Anteros, he returned to his baby form. Often Anteros and Eros were portrayed striving to seize a palm tree from one another, to symbolize that true love endeavors to overcome by kindness and gratitude. Anteros and Eros were always portrayed in Greek academies as a symbol that students should love their teachers. Anteros is cited in Pausanias' *Description of Greece*.

0269

Antero Vipunen. In the Finnish epic poem *The Kalevala* (rune 17), primeval giant who gave charms to the culture hero Vainamoinen.

Once, wanting to build a boat, Vainamoinen asked Tapio, the forest god, to supply him with the necessary woods. But all of the trees except the oak refused to offer themselves. Vainamoinen began to construct the boat but discovered he lacked the necessary magic words to complete the project. After vainly seeking the words among birds and animals, he journeyed to Tuonela, the land of the dead. He was told the magic words were possessed by the giant Antero Vipunen, and Vainamoinen went to seek him. Awaking Antero Vipunen from his long sleep underground, Vainamoinen opened the giant's mouth, forcing him to speak, but in the effort he slipped into the giant's mouth. Not wishing to remain the giant's guest, Vainomoinen set up a forge, which caused intense pain to Antero Vipunen. When the culture hero demanded the magic words as payment for stopping the forge, the giant supplied them and let him out. With the magic words Vainamoinen finished the boat, which was self-propelling. It carried him to Pohjola, the Northland, where he wooed the Maiden of Pohjola, who refused his advances.

The name Antero is derived from St. Andreus, or Andrew, and Vipunen signifies the cross of the saint, revealing the Christian influence on the final form of the Finnish epic poem.

Variant spelling: Wipunen.

0270

Anthony of Padua, St. (praiseworthy, priceless). 1195–1231 C.E. In Christian legend, Doctor of the Church. Invoked to find lost property. Feast, 13 June.

Born in Portugal, Anthony wished to become a missionary. He went to Italy, where he became a follower of St. Francis of Assisi. He was noted for his preaching and knowledge of the Bible. There are numerous legends associated with him, some contained in *The Little Flowers of St. Francis*, a collection of medieval tales and legends of St. Francis and his companions. According to that source, one day as Anthony was preaching before the pope and cardinals, he spoke so eloquently, "so sweetly, so clearly, and in a manner so efficacious and so learned, that all those who were in the Consistory, though they spoke different languages, understood what he said as perfectly as if he had spoken the language of each."

Another legend in the same collection tells how he preached to the fishes in Rimini after some heretics had refused to listen to him. He went to the seashore and placed himself on a bank and "began to speak to the fishes . . . who kept their heads out of the water" and looked attentively at the saint. When the townspeople heard what was happening, they came to see, and the heretics among them were converted by Anthony's preaching.

Once the saint preached at the funeral of a very rich and avaricious man. He condemned the man, saying his heart would be found in his treasure chest. The man's relatives discovered that his heart was missing from his body.

Another legend tells how the saint was asked by a heretic to prove that Christ was really present in the Holy Eucharist. The man's mule bowed down as Anthony carried out the Sacrament and remained so until he passed. A 17th-century legend tells of the Christ Child appearing to the saint, standing on a book.

In Christian art St. Anthony of Padua is portrayed as a young Franciscan, often with a lily or crucifix in his hand, or in later paintings, with the Christ Child standing on a book or carried by the saint in his arms.

0271

Anthony the Abbot, St. (praiseworthy, priceless). 251–356 C.E. In Christian legend, patron saint of basket makers. Invoked against erysipelas (or St. Anthony's fire). Feast, 17 January.

St. Anthony the Abbot

St. Anthony was among the first "desert fathers" of the Christian Church. The list includes such saints as Pachomius, Simeon Stylites, Hilarion, and Jerome. His life, written in the fourth century by St. Athanasius, bishop of Alexandria, is believed to be the first example of an extended or full-length biography of a saint. It set the style for the saints' lives that were written later. It tells of numerous miracles and the proverbial combat with the devil, which became a standard literary device in writing about the lives of the saints.

Born in Alexandria, Anthony was an orphan. He divided his inheritance with his sister, sold his portion, and went to live among the hermits in the desert. But as St. Athanasius writes, "the devil, the envier and enemy of all good, could not bear to see such a purpose in so young a man" and sent many temptations to the saint. The devil "would assume by night the form and imitate the deportment of a woman, to tempt Anthony." The saint, however, overcame all of the sensual assaults. The devil then assumed the forms of various monsters, serpents, and poisonous animals to torment Anthony. Again, the saint overcame them.

After Anthony had lived for 75 years in the desert, he had a vision of St. Paul the Hermit, who had been living in penance for 90 years. So Anthony set out across the desert. After journeying several days and meeting on the way a centaur and a satyr, he came at last to a cave of rocks where St. Paul the Hermit lived beside a stream and a palm tree. The two men embraced. While they were talking, a raven came, bringing a loaf of bread in its beak. St. Paul said the raven had come every day for the last 60 years, but that day the portion of bread was doubled. St. Paul asked Anthony to fetch a special cloak, for he was about to die and wished to be buried in it. Anthony set out to get the cloak (it was in a monastery some distance away), but as he went he had a vision of St. Paul ascending to heaven. When he returned to the cave, he found St. Paul dead. Anthony had no strength to dig a grave, but two lions came and helped him. St. Anthony died 14 years later and was buried secretly, according to his wish.

St. Anthony is portrayed as a very old man, in his monk's habit, often with a crutch and an asperges or a bell to exorcise demons; a pig, the ancient symbol of the Egyptian gods Osiris and Set ; and a Tau cross. Perhaps the most striking paintings of the saint's life were done by Mathias Grüenwald in his Isenheim altarpiece. In *The Temptation of St. Anthony*, one of the panels of the altarpiece, the saint is shown assaulted by demons and with the rotted body of a man suffering from St. Anthony's fire. Another panel of the altarpiece, *The Meeting of St. Anthony and St. Paul the Hermit*, portrays the saints awaiting the arrival of the raven with the bread in its beak. The Isenheim altarpiece inspired Paul Hindemith's opera *Mathis der Maler*, based on the life of Mathias Grüenwald. The music from the opera was used by the composer in a symphonic suite, made up of "The Concert of the Angels," "The Entombment," and *The Temptation of Saint Anthony.*" Gustave Flaubert wrote *La Tentation de Sainte Antoine*, a prose poem based on the legend of the saint.

0272
Antigone (in place of a mother). In Greek mythology, daughter of Oedipus and his mother, Jocasta (or Euryganeia); sister of Eteocles, Esmene, and Polynices. Antigone accompanied her blind father into exile in Attica, and after his death, she returned to Thebes. In defiance of her uncle Creon, she attempted to bury the body of her brother Polynices, which Creon had cast outside the walls of the city because Polynices had died trying to usurp his brother Eteocles' throne. Creon sentenced her to be entombed alive.

Sophocles, in his play *Antigone*, pictures her as defiant in defending her ministrations to her dead brother. Sophocles has her say, "And what law of heaven have I transgressed? . . . if these things are pleasing to the gods [to be punished for ministering to her dead brother], when I have suffered my doom, I shall come to know my sin; but if the sin is with my judges, I could wish them no fuller measure of evil than they, on their part do wrongfully to me." Antigone then hangs herself, while her betrothed, Haemon, the son of Creon, stabs himself beside her body.

In a variant myth Antigone and Argeia, the widow of Polynices, try to bury Polynices and are seized by Creon's guards. They are handed over to Haemon for execution, but Haemon hides Antigone in a shepherd's hut, and the two live together secretly for years. Antigone bears a son who, when he grows up, engages in some funeral games in Thebes and is recognized by a birthmark peculiar to the family. He is revealed to be the child of Antigone and Haemon, who were secretly among the spectators. Creon orders them put to death. To escape Creon's vengeance, Haemon kills Antigone and himself.

In addition to Sophocles' play, Antigone has inspired numerous others, including those of Cocteau, Anouilh, and Brecht. Cocteau's play (1922) forms the basis for Honegger's opera *Antigone* (1927). Carlos Chávez's Symphony Number 1 (1933) is subtitled *Sinfonia de Antigona* and is based on incidental music to Cocteau's version of Sophocles' play. A German translation of Sophocles is used by Carl Orff for his "tragic play with music" *Antigono* (1948) and the earlier opera *Antigono* (1756) by Gluck uses an Italian translation of the Greek play.

0273
Antilochus (lying in ambush against). In Greek mythology, a hero, the eldest son of Nestor and Anaxiba (or Eurydice); brother of Aretus, Echephron, Paeon, Peisidice, Peisistratus, Perseus, Polycaste, Stratius and Thrasymedes; possibly the father, not brother, of Paeon. Antilochus accompanied his father to the Trojan War and was distinguished for his beauty and bravery. Homer, in *The Iliad*, calls him a favorite of Zeus and Poseidon. After Patroclus he was closest to Achilles. Antilochus was chosen by the Greeks to tell Achilles that Patroclus had been slain by Hector. In later myth, when Memnon attacked the elderly Nestor, Antilochus threw himself in the way and was killed as a result. His death was avenged by Achilles. The ashes of Antilochus, Patroclus, and Achilles were laid together in the same grave. In the underworld Odysseus saw the three heroes pacing the asphodel meadow. Sacrifices were offered to all three as semidivine beings.

0274
Antinous (hostile mind). c. 110 C.E. In Roman history and legend, the Emperor Hadrian's male lover, drowned in the Nile. Whether Antinous drowned himself or was murdered is not known. Hadrian had his lover deified and founded the city of Antinoöpolis at the site of his death. Coins and statues of Antinous as a handsome youth also were produced, one of the most beautiful statues being the Farnese Antinous. Marguerite Yourcenar's novel *Memoirs of Ha-*

drian, deals in part deals with Hadrian's love for Antinous.

0275

Antiope (with face confronting). In Greek mythology, the daughter of the Boetian river god Asopus and Metope, or of Nycteus of Thebes and Polyxo; mistress of Zeus, by whom she was the mother of Amphion and Zethus. When her father discovered that Zeus, in the form of a satyr, had seduced Antiope, he threatened to punish her. Antiope fled her father and went to Epopeus of Sicyon, but he had been killed by her uncle Lycus. The girl was brought back and bore twin sons, Amphion and Zethus. Nycteus ordered the boys exposed on a mountain to die, but the babies were saved by a shepherd. In the meantime Antiope was kept a prisoner by Dirce, the wife of Lycus. Eventually Antiope escaped, found her sons, and took her revenge on Dirce by having her tied to the tail of a wild bull, which dragged her until she died.

Antiope's seduction by Zeus has for centuries fascinated European artists, among them Pinturicchio, Correggio, Titian, and Watteau.

Another Antiope, also called Melanippe, was the sister of Hippolyte, queen of the Amazons. She was given as a prize to Theseus and bore him a son, Hippolytus; she was killed by Theseus when he wanted to marry Phaedra. In a variant account she was given to Pirithous.

0276

Anu. In Celtic mythology, goddess of prosperity and abundance who appears in Celtic folklore as Aine, a powerful fairy, queen of South Munster. Two mountains located near Killarney, called The Paps, were once called the Paps of Anu.

0277

Anu (lofty; sky). In Near Eastern mythology (Sumero-Akkadian), sky god, head of a triad of gods made up of Anu, Enlil, and Ea. Anu's wife was Antum; his daughter the goddess Bau. In the Babylonian creation epic poem *Enuma Elish*, Anu is the son of the primeval god Anshar. In Hittite mythology Anu is called Anus. In one myth he ousted his father, Alalus, from the throne. He was in turn dethroned by his son Kumarbi, who emasculated Anus by a single bite of his penis. Kumarbi then spit out the penis and three gods: Teshub, the storm god; Tasmisus, the god's attendant; and a river god. Teshub in turn dethroned Kumarbi and was father of the giant Ullikummi, who was destroyed by the god Ea. Anu's symbols are a horned cap and star.

Variant spellings: An, Ana, Anos, Dana, Danu, Nanu.

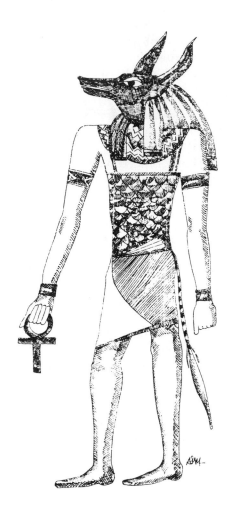

Anubis

0278

Anubis. In Egyptian mythology, Greek name for the jackal-headed god of the dead, called Anpu by the Egyptians. Although the jackal was known to prowl the ancient cemeteries as a scavenger, the early Egyptians turned him into a god who protected rather than pillaged tombs. According to one myth, Anubis was the son of the goddess Nephthys, who had tricked her brother, the god Osiris, into adulterously sleeping with her. Nephthys abandoned Anubis at birth, and he was found and raised by Osiris's sister-wife, the goddess Isis. He accompanied Osiris on his conquest of the world, and when Osiris was murdered and dismembered, Anubis helped find his body and then embalmed it so well it resisted the influences of time and decay. Thus, it was said, the burial rites were invented.

Subsequently, Anubis presided over funerals and guided the dead through the underworld into the kingdom of Osiris. In Anubis's function as guide of the dead he assimilated the character of the earlier Egyptian god Wepwawet (he who opens the ways). Anubis's cult continued during Greek and Roman times. According to Plutarch, the Egyptian jackal god was common to both the celestial and infernal regions.

This dual role was reinforced in Roman times by Apuleius's Latin novel *The Golden Ass* (book 11), which describes a procession of the goddess Isis in which Anubis appears with his dog's head and neck, a "messenger between heaven and hell, displaying alternately a face black as night and golden as day." Anubis is the Greek form of the Egyptian name Anpu.

0279

Anunnaki. In Near Eastern mythology (Babylonian), gods or spirits of the underworld, opposed to the Igigi, the heavenly gods. In the ancient narrative poem *Inanna's Journey to the Underworld* the Anunnaki are the seven judges of the underworld. Sometimes, however, they are listed as gods. In the *Enuma Elish*, the epic of creation, they are the defeated rebel gods who build the city of Babylon for the hero god Marduk.

Variant spellings: Anunna, Anunnake, Ennuki.

0280

Anuruddha. Fifth century B.C.E. In Buddhist legend, a disciple of the Buddha who was present at his death. He is mentioned in the Pali sacred writings. Physically blind, Anuruddha was famous for his spiritual insight.

0281

Apauk-kyit Lok. In Burmese mythology, an old man responsible for bringing death into the world.

Though old, Apauk-kyit Lok had renewed his life nine times because there was no death in the world. One day he went fishing and saw an animal (either a monkey or squirrel) that had fallen asleep on a branch and was floating in the river. He placed the animal in a basket and covered it with his clothes; then he disappeared. It was announced (though the myth does not tell us how) that he was dead. All of his neighbors came to see, but no one dared remove the coverings. When the lord of the sun heard what had happened, he sent some messengers to investigate. They took the form of dancers at the funeral. As they danced, they removed the clothes that covered the basket, revealing the fraud. Because of this the lord of the sun caused Apauk-kyit Lok to die and people have been dying ever since.

0282

Ape or monkey. Any mammal of the primates except humans, seen as a symbol of both beneficence and evil. In ancient Egypt a dog-headed ape assisted the god Thoth when the soul of a deceased person was weighed on the scales. Apes were embalmed when they died. In Hindu mythology Hanuman, who helps the hero Rama, is an ape or monkey god. In China a whole cycle of monkey tales developed around the adventures of a seventh-century Buddhist monk who traveled from China to India with his companion monkey and brought back sacred books.

In contrast to the beneficent aspect of the ape or monkey, the ancient Jewish rabbis said that if one saw a monkey it was a sign of bad luck. One Jewish tale says three classes of men built the Tower of Babel, one of which turned into apes as punishment from God. Some Moslems still believe that the ancient Jews who lived in Elath on the Red Sea were turned into monkeys or apes as a punishment from Allah for having fished on the Sabbath. In medieval Christian folklore the monkey was seen as shameless and lustful. One bestiary of the 12th century says that while the monkey's whole physical being is "disgraceful, yet their bottoms really are excessively disgraceful and horrible."

Venus (Aphrodite)

0283

Aphrodite (foam-born). In Greek mythology, one of the 12 Olympian gods; a form of the Great Mother goddess; the goddess of sensual love; daughter of Zeus and Dione; or born of the foam of the sea when the severed genitals of Uranus were cast into the sea; still other accounts say Eileithyia was her mother; identified by the Romans with Venus. Aphrodite often appears as the wife of Hephaestus, the smith god. Her erotic adventures with Ares produced Eros, Anteros, and Harmonia, wife of Cadmus; as well as Deimos and Phobos (fear and alarm), attendants to their father, Ares. By the mortal Anchises, Aphrodite was the mother of Aeneas, the Trojan hero. A passage in the Homeric Hymns (not by the poet Homer) describes Aphrodite's encounter with Anchises. Zeus himself inspired Aphrodite with the desire to lie in the arms of a mortal man so that she might be practiced in the art of "mingling goddesses in love with mortal men."

By Hermes she bore Hermaphroditus; by Poseidon she bore Eryx; by Dionysus she bore Priapus; and by Adonis a boy and a girl.

Aphrodite's main adherents were in Paphos, Amathus, and Idalion (all in Cyprus), in Cindus in Dorian Asia Minor, in Corinth, on the island of Cythera, and in Eryx in Sicily. As mother of Harmonia, Aphrodite was the guardian deity of Thebes. Among plants, the myrtle, the rose, and the apple were sacred to her as goddess of love; among animals the ram, he-goat, hare, dove, and sparrow; as sea goddess, the swan, mussels, and dolphin; as Urania, the tortoise. The goddess appears in Homer, Hesiod, Ovid, Vergil, Pausanias, and Euripides among other ancient authors.

The best-known statue of Aphrodite in the ancient world was the Aphrodite of Cnidos by Praxiteles, made about 350 B.C.E. It is known to us by Roman copies. Other works are the Capitoline Venus in Rome and the Aphrodite of Melos, called the Venus di Milo.

In Western literature and art the name Aphrodite rarely appears; the more common Roman form, Venus, is used. However, Pierre Louÿs wrote a novel *Aphrodite*, which was made into a five-act opera by Erlanger, published in 1906.

There is a ballet *Aphrodite* (1930) by Nikolay Nabokov; a setting for women's chorus and orchestra of *Sappho's Ode to Aphrodite* (1946) by Albert Moeschinger; and a symphonic poem, *Aphrodite* (1910), by the American composer George Chadwick.

Aphrodite had many epithets, among them Aphrodite Acrae (of the height), Doritis (bountiful), Epistrophia (she who turns men to love), Euploia (fair voyage), Limenia (of the harbor), Pontia (of the deep sea), Area (warlike), Aphrodite Migonitis (uniter), Aphrodite Nymphaea (bridal), Aphrodite Melaenis (black), Scotia (dark one), Androphonos (man slayer), Epitymbria (of the tombs), Pandemos (common to all), Aphrodite Urania (heavenly), Pasiphae (shining one), Asteria (starry), Apostrophia (rejecter), and Aphrodite Morpho (shapely).

Venus (Aphrodite)

0284

Apis. In Egyptian mythology, Greek name for the sacred bull, Hapi, associated with the god Ptah of Memphis and regarded as his earthly manifestation during the Ramesside period (1320–1085 B.C.E.). When an Apis bull died, it was given great honors, similar to those for a dead pharaoh. The animal was buried at Memphis in the Serapeum, a vast system of catacombs cut into the limestone beneath the desert sands. A committee of priests was then appointed to search throughout Egypt for another Apis bull to replace the dead one. The replacement had to have 29 marks, the most important being a rich black coat intermingled with white patches and a triangular blaze on the forehead. Once chosen, the new Apis was enthroned in his own palace, or *sikos*, located to the south of the temple of Ptah at Memphis.

Apis was also associated with Osiris, the major god of the dead. In one myth Apis assisted Isis, Osiris's wife, in searching for the body of Osiris. It was believed by the ancient Egyptians that the bull's fecundity and generative powers could be transferred to the deceased, ensuring him or her rebirth in the next life.

0285

Apis (long ago). In Greek mythology, a son of Phoroneus and the nymph Teledice, or of Apollo Apis was credited with driving monsters, plagues, and snakes from Argos and was given the power to heal illness by Apollo. St. Augustine, in commenting on the tale, believed Apis went to Egypt and

Apollo pursues Daphne (A. Beardsley)

founded a colony of Greeks, who later worshiped Apis as the god Serapis.

Apizteotl (hungry god). In Aztec mythology, god of famine. When a sacrifice was offered and human flesh eaten as part of the rite, those who did not then wash in a fresh-running river or spring were said to be "addicted to the god of famine," according to Fray Diego Durán in his book *The Ancient Calendar*, which describes Aztec feasts and festivals.

0286

Apocatequil (chief of the followers of the moon). In the mythology of the Huamachuco Indians of Peru, god of night, twin brother of the god Piguero (white bird), who represents day.

0287

Apocatequil was the son of Guamansuri, the first man to descend to earth. Guamansuri came down and lived underground with a people called Guachimines. He seduced their sister and as a result was killed along with the girl. Their offspring, born from two eggs, survived and were the twins Apocatequil and Piguerao. Apocatequil, with the aid of a creator god, Atagudu, brought his mother back to life and killed the other Guachimines. With a golden spade he made an aperture in the earth through which the race of Peruvians emerged and took possession of the land.

Apocatequil was called Prince of Evil, though this title may stem from his association with night.

Apoiaueue. In the mythology of the Tupi Indians of Brazil, rain spirits who cause rain when the land is dry.

0288

Apollo (destroyer, apple man). In Greek mythology, one of the 12 Olympian gods; god of prophecy, healing, archery, music, youth, plastic arts, science and philosophy; son of Leto and Zeus and brother of Artemis. Apollo was also the protector of flocks and herds and patron of the founding of cities and colonies.

0289

The *Hymn to Apollo* (one of the Homeric Hymns falsely ascribed to Homer) describes how the island of Delos was raised up out of the sea by Zeus for the special purpose of becoming the birthplace of Apollo. Leto, Apollo's mother, says:

Delos, would that thou were minded to be the seat of my Son, Phoebus Apollo, and to let him build therein a rich temple! No other God will touch thee, nor none will honor thee, for I think thou art not to be well seen in cattle or in sheep, in fruit or grain, nor wilt thou grow plants unnumbered. But were thou to possess a temple of Apollo the Far- darter; then would all men bring thee hecatombs, gathering to thee, and ever will thou have savor of sacrifice . . .

from others' hands, although thy soil is poor. (Andrew Lang translation)

The island then speaks directly to Leto, lamenting its bleak and barren terrain and fearing that Apollo, who will be lord over men and the grain-giver (earth), will disdain Delos and cause a tidal wave to wipe out the island. Delos therefore asks Leto to promise that Apollo will build a temple on the island so that it would be forevermore sacred to Apollo and thus protected from destruction. Leto gives her oath: "Bear witness, Earth, and the wide heaven above, and dropping water of Styx—the greatest oath and the most dread among the blessed Gods—that verily here shall ever be the fragrant altar and the portion of Apollo, and thee will he honor above all."

Apollo had numerous love affairs with both men and women. Among the most famous (and the offspring they produced) are the following: Acacallis (Amphithemis and Miletus); Arsinoe (Erioris); Calliope (Orpheus); Calaeno (Delphus); Chione (Philammon); Chrysorthe (Coronus); Coronis or Arsinoe (Asclepius); Cyrene (Autychus, Idom, and Aristaeus); Dryope (Amphissus); Evadne (Iamus); Hecuba (Troilus, possibly); Ocyrrhoe (Phasis); Parthenone (Lycomedes); Pythia (Dorus, Laodocus, and Polypoetes); Procleia (Tenes); Psamathe (Linus); Rhoeo (Anius); Stilbe (Centaurus and Lapithus); Syllis (Zeuxippus); Thyia (Delphus); Thyria (Cycnus and Phylius). Other lovers included Acantha, Bolina, Clymene, Daphne, Issa, and Leucothoe. His favorite male lover was Hyacinthus.

Numerous symbols were attached to Apollo. The most common were the lyre and the bow, symbols of his role as god of song and as the far-darter archer. In his role as Pythian Apollo, he is portrayed with the tripod, which was also the favorite offering at his altars. Laurel trees were planted around his temples since the leaf of the laurel, the bay leaf, was used for expiation of sins. Bay leaves were plaited into garlands of victory at the Pythian Games. The palm tree was also sacred to Apollo, for it was under the palm tree that he was born in Delos.

Among animals sacred to Apollo were the wolf, the dolphin, and the snow-white and musical swans. The hawk, raven, crow, and snake were symbols of Apollo as prophet.

In ancient art he was portrayed as a handsome youth. The Apollo Belvedere is a marble copy of a Hellenistic bronze found in Rome in the late 15th century; it is now in the Vatican Museum. The German artist Dürer based his proportions for the "ideal male" on the statue. Lord Byron wrote of it in *Childe Harold's Pilgramage*:

The God of life, and poesy, and light—
The Sun in human limbs array'd and brow
All radiant from his triumph in the fight . . .

Apollo appears in numerous paintings from ancient times to the 19th century. During the Middle Ages he was portrayed as a doctor or scholar in contemporary medieval dress. During the Renaissance he appears as a handsome youth. The Galérie d'Apollon in the Louvre was painted by Le Brun for Louis XIV, whose emblem was Apollo, le Roi Soleil.

In music and dance the best-known ballet about Apollo is Stravinsky's *Apollon Musagète* (1928), which is sometimes called simply *Apollo*. The ballet depicts Apollo, leader of the Muses, preparing himself for his duties as a god. Supported by the Muses, he ascends Olympus to drive his sun chariot across the heavens. There are also more than 20 operas with Apollo as the subject.

In English literature, Shelley's *Hymn to Apollo* reflects the poet's view of the god:

I am the eye with which the Universe
Beholds itself and knows itself divine;
All harmony of instrument or verse.
All prophecy, all medicine are mine,
All light of art or nature o my song
Victory and praise in their own right belong.

Swinburne, in his poem *The Last Oracle*, sees Apollo as the god who triumphs over the Christian god.

Apollo had many epithets; among them, in his role as god of healing, Alexicarus (averter of evil) and Paean (healer); before setting out on a journey, Apollo Embasius (Apollo of embarkations); in his role of removing a plague of locusts from Attica, Apollo Parnopius (locust god). In his role as seer Apollo was called Loxias (crooked, ambiguous) because many of his oracles were difficult to understand. As god of music, poetry, and dance he was called Musagetes (leader of the Muses). He was also Phoebus (bright or pure god).

0290

Apollodorus. c. 140–115 B.C.E. Greek writer on mythology, history, and grammar whose best-known work is the *Bibliotheca* (Library), which presents the deities and myths of the Greeks. The extant works of the book belong to the first or second century of our era. James G. Frazer, who translated it into English, wrote, "It is a history of the world as it was conceived by the Greeks."

0291

Apollonia, St. (of Apollo). Third century. In Christian legend, patron of dentists and their patients. Feast, 9 February.

Apollo Musagetes

The life of the saint is recorded in *The Golden Legend*, a collection of saints' lives written in the 13th century by Jacobus de Voragine. Apollonia was the daughter of rich parents in Alexandria, Egypt. She was a virgin "far advanced in years" and noted for her "chastity, purity, piety and charity." All of these virtues, however, did not deter a pagan mob from attacking her house because it was a refuge for Christians. Apollonia was dragged out, and the mob began "tearing out all her teeth." When that was done the saint was burned. In a variant account of her life she was killed with a sword.

In Christian art St. Apollonia is usually shown with a pair of pincers, occasionally holding a tooth. One work, ascribed to Piero della Francesca, portrays the saint holding her symbol and looking quite determined if not angry.

0292

Apollyon (destroyer). In the Bible, N.T., angel of the bottomless pit (Revelation 9:11). Apollyon is a Greek translation of the Hebrew word *Abaddon*, a poetic name for the land of the dead in the Old Testament. In early Christian literature Apollyon is a name for the devil. John Bunyan's *Pilgrim's Progress* calls Apollyon an evil monster, "hideous to behold," with "scales like a fish," "wings like a dragon," bear's feet, and a lion's mouth. Christian, the hero of Bunyan's work, battles Apollyon and wounds the monster with his two-edged sword. In later Christian writings Apollyon is often identified as the angel of death.

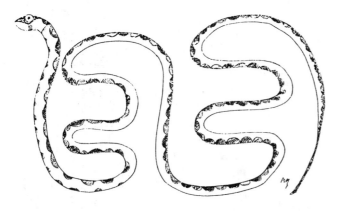

Apophis

0293

Apophis. In Egyptian mythology, Greek name form of the Egyptian Apep, or Aaapef, giant serpent and night demon. According to some ancient accounts, Apophis was a form of Set, god of evil and darkness. Each night Apophis battled with the sun god Ra, whose spells and flames eventually destroyed the serpent. This nightly combat took place right before Ra's ascension from Duat, the underworld. In the ancient Egyptian ritual text *Books of the Overthrowing of Apophis*, a rite was to be recited in the temple of the sun god, cataloging in great detail the destruction that was to befall Apophis. The monster's statue or representation was to be speared and gashed and every bone of his body cut by knives. His head, legs, and tail were to be scorched, singed, and roasted until the whole was consumed by fire. The same fate awaited Apophis' monstrous helpers, Sebau and Nak, as well as other shadows and offspring of night.

0294

Apostle (ambassador, messenger, envoy). In the Bible, N.T., title given to the 12 chief disciples of Jesus. The names given in the Gospels and Acts vary, a fact often explained by the custom of calling the same person by different names; thus, Peter is also known as Simon Peter or just Simon, and Bartholomew is sometimes called Nathanael. In general, the Twelve Apostles are Simon, called Peter or Cephas (rock); Andrew; James the Greater (or Elder or Major); John; James the Less (or Younger or Minor); Jude, also called Thaddaeus; Philip; Bartholomew, also called Nathanael; Matthew, surnamed Levi; Thomas, surnamed Didymus or the Twin; Simon, the Cananean or Zealot; Judas, surnamed Iscariot.

After the suicide of Judas, his place was taken by Matthias, who was then called Apostle. The term also was applied to St. Paul, who is the Apostle to the Gentiles, and to saints who in legend are responsible for the conversion of countries to Christianity. Thus, St. Patrick is the Apostle to Ireland, and SS. Cyril and Methodius are Apostles to the Slavs.

The earliest paintings of the Twelve Apostles are in the Roman catacombs of Domitilla (fourth century C.E.). They are pictured seated in a semicircle around Christ. In two Ravenna baptisteries of the mid-fifth century and early sixth century they are seen walking in procession around the cupola of the building. Sometimes the Apostles are portrayed as 12 lambs around Christ, the Good Shepherd, as in St. Clement's Church in Rome (twelfth century C.E.). Sets of the 12 Apostles in later Christian art were painted by Raphael and engraved by Marc Antonio, Lucas van Leyden, Parmigiano, El Greco, and Albert Dürer. However, not all of the Dürer set survive.

Edward Elgar, the English composer, planned a sequence of oratorios dealing with the calling of the apostles and their mission to convert the world. The first part of the project was called *The Apostles* and the second part, *The Kingdom*; the third part was never finished.

0295

Apple. A fruit tree common throughout the temperate regions of the world; in world mythology and folklore, a symbol of fertility and love. In Christian folklore the apple is often identified as the fruit eaten by Adam and Eve, though the actual fruit is not named in Genesis. Thomas Otway, in his play *The Orphan*, tells of how Eve "for an apple damned mankind." Often a golden apple is a prize; in Greek mythology it was cast into a gathering of the gods to cause dissension among them. It was to be awarded to the goddess who won the love of the youth, Paris, and Aphrodite, the goddess of sexual love, won it. In Greek custom, tossing an apple to the object of one's desire was an invitation to sexual intercourse. The apple or apple tree was sacred to Nemesis, Artemis, and Apollo. In Aristophanes' play *The Clouds* young men are told not to frequent houses of dancing girls where "while they are gaping at some cute strumpet, she might get them involved by tossing an apple at them." In one of Lucian's dialogues, *Conversations of the Courtesans*, a courtesan complains that her lover is not paying attention to her, but "throwing apples" at another girl. In present-day custom boys and girls dunk for apples at Halloween, mostly unaware of the rich symbolism of the fruit, which, according to European folklore, could induce pregnancy.

0296

Apple of Discord. In Greek mythology, a golden apple with the inscription "For the fairest." Eris, the goddess of discord, threw it into an assembly of the gods at the wedding of Thetis and Peleus. Aphrodite, Hera, and Athena each claimed the apple. None of the gods could decide who should have it, so Zeus chose Paris of Troy to be the judge. Paris gave the apple to Aphrodite, who then promised him Helen, the most beautiful woman in the world. The result: the Trojan War. The event is frequently painted as *The Judgment of Paris* and was popular with artists from the Middle Ages to the 19th century.

0297

Appomattox Apple Tree. In American history and folklore of the Civil War, tree under which General Lee surrendered to General Grant. According to legend, General Lee mistook General Grant (who was far from neat) for an orderly and handed him his sword to clean, thus surrendering by mistake. In actuality, nothing took place under the Appomattox Apple Tree; the surrender was made at the house of Major Wilmer McLean on 9 April 1865.

0298

Apricot. A tree that bears fruit similar to the peach. In European folklore the apricot was believed to be a stimulant to sexual activity. In Shakespeare's *Midsummer Night's Dream* (3.1) when Titania fell in love with Bottom, the weaver turned into an ass, she ordered her elves to feed him "apricocks." In English folklore to dream of an apricot means good luck, health, and pleasure. In Chinese belief, however, the apricot symbolizes death and timidity.

0299

Apsu (the abyss). In Near Eastern mythology (Babylonian), primordial god of fresh water, husband of Tiamat, or chaos.

In the Babylonian epic of creation *Enuma Elish*, Apsu's nature is described:

There was a time when above the heaven was not named
Below, the earth bore no name.

Apsu was there from the first, the source of both.
And raging Tiamat the mother of heaven and earth.
But Apsu and Tiamat were gathered together in a mass.

Apsu represents the male and Tiamat the female principle of the primeval universe. In the poem, however, Ea, the son of Apsu, castrates his father and takes over his role as god of fresh water. The worship of Ea, as god of fresh water, was even found in the temple of King Solomon, where water jars stood near the great altar in the large court. The great basin in the court was called Apsu.
Variant spellings: Absu; Apason; Apsu-Rishtu.

0300

Aqhat. In Near Eastern mythology, a Canaanite hero restored to life.

Aqhat was the son of Daniel. He had been given to his father as a gift by the god El for the father's prayers. Aqhat was perfect in all things. One day Daniel gave Aqhat a bow made by the divine smith of the gods. However, the war goddess, Anath, coveted the boy and made an offer to Aqhat.

"Ask for everlasting life and I will give it to you," the goddess said to Aqhat.

"How can a mortal live forever?" Aqhat asked.

His question so angered the goddess that she sent a hired killer, Yatpan, to murder Aqhat. After his death Aqhat was restored to life by the goddess, who felt remorse for her evil deed. This ending, however, is only conjectural, because the myth, found on tablets from the ancient city of Ugarit in 1930 and 1931, is not complete.

0301

Aquarius. The eleventh sign of the Zodiac. Aquarius rises in 20 January and sets in February. Aquarius is the water-bearer constellation said to represent Ganymede, the young-boy lover and cupbearer of the Greek god Zeus. Other accounts say it represents Deucalion or Cecrops.

0302

Ara. In Armenian mythology, a handsome hero who died in battle and was restored to life. An evil queen, Semiramis, heard how handsome Ara was and sent messengers to propose that he marry her. Ara rejected the offer because he was married to Nvard, whom he deeply loved. Semiramis, upset by the refusal, sent an army against the hero, and he was killed in battle. His lifeless body was taken to Semiramis and placed in an upper chamber, where she prayed to her gods to restore it to life.

0303

Arachne (spider). In Greek mythology, daughter of the Lydian cloth dyer, Idmon, and Colophon.

Arachne challenged Athena to a weaving match in which she wove a tapestry portraying the erotic activities of the gods. Athena was offended by the work and destroyed it. Arachne then hanged herself, and Athena changed her into a spider. The myth is told in detail in Ovid's *Metamorphoses* (book 6) and by the English poet Spenser in *Muiopotmos*. A magnificent painting depicting the weaving contest is *The Competition between Arachne and Pallas Athene* or *The Spinners* by Velasquez.

0304

Arae. In Roman mythology, rocks in the Mediterranean between Africa and Sardinia. Vergil's *Aeneid* (book 1) tells how Aeneas lost most of his fleet there. It is also the place where Aeneas and the Africans ratified a treaty.

0305

Aralu. In Near Eastern mythology, the Babylonian land of the dead, ruled over by the goddess Ereshkigal and her husband, the god Nergal.

Aralu was pictured as a vast place, dark and gloomy. Sometimes it was called a land, sometimes a great house. It was difficult to approach because it lay in the lowest part of a mountain. Aralu was surrounded by seven walls and guarded so that no living persons could enter it. If they did, they would never come out. A second name for the land of the dead in Babylonian mythology was Ekur (the bright mountain house), a third was Shalu (to ask), a fourth was Ganzir, a name whose meaning is uncertain. In numerous incantations used in cultic rites the names of the dead were avoided and the place was often described as "land of no return," "dark dwelling," or "great city."

Variant spellings: Arallu, Irkalla.

0306

Aram. In Armenian folklore, hero who conquered Barshamina, the giant. Barshamina ruled a great land, which Aram conquered; Aram made himself king and forced the people to learn Armenian. Some scholars believe that Aram was originally an Armenian war god, Aremenius; and the giant Barshamina was none other than the Syrian god Ba'al Shamin, the lord of heaven, imported into Armenian mythology and demoted into a giant in later legend.

0307

Aramazd. In Armenian mythology, supreme god, derived in part from the Persian good god, Ahura Mazda. Aramazd was the giver of prosperity, abundance, and fatness to the land. He made the fields fertile and may therefore have been a rain god. He was the father of the gods Anahit, Nane, and Mihr.

0308

Arcadia (bean). In Greek mythology, a mountainous region in the Peloponnesus, the central district of Greece, associated with pastoral life in much poetry and art; named after Arcas, king of the Arcadians. Ancient authors such as Theocritus and Vergil used Arcadia to portray an ideal state, and it has been used by poets and artists ever since. One of the most popular works was *Arcadia* (1481) by the Italian Sannazaro, a collection of poetic eclogues connected by prose passages. Other works in literature are Spenser's *Shepherd's Calendar* and Sir Philip Sidney's prose romance *Arcadia*. The use of Arcadia to denote a pastoral state that never existed except among the poets was attacked by the English poet William Cowper in his poem *Hope*:

> The poor, inured to drudgery and distress,
> Act without air, think little, and feel less,
> And no where, but in feign'd Arcadian scenes
> Taste happiness, or know what pleasure means.

The saying *Et in Arcadia ego* (even in Arcadia I am found) refers to death and was used by Poussin as the title for a painting of Arcadian shepherds looking at a skull and tomb. Often, however, the lines are mistranslated as "I too have lived in Arcadia."

0309

Arcas (bear). In Greek mythology, a culture hero, king of Arcadia; a son of Zeus and Callisto; married the Dryad Erato; father of Azan, Apheidas, Elatus, Hyperippe and the illegitimate Autolaus. Arcas taught the Arcadians agriculture and the art of spinning wool. He was turned into a star, the Little Bear (Arcturus), located behind his mother, Callisto, who was turned into the Great Bear by Zeus. Arcas is cited in Apollodorus' *Bibliotheca* (3), and Pausanias' *Description of Greece*.

0310

Archangels. In Jewish, Christian, and Islamic mythology, order of angels.

In the Old Testament Apocrypha Book of Tobit (12:15) the archangel Raphael says he is "one of the seven holy angels, which present the prayers of the saints, and which go in and out before the glory of the Holy One." Influenced by this verse, the author of the Book of Revelation (8:2) has seven angels who stand before God. However, the names of the seven are not given in either text. Judaeo-Christian tradition has supplied a list: Michael (who is like unto God), Raphael (God has healed), Gabriel (God is my strength), Uriel (the light of God), Chamuel (he who seeks God), Zophiel (the beauty of God), and Zadkiel (the righteousness of God). There are numerous variant spellings of the names, often making it difficult to know which angel is spoken of in a particular text. The first three on the list, however, are most often represented in Western medieval art and literature.

Islam does not have seven archangels but four. They are Michael, Gabriel, Azazel (the angel of death), and Israfel (the angel who will sound the trumpet on the Last Day when everyone will be judged by Allah). Michael and Gabriel are named directly in the Koran; the other two names are not given but are supplied by Islamic tradition.

0311

Ardhananari. In Hindu mythology, epithet of the god Shiva, meaning half man. Often it signifies Shiva as an androygne or as a composite god made up of his male element, Shiva, and his female form, Parvati.

0312

Ares (male-warrior). In Greek mythology, one of the 12 Olympian gods, the war god, son of Zeus and Hera; lover of Aphrodite; father of Deimos and Phobos (or Pavor) (gods of tumult and terror) Enyo (goddess of battle) and Eris (goddess of discord); equated by the Romans with their god Mars.

Ares was "the blood-stained bane of mortals," according to Homer in *The Iliad* (book 5). He was hated by the other gods and even disliked by his parents, Zeus and Hera, as demonstrated in a passage from Homer's *Iliad* (book 5) in which the god is wounded. Zeus says to Ares, "You are to me the most hateful of the gods who dwell upon Olympus. For dear to you always are strife and wars and battles. You have your mother Hera's intolerable, unyielding spirit. Hardly can I restrain her with words. Therefore I think that it is at her prompting that you suffer thus. But still I will not long endure that you suffer pain, for you are my offspring and your mother bore you to me. If you had been born so insolent of any other of the gods, long ago would you have been lower than the sons of heaven" (translated by Chase and Perry).

The *Hymn to Ares*, one of the Homeric Hymns (works ascribed to Homer but not by the poet), gives a contrasting image of the god and portrays Ares as a benign protector as well as a patron of bravery:

. . . O defence of Olympus, father of warlike Victory, ally of Themis, stern governor of the rebellious, leader of righteous men, sceptred King of manliness....helper of men, giver of dauntless youth! Shed down a kindly ray from above upon my life, and strength of war, that I may be able to drive away bitter cowardice from my head and crush down the deceitful impulses of my soul....O blessed one, give you me boldness to abide within the harmless laws of peace, avoiding strife and hatred and the violent

Diomedes casting his spears against Ares (John Flaxman)

fiends of death. (Translated by Hugh G. Evelyn-White)

Among his many loves (and the offspring produced) were Aerope (Aeropus); Agraulos (Alcippe); Althaea (Meleager); Astynome (Calydon); Astyoche (Ascalaphus and Ialmenus), Atlanta (Parthenopapaeus); Asterope or Harpina (Oenomaus); Chryse or Dotis (Phlegyas); Cyrene or Asterie (Diomedes); Demonice or Alcippe (Evenus, Molus, Oeneus, Pylus, and Thestius); Otrera (Antiope, Hippolyte, and Penthesilea); Pelopia or Pyrene (Cycnus) and Protogeneia (Oxylus).

Ares was worshiped by the Spartans, who sacrificed dogs to him. The vulture also was sacred to Ares. He had sanctuaries under the name of Enyalius in several places. The Spartans also called him Theritas (wild beast). Among his other names were Gradiuus (leader of armies) and Ares Gynaecotheonas (he who entertains women), the latter because, according to one myth, the women of Tegea armed themselves and drove out the Spartans who had attacked them. The god was also called Aphneius (abundant), referring to the myth of Aerope, a daughter of Cepheus. Ares loved her, but she died giving birth to a child, who clung to her breast even after she was dead. Through the power of Ares, the child still sucked great amounts of milk from its mother's breasts. The Areopagus (hill of Mars), northwest of the Acropolis in ancient Athens, was the meeting place for elders, who tried treason and homicide cases. Ares was the first to be tried by the Areopagitae, the court, for the murder of Halirrhotius, son of Poseidon, who had raped Ares' daughter Alcippe. Orestes was also tried at this court. The Areopagus is the "Mars" Hill cited in Acts (17:22) from which St. Paul tried to convince the Athenians of the merits of Christianity over their pagan gods.

Ares appears in Homer's *Iliad* and *Odyssey* (he sides with the Trojans), Vergil's *Aeneid* (book 8), Hesiod's *Theogony*, The Homeric Hymns, and Apollodorus' *Bibliotheca* (Library), among other works.

In ancient works of art Ares is portrayed as a young and handsome man. One of the best-known statues of him portrays him seated with his son Eros at his feet.

0313

Arethusa (the waterer). In Greek mythology, a nymph of Elis (or Achaed); daughter of Oceanus. Arethusa was a follower of Artemis, who turned her into a fountain. One day she bathed in the stream of the river god Alpheus, who fell in love with her. She fled his sexual advances and was transformed by Artemis into a spring on the island of Ortygra near Syracuse. But Alpheus, following under the sea, was united with the fountain. Ovid's *Metamorphoses* (book 5) and Shelley's poem *Arethusa* (1824), as well as *Arethusa*, a "Symphonic Myth" by Alex Voormolen, all deal with the myth. The Fontana Arethusa still exists today, though it is now a saltwater stream.

0314

Aretos. In Greek mythology, a hero; the name of a son of Nestor mentioned in Homer's *Odyssey* (book 3), as well as the name of a son of Priam killed by Automedon, according to Homer's *Iliad* (book 17). Aretos was also the name of a warrior who used as his weapon an iron club. He was slain by Lycurgus, king of Arcadia, according to Pausanias' *Description of Greece*.

0315

Arge (brightness). In Greek mythology, a female hunter who was transformed into a stag by Apollo. Arge is also the name of one of the Cyclopes according to Hesiod's *Work and Days*, as well as the name of a daughter of Heracles by Thespius and of a nymph daughter of Zeus and Hera, sister of Ares, Elleithyia, Hebe, Eris, and Hephaestus, according to Apollodorus' *Bibliotheca* (Library).

0316

Argeia. In Greek mythology, daughter of Adrastus and Amphithea; sister of Aegialeia, Aegialeus, Deipyle, Cyanippus, and Hippodameia; mother of Thersander and another Adrastus. Argeia was the wife of Polynices, whom she loved very dearly. Together with Antigone, she tried to bury Polynices' body, and Creon had her killed for the deed. Theseus, in turn, killed Creon. The name Argeia is also given to the mother of Argos, who built the first ship, *Argo*, for the hero Jason.

0317

Argives. The ancient inhabitants of Argos and Argolis. Homer and other early poets called the people of Greece Argives. Homer's *Iliad* does not use the term *Greek*, but Argives, Achaeans, or Danaans. Later writings use *Greek* to cover all tribes.

0318

Argo (bright). In Greek mythology, the 50-oared ship in which the Argonauts sailed with Jason to Colchis to capture the Golden Fleece. The *Argo* was built by Argus, son of Argeia. Its prow contained magic wood, given by Athena, from the sacred talking oak of Dodona. While at sea, sometimes the beam would speak oracles to the crew. The *Argo*, according to some accounts, was the first ship. It appears in Apollonius Rhodius' epic, *Argonautica*, and William Morris's *Life and Death of Jason*.

The building of the *Argo*

Argonauts. In Greek mythology, the name given to   0319
Jason and his 55 companions who sailed the *Argo* to
capture the Golden Fleece. The list of heroes varies
from source to source. The Argonauts according to
Apollonius Rhodius's epic poem, *Argonautica* are
Acastus, son of King Pelias of Iolcus Admetus,
prince of Pherae, son of Pheres Aethalides, son of
Hermes Amphidamas, son of Alcus, from Arcadia
Amphion, son of Hyperasius, from Pellene Ancaeus,
son of Lycurgus, from Arcadia Ancacus, a steersman,
son of Poseidon, from Tegea Areus, a son of Bias Argus, builder of the *Argo* Asterion, son of Cometes Asterius, brother of Amphion Augeas, son of Helius,
from Elis Butes, son of Teleon, from Athens
Canthus, son of Canethus, from Euboea Calais,
winged son of Boreas and Orithyia Castor, one of
the Dioscuri, from Sparta Cepheus, son of Aleus,
from Arcadia Clytius, son of Eurytus, from Oechalia
Coronus, son of Caenus, a Lapith from thessaly Echion, herald of the Argonauts, son of Hermes Erginus,
son of Poseidon, from Orchomenus Eribotes, son of
Teleon, from Athens Erytus, brother of Echion, from
Alope Euphemus, son of Poseidon, from Taenarus
Eurydamas, son of Ctimenus, a Dolopian Eurytion,
son of Irus Heracles, son of Zeus, from Tiryns Hylas,
squire of Heracles Idas, son of Aphareus, from Arene
Idmon, a seer, son of Apollo, from Argos Iphiclus,
son of Thestius, from Aetolia Iphiclus, son of Phyla-
cus, from Phylace Iphitus, brother of Clytius Iphitus,
son of Naubolus, from Phocis Jason, son of Aeson,
captain of the expedition Laocoön, uncle of Meleager Leodocus, brother of Areus Lynceus, brother of
Idas Meleager, son of Oeneus, from Calydon Menoetius, son of Actor Mopsus, son of Ampycus, a Lapith Nauplius, son of Clytonaeus, from Argos
Oileus, father of Ajax the Lesser, from locris Or-

pheus, the musician and poet, from Thrace Pala-
emonius, lame son of Hephaestus, from Actolia
Peleus, father of Achilles, from Phthia Periclymenus,
son of Nestor, from Pylus Phalerus, archer from
Athens Phlias, from Araethyrea Polydeuces, one of
the Dioscuri, from Sparta Polyphemus, son of Elatus,
from arcadia Tacnarus, son of Poseidon Talaus,
brother of Areus Telamon, father of Great Ajax,
from Salamis Tiphys, the steersman, son of Hagnias,
from Boeotia Zetes, winged brother of Calais

Others sometimes listed as Argonauts include
Actor, son of Deion, from Phocis Amphiaraus, the
seer, from Argos Ascalaphus, son of Ares, from
Orchomenus Atalanta, the virgin huntress, from
Calydon Caeneus, the Lapith, father of Coronus
Euryalus, son of Mecisteus, one of the Epigoni
Iphitus, from Mycenae Laertes, son of Acrisius, from
Argos Melampus, son of Poseidon, from Pylos
Peneleus, son of Hippalcimus, from Boeotia Phanus,
son of Dionysus, from Crete Poeas, father of
Philoctetes Staphylus, brother of Phanus.

The myth of the Argonauts, which predates
Homer, has inspired numerous ancient and modern
works in addition to the *Argonautica*, including
Euripides' play *Medea*, Pindar's *Pythian Ode*. Chaucer
tells the tale in his *Legend of Good Women*. The longest
reworking of the myth is found in William Morris's
Life and Death of Jason (1867), a poem of 7,500 lines.
Robert Graves wrote a novel on the theme called
Heracles, My Shipmate (1944). Other versions of the tale
include Hawthorne's *Tanglewood Tales* (1851) and *The
Heroes* (1855) by Charles Kingsley; both were written
for children and reflect more of the 19th century
than of ancient Greece.

Argus (bright). In Greek mythology, the name of the   0320
100-eyed giant who guarded Io on the orders of
Hera. The myth is told by Ovid in the *Metamorphoses*
(book 1). Argus is also the name of Odysseus' dog in
Homer's *Odyssey* (book 17), as well as the name of the
builder of the ship *Argo* used by Jason to capture the
Golden Fleece. Others in Greek mythology with the
same name are a king of Argos who reigned for 70
years; a son of Agenor, a son of Zeus and Niobe
(Zeus' first child by a mortal); one of the dogs of Actaeon, a son of Jason and Medea; and a grandson of
Aeëtes, king of Colchis.

Arhat (to deserve, to be worthy). In Theravada Bud-   0321
dhism, one who has reached the end of the Eightfold
Path. Their number varies in Buddhist works from
16 to 500. Often they are portrayed seated along the
eastern and western walls of the principal hall in a
Buddhist temple. An arhat is often seen in contrast

to the Bodhisattva of Mahayan Buddhism, in which the Enlightened One delays entrance into Nirvana to teach the way to others.

In China the term *lohan* is used; in Japan, *rakan*. In Pali the term is Romanized as *arahat*.

Ariadne

Ariadne (purest, high fruitful mother of barley). In Greek mythology, daughter of Minos and Pasiphae; sister of Acacallis, Andiogeus, Catreus, Deucalion, Euryale, Glaucus, Lycastus, Phaedra, and Xenodice. Ariadne fell in love with Theseus when he came to Crete to kill the Minotaur. She gave him yarn to mark his path into the labyrinth so that he could find his way back after slaying the Minotaur. Ariadne then eloped with Theseus. Homer's *Odyssey* (book 11) says Ariadne was killed by the goddess Artemis in the Island of Dia, near Crete, at the request of Dionysus. Later, post-Homeric myth shifts the scene to the Island of Naxos, where the slumbering Ariadne is deserted by Theseus. Waking up, she is on the brink of despair, when Dionysus comes and makes her his wife. Zeus grants her immortality and sets her bridal gift, a crown, among the stars.

Ariadne was accorded godlike honors. At Naxos her festivals portrayed her life. At Athens in the autumn a festival in the honor of Dionysus and Ariadne was celebrated. In Italy Dionysus was identified with the ancient Italian wine god Liber, and Ariadne with the wine goddess Libera.

Ariadne's abandonment by Theseus inspired a poem by the Roman poet Catullus. She is also the subject of one of Ovid's *Heroides*, and appears in Chaucer's *Legend of Good Women*. Tintoretto, Raphael, Titian, and Poussin all deal with the subject in paintings. Richard Strauss's opera *Ariadne auf Naxos* (1912) has a libretto by Hugo von Hofmannsthal. An earlier opera, *Ariadne auf Naxos* by Georg Benda, was much admired by Mozart.

0323

Arianrod (silver circle). In Celtic mythology, a goddess married to the British king and magician Gwydion. Their sons were Lleu Llaw Gyffes, the culture hero, and the sea god Dylan, who at birth plunged into the sea.

0324

Ariel (lion of God or hearth of God). In the Bible, O.T., symbolic name for Jerusalem in Isaiah (29:1–2). In occult medieval literature, the name of a water spirit under the leadership of the archangel Michael.

Ariel figures rather prominently in English literature. In *The Tempest* Shakespeare lists Ariel as an "airy spirit," who is rescued by Prospero from imprisonment in a cloven pine and becomes a servant of the magician. At Prospero's bidding he causes the storm and shipwreck. He lures Ferdinand to a meeting with Miranda, singing "Come unto these yellow sands." He also awakens Gonzalo in time to frustrate the murder of the king. At the end of the play, after Ariel has provided a calm sea and a good wind for a voyage to Milan, Prospero frees the spirit.

Whereas Shakespeare's Ariel is airy and mischievous, Milton's Ariel in *Paradise Lost* is part of the "atheist crew" of fallen angels. The mischievous Ariel returns in Pope's brilliant poem *The Rape of the Lock*, in which Ariel is a sylph assigned to protect Belinda, the heroine, as long as she does not let love for a man enter her heart. Ariel is chief of the "light Militia of the lower Sky," a place inhabited by other sylphs. He rules over other fairies like an epic hero and takes the most dangerous position, guarding Belinda's lapdog. Although he is brave, loyal, and heroic, he cannot help Belinda once she falls in love.

Percy Bysshe Shelley, the English Romantic poet, often called himself Ariel. One biography of Shelley, written by André Maurois, is titled *Ariel*. In music, Ariel is depicted in Tchaikovsky's symphonic poem *The Tempest* and in Sibelius' incidental music for Shakespeare's *The Tempest*.

0325

Arimaspi. In Greek mythology, a fantastic one-eyed people of Scythia, according to Herodotus' *History* (book 4). They were said to be constantly fighting with griffins for the gold the griffins guarded. Milton in *Paradise Lost* (book 2.943-5) cites them.

0326

Arinna. In Near Eastern mythology (Hittite), sun goddess and goddess of fecundity. Arinna was the most important deity in the Hittite pantheon, being addressed in masculine terms as "sun god of heaven." Her symbols were the lion and the dove.

Variant spelling: Arinniti.

Arioch (lion-like). In the Bible, O.T., name given in the Book of Daniel (2:14) for the captain of Nebuchadnezzar and also used in Milton's *Paradise Lost* for a fallen angel.

0327

Aristaeus (the best). In Greek mythology, god of beekeeping and protector of fruit trees; a son of Apollo and a Lapith girl, Cyrene; half-brother of Orpheus. Though he was married to Autonoe, daughter of Cadmus, he fell in love with his sister-in-law Eurydice and pursued her. When he accidentally caused her death by snakebite, the gods punished him by killing his bees. His mother advised him to sacrifice cattle to placate the gods. Nine days after the sacrifice he found swarms of bees in the cattle carcasses. He disappeared near Mount Haemus. Vergil's *Fourth Georgic* tells the tale, and it is his version of Eurydice's death that Niccolo dell' Abbate followed in his painting *The Story of Aristaeus*.

0328

Aristotle (best thinker). 384–322 B.C.E. Greek philosopher, accepted as "the philosopher" by such medieval writers as Dante and St. Thomas Aquinas.

One medieval legend places Aristotle in a bad light. According to the legend, Aristotle, in an attempt to end the relationship between his pupil Alexander the Great and his mistress Campaspe, warned Alexander of the evil of being ruled by a woman. To revenge herself on the philosopher, Campaspe aroused Aristotle to lust. She asked as proof of his love that she be allowed to ride his back. She mounted the old man, who went about the room on all fours. Alexander witnessed the scene and learned to mistrust women.

0329

Arjuna (white; bright; silvery). In the Hindu epic poem *The Mahabharata*, a hero, third of the five Pandu princes/brothers.

Arjuna's father was the storm god, Indra, and he was taught the use of arms by Drona. His skill was so great that he won the girl Draupadi at her *svayamvara* (self-choice), a contest of arms at which a girl chose her husband. However, Arjuna's mother, Kunti, not knowing Arjuna had just acquired a bride, commanded him to share his acquisition with his brothers; thus, Draupadi became the joint wife of all five Pandu brothers. They all agreed that when one of them was making love with Draupadi no other brother was to enter the room. One day, Arjuna,

0330

looking for some weapons, walked into the room when his brother Yudhi-shthira and Draupadi were making love. As a punishment Arjuna went into exile. (At the same time, however, Arjuna kept an entire harem.)

While in exile Arjuna experienced many adventures, among which was winning as a gift from the fire god, Agni, the magic bow, Gandiva. Arjuna's exile over, he returned home, only to find that his brother, Yudhi-shthira, had lost the kingdom in a gambling match. As a result all five Pandu brothers had to go into exile for 13 years. At one time during the long exile Arjuna went on a pilgrimage to the Himalayas to ask the gods to give him celestial weapons to use against the enemy, the Kauravas. At another time Arjuna took a journey to the heaven of his father, Indra.

In the great battle with the Kauravas, Arjuna obtained the help of Krishna (an incarnation of the god Vishnu), who acted as his charioteer. Their great dialogue, which has been inserted into *The Mahabharata*, is called the *Bhagavad-Gita*

On the 10th day of the great battle Arjuna wounded the hero Bhishma; on the 12th day he defeated Susarman and his four brothers; on the 14th day he killed Jayadratha; on the 17th, he argued with his brother Yudhi-shthira and would have killed him had it not been for the interference of Krishna, who stopped the fight. Finally, Arjuna and the other Pandavas were victorious over the Kauravas.

Numerous other adventures as well as love affairs of Arjuna are narrated in the epic. In the end he retired to the Himalayas.

In the epic Arjuna is called Aindri because his father was Indra; also Bibhatsu (supercilious); Dhananjaya (wealth-winning); Gudakesa (tufted hair); Jishu (victorious); Kapidhvaja (ape standard) because his flag bore an ape as a symbol; Kiritin (diademed); Paka-sasana (punisher of the demon Paka); Partha (descent of Pritha); Phalguna because he was born in the month of Phalguna; Savya-sachin (ambidextrous); and Sveta-vahana (white-vehicled).

Ark of the Covenant or Testimony. In the Bible, O.T. (Exod. 25:10–22), a chest some 3 feet 9 inches long, 27 inches broad and deep, made of acacia wood and overlaid with gold, fitted with staves and rings for handles. It was covered with a golden lid called the Mercy Seat, which bore the figures of two cherubim, griffinlike beings derived from Near Eastern mythology. The Ark was a fetish and may have originally contained a live snake god, then an image of a snake, and later the Ten Commandments. It was placed in the Holy of Holies in the temple but later

0331

Ark of the Covenant

disappeared. It may have been carried away or destroyed as an idol. In medieval Christian symbolism the ark symbolized the Virgin Mary, who bore, or sheltered, Christ. Many medieval statues of the Virgin would open to show the infant Christ or the crucified Christ inside. The Hollywood movie *Raiders of the Lost Ark* tells of an attempt to find the ark.

0332

Armageddon (the mount or city of Megiddo). In the Bible, N.T., name given in the Book of Revelation (16:16) to the site of the last battle between Good and Evil before the Day of Judgment. The word is now used for any great battle.

0333

Armida. In the Charlemagne cycle in medieval legend, a beautiful sorceress. In Torquato Tasso's poem *Jerusalem Delivered* Rinaldo falls in love with Armida and wastes his time in voluptuous pleasure. After his escape from her, Armida followed him and, unable to lure him back, set fire to her palace. She then rushed into the midst of a battle and was killed. When she made love, she wore an enchanted girdle, which "in price and beauty" surpassed all of her other ornaments.

In 1806, when Frederick William of Prussia declared war on Napoleon, his young queen rode about in military costume to arouse popular support. When Napoleon was told, he said, "She is Armida, in her distraction setting fire to her own palace." Armida is the central character of Gluck's opera *Armide*, Haydn's opera *Armida*, Rossini's opera *Armida*, and Dvořák's last opera, *Armida*. She appears in Anthony Van Dyck's *Rinaldo and Armida*, one of his most erotic paintings.

0334

Armilus. In Jewish legend, false Messiah, offspring of Satan and a beautiful marble statue of a woman in Rome. Armilus will claim to be the Messiah, gaining some followers, but he will be defeated by God or the true Davidic Messiah. In one medieval text he is described as bald, leprous, deaf in one ear, and maimed in his right arm.

0335

Army of the Dead. In American folklore of the Civil War, ghosts of Confederate soldiers who still march through certain streets of Charleston, South Carolina. It was believed they were the souls of those dead who could not find rest. This folk belief was fostered by the Ku Klux Klan to frighten blacks, who were told that the white-hooded figures were the spirits of the dead.

0336

Arne (ewe lamb). In Greek mythology, daughter of Aeolus, king of Magnesia in Thessaly, and Thea, daughter of Chiron the centaur. Poseidon transformed himself into a bull in order to have sexual intercourse with her. On discovering she was pregnant, her keeper Desmontes blinded and placed her in prison. Arne bore two sons, Aeolus and Boeotus. Ovid's *Metamorphoses* (book 6) tells the tale.

0337

Aroteh and Tovapod. In the mythology of the Tupi Indians of Brazil, two primeval magicians who brought the first men and women up from under the earth.

In the beginning there were no men or women on the face of the earth, for they all lived underground. They had long canine teeth like a wild boar's. Their hands and feet were webbed like the duck's. There was little food underground for them to eat. One day the men and women discovered a way out to the upper earth. Above ground they found two primeval magicians, Aroteh and Tovapod, and stole peanuts and maize from them. At first the magicians believed some animal had taken the food, but when they followed the tracks, they found the hole where the people had come up. They began digging around it and heard screams from the underground. As people emerged from the hole, the two magicians snapped off their tusks and shaped their hands and feet, making them look as humans look today.

Though many men and women came to the earth's surface, some remained underground. When the descendants of all those who came up have died, the underground people, the *kinno*, will then come up and repopulate the earth.

Variant spellings: Aricoute, Timondonar.

0338

Aroundight. In Arthurian legend, the sword of Lancelot of the Lake. Longfellow wrote, "It is the sword of a good knight."

0339

Artemis (high source of water?). In Greek mythology, one of the 12 Olympian gods; goddess of the moon, hunting, childbirth and patroness of chastity and unmarried girls; daughter of Zeus and Leto and twin sister of Apollo. The Romans equated her with their goddess Diana.

One of the Homeric Hymns (works ascribed to Homer but not written by him) praises her role as female twin to Apollo:

> . . . Goddess of the loud chase, a maiden revered, the slayer of stags, the archer, very sister of Apollo of the golden blade. She through the shadowy hills and the windy headlands rejoicing in the chase draws her golden bow, sending forth shafts of sorrow. Then tremble the crests of the lofty mountains, and terribly the dark woodland rings with din of beasts, and the earth shudders, and teeming sea. (Translated by Andrew Lang)

The various epithets of the goddess reflect her many roles. She was called Orthia (upright) and Lygodesma (willow bound) because of an image of the goddess that was said to have been found in a thicket of willows and was held upright by willow fronds that twined around it. Artemis was Agrotera (huntress), Coryphaea (of the peak), Limnaea and Limatis (of the lake), Daphnaea (of the laurel), Lyceia or Lycea (wolfish), Aeginaea (goat goddess), Caryatis (of the walnut tree), Ariste (best), Calliste (fairest). Her most famous title was Artemis Plymastus (many-breasted); she appeared in this form at Ephesus. In the New Testament Artemis is called Diana. In Acts 19 the famous temple of Diana of the Ephesians is the great Artemisium at Ephesus, one of the Seven Wonders of the Ancient World. Most literary allusions to the goddess use her Roman name, Diana.

King Arthur and Guenever

0340

Arthur (bear, hero). In medieval legend, king of Britain. According to various medieval sources, King Uther Pendragon and Igraine were the parents of King Arthur. Merlin, the magician, built a beautiful castle for Uther Pendragon and placed in it the Round Table, in imitation of the one Joseph of Arimathea had once instituted. The table had places for many knights (the number varies) and a special place was reserved for the Holy Grail, the cup that Christ used at the Last Supper. The Holy Grail had disappeared from Britain because of the sinfulness of the people.

A great festival was announced for the institution of the Round Table. All of the knights came to Carduel (Carlisle), accompanied by their wives. Among the latter was Igraine, wife of Gorlois, lord of Tintagel in Cornwall. When Uther Pendragon saw Igraine he fell in love with her. Igraine already had three or four daughters, famous in Arthurian legends as mothers of the knights Gwaine, Gravain, and

Ywaine. One of the king's counselors, Ulfin, told of Uther's passion for Igraine, and she told her husband. Indignant at the insult, Gorlois left the court, locked up his wife in the fortress at Tintagel, and gathered an army to fight Uther Pendragon.

The day before the battle Merlin used his magic to change Uther Pendragon into the form of Gorlois. Merlin also transformed himself and Ulfin into the squires of the duke of Cornwall. In this guise the three went to Tintagel, where Igraine opened the gates and received Uther, thinking he was her husband.

The next morning the battle took place. Gorlois was killed. Not long afterward Uther married Igraine, who never suspected that the child soon to be born was not the son of Gorlois. When Arthur was born, he was given to Merlin, who entrusted him to Sir Hector, who brought up Arthur with his own son, Sir Kay. Sir Hector, however, had no idea whose son Arthur was because Merlin never informed him.

Two years later Uther died. His noblemen, not knowing whom to choose as his successor, consulted Merlin, promising to abide by his decision. By Merlin's advice they all assembled in St. Stephen's Church in London on Christmas Day. When Mass was over, they saw a large stone that had mysteriously appeared in the churchyard. The stone was surmounted by an anvil in which the blade of a sword was deeply sunk. Drawing near to examine the sight, they read an inscription on the jeweled hilt. It said that the man who could withdraw the sword was the rightful king. All of those present attempted to pull the sword from the stone, but all failed.

Several years had passed when Sir Hector came to London with his son Sir Kay and his foster son Arthur. Sir Kay, who was to take part in his first tournament, discovered that he had forgotten to bring his sword. Arthur volunteered to ride home to fetch the sword; however, he found the house closed. So he went to the churchyard of St. Stephen, saw the stone with the sword in it and easily drew it from the anvil.

This mysterious sword was given to Sir Kay by Arthur. Sir Hector, however, recognized the sword and asked Arthur how he had obtained it. At first he refused to believe that Arthur had removed it by himself, but after Sir Hector witnessed Arthur place the sword back in the stone and then withdraw it, he believed.

Because Merlin was known to be an enchanter, rumors spread that Arthur was not Uther Pendragon's son but a child from the sea, who had been brought up on the ninth wave and cast ashore at Merlin's feet. Many people, therefore, mistrusted Arthur at first and refused to give him their allegiance. Among the unbelievers were some of the king's own family, notably his four nephews, Gwaine, Gaharin, Agravaine, and Garath. Arthur was forced to declare war against them. Although Gwaine's strength increased from 9 to 12 in the morning, and from 3 to 6 in the afternoon, Arthur succeeded in defeating him by taking advantage of his weak moments, as Merlin advised.

With Merlin's aid Arthur ruled over the land and established peace and justice. But one day, having drawn his blade on Sir Pellinore without reason, the sword suddenly failed and broke. Left without any means of defense, Arthur would have perished had not Merlin used his magic to put Sir Pellinore to sleep and remove Arthur to a safe place.

Deprived of his magic sword, Arthur was at a loss as to what to do. While standing by a lake, he saw a white-draped hand and arm rise out of the water, holding aloft a jeweled sword that the Lady of the Lake, who appeared beside Arthur, told him was intended for his use.

Arthur rowed out to the middle of the lake and secured the sword, which was known as Excalibur. He was then told by the Lady of the Lake that the sword possessed magic powers. As long as the scabbard remained in Arthur's possession he would not be defeated by anyone.

Thus armed, Arthur went back to his palace and defeated the Saxons who had invaded his land. Arthur then came to the aid of Leodegraunce, King of Scotland, who was threatened by his evil brother Ryance, King of Ireland. Ryance was determined to complete a mantle furred with the beards of kings and wanted to secure Leodegraunce's for the last one. Arthur not only killed Ryance but took the mantle and carried it away as a trophy.

Later Arthur returned to Leodegraunce's court and fell in love with Guinever, the king's daughter. Merlin objected to the marriage unless Arthur first had a successful campaign in Brittany. When the king returned in triumph a wedding was celebrated at Camelot (Winchester) at Pentecost. Arthur received the Round Table as a gift. Earlier Arthur had successfully defeated the 12 kings who had revolted against him. Their remains had been interred at Camelot by his order. There Merlin erected a castle containing a special hall for the reception of the Round Table. The hall was adorned with lifelike statues of all of the conquered kings, each holding a burning taper which Merlin said would burn brightly until the Holy Grail should appear.

The variant legends range from 12 (the mystical number of Christ's Apostles) to over 100 knights of the Round Table.

Among the many knights connected with the Round Table, Lancelot was the handsomest. He fell in love with Guinever, and the queen returned his love. In time the queen was accused of adultery, and Lancelot, who had disappeared for some time, returned to the court to defend her honor, then left for Brittany. Arthur pursued Lancelot, leaving Guinever in the care of Mordred, his nephew, or as some accounts say, his son.

Sir Mordred (H. J. Ford)

Mordred immediately took advantage of Arthur's absence and seized the throne, saying that Arthur had been killed. He then tried to force Guinever to marry him. At first she refused, but finally consented for fear of her life. However, she asked Mordred permission to go to London to buy some wedding garments. When the queen arrived in the city she went to the Tower and sent word to Arthur of what had happened. Without delay Arthur abandoned the siege of Lancelot's castle and, crossing the channel, encountered Mordred's army near Dover.

Negotiations took place, and it was agreed that Arthur and a certain number of knights should meet Mordred with an equal number to discuss peace terms. No weapons were to be drawn. A serpent, however, was lurking in the grass when the knights met, and one of them drew his sword to kill it. His drawn sword was taken as a signal to begin the battle. On both sides the slaughter was terrible, and nearly all of the knights were slain. Arthur then encountered Mordred. Summoning all of his strength, the exhausted king finally slew the usurper but not before Mordred dealt Arthur a mortal blow.

This never would have happened if Morgan le Fay, Arthur's evil sister, had not stolen his magic scabbard and substituted another. All of the enemy's army had perished, and of Arthur's knights only one man remained alive, Sir Bedivere. He hastened to Arthur's side, and Arthur, giving him his sword, asked him to cast it into the lake. At first Bedivere refused but finally did as Arthur asked. As the magic sword touched the waters, Sir Bedivere saw a hand and arm rise up from the depths of the water to seize it, brandish it three times, and disappear.

Arthur gave a sigh of relief when he heard this report. He then told his faithful knight that Merlin had said Arthur would not die. He asked Sir Bedivere to place him on a barge hung with black. Sir Bedivere obeyed, then seeing Arthur about to leave him, he asked permission to accompany him. However, Arthur could not grant the wish because he had to go to Avalon to be cured of his wound and wait to return one day to his sorrowing people.

King Arthur's legend is one of the high points of medieval imagination, representing a portrait of the ideal Christian hero, whose life and deeds often parallel those of his master, Jesus. Some of the analogies to Jesus' life that run through the complex legend are Arthur's birth under mysterious circumstances; his betrayal by a loved one, Guinever; his death at the hands of his enemies; his triumph over death, when he is taken to Avalon, the land of bliss; and finally, the belief that he will return when Britain is in most need.

Around this thread medieval imagination wove a rich tapestry of legends that are still potent today, as witnessed by the success of T. H. White's novel *The Once and Future King* and Lerner and Lowe's Broadway musical *Camelot*, both dealing with Arthur and his legend.

Did King Arthur actually exist? Scholars disagree. Some medievalists believe that King Arthur's legend is based on Artorius, a British war chief, leader of the Romanized Britons against Saxon war bands that invaded Britain from about 450 onward.

The *Cambrian Annals*, written in the 10th century, say Arthur defeated the Saxons at Mount Badon in

516. According to the same work, he fell in battle with Mordred in 537. In 1113 a medieval chronicle mentions a quarrel between a Cornishman and some French monks about whether King Arthur actually existed at all. But in 1125 the historian William of Malmesbury defended the belief in the historical Arthur. In the first half of the same century, on a portal of the cathedral of Modeno in Italy, masons portrayed a siege of a castle by Arthur and his Knights of the Round Table.

An entire literature, both prose and poetry, grew up in medieval Europe around King Arthur. One of the first accounts is in Geoffrey of Monmouth's Latin work *History of the Kings of Britain*, written in the 12th century, which inspired an account by Wace, a French poet, who turned the chronicle of Geoffrey into some 14,000 lines of French verse. This version was used by Layamon, a priest, for his version of Arthur and British legends, running to some 32,000 lines of alliterative verse. Additions were made by successive writers.

Chrétien de Troyes, who lived in the 12th century at the court of the countess of Champagne in Troyes, based his poem about Arthur (so he said) on earlier written texts, which have not survived. In Geoffrey of Monmouth's telling of Arthur's legend the emphasis is on the hero, but in Chrétien's poems Arthur recedes into the background, and the adventures of Gwaine, Yvain, Erec, Lancelot, and Perceval are told.

Chrétien also tells of the love affair between Lancelot and Guinever, King Arthur's wife, and how Arthur was cuckolded. Arthur as the duped husband figures in many later tellings of the legends. The work of Chrétien was followed by Robert de Borron's *Merlin*, written about 1200, in which Arthur's birth, his upbringing, and the drawing of the sword are narrated. The poem *Mort Artu* (Arthur's Death) tells of the disappearance of Arthur's sword Excalibur into a magic lake when Arthur is carried away to Avalon.

Sir Thomas Malory's *Morte d'Arthur*, though having a French title, is a masterpiece of English prose of the 15th century in which all of the previous legends were used.

Malory's work was not the last to deal with the King Arthur legends. Tennyson's *Idylls of the King* owes much to Malory's work, but his approach is different. The poet makes the adultery of Lancelot and Guinever the evil cause of the failure of the Round Table. Arthur tends to be more a symbolic figure in Tennyson than a flesh-and-blood creation. Other 19th-century poets, such as William Morris, Swinburne, and Matthew Arnold, also treat the legends. In the 20th century the best versions are those of the American poet Edwin Arlington

Robinson whose *Tristram*, *Merlin*, and *Lancelot* form a trilogy on Arthurian legends. Mark Twain's *Connecticut Yankee in King Arthur's Court* treats the legends in a less than respectful manner.

0341

Aruru. In Near Eastern mythology (Babylonian-Assyrian), a creator goddess who, together with the hero god Marduk, created man. In the epic poem *Gilgamesh* she creates Gilgamesh's rival and companion, Enkidu, by washing her hands and taking a bit of clay, which she throws on the ground. In a variant tradition the god Ea is credited with the creation of mankind.

0342

Asanga. In Hindu legend, author of some hymns in the *Rig-Veda*, a collection of hymns to the gods. As a result of a curse by the gods, Asanga was changed into a woman but recovered his male form after repenting.

0343

Ascanius (tentless). In Roman mythology, the son of Aeneas and his wife Creusa. He escaped with his parents and his grandfather, Anchises, from burning Troy. Later Roman mythology makes him the son of Lavinia, a Latin princess. Ascanius succeeded his father as second king and moved the kingdom from Lavinium to Alba Longa, where he and his descendants reigned for 420 years, until the reign of Numitor, son of the Alban king Procas. Ascanius was also called Iulus or Ilus, as well as Julus. The family of Julius Caesar claimed descent from him. Vergil's *Aeneid* (book 1) tells part of his tale.

0344

Asclepius (unceasingly gentle). In Greek mythology, god of healing and medicine, son of Apollo and Coronis, who was the daughter of a Thessalian prince Phlegyas (or Arsinoe). The wife of Asclepius was Epione (soother), and his most celebrated daughters were Hygieia (fullness bringer), goddess of recovery, Acesis (remedy), Aegle, Iaso (cure), Janisais, and Panacea (all-healing). In Roman mythology he was called Aesculapius. One of his titles was Paean (healer).

Coronis was killed by Artemis for unfaithfulness. Her body, pregnant with Asclepius, was about to be burned on a pyre when Apollo snatched the boy out of her womb and handed him over to the wise centaur Chiron. The centaur instructed Asclepius in all of the healing arts. In a variant myth Coronis accompanied her father on a campaign to the Peloponnesus and bore the child secretly. She exposed it on a mountain to die, but Asclepius was nursed by a herd of goats. When he grew up, his fame as a healer spread. He even brought the dead back to life. Zeus killed Asclepius with a thunderbolt either in fear of his setting men free from death or on a complaint from Hades, god of death. In revenge Apollo slew all of the Cyclopes who forged the thunderbolts. For this insult to Zeus, Apollo had to serve Admetus for a time as a shepherd.

In Homer and Pindar, Asclepius is only a hero doctor and the father of two heroes, Machaon and Podalerius. Asclepius had a widespread cult in the ancient world. Cocks were sacrificed to him. Plato has Socrates say, as his last words, that he owes a cock to Asclepius, the sacrifice for a cure. It was Socrates' ironic way of saying death was the supreme "cure" for life. Asclepius was worshiped as god of healing in groves, beside medicinal springs, and on mountains. The seats of his worship served also as places of cure, where patients left thank offerings and votive tablets describing their complaints and the manner of the cure. Often the cure was effected through the dreams of the patients, who were required to sleep in the sacred building, in which there sometimes stood a statue of Sleep or Dreaming. Asclepius' worship extended all over Greece and its islands and colonies.

At Rome the worship of the god was under the name Aesculapius. His cult was introduced by order of the Sibylline books when a plague in 293 B.C.E. devastated the area. The god was brought from Epidaurus in the shape of a snake. The animal was sacred to the god, and snakes were kept in his temples.

In later times Asclepius was confused with the Egyptian composite god, Serapis. He appears in art as a bearded man holding a staff with a serpent coiled around it.

Variant spelling: Asklepios.

0345

Asgard (home of the gods). In Norse mythology, home of the Aesir gods. Asgard consisted of many palaces, such as Valaskjalf, a hall roofed with silver in which the god Odin lived. Valaskjalf contained a room, Valhalla, the hall of the slain, where those who had died in battle were feasted by the gods. Asgard was encircled by a wall built by the giant Hrimthurs to protect it from the frost giants. Heimdall was the watchman at the gate to Asgard, which could be reached only by crossing Bifrost Bridge. It was believed that Asgard would be destroyed at the end of the world, Ragnarok, but finally restored to even greater glory.

0346

Asgardreia. In Northern legend, a name for the Wild Hunt, also known as Woden's Hunt, which people believed was the souls of the dead let loose during a storm.

0347

Asgaya Gigagei. In North American Indian mythology (Cherokee), bisexual deity, either the Red Man or the Red Woman. Believed originally to have been a thunder deity, Asgaya Gigagei is invoked by the medicine man to cure sickness. The sex of the deity varies with the sex of the supplicant.

0348

Ash. A tree of the olive family. In world mythology the ash tree is often the Cosmic Tree or World Tree; in Norse mythology it is called Yggdrasil. In Hesiod's *Work and Days* the poet tells how Zeus created the "third generation of men" (that is, the Bronze Age) "from ash spears." In North American Indian mythology the Algonquins believed that the creator god shot an arrow into an ash tree, from which the first human beings emerged.

0349

Asherah. (grove?) In Near Eastern mythology (Canaanite), sea goddess, mother of the gods; her son was Ashtar, a Ugaritic god. At ancient Ugarit, Asherah was the mother-goddess, consort of El, and mother of 70 gods, including Baal. She appears as a rival of Yahweh, the Hebrew god, in the Old Testament. She was represented by a plain pole, a carved pole, a triangle on a staff, a cross, a double ax, a tree, a tree stump, a headdress for priests, and a wooden image. Asherah is seen in some texts to be a variant of the Great Mother goddess Ishtar.

0350

Ashta-mangala. In Buddhism, the Eight Glorious Emblems. They are found in numerous Oriental art works. They are the Wheel of the Dharma, the Conch Shell, the Umbrella, the Canopy, the Lotus, the Vase, the Paired Fish, and the Entrails, or Endless Knot. Sometimes a bell is substituted for the Wheel of the Dharma. In Chinese the Eight Glorious Emblems are called *Pa Chi-hsiang*.

0351

Ashtavakra (crooked limbs). In Hindu legend, a priest who was cursed by his father before birth and was born deformed.

Kahoda, the father of Ashtavakra, paid so little attention to his wife and her pregnancy that the still unborn child, Ashtavakra, rebuked him for his neglect. Kahoda, angry at the child's impertinence, condemned him to be born deformed. Despite this, when his father was killed, Ashtavakra went to seek vengeance on the sage who had committed the crime. When he got the better of the sage and was ready to throw him into a river (his father had been drowned), the sage told him that he was the son of the god of the waters and had thrown people into the water in order to obtain priests for the cult. Then Ashtavakra was told by the sage to bathe in the waters and he would be healed. He did, and his deformity disappeared.

In a variant of the legend Ashtavakra was standing in water performing penances when he was seen by some Apsaras, water nymphs, who worshiped him. He was so pleased that he told them to ask him for any gift. They asked for the best of men as husbands. Ashtavakra came out of the water and offered himself. When they saw his crooked body, they laughed at him. He was angry but could not recall the blessing he had given them. He did say, however, that after obtaining the blessing they should fall into the hands of some thieves.

0352

Ashur. In Near Eastern mythology (Assyrian), war god married to the chief goddess, Ishtar. Ashur was the patron god of the city of Ashur, a military city situated on the Tigris. It is believed to have been the first city to employ cavalry, horse-drawn chariots, and siege machinery. Ashur was symbolized by a winged disk that enclosed a human figure shooting an arrow. Sometimes he appeared eagle-headed. Other animals associated with Ashur were the bull, the ox, and the lion. His standard was carried into battle to indicate his presence among his faithful followers.

Variant spellings: Ashir, Ahshur, Asir, Asshur, Asur.

0353

Ashva-medha. In ancient Hindu ritual, a horse sacrifice performed in Vedic times.

In the Hindu epic poem *The Mahabharata*, the Ashva-medha is given great importance. It was performed only by kings, and its performance indicted that a king was a great conqueror. One hundred Ashva-medhas would enable a mortal king to overthrow the throne of Indra, making the mortal the ruler of the entire universe.

During the rite a horse of a particular color was consecrated by the priests, then allowed to wander at will for a year. The king or his representative followed the horse with an army. When the horse entered a foreign country, the ruler of the country was bound either to fight with the invading army or submit. If the king who followed the horse conquered all other kings whose territory he entered, he would return in triumph, ordering a great festival, at which the horse was sacrificed. In some cases, however, the horse was only symbolically sacrificed.

0354

Ash Wednesday. In Christianity, the first day of Lent in the Western church, observed since the sixth century C.E. The name comes from the ceremony of placing blessed ashes in the form of a cross on the foreheads of the faithful. The priest pronounces the words *Memento homo quia pulvis es et in pulverem reverteris* (Remember, man, that thou art dust, and to dust thou shalt return.) The ashes used in the ceremony are obtained from burning the palms used on the previous Palm Sunday.

Originally, the service was connected with public penance. Sinners would approach the priest shortly before Lent and accuse themselves. The priest then would bring them before the bishop. The sinners, dressed in sackcloth, were assigned acts of penance. Afterward they went into the church and had the ashes imposed on them. The sinners were not allowed to reenter the church until Holy Thursday, when they were reconciled. As part of their penance they had to go barefoot, sleep on straw, and not bathe or cut their hair.

By the end of the 11th century the rite of public penance had been adopted by many of the faithful. Medieval ritual was done away with at the time of the Protestant Reformation, but the Church of England, by special proclamations in 1538 and 1550, continued its use. However, the Puritans objected to any ritual that seemed pagan, and in time it was dropped. *The Book of Common Prayer*, therefore, had no service for the imposing of ashes until the revision of the American prayer book in 1979. The prayer said when ashes are imposed: "Almighty God, you have created us out of the dust of the earth: Grant that these ashes may be to us a sign of our mortality and penitence, that we may remember that it is only by your gracious gift that we are given everlasting life; through Jesus Christ our Savior. Amen."

The ashes are imposed, the Celebrant saying: "Remember that you are dust, and to dust you shall return."

Eastern Orthodox churches do not observe Ash Wednesday. Their Lent begins on Monday before Ash Wednesday, which is called Clean Monday. The name refers not only to the cleansing of their souls but also to the washing and scrubbing of cooking utensils to remove for the season any trace of meat or fat, which is not allowed to be eaten.

During the Middle Ages in England, France, and Germany à Lenten cloth was used at the altar during Lent. It was made of a large piece of white or purple cloth decorated with crosses or other symbols of the Passion of Christ. Suspended in front of the sanctuary, it was parted in the middle to symbolize the casting out of the penitent congregation from the sight of the altar and was drawn apart only during the main part of the mass. It was removed during the reading of the Passion on Wednesday of Holy Week.

T. S. Eliot's *Ash Wednesday* (1930) is an example of his Anglican High Church beliefs, stressing the joy found in traditional Christianity.

0355

Ashwins (horsemen). In Hindu mythology, twin brother gods who preceded Ushas, the dawn. They are young and handsome, bright with golden hair, and ride in a golden chariot drawn by horses or birds. In the Rig-Veda they are "destroyers of foes" and "send adorable light from heaven to men." Some Hindu texts, however, make them into day and night or physicians to the gods. In their role as physicians they are called Dasras and Nasatyas. According to some accounts their mother was Saranyu (fleet runner), who bore them to her husband Vivaswat and then fled, leaving in her place another woman who looked just like her. In a variant account Saranyu took the form of a mare and was mated by Vivaswat, who took the form of a horse. In their haste, however, Vivaswat's semen fell to the ground. Saranyu smelled it, and from the act of smelling it the Ashwins were born.

Variant spelling: Ashwin.

0356

Asita. In Buddhist legend, a sage who told the father of the Buddha that the child born to him would "bring deliverance to the whole world."

0357

Ask and Embla (ash and elm). In Norse mythology, the first man and woman. Odin, Vili, and Ve (or as a variant account lists them Odin, Hoenir and Lodehur) were walking along a beach when they found "two stems of wood, out of which they shaped a man and woman," according to the account in the *Prose Edda*. Odin infused them with life and spirit; Vili, with reason and the power of motion; and Ve, with speech and features, hearing and vision. From Ask and Embla descended the whole human race. Ask and Embla (the latter also spelled Emla or Emola) appear in the *Poetic Edda*.

0358

Asmodeus (destroyer). In Jewish and Christian mythology, demon of lust, sometimes identified with the Persian demon Aeshma, "friend of the wounding spear."

Asmodeus is not mentioned in the Hebrew Scriptures, but he is found in many Jewish folktales and the Old Testament Apocryphal Book of Tobit. In Tobit he is in love with Sarah, daughter of Raguel. She had been given seven husbands and "the evil Asmodeus had slain each of them before he had been

with her as a wife" (Tobit 2:8 RSV). Tobias wished to marry Sarah aided by the archangel Raphael, "took the live ashes of incense and put the heart and liver of the fish upon them and made a smoke." When Asmodeus smelled the odor he fled to the remotest part of Egypt, where Raphael made him a prisoner.

The Latin translation of the Book of Tobit adds the fact that Tobias and Sarah defeated the demon because, aside from using the fish spell, they remained chaste for the first three nights of their marriage. "Tobias nights" later became a custom in some parts of Europe. The husband and wife were not allowed to have sexual intercourse for three nights after the wedding. In medieval France, however, the Church allowed husbands to buy a license to disregard the custom.

According to various Jewish sources, Asmodeus was the son of Naamah, a mortal woman by either a fallen angel or by Adam before Yahweh had created Eve. Asmodeus was responsible for the drunkenness of Noah in one Jewish tale and the construction of the Temple of Solomon in another. By the use of his magic ring King Solomon forced Asmodeus and his devil cohort to work on the massive undertaking. Asmodeus was not happy, and he devised a plan to get the better of Solomon. One day Solomon foolishly allowed the demon to seize his magic ring. The devil hurled the ring into the bottom of the sea, sent the king into exile, and then ruled in his place. However, Solomon recovered the ring when he found it in the belly of a fish. As punishment for his evil deed, Asmodeus was imprisoned with his demons in a large jar.

In a romance by Le Sage, *Le Diable Boiteux* (The Lame Devil), Asmodeus is released from his bottle or jar by Don Cleofas Zambullo. As a reward for his release, Asmodeus lets his master see into the various lives of people by lifting off the rooftops of their homes. At the end of the romance Don Cleofas marries Serafina with the help of the demon. Le Sage's romance was continued in English by W. Comb in *The Devil upon Two Sticks in England*.

The *Lemegeton*, a textbook of ceremonial magic and conjuration, written in the 17th century and often called the *Lesser Key to Solomon*, says that when Asmodeus appears to humans, he rides a dragon, carries a spear, and has three heads: a ram's, a bull's and a man's. All three, of course, are noted for lechery.

0359

Asoka. Third century B.C.E. In Buddhist history and legend, king of the Mauryan empire in North India, perhaps converted to Buddhism. In Buddhist works he is portrayed as a king who wished to spread Buddhism throughout his empire. He is said to have had 64,000 Buddhist monks in his palace and to have had more than 80,000 Buddhist shrines constructed.

Variant spelling: Ashoka.

0360

Asopus (never silent). In Greek mythology, a river god, son of Poseidon or of Oceanus and Tethys. His wife was Metope, daughter of Ladon. Their children included Pelagon, Pelagus, and Ismenus, and many daughters, who were often abducted and raped by the gods; among them Aegina, Antiope, Cleone, Corcyra, Plataea, Salamis, and Thebe. When his daughter Aegina was carried off by Zeus, Asopus was determined to have his revenge. Asopus chased Zeus and found him in a forest. Zeus, not armed with his thunderbolts, changed himself into huge stone, and Asopus lost him. Zeus then went to Olympus, where he hurled thunderbolts at Asopus, wounding and laming the river god. According to the ancient Greeks, the reason the Asopus River flowed so slowly was that the thunderbolts hurled by Zeus left charcoal in the river bed.

0361

Aspen. A poplar tree with quivering leaves. In Christian folklore the aspen trembles because it refused to bend to the Christ when the Holy Family made the Flight into Egypt. The Child Jesus, according to one medieval text, looked at the tree in such a way that "she trembles evermore." In a variant account the aspen was used to make the True Cross, the cross on which Jesus was crucified, and has trembled ever since.

0362

Asphodel Fields. In Greek mythology, the meadow of the dead. According to Homer's *Odyssey* (book 14), Odysseus saw the dead heroes Achilles, Patroclus, and others in the Asphodel Fields. The asphodel was the flower of the underworld (or Hades).

0363

Ass. Horselike mammal with large ears, erect mane, and dark stripe along the back. Noted for its stupidity, obstinancy, lewdness, and patience, the ass appears in world folklore and mythology. In Egyptian mythology the ass is associated with the evil god Set. Greek mythology associates the animal with Dionysus, Typhon, Priapus, and Cronos. In the Old Testament, as in Aesop's fables, asses talk (Num. 22:4–24:25). Yahweh, the Hebrew god, talks through the ass to Balaam, a Midianite magician who had set out to curse the Israelites but ended by blessing them. The biblical account does not say what happened to the speaking ass. According to later Jewish legend, an angel slew the animal to make sure the Hebrews would not be tempted to worship it as they had earlier worshiped the golden calf. Ancient Roman authors accused the Jews of worshiping an ass-headed god, and the Jesuits in the 17th century accused the Masons of the same crime. One medieval bestiary equates the ass with the devil because the ass "brays about the place night and day, hour by hour, seeking its prey." During the Middle Ages, however, at the Feast of Fools, the ass on which Jesus made his triumphal entry into Jerusalem was honored. The congregation, upon reaching the end of each prayer, would bray instead of saying "Amen."

0364

Ass in the Lion's Skin, The. Aesopic fable found throughout the world.

Once upon a time an ass found a lion's skin and put it on. In this disguise he roamed about, frightening all the silly animals he met. When a fox came along, the ass in the lion's skin tried to frighten him too. But the fox, having heard his voice, said: "If you really want to frighten me, you will have to disguise your bray."

Moral: Clothes may disguise a fool, but his words will give him away.

The fable is found in the *Jatakas, or Birth-Stories of the Former Lives of the Buddha*. The ass in the *jataka* is dressed every morning by his master in the lion's skin, so as to obtain free pastureage by frightening away the villagers. The same story is told of a hare in South Africa, and Thackeray includes a reference to it in the prologue to his novel *The Newcomers*.

0365

Ass's Brains. Aesopic fable found in various collections throughout the world.

A lion and a fox went hunting together. The lion, on the advice of the fox, sent a message to the ass, proposing to make an alliance between their two families. The ass came to the place of meeting, overjoyed at the prospect of a royal alliance. But when he arrived the lion simply pounced on the ass and said to the fox: "Here is our dinner for today. Watch you here while I go and have a nap. Woe betide you if you touch my prey." The lion went away and the fox waited. Finding that his master did not return, he ventured to take out the brains of the ass and eat them. When the lion came back, he soon noticed the absence of the brains. He asked the fox, "What have you done with the brains?"

"Brains, Your Majesty! It had none, or it would never have fallen into your trap."

Moral: Wit has always an answer ready.

The fable appears in the great Indian collection *The Panchatantra*, as well as in a rabbinic commentary on Exodus. In both the Indian version and the Greek original the animal loses its heart, which was regarded as the seat of intelligence.

Astarotte. In the Charlemagne cycle of legends, a friend who by magic conducts Rinaldo from Egypt to Roncesvalles in just a few hours. He appears in Pulci's epic *Il Morgante Maggiore*.

0366

Astarte. In Near Eastern mythology, Great Mother goddess worshiped throughout the ancient Near East, identical with the goddess Ishtar.

0367

Astarte was one of the most popular goddesses in the entire pantheon of the Near East; in the Old Testament she was the great rival of Yahweh, the Hebrew deity, in the affections of the people. The Book of Judges (2:12) tells how the Jews "forsook the Lord God of their fathers, which brought them out of the land of Egypt, and followed other gods, of the gods of people that were round about them, and bowed themselves unto them . . ." Of these many strange gods, often connected with fertility rites, Astarte was the leading female deity. King Solomon built "high places" or sanctuaries "on the right hand of the mountain of corruption . . . for Ashtoreth [a variant of her name] the abomination of the Zidonians" (2 Kings 23:13). Later we are told how the evil King Ahab and his wife, Jezebel, were devoted to the goddess, maintaining some 400 prophets in her honor.

The rivalry between Astarte and Yahweh was in part due to the goddess's role as promoter of fertility in plants, animals, and men. Part of her cult consisted of male and female prostitution. Astarte was so popular that her worship spread to Rome, where it was eagerly accepted. The Roman writer Apuleius, in his novel *The Golden Ass*, cynically describes the priests of Astarte with "their faces daubed with rouge and their eye sockets painted to bring out the brightness of their eyes." Ironically, during the Middle Ages the Christians turned the goddess into a male demon, Astaroth, and connected him with the archdemon Asmodeus. In 1637 Madame de Montespan sacrificed children to Astarte and Asmodeus, "princes of amity," in her attempt to maintain her hold on the affection of Louis XIV.

The goddess has appealed to poets. Milton in his *Ode on the Morning of Christ's Nativity* makes reference to:

. . . mooned Ashtaroth,
Heaven's Queen and Mother both . . .

In *Paradise Lost* (book 1) he again mentions the goddess, spelling her name differently:

With these in troop
Came Astoreth, whom the Phoenicians called
Astarte, Queen of Heaven with Crescent horns.

Milton believed the "crescent horns" referred to the goddess in her role as moon deity, though some scholars associate the horns with the cow, as a symbol of fertility.

Byron, in his poetic drama *Manfred*, gives the name Astarte to the beloved of the suffering hero, Manfred. D. G. Rossetti, the English poet-artist, painted *Astarte Syriaca*, in which the goddess has all of the decking of a pre-Raphaelite beauty—heavy lips and long, waving hair.

The oldest known image of Astarte, at Paphos, portrayed the goddess in the form of a white conical stone. In Canaan and Phoenicia she assumed the form of a cow or had the head of a cow or bull. Later she was symbolized by a star. In later art she was portrayed as the Queen of Heaven, and the lion was her symbol. One statue from Mesopotamia (c. 2000 B.C.E.) portrays a nude woman with a horned headdress, wearing earrings and necklace. Cypress groves were sacred to the goddess.

Variant spellings: Aserah, Asherah, Asherat, Ashtart, Ashtoreth.

Asteria. In Greek mythology, a daughter of Ceus (Coeus) and Phoebe, both Titans. Asteria was the mother of Hecate by Perses and sister of Leto. (In some accounts Hecate is another form of Artemis.) Asteria was pursued by Zeus against her will; she transformed herself into a quail and leaped into the sea to escape his sexual advances. She then turned into an island, Ortygia. The island later became the birthplace of Apollo and Artemis when Leto, their mother, sought refuge there. Four pillars arose from the sea; the island became anchored and was then called Delos (Asteria). Asteria's fate is narrated in Ovid's *Metamorphoses* (book 6).

0368

Astolat. In Arthurian legend, a town identified in Malory's *Morte d'Arthur* as Guildford in Surrey. The Fair Maid of Astolat was Elaine le Blank, who died for love of Lancelot. Tennyson's early poem *The Lady of Shalott* and his longer poem, *Lancelot and Elaine*, tell the tale. Edward MacDowell's symphonic poem *Lancelot and Elaine* is based on Tennyson's poem.

0369

Astolpho. In the Charlemagne cycle of legends, one of the 12 Paladins of Charlemagne. Astolpho was an English duke who joined Charlemagne in his struggle with the Saracens (Moslems). He was a great braggart but very generous, courteous, and hand-

0370

some. In Ariosto's *Orlando Furioso* he is carried to Alcina's magic isle on the back of a whale. When the enchantress becomes bored with him sexually, she transforms him into a myrtle tree. Astolpho is later disenchanted by Melissa. He also descends to the underworld and takes a trip to the moon to find the wits, or brains, of Orlando (Roland), bringing them back in a vial to cure Orlando of his madness. Logistilla gives Astolpho a book called *Astolpho's Book*, which will direct him on his journeys. He also has a horn, another gift from Logistilla. Whenever it is sounded, any human or animal within hearing distance is seized with panic and becomes an easy prey of Astolpho.

Astraea (starry). In Greek and Roman mythology, goddess of justice; daughter of Zeus and Themis; sister of the Moerae and the Horae; sometimes called Dike; she lived on earth during the Golden Age but fled when men became wicked. She was placed among the constellations of the Zodiac as Virgo. Vergil refers to the goddess in his *Fourth Eclogue*, "Now returns the Virgin, too, the Golden Age returns." Dryden, the English poet, wrote *Astraea Redux* (1660) to celebrate the return of Charles II after the harsh rule of Cromwell. Alexander Pope also used the image in his poem *Messiah*, which deals with the coming of Christ. Pope used the name directly in *Imitations of Horace* (First Epistle, Second Book) when he writes:

> The stage how loosely does Astraea tread,
> Who fairly puts all characters to bed.

The lines refer to Mrs. Aphra Behn, who used the *nom de plume* Astraea. She wrote plays in which women often had to resort to sex to win their ends. In *The Faerie Queene* by Spenser the knight of Justice, Artegall, is brought up by Astraea.

Astraeus (starry). In Greek mythology, a Titan, son of Crius and Eurybia; brother of Pallas and Perses. He was the father by Eos, the goddess of dawn, of the stars and winds—Boreas, Hesperus, Notus, Phosphorus, Zephyrus, and, according to some accounts, Aura. He was also an enemy of Zeus.

Astyanax (king of the city). In Greek mythology, a young son of Hector and Andromache. He was saved from burning Troy by his mother, only to be thrown from its towers by the Greeks, who feared he would grow up to avenge the death of his father, Hector. Odysseus advised that the child be killed. In some variant accounts Menelaus is said to have killed the boy or Achilles' son Pyrrhus (Neoptolemus). As-

tyanax appears in Homer's *Iliad* (book 6), Vergil's *Aeneid* (book 2), and Ovid's *Metamorphoses* (book 13). Astyanax was also known as Scamandrius.

Asuras (divine beings). In Hindu mythology, demons often in combat with the gods. In the epic myths contained in the *Puranas* and other late Hindu writings, the Asuras are powerful evil beings. In the earlier *Vedas*, however, the name Asuras is often applied to the gods themselves, rather than to their enemies, the demons.

Ataensic. In North American Indian mythology (Iroquois), sky woman, creator goddess, mother of twin brothers, Hah-gweh-di-yu and Hah-gweh-da-et-gah, one good and one evil.

Long ago there grew one stately tree that branched beyond the range of vision. Perpetually laden with fruit and blossoms, the air was fragrant with the tree's perfume. People gathered under its shade when councils were held. One day the Great Ruler said to his people: "We will make a new place where another people may grow. Under our council tree is a great cloud sea that calls for our help. It is lonesome. It knows no rest and calls for light. We will talk to it. The roots of our council tree point to it and will show the way."

Having commanded that the tree be uprooted, the Great Ruler peered into the depths where the roots had grown. He then summoned Ataensic, the sky woman, who was with child, and asked her to look down. She saw nothing. The Great Ruler, however, knew that the sea voice was calling and bidding Ataensic to carry light to it. He wrapped a great ray of light around Ataensic and sent her down to the cloud sea.

When the animals saw the blinding light they became frightened.

"If it falls, we will be destroyed," they said.

"Where can it rest?" asked Duck.

"Only the *oeh-da* [earth] can hold it," said Beaver, "the *oeh-da*, which lies at the bottom of our waters. I will bring it up."

The beaver went down but never returned. Then Duck ventured, but soon his dead body floated to the surface.

Many other divers also failed. Then Muskrat, knowing the way, volunteered. He soon returned bearing a small portion of mud in his paw.

"But it is heavy and will grow fast," he said. "Who will bear it?"

Turtle was willing, and *oeh-da* was placed on his hard shell. Hah-nu-nah, the turtle, then became the earth bearer. The *oeh-da* grew, and Ataensic, hearing the voices under her heart—one soft and soothing, the other loud and contentious—knew that her mission to people the island was nearing. Inside Ataensic were the twin brothers, Hah-gweh-di-yu, who was good, and Hah-gweh-da-et-gah, who was evil. Hah-gweh-da-et-gah, .discovering that there was some light coming from his mother's armpit, thrust himself through it, causing Ataensic's death. Hah-gweh-di-yu, however, was born in the natural manner. Foreknowing their power, each claimed dominion over the other. Hah-gweh-di-yu claimed the right to beautify the land whereas Hah-gweh-da-et-gah was determined to destroy it.

Hah-gweh-di-yu shaped the sky with the palm of his hand and created the sun from the face of his dead mother, saying, "You shall rule here where your face will shine forever."

But the evil brother set darkness in the western sky to drive the sun down before it.

The good brother then drew forth the moon and the stars from the breast of his mother and led them to the sun as its sisters who would guard the night sky. He gave to the earth her body, its Great Mother, from whom was to spring all life.

The two then created all that is on the the earth. Hah-gweh-di-yu created mountains, valleys, forests, fruit-bearing trees, and good animals, such as the deer. Hah-gweh-da-et-gah, the evil one, created monsters that dwell in the sea, hurricanes, tempests, wild beasts that devour, grim flying creatures that steal life from helpless victims, and creeping poisonous reptiles.

When the earth was completed, Hah-gweh-di-yu bestowed a protecting spirit on each of his creations. He then asked his evil brother to make peace, but Hah-gweh-da-et-gah refused and challenged Hah-gweh-di-yu to combat, the victor to be ruler of the earth.

Hah-gweh-da-et-gah proposed weapons that he could control— poisonous roots strong as flint, monster's teeth, and fangs of serpents. But these Hah-gweh-di-yu refused, selecting the thorns of the giant crabapple tree, which were arrow pointed and strong.

They fought with the thorns, and Hah-gweh-da-et-gah was defeated. Hah-gweh-di-yu, having become ruler of the earth, banished his brother to a pit under the earth, whence he cannot return. But he still retains servers, half human and half beasts, whom he sends to continue his destructive work. They can assume any shape or form. Hah-gweh-di-yu the good, however, is continually creating and protecting.

0376
Atago-Gongen. In Japanese Buddhist mythology, god worshiped on Mount Atago in the province of Yamashiro; he is the patron god of fire. His temple, built in the eighth century C.E., became popular with the military caste, and numerous warriors came to pray to the god, who is portrayed as a Chinese warrior on horseback.

0377
Atai. In African mythology (Efik of Nigeria), wife of the sky god Abassi who sent death into the world. Abassi placed the first couple on earth but forbade them to work or produce children for fear they would become more powerful than he. But the couple produced food and children, provoking Abassi to ask his wife Atai to punish them. She sent death and discord into the world to plague humankind.

0378
Atalanta (unswaying). In Greek mythology, two women— Atalanta of Arcadia, a virgin huntress, supposed daughter of Iasus and Clymene; and Atalanta of Boeotia, daughter of Schoeneus, king of Scyros. Some scholars, however, regard the two as one person.

Atalanta of Arcadia was the supposed daughter of Iasus of Arcadia, though her real father was Zeus. Iasus wanted a son, and when Atalanta was born he exposed the girl on a mountain to die. (It was a common practice of the Greeks to let their female infants die.) Artemis, however, protected the child by sending a she-bear to nurse Atalanta until the child was found by a band of hunters, who rescued her and brought her up. Atalanta was told that if she married she would be unhappy, so she avoided men. She devoted her time to hunting and became so skilled that she killed two centaurs who had attempted to rape her. Some ancient accounts say Atalanta was with the Argonauts in the quest for the Golden Fleece.

Meleager of Calydon fell in love with her and invited her to join the Calydonian boar hunt. The men, however, objected. Meleager said he would leave if Atalanta was not accepted, and the men reluctantly accepted her. Atalanta was the first to draw blood from the boar. Ancaeus, another hunter, said he would teach her how to kill a boar. He attacked the boar and was disemboweled by the boar's tusks. Meleager then struck the fatal blow and presented Atalanta with the boar's hide and tusks. The men of the hunt were insulted by his presenting the prize to a woman.

According to some accounts, Atalanta and Meleager had a son, Parthenopaeus, who was exposed by his mother on a mountain to die. She then pretended she had never married and was a virgin. Atalanta returned home and was welcomed by her father, who now wished to see her married. She remembered the oracle that said she would be unhappily married and devised a means to defeat her father's schemes. She informed her suitors that whoever wanted to marry her must first beat her in a foot race, but whoever lost to her in the race must die. Many suitors died as a result, but they still came. One, Hippomenes (or Melanion), prayed to Aphrodite, goddess of love, to help him win Atalanta. The goddess brought three golden apples from her garden on the island of Cyprus and gave them to Hippomenes with directions for their proper use. The race was begun and Atalanta was about to pass Hippomenes when he dropped one of the golden apples. Atalanta slowed down to pick it up. Hippomenes then dropped the second and third apple and won the race. At first Atalanta did not want to honor her bargain, but eventually she did. The two were so happy that they forgot to thank Aphrodite. The goddess then made them offend Zeus or Cybele by causing them to make love in the deity's temple. Because of the sacrilege, Atalanta was transformed into a lioness and Hippomenes into a lion. The two were then yoked to Cybele's chariot to draw it for eternity. The other Atalanta, of Boeotia (or perhaps the same one), was the daughter of the king of Scyros. She married Hippomenes (or Melanion).

Atalanta's myth is told in Ovid's *Metamorphoses* (book 10) in which Venus narrates the tale to Adonis. This was the version painted by Poussin. The tale is also told in *The Earthly Paradise* by William Morris and in Swinburne's play *Atalanta in Calydon*.

Atar. In Persian mythology, fire god, protector against demons; son of the good god, Ahura Mazda. Atar watched over pregnant women and bitches and blessed those who brought him dry wood for the fire sacrifice. One myth records his battle with the demon Azhi Dahaka. The demon tried to seize the Divine Glory by rushing toward it and trying to extinguish it. (It would seem to be some form of fire or light.) However, Atar cursed Azhi Dahaka, saying he would burn his "hinder part" if he did not give in. Threatened with such violence to his person, the demon relented.

Variant spelling: Ataro.

Atargatis. In Near Eastern mythology (Syrian), mother goddess, associated with the moon and fertility.

Atargatis was born from an egg that the sacred fishes found in the Euphrates and pushed ashore.

Her shrine at Ascalon had a pool near her temple that contained sacred fish. The Old Testament Apocrypha book 2 Maccabees (12:26) tells how Judas Maccabeus "marched forth to Carnion, and to the temple of Atargatis, and there he slew five and twenty thousand persons." A marginal note to the King James Version says in reference to Atargatis, "That is, Venus."

Atargatis's cult was very popular in the Near East, and she was known under various names. The Phoenicians called her Dereto, and some scholars believe the goddess Atheh, worshiped at Tarsus, was another version of the goddess. The Romans called her Dea Suria, and the Greeks identified her with Aphrodite.

In art Atargatis was sometimes portrayed as half woman and half fish. Doves were sacred to her, and fish were used in her worship.

Variant spellings: Atarate, Atargate, Atharate.

Atchet (the nurse?). In Egyptian mythology, goddess associated with the sun god Ra and in some texts considered the female counterpart of the sun god. Atchet may have been a deity associated with nursing children.

Ate (mischief). In Greek mythology, goddess of discord, evil, mischief, and infatuation and the personification of moral blindness; daughter of Zeus and Eris; identified by the Romans with their goddess Discordia. Ate was cast out of heaven by Zeus because she had misled him. One day, according to Homer's *Iliad* (book 19), Zeus, tricked by Ate, boasted among the gods that on that day a man should be born, mightiest of his race, who should rule over many. Hera saw an opportunity to deceive Zeus, who was waiting for the birth of Heracles by one of Hera's female rivals. After getting Zeus to make an oath that he would keep his word, Hera persuaded the goddess of childbirth to delay Heracles' birth and hasten that of Eurystheus, who then had power even over Heracles. Ate was not invited to the marriage of Peleus and Thetis. Angry, she wrote "For the fairest" on the Golden Apple and rolled it into the midst of the gathering. The goddesses all claimed it. Zeus refused to make judgment, and the matter was given to Paris. His choice of Aphrodite caused the Trojan War. Behind Ate go the Litai (prayers), the lame, wrinkled, squinting daughters of Zeus. They can heal the evils of Ate, but they bring new evils upon the stubborn. Hesiod's *Theogony* mentions the goddess.

Atea and Papa (sky and flat). In Polynesian mythology, the sky and the earth, who were later made into gods. In one myth the couple held themselves in such a tight sexual embrace that none of their children could free themselves. Finally, the children conspired to kill their mother and father, but one of the children, Tane, suggested that the two be separated. This was done, forming the sky and earth.

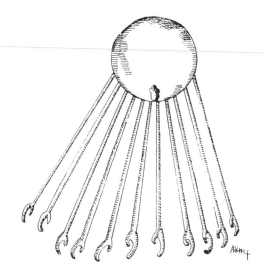

Aten

Aten. In Egyptian mythology, the sun disk worshiped by Akhenaton (1372–1355 B.C.E.). One hymn to Aten by the pharaoh has been preserved. It opens:

> Thy rising is beautiful in the horizon of heaven,
> O thou Aten, who hadst thine existence in primeval time.
> When thou riseth in the eastern horizon thou fillest every land with thy beauties.
> Thou art beautiful to see, and art great, and art like crystal, and art high above the earth.
> Thy beams of light embrace the land, even every land which thou hast made.
> Thou art as Ra, and thou bringest thyself unto each of them,
> And thou bindest them with thy love.
> Thou art remote, but thy beams are upon the earth.

Although this extract from the hymn gives some idea of Akhenaton's views and those of his followers concerning the Aten, it is still impossible to gather precise information about the details of cult and belief. Incense was burned several times a day, and hymns were sung to the Aten, accompanied by harps and other instruments. Offerings to the deity consisted of fruits and flowers, with no animal sacrifice. Worship was joyous. Mika Waltari's novel *The Egyptian* deals with the failure of Akhenaton to convince the priests to worship the Aten over other gods

Variant spellings: Aton, Adon, Eton.

Athaliah (Yahweh is exalted). In the Bible, O.T., queen, the daughter of Ahab and Jezebel and the wife of Joram, king of Judah. After Joram's death, Athaliah's son Ahaziah took the throne after killing the princes of King David's house. Athaliah ruled for six years. When Joash, who had escaped massacre, was proclaimed rightful king, Athaliah entered the temple, where she was killed by the mob (2 Kings 11). Jean Racine's play *Athalie* uses the biblical legend. Mendelssohn wrote incidental music for the play.

Athamas (reaper on high). In Greek mythology, a king of Achaea, Orchomenus, Phthiotis, or Thebes (ancient accounts vary); son of Aeolus and Enarete; husband of Nephele; father of Phryxus and Helle. Anthamas later married Ino, daughter of Cadmus, and the couple had two sons, Learchus and Melicertes. His children fled to Colchis on a golden ram to escape the wrath of their jealous stepmother, Ino, who resented Athamas' preference of them over her own children. Athamas accidentally killed his son Learchus, mistaking him for a stag.

Athanasius, St. (immortal). c. 296–373 C.E. In Christian legend, bishop of Alexandria; one of the Greek Doctors of the Church. Feast, 2 May.

A pupil of St. Anthony the Abbot, Athanasius wrote what is considered the first full-length biography of a saint. He is best known for the Athanasian Creed, which scholars now say was not composed by the saint, though the saint was a staunch defender of orthodoxy over Arianism, a heresy of the early church. In Christian art he is portrayed as old, bald and with a long white beard, wearing vestments of the Greek church.

Atheh. In Near Eastern mythology, goddess worshiped at Taraus, portrayed wearing a veil and seated on a lion. Some scholars believe Atheh to be another version of the Syrian mother goddess, Atargatis.

Athena (queen of heaven). In Greek mythology, one of the 12 Olympian gods; goddess of wisdom, skill, and warfare; identified with Minerva by the Romans. Athena was born, full grown, out of the head of Zeus, who had swallowed his first wife Metis (counsel) for fear that she would bear a son superior to himself. Hephaestus (or Prometheus) opened Zeus' head with an ax, and Athena sprang forth clad in armor. Her ancient epithet Tritogeneia (born of Triton or the roaring flood) would seem to indicate that she was the daughter of the ocean. Oceanus, according to Homer, was the origin of all things, all gods and goddesses.

Athena had a prominent place in ancient Greek religion. When solemn oaths were to be taken, her name was invoked along with those of Zeus and Apollo. Athens, named for her, was the most important seat of her worship. The names of Athena's earliest priestesses, the daughters of Cecrops—Aglaurus, Pandrosus, and Herse—signify the bright air, the dew, and the rain.

Athena was important in agriculture. The sowing season was opened in Attica by three sacred rites of plowing, two of which honored Athena as inventor of the plow. It was Athena who taught man to attach oxen to the yoke, and it was she who gave man the olive tree. Her chief feast was the *Panathenaea*, which was originally a harvest festival but later became a festival to honor the intellectual gifts of Athena.

Athena's birth story influenced Milton's *Paradise Lost* (book 2) in which the poet describes the birth of Sin from the head of Satan.

Among art works inspired by Athena, one of the best-known statues was the Palladium, an image that was believed to have fallen from heaven. A priestly family in Athens had charge of the sacred image. It was believed that as long as the statue was safe, the city of Athens was safe. The Trojans had the statue earlier, and the fall of Troy is is sometimes attributed to its removal, either by Odysseus and Diomedes or by Aeneas when he left the city. Athens, Argos and Rome all claimed to have the real statue. Matthew Arnold's poem *Palladium* contains the lines:

> And when it fails, fight as we will, we die;
> And while it lasts, we cannot wholly end.

Another famous image, contained in the Parthenon, was the gold-and-ivory statue by Phidias, of which we have only small copies. Another statue by Phidias, a 30-foot bronze of Athena the warrior, stood by the Propylaea, the great marble gateway at the west end of the Acropolis.

In works of art Athena is usually portrayed with a shield and a spear and holding the bleeding head of Medusa. The olive, the cock, the owl (late classical times), the crow, and the serpent were sacred to her.

Athena repressing the fury of Achilles (John Flaxman)

Among Athena's epithets were Athena Polias (of the city), Poliatas (keeper of the city), Ergane (worker) as patroness of workers in the decorative arts, Athena Leitis (goddess of beauty), Paeonia (healer), Athena Zosteria (girder) when she armed for battle, Athena Anemotis (of the winds) as goddess of winds and rains, Promachorma (protector of the anchorage), Pronaea (of the foretemple), Pronoia (forethought), Xenia (hospitable), Larisaea (of Larisa), Ophthalmitis (of the eye), Cissaea (ivy phasium), Aeantis (Ajacian), Aethyia (Gannet), Agoraea (of Hippola), Athena Nike (victory) for her special temple on the Acropolis at Athens, Parthenon (virgin or maiden) and Athena Promachus (champion), which inspired the statue by Phidias. Among the myths associated with Athena are the giving of the magic bridle to Bellerophon, helping Perseus kill Medusa, teaching Argus to build the ship *Argo*, teaching Epeius to build the wooden horse (she sided with the Greeks), giving dragon's teeth to Cadmus and Aeetes, and helping Heracles, Diomedes, Odysseus, and Tydeus. Athena appears in Homer, Vergil, the Homeric Hymns, Pausanias, Ovid, Aeschylus, Sophocles, and in English literature often, though generally under the Roman form of her name, Minerva.

Variant spelling: Athene.

Athena (Minerva)

0390

Atlacamanc. In Aztec mythology, a storm god, often identified as the male counterpart of Chalchihuitlicue, the Aztec storm goddess.

0391

Atlantes. In the Charlemagne cycle of legends, a wizard who educated Ruggiero in all of the manly arts. He appears in Ariosto's *Orlando Furioso*.

0392

Atlantis. In European mythology, an island in the western sea that was destroyed by a tidal wave or earthquake. Supposedly, the island of Atlantis had attempted to enslave its neighbors but was defeated by Athens, then destroyed. Plato in *Timaeus* and *Critias* tells of the civilization. Francis Bacon called his concept of the ideal society *The New Atlantis*.

0393

Atlas (he who dares or suffers). In Greek mythology, son of the Titan Iapetus and Clymene (or Aisa); brother of Menoetius, Prometheus, and Epimetheus. Atlas was a Titan who sided with the Titans against Zeus and was condemned by Zeus to stand in the west holding up the sky on his shoulders. His burden was relieved by Heracles while Atlas fetched for Heracles the golden apples of the Hesperides. In one early myth Atlas was visited by Perseus and was in-

hospitable. Perseus turned him into stone by showing him the Gorgon's head. The stone became Mount Atlas in northwestern Africa. Homer makes Atlas the father of Calypso. Other accounts say the Pleiades are his daughters. Because he was associated with the sky, it was believed during the Middle Ages that Atlas had taught man astrology. A book of maps is called an atlas because the figure of Atlas with the world on his shoulders was used by the 16th-century mapmaker Mercator on the title page of his book.

Atlantiades (offspring of Atlas) was a patronymic of Hermes, the Pleiades, and the Hesperides. The seven daughters of Atlas, the Pleiades, were Alcyone, Celaeno, Electra, Maia, Merope, Sterope or Asterope, and Taygete. Atlas appears or is mentioned in Vergil's *Aeneid* (book 4), Hesiod's *Theogony*, and Ovid's *Metamorphoses* (book 4). Heinrich Heine's poem on Atlas was set to music by Franz Schubert. The Titan also appears in Rockefeller Center, New York, in a rather gross statue.

Atlatonan. In Aztec mythology, goddess "of the leprous and maimed," according to Fray Diego Durán in his *Book of the Gods and Rites* (c. 1576), dealing with Aztec mythology and ritual.

0394

Atlaua (water, arrow). In Aztec mythology, a water god, also associated with arrows.

0395

Atman (Sanskrit root *an*, "to breathe"). In Hinduism, the essence of life, often translated as soul, spirit, ego, world spirit, or world soul.

0396

Atnatu. In Australian mythology, self-created god who punished some of his children by casting them out of heaven through a hole in the sky.

0397

Atreus (fearless). In Greek mythology, king of Mycenae; son of Pelops and Hippodameia; brother of Alcathous, Astydameia, Chrysippus, Copreus, Lysidice, Nicippe, Pittheus, Thyestes, and Troezen; married to Aerope; father of Agamemnon, Menelaus, and Anaxibia; grandson of Tantalus. Atreus, with the help of his brother Thyestes, murdered his step-brother Chrysippus. To escape the wrath of their father, the two took refuge with their brother-in-law Sthenelus, king of Mycenae, who gave them the kingdom of Media. Eurystheus, the brother of Sthenelus, was killed in a battle, and his kingdom, Argos, was taken over by Atreus, who ruled with the scepter made by the god Hephaestus and given him by his father, Pelops. Atreus' first wife was Cleola, who died in childbirth after delivering a son, Plisthenes. Atreus then married Aerope. Their children were Agamemnon, Menelaus, and Anaxibia. Hermes had given Atreus a horned lamb with a golden fleece which was to be sacrificed to Artemis. Instead Atreus killed the lamb and had it stuffed and mounted. He proclaimed that whoever possessed the golden lamb possessed the right to the throne. Thyestes, with the aide of Aerope, conspired against Atreus and stole the lamb. Thyestes was thereupon acknowledged king. Atreus then made a bargain with Thyestes that if he, Atreus, could cause the sun to reverse its path in the heavens, his throne would be restored to him. With the aid of Zeus and Eris the feat was accomplished, and Atreus was res-

0398

tored. This, however, did not please Thyestes, and he arranged for the murder of Plisthenes, Atreus' son. To avenge Plisthenes' death, Atreus killed one of Thyestes' sons and invited Thyestes to a banquet. After he had eaten, Atreus told him he had eaten the flesh of his own child. Thyestes then placed a curse on the house of Atreus and went into exile, where he met and raped Pelopia, not knowing she was his daughter. A famine in the kingdom had followed Thyestes' curse, and and an oracle told Atreus he must bring back Thyestes in order to end it. Atreus cast the unfaithful Aerope into the sea and went in search of Thyestes. He came upon Pelopia at about the time she was to deliver Thyestes' son, Aegisthus, whom she exposed to die on a mountain. Atreus rescued Aegisthus and brought him up as his own son. Years later Atreus succeeded in bringing Thyestes back and putting him in prison. He then instructed Aegisthus to kill Thyestes. When Thyestes discovered that Aegisthus was the son of Pelopia, he knew that he was the boy's father. He revealed his identity to his son, and the two plotted against and killed Atreus.

The tale of the House of Atreus, made of the stories of Agamemnon, Menelaus, Clytemnestra, Helen, Aegisthus, Orestes, Electra, and Iphigenia, inspired 8 of the 33 surviving Greek tragedies and also inspired modern dramatists and poets such as Eugene O'Neill and T. S. Eliot.

Attila (fatherlike). 404–453 C.E.. In medieval history and legend, king of the Huns, known as the Scourge of God, who was stopped by Pope Leo I. Attila and his army ravaged the eastern Roman Empire for several years, then made peace with Emperor Theodosius. The Hun then turned toward the western Empire and was defeated by Aetius, the Roman general, in 451. Undaunted, Attila then invaded northern Italy as far as the Po River. He was met by Pope Leo I, who came to plead with the invader to spare Rome from destruction. To the amazement of everyone, Attila removed his army. When asked why, he said, "While Pope Leo was speaking, I distinctly saw two shining beings of venerable aspect, and manifestly not of this earth, standing by his side. They had flaming swords in their hands, and menaced me with death if I refused to withdraw the army." The two beings, according to the account of Damasus in his *Lives of the Popes*, were St. Peter and St. Paul. But the truth is that Attila agreed to leave Italy in return for the Princess Honoria and her vast dowry, according to Gibbon in his *Decline and Fall of the Roman Empire*. The medieval legend inspired Raphael's fresco in the Stanza d'Eliodoro in the Vatican Museum, *The Encounter of Attila and Leo I*, Delacroix's

0399

mural *Attila Tramples Italy and the Arts*, and William von Kaulbach's *Hunnenschlacht* (The Battle of the Huns), which in turn inspired Franz Liszt's symphonic poem of the same name. Attila appears in Corneille's play *Attila* and Verdi's opera *Attila*. He also appears as the character Etzel in the medieval epic *Nibelungenlied* as well as the earlier work, *Volsunga Saga*, in which he is called Atli.

0400

Attis (luckless). Phrygian god of death and resurrection, annually mourned and rejoiced over at a festival in spring. Attis was a handsome young shepherd who was loved by the goddess Cybele, mother of the gods. Cybele's chief shrine was at Phrygia, the name given to a large area in ancient Asia Minor. Some myths say Attis was the son of Cybele, though most texts give Nana, a virgin, as his mother. She conceived him by putting a ripe almond or pomegranate in her bosom. His death, however, was the major motif of his myth. In one account he was killed by a boar. According to a variant text, Attis castrated himself under a pine tree and bled to death on the spot. Worship of Attis and Cybele spread to Rome in the second century B.C.E. Attis, in the form of a pine log, covered with violets, was annually mourned, as were Tammuz and Adonis, at a spring festival, part of which consisted of self-mutilation of Cybele's priests. The Roman poet Catullus, in his *Carmina*, tells of one priest, named after the god, who castrated himself and then lamented his rash act. Catullus reflects the rites in such a way that the priest of the poem is literally possessed with a religious frenzy of unbridled proportions, which is so strong that it compels him to commit the castration. It is only after the heat of the moment has sufficiently subsided that the priest realizes the effect of his actions.

Variant spelling: Atys, Attes

0401

Audhumla (rich, hornless cow). In Norse mythology, the primeval cow at creation, formed from vapors. She fed the primeval giant Ymir and lived by licking the salt from stones. On the first day she licked the stones, the hairs of a man appeared. On the second day a human head appeared. On the third day "an entire man appeared, who was endowed with beauty, agility and power," according to the *Prose Edda*. The man was Bur, father of Bor, who married the giantess Besla; she bore three gods, Odin, Vili, and Ve.

Variant spellings: Audhumbla, Audumla.

0402

Auge (radiance). In Greek mythology, a goddess of childbirth, an Arcadian princess, priestess of Athena; daughter of Aleus, king of Tegea, and Naera. She was raped by Heracles and bore him a son, Telephus. Auge's father, Aleus, did not believe Heracles to be the father of her child and ordered Nauplius to drown Auge and expose the baby on Mount Parthenius to die. Instead of drowning Auge, Nauplius sold her to King Teuthras, who adopted her as his daughter. Telephus was rescued by a shepherd and reached manhood. When King Teuthras' kingdom of Mysia was invaded, it was Telephus, directed to Mysia by an oracle, who drove out the invaders. His mother's identity was then made known to him by Heracles.

Variant spellings: Auga, Augea.

0403

Augeas (bright ray). In Greek mythology, son of Helios (or Phorbas) and Hyramina; brother of Actor and Tiphys; the king of the Epeians in Elis and one of the Argonauts. He possessed 3,000 sheep and oxen, among which were 12 white bulls consecrated to the sun. The cattle were blessed by the gods and never sickened or died of disease, and they were extremely fertile. They were kept in a stable that had not been cleaned for 30 years. Heracles' sixth labor, given him by Eurystheus, was to clean the stable. Augeas agreed to pay Heracles one-tenth of his herd if he fulfilled the task in one day. Heracles diverted the rivers Alpheus and Peneus to wash away the dirt, but Augeas refused to pay, so Heracles killed him and all of his sons, except for Phyleus, whom he made ruler of the kingdom. The term "Augean stables" is now applied to anything filthy.

0404

Augures (to tell, declarers, tellers). In ancient Roman cult, a group of priests established, according to tradition, by Romulus. Their function, important in Roman life, was not to predict the future but, by observing natural signs, to determine if the gods approved of a specific action. They wore a state dress with a purple border and carried a staff without knots and curled at the top. Roman augury was based chiefly on written works such as the *Libri Augurales*, a book on the techniques of augury, and the *Commentarii Augurales*, a collection of answers given to inquiries of the Roman senate. Magistrates would commission augurs to provide answers to specific questions by observing omens of birds. They would consecrate the observation place with the following rite: Immediately after midnight or at dawn, the augur, in the presence of the magistrate, selected an elevated spot with a view as wide as possible. Taking his station, he drew with his staff two straight lines crossing one another—one north to south, the other east to west. He then enclosed this cross in a rectangle, forming four smaller rectangles. The augur then spoke the ritual words consecrating the marked space. This space within the rectangle as well as the space upward to the sky was called the *templum*. At the point of the intersection in the center of the rectangle was erected the *tabernaculum*, which was a square tent with its entrance looking south. Here the augur, facing south, sat down, asked the gods for a sign according to a prescribed formula, and waited for an answer. Complete quiet, a clear sky, and an absence of wind were necessary conditions for the rite. The least noise was sufficient to disturb it, unless the noise was an omen of terror, called *diroe*.

The Romans regarded signs on the left side as propitious omens, signs on the right side as unlucky. The east was the region of light, and the west was that of darkness. The reverse was the case in ancient Greece, where the observer looked northward.

The augur watched the birds for omens. Eagles and vultures gave signs by their manner of flying; ravens, owls, and crows by their cry as well as their flight. Some bird species were held sacred to particular gods, and the appearance of those birds were omens of good or evil. The augur's report was expressed in the words "the birds allow it" or "on another day," meaning postponement.

0405
Augustine of Canterbury, St. (venerable). Died 605 C.E. In Christian legend, first archbishop of Canterbury. Feast, 26 May.

The legend of St. Augustine of Canterbury is told in St. Bede's *Ecclesiastical History of the English People*. Augustine was sent by Pope St. Gregory the Great as a missionary to Kent in England. The queen, Bertha, was already a Christian, but her husband, Ethelbert, was not. However, Ethelbert permitted Augustine and his followers to enter Canterbury, which they did, singing praises and carrying an image of Christ. The king was so moved that he consented to be baptized along with his people. The saint then wished to speak with others on the island, the Britons, who had been converted to Christianity earlier but followed different customs from those of the Roman church. A meeting was held during which they debated the date of Easter and some other customs. To prove that God was on his side in the matter, a blind man was brought in and immediately "received sight, and Augustine was by all declared the preacher of the Divine Truth." However, the Celtics or Britons, said they had to get the "consent and leave of their people," and they asked for a second conference. This was arranged and seven Celtic bishops arrived.

"If he is a man of God, follow him," a holy man said.

"How shall we know that?" the bishops asked.

"If at your approach he shall rise up to you," he said, "hear him submissively, being assured that he is the servant of Christ; but if he shall despise you, and not rise up to you, whereas you are more in number, let him also be despised by you."

When they arrived, Augustine remained in his chair, and the conference fell apart. Augustine, however, had the last word. He cursed the group, saying they would fall under the judgment of death. This prediction came true after St. Augustine's death, for some 2,000 monks who followed the Celtic church were killed by Ethilfrid, king of the pagan Northern English.

In Christian art Augustine is shown either as a Benedictine with a staff or as a bishop with a pallium, wearing a cope and miter.

St. Augustine

0406
Augustine, St. (venerable). 354–430 C.E. In Christian legend, bishop of Hippo (modern Bône, Algeria) in Africa; Doctor of the Church; author of *The City of God*, a defense of Christianity against pagan philosophy, and an autobiography, *The Confessions*. Feast, 28 August.

Augustine's father was a pagan, but his mother, Monica, was a Christian. As a young man Augustine devoted his life to the pursuit of pleasure (he had numerous mistresses) and the study of philosophy. As he was interested only in some heretical sects, his mother prayed for his conversion to Catholic Christianity. Eventually, her prayers were answered; Augustine was baptized by St. Ambrose, bishop of Milan.

The most famous legend regarding the saint is called the vision of St. Augustine and is frequently portrayed in art. While Augustine was busy writing his *Discourse on the Trinity*, he wandered along the seashore, lost in meditation. Suddenly he saw a child who had dug a hole in the sand and was bringing water from the sea to fill it. Augustine stopped and asked the boy what he was doing. The boy replied that he wanted to empty into the hole all of the water of the sea.

"Impossible," the saint replied to the child.

"Not more impossible than for thee, O Augustine, to explain the mystery of the Trinity," the child answered.

St. Augustine is often portrayed in his episcopal vestments, carrying a book and a heart, symbol of his love and learning. Sometimes he is shown as a young man, before his conversion, reading or disputing with his mother, St. Monica. He is also sometimes painted in the black habit of the Augustinian Order, which legend credits him with founding.

Augustus (consecrated by augury). Honorary Latin title and given in 27 B.C.E. to Octavian, great nephew and adopted son of Julius Caesar. The title was not hereditary but was taken by succeeding emperors as bestowed by the senate. The title of Augustus was reserved exclusively for the emperor, but the corresponding feminine style of Augusta was assumed by great ladies of the imperial house. The title was used by Christian emperors of the Holy Roman Empire.

0407

Aunyain-á. In the mythology of the Tupi Indians of Brazil, an evil magician from whose body iguanas, lizards, and other animals were produced. Aunyain-á had tusks like a boar's and ate children. The people, wishing to rid the land of him, climbed up a creeper vine to heaven, knowing he would follow. When Aunyain-á began climbing, a parrot flew ahead of him and gnawed through the vine, so that Aunyain-á fell back to earth. From his arms and legs caymans and iguanas grew; from his fingers and toes, other lizards. What was left of his body was then eaten by vultures.

0408

Aurora (dawn). In Roman mythology, the dawn; daughter of Hyperion and Thia (or Thea); married to Astraeus; mother of the wind and the stars; called Eos by the Greeks. Aurora's chariot, drawn by white horses, raced across the heavens and caused the constellations to disappear at her approach. The subject is found frequently in Baroque paintings, including works of Carracci, Guercino, and Guido Reni. In literature, Shakespeare refers to the dawn in *A Midsummer Night's Dream*, as "Aurora's harbinger," (3.2.380), and Spenser in *The Faerie Queene* (book 1) writes: "And fayre Aurora from the deawy bed/ Of aged Thitone gan herselfe to reare" Thitone is Spenser's spelling of Tithonus, the old lover of the goddess. Ancient references are found in Homer's *Odyssey* (book 10), Vergil's *Aeneid* (book 6), and Ovid's *Metamorphoses* (book 3).

0409

Ausonia. An ancient name for Italy, derived from Auson, a son of the Greek hero Odysseus and Calypso. In Vergil's *Aeneid* (book 3) Aeneas speaks of Ausonia.

0410

Auster. In Roman mythology, the southwest wind; called Notus in Greek mythology.

0411

Autolycus (very wolf). In Greek mythology, a son of Hermes and Chione or Philonis; father of Anticleia; maternal grandfather of Odysseus. Autolycus was a noted thief, having the gift of being able to change his form and that of his stolen goods at will. Autolycus stole the cattle of Sisyphus, who, after he found the cattle, raped Anticlea, Autolycus' daughter. Autolycus also stole the cattle of Eurytus of Oechalia. After changing their color, he sold them to Heracles. In *The Winter's Tale* Shakespeare uses the name Autolycus for the rogue in the play. Autolycus is also the name of one of the Argonauts, cited in Homer's *Odyssey* (book 14) and Ovid's *Metamorphoses* (book 1).

0412

Automedon (independent ruler). In Greek mythology, a hero, son of Diores; he sailed for Troy with ten ships. He was Achilles' charioteer and later Pyrrhus'. Automedon is mentioned in Homer's *Iliad* (book 9) and Vergil's *Aeneid* (book 2).

0413

Autonoe (with mind of her own). In Greek mythology, daughter of Cadmus and Harmonia; sister of Agave, Illyrius, Ino, Polydorus, and Semele. She was the wife of Aristaeus and mother of Actaeon and

0414

Macris. Autonoe was driven insane, along with her other sisters, for their ill treatment of Semele. Ovid's *Metamorphoses* (book 3) tells the tale.

0415

Av. Fifth month in the cultic calendar of the ancient Babylonians. Av corresponds to parts of July and August. The month is also sacred in Judaism, often being called Menahem (comforter). As comfort must arise from despair, according to Jewish tradition, so on the ninth month, during which the temple was destroyed by the Babylonians under Nebuchadnezzar in 586 B.C.E. and the Second Temple under the Roman Titus, the Messiah will be born. On that date a fast is held, ornaments are removed from synagogues, and the Book of Lamentations is read. The commemoration has been used in recent times in memory of the Jews killed by the Nazis.

Variant spelling: Ab.

0416

Avalokiteshvara (he who hears the groanings of the world). In Buddhism the Bodhisattva who appears in any appropriate form to help suffering beings. In China and Japan he has many female forms. In Mahayana Buddhism he is either one of the five Dhyani-Bodhisattvas who is noted for his compassion or a Bodhisattva in his own right.

Avalokiteshvara appears in numerous forms throughout Buddhism. In the form of the Bodhisattva of Infinite Compassion with 11 heads and 8 or 1,000 arms, he looks in every direction to save all creatures. The nine heads in three tiers have a benign expression, the 10th head shows anger, and the 11th is that of Amitabha, the father of Avalokiteshvara, shown with a *cintamani*, a sacred pearl. Some of his hands are in prayer; others hold a lotus, a vase of ambrosia, a rosary, a bow, and the *cakra*, Wheel of the Dharma. One hand, the lower right, is the *mudra* gesture of charity.

Another well-known icon is that of Avalokiteshvara as the Four-Armed Bodhisattva of Infinite Compassion. One pair of hands is in the gesture of prayer. The upper right hand holds a rosary; the upper left, a lotus. The top of the head is surmounted by a representation of Amitabha, his spiritual father. An antelope skin drapes the left shoulder.

0417

Avalon (island of apples). In Arthurian legend, the place of the blessed dead, where, according to some accounts, King Arthur still lives. Some scholars believe Avalon is derived from *Yns Avallon* (Avallon's Island), the realm of the Celtic god Avallach.

0419

Avaricious and Envious, The. Aesopic fable found in various collections throughout the world.

Two neighbors came before Zeus and asked him to grant their heart's desire. One was full of avarice, and the other was eaten up with envy. To punish them both, Zeus granted that each might have whatever he wished for himself, but only on condition that his neighbor had twice as much. The avaricious man prayed to have a room full of gold. No sooner said than done, but all of his joy was turned to grief when he found that his neighbor had two rooms full of the precious metal. Then came the turn of the envious man, who could not bear to think that his neighbor had any joy at all. So he prayed that he might have one of his own eyes put out, by which means his neighbor would be made totally blind.

Moral: Vices are their own punishment.

This is one of the most popular Aesopic fables. It occurs in the Indian collection *The Panchatantra* and in various collections of the Middle Ages. It is told by Hans Sachs, the German poet and dramatist of the 16th century, and by John Gower, the English poet and friend of Chaucer, in his *Confessio Amantis* (book 2:2).

0420

Avatar (a descent). In Hindu mythology, the incarnation of a god in some form, often applied to Vishnu.

0421

Avernus (no birds). In Roman mythology, a deep sulfurous lake in southern Italy in a crator of an extinct volcano west of Naples, believed by the ancients to be one of the entrances to the underworld, the land of the dead. No birds were ever seen in its area. Vergil's *Aeneid* (book 6) tells how the hero Aeneas was told by the Sibyl of Cumae to enter the underworld through Avernus. It is still called Lago Averno today.

0422

Avesta (basic text, wisdom, or injunction). Sacred book of ancient Persia (Iran), containing the teachings of the prophet Zarathustra as well as pre-Zoroastrian myths from Persian mythology.

The *Avesta* proper consists of the following:

Gathas, a collection of hymns, some ascribed to the prophet Zarathustra and others believed to have been written earlier and adapted for the work.

Yashts, hymns to the individual gods, as well as some material on earlier Persian mythology.

Yasna, liturgical texts in prose and verse.

Vendidad, a miscellaneous collection of writings in prose.

The original *Avesta* is believed to have been lost during the time of Alexander the Great (fourth century B.C.E.). From the third century to the sixth century C.E. magi (Zoroastrian priests) compiled a collection of sacred writings consisting of some 21 *nasks*, or books, of which only a small part contained material from the original *Avesta*. The *Zend Avesta*, the term usually applied to the sacred writings of Persia, is actually a zend (commentary) on the parts of the original *Avesta*, containing quotes from the original lost text.

0423

Awonawilona (maker and container of all). In North American Indian mythology (Zuni), bisexual creator deity. In the beginning Awonawilona was alone in a dark void, "though outward in space," according to *Report of the Bureau of American Ethology* (Cushing), "whereby mists of increase, steams potent of growth, were evolved and uplifted. Then Awonawilona became the sun and mist formed creating Awitelin Tsita (four-fold containing Mother-earth) and Apoyan Ta'chu (all-covering Father-sky)." The two then had sexual intercourse and "terrestrial life was conceived; whence began all beings of earth, men and the creatures." Among the first men was Poshaiyangkyo, who led the people from the darkness to the light.

0424

Ayesha. c. 610–677 C.E.. In Islamic legend, favorite wife of Muhammad, married to the prophet when she was a child. At one time she was suspected of being unfaithful to Muhammad, but the prophet defended her honor. He ultimately died in her arms. At his death she helped her father, Abu-Bakr, to become the first caliph, and he reigned for two years. She was defeated in 656 when she tried to gain more power from Ali.

0425

Ayida. In Haitian voodoo, the rainbow, female counterpart of Danbhalah Houé-Do. A form of the goddess Erzulie Ayida is also called Aida Wédo.

0426

Aymon, The Four Sons of. In medieval French legend, the sons of Aymon: Renaud (Rinaldo), Alard, Guichard, and Richard. They appear in the medieval French romance, *The Four Sons of Aymon*, as well as Bolardo's *Orlando Innamorato*, Ariosto's *Orlando Furioso*, Tasso's *Rinaldo*, and *Jerusalem Delivered*.

0427

Aynia. In Celtic folklore, the most powerful fairy in Ulster, Ireland, thought to be derived from Anu, the goddess who presided over prosperity and abundance.

0428

Azaca Mede. In Haitian voodoo, the loa (deified spirit of the dead) of gardens and mountains, who is offered goats in sacrifice. Often the goats are black.

0429

Azariel (God has helped). In Jewish folklore, angel of the earth waters, invoked by fishermen to obtain a good catch.

0430

Azazel (goat that departs?). In the Bible, O.T., a scapegoat, an evil spirit or demon.

In Leviticus (16:8) the high priest Aaron casts lots "upon two goats, one lot for the Lord and the other lot for Azazel." The one chosen for the Lord was sacrificed as an offering for sins, and Azazel was driven into the desert. Originally, Azazel was a Semitic satyr or god of flocks who was incorporated into Hebrew ritual.

In medieval Jewish folklore Azazel is credited with being one of the angels who came down from heaven to have intercourse with the daughters of men, teaching men witchcraft and warfare.

In Islam, Elbis (the equivalent of Satan) is considered to be the Islamic form of Azazel.

In *Paradise Lost* (book 1:534) Milton describes Azazel as a "Cherub Tall" who holds the "glittering staff" of the fallen angels. In Collin de Plancy's *Dictionnaire Infernal*, Azazel is portrayed as a fat, naked man with horns holding a pitchfork-type banner on which a frog is shown. In his other hand he holds a goat. The English Pre-Raphaelite artist William Holman Hunt painted *The Scapegoat*, which portrays the goat with photographic accuracy.

0431

Azeto. In Haitian voodoo, an evil loa (deified spirit of the dead), either a male or female werewolf or vampire.

0432

Azhi Dahaka. In Persian mythology, archdemon with three heads, six eyes, and three jaws, who is defeated by the hero Traetaona.

Azhi Dahaka is under the control of the evil spirit, Ahriman. His greatest battle was with the hero Traetaona. The two fought in Varena (the heavens). Traetaona clubbed Azhi Dahaka in the head, neck, and heart, but the demon refused to die. Finally, Traetaona took a sword and plunged it into the monster's breast. Out of the wound came a host of ugly animals: snakes, toads, scorpions, lizards, and frogs. Frightened that more of such animals were inside the demon, Traetaona took the body and imprisoned it in Mount Demavend. Here the demon is to stay for a time; then he will escape to cause havoc in the world until he is slain by the hero Keresaspa, who will usher in a new world order.

In Firdusi's epic poem *Shah Namah* the character of the evil king, Zahhak, is modeled on that of Azhi Dahaka.

Variant spellings: Asi Dahak, Az-i Dahak, Dahhak.

0433

Azrael (whom God helps). In Jewish and Islamic mythology, an angel of death, often identified with Gabriel in Jewish writings and with Raphael in Islamic works.

Azrael keeps a roll containing the name of every person born in the world. The time of death and whether the person is saved or damned is not known to Azrael. When the day of death approaches, Allah lets a leaf inscribed with the person's name drop from his majestic throne. Azrael reads the name and within 40 days must separate the soul from the body. If the person makes a struggle, Azrael flies back to the throne of Allah and informs him. Then Allah gives him an apple from paradise on which the *basmala*, the Name of God, "the merciful and compassionate," is written. When the person reads the Name of God, he then gives up his life to the angel of death.

However, if the person is an unbeliever and lost, Azrael tears the soul from the body in a rough manner. The gate of heaven closes, and the person is cast into hell.

Azrael is variously described in Islamic writings. In general he has some 70,000 feet and 4,000 wings. He has four faces and as many eyes and tongues as there are men in the world.

Longfellow, in one of his metrical poems included in *Tales of a Wayside Inn*, has a Spanish Jew tell a tale of Azrael and King Solomon. The king is entertaining a "learned man" who is a rajah. As they walk, a white figure in the twilight air is gazing intently at the man. The rajah asks Solomon:

What is yon shape, that, pallid as the dead,
Is watching me, as if he sought to trace
In the dim light the features of my face?

The king calmly tells his guest that it is the angel of death, Azrael. The man then asks Solomon to get him as far away from Azrael as possible. The king, with his magic ring, sends him off to India. The angel of death asks Solomon who the man was who left so suddenly. The king gives Azrael the name, and Azrael thanks the king for sending the man off the India, since he was on his way "to seek him there."

Variant spelling: Izrail.

B

Ba (soul). In Egyptian mythology, the soul, or that part of a person that had eternal existence after death, represented as a human-headed bird. The *ba* was closely associated with the *ka*, a person's double, and the *ib*, or heart, and constituted one of the principles of a person's life. After death the *ba* was believed to visit its body in the tomb. In the pyramids of Meroë openings were left in the stone covering the apex so that the *ba* might enter, and a ledge was placed beneath each opening for the *ba* to stand on. A small figure of the *ba* made of gold and inlaid with some precious stones was placed on the breast of the mummy in the hope of preserving it from decay, because the ancient Egyptians believed there was to be a final union of all souls with their bodies.

0434

Baal (lord, owner, possessor). In Near Eastern mythology, generic name for numerous gods of rain, agriculture, and fertility.

0435

Many Baals or Baalim, as the Old Testament calls them, were worshiped in the ancient Near East. Usually a god was called Baal when his worshipers had taken "possession" or "ownership" of land by settling it. Many place names in the Old Testament indicate that a local form of Baal was worshiped in the land: thus Baal-peor (Num. 25:3) and Baal-hermon (Judg. 3:3). The influence of Baal worship, with its fertility rites, left its mark on the worship of the Hebrew deity Yahweh, since at one time the two gods were worshiped together. Yahweh, however, eclipsed the worship of Baal, and the latter was denounced by the later Hebrew prophets. Yet the titles assigned to Baal were often also assigned to Yahweh. Baal was "he who mounts the clouds," whereas Yahweh, the god of Jerusalem, was he "who rideth upon the heavens" (Deut. 33:26).

Among the most famous Baals worshiped in the Near East were Baal Berith, Baal-hermon, Baal-macod, Baal-peor, Baalsamin, Baalzebub, and Baalzephon.

Variant spellings;: Ba'al, Ball.

Baba Yaga (old woman). In Russian folklore, cannibalistic ogress who kidnaps children, then cooks and eats them.

0436

Baba Yaga usually lives in a hut that stands on hens' legs. Sometimes it faces the forest, sometimes the path, and sometimes it moves about from place to place. In some Russian folktales Baba Yaga's hut is surrounded by a railing made of sticks surmounted by human skulls, which glow at night from candles placed inside them.

One Russian folktale, simply titled "Baba Yaga," tells of an evil stepmother who attempted to have her daughter eaten by Baba Yaga. The girl was saved when a magic comb thrown in Baba Yaga's path made it impossible for the ogress to catch the girl as she escaped. In a variant tale, however, the girl was broken into little pieces and placed in a basket.

Anatol Liadov's short symphonic poem *Baba Yaga* deals with the ogress, as does one section of Modest Moussorgsky's *Pictures at an Exhibition*, also titled "Baba Yaga," originally written for piano and transcribed for orchestra by Ravel in 1923.

Variant spelling: Baba Jaga.

Tower of Babel

Babel, Tower of (confusion). In the Bible, O.T., a ziggurat erected on the plains of Shinar by the descendants of Noah when they reached Babylonia. Genesis (11:1–9) says the plan was to build a tower that would reach to heaven. Yahweh, the Hebrew cult god, said "Go to, let us go down, and there confound their language, that they may not understand one another's speech" (Gen. 11:7). This accounts for the variety of languages in the world. The ziggurat is believed to have been of the god Marduk's temple in Babylon, which consisted of six square stages, one on top of the other, the last with a small room for the

0437

god. Numerous paintings on the subject exist. One of the most famous is by Brueghel; another is by Marten van Valckorborch.

0438

Babes in the Wood. Popular title of the English ballad *Children in the Wood*, found in Percy's *Reliques*. The master of Wyland Hall, Norfolk, leaves a little son and daughter to the care of his wife's brother. Both children were to inherit money, but if they died, the money would go to the uncle. After 12 months the uncle hired two men to murder the children. One of the murderers relented and killed his fellow, leaving the children in the wood. They died during the night and were covered with leaves by Robin Redbreast. The uncle eventually died after seeing his children die and his wealth destroyed. After seven years the murderer was caught, and confessed. A play by Robert Farrington (1599) tells the tale.

The phrase "babes in the wood" is often used for simple, trusting people, never suspicious and easily fooled.

0439

Babe, the Blue Ox. In American folklore, a giant ox, companion of Paul Bunyan. He created Lake Michigan when he sank knee-deep into solid rock. He died when he accidentally ate a stove instead of the batch of hotcakes on it.

0440

Baboon. A large monkey of Arabia and Africa, with a short tail and doglike muzzle. In Egyptian mythology the baboon was sacred to the moon god Thoth, who was sometimes portrayed as a baboon. In the Egyptian *Book of the Dead* the dead person's heart is shown placed on a scale, on top of which sits a baboon. The baboon was to report to Thoth when the pointer was in the middle, indicating a balance of the person's deeds so he or she could be judged. Sacred baboons were kept in various Egyptian temples that were dedicated to moon gods. The baboons were believed to be the spirits of the dawn who had been transformed into baboons as soon as the sun arose when they sang a hymn in the sun's honor.

0441

Bacabs (erected, set up). In Mayan mythology, four giant brothers who supported the four corners of the heavens, blowing the winds from the four cardinal points. Each was identified with a particular color and cardinal point, thus Hobnil (belly) was associated with the south and the color yellow. The remaining three were red, assigned to the east; white, to the north; and black, to the west. The winds and rains were said to be under the control of these Bacabs.

As each year in the Mayan calendar was supposed to be under the influence of one of the brothers, one Bacab was said to die at the close of each year. After the nameless or intercalary days had passed, the next Bacab would come alive. Each computation of the year began on the day Imix, which was the third before the close of the Mayan week; this was said to be figuratively the day of death of the Bacab of that year. It was not until three or four days later that a new year began, with another Bacab, who was said to have died and risen again. *The Ritual of the Bacabs*, an ancient Mayan book containing incantations, was so named because of its frequent mention of the Bacabs.

0442

Baca, Elfego. 1865–1945. In American history and folklore, Mexican-American hero. When Baca, at 19, was told that a band of Texans had publicly castrated a Mexican and used another for target practice, he borrowed a lawman's badge and set out for Frisco (now Reserve), New Mexico. When he got there, some cowboys were still causing trouble, and Baca promptly arrested one who had shot off Baca's hat. The next day some 80 cowboys arrived to teach Baca a lesson; a gunfight ensued in which some 4,000 rounds of ammunition were fired during a 36-hour period. At the end, four Texas cowboys were dead. Baca was brought to trial but acquitted; he became a lawyer and owner of a detective agency in later life. He was known as hero of the people, and his legend continued in his lifetime.

0443

Bacalou. In Haitian voodoo, an evil loa (deified spirit of the dead), represented by a skull and crossbones.

0444

Bacchants (raving women). In Greco-Roman cult, women who followed the god Dionysus, who was also called Bacchus. His followers, also called Maenads, were said to tear human flesh and even eat their own children. The cult was banned by the Roman Senate in 186 B.C.E. Euripides play *The Bacchae* deals with the cult. Numerous paintings depict the *Bacchanalia*, the festival held in honor of the god. Among the most famous are those by Rubens and Poussin. Picasso "repainted" the Poussin work.

Variant spellings: Bacchantes, Bacchae.

0445

Bacchus (raging). In Greek and Roman mythology, a title for Dionysus, son of Zeus and Semele, who was a daughter of Cadmus; also called Liber. Numerous art and music works identify the god Dionysus as Bacchus, such as *The Young Bacchus* by Caravaggio, which portrays one of the artist's male lovers; Ti-

Priest of Bacchus

tian's great *Bacchus and Ariadne*, depicting the god jumping from his chariot; and Roussel's two-act ballet, *Bacchus et Ariane* (1930). Ovid's *Fasti* (book 3) supplied most of the imagery for the paintings.

0446

Bachúe (she of the large breasts). In the mythology of the Chibcha Indians of Colombia, mother goddess and protector of crops. After the supreme god Chiminigagua had created light, the goddess Bachúe emerged from a mountain lake with a three-year-old child. She went to live in a nearby village, Iguaque, and brought up the child. When he was of age, she married him and bore four or six children, who populated the land. With her task finished, Bachúe and her husband left for the mountains and finally reentered the sacred lake as snakes. In some accounts the name of the goddess is given as Fura-chogue, "the beneficent female."

0447

Bacon, Roger. 1214–1292. In medieval history and legend, English monk, believed to be a wizard.

Bacon did numerous scientific experiments, which earned for him a reputation as being in league with Satan. One legend, cited numerous times, tells of the Brazen Head. The monk had a head made of bronze, which he often consulted. He had his attendant Miles watch the Brazen Head while he slept. Once, while Miles was watching the head, it spoke to him.

"Time is," it said. A half hour later it said, "Time was." In another half hour it said, "Time's past." Then the Brazen Head fell to the ground and broke to pieces.

Byron in his mock epic poem *Don Juan* (book 1), uses the lines:

Like Friar Bacon's brazen head, I've spoken
"Time is," "Time was," "Time's past."

Earlier the English poet Alexander Pope had written in his mock epic *The Dunciad* (book 3): "Bacon trembled for his brazen head." The monk is the subject of a play by Robert Greene, *Friar Bacon and Friar Bungay*.

0448

Badal (substitute; double). In Islamic folklore, spirit of a man. The *badal* are known only to Allah. The number of badals varied. Some Islamic accounts give 40, some 30, others just 7. It is believed that when a holy man or saint dies, his *badal*, or "substitute," immediately fills his place. Some Islamic writers explain *badal* as "one who, when he departs from a place, has the power to leave his double behind him." Others say the *badal* is "one who has experienced a spiritual transformation."

Variant spelling: Abdal.

0449

Badessy. In Haitian voodoo, loa (deified spirit of the dead) of the winds.

0450

Badi (mischiefs). In Malayan mythology, demons that inhabit animate and inanimate objects. Various accounts are given of their origin. One says they sprang from three drops of blood spilled by Adam on the ground; another account says they are the offspring of the djinn; still another credits their origin to the yellow glow at sunset. There is disagreement on their total, which is either 190 or 193. Various charms and ceremonies are used in Malaya to cast out badi from people, animals, plants, and objects.

0451

Bagadjimbiri. In Australian mythology, twin culture heroes of the Karadjeri in northwestern Australia. At first they appeared in the form of dingos; they created water holes and sexual organs for humankind and instituted the rite of circumcision. The two brothers were killed when, having become gigantic men, they annoyed the cat man Ngariman with their loud laughter. He gathered together his relatives, and they speared the twins to death. Distraught at this, Dilga, their mother, the earth goddess, caused milk to flow from her breasts, which drowned the killers and revived her sons. When the

Bagadjimbiri decided to leave earth, their dead bodies became water snakes, and their spirits ascended to the sky.

Baginis. 0452 In Australian mythology, half human and half animal female beings who have lovely faces but claws instead of fingers and toenails. They capture men and rape them. After they are satisfied, the men are freed.

Bahram fire. 0453 In Persian mythology, sacred fire that represents all fires and shoots up before the good god, Ahura Mazda. It is composed of 16 different kinds of fire and is the earthly representative of divine fire.

Variant spelling: Berezisauanh.

Bahram Gur. 0454 In Persian mythology, a hero king appearing in the epic poem *Shah Namah* by Firdusi, as well as in the poem *Haft Paykar* (seven portraits) by another Persian poet, Nizami.

Bahram Gur is met with frequently in Persian poetry and legend. He is credited with the invention of Persian poetry and appears in many tales as a "great hunter." In Firdusi's epic Bahram Gur married seven princesses, daughters of the king of the Seven Climates, each of whom told him a story at night before retiring. Each night Bahram Gur slept with a different wife and heard a different tale.

Often Bahram Gur is depicted in Persian art hunting with his mistress Azada. One scene often portrayed is that of the hero meeting a shepherd who has hung his dog on a tree because the dog let the wolf steal lambs from his flock.

Some scholars believe Bahram Gur is a portrait of a Sassanian king of Persia who lived in the fifth century C.E.

Variant spellings: Bahramgor, Bahram Gor.

Baiame. 0455 In Australian mythology, the totemic ancestor of the Kamilaron tribe of New South Wales who taught the people customs and sacred rites. His wives are Cunnembeille, who bore him children, and his favorite, Birrahgnooloo, who did not. Birrahgnooloo, however, sends floods upon the earth; Baiame is invoked for rain.

Bailiff's Daughter of Islington. 0456 English ballad found in Percy's *Reliques*. A squire's son loved the bailiff's daughter, but she gave him no encouragement. His friends sent him to London, "an apprentice for to binde." After seven years, the bailiff's

daughter, "in ragged attire," set out to walk to London, "her true love to inquire." The young man, on horseback, met her but did not recognize her. When he asked after the bailiff's daughter of Islington, she at first said she was dead but later told the truth, revealing her identity.

Bajang. 0457 In Malayan mythology, an evil spirit whose presence foretells disaster and brings illness. Generally, it takes the form of a polecat and disrupts the household by mewing like a great cat.

The *bajang* is considered very dangerous to children, who are sometimes provided with amulets of black silk threads, called bajang bracelets, which are supposed to protect them against the evil influence of the *bajang*. In Perak and some other parts of the Malay Peninsula, the *bajang* is regarded as one of several kinds of demons that can be enslaved by man and become familiar spirits.

Such familiars are handed down in certain families as heirlooms. The master of the familiar is said to keep it imprisoned in a *tabong*, a vessel made from a joint of bamboo closed by a stopper made from leaves. Both the case and the stopper are prepared by certain magic arts before they can be used. The familiar is fed with eggs and milk. When its master wishes to make use of it, he sends it forth to possess and prey on the vitals of anyone whom his malice may select as victim. The victim is at once seized by a deadly and unaccountable ailment that can be cured only by magic.

If the *bajang* is neglected by its keeper and is not fed regularly, it will turn on its owner, who will thereupon fall victim to the *bajang*.

Variant spelling: Badjang.

Baka. 0458 In Haitian voodoo, a very evil loa (deified spirit of the dead). Black roosters and black goats are sacrificed to appease his anger. Sometimes instead of the blood sacrifice he will accept a virgin girl for sexual intercourse. His symbol is two broken crosses.

Variant spelling: Babako.

Bakemono. 0459 In Japanese folklore, a generic name for evil spirits or ghosts. They are often portrayed without feet and with long straight hair.

Balaam(destroyer of the people). 0460 In the Bible, O.T., a Midian prophet or seer, called on to curse the Hebrews by Balak, King of Moab (Num. 22–23). On his journey an angel of Yahweh, the Hebrew god, invisible to Balaam, barred the way, causing his ass to turn

mysterious package was never opened. It was called the Bundle of Greatness.

Balan and Balin. In Arthurian legend, two brothers: Balan, the wiser and more even-tempered, and Balin, the hot-tempered. Through some mistake the two meet in battle, and both are killed. They are the subject of Tennyson's narrative poem *Balin and Balan* in *Idylls of the King*.

0462

Balaam

aside (the ass could see the angel). Balaam then beat his ass, and the animal spoke to him, asking him why he was doing it since an angel was in the way. In medieval Christian belief the conversion of Balaam by the angel was regarded as a prefiguration of the appearance of the risen Christ to the Apostle Thomas. The theme is often found in Romanesque and Gothic church decorations. Medieval Christians believed that the ass Jesus rode into Jerusalem was a direct descendant of Balaam's ass and that after Jesus' death it was taken to Verona, Italy, and died later of old age. Its bones were set aside as relics and preserved in the city's cathedral. Rembrandt painted *Ballaam, the ass, and the angel.*

Balarama

Balam-Quitzé (smiling tiger). In Mayan mythology, first man and a culture hero in the *Popol Vuh*, the sacred book of the ancient Quiché Maya of Guatemala.

0461

Balam-Quitzé was the first man, created by Hurakán. He was followed by Balam-Agag (nocturnal tiger), Mahucutan (famous name), and Iqui-Balam (moon tiger). These four were the ancestors of the Quiché, providing them with skills and knowledge.

The *Popol Vuh* tells how Balam-Quitzé provided fire for his people. One day the god Tohil appeared to Balam-Quitzé, who took the god and "put him on his back" in a wooden chest he carried. As yet there was no fire, and the hero asked Tohil to provide him with it. The god gave Balam-Quitzé fire, which the culture hero then took to his people.

After the four men had completed their task of educating the people, they departed from the land and disappeared on Mount Hacavitz. Before the departure Balam-Quitzé left behind the Pizom-Gagal, a package that "was wrapped up and could not be unwrapped; the seam did not show because it was not seen when they wrapped it up." The

Balarama (strong-armed Rama). In Hindu mythology, brother of Krishna. He is often regarded as an avatar or incarnation of the serpent Sesa, upon which Vishnu reclines.

0463

The Hindu epic poem *The Mahabharata* tells how the god Vishnu took two hairs, one black and one white, and they became Krishna and Balarama. Krishna was of dark complexion and Balarama light. Once when Balarama was drunk, he called on the Yamuna River to come to him that he might bathe himself. The river did not listen to him, so he dragged its waters until they assumed a human form and asked Balarama for forgiveness. This action gained for Balarama the title Yamuna-bhid (breaker; dragger of the Yamuna).

Another important episode in the life of Balarama tells how he killed the demon Dhenuka. As boys Krishna and Balarama picked some fruit from a grove belonging to the demon. Dhenuka took the form of an ass and began to kick Balarama. The young hero seized Dhenuka by the heels, whirled him around till he was dead, and then threw his body on top of a palm tree. Several other demons came to the assistance of Dhenuka, but they were also thrown to the top of palm trees until "the trees were laden with dead asses."

Balarama also fought an apelike demon, Dwivida, who had stolen Balarama's plowshare. Dwivida was thrown to the earth, and "the crest of the mountain on which he fell was splintered into a hundred pieces by the weight of his body."

In Indian art Balarama is portrayed with a fair complexion. His weapons are a club, plowshare, and pestle, and his emblem is the palm tree.

0464

Baldak Borisievich. In Russian legend, a hero who defeated the Turkish sultan. One day Baldak Borisievich, with 29 other young men, went directly to the Turkish sultan to "take from him his steed with the golden mane." They accomplished the deed, and in the process they killed the sultan's cat; spat in the sultan's face, and hanged the sultan with a silken noose, his favorite pasha with a hempen noose, and his youngest daughter with a bast (rope of tree bark) noose.

Baldur (W.G. Collingwood)

0465

Baldur (lord). In Norse mythology, god of light, the sun, who always spoke the truth; son of Odin and Frigga; husband of Nanna; father of Forseti. Baldur's myth, told in the *Prose Edda*, is one of the most complete in Norse mythology. Baldur was tormented by terrible dreams, indicating that he was to die. He told the gods of his evil dreams, and they resolved to "conjure all things to avert from him the threatened danger." Frigga exacted an oath from fire, water, iron, metals, stones, earths, diseases, beasts, birds, poisons, and creeping things so that none of them would harm Baldur. When this was done the gods passed their time hurling darts, swords, and battle-

axes at Baldur, knowing he could not be harmed. When the evil god Loki saw that Baldur remained unhurt, he transformed himself into a woman and went to Frigga's home, Fensalir. Loki, in disguise, asked Frigga why the gods were throwing stones at Baldur. She replied that he could not come to any harm. "Neither metal nor wood can hurt Baldur," she said, "for I have exacted an oath from all of them."

"What!" exclaimed Loki. "Have all things sworn to spare Baldur?"

"All things," replied Frigga, "except one little shrub that grows on the eastern side of Valhalla. It is called mistletoe, and I thought it too young and feeble to ask an oath from it."

As soon as Loki heard this he went away. Resuming his natural shape, he cut off a twig of mistletoe and went to the assembly hall of the gods. Hodur, the blind god, was asked by Loki why he wasn't throwing anything at Baldur.

"Because I'm blind," Hodur said, "and can't see where Baldur is standing. Also, I haven't anything to throw at him."

"Come then," said Loki, "do as the rest of the gods. Show honor to Baldur and throw this twig at him. I'll direct your arm toward the right place."

Hodur took the mistletoe, and under Loki's guidance, hurled it at Baldur, who was pierced through and fell dead to the ground. The gods were stunned and began to lament. Frigga then said she would give all of her love to anyone who would ride to Hel to find Baldur and offer Hela, goddess of death, a ransom for the god's return to Asgard. Hermod volunteered. He arrived in Hel and found Baldur occupying the most distinguished seat in the hall of the dead. He then asked Hela to let Baldur ride home with him, saying that the whole world was lamenting the god's death.

"If all things in the world both living and lifeless weep for him, then I will let him return," she said, "but if any one thing speak against him or refuse to weep, he shall be kept in Hel."

The gods then sent messengers throughout the world asking everything to weep for Baldur. All things complied. As the messengers were returning, believing their mission a success, they found an old hag named Thaukt sitting in a cavern. They asked her to weep for Baldur so the god could return. She refused.

The *Prose Edda* ends the account with "It was strongly suspected that this hag was no other than Loki himself who never ceased to work evil among the gods."

Baldur's myth was the inspiration for Matthew Arnold's long narrative poem, *Balder Dead*.

Variant spellings: Balder, Baldr, Balldr.

Baldwin of Flanders. 1058–1118. First titular Christian king of Jerusalem after the city was captured by Crusaders. Technically, Godfrey of Bouillon was the first king, but he refused to wear the crown, saying he would not wear a golden crown in the city where his Savior had worn one of thorns. Godfrey therefore accepted only the title of count. Baldwin of Flanders succeeded Godfrey on his death in 1100.

Ballad. A narrative folk song, believed to have been developed during the Christian Middle Ages and found throughout Europe. The most famous collection in English is F. J. Child's *English and Scottish Popular Ballads* (1882–1885) in five large volumes. Numerous poets have written literary ballads; Goethe and Longfellow are among the most famous.

Balmung. In Norse mythology, a magical sword forged by Völund the Smith (Wayland the Smith). Balmung appears in the sagas relating to the adventures of the Norse Sigmund, called Siegfried in Germanic myth. The sword was placed in the Branstock tree by Odin, chief of the gods. Odin said that the weapon would belong only to the warrior who could pull it out of the tree. The sword then would assure its owner victory in battle. Nine Volsung princes and others tried to remove the sword and failed. Sigmund, the tenth and youngest, laid a firm hand on the sword's hilt and easily removed it from the Branstock tree. The episode is vividly recreated in William Morris's narrative poem *Sigurd the Volsung and the Fall of the Niblungs*. According to other sources, Balmung was later destroyed by Odin, restored, and used by Sigurd (Siegfried) to kill the dragon Fafnir.

Balor. In Celtic mythology, a god-king of the Fomors, a group of deities connected with darkness and evil; grandson of Net; son of Buarainech; husband of Cathlionn. Balor had one eye, poisoned in his youth, but it retained the power of striking dead anyone it looked at. The eye was opened by four men who lifted the eyelid. In the war with the beneficent gods Balor slew Nuada but was killed by the god Lugh, who finally destroyed his fatal eye with a magic missile. In James Joyce's novel *Ulysses*, the god is called Balor of the Evil Eye.

Bamapama. In Australian mythology, trickster of the Murngin in Northern Australia, often called the "crazy man" because he violates various taboos, especially those involving clan incest.

Bamboo. A plant with hollow reeds that grows in tropical and semitropical regions. In Chinese mythology, the bamboo is a symbol of longevity because of its durable, evergreen qualities. In the Philippine Islands, Christian crosses made of bamboo are set up in the fields to ensure that the crops will grow. The Aka-Bo of the Andaman Islands believed that the first man, called Jutpu, came to life inside a large bamboo.

Bana. In Hindu mythology, a demon giant with 1,000 arms, who was a friend of the god Shiva and an enemy of the god Vishnu. Bana is sometimes called Vairochi.

Banaidja. In Australian mythology, ancestral figure, son of Laindjung. He taught the Arnhem Landers their totems and sacred rituals and was killed by those who doubted his gifts.

Banba. In Celtic mythology, a goddess representing Ireland, as well as one of the ancient names for the country. Banba is cited in James Joyce's novel *Ulysses*, in which the novelist writes: "Wail, Banba, with your wind. . . ." In a variant myth influenced by Christianity, Banba was said to be a daughter of Cain who lived in Ireland before the Flood recorded in Genesis (6:5–8:22).

Ba-neb-djet (soul, lord of Busiris). In Egyptian mythology, ram god of Mendes, portrayed as a ram with flat, branching horns surmounted by a uraeus. As with the Apis bull, a live ram was used in worship and believed to have within him the soul of a god. Ba-neb-djet was believed to have the souls of Ra, Osiris, Geb, and Shu. The ancient Greeks identified the Egyptian deity with their Priapus and Pan.
   Variant spellings: Ba-neb-Tatau, Ba-neb-Tet, Benedbdetet.

Banjo. In American folklore, a guitarlike stringed instrument said to have been invented by Ham, a son of Noah, when the family was on the Ark. It is also said that the gift of making music on the banjo is granted to those who meet the devil at a crossroads "where men are hanged and suicides buried."

Bannik (bath spirit). In Slavic folklore, bathhouse spirit, portrayed as a small old man with a large head and lots of disheveled hair.

Bannik (I. Bilibin)

Bannik is either beneficent or demonic, depending on his mood. He guards the entrance to the bathhouse and allows three groups of bathers to enter unharmed, but the fourth group is his to do with as he wishes. If he is angry, he pours scalding water over a bather's head or, even worse, strangles the bather to death. Sometimes he invites devils and forest spirits into the bathhouse.

To pacify him, peasants leave some water for him to bathe in. If one wishes to discover the future, Bannik gives the answer but only if he is in the right mood. Before entering one has to put his naked back through a half-open door of the bathhouse. If Bannik touches the person with his claws, it is a bad omen; but if he touches the person with the soft part of his hand, it is a good omen.

0478

Banshee (English spelling of *bean-sidhe*, Celtic for "woman fairy"). In Celtic folklore, an attendant fairy that follows a family and wails, foretelling the death of one of its members. The Caoine, the funeral cry of the Irish peasants, is said to be an imitation of the cry of the banshee. When more than one banshee is present and they wail and sing in chorus, it is for the death of some very holy or great person. An omen that sometimes accompanies the banshee is the Coach-a-bower, an immense black coach mounted with a coffin and drawn by headless horses. If this funeral entourage arrives at a house and the householder opens the door, a basin of blood will be thrown in his or her face. Various tales of the ban-

shee are found in William Butler Yeats's collection of *Irish Folk Stories and Fairy Tales*.

Baphomet

0479

Baphomet. In medieval Christianity, idol said to have been worshiped by the Order of Knights Templar. Some scholars believe that Baphomet is a corruption of the medieval French spelling of Mahomet, who was accused of being a devil by the Christians. The Order of Knights Templar was charged with both heresy and homosexuality by King Philip IV in 1307. Whether the charges were true or false is still debated by historians. Baphomet's idol was a small figure with two heads, one male and one female. The body was that of a woman.

0480

Baphyra. In Greek mythology, the name assumed by the Helicon River when it refused to wash away the blood the Bacchants (or Maenads) had spilled when they tore Orpheus limb from limb. To avoid complicity in the crime, the river submerged itself and reemerged miles away, taking the name Baphyra.

0481

Baptism (to dip or to dunk). In Christian ritual, sacrament of initiation by immersion or sprinkling with water. It was one of the seven sacraments of Christianity during the Middle Ages.

The rite of baptism was not originally connected with the followers of Jesus but with those of St. John the Baptist. When Jesus' followers absorbed those of John, the rite was taken over into Christianity. In John's baptism the sinner was made aware of his sinfulness, but in Christian baptism the sinner was cleansed from Original Sin, the mark of Adam, which, according to Christian dogma, had descended on all men and women. Thus, the Church Council of Orange, held in 529, decreed: "With the grace received through baptism aiding and cooperating, all those are baptized in Christ can and ought, if they will strive faithfully, to fulfill what pertains to the salvation of the soul." Part of the medieval rite of baptism contained an exorcism. The priest would say over the person or child to be baptized:

> I exorcise you, unclean spirit, in the name of the Father, and of the Son, and of the Holy Spirit. Come out and leave this servant of God [name]. Accursed and damned spirit, hear the command of God Himself, he who walked upon the sea and extended his right hand to Peter as he was sinking. Therefore, accursed Devil, acknowledge your condemnation; pay homage to the true and living God; pay homage to Jesus Christ, his Son, and to the Holy Spirit, and depart from this servant of God, [name], for Jesus Christ, Our Lord and God, has called [him/her] to his holy grace and blessing, and to the font of Baptism.

This formula is still used today in the English versions of the Roman rite of baptism.

A medieval baptismal rite used in northern countries contained the following recitation by priest and candidate:

> Q Forsaketh thou the Devil?
> A I forsake the Devil!
> Q And all the Devil guilds?
> A And all Devil guilds.
> Q And all Devil works?
> A And I forsake all Devil works, and words.
> Thor and Woden [pagan Norse gods] . . . and all the evil ones that are his companions.

This formula took for granted that the Northern pagan gods actually existed and were devils.

0482
Barabbas (son of Abba). In the Bible, N.T., the robber and insurrectionist leader whom Pilate freed from prison instead of Jesus (Matt. 27:15, Mark 15:7, Luke 23:18, John 18:40). The incident, which has no historical basis, is an attempt to place the blame for Jesus' death on the Jews instead of the Romans, who were responsible for his trial and execution. A novel, *Barabbas*, by Par Lagerkvist, tells the story of what happened after the Crucifixion.

0483
Barada, Antoine. d. 1887. In American history and folklore, son of an Indian woman and a Parisian count. According to legend, he once stuck a post into the ground, which caused a geyser to shoot 50 feet into the air. In order to stop it, he sat on it.

0484
Barbara Allen. Literary ballad by Allan Ramsay (1724), included in Percy's *Reliques* (1756). Sir John Grehme was dying because of his love for Barbara Allen. Barbara was sent to see him, and drawing aside the curtain, said, "Young man, I think ye're dyan." She then left him. She had not been long gone when she heard the death bell toll. She repented of her cruel action and said:

> O mither, mither, mak' my bed . . .
> Since my love died for me to-day,
> I'll die for him to-morrow.

0485
Barbara Frietchie. In American legend, a heroine of John Greenleaf Whittier's poem of the same title, published in 1864, that tells how Barbara Frietchie raised the Union flag when the Confederate general Stonewall Jackson entered Frederick, Maryland. Barbara says in the poem:

> Shoot if you must, this old gray head,
> But spare your country's flag, she said.

Whittier, however, confused the facts. A Mrs. Mary S. Quantrell waved the Union flag at the Confederate general. Barbara waved the Union flag when General Burnside, a Union officer, came into the town after Jackson's men left.

0486
Barbara, St. (strange, foreign). Third century C.E. In Christian legend, martyr. Patron saint of architects, builders, and fireworks makers. Invoked against thunder and lightning and all accidents arising from explosions of gunpowder. Feast, 4 December.

One of the most popular saints during the Middle Ages, St. Barbara's life is told in *The Golden Legend*, a collection of saints' lives written in the 13th century by Jacobus de Voragine. Barbara was the daughter of Dioscorus, a rich pagan nobleman. He loved her dearly but did not want her to be married, so he shut her up in a solitary tower. There she began to contemplate the meaning of life and came to the realization that the gods worshiped by her father—the sun, moon, and stars—were false. Seeking some answer to the mystery of life, she called upon

Origen, the Christian writer, to instruct her in the Christian faith. Origen sent her one of his disciples disguised as a physician. Barbara was taught and was baptized a Christian.

One day, before Dioscorus left on a journey, he "sent skillful architects to construct within the tower a bath-chamber of wonderful splendor. One day Saint Barbara descended from her turret to view the progress of the workmen." She saw they were constructing two windows and ordered that they make three instead. When her father returned, he asked why she had changed his orders.

"Know, my father," said Barbara, "that through three windows doth the soul receive light, the Father, the Son and the Holy Ghost; and the Three are One."

Dioscorus was not at all pleased by his daughter's theological explanation of the three windows. In a fit of anger he "drew his sword to kill her," but she fled and was hidden by angels. A shepherd betrayed her by pointing silently to the place of her concealment. Her father dragged her by the hair, beat her, and shut her up in a dungeon. After she had been tortured by the proconsul Marcian, her father "carried her to a certain mountain near the city, drew his sword, and cut off her head with his own hands." As he descended from the mountain, a "most fearful tempest, with thunder and lightning, and fire fell upon this cruel father and consumed him utterly, so that not a vestige of him remained."

This gruesome tale found great acceptance during the Middle Ages, when statues of St. Barbara were frequently placed in churches and at shrines. In some sections of Central Europe it is the custom to break a branch off a cherry tree on St. Barbara's feast day, place it in a pot of water in the kitchen, and keep it warm. When the twig bursts into bloom at Christmastime, it is used for decoration. The girl who tends the twig, according to the belief, will find a good husband within the year if she succeeded in producing the bloom exactly on Christmas Eve.

In medieval Christian art St. Barbara is often portrayed with her tower. Sometimes she is shown holding a feather in her hand. This refers to an old medieval German legend that when she was scourged by her father, angels changed the rods into feathers.

As the patron saint connected with firearms, an effigy of St. Barbara is often found on shields, great guns, and fieldpieces. During World War I, however, St. Joan of Arc was considered the patron of firearms among the French.

Bardo Thodol. In Buddhism, the Tibetan Book of the Dead, or the "After-Death Experiences of the
0487

Bardo Plane, according to Lama Kazi Dawa-Samdup's English rendering." Published in English translation in 1927, compiled and edited by W. Y. Evans-Wentz, it is a guide for a dying man to pass through death and rebirth. In his second preface the editor writes that the message of the work is "that the Art of Dying is quite as important as the Art of Living . . . of which it is the complement and summation; that the future of being is dependent, perhaps entirely, upon a rightly controlled death. . . ." Traditionally composed by Padmasambhava, its full Tibetan title literally means "the Dharma that liberates the hearer in the Bardo just by being heard." The *Bardo* is any intermediate state of confusion, not necessarily that between lives.

0488
Bariaus. In Melanesian mythology, spirits who inhabit old tree trunks. They are often shy and run away when approached by people.

0489
Barlaam and Josaphat. Eighth-century legend by St. John of Damascus, a Syrian monk. It tells how Barlaam, a monk living in the Sinai, converted Josaphat, the son of a Hindu king, to Christianity. The basis for the legend is the life of Buddha, which filtered into medieval Christian sources from the East. The work contains the tale of the three caskets, which was used by Shakespeare in *The Merchant of Venice*.

0490
Barnabas, St. (son of consolation). First century C.E. In the Bible, N.T., companion of St. Paul who, according to Christian tradition, was martyred either by burning or being stoned to death. He is invoked against hailstorms and as a peacemaker. Feast, 11 June.

0491
Barnum, Phineas Taylor. 1830–1891. In American history and folklore, a showman who was called the "Prince of Humbug." In 1835 he exhibited a black female slave, Joice Heth, who he claimed was 161 years old and had been George Washington's nurse. Actually, she was only 80 years old. In 1881 he merged his circus with that of his rival James A. Bailey, forming the circus company Barnum and Bailey. He introduced to America General Tom Thumb, a midget, and Jenny Lind, the Swedish soprano. On his deathbed he is reported to have asked how much money the circus pulled in that day. He is credited with saying, "A sucker is born every minute," but it is believed he said, "The American people like to be humbugged." The American composer Douglas Moore's symphonic work *Pageant of P. T. Barnum* tries to capture Barnum's spirit.

St. Barnabas

Baron Samedi. In Haitian voodoo, a loa (deified spirit of the dead), lord of the cemeteries and god of the crossroads. Baron Samedi is also known as Baron Cimitière.

0492

0493

Barsisa. In Islamic legend, a man who bargains with the devil and loses. There are various versions of the legend, which is based on a verse in sura 59 of the Koran.

A monk or devotee, living in a cell for some 60 years, is continually tempted by the devil. To win the monk the devil brings a girl (who is variously described as a shepherdess, a neighbor's daughter, a princess) to the monk. The monk has intercourse with the girl, and she becomes pregnant. To cover his sin, he kills the girl and buries the body. Of course, the devil makes the crime known and the man is arrested and sentenced to die. The devil reveals himself to the monk, offers to save him, and gives his condition: the monk must worship him. The monk agrees but the devil, in an ironic tone, quotes a verse in sura 59 of the Koran: "Verily, I am clear of thee! I fear Allah the Lord of the Worlds!"

A more elaborate version of the tale is found in the 15th-century Turkish collection *History of the Forty Viziers*. From the Turkish collection the tale passed into European literature, finding its best-known Western expression in Matthew Gregory Lewis's Gothic novel *Ambrosio, or The Monk*. The novel was so popular that it earned the author the nickname "Monk Lewis."

Ambrosio, the superior of the Capuchins in Madrid, is known for his holy life. Matilda, a young noblewoman (who is actually a demon in disguise), enters the monastery dressed as a young novice. She entices Ambrosio and the two go from one crime to another (described with relish by the author), including the seduction and murder of a young girl by the monk. The crimes are brought to light and Ambrosio is tried before the Inquisition. He bargains with the devil to free him, and the devil agrees, releasing Ambrosio in a desert waste. When the lost monk realizes what he has done and wants to repent, the devil dashes him to pieces against a rock.

0494

Bartek and Pies. In Polish folklore, a king and his jester who exchange places in order to discover a person's true feelings. One day King Bartek, in the clothes of his jester, with the jester in royal robes, went to meet the king's prospective bride, Bialka, and her sister Spiewna. Of course Bialka thought the jester, Pies, was the king and fawned over him, but Spiewna showed she cared for Bartek even though she did not know he was the king. The tale ends with the marriage of Spiewna to the king and her sister Bialka married to an old organist.

0495

Bartholomew, St. (son of Tolmai). First century C.E. In the Bible, N.T., one of the Twelve Apostles of Jesus. Patron saint of Florentine salt and cheese merchants, bookbinders, butchers, corn chandlers, dyers, furriers, leather workers, shoemakers, tailors, and vine growers. Invoked against nervous diseases and twitching. Feast, 24 August.

Bartholomew's name appears on all four lists of the Twelve Apostles given in the Gospels. Some scholars believe he and Nathanael, mentioned in the Gospel according to Saint John, to be one and the same person. Bartholomew, they contend, is the patronymic, or surname, by which Nathanael is specified as the son, or *bar*, of Tolmai or possibly Ptolemy.

In an early Christian legend (not included in the New Testament), Bartholomew was the son of Prince Ptolomeus (a corruption of Tolmai or possibly Ptolemy). After the Ascension of Christ, according to that legend, Bartholomew preached the gospel in India and Armenia.

He was martyred, but the accounts of his death do not agree. In the Middle Ages various accounts circulated. *The Golden Legend*, a collection of saints' lives written in the 13th century, says that "some say he was crucified and was taken down ere he died, and for to have greater torment he was flayed and at the last beheaded." *The Golden Legend* always tried to reconcile differing accounts and may have combined three different legends that variously said Bartholomew was crucified, flayed, or beheaded.

Medieval Christian art often portrays the saint carrying a large knife, symbol of one form of his martyrdom. Sometimes St. Bartholomew is portrayed with his skin hanging over his arm, as in Michelangelo's *Last Judgment*, in which the saint defiantly holds a knife in one hand and his flayed skin in the other.

Basilisk

Basilisk (little king). Fantastic lizardlike creature believed to be able to kill with its look or breath; often equated with the cockatrice.

Pliny's *Historia Naturalis* recounts the myth of the basilisk, saying it is hatched from the egg laid by a toad or a cock. Its look or breath can cause instant death. To avoid being killed by the animal, travelers were advised to carry a mirror with them or a cock or a weasel, two mortal enemies of the beast. It was

believed that if the basilisk saw its own reflection in the glass it would instantly die. Early Christian belief saw the basilisk as a symbol of the devil or of Antichrist. A statue in the cathedral at Amiens, France, portrays Christ treading on a basilisk, referring to Psalm 91:13: "thou shalt tread upon the adder and the basilisk, and trample under foot the lion and the dragon" (Douay version). Chaucer, Spenser, and Shakespeare all refer to the fantastic creature. When Richard III attempts to woo Ann, Edward's widow, he cites the beauty of her eyes. She replies, "Would they were basilisks to strike you dead." In *Romeo and Juliet* (3:2) Shakespeare uses the word cockatrice, meaning basilisk:

> . . . say thou but "I,"
> And that bare vowel "I" shall poison more
> Than the death-darting eye of cockatrice.

Basil the Great, St. (kingly). 328–379 C.E. In Christian legend, one of the Four Doctors of the Greek church. Feast, 14 June.

Basil was made bishop of Caesarea in 370 and came into conflict with the Emperor Valens, who was an Arian Christian. Though threatened with death by the emperor, Basil remained steadfast and later even gained some concessions for the Catholics. Robert Southey took a legend from the saint's life and used it for one of his narrative poems, *All for Love or A Sinner Well Saved*. Elëemon, a freedman, makes a compact with Satan that if he can marry his master's daughter, Cyra, he will give Satan his soul. The compact is agreed on and the devil delivers the girl to Elëemon; the two stay married for 12 years. Then the ghost of Cyra's father reveals the compact. Elëemon flees to St. Basil, who imposes penance on the sinner. When Satan comes to collect Elëemon, the saint enters into a debate with Satan, proving that the deal is no longer valid.

In Christian art St. Basil is often pictured with the Four Doctors of the Greek Church.

Bass, Sam. 1851–1878. In American history and folklore, a bandit who started out as a deputy sheriff and became a robber. According to legend, he often gave his stolen money to the poor. He was killed by one of his own men, who informed the Texas Rangers of a projected bank robbery. A folk song "The Ballad of Sam Bass," makes him into a Robin Hood. For years a legend persisted about gold he had hidden and never recovered.

Bast

Bast. 0499

In Egyptian mythology, cat goddess worshiped at Bubastis. Bast, who loved music and dance, was the protector of pregnant women and also protected men against disease and evil spirits. Generally, she was considered the personification of the beneficial, fertilizing power of the sun; whereas her counterpart, Sekhmet, the lion goddess, represented the fierce, destructive power of the sun.

Bast became an important national deity about 950 B.C.E., and her festival was among the most popular in Egypt. According to Herodotus' *History* (book 2), vast numbers of men and women came to her festival by barge, singing and dancing, clapping their hands, and playing the castanets. On their way the women would shout abuses and even expose themselves to those along the shore. At Bubastis the feast was celebrated with abundant sacrifices and festivities. Dead cats were carefully mummified and buried. It was said that more than 700,000 devotees attended Bast's yearly festival and that more wine was consumed than in all of the rest of the year besides.

In the Bible the Hebrew prophet Ezekiel (30:17) refers to Bast's city, which he calls Pibeseth, and says of Bast's worshipers that the young men will "fall by the sword" for their worship of her.

Egyptian art usually portrays Bast as a woman with the head of a cat. She holds in her right hand a sistrum for her music and in her left a shield with the head of a cat or lioness at the top.

Variant spellings: Bastet, Pasht.

Bat. 0500

Any nocturnal flying mammal having modified forelimbs that serve as wings; symbol of both good and evil in world mythology and folklore. In ancient China and Japan the bat was a symbol of good fortune. Five bats in Chinese belief are symbolic of the five blessings: wealth, health, old age, love of virtue, and a natural death. It is said the Chinese eat bats to ensure all of these blessings. In contrast, the bat was considered a demonic creature during the Christian Middle Ages, being identified with witches and the devil. This belief in part stems from the Old Testament, where the prophet Isaiah (2:20) tells of a time when sinners will cast their idols "to the moles and to the bats." The animal is also listed among the unclean ones in the Old Testament. Some cultures believe that bats contain the souls of the dead. In popular movies and comic books the heroes Batman and Robin seem to see the animal as a beneficent symbol.

Batara Guru. 0501

Name of the Hindu god Shiva used in the Malay Peninsula, Bali, Java, and Sumatra. Batara Guru is often identified with the spirit or god of the sea, Si Ray or Madu-Ray. The god rules over the sea from the low-water mark (at the river's mouth) to midocean. His home is in Pusat Tassek, the navel of the lake. In this mysterious home lives a gigantic crab. When the crab goes out for food at certain times during the day, he displaces the water in Pusat Tassek, causing the ebb and flow of the tides. From the center of Pusat Tassek springs a gigantic magic tree, Pauh Jangi, in whose boughs perches the roc, a large bird able to lift an elephant (found also in *The Thousand and One Nights* in the story of Sinbad the Sailor). Batara Guru has a wife, Madu-ruti, and two children, Wa' Ranai and Si Kekas (the scratcher).

Variant spelling: Betara Guru.

Bato Kanzeon (horse-headed Kanzeon). 0502

In Japanese Buddhist mythology, a form of Avalokitesvara, the Bodhisattva of compassion, guardian of horses, farm animals, and travelers. Usually Bato Kanzeon is portrayed wearing a crown or hat on which is a small horse's head. Some Japanese art works portray him with three faces, each having three eyes. Most images portray him seated, though some show him on a horse. Often his image is placed beside roads and near mountain passes.

Battus (stammer). 0503

In Greek mythology, a shepherd of Pylos who saw Hermes steal the cattle of Apollo. Battus promised not to divulge the theft but broke his promise and was turned into stone. The story of Battus' transformation is told in Ovid's *Metamorphoses* (book 2). The name is also borne by a king of Cyrene, son of Polymnestus, a Theraean noble, and Phronime, daughter of Etearchus. That Battus founded Cyrene in Libya and was cured of his stammer when he was frightened by a lion.

Batu Herem. 0504 In Malayan mythology, the stone pillar that holds up the sky.

Bau. 0505 In Near Eastern mythology (Babylonian), goddess of abundance and fertility worshiped in Babylon before 2300 B.C.E. In various inscriptions Bau is called the chief daughter of Anu, the god of heaven. Among her titles, the one most frequently given is that of "good lady." She was the mother who fixed the destinies of men and provided abundance for the tillers of the soil. On the feast of Zag-Muk (New Year), bridegrooms offered presents to their prospective brides in honor of Bau.

Baucis and Philemon 0506 (over-modest and friendly slinger). In Greek mythology, an old couple rewarded for their hospitality to Zeus and Hermes.

Zeus and Hermes—in human form—found themselves in Baucis and Philemon's country, Bithynia, without shelter for the night. They sought lodging at every house, but it was late, and the householders refused to accommodate the travelers. At last they came to the house of Baucis and Philemon, a poor couple who had grown old together. Baucis and Philemon welcomed the travelers, raked up the coals into a fire and prepared food. When the wine was poured out for the visitors, the couple saw that its level in the pitcher had not gone down but the wine had replenished itself. They realized that their visitors were gods and, becoming fearful, apologized for the poor quality of their hospitality. But Zeus said: "We are gods. This inhospitable village shall pay the penalty of its impiety; you alone shall go free from the chastisement. Quit your house, and come with us to the top of yonder hill."

They hastened to obey, and staff in hand, labored up the steep ascent. When they turned and looked back down at their village, they saw that it had been submerged in a lake, with only their own house standing on a small island of dry ground. Suddenly, before their eyes, their house was transformed into a magnificent temple. Their reward for their hospitality to the gods was to become priest and priestess in the temple for the rest of their lives. Their final prayer to the gods was that when the time came for them to die, they should both die at the same hour so that they should never be without each other.

Ovid's *Metamorphoses* (book 8) tells the myth, which was also translated into French by La Fontaine

and into English by Dryden, who translated part of the entire *Metamorphoses*. The myth was used by Rembrandt for his *Philemon and Baucis*, in which he portrays the couple and the gods at dinner. Rubens also painted the scene. There are some ten operas on the subject. One, *Philémon et Baucis* (1860), is by Charles Gounod, the composer of *Faust*.

Baugi. 0507 In Norse mythology, an evil giant; brother of Suttung; killed by Odin, chief of the gods. Baugi had attempted to kill Odin, but the god overpowered him. Odin married Baugi's daughter Gunlod. She bore Odin a child, Bragi, the god of poetry and eloquence. Baugi appears in the *Prose Edda*.

Bavon, St. 0508 Seventh century C.E. In Christian legend, patron saint of falconers and of the cities of Ghent and Haarlem. Feast, 1 October.

Born a nobleman, Bavon was converted to Christianity by St. Amand of Belgium, first bishop of Maestricht. This happened when Bavon was nearly 50 years old, a widower who had led a life of considerable dissipation, spending most of his time hunting with his falcon. After his conversion he gave all of his possessions to the poor and was placed in a monastery by St. Amand in Ghent. Not satisfied with the way the monastery was ruled, Bavon decided to live alone as a hermit in the forest. He found a tree with a large opening and set up house, living off herbs. One legend says that when he became a Christian he was so guilt-ridden because of his past life that he asked a former slave to beat him and then cast him into prison. The servant refused the second part of the wish, but he did beat the saint.

In Christian art Bavon appears with his falcon. Sometimes he is portrayed as a hermit, living in a tree, other times as a well-dressed prince holding the falcon. In Hieronymus Bosch's *The Last Judgment* the saint is shown with a falcon on his left hand, while his right hand reaches for money to distribute to the poor. Bavon is also known as Allowin.

Bayard 0509 (ruddy, red-haired). In the Charlemagne cycle of legends, a horse of incredible swiftness given by Charlemagne to the four sons of Aymon. If only one of the sons mounted, the horse was of ordinary size. But if all four mounted, its body became elongated to accommodate the extra riders. It appears in Boiardo's epic *Orlando Innamorato* and Ariosto's *Orlando Furioso*.

Bean. 0510 A legume. The bean was sacred to the Egyptians, who therefore did not eat it. The Greek philosopher Pythagoras was said to believe that the souls of the dead were lodged within beans, and ancient Roman legend held that ghosts of the dead, *lemures*, threw beans at houses at night and brought bad luck to the inhabitants. To placate these ghosts the Romans held festivals in which beans were placed or burned on graves.

Bean festivals are common in world rituals and tradition. Native American Hopi and Iroquois both celebrate the bean in ritual, and bean festivals in Europe celebrated Epiphany, or Twelfth Night, at which a king and queen were chosen. The king was elevated three times in honor of the Trinity and then held up to the ceiling while he made crosses on the rafters with chalk to protect the house from evil. Bean cakes were baked for the feast and portioned out; one for God, one for the Virgin, one for each member of the family, and one for the poor.

Bean, Judge Roy. c. 1825–1903. In American history and folklore, self-proclaimed "law west of the Pecos." Roy Bean ran a saloon and courtroom in Langtry, Texas, where he meted out his type of justice. When a man was accused of killing a Chinese worker, Bean let the man go free because he couldn't find in his law book "any place where it is named an offense for a white man to kill a Chinaman." In another case, in which he acted as the town coroner, he fined a dead man $40 for having a concealed weapon found on his person. He also owned the saloon. It was the custom in those days for a beer salesman to buy drinks for the whole crowd present, then the empty bottles were counted and paid up. Bean always added old empties to the lot. One day a salesman questioned him about the large amount he was being charged and the fact that some of the beer bottles did not look freshly emptied. Bean replied, "It does look fairly dry, but it's the way of drinking that some of the boys has. They don't often get good beer, and when they do, they not only drink the bottle dry but they sop it out. Purty good vouch for yore beer, son." Hollywood deals with the legend in *The Life and Times of Judge Roy Bean*, starring Paul Newman and Ava Gardner.

0512

Bear. A large mammal with massive body and heavy fur; symbol of both good and evil in world mythology and folklore.

American Indians regard the bear with awe and respect. When an Indian killed a bear, he would beg its pardon and often smoke a peace pipe so that the bear's spirit would not be angry. This respectful approach reflects the belief that the bear possessed curative powers, and American Indian shamans in

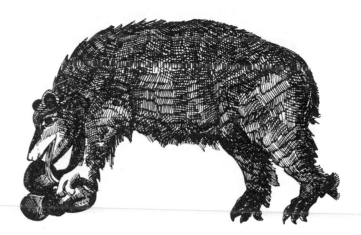

Bear

some tribes would imitate the bear in order to possess those powers. It was believed by many American Indian tribes that shamans could transform themselves into bears and that when they died they went to the heaven of bears. In Greek mythology the bear was sacred to the goddess Artemis. At her shrine in Arcadia girls between five and ten years, called "brown bears," would dance in honor of the goddess. In the Old Testament the bear is a symbol of evil and cruelty, representing the kingdom of Persia in the Book of Daniel (7:5). Medieval Christians believed that a bear was born as a shapeless white lump of flesh, a little larger than a mouse, without eyes or hair, and that the mother bear would lick this mass into shape, eventually forming a bear cub. The legend was seen as a symbol of the Christian church converting the unbeliever to the "true faith." In today's American popular symbolism, the bear is both good, as in Smokey the Bear, and demonic, as the symbol of Soviet Russia.

0513

Beast Epic. In European medieval literature, a series of linked tales grouped about animal characters. The tales are often used to make satirical comment on the church or the court. The best-known beast epic is the *Roman de Renart*, about Reynard the Fox. An excellent example of the beast epic in English is found in Chaucer's *Canterbury Tales* in *The Nun's Priest's Tale*.

0514

Beatrix (bestower of the blessings). In medieval legend, a nun devoted to the cult of the Virgin Mary, to whom she offered daily prayers. One day a clerk spotted her and wanted her for his mistress. He tempted her until the "old serpent enkindled her breast so vehemently that she could not bear the flames of love," according to one medieval account. Beatrix went to the statue of the Virgin and said, "Mistress, I have served thee as devoutly as I could;

behold, I resign thy keys to thee. I cannot longer withstand the temptations of the flesh." She then left the convent to live with her lover, but he abandoned her after a few days. Ashamed to return to the convent, she became a whore for some 15 years. One day she returned to her convent and asked the doorkeeper, "Did you know Beatrix, formerly custodian of this oratory?" The man replied, "I know her well. For she is an honest and holy woman, and from infancy even to the present day has remained in this convent without fault." When Beatrix heard this, she wanted to run away. Suddenly, the Virgin Mary appeared to her. "During the fifteen years of thy absence, I have performed thy task: now return to thy place and do penance; for no one knows of thy departure." There are various medieval retellings of the legend, the most famous being a Dutch version.

Beauty and the Beast.   0515
Popular folktale found in many parts of the world, telling how a woman's devotion frees a prince who had been magically transformed into a beast.

Beauty, the heroine, is the youngest daughter of a merchant who has lost his fortune. As he departs on a journey, he asks his daughters what they want him to bring them. His two elder daughter ask for expensive gifts, but Beauty asks for a rose. The merchant's trip is a failure, and he is unable to buy gifts for his daughters. As he approaches home, he passes a garden and remembers Beauty's request. Impulsively he plucks a rose. Suddenly the Beast appears and confronts the merchant for stealing the rose. He tells the merchant that to avoid punishment he must send the Beast one of his daughters to be a hostage.

Beauty volunteers to go to the palace and serve as hostage to the Beast. While she is there, she begins to realize that the Beast is really a kind and generous being. She asks permission to go home to see her father, who is now sick, and promises to return soon. When she overstays, the Beast begins to grow sick and is in danger of dying. She discovers this by looking into a magic mirror, and she returns to the Beast's palace. She tells the Beast that she loves him, thus breaking the spell and freeing the prince.

The most famous telling of the tale is by Mme Leprince de Beaumont, though Perrault's *Riquet a la houpee*, the Grimms' *Frog Prince*, and the British *The Well at the World's End* are other well known versions. The folktale is found in Basque, Swiss, German, English, Italian, Portuguese, Lithuanian, Indian, and Kaffir collections. Ravel's ballet *Mother Goose* has a Beauty and Beast episode. Cocteau's film *Beauty and the Beast*, with music by Georges Auric, is the best known film version.

Beaver.   0516
Gnawing mammal with a broad, flat, naked tail and webbed hind feet. In ancient Roman folk belief, as recorded in Pliny's *Historia Naturalis*, the beaver would castrate itself when pursued by a hunter, knowing that the hunter only wanted its testicles, which contained a magical medicine. Medieval Christians who read Pliny's work took up the belief and gave it symbolic meaning. For them the beaver symbolized the sinner who should cut off his sinfulness (testicles) and throw them at the devil (the hunter).

Bede the Venerable, St.   0517
(prayer). 673–735 C.E. In Christian legend, Doctor of the Church. Author of the *Ecclesiastical History of the English People*, a record of the conversion of England to Christianity as well as a secular history of the island. Feast, 27 May.

In the conclusion to his major work (he also wrote saints' lives and commentaries on the Bible) Bede says he was a "priest of the monastery of the blessed apostles, Peter and Paul, which is at Wearmouth and Jarrow." He was born in the neighborhood of the monastery and was sent there to live at the age of seven. He "wholly applied" himself to study of the Bible and "took delight in learning, teaching, and writing." When he was 19 years old he was made a deacon and became a priest when he was 30 years old.

According to legend, Bede died while dictating the last words of his translation of the Gospel according to St. John. His title "Venerable" is a term of respect often bestowed on members of religious orders in his time. There is a legend, however, with a different accounting for the title. A priest, wishing to put an inscription on his tomb, left out a word since he could not find a suitable one. At night an angel came and wrote *venerabilis* (venerable). In *The Divine Comedy* (Heaven, canto 10) Dante places St. Bede, together with St. Isidore of Seville and St. Richard, among the great Doctors of the Church in the Heaven of the Sun.

In Christian art St. Bede is portrayed as an old monk writing at his desk with a quill.

0518
Bedivere, Sir (birch hero). In Arthurian legend, a knight of the Round Table, who was present at the last battle between King Arthur and Mordred. At the request of the dying king, Bedivere threw the sword Excalibur into the lake. Afterward he bore the king's body to the three fairy queens who set it on a barge for Avalon.

0519
Bee. Any of a large group of four-winged insects, usually with a sting, sacred to many gods and goddesses in world mythology.

In Greek mythology Zeus, the sky god, was sometimes called Melissaios (bee-man) in the myth that he had a son by a nymph, who fleeing the wrath of Hera, Zeus's wife, hid their child in the wood, where his father sent him food by bees. The bee was also sacred to the Greek goddess Artemis in her role as orgiastic nymph. It was identified with Demeter in Greek mythology and with Cybele in Roman mythology as a sign of productivity. Vishnu, Krishna, and Indra in Hindu mythology are called Madhava (nectar-born ones) and are often portrayed with a bee resting on a lotus flower. Karma, the Hindu god of love, has a bowstring made of bees. Christianity also adopted the bee as a symbol. St. John Chrysostom (golden-mouthed) was born, according to legend, with a swarm of bees hovering around his mouth to symbolize the sweetness of his preaching. The same legend is told of St. Ambrose and St. Bernard of Clairvaux, both noted preachers.

Various accounts are given of the bee's origin in world folklore. Medieval German Christians believed that bees were created by God to supply wax for church candles. In a Breton belief, bees were created from the tears of Christ on the cross. The most common myth, however, given in Vergil's *Fourth Georgic*, is that bees are produced from decaying oxen. This belief, also expressed by Aristotle, arose because the rib cage of a dead ox provided a perfect natural frame for a beehive.

Another common belief is that bees had to be informed of the death of their keeper or they would leave or die. In Mark Twain's *Huckleberry Finn* Jim tells Huck: "If a man owned a beehive and the man died, the bees must be told it before sun-up next morning, or else the bees would all weaken down and quit work and die." This belief may stem from the ancient belief that bees were the messengers of the gods, announcing the arrival of the dead in the underworld.

0520
Beetle. An insect having hard, horny front wings that cover the membranous flight wings. In Egyptian mythology, the beetle, or scarab, is a common symbol of spontaneous creation and regeneration, often associated with the great god Ra and his various manifestations. In Christian belief, the beetle has often been identified with the devil. Irish Christians, for example, see the darbhodaol, a species of long black beetle, as a devil that has eaten the souls of sinners.

0521
Befana. In medieval Italian folklore, a spirit who gives gifts to children on Epiphany, 6 January, or Twelfth Night. Her name is a corruption of the word *Epiphany*. According to legend, Befana was too busy with house affairs to look after the Magi when they passed on their way to visit the Christ Child. She said she would wait for their return, but they went another way. Every Twelfth Night she watches, hoping to see them. In accordance with folkloric custom, on Twelfth Night after the children are in bed, someone enters their rooms, leaving the gifts, and the children say, "*Ecco la Befana.*"

0522
Begochiddy (the love a mother gives her child). In North American Indian mythology (Navaho), great creator god.

0523
Bego Tanutanu (Bego the maker). In Melanesian mythology, creator god and culture hero who formed the land and taught various arts. Bego's wife put limits to the sea, but when she was seen by her grandsons, she caused a flood.

0524
Behdety (he, i.e., Horus, of Behdet). In Egyptian mythology, the winged sun disk, combining the sun with the falcon as the two highest soaring bodies known to the ancient Egyptians. Later assimilated with the god Horus, the winged sun disk is a frequent motif found at the top of funerary stelae. The cult was localized in the district of Edfu, called Apollinolis Magna by the ancient Greeks, who equated this disk with their god Apollo.

0525
Bel (lord, master). In Near Eastern mythology (Babylonian-Assyrian), earth god; a form of the title Baal (lord) applied to various gods, especially to Enlil, the lord of the underworld, and to Marduk, the patron god of Babylon.

Bel, as god of the earth, was associated with Anu, as god of heaven, and Ea, as god of the watery deep, forming a triad that embraced the whole universe. When the three gods were invoked, it was equivalent to naming all of the powers that influenced the fate of man. Bel's wife was the goddess Belit.

The tale of *Bel and the Dragon*, which is part of the Old Testament Apocrypha, tells how the Hebrew prophet Daniel proved to King Cyrus of Persia that a statue of Bel could not possibly eat the food provided for it.

Every day, according to the tale, the statue of the god was provided with "twelve great measures of fine flour, and forty sheep, and six vessels of wine." The king would come to the temple and worship the idol. One day he said to Daniel, "Why dost not thou worship Bel?"

Daniel replied: "Because I may not worship idols made with hands, but the living God, who hath created the heaven and the earth, and hath sovereignty over all flesh."

"Thinkest thou not that Bel is a living god?" said the king. "Seest thou not how much he eateth and drinketh every day?"

Then Daniel laughed, saying the king was deceived, that the idol did not eat any food because it was made of clay and brass. The king then got angry and called his priests.

"If ye tell me not who this is that devoureth these expenses, ye shall die. But if ye can certify me that Bel devoureth them, then Daniel shall die; for he hath spoken blasphemy against Bel."

The priests and Daniel agreed to a contest. Food and wine were brought to the chamber. The priests, however, had a private entrance under the table by which each night they entered with their wives and children, eating all of the food. Daniel knew of this and asked that his servants bring ashes and strew them throughout all of the temple in the presence of the king alone before the room was sealed. When they went out, the door was sealed with the king's signet.

That night the priests came with their wives and children and ate the food. When the king and Daniel returned the next morning they opened the seal. The king looked it the table and said, "Great art thou, O Bel, and with thee is no deceit at all."

Then Daniel said to the king: "Behold now the pavement, and mark well whose footsteps are these."

"I see the footsteps of men, women, and children," the king replied.

Angry at being deceived by his priests, "the king slew them, and delivered Bel into Daniel's power, who destroyed him and his temple."

According to ancient historians, however, it was not Daniel, the Hebrew prophet, but King Xerxes, a pagan, who destroyed Bel's temple.

Belial

Belial (worthless, useless). In the Bible, O.T., a good-for-nothing or scoundrel is called a "man of Belial" (1 Sam. 20:1, 30:22). In the New Testament, however, the term is used for the opponent of Christ, or the devil (2 Cor. 6:15).

St. Paul in 2 Corinthians (6:15) writes: "And what concord hath Christ with Belial." Most biblical commentators assume the reference to Belial to be another name for Satan, since various apocryphal books use Belial as the name of a demon or the name of Antichrist. In *Das Buch Belial* by Jacobus de Theramo, Belial is the official lawyer of the devils. He appears before God and demands that the deeds of Christ be investigated. King Solomon, who was noted for his wisdom, is chosen by God to be the judge of the case. Moses is chosen by Jesus as the lawyer to defend him. Belial accuses Jesus of tampering with the infernal machinery of the world, usurping the powers of the devil, since not only hell but the seas, the earth, and "all beings that inhabit it" are under his control now. To influence his case Belial does a dance for King Solomon. The king, unmoved, favors Jesus. Belial does not give up; he appeals the case, and with Joseph, the patriarch of the Old Testament, as judge, Christ is found guiltless, but Belial is given power over the damned on Judgment Day.

In Milton's *Paradise Lost* (book 1:490–492) Belial is as a "lewd" spirit who loves "vice for it self." Victor Hugo, in his novel *The Toilers of the Sea*, credits Belial with being hell's ambassador to Turkey.

0527

Belin (bright?). In medieval British legend, the 21st of the mythical kings of Britain. Belin fought with his brother Brennius over the inheritance of the kingdom, but their mother, Conwenna, persuaded them to join forces to fight against the Romans. Belin is credited with building the Tower of London. His ashes are said to have been placed in a golden urn at the top of the tower.

0528

Belinus. In Celtic mythology, a British sun god; son of Ana; husband of Don; father of Caswallacon, Llevelys, Lludd, and Nynnyan; who in later medieval legend is called King Belinus and appears in Geoffrey of Monmouth's *History of the Kings of Britain.* Belinus may be a variant of Bile, a Celtic god of the dead, to whom human sacrifices were made.

Variant spelling: Belenos.

0529

Belisama. In Celtic mythology, among the British Celts, tutelary goddess of the river Ribble. The name was given to the goddess by ancient Roman writers, who identified her with their goddess Minerva.

0530

Belisarius. Sixth century C.E. In Eastern history and legend, general of the Emperor Justinian who defended the Roman Empire against Vandals and Goths. He was charged by his enemies with conspiracy, imprisoned, and later freed. Legend, however, says that he died blind and a beggar. David's painting *Give Belisarius a Penny* is based on this legend. Robert Graves's novel *Count Belisarius* also deals with the general.

0531

Belit. In Near Eastern mythology (Babylonian-Assyrian), wife of the great god Bel. Among her many titles were Nin-khar-sag (lady of the high or great mountain), referring to the mountain of the gods; Nin-lil (mistress of the lower world); Nunbar-Segunnu, goddess of agricultural fertility; Nisaba, goddess of wisdom; and Haya, goddess of direction. Belit was often equated with Ishtar.

0532

Bellerophon (he who appears in the clouds, he who slays the cloudy monster). In Greek mythology, a hero, son of Glaucus of Corinth or Poseidon and Eurymede; brother of Deliades; grandson of Sisyphus; married Philinoe; father of Deidameia, Hippolochus, Islander, and Laodameia.

Bellerophon was a virtuous man who was betrayed by a spurned love. According to Homer's *Iliad* (book 6), Antaea, wife of King Proteus, had a mad passion for Bellerophon; but Bellerophon, being a man of honor, would not have an affair with another man's wife. Antaea, furious at the rejection, told her husband lies about Bellerophon, that he had attempted to rape her, and she begged the king to have Bellerophon killed. Proteus, who abhorred violence, demurred, but to placate Antaea, he agreed to send Bellerophon to her father, king of Lycia, to be dealt with. Bellerophon was sent to Lycia with sealed letters to the king, telling of his alleged crime and begging Antaea's father to see to his punishment. Accordingly, Bellerophon was sent out to slay the Chimera, a fire-breathing monster— lion in front, serpent behind, and goat in the middle. Bellerophon succeeded with the aid of his winged horse, Pegasus. He then went on to conquer the Solymi and the Amazons. Later he married Philline and had children. Pindar adds to the Homeric account by telling how Bellerophon, proud of his feats, wanted to mount to heaven on Pegasus, but Zeus drove the horse insane with a gadfly, and Bellerophon fell to earth and died.

Bellerophon appears in Edward Young's *Night Thoughts*, William Morris's *Earthly Paradise* and George Meredith's *Bellerophon*. In *Paradise Lost* (book 7) Milton asks his Muse Urania, who has helped him soar "above the flight of Pegasean wing," to descend again:

> . . . up led by thee
> Into the Heav'n of Heav'ns I have presum'd
> An earthlie Guest, and drawn Empyreal Aire,
> Thy tempring; with like safeties guided down
> Return me to my Native element:
> Lest from this flying Steed unrein'd, (as once
> Bellerophon, though from a lower Clime)
> Dismounted, on th' Aleian Field I fall
> Erroneous, there to wander and forlorne.

The phrase "letters of Bellerophon" is sometimes applied to documents that are dangerous or prejudicial to the bearer.

0533

Belle Starr. 1848?–1889. In American history and folklore, popular name of Myra Belle Shirley, the Queen of the Bandits and Petticoat of the Plains. The leader of a band of cattle rustlers, horse thieves, and bank robbers, she was ambushed and killed. Her boyfriend was Cole Younger, a member of Jesse James's gang of robbers. Her life and legend appeared in Richard E. Fox's *Belle Starr, the Bandit Queen: or, the Female Jesse James* as well as a Hollywood movie *Belle Starr*, with Gene Tierney, which presents a laundered version of her life.

0534

Bellona (war, to fight). In Roman mythology, ancient Italian war goddess, wife or sister of Mars (or Quirinus), identified by the Greeks with Enyo. Bellona's temple, which was situated on the Campus Martius, was used for meetings of the senate when it dealt with foreign ambassadors or Roman generals who claimed a triumph (a festal procession, the highest honor accorded a commander) on their return from war. Without permission the generals were not allowed to enter the city. The *Columna Bellica* (pillar of war) stood nearby. It was from near Bellona's temple that the *Fetialis* threw his lance when declaring war. The cult of the war goddess Bellona, however, seems to have been confused with another Bellona, a goddess brought from Comana in Cappadocia towards the beginning of the first century B.C.E. This goddess was worshiped in a different locality and with a service conducted by Cappadocian priests and priestesses. During the festivals of the goddess these Bellondrii moved through the city in procession, dressed in black and shedding their blood by wounding themselves in the arms and loins with a two-edged ax. Drums and trumpets were part of the ritual. Her festival date was 3 June. Bellona appears in Vergil's *Aeneid* (book 8).

0535

Belly and Its Members, The. Aesopic fable found in various collections of the fables throughout the world.

It is said that in former times the various members of the human body did not work together as amicably as they do now. On one occasion the members began to be critical of the belly for spending an idle life of luxury while they had to spend all of their time laboring for its support and ministering to its wants and pleasures.

The members went so far as to decide to cut off the belly's food supplies for the future. The hands were no longer to carry food to the mouth, nor the mouth to receive, nor the teeth to chew it.

But, lo and behold, it was only a short time after they had agreed on this course of starving the belly into subjection that they all began, one by one, to fail and flop, and the whole body started to waste away. In the end the members became convinced that the belly also, cumbersome and useless as it seemed, had an important function of its own and that they could no more exist without it than it could do without them.

Moral: As in the body, so in the state, each member in his proper sphere must work for the common good.

The fable occurs in Plutarch's life of Coriolanus and is important in the second scene of

Shakespeare's play *Coriolanus*, based on Plutarch. Similar fables occur in Egypt and India (in the great epic poem *The Mahabharata*), in Buddhistic sources and Jewish ones, where it is told in a rabbinic commentary on Psalm 39. St. Paul may have had a similar fable in mind when he wrote 1 Corinthians, in which he compares the church to the body of Christ (12:12–26).

0536

Belshazzar (may Bel protect the king). In the Bible, O.T., last Babylonian king, killed in the sack of the city by Cyrus II in 539 B.C.E. Belshazzar gave a great feast (Dan. 5) for his court, using golden vessels that his father Nebuchadnezzar had taken from the temple in Jerusalem. As the party progressed, a hand wrote on the wall: *Mene, mene, tekel, upharsin.* Wanting to know what these words meant, the king called his astrologers, magicians, and soothsayers. None of them could translate the words. Then Daniel, the Hebrew prophet, was called in. He told Belshazzar the words meant that he was "weighed in the balances and art found wanting" (Dan. 5:27), and his kingdom would be destroyed. That night the Medes invaded the city, killing Belshazzar, and Darius the Persian came to the throne. Our common expression "the writing on the wall" comes from this passage. The legend inspired Rembrandt's painting *Belshazzar's Feast*, Handel's oratorio *Belshazzar*, and William Walton's *Belshazzar's Feast*.

0537

Beltaine. In Celtic mythology, a feast held at the spring equinox in early May. Part of the rituals associated with the day consisted of bonfires and the sacrifice of a man who represented the Oak King. In Ireland the feast was called Samradh or Cetsamain; in Wales it was Cytenfyn.

Variant spellings: Beltane, Baltein, Bealtuinn, Beltan.

0538

Bendis. In Greek mythology, a Thracian goddess of the moon, identified by the Greeks with Artemis, Hecate, and Persephone. Bendis' worship was introduced into Attica by Thracians and was very popular during Plato's time. A public festival called the *Bendideia* was held annually at which there were torch races and a solemn procession of Athenians and Thracians at the Piraeus, a promontory outside Athens.

0539

Benedict, St. (blessed). 480–543 C.E. In Christian legend, father of Western monasticism. Patron saint of coppersmiths and schoolchildren. Invoked against fever, gallstones, nettle rash, poison, and witchcraft, by servants who have broken their employer's possessions, and by the dying. Feast, 21 March.

Benedict was born of a noble family in Spoleto and sent to study in Rome, where he showed great scholarly promise. However, he was disgusted by the life of the clergy, who lived in debauchery. To escape, he became a hermit at the age of 15. His nurse, Cyrilla, who was always with him, tried to follow; but Benedict escaped, hiding in the wilderness of Subiaco. Here, according to numerous legends, he underwent many temptations from the devil. Once the devil tried to distract him with the vision of a beautiful woman, but the saint, to avoid falling into sin, threw himself on a thicket of briars and arose "bleeding, but calm." Another time the devil transformed himself into a blackbird and began to flutter around Benedict. Although the saint was hungry, he did not reach out for the bird. In fact, he was suspicious of the creature and made the sign of the cross. The bird instantly disappeared.

Despite the annoyances from the devil, the saint founded 12 monasteries with the help of St. Maurus and St. Placidus, sons of Roman senators. Both afterward became famous. St. Maurus introduced the Benedictine Rule in France; St. Placidus brought it to Sicily, where his sister St. Flavis joined him and was martyred with him.

St. Gregory the Great, in his *Dialogues* (book 2), records a legend about Mount Cassino (destroyed in World War II by Allied bombers because it was a Nazi stronghold). The devil, since he could not get anywhere tempting the flesh of St. Benedict, decided he would obstruct his efforts to build a monastery on the site of the Temple of Apollo. One day the builders went to carry a stone prepared for a certain part of Mount Cassino, but when they attempted to lift it, they found it was too heavy. They went to Benedict, who immediately saw that the devil was holding the stone down. He made the sign of the cross over the stone and picked it up all by himself. The stone, St. Gregory informs his readers, can still be seen at the monastery.

Another legend recorded by St. Gregory tells how a novice, in clearing the banks of a lake, accidentally lost his ax head, which flew off its handle and into the water. Benedict went at once to the lake and held the wooden handle in the water; the iron ax head rose to the surface and fitted itself firmly onto the handle. The miracle is similar to that of Elisha in the Old testament (2 Kings 6:5–7).

A much later legend tells how he healed Bruno, later Pope Leo IX, of toad poison by touching the boy's lips with a crucifix.

In Christian art St. Benedict is usually shown bearded, generally in a black Benedictine habit but sometimes the white one of the reformed order. He holds an asperges for sprinkling holy water on people possessed by demons, or a pastoral staff, signifying his position as an abbot. Sometimes a raven is shown, referring to the legend, or a piece of crockery, which the saint miraculously put together after it had accidentally been broken by a servant.

0540

Benini. In Near Eastern mythology (Babylonian), a monster with the face of a bird or raven. Benini, along with his evil mother, Melinni, and a host of demonic birds, once attacked Babylon. They were finally defeated when the proper prayers were said and the proper sacrifices offered to the gods.

Benjamin

0541

Benjamin (child of fortune or son of the right). In the Bible, O.T. (Gen. chap. 35ff), youngest son of Jacob and Rachel, who died giving him birth; brother of Joseph. Benjamin's descendants became the tribe of Benjamin. Saul, the first king of Israel, and St. Paul both descended from the tribe.

0542

Benkei. 12th century C.E. In Japanese legend, a hero, often called Oniwaka (young demon).

Benkei was the son of a priest of Kumano in Kii. Because of his boisterous nature he gained the nickname Oniwaka. When he was 17 years old, he became a wandering priest and is sometimes portrayed with his head partly shaven and wearing a hexagonal cap. Often he is shown blowing on a huge conch shell or inside a conch shell drinking sake. His most common form in Japanese art, however, is fighting the Yamabushis (mountain warrior-priests) or capturing a huge fish in a waterfall. Benkei was said to be eight feet tall and as strong as 100 men.

Benten. In Japanese Shinto-Buddhist mythology, goddess of love, beauty, music, and other arts; one of the Shichi Fukujin, gods of good luck or fortune. Benten was originally derived from the Hindu goddess Sarasvati, who was also associated with love; but when her cult reached Japan, her nature was somewhat changed. Benten is frequently portrayed with a Hakuja, a white serpent, and is known as the White Snake Lady. The snake, aside from being a symbol of fertility and sexuality, is also one of the symbols of the sea and thus connects Benten's worship with rivers, seas, and water in general. The goddess is also invoked for the growth of rice. Her main seat of worship is a shrine on Enoshima, near Kamakura, and at Itsukushima, on Miyajima near Hiroshima.

Benten is portrayed with four or eight hands, each holding a different symbol, such as a sword, wheel, ax, rope, bow and arrow, tama (symbolic jewel of purity), and key. Her crown varies. Sometimes it has a phoenix on top, sometimes three flaming jewels or a coiled white snake with the face of an old man. Often the goddess is shown playing a *biwa*, a Sino-Japanese instrument resembling a lute. Benten is also called Kotokuten (goddess of meritorious works) and Ako Myo-on-ten (goddess of the marvelous voice). She is also the mother of 15 sons, the Jiugo Doki.

Variant spellings: Bensaiten; Benten Sama; Dai Bensaiten.

Benu. In Egyptian mythology, bird identified by the Greeks with the phoenix. The benu was said to have created itself from fire that burned at the top of the sacred persea tree of Heliopolis. It was essentially a sun bird, symbol of both the rising sun and the dead sun god, Osiris, from whose heart, in one account, the bird sprang. The benu not only signified the rebirth of the sun each morning but became a symbol of the resurrection of man. *The Book of the Dead* provides a formula for enabling the deceased to take the form of the benu. According to the Greek historian Herodotus (book 2), the benu made its appearance once every 500 years. Its plumage was partly golden and partly red, and in size and form it resembled an eagle. It came from Arabia and brought with it the body of its father (which it had enclosed in an egg of myrrh) to bury at the temple of the sun.

Beowulf (wolf-of-croft, bear's son; Anglo Saxon corn god Beow). In medieval British legend, hero of the epic poem *Beowulf*, recorded by an unknown monk of Northumbria early in the eighth century,

The death of BEOWULF

Beowulf (H.J. Ford)

combining pagan and Christian myths and legends. In the poem Heorot, the palace of Hrothgar king of the Danes, is visited nightly by a monster named Grendel, who devours the king's thanes as they sleep. Beowulf, the nephew of Hygelac, king of the Geats (a tribe in southern Sweden or, according to some scholars, the Jutes), comes across the sea with 14 followers to free the Danes from this scourge. After a cordial welcome by Hrothgar and his court the visitors are left alone in the hall for the night. As they sleep, Grendel enters and devours one of the Geats. Though invulnerable to weapons, Grendel is seized by Beowulf and held in a mighty grip, from which he breaks away only with the loss of his arm, and he flees to his cavern beneath the lake to die.

There is great rejoicing in Heorot at Grendel's death. The minstrels sing lays to honor Beowulf, and the king loads him with gifts. But another monster,

Grendel's mother, still lives, and she comes to the hall that night to avenge her son's death. She finds Hrothgar's followers asleep and carries off one of them, Aeschere, and eats him. Beowulf pursues the monster to the depths of the lake. She grapples with Beowulf and drags him into the cavern beneath the water. A desperate struggle ensues, in which Beowulf loses his sword; but the hero finds a magic sword in the cave and kills Grendel's mother. Beowulf cuts off her head and returns to the shore. Again he is thanked by Hrothgar, and after many ceremonial speeches, he returns to the palace of Hygelac.

A long interval ensues, in the course of which Hygelac and his son Heardred are killed in battle, leaving the kingdom to Beowulf, who rules it for 50 years. Then a dragon with a fiery breath devastates the kingdom. Going out with 12 followers to kill the monster, Beowulf is wounded and deserted by all but one of his comrades. He finally kills the dragon but at the cost of his own life. His body is burned by the Geats on a funeral pyre, and the ashes are enclosed in a barrow.

The burial of Beowulf inspired American composer Howard Hanson's *Lament for Beowulf* for chorus and orchestra. Hanson used the translation of William Morris, the 19th-century English poet.

0546

Berenice. Third century B.C.E. In Roman history and legend, wife of Ptolemy III. She dedicated a lock of her hair to ensure her husband's safe return from a war in Syria. The lock then disappeared. It was later seen as a group of stars by the royal astronomer. The "lock of Berenice" is referred to by Catullus (poem 66) and inspired Pope's mock epic, *The Rape of the Lock*, in which the heroine's curl of hair is also made into a star at the poem's conclusion. Berenice also is the name of a daughter of Herod Agrippa, born 28 C.E., who married her uncle and lived incestuously with her brother. Later she became mistress to Titus, emperor Vespasian's son. When Titus became emperor, he dismissed her. Berenice appears in the Acts of the Apostles at St. Paul's trial (chap. 25) as Bernice, in Corneille's *Tite et Berenice*, and in Racine's *Berenice*.

0547

Bergelmir (mountain old, i.e., the old man of the mountain). In Norse mythology, a giant from whom all the frost giants descended. After the original giants were destroyed at the death of the primeval giant Ymir, only Bergelmir survived. He and his wife climbed up to his boat made of a hollow tree trunk, according to the *Prose Edda*. Matthew Arnold refers to the incident in his narrative poem *Balder Dead*, saying that Bergelmir "on shipboard fled."

Variant spelling: Bergelmer.

St. Bernardino of Siena

0548

Bernardino of Siena, St. (bear-brave). 1380–1444. In Christian legend, patron saint of wool weavers. Invoked against diseases of chest and lungs. Feast, 20 May.

One of the most notable preachers of the 15th century, St. Bernardino held aloft a tablet with the carved monogram IHS encircled by rays when he preached. The *Life of St. Bernardino* by his contemporary, Barnaby of Siena, tells how the saint walked on water. Bernardino had to cross a river to reach Mantua, where he was to preach. He did not have the money for the crossing and the ferryman refused to take him. The saint took his cloak, cast it on the water and sailed away.

In Christian art St. Bernardino is usually shown with the IHS monogram, as in El Greco's painting of the saint. Bernardino is a form of the name Bernard.

0549

Bernardo del Carpio. In medieval Spanish legend, hero who fought against Charlemagne, appearing in many Spanish ballads.

Bernardo del Carpio was the illegitimate son of Doña Ximena, sister of King Alfonso II who came to the Visigoth throne about 795. The king, known as the Chaste, because he did not have intercourse with his wife, had Ximena locked up in a convent for giving birth illegitimately; and the father of her son, Sancho Diaz, Count of Saldana, was imprisoned and blinded. (Some Spanish chroniclers gloss over the cruel incident, alleging that a private marriage took place between the lovers.)

When Bernardo was grown, Alfonso, according to the Spanish chronicles, invited the Emperor Charlemagne into Spain to eventually become king of Spain, Alfonso being childless. The Spanish nobility, headed by Bernardo, opposed the alliance, and the king finally gave in to their wishes. Charlemagne, however, came to Spain to expel the Moors and found that Alfonso had united with the Moors against him. A battle took place at Roncesvalles in which the French were defeated and the hero Roland was slain. The victory, which in the *Chanson de Roland* is credited to the Moors, was chiefly due to Bernardo del Carpio.

A Spanish ballad, *The March of Bernardo del Carpio*, describes the enthusiasm among his men when Bernardo first raised the standard to oppose Charlemagne's army.

"Free were we born,—" 'tis thus they cry—
"though to our King we own
The homage and the fealty behind his crest to go;
By God's behest our aid he shares, but God did ne'er command
That we should leave our children heirs of an enslaved land."

(John Gibson Lockhart translation)

Another Spanish ballad, *The Complaint of the Count of Saldana*, narrates the imprisonment of Don Sancho, Bernardo's father; another, *The Funeral of the Count of Saldana*, narrates the gruesome death of Don Sancho, who was mounted on his horse after his death and sent to his son, who did not know his father had been killed at the orders of King Alfonso. When Bernardo saw his father he cried out:

"Go up, go up, thou blessed ghost, into the hands of God;
Go, fear not lest revenge be lost, when Carpio's blood hath flowed;
The steel that drank the blood of France, the arm thy foe that shielded,
Still, father, thirsts that burning lance, and still thy son can wield it."

(John Gibson Lockhart translation)

A ballad titled *Bernardo and Alfonso* recounts events taking place after the funeral of Bernardo's father. Bernardo argues with King Alfonso and leaves the court, going over to the Moors. The actual end of Bernardo del Carpio, however, is not known.

Bernardo de Balbuena wrote an epic poem, *El Bernardo, la Victoria de Roncesvalles*, in which Bernardo is the main hero. The poem is an imitation of Ariosto's *Orlando Furioso*. Balbuena was born in Spain but went to Mexico as a child. He was made bishop of Puerto Rico in 1620.

0550

Bernard of Clairvaux, St. (bear-brave). 1090–1153 C.E. In Christian legend, patron saint of beekeepers and wax melters. Doctor of the Church. Feast, 20 August.

Born of noble parents near Dijon, Bernard studied at the University of Paris and entered the Benedictine Monastery of Citeaux when he was 20 years old. A few years later, at the abbot's bidding, he set out with 12 monks and founded another monastery at Clairvaux. He became one of the most important preachers of the age. He was in part responsible for the Second Crusade, which killed more European Jews than Muslims in the Holy Land. He was known to have had a fierce debate with Abelard, whom he hated intensely. Among his numerous works, *On the Love of God* and his *Commentary on the Song of Songs* are the best known.

According to legend, when he was writing his commentary on the Song of Songs in praise of the Virgin Mary, to whom he was dedicated, she appeared to him. She moistened his lips with milk from her bosom, and from that day he had a supernatural eloquence. Legend also says the white habit of the Cistercians was chosen by the Virgin Mary herself.

In Christian art St. Bernard is shown in the white habit of the Cistercians, carrying a book or writing one. Sometimes he is shown presenting his works to the Virgin Mary or being inspired by her to write them, as in Fra Filippo Lippi's painting *The Vision of St. Bernard*.

0551

Berserks (bear-shirt?). In Northern countries, warriors possessed by battle fury. They were dedicated to the god Odin and believed to be under his control or "possession." They would enter battle, seemingly impervious to wounds and danger. One medieval Nordic source says they "went without mailcoats, and were frantic as dogs or wolves; they bit their shields and were as strong as bears or boars; they slew men, but neither fire nor iron could harm them." This behavior was known as "running berserk." In Scandinavian society berserks were viewed as holy because they were sacred to Odin. However, the god would at his will desert them in battle. For this reason Odin was often called the Arch-Deceiver.

0552

Bertha (bright). In Germanic legend, one of the names by which the Norse goddess Frigga is known. Bertha, sometimes called Brechta (the white lady) or Perchta, is said to live in the hollow of a mountain in Thuringia, where she keeps watch over the souls of unbaptized children. She also watches over plants. She is said to be the ancestor of numerous European noble families. Charlemagne's mother was called *Berthe aux grande pieds* (Bertha with the large feet) because the continual working of the foot-treadle on her spinning wheel caused her feet to flatten, according to medieval legend. She appears in a 13th-century *chanson de geste* by Adenet le Roi.

Bertha is believed to appear as the White Lady before the death or misfortune of a family. At Christmastime Bertha is said to pass through village streets during the 12 nights between Christmas and Epiphany to see whether spinning is being done. She rewards some with golden threads or a distaff of extra-fine flax and punishes those who do not honor her.

0553

Bertoldo. In Italian legend, a clown whose life is told in *Vita di Bertoldo* by Giulio Caesare Croce, written in the 16th century. His antics and those of his son Bertoldina and his grandson Cacasenno frequently appear in Italian tales.

0554

Bes. In Egyptian mythology, a patron god of art, music, and childbirth as well as a god of war and a strangler of antelopes, bears, lions, and serpents; derived from a lion deity. The dual nature of Bes in Egyptian belief is reflected in the various images of the god. Usually he is portrayed as a dwarf with a huge bearded head, protruding tongue, flat nose, shaggy eyebrows and hair, large projecting ears, long thick arms, and bowed legs. Around his body he wears an animal skin whose tail hangs down, usually touching the ground behind him. On his head he wears a tiara of feathers, which suggests his primitive nature.

In later Egyptian art, however, Bes is given a handsome body because he absorbed the character of the sun god and became identified with Horus the Child as well as Ra and Temu. As Horus he wore a lock of hair on the right side of his head, which is the symbol of youth. All of these images suggest the various phases of the sun during the day.

Bes was frequently portrayed on steles, vases, and amulets, often in ithyphallic form. His image was hung over headrests as a charm to keep away evil spirits. His female counterpart was Beset.

0555

Bestiary. A book of beasts, popular during the Middle Ages, containing natural history and lore. The bestiary in one form or another is found in major languages: Old English, Arabic, Armenian, English, Ethiopic, French, German, Icelandic, Provençal, and Spanish. For medieval man a bestiary was a serious work of natural history, not a collection of myths and legends. What information is contained was believed to be factually true. Yet the medieval mind was not satisfied with mere facts. They had to be interpreted. Thus, bestiaries contain symbolic meanings. In Guillaume's *Le Bestiaire Divin* we have an excellent example:

> The unicorn represents Jesus Christ, who took on him our nature in the Virgin's womb, was betrayed by the Jews, and delivered into the hands of Pontius Pilate. Its one horn signifies the Gospel truth, that Christ is one with the Father.

0556

Bestla. In Norse mythology, giantess, wife of Bor; daughter of the giant Bolturon; mother of the gods Odin, Vili and Ve. Bestla appears in the *Prose Edda*.

0557

Bevis of Hampton (dear son). In medieval legend, an English hero who converts his pagan wife, Josian, to Christianity, defeats a host of enemies, and converts the giant Ascapart (Asclopard) to Christianity. Bevis's magic sword is called Morglay. His tale is told in the 14th-century English romance *Bevis of Hampton*.

0558

Bhaga. In Hindu mythology, a god who bestows wealth and presides over marriage. Bhaga is mentioned in the sacred *Vedas*, though his personality and powers are rather indistinct.

0559

Bhagavad-Gita (song of the divine one). A dialogue between the hero Arjuna and the god Krishna, forming part of the Hindu epic poem *The Mahabharata*.

Though part of a vast epic poem, the longest in the world, the *Bhagavad-Gita* is frequently found in separate editions. It is the most popular sacred book of India, even though it is not part of *shruti*, or revealed writings, but belongs to *smriti*, or traditional works. The main theme of the dialogue between Arjuna and his charioteer, Krishna (who is an incarnation of the god Vishnu), concerns the role Arjuna must play in the coming battle with the Kauravas, his enemies but also his relatives. Krishna assures Arjuna that he should not hesitate to slay his foes because he is just killing their bodies, which does not affect the vital principle that inhabits the body. Throughout the dialogue Krishna touches on various Hindu beliefs, often found expressed in the *Upanishads*. Arjuna, as a member of the warrior caste, must fulfill his role in the world, since God himself is tirelessly engaged in works in order to keep the universe going.

One of the most important sections of the poem is that in which Arjuna asks Krishna to reveal himself. There takes place a transfiguration of All-Form-Vision (book 9), in which Krishna displays his true, godlike nature.

"In him was the whole universe centered in one," says the *Bhagavad-Gita*. "Endowed with countless eyes and numberless mouths, and innumerable faces turned in every quarter, and blazing with the glory of a thousand arms, with celestial ornaments and fierce weapons; with many hands, feet, and organs, with countless stomachs and fierce and fearful tusks terrible to behold."

Arjuna then sees the Kauravas, his enemies, in Krishna's mouths, with their hands crushed to powder. Krishna tells Arjuna to worship him by fixing his heart and thought on Krishna. At the conclusion of the work (book 18) Arjuna says:

> Trouble and ignorance are gone! The Light
> Hath come unto me, by Thy favor, Lord!
> Now am I fixed! My doubt is fled away!
> According to Thy word, so will I do!
>
> (Edwin Arnold translation)

There is a version of the *Bhagavad-Gita* in which the name Ganesha, the elephant-headed god of wisdom and good fortune, is substituted for that of Krishna. It is called *Ganesha-Gita* and is used by the Ganapatyas (worshipers of Ganesha), who see their god as the supreme being.

Bhakti (devotion). In Hinduism the love existing between the human soul and the divine. Bhakti yoga is one of the ways of achieving this union.

0560

Bharata. In Hindu mythology, a king devoted to the worship of the god Vishnu. He abdicated his throne to continue in constant meditation on the god.

0561

While Bharata was at his forest retreat, he went to bathe in the river and saw a pregnant doe frightened by a lion. Her fawn, which was born suddenly, fell into the water, and Bharata rescued it. He brought up the animal, becoming very fond of it, and forgetting his worship of Vishnu. When Bharata died, he was transformed into a deer, with the faculty of remembering his former life as a punishment for forgetting to honor Vishnu. Bharata continued in his deer form and atoned for his sin, being born again as a priest, who was ungainly and looked as if he were a madman. In his new life he constantly worshiped Vishnu and as a result was exempt from future births.

Another Bharata is the ancestor of the warring sides, the Pandavas and Kauravas, in the Hindu epic poem *The Mahabharata*.

Bhavacakra (the wheel of becoming). In Buddhism, the Wheel of Life or Existence, used to bring before the mind the nature of existence. The wheel is portrayed as being whirled around by a monster, who symbolizes the limitations of human existence. Outside the wheel the Buddha is portrayed to show the release.

0562

In some versions the Buddha is also portrayed within the wheel, symbolizing the accessibility of Buddhist teachings to all beings. The segments of the wheel depict the levels of rebirth as a human, an animal, a god, or other form of life.

Bhikkhu (Pali) or **Bhikshu** (Sanskrit). In Buddhism, one who has devoted his life to the following of the Eightfold Path by renunciation and relies for his livelihood on gifts of lay disciples, in return for which he preaches and gives counsel. Often the term is translated into English as monk, mendicant, friar, or priest. The female equivalent is *bhikkhuni* or *bhikshuni*.

0563

Bhima (the terrible). In the Hindu epic poem *The Mahabharata*, a hero, second of the five Pandu brothers. Bhima, the son of Vayu, the wind god, had great strength but was of a fierce and often cruel nature. His coarse manners earned for him the title Vrikodara (wolf's belly) because he ate more food than all of his brothers combined. One episode in *The Mahabharata* tells how Bhima kicked the head of his prostrate enemy, Dur-yodhana, earning him the title Jihma-yodhin (the unfair fighter).

0564

Bhishma (the terrible). In the Hindu epic poem *The Mahabharata*, a hero, commander-in-chief of the Kauravas in the war with the Pandavas.

0565

Bhishma taught the children of both sides, the Kauravas and Pandavas, but when the war broke out

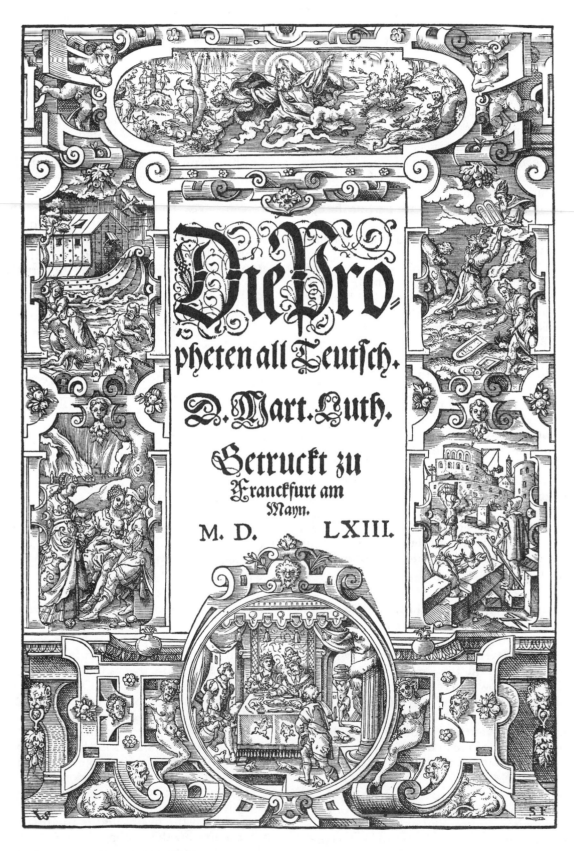

Decoration from a 1563 edition of the Bible

between the two sides, he took the part of the Kauravas. He laid down some rules for mitigating the horrors of the war, stipulating that he should not be called on to fight Arjuna, the Pandu prince and main hero of the poem. However, Bhishma was goaded by one of the Kauravas to fight against Arjuna; their encounter took place on the 10th day of battle. Bhishma was pierced with so many arrows that there was no space for a finger's breadth. When he fell from his chariot, he was held up from the ground by the arrows in his body. He lived for some 58 days more because he had determined the hour of his death. During that time he delivered several long didactic discourses, which make up part of the epic poem.

Bhishma is also called Tala-ketu (palm banner), referring to his banner symbol.

Bhrigu. In Hindu mythology, a Prajapati, a son of the god Brahma, sent by the priests to test the characters of various gods. Bhrigu could not get to see Shiva because the god was making love to his wife. As a result, Bhrigu, "finding him, therefore to consist of the property of darkness," sentenced Shiva "to take the form of the Linga (phallus), and pronounced that he should have no offerings presented to him, nor receive worship of the pious and respectable." Bhrigu's next visit was to his father, Brahma, whom he saw surrounded by sages and so much inflated by his own importance as not to pay any attention to Bhrigu. Brahma was therefore excluded from worship by the priests. Next Bhrigu went to Vishnu and found the god asleep. Bhrigu stamped on Vishnu's chest with his left foot and awoke the god. Instead of being offended, Vishnu gently pressed Bhrigu's foot and said he was honored. Bhrigu, pleased by the god's humility, proclaimed Vishnu as the only being to be worshiped by men or gods.

Bhuta. In Hindu mythology, a ghost, imp, or goblin. Bhutas are malignant and haunt crematoria, lurk in trees, animate dead bodies, and delude and devour humans. According to the *Vishnu Purana*, a text in honor of the god Vishnu, they are "fierce beings and eaters of flesh" who were created when the Creator was angry. In another text their mother is said to have been Krodha (anger). The Bhutas are attendants on the god Shiva, their lord. The term *Bhutesa* (lord of beings; lord of created things) is applied to the gods Vishnu, Brahma, and Krishna (an incarnation of Vishnu).

Bible, The. In Christianity, sacred writings compiled from the Hebrew Scriptures and various early Christian works. The word *bible* is derived from the Greek *biblos*, part of an ancient plant used in making books.

The Greek word *biblia*, meaning "the books," referred to the Scriptures. The Greek *biblia* (plural) became the Latin *biblia* (feminine singular), from which came the English word *bible*.

The Catholic church in the third century took the Hebrew Scriptures—both the Hebrew books accepted by all Jews and those written in Greek and used by some Jews in various parts of the world—then added various Christian works, forming the Bible.

The King James, or Authorized Version, completed in 1611, is the best-known translation of the Bible into English, though numerous other versions exist. During the Middle Ages the common Bible was the Latin translation called the Vulgate, made by St. Jerome in the fourth century. It contained books later rejected by Protestants at the Reformation and placed in the Apocrypha.

Translations of the Vulgate into some European languages were made during the Middle Ages. One of the first is ascribed to Caedmon about 650. St. Bede the Venerable made a translation of the Gospel According to St. John about 735. In 825 Anglo-Saxon glosses (marginal annotations) were made of the Vulgate Gospels and psalters. Between 890 and 900 King Alfred made various translations of selected passages of the Bible. In the year 1000 the earliest extant English translation of the Four Gospels appeared. In 1320 William of Shoreham made an English translation of the Psalms, and Richard Rolle made an English translation of the Psalms in 1340. The first Wycliffe translation of the whole Bible appeared in 1384 but was condemned by the church. A revised version by John Purvey was made about 1396. Numerous English versions followed the Reformation, the most famous, because of its influence on English literature and life, being the King James Version of 1611.

The Bible has two major divisions, the Old Testament, containing the pre-Christian Jewish Scripture, and the New Testament, containing writings of the early Christian era. Each division of the Bible consists of many different books, written by various authors over a long period of history. In the King James Version the Old Testament consists of 39 books; the New Testament, 27. Roman Catholic Bibles contain the Apocrypha within the Old Testament. For example, the Catholic New American Bible contains 46 books within the Old Testament and the same New Testament books found in the King James Version.

The following books of the Bible as found in the King James Version:

Genesis (in the beginning) is the first book of the Bible, narrating the myths and legends of the ancient Hebrews from the Creation to the story of Joseph in

Egypt. Genesis forms the first part of the Law, or Torah or Pentateuch (five-volume document), which consists of the first five books of the Bible. The major themes of Genesis are primeval legends and myths of humankind (1–11:19); and accounts of the patriarchs (11:28–50:26), including the legends of Abraham (11:26–25:10), Isaac (25:11–26:35), Jacob (27–36), and Joseph (37–50).

Exodus (going out) continues the tales, legends, myths, and history of the Hebrews. The main themes of Exodus are oppression and deliverance (1–18), including Moses' call (2–4), escape from Egypt (5– 14), and the Wilderness (14–18); imposing the law through delivering the Ten Commandments (20); forming the Covenant between God and Israel (21– 23) and giving details and specific laws of the tribes; the Tabernacle at Sinai and the construction of the Ark (24–40).

Leviticus consists of ritual laws; its title comes from the tribe of Levi, the hereditary priests.

Numbers is so named because of the two numberings of the people. It focuses on Moses, the leader and prophet. The book narrates the legends of the Hebrews from their second year in the Wilderness to the arrival on the borders of Moab, close to the Promised Land.

Deuteronomy (second law) is the last book of the Pentateuch; the title refers to the repetition by Moses of Yahweh's commandments. The book consists almost entirely of discourses ascribed to Moses by later Hebrew legend. It narrates a resume of the Wilderness events (1–4), the Decalogue and other laws (5–26), the written law (27–28), Moses' farewell speech and his charge to Joshua (29:1–31:13), and Moses' last days and death (31:14–34:12).

Joshua the last of the first six books of the Bible, called the Hexateuch, is named for the successor of Moses, who led the Israelites into Canaan. Its main themes are the conquest of Canaan (1–12), division of the land (13–22), and Joshua's last speech and death (23–24).

Judges deals with the activities of the "judges" or tribal leaders who ruled between the entry into Canaan and the establishment of the monarchy. Its main divisions are introduction (1–2:5); the legends of the judges (2:6–16:31) telling of Othniel, Ehud, Deborah, Gideon, Abimelech (antihero), Tola, Jair, Jephtah, Ibzan, Elon, Abdon, and Samson; the conquest of Laish by the Danites, who renamed it Dan; the sexual abuse of a Levite's concubine by Benjamites of Gibeah, resulting in her death and the subsequent war of vengeance by the rest of the tribes of Israel (17–21).

Joshua at Jericho

Ruth tells a story of the days of the judges concerning the family of a man of Bethlehem who was forced by a famine to migrate to Moab; his Moabite daughter-in-law Ruth became the ancestress of King David and, according to New Testament accounts, also of Jesus.

1 Samuel records the events leading to the establishment of the kingdom of Israel and the reign of Saul, the first king. Its main themes are legends of Samuel (1–12) and the reign of Saul (12–31), telling of the conflict of David, who later became king, and ending with the killing of Saul and his sons at Gilboa by the Philistines.

2 Samuel continues the narrative, telling of David, who became first king of Judah and later of all Israel. Its main themes are David's attainment of the monarchy (1–10), David and Bathsheba (11–12), David and his rebel son Absalom (13–19), and the last events in David's life (20–24).

1 Kings tells of the death of David and the succession and reign of his son Solomon (1–11); then of the legends, history, and myths of Israel and Judah (12–22) after the split of Israel. Important figures are Ahab, Elijah, and Elisha.

2 Kings continues 1 Kings, narrating the end of the northern kingdom, the reign of Hezekiah in Judah, and legends and tales of Elisha. The book ends with the destruction of the southern kingdom and tells of Josiah and the conquest of Judah by Babylon.

1 and 2 Chronicles recapitulate previous books, often contradicting information in them.

Ezra tells of Ezra and Nehemiah, who came back from Babylon with the Jews to rebuild the Temple.

Nehemiah continues the legends recorded in 1 and 2 Chronicles as well as in Ezra.

Esther is a folktale about the Jewess Esther who married Xerxes, king of Persia, and saved the Jews from a pogrom. The Jewish feast of Purim was established to celebrate this deliverance.

The next major division of the Bible consists of the five poetical books; Job, Psalms, Proverbs, Ecclesiastes, and the Song of Solomon or Song of Songs.

Job tells of a man punished by God, though he is guilty of no sin. The book explores the question "Why do the righteous suffer?" but produces no answers.

Psalms is a collection of prayers, poems, and hymns recited and sung in both Jewish and Christian worship.

Proverbs is a book of sayings illustrating general truths, using pithy and colorful language. It was traditionally ascribed to Solomon but is written by many other hands. *Ecclesiastes* is filled with skepticism and pessimism about the world and its creator. After it was included in the Bible, it was edited to soften its harsh message.

Job

The next major division of the Old Testament contains the Major and Minor Prophets.

Isaiah is named for a prophet who warned Israel of its sin and promised a messiah to deliver her from her enemies. Isaiah also was a preacher who used parables, as Jesus did much later. Jesus was probably greatly influenced by Isaiah and his preaching, since Christians consider the central message of his prophecy to be the coming of Jesus. Much of the text of Handel's *Messiah* was taken from the Book of Isaiah. It is now agreed by scholars that Isaiah wrote only part of the book; his followers wrote some sections.

Jeremiah is named after the prophet. It includes his prophecies as well as considerable biographical material.

Lamentations consists of five poems that have been ascribed to Jeremiah but were not written by him. They tell of the siege of Jerusalem by the Babylonians and are used extensively in Christian liturgy.

Ezekiel is a long, often tedious work, but it contains some passages of greatness. Ezekiel claimed he was commanded to warn Israel about its rebellion against God. Much of his prophecy he received through visions, the best known being his vision of the fiery wheels.

Daniel contains legends about the prophet for whom it is named. Daniel was an Israelite in the land of Persia and came into conflict with Persian officials when he refused to worship Persian idols. He was cast into a lion's den for his refusal, but the God of Israel protected Daniel and he emerged unharmed. It was also Daniel who correctly interpreted the "writing on the wall" for King Belshazzar, which predicted the king's destruction.

Daniel

Hosea the 28th book and the first of the Minor Prophets, uses symbolic language, telling of Hosea's marriage to a whore, who represents faithless Israel.

Joel the second of the Minor Prophets, consists of only three chapters in three discourses. It contains no Bible stories in the usual sense but is largely a series of exhortations for Israel to repent its sins.

Amos is the first prophetical book compiled. It denounces wealth and luxury.

Obadiah is only 21 verses long. It is a violent attack on Edom, Israel's enemy.

Jonah is a short folktale about the prophet, in which Jonah causes a tempest at sea when he flees from God in a boat. When he confesses he is the cause of the tempest, the mariners cast him overboard, and he is swallowed by a giant fish. After Jonah repents, the fish vomits him out on dry land, and Jonah fulfills his promise to God and becomes a prophet.

Micah is ascribed to the prophet Micah, a contemporary of Isaiah in Judah. Micah laments the degeneracy of the house of Jacob and warns against false prophets.

Nahum is a collection of oracles written by Nahum, the Elkoshite about 700 B.C.E. He warns of punishment for Nineveh for the sins of its people and predicts that God will rout the enemies of Israel.

Habakkuk concerns the threat of the Babylonians to Judah's security. The prophet rebukes the Chaldeans for their sins.

Zephaniah speaks of the sins of Judah and predicts God's severe punishment. He ends with the vision of the dispersed people of Judah returning to their own land.

Haggai is the prophet chosen by God to encourage the rebuilding of the Temple. He tells the people that sin impedes their work.

Zechariah stresses temple worship. He warns the people of Jerusalem of their possible destruction and of the vengeance of God against the enemies of the city.

Malachi is the last of the Old Testament prophets. He tells of a time when the prophet Elijah will return.

The next section of the Bible, which is often omitted, contains the Apocrypha, those books rejected by Protestants as not belonging in the Hebrew Bible because they were written in Greek and used by Greek-speaking Jews, not by the Jews in Jerusalem. All the books influenced Christian art, which has used many of their legends and tales. The 15 books of the Apocrypha are the following:

1 and 2 Esdras is a Greek reworking of the books of Ezra and Nehemiah.

Tobit is a tale beloved by Martin Luther that tells of a demon who possesses various people and of how the angel of the Lord frees them.

Judith is a short novel of a Jewess who destroys the enemy by cutting off the head of their leader.

The Rest of Esther consists of additions to the Hebrew Book of Esther in the Bible, giving more details and dwelling on God and Israel. The Hebrew Book of Esther never mentions God.

Wisdom of Solomon is a collection of proverbs, similar to the book of Proverbs in the Old Testament.

Ecclesiasticus is another wisdom book.

Baruch is a short book ascribed to the secretary of the prophet Jeremiah.

Letter of Jeremiah, a short letter ascribed to the prophet, ridicules idolatry.

Prayer of Azariah and the Song of the Three Young Men gives their prayer, which is not found in the biblical Book of Daniel.

Susanna

Susanna is a short folk tale of a woman vindicated by the prophet Daniel.

Bel and the Dragon is a short tale of Daniel in which he shows that idols are not really gods.

Prayer of Manasseh, a short prayer, is still used in the Anglican church.

1 and 2 Maccabees are two books of legends and history of the Jews.

The next major division in the King James Bible is the New Testament, which consists of 27 books, all accepted by Christians today.

The first four books are called Gospels (good news) and are the Early Church's view of the person of Jesus as Messiah and the Son of God. They are not concerned with history but with faith, and they rearrange information to suit the needs of the believing Christians at the time they were compiled. The Four Gospels are Matthew, Mark, Luke, and John.

Matthew, the first but not the oldest Gospel, is arranged as a teaching manual. Matthew mentions many Jewish customs and stresses that Jesus is the Jewish Messiah. The main divisions of his account are as follows: Jesus' birth and childhood (1–2); Jesus' baptism (3); Jesus' temptation (4:1–11); the beginning of Jesus' work in Galilee (4:12–25); the Galilean ministry (5–13), including the Sermon on the Mount; miracles and teachings (14–20), journey to Jerusalem (21–25); the trial, passion, death, and Resurrection (26–28).

Mark, the second Gospel but the earliest, is very short. It was used by Matthew and Luke when they compiled their own accounts. It breaks down as follows: Jesus' baptism and temptation (1:1–13); Galilean ministry (1:14–6:6); ministry outside Galilee (6:7–8:21); labors and instructions (8:22–13:37); passion and Resurrection (14–16).

Luke, the third Gospel, is written in better Greek than that of either Matthew or Mark. It gives more details but softens harsh aspects of the legend. It breaks down as follows: introduction (1:1–4); birth and childhood of Jesus (1–2); baptism and temptation (3:1–4:13); Galilean ministry (4:14–9:50); journey to Jerusalem (9:51–21:38); trial, passion, death, Resurrection, and Ascension (22–24).

These first three Gospels are called synoptic because they often use the same material, though they shift it about for different emphasis.

John, the last Gospel, is completely different in character. In it Jesus speaks like a Greek philosopher, and little is told of the historical Jesus. It breaks down as follows: prologue (1:1–18); narrative demonstrating the Incarnation (1:19–12:11); trial, passion and Resurrection (12:12–21:25).

Acts of the Apostles, written by the author of Luke's Gospel, tells the history of the Early Church and the lives of St. Peter and St. Paul.

The next division of the New Testament contains Epistles, or letters, the majority ascribed to St. Paul. They are *Romans, 1 and 2 Corinthians, Galatians, Ephesians, Philippians, Colossians, 1 and 2 Thessalonians, 1 and 2 Timothy, Titus,* and *Philemon.*

Hebrews, ascribed to St. Paul in the King James Version, was not written by him.

The other letters are *James,* which contradicts St. Paul's teaching regarding faith and works; *1 and 2 Peter; 1, 2,* and *3 John* and *Jude.*

The last book of the Bible is *Revelation,* the only prophetic book in the New Testament. It deals with the end of the world, the punishment of sinners, and the vindication of the righteous.

0569
Bicorn and Chichevache. In medieval French folklore, two animals, one fat and the other thin. Chichevache (lean cow) lived on patient wives and was therefore very thin, whereas Bicorn lived on patient husbands and was well fed. Chaucer's Clerk mentions Chichevache in the conclusion of his story in *The Canterbury Tales.*

0570
Bidental (struck by lightning). In Roman cult, a consecrated spot where lightning had passed into the ground.

0571
Bifrost (rainbow or quivering roadway). In Norse mythology, rainbow bridge, made of fire, water, and air, that led from Asgard, home of the Aesir gods, to the well of Urd. The *Prose Edda* tells how the gods made "a bridge from earth to heaven . . . constructed with more art than any other work. But, strong though it be, it will be broken to pieces when the sons of Muspell [the frost giants], after having traversed great rivers, shall ride over it." To delay as much as possible the end of their existence and that of the world, the gods ordered the god Heimdall to be a watchman and inform them when the frost giants were on their way.

Variant spellings: Bilrost; Bif-raust.

0572
Biggarro. In Australian mythology, the wombat snake who aids man to the spirit land. He is the opposite of the evil carpet snake, Goonnear.

0573
Big Harpe. In American folklore, a sadistic outlaw who killed men, women, and children for pleasure. He was finally caught by a man who had witnessed

him murder his wife and child. When the man grabbed Harpe's hair and proceeded to cut off his head, Harpe cried out: "You're a damned rough butcher, but cut on and be damned." Big Harpe's head was then stuck in the fork of a tree.

Big Owl. In North American Indian mythology (Apache), cannibalistic monster who transfixes his victims with a stare, takes them home, and eats them. In other accounts he is the evil son of the sun. He kills many people and is killed in turn by his brother.

0574

Bik'eguidinde (according to whom there is life). In North American Indian mythology (Mescalero Apache), creator god.

0575

Bil and Hjuki. In Norse mythology, the waxing and the waning moon. The *Prose Edda* says, "One day he [the moon] carried off from the earth two children, named Bil and Hjuki, as they were returning from the spring called Byrgir, carrying between them the bucket called Saegr, on the pole Simul. Vidfinn was the father of these children, who always follow Mani [the moon], as we may easily observe even from the earth." The image of Bil and Hjuki, holding their pails, were said to be darkly outlined on the moon.

0576

Billy Blin. In English and Scottish folklore, a household spirit who protects the family. He appears in some Scottish ballads and also is called Billy Blind, Belly Blin, and Blind Barlow.

0577

Billy Potts. In American folklore, a murderer and robber, said to be a member of the Cave-in-Rock gang in the Ohio and Mississippi River area. The gang consisted of Billy, his mother, and his father. After one killing, Billy's father told him to flee and hide out for a time. When he returned, he was shot by his father, who didn't recognize him with his new beard and added weight.

0578

Billy the Kid. 1859–1891. In American history and legend, bandit; popular name of William H. Bonney. Born in New York City, his family moved to Kansas and then to New Mexico when he was a child. By the time he was 16 he was credited with killing 16 men, and at his death the total was past 20. His personality affected people differently. To some, he was "a nondescript, adenoidal, weasel-eyed, narrow-chested, stoop-shouldered, repulsive looking crea-

0579

ture with all the outward appearance of a cretin," whereas others called him "the darling of the common people." Pat Garrett, the sheriff who finally killed Billy, wrote in his *Authentic Life of Billy the Kid* that "the Kid had a lurking devil in him. It was a good-humored, jovial imp, or a cruel and blood-thirsty fiend, as circumstances prompted. Circumstances favored the worser angel, and the Kid fell." Despite the fact that he was no angel, folklore tends to see Billy the Kid in a kind light. Two Hollywood films, both called *Billy the Kid*, present romanticized views of the murderer. Other movies are *Dirty Little Billy* and *Pat Garrett and Billy the Kid*. Aaron Copland's one-act ballet *Billy the Kid* presents the life of Billy the Kid against the ongoing push of the pioneers, who had to put down Billy's lawlessness to achieve civilization.

Bimbo. In Japanese legend, a poor farmer who was given a son by Raiden, the thunder god. After 20 years of toil Bimbo owned barely three-quarters of an acre of land. He had no son and wished to adopt one. One day, as he was leaving the field, a storm broke, and the lightning dazzled him. After many invocations to the gods he started home; then he noticed a little rosy boy lying on the ground. He picked up the child and took him to his wife. They called the child Raitaro in honor of Raiden, the god of thunder, who had give them this gift. Prosperity followed their adoption of the child. When Raitaro was 18 years old, he took the shape of a dragon and flew away to a castle formed of clouds, above the hills. When Bimbo and his wife died, their grave was marked with the shape of a dragon.

0580

Birch. A hardwood tree with thin, layered bark. According to one Slavic folk custom, the birch tree was used to placate forest spirits. The celebrants would gather in the forest, cut down a small birch, form a circle—each in turn stepping on the stump of the tree— and call upon the spirit. The spirit indicated its presence through the trembling of the birch leaves. In ancient Rome birch bundles wrapped around an ax were symbols of authority.

The birch was sacred to the Nordic god Thor and was later associated with the switches used to scourge Christ during his Passion. In Scandinavia a birch branch protected against the evil eye, lightning, gout, and barrenness. In Victorian England the birch symbolized grace and meekness.

0581

Birds. Warm-blooded vertebrate having a body covered with feathers and forelimbs modified with wings. Because birds fly they have often been sym-

0582

bols of the soul leaving the body at death. In ancient Egyptian mythology the *ba* (soul) was portrayed as a bird with the head of a human being. Bird features were also assumed by various gods: the hawk was associated with Horus, Ra, and other sun deities; the ibis with the god Thoth; the goose with Geb, and the swallow with Isis. The *ba* abandoned the body at death and hovered over the mummy to protect it from decay until it reentered the body. In Hindu mythology birds are also symbols of the soul or contain the souls of humans. In Jewish folklore the hoyl bird was believed to be the only creature that refused to eat the forbidden fruit when Adam gave it to all the animals after he and Eve had eaten it. The hoyl, therefore, does not know death but like the phoenix goes to sleep, a divine fire consuming it and its nest. All that remains is an egg, which miraculously hatches a new, full-grown hoyl.

One of the most persistent motifs regarding birds in nearly all mythologies and folklore is their ability to speak and to be understood by humans. In Christian legend St. Rose of Lima sang to the birds, and they answered her. In Norse mythology Sigurd tastes dragon's blood and then understands the language of birds. In the Grimm folktale *The White Snake* a servant eats a part of the king's supper and then is able to understand the language of birds and other animals.

0583

Bisan. In Malayan mythology, the female spirit of camphor, who assumes the form of a cicada.

0584

Bishamon. In Japanese Buddhist mythology, war god and a god of riches; one of the Shichi Fukujin, seven gods of good luck or fortune. Often he is portrayed dressed in armor and carrying a pagoda in his left hand and a scepter, lance, or three-pointed halberd in his right hand. He is one of the Jiu No O, 12 Japanese Buddhist gods and goddesses adopted from Hindu mythology. Bishamon is derived from the war god Skanda or Vaiśrávana.

0585

Bith and Birren. In Celtic mythology, husband and wife in the myth of the great flood. Bith, his wife, Birren, their daughter Cesara and her husband, Fintaan, with their son Lara and his wife, Balma, escaped by ship to Inisfail when the great flood came upon the earth. A short time later, however, the moon, blood red, broke into hundreds of pieces, killing the whole family.

0586

Biton and Cleobis (wild ox and famous life). In Greek mythology, two heroes of Argos. They were sons of Cydippe, a priestess of the goddess Hera. When no oxen could be found to draw their mother's chariot, they pulled it several miles to the temple of the goddess. There Cydippe prayed that they receive the best possible gift as a reward for their filial duty. In response the goddess let them die in her temple, indicating that death is the only truly happy event for humankind.

0587

Black Bart. 1830–1917? In American history and legend, popular name of Charles E. Boles, the bane of Wells Fargo. Black Bart was a Union soldier and a schoolteacher before he took up stealing. He is credited with more than 30 robberies without ever firing a shot. Often he would leave a poem as a reminder of his visit, such as:

> I'll start out to-morrow
> With another empty sack.
> From Wells Fargo I will borrow
> But I'll never pay it back.

The poems were signed: "Black Bart, Po. 8." When he was released from jail after having been caught and convicted, the warden asked him if he was finished with a life of crime. Black Bart replied he was. "What are you going to do then, Bart?" the warden asked. "Are you going to write poetry for a living?" "Warden," Bart replied, "didn't I tell you I wasn't going to commit any more crimes." When he was old, Bart was given a pension of $200 a month not to rob Wells Fargo. All he had to do was report every week to the authorities to let them know his whereabouts. He appears in the Hollywood movie *Black Bart*, in which Lola Montes falls in love with him.

0588

Blackbeard. d. 1718. In American history and legend, popular name of the sadistic English pirate Edward Teach, who wore black, braided whiskers. Preying on ships and coastal towns from the West Indies to the Atlantic coast of North America, Blackbeard's activities were overlooked by the governor of North Carolina, who shared in his booty. But eventually the British sent troops from Virginia to capture the pirate. When he was beheaded, according to legend, his headless corpse swam around the ship three times before it sank, and his head was later made into a drinking cup.

0589

Bladud. In British mythology, the 10th king of Britain, father of King Lear. Bladud built Bath "and fashioned hot baths therein, meet for the needs of men, in which he placed under the guardianship of the deity Minerva," according to Geoffrey of Monmouth's *History of the Kings of Britain*. Bladud practiced sorcery and attempted to fly with artificial wings but fell on the Temple of Apollo and was dashed to pieces.

0590

Blain (Ymir's bones?). In Norse mythology, a giant, often identified with Ymir, the great giant from whose body the earth was formed. The name appears in the *Prose Edda*.

St. Blaise

0591

Blaise, St. (crippled, stammering). Fourth century C.E. In Christian legend, bishop, patron saint of physicians, wax chandlers, and wool combers. Invoked against throat infections. Feast, 3 February.

Blaise was a physician before he became a bishop in Armenia. He suffered beheading after his flesh was torn with iron combs used for carding wool. One legend tells that while the bishop was in prison awaiting his martyrdom, he miraculously cured a little boy who nearly died because a fishbone was stuck in his throat.

During the Middle Ages, St. Blaise was one of the most popular saints. In Central Europe and in Latin countries people are still given *pan bendito* (St. Blaise sticks), which they eat when they have a sore throat. One of the most popular customs of the Roman church is the blessing of throats, held on St. Blaise's feast day. A priest holds crossed candles against the head or throat of a person, saying: "Through the intercession of St. Blaise, bishop and martyr, may the Lord free you from evils of the throat and from any other evil." In certain parts of Italy priests touch the throats with a wick that has been dipped into blessed oil.

0592

Blanchefleur (white flower). In medieval French legend, a Moorish slave girl rescued by a Christian. The heroine appears in a French metrical romance, *Flore et Blanchefleur*. She also appears in works by Boccaccio and Chaucer.

0593

Blánik. In Czech legend, name of a hillside where a troop of sleeping Hussites wait to answer the call of their country in its time of need. The 15th-century legend inspired Smetana's symphonic poem *Blánik*, last in his cycle of six symphonic poems included in *Má Vlast* (My Country). Smetana uses the old Hussite hymn "Ye Are the Warriors of God" in the work to express, according to the composer, "the resurrection of the Czech people."

0594

Blathnat (little flower). In Celtic mythology, daughter of Mider, king of the Gaelic underworld; she helped the hero Cuchulain steal her father's magic caldron, which was guarded by her husband, Curoi Mac Daire. She helped Cuchulain murder her husband. Her counterpart in Welsh legend is Blouderwedd (flower maiden), who also betrayed her husband and as a punishment was changed into an owl.
Variant spelling: Blathine.

0595

Bluebeard. In European folktales, a villain who marries, one after the other, three or seven women, killing each of them, but he himself is killed by his last wife. Bluebeard may appear as a king, merchant, or sorcerer. In the general outline, Bluebeard gives his wife the keys to his castle or house, telling her not to open one certain door. Of course, the wife opens the door and discovers either a number of dead wives or a basin of blood. When Bluebeard returns, he either kills his wife or locks her in a dungeon to eat only human flesh. This happens to all of his wives except the last, the youngest, who either kills Bluebeard with a saber or is saved by a young man; in some tellings she outwits Bluebeard and has her brothers kill him. The most famous telling of the tale is Charles Perrault's version in his *Contes de ma mère, l'oye'* (1697), often translated as *Tales of Mother Goose*. Béla Bartók's *Prince Bluebeard's Castle* is an operatic version of the folktale.

0596

Blunderbore. In British legend, a giant who is tricked by Jack the Giant Killer into cutting open his own stomach. Blunderbore offered Jack the Giant Killer a bed for the night, hoping to club him to death while he slept. Jack, suspicious, placed logs under the bed covers and crept underneath the bed. Blunderbore came into the room and thoroughly pounded the bed with his club. Next morning Jack appeared at breakfast, and the giant was thoroughly surprised, believing he had killed Jack the night before. As they ate their breakfast of hasty pudding, Jack seemed to be consuming vast quantities of it; but in reality he was surreptitiously stuffing the pudding into a bag hidden underneath his clothing. The giant, trying to keep up with Jack, stuffed himself with more and more pudding. Jack then put a knife into the bag and let out some of the pudding. The giant, seeing this, put a knife into his stomach, killing himself.

0597
Boabdil. d.c. 1533. In Spanish history and legend, last Moorish king of Granada, subject of numerous Spanish ballads. Boabdil, also called El Chico (the young one), dethroned his father, but was later forced to give up his throne and city to King Ferdinand of spain. The Spanish ballad *The Flight from Granada* tells the legend of his escape. José Zorrilla y Moral's literary ballad *Boabdil* tells the legend of the king's love for a Christian lady to whom he would give all Granada, and Washington Irving's *The Conquest of Granada* deals with Boabdil's history and legend.

0598
Boadicea (victorious). First century C.E. British queen who led a revolt against the Romans, failed, and poisoned herself.

Boadicea was the wife of Prasutagus, king of the Iceni. On his death the Romans seized the territory, and according to Tacitus in *Annals* (book 14), "Boadicea was flogged and her daughters raped." However, she rallied and appeared riding in a chariot with her daughters in front of her. She cried out: "We British are used to woman commanders in war. I am descended from mighty men! But I am not fighting for my kingdom and wealth now. I am fighting as an ordinary person for my lost freedom, my bruised body, and my outraged daughters."

Boadicea raised a revolt but eventually lost and poisoned herself. Her story forms the theme for a play *Bonduca* (Boadicea) by John Fletcher, produced in 1619; a literary ballad by William Cowper, *Boadicéa: An Ode*; and Tennyson's poem *Boädicea*. John Milton, in his *History of Britain*, rejects the legend, saying it was written to prove that "in Britain women were men, and men women."

0599
Boann (cow-white goddess?). In Celtic mythology, water goddess, wife of Nechtan or Ecmar, mistress of the god Daga and mother of Aengus, god of love and beauty. After her affair with Daga, she attempted to prove she was chaste by walking around Connla's well or Nechtan's well. But three waves arose. One took off her thigh, another a hand, and the third, an eye. Boann fled and was drowned by the pursuing

waves, which became the river Bogne. Near it lived the magic Salmon of Knowledge, who was fed by nuts dropped from the nine hazel trees at the water's edge.

0600
Bochica. In the mythology of the ancient Chibcha Indians of Colombia, chief god and culture hero. He came from the east, traveling across the country disguised as a bearded old man, teaching moral laws and arts to man. In one myth Bochica saved the people when a flood inundated the plain of Botgotá. He appeared and cleaved the mountains with his golden scepter, opening a passage for the waters into the valley below. Bochica's wife was Cuchaviva, the rainbow goddess, who watched over women in childbirth and made the fields fertile. Bochica was sometimes worshiped as Zuhe (sun) or Xue (lord) or was identified with the culture hero Nemterequeteba or Chimizapagua.

0601
Bodhi. In Buddhism, term meaning enlightenment or awakening. *Buddha* means "one who has attained *Bodhi.*"

0602
Bodhidharma. Fifth century C.E. In Buddhism, sage who introduced Buddhism to China where he is called P'u-T'i-Ta-Mo, often abbreviated Ta-Mo. In Japanese legend he is called Daruma.

0603
Bodhisattva (Sanskrit) or **Bodhisatta** (Pali). In Buddhism, one who aspires to *Bodhi* (enlightenment), a potential Buddha, a Buddha-to-be. When a Mahayana Bodhisattva has achieved stage seven on the Path and is entitled to enter lesser Nirvana, he refuses, renouncing it in favor of greater enlightenment. In the Avatamsaka Sutra the reason is stated: "Forasmuch as there is the will that all sentient beings should be altogether made free, I will not forsake my fellow creatures." There are, according to the Lotus of the Good Law (chapter 20), "hundreds of thousands of myriads of Bodhisattvas who equal in number the atoms contained in the thousand worlds. . . ." In Buddhist art the Bodhisattvas are portrayed crowned and loaded with jewels, whereas the Buddha himself, who is in the center, is simply adorned. Among the best-known Mahayana Bodhisattvas are Avalokiteshvara, Manjushri, Samantabhadra, Kshitigarbha, and Mahasthamaprapta. The term Bodhisattva also is used in the Pali texts for the Buddha before he reached his Enlightenment, and the term is applied in the Jatakas, folktales of the former existences of the Buddha.

Bodhi-Tree. In Buddhism, tree under which the Buddha gained Enlightenment. The tale of the tree is told in the *Mahabodhi-Vamsa* (The Great Bodhi Chronicle), written in the 11th century and ascribed to Upatissa. The tale tells of the various fortunes of the tree from before the time of the Buddha and after his Enlightenment. The tree is a specific example of the *pipal*, or sacred fig, a very common species in India, sacred to Hindus as a source of fertility and/or gnosis.

0604

Bogy. In English and Scottish folklore, a hobgoblin. The word appeared in use in the early 19th century and may be related to the Scottish word *bogle* and with the obsolete word *bug*.

0605

Bomazi. In African mythology (Bushongo of the Congo), lord of Bushongo, father of the male twins Woto and Moelo. Once the fair-skinned Bomazi told an old couple that they would bear a child. In time they had a daughter, whom Bomazi married. She bore him five sons, two of whom were the twins Woto and Moelo. Woto later became the founder of the Bushongo people.

0606

Bona Dea (the good goddess). In Roman mythology, the ancient Italian goddess, also called Fauna, who was patron of chastity and fruitfulness; married to Faunus, who was the only being who saw her after their marriage. Her worship was conducted by vestal virgins. The festival of the founding of her temple was held on 1 May. Prayers were then offered for the averting of earthquakes. A secret festival also was held in the house of the chief city official by matrons and vestal virgins on the nights of 3 and 4 May. The mistress of the house presided over the rites, from which men were barred. After offering a sacrifice of suckling pigs, the women performed a dance accompanied by stringed and wind instruments. In Roman art Bona Dea was portrayed with a scepter in her left hand, a wreath of vine leaves on her head, and a jar of wine at her side. Near her image was a consecrated serpent. Tame serpents were kept in her temple, located on the slope of the Aventine in Rome, and healing plants were preserved at her shrine. No men were allowed to enter. Cicero gave details of the rites when he wrote about his political archenemy, Clodius, notorious for sacrilege, attempting to take part in the secret rites dressed as a woman. Ovid's *Ars Amoris* also cites the goddess.

0607

Bonaventura, St. (good fortune). 1221–1274 C.E. In Christian legend, the Seraphic Doctor. Feast, 14 July.

0608

Born Giovanni Fidanga in Tuscany, he was so ill as a child that his mother took him to St. Francis of Assisi to be healed. When St. Francis saw him he said, "O, buona venturai" (Oh, good fortune). His mother then named the child Bonaventura and dedicated him to God. At 22 he became a Franciscan and went to Paris to study theology.

Legend says that when he did not come to receive Holy Communion, feeling himself unworthy, an angel brought it to him. Though he was known for his humility, he was greatly honored by St. Louis, king of France, and made general of the Franciscan order in 1256. Some years later he was made cardinal and bishop of Albano.

According to legend, when two nuncios came from Pope Gregory X to present him with the cardinal's hat, they found him in the garden of a convent near Florence, washing his plate after dinner. He told them to hang the hat on a tree until he had finished. The great council at Lyons (1274), held to reconcile the Greek and Latin churches, in which he took part, exhausted the saint, and he died shortly afterward. Some claim, however, that he was poisoned. He was buried in the Church of the Franciscans at Lyons. In 1562 Calvinists broke open his shrine and threw his ashes into the Saône.

In Christian art St. Bonaventura is shown in a Franciscan habit, sometimes wearing a miter or cardinal's hat, or with one hanging on a tree. Often he carries the Host (communion wafer), or an angel is giving one to him.

St. Boniface

Boniface, St. (of good fate). c. 675–754 C.E. In Christian legend, Apostle of Germany. Patron saint of brewers and tailors. Feast, 5 June.

0609

Born Winfred in Devonshire, England, he taught in a Benedictine abbey near Winchester. In his middle age he had a great desire to preach the gospel in Germany, and went to Rome to gain the support of Pope Gregory II. Here he changed his name to Boniface. He then started on his mission, visiting Thuringia, Bavaria, and Saxony. In 732 he was made primate of all Germany and soon afterward first bishop of Mainz. When he was 74, he was sent out on another missionary journey, carrying a copy of St. Ambrose's *De Bono Mortis* under his cloak. He got as far as Friesland, where he was murdered by some pagans. For centuries his bloodstained book was exhibited as a relic in Fulda.

In Christian art he is portrayed as a bishop—in one hand, a crosier and in the other, a book pierced by a sword. Sometimes he is shown baptizing a convert, with one foot on a fallen oak, the symbol of Druidism, which he overthrew by his preaching.

0610

Bonten. In Japanese Buddhist mythology, a god derived from the Hindu god Brahma, in art portrayed standing on a lotus leaf. He has three heads of equal size with three eyes each, surmounted by a smaller head with two eyes only. One hand holds a lotus; another, a trident; and a third, a drinking vessel. The fourth and last one is directed downward with open palm and fingers extended in the *mudra*, or gesture of charity. He is one of the Jiu No O, 12 Japanese gods and goddesses adopted from Hindu mythology.

0611

Book of the Dead, The. Popular title given to a collection of ancient Egyptian funerary texts composed for the benefit of the dead. The collection consists of incantations, hymns, prayers, and magic words and formulas that were found cut or painted on the walls of pyramids and tombs and on rolls of papyrus. The texts do not form a connected work, nor do they belong to any one period. They are miscellaneous in character and tell nothing of the lives or works of the dead with whom they are buried.

The Egyptians possessed many funerary works, but none of them bore a name that could be translated *The Book of the Dead*. This title was given in the early 19th century by tomb robbers, who discovered buried with the mummies rolls of papyrus, which they called *Kitâb al- Mayyit* (book of the dead man) or *Kitâb al-Mayyitun* (book of the dead). The robbers, however, knew nothing of the contents of the rolls; they were merely saying that what they found in the coffin was a "dead man's book."

0612

Boone, Daniel. 1734–1830. In American history and legend, a frontiersman. Boone began his life as a backwoods trailblazer, an agent for the Transylvania

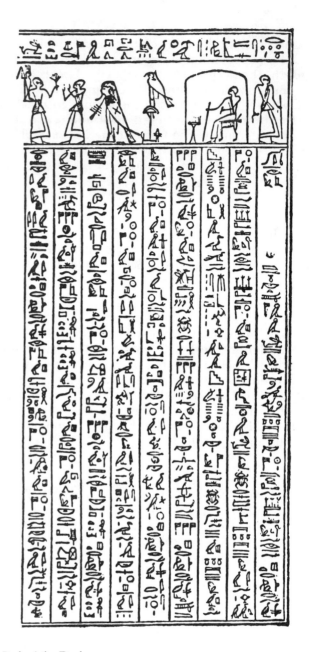

Book of the Dead

Company in Kentucky. He became a land speculator but lost many of his holdings and later moved westward to Missouri. His fame in American folklore began with the publication of John Filson's *Discovery, Settlement and Present State of Kentucky*, which was a supposedly autobiographical account of Boone's life. One legend says that in later years Boone kept a coffin under his bed, and when the mood came upon him, he would try it on for size. According to another legend, he died alone in the wilderness. In reality he died with his family around him. The state legislature of Missouri even wore mourning crepe for 20 days after his death. In art, a lithograph published by Currier & Ives portrayed Boone defending his family against an Indian attack. Charles F. Wimar's *The Abduction of Daniel Boone's Daughter* portrays his daughter Jemina being abducted by Chief Hanging Maw. Hollywood has used Boone's legend in *Daniel Boone, Young Daniel Boone*, and *Daniel Boone, Trail Blazer*, and television had a long running series, *Daniel Boone*, which began in 1964.

0613

Boorala. In Australian mythology, tribal name for a creator god. Those who are good go to Boorala's home when they die.

0614

Borak (lightning). In Islamic mythology, fabulous animal that the prophet Muhammad mounted on the night of his ascension to heaven.

The Koran (sura 17) tells of a vision the prophet had in which he was borne from Mecca to Jerusalem and then on to the various heavens. The animal that carried him is neither described nor named in the text. Islamic legend, however, has embellished the story, and *The Ascension of Muhammad* tells of the prophet's journey to the heavens. Borak is described as "smaller than a mule and larger than an ass, his face was like that of a human being, while his tail and hoofs were like those of a cow." (In another telling the tail and hoofs resembled a goat's.) "He had the rump of a horse, and carried an emerald green saddle, a harness of pearls, and turquoise stirrups." When Borak took a stride, it "was as far as the eye could reach."

In Islamic art the fabulous animal is often portrayed with the head of a veiled woman and a peacock's tail. His saddle is shown to pilgrims in the mosque of al-Sakhra in Jerusalem.

Variant spellings: Al Burak, Alborac, Al-borach and Al-Buraq.

0615

Borden, Lizzie. 1860–1927. In American history and legend, a woman accused of murdering her father and stepmother on 4 August 1892 in Fall River, Massachusetts. When Lizzie was brought to trial, she displayed little or no emotion over the event, but she was found innocent of the crime. However, a popular American ballad *Lizzie Borden* finds her guilty:

Lizzie Borden took an ax
And gave her mother forty whacks;
When she saw what she had done,
She gave her father forty-one.

Morton Gould's ballet *Fall River Legend* deals with the story in flashbacks, finally ending with Lizzie's hanging for murder.

Boreas carrying off Orithyia

0616

Boreas (north wind, devouring). In Greek mythology, the North Wind; son of Astraea and Eos, brother of the Winds, Zephyrus, Eurus, and Notus; called Aquilo in Roman mythology. His home was in the Thracian Salmydessus on the Black Sea. He carried off and raped Orithyia after her father Erechtheus, king of Athens, had refused to give her to Boreas in marriage. Their children were Calais and Zetes, the Boreadae; Cleopatra, the wife of Phineus; and Chione, the beloved of Poseidon. Vergil's *Aeneid* (books 10, 12) cite Boreas, as does Shakespeare's *Troilus and Cressida* (1.3.37) In Western Renaissance art, Boreas appears in allegories of the Four Seasons as the personification of Winter. He is shown as an old man with flowing gray locks and wings.

0617

Bori. In Australian mythology, invisible spirit who kills his victims by injecting them with incurable diseases.

0618

Boris and Gleb, SS. (fight). 11th century C.E. In Christian legend, martyrs. In Russia patrons of brotherly love and devotion. Feast, 24 July.

They were the sons of St. Vladimir, ruler of Kiev. At Vladmir's death the throne was to be divided among them and their elder brother, Sviatopolk. The elder brother, however, decided he wanted the throne for himself and planned the murder of both of his brothers. As the *Primary Chronicle* or *The Tale of Bygone Years*, compiled by various hands from about 1040 to 1118, tells it, Sviatopolk "was filled with lawlessness," and he hired men to kill Boris. Boris was attacked and wrapped in a canvas, loaded into a wagon, and dragged off, though "he was still alive." A knife was then plunged into his heart. His brother Gleb was attacked by Sviatopolk's men, but Gleb's cook, fearful he would be killed, murdered Gleb to appease the assassins.

From about 1200 the two saints were honored in the Cathedral of St. Sophia at Constantinople, where their icon stood to the right of the altar at which the Byzantine emperors were consecrated. In Russia the saints were extremely popular and frequently painted on icons. In a 13th-century icon of the Moscow school, the two saints hold swords, crosses and emblems of their rank. The two are usually dressed alike but in different colors.

Boris Godunov. 1552–1605. In Russian history and legend, czar of Russia who became part of Russian legend because of his supposed murder of Ivan IV's younger son, Dmitri.

Boris came to the throne in 1598, having been regent since 1584. Ivan IV's son Dmitri had been banished to the upper Volga, where he died. It was believed he had been murdered by order of Boris. A pretender, claiming to be Dmitri, said he had escaped the assassins and was the rightful heir to the throne. Supported by an advancing army, Dmitri was crowned in 1605, but Boris died suddenly, avoiding a dethronement.

Influenced by the legend of Boris and by his reading of Shakespeare, Pushkin wrote a dramatic play, *Boris Godunov*, which was later used by Moussorgsky for his opera *Boris Godunov*. The opera is considered one of the cornerstones of Russian and modern opera, and is performed in numerous musical arrangements, the best-known being Rimsky-Korsakov's 1908 version.

Borvo (boil). In Celtic mythology, a god who presided over healing hot springs and health resorts in central France. He was identified by ancient Roman writers with their god Apollo; he was called Bormanus in Provence and Bormanious in Portugal. Borve, the king in Celtic mythology whose children were turned into swans by his evil second wife, Aeife, is believed to be derived from the god.

Variant spelling: Bormo.

Boyde, Rebel Belle. 1844–1900. In American history and Civil War folklore, a Southern woman whose charm captivated the Yankees. When she killed a Yankee soldier who, she said, was attacking her mother, the Yankee captain not only thought what she did was honorable but gave her a small revolver so she could better protect her mother and herself in the future. Belle was courted by Union soldiers but spied on them, finally being arrested in 1862 and escorted to jail by nearly In prison she gained the

friendship of all of the jailers and was out in a month. She wrote *Belle Boyde in Camp and Prison* and gave lectures on her Civil War adventures.

Bragi (to shine, leader). In Norse mythology, Aesir god of eloquence and poetry; son of Odin and Gunlod; married to Iduna. Some scholars believe that Bragi might be a deified ninth-century poet named Bragi Boddason or merely another name for Odin, chief of the gods, since both Odin and Bragi are called Long-Bearded. Both are associated with the cult of the dead. When a king died, a feast was held and a cup, called Bragarfull (cup of Bragi), was drunk from in his honor. Each guest pledged some great deed at the time. Some connect Bragi's name with the English "to brag." Northern poets were often called Braga-men and priestesses Braga-women. Bragi was portrayed as an elderly man with a long white beard, holding a harp. At the sound of his music trees bloomed. Bragi greeted the slain heroes in Valhalla.

Brahma

Brahma (swelling, growth). In Hinduism, creator god in the triad of deities called Trimorti, including also Vishnu and Shiva.

Brahma in present-day Hinduism is often called the first of the gods, the framer of the universe, and the guardian of the world. In the ancient *Vedas*, however, he is not named; there the creator is called Hiranya-garbha (the golden egg) or Prajapati (lord of creatures). Prajapati was later used as a title for Brahma and also for his sons, who in Hindu mythology are progenitors of the human race.

Various accounts, which differ considerably, are given of Brahma's origin. In the Hindu epic poem *The*

Mahabharata Brahma is said to have issued from the lotus that sprang from the navel of the god Vishnu. In another text Brahma is said to have lived in a cosmic egg for 1,000 years and then burst out. Seeing that the earth was sunk beneath the waters, Brahma assumed the form of a boar (in later Hindu writings the role is assigned to Vishnu in one of his avatars, or incarnations) and diving, raised the earth on his tusks. After this Brahma continued the work of creation. Concerning this role as supreme creator of the universe, Ralph Waldo Emerson wrote in his poem *Brahma*:

> If the red slayer think he slays,
> Or if the slain think he is slain,
> They know not well the subtle ways
> I keep, and pass, and turn again.
> Far or forgot to me is near;
> Shadow and sunlight are the same;
> The vanished gods to me appear;
> And one to me are shame and fame.
> They reckon ill who leave me out;
> When me they fly, I am the wings;
> I am the doubter and the doubt,
> And I the hymn the Brahmin sings.
> The strong gods pine for my abode,
> And pine in vain the sacred Seven;
> But thou, meek lover of the good!
> Find me, and turn thy back on heaven.

Emerson was questioned about the meaning of his poem because many readers were upset by the imagery and reference to an alien god. He said to his daughter: "Tell them to say Jehovah instead of Brahma."

Numerous myths are told of the god in various Hindu texts. Once Brahma, as Apava (who sports in the waters), formed two beings from his body—a male, Viraj, and a female, Shatarupa (the hundred-formed). After creating Shatarupa, Brahma lusted for her. "How beautiful you are," he said to his daughter.

Shatarupa turned to avoid Brahma's lustful look, but the god sprouted a second head. As she passed to the left, two other heads appeared. At last Shatarupa sprang up to the sky, and Brahma grew yet another head to view her. Shatarupa then came down, and the two made love, producing offspring that later populated the earth. She was then made Brahma's wife.

Brahma, however, did not keep his fifth head, for it was cut off by the god Shiva. Once when the holy sages were assembled at Brahma-pura, the heavenly city of Brahma on Mount Meru, they asked Brahma to display his true nature. Brahma, influenced by delusion brought on him by a demon and obscured by spiritual darkness (both gods and people in

Hindu mythology often share the same virtues and faults), said: "I am the womb of the universe, without the beginning or end, and the sole and self-existent lord; and he who does not worship me shall never attain beatitude."

On hearing this reply Kratus (a form of the god Vishnu) smiled and said: "Had thou not been misled by ignorance, thou would not have made an assertion contrary to truth; for I am the framer of the universe, the source of life, the unborn, eternal and supreme. Had I not willed it, creation would not have taken place."

The two gods then fought, finally agreeing to let the sacred writings, the *Vedas*, decide the issue. The *Vedas* declared that Shiva was the creator, preserver, and destroyer. Shiva then appeared and Brahma's fifth head asked Shiva to worship him. Shiva then assumed a horrible form and cut off Brahma's fifth head with the thumb of his left hand.

Brahma is also called Srashtri (creator), Ka (who), Dhatri and Bidhatri (sustainer), Pitamaha (the great father), Lokesa (lord of the world), Parameshta (supreme in heaven), Adikavi (the first poet), Drughana (the ax, the mallet), and Hiranya-garbha (the golden egg), referring to the myth that Brahma "continued a year in the egg" and then "divided it into two parts by his mere thought, and with these two shells he formed the heavens and the earth."

The four mind-born sons of Brahma are Sanaka (the ancient), Sananda (joyous), Sanatana (eternal), and Sanatkumara (eternally a youth).

0624

Brahman (swelling, growth). A term used in Hinduism for ultimate reality, as well as for the priestly caste.

Brahman is a neuter term (the masculine form is Brahma, which is also the name of the Hindu god but is distinct from the term *Brahma*). It refers to the sacred powers implicit in and created through sacrificial ritual by the priests who are called Brahmans. A Brahman is believed to be a god. In the sacred book *Satapatha Brahmana* a Brahman is defined thus: "There are two kinds of gods; first the gods, then those who are Brahmans, and have learnt the *Veda* and repeat it: they are human gods." Of course, this sentence was written by a Brahman and was used to reinforce his authority and position in Indian society. Some Hindu texts equate the terms *Brahman* and *Atman*, both being used for "ultimate reality" or "world spirit."

The term *Brahmin* in English and American literature has come to mean a socially exclusive person who considers himself better than those not of his own class. It was applied to many rich families in New England during the 19th century, and the term *Boston Brahmin* is still occasionally heard.

0625

Bran. In Celtic mythology, god who presided over poetry and, according to some scholars, was lord of the underworld in Welsh mythology because his totem was a crow or raven, both connected with death. Bran, according to myth, invaded Ireland to redress a wrong done by King Matholwch, who was married to Branwen, sister of Bran and goddess of love. When he and his host of men were defeated, his head was cut off, carried to White Tower Hill in London and buried with the eyes looking toward France, as a spell against foreign invasion. King Arthur, according to medieval legend, unearthed the head, which was called Uther Ben (wonderful head), saying Britain would remain a power by virtue of her own strength. In some medieval Christian legends Bran is transformed into Bran the Blessed and credited with bringing Christianity to Britain. Bran appears under various names in medieval lore, among them Brandegore, Sir Brandel, and Ban of Belwik Leodegrance.

0626

Branwen. In Celtic mythology, goddess of love, wife of King Matholwch and sister of Bran, god of poetry.

0627

Breidalblick (broad blink, wide glancing). In Norse mythology, the palace of the god Baldur, who was murdered by a scheme of the evil god Loki. Matthew Arnold, in his narrative poem *Balder Dead*, describes the palace where engraved on the columns were "enchantments that recall the dead to life."

Variant spelling: Breithablik.

0628

Brendan, St. (stinking hair, dweller by the beacon?). Sixth century C.E. In Christian legend, patron saint of seafarers and travelers. Feast, 16 May.

The best-known legend of St. Brendan concerns his fantastic voyage to find the Earthly Paradise, narrated in the *Navigatio Sancti Brendani*. The work, which appeared in numerous European languages during the Middle Ages, is filled with adventures, many based on earlier Irish pagan sagas, such as *The Voyage of Bran*. Before St. Brendan reaches the Earthly Paradise, which is an island, he encounters on his way the arch-traitor Judas on a lonely rock on Christmas night. Here Judas is allowed to cool himself on certain feast days for the one kind act he performed during his life. The episode inspired Matthew Arnold's poem *St. Brandan*, in which the poet changes the rock to an iceberg and Judas's relief to but one hour annually at Christmas. Dante is

believed to have read one version of the voyages of the saint before writing *The Divine Comedy*. Maps as late as the 18th century marked St. Brendan's Island, or the Earthly Paradise, to the west of Ireland, inspiring many Spanish and Portuguese expeditions to go in search of the island.

0629

Br'er Fox. In American folklore, the wily fox of Joel Chandler Harris's *Uncle Remus: His Songs and His Sayings*. One fable tells how Br'er Fox outwitted and ate Ole Sis Goose. Br'er Fox caught Ole Sis Goose sailing on his lake and said he would take her to court and then eat her. She protested. But when they arrived at court, the sheriff, the judge, and all of the jury were foxes. "And they tried Ole Sis Goose and convicted her and executed her and they picked her bones," the fable ends. Br'er Fox appears in Walt Disney's movie *Song of the South* (1947), which combines live actors and cartoon animation.

0630

Br'er Rabbit. In American folklore, the trickster rabbit of Joel Chandler Harris's *Uncle Remus: His Songs and His Sayings*. In Harris's tales Br'er Rabbit always outwits Br'er Fox and most of the other dull-witted animals. The most famous tale, variants of which are found in African folklore, is that of the tar baby with which Br'er Fox traps Br'er Rabbit by molding a life-size doll out of tar and placing it in Br'er Rabbit's way. When the tar baby doesn't answer Br'er Rabbit's greeting, he becomes annoyed and slaps the creature. His hand sticks to the tar baby, and in his effort to free himself by kicking and hitting it, he becomes completely entangled. Br'er Fox, pondering the cruelest fate for his captive, is begged by Br'er Rabbit to do anything to him except "please don't throw me in the briar patch." Br'er Fox then tosses Br'er Rabbit into the briar patch, thinking it the fate Br'er Rabbit dreads most. As Br'er Rabbit scampers away to freedom he calls back to Br'er Fox, "I was born and raised in the briar patch." Br'er Rabbit appears in Walt Disney's movie *Song of the South* (1947), which combines live actors and cartoon animation.

0631

Bress (beautiful). In Celtic mythology, a sun god; son of Fomer and Eri, air goddess; married to Brigit; king of the Tuatha de Danann, the good people descended from the goddess Danu (Anu). Though handsome, he was disliked because he oppressed his people with labor and high taxes. Eventually he was murdered.

0632

Brewins. In Australian mythology, invisible evil spirits who cause disease. They can be driven away by a medicine man, who uses foul language against them and sucks the parts of the victim's body that have been attacked.

Brian (strong). In Celtic mythology, a wind god or god of knowledge, son of Tuirenn and Danu or Buan Ann, brother of Iuchon and Iuchurba. The tree brothers married three princesses, Banbha, Eire, and Fodhla.

0633

St. Bridget (Dürer)

0634

Bridget of Sweden, St. (the high one, strength) d. 1373 C.E. In Christian legend, mystical writer, founder of Brigittine Order. Feast, 8 October.

Daughter of a wealthy family in Sweden, she married at 13 (not uncommon for the time) and had eight children. She made a journey to the shrine of St. James at Compostela with her husband. At his death she founded a monastery at Wastein for 60 nuns and 24 monks under the rule of St. Augustine. In 1349 she went to Rome to obtain confirmation for her order from the pope. She also traveled to the Holy Land. Her most famous work, *Revelations*, about the Birth and Passion of Christ, had a deep influence on Christian symbolism and art.

In Christian art she is shown as an abbess holding a crosier. She may have a pilgrim's staff with wallet in reference to her journeys to the Holy Land, or a book and pen for her mystical writings. Sometimes she is shown with a candle, which according to legend, she let drip on her hand to imitate the wounds of Christ.

0635

Brigit (the high one, strength). In Celtic mythology, goddess of knowledge, fire, the hearth, and poetry. Brigit is a culture goddess, her name being found in various forms throughout Britain as well as the Continent. When the Irish became Christian, Brigit was, according to some scholars, metamorphosed into Saint Brigit. Her sacred shrine at Kildare was guarded by 19 nuns, and men were not permitted to enter. Among some of the variant names by which the goddess was known in Celtic mythology are Berecyntia, Briganta, and Brigindo.

Variant spellings: Brigid, Brid, Bride, Bridget, Brigindo.

0636

Brigit, St. (the high one, strength). Seventh century C.E. In Christian legend, abbess of Kildare. Feast, 1 February.

Brigit was born at Faughart, near Dundalk, a few years after St. Patrick arrived on his mission to convert the Irish. One day, after milking the cows, Brigit gave the contents of her pail to some poor people who were passing. Then realizing that her mother would be angry at her for giving away the milk, Brigit asked God to make good the loss. On reaching home Brigit's milk pail was found to be full.

According to another medieval legend, she once sat with a blind nun, Dara. They talked and the night passed and the sun rose. Brigit passed her hands over the eyes of Dara, and the nun gained her sight. The nun looked around and then said to Brigit, "Close my eyes again, dear Mother, for when the world is so visible, God is seen less clearly to the soul."

Brigit was called the Mary of Gael because one monk said he had seen a vision of the Virgin Mary, who said she would appear to him again the next day. When he happened to see Brigit, he called out that she was the woman he had seen in his vision.

Some legends attached to the saint derive from her namesake, Brigit, the pagan Celtic goddess of knowledge, fire, the hearth and poetry. When the Irish became Christian, they transferred some of the tales of the goddess to the saint.

0637

Brihaspati (lord of sacred speech). In Hindu mythology, originally an epithet of Indra, or Agni. It later evolved into a separate god who instructed the other gods; he is equated with the planet Jupiter. A myth records how his wife, Tara, was kidnapped and raped by the moon god Soma and later bore a son, Budha (wise), who is the planet Mercury.

0638

Brimir (the bloody moisture). In Norse mythology, a giant, sometimes believed to be identical with the primeval giant Ymir. In the *Grimnismal*, one of the poems of the *Poetic Edda*, Brimir is the name of a sword.

0639

Britomartis (sweet maid?). In Greek mythology, a Cretan goddess, daughter of Zeus and Carme (or Charme or Leto). Britomartis was often identified with the goddess Artemis, patroness of hunters, fishermen, and sailors, and she also was goddess of birth and chastity. In her role as sea goddess Britomartis was called Dictynna (lady of the net?). Minos loved her and pursued her for nine months. Britomartis leaped into the sea from a high rock to avoid his advances. According to one myth she was saved by Artemis, who caught her in a net. Artemis then made Britomartis a goddess. In Aegina she was known as Aphaea.

0640

Brizo (charmer, soother). In Greek mythology, a goddess worshiped at Delos and honored by women as the protector of mariners. Food offerings (no fish) were set before the goddess in little boats. Brizo presided over an oracle that was consulted on matters relating to navigation and fishing. The answers were given in dreams.

0641

Brok (hunchback). In Norse mythology, dwarf, brother of Sindri. Brok blew the bellows for the dwarf sons of Sindri, who were the gold workers. Loki, the evil god, tormented him by taking the form of a fly and buzzing around him. Brok appears in the *Prose Edda*.

Variant spelling: Brokk.

0642

Brontes (thunder). In Greek and Roman mythology, son of Uranus and Gaea; one of the three Cyclopes, the other two being Arges (the lightning bolt) and Steropes (the lightning flash).

0643

Brownie. In Celtic mythology, a Scottish goblin, who may have earlier been some Celtic god. At night he is supposed to busy himself on little jobs for the family over which he presides. Brownies are brown or tawny spirits. In England they are called Robin Goodfellow or Puck.

0644

Brown, John. 1800–1859. In American history and folklore, an abolitionist. The most famous episode in Brown's life is his raid on Harper's Ferry, now in West Virginia, on 16 October 1859 when he and 21 followers crossed the Potomac and captured the U.S. Arsenal. Eventually Brown was caught and hanged on 2 December 1859. His courage and devotion to freeing the slaves had great impact on American folklore. One of the most popular Civil War ballads was "John Brown's Body," which is also the title of Stephen Vincent Benét's long narrative poem. Whittier's poem *John Brown of Osawatomie* also deals with the man, as does Edmund Stedman's *How Old Brown Took Harper's Ferry* and Leonard Ehrlich's novel *God's Angry Man*.

0645

Bruce, Robert. 1272–1329. In Scottish history and legend, national hero, crowned Robert I at Scone in 1306. He died of leprosy. He appears in numerous legends as a hero. The most famous tale deals with a spider. While lying concealed from the English on the island of Rathlin, Bruce one day watched a spider making repeated attempts to attach its web to a ceiling beam. At last the spider succeeded in its task. Encouraged by this example, Bruce left the island in 1307, landed at Carrick with some followers, and drove the English from Scotland. His life is told in the epic poem *The Bruce* by John Barbour, written about 1375.

0646

Bruno, St. (brown). c. 1033–1101. In Christian legend, founder of the Order of Carthusians. Invoked against carbuncles. Feast, 6 October.

Born in Cologne, St. Bruno became chancellor of the diocese of Rheims but left after denouncing the archbishop for simony. With six companions he opted for the solitude of La Chartreuse in the mountains near Grenoble, where he founded the first Carthusian community. St. Bruno was never formally canonized but his feast was extended to the whole Latin church in 1674.

Though his life is not filled with miracles, Bruno has been painted frequently. Some scenes portray the death of Raymond Diocres, Bruno's teacher, who said on his deathbed, "By the justice of God, I am condemned." This statement, according to various accounts, made a deep impression on the saint. Other scenes portray St. Bruno praying in the desert of the Grande Chartreuse, refusing a bishopric, and dying surrounded by monks of his order.

0647

Brut (heavy). In British mythology, the first king of the Britons, son of Sylvins, grandson of Ascanius and great-grandson of Aeneas, the Trojan hero. The name Britain is derived from Brut (Brute). At 15, according to the myth, Brut accidentally killed his father with an arrow while out hunting. Banished from his home, he sought refuge in Greece with a band of Trojan exiles. After several encounters with the Greeks, Brut captured the Greek king. In exchange for his freedom the Greek king offered Brut his daughter Imogen. After the marriage Brut and his men set sail, arriving at a deserted island, where Brut saw the ruins of the Temple of Diana and called on her for guidance. She answered him, telling him there was an island past the realms of Gaul in which he was to settle with his people. The island was Britain, which Brut and his army settled. Brut had *Trojanova* (new Troy) built, which later became London. He was the progenitor of a host of kings— Bladud, Gorboduc, Ferrex, Porrex, Lud, Cymbeline, Coel (Cole), Vortigern, and Arthur. Brut's myth is told in Layamon's *The Brut*, written between 1189 and 1205.

0648

Brutus, Lucius Junius. 509 B.C.E. In Roman history and legend, the first consul of Rome, who is said to have held office in 509 B.C.E. Brutus condemned to death his own sons for joining a conspiracy to restore the banished Tarquin to the throne. Brutus was, according to James Thomson in his poem, *Winter* (1726- 1730):

The public father who the private quelled,
And on the dread tribunal sternly sat.

The Italian dramatist Alfieri wrote a play on the subject in 1783, and Rembrandt painted the scene, as did David in his neoclassical style.

0649

Brutus, Marcus Junius. 85–42 B.C.E. In Roman history and legend, Julius Caesar's friend, perhaps his natural son. Brutus joined the conspiracy to murder Caesar. He committed suicide after his defeat in battle at Philippi. Shakespeare, in *Julius Caesar*, calls Brutus "the noblest Roman of them all." Dante, seeing Brutus differently, placed him, along with Cassius and Judas Iscariot, in the lowest circle of Hell in *The Divine Comedy* (Inferno, canto 34).

Brynhild

0650

Brynhild (warrior in coat of mail). In Norse mythology, a Valkyrie, daughter of Odin. Brynhild appears in numerous Northern legends and myths. In the *Volsunga Saga* she is chief of the Valkyries. When she disobeys Odin by siding with Sigmund (Sigurd's father), Odin punishes her by putting her to sleep surrounded by a ring of fire. Only a hero brave enough to ride through the flames could awaken her, a feat accomplished by Sigurd. On waking she fell in love with the hero, and he gave her a magic ring. Sigurd then rode off to the land of the Nibelungs. Here he was given a magic drink that made him forget his love for Brynhild, and he married Gudrun. In time he urged his brother-in-law Gunnar to seek the hand of Brynhild. Gunnar made two attempts but failed to break through the circle of fire. Sigurd, disguised as Gunnar, rode again through the fire and received from Brynhild the magic ring he had previously given her. Thinking it was Gunnar who had broken the ring of fire to reach her, she married him and plotted Sigurd's death. After his death, however, she was overcome with remorse, killed herself, and was burned on Sigurd's funeral pyre.

The Germanic *Nibelungenlied*, in which she is called Brunhild, recounts her story differently. Gudrun is called Kriemhild, Gunnar is known as Gunther, and Sigurd is called Siegfried. The events are more elaborately drawn out and the tragic elements form an important part of the work.

Richard Wagner, in his four music dramas, *Der Ring des Nibelungen*, for the most part uses the names in the *Nibelungenlied*; however, he generally follows the plot of the *Volsunga Saga*. Arthur Rackham portrays Brynhild in his illustrations for Wagner's Ring Cycle.

Variant spellings: Brünnhilde; Brunhild; Brunhilda.

0651

Bucephalus (bull-headed). In Greek history and legend, the horse of Alexander the Great. Plutarch, in his *Parallel Lives*, tells the legend of how the horse was given to Alexander by his father, Philip of Macedon, because the boy was the only person who could tame the animal. Bucephalus died after the battle of Hydaspes (326 B.C.E.) and was buried with honors. The city of Bucephala (modern day Jhelum in Pakistan) was named after the horse.

0652

Buchis. In Egyptian mythology, the sacred bull worshiped at Hermonthis, believed to be an incarnation of the war god Menthu.

Variant spellings: Bacis, Bkha.

0653

Buddhas (enlightened ones). In Buddhism, those who have achieved *Bodhi* (Enlightenment). Aside from the historical Buddha, Gotama, there are, according to Theravadias, numerous other Buddhas who existed before the historical Buddha and Buddhas who will come. The Mahayanists believe in an infinite number of Buddhas. The *Aparimita-Dharani* says, "The Buddhas who have been, are, and will be, are more numerous than the grains of sand on the banks of the Ganges." In Nepal, for example, there was a system where some 1,000 Buddhas were honored. However, the number is greatly reduced in some other Buddhist mythologies. There is a group of 25, beginning with Dipankara Buddha and ending with the historical Buddha, Gotama. Sometimes the last 7 of the 25 are recognized as the Principal Buddhas, with the Buddha Maitreya (the Buddha of the Future) as number 8, a sacred number of the Buddhists.

All Buddhists believe in the existence of numerous Buddhas. Theravadias hold that there is only one Buddha at a time; Mahayanists hold to the simultaneous existence of many Buddhas in different world systems.

Buddha

0654

Buddha, The (enlightened one; awakened one). c. 566–486 B.C.E. Title of Siddhartha Gautama (he whose aim is accomplished; of the lineage of Gotama), founder of Buddhism.

Most scholars accept the fact that Siddhartha Gautama was a historical person, and as in the case of Jesus, that many mythical and legendary events have been attached to the historical being, making it impossible to disentangle history from myth and legend. The events in the Buddha's life are usually arranged in a set order, as depicted in literature and art.

The first event is Maya's Dream. Maya was the mother of the future Buddha. She is portrayed as a woman asleep on a couch, with a small white elephant, sometimes ridden by a child, coming down to impregnate her.

The next event is the Buddha's birth. When Maya was ready to give birth, she asked her husband, Shuddhodana, "to send her home to her parents; and Shuddhodana, anxious about his wife and the child she would bear him, willingly granted her request. While she passed through the gardens of Lumbini, the hour arrived; her couch was placed under a lofty satin-tree and the child came forth from the womb like the rising sun, bright and perfect."

This event is usually portrayed in Buddhist art as a woman standing with one hand against a tree trunk, while an attendant receives the child from Maya's side. Sometimes accompanying the Buddha's birth is his bath, in which the Nagas make a screen for the child's back. Occasionally the scene will show a small bathtub or fountain near the child.

The next event is the Buddha's First Seven Steps. This scene portrays the infant pacing forward to each of the cardinal points to which he had announced the end of birth, old age, sickness, and death. Each place is marked by a lotus flower. Being a prince, the future Buddha had to marry when he became a young man. For his wife he chose Yashodhara, his cousin. Their union produced a son, Rahula.

The Four Encounters are the next episode often portrayed in Buddhist art and literature. All the happiness one could expect was enjoyed by the prince. "All sorrowful sights, all misery, and all knowledge of misery were kept away from Siddhartha, and he knew not that was evil in the world," according to the Buddhist texts. But the prince ventured out on four occasions to meet for the first time old age (a man leaning on a staff), sickness (a man lying in a bed), death (a man in a shroud), and finally poverty (a man shorn and shaved carrying an alms bowl). These encounters changed his outlook. He said, "I see everywhere the impression of change; therefore, my heart is heavy. Men grow old, sicken, and die. This is enough to take away the zest of life."

The next main event in the Buddha's life is called the Great Renunciation. Buddhist art often portrays this as the prince mounted on his horse Kantaka, riding away from the city with his servant Chandaka. "Thus," say the Buddhist texts, "the prince renounced worldly pleasures, gave up his kingdom, severed all ties, and went into homelessness." Sometimes Buddhist art portrays the scene of the future Buddha sending his horse or his servant back to his home at Kapilavastu. The horse is often shown kneeling before the future Buddha.

The future Buddha than went in search of a system to free himself. He practiced intense mortification but found it futile. He then sat himself underneath the Bodhi Tree and was attacked by Mara, who was supreme god of desire, and thus evil for one seeking release from desire. The scene portrays the future Buddha seated under the Bodhi Tree with demons on either side of him. Along with the demons are beautiful women, meant to seduce the future Buddha from his aim; however, he remains unmoved. Often the future Buddha is portrayed in the *bhumisparsa mudra*, or the earth-touching gesture. It shows his arm fully extended, his hand palm downward with the tips of the fingers just touching the earth. It symbolizes the call to witness of the earth goddess of the future Buddha's right to sit under the Bodhi Tree, the Tree of Wisdom.

Having defeated Mara, the Future Buddha became a Buddha, and Enlightened One. He saw the Four Noble Truths: (1) existence is unhappiness; (2) unhappiness is caused by desire; (3) desire and craving can be overcome by (4) following the Eightfold Path.

The Eightfold Path is (1) right understanding; (2) right purpose; (3) right speech; (4) right acts; (5) right way of earning a livelihood; (6) right efforts; (7) right thoughts; (8) right concentration or the right state of a peaceful mind.

The Buddha then went out to make disciples for his belief. The next episode in the Buddha's life is called Preaching the Law or the Sermon in the Deer Park at Benares. Gathered around him were men who at first came to laugh at the Buddha. But as they listened to his discourse, they were converted. In traditional Buddhist texts the following are examples from the sermon:

> The spokes of the wheel are the rules of pure conduct; justice is the uniformity of their length; wisdom is the tire; modesty and thoughtfulness are the hub in which the immovable axle of truth is fixed. . . .
>
> He who recognizes the existence of suffering, its cause, its remedy, and its cessation has fathomed the four noble truths. He will walk in the right path. . . .
>
> Right views will be the torch to light his way. Right aims will be his guide. Right words will be his dwelling-place on the road. His gait will be straight, for it is right behavior. . . .
>
> Whatsoever is originated will be dissolved again. All worry about the self is vain; the ego is like a mirage, and all the tribulations that touch it will pass away. They will vanish like a nightmare when the sleeper awakes. . . .

He who has awakened is freed from fear; he has become Buddha; he knows the vanity of all his cares, his ambitions, and also of his pains. . . .

Happy is he who has overcome all selfishness; happy is he who has attained peace, happy is he who has found the truth. . . .

The truth is noble and sweet; the truth can deliver you from evil. There is no savior in the world except the truth.

Buddha preaching the law

In Buddhist art the Preaching of the Law (Dharma) usually portrays the Buddha seated with his hands in the *dharmacakra mudra*. The hands are together before the breast; the index finger of the left hand touches the right hand, the finger and thumb of which are joined at the tip. Sometimes called "Turning the Wheel of the Law," the gesture is symbolic of the Buddha's preaching. The Buddha may be seated on a lotus throne or supported by lions. There also may be a pair of deer, symbolic of the Deer Park.

The last scene or episode in the Buddha's life often is that of the *Parinirvana* (complete disappearance). It portrays the Buddha apparently asleep, sometimes with mourning figures around him. After the Buddha's death his body was burned, and the relics were recovered for his followers. An ordinary person's cremation is believed to leave only ashes. A holy person's, according to Buddhist belief, leaves spherical crystalline objects, *sharira* (body), suitable for veneration.

The historical Buddha (anyone who follows the Eightfold Path can become a Buddha) is often called

Shakyamuni (The Holy One of the Shakyas)—his clan name plus *muni*, which means holy man or monk. One of the few titles applied by the Buddha to himself was Bhagavat (the Blessed One).

Buddha's death

0655

Bue. In Micronesian mythology, culture hero of the Gilbert Islands who ascended to the sky and brought back fire to humankind. Bue also taught people how to construct boats and houses and to sing and dance.

0656

Buffalo Bill. 1846–1917. In American history and legend, the popular name of William Frederick Cody, scout and showman. Born in Iowa, Buffalo Bill's family moved West, where he had various jobs as "herder, hunter, pony express rider, stage driver, wagon master in the quartermaster's department, and scout of the army," to quote from his press agent. In 1883 he organized Buffalo Bill's Wild West show, which increased his reputation, as did a series of dime novels by Prentise Ingraham that totaled nearly 200. More a product of publicity than of folklore, the hero appears in two Hollywood films. *Buffalo Bill* and *Buffalo Bill and the Indians, or Sitting Bull's History Lesson*, in which Buffalo Bill and his friends discuss his legend and life.

0657

Buga (god). In Siberian mythology, creator god among the Transbaikal Tungus. Buga took materials from the four quarters of the earth. The east supplied

him with iron; the south, with fire; the west, with water; and the north, with earth. Out of the earth he created flesh and bones for the first two people; out of the iron, the heart; out of the water, blood; and out of fire, warmth.

0658

Bulla (a round swelling). In Roman cult, a round or heart-shaped box containing an amulet, worn around the neck by freeborn Roman children. To wear a golden *bulla* was originally a privilege of the patricians but later was extended to rich and distinguished nonpatrician families. Leather *bulloe* were worn by children of poor families and of freedmen (former slaves). Boys ceased to wear the *bulla* when they assumed the *toga virilis*. The *bulla* was then dedicated to the Lares, household gods, and hung up over the hearth. Girls, it is believed, removed the *bulla* at marriage. It was sometimes worn by adults on special occasions as a protection against the evil eye.

0659

Bumba. In African mythology (Bushong of the Congo), creator god; a gigantic white being in human form.

Bumba existed alone in the universe when there was nothing but water. One day he felt severe internal stomach pains and vomited up the sun, moon, and stars, thus giving light to the world. The heat from the sun's rays dried up the water, and sand banks began to appear. Bumba then vomited up eight living creatures: a leopard, a crested eagle, a crocodile, a small fish, a tortoise, a white heron, a beetle, and a goat. Then Bumba created humankind, among whom were three of his sons. The human race was given laws and customs to follow as well as rulers. When Bumba felt he had finished his work, he left for his home in the sky. Now he communicates with men through dreams and visions.

0660

Bunjil. In Australian mythology, creator sky god and culture hero. According to one version of the creation myth, Bunjil formed rivers, trees, plants, and hills from the bare land. At first there were only animals; then Bunjil created the first men out of clay. His brother, the Bat, created woman from the mud in the depths of the water. After the creation, Bunjil taught the people the sacred rites and customs, then left for his home in the sky. In Australian ground reliefs Bunjil is portrayed as a man with a large phallus and a mouth filled with a quartz crystal. Though Bunjil is one of the most common names for the creator god in Australia, other names also are assigned to him, such as Daramulum, Baiame, Nurrundere, or Ngurunderi. As Daramulum, he is said to be the son of Baiame and the husband of Ngalalbal. In Daramulum's creation myth he leaves the earth after a great flood and returns to the sky.

Bunyip. 0661 In Australian mythology, an evil water monster who lives in mud at the bottoms of lakes. He pulls his victims down and drowns them.

Burkhan. 0662 In Siberian mythology, a creator god in a myth told by the Buriat. Burkhan created a man completely covered by hair but in need of a soul or spirit to bring him to life. Burkhan left a dog to guard the body while he went off to heaven to fetch the soul. The dog, tricked by Shulman, the devil, let the devil remove all of the hair from man's body except for certain parts. If the devil had not touched man, he would never get sick.

Variant spelling: Burkhan-Bakshi.

Busiris 0663 (grave of Osiris). In Greek mythology, a king of Egypt, the son of Poseidon and Lysianassa, a daughter of Epaphus. According to one myth, Busiris, country had been in the midst of a nine-year series of crop failures when Phrasius of Cyprus, a prophet, told Busiris to sacrifice a stranger every year to Zeus. The king made Phrasius the first sacrificial victim. When Heracles came to Egypt during his quest for the apples of the Hesperides, he allowed himself to be bound and taken to the altar as a victim. Then he broke his bonds and killed Busiris, as well as the king's son Amphidamas and all of his followers.

Bussumarus 0664 (the large-lipped). In Celtic mythology, a god, worshiped by the continental Celts, identified by ancient Roman writers with their god Jupiter.

Bustan, The 0665 (the orchard). Didactic poem, consisting of numerous fables, by the Persian poet Sadi, written in 1257.

The Bustan is a mystical book by a Sufi poet consisting of "dissertations of Justice, good government, beneficence, earthly and mystic love, humility, submissiveness, contentment and other excellencies." It was translated into Latin and became known in Europe. Jeremy Taylor, an Anglican divine who lived in the 17th century, retold a fable from *The Bustan* in one of his works. Benjamin Franklin came upon the fable in Taylor's work and, as a hoax, passed it off as a missing chapter from the Book of Genesis in the Old Testament.

Three fables bring out the mystical element in the work. "The Moth and the Flame" is one of the best known.

One night a moth, flying near a burning candle, said, "Ah, my beloved, I am your lover and weep with desire, and burn with pleasure; that is expected of me, but why do I see you weeping?"

"The honey of my life melts from my brow," the flame answered. "You fly near my naked flame, desiring, yet afraid of your desire, but I consume, exhale, glow, and expire."

A man then came and put out the flame.

"Look, lover," the dying flame said. "Love now ends. Dying thou gainest love's best ecstasy!"

"The Sufi and the Slanderer" brings out the wisdom of a Sufi.

One day a man said to a Sufi, "You do not even know how they talk behind your back."

"Silence," said the Sufi. "It is best not to know what your enemies say behind your back." Sadi's moral is:

A talebearer gives to old war a fresh life,
And urges a good, gentle person to strife.
Fly away from that comrade, while strength in you lies!
(Davie translation)

"The Tale of the Pearl" has an almost New Testament cast to it.

A droplet of rain descended from a cloud to the sea, but it was ashamed when it saw how vast the sea was.

"Who may I be," the droplet said, "when the sea is so vast. If the sea has existence, then I have none."

But Sadi adds the moral conclusion:

Since in its own eyes the drop humble
    appeared,
In its bosom, a shell with its life the
    drop reared;
The sky brought the work with success to
    a close,
And a famed royal pearl from the rain drop
    arose
Because it was humble it excellence
    gained;
Patiently waiting till success was
    obtained.

(Davie translation)

Variant spelling: Bostan.

Butch Cassidy. 0666 1866–1911? In American history and legend, assumed name of Robert Leroy Parker, leader of the Wild Bunch, an outlaw gang consisting of Kid Curry, Harry Longbaugh (the Sundance Kid), Ben Kilpatrick (the Tall Texan), Harry Tracy, Elza Lay, Deaf Charley Hanks, and other criminals. According to one account, Butch Cassidy and the Sundance Kid were killed by Bolivian troops in 1911 in the village of San Vicente. But legend says they both escaped death. Cassidy is said to have returned to the United States and died in 1937, and the Sundance Kid is said to have lived to 1957. Their romantic legend as thieves was used in the Hollywood movie *Butch Cassidy and the Sundance Kid*, starring Paul Newman and Robert Redford.

0667
Butes (herdsman). In Greek mythology, a Thracian, the son of Boreas. His brother Lycurgus, whom he had tried to murder, banished him, and he settled on the island of Strongyle (or Naxos). Finding no women there to marry, he went to Thessaly and carried off some of the women while they were celebrating a sacrifice to Dionysus. One of these, Coronis, whom he raped and forced to be his wife, prayed to Dionysus for vengeance. In retaliation Dionysus drove him mad and Butes threw himself into a well.

Butes is also the name of an Athenian hero, son of the Athenians Pandion and Zeuxippe. He was a tiller of the soil and a priest of Athena and Poseidon. He was believed to be the ancestor of the priestly caste of the Butadae and Eteobutadae. He was worshiped at an altar in Erechtheum with Poseidon and Hephaestus. Variant myths say he was the son of Teleon and Zeuxippe and took part in the expedition of the Argonauts.

Another Butes, a Sicilian hero, was also on the *Argo*. He was enticed by the Sirens' song and leaped into the sea but was rescued and brought to Lilybaeum in Sicily by Aphrodite. He became the father of Eryx by Aphrodite.

0668
Buto. In Egyptian mythology, Greek name for the cobra, or uraeus, goddess Utachet (Wadjet, Inadjet, Edjo), protector of Lower Egypt. Her twin sister, Nekhebet the vulture, was the goddess of Upper Egypt.

Buto helped the goddess Isis hide from the demonic god Set, the murderer of Isis' brother-husband, Osiris. Isis retreated to the papyrus swamps to give birth to her son Horus, who would in time avenge his father's death. Set never succeeded in finding her hiding place because Buto caused the papyrus and other plants to screen Isis from view. She further helped to camouflage Horus by shaking her hair over him.

In *The Book of the Dead* Utachet generally plays the part of destroyer of the foes of the deceased. During

the ceremonies connected with embalming, the priest addresses the mummy, saying, "The goddess Utachet [Buto] cometh unto thee in the form of the living uraeus, to anoint thy head."

Egyptian art portrays Buto as a woman wearing on her head the crown of Lower Egypt. In one hand she holds the papyrus scepter, around which is sometimes twined a snake. In some pictures she bears the crown of Lower Egypt in her right hand, about to place it on the head of the king. Occasionally, she appears as a winged serpent with the crown of the north, or Lower Egypt, on her head.

Variant spelling: Bouto.

0669
Butterfly. Any of numerous diurnal insects with a slender body and broad, often brightly colored wings. In Christian symbolism the butterfly is a sign of the Resurrection of Christ, based on its natural order of caterpillar, chrysalis, and then butterfly—life, death, and resurrection. However, some ancient mystical groups, such as the Gnostics, saw the butterfly as a symbol of corrupt flesh. The Angel of Death in Gnostic art works was portrayed crushing a butterfly. In Slavic countries it was believed that butterflies were symbols of the soul, issued from the mouths of witches to invade living bodies when the true soul was absent.

0670
Buurt-kuuruk. In Australian mythology, an evil spirit in the form of a woman as tall as a gum tree, which can range to 50 feet in five years.

0671
Byelobog and Chernobog (white god and black god). In Slavic mythology, one white and one black god, representing the dual nature of good and evil in the world.

Byelobog went about in daytime helping lost travelers find their way out of the dark forest. He also bestowed wealth and fertility and helped with the harvest. In White Russian popular legends he was called Belun (Byelun) and was portrayed as an old man dressed in white with a white beard. His evil counterpart, Chernobog, represented darkness and evil. In western Slavic folklore, which had contact with Christianity, Chernobog acquired many of the traits of the Christians' devil.

Variant spellings: Byelbog, Cernobog, Zcernoboch.

0672
Byggvir (barley?). In Norse mythology, a barley god, husband of Beyla; servant of Frey. He appears in the *Prose Edda* in the poem *Loki Asena* (Loki's mocking).

0673

Byleipt (raging fire). In Norse mythology, brother to the fire-trickster god Loki, or merely another name for the god. He appears in the *Prose Edda*.

0674

Byliny (past event). In medieval Russia, oral heroic songs or poems, originally sung by court minstrels and in recent centuries by *skaziteli*, peasant bards.

The *byliny* are usually about 300 lines long. Many tell of the exploits of the *bogatyrs*, or epic heroes, such as Ilya Muromets, Potok-Mikhailo-Ivanovich, Syyatogor, Volkh, Mikula, and Aliosha Popovich. All of these *bogatyrs* were men of superhuman strength who used their physical power as well as their cunning to defend Russia from the "infidels" and foreign invaders. Their adventures usually took place around the city of Kiev, under the rule of Prince Vladimir, sometime in the 11th or 12th century. Another cycle of *byliny*, centering around the city of Novgorod, tell of the merchant *bogatyr* Sadko. They are dated somewhat later, perhaps the 13th to the 15th century, though scholars differ.

The *byliny* "Why There Are No More Bogatyrs in Holy Russia" tells how, after a successful battle one of the *bogatyrs*, Ilya Muromets pridefully said he could conquer any enemy. God first sent two men who, when sliced in half, multiplied into four, and so on until they became a large army and attacked Ilya Muromets. The battle lasted "for three days, three hours and three brief minutes." Out of fear the *bogatyrs* fled to a mountain, where they were all turned to stone.

C

Cabauil. Among the Quiché Maya of Guatemala, generic name for god, sometimes erroneously translated as "idol." 0675

Cabbage. A plant of the mustard family that forms a head and is eaten as a vegetable. In some European folk belief babies are found under cabbage leaves. 0676

In Irish folklore cabbage stalks serve fairy spirits as steeds. One folktale tells of a farmer near Cork who was believed to be under the control of fairies in his garden. For a long time he suffered from the "falling sickness" (epilepsy) owing to the long journeys he was forced to make with the fairy folk, night after night, on one of his own cabbage stalks.

Cabeiri (the great, the mighty). In Greek and Roman mythology, ancient deities worshiped with secret rites along the coast of the Aegean Sea and on the Aegean islands. Cabeiri is also the name of the children of Uranus, according to some accounts the first people; or children of Camillus, son of Cabeiro, who had three daughters, called Caberides, and three sons, Cabeiri; or sons of Zeus and Calliope, called the Cabeiri of Samothrace. 0677

Caca. In Roman mythology, ancient Italian goddess of the hearth whose cult was supplanted by Vesta, also a Roman hearth goddess. Caca was the daughter of Vulcan and Medusa and the sister of Cacus, a fire-breathing giant with three heads who lived in a cave on Mount Palatine in Rome. He was killed by Heracles. Caca was also said to be the goddess of excrement, and the word is sometimes used in present-day vulgar Italian for excrement. 0678

Cacce-jielle and Cacce-jienne. In Lapland mythology, water gods. Cacce-jielle appeared in various forms—an old man, a beautiful woman, a naked child, or a fish. When he appeared as a fish in a piece of bread, a coin or brandy was offered to appease his evil spirit. His companion, Cacce-jienne, the water mother, appeared as a naked woman emerging from the water to comb her hair, often enticing men to fall in love with her and then drowning them. Other water spirits were Jengk-tongk, Vit-khan, Vu-murt, 0679

Kul, Vasa, Vut-oza, Vut- kuguza, Vut-kuva, Vederaj, Vesta-erag, Veeneiu or Mereneiu, and Vetehinen.

Cachimana. In the mythology of the Orinoco Indians of South America, the great spirit who regulated the seasons and harvests. He was opposed by an evil spirit, Iolokiamo, who was less powerful but cleverer and more active than Cachimana. 0680

Cacus (bad). In Roman mythology, a fire-spitting giant, son of Vulcan and Medusa; brother of Caca, who was goddess of excrement. 0681

When Heracles, with the cattle of Geryon, wandered into the vicinity of Cacus' cave, Cacus stole some of the cattle while Heracles was sleeping. Cacus dragged them backward into his cave so that their hoof prints would seem to be going in the opposite direction. He then closed the entrance to the cave with a rock so heavy that ten pairs of oxen could not budge it. The lowing of the cattle in the cave guided Heracles to their hiding place. He moved the rock, opened the cave, and killed Cacus with his club. At the site of the cave Heracles then built an altar to Jupiter, under the title Pater Inventor (the discoverer). He then sacrificed one of the cows on the altar.

Vergil's *Aeneid* (book 8) locates the cave of Cacus on the Aventine in Rome. Medieval Christian writers saw Heracles' triumph over the giant Cacus as a symbol of the forces of evil being vanquished by those of good. The French artist Poussin painted the scene, as did Domenichino. There is an engraving by Dürer on the subject. In literature Cacus was the standard for thievery. Cervantes wrote: "There you will find the Lord Rinaldo of Montalban, with his friends and companions, all of them greater thieves than Cacus." The English novelist Sir Walter Scott wrote: "Our hero, feeling his curiosity considerably excited by the idea of visiting the den of an Highland Cacus, took however, the precaution to inquire if his guide might be trusted."

Cadmus (from the east). In Greek mythology, culture hero, king of Thebes; son of Agenor of Phoenicia and Argiore (or Telephassa); brother of Cilix, Electra, Demodoce, Phineus, Thasus, Europa, and 0682

Europa

Phoenix; married Harmonia; father of Agave, Autonoe, Illyrius, Ino, Polydorus, and Semele. Cadmus' sister Europa was carried off and raped by Zeus. Cadmus and his brothers Phoenix and Cilix were sent out with the command to find Europa. They were forbidden to return to Phoenicia without their sister. In the course of their wanderings they arrived in Thrace, where Cadmus' mother, who had accompanied him so far, died. Cadmus then asked the Delphic oracle what he should do. He was told to cease his search for Europa and follow a certain cow and to establish a city on the spot where the cow would lie down. The cow met Cadmus in Phocis and led him to the site that was to become Boeotia. Cadmus wanted to sacrifice the cow to Athena, so he sent his companions to a nearby spring to bring water for the rites. The spring was guarded by a dragon-serpent, the offspring of Ares and the Erinys Tilphosa. When the men did not return in a short time, Cadmus went in search of them. He found the dragon-serpent feeding on their flesh, and he killed the monster. (Medieval European paintings show the beast with wings.) Athena then advised Cadmus to sow the teeth of the dragon like seeds. He did so, and immediately a crop of armed warriors sprang up. Cadmus then flung a stone into their midst. A battle broke out, and all but five of the men killed each other. The five were called Spartoi (sown men). They were Echion (snake man), Udaeus (ground man), Chthonius (earth man), Hyperenor (superman or overbearing) and Pelorus (monster).

The price Cadmus had to pay for killing the dragon of Ares was to serve the god for an "eternal" year—about eight years, the period of banishment for a homicide. Afterward Athena made him ruler of Thebes. Zeus gave Harmonia, the daughter of Aphrodite and Ares, to Cadmus as his wife. Cadmus gave Harmonia an outer-robe or cloak, and a necklace made by the craft god Hephaestus.

As further punishment for killing Ares' dragon-serpent, many of the children of Cadmus and Harmonia died. Childless, the couple left Thebes and settled in the country of the Enchelians. The people received them kindly, making Cadmus their king. One day Cadmus said, "If a serpent's life is so dear to the gods, I would I were myself a serpent." No sooner had Cadmus uttered the words than he began to change into a snake. When Harmonia saw him, she asked the gods to grant her the same. The two became serpents. When they died, they went to Elysium.

Later Greek mythology credits Cadmus with the invention of the Greek alphabet and the art of mining and with the introduction of the worship of Dionysus. Lord Byron refers to the belief that Cadmus invented the alphabet:

> You have the letters Cadmus gave
> Think you he meant them for a slave?

In *Paradise Lost* (book 9.503–506) Milton refers to the changing of Cadmus and Harmonia into serpents:

> . . . pleasing was his shape,
> And lovely: never since of serpent kind
> Lovelier; not those that in Illyria changed
> Hermione and Cadmus. . . .

(Milton confused Hermione with Harmonia.) Matthew Arnold's play *Empedocles on Aetna* refers to Harmonia and Cadmus' tale:

> . . . Two bright and aged snakes
> Who once were Cadmus and Harmonia,
> Back in the glens or on the warm sea shore,
> In breathless quiet after all their ills.

Ovid's *Metamorphoses* (book 3), Chaucer's *Knight's Tale*, and Alexander Pope's *Thebais* all refer to the myth.

0683

Caduceus (herald staff). In Greek and Roman mythology, a magic wand consisting of a rod topped by wings and intertwined by two snakes; called kery keionin in Greek. The caduceus was carried by Hermes in Greek myths and Mercury in Roman mythology. Originally, the caduceus was represented as a simple staff wound about with two white ribbons. It was a symbol of authority and inviolability and protected the herald who carried it. In Homer's *Iliad* and *Odyssey* the caduceus is often mentioned as a type of magic wand by which Hermes opened and closed the eyes of mortals. It was therefore connected with death and the journey through the underworld. Later myth says Hermes once threw his magic wand at two snakes fighting on the ground. The snakes became entangled in the magic wand and have been attached to it ever since. The wings at the top were added in later Greek and Roman art. In Vergil's *Aeneid* (book 4) the caduceus is said to have been given to Mercury by Apollo in exchange for the lyre. Milton, calling it Hermes' "opiate rod" in *Paradise Lost* (book 11.133), refers to the belief that the caduceus can induce sleep. Today the caduceus is associated with medicine because it was one of the symbols of Asclepius, the god of medicine for the ancients. Le Sage, in *Gil Blas* (1715) writes: "I did not think the post of Mercury-in-chief quite so honorable as it was called . . . and resolved to abandon the Caduceus [give up the medical profession] for ever."

0684
Caeculus. In Roman mythology, a son of Vulcan and the sister of the Frates Delpidii; ally of Turnus in the war against the Trojans. Caeculus' mother became impregnated by Vulcan when a spark from heaven fell into her bosom. Her son Caeculus, however, became a robber. In time he built the city of Praeneste and wanted to find citizens to inhabit it, but no one would consent to live there. Caeculus then prayed to Vulcan, asking him to show the gathered crowd that the god was his father. A flame suddenly shot up, and the mob, moved by the miracle, consented to become citizens of Praeneste. Vergil's *Aeneid* (book 7) says Caeculus was born among herds in the country, exposed by his mother to die, and later found near the hearth at a shrine of Jupiter.

one knows where he went. The northern Bushman call him Cagn or Kang, and the southern Bushmen call him Thora.

0687
Cahá-Paluna (standing water falling from above?). In Mayan mythology, wife of the first man and culture hero, Balam-Quitzé, of the Quiché Maya of Guatemala. Cahá-Paluna is called a "distinguished woman" in the *Popol Vuh*, the sacred book of the Quiché.

0688
Caicas. In Greek mythology, the northeast wind, son of Eos and Astraeus.

0685
Caeneus (new). In Greek mythology, a Lapith chieftain who was born a girl, Caenis, daughter of the Thessalian king Elatus and Hippea, and later transformed into a man. He was the father of Coronus and the brother of Polyphemus and Ischys. As a girl, Caeneus was very beautiful and caught the eye of Poseidon, who raped her. The god then offered to grant her any wish. She chose to be turned into a man so she could not be raped again. The god granted her request. Caeneus then became the leader

Cain and Abel

of the Lapiths. When the Lapiths and centaurs had their great battle at the wedding of Peirithous and Hippodameia, Caeneus killed several of the foe. However, he offended Zeus and was beaten on the head with fir trees or else buried beneath a pile of them. Ovid's *Metamorphoses* (book 12) says Caeneus was finally changed into a bird.

0686

Cagn. In African mythology (Bushman), creator god who often appears as a mantis or caterpillar. His wife, Coti, bore him two sons, Gogaz and Gowi, both culture heroes, who taught the people how to make digging tools with sharp stone points. Cagn's mysterious power was believed to reside in his tooth, which he sometimes lent to others who wanted added strength. After he created the world, Cagn became annoyed with man's stupidity and left.

0689

Cain and Abel (smith and meadow? breath?) In Jewish, Christian, and Islamic mythology, first children of Adam and Eve.

In the Old Testament (Gen. 4:1–16) Cain murdered his brother Abel (the reason is not given) and became a "fugitive and a vagabond" on the earth (Gen. 4:12).

God marked Cain with a sign to protect him from the vengeance of others for the murder, though the term "mark of Cain" has come to signify a stigma for an outlaw (Gen. 4:15). In medieval Christian belief Abel was the first martyr, a prefiguration of Christ because he suffered an unjust death. In Islamic legend, Cain and Abel are called Kabil and Habil. Kabil (Cain) and Habil (Abel) each had a twin sister. Kabil's twin sister was Aclima and Habil's twin was Jumella. Adam wanted Kabil to marry Jumella and Habil to marry Aclima. Kabil, however, rejected the idea. Adam then said God would be asked through a sacrifice to decide. Sacrifice was made, and Kabil's offering was rejected, signifying that God did not approve of Kabil's rejection of the marriage. In a fit of anger Kabil killed Habil. For some time Kabil carried around the dead body of his brother, until he saw a raven scratch a hole in the ground to bury a dead bird. Kabil took the hint and buried Habil in the ground.

Medieval Christian belief held that Cain had a yellowish or sandy-red beard, which then became a symbol of murder and treason and was used in medieval art to depict Cain, Judas, and the Jews. (Yellow became a color for anti-Semitic propaganda.) Shakespeare in *The Merry Wives of Windsor* (act 1, sc. 4, line 22), writes: "He hath but a little wee face, with a little yellow beard, a Cain-colored beard."

The biblical account inspired Samuel Taylor Coleridge's prose poem *The Wanderings of Cain* and Lord Byron's poetic drama *Cain, A Mystery*, in which Cain's wife is called Adah (adornment).

0690

Calais (a changeful hue). In Greek mythology, an Argonaut; son of Boreas and Orithyia; twin brother of Zetes (searcher). Calais and Zetes aided Jason as Argonauts. Both were given wings for recovering Phineus from the Harpies in Bithynia. When they were killed, they were transformed into birds. Ovid's *Metamorphoses* (book 8) gives the myth.

0691

Calamity Jane. c. 1852–1903. In American history and folklore, popular name for Martha Jane Canary, noted for her marksmanship, who dressed as a man. Some accounts allege that she was a Lesbian and that her affair with Wild Bill Hickok was a coverup, because he was said to be a homosexual. But Hollywood's movie *Calamity Jane*, starring Doris Day and Howard Keel, tells how Calamity Jane wins the love of Hickok.

0692

Calchas (brazen). In Greek mythology, a soothsayer, son of Thestor and Megaera; brother of Alcmeon, Leucippe, and Theonoe; father of Cressida. Calchas was an Argonaut who accompanied Agamemnon's army in the Trojan War. Homer, in the *Iliad* (book 1), says that Calchas was the "most excellent of augurs, who knew of things that were and that should be and that had been before." In post-Homeric myth, it was Calchas whose predictions demanded the sacrifice of Iphigenia as well as the building of the wooden horse. He died when he met another soothsayer, Mopsus, who beat him at guessing how many figs were in the branches of a certain fig tree. Some accounts say he died of grief; others say he took his own life. Another myth tells that he died laughing when, as he raised a cup of wine, someone said he would never live to drink it.

0693

Caleuche. In the folklore of the Araucanian Indians of Chile, a witch boat, seen illuminated at night, carrying fishermen to the treasure stores at the bottom of the sea.

0694

Callidice (fair justice). In Greek mythology, queen of Thesprotia and a wife of Odysseus after the Trojan War. According to some accounts, when Odysseus was returning to Ithaca, he stopped off at Thesprotia and married Callidice, who bore him a son, Polypoetes. When Callidice died, Odysseus continued on his journey and left the kingdom to Polypoetes.

Calliope (beautiful voice, fair face). In Greek mythology, one of the nine Muses, the Muse of epic or heroic poetry; daughter of Zeus and Mnemosyne; mother of Orpheus and Linus by the Thracian king Oeagrus (or by Apollo). She is portrayed in Western art with a tablet and stylus or a trumpet. Often she holds a laurel crown. In 17th-century paintings, books such as the *Iliad, Odyssey*, and *Aeneid* are shown as part of her attributes.

0695

Callirrhoë (fair flowing). In Greek mythology, daughter of the river god Achelous; sister of Castalia and Peirene; who unwittingly sent her husband Alcmaeon to his death by persuading him to obtain Harmonia's necklace and robe from Alphesiboea. When Alphesiboea's brothers discovered the attempt, they murdered him. Callirrhoë is also the name of a daughter of Oceanus and Tethys and the mother of the three- headed cowherd Geryon, Cerberus, and Echidna, according to some accounts. The name is also that of a daughter of the Trojan river god Scamander; she was married to Tros and mother of Assaracus, Cleopatra, Ilus, and Ganymede. She killed herself, and a fountain in Attica is named after her.

0696

Callisto (fairest). In Greek mythology, an Arcadian nymph, follower of Artemis; daughter of Lycam and Cyllene (or Nycteus or Cereus); sister of Pallas; mother of Arcas by Zeus. Callisto was transformed into a bear and placed in the heavens as the Great Bear along with her son Arcas, as the Little Bear.

Callisto was a follower of Artemis and had taken a vow of chastity. Zeus, ever lustful, saw her one day resting alone in the woods. Disguising himself as the goddess Artemis, he began caressing Callisto. Before the girl was fully aware of what was happening, he raped her. In order to keep his adultery a secret from his wife, Hera, the god changed Callisto into a bear. A variant account says Artemis discovered the girl was pregnant and metamorphosed her into a bear. Another account says that Hera changed the girl into a bear when she discovered Zeus' infidelity.

The story's ending also varies considerably in the ancient accounts. In some versions Artemis shoots Callisto while she is out hunting with Hera, who points out the bear. Zeus sends Hermes to save the baby Arcas, who is then brought up by Maia, Hermes' mother. Another story is that Arcas, when grown up, saw the bear in the woods and, not knowing the bear was his mother, killed it. Still

0697

another variation tells how the bear wandered into the sacred shrine of Zeus Lycaeus and was killed for sacrilege.

The fate of Callisto, however, finds all of the accounts in agreement. Zeus transported her to the stars as the constellation Arctos, the Great Bear. Either at the same time or later he placed their son Arcas as the nearby constellation Arctophylax, which appears to be guarding the Great Bear. Hera, however, was not at all happy at this and appealed to Tethys, the sea goddess and Hera's old nurse. She asked that Tethys and her husband, Oceanus, never permit Callisto to enter their realm. They agreed, and that is why the Great Bear is doomed to revolve ceaselessly about the North Star. The ancient Arcadians showed visitors a tomb of Callisto on a hill, the top of which contained a sanctuary of Artemis Calliste, indicating that Callisto was another form of the goddess Artemis. The she-bear was the animal associated with the cult of Artemis Calliste.

Sources for the myth of Callisto are Ovid's *Metamorphoses* (book 2), Hyginus' *Fabulae* and *Poetica Astronomica*, and Apollodorus' *Bibliotheca* (Library).

The rape of Callisto is the theme of the painting *Jupiter and Callisto* by François Boucher, the French artist. He shows Jupiter in his female disguise as Artemis. Titian painted *Diana and Callisto*, portraying the goddess discovering that Callisto is pregnant.

Calydon. In Greek mythology, son of Thestius, accidentally killed by his father; also the name of the son of Aetolus and Pronoe; the brother of Pleuron; husband of Aeolia; and father of Epicasta and Protogeneia. Calydon is also the name of a son of Ares and Astynome, turned into stone for seeing the goddess Artemis bathe. Finally, Calydon is the city of Aetolla, Greece, founded by Calydon and Pleuron, the setting for the Calydonian boar hunt.

0698

Calydonian Boar Hunt. In Greek mythology, the Calydonian boar was sent by Artemis to ravage the territory of King Oeneus of Calydon because Oeneus had offended Artemis by not offering proper sacrifice. Meleager, the son of Oeneus, was sent to kill the boar. Heralds were sent all over Greece summoning sport-and adventure-loving heroes to aid in the task. Castor and Polydeuces came from Sparta, and Idas and Lynceus came from Messene. Theseus of Athens, his friend Peirithous, and Jason and his cousin Admetus came. Peleus, the father of Achilles, and Telamon, the father of Ajax, also responded to the summons. From the royal family of Arcadia came Ancaeus and Atalanta. Atalanta was the only

0699

Meleager

The myth is told in Ovid's *Metamorphoses* (books 8, 10), William Morris's *Earthly Paradise*, and Swinburne's poetic drama *Atalanta in Calydon*.

A late Roman sarcophagus in the Capitoline Museum, Rome, portrays the hunt. Meleager stands in the center of the piece thrusting his spear into the boar. To his right is Atalanta with her bow. Poussin based his painting on Ovid's account.

0700

Calypso (hidden, hider). In Greek mythology, daughter of Atlas and Pleione or of Oceanus and Tethys; sister of Hyas, the Hyades, the Hesperides, Maia, and the Pleiades. Calypso received Odysseus on her island, entertained him, became his mistress, and bore him two children, Nausinous (cunning sailor) and Nauisithous (in the service of the sea goddess). Odysseus remained with Calypso for seven years. Calypso at last received the command of Zeus to dismiss him. Hermes brought the message to Calypso and found her in her grotto. With much reluctance, Calypso obeyed the command of Zeus. She supplied Odysseus with means for constructing a raft, provisions, and a favorable wind.

Fénelon, the French writer, in his romance *Telemachus*, which tells of the adventures of Odysseus' son, has Telemachus visit the island of Calypso. As with his father, she offered him immortality (it is believed she was originally a goddess connected with death), but the lad refused. Minerva (Fénelon uses the Latin names of the Greek gods), in the shape of Mentor, Telemachus' friend, escaped with Telemachus by leaping from a cliff into the sea. They both reached a boat offshore. Lord Byron, in his long poem *Childe Harold* alludes to this incident when he writes: "But not in silence pass Calypso's isles." It is believed that Goza was the isle of the goddess.

0701

Camahueto. In the folklore of the Araucanian Indians of Chile, a sea monster who wrecks large boats.

0702

Camazotz. In Mayan mythology, vampire-bat god of the Quiché Maya of Guatemala. He is often portrayed with a sacrificial knife in one hand and his victim in the other.

Variant spelling: Camalotz.

0703

Camel. A large ruminant found in desert countries and used as a beast of burden. In medieval Christianity the camel was a symbol of temperance because it could go without water for long periods. It was also a symbol of humility because, as Christ carried the burden of the world's sins, the camel carried

woman in the hunt. These heroes and others were entertained for nine days by King Oeneus before the hunt began. It was his son Meleager who finally killed the wild boar after it had been first wounded by Atalanta.

The prize—the boar's skin—became the object of a quarrel after Meleager had given it to Atalanta. A battle ensued in which, according to some accounts, Meleager was the victor. In a later myth, Meleager died after the hunt because of the anger of his mother, Althaea. When Meleager was born, the two Fates predicted he would be a brave warrior but that he would die when a stick, in a fire burning at the time of his birth, was consumed. Althaea, Meleager's mother, hid the stick, but when Meleager killed her brothers in the battle over the boar's skin, she took the stick and had it burned. Meleager then died agonizingly in the fighting when the Curetes attacked the Calydonians after the boar had been killed. After his death he was changed into a guinea fowl by Artemis.

man's physical burdens. St. John the Baptist "was clothed with camel's hair, and with a girdle of a skin about his loins." (Mark 1:6) as a sign of penitence. In art works of the Christian Middle Ages and the Renaissance the camel is shown in paintings of Joseph and his brothers, Rebecca at the well, the Exodus from Egypt, and the Adoration of the Magi.

In Islam the Camel of Seleh is one of the ten animals admitted into heaven. The camel also had its detractors. Aristotle wrote that camels spend nearly the whole day copulating, and Leviticus (11:4) calls the camel an unclean animal.

0704
Camelot. In Arthurian legend, the home of King Arthur and his knights. It has been variously identified as Caerleon- upon-Usk in Wales, Camelford in Cornwall, and by Malory in *Morte d'Arthur* as Winchester, England. Lerner and Lowe's Broadway musical about King Arthur is titled *Camelot*.

0705
Camilla. In Roman mythology, a virgin queen of the Volsci (Volscians) and a daughter of Metabus and Casmilla; she fought against Aeneas. Camilla was dedicated to the goddess Diana and fought with one breast exposed to give greater freedom to her bow arm. Camilla was killed by Aruns' spear in an ambush, according to Vergil's *Aeneid* (book 7).

0706
Camillus (attendant at religious services?). In Roman cult, the Latin name for the boys and girls who served the priests and priestesses during the performance of their religious functions. The children had to be below the age of puberty with both parents living.

0707
Camillus, Marcus Furius. In Roman history and legend, conqueror of the Gauls. Camillus cast them out of Rome in 387 B.C.E. He was noted for his sense of justice. One legend tells how he reprimanded a schoolteacher. When the Romans were attacking Falerii, the local schoolteacher brought the children in his charge to Camillus and offered them as hostages. Shocked at the schoolteacher's treachery, Camillus sent the children back but not before he had the schoolmaster whipped in front of them. Poussin's *Camillus and the Schoolmaster of Falerii* depicts the legend. Both Livy's *History of Rome* and Plutarch's *Parallel Lives* have biographies of him with legendary material.

0708
Campus Martius (field of Mars) A plain lying to the north of Rome, outside the Pomerium, between the Tiber, the Quirinal and the Capitoline Hills. Campus Martius was dedicated to Mars, the god of war. Roman youths performed exercises in its field.

0709
Camulos. In Celtic mythology, a war god worshiped in Colchester, England, who possessed an invincible sword; called Camolundunum by the ancient Romans. Some scholars believe he is the original for the King Cole who figures in children's nursery rhymes.
Variant spelling: Camulus.

0710
Canace (barking). In Greek mythology, daughter of Aeolus and Enarete; she committed incest with her brother Marcareus, had a child, and then killed herself at her father's command. Marcareus also committed suicide. In variant accounts texts Canace is the mother of Hopleus, Nireus, Epopeus, Aloeüs and Tripoas by Poseidon. Canace is one of the heroines in Ovid's *Heroides* (11).

0711
Cancer. One of the 12 signs of the Zodiac. Cancer is called the Crab. It appears when the sun has reached its highest northern limit and begins to go backward toward the south. Like a crab, the return is sideways. The dates generally are 21 June to 23 July. In Greek mythology Hera sent Cancer against her enemy Heracles when he fought the Hydra. Cancer bit Heracles' foot, but the hero killed the animal. However, Hera rewarded the crab by making it the constellation of Cancer.

0712
Candlemas Day (Candlemass). Christian feast celebrated on 2 February, also called the Feast of the Purification of the Virgin Mary, or Presentation of Our Lord. During the Middle Ages candles that were to be used during the Church year were consecrated on this day, symbolizing Jesus Christ, "the light of the World." The feast is still observed in Roman and Anglican churches. The ceremony of the candles may stem from the pagan Roman custom of carrying lighted torches to honor Juno Februata.

An old verse for the feast day of Candlemass went:

If Candlemass Day be fair and bright,
Winter will have another flight;
If Candlemass Day be shower and rain,
Winter is gone and will not come again.

In secular custom, we have Groundhog Day on February 2, which is a replacement of the Christian folk belief by a secular one.

0713

Canens. In Roman mythology, a nymph, the daughter of Janus and Venilia. She pined away when her husband, Picus, was lost. Picus was a handsome youth and Canens a nymph who attracted trees and rocks by her voice, soothed wild beasts, detained the birds, and halted rivers in their courses. One day Circe made sexual advances toward Picus. The youth refused, and the angry Circe turned him into a woodpecker. Canens searched for Picus for six days and nights. At last, melting with grief, she pined away, and by degrees vanished into the air. Ovid's *Metamorphoses* (book 14) tells the tragic tale of Canens and Picus.

0714

Capaneus (charioteer). In Greek mythology, one of the Seven against Thebes; son of Hipponous and Astynome, married to Evadne, and father of Sthenelus. Capaneus boasted that not even Zeus could stop him from entering Thebes. The god, of course, sent a thunderbolt and killed Capaneus. Some accounts say Asclepius, the god of medicine, resurrected Capaneus. Other accounts say he was the inventor of the scaling ladder.

0715

Caphaurus (camphor). In Greek mythology, a Libyan shepherd, son of Amphithemis and Tritonis; brother of Nasamon; he killed the Argonauts Canthus and Eribotes for attempting to steal his sheep. He was in turn killed by other Argonauts. Cape Capharus is a rocky promontory in southeast Euboea, where Nauplius lit beacons to lure returning Greek ships to their doom on the rocks.

Variant spelling: Cephalion.

0716

Capitol. The southern summit of the Capitoline Hill at Rome, separated from the northern summit by a saddle. On the highest point of the southern tip was the temple of Jupiter Optimus Maximus, begun by the Tarquins but not finished until the first year of the Republic in 509 B.C.E. In 83 B.C.E. the whole temple burned down to the vaults where the Sibylline books and other consecrated objects were preserved. A new temple was consecrated in 69 B.C.E. A statue of Jupiter in ivory and gold, on the model of the Olympian Zeus of Apollonius, was substituted for the old terra-cotta image of the god. One hundred years later the temple again burned. Vespasian restored it, but the new structure was destroyed by fire in 80 C.E. In 82 C.E. a new temple was erected by Domitian that survived until the fifth century C.E. It was gradually destroyed by the Christians and Barbarians during the Middle Ages.

0717

Capricorn. The goat, the tenth sign of the Zodiac, which the sun enters on 22 December. Capricorn's form combines the upper half of a goat with the lower half of a fish. According to some ancient texts, it represents Aegipan, son of Zeus and Aex (Aega), a nymph, or of Boetis, a goat. In Greek mythology Aegipan was immortalized by Zeus for helping the god recover his stolen sinews, which the evil Typhon had severed and hidden with the monster Delphyne. Aegipan also taught the Greek gods to change their shapes into animal forms to escape from Typhon. Many Greek texts identify Aegipan as a form of the goat god Pan. Other accounts say the goat is Amalthea, who fed Zeus with her milk when he was an infant.

0718

Captain Kidd. 1645?–1701. C.E. In British and American history and folklore, popular name of William Kidd, privateer. Born in Scotland, Kidd came to New York City, where he ran a thriving ship business. He worked for the British government in their fight against French privateers, but in 1696 he turned pirate himself. He returned to Boston in the hope of being pardoned but was sent to England and hanged. After his death various ballads were circulated, such as "Dialogue Between the Ghost of Capt. Kidd and the Kidnaper." Legend grew up around his life and about where he had hidden his vast treasure, inspiring various hoaxes about the burial site. According to legend, his spirit hovers over his treasure. Captain Kidd's treasure appears in Edgar Allan Poe's tale *The Gold Bug*, set on Sullivan's Island near Charleston, South Carolina. Poe's tale influenced Robert Louis Stevenson's novel *Treasure Island*. Hollywood's *Captain Kidd*, starring Charles Laughton deals with the legend.

0719

Capys (gulper, snatcher). In Greek and Roman mythology, son of Assaracus and Hieromneme; father of Anchises and Laocoön by his cousin Themiste. Capys is also the name of a Trojan hero who warned against bringing in the wooden horse. He advised casting it into the sea, but his advice was not heeded. When Troy fell, Capys fled with Aeneas. He founded Capua in Italy with Aeneas after the Trojan War.

0720

Caractacus. First century C.E. In British history and legend, son of Cymbeline, a king who fought against Rome for nine years but was betrayed by Carthismandu, queen of the Brigantes, and captured by the Romans but spared his life by the Emperor Claudius who admired his courage. Edward Elgar's cantata *Caractacus* deals with the legend.

Variant spelling: caradoc.

0721

Carausius. Third century. C.E. In British history and legend, a hero who fought successfully against Rome, became ruler of Britain with full Roman approval, and later was murdered. MacPherson's Ossianic poem *Caros*, the name he gives Carausius, tells the legend.

0722

Cardea (hinge). In Roman mythology, tutelary virgin goddess of thresholds and door pivots. Cardea warded off evil spirits, especially the Strigoe, who were believed to suck the blood of children by night.

0723

Carlos, Don. 1545–1568. In Spanish history and legend, son of Philip II of Spain by his wife, Maria of Portugal. The historical picture of Don Carlos varies widely from the legendary one. According to most historical accounts, he plotted the death of his father, Philip II, was arrested, and died in prison. He is described in numerous contemporary accounts as brutal, intolerable, devilish, ill-tempered, vicious, and vindictive. One source tells how he roasted a rabbit alive; in another he forced a shoemaker to eat a pair of shoes. But the legend says Don Carlos was a handsome prince (he was actually short and ugly), who died in the cause of freedom, fighting against the dictatorship of his father, Philip II. To add to his charm he was also supposed to be in love with his father's intended wife, Elisabeth of Valois. The most famous play treating the legend is Schiller's *Don Carlos*, which was used as the basis for Verdi's opera *Don Carlo*.

0724

Carme. In Greek mythology, a nymph, daughter of Eubulus and the mother of Britomartis by Zeus. Carme was an attendant of the virgin goddess Artemis and was nursemaid to Scylla.

0725

Carmenta (Car the wise). In Roman mythology, one of the Camenae, goddesses and water deities identified with the Muses. Carmenta was an ancient Italian goddess of prophecy who protected women in childbirth. In Rome she had a priest attached to her cult and a shrine near one of the gates of Rome, the Porta Carmentalis, near the capitol. On this spot Roman women celebrated the festival of *Carmentalia* in her honor. She was worshiped along with her sisters, Porrima (or Antevorta) and Postvorta. According to Roman myth, Carmenta was the prophetic mother,

by Mercury, of the Arcadian stranger Evander. Other accounts say she was Evander's wife. Carmenta was the Roman counterpart of the Greek Themis and also was known as Nicostrata.

0726

Carna (flesh). In Roman mythology, goddess of hearts and other body organs. She had a shrine on the Caelian Hill in Rome. Her festival, at which the worshipers ate beans and bacon and made offerings of them to the goddess, was held on 1 June.

0727

Carnation. A large white, pink, yellow, or red flower with fringed petals; a symbol of Mother's Day, celebrated in the United States on the second Sunday in May. In Christian legend the carnation is associated with the Virgin Mary; when she witnessed her son carrying the cross, she shed tears that turned into carnations when they touched the ground.

Indians in Mexico call the carnation the "flower of the dead" and mass the flowers around corpses in preparation for burial. In Korean legend a cluster of three carnations is placed on the hair; if the top flower withers first, the last years of life with be difficult; if the second, one will suffer in youth. In the Victorian language of the flowers the carnation symbolized admiration.

0728

Carpo (withering). In Greek mythology, goddess of autumn, daughter of Zeus and Themis, and one of the Horae, who were goddesses of the seasons.

0729

Cartwright, Peter. 1785–1872. In American history and legend, a Methodist circuit rider in the South and Middle West who preached against slavery. One legend says he held a man under water for advocating slavery, saying he would let him go free if the man recited the Lord's Prayer every morning and night and attended every sermon delivered anywhere within five miles. Cartwright also made the man promise to give free rides on his ferry to Methodist ministers. In his *Autobiography* he recounts many of his adventures, which place him more in the realm of legend than history.

0730

Carya (nut tree). In Greek mythology, a girl loved by the god Dionysus. After her death she was turned into a walnut tree, and a city in Laconia was named after her. Artemis, who reported the death of Carya, was called Caryatis (of the walnut tree).

0731

Caryatis (of the walnut tree). In Greek mythology, Carya, a girl loved by Artemis who died and was transformed into a walnut tree. Artemis repented Carya's death and was given the epithet Caryatis. Caryatids, female-form statues used for support, are said to be based on Caryatis. In a variant myth Caria, a Greek state, supported the Persians in their war against the Greeks. When the Persians were defeated, the Greeks killed off all the Carian men and enslaved the women. Greek builders' use of statues of the women as building supports was symbolic punishment. Examples of caryatids are found in the ruins of Cnidos and Siphnos at Delphi. The *salle des Caryatides*, a 16th-century room in the Louvre, Paris, also uses the motif.

0732

Casey at the Bat. American literary ballad, published in 1888 by Ernest Lawrence Thayer, which tells how the mighty Casey of the Mudville baseball team strikes out and loses the game. William Schuman's opera *The Mighty Casey* deals with the hero.

0733

Casey Jones. In American history and legend, popular name of John Luther Jones (1864–1900), a train engineer believed to be responsible for one of the worst train wrecks in history. The ballad "Casey Jones," published in 1909, but known earlier, opens:

Come all you rounders for I want you to hear
The story told of a brave engineer;
Casey Jones was the rounder's name
On a heavy six-eight wheeler he rode to fame.

The ballad then goes on in detail, telling how Casey stayed on the train, even though warned that a wreck was about to take place. In 1948, a "Mrs. Casey Jones" was interviewed about her late husband. She said: "He was a lovable lad—6 feet 4½ inches in height, dark-haired and gray-eyed. Always he was in good humor and his Irish heart was as big as his body. All the railroaders were fond of Casey. . . ." Aside from the ballad, Casey Jones appears in a play by Robert Ardrey.

0734

Casilda, St. Eleventh century. In Christian legend, Spanish saint of Moorish descent invoked against bad luck, hemorrhage, and sterility. Daughter of a Moorish king, she secretly sympathized with Christian captives. She took bread to the starving prisoners, which then turned to roses at the approach of the guards. She is portrayed by Francisco de Zurbarán as an elegant Spanish woman holding roses.

0735

Casimir of Poland, St. (proclamation of peace). Died 1483 C.E. In Christian legend, prince often portrayed

in ecstasy with a lily and crown nearby; a patron saint of Poland and Lithuania. Feast, 4 March.

0736

Cassandra (she who entangles men). In Greek mythology, prophetess, daughter of King Priam and Queen Hecuba; sister of Aesacus, Creusa, Hector, Helenus, Paris, Polyxena, and Troilus, among others. Cassandra is sometimes called Alexandra.

According to some ancient accounts, Cassandra and Helenus, her twin, as children fell asleep in a temple of Apollo while their parents were taking part in the sacred rites. Sacred serpents, kept in the temple, licked the ears of the children while they were asleep. When Hecuba saw this, she screamed, and the serpents fled. However, since the serpent was sacred to Apollo, the children were given the gift of prophecy from the archer god.

In a variant account Apollo fell in love with Cassandra. He promised her the gift of prophecy if she returned his love. Cassandra, who was the most beautiful of all King Priam's daughters, agreed. However, when it came time for her to return Apollo's love, she refused. In anger Apollo, who could not take back his gift, cursed Cassandra: she would tell the future correctly, but no one would ever believe what she said.

Cassandra warned the Trojans about the wooden horse but was silenced. When the Greeks took the city, Cassandra was given as a prize to Agamemnon. She warned him that he would be killed by his wife, but this prophecy, like all her prophecies, was ignored. Both Cassandra and Agamemnon as well as their sons, were killed by Clytemnestra and her lover.

Cassandra appears in Homer's *Iliad* (books 6, 13) and *Odyssey* (book 4); she is a character in Vergil's *Aeneid*, Ovid's *Metamorphoses*, Chaucer's narrative poem *Troilus and Crisyde*, Byron's *Don Juan*, Shakespeare's play *Troilus and Cressida*, Meredith's poem *Cassandra*, Dante Gabriel Rossetti's poem *Cassandra*, Schiller's poem *Kassandra*, Tennyson's *Oenone*, and Robinson Jeffers's *Cassandra*.

0737

Cassiopea (cassia juice). In Greek mythology, the wife of Cepheus, king of Ethiopia; mother of Andromeda and of Atymnius by Zeus. Cassiopea boasted that she and her daughter were more beautiful than the Nereids. This angered the sea god Poseidon, who sent a monster to devastate the land. To appease the god an oracle had demanded that Andromeda be placed on a rock in the sea, exposed to the monster. After being tied to the rock by her father, the girl was freed by the hero Perseus, whom she then agreed to marry. Cassiopea, however, objected to Andromeda marrying Perseus and broke in on the wedding festivities. Perseus then turned Cassiopea and Phineus (whom Cassiopea wanted Andromeda to marry) into stone by showing them the head of Medusa. For further revenge Poseidon placed Cassiopea in the heavens as a constellation where at certain times, she appears to be hanging upside down. Cassiopea is a northern constellation containing 13 stars. Five of the brightest resemble a chair and have been given the name, Cassiopea's Chair. Ovid's *Metamorphoses* (book 4) tells the myth.

Variant spellings: Cassipea, Cassiopc, Cassiopeia.

0738

Castalia. In Greek mythology, daughter of the river god Achelous and sister of Callirrhoë and Peirene. Castalia was chased by Apollo and turned into a spring at Mount Parnassus at Delphi. The spring, called Castalia, then became sacred to Apollo and the Muses. Castalides was an epithet applied to the Muses because of their connection with the sacred spring.

0739

Castor and Polydeuces (beaver and much sweet wine). In Greek mythology, twin brothers, sons of Leda and Tyndareos; often called Dioscuri (sons of Zeus); brothers of Phoebe, Philonoe, Timanda, and Clytemnestra; half-brothers of Helen.

The myths of Castor and Polydeuces (called Pollux in Latin) vary. In Homer, they are said to be the sons of Leda and King Tyndareos and are called Tyndaridae (sons of Tyndareos). They died sometime between the rape of Helen and the Trojan War and were buried in Lacedaemon. But even in death they were said to live because Zeus, the king of the gods, honored them. Thus, it was believed that they lived and died on alternate days—the day Castor was on earth, Pollux was in the underworld. Their positions were reversed the following day.

In a later variant myth only Polydeuces is said to be a son of Zeus. Polydeuces was born after Zeus, disguised as a swan, raped Leda. In the later account they freed their sister Helen, whom Theseus had abducted. They also took part in the Argonauts' search for the Golden Fleece. Castor, in the later myth, died in a contest with Idas and Lynceus, the sons of their paternal uncle Aphareus. The fight arose in a quarrel over some cattle which Castor and Polydeuces had carried off. In a variant myth, the quarrel was about the rape by Castor and Polydeuces of two daughters of another uncle, Leucippus, who were betrothed to the sons of Aphareus. When Castor died, Polydeuces, the immortal one of the pair, prayed to Zeus to let him die also. Zeus permitted Polydeuces to spend one day among the gods, the other in the underworld with his beloved brother.

According to another variant myth, Zeus rewarded the two for their brotherly love by placing them in the heavens as the constellation Gemini (the twins). They never appear together; when one rises, the other sets. The sun enters the constellation 21 May. The pair was worshiped at Sparta and Olympia, along with Heracles and other heroes. At Athens they were honored as gods under the title Anakes (lords or protectors). They were also regarded as gods of the sea. When sailors saw a flame at the masthead of a vessel, they believed Castor and Polydeuces were present. White lambs were sacrificed to the two.

Roman cult also honored Castor and Polydeuces. A temple was built in their honor in the Roman Forum in 414 B.C.E. in honor of their help during the battle of Lake Regillus 12 years earlier. Macaulay's *Lays of Ancient Rome* tells of the battle. On 15 July Roman *equites* (army divisions) passed in solemn review in honor of the battle. Castor's and Pollux's images were found on the oldest Roman coins. They were also regarded as patrons of horses; their horses being Xanthus (Yellow) and Cyllarus.

They are cited in Vergil's *Aeneid* (book 6), Ovid's *Metamorphoses* (book 6), Euripides' *Helen*, the Homeric Hymns, and Spenser's *Prothalamion*.

In the New Testament (Acts 28:11) Saint Paul sails from Malta in a ship "whose sign was Castor and Pollux." They are the subject of Rameau's opera, *Castor et Pollux*.

0740

Caswallawn (war king). In Celtic mythology, a war god worshiped in Britain; son of Beli; brother of Penardon, Llevelys, Lludd, Nynnyaw, and Peiban. He was noted for his cloak, which made him invisible. Caswallawn reigned when Julius Caesar first invaded Britain.

Variant spellings: Cassibellawn, Cassivelaonus.

0741

Cat. A domesticated carnivore, associated in many legends and myths with female goddesses and witches. In ancient Egypt the people were forbidden on pain of death to harm a cat. When a cat died, the bereaved family would shave off their eyebrows as a mark of mourning. The cat was then mummified, and a grand funeral procession took place. With weeping and lamentation the cat, along with its favorite toys and saucers of food, was placed in a tomb. This ceremony was the rule, not the exception. Many cats were brought to Europe by Roman soldiers returning from Egypt, even though Julius Caesar hated the animal intensely. But his dislike in no way affected the beliefs of the people.

Cat

Bast, the Egyptian goddess, as well as the Greek goddesses Demeter and Artemis, were identified with the cat.

The cat population of Europe increased during the Christian Middle Ages when Crusaders returned with them from their pillage of the Holy Land. During the 15th century there was a resurgence of the cult of the Norse goddess Freya, whose chariot was drawn by black cats. In Christian Europe the church made an effort to suppress witchcraft, and the cat came to be identified with witches. Many women were killed along with their cats. Cats, as demons, were burned, usually in a rite on Shrove Tuesday, the day before Ash Wednesday.

The ancient Jews disliked cats. Only one mention of a cat is given in the Epistle of Jeremy (v.22), part of the Old Testament Apocrypha but not included in the Jewish Scriptures today. The Arabs, along with the Jews, disliked cats, but Muhammed was said to have had a cat named Muezza. If a cat enters a mosque, it is considered a sign of good fortune even today.

In Buddhist folklore the cat is disliked. One tale tells that when the Buddha was sick a rat was sent to

obtain medicine to cure him, but a cat captured the rat and ate him. In Thailand and Burma the soul of a person who at death has attained a degree of spiritual enlightment enters the body of a cat. The soul is believed to stay with the cat until the animal dies and then the soul proceeds to heaven. In an ancient Thai burial custom, when a member of the royal family died, a live cat was buried along with the body. Small holes were strategically placed in the burial site so the cat could eventually get out. When the cat escaped, the temple priests declared that the soul of the dead person had passed into the cat.

0742

Catequil. In Inca mythology, thunder and lightning god, attendant on Inti, the sun, and Mama Quilla, the moon, and portrayed as carrying a sling and a mace. Children were sacrificed to Catequil.

Variant spelling: Choke Illa.

St. Catherine of Alexandria

0743

Catherine of Alexandria, St. (pure, clean). Third century C.E. In Christian legend, patron saint of theologians, philosophers, saddlers, spinsters, students, and rope-makers. Invoked against diseases of the tongue. Feast, 25 November.

The life of St. Catherine of Alexandria is found in *The Golden Legend*, a collection of saints' lives written in the 13th century by Jacobus de Voragine. Catherine was the daughter of Costis, a brother of Emperor Constantine the Great, and of Sabinella, daughter of the king of Egypt. At 15 Catherine was conversant with the works of Plato and was considered wiser than the Seven Wisest Men of her day. Her father died at this time and she was made queen. Nevertheless, she continued to study, even though her people objected. Finally, she refused to marry until a prince possessing all of the virtues should woo her.

A vision then appeared to an old hermit in the desert near Alexandria, in which the Virgin Mary told him to go to Catherine and tell her that the Savior of the world would come to be her bridegroom. That same night Christ appeared to Catherine and placed a wedding ring on her finger.

While Catherine was busy with her spiritual life, Maxentius came to the throne and started a persecution of Christians. Catherine argued so forcibly with him that he called together 50 of the most learned philosophers, promising them great rewards if they could refute her arguments. One by one they renounced their belief and accepted Christianity. Maxentius had them all burned to death, but he saved Catherine, who was beautiful, for himself. She, however, could not be moved. When she was locked in prison, her steadfastness so impressed the empress and a minion of the emperor that they both became Christians. The emperor then ordered Catherine bound on the sharp points of four revolving wheels, which when turned would tear her to pieces. The saint went gladly to her death, but an angel came and broke the wheels, the fragments of which killed many of the onlookers. Catherine was then carried outside the city, tortured, and finally

beheaded. Angels came and carried her body to the top of Mount Sinai.

In medieval Christian art St. Catherine has proved an almost inexhaustible subject. She is usually shown as a young, beautiful girl with a palm, book, or sword in her hand. Her most distinguishing attribute is her spiked wheel, often shown broken. In pictures of the Mystical Marriage of St. Catherine, Christ is portrayed as a child in the lap of his mother, the Virgin. This convention arose from the reluctance of medieval Christians to portray an adult Christ placing the wedding band on the finger of the female saint. In 1969 she was dropped from the liturgical calendar of the Roman Church.

0744
Catherine of Siena, St. (pure, clean). 1347–1380 C.E. In Christian legend, mystical author, patron saint of Italy. Feast, 30 April.

Cat and mouse

Catherine was the youngest child of a rich dyer of Siena. At an early age she displayed an intense religious sensibility, often causing her to go into a trancelike state. Her family was displeased with her and attempted to have her married off, but the girl had taken a vow of virginity. In her teens she sought admission to the Daughters of Penance of St. Dominic's Order of Preachers. Since she did not have to live in a convent, she chose a room in her father's house where she stayed for three years, suffering from great temptation. Finally, she had a vision of Christ, who set a ring on her finger and married her.

"Behold," he said to her, "I hereby espouse thee to myself in faith, which shall adorn thee from this time forward evermore . . . until . . . thou shalt celebrate with me in heaven the eternal wedding feast."

Catherine left her room and entered the world of political and religious intrigue, fighting to force the pope into leaving his residence at Avignon and returning to Rome. In 1375, according to legend, she received the stigmata, the wounds of Christ. They did not show on her body, however, until after her death. She died in Rome and was buried in the Minerva Church. Her head was removed and carried to Siena, where it is venerated as a sacred relic.

Among her writings, the *Dialogue*, dedicated in 1378 is considered a masterpiece of mystical writing, whereas her letters display another side to her complex personality.

In medieval Christian art St. Catherine of Siena is portrayed in the habit of her order, with the stigmata, holding a lily or crown of thorns.

Cat Maiden, The. Aesopic fable found in various collections throughout the world.   0745

A beautiful cat fell in love with a young man. Naturally, the young man did not return the cat's affections, so she prayed to Venus, the goddess of love and beauty, for help. The goddess, taking compassion on her plight, changed her into a fair damsel.

No sooner had the young man set eyes on the maiden than he became enamored of her beauty and in due time led her home as his bride. One evening a short time later, as the young couple were sitting in their chamber, the notion came to Venus to discover whether in changing the cat's form she had also changed her nature. So she set down a mouse before the beautiful damsel. The girl, reverting completely to her former character, started from her seat and pounced on the mouse as if she would eat it on the spot, while her husband watched her in dismay.

The goddess, provoked by such clear evidence that the girl had revealed her true nature, turned her into a cat again.

Moral: What is bred in the bone will never be absent in the flesh.

A similar fable is told in the great Indian collection *The Panchatantra*. A Brahmin saves a mouse and turns it into a girl, whom he determines to marry to the most powerful being in the world. The mouse maiden objects to the sun as a husband, as being too hot; to the clouds, which can obscure the sun, as being too cold; to the wind, which can drive the clouds, as too unsteady; to the mountain, which can withstand the wind, as being inferior to mice, which can bore into its entrails. So the Brahmin goes with her to the mouse king. The mouse maiden says: "Papa, make me into a mouse, and give me to him as a wife."

Cato the Younger, Marcus Porcius. 95–46 B.C.E.) In Roman history and legend, great-grandson of Cato the Elder and supporter of Pompey. Cato committed suicide at Utica when he learned Caesar had defeated Pompey. Lucan's epic *Pharsalia* pictures him as a hero. Dante's *Divine Comedy* makes Cato guardian of the approach to Mount Purgatory because of Cato's devotion to liberty. One of Plutarch's *Parallel Lives* and Joseph Addison's tragedy *Cato* deal with the Roman hero.

Catreus (down-flowing). In Greek mythology, son of King Minos of Crete and Pasiphae; brother of Acacallis, Androgeus, Ariadne, Deucalion, Euryale, Glaucas, Lycastrus, Phaedra, and Xenodice. Catreus was the father of three daughters, Aerope (the mother of Agamemnon and Menelaus), Clymene, and Apemosyne. Catreus had one son, Althaemenes, who, an oracle predicted, would kill his father. Many years later when Catreus went to Rhodes to visit him, Althaemenes mistook him for a pirate and killed him.

Cattle of the Sun. In Greek mythology, cattle living on the island of Thrinacia that were sacred to Apollo. Odysseus warned his men not to eat the cattle, but they paid no attention. As a result, Apollo sank their ship, and all of the men drowned except Odysseus. The episode is in Homer's *Odyssey* (book 12).

Caucasus. Mountain range where the Greek god Zeus chained Prometheus as a punishment. Each day Prometheus' liver was devoured by an eagle or a vulture. Vergil's *Aeneid* (book 4) says that Mount Caucasus burned when Phaethon's chariot came too close to earth.

0750

Caunus and Biblis. In Greek and Roman mythology, brother and sister, children of Miletus and Cyanee. Biblis fell in love with her brother and wrote him a letter telling of her sexual passion. Caunus fled in horror to Caria. Biblis followed him, but eventually she wearied of the chase and dissolved in her tears and changed into a fountain. Ovid's *Metamorphoses* (book 9) tells the tale.

0751

Cavall. In Arthurian legend, the dog of King Arthur. In Tennyson's poem *Enid*, part of *Idylls of the King*, he is described as "King Arthur's hound of deepest mouth."

0752

Cecilia, St. (blind). Third century C.E. In Christian legend, patron saint of music and musicians. Feast, 22 November. One of the most popular saints in Christianity.

In *The Canterbury Tales* Chaucer has the Second Nun narrate the life of the saint. The poet based his telling on *The Golden Legend*, a collection of saints' lives written in the 13th century by Jacobus de Voragine.

Cecilia was born of noble Roman parents during the reign of the Emperor Severus. Both parents were Christian, and the girl was brought up in that faith. She always carried a copy of the Gospels concealed in her robe, and she pledged herself to Christ and chastity. She was noted for her gift of music. She composed and sang hymns so sweetly that angels came down from heaven to listen to her. Because the instruments employed in secular music were insufficient for the music of her soul, she invented the organ, according to legend.

Her parents wanted her to marry a young Roman noble, Valerian, when she was about 16 years old. She persuaded the young man to respect her vows of chastity and even converted him to Christianity. The young man went to St. Urban in the catacombs and was baptized by him. When he returned, he found his wife Cecilia with an angel, who crowned them both with roses from Paradise. Valerian, in response to the angel's offer to grant any request of him, asked that his brother Tiburtius might also be converted to Christ. Soon after Tiburtius came in and noticed the scent of roses, though he could not see them. When he was converted by the words of Cecilia, he too saw the roses. The two men and Cecilia then went about doing good among the poor and sick. This came to the notice of the authorities, who had the two men arrested and executed for being Christians. Cecilia buried their bodies and was also arrested. Thrown

into a boiling bath, she emerged alive. She was then given three wounds in the neck and breast and was left for dead. After three days she died.

When the Academy of Music was founded at Rome in 1584 Cecilia was adopted as the patroness of church music. Ironically, the patronage arises from a medieval misunderstanding that associated her with the invention of the organ. Actually, the earliest known organ was the *Hydraulos*, built by the ancient Greeks about 250 B.C.E. Both John Dryden and Alexander Pope wrote odes in honor of St. Cecilia. Dryden's work, *Ode for St. Cecilia's Day*, was set to music by Handel in 1739. Liszt composed a legend for chorus and orchestra, *Die heilige Cäcilia*. In Christian art St. Cecilia is portrayed with a palm; sometimes she is crowned with roses. She is easily distinguished from other virgin martyr saints by her organ or other musical instrument or roll of music.

Cecrops

0753

Cecrops (face with a tail). In Greek mythology, a culture hero, son of Gaea; married Agraulos; father of Erisichthon, Herse, and Pandrosos. Cecrops was half man, half serpent with the torso of a man and the lower body of a serpent.

According to some accounts, Cecrops was the first king of Attica, which was called Cecropia in his honor. He built temples, established the worship of the gods, abolished human sacrifice, and introduced the art of writing.

When Poseidon and Athena were contending for possession of the land, Poseidon struck the rock of the Acropolis with his trident, and water (or, according to a variant myth, a horse) sprang forth. Athena, however, planted the first olive tree. Cecrops, who had to decide which god would have the land, conferred the honor on Athena because the olive branch was a sign of peace, whereas the horse was a symbol of war. Pandrosos (all dewy), his daughter, was the first priestess of Athena and had a shrine of her own, the *Pandroseum*, in the temple of Erechtheus on the Acropolis. She was invoked in time of drought. In her temple stood the sacred olive tree that Athena had created.

Cecropia was the original name for Athens, in honor of Cecrops. The word was used for Attica, and Athenians were called Cecropidae.

0754
Cedalion (he who takes charge of sailors). In Greek mythology, a man sent by Hephaestus to carry the blind Orion from Lemnos to the sun, where Apollo restored Orion's sight.

0755
Cedar. A fragrant evergreen tree; in world mythology and folklore, often a symbol of fidelity, manly strength, and fatherhood. In Near Eastern mythology the hero king was often represented by the cedar. In Assyria the cedar was under the protection of the god Ea, who personally watched over the fortunes of the sacred king. In Ezekiel (31) the cedar is used in a messianic allegory and represents strength and greatness. In Christian writing the cedar is often used as a symbol for Christ.

0756
Ceiuci. In the mythology of the Tupi Indians of Brazil, a cannibalistic witch.

One legend recounted by José Viera Couto de Magalhaes in his *O Selvagen* (1874), tells how Ceiuci caught a young man to eat. One day Ceiuci came to fish and saw a young man's shadow near the water. She cast her line into the water and saw the young man laugh. She looked up and said, "Descend," but the young fellow refused. She then sent biting ants after him. When he jumped into the water, she caught him and took him home, intending to eat him. While she was fetching wood, her daughter came upon the captive. He persuaded her to hide him. When Ceiuci returned, the two fled, dropping palm branches on the way; these were transformed into animals that the witch stopped to eat. Eventually, the young man reached the hut of an old

woman who was his mother. By this time he was an old man himself.

0757
Celaeno (swarthy). In Greek mythology, one of the seven Pleiades (a constellation), daughter of Atlas and Pleione. Celaeno was the mother of Lycus and Chimaereusc by Poseidon and, according to some accounts, the mother of Delphus by Apollo. Celaeno is also the the name of one of the Danaides (the 50 daughters of King Danaus), the name of a daughter of Poseidon and Ergea, and the name of one of the Harpies.

0758
Cenn Cruaich (lord of the mound). In Celtic mythology, idol worshiped in Ireland by the sacrifice of firstlings. According to ancient accounts, his image was made of gold and surrounded by 12 stones, stood on the plain of Mag Slecht in Ulster. When St. Patrick came to Ireland, according to Christian accounts, the Idol of Cenn Cruaich bent down to honor the saint and was called Cromcruaich (the bowed-one Cruaich).

The centaur Chiron

0759
Centaur (one-hundred strong). In Greek mythology, a half-man, half-horse creature, living principally in Thessaly; offspring of either Ixion and Nephele, a cloud, or Apollo's son Centaurus and Silbia, or Cen-

taurus and the mare Magnesian. Centaurs, noted as rapists and drunkards came to the marriage of Hippodameia and Pirithous, king of the Lapiths, as invited guests and attempted to rape the women and kill the men. Pirithous and his friend Theseus killed many centaurs at the wedding and drove the rest out of Thessaly. But not all centaurs were lascivious drunkards. The centaur Chiron, son of Cronus and an Oceanid, was a friend of man, teaching him the arts of healing, hunting, and music. He was the tutor of Asclepius, the god of medicine, and also of Jason, Achilles, and Heracles. During a fight with some other centaurs one of Heracles' poisoned arrows accidentally struck Chiron, who was immortal. To avoid suffering from the wound for eternity, Chiron asked Zeus to let him die. Zeus then presented his immortality to Prometheus, and out of pity placed Chiron in the heavens as the constellation Sagittarius, the archer, the ninth sign of the Zodiac. In general, the Greeks used centaurs in their art and literature to represent barbaric civilization. They are often portrayed on vases and appear on the metops of the Parthenon and as sculptures on the west pediment of the temple of Zeus at Olympia. In Roman art they are portrayed in Pompeii at the House of the Centaur. In medieval Christian art they represent man's animal nature. For example, a centaur is portrayed on one of the capitals of Winchester Cathedral in England. Vergil's *Aeneid* (book 6.618) and Ovid's *Metamorphoses* (book 12), which describes the battle of the Lapiths and centaurs, inspired Spenser's *Faerie Queene* (4.1.23), which tells of the battle of the centaurs with Heracles as well as the Lapith-centaur battle.

Sagittarius

0760
Ceridwen (poetry, fair). In Celtic mythology, a Welsh fertility goddess; daughter of Ogyrven; wife of Tegid the Bold; mother of Crerwy, the most beautiful girl in the world, and Avagdu, the ugliest boy. She possessed a magic caldron called Amen. The caldron contained a magic drink called greal, made from six plants. When the greal was drunk, it gave inspiration and knowledge. The caldron was used by the goddess as some form of compensation for the ugliness of her son Avagdu. It was stolen by Gwion, and Ceridwen pursued him. He first changed into a hare and she into a greyhound; he became a fish and she an otter; he became a bird and she a hawk; he became a grain of corn and she a hen--and finally she ate him. She then gave birth to him and threw him into the sea, and he became the bard Taliesin.
Variant spellings: Cerridwen, Keridwen.

0761
Cernunnos. In Celtic mythology, the "lord of animals"; he was portrayed horned, sitting cross-legged, and flanked by various animals. Cernunnos was associated with fertility and prosperity, causing ancient Roman writers to equate him with Mercury, their god of commerce and leader of the souls of the dead. In later medieval Christian legend Cernunnos became a symbol of Antichrist.

0762
Cessair. In Celtic mythology, one of the tribal goddesses of the peoples who preceded the Celts in Ireland. In medieval legend Cessair was regarded as a daughter of the biblical Noah and the first person to set foot in Ireland.

0763
Chabriel (dryness). In medieval Jewish folklore, the angel credited with drying up the waters of the flood mentioned in Genesis (8:13). In the biblical account, however, Yahweh, the Hebrew God, is responsible.

0764
Chac. In Mayan mythology, four-part god of rain and thunder, patron of the number 13. Each part of Chac was connected with a cardinal point and a color. They were Chac Xib Chac (the red man), Chac of the east; Sac Xib Chac (the white man), Chac of the north, Ek Xib Chac (the black man), Chac of the west; and Kan Xib Chac (the yellow man), Chac of the south.

In Mayan art Chac appears more frequently than any other god. He is portrayed with a long truncated nose and two curling fangs protruding downward out of his mouth. Paul Schellhas, when classifying the gods in some Mayan codices, gave Chac the letter *B*, and the god is sometimes referred to as God B.

0765

Chachalmeca. In Aztec ritual, high-ranking priest in charge of sacrifices. Aztec priests were not allowed to marry, and they lived in a cloisterlike compound. As part of their initiation they were castrated and blood was drawn from their penises, ears and tongues by a *chaichiutzli*, a ritual stone.

0766

Chad, St. (battle). Seventh century. In Christian legend, bishop of Lichfield, England. Feast, 2 March.

Chad became abbot of the Priory of Lastingham in 659, which had been founded by his brother, St. Cedd. King Oswy then appointed Chad to the see of York, but he was removed by St. Theodore in favor of St. Wilfrid. Theodore was impressed by Chad, however, and arranged for him to be bishop of Mercia. Chad moved the episcopal seat from Repton to Lichfield, "the field of the dead." He built a church and lodging. After some two years he had a vision in which he was warned of his approaching death. He saw his brother, St. Cedd, with a troop of angels. They sang and called him to follow them to God as they ascended to heaven. Shortly afterward Chad died. In art he is shown holding a model of the cathedral of Lichfield.

0767

Chagan-Shukuty. In Siberian mythology, a creator god who formed the earth with the aid of Otshirvani, another creator god.

The two companions one day descended from heaven. They saw a frog or turtle diving into the water. Chagan-Shukuty raised the animal and placed it on the water. Otshirvani then sat on the animal's stomach. Otshirvani asked Chagan-Shukuty to dive to the bottom of the water and bring up what he found. On the second try Chagan-Shukuty came up with a piece of dirt, which was sprinkled on the stomach of the animal. By now both gods were sitting on the animal. The animal then sank out of sight, and only the earth remained visible on the surface of the waters. The two gods fell asleep, and the devil decided to drown them. But when he attempted to seize the edge of the earth he no longer saw the water, for the earth kept growing. He then seized the two gods under his arm and began to run toward the shore, but the earth kept ahead of him. Realizing he could not accomplish his task, he dropped the gods and escaped.

0768

Chalchihuitlicue (lady precious green, precious wound). In Aztec mythology, storm goddess, per-

sonification of whirlpools and youthful beauty; wife of Tlaloc, the god of rain and water.

According to Fray Bernardino de Sahagún in his *Historia general de las cosas de Nueva España*, the goddess "had power over the sea and the rivers, and could drown those who navigated on the waters, causing tempests and whirlwinds that would flood the boats and barges and other vessels happening to be on the water." However, Lewis Spence, the Scottish anthropologist, observed that Shagún's description "appears inexact" since the "Mexicans were not a seafaring people." In art Chalchihuitlicue was portrayed as a bare-breasted woman wearing a coronet of blue paper surmounted by green feathers. Her dress was of a green-blue tint. In her left hand she carried a large water plant, in the right a vase surmounted by a cross, symbol of the four points of the compass, from which the rain comes.

Variant spellings: Chalchiuhtliycue, Chalchiuhcihuatl, Chalchiuhtlicue.

0769

Chalmecaciuatl. In Aztec mythology, paradise for children who died before they reached the age of reason. The concept is similar to the Christian limbo and may merely be an Aztec reworking of the Christian belief prompted by Spanish missionaries.

0770

Chamalcán. In the mythology of the Cakchiquel Indians, a bat god, mentioned in the *Popol Vuh*, the sacred book of the ancient Quiché Maya of Guatemala.

0771

Chamuel (he who seeks God). In Jewish and Christian folklore, one of the seven archangels. In Jewish folklore Chamuel is the name given to the angel who wrestled with Jacob (Gen. 32:24–32) but who is not named in the biblical text. In Christian folklore Chamuel is name of the angel who comforted Jesus in the Garden of Gethsemane (Luke 22:43) but not is named in the text.

Variant spellings: Camael, Camial, Camniel, Cancel, Chamael, Kemuel, Khamael.

0772

Chandra (moon). In Hindu mythology, moon god, source of fertility, often identified with the magic drink of the gods, Amrita or Soma. Chandra was the ancestor of the Chandra-vansa, the lunar race, which was divided into two branches, the Yadavas and the Pauravas. Krishna (an incarnation of the god Vishnu) was descended from the Yadavas.

Wilkie Collins, the English writer, in his novel *The Moonstone*, tells of the Chandra-kanta (the moonstone), an enormous diamond placed in the head of a statue of Chandra. The moonstone is guarded by three priests who are killed by an Englishman, John Herncastle. The novel then traces the life of the gem and the evil it brings on each person who comes into contact with it.

Another magic gem in Hindu lore, the Chintamani (the wish gem) grants the owner all he or she desires. It belongs to the god Brahma, who is sometimes called by its name. Other traditions ascribe it to Indra, as part of his crown, or say it is the third eye of a snake god.

0773

Chang Chiu. In Chinese legend, a deified Taoist sage who wore thin, unlined clothes, even in the depths of winter. Once Chang Chiu was invited to the emperor's court to exhibit his magical powers. He cut his clothes into small pieces and transformed them into butterflies. They resumed their original shape when he clapped his hands.

Chang Hsien

0774

Chang Hsien (Chang the immortal). In Chinese legend, a deified mortal, patron god of childbearing, often portrayed as an old man. He holds in his hand a bow and arrow, with which he shoots at the Dog Star.

0775

Chang Kuo-lao. Eighth century C.E.? In Chinese Taoist legend, one of the Pa-Hsien, the Eight Immortals. He was a noted magician who could become invisible. He rode a magic mule which, when not in use, was folded up and put in his wallet. When the mule was needed, water was poured into Chang Kuo-lao's wallet and the mule reappeared. He is portrayed often with a bamboo tube drum, carried in either arm; its sounds announced his arrival in a community.

In Japanese legend Chang Kuo-lao is called Chokaro.

0776

Channa. In Buddhist legend, the faithful charioteer of the Buddha who accompanied him when he went out to see the world. He does not appear in Buddhist legend, however, as a convert to Buddhism.

0777

Chanson de geste (song of deeds). Old French epic, often telling of the deeds of such heroes as Charlemagne, Roland, and Huon de Bordeaux. The most famous chanson de geste is the 11th century *Chanson de Roland*.

0778

Chanticleer (sing clear?). In medieval folklore, a clever rooster, always pursued by the fox. Chaucer's *The Nun's Priest's Tale*, part of *The Canterbury Tales*, narrates one of the tales associated with the cock. One day the fox, Dan Russell, came to the poultry yard and told Master Chanticleer he could not resist Chanticleer's singing. Flattered by the fox, Chanticleer closed his eyes and began to sing. The fox immediately seized Chanticleer and ran off. "I would recommend you eat me at once for I think I can hear your pursuers," Chanticleer said to the fox. When the fox opened his mouth to reply, Chanticleer flew out.

0779

Charlemagne (Charles the great). c.742–814. C.E. In medieval history and legend, king of the Franks, first Holy Roman Emperor, who appears in medieval legends and French *chansons de gestes*.

Charlemagne was the son of Pepin the Short and Bertha the Largefooted. Pepin died in 768, and his Frankish kingdom was willed to his sons Carloman and Charles. Three years after the accession of the brothers Carloman died, and Charles took possession of his dominions. During his long reign of nearly half a century Charlemagne extended his boundaries until they embraced the larger part of Western Europe. He conducted more than 50 military campaigns, among which were those against the Lombards, the Saracens, and the Saxons. He was crowned by the Pope in 800 as Holy Roman Emperor.

His rule as emperor lasted 14 years. During that time he called synods or councils of the clergy in his dominions, presided at these meetings, and addressed words of admonition to abbots and bishops. Education was important to Charlemagne. In his old age he tried to learn to write but found it beyond his powers. Distressed by the ignorance of his people, he established schools and had numerous manuscripts copied. He invited Alcuin, one of the finest scholars of his day, to come from England to his court and help him organize a palace school. Numerous legends grew about his person, forming an important part of medieval folklore.

In one legend Charlemagne, having built for his own use a new castle overlooking the Rhine, was awakened from his sleep during the first night he spent there by the touch of an angel. The heavenly messenger told Charlemagne to go out into the night and steal something. So the ruler saddled his horse and rode off. He had not gone far when he met a knight unknown to him. A challenge ensued, and Charlemagne unhorsed his opponent. When he learned that he had disarmed Elbegast (Alberich), the notorious highwayman, he promised to let him go free if he would only help him steal something that night.

Guided by Elbegast, Charlemagne secretly went to the castle of one of his ministers. With Elbegast's aid he got into the bedroom of his minister unseen. There, crouching in the dark, Charlemagne overheard his minister confide to his wife about a plot to murder the emperor the next day. Patiently biding his time until they were sound asleep, Charlemagne took a worthless trifle and noiselessly made his way out, returning to his castle unseen. The next day he foiled the plot and later forgave the conspirators when they swore allegiance to him. Elbegast was so impressed by Charlemagne that he renounced his dishonest profession and joined the emperor's service.

Grateful to the angel, Charlemagne named his new castle Ingelheim (angel home). This episode is often alluded to in later legends of chivalry, in which knights, called on to justify their unlawful appropriation of another's property, disrespectfully remind the emperor that he too was once a thief.

When Charlemagne's third wife died, he married a beautiful Eastern princess, Frastrada, who with a magic ring soon won Charlemagne's complete devotion. The new queen, however, did not long enjoy her power, for a dangerous illness overcame her. At the point of death, she feared the ring might be worn by another, and she slipped it into her mouth and died. Solemn preparations were made to bury her in the cathedral of Mayence, but the emperor refused to part with her body. Neglectful of all matters of state, he remained in the mortuary chamber day after day. Turpin, his archbishop and advisor, slipped into the room while the emperor, exhausted with fasting and weeping, was asleep. After carefully searching for the magic ring, Turpin discovered it in the queen's mouth. The archbishop slipped on the ring and was about to leave the room when Charlemagne awoke. The emperor flung himself on Turpin's neck, saying he needed him to be near. Taking advantage of the ring's magic power, Turpin told Charlemagne to eat and drink and after the funeral to resume his affairs of state.

Although old, Turpin was now forced by the magic ring (which he never took off for fear it would fall into the wrong hands) to accompany Charlemagne everywhere. One moonlit night he stole noiselessly out of the emperor's tent and wandered alone in the woods, thinking how he could get rid of the ring without exposing Charlemagne to danger. As he walked, he came to a glade in the forest and saw a deep pool. He cast the ring into the pool and went back to his tent. The next day he was delighted to see that the magic spell of love was broken and that Charlemagne had returned to his own self. Charlemagne, however, seemed restless and soon went out to hunt. He lost his way and came to the pool where Turpin had thrown the ring. He was so charmed by the spot that he gave orders later that a castle should be erected there. The castle was to become Aix-la-Chapelle (Aachen).

Charlemagne gathered around him twelve paladins, among them Roland (his nephew), Rinaldo, Namo, Salomon, Astolpho of England, Florismart, Malagigi, Ganelon (the traitor), Ogier the Dane, Fierambras, Oliver, and Archbishop Turpin. (Other names given in various legends are Ivon, Ivory, Otton, Berengier, Anseis, Gerin, Guarinos, Engelier, Samson, and Gerard.)

Another legend tells how St. James the Greater appeared to Charlemagne, telling him to free Spain from the Moors. The emperor went to Spain with a large army and attacked Pamplona. For two months they were beaten back; then they prayed for God's help, and the walls of the city fell like those of Jericho. All of the Moors who converted to Christianity were spared, but the remainder were slaughtered. Afterward the emperor went to the shrine of St. James at Santiago de Compostela to pay his devotions and later returned to France.

Once Charlemagne was challenged to single combat by Ferracute, a giant. Although Charlemagne is described as 20 feet tall in most legends, the emperor felt himself no match for the giant, so he sent Ogier the Dane to fight him. Ogier failed, as did Renaud de Montauban, and finally Roland took the field. The two fought, with Roland trying to convert Ferracute to Christianity. With heavenly aid, Roland dealt a death blow. The giant fell, calling on Muhammad, while Roland laughed.

Later Roland was killed at the battle of Roncesvalles, the subject of *The Song of Roland*. The defeat was the result of Ganelon's betrayal of Charlemagne's forces. On his return Ganelon was convicted of treason and sentenced to be drawn and quartered.

Another legend, which sometimes appears in European art, relates to St. Giles. Charlemagne had an unconfessed sin (perhaps an incestuous relationship with his sister). One day Giles was celebrating Mass in the emperor's presence when an angel appeared above the altar bearing a scroll on which the sin of the emperor was written. Charlemagne then confessed his sin and was given absolution by the saint.

When Charlemagne is portrayed as a devotional figure in Christian art, he often stands next to Constantine the Great. He generally wears armor and a cloak lined with ermine. He also wears the Iron Crown of Lombardy and holds an orb and scepter, a book, or a model of a cathedral, signifying Aix-la-Chapelle, where his relics lie. His cult as a saint was advanced by Frederick Barbarossa and the antipope Paschal III in 1166. Though he was not officially canonized as a saint, he was given the title "Blessed" by Pope Benedict XIV. His feast day is 28 January. In 1475 his feast was made obligatory in France, but today it is observed only in Aix-la-Chapelle and two Swiss abbeys.

0780

Charon (fierce brightness). In Greek mythology, ferryman of the Styx, who carried the dead to the underworld. Each dead person was buried with a coin in his mouth or on his eyelids to pay for the crossing.

0781

Charter Oak. In American history and folklore, a large tree once standing near Hartford, Connecticut. Supposedly, the oak was the place where the colonial charter of 1687 was hidden when it was demanded by the royal governor Sir Edmund Andros. King James II had appointed Andros governor over all New England, with the intent of declaring all the previous royal charters void. When Andros demanded the Connecticut charter at a Colonial Assembly meeting where it was displayed, its members held him off for a long debate. It continued into the night, and candles had to be lit. Then suddenly all of the candles went out; when they were relit, the charter had disappeared. According to legend, it was hidden in the oak by Captain Joseph Wadsworth.

The tree lived until 1856 when it was destroyed by a storm.

0782

Chasca. In Inca mythology, the planet Venus, known as the "youth with the long and curling locks." Chasca was worshiped as a page of the sun (Inti), whom he attended in his rising and setting. He was sometimes mistakenly thought to be a goddess.

0783

Chay. In the mythology of the Cakchiquel Maya, obsidian stone from which they made their cutting tools and ornaments; worshiped as a god. *The Annals of the Cakchiquels*, written at the end of the 16th century, tells how the Indians "gave homage to the Obsidian Stone" and how it spoke to them, telling them where to settle for a happy and good life.

0784

Chelm Goat, The. Jewish folktale about how the disciples of the rabbi of Chelm were tricked by an innkeeper.

Once the rabbi of Chelm became ill. He was told that only goat's milk could cure him, so his disciples went to another town to buy a nanny goat. On their way home they stopped at an inn. The innkeeper switched his billy goat for the nanny goat while the men drank. When they arrived home and tried to milk the goat they discovered it was a billy goat. They returned to the trader, thinking he had tricked them, and again they stopped at the inn for a drink. The innkeeper again switched the goats, so they arrived at the trader with the nanny goat and complained that it was a billy goat. The trader demonstrated that the goat was indeed a nanny capable of giving milk. The rabbi of Chelm asked the disciples to get a certificate from Rabbi Shmul in the trader's town, warranting that they were sold a nanny goat. They obtained the document and returned to Chelm, but the goats were once again switched at the inn and they arrived with the billy goat. They now believed they had been bewitched. The rabbi of Chelm replied, "Rabbi Shmul is a wise and upright man. He never writes anything that is not true. If he tells us that the goat is a nanny you can believe that it is not a billy. Now you will ask: how is it that the goat he says is a nanny turns out to be a billy goat? A good question. The answer is simple. The goat he saw was a nanny, but we have such bad luck in Chelm that by the time the goat reached our town it was turned into a billy goat."

This folktale was used by Sholom Aleichem in his Yiddish short story "The Enchanted Tailor," included in his book *The Old Country*.

Chemosh. In Near Eastern mythology (Moabite), a god of Moab; enemy of Yahweh, the Hebrew god, in the Old Testament. Nothing specific is known about the cult of Chemosh, though King Solomon, beguiled by his foreign wives, built "an high place for Chemosh, the abomination of Moab, in the hill that is before Jerusalem" (2 Kings 11:7). This shrine to the god was destroyed by the religious reforms of King Josiah (1 Kings 23:13). In Milton's *Paradise Lost* (book 1), Chemos is a fallen angel, listed in a catalog of demons enumerated by the poet. Milton's line "Next Chemos, th' obscene dread of Moab's sons," indicates that Milton believed that human sacrifices of young men were made to Chemos. St. Jerome, commenting on some biblical verses that mention Chemosh, equated the name with Baal-peor, another Moabite god, whom the Israelites adopted in their worship of foreign gods and goddesses.

0786

Cheng San-kung. In Chinese legend, a deified mortal honored as patron god of fishermen. Cheng San-kung, Hou Erh-kung, and Keng Ch'i-kung all fished together, as sworn brothers. One day they saw a yellow rock protruding out of the water. A spirit told them it was made of gold. They rowed to the rock and tried to pick it up, but it was too heavy to move. Then they prayed to Buddha, promising to build a temple in exchange for the golden rock. Their prayers were answered: the rock became light, and they took it home. In return, they built a temple to Buddha.

0787

Ch'en Nan. In Chinese legend, a sage who had the power to cause rain; he lived 1,350 years, mostly on dogs' flesh. Once, passing through a village, he found people praying for rain. Detecting a dragon (maker of rain) hidden in the mud, he forced the animal to come out, which made it rain. Ch'en Nan is often portrayed in Chinese and Japanese art evoking a dragon from a gourd or bowl, or sailing on a large hat, which he used once to cross a river when there was no one to ferry him.

In Japanese legend, Ch'en Nan is called Chinnan.

0788

Chenuke. In the mythology of the Ona Indians of Tierra del Fuego, an evil spirit. The hero hunter Kwanyip defeated him.

0789

Che Puteh Jambai. In Malayan legend, a poor man who was told in a dream to murder his wife if he wished to get rich.

Che Puteh Jambai and his wife were so poor they could not afford clothes for both of them. When one left the house, the other stayed at home naked. In a dream Che Puteh was told to kill his wife and he would then be rich, so the man told his wife to prepare for death. She, being a faithful wife according to Oriental beliefs, just asked permission to go down to the river to wash herself with some lime juice. At the river she divided the limes with her knife, cutting herself in the process, and blood dripped onto the rocks and into the river. As each drop was carried away by the current, a large jar immediately rose to the surface and floated upstream. When each jar reached her, Che Puteh's wife tapped it with her knife and pulled it in to the edge of the rocks. When she found the jars full of gold, the ever-faithful wife went in search of her husband. He kept the gold and decided it was best to keep his wife as well.

They lived happily together for many years, and a beautiful daughter was born to them. All the rajahs and chiefs wanted her for a wife. The couple, however, hid all of their gold and disappeared. They have not been seen since, nor has their treasure ever been found.

0790

Cheron, St. (dear one?) Third century. In Christian legend, bishop of Chartres, France. On his way to visit his teacher, St. Denis, Cheron was attacked by robbers who struck off his head. Taking his head into his hand, he continued his journey from Chartres to Paris. One of the windows in the cathedral of Chartres portrays the legend of the saint.

0791

Cherruve. In the folklore of the Araucanian Indians of Chile, the spirits of shooting stars.

0792

Cherry. A fruit tree; in world mythology and folklore, often a symbol of female sexuality. In the Finnish epic poem *The Kalevala* (rune 50), the Maiden of the Air, Marjatta, swallows a cherry and becomes pregnant. In China the cherry is identified with female beauty and female power. In Japanese folklore the cherry symbolizes prosperity and riches. In English folklore, however, dreaming of a cherry tree means ill fortune is on the way. In Germany it was considered inadvisable to eat cherries with princes because the ruler might use the pits to gouge out one's eyes; no reason can be traced for this outrage.

0793

Cherubim (intercessor). In Jewish, Christian, and Islamic mythology, an order of beings or angels derived from griffinlike monsters in Near Eastern mythology. In Western European art they are usually portrayed as chubby-faced babes with small wings.

In the Old Testament cherubim are spirits in the service of Yahweh (a Hebrew cult name of God). They are not, strictly speaking, angels, since they do not deliver any messages from Yahweh. In Genesis (3:24), for example, they stand guard over the way to the Tree of Life, guard the Ark of the Covenant (Exod. 25:18–20), and serve as the mount of Yahweh (2 Sam. 22:11).

In medieval Jewish folklore cherubim were thought of as beautiful men. Christianity in the baroque age reduced them to chubby-faced children, who often appear in paintings such as those by Rubens. The singular of cherubim is cherub.

0794

Chia-Lan. In Chinese Buddhism, generic name for tutelary gods who protect monasteries.

0795

Chibcachum. In the mythology of the Chibcha Indians of Colombia, patron god of laborers and merchants.

Once Chibcachum became angry with the people and sent a flood over the land. They called on Pochica, chief of the gods, to save them. He appeared as a rainbow near the town of Soacha. As the sun, he dried the waters; then with his staff he opened a deep chasm in the rocks so that the flood waters could recede. From this the great waterfall Tequendama was formed. Chibcachum went underground, and from that time he has supported the earth. Earthquakes occur when Chibcachum shifts his burden from one shoulder to another.

Variant spelling: Chicchechum.

0796

Chiconquiahuitl (seven rain). In Aztec ritual a god who was impersonated by a slave during the feast of the god Xolotl Huetzi, the lord of the evening star. The slave who represented Chiconquiahuitl and slaves who represented other gods, such as Yacatecutli (he who goes first), Cauhtlaxayanh (eagle face), Coatlinahual (weresnake), and the goddess Chachalmecacihuatl (lady of the Chachalmec people?), were "honored as if they had been the gods themselves," according to Fray Diego Durán in his *Book of the Gods and Rites* (c. 1576), describing Aztec ritual. On the feast day the impersonators were "cast alive into the fire" and pulled out "half-roasted." Their chests were then opened.

0797

Ch'ih Ching-tzu (son of red essence, red spirit). In Chinese mythology, the spirit of fire, who made himself clothes from red leaves. He is one of the Wu Lao, the five spirits of natural forces.

0798

Chih Nu. In Chinese mythology, the goddess of weavers.

0799

Ch'i Ku-tzu. In Chinese mythology, seven deified young women, invoked in times of drought, flood, and other natural disasters.

0800

Chimaera (she-goat). In Greek mythology, a fantastic fire- breathing creature with the head of a lion, the body of a goat, and the tail of a serpent or dragon; offspring of Typhon and Echidna. Homer's *Iliad* (book 6), Vergil's *Aeneid* (book 6), the visit to the underworld, and Ovid's *Metamorphoses* (book 9.647) describe the beast. Spenser's *Faerie Queene* (6.1.8) makes the Chimaera and Cerebus the parents of the Blatant Beast, the evil monster of the poem. Milton's *Paradise Lost* (book 2.624–8) places Chimaeras in hell. In Greek mythology the hero Bellerophon destroyed the Chimaera by mounting his winged horse, Pegasus, and shooting the monster with his arrows. There is a famous fifth-century B.C.E. Etruscan bronze Chimaera which is now housed in Florence.

0801

Chiminigagua. In the mythology of the Chibcha Indians of Colombia, a creator god. Chiminigagua held light inside his being. When it burst forth, creation began.

He first made gigantic black birds that covered the mountain, bringing light. Chiminigagua's cult was unimportant among the Chibcha because they considered the sun (Zuhe) and the moon (Chia) more beautiful and therefore more deserving of honor and worship.

Variant spelling: Chimizigagua.

0802

Chin. In the mythology of the Muysca Indians of Bogotá, Colombia, moon goddess representing the power of female destructiveness. In one myth she was credited with flooding the earth when she was displeased. In order to pacify her, men would dress up in women's clothes and perform women's duties in the hope that the goddess would not punish them for being men.

0803

Ching Tu (the pure land). In Chinese Buddhism, the dwelling place of those liberated who have prayed to A-mi-t'o Fo, the Buddha of Infinite Light. Sometimes it is called *Hsi fang chi-lo-shih-chieh* (the paradise in the west).

Ch'in-kuang wang. In Chinese mythology, ruler of the first hell of Ti Yü, the underworld.

0804

Chinvat. In Persian mythology, a bridge over which all souls of the dead must pass on their way to heaven or hell. According to one Zoroastrian text, Chinvat "is like a beam of many sides, of whose edges there are some which are broad, and there are some which are thin and sharp; its broad sides are so large that its width is twenty-seven reeds, and its sharp sides are so contracted that in thinness it is like the edge of a razor." Both the good and the wicked come to the bridge, but it "becomes a narrow bridge for the wicked, even unto a resemblance to the edge of a razor.... He who is of the wicked, as he places a footstep on the bridge . . . falls from the middle of the bridge, and rolls over head-foremost" to hell. The good, however, pass over the bridge easily.

Variant spellings: Chinvad, Kinvad.

0805

Chipiripa. In the mythology of the Indians living in the Isthmus of Panama, a rain god.

0806

Chiu-t'ien Lei Kung. In Chinese mythology, a thunder god, invoked against disasters.

0807

Chonchon. In the folklore of the Araucanian Indians of Chile, a vampire with a human head and huge ears. It uses its large ears for wings to fly about seeking its prey.

0808

Christina the Astonishing, St. (I anoint, the anointed). 1150– 1224 C.E. In Christian legend, patron saint of psychotherapists. Feast, 24 July.

Born at Brusthem in the diocese of Liège, Christina at 15 was left an orphan with her two elder sisters. At the age of 22 she had a seizure and was pronounced dead. Her coffin was carried to the church and a Requiem Mass was begun. Suddenly, after the *Agnus Dei*, Christina sat up in her coffin and soared to the beams of the ceiling "like a bird," according to one account, and perched there. The congregation, except for her elder sister, who stayed for the end of the Mass, fled from the church. The priest then called Christina to come down from the beams. She cried out that she was up in the beams because she could not stand the smell of sinful human flesh. She then said she had died, gone down to hell, visited purgatory, and had a trip to heaven. God had offered her the choice of staying in heaven or returning to earth to help the poor souls in

0809

purgatory by her prayers. Christina decided to come back to life and help the dead. She said that by the time the *Agnus Dei* had been said the third time, her soul had been restored to her body.

After Christina came back to life, her day-to-day activities became abnormal. She would flee to remote places, climb trees, towers, and rocks, and crawl into ovens to escape the smell of human flesh. She would handle fire, rush into a river in the depth of winter, or jump into a millrace and be carried away unharmed under the wheel. She liked to pray by balancing herself on the top of a hurdle or curled up on the ground looking like a ball.

Though the medieval mind was understanding of many oddities, her actions made some accuse her of being possessed by devils. Attempts were made to confine her, but she always broke loose. One time a man attacked her, broke her leg, and tied her up. A doctor came to mend the leg but chained her to a pillar for safety. No sooner had he left than Christina escaped. Another time a priest refused to give her Holy Communion, and she jumped into the Meuse river and swam away. She kept herself alive by begging. She dressed in rags, frightening the populace. However, when she sat in water blessed for baptism, "her way of living was more conformed to that of men, she was quieter, and better able to bear the smell of human beings," writes her Dominican biographer, Thoma de Cantimpré, who had known her personally.

Christina's last years were spent in the Convent of St. Catherine at Saint-Trond where many nobles came to her for advice.

Christmas (Christ's Mass). Feast of the Nativity of Jesus, celebrated on 25 December. The date of Christmas was chosen in 440 C.E. to coincide with the winter solstice and a pagan festival in honor of the sun god. The actual birth date of Jesus is not known, and the Early Church paid little attention to the matter. St. Leo, however, writing in the fifth century, describes the importance of Christmas: "When adoring the Birth of Our Savior, we are celebrating our own true origin. For indeed this generation of Christ in time is the source of the Christian People, and the birth of the Head is, too, that of his Mystical Body."

Numerous legends arose during the Middle Ages regarding the Christmas season. At time of Jesus' birth (the Gospels do not mention this, but tradition assigned the time), all of the animals in the stables, such as cattle, and deer in the field kneel down to honor Christ. Bees were believed to awake from sleep and hum a song in praise of the Child, but the song could be heard only by those chosen by Jesus. The birds were believed to sing all night at

0810

Christmas. In addition to kneeling in adoration of the Christ Child, the animals were gifted with speech on the sacred eve. One French medieval play portrays the belief. The animals, it seems, preferred to speak in Latin.

Crow: *Christus natus est* (Christ is born)
Ox: *Ubi?* (Where?)
Lamb: *Bethlehem*
Ass: *Eamus* (Let us go).

Central Europeans believed, and some still do, that the animals also discuss the virtues and faults of various people since they hear all conversations during the year.

The medieval ages believed in a host of devils, ghosts, witches and assorted malignant spirits, and it was believed that their power was suspended during the Christmas season. Since the Christ Child was present, no harm could be worked by the demons of darkness. Shakespeare in *Hamlet* (act 1, sc.1, lines 158– 163) alludes to this belief:

Some say that ever 'gainst that season comes
Wherein our savior's birth is celebrated,
The bird of dawning singeth all night long:
And then, they say, no spirit dare stir abroad!
The nights are wholesome; then no planets strike,
No fairy takes, no witch has power to charm.

If you were lucky enough to die at midnight on Christmas, you could enter heaven at once. Children born on Christmas were blessed with the power of seeing spirits and even controlling them, according to some medieval accounts. But in some other accounts a child born on Christmas was cursed because it was born at the same time as Jesus.

One legend that constantly reappeared in different guises during the Middle Ages relates to the Christmas Angel. Every year the Virgin Mary selected a number of angels and sent them out from heaven into different parts of the world. Each angel awakened a little child from its first sleep and carried it to heaven to sing a carol to the Christ Child. When the children returned to earth, not everyone would believe their story, but those blessed by God would know that the children had been specially chosen.

The first hymns in honor of Christmas were written in the fifth century, soon after the Christmas feast was established in the medieval church. The birthplace of the Christmas carol was Italy. In the 13th century St. Francis of Assisi wrote a hymn in

Latin, *Psalmus in Nativitate*. Franciscans then composed hymns in Italian, among them, one that opens:

In Bethlehem is born the Holy Child,
On hay and straw in the winter wild
O, my heart is full of mirth
At Jesus' birth

From Italy the carol spread to other European countries, such as France, Spain, Germany, and England. The earliest English carol was written at the beginning of the 15th century.

One of the most important folk customs of Christmas is that of the crèche, which portrays the Christ Child, the Virgin Mary, St. Joseph, and the Wise Men, or Magi. Legend also credits it to St. Francis of Assisi. His biographer, Thomas of Celano, writes of how the custom came about:

It should be recorded and held in reverent memory what Blessed Francis did near the town of Greccio, on the Feast Day of the Nativity of Our Lord Jesus Christ, three years before his glorious death. In that town lived a certain man by the name of John (Messer Giovanni Velitta) who stood in high esteem, and whose life was even better than his reputation. Blessed Francis loved him with a special affection because, being very noble and much honored, he despised the nobility of the flesh and strove after the nobility of the soul.

Blessed Francis often saw this man. He now called him about two weeks before Christmas and said to him: "If you desire that we should celebrate this year's Christmas together at Greccio, go quickly and prepare what I tell you; for I want to enact the memory of the Infant who was born at Bethlehem, and how He was deprived of all the comforts babies enjoy; how He was bedded in the manger on hay, between an ass and an ox. For once I want to see all this with my own eyes." When the good and faithful man had heard this, he departed quickly and prepared in the above mentioned place everything that the Saint had told him.

The joyful day approached. The brethren (Franciscans) were called from many communities. The men and women of the neighborhood, as best they could, prepared candles and torches to brighten the night. Finally the Saint of God arrived, found everything prepared, saw it and rejoiced. The crib was made ready, hay was brought, the ox and ass were led to the spot. . . . Greccio became a new Bethlehem. The crowds drew near and rejoiced in the novelty of the celebration.

Also associated with Christmas was the Yule log, believed to be derived from pagan Northern ritual. The log was burned in an open hearth during the Christmas season. Its unburned parts were put away until the following year, when they were used to light the new Yule log. Closely connected with the Yule log is the Christmas tree. It is believed to be in part derived from the pagan Yule log and the paradise tree, which appeared in medieval miracle plays about Adam and Eve. The paradise tree had apples and wafers later candy hung from it, and it signified both the Tree of Sin and Death and the Tree of Life, the wafers representing the Holy Eucharist. The modern Christmas tree is, however, credited to Martin Luther, the Protestant reformer, who saw a fir tree in the forest lit by stars and was inspired to invent the Christmas tree.

The custom of giving gifts during the Christmas season derives from an old pagan Roman custom called *strenae* when the people gave gifts of pastry, lamps, precious stones, and coins as tokens of good wishes for the new year. The giver of the gifts for Christmas varies from one Christian country to another. In Italy it is Lady Befana, a fairy queen or witch, who gives the gifts on Epiphany (6 January), when the Magi were believed to have given their gifts to the Christ Child. Her name, Befana, is actually a corruption of the word Epiphany. In Russia Babushka (grandmother) gives the gifts. The most famous gift giver in European folklore, however, is Santa Claus, who is derived in part from St. Nicholas and the pagan god Thor. When the Protestants abolished the feast of St. Nicholas (6 December), who was the patron saint of children, a composite figure, made up of the bishop saint and the pagan god, emerged and was responsible for giving gifts.

Christmas was not just one day during the Middle Ages but a season that consisted of 12 days, from Christmas to Twelfth Night, or Epiphany. It was a time of rest for domestic animals, horses, and most servants, who often celebrated various feasts such as one dedicated to fools which had a Bishop of Fools and a Pope of Fools. All of this was abolished by the Reformation, since few of the reformers had any sense of humor or fun. In the United States Christmas was outlawed in Boston during a large part of the 19th century. Schools and businesses were open, and people were fired if they refused to work.

0811
Christopher, St. (Christ bearer). Third century? C.E. In Christian legend, patron saint of travelers. Feast, 25 July.

Although officially removed in 1969 from the Roman Catholic calendar of saints, St. Christopher still maintains his popularity with the faithful. His legend, based on Eastern sources, came to Western Europe about the ninth century. One tradition says that before his conversion to Christianity he had the head of a dog (he is sometimes portrayed with one in

St. Christopher

Eastern art); others say he was a prince who, through the intercession of the Virgin Mary, was born to a heathen king. Some sources say he was born in Syria; others, Canaan; and still others, Arabia. His name before his conversion is given as Offerus, Offro, Adokimus, Reprobus, or Reprebus.

According to *The Golden Legend*, a series of saints' lives written in the 13th century, St. Christopher was called Reprobus and was a Canaanite. He was of "prodigious size, being twelve cubits in height, and fearful of aspect." He was so proud of his size and strength that he swore he would enter the service of the most powerful monarch in the world. So he went searching and came to the court of a great king. He served that monarch until he noticed that the king made the sign of the cross at the mention of the devil. He therefore went in search of Satan, assuming that he must be more powerful than the king. He found Satan and his host of followers, but in their travels he noticed that Satan trembled when they came upon a wayside cross. Christopher asked the devil why he was afraid. He was told that the cross symbolizes Christ. Christopher then went in search of Christ, who was an even greater king than the devil.

Christopher found a hermit who instructed him in the Christian faith, but the saint refused to be bound by prayers and fastings. So the hermit told him that if he could not worship in the acceptable manner he could serve Christ another way. He sent him to a certain river where there was a ford and told him to carry over on his shoulders all who wished to cross. Christopher uprooted a palm tree for a staff. Day and night he carried across all who came to the river.

After many days, as he slept in his hut, he heard a child's voice calling him and saying, "Christopher, come out and carry me across the river."

He ran out of his hut and found no one, so he returned. But again he heard the child's voice, and again no one was outside. At the third call he went out and found a child who asked to be ferried across the water. Christopher took the child on his shoulders and, taking his staff, set out. Little by little, the child grew heavier, until Christopher thought he would fall into the stream.

"Child, why have you put me in dire peril? You weigh so heavily on me that if I had borne the whole world on my shoulders, it could not have burdened me more heavily."

"Wonder not," said the child, "for you have not only borne the world on your shoulders but him who created the world. For I am Christ the King."

The Christ Child then told Christopher to plant his staff, and the next morning it was filled with flowers and fruits. After many adventures Christopher was finally beheaded as a martyr.

In Christian art St. Christopher is portrayed as a very tall and strong man fording a river with his huge staff in his hand, carrying the Christ Child on his shoulders. Sometimes the hermit's hut is seen in the distance. Often inscribed near his image is the inscription: "Whoever shall behold the image of St. Christopher shall not faint nor fail on that day." Liszt composed *Sankt Christoph*, a legend for baritone, female chorus, piano, harmonica, and harp, but the work remains unpublished.

0812

Chthonian Gods (earth gods). In Greek mythology, deities who ruled under the earth or were connected with Hades, the underworld, such as Hades, Pluto, Persephone, Demeter, Dionysus, Hecate, and Hermes.

0813

Chuang Tzu (Master Chuang). c.399–295 B.C.E. Title given Chuang Chou, Chinese Taoist philosopher, whose work contains fables, parables, and anecdotes.

Chuang Tzu's basic premise in his work is that the Tao is the universal way of everything, pervading the entire universe. One becomes free only when one identifies with the Tao. There is no right or wrong because such concepts always stem from a point of view. For example, life is good and desirable and death is evil only from the point of view of the living. How does one know that the reverse is not true?

One of the most famous episodes in his work is the account of his mourning for his wife. When

Chuang Tzu's wife died, Hui Tzu went to console him. He found the widower sitting on the ground with his legs spread out at a right angle, singing and beating time on a bowl.

"To live with your wife," said Hui Tzu, "and see your eldest son grow up to be a man, and then not to shed a tear over her corpse—this would be bad enough. But to drum on a bowl and sing; surely this is going too far."

"Not at all," replied Chuang Tzu. "When she died, I could not help being affected by her death. Soon, however, I remembered that she had already existed in a previous state before birth, without form, or even substance; that while in that unconditioned condition, substance was added to spirit; that this substance then assumed form; and that the next stage was birth. And now, by virtue of further change, she is dead, passing from one phase to another like the sequence of spring, summer, autumn, and winter. And while she is thus lying asleep in eternity, for me to go about weeping and wailing would be to proclaim myself ignorant of these natural laws. Therefore I refrain."

Variant spelling: Kwuang-zze.

0814

Chu Jung. In Chinese legend, a deified mortal, nicknamed Ch'ih Ti (the red emperor), honored as the god of fire, which he taught men how to use. He is also regarded as the spirit of the Southern Sea. He helped break the link between heaven and earth and was appointed to keep men in their right positions in the established order. He is sometimes portrayed seated on or riding a tiger, or as an animal with a three-eyed human face, the extra eye in the center of his forehead. He is surrounded by his servants and fire symbols, a fiery serpent and a fire wheel—plus a pen and pad to list the places he intends to burn. He is invoked both to prevent and to cause fire.

0815

Chu-ko Liang. Third century C.E. In Chinese legend, a deified mortal, who in life was noted for his wisdom. Chu-ko Liang, who was eight feet tall, was called by the emperor to be his general. At the time human sacrifices were made to the gods, but Chu-ko Liang put an end to the practice by substituting clay figures. When he saw his death approaching, he lit 49 candles, which burned for seven days on a heap of rice. When he was informed of the defeat of an enemy, he accidentally kicked over the candles and fell dead. Before dying, however, he ordered that seven grains of rice should be put in his mouth so that his body might be kept unchanged forever. He also asked that his body be placed on the battlefield with two pigeons sewed into his sleeves. When the enemy saw the sleeves of Chu-ko Liang's garment moving, they assumed he had come back to life, and fled in terror.

In Japanese legend, Chu-ko Liang is called Komei.

0816

Chu-lin Chi'i-Hsien (seven immortals of bamboo grove). In Chinese legend, seven men who drank and conversed together in a bamboo grove, or in a place called Bamboo Grove, about 275 B.C.E. They are called the Seven Immortals and were known for getting drunk and challenging Confucian beliefs. They are Juan Chi and his nephew, Juan Hsien; Liu Ling; Hsiang Hsiu; Wang Jung; Shan T'ao; and Hai K'ang.

0817

Chunda. In Buddhist legend, a smith who invited the Buddha to his house and offered him a meal. It was the last meal eaten by the Buddha.

0818

Chung-li Ch'üan. Second century B.C.E. In Chinese Taoist mythology, one of the Pa-Hsien, the Eight Immortals. In one legend he was forced by an old man to pick up a shoe that had fallen, and in another he is said to have done it of his own free will. In art he is often portrayed as an extremely fat person, with a bare stomach, carrying a peach, symbol of immortality, and a fan, by which he revives the dead. He is believed to have found the elixir of life.

In Japanese legend he is called Chorio.

Variant spelling: Chang Liang.

0819

Chun T'i. In Chinese mythology, goddess of dawn and light, protector against war; she is portrayed with eight arms, two of which hold the sun and moon.

0820

Churinga. In Australian mythology, sacred objects of stone or wood in which the spirits of ancestors come to dwell; also a mnemonic device for storytelling.

Variant spelling: Tjuringa.

0821

Churning of the Ocean. In Hindu mythology, term used for the cosmic struggle between the demons and gods over the Amrita, the water of life, often identified with Soma juice.

Durvasas (ill-clothed), a Hindu sage and an incarnation of the god Shiva, offered Indra a garland as a gift, which Indra ignored. Because of this affront, Durvasas cursed Indra, saying that "his sovereignty over the three worlds should be subverted." Under the curse Indra and the gods grew weak and were on their way to destruction. The Asuras, or demons, seeing an opportunity, used all of their powers to finish off the gods and gain control of the three worlds.

In desperation some of the gods fled to Brahma, asking him for protection. He advised them to seek the aid of Vishnu.

"I will restore your strength," Vishnu replied, "but you must do as I command you. Cast into the Milky Sea some magic herbs, then take Mount Mandara for a churning stick, the serpent Shesha for a rope, and churn the ocean to obtain the Amrita, the water of life. To do this you will need the help of the Asuras. Promise them some of the Amrita, but I will make sure they have no share of it."

The gods listened to Vishnu and entered into an alliance with the Asuras, the demons, to set about the task of obtaining the Amrita. They cast the magic herbs, took Mount Mandara for a churning stick and Shesha the serpent for a rope. (In India a churning stick is a stick with a long rope twisted around it. The rope, held at both ends, keeps the stick in a vertical position, while the turning caused by pulling the rope accomplishes the churning.) The gods grabbed the serpent's tail while the Asuras pulled its head. Vishnu took the form of Kurma, a tortoise, his second avatar, or incarnation, and became a pivot as the mountain twirled around.

Vishnu was also present but unseen among the gods and demons pulling the serpent back and forth, as well as present on top of the mountain. Vishnu thus sustained the gods with his powerful energy. When the venom from the serpent Shesha burned the faces of the Asuras, Vishnu protected the gods from the same fate by sending up clouds with rain that drifted toward the serpent.

First, the wish-bestowing cow, Surabhi, arose from the sea. Next came the goddess of wine, Varuni, with rolling eyes. Suddenly the magic tree Parijata appeared. It was "the delight of the nymphs of heaven, perfuming the world with its blossoms." (Later the tree was kept in Indra's heaven and was the pride of one of his wives, Sachi. When Krishna visited Indra he carried away the tree, causing a war between the two, which Indra lost. After Krishna's death, however, the tree was returned to Indra.) After the appearance of the Parijata there came the Apsaras, water nymphs, then the moon, which Shiva took and placed on his brow. Next came a draft of deadly poison, which Shiva drank, lest it should destroy the world. The bitter poison turned the god's throat blue, earning for him the epithet Nilakantha (blue throat). Next came Dhanvantari, physician of the gods, holding in his hands a cup of the Amrita. Then the goddess Sri appeared seated on an open lotus. She came to the god Vishnu's breast to rest. A fabulous jewel, Kaustubha, also appeared, which Vishnu placed on his breast.

The demons now took the opportunity to steal the cup from Dhanvantari and were ready to drink the water of life. Vishnu then appeared as a ravishing woman, Mohini (the enchantress), which made the demons so lustful that they forgot to protect the cup of Amrita. While they disagreed among themselves, Vishnu took the cup and gave it to the gods.

The Amrita, or Soma, as it is identified in some tellings of the myth, has been interpreted as the life-giving genital semen produced by the rubbing of the snake (phallus) at the base of the mountain.

0822

Chyavana. In Hindu legend, a sage, opponent of Indra, restored to youth by the twin gods, the Aswins.

The *Rig-Veda*, the ancient collection of hymns to the gods, tells how Chyavana was restored to his youth, "making him acceptable to his wife, and the husband of maidens," by the twin gods, the Aswins. This miracle made Chyavana devoted to the Aswins and, according to the Hindu epic poem *The Mahabharata*, he asked Indra to allow them to drink the magic Soma juice. Indra objected, however, and Chyavana began a sacrifice that found acceptance before the gods. In a rage Indra rushed at Chyavana with a mountain in one hand and a thunderbolt in the other, but Chyavana stopped the god by sprinkling him with water. He then "created a fearful open-mouthed monster called Mada, having teeth and grinders of portentous length, and jaws one of which enclosed the earth, the other the sky; and the gods, including Indra, are said to have been at the root of his tongue like fishes in the mouth of a sea monster."

In this predicament "Indra granted the demand of Chyavana, who was thus the cause of the Aswins becoming drinkers of the Soma."

0823

Cid, El (lord; master). In medieval Spanish legend, a hero, Rodrigo Díaz de Bivar (1040–1099), whose victories over the Moors inspired ballads, chronicles, and the national epic poem, *Poema del Cid* (*Cantar de mio Cid*). There are some 200 Spanish ballads that treat El Cid's legend, forming, as it were, an introduction to the epic.

Rodrigo, also called *El Compeador* (the champion), was a young man when he avenged an insult to his father, Don Diego Laynez, by Don Gómez. The young hero challenged Don Gómez and killed him, cutting off his head and presenting it to his father as proof that the wrong had been avenged. Don Diego then took his son to court, but the young man did not please King Ferdinand, who banished him from

his presence. Rodrigo then left with 300 knights, encountered the Moors, who were invading Castile, and defeated them, taking five of their kings prisoner. He released them only after they promised to pay him tribute and refrain from further warfare. They were so grateful for their liberty that they pledged themselves to his will, calling him *El Cid*. After Rodrigo had delivered the land from the Moors, King Ferdinand restored him to favor at the court.

Shortly after this, Doña Ximena, daughter of Don Gómez, the man El Cid had killed, demanded vengeance for the murder of her father. When her pleas to the king came to no avail, she asked that the king order El Cid to marry her instead. To win Doña Ximena's love El Cid said he would not rest until he had won five battles for her. Before he left he went on a pilgrimage to Santiago de Compostela, the shrine of St. James the Greater, where he had a vision of Lazarus, the leper beggar (Luke 16:19–31) and as a result established a leper house in St. Lazarus's honor.

When King Ferdinand died, his relatives fought over the succession. Finally Don Alfonso came to the throne, but the king hated El Cid. *The Poema del Cid* opens with King Alfonso's banishment of El Cid from court. El Cid was given nine days to leave Castile. He and his men left and were supported by admirers to whom El Cid was a hero. Once again El Cid went into battle against the Moors and again defeated them. The king restored El Cid to favor, but the reconciliation was not to last. There was a misunderstanding between El Cid and the king. El Cid left the court again, and during his absence the Moors took Valencia. Hearing of this, El Cid promptly returned, captured the city, and established his headquarters there. He asked King Alfonso to send his wife and daughters. As master of Valencia, El Cid was enormously rich, and therefore his daughters Doña Elvira and Doña Sol were much sought after as brides. Among the suitors were the counts of Carrion, whose proposals were warmly encouraged by King Alfonso. El Cid, in obedience to the king had his daughters married to the counts, but the results were not happy.

Once a lion broke loose from El Cid's private menagerie. It entered the hall where he was sleeping while his guests were playing chess. His sons-in-law fled, one falling into an empty vat, the other hiding behind El Cid's couch. Awakened by the noise, El Cid seized his sword, twisted his cloak around his arm, and grasping the lion by its mane, thrust it back into its cage. He then calmly returned to his palace. The two men, however, were angered by the humiliation of their cowardly behavior and asked to leave with their wives. After traveling some time with their brides and an escort named Felez Muñoz, the counts of Carrion camped near Douro. Early the next day they sent all of their suites ahead, and being left alone with their wives, stripped them of their garments, lashed them with thorns, kicked them with spurs, and finally left them for dead on the bloodstained ground. They then rode on. The brides were rescued by Felez Muñoz and taken home. El Cid demanded vengeance, and the king summoned the counts. A battle was arranged, and the counts of Carrion were defeated and banished. The daughters were then married to counts from Navarre.

The *Poema El Cid* ends here with a statement of El Cid's death. Ballads continue the tale. In one the Moors, under the leadership of Cucar, King of Morocco, returned to besiege Valencia. El Cid was preparing to do battle when he had a vision of St. Peter. The saint predicted his death within 30 days but assured him that, even though he would be dead, he would still triumph over the enemy.

El Cid then prepared to die. He appointed a successor, gave instructions, and directed that his body be embalmed, set on his horse, Babieca, with the sword Tizona in his hand, and sent into battle. When these instructions had all been given, he died at the appointed time. The successor and El Cid's wife, Ximena, carried out his wishes. A sortie was planned against the Moors, and El Cid, fastened onto his warhorse, rode in the van. Such terror was created by his presence that the Moors fled.

King Alfonso ordered El Cid's body placed in the church of San Pedro de Cardena, where it remained for ten years seated in a chair of state in plain view of all. Such respect was paid the body that no one dared touch it, except one person who, remembering El Cid's proud boast that no man had ever dared lay a hand on his beard, attempted to do so. Before he could touch the beard, however, El Cid's lifeless hand clasped the hilt of Tizona, his sword, and drew it a few inches out of its scabbard. The man fled.

The legend of El Cid inspired the two-part play by Guillén de Castro, *Las Mocedades del Cid* (the youth of the Cid), which in the first part centers around his wedding. The French playwright Corneille used Part 1 of the Spanish drama for his play *Le Cid*, which in turn was made into an opera by Jules Massenet. The English poet Leigh Hunt wrote a verse play, *A Father Avenged*, based on El Cid and his father. A movie starring Charlton Heston as El Cid and Sophia Loren as his wife, Doña Ximena, was also based on the legends.

0824

Cigouaves. In Haitian voodoo, a demon who comes at night and castrates men. To avoid this, genital organs of animals are offered to the demon.

0825

Cincinnatus, Lucius Quinctius. 458 B.C.E.) In Roman history and legend, a hero who left his farm and aided the Roman army, which was besieged in the Apennines by the Aequi. Cincinnatus was elected dictator but resigned his office and returned to his farm after 16 days. Livy's *History of Rome* (book 3) tells the tale as an example of old-fashioned Roman virtue.

Cinderella (A. Beardsley)

0826

Cinderella (ash girl). Popular name for a folktale found throughout the world; the earliest known version has been traced to the ninth century C.E. in China. The best-known version is the one by Charles Perrault included in his *Contes de ma mère l'oye* (Tales of Mother Goose) of 1697. Perrault's version tells how Cinderella's cruel stepmother and wicked stepsisters force her to do all of the housework. Cinderella never complains but even helps prepare her three ugly stepsisters for a ball. However, after they leave, she begins to cry over her sad fate. Her fairy godmother appears and promises her that she too will go to the ball. With her wand she transforms

Cinderella's ragged housedress into a beautiful ball gown, six mice into white horses, and a pumpkin into a coach. Cinderella's ugly sandals are transformed into beautiful glass slippers. The godmother then transforms some other rodents into footmen and tucks Cinderella into the coach, giving her one admonition: she must be home by midnight, for at the stroke of 12 her coach will turn back into a pumpkin and her ball gown into rags.

At the ball Cinderella enchants everyone with her beauty and mystery, including the prince, who is just about to ask her to dance when the clock begins to strike. Jolted back to reality, Cinderella runs for her coach, losing one of her glass slippers as she climbs aboard and rushes away. The prince, left holding her slipper, declares he will marry the girl who lost the slipper. The prince tries the slipper on every young girl in the kingdom, including Cinderella's wicked stepsisters. It fits none of them. He finally tries it on Cinderella's foot. The shoe fits, and Cinderella weds the prince and forgives everybody.

Perrault's version, though the most popular, is but one of the 500 or more European versions of the tale. Marian Emily Roalfe Cox (1860– 1916) made a study of the Cinderella tale, published in 1893 as *Cinderella*, in which she presented comparative and analytical notes to the tale with its many variants. Rossini's opera *La cenerentola* is a witty presentation of the tale. Other treatments include Massenet's *Cendrillon*, Edvard Poldini's *Aschenbrödel*, Wolf-Ferrari's *La cenerentola*, Prokoviev's ballet *Cinderella*, and Walt Disney's movie *Cinderela*, a somewhat sentimental version of the tale.

0827

Citipati. In Mahayana Buddhism, two skeletons, one of a man and one of a woman, often portrayed with arms and legs interlaced, dancing on two corpses. According to Buddhist legend, they were two ascetics who were deep in meditation and did not notice that a thief had cut off their heads and thrown them into the dust. Because of this they are the enemies of thieves. Often they carry a scepter topped by a skull.

0828

Ciuateteo. In Aztec mythology, the spirits of women who died in childbirth. They would leave their paradise of the West, called Tamoanchan, coming back to bring disease to children. On the days that the Ciuateteo were believed to descend, parents would not allow their children outdoors. To placate the evil spirits, temples were built at crossroads, and offerings of bread, sometimes in the form of butterflies, were made. The Ciuateteo were portrayed with

blanched white faces, and their hands, arms, and legs were whitened with powder. To die in childbirth, however, was considered honorable and good by the Aztecs.

Variant spelling: Ciuapipiltin.

St. Clare

0829

Clare, St. (bright, illustrious). 1194–1253? C.E. In Christian legend, founder of the Order of Poor Clares. Feast, 12 August.

Clare, the oldest daughter of a noble family of Assisi, wanted to devote herself to a religious life. Her parents objected, but Clare fled from her father's house to the Chapel of the Porzioncula one Palm Sunday. There she met St. Francis of Assisi and placed herself under his care. In vain her parents tried to win her back. They also lost another daughter, Agnes, to religious life. The Order of the Poor Clares was founded in 1212 by St. Francis for Clare. (The order is also called Clarisses, Minoresses, or Nuns of the Order of St. Francis.)

Legend credits St. Clare with stopping the Moors when they overran Assisi. They approached her convent when the saint was bedridden. She rose up and, taking the pyx (which contains the consecrated Host from the Mass), placed it on the threshold of the doorway. Upon seeing the pyx, the enemy fled.

Medieval Christian art portrays St. Clare as a nun in a gray habit with a cord, holding a cross or a lily. Her distinctive attribute is the pyx. The great Italian artist Giotto portrayed the saint in frescoes in the Santa Croce in Florence and in the Upper Church of St. Francis in Assisi.

0830

Clement, St. (merciful). First century C.E. In Christian legend, third bishop of Rome. Feast, 23 November.

According to legend, St. Clement was a disciple of St. Peter and St. Paul. During the reign of Trajan he was banished, together with other Christians, to an island where there was no water. St. Clement prayed, and a lamb appeared to him on a hill. He dug a hole where the lamb stood, and a stream flowed from it. As a punishment for providing water to the Christians he was thrown into the sea with an anchor around his neck. But the waters drew back for three miles and the people could then see a ruined temple that the sea had covered. In it was found the body of the saint with the anchor around his neck. For many years at the anniversary of his death the sea retreated for seven days, and pilgrimages were made to his tomb. Once a woman came with her child to pray at the tomb. The baby fell asleep, and the woman became absorbed in prayer. Suddenly the waters arose, and the woman fled, forgetting her child. The next year, when she returned to the tomb when the waters had retreated, she found her child sleeping safely.

The Church of San Clemente in Rome contains his supposed relics as well as scenes illustrating his life.

0831

Clem of the Clouth (Clement of the cliff). In British legend, an outlaw hero who appears in ballads along with Adam Bell and William of Cloudesly. He is mentioned in Ben Jonson's play *The Alchemist*.

0832

Clootie (one division of a cleft hoof). In Scottish folklore, one of the names of the devil. It was a custom to leave an untilled section of land, or one that could not be tilled, as a gift to Old Cloots or Clootie.

0833

Clotilda, St. (loud battle). Sixth century C.E. In Christian legend, wife of Clovis, king of France. Feast, 3 June.

When in danger of defeat by the Huns, King Clovis, who was a pagan, asked his queen, Clotilda, to pray to her god to bring him victory. When he defeated the Huns in battle, he ascribed it to the Christian god and was baptized by St. Remi. At the king's baptism, according to legend, the oil was brought from heaven by a dove, and an angel came down bearing three lilies, which he gave to St. Remi. The saint in turn gave them to Clotilda, who then changed the arms of France from the three toads, or *crapauds* to the fleurs-de-lis, emblems of purity and regeneration.

In Christian art St. Clotilda is portrayed in royal robes, with a long white veil and jeweled crown, either kneeling in prayer or bestowing alms. Sometimes she is attended by an angel holding a shield bearing the three fleurs-de-lis.

0834

Clover. A forage plant with trifoliate leaves. In Christian symbolism the clover is used to explain the Trinity (three leaves yet one clover; three persons yet one God). St. Patrick is said to have converted the pagan Irish with this explanation when confronted by King Leoghaire. In Druid belief the clover was a sacred plant, sign of both good and evil. In English folklore, if one dreams of a clover, it means a happy marriage filled with wealth and prosperity. According to the Victorian language of flowers the clover is a symbol of fertility.

0835

Cluricane. In Celtic folklore, an elf who often appeared as a wrinkled old man. Cluricane was noted for his ability to find hidden treasure.
Variant spellings: Cluralan, Cluricaune.

0836

Coachman Legends. In Hungarian folklore, a series of tales around the figure of a coachman endowed with supernatural knowledge and powers. Often the coachman is in the service of some country squire, and there is a younger coachman who wishes to discover how the older man can perform all of his duties seemingly without doing any work. The younger coachman often achieves the knowledge by performing some magical rite or is told the secret by the older coachman, who cannot die unless he passes on his knowledge. The older coachman's powers are ascribed to an evil spirit with whom he has had contact.

0837

Coal-Oil Johnnie. 19th century. In American history and folklore, popular name of John W. Steel, who inherited oil money on his 21st birthday. He left his wife, job, and child and spent lavishly. When he had used up all of his cash, he returned home to his wife and family.

0838

Coatlicue (the serpent lady, robe of serpent). In Aztec mythology, mother goddess, appearing in numerous forms throughout Aztec mythology as both beneficent and demonic.

According to Fray Bernardino Sahagún in his *Historia general de las cosas de Nueva España*, Coatlicue was responsible for giving people "poverty, mental depression, and sorrows." She would often appear in the marketplace dressed as a lady of rank and leave a cradle in which was found a lance point later used in human sacrifices.

Fray Diego Durán in his *Historia de las Indias de Nueva España e islas de tierra firme* relates that Montezuma II sent representatives to find the origin of his ancestors. They discovered a hill containing seven caves. A priest appeared and introduced them to an old woman, ugly and dirty, whose "face was so black and covered with filth that she looked like something straight out of Hell." The woman was Coatlicue. She welcomed the ambassadors and said she was the mother of the god Huitzilopochtli. She had been fasting since the day the god left and not washing or combing her hair, waiting for his return from the Aztec land. As the messengers prepared to leave, she called to them, telling them that in her land no one grew old. She then told them to watch as one of her servants ran down a hill and became younger as he reached the bottom. The ambassadors watched the man become younger as he descended and old again when he ascended the hill.

One of the most prominent manifestations of Coatlicue was as the deity of grain, in which role she would appear in both male and female forms under the name of Centeotl. Centeotl was often portrayed as a frog with numerous breasts, symbolic of the wet earth, according to some commentators. Her face was painted yellow, the color of corn. During her festivals the priests wore phallic emblems in the hope of inducing Centeotl to provide crops for the coming year.

Another important manifestation was as an earth goddess. She appeared with a huge open mouth and ferocious teeth, and was dressed all in white. Durán says that when the Aztecs won a great victory under the leadership of Montezuma II, Prince Cihuacoatl, who was named after the goddess, "attired himself in the garb of the goddess Cihuacoatl. These were the female clothes which were called ''eagle garments.'''

An Aztec statue of Coatlicue in the Mexican Anthropological Museum portrays the cosmic aspects of the goddess as the great mother, who brings life and death.

Coatlicue was also known as and identified with Tonantzin (our mother), Ilamatecuhtli (old goddess), Tlatecutli (earth toad swallowing stone knife), Temazalteci (grandmother of the sweat bath), Itzpapalotl (obsidian butterfly), and as goddess of fate, portrayed as a beautiful woman with the symbols of death on her face.

Variant spellings: Ciuacoatl, Civocoatl, Cihuacoatl, Coatlantona, Conteotl.

0839
Cock. A male bird, usually the domestic rooster. The shrill crow of the cock in world mythology and folklore is often a symbol of the rising sun. The Greeks identified the bird with Apollo in his role as sun god, but it was also associated with Demeter and her daughter Persephone as a symbol of fertility. Cocks were often used as sacrifices to various deities. In Aztec ceremonies a cock could often be substituted for a human victim. Cocks were sacrificed by the Romans and were sacred to Mars, the god of war, because of their fighting nature. But along with the snake they were also sacred to Asclepius, the god of medicine, for their believed curative properties. In Christian legend the cock is associated with St. Peter's denial of Jesus as narrated in the Gospels. Jesus said: "Before the cock crow, thou shalt deny me thrice" (Matt. 26:75). But the cock is also a symbol of Christ's Resurrection and placed on the top of churches. Shakespeare's *Hamlet* (1.1) alludes to the belief that the cock crows all night on Christmas Eve so as to drive away every malignant spirit and evil influence.

0840
Cockaigne, Land of. In medieval European folklore, an imaginary land of pleasure, wealth, luxury, and idleness. The 13th century Middle English poem *The Land of Cockayne* describes it as having houses made of barley sugar and cakes, streets paved with pastry, and shops with an unending supply of goods. In the satiric novel *Jurgen* by American writer James Branch Cabell, the hero visits Cockaigne, which is described as a land of curious delights. Edward Elgar's *Cockaigne Overture* is a musical description of London, which in some accounts was identified as the land of Cockaigne.

Variant spelling: Cocagne, Cockayne.

0841
Cock and the Pearl, The. Aesopic fable found in various European collections such as those of Luther, La Fontaine, Lessing, and Krilof.

A cock was strutting up and down the farmyard among the hens when suddenly he saw something shining amid the straw.

"Ho! ho!" he said. "That's for me." And soon rooted it out from beneath the straw. What did it turn out to be but a pearl that by some chance had been lost in the yard. "You may be a treasure," said Master Cock, "to men that prize you, but for me I would rather have a single barleycorn than a peck of pearls."

Moral: Precious things are for those who can prize them.

The fable is quoted by Rabelais, Bacon in his *Essays* (13), and R. L. Stevenson in *Catriona*, his sequel to *Kidnapped*.

0842
Coffee. A bean used to brew a strong caffenic drink. Various world legends account for the origin of coffee. In an Ethiopian tale the bean was discovered by a goatherd named Kaldi. He kept noticing that his

charges were especially lively after they had eaten berries from a certain bush. Curious about their behavior, Kaldi ate some of the berries himself and found them stimulating. Excited by his discovery, he took some of the beans to his religious leader (he was a Moslem), who decided that this might be an ideal way of keeping the faithful awake during the long evening prayers. In European versions of the tale the shepherd is a monk and the goats are sheep. Various forms of the tale are found in South America.

0843
Coffin Texts. In ancient Egypt, magic formulas found inside wooden coffins of the Middle Kingdom. They were derived from spells used during the Old Kingdom to guarantee the deceased king's entry into the hereafter and were first carved into the walls of the pyramids at Saqqara. The right to use these texts or spells, known collectively as the Pyramid Texts, in time was granted to individuals of non-royal status. During the time of the Middle Kingdom, these Coffin Texts, loosely based on the Pyramid Texts, began to appear inside coffins. In the New Kingdom a somewhat modified form of these texts became known as *The Book of the Dead*.

0844
Colbumatuan-kurrk. In Australian mythology, an evil female spirit who kills people by throwing tree limbs at them.

0845
Columba, St. (dove). 521–597 C.E. In Christian legend, Apostle of Scotland, abbot of Iona. Feast, 9 June.

Born the son of Feidilmid, an Ulster chief, Columba with 12 companions landed on the island of Iona in 563 C.E., having made the passage in a wicker boat covered with hides. The Druids who occupied the island tried to prevent the Christians from forming a community, but Columba persisted and built a monastery on Iona, of which he was made the abbot. The members of Columba's community were not bound by celibacy or poverty, only obedience. They were allowed to marry, though their wives were not allowed to live with them but had special quarters on an adjacent property, called *Eilen nam ban* (Woman's Island). The monks, however, were allowed to visit their wives from time to time.

The followers of Columba's rule were called Culdees. Thomas Campbell,, the Scottish poet, alludes to them in his *Reullura*:

. . . The pure Culdees
Were Albyn's earliest priests of God,
Ere yet an island of her seas

By foot of Saxon monk was trod,
Long ere her churchmen by bigotry
Were barred from holy wedlock's tie.

The Irish poet Thomas Moore, in his *Irish Melodies*, tells the legend of St. Senanus and a lady who sought shelter on the holy island but were told to leave.

The relics of St. Columba were transferred to Ireland in 878 but were destroyed by the pagan Danes in the 12th century.

Confucius

0846
Confucius (Latinized form of the Chinese K'ung Fu-Tzu, Master K'ung). 551–479 B.C.E. Chinese philosopher.

Confucius was born of a poor family, but he received a good education. He married at the age of 19 and had a son. Deeply interested in the Chinese past, he acquired an extensive knowledge of the ancient traditions and worked as a teacher, passing this knowledge on to his followers. Though he did some government work, at which he failed, most of his life was nomadic.

According to legend, he was raised to the status of a shen (spirit) in 195 B.C.E. when the emperor of China offered animal sacrifice at his tomb. In 555 C.E. separate temples for worship of Confucius were ordered at the capital of every prefecture in China. Even in 1914 the worship of Confucius was continued by Yuan Shih'iai, the first president of the Republic of China.

This is ironic because the attitude of Confucius himself toward deities and spirits is uncertain. He constantly referred to heaven as if it were a semipersonal moral overseer but only once used the more distinctly personal title Shang-ti

(the emperor above). In the *Analects* (3:12) he counseled the worship of spirits as if they were present but made no decision on whether or not they existed. The emphasis here is on the value of ceremony, which for Confucius was not separable from morality. Proper ceremony is morally edifying; proper morals are expressed in ceremony. Thus, for him it was not important whether the spirits existed, but it was essential that they be worshiped. Later, therefore, the worship of Confucius' spirit does not necessarily imply that he was regarded as having a spirit that could be worshiped. Traditionally, the mandarins have been skeptical or agnostic and have regarded religion as an affair of the peasants.

0847

Coniraya. In the mythology of the Huarochiri (Warachiri) Indians on the western side of the coastal Cordillera of Peru, a creator god, the all-wise god who knew the thoughts of both men and gods. Coniraya's myths are told by Francisco de Ávila, a Roman Catholic priest, in his *A Narrative of the Errors, False Gods, and Other Superstitions and Diabolical Rites . . . [of] the Indians* (1608). Coniraya once appeared dressed as an old beggar. He fell in love with the virgin Cavillaca, who sat weaving under a lucma tree. The god dropped a ripe fruit containing his seed near the girl, and she ate the fruit and became pregnant. Determined to find out who was responsible for fathering the child, she called together the "principal idols of the land" and watched as her child crawled to Coniraya, who was still disguised as a beggar. Disgusted at seeing who the father of her child was, she took the baby and fled to the sea. Coniraya now dropped his disguise. He "put on magnificent golden robes, and leaving the astonished assembly of the gods" ran after her, crying out: "O my lady Cavillaca, turn your eyes and see how handsome and gallant am I."

However, the girl continued her flight and jumped into the sea. When Coniraya came to the coast he found that Cavillaca and her son had "turned to stone."

Coniraya then met two daughters of Pachacamac, the supreme god of the Incas. Since their mother, Ursihuachac, was away, "Coniraya had intercourse with the elder daughter and wished to do the same with the other, but she turned into a pigeon and flew away."

Coniraya then went to Cuzco, taking with him the Inca monarch Huayna Capac. He told the king to send a commission to the lowlands of the West. The commission was made up of descendants of the condor, the falcon, and the swallow. "After five days one of the descendants of the swallow reached his journey's end. There he was given a coffer with instructions that it was to be opened by the Inca in person." Of course the coffer was opened by the messenger, who found "inside a radiantly beautiful woman with hair like gold and dressed as a queen." This vision disappeared.

When Coniraya arrived before Huayna Capac, the monarch "spared his life because he was descended from the swallow and sent him back to the highlands. This time he brought the coffer intact into the hands of the Inca, but before the latter could open it Coniraya said to him: 'Inca, we must both leave this world. I go to [the] other world and you shall go to another in the company of my sister. We shall not see each other again.' When the coffer was opened an immediate splendor covered the world. The Inca determined not to return to Cuzco. 'Here I will stay with my princess,' he said, and sent back one of his relations to Cuzco in his place with the command: 'Go thou to Cuzco and say that your are Huayna Capac.' In that moment the Inca disappeared with his spouse, as did Coniraya."

0848

Constans. In British mythology, an early king, eldest of the three sons of the Emperor Constantine. His two brothers were Aurelius Ambrosius and Uther Pendragon, who was the father of King Arthur. Constans was a monk, but at the death of his father he laid aside the cowl for the crown. Vortigern, however, had him assassinated and then took the throne. Aurelius Ambrosius succeeded Vortigern, and he was followed by Uther Pendragon.

0849

Constantine the Great (firm, constant, persevering) c. 280–337 C.E. Roman emperor (306–337) who granted toleration to the Christians.

The historical Constantine bears little resemblance to the legendary one found in such works as Eusebius' *Life of Constantine* and the *Vita Beati Silvestri*. According to legend, Constantine had a dream in which he was told he would be victorious over his rival, Maxentius, if he would adopt the sign of the cross. He saw in the sky a luminous cross with the words *In hoc signo vinces* (By this sign thou shalt conquer). The emperor, after defeating Maxentius, then adopted the standard, the *chi-rho* monogram, to replace the imperial eagles.

Another legend is that while Constantine was a pagan he suffered from leprosy. His priests said he should bathe in the blood of some 3,000 children and he would be cured of his disease. The children were rounded up, but after hearing the pleas of their mothers, the emperor decided against the sacrifice.

"Far better it is that I should die, than cause the death of these innocents," he said.

That night St. Peter and St. Paul appeared to him and told him that Christ had sent them to him because he had spared the innocent children. They told him to send for Sylvester, the bishop of Rome, who would show him a pool in which he could wash and be healed of his sickness. When this happened, he should then stop his persecution of the Christians and adopt the faith of Jesus Christ.

Sylvester was found hiding in a cave near Monte Calvo when the emperor's men came for him. He had hidden there in fear of his life. When he appeared before Constantine the ruler asked him who were the two gods he had seen in a vision the night before. Sylvester said they were not gods but the Apostles of Jesus Christ, the only true God. Constantine then asked to see an image of the Apostles to see if they were the same as the two men in his vision. When the images agreed with what he had seen, he asked to be baptized. Bishop Sylvester performed the rite.

The historical Constantine, however, was not baptized by Sylvester, as the legend says, but by an Arian bishop of Nicomedia, as he lay on his deathbed. Sylvester had been dead some 18 months before the event.

When Helena the mother of Constantine (who later went in search of the True Cross), heard that her son had become a Christian, she said she would rather be a follower of the Jewish god than the Christian one. Constantine then asked his mother to bring all of the most learned Jewish rabbis to debate with his bishop. One hundred forty rabbis came and debated with Sylvester, who defeated them all in argument except for Zambri, a magician. Zambri said he could whisper the secret name of God into a bull's ear, and the animal would die. A bull was brought forth, the magician whispered into its ear, and the animal fell dead. Sylvester, not flustered, said he would raise the bull to life. He called on Christ, the god of the living, and the bull arose.

Later legend says that Constantine was so impressed by Sylvester that he gave him and his successors (the popes) the territory of central Italy as well as primacy over all other bishops in the church. The *Donation of Constantine*, as the document proving Constantine's gift was called, was proved a forgery by Lorenzo Valla, a 15th-century Italian scholar, though it had been used by the Roman church to support its claims for secular authority.

In art Constantine and St. Sylvester are sometimes portrayed together. Sylvester is seen receiving the deed from the emperor. When Sylvester is portrayed alone, he is seen with a bull. He is easily distinguished from St. Luke, who is also portrayed with a bull, by his rich pontifical robes. Piero della Francesca painted the *Dream of Constantine*, which portrays the emperor asleep with the angel hovering overhead, as well as the *Victory of Constantine over Maxentius* for the choir of the Church of San Francesco in Arezzo, Italy. Rubens also painted the victory of the emperor.

0850
Conwenna. In British mythology, the wife of King Dunwallo, the first king to wear a gold crown. In William Blake's poem *Jerusalem* she appears and "shines a triple form over the north with pearly beams, gorgeous and terrible."

0851
Cophetua. In British mythology, a mythical king of Africa, who fell in love with a beggar maid, Penelophon, and married her. She is mentioned as Zenelophon in Shakespeare's *Love's Labour's Lost*, Tennyson's poem *The Beggar Maid*, and in a ballad, "King Cophetua and the Beggar Maid," included in Percy's *Reliques*. The subject was used by Edward Burne-Jones, the 19th-century painter and designer.

0852
Corey, Giles. 1612–1992. In American history and legend, one of the victims of the Salem witchcraft trials, pressed to death under heavy weights. Hundreds were tried and 19 executed, including Corey's wife. In legend Corey is said to reappear before times of disaster in Salem. Corey appears in a good light in Robert Calef's *More Wonders of the Invisible World*, which attacks Cotton Mather, whose writings were in part responsible for the trials. Longfellow's poetical play *Giles Corey of Salem Farms*, part of his *New England Tragedies*, has Corey as a hero, as does Arthur Miller's play *The Crucible*, which was used as the basis of Robert Ward's opera *The Crucible*.

0853
Corn. In Europe, seed of any cereal grass used for food (wheat, oats, maize, barley), and in America, Indian corn, *Zea Maya*, native to the American continent.

In European folklore corn is often personified as the corn mother or corn maiden. In Germany peasants would cry out as the grain waved in the wind: "There comes the corn mother" or "The corn mother is running over the field." Children were told not to pull cornflowers or red poppies in the field because the corn mother was sitting in the corn and would catch them.

Sometimes the last sheaf of grain was called the harvest mother, great mother, or grandmother. In Germany the last sheaf was dressed as a woman, and harvesters danced around it. It was believed that whoever got the last sheaf would be married by the following year, though the spouse would be old. If a woman got it, she would marry a widower; if a man, an old crone.

The North American Ojibwa Indians have a myth about Mondamin, who came to earth and battled a hero. He was defeated and buried, and from his body the corn grew—a gift to man. The tale is told in Longfellow's poem *The Song of Hiawatha*.

The Holy Eucharist

0854
Corpus Christi (Christ's body). Medieval Christian feast of the Holy Eucharist, celebrated on the Thursday after Pentecost; instituted by Pope Urban IV in 1264 C.E. The feast was first suggested by St. Juliana (13th century), who was the prioress of Mont Cornillion in Liege, Belgium. She said she frequently had visions in which the full moon appeared to her in a brilliant light, except for one spot, which was black. The dark spot, she said Christ told her, was the lack of a feast in honor of the Holy Eucharist. One man who supported Juliana in her efforts to institute the feast was Jadques Pantaleon, the archdeacon of Liege, who later became Pope Urban IV.

Thomas Aquinas's hymn, *Adoro Te Supples, Latens Dietas*, "Godhead here in hiding, whom I do adore," was written for the feast. Other hymns he composed for the feast were *Lauda, Sion* and *Pangue Lingua*. Part of the celebration consisted of miracle plays, which were performed in York, Coventry, and Chester in England until the Reformation, when they were banned. In Spain *Auto sacramental*, (sacramental act), one-act verse plays, were performed. Calderón wrote more than 70 such plays.

Two English colleges, one at Cambridge and one at Oxford, are named after the feast. Corpus Christi,

Texas, and Sacramento, California also are named in honor of the Holy Eucharist.

0855
Corydon. In Roman mythology, common name given to Arcadian shepherds. Vergil's second *Eclogue* tells of the love of Corydon for his faithless male lover, Alexis. André Gide's dialogue *Corydon* uses the shepherd's name in his defense of homosexuality.

0856
Cosmas and Damian, SS. (order, tamed, tamer). Third century C.E. In Christian legend, patron saints of barbers, apothecaries, and physicians. Feast, 27 September.

Their legend, from the East, became a part of Western Christian lore in the early ages of the church. Cosmas and Damian were brothers born in Cilicia. Their father died when they were young, and their mother, Theodora, brought them up as Christians. They became physicians to help the sick, whether rich or poor, and to help animals. They were eventually arrested for being Christian and thrown into prison. At first they were to be drowned at sea, but an angel saved them. Then they were to be burned to death, but the fire refused to consume them. They were then bound to two crosses and stoned, but the stones, instead of pelting them, fell on those who threw them. The proconsul, believing them to be enchanters, then had them beheaded.

One tale in *The Golden Legend*, a collection of saints' lives written in the 13th century by Jacobus de Voragine, tells how the saints replaced the diseased leg of a patient. They took the black leg of a dead Moor and used "celestial ointment" to attach it to the white man. The operation was a success.

Among Greek Christians the saints displaced the worship of Asclepius, the Greek god of medicine. They were called *Anargyres* (without fees), since it was as rare then as now for a doctor not to charge for his services.

In Christian art the two are portrayed in loose dark robes, trimmed with fur. In *The Canterbury Tales* Chaucer describes the dress of a physician of his time as a "scarlet gown, furred well." Often they hold a box of ointment in one hand and a lancet or some surgical instruments in the other. Sometimes they hold a pestle and mortar.

Stravinsky's *Les Noces* (The Wedding), a piece for dancers and chorus with various Russian texts, invokes the names of SS. Cosmas and Damian because they are recognized in Russia as wedding saints who watch over fertility of the couple.

0857
Cow. Female ruminant, symbol of the Great Mother and creation in world mythology. The cow was sa-

cred to Hathor and Isis in Egyptian mythology. In Nordic mythology, as told in the *Prose Edda* and the *Poetic Edda*, Audhumla, a cow, licked the salt of the earth and created the first man.

0858

Coyolxauhqui (golden bells). In Aztec mythology, goddess, the moon lady, sister of the god Tezcatlipoca, who cut off her head, which now lives in the sky.

0859

Coyote. A carnivorous wolflike mammal of western North America that frequently appears in American Indian tales as a trickster and creator. In one myth Coyote prevented the creator god from turning some wooden dummies into animals. In anger the creator god left, and Coyote took the wooden dummies, planted them, and the first Indians sprouted up. In another myth Coyote plants some bird feathers that sprout into humans. Sometimes, however, he is a victim, as when Coyote's entire family is killed by Porcupine because he had cheated the animal out of his share of some buffalo meat.

0860

Crab. A crustacean having a short, broad, flattened body. In Greek mythology the crab obstructs Heracles in his battle with the nine-headed monster, the Hydra of Lerna. In Japanese folklore the facelike form or imprint on the back of a crab is that of the Heike, a family of warriors who in the 12th century engaged in a massive battle with another Japanese family, the Genji. The Heike lost and committed mass suicide by throwing themselves into the sea, where they were turned into crabs. Their faces were impressed on the backs of the crab shells. In Siamese folklore the crab is a symbol of sleeplike death. As one of the signs of the Zodiac, Cancer, the crab signifies the oblique, sideways movements of the sun during the summer solstice.

0861

Cradlemont. In Arthurian legend, king of Wales, subdued by King Arthur, mentioned in Tennyson's *The Coming of Arthur*, one of the *Idylls of the King*.

0862

Cradock. In Arthurian legend, the only knight who could carve the boar's head that no cuckold could cut, or drink from a bowl that no cuckold could drink from without spilling. His lady was the only one in King Arthur's court who could wear the mantle of chastity.

0863

Crane. A long-necked, long-legged bird. The crane is often a messenger of the gods in Chinese,

Crane

Japanese, and Greek mythologies. In medieval Christianity the crane is a symbol of vigilance, loyalty, and good works.

0864

Credne. In Celtic mythology, culture hero and bronze worker, who aided the Tuatha de Danann (the good people of the goddess Danu) with weapons in their fight against the evil Fomors.
Variant spelling: Creidne.

0865

Crispin and Crispinian, SS. (curly haired). Third century C.E. In Christian legend, patron saints of shoemakers. Feast, 25 October.

The saints were brothers who went with St. Denis from Rome to preach in France. They supported themselves by making shoes. According to one legend, angels supplied them with leather to make shoes for the poor. This upset the Roman authorities, who had the two beheaded at Soissons.

According to a Provençal legend, St. Crispin is responsible for the practice of the craft of shoemaking by cripples and hunchbacks. The saint was so pleased with his first feast day that he asked that God grant the shoemakers a glimpse of paradise. A ladder was lowered from heaven, and some of the shoemakers mounted it. When they reached heaven, there was a celebration for St. Peter, and everyone was singing the *Sursum corda*. St. Paul, who was deaf, mistook the words that were sung and cut the rope holding the ladder. The shoemakers fell to earth, causing many of them to become cripples.

St. Crispin's Day, 25 October, is the anniversary of the transfer of the relics of the two saints from Soissons to Rome in the ninth century. The date is the same as the battle of Agincourt. Shakespeare makes Crispin and his brother Crispinian into one person, Crispin Crispian, in *Henry V*.

Crockett, Davy. 1786–1836. In American history
and folklore, Tennessee-born frontiersman. Crockett served as a scout under Andrew Jackson in the
Creek Indian War. He entered political life and was
elected three times as a U.S. Congressman. Known as
the "Coonskin Congressman," Crockett opposed the
policies of President Jackson and eventually lost his
seat. He left for Texas, where he died defending the
Alamo. His legend, partly of his own making, began
during his lifetime and told how he spoke the language of animals, whipped wildcats, and killed as
many as 100 bears in less than 9 months. *A Narrative
of the Life of David Crockett*, attributed to him, helped
spread his legend, as did the *Crockett Almanacs*, which
began to appear about 1835 and were published long
after his death. An example from one of the almanacs says: "Friends, fellow citizens, brothers and
sisters! Jackson is a hero and Crockett is a horse!
They accuse me of adultery; its a lie—I never ran
away with any man's wife that was not willing, in
my life." A popular television series based on his life
and legend was later made into a Walt Disney
movie, *Davy Crockett*.

Crocodile. An amphibious reptile, both beneficent
and demonic in world mythology; the crocodile is
identified with Sebek, Set, and Horus in Egyptian
mythology. A sacred, tamed crocodile was kept in an
artificial lake by Egyptian priests and fed cakes,
meat, and wine. Some of the priests would open its
mouth while others put in cakes and other food. The
meal would end with a mixture of milk and honey.
In the Middle Ages in some Arab countries, accused
criminals were thrown into a lake of crocodiles. If
the crocodiles ate the accused, he was pronounced
guilty; if not, innocent. In West African belief crocodiles are reincarnations of murder victims, and in
Hindu mythology they are the reincarnations of
murdered Brahmins. In European folklore the crocodile is best known for the tears it is supposed to shed
over its victims. Shakespeare's *Othello* (4:2) cites the
belief and the English poet Robert Herrick in his
poem *To Mistress Ann Potter* refers to the belief that the
beast has no tongue: "True love is tongueless like a
crocodile."

Cross. Major symbol of the Christian faith. Numerous references are made to the cross in the writings
of the Early Christian Church. The legend of the
True Cross, as it was known in the Middle Ages, was
one of the most popular in Western art and
literature. It was frescoed on the choir walls of the
Church of Santa Croce in Florence by Agnolo Gaddi,
and by Piero della Francesca in the Chapel of the
Bacci, Church of San Francesco in Arezzo.

The tale is told in *The Golden Legend* by Jacobus dé
Voragine, source of much of the lore surrounding
saints' lives and Christian festivals. When Adam
was banished from the Garden of Eden, he lived a
life of penitence, toiling day and night and praying
to God. When he reached old age and felt death
approaching, he called his son Seth.

"Go, my son," he said, "to the Garden of Eden and
ask the Archangel who keeps the gate to give me a
balsam that will save me from death. You will easily
find the way, for my footsteps scorched the soil as I
left the garden."

And Seth went to carry out his father's command.
As he drew near, he saw the flaming sword in the
hand of the Archangel guarding the gate, and his
wings were spread to block entrance to the garden.
Seth prostrated himself before him, unable to utter a
word.

"The time of pardon is not yet come," said the
Archangel. "Four thousand years must roll away ere
the Redeemer shall open the gate to Adam which
was closed by his disobedience. But as a token of
future pardon, the wood on which redemption shall
be won shall grow from the tomb of your father
Adam.

"I will give you three seeds from this tree. When
Adam is dead, place them in his mouth and bury
him."

Seth took the seeds and in the course of time did
as the Archangel instructed. Three trees grew at his
father's grave—a cedar, a cypress, and a pine. They
touched and mingled with one another, finally
becoming a single trunk. It was beneath this great
tree that King David sat when he bewailed his sins.

King Solomon attempted to use this tree in the
building of his palace, but the tree would not
cooperate, so he cast it out where it would be
trampled. The Queen of Sheba found it and caused
its trunk to be buried on the spot near where the pool
of Bethesda would be placed, and the tree acquired
miraculous properties.

When the time of the crucifixion of Christ drew
near, the wood rose to the surface and was brought
out of the water. The executioners, seeking a suitable
beam for his cross, found it there. After the
Crucifixion, the wood was buried on Calvary, but
according to legend was uncovered on May 3, 328 C.E.
by the Empress Helena, mother of Constantine the
Great. The cross was carried away by Chosroes, King
of Persia, at the destruction of Jerusalem but
recovered in the year 615, on September 14, a day
that has since remained in the Christian calendar as
the Feast of the Exaltation of the Cross.

0869

Crow. A large bird having a lustrous black plumage, often associated with the devil in Christian symbolism. English folklore says the crow visits hell in mid-summer each year and makes payment to the devil by giving its feathers. The birds do molt in midsummer, and since they are usually absent from their regular haunts during that time it was easy for people ignorant of bird migrations to believe. Plutarch, the Greek author, uses the crow in one of his essays dealing with chastity. The crow is cited for its faithfulness to its mate because, according to Plutarch, it does not remarry for nine human generations. "Can Penelope match that?" Plutarch asks.

0870

Cuchulain (the hound of Cullan). In Celtic mythology, great Irish hero of Ulster.

Cuchulain, who is believed to have lived in the first century C.E., was the son of the sun god, Lugh, and Dectera, though his reputed father was Sualtam. As a child he was called Setanta (the little); he received the name Cuchulain (the hound of Cullan) when he killed the watchdog of the smith Cullan and compensated the owner by undertaking to guard his house in the dog's place. Later, when the men of Ulster asked Cuchulain to take a wife, he said he loved Emer, daughter of Forgall. He set out in his chariot for Forgall's home, only to learn that Emer would not marry him until he had slain hundreds of men. Cuchulain went to the war goddess Skatha for advice and lived with her for a year and a day, learning how to use the Gae Bolg, a magic deadly weapon.

Skatha then made war with Aifa, the strongest woman in the world. However, the goddess did not wish Cuchulain to enter the battle because he was very young. She therefore gave him a sleeping potion that was to last 24 hours. However, he awoke one hour later and attacked the enemy, causing havoc and death. Finally, Aifa incited Skatha to single combat. Cuchulain accepted the challenge for himself and by his victory made an end of the war. Aifa then became his friend and lover. Before he left her, Cuchulain gave Aifa a ring to give their son if a child should be born of their union. A son called Connla was born; however, he did not know his real father and was later killed by Cuchulain, who learned too late that he had killed his own son.

Cuchulain then fought the sons of Nechtan, whom he slew, fastening their heads to his chariot's rim. He returned to battle with 16 swans and 2 stags also yoked to his chariot. Cuchulain then went to fight Forgall and his men, all of whom he defeated, thus winning Emer as his wife. When Cuchulain was born, the Druid priest Morann had said: "His praise will be in the mouths of all men. Charioteers and warriors, kings and sages will recount his deeds. He will win the love of many."

The most famous deed of the hero is contained in the saga *Táin Bó Cualgne* (The Cattle Raid of Cooley), written in the eighth or ninth century. The epic opens with Queen Maev (Medb) of Connacht and her henpecked husband, Ailill, arguing over who had greater possessions. The queen discovers she has possessions equal to those of her husband, except for one bull owned by Ailill, the White Horned Bull of Connacht. Maev determines to correct this imbalance by obtaining the bull from the Donn of Cooley. She asks Daire, a chief of Ulster, to lend her the bull. He refuses and she then sends an army to invade Ulster. The warriors of Ulster, however, are under a curse; only Cuchulain is free of it. All alone he withstands the enemy. Once during the various battles Cuchulain is compelled to fight his dear friend Ferdiad, who made a bold challenge to him while drunk. For three days they fight, until Cuchulain finally kills Ferdiad. Eventually a truce is made between Cuchulain and Queen Maev, but she breaks it, sending her men to steal the bull. They are defeated, and the White Horned Bull of Connacht is killed by the donn of Cooley, who later dies when his heart bursts.

According to other accounts, Queen Maev waited for her time to avenge herself on Cuchulain for his victory. Maev sent the posthumous three sons of the three daughters of the wizard Catlin against Cuchulain. He became ill and was tended in his despondency in a solitary glen by Niam, the wife of Connel, and other princesses. Then Bave, Catlin's daughter, took the form of Niam and beckoned him forth to battle. At the touch of his lips, the wine that his mother, Dectera, gave him turned to blood. When he reached the ford on the plain of Emania, he saw a maiden weeping and washing bloody garments and arms—they were his own. Then breaking his geis, or taboo, Cuchulain ate the roasted dog offered him by Catlin's three daughters and went forth again to battle. He bound himself with his belt to a pillar so that he might die standing. Cuchulain was killed by Curoi's son, whose father had earlier been killed by Cuchulain. The age of the hero was 27.

Cuchulain's legends were used by W. B. Yeats in *The Death of Cuchulain*, as well as in another poem, *Cuchulain's Fight with the Sea*. Lady Gregory compiled the legends and myths in *Cuchulain of Muirthemne*.

0871

Cuckoo. Slender-bodied, long-tailed bird with downcurved beak and pointed wings.

In Greek and Hindu mythology the cuckoo is noted for its sexual appetite. Both the Greek sky god Zeus and the Hindu sky god Indra at one time transformed themselves into cuckoos in order to take advantage of some maiden. The ancient Romans called an adulterer a cuckoo. Shakespeare's song in *Love's Labour's Lost* (5.2.87–90) expresses the European belief:

> The cuckoo then, on every tree,
> Mocks married men; for thus sings he,
> "Cuckoo!
> Cuckoo, cuckoo! O word of fear,
> Unpleasing to the married ear!"

In European folk belief a man's fancy turns toward love in springtime, and the cuckoo is popularly known as the herald of spring. Delius' symphonic poem *On Hearing the First Cuckoo in Spring* captures the mood of springtime.

Cuckoo and the Turtledove, The. Satirical verse fable by Ivan Krylov.   0872

A cuckoo sat on a bough, bitterly complaining. "Why are you so sad, dear friend?" cooed the turtledove sympathetically from a neighboring twig. "Is it because spring has passed away from us, and love with it; that the sun has sunk lower, and that we are nearer to winter?"

"How can I help grieving, unhappy one that I am?" replied the cuckoo. "You yourself shall be the judge. This spring my love was a happy one, and after awhile, I became a mother. But my offspring utterly refuse even to recognize me. Was it such a return that I expected from them? And how can I help being envious when I see how ducklings crowd around their mother—how chickens hasten to the hen when she calls to them? Just like an orphan I sit here, utterly alone, and know not what filial affection means."

"Poor thing!" said the dove. "I pity you from my heart. As for me, though I know such things often occur, I should die outright if my dovelets did not love me. But tell me, have you already brought up your little ones? When did you find time to build a nest? I never saw you doing anything of the kind. You were always flying and fluttering about."

"Yes, indeed!" said the cuckoo. "Pretty nonsense it would have been if I had spent such fine days in sitting on a nest! That would indeed have been the highest pitch of stupidity! I always laid my eggs in the nests of other birds."

"Then how can you expect your little ones to care for you?" asked the turtledove. In English the fable is sometimes called "The Cuckoo and the Wood Pigeon."

Culture hero. In world myth and legend, a human, animal, or combination who gives to his people all good and useful things, for example teaching them how to gather food. He may give them the gift of fire and some forms of medicines to heal themselves. In many cultures, when the culture hero has accomplished his task, he departs, and his people wait for the time when he will return to them.   0873

Cun. In the mythology of the Andes Indians near Lake Titicaca, a thunder god who lived in the mountains high above the snow peaks. He had no bones, muscles, or members, though he was as swift as the wind. His nature was irritable, and he was not interested in human affairs.   0874

Variant spelling: Con.

Cupay. In Inca mythology, an evil spirit, equated with the devil by Christian Indians of Peru and Bolivia today.   0875

W. H. Prescott, in *The History of the Conquest of Peru*, wrote that no sacrifices were made to Cupay. He "seems to have been only a shadowy personification of sin, that exercised little influence over the daily lives of the people." But Max Fauconnet, in his discussion of Cupay in the *New Larousse Encyclopedia of Mythology*, wrote that he was "a god of death . . . who lived inside the earth." He was a "dreary and greedy god, always longing to increase the number of his subjects, so he must be placated, even at the cost of painful sacrifices. Thus, every year a hundred children were sacrificed to him."

Variant spellings: Supay, Supai.

Curtana (short). The Sword of Mercy in England borne before English kings at their coronation. The sword, according to medieval legend, belonged to St. Edward the Confessor. Curtana has no point and thus symbolizes mercy.   0876

Curtius, Marcus. Fourth century B.C.E. In Roman legend, a hero who killed himself to close a chasm. According to the legend, a gigantic chasm opened and could be closed only if Rome's greatest treasure were cast into the pit. Mounting his horse, Curtius leaped in, and the chasm closed.   0877

Cuthbert, St. (famous, bright). Died 687 C.E. In Christian legend, patron saint of shepherds and seafarers. Invoked against plague. Feast, 20 March.   0878

Curtius riding into the pit

The legends of the saint were written by St. Bede as *The Life and Miracles of St. Cuthbert, Bishop of Lindisfarne*, in the seventh century. Cuthbert was a young shepherd in the valley of Tweed. One day an angel appeared to him and told him to lead a holy and pious life. He therefore went to be instructed at the monastery of Melrose near his home, which was run by St. Aidan. One night, as Cuthbert tended his flocks, he saw a dazzling light and, looking up, beheld angels bearing St. Aidan to heaven. He then entered the monastery and became abbot. He was noted for his preaching as he wandered among the mountainous regions. Later he went to live on an island off the coast of Northumberland called Lindisfarne (Holy Island). Numerous miracles are recorded by Bede in his life of the saint; for example one night, when the saint lay on the cold shore, exhausted by his penance, two otters licked him and revived his benumbed limbs.

His main attribute, however, is the head of King St. Oswald, which was buried in the tomb of St. Cuthbert when the king was slain in battle.

0879

Cuthman, St. (famous). Died c. 900. In Christian legend, builder of the first Christian church in Sussex, England. Feast, 8 February.

Cuthman lived with his mother at Steyning in Sussex. One medieval legend concerns the Devil's Dyke at Brighton. One day St. Cuthman was walking over the South Downs, thinking of how he had saved the whole country from paganism. Suddenly, the devil appeared.

"Ha, ha," said the devil, "so you think that by building churches and convents you can stop me. Poor fool! Why, this night I will flood the whole land and destroy all the churches and convents."

"Forewarned is forearmed," said St. Cuthman to himself as he calmly left the devil to his ranting. Cuthman went to his sister Cecilia, mother superior of a convent that stood on the present site of Dyke's House.

"Sister," said the saint, "I love you very much. This night, for the grace of God, keep lights burning at the convent windows from midnight to daybreak, and let Masses be said."

At sundown the devil came with a pickax, spade, mattock, and shovel and set to work to let the sea flow into the downs. But the sound of the nuns' singing at Mass made it impossible for the devil to continue his work, and he became paralyzed. When the candles were lit by the nuns, the cock, thinking it was morning, began to sing, and the devil, who could only work at night, fled as fast as he could. Before he fled, however, he had dug a small hole, which is called Devil's Dyke to this day.

0880

Cuycha. In Inca mythology, rainbow god who attended the sun, Inti, and the moon, Mama Quilla.

0881

Cyhiraeth. In Celtic mythology, a goddess of streams who appears in Welsh folklore as a species of spectral female, haunting woodland brooks. Her blood-freezing shriek foretells a death.

0882

Cymbeline. In British legend, a king who reigned for 35 years under Roman rule. In Holinshed's *Chronicles* he is said to have been "brought up in Rome, and there made a knight by Augustus Caesar." He had two sons, Guiderius and Arviragus. Shakespeare used the reference to Cymbeline in *Chronicles* as well as the story of Imogen from Boccaccio's *Decameron* for the plot of his play *Cymbeline*. In some accounts, Cymbeline is identified with King Cunobeline, after whom the city of Camalodunum or Colchester is named.

0883

Cyril and Methodius, SS. (lord). Ninth century C.E. In Christian legend, Apostles of the Slavs. St. Cyril's feast, 9 March in the Greek church; St. Methodius, 11 May. In the Latin church both are honored on 9 March.

Cyril was a philosopher and Methodius an artist; both belonged to the Order of St. Basil. They were sent by the Patriarch of Constantinople as Christian missionaries to the people who lived on the borders of the Danube. One legend tells how Bogaris, the King of Bulgaria, asked Methodius to paint a picture in his palace hall that would impress his subjects. Methodius painted the Last Judgment with Christ enthroned and surrounded by angels, and also panels portraying the punishment of hell and the rewards of heaven. Impressed by the work, Bogaris became a Christian and adopted the religion for his country. Cyril and Methodius then went among the surrounding nations preaching the gospel. St. Cyril, according to legend, invented the Cyrillic alphabet and translated parts of the Gospels.

The two saints are portrayed together in most icons. St. Cyril holds a book and St. Methodius has a tablet on which he is painting.

D

Da. In African mythology (Fon of Benin), serpent god, who symbolizes life and movement.

0884

Dabaiba. In the mythology of the Indians of the isthmus of Panama, the region joining the South American continent, a rain goddess and mother of the creator god.

0885

Dabaiba was worshiped near a river of the same name. Human sacrifices were made to her, perhaps in the hope that she would never again send a drought such as a previous one that nearly destroyed the population. In a myth of the Antioquians, Dabaiba appears as the goddess Dabeciba, and her son is Abira, the creator god.

Dadak. In Tibetan Buddhism, a guardian deity, associated with the hero and founder of Buddhism in Tibet, Padmasambhava.

0886

Dadhyanch. In Hindu mythology, a sage who was taught certain sciences by Indra but was not allowed to pass on his knowledge to anyone else without punishment. However, Dadhyanch gave some of the knowledge to the Aswins, the twin gods. When Indra discovered this he set out to cut off Dadhyanch's head. The Aswins, however, removed Dadhyanch's head and replaced it with a horse's head. When Indra cut off Dadhyanch's horse head, the Aswins then replaced it with Dadhyanch's real head.

0887

Variant spellings: Dadhica, Dadhicha.

Daedala (wooden image). In ancient Greek cult, a festival in honor of Hera held by the Boetians. It commemorated the myth about Hera leaving Zeus and hiding. The god said he would then marry another and had a wooden image dressed up as his bride. When Hera believed Zeus was to marry another, she reappeared and attacked the "bride," only to discover it was a wooden statue. Part of the rites of the festival consisted of dressing a statue and offering a goat to Zeus and a cow to Hera.

0888

Daedalion (bright). In Greek mythology, a young man, son of Phosphorus; brother of Ceyx; father of Chione (Philonis). He was loved by the gods Apollo

0889

and Hermes. His daughter Chione slept with both Apollo and Hermes and gave birth to twins. When she was turned into a hawk by Artemis for rejecting her love, Daedalion jumped from the summit of Mount Parnassus. Apollo then changed him into a hawk. The myth is told in Ovid's *Metamorphoses* (book 11).

Daedalus (bright, cunningly wrought). In Greek mythology, a culture hero, son of Eupalamus (or Metion) and Alcippe (or Merope); brother of Perdix and Sicyan; father of Icarus. Instructed by the goddess Athena, Daedalus was inventor of the ax, awl, and level. He was exiled from Athens after he murdered his nephew, Talus (sufferer?), whom Daedalus envied because Talus showed promise of becoming as great as Daedalus. He escaped to Crete, where he built the famous labyrinth with a thousand turnings for King Minos. Inside the labyrinth lived the Minotaur, the offspring of Minos' wife, Pasiphaë, and the Cretan bull. Daedalus, along with his son Icarus, was imprisoned in the maze as punishment for giving Ariadne directions for guiding Theseus out of the maze. To escape, Daedalus fashioned wings out of wax and feathers for himself and Icarus. During their escape Icarus flew too close to the sun, the wax in his wings melted, and he fell onto the island of Icaria. Daedalus flew to Sicily. The Sicilian king Cacalus refused a request to return Daedalus to Crete.

0890

The scene of the fall of Icarus is frequently found in paintings. Daedalus and Icarus are a motif in the writings of James Joyce, whose hero is Stephen Daedalus. Ovid's *Metamorphoses* (book 8) tells the myth of Daedalus and Icarus. Socrates claimed descent from Daedalus. English poets borrowed from Greek the adjective *daedal*, which means "cunningly wrought." Both Keats and Shelley use the word. Other English poets who mention Daedalus are Chaucer, Shakespeare, and Auden.

Daemon. In Greek mythology, a supernatural being, part god and part man; called Genius by the Romans. Daemons were believed to be guiding spirits of people assigned to them by Zeus. Agathodaemas (good demon) was the name of the good spirit of rural prosperity and of vineyards. The word is the source for the English word *demon*.

0891

Daena. In Persian mythology, an angel, the personification of Zoroastrian law and religion, who presides over the 24th day of the month.   0892
Variant spellings: Din, Dino.

Dagda (good god?). In Celtic mythology, Irish god of fertility, husband of Brigit or a goddess with three names—Breg (lie), Meng (guile), and Meabel (disgrace)—who bore him a daughter named Brigit, and Bodb the Red, Ceacht, Midir, and Ogma. He possessed a magic caldron, Undry, that could feed the whole earth. Sometimes he is called the Lord of Great Knowledge because he possessed all wisdom. He was forced from his throne as king of the Tuatha de Danann (people of the goddess Danu) by his son Oengus. Dagda was portrayed holding a large club or fork, symbol of his dominion over the food supply.   0893
Variant spelling: Daghda.

Dagon (corn, grain). In Near Eastern mythology (Canaanite), vegetation god worshiped by the Philistines.   0894

The Old Testament records three incidents that portray the encounter between the worship of Dagon and of the Hebrew deity Yahweh. The first (Judg. 16:29–30) tells how the hero Samson destroyed the temple of Dagon by taking "hold of the two middle pillars upon which the house stood, and on which it was borne up, of the one with his right hand, and of the other with his left. . . . And he bowed himself with all his might; and the house fell upon the lords, and upon all the people that were therein."

The second episode (1 Sam. 5:3–4) tells how the Philistines at Ashdod were killed when the ark of God, which contained the tablets of the law, was taken into the temple of Dagon and placed by Dagon's image.

"And when they of Ashdod arose early on the morrow, behold, Dagon was fallen upon his face to the earth before the ark of the Lord. And they took Dagon, and set him in his place again. And when they arose early on the morrow morning, behold, Dagon was fallen upon his face to the ground before the ark of the Lord; and the head of Dagon and both the palms of his hands were cut off upon the threshold; only the stump of Dagon was left to him."

In *Paradise Lost* (book 1) Milton refers to this biblical episode when he turns Dagon into a fallen angel:

> Next came one
> Who mourn'd in earnest, when the captive Ark

> Maim'd his brute image, head and hands lopt off
> In his own Temple, on the grunsel edge,
> Where he fell flat, and sham'd his Worshipers:
> Dagon his Name, Sea Monster, upward Man
> And downward Fish:

Milton's description of Dagon as half fish, half man is incorrect. The poet may have borrowed it from an earlier work by Alexander Ross called *Pansebeia, or A View of All Religions of the World*, which gives such a description. Modern scholars, however, discredit this image of the god, which goes back to St. Jerome, who believed the word *Dagon* was related to "fish," not "grain" as is now known.

First Chronicles (10:10) supplies the last Old Testament episode. It tells how King Saul was killed at Mount Gilboa and his head fastened "in the temple of Dagon."

Dagonet. In Arthurian legend, King Arthur's fool. One day Sir Dagonet came to Cornwall with two squires. As they drew near a well, Sir Tristram soused them and made them mount their horses and amid jeers ride off dripping wet. Malory in *Morte d'Arthur* writes that "King Arthur loved Sir Dagonet passing well, and made him a knight, with his own hands; and at every tournament he made King Arthur laugh." Tennyson, however, in *The Last Tournament*, one of the *Idylls of the King*, says Sir Gwaine made Dagonet "mock-knight of Arthur's Table Round."   0895

Dagr (day). In Norse mythology, the day, son of Nott (night) and Delling (dayspring), whose horse is Skinfaxi. He appears in the *Prose Edda*.   0896

Daibutsu (great Buddha). In Japanese Buddhist art, name given to several large bronze images of the Buddhas; the most famous, Amida Buddha, some 49 feet, 7 inches in height, located at Kamakura. The work was erected in 1252 and housed in a temple. The temple has been destroyed twice; after the second destruction it was not rebuilt.   0897

Daikoku. In Japanese Shinto-Buddhist mythology, god of wealth, portrayed as a short, stout man standing or sitting on two bales of rice, with a large wooden mallet in his right hand and a bag slung over his left shoulder. The god's "lucky mallet" is capable of bestowing wealth with one stroke. He is one of the Shichi Fukujin, the seven gods of good luck or fortune.   0898

Dai Mokuren. In Japanese mythology, one of the disciples of the Buddha. Seeing the soul of his   0899

Amida Buddha

Daisy (Walter Crane

mother in the Hell of Hungry Spirits, Dai Mokuren sent her some food, which became transformed into flames and blazing embers as she lifted it to her lips. He asked the Buddha for an explanation and was told that in her previous life his mother had refused food to a wandering mendicant priest. The only way to obtain her release from perpetual hunger was to feed, on the tenth day of the seventh month, the souls of all of the great priests of all countries. Notwithstanding the difficulty of this undertaking, Dai Mokuren succeeded, and in his joy at seeing his mother relieved, he started to dance. This performance is said to be the origin of the Japanese *Bon Odori*, dances that take place during the Festival of the Dead, variously scheduled in different regions but usually mid-July and mid-August.

0900
Daisy. A small wildflower with white and yellow blossoms. In Roman mythology the daisy was formed when the nymph Belides escaped being raped by Vertumnus, god of orchards, by being transformed into a daisy. In Christian legend St. Mary Magdalene, repenting her sinful life, shed tears that fell to earth and became daisies. In European folk medicine the daisy was used to cure ulcers, madness, and chest wounds.

0901
Daityas. In Hindu mythology, demon-giants, descendants of Diti by Kasyapa.

0902
Dajoji. In North American Indian mythology (Iroquois), the panther, god of the west wind; his snarl makes even the sun hide its face.

0903
Dakhma. Tower of Silence in Zoroastrian funeral rites, where the bodies of the dead are left to be eaten by vultures. A corpse is regarded as unclean and therefore not fit to be buried in the earth, which it would defile, or burned in fire, which would also be defiled.
   Variant spelling: Dahkma.

0904
Dakinis (sky goer). In Tibetan Buddhism, eight goddess assistants. They are Lasya, of white complexion, holding a mirror in a coquettish attitude; Mala, of yellow color, holding a rosary, called *pren-ba-ma*; Git, of red color, holding a lyre; Gar-ma, of green color, dancing; Pushpa, of white color, holding a flower, also called Me-tog-ma; Dhupa, of yellow color, holding an incense vase, also called bDug-spos ma; Dipa, of red color, holding a lamp; Gandha, of green color, holding a shell vase of perfume, also called Dri-ch'a-ma.

0905
Daksha (able). In Hindu mythology, a Prajapati, one of the sons of the god Brahma; he sprang from his father's right thumb. Daksha's first attempt at popu-

lating the world was unsuccessful. A thousand sons were born to him by his wife, Asikni, but they did not produce any offspring. Another thousand sons, by the same wife, also did not produce any offspring. In all, 5,000 children were born, called Haryaswas. Sixty daughters were then born, who married and had children.

In Indian art Daksha is portrayed with a goat head. One day, according to one account, he insulted the god Shiva, who was his son-in-law. Shiva, in anger, changed Daksha's head to that of a goat, a perpetual sign of stupidity. Ironically Daksha's name means "able," "competent," or "intelligent."

0906
Dalai Lama (great ocean Lama). In Tibetan Buddhism, the spiritual and temporal head, who is regarded as an incarnation of Avalokiteshvara, one of the five Dhyani-Bodhisattvas. He is called in Tibet *Gyal-wa Rin-po-che'e* (the gem of majesty; victory). The Panchen Lama (learned Lama) ranks second after the Dalai Lama and is considered an incarnation of Amitabha, the Buddha of Infinite Light. The Panchen Lama, being a Buddha, is spiritually superior to the Dalai Lama. But since a Buddha is not involved in the temporal process, but a Bodhisattva is, the Dalai Lama is temporally superior to the Panchen Lama. Together, each has the superiority of *primus inter pares* as did the kings of old Tibet.

0907
Dambhodbhava. In the Hindu epic poem *The Mahabharata*, a king who was punished for his pride.

Dambhodbhava had an overweening conceit about his own powers. He was told, however, by his priests that he was no match for two sages, Nara and Narayana, who were living as ascetics on the Gandha-madana Mountain. Puffed up with pride, the king went with his army and challenged Nara and Narayana. Nara at first tried to disuade Dambhodbhava, but the king insisted on fighting. Nara then took a handful of straws and, using them as missiles, sent them through the air, penetrating the eyes, ears, and noses of the king's army. Defeated, Dambhodbhava fell at Nara's feet and begged him for peace.

0908
Damkina (lady of the earth). In Near Eastern mythology (Babylonian-Assyrian), earth goddess married to Ea, god of sweet waters and the earth.
Variant spellings: Dauke; Dawkina.

0909
Damon and Pythias. Fourth century B.C.E. In Greek legend, two male lovers, believed to be Pythagorean philosophers. Pythias plotted against the Sicilian tyrant Dionysius and was condemned to death. He was allowed to return home first to arrange his affairs. Damon then offered to take his place as a hostage, even to suffer death if necessary. Dionysius was so moved by this offer that he pardoned the two men.

0910
Danaans (judge?). In Greek mythology and legend, name given to the subjects of King Danaus of Argos. The name was then applied to all Greeks. Homer never uses the word *Greek* in his writings but calls the people Achaeans, Argives, and Danaans. Sometimes Ovid and Vergil use *Danai* for Greeks.

0911
Danaë (she who judges, parched). In Greek mythology, mother of the hero Perseus; daughter of King Acrisius of Argos and Eurydice; sister of Evarete. Acrisius had been told by an oracle that one day his daughter would bear a son who would kill him. Acrisius locked Danaë in a bronze chamber, either in a tower or under ground. Zeus, always ready to sleep with a beautiful young girl, came to Danaë in the form of a golden shower (urine) and fathered Perseus. The king, however, refused to believe his daughter's son was fathered by Zeus. He shut Danaë and the boy in a chest and had it cast into the sea. It floated safely to the island of Seriphus and was found by Dictys, a fisherman. He took care of Perseus until the lad was grown. Polydectes, brother of Dictys and king of the island, fell in love with Danaë, who did not return his love. To more easily pursue Danaë, Polydectes sent Perseus to fetch the head of Medusa, hoping the young man would be killed. Danaë went into hiding until Perseus returned with Medusa's head. In anger at being sent on the expedition, Perseus showed the head to Polydectes and his guests at a banquet, and they all turned to stone. He then took his mother back to Argos. Homer's *Iliad* (book 14), Vergil's *Aeneid* (book 7), and Ovid's *Metamorphoses* (book 10) all cite the myth. Numerous Renaissance paintings portray Danaë and the Golden Shower as an opportunity to be both erotic and learned. Among the artists who treated the subject are Titian, Correggio, Tintoretto, and Rembrandt. Richard Strauss's opera *Die Liebe der Danaë* also deals with the myth.

0912
Danaidae (judge?) In Greek mythology, the 50 daughters of Danaus who married the 50 sons of Aegyptus, Danaus' brother. Among the women were Calaeno, Exato, Eurydice, Glauce, and Hypermnestra. On their wedding night, 49 of the women killed their husbands. As punishment they were condemned to draw water with a sieve in Hades. Only one, Hypermnestra, saved her husband, Lynceus.

Aeschylus' *The Suppliant Maidens* and Chaucer's *Legend of Good Women* draw on the myth.

Danavas. In Hindu mythology, demon-giants who warred against the gods. They are descendants of Danu by Kasyapa.

0913

Danbhalah Houé-Do. In Haitian voodoo, major serpent god, the oldest of the loas (deified spirits of the dead). His symbol is a snake, arched in the path of the sun as it travels across the sky. Sometimes half of the arch is made up of his female counterpart, Ayida, the rainbow. He is often identified in Haitian voodoo belief with St. Patrick of Christian legend because the saint is often pictured with a snake at his feet.

Variant spellings: Damballa, Damballah, Damballa Wédo, Dan-Gbe.

0914

Dance of Death

Dance of Death. A medieval series of woodcuts or paintings depicting Death claiming his victims.

0915

The series portrays Death taking people from all walks of life, from peasant to pope. The theme became popular in the late 14th century in Germany and spread to other European countries. A series of woodcuts by Hans Holbein the Younger was published in 1538. Liszt's *Totentanz* (dance of death) is a work for piano and orchestra that uses the medieval sequence "Dies Irae" as its theme. Saint-Saëns's symphonic poem *Danse Macabre* is a short work dealing with the subject. An Ingmar Bergman film, *The Seventh Seal*, also used the motif.

Danh. In Haitian voodoo, a loa (deified spirit of the dead) who brings good fortune and money; symbolized by a horned and coiled snake.

0916

Daniel (God is my judge). In the Bible, O.T., one of the Four Major Prophets, the others being Isaiah, Jeremiah, and Ezekiel. Title of one of the books of the Bible, placed among the *Hagiographa* (sacred writings) in Hebrew Scriptures but among the prophets in the King James Version.

0917

Daniel was a captive at the court of Nebuchadnezzar and was called Belteshazzar. He interpreted Nebuchadnezzar's dream by telling the king that the great beast of gold, silver, brass, iron, and clay in the dream represented the gradual disintegration of the kingdoms to come after him. Interpreting another dream, Daniel told Nebuchadnezzar of his future madness. Through his skill Daniel, as well as his friends Shadrach, Meshach, and Abednego, rose in power in the court. Because they were Jews, they refused to worship Nebuchadnezzar's golden idol, and Daniel's three young friends were cast into the fiery furnace but were not consumed by the flames. Later Daniel interpreted the writing on the wall for King Belshazzar, Nebuchadnezzar's son, in which the king's death was predicted. The king's successor, Darius, gave Daniel a high position in his court. Other courtiers, jealous of Daniel, persuaded Darius to have Daniel thrown into the lion's den, but God closed the mouths of the lion and Daniel remained unharmed. Daniel also appears in the Old Testament Apocrypha in the tales of Bel and the Dragon and Susanna. In Christian art Daniel is seen as the prophet of justice. Daniel also had visions, which are recounted in the second half of the Book of Daniel. Rembrandt painted *The Vision of Daniel.*

Danu. In Celtic mythology, mother goddess, sometimes identified with the goddess Anu (Ana) among the Irish Celts. Danu was the daughter of King Dagda and ancestress of the Tuatha de Danann, the people and gods of the goddess Danu. In British Celtic mythology Danu is known as Don, her children as the Children of Don. When she is identified with the goddess Anu (scholars do not agree on whether the two are the same goddess), she is known as a goddess of prosperity and abundance to whom human sacrifices were made. The name Anu clings to two mountains near Killarney, Ireland, which are called the Paps of Anu, indicating her role as a mother goddess.

0918

Daphne (bay, laurel). In Greek mythology, a mountain nymph, daughter of the river god Peneus (or Ladon). She was dedicated to Artemis, the virgin goddess, and spurned all men. Apollo fell in love with her, pursued her, and lost her when she cried for help and her father transformed her into a laurel. Embracing its trunk, Apollo said its leaves would be ever green, and later he wore laurel leaves as a crown. The myth is told in Ovid's *Metamorphoses* (book 1), alluded to by Chaucer and Milton, painted by Giorgione, Pollaivolo, Poussin, and Tiepolo, and sculptured by Bernini. Richard Strauss also told the story in his opera *Daphne*.

0920

Daphnis (laurel). In Greek mythology, inventor of bucolic poetry; a son of Hermes by a Sicilian nymph. He was exposed to die but was saved by shepherds and taught by Pan to play the flute and sing. Daphnis fell in love with Piplea (variant names for the nymph are Lyce, Nais, Nomia, and Xenea), entered a contest to win her hand, and was about to lose when Heracles killed his rival, Lityerses. In a variant myth, Daphnis promised Piplea he would never fall in love with another woman. Daphnis broke his promise and was punished by the Muses with blindness. He died when he refused to eat after his five hunting dogs died. He has no connection with the myth of Daphnis and Chloe.

0921

Daphnis and Chlöe (laurel and young green shoot). In Greek and Latin mythology, a young shepherd, and Chlöe, a shepherdess. They lived on the island of Lesbos. The tale is a pastoral story about the maturing of love. The tale is told by Longus (third-century C.E.) of Daphnis. The theme was a favorite in 17th- and 18th-century France and England and inspired Ravel's ballet Daphnis and Chlöe (1910). Daphnis is also the name of a Sicilian shepherd in pastoral poetry, credited with the invention of the genre. He was blinded by the Muses and later died for love. He appears in Theocritus and in Vergil's *Eclogues*. Daphnis is also the name of a shepherd on Mount Ida transformed to stone by a jealous nymph. Ovid's *Metamorphoses* (book 4) tells the tale.

0922

Darana. In Australian mythology, the rainmaker who causes rain to fall by singing.

Once when Darana sang, so much rain fell that the earth was flooded. He placed his throwing stick in the waters, and they receded. As a result of the rainfall, flowers and witchetty grubs bloomed in the desert. Darana picked them, placed them in bags, and hung them on trees. Finished with his work, he went on a journey. But two youths, the Dara-ulu, spotted the bags and threw their boomerangs at them, causing them to break and scatter to the winds. Dust seemed to cover the whole earth and obscure the sun. When the Muramura spirits saw what was happening, they came down and killed the two boys. Darana restored the youths to life, only to have them killed a second time and transformed into heart-shaped stones. Heart-shaped stones are still used in rainmaking ceremonies. It is believed that if these stones are destroyed the earth would be covered with red dust.

0923

Dardanus (burner-up). In Greek mythology, prime ancestor of the Trojans, son of Zeus and Electra; brother of Iasim; married to Chryse and after her death to Bateia (Arisbe); father of Erichthonius and Ilus and of Herophile by Neso. He founded Dardania, which later became Troy, at the foot of Mount Ida. He is mentioned in Vergil's *Aeneid* (book 5) and Homer's *Iliad* (book 20). The mares of Dardanus are mares from which Boreas, who changed himself into a horse, later fathered 12 steeds that could not be overtaken.

0924

Dares Phrygius. In medieval legend, an ancient Trojan priest of the god Hephaestus, believed to be the author of a popular account of the Trojan War called *De Excidio Troiae Historia*, which favors the Trojan viewpoint. An account credited to Dictys Cretensis called *Ephermiris Belli Trojani*, also popular during the Middle Ages, gives a pro-Greek account of the war. Both works were forgeries but kept alive much Greek and Trojan mythology during the Middle Ages.

0925

David (beloved, friend?) c. 1085–1015 B.C.E. In the Bible, O.T., second king of Israel, youngest son of Jesse, of the tribe of Judah, settled in or near Bethlehem. David was a handsome youth who was chosen by Yahweh (the Hebrew cult god) to replace King Saul, with whom Yahweh was displeased. Samuel the Prophet anointed David with his horn of oil in the midst of his other brothers. David first won a place at Saul's court by playing the harp to ease Saul, who was being tormented by an evil spirit sent by Yahweh. Later, David killed the giant Goliath with a single stone from his slingshot. After cutting off the giant's head, David brought it to Saul as a trophy. When Jonathan, Saul's son, saw David, he fell in love with him and defended him when Saul wanted to have him murdered. David fled and gathered a following of men after Saul himself tried to murder him with a javelin. David's wife, Michal, one of Saul's daughters, let David out through the window of their house. She put a pillow of goat's hair in the bed and pretended David was sick. Fleeing to the fields, he met Jonathan, who warned him he must flee for his life. The two men parted, promising love and friendship forever. From then until Saul's death, David lived the life of an outlaw. Three times David had the opportunity to kill Saul but refused. Saul was "the anointed king of God." (This passage was used by later Christian kings as authority against any form of sedition.) Finally, Saul and his son Jonathan were killed by the Philistines, and David lamented their deaths, saying, "I am distressed for thee, my brother Jonathan: very pleasant hast thou been unto me: thy love to me was wonderful, passing the love of woman" (2 Sam. 1:26). David then recaptured the Ark (in which Yahweh lived) and brought it to Jerusalem amid shouts of great joy. David even danced before the Ark, which upset his wife Michal, whom he then had locked up, never sleeping with her again. One of David's hero warriors, Uriah the Hittite, had a wife, Bathsheba, whom David saw bathing from his rooftop. David lusted after her and committed adultery with her. He then caused her husband's death by sending him into battle and then took Bathsheba as one of his wives. As

punishment for David's sin, Yahweh caused the first child of David and Bathsheba to die. After David's penitence, a second child was born and was named Solomon. When David grew old and was no longer able to have sexual intercourse, a successor was sought, and after much court intrigue Solomon was chosen.

Medieval Christianity took the various incidents from David's life and tied them into Christian belief. David was viewed as a type of prefiguration of Christ, who descended from David. Various events in David's life were given a Christian interpretation. David's slaying the lion and bear (1 Sam. 17:32–37) was seen as a prefiguration of Christ's victory over Satan. David's slaying of Goliath (1 Sam. 17:38–51) was a prefiguration of Christ's temptation in the desert by the devil, and the triumph of David after Goliath's defeat (1 Sam. 18:6–7) was viewed as a prefiguration of Christ's entry into Jerusalem. Even the episode of David and Bathsheba (2 Samuel 11:4, 5) was seen as a prefiguration of Christ (David) and the Church (Bathsheba).

Medieval art usually portrayed David playing the harp. Among some famous works are Michelangelo's statue, Caravaggio's *David with the Head of Goliath*, Rembrandt's *David Playing the Harp for*

Bathsheba

Saul, and Honegger's cantata *Le Roi David*, a popular musical setting of part of David's legend. In Islamic legend David is called Dawvd, the king to whom Allah revealed the Zabur, or Book of Psalms.

0926

David of Sassoun (beloved, friend?). Armenian epic poem compiled in the 19th century from oral and written sources. The epic consists of four cycles:

Sanassar and Baghdassar: Once King Senakerim besieged the city of Jerusalem, but his troops were killed by angels sent by God to punish the pagan king. He vowed that if he could safely escape the city, he would sacrifice his own sons when he reached his native land. Senakerim's wife, who was secretly a Christian, learned of the vow and warned her two sons, Sanassar and Baghdassar. They fled the country disguised as servants. They found a place to stay with the king of Kraput-Koch. One day, to test the young men, the king asked them to fight his soldiers. Accepting the challenge, Sanassar and Baghdassar defeated the men, and as a result they were told to leave the land. They would not leave unless the king granted them land and workmen to build a city. The wish was granted, and they built Sassoun. The king also gave his daughter as a wife to Sanassar.

The god of King Senakerim, however, would not let the king forget his vow of sacrificing his two sons. Each night the god appeared to the king in his sleep in the form of a goat. Knowing what the king would do, Baghdassar decided to return home. When he arrived, his father took him to the idol of the god to sacrifice him. Baghdassar asked Senakerim to show him how to bow to the god. Complying, the king knelt down, whereupon the son cut off his head. Baghdassar was then crowned king.

David of Sassoun: The main hero of the poem, David of Sassoun, is one of the sons of King Baghdassar. He is noted for his strength and for the oaken stick with which he performs many feats.

David, along with a friend, took care of the calves. One day the devs, half-demon, half-men monsters, came and drove away the calves. David followed their tracks to the entrance of a cave and paused. He cried out with so loud a voice that the devs became frightened and "were as full of fear as is the devil when Christ's voice is heard in hell."

When the leader of the devs heard the voice, he said: "That is surely David, the son of Baghdassar. Go receive him with honor, else he will strike us dead."

They went out, one by one, and David struck them with his oak cudgel as they passed, so that their heads fell off. He then cut off the ears of all 40 devs and buried them at the mouth of the cave.

When he entered the cave, he found heaps of gold and silver.

Numerous other exploits of the hero are narrated. David was killed by one of the illegitimate children of his father, Baghdassar, a girl who was not a Christian but a Muslim.

Lion-Mher: This cycle tells of the hero Lion-Mher, who fought single-handed against the Turks.

Davith-Mher: This cycle contains the tale of Davith-Mher, who married the queen of Egypt and had a son, Misra-Malik.

0927

David, St. (beloved, friend?). Sixth century C.E. In Christian legend, patron saint of Wales. Feast, 1 March.

David was the son of Xantus, prince of Cereticu (Cardiganshire), but he was brought up a priest and became an ascetic on the Isle of Wight. He established a strict rule, founded some 12 monasteries, and even visited Jerusalem. He was a defender of the Catholic faith against the monk Pelagius who denied Original Sin and said men could be good without grace from God. Various legends surround the saint. One is that when the blind priest who baptized David was touched with some of the baptismal water, which David splashed in his eyes, the priest regained his sight. Another tells how a hill on which he stood rose so that all of the crowds could hear him preach. A white dove is said to have appeared on his shoulder. He lived on leeks and water and was called "the waterman." Geoffrey of Monmouth, in his *History of the Kings of Britain* writes that David was the uncle of King Arthur. David's name is also given as Dewi Sant.

0928

Dayunsi (beaver's grandchild). In North American Indian mythology (Cherokee), the little water beetle who helped form the earth. The earth was a great island floating in a sea of water. It was suspended at each of the four cardinal points by a cord hanging down from the sky vault, which was of solid rock. When all was water, the animals were above, in Galunlati, beyond the arch. But it was very crowded, and there was no more room. They wondered what was below the water. At last Dayunsi offered to go and see what he could learn. He darted in every direction over the surface of the water but could find no firm place to rest. Then he dived to the bottom and came up with some soft mud, which began to grow and spread on every side until it became an island that is now the earth. It was afterward fastened to the sky with four cords.

0929

Dazhbog (giving god). In Slavic mythology, sun god, son of Svarog, the sky god, and brother of Svarogich, the fire god.

According to one myth, Svarog became tired of reigning over the universe and passed on his power to his sons, Dazhbog and Svarogich. Dazhbog lived in the East, the land of eternal summer, in a golden palace from which he emerged every day in a chariot drawn by white horses that breathed fire. Some accounts say the chariot was drawn by 3 horses, others say 12. The chariot is described as golden with diamonds, and the horses as white with golden manes.

Among the Serbians, Dazhbog was believed to be a handsome young king who lived with two beautiful maidens, the Zoyra. One maiden was the Aurora of the Dawn; the other, the Aurora of the Evening. In some myths the two sisters were accompanied by two stars—the morning star, Zvezda Dennitsa, and the evening star, Vechernyaya Zvezda—who help the Zorya in tending the horses of the sun god. In the Russian epic poem *The Lay of Igor's Army*, Prince Vladimir and the Russians call themselves the "grandchildren of Dazhbog." In other Slavic folklore, however, Dabog or Dajbog, variants of Dazhbog, are names applied to a devil-like creature that opposes God. Sometimes Dazhbog is identified with Chors, a Russian sun god.

Variant spellings: Dazbog, Dazdbog.

0930

Deborah (a bee). In the Bible, O.T., a Hebrew prophetess and judge of Israel (Judges 4:4), wife of Lapidoth. She called Barak to fight against King Jabin, prophesied success, and accompanied him in the battle against Sisera, captain of Jabin's army. Her triumphant song (Judges 5) is one of the oldest writings in the Bible. Handel's oratorio *Deborah* deals with the prophet.

0931

Decius Mus. Fourth century B.C.E. In Roman history and legend, general who sacrificed his life to save his army. Decius dreamed that to win a battle the general of one army had to kill himself. To save his army he went into battle alone and was killed. Livy's *History of Rome* (book 8) tells the tale. Rubens left a series of oil sketches of the legend.

0932

Deert. In Australian mythology, the moon god, who punished animals with death. Only he, Deert, would be able to die and return to life again.

0933

Deianira (stringer together of spoil). In Greek mythology, second wife of Heracles; daughter of Dionysus (or Oeneus) and Althaea; half-sister of Gorge, Meleager, and Toxeus; mother of Ctesippus, Hyllus, and Macaria. She accidentally killed Heracles when she sent him, by the centaur Nessus, a garment soaked in poisoned blood, which she believed would renew Heracles' love for her. Ovid's *Metamorphoses* (book 9) and Chaucer's *The Monk's Tale*, part of *The Canterbury Tales*, all refer to the myth.

0934

Deidamia (taker of spoil). In Greek mythology, mistress of Achilles; daughter of Lycomedes, king of Scyros; mother of Neoptolemus (Pyrrhus). She was seduced by Achilles when he hid on the island of Scyros disguised as a woman. A second Deidamia was the daughter of Bellerophon and Philonoe; sister of Hippolochus, Isander, and Laodameia; married to Evander; and mother of Dyna, Pallantia, Pallas, Roma, and Sarpedon II. A third bearing the name was a daughter of Amyntor and Cleobule; sister of Crantor and Phoenix.

0935

Deino (terrible). In Greek mythology, daughter of Phorcys and Ceto; one of the three Graeae—the others being Enyo and Pephredo—who were guardians of the Gorgons. They had one eye and one tooth among the three of them.

0936

Deirdre (fear, one who rages). In Celtic mythology, a great heroine.

Felim, a lord of Ulster, invited King Conor (Conchuber) to a feast. During the festivities a messenger brought word of the birth of a daughter to Felim. Then Cathbad, the king's Druid, said: "The infant shall be fairest among the women of Erin and shall wed a king, but because of her, death and ruin shall come on the prince of Ulster."

King Conor sought to avert the doom by sending the child, called Deirdre, with her nurse, Lavarcam, to a solitary place in the wood. Here she was visited by the king, who intended to wed her when she was of marriageable age. The girl saw no other except the Druid, Cathbad.

One winter's day, however, near the bridal day, Deirdre saw upon the white snow the blood of a newly slain calf and a raven lapping it. She told her nurse that she wished to wed a man with hair as black as the raven's wing, a cheek as red as the calf's blood, and skin as white as the snow. Her description fit Naisi (Naois), a member of the Red or Ulster branch of King Conor's household. The nurse then, upon the pleading of Deirdre, took the girl to meet Naisi. Deirdre's beauty so overwhelmed Naisi that he fled with her to Scotland. Naisi then took service with the king of the Picts. However, after seeing Deirdre, the king wanted her for himself. Therefore, Deirdre, Naisi, his two brothers, Arden and Allen, and the nurse fled to shelter in Glen Etive.

Years passed, and King Conor, promising not to avenge the wrong done to him, invited Naisi, his brothers, and Deirdre to return. With misgivings, Deirdre came. Naisi and his two brothers were killed by Owen, who cut off their heads. Deirdre was then taken by the king to live at Emain Macha. A year passed, and the king asked Deirdre what she hated most.

"Thou thyself and Owen," she replied. So King Conor sent Deirdre to Owen for a year, but on the way she threw herself from the chariot against a rock and died.

In one variant of the myth, Deirdre sees the bodies of the three dead brothers being buried. She sits on the edge of the grave, constantly asking the grave diggers to dig the pit wide and free. When the bodies are put in the grave, she says:

Come over hither, Naisi, my love,
Let Arden close to Allen lie;
If the dead had any sense to feel,
Ye would have made a place for Deirdre.

The men do as she asks them. She then jumps into the grave and dies.

Two great Irish playwrights took up the myth of Deirdre. William Butler Yeats wrote a tragedy, *Deirdre*, about the last day in the life of the lovers, and John Millington Synge wrote *Deirdre of the Sorrows*.

Variant spellings: Deidrie, Deidra, Deidre, Dierdrie.

Dekanawida (two river currents flowing together). 0937
16th century C.E. In North American Indian history and legend, hero, one of the founders of the Iroquois confederacy with Hiawatha, credited with supernatural powers. According to legend he was born of a virgin mother. Warned before his birth that he would bring ruin upon her people, the Hurons, Dekanawida's mother tried three times to drown her child. Each time she threw the child through a hole in the ice, the next morning she would find him lying next to her, safe and sound. Dekanawida grew to manhood quickly and left home. Before he left, he placed an otter skin on the wall, hanging by its tail. He told his mother that if he died a violent death the skin would vomit blood.

Hiawatha enlisted Dekanawida's help in his plan for the unity of Indian nations, and the two worked until it was achieved. In some accounts Dekanawida is credited with the idea.

Delilah (flirt). In the Bible, O.T., a Philistine woman 0938
who seduced Samson into revealing the secret of his strength, which lay in his hair. She then cut his hair so that he could be captured by the Philistines

(Judges 16). Delilah appears in Rembrandt's painting of Samson as well as in Saint-Saëns' opera *Samson et Dalila*.

Delos. In Greek legend, a small island in the Cy- 0939
clades, where Apollo and Artemis were born on Mount Cynthos. Poseidon raised it from the sea as a place of refuge for their mother, Leto, to escape the wrath of Hera, the ever-jealous wife of Zeus. Referring to their birthplace, Apollo was sometimes called Delius, and Artemis was called Delia. Delos' king was Anius.

Delphi (from Delphus, a son of Apollo). In Greek 0940
history and mythology, a town (now Kastri) of Phocis at the foot of Mount Parnassus. Delphi was famous for its oracle and temple to Apollo. Delphi was believed to be the center of the earth. The *omphalos* (navel stone) was kept there. At Apollo's temple was the inscription "know thyself," which came to mean self-understanding, though originally it meant: "Know that I, Apollo, am immortal, and you are mortal and must die." According to Greek myth, Apollo killed Python, the Chthonic deity who guarded the site, and then set up a shrine to himself. It is believed that the various buildings of Delphi were destroyed by Alaric and the Goths in 396 C.E. The Homeric *Hymn to Apollo* (a work ascribed to Homer but not by him) describes the contest between Apollo and Python. Pausanias' *Description of Greece* (book 10) describes the site. Often in English poetry Delphi is confused with Delos, the smallest island of the Cyclades, sacred to Apollo, who was born there along with his sister Artemis. Milton's *Ode on the Morning of Christ's Nativity* compounds Delphi and Delos into Delphos. This was a common mistake of writers of the Middle Ages and passed on to later writers.

Dem Chog. In Tibetan Buddhism, a tutelary deity, 0941
the chief of happiness, also known as Samvara. In general, the terms devil and demon are products of early Western misunderstanding of the wrathful aspect of Tibetan deities, an obverse of their pacific aspect.

Demeter (barley-mother). In Greek mythology, 0942
Great Mother goddess, one of the 12 Olympian deities, daughter of Cronus and Rhea; mother of Plutus by Iasim and mother of Persephone by her brother Zeus; called Ceres by the Romans. Demeter was worshiped as provider of harvest and fertility. Her daughter Persephone was raped by Hades and

came to represent the time of the year when Demeter, grief-stricken over the absence of her daughter, let plant life wither. The mysteries of Eleusis were dedicated to Demeter.

Demeter appears in Hesiod, the Homeric Hymn to Demeter, Vergil's *Aeneid* (book 1), Ovid's *Fasti* (book 4), *Metamorphoses* (book 5). Among English poets, Tennyson's *Demeter and Persephone* is best known, but Pope, Spenser, Shakespeare, Milton, Keats, Shelley, Arnold, and Swinburne all cite the goddess, often under her Latin name form, Ceres.

In Greek and Roman art, Demeter was always portrayed as a mature, clothed woman, often drawn in her chariot by serpents. The honeycomb, fruit, cow, and sow were sacred to her. Other attributes

Demeter (Ceres)

brought to the underworld as his bride. Demeter, not knowing Persephone's fate, went in search of her. She searched for nine days before she was told by Helios, the all-seeing sun god, that Hades had abducted Persephone. Furious with Zeus for allowing the rape, Demeter, disguised as an old woman, left Olympus to seek Persephone. When she arrived at Eleusis, she was welcomed by Queen Metanira and King Celeus and tended their son Demophon. One night she held the child over a fire in order to give him immortality but was surprised in the act by the king. She then revealed her identity and commanded King Celeus to build a temple in her honor. In the meantime, Zeus sent Iris to ask Demeter to return, but she refused. Finally, Zeus sent Hermes to the underworld to fetch Persephone, but already the girl had eaten four pomegranate seeds (fruit of the underworld), so she was allowed to spend only eight months of the year in the upper world. Returning to Olympus, Demeter left the gift of corn and the holy mysteries at Eleusis with King Celeus. She sent Triptolemus, Celeus' son, around the world to spread the knowledge of agriculture and cult. Fall and winter

Priestess of Demeter

were poppies, symbolizing sleep and death; ears of corn; wheat; a basket of fruit; a torch; or a serpent shedding its skin, symbol of rebirth.

0943

Demophon (voice of the people). In Greek mythology, joint king of Melos; son of Theseus and Phaedra or of Theseus's mistress, Antiope; half-brother or brother of Acamas; and in some accounts father of Munitus by Laodice, a daughter of King Priam. Demophon was one of the Greeks hidden in the wooden horse, and he helped steal the Palladium from Troy. After Troy's fall he fell in love with Laodice, but on the way home from Troy he visited Thrace and fell in love with with Phyllis, daughter of the king of Thrace. When he deserted her to live in Athens, she either hanged herself or was turned into an almond tree by Athena. Ovid's *Heroides* (book 2) and Chaucer's *Legend of Good Women* deal with her sad fate.

0944

Dendan. In Arabic legend, a monstrous fish that dies when it eats human flesh or hears a human voice. In the tale "Abdallah the Fisherman and Abdallah the Merman" in *The Thousand and One Nights* (nights 940–946), the fat from a dendan is made into an ointment to cover Abdallah the Fisherman's body so he can live under the water when he visits his friend Abdallah the Merman. While they are undersea, a black dendan, bigger than a camel, comes near Abdallah the Fisherman, whose immediate shout in his human voice causes the monstrous fish to die instantly.

0945

Deng. In African mythology (Dinka of Eastern Sudan), sky god, ancestor of the Dinka. The Dinka believe that in the beginning the sky was very low, so low that man had to be extremely careful when hoeing or pounding grain so as not to hit the sky. One day the greedy woman Abuk pounded more grain than she was allotted, using an especially long pestle. Deng was so angered by this that he cursed mankind, saying people would have to work harder for the fruits of the earth and in the end would also have to die.

Lightning is Deng's club, and rain and birth are manifestations of his presence. If one is struck by lightning, one is not to be mourned because it is believed that Deng has taken that person directly to himself.

0946

Denis of France, St. (lame god, Dionysos). First century? C.E. In Christian legend, patron saint of Paris,

along with St. Geneviève. Invoked against frenzy, headache, and strife. Feast, 9 October.

St. Denis of France is often confused with Dionysius the Areopagite, a follower of St. Paul, and Pseudo-Dionysius, a mystical writer whose dates are unknown. His legend therefore combines three personalities into one.

Dionysius was an Athenian philosopher who went to study astrology in Egypt. While he was at Heiliopolis, Christ was crucified, and he witnessed the darkness over the face of the land for three hours. He went to inquire why this had happened and eventually was converted to Christianity by St. Paul. (The time sequence in the legend makes no actual sense.) According to legend, he was present at the death of the Virgin Mary in Jerusalem as well as the martyrdom of St. Paul in Rome.

From Rome he was sent by Pope Clement to preach the gospel in France. He left with two deacons, Rusticus and Eleutherius. When he arrived in France, his name was changed to Denis. (Here again the legend tries to connect the three men.) After preaching for some time and winning many converts he was arrested along with his two deacons. At the place of execution all three were beheaded, but St. Denis took his severed head and walked all the way to *Montmartre* (Mount of Martyrs). Angels sang as the saint held his head. Later he was buried by St. Geneviève.

In Christian art he is portrayed as a bishop, holding his severed head in his hand.

0947

Deohako. In North American Indian mythology (Seneca), three sisters, spirits of corn, beans, and squash. They all lived on one hill. One day Onatah, the corn spirit, left in search of moisture but was attacked by the evil spirit Haghwehdaetgah, who took her to the underground. He then sent winds to destroy the two remaining sisters, who also fled. Finally, the sun saved Onatah, but she must now stand in the field, through rain and drought, never to leave again.

0948

Dervish and the King, The. Moral fable by the Persian mystic poet Sadi, in *The Gulistan* (chapter 1, story 28).

A solitary dervish (holy man) was sitting in a corner of the desert when a king passed by, but he took no notice of the king. The king became angry, saying to his prime minister, "This tribe of rag weavers resembles beasts." The prime minister went to the dervish. "The king has passed near you," he told the dervish. "Why haven't you shown him homage and respect?"

"Tell the king," the dervish replied, "to look for homage from a man who expects to benefit from him. Kings exist for protecting subjects. Subjects do not exist for obeying kings."

Deucalion and Pyrrha

Deucalion and Pyrrha (new-wine sailor and fiery red). In Greek mythology, hero and heroine of the Deluge, or Flood. Deucalion was the son of Prometheus and Hesione; married Pyrrha; father of Amphictyon, Hellen, Pandora, Protogeneia, and Thyia. Hellen was the ancestor of the Hellenes, or Greeks. Deucalion and his wife, Pyrrha, survived the world flood. They repeopled the earth by casting stones behind them that were transformed into people. Ovid's *Metamorphoses* (book 1) tells the myth. Reference is made to the myth in Giles Fletcher's *Christs Victorie and Triumph*, Milton's *Paradise Lost* (book 11), and Spenser's *Faerie Queene* (book 5).

0950
Deva. In Hindu and Buddhist mythology, a term for a deity or divine being, from the Sanskrit root *div*, to shine.

0951
Devadasi (female slaves of the gods). In Hinduism, dancers and courtesans who are connected with various ceremonies devoted to images of the gods, such as singing, dancing before the god when he is carried in procession, and purifying the temple floor with cow dung and water. They are considered married to the god.

0952
Devadatta. Fifth century B.C.E. In Buddhist legend, cousin of the Buddha, who at first was converted by the Buddha but later became his archrival. Devadatta attempted to kill the Buddha numerous times.

0953
Devak. In Hindu folklore, a guardian deity or spirit, such as an animal, tree, or implement of trade. Those people having the same *devak* cannot marry, possibly suggesting that once the *devak* was a totem of a clan.

0954
Devala. In Hindu mythology, the personification of music as a female. The name also is used for several sages who, legend says, composed hymns for the *Rig-Veda*, the ancient collection of hymns to the gods.

0955
Devarshis. In Hinduism, sages or holy men who have attained perfection on earth and have been exalted to demigods. They live in the region of the gods.

0956
Devils. Demons and evil spirits, which abound in medieval Jewish, Christian, and Islamic mythology.

In the Hebrew Old Testament, Satan is not the devil. He is the "adversary," part of God's heavenly host. This is shown in the Book of Job. Satan tempts Job, destroying his family and goods, but only with the permission of God. When Job cries out for justice, he does not condemn Satan, but God himself (Job 9:21–24). As Judaism developed, coming into contact with many pagan cults, Satan took on more of the attributes we know as belonging to the devil. By the time of the New Testament, Satan was generally regarded as an evil demon or ruler of demons (Matt. 12:24–28). He not only controls the body but also has power over spiritual nature, being called "prince of the world" (John 16:11) and even "god of the world" (2 Cor. 4:4). All of these New Testament quotes reflect the Jewish belief of that time.

In Christianity the belief in the corporeal existence of the devil assumed its greatest force during the Middle Ages. The great St. Thomas Aquinas believed in devils, witches, incubi, and succubi. When he wrote a commentary on the Book of Job, he identified the monster Behemoth as the devil and concluded that the devil could have intercourse with humans. When the devil assumed a female form (succubus), he seduced men. When he assumed a male form (incubus), he impregnated women. The result of this sexual union produced, according to Aquinas, a human being, though the child would be more cunning than children of an ordinary human couple.

Aquinas's many explanations of Christian doctrines find their full expression in Dante's *The Divine Comedy*. In this massive work the entire universe is ordered according to scholastic teaching. The poem, divided into three sections—Hell,

Purgatory, and Heaven—contains many descriptions of demons and, of course, Satan. Dante describes the three-faced Satan as a parody of the Christian Trinity and portrays him chewing on three sinners: Judas Iscariot, who betrayed Jesus, and Brutus and Cassius, who betrayed Julius Caesar. Dante leaves out Pontius Pilate because, to placate the Roman Empire, Christianity forgave Pilate's part in the murder of Jesus. In fact, one branch of the Eastern Orthodox church lists Pilate among its saints.

The medieval belief in demons passed on to the Protestant Reformation. Luther, like Aquinas, believed in the devil's evil power to assist wizards and witches. Following St. Augustine's authority, Luther had come to believe in incubi and succubi, since Satan in the form of a handsome man loves to decoy young girls. Luther also believed in changelings, children of the devil who replace human children.

Islam, which is in part based on Jewish and Christian beliefs, calls Satan Iblis. He is mentioned in the Koran, as are the djinn (plural of genie), his offspring.

Djinn are divided into different categories, although Islamic folklore is not always clear in its distinctions, many names being just different words for a demonic being. The orders are jann, the lowest and weakest; the djinn proper, who often appear in animal form; the shaitan or sayatin; ifrits; and the marida, djinn of the most powerful class. In all there are some 40 troops of 600,000 djinn, according to one count.

When King Solomon (who often appears in Islamic legend) first saw the djinn, he was horrified at how ugly they were. He used his magic ring to gain mastery over them, forcing them to help build his great temple. A modern Islamic tale tells of a family so tormented by djinn, which appeared in various animal shapes, that the family went into the desert, the home of the djinn, and killed all of the animals they could capture. This so reduced the population of djinn that Allah (who wanted to maintain a balance in His order of nature) had to intervene, and a truce was made to insure that the djinn would not be wiped out entirely.

The Koran (sura 6) tells that the djinn "in their ignorance" believed Allah had "sons and daughters." Some, however, were later converted by Muhammad to Islam and are diligent followers of its rites. These djinn often appear as "household serpents" who protect the family, much in the manner of the *genii* in Roman mythology.

The shaitans are a more dangerous breed of spirit than the djinn proper. Allah created al-Shaitan, perhaps another name for Iblis, who then produced eggs from which other demons were hatched. In a variant legend, Allah created not only al-Shaitan, but a wife, who produced three eggs. When hatched, the children were all ugly, having hoofs instead of feet. Shaitans are even uglier in their eating habits. They like excrement and other dirt and waste and prefer the shade to sunlight. It is believed that every man has a personal shaitan or demon, just as he has a personal guardian angel. Sometimes the shaitan is considered the muse of poetic inspiration.

Ifrits, or afrits, are an even more dangerous group than the shaitans. Originally the word may have meant one who overcomes an antagonist and rolls him in the dust. In time the term was applied to a very powerful and always malicious djinn. The Koran (sura 27) makes brief mention of the spirit as an "ifrit, one of the djinn," and Islamic legend has added to this brief Koranic mention. In Egypt, ifrit has come to mean the ghost of a murdered man or one who died a violent death. Yet the female version of the ifirt, the ifriteh mentioned in *The Thousand and One Nights*, is a benevolent djinn. In fact, in *The Second Old Man's Story* (night 2) a pious woman is turned into an ifriteh and carries the hero to an island to save his life. In the morning she returns and says: "I have paid thee my debt, for it is I who bore thee up out of the sea and saved thee from death, by permission of Allah. Know that I am of the djinn who believe in Allah and his Prophet."

Of the other demons in Arabic and Islamic folklore, perhaps the most dreaded is the Ahl-at-Tral, who live below the Sahara desert and appear as whirling sandstorms, drying up the wells before caravans arrive.

There are numerous variant spellings of the demons in Islamic mythology. Djinn sometimes appears as jinn and jinniyeh (feminine). Ifrit is also spelled efreet, alfrit, afrit; for the female, ifriteh and afriteh.

0957

Devi or Mahadeve (the goddess and the great goddess). In Hindu mythology, the great goddess, sometimes regarded as the wife of Shiva. She has both a gentle and a fierce nature.

Devi is one of the most ancient deities worshiped in present-day Hinduism. Traces of her worship date back to prehistoric times. She was taken into the Hindu pantheon and wedded to the god Shiva, being made his *shakti*, or female energy. Among the many roles she assumes in Hindu mythology are the following:

Sati (the good woman), daughter of Daksha. She married the god Shiva, even though her father opposed the match. To prove her love for Shiva she burned herself alive at Jwala-mukhi (mouth of fire), a volcano in the lower Himalayas, north of Punjab.

Kali

Today the place is a pilgrimage site. When Shiva embraced the body of his wife, it took the god Vishnu to cut her out of Shiva's hold. Fifty pieces of her bodily remains were then scattered, each becoming a place of worship for the *yoni* (womb), the female organ, along with Shiva's *linga* (phallus).

Parvati (the mountain girl). Devi is the constant companion and loving wife of Shiva, often engaging in lovemaking. On one occasion Shiva reproached Parvati for the darkness of her skin. She was so upset by the reproach that she went to live alone in the forest, where she performed austerities. The god Brahma said he would grant her any wish as reward for her austerities.. Parvati asked that her complexion be golden. She was then called Gauri (yellow, or brilliant) and became regarded as the goddess of crops (the harvest bride) or Uma (mother), the golden goddess, personification of light and beauty; as Sandhya (joint) she is viewed as twilight personified. In some texts Sandhya is believed to be the daughter of the god Brahma.

Jaganmata (the mother of the world), the goddess as the great mother. This name recalls early worship of her.

Durga (the inaccessible), one of the most popular manifestations of the goddess. The title was given her when she fought the great buffalo demon, Mahisha. The demon, having performed penance, obtained great power and took control of the three worlds, dethroning Indra as well as sending the other gods fleeing to Brahma for help.

At a meeting of the gods, their united energies produced a woman, Durga, "more dangerous than all the gods and demons." (In a variant account Durga already existed as the wife of Shiva and came to the aid of the gods.) Durga now set out to destroy the buffalo demon. At first she sent Kalaratri (dark night), a female whose beauty bewitched the three worlds. Mahisha, even though moved by her charms, came after Kalaratri, who, of course, was a form of Durga, but "she took the unassailable form of fire." When the demon in the form of a buffalo saw her standing before him, blazing with her great magic power of illusion, he made himself as large as Mount Meru. He sent an army, but it was reduced to ashes by the fire.

Mahisha then sent 30,000 giants, and they made Kalaratri rush to Durga (the goddess can be in two places at the same time as well as be two beings). The demon's troops hurled arrows as thick as raindrops in a storm at Durga as she sat on Mount Vindhya. In return Durga threw weapons that carried away the arms of many of the giants. Mahisha then hurled a flaming dart at the goddess, which she turned aside. He sent another, and she stopped it by 100 arrows. His next arrow was aimed at Durga's heart, but this was also stopped. At last the two came together, and Durga seized Mahisha, setting her foot on his chest. However, he managed to disengage himself and renew the battle.

The battle continued for some time, until Durga pierced Mahisha with her trident. He reeled to and fro and again assumed his original form, that of a giant with 1,000 arms, a weapon in each. He approached Durga, who seized him by his arms and carried him through the air. She then threw him to the ground. Seeing that the fall did not kill him, she pierced him in the chest with an arrow. Blood began to flow from his mouth, and he died.

In Indian art Durga is often portrayed as a golden-colored woman with ten arms, called Dashabhuja (ten-armed). In one hand she often holds a spear, which is piercing Mahisha. With another hand she holds the tail of a serpent, with another the hair of Mahisha, whose chest the snake is biting. Her other hands are filled with weapons, and a lion, tiger, leopard, or other large cat leans against her right leg.

Durga's battle with Mahisha is but one of many fought by the goddess against various demons. Often she gained the title or name of the demon because of her encounter with him. One epic myth describes such an incident: "From the forehead of the goddess contracted with wrathful frowns, sprang swiftly forth a goddess of black and formidable aspect, armed with a scimitar and noose, robed in the hide of an elephant, dry and withered and hideous, with yawning mouth, and lolling tongue, and bloodshot eyes, and filling the regions with shouts." When the goddess in this form killed the two demons Chandra and Munda, she returned to herself and was called by a contraction of the two demon's names, Chamunda.

Devi is also known as Kali (the black woman). Devi was sent to earth to destroy a host of demons, but in her rampage of death and destruction she also killed men and women. The gods, horrified and fearing that if she was not stopped all life would cease, pleaded with her but to no avail. Finally Shiva, her husband, threw himself down amid the bodies of the dead. When Kali realized she was trampling on her husband, she regained her senses. As a sign of shame she stuck out her tongue. Kali is often portrayed in this manner in Indian art. Another account says that she fought a demon who could restore himself from a drop of blood that hit the ground; Kali therefore stuck out her tongue from her many heads to lick up the blood.

Other attributes of Kali are fanged teeth, matted hair, red eyes, and four eyes. In two arms she holds the symbols of death: a noose to strangle her victims and a hook to drag them. In her other hands she holds the symbols of life, a prayer book and prayer beads. Kali also wears a necklace of skulls and corpse earrings and is surrounded by serpents, showing her mastery over the male, according to some interpretations.

Calcutta, India, receives its name from Kalighat (the steps of Kali), where her worshipers descend into the sacred Ganges. In earlier times human sacrifices were made to the goddess. Today black goats are sacrificed to her. Thugs (a Hindi word that has passed into English) robbed and strangled their victims before sacrificing them to the goddess.

Devs and Hambarus. In Armenian mythology and folklore, demonic spirits.

The Devs are male and female spirits, often appearing as humans, such as old women, or in animal guise. One Armenian folktale, "The Sheep Brother," tells how a girl encountered a Dev. She stepped into a cavern and saw a thousand-year-old Dev lying in a corner.

The Dev said, "Neither the feathered birds nor the crawling serpent can make their way in here; how then hast thou, maiden, dared to enter?"

The girl thought quickly and said, "For love of you I came here, dear grandmother."

The Dev then took a liking to the girl and rewarded her with golden hair and a golden dress.

The Hambarus, cousins to the Devs, are spirits who live in desert places and also reward or punish at will. For a passage in Isaiah (13:21) in which the King James Version of the Bible reads "satyrs" and "owls," the Armenian translation uses "Hambarus" and "Devs."

⁰⁹⁵⁹
Dhammacakka. In Buddhism, the Wheel of the Dharma, which was set into motion when the Buddha preached his first sermon in the Deer Park near Benares.

⁰⁹⁶⁰
Dhammapada, The (verses on Dhamma). A Buddhist sacred book in 26 divisions, consisting of 423 verses attributed to the Buddha. Each aphorism is encapsulated in a legendary incident, which is told in the *Dhammapadattha-katha* (Dhammapada commentary) collected in the fifth century C.E. Another version exists in Chinese, translated from the Sanskrit, and a partial manuscript of still another version, in Gandhari (a language related to Sanskrit), has been recovered.

⁰⁹⁶¹
Dhanvantari (moving in a curve). In Hindu mythology, physician of the gods, who was produced at the churning of the ocean when the gods and demons fought for the Amrita, the water of life.

⁰⁹⁶²
Dharma (Sanskrit) or **Dhamma** (Pali). Term in Hindu and Buddhist works variously translated as truth, law, religion, doctrine, righteousness, virtue, or force-factor. For Buddhism it often means the doctrine of the Buddha as found in the sacred writings and a momentary, irreducible component of the perceived universe. It is the Buddhist term for Buddhism.

⁰⁹⁶³
Dharmapala (Dharma protector). In Mahayana Buddhism, the Eight Terrible Ones, defenders of the Dharma, who wage war against demons and enemies of Buddhism. They are Lha-mo, a female goddess, portrayed on a mule with a sword and mace; Ts'angs-pa Dkar-po, often portrayed on a white horse, with a sword, and sometimes carrying a banner; Beg-Ts'e, god of war and protector of horses, carrying a sword with a shrimp-shaped handle and wearing Mongolian boots; Yama, the Hindu god of the dead, who is also found among the Buddhists; Kuvera, god of wealth and guardian of the North, borrowed from Hindu mythology, among whose symbols are a mongoose vomiting jewels, a trident, a banner, and an elephant or lion; Mahakala, the great black one, often portrayed with a trident, possibly derived from the Greek god Poseidon or a variant of Kuvera or Shiva; Hayagriva, the horse-necked one, also derived from Hindu mythology, portrayed with a chopper and skull cap.

Dhyani-Bodhisattvas (Bodhisattvas emenated by thought, reflection, meditation). In Mahayana Buddhism, five Bodhisattvas emanating from the five Dhyani-Buddhas. They are Samantabhadra, Vajrapani, Ratnapani, Avalokiteshvara, and Vishvapani. Also, there are eight Bodhisattvas who act as protectors. They are Samantabhadra, Vajrapani, Avalokiteshvara, Manjushri, Maitreya, Akashagarbha, Kshitigarbha, and Sarvanivaranavishkambhin.

Avalokitesvara

Dhyani-Buddhas (Buddhas emanated by thought, reflection, meditation). In Mahayana Buddhism, five Buddhas who come from Adi-Buddha, the primordial Buddha. They are Vairocana, Akshobhya, Ratnasambhava, Amitabha, and Amoghasiddhi. They have in turn five Dhyani-Bodhisattvas who are Samantabhadra, Vajrapani, Ratnapani, Avalokitesvara, and Vishvapani.

Diab. In Haitian voodoo, a male demon who controls sexual passions in men. He is symbolized by a penis.

Diablesse. In Haitian voodoo, a female demon who controls sexual passions in women. She is symbolized by a vagina.

Diamond Jim Brady. 1856–1917. In American history and legend, popular name of James Buchanan Brady, American financier and philanthropist, noted for his passion for diamonds. He wore them on his fingers, cuffs, and shirt fronts and is believed to have had some diamonds in his bridgework. He was also noted for his immense appetite for food. He is said to have habitually eaten three dozen oysters, a dozen crabs, and some lobsters before sitting down to the main course. His stomach, so legend goes, was replaced by that of an elephant by doctors at Johns Hopkins Hospital in Baltimore. He did give money to the institution in 1912 to found the James Buchanan Brady Urological Institute. A Hollywood movie, *Diamond Jim*, starring Edward Arnold and Jean Arthur, deals with his love for Lillian Russell.

Diana

Diana (belonging to the divine). In Roman mythology, an ancient Italian goddess honored in central Italy; identified with the Greek goddesses Artemis and Selene. The Italian Diana was the guardian of those treaties by which peaceful relations were begun. In her sacred grove at Aricia she presided over the league of Latin cities. Her worship moved to Rome when it became the center for treaties. Diana also was the patron goddess of women and their protector in childbirth. Diana was often associated with Apollo, and during the reign of Augustus the two deities became patron gods of the new imperial residence on the Palatine during a special festival. During the Christian Middle Ages the name Diana was often used for the leader of the witches, along with Hecate. In George Meredith's novel *Diana of the Crossways* (1875) the heroine complains of her "pagan" name, saying, "to me the name is ominous of mischance."

Diana

0970

Diancecht (swift in power). In Celtic mythology, god of medicine and healing. At the battle of Magtured he sat by a stream that possessed magic healing properties. There he bathed the mortally wounded, hence his association with healing wells. In Christian medieval legend he appears as an enchanter.

0971

Dido (the wanderer). In Roman mythology, queen of Carthage, mistress of the Trojan hero Aeneas; daughter of Mutto or Belus, a king of Tyre; or of Agenor; sister of Anna and Pygmalion. Dido's husband, Acherbas, Acerbas, or Sychaeus, was murdered by his brother Pygmalion. Dido (also called Elissa of Belus) fled to North Africa where she was allowed to buy as much land as a bull's hide could cover. The hide was cut into thin strips and used to outline a large section of land. On that site Dido founded Carthage and became its queen. When Aeneas landed in Carthage, she entertained him, and the two fell in love. When Mercury reminded Aeneas of his mission to found a new city for the Trojans, pious Aeneas deserted Dido. In complete despair she threw herself on a funeral pyre. Some variants of the myth, however, say her sister Anna killed herself for love of Aeneas. In Vergil's *Aeneid* (book 6) the hero visits the underworld, sees Dido and calls out to her, but she turns her back on him and does not answer. Aside from Vergil's *Aeneid*, Dido appears in Ovid's *Heroides* (7); Dante's *Divine Comedy* (Inferno, canto 5), in which she is one who died for love; Chaucer's *Legend of Good Women*, in which the tale is based on Vergil and Ovid; Marlowe's play *Dido, Queen of Carthage* (1689); Shakespeare's *The Merchant of Venice* (5.1.9–12), which alludes to Dido's death; Purcell's one-act opera *Dido and Aeneas* (1689), which contains the great aria, "When I Am Laid in Earth"; and Berlioz's *Les Troyens* (1858), based on Vergil. Liberale de Veroan's painting *Dido's Suicide* portrays the queen on the funeral pyre about to stab herself to death.

0972

Diego d'Alcalá, St. (James). 1400–1463. In Christian legend, patron saint of cooks. Feast, 13 November.

Diego was a cook in a monastery. One day he was caught giving away some bread to the poor and was reprimanded by his religious superior. But when he opened his tunic, the hidden bread had turned into roses. He was canonized at the request of King Philip II of Spain, who believed that his son Don Carlos had been healed of a serious wound by the prayers of the saint. About 1600 a wealthy Spaniard living in Rome dedicated a chapel to the saint in the Church of San Giacomo degli Spaguuoli. Frescoes were painted by Annibale Carraci and Albano, his pupil. Diego's name is also given as Diadacus or Didace.

0973

Dietrich of Bern (people, rule). In medieval legend, hero of numerous poems, ballads, and chronicles, identified with Theodoric the Great (c.454–526 C.E.), king of the Ostrogoths.

Dietrich's name is spelled at least 85 different ways in various medieval manuscripts. He was the son of Dietmar and Odilia, the heiress of the conquered duke of Verona. As a child he was gentle and generous when things went his way, but when he was angry, flames would shoot out of his mouth and consume any flammable object nearby.

When Dietrich was five, his training was entrusted to Hildebrand, son of Herbrand, one of the Volsung race. In a short time Dietrich was an accomplished fighter and a close friend of Hildebrand. In one of their first adventures the two went out to seek the giant Grim and the giantess Hilde. On their way they came to a forest and met a dwarf, Alberich (Alferich, Alpris, or Elbegast; the name varies). They bound the dwarf and told him they would free him only when he told them where the giants lived.

The dwarf not only told them where the giants lived but gave Dietrich the magic sword Nagelring, which alone could pierce the giants' skin. The giants' hiding place was found, and after an intense battle Grim was killed by Dietrich with the magic sword. But Hilde, though cut in half, was still not defeated because her body knit together again. To prevent this the next time, Dietrich cut her in two and placed his sword between the severed parts, knowing that the magic steel would annul any magic of the giantess.

The two men returned home, Dietrich with his magic sword, Nagelring, and with Hildegrim, a magic helmet he had taken from the giants. But though Dietrich believed he had undone all of the giants, he was mistaken. More battles ensued. One giant, Sigenot, would have defeated Dietrich had it not been for Hildebrand's coming to his rescue.

Alberich appears again later in legends of Dietrich. Dietlieb, a close companion of Dietrich, went to his master to inform him that his only sister, Kunhild (Similde or Similt), had been carried away by Alberich, who now kept her a prisoner in the Tyrolean mountains, not far from his rose garden. This garden was surrounded by a silken thread and guarded by Alberich, who exacted the left foot and the right hand of any knight venturing to enter or breaking a single flower from its stem.

As soon as Dietrich heard the tale, he set out to rescue Kunhild. He was accompanied by Dietlieb, Hildebrand, Wittich, and Wolfhart. As they came to the rose garden, all of the men except Dietrich and Hildebrand began to trample on the flowers and break the silken thread. Alberich put on his shining girdle of power, which gave him the strength of 12 men, and brandished a sword that had been tempered in dragon's blood and could cut through iron and stone. He also put on his ring of victory and

the Tarnkappe (Helkappe), which allowed its wearer to work magic.

Dietrich, following Hildebrand's instructions, struck off Alberich's cap and took his girdle and ring. The dwarf promised to return Kunhild unless she wished to stay as his wife. An agreement was made, and the knights were treated to a supper. Alberich had drugged the wine, and soon they all fell asleep and were bound and cast into a prison. When Dietrich awoke at midnight and saw his condition, he opened his mouth, and his fiery breath burned all the ropes. He then released Kunhild. Noiselessly, she brought them all back to the great hall, where they took their arms and were given magic rings made by the dwarfs. These rings enabled them to see their tiny foes, who otherwise were invisible to the naked eye.

A terrible battle ensued in which Dietrich's men were the victors. Now Kunhild pleaded for Alberich's life, asking Dietrich to set the dwarf free if he promised to be good. Of course Alberich agreed. The two were then married and went to live in the rose garden and the underground palace.

In his old age Dietrich, weary of his life and his various wives, ceased to have any pleasure except in hunting. One day while he was bathing in a stream, his servant came to tell him that there was a stag in sight. Dietrich immediately called for his horse, and as it did not arrive quickly, he jumped on a coal-black steed standing nearby and was quickly borne off, and disappeared.

Numerous other adventures are recorded of the hero in other Middle High German poems, such as *Das Heldenbuchs* (book of heroes). He also appears in *The Nibelungenlied* as a liegeman of King Etzel.

0974

Dilmun. In Near Eastern mythology (Sumerian), paradise, the place where the sun rises and the land of the living. At one time Dilmun lacked fresh water, which was supplied by Enki, the water god. Eaki ordered Utu, the sun god, to fill the land with fresh water taken from the earth. Dilmun was then turned into a divine garden. Dilmun appears in the epic poem *Gilgamesh* as the home of Utnapishtim and his wife, who were granted immortality after the great flood. Some scholars locate Dilmun in the Persian Gulf.

0975

Dilwica (Diana?). In Slavic mythology, Serbian goddess of the hunt, portrayed as a young girl mounted on a swift horse and accompanied by steeds. She galloped through the forests with her retinue. Dilwica was called Devana by the Czechs and Dziewona by the Poles, indicating that her myth may have been derived from that of the Roman goddess Diana. Areas of her worship came into contact with Teutonic races, who had absorbed some Greek and Roman mythology in their religious beliefs.

Dimbulans. [0976] In Australian mythology, large, and strong creatures who approach women in a friendly way but later rape them. They then allow their victims to return home.

Dinah (judged). [0977] In the Bible, O.T. (Gen. 34:1–31), daughter of Jacob and Leah, who married Shechem, a Hivite, the man who had raped her. Dinah's brothers were so incensed that they killed Shechem and all of his men and destroyed their city.

Diomedes (godlike cunning of Argos). [0978] In Greek mythology, hero, king of Argos, son of Tydeus and Deipyle; companion to Achilles in the siege of Troy. He was a favorite of Athena, who constantly protected him, especially since he wounded both Ares and Aphrodite (Venus) who sided with the Trojans. He entered Troy in the wooden horse. Diomedes appears in Homer's *Iliad* (books 2, 5, 6, 10, 23), Vergil's *Aeneid* (book 1), Ovid's *Metamorphoses* (book 14), and Dante's *Divine Comedy* (Inferno), in which he is placed, along with Ulysses (Odysseus), as one of the "counselors of fraud" in the Eighth Circle of Hell. Ingres' *Venus Wounded by Diomedes* deals with one episode of his life.

Dionysus (lame god). [0979] In Greek mythology, one of the 12 Olympian gods; god of fertility, ecstasy, and wine; son of Zeus and Semele; called Bacchus by the Romans. Zeus's wife, Hera, angry that her husband had another mistress, persuaded Semele to let Zeus appear to her in all his splendor. When Zeus appeared with thunder and lightning, Semele was burned to ashes by the splendor of the vision. Before she was completely consumed, Zeus seized her unborn child, Dionysus, and implanted the child in his own thigh until the child was ready to be born; thus, Dionysus is sometimes called *Dithyrambus* (twice born). The young god was taken to Mount Nysa in India where he was raised by Ino, his mother's sister, and by nymphs. The uses of wine was taught to him by Silenus, a son of Pan, and by the satyrs. He was also taught the mystery of ivy, a mild intoxicant when chewed and a symbol of everlasting life. Always angry with him, Hera drove Dionysus mad, sending him wandering around the world. The god was restored to his senses by the earth goddess Rhea. Dionysus then went on to teach humankind the cul-

Reception of Bacchus

tivation of the vine and the uses of wine. Once during his travels he was captured by sailors who wanted to sell him into slavery in Egypt. During the voyage to Egypt, Dionysus had vines grow up out of the sea, entwining the mast of the ship. Then the god appeared in all his splendor, surrounded by wild beasts and crowned with ivy. All of the sailors except Acetes, who had befriended Dionysus, were transformed into dolphins. Acetes piloted the ship to Naxos, where Dionysus found Ariadne, who had been deserted by Theseus. Dionysus fell in love with her and asked Zeus to grant her immortality. Ariadne's wedding gift, a golden crown, appears in the constellation of Taurus and is called the Corona Borealis.

Dionysus' cult was one of the most important in Greece and later in Rome, where at first it was forbidden because its ceremonies sometimes culminated in the ritual killing of animals or even human victims. One myth tells how King Pentheus opposed the worship of the god and Dionysus had him torn to pieces by his own mother when the king attempted to stop the Dionysian rites on Mount Cithaeron. In another myth, when King Lycurgus of Thrace opposed worship of the god, Dionysus drove the king mad, having him kill his own son, who the king believed was a vine in need of pruning.

Dionysus was closely associated with Demeter as a season divinity; his festivals were celebrated in winter (when the god was believed to suffer) and in spring (when the god arose from his deathlike sleep). Often the celebrations took the form of orgiastic rites, but these were somewhat tamed down when Dionysus' cult was accepted by Apollo at Delphi. Greek drama stems from the great spring festival, the *Great Dionysia*, held in honor of the god, who was a patron of the drama in association with Apollo and the Muses. Comedies and tragedies were played at the theater of Dionysus in Athens. Plato's *Ion* has Socrates say that "all good poets, epic as well as lyric, compose their poems not by art, but because they are inspired and possessed by a god, namely Dionysus. The release of powerful irrational impulses through ritual drama was seen as a necessary catharsis, according to Aristotle's analysis of the effect of tragedy in his *Poetics*.

Bacchanalian reclining on a couch

In Greek art Dionysus appears as a handsome, strong man, crowned with ivy leaves and holding a bunch of grapes in one hand and a cup in the other. Often surrounding him are tigers, panthers, and other wild animals. His staff, Thyrsus, is tipped with a pine cone.

Dionysus' female followers are called Maenads, Bacchantes, or Bassairds. The term Dionysian is now generally used to express sensual and irrational impulses in man, as opposed to Apollonian, the rational, according to Nietzsche in his discussion of the Greeks. Dionysus appears in the Homeric *Hymn to Dionysus*, which tells the myth of the sailors; in Ovid's *Metamorphoses* (book 3); and in Euripides' *Bacchae*, which tells of the killing of Pentheus. He also appears in various English and American poems, including Spenser's *Shepheardes Calendar*; Milton's *Paradise Lost* (book 7.31–33), in which the poet condemns the god; Keats's *Ode to a Nightingale*, which rejects the irrational power of the god, and also *Endymion* (book 4.193– 267), in which the poet describes a Bacchanalian procession; Matthew Arnold's *Bacchanalia: or, The New Age*; Ralph Waldo Emerson's *Bacchus*; Shelley's *Ode to the West wind* (20–23), which describes the Maenads; Swinburne's *Atalanta in Calydon*, in which the female devotees of the god are described; and Albert Noyes's *Bacchus and the Pirates*. In music Richard Strauss's opera *Ariadne auf Naxos* and Albert Roussel's ballet *Bacchus et Ariadne* deal with the god. In art Michelangelo's statue of *Bacchus*; Titian's *Bacchus and Ariadne*; Correggio's *Bacchus*; Piero di Cosimo's *Discovery of Wine*; Poussin's *Bacchanalian Revel*; the frieze in the Villa dei Misteri at Pompeii, which shows scenes from the mystery cult of the god; and the reclining Dionysus of the Elgin Marbles are some of the art works inspired by Dionysus.

0980
Dipankara Buddha (light-bringer Buddha). In Buddhism, the Buddha of Fixed Light, who is portrayed in the *mudra* of "blessing of fearlessness" and that of charity and love. Dipankara lived some 100,000 years on earth, some 3,000 years before anyone was found worthy to hear his message. When he was born there was a miracle—a large number of lamps were suddenly lit—thus his name. In Tibet he is called Mar-me-mdsad; in China, Ting-kuang-fo.

0981
Dirona. In Celtic mythology, a mother goddess whom ancient Roman writers associated with the consort of their god Mercury.
Variant spelling: Sirona.

Temptation of Sakyamuni

0982
Dismas. In medieval Christian legend, the name usually given to the Penitent Thief who, however, is not named in the Gospels (Luke 23:41). The impenitent thief is usually called Gesmas or Gestas.
Variant spellings: Dysmas, Dimas.

0983
Diti. In Hindu mythology, mother of the Dityas, a race of demon giants, and the Maruts, the wind gods.

Diti was married to the sage Kasyapa and through him was the mother of the Dityas. Indra, however, objected to the demons and cast them down into the ocean depths. Upset by the loss of her children, Diti asked her husband, Kasyapa, for a child who would destroy Indra. The wish was granted but with one condition.

"If, with thoughts wholly pious and person entirely pure," her husband said, "you carefully carry the babe in your womb for a hundred years."

Following this condition, Diti went through 99 years. In the last year, she went to bed one night without washing her feet, which was a ritual necessity. Indra then cast a thunderbolt into Diti's womb, dividing the unborn child into seven. The children then began to cry. Indra said, *"Ma rodih"* (weep not), but this was to no avail. Indra divided each of the seven into another seven, thus creating 49 Maruts.

Another explanation for the origin of the Maruts is that 49 lumps of flesh were made into boys by the god Shiva at the request of his wife, Parvati. In this telling they are called Rudras because Rudra has come to be another name for the god Shiva.

0984

Divali. A Hindu festival celebrated for five days in October and November. Originally, Divali was a fertility festival, and up to the end of the last century farmers would go to dung heaps and worship them by placing flowers, fruit, other offerings, and lights on them. Today it is a sort of All Fools' Day, when servants are allowed to play practical jokes on their masters, and people joyfully throw water, colored powder, and excrement at each other.

0985

Dives (rich). In medieval Christian legend, the name given to the unnamed rich man in Jesus' parable of the rich man and Lazarus (Luke 16:19–31). *Dives* is the Latin for "rich" and appears in the Vulgate translation of the Bible.

0986

Divji Moz (wild men). In Slovenian folklore, wild men who inhabit the forest. They have enormous strength, and the peasants are generally fearful of them, but often the Divji Moz help by offering advice on how to work in the forest. In return the peasants offer them food. Sometimes, when not in a good mood, the Divji Moz cause peasants to lose their way in the forests or, worse, tickle them to death.

0987

Djanbun. In Australian mythology, a human being who turned into a platypus. One day a man named Djanbun came out of Washington Creek and was traveling alone across great mountains. He was carrying a fire stick and trying to get it to burst into flame. As he blew and blew on the sparking end, some glowing chars fell from it and turned into gold. But still the stick would not turn to flame. As he blew harder, he felt that his mouth was growing larger. Djanbun threw the stick down to the ground and jumped into the water. As soon as he did, he turned into a platypus. To this day natives warn of blowing too hard on fire sticks for fear that, like Djanbun, one just might turn into a platypus.

0988

Djanggawul. In Australian mythology, primeval beings, two sisters and a brother and their companion Bralbral, who traveled across the earth. Always pregnant by their brother, the two sisters peopled the land, teaching various rituals and customs to the people. At first the two sisters had elongated genitals, embodying both male and female aspects. However, their brother cut off the "excess," making them proper women according to the myth. This belief is used to explain why men now control the sacred ceremonies that were once believed to have been the property of women alone.

0989

Djokhrane. In Islamic legend, Berber folk hero who fought against the Romans. Djokhrane led a rebellion against Rome, finally ending in hand-to-hand combat with one Roman soldier. He was losing the battle when a jaybird flew down and pecked out the eyes of the Roman soldier. Djokhrane told his children: "As long as you live, never eat this bird. If anyone brings you one to eat, buy it and set it free."

The Romans had a similar legend concerning a raven. Marcus Valerius, a Roman hero, was fighting a Gallic warrior when a raven swooped down and pecked out the eyes of Marcus's adversary.

0990

Dockalfar (dark elves). In Norse mythology, the dark elves or dwarfs who live underground. They tend to be evil by nature but often can be appeased.

0991

Doctors of the Church. In Christianity, title used since the Middle Ages for certain Christian writers noted for their theological works, which are considered the foundation of most Christian theology. In the Western church the Four Doctors are St. Jerome, St. Ambrose, St. Augustine, and St. Gregory the Great.

In the Eastern church the Four Doctors are: St. John Chrysostom, St. Basil the Great, St. Athanasius, and St. Gregory Nazianzen.

In medieval Western art the Four Western, or Latin, Doctors are often grouped around the Virgin and Child. The Eastern, or Greek, Doctors are rarely found in Western medieval art. However, they appear, in the central dome of the baptistery of St. Mark's in Venice, the work having been done by Greek artists of the 12th and 13th centuries.

The term Fathers of the Church is also used for Doctors of the Church. During the Middle Ages the Schoolmen, theologians who lectured in the cloisters and cathedral schools, also were called doctors. Many of them became known under special titles such as Angelic Doctor for St. Thomas Aquinas, Mellifluous Doctor for St. Bernard, and Seraphic Doctor for St. Bonaventura.

0992

Dodona. In Greek cult, the site of the oracle of Zeus, built by Deucalion after the deluge and located in northwestern Greece. At Dodona there were priestesses called Peleiades (pigeons) who made known the will of Zeus. A large oak, sacred to Zeus, was the home of the real pigeons, and the god revealed himself by the rustling or markings of the leaves, and the murmuring of a nearby brook. The priests of the shrine were called Selloi according to Homer's *Iliad* (16). In later times oracles were taken from lots and the ringing of a gong or basin. In front of the gong was an iron statue of a boy with a whip made of three chains, from which hung some buttons that touched the gong. If the whip moved in the breeze, the buttons sounded against the gong. The shrine of Zeus gave way to that of Delphi, dedicated to Apollo, though it continued until about the fourth century C.E.

Dog. A domesticated carnivorous mammal; in world mythology and folklore, symbol of both demonic and beneficent forces. In the Buddhist hell, dogs inflict punishments; and the Hindu god of death, Yama, has two dogs that are sent out to bring back wandering souls. A red dog was sacrificed by the Aztecs to help carry the soul of the dead king across a stream or to announce his arrival in the other world. The dog is referred to some 40 times in the Bible. Deuteronomy (23:18) sums up the Hebrew attitude: "Thou shalt not bring the hire of a whore, or the price of a dog, into the house of the Lord thy God for any vow: for even both are abomination unto the Lord thy God." "Dog" was a term used for a male homosexual dedicated to pagan gods who took part in sexual rites. In the book of Tobit (5:16), part of the Old Testament Apocrypha and not included in the Hebrew or Protestant Bible, there is a positive mention of Tobit's dog, reflecting a different attitude.

In many ancient and modern tales dogs help solve crimes. Plutarch, the Greek writer, reports a tale of how King Pyrrhus came upon a dog on the road, guarding the body of a dead man. The dog was taken back to the king's palace, fed, made comfortable. One day while the king was reviewing his troops, the dog began to growl and bark at some soldiers. The men were arrested, questioned, and found guilty of the murder of the dog's master.

European medieval legend tells of Aubry of Montdidier, who was murdered in 1371. His dog, Dragon, always snarled and went for the throat of a man named Richard of Macaire. Years later Richard was condemned to judicial combat with the dog. He lost, and with his dying breath Richard admitted he had killed Aubry. Based on tales of this type, medieval Christianity saw the dog as a symbol of conscience. Francis Thompson's ode *The Hound of Heaven* portrays the soul's flight from God and God's unrelenting houndlike pursuit. Walt Disney's Pluto combines the beneficent aspect of the dog with a demonic name, since Pluto is the Latin form of Hades, the god of the underworld, whose dog was Cerberus. Snoopy, of the *Peanuts* cartoon, is also beneficent. In fact, he often sounds like a Midwestern preacher.

0994
Dog and His Shadow, The. Aesopic fable found in various European and Oriental collections.

A dog stole a piece of meat from a butcher shop. On his way to a safe place where he could eat it without interruption he had to cross a footbridge over a clear stream. Looking down, he saw his own reflection in the water.

Thinking that the reflection was another dog with another piece of meat, and being a greedy dog, he made up his mind to have that also. So he snarled and made a grab for the other dog's meat.

As his greedy mouth opened, out dropped the piece of meat, which fell into the stream and was lost.

Moral: Grasp at the shadow and lose the substance.

In one Indian version of the fable, the tale is somewhat expanded. An unfaithful wife eloping with her lover arrives at the bank of a stream. There the lover persuades her to strip herself so that he may carry her clothes across the stream. He does so but never returns. The god Indra, seeing the woman's plight, changes himself into a jackal bearing a piece of flesh in his mouth and goes down to the bank of the stream. When the god, transformed into a jackal, sees the fish sporting in the water, he lays aside the meat, and plunges in after them. A vulture hovering nearby seizes the meat and bears it off. The jackal, returning unsuccessfully from his fishing, is taunted by the woman, who cries out:

"The fish swims in the waters still, the vulture is off with the meat. Deprived of both fish and meat, Mistress jackal [here the god is addressed as a woman], whither away?"

The jackal replies:

"Great as is my wisdom, thine is twice as great. No husband, no lover, no clothes, lady, whither away?"

Thus, in the Indian version the loss of the meat is a deliberate plan of the god Indra to read a lesson to the unfaithful wife.

Juan Ruiz, the archpriest of Hita, in his *El Libro de Buen Amor* (The Book of Good Love), also tells the fable, with the moral: "The same thing happens every day to the servant of cupidity. He expects to realize a profit with your help, and he loses his capital. From this evil root springs all evil; cupidity is truly a deadly sin. Man should never abandon goods of great value, already secure, and held free and clear, for an empty dream; he who abandons what he has strikes a very bad bargain" (translated by Rigo Mignani and Marie A. Di Cesare).

Dolphin. A marine mammal resembling a small whale with an elongated head; in world mythology and folklore, often appearing as a friend of man. One Greek myth tells how Arion, a poet of the sixth century B.C.E. was saved by dolphins when he was cast overboard from a ship. In a similar myth Telemachus, son of the Greek hero Odysseus, was saved from drowning by a helpful band of dolphins that carried him safely to shore. In gratitude Odysseus engraved a dolphin on his ring and emblazoned one on his shield. The Roman emperor Titus had a portrait of a dolphin twisted around an anchor to symbolize the mean between the dolphin's swiftness and the anchor's heaviness. Many early Christian paintings and carvings portray a dolphin swallowing Jonah. In later European heraldry the device of a dolphin was often used with the motto *Festina lente* (hasten slowly). In medieval Christian folklore the dolphin was believed to carry the souls of the blessed to the isle of the dead.

Domitilla, Nereus, and Achilleus, SS. First century. In Christian legend, martyrs. Feast, 12 May.

The Golden Legend, a collection of saints' lives written in the 13th century by Jacobus de Voragine, contains the lives of the Roman martyrs. The two men were chamberlains to Flavia Domitilla, a rich woman. They not only converted her to Christianity but made her take a vow of chastity. When her betrothed, Aurelian, heard of her vow, he ordered her servants to sacrifice to the Roman gods, knowing they would refuse and be executed. They refused, and their heads were "smitten off." Aurelian then decided he would marry Domitilla. He sent two men and two women to obtain her consent by magic, but she converted them also. When he realized that his scheme had failed, he came to her room, asking "the enchanters to sing, and commanded the others to dance with him as he would defoul Domitilla, but the jugglers left singing, and the others dancing, and he himself ceased not to dance two days continually, unto the time that he expired and died."

When Aurelian's brother Luxurius heard what had happened, he set fire to the palace and burned all of the Christians, Domitilla among them. Rubens painted *St. Domitilla, St. Nereus and St. Achilleus* as part of a triptych for the Oratorians of the Chiesa Nuova in Rome. The Oratorians rejected the first version of the work but accepted the second, which portrays Domitilla richly dressed, holding a palm, with the two male saints on either side.

Domnu (abyss, deep sea). In Celtic mythology, a goddess of the Fomors, the evil deities who were defeated and replaced by the Tuatha de Danann, people of the goddess Danu.

Domovoi (house spirit). In Slavic folklore, a house spirit, often called grandfather or master of the house.

According to one myth, when God created the heavens and the earth, one group of spirits revolted against him. God cast out the rebellious spirits from heaven; some fell into the water or forests, and others fell onto housetops or in backyards. Those that fell onto housetops or in backyards became good because of their contact with humans; the others remained wicked. It is believed by some Russians that when someone is about to die in a house, the Domovoi will cry. Domovoi likes living near the stove in a house, while his wife, Domovikha, likes to live in the basement. Some accounts say his wife is Kikimora.

Variant names for the house spirit in Slavic folklore are Iskrzychi (Galicia and Poland), Syenovik (Montenegro), Tsmok (White Russia), and Djadek (Czechoslovakia).

Variant spellings: Domoule, Domovik, Domovoj, Domovoy.

Donato of Arezzo, St. (given). Fourth century. In Christian legend, bishop and martyr. Feast, 7 August.

Born of a noble family, Donato studied with his companion, Emperor Julian. When Julian gave up Christianity and became known as Julian the Apostate, he put Donato's father to death for being a Christian. Donato fled from Rome to Arezzo along with his companion, the monk Hilarion. They preached and performed many miracles.

One legend tells how helped find hidden money. A tax collector went on a journey and left money with his wife, Euphrosina. She died suddenly, having told no one where she had hidden the money. When the tax collector returned, he was afraid he would be thought a thief. He called Donato to help him. They went to Euphrosina's tomb and called to her, and her voice told them where the money was hidden. Since many others were present at the miracle, a vast number of people were converted. Donato was made bishop of Arezzo. Once when he was saying Mass, the chalice of wine (which was made of glass) was broken by some idolaters. Donato prayed over it, and it was restored, with not one drop spilled. Again, because it was witnessed by so many people, many pagans were converted. This caused the authorities to arrest Donato and Hilarion. Donato was beheaded, and Hilarion was scourged to death.

Their bodies lie under the high altar of the cathedral of Arezzo, where their shrine has sculptures by Giovanni di Francesco of Arezzo and Betto di Francesco of Florence, completed in the 14th century.

1000

Don Juan Tenorio. 14th century. In late medieval legend, libertine Spanish nobleman who is taken off to hell for his sins. Don Juan, the son of a leading family in Seville, killed the commandant of Ulloa after seducing his daughter. To put an end to his debaucheries the Franciscans enticed him to their monastery and killed him, telling the people that he had been carried off to hell by the statue of the commandant, who was buried on their monastery grounds. The legend of Don Juan is believed to have originated in various Spanish ballads in which insult to the dead and invitation to join the living at a banquet frequently appear. Don Juan first appears on the stage in Tirso de Molina's play *El burlador de Sevilla y convidado de piedra* (The Playboy of Seville and the Stone Guest). The French took up the subject with plays by Dorimon, De Villiers, and Molière. The most important opera on the theme is Mozart's *Don Giovanni*, with a libretto by Da Ponte. Other musical works are Dargomijsky's *Kamjennyi Gost* (The Stone Guest) with a Pushkin text, Gluck's ballet *Don Juan*, and Richard Strauss's tone poem *Don Juan*. Later plays on the subject are Zorrilla's *Don Juan Tenorio*, in which the don is saved, and Shaw's *Man and Superman*. Byron's long narrative poem *Don Juan* recasts the Don into an agreeable young man, passively amoral rather than actively evil.

1001

Doodang. In American folklore, a mythical creature who wished to swim and then fly and was never satisfied. Finally, given wings, he flew, failed, and died.

1002

Doris (bountiful). In Greek mythology, a sea goddess, daughter of Oceanus and Tethys; sister of Eidyia, Electra, Clymene, Meliboea, Metis, Perseis, Pleione, Proteus, Styk, Europa, Clytia, and Callirrhoë, the rivers and fountains; wife of the sea-god Nereus; mother of 50 daughters, called Nereids, and in some myths mother of Amphitrite, Galatea, and Thetis.

1003

Dorothy, St. (gift of God). Third century? C.E. In Christian legend, patron saint of brewers, brides, flo-

St. Dorothy

rists, gardeners, midwives, and newly married couples. Feast, 6 February.

Her life is contained in *The Golden Legend*, a collection of saints' lives written in the 13th century by Jacobus de Voragine. Dorothy was tortured by Fabricius, governor of Caesarea, Cappadocia, for refusing to marry and to worship idols. As she was on her way to execution a young lawyer, Theophilus, mocked her, "Send me some of the fruit and flowers from that garden you speak of," he said, "where you are going to your bridegroom!" "Thy request is granted," the young saint replied.

When she was about to die, an angel or the Christ Child appeared to her with a basket of three apples and three roses. She then asked that they be carried to Theophilus as she had promised. The angel or the Christ Child appeared to Theophilus and gave him the basket. Theophilus then became a Christian and later met his death for being one.

In Christian art St. Dorothy is portrayed with the Christ Child and the basket of fruit and flowers as in Francesco di Giorgio's charming painting of the subject.

1004

Dosojin (earth ancestor god, road ancestor god). In Japanese Shinto mythology, phallic god, protector of roads and travelers, invoked to ensure abundance in agriculture and human reproduction. One of his most popular forms is as Saruta-hiko (monkey rice field prince).

1005

Douban. Physician who killed King Younan in the "Story of the Physician Douban," a tale in *The Thou-*

sand and One Nights (nights 4, 5, and 6, with interruptions from other tales in the collection).

A physician named Douban cured a Persian king, Younan, of leprosy. But because of the whispers of a vizier, the king suspected that the physician wished to kill him. When he ordered the death of the physician, the man pleaded for some time to straighten out his home and books, many of which were valuable. The king agreed. The next day, after the amirs and viziers and chamberlains had gathered at the court, the physician entered, "bearing an old book, and a small pot full of powder." He told the king that when his head was cut off it would speak to the king if the king placed the head on the powder to stop the bleeding. the king should then open the book and read from where the head directed him. The king took the book and gave the signal to the executioner, "who rose and struck off the physician's head and set it on the dish, pressing it down on the powder." The blood immediately ceased to flow. The head opened its eyes and said: "Open the book, O King!"

Younan opened the book and found the leaves stuck together, so he put his finger to his mouth, taking his "spittle and loosened them therewith and turned over the pages in this manner, one after another." Eventually, he cried out that there was nothing there to see. The head said: "Open more leaves." The king wet his finger and continued. The leaves of the book were poisoned and before long the poison began to work upon the king. He fell back in convulsions crying out: "I am poisoned!"

1006

Dove. A small bird resembling a pigeon, often used as a symbol of peace (secular) or the Holy Spirit (religious). The Near Eastern goddess Astarte and the Greek goddess Aphrodite had doves sacrificed to them in their temples. One Greek myth tells of the origin of the doves that drew Aphrodite's chariot. Eros and Aphrodite were picking flowers in a contest to see who could pick the most. Eros was winning when two nymphs began to aid the goddess. Indignant, Eros changed the nymphs into doves. Aphrodite then had them draw her chariot as a reward.

In early Christian legend a dove descended on the staff of St. Joseph to indicate that he was to be the husband of Mary. In another early Christian legend Joachim and Anna, parents of the Virgin, dreamed of a dove before her birth. In the Gospel According to Mark (1:9–11) a dove descends to Jesus when he is baptized, and the dove is the Holy Spirit. As symbol of the Holy Spirit the dove is often seen in art portraying saints noted for their spiritual writings. It also appears in paintings of the Annunciation to the Blessed Virgin. In Moslem folklore the dove is also a symbol of the Holy Spirit. According to one legend, a dove used to feed out of the ear of Muhammed. His followers said it was the Holy Spirit giving the prophet advice. Shakespeare's *Henry VI, Part I* (1.2.40) refers to this belief in a mocking tone: "Was Mahomet inspired with a dove?"

1007

Drac. In French folklore, a spirit in human form who lives in the caverns of rivers. Sometimes *dracs* will float like golden cups along a stream to entice bathers, but when the bather attempts to catch one, the *drac* draws him under water.

1008

Dracula. c. 1431–1476. In Eastern European history and legend, popular name of Vlad the Impaler, a Rumanian tyrant who is known in folklore and literature as a vampire.

Various theories have been advanced about the truth of Vlad the Impaler, or Vlad Tepes. According to an official Rumanian Communist government tourist agency: "The real Dracula fought for the cause of the Rumanian people." Older legend has credited this "hero" of the people with the most horrendous deeds. In German, Russian, Hungarian, and Italian folklore, the deeds of Dracula are copiously recorded, though no mention is made of his vampirism.

A few of the legends surrounding the sadistic tyrant tell how he punished those who in any way offended him. For example, when a group of Turkish envoys did not remove their turbans in his presence, he had their turbans nailed to their heads. Dracula often dined outdoors amid the screams of his impaled victims, hung on stakes around the dinner table. Once a guest complained of the stench of the decaying bodies. Dracula had the guest impaled on a stake much higher than the other victims, so that he might die out of the range of their stench. Another tale tells how Dracula invited some beggars into his castle, fed them, and told them he could end all of their troubles if they wished. They agreed, and he had them shut indoors and burned alive.

However, in modern folklore Dracula is noted for his vampirism, tales of which stem from Bram Stoker's novel *Dracula*.

Stoker's novel was used as the basis of numerous films, beginning with a silent film, *Nosferatu*, and continuing through many versions, including the classic *Dracula*, starring Bela Lugosi, who became identified with the role in movies. *The Fearless Vampire Killers* by the Polish director Roman Polanski gives Dracula the name Count Von Krolock, but he still retains all of the characteristics of the old vampire count.

Dragon

Dragon. A fantastic beast that appears in world mythology and folklore as either demonic or beneficent.

In most European mythologies the dragon is viewed as a demonic beast. In Christian symbolism the dragon is the devil, as in the Book of Revelation (20:2). The Christian devil is derived from the dragon in the Old Testament, who in turn is derived from Tiamet, the Babylonian female dragon monster. The most famous encounter between a Christian and dragon is that of St. George and the dragon. He slays the dragon or tames the animal and frees the maiden. In Norse mythology the dragon appears as Fafnir, a giant who changed himself into a dragon to guard the gold that he had stolen.

In Oriental mythologies the dragon is seen as a beneficent animal. In China the emperor's throne was referred to as the Dragon's Throne and his face as the Dragon's Face. At the emperor's death it was said he ascended to heaven like a dragon. As a dragon ascends to heaven, the pressure of its feet on the clouds causes rain. Lung Wang is the Chinese dragon-king and supernatural rainmaker. One of the most common motifs in Chinese art is the dragon with its claws outstretched, reaching for a disk. Some explain the disk as the sun, which the dragon tries to swallow; being a watery creature, it wishes to drown the heat of the day. Others see the disk as a pearl or the moon. The dragon is one of the four constellations in Chinese astronomy.

Draupadi. In the Hindu epic poem *The Mahabharata*, the common wife of the five Pandu princes.

Draupadi, daughter of King Draupada of Panchala, was of dark complexion and great beauty, "as radiant and graceful as if she had descended from the city of the gods." (In a former existence she had been the daughter of a sage.) She performed a most severe penance in order that she might have a husband. The god Shiva, pleased with her devotion, said: "You shall have five husbands; for five times you said, 'Give me a husband.' " Her father, King Draupada, held a *svayamvara*, a tournament in which the princess would choose for herself a husband from among the contestants. Arjuna was selected from among the many suitors on account of his skill in archery.

When he and his four brothers returned home, they told their mother, Kunti, that they had made a great acquisition. Kunti replied that they should share it among themselves. The command of a mother could not be opposed, so the sage Vyasa settled the matter by having Draupadi "become the wife of all of the brethren." It was arranged that she should stay two days in the house of each brother, and no other brother should enter that house while she was there. Although she was shared by all the brothers, Draupadi loved Arjuna and displayed jealousy when he married Su- bhadra.

Dreamtime. In Australian mythology, the primeval past when spirits, gods, and ancestors walked on earth.

Drithelm, St. Died c. 700. In Christian legend, monk. Feast, 1 September. Drithelm was seized with a fatal illness and died in 693, but before he was buried he arose from the dead and told his wife and children he had visited hell, purgatory, and heaven. He then left his family and went to live as a monk. St. Bede tells his tale in his *History of the English People*.

Drona (a bucket). In the Hindu epic poem *The Mahabharata*, a priest who was generated in a bucket by his father, Bharadwaja. Drona taught archery to both the Pandavas and the Kauravas. When the great war broke out, however, Drona sided with the Kauravas, eventually becoming commander-in-chief. When he received news that his son had been killed, he was so upset that an enemy cut off his head while he was distracted with grief.

Drugaskan. In Persian mythology, section of hell filled with darkness and evil. Located "at the bottom of the gloomy existence," it is the lowest section of hell. Drugaskan is also the name of the son of the evil spirit, Ahriman, in Persian mythology.

Druids (tree). Priests of Druidism, the name given to the religion of the ancient Celts as practiced in Gaul and Britain. [1015]

The function of a Druid was described by Julius Caesar in *The Gallic Wars* (book 6). He wrote that Gallic society had two main classes: the warriors, or knights, and the Druids. The Druids "officiate at divine worship, regulate sacrifices public and private, and expound questions of ritual. Numbers of young men resort to them for study and hold them in high respect. They are judges in nearly all disputes, whether public or private, and in cases of crimes or murders or disputes about inheritances or boundaries, they settle the matter and fix awards and penalties. And who do not abide by their decision, whether an individual or a tribe, they excommunicate, and this is their severest penalty.... As a rule Druids keep aloof from war, and do not pay taxes with the rest. They are exempt from military service and all obligation." As to the worship of the Druids, Caesar writes of their human sacrifices: "They have images of immense size, the limbs of which are framed with twisted twigs and filled with living persons. These being set on fire, those within are encompassed by the flames."

They had many gods, but Dis Pater was the father god from whom the Gauls claimed descent. The Druids observed two festivals each year. One, Beltaine (fire of god), was in honor of the sun and was held at the beginning of May; at the other, Samh'in (fire of peace), at the beginning of November, judicial functions were dealt with.

The concept of the Druids in literature and music has very little to do with any of the known facts culled from ancient sources. During the 18th century Druidism was greatly romanticized, with some English writers claiming that the Druids were descendants of Ashkenaz, eldest son of Gomer and great grandson of the biblical Noah. Others believed that the Druids were one of the ten lost tribes of Israel. William Blake, the English poet and painter, found many of these ideas congenial to his own mythmaking. He wrote in *Jerusalem* that Adam, Noah, and other patriarchs were actually Druids, with Britain being "the Primitive Seat of the Patriarchal Religion," to which the Druid temples and oak groves in Britain were a "witness to this day." In the same poem Blake credits the Druids with inventing "female chastity." This concept of Druid vestal virgins is best known through the Italian opera *Norma* by Vincenzo Bellini with a libretto by Felice Romani. The work tells how Norma, the high priestess of the Druid temple of Esus, breaks her vow of virginity by bearing the Roman soldier, Pollione, two sons. At the end Norma confesses her sin to her people, saying she must be sacrificed. Both Norma and Pollione then enter the funeral pyre. In modern literature James Joyce mentions the Druids several times in his novel *Ulysses.*

Dryads (oak nymphs). In Greek mythology, wood nymphs, who lived in trees; also called hamadryads. They died when the tree died. Pope's *Moral Essays* (book 4.94) and Keats's *Ode to a Nightingale* cite the dryads. [1016]

Dryope (oak tree). In Greek mythology, a name for various women. According to the *Homeric Hymn to Pan* (attributed to Homer but not by him), one, a nymph of Arcadia, was the mother of Pan by Hermes. In Ovid's *Metamorphoses* (book 9) Dryope was a woman married to Andraemon, and she was raped by Apollo. The god first appeared as a turtle that Dryope picked up, but suddenly it was transformed into a serpent, which frightened the hamadryads who were companions of Dryope. Apollo then appeared in his human form and seduced Dryope. Their child was Amphisusus. When a year old the child was transformed, along with Dryope, into a lotus as a punishment for picking flowers from a tree that was the home of the nymph Lotis. Another Dryope was a nymph, mother of Tarquitus by Faunus in Vergil's *Aeneid* (book 10). Dryope was also the name of a woman of Lemnos whose shape the goddess Aphrodite assumed to persuade the women on the island to murder all of the men. [1017]

Dsajaga. In Siberian mythology, spirit who rules over the fate of the individual. It is closely connected with the sky god Tengri, who also watches over the fate of man. In *The Chronicle of Ssangang Ssetsen* Ghengis Khan is said to have been born through "the Dsajaga of the blue, eternal sky." Not only rulers were born under Dsajaga, however, but peasants as well. In laws written by Mongolian rulers, the phrase "by the Dsajaga of the eternal sky" is used, instead of the formula "by the Grace of God," so often found in Western documents. Each person is believed to have a special ruler over his life, called Dzajagatsi. Often the term Dzajagatsi Tengri is used. [1018]

Duat. In Egyptian mythology, the underworld or other world. [1019]

Originally, Duat signified the place through which the sun god Ra passed each evening after his setting, or death, on his journey to that portion of the sky where he would appear the next morning. Although generally called the underworld, Duat was not believed to be situated under the earth but rather away from the earth, in a part of the sky where the gods resided. It was the realm of the great god Osiris, who reigned over all other gods of the dead as well as the dead themselves. Duat was separated from the world by a range of mountains that surrounded it, forming a great valley. On one side the mountains separated the valley from the earth and on the other side, the valley from the heavens. Through Duat ran a river that was the counterpart of the Nile in Egypt and of the celestial Nile in heaven, and on each bank of this river lived a vast number of beasts and devils who were hostile to any being that invaded the valley. Duat was further divided into 12 sections, or *nomes*, each of which corresponded to one of the hours of the night.

According to one Egyptian text, *The Book of Pylons*, Duat is a long, narrow valley with sandy slopes, divided into two equal parts by a river on which the boat of the sun sails. Each of the 12 sections, or *nomes*, of the valley has its own demons, or ordeals, that the deceased has to pass in order to be worthy of life with Osiris. The same concept is used in Mozart's opera *The Magic Flute*, in which the hero, Tamino, undergoes a series of ordeals instituted by the high priest Sarastro in order to be worthy to praise Isis and Osiris.

Duat is sometimes called Ta-dchesert (the holy land), Neter- khertet, or Khert Neter (divine subterranean place).

Variant spelling: Tuat.

Dudugera. In Melanesian mythology, the sun, according to a myth from New Guinea. Once a woman played with a fish that rubbed itself against her leg. In time her leg swelled, and when it was cut open, a baby, Dudugera, appeared. The young Dudugera did not get along with his playmates, so one day his great fish father came and took him away. Before he left, he told his mother and relatives to hide under a big rock because he was going to climb up to the sky on a plant and become the sun. They did as he asked. When Dudugera became the sun, his heat rays were destroying all plant and animal life until his mother threw some lime juice in his face. From that day clouds appear, relieving the earth from the sun's heat.

Dugong. In Islamic mythology, herbivorous aquatic man of the Red Sea, the Indian Ocean, and the waters around Australia. In Malay mythology it is be-

Mermaid and merman

lieved to have sprung from the remains of a pig on which Muhammad himself had dined before he pronounced pork to be cursed. It was cast into the sea by the prophet but revived and took the shape of the dugong. The tears of the dugong are believed to be a strong love charm. The dugong is also called a sea cow and may be an origin of mermaids in mythology.

Dumah (silence?). In Jewish folklore, an angel of death, to whom one has to give account. Isaac Bashevis Singer, in his short story "Short Friday," tells of a husband and a wife who discover they have died and are thinking about what is going to happen to the Sabbath meal they have just prepared. They realize, however, that they have to wait for the angel Dumah "with his fiery staff" and "give an account" of themselves to him. In their stillness they hear "the flapping of wings" and a "quiet singing" as they are taken to paradise. In Genesis (25:14) Dumah is a son of Ishmael and the presumed ancestor of an Arabian tribe.

Dumah is also the name given to the guardian of the 14th gate, through which the goddess Ishtar passed on her journey to the underworld in Babylonian mythology.

Variant spelling: Douma.

1023

Dun Cow. In British legend, a fantastic cow, slain by Sir Guy of Warwick on Dunsmore Heath. The Dun Cow was kept by a giant in Mitchel Fold (middle fold), Shropshire. Its milk was inexhaustible. One day an old woman who had filled her pail with its milk wanted to fill her sieve also, but this so enraged the cow that it broke away and wandered to Duns-more, where it was killed.

1024

Duns Scotus, Joannes. 1265–1308? C.E. In Christian legend, Franciscan theologian who supported the doctrine of the Immaculate Conception (that the Virgin Mary was born without Original Sin) against St. Thomas Aquinas, who opposed the doctrine. The term Dunsmen or Dunses, a name for his followers, passed into the language as *dunce* because so much time was spent in his scholastic philosophy on "nonsense." Duns Scotus is also known as Doctor Subtilis.

1025

Dunstan, St. (hill stone) 909–988 C.E. In Christian legend, archbishop of Canterbury, patron saint of blacksmiths, armorers, goldsmiths, locksmiths, musicians, and the blind. Feast, 19 May.

A monk of Glastonbury, Dunstan was a noted scholar, musician, painter (his self-portrait at the foot of Christ is still preserved at the Bodleian Library, Oxford), and metalworker. As a young man he was a great favorite of King Edmund, who admired his musical talents. He had such a strong influence over the king that he was accused of sorcery and driven from the court. One day, as the king was stag hunting, his dogs leaped over a precipice. The king thought he would be unable to rein his horse and would also fall. He prayed and thought of his ill treatment of Dunstan, and the horse stopped on the brink. The king then begged Dunstan to return to his court.

One legend tells how Dunstan outwitted the devil. He was making a chalice to use at Mass when the devil suddenly appeared before him. The saint, however, was not afraid. He took the pincers out of the fire and seized the nose of the devil, who ran off howling and never again bothered the saint. An old poem commemorates the event:

St. Dunstan, as the story goes,
Once pulled the devil by the nose
With red-hot tongs, which made him roar
That he was heard three miles or more.

In Christian art St. Dunstan is portrayed as a bishop holding a pair of tongs.

1026

Duppies. In Haitian voodoo, evil spirits of the dead.

1027

Durán, Fray Diego. c. 1537–1588 C.E. Spanish historian who did missionary work in Latin America. Author of three works dealing with Aztec history and mythology: *Book of the Gods and Rites*, giving a detailed description of Aztec gods; *The Ancient Calendar*, a guide to the Mesoamerican system of counting time; and *Historia de las Indias de Nueva España y islas de tierra firme*, which tells the history of the Aztecs from their beginnings to their fall in 1521 at the hands of the Spanish. The *Historia* also contains numerous references to the religious and mythological beliefs of the Aztecs.

1028

Duranki (the bond that unites heaven and earth). Ancient name for Nippur, a Sumerian city sacred to the god Enlil. According to myth, Enlil split the earth's crust with his pickax at Nippur so that the first man could break through to the upper earth.

1029

Dur-yodhana (hard to conquer). In the Hindu epic poem *The Mahabharata*, a leader of the Kauravas against their enemies, the Pandavas. Dur-yodhana battled Bhima, one of the five Pandu princes. Bhima kicked Dur-yodhana in the head and left him mortally wounded. Dur-yodhana then asked his men to slay all of the Pandavas and bring Bhima's head to him before he died. Some Kauravas entered the Pandava camp and killed five young sons of the Pandavas. Their heads were brought to Dur-yodhana, who was told they were the five Pandu princes. In the twilight Dur-yodhana was unable to tell the difference. When he asked for Bhima's head, one of the children's heads was given to him, and he crushed it. Because it was so easily crushed, he knew it could not be the head of Bhima. He cried out: "My enmity was against the Pandavas, not against these innocents." Dur-yodhana died shortly afterward of the wound inflicted by Bhima. Dur-yodhana was also called Su-yodhana (good fighter).

1030

Dushan the Mighty. c. 1308–1355. In Serbian legend, greatest czar. Stephen Dushan, who conquered Bulgaria, Macedonia, and Albania, became an important folk hero in Serbian ballads.

1031

Dustin, Hannah. 1657–after 1729. In American history and folklore, New England pioneer woman captured, along with her young son, by Indians in 1697. Eventually she and her son escaped after having killed and scalped ten of their captors. In Robert P. Tristram Coffin's ballad "The Lady of the Tomahawk" she scalps 20 braves.

1032

Dvalin. In Norse mythology, a dwarf who gave to the dwarfs magic runes that made them skillful in crafts. Dvalin, along with Alfrigga, Berling, and Grerr, possessed the magic necklace of the Brislings, which the goddess Freyja wanted. She agreed to sleep one night with each dwarf to gain the necklace. In some accounts Dvalin is said to be the father of the Norns, who dispense fate. Dvalin is also the name of one of the harts at the foot of the world or cosmic tree, Yggdrasill.

1033

Dwyvan and Dwyvach. In Celtic mythology, the man and woman who built the ark *Nefyed Nevion* in the Welsh account of the flood. The flood was caused by the monster Addanc.

1034

Dyaus and Prithivi (shine and broad). In early Hindu mythology, the sky god and the earth goddess; Dyaus is often called the "vigorous god" and Prithivi, "the heroic female." In many texts they are represented as the universal parents, not only of men but of the gods. Among their offspring were the storm god, Indra; Ushas, the dawn; and Agni, the fire god.

1035

Dybbuk (attachment). In Jewish folklore, the disembodied spirit of a dead person who cannot find rest, often owing to his sin. The most famous dramatic work on the subject is *The Dybbuk* by S. Ansky. In it a rabbinical student, Khonnon, turns into a dybbuk when he dies because he invoked Satan in order to win his love, Leye. He had been forbidden by her father, Sender, to marry her because he did not possess wealth. At the end of the play Leye, who has been possessed by Khonnon's spirit, is freed; she dies, and her spirit joins Khonnon's. A ballet by Leonard Bernstein, titled *The Dybbuk*, also deals with the folkloric spirit.

1036

Dylan (son of the wave). In Celtic mythology, a sea god, son of Gwydion and Arianrhod, twin brother of Llewllaw. Dylan was slain by his uncle, Govannon, and a loud lament was made for him by the waves, his burial place being where their murmur sounds sullenly along the seacoast.

1037

Dzelarhons. In North American Indian mythology (North Pacific Coast Indians), heroine who, accompanied by six canoes filled with people, came to marry and settle with Kaiti, the bear god, chief of the Grizzlies. However, her husband did not have sexual intercourse with her for the first four nights of their marriage. When her uncle Githawn (salmon eater) was told of this, he made war on Kaiti and his tribe. When Githawn searched for Dzelarhons, all he found was a stone statue of her. Dzelarhons is called the Copper Woman, Volcano Woman, Frog Woman, or Copper Frog, depending on which tribe tells the story.

1038

Dziady (ancestors). In Slavic folklore, ancestor spirits. The White Russians honor the Dziady four times a year, at home or at churchyard ceremonies. The autumn celebration is connected with the harvest and the spring celebration with Easter, when eggs (symbols of resurrection) are rolled and Christian priests bless the graves. In Bulgaria the ancestor spirits are called Zadusnica.

1039

Dziwozony (wild women). In Polish folklore, wild women who have cold hearts but are extremely passionate. They are tall with thin faces and long disheveled hair. They fling their breasts over their shoulders in order to run. If they come upon an adult in the forest, the Dziwozony usually tickle the person to death. Younger people are often made their lovers. The Diva-ta-Zena in Bulgarian folklore is similar to the Polish version. She, however, throws her breasts over her shoulders to nurse her children. Sometimes the Dziwozony will substitute a *premien*, or changeling, for a human child.

1040

Dzoavits. In North American Indian mythology (Shoshonean), an evil monster. Dzoavits stole two of Dove's children. With the aid of Eagle, Dove saved the two, but Dzoavits would not give up and continued to pursue the group. Dzoavits was close upon them when Badger intervened. He dug two holes and had Dove and his children hide in one. When Dzoavits asked Badger where Dove and his children were, Badger pointed to the other hole. The monster quickly went into the hole, and just as quickly, Badger threw in some hot rocks and then sealed the hole with a stone.

E

1041

Ea. In Near Eastern mythology (Sumero-Akkadian), god of sweet waters, earth, and wisdom; patron of the arts; and one of the creators of mankind; also called Enki.

In the Babylonian epic poem *Enuma Elish*, Ea is given credit for creation:

> Who but Ea created things?
> And Ea knoweth everything.

In a much later text the myth of Ea's appearance to help mankind is told. The god appeared as "an animal endowed with reason," having a body "like that of a fish; and had under a fish's head another head, and also feet below, similar to those men, subjoined to the fish's tail." This mysterious animal was "articulate" and spoke like a human, teaching men "every kind of art. He taught them to construct houses, to found temples, to compile laws, and explained to them principles of geometrical knowledge." Ea also taught mankind how to till the earth and "how to collect fruits . . . he instructed them in everything which could tend to soften manners and humanize mankind."

Ea's chief seat of worship was at Eridu, an old Sumerian city at the top of the Persian Gulf. His wife was the goddess Damkina, and his son was Marduk. In art his symbol was either a ram's or a goat's head, with the body of a fish. Copper was his metal. Ea was also known an Enki, "lord of the world," and Oannes.

Variant spellings: Hea, Hoa.

1042

Eagle. A large bird of prey noted for its strength and vision, often associated with sky gods. In Greek mythology the eagle was sacred to the sky god Zeus, who often took eagle form in his sexual adventures. When Zeus fell in love with the Trojan boy Ganymede he took the form of an eagle, swooped down, and abducted the boy. The eagle was also adopted as a symbol of the Roman sky god Jupiter or Jove. The eagle as an imperial symbol appeared on Austrian and Russian heraldic devices. When the United States chose the bald eagle for the new nation's symbol, Benjamin Franklin disagreed with the choice. He wrote to his daughter that the bird was a "rank coward" and had a "bad moral character; he does not get his living honestly." Franklin wanted the turkey to be chosen instead. The eagle is also a symbol of the Aztec god Tonatiuh and the Norse god Odin. In Christian symbolism the eagle is often a symbol of Christ. Dante's *The Divine Comedy* calls the eagle the bird of God. St. John the Evangelist is often portrayed as an eagle or with an eagle companion because his Gospel account was considered by the Church Fathers the most elevated and spiritual of all four accounts. Nietzsche, the 19th-century German philosopher and despiser of Christianity, chose the eagle as one of the animal companions of the Solitary Sage in *Thus Spake Zarathustra*. The other animal companion is the snake. Nietzsche calls the eagle and the snake the "proudest and the shrewdest among animals." Both animals appear on the Mexican flag.

1043

Eagle and the Arrow, The. Aesopic fable found in various collections throughout the world, possibly of Eastern origin.

One day a bowman saw an eagle soaring lazily in the sky. Quickly, he notched an arrow and sent it whizzing after the bird. It found its mark, and the eagle felt itself wounded to death. As it slowly fluttered down to earth, it saw that the haft of the arrow that had pierced its breast was fitted with one of its own feathers.

Moral: How often do we supply our enemies with the means of our own destruction!

Byron, in his *English Bards and Scotch Reviewers*, a satirical poem in heroic couplets that lambastes such poets as Southey, Scott, Wordsworth, and Coleridge and praises Pope and Dryden, has an allusion to the fable of *The Eagle and Arrow*:

> So the struck eagle, stretch'd upon the plain,
> No more through rolling clouds to soar again,
> View'd his own feather on the fatal dart,
> And wing'd the shaft that quiver'd in his heart.

Byron got the idea from Edmund Waller's poem *To a Lady Singing a Song of His Composing*. The fable is also told in La Fontaine's collection.

1044

Earthly Paradise, The. In medieval European mythology, a land or island where everything was beautiful and restful, where death and decay were unknown. The Earthly Paradise was usually located far away to the east. William Morris's long poem *The*

Earthly Paradise tells how a party of adventurers leave a Scandinavian port during a pestilence to search for the Earthly Paradise. After many adventures the remnant of the band discovers the land.

1045

Easter. In Christianity, feast celebrating the Resurrection of Christ from the dead.

The English name Easter was explained by St. Bede the Venerable as coming from the Anglo-Saxon goddess *Eostre*, who was associated with the season of new birth. Some modern scholars, however, contend that St. Bede misread the Anglo-Saxon word for spring, thinking it was an ancient pagan goddess.

Easter falls on the first Sunday after the full moon that occurs on the day of the vernal equinox (21 March) or on any of the next 28 days. Easter Day cannot be earlier than 22 March or later than 25 April. The date for Easter was fixed by the Council of Nicaea in 325 C.E., though various Christian groups still celebrate it at different times. Until the Roman church made headway in Britain during the Middle Ages, the Celtic church celebrated Easter at a time different from that of the Roman observance. Numerous battles were fought over the proper date, but eventually the stronger Roman position (it was backed by the pope and the rest of Western Christendom) won out.

Medieval documents often mention Easter as the beginning of the new year, especially in France, where it was so until 1563. At Easter time the Roman emperors, starting with Valentinian in 367, released nondangerous criminals from prison. This custom was followed by medieval popes, emperors, and kings for centuries.

The preparation for Easter season, beginning on Ash Wednesday and continuing for a week after Easter Day, was filled with pagan customs that had been revised in the light of Christianity. Germanic nations, for example, set bonfires in spring. This custom was frowned on by the Church, which tried to suppress it. But when Irish monks in the sixth and seventh centuries came to Germany, they brought their earlier pagan rites and would bless bonfires outside the church building on Holy Saturday. The custom spread to France, and eventually it was incorporated into the Easter liturgy of Rome in the ninth century. Even today the blessing of the new fire is part of the Vigil of Easter.

It was a custom during Easter celebration in the Middle Ages to raise the Host, or the cross, from the shrine of the sepulcher during the night of Holy Saturday. A figure of the dead Christ was also kept in the Church from Holy Thursday until Holy Saturday, and the faithful would sit with it as at a wake.

Medieval celebrations of Easter began at dawn. According to one old legend, the sun dances on Easter morning or makes three jumps at the moment of its rising, in honor of Christ's Resurrection. The rays of light penetrating the clouds were believed to be angels dancing for joy.

Part of the medieval Easter rites consisted of the Sequence *Victimae Paschali Laudes*, (Praise to the Paschal Victim), written by Wipo, a priest who about 1030 was court chaplain of the Emperor Conrad. The poem, which was placed in the Latin Mass for Easter, is believed to have been the inspiration for miracle plays that developed from the tenth century on. (However, scholars still debate the origin of medieval drama.)

In time plays dealing with Christmas, Epiphany, and other Christian feasts were written.

Some Easter folk traditions that have survived today are the Easter egg, rabbit and lamb. During medieval times it was a tradition to give eggs at Easter to servants. King Edward I of England had 450 eggs boiled before Easter and dyed or covered with gold leaf. He then gave them to members of the royal household on Easter day. The egg was an earlier pagan symbol of rebirth and was presented at the spring equinox, the beginning of the pagan new year.

The Easter rabbit is first mentioned in a German book of 1572 and also was a pagan fertility symbol. The Easter lamb goes back to the Middle Ages; the lamb, holding a flag with a red cross on a white field, represented the resurrected Christ. A prayer for blessing lambs can be traced to the seventh century in Italy. In the ninth century Rome adopted the prayer and a roasted lamb was part of the pope's dinner for Easter. It was believed lucky to meet a lamb during Easter time because the devil could assume any animal shape but one, the lamb, for the lamb was a symbol of Christ. Medieval Easter week was one long celebration. One Spanish missal of the ninth century has mass texts for three masses each day of the Easter Octave. Gradually, however, the church reduced the celebration to three days. Since many people were baptized on Holy Saturday, they wore new white garments, from which we still have the custom of new clothes for Easter.

Monday and Tuesday of Easter week in Northern countries were the traditional days of "drenching" and "switching," customs based on pagan fertility rites. The drenching custom consisted of the boys dousing the girls with buckets or bottles of water. In the switching ceremony the boys switched the women with pussy willow or leaved branches.

1046

Ebba of Codingham, St. (boar protection). Ninth century. In Christian legend, martyr, abbess. Feast, 2 April. When the Danes invaded her land, Ebba, fearful that all of her nuns would be raped, cut off her nose and upper lip to make herself unattractive. Her nuns followed her example and also cut off their noses and disfigured themselves. When the Danes arrived and saw the noseless nuns, their anger flared, and they set the convent on fire, burning the nuns inside.

1047

Ebisu. In Japanese Shinto-Buddhist mythology, god of daily food, who was born deformed, having no legs and also being deaf. He is the god of honest dealing and is portrayed with a beard, wearing a two-pointed hat, laughing, and holding a fishing pole. Sometimes he is called Hiruko. He is one of the Shichi Fukujin, the seven gods of good luck or fortune.

1048

Echidna (she-viper). In Greek mythology, half-woman, half-serpent monster, child of Chrysaor and Callirrhoë, the daughter of Oceanus (or Phorcys and Ceto). Echidna was the mother, by the monster Typhon, of Orthus, Geryon's hound, Cerberus, the Hydra, and the Chimaera. By Orthus she was the mother of the Sphinx and the Nemean Lion. According to Herodotus *Histories* (book 3) the hero Heracles had three children by her, Agathyrsus, Gelonus, and Scytha. Echidna appears in Hesiod's *Theogony* (295 ff.) and Ovid's *Metamorphoses* (book 9).

1049

Echo (echo). In Greek mythology, a nymph of Mount Helicon; daughter of Gaea. Echo was deprived of speech by the ever-jealous Hera because she was a confidant of Zeus' many love affairs. She wasted away when Narcissus, whom she loved, did not return her love. Ovid's *Metamorphoses* (book 3) tells the tale. Juliet in Shakespeare's *Romeo and Juliet* (2.2.162–4) says:

> Else would I tear the cave where Echo lies,
> And make her airy tongue more hoarse than mine,
> With repetition of "My Romeo!"

English poets who have used or referred to the tale of Echo are Chaucer, Spenser, Marlowe, Milton, Shelley, and Keats.

1050

Edith of Wilton, St. (prosperous war). In Christian legend, daughter of King Edgar of England. Feast, 16 September.

Edith's mother was a beautiful nun, Wilfrida, who was taken by the king to be his mistress. As soon as she could, Wilfrida escaped and returned to her nunnery, but she bore a child, Edith. The girl stayed with her mother in the convent but spent most of her time dressing up in costly array. St. Ethelwold, who often visited the convent, rebuked the girl for her dress. She replied, "Pride may exist under the garb of wretchedness and a mind may be pure under these rich garments as under tattered ones."

1051

Edmund, St. (prosperity, guardian). 841–870. King and martyr, invoked against plague. Feast, 20 November.

When the Danes invaded East Anglia in 870, they slew King Edward, who had been crowned king of the East Angles in 855. The king was shot with arrows and then beheaded. According to legend, when his followers sought his body, they found a huge gray wolf reverently watching over it. They bore it away, the wolf quietly following, and interred the saint in a town now known as Bury St. Edmund's.

In Christian art St. Edmund is portrayed with an arrow in his hand. Sometimes a gray wolf crouches at his feet.

1052

Edyrn. In Arthurian legend, son of Nudd, who ousted Yniol from his earldom and tried to win Enid, the earl's daughter. He was overthrown by Geraint and sent to the court of King Arthur, where he became a gentle person. He appears in Tennyson's narrative *Marriage of Geraint*, one of the *Idylls of the King*, and in *Geraint* in Lady Charlotte Guest's translation of the Welsh collection of tales, *The Mabinogion*.

1053

Efé. In African mythology (Pygmy), the first man whom God created. After God created Efé, he wanted him to return to heaven so that he could hunt for Him. Efé served God well in heaven, but in time he wanted to return to earth. All of the Pygmies came out to greet him on his return, but because he had been away so long, no one was able to recognize him, not even his brother. When asked if God was still alive in the sky, Efé said that he was, and as presents he gave the people three spears he had used for hunting in heaven.

1054

Egeria (of the black poplar). In Roman mythology, protector of unborn babies; wife of Numa Pompilius, second king of Rome. She melted into tears when Numa died and was transformed into a fountain by the goddess Diana. Ovid's *Metamorphoses* (book 15) tells her tale.

Egil. In Germanic mythology, peasant whom the god Thor visited several times. Thor would often leave his goats and chariot for the night. Once he saw that Egil's family had no food and told them to kill the goats but to make sure they put the bones back into the skin when they had finished. The evil god Loki, however, convinced Egil's son Thialfi to break one of the bones and eat its marrow. When Thor returned, he brought the goats back to life, but one of them was missing a leg. To appease the god, Egil gave Thialfi and his sister Roskova as gifts to the god. Egil is also the name of a hero who along with his two brothers Slagfin and Volund, married three Valkyries by stealing their swans after bathing. After nine years of marriage, however, the women returned to their swan shapes. The myth is told in the *Poetic Edda* in the *Song of Volund*.

Ehecatl. In Aztec mythology, wind god, a manifestation of the god Quetzalcoatl. One day Ehecatl realized that besides the fruits of the earth man also needed sexual love. He therefore went in search of a maiden, Mayahuel, who was in the underworld under the guardianship of Tzitzimitl. The maiden agreed to go with Ehecatl to the upper world, the earth, and there they had sexual intercourse. As the two touched the ground, a beautiful tree with two great branches shot up. The sound of the wind in the trees was feared by the ancient Mexicans, who offered sacrifices to Ehecatl, going so far in some cases as to "bleed" the genital organ "by passing cords as long as fifteen to twenty yards through it," according to Fray Diego Durán in his *Book of the Gods and Rites*.

Eikthyrnir (oak-thorned). In Norse mythology, the hart or stag that eats from the branches of the cosmic or world tree, Yggdrasill. The *Prose Edda* states that "whilst he is feeding so many drops fall from his antlers down into Hvergelmir that they furnish sufficient water for the rivers that issuing thence flow through the celestial bodies."

Eirene. In Greek mythology, goddess of peace and wealth, daughter of Zeus and Themis; called Pax by the Romans. In Greek art she was portrayed as a young woman with the infant Plutus, god of wealth, in her arms. Other attributes are the cornucopia, the olive branch, Hermes' staff, and ears of corn on her head.

Eka Abassi. In African mythology (Ibibios of southern Nigeria), wife of Obumo, the thunder god; in some accounts she is said also to be the mother of Obumo. She is believed to be the mother of God and is regarded as the divine creatress. She is also believed to have conceived Obumo, her first-born, without the aid of a husband.

Ek Balam (black jaguar?). In the mythology of the ancient Indians of Yucatán, a god who may have been worshiped as a jaguar.
Variant spelling: Equebalam.

Ek Chauah. In Mayan mythology, a god of war, of cacao, and of traveling merchants; he is portrayed with a lance in one hand or in combat with another war god. In his role as god of traveling merchants, Ek Chauah is portrayed with a bundle of merchandise on his back. Paul Schellhas, when classifying the gods in some Mayan codices, gave Ek Chauah the letter *M*, and Ek Chauah is sometimes referred to as God M.

Ekkekko. In the mythology of the Peruvian highland Indians, domestic god of good luck. Ekkekko is portrayed as a small figure with a pot belly; he is covered with toy household utensils. To this day *alacitas* (fairs) in Bolivia sell objects in miniature in his honor. Thus, a woman will buy a miniature house in the hope that she will obtain a husband and a house of her own.
Variant spellings: Ekeko, Ekako, Eq'eq'o.

El. In Near Eastern mythology, basic Semitic word for a god, often used to designate a supernatural power. Among the Canaanites and Phoenicians, El was the king of the gods, "creator of creation," the all-wise judge of humankind. In the Old Testament El and Elohim are often used to designate a god or the Hebrew god. Among the most frequent titles found in the Old Testament are the following: El Shadday (God, the one of mountains), translated as God Almighty in the King James Version; El'Elyon (Exalted One, Most High); Melchizedek (Gen. 14:18), is a priest of the "most high God"; El Olam (God of Eternity), originally a title of a Canaanite god worshiped at Beer-sheba and later applied to the Hebrew god, Yahweh, translated as "the Lord, the everlasting God" in the King James Version; El-Bethel (God of Bethel), the god who revealed himself to Jacob (Gen. 35:7); El Berith (God of the Covenant), appearing in Judges (9:46); El elohe-Yisrael

Elaine (A. Beardsley)

(El, God of Israel), the god to whom Jacob (Gen. 33:19–20) built an altar in Shechem; and Elchim (god or gods), often appearing in the Old Testament.

In Genesis, the King James translators substitute God for *Elohim*.

1064

Elaine (the bright one, the shining one). In Arthurian legend, the name of two women, both of whom were in love with Lancelot.

The first Elaine was the daughter of King Pelles and the mother of Galahad by Lancelot. When Lancelot refused to marry her, Elaine used magic and assumed the form of Queen Guinever, who was loved by Lancelot. Through this deception, the first Elaine became the mother of Galahad.

The second Elaine was known as the Lily of Astolat. Lancelot did not return her love, and she died. By her request her body was placed on a barge. In her right hand was a lily and a letter avowing her love for Lancelot. An old servant rowed the barge until it reached the palace of King Arthur, where the king asked that the letter be read and then commanded the woman be buried as a queen. She is the subject of Tennyson's poem *The Lady of Shalott*.

1065

El Dorado (the gilded man). In Central and South American legends, a fantastic city and its king. The earliest form of the legend tells of a priest-king who once a year covered his body with oil and gold dust and bathed in a river, offering the gold to the river spirits. When the Spaniards came to the New World, the Indians told them of the city where the king lived (it was called Omagua, Manoa, Paytiti, or Enim). They usually located it far from their own cities, in the hope that the Spanish greed for gold would encourage the conquistadores to move on.

In 1530 a German knight, Ambros von Alfinger, went in search of El Dorado, chaining his native carriers to one another and cutting of the heads of any who died, to avoid having to break the chains. This sadist was eventually killed by an arrow shot into his neck. Others who sought the city were Diego de Ordaz (1531), Philip von Hutten (1540–1541), and Sir Walter Raleigh (1595). One of the most interesting was a group under the leadership of Don Pedro de Ursúa that set out from Peru in 1559. Though Don Pedro was a gentleman, his men were a band of cutthroats. By the end of the journey most of them had been killed by the others. Another seeker, Lope de Aguirre, proclaimed himself prince and king of Tierre Firme; he was murdered by one of his men. His name continues in Venezuelan folklore, in which the phosphorescence of a swamp is called *fuego de Aguirre* (Aguirre's fire).

Electra mourning for Orestes

The term El Dorado has come to be a metaphor for any place that offers unrealistic hope of quick riches. Voltaire, in his satirical book *Candide*, had the hero discover the country of El Dorado. Candide is told by a 172-year-old man that El Dorado was the ancient country of the Incas, "who left it very indiscreetly, in order to conquer one part of the world; instead of doing which, they themselves were all destroyed by the Spaniards." He tells Candide that "the Spaniards have some confused idea of this country and have called it El Dorado." Candide and his associate Cacambo are entertained in the kingdom, given gold (which is of no value to the inhabitants), and then placed on a specially constructed machine that carries them out of the country. Edgar Allan Poe's poem *Eldorado* also invokes the legend.

1066

Electra (amber). In Greek mythology, daughter of Agamemnon and Clytemnestra; sister of Orestes, Iphigenia, and Chrysothemis. Electra convinced her brother Orestes to murder their mother, Clytemnestra, and Aegisthus, their mother's lover, in retaliation for the murder of their father, Agamemnon. In later life she married Pylades and was mother of Medon and Strophius. Electra is also known as Laodice. Electra appears in Sophocles' *Electra*, Euripides' play *Electra*, Richard Strauss's one-act opera *Electra* (1909), Giraudoux's *Electre* (1939), Eugene O'Neill's *Mourning Becomes Electra* (1931), which later was filmed, and Cacoyannis' film *Electra*. The term Electra complex is sometimes used to describe the pathological relationship of a woman with men, based on her unresolved conflicts with her father.

1067

El El. In the mythology of the Puelcho Indians of the Patagonian pampas in South America, El El is the leader of a host of demons, called Quezubu, who are bent on destroying mankind.

1068

Elephant. A large mammal with large floppy ears, ivory tusks, and flexible trunk, found in India and Africa. In Hindu mythology the elephant is a manifestation of Ganesha, the friendly god who brings good luck to his worshipers. No venture or undertaking is begun without prayers being offered to the elephant deity. In Hindu folklore it is also believed that white elephants attract white clouds and thus cause rain. If a ruler did away with a white elephant, his people would feel betrayed. In Buddhist folklore one tale in the *Jataka*, a collection of tales on the previous births or lives of the Buddha, tells how the future Buddha gave away his father's white elephant to bring rainfall to a nearby country suffering from drought and famine. The king's subjects felt betrayed and forced the future Buddha into exile. Buddha's birth is connected with a white elephant. Buddha's mother, Queen Maya, had a dream of a white elephant who entered her body. When she told her dream to the soothsayers, they said she would bear a son who would either rule the world or save it. She bore the latter, the Buddha.

In Chinese folklore the elephant is a symbol of sagacity and prudence, as well as strength. In Roman belief the elephant was said to be a religious animal, one who worshiped the sun and stars. In medieval Christian folklore it was believed the elephant could not bend its knees and had to lean against a tree to sleep. If the tree broke, the elephant would fall and could never get up. In modern folklore Dumbo and Babar, both children's book characters, portray the elephant as a sweet, lovable animal.

1069

Eleusinian Mysteries. In ancient Greece, sacred rites initiated by Eumolpus and Celeus in honor of the goddess Demeter and her daughter Persephone; held at Eleusis, a city 14 miles west of Athens, near the Isthmus of Corinth. Celebrated in February and September, the rites consisted of purifications, fasts, and dramas, but the exact particulars of each are not known. Their purpose was to ensure rebirth and immortality. Because such rites conflicted with Christianity, they were abolished by Emperor Theodosius at the end of the fourth century C.E. Swinburne's *At Eleusis*, Shelley's *Song of Proserpine, While Gathering Flowers on the Plain of Enna*, Tennyson's *Demeter and Persephone*, and George Meredith's *The Appeasement of Demeter* all deal with Demeter and Persephone.

1070

Elfthryth. In medieval British legend, a queen noted for her beauty.

King Edgar sent Aethelwald, his friend, to ascertain if Elfthryth was really as beautiful as she was reported to be. When Aethelwald saw Elfthryth, he fell in love with her. Reporting to the king, he said she was not beautiful enough for the king but was rich enough to make an eligible wife for himself. The king agreed to the match and became godfather to the first child, Edgar. One day the king told his friend he intended to pay him a visit to see his wife for the first time. Aethelwald then told his wife the truth and begged her to make herself as ugly as possible. Indignant, she appeared in all her beauty. When the king saw her, he fell in love with her, slew his friend Aethelwald, and married Elfthryth.

A similar tale is told in the *Histories* of the Greek writer Herodotus, with Prexaspes as the name of the woman and Kambyses that of the king.

1071

Elgin Marbles. Popular name given to Greek sculptures from the Parthenon at Athens, portraying Theseus, Lapiths, Centaurs, Three Fates, Iris, and others. They were removed from the ruins by the seventh earl of Elgin in 1801–1803. The sculptures, displayed in the British Museum, are the work of Phidias (c. 490–415 B.C.E.) or his studio and pupils.

1072

Elidure. In British mythology, a king who was placed on the throne three times. He first came to the throne when he believed his brother Artegal was dead. At the return of Artegal he stepped down. Ten years later Artegal died, and Elidure again was made king. Shortly afterward he was deposed by two younger brothers. Finally, they both died, and he was made king for the third time. He appears in Geoffrey of Monmouth's *History of the Kings of Britain*, in the poet Milton's *History of Britain*, and in William Wordsworth's poem *Artegal and Elidure*, which was inspired by Milton's and Monmouth's accounts of the king.

Elijah

Elijah (my god is Yahweh) Ninth century B.C.E. In the Bible, O.T., prophet taken up to heaven in a chariot of fire. Elijah prophesied during the reigns of Ahab and Jezebel. One of his major battles was against the worship of Baal as instituted by Jezebel. In a competition on Mount Carmel, Elijah called on Yahweh, the Hebrew god, to set fire to the altar sacrifice, winning the contest when Baal's priests could not muster their god to do the same. Though he won, Elijah had to flee from Jezebel. He went to Mount Horab (Mount Carmel), where he was fed by an angel, as earlier at Cherith he had been fed by ravens. While on the mountain he heard or felt the presence of Yahweh in "a still small voice"(1 Kings 2:11). As he was being taken to heaven, his mantle fell on his successor Elisha (2 Kings 2:13). In the New Testament, Elijah appears at the Transfiguration of Jesus, along with Moses. A place for the prophet is set aside at every Passover meal. The Carmelite religious order claims Elijah as its founder because he lived a solitary life in a cave on Mount Carmel. Dieric Bouts (c. 1415–1475) painted an *Elijah Comforted by an Angel*, and Giovanni Battista Piazzetta (1682–1754) painted *Elijah Taken Up to Heaven in a Chariot of Fire*. Mendels-

sohn's oratorio *Elijah* also deals with the prophet. Elias is the Greek form of his name.

Elisha

Elisha (God is salvation) Ninth century B.C.E. In the Bible, O.T., attendant and disciple of the prophet Elijah. Among his miracles, the influence of which can be seen in New Testament writings, are the purification of Jericho springs (2 Kings 2:19–22), the multiplication of the widow's oil (2 Kings 4:1–7), returning a woman's son to life (2 Kings 4:8–37), increasing loaves (2 Kings 4:42–44), and the cleansing of Naaman, army chief of the king of Syria (2 Kings 5:1–14).

Elivagar (rivers whipped by passing showers). In Norse mythology, a river filled with venom which froze over the icy banks of Ginnungagap, the abyss from which the primeval giant Ymir was born. Elivagar is mentioned in the *Prose Edda*.

Elizabeth of Portugal, St. (God is an oath?). 1271–1336. In Christian legend, patron saint of peacemakers. Feast, 8 July.

Unhappily married to King Denis of Portugal, Elizabeth devoted her time to negotiating peace between rival elements in her society, such as Ferdinand IV of Castile and his cousin and Ferdinand and James II of Aragon. After the death of her husband she retired to a convent and became a Poor Clare. Schiller's poem *Fridolin* recounts a legend in which St. Elizabeth saved her servant from being murdered by her husband. In the poem, however, the setting is Germany, and the saint is called *Die Gräfin von Savern* (The Countess of Savern). In Spanish her name is Sant' Isabel de Paz.

Elizabeth, St. (God is an oath?). In the Bible, N.T., mother of John the Baptist, wife of Zacharias, and cousin of the Virgin Mary (Luke 1:11–13). Feast, 5 November. Although an old woman, she bore John the Baptist. When Mary knew she was pregnant by the Holy Spirit, she went to visit Elizabeth, who greeted her with "Whence is this to me, that the mother of my Lord should come to me?" (Luke 1:43). This scene, called the Visitation, is frequently painted in Christian art.

El-lal. In the mythology of the Tehuelche Indians of the Patagonian pampas in South America, a creator-hero god.

El-lal's father, Nosjthe, wanted to eat his son and snatched him from his mother's womb. A rodent saved the child and carried him to a cave that Nosjthe was unable to enter. The rodent taught El-lal the secrets of plants and the different paths in the mountains. El-lal then invented the bow and arrow, and with these he learned how to hunt wild animals. El-lal did not hold a grudge against his father but taught him all he knew, and Nosjthe acted "as master of it" even while still plotting to kill his son. He followed El-lal across the Andes, but when he was about to kill him a dense forest arose between the two, saving El-lal. The hero descended to the plain, which in the meantime had become populated with men and women. Among the group was also a giant, Goshy-e, who liked to eat children. El-lal fought against the giant, but his arrows were useless. He then transformed himself into a gadfly and, entering the stomach of the giant, wounded Goshy-e fatally with his sting. After numerous other heroic feats El-lal wanted to marry the daughter of the sun, but she refused. El-lal left the earth, borne on the wings of a swan, and found eternal rest "in the verdant island that rose among the waves at the place where arrows shot by him had fallen on the surface of the water," according to Ramón Lista in *Los Indios Tehuelches*.

Ellora. Site in Maharashtra, India, associated with the deeds of many gods and heroes, as well as with ancient blood sacrifices. There are numerous Hindu, Jain, and Buddhist cave temples in the area.

Eloy of Noyon, St. 588–659 C.E. In Christian legend, patron saint of metal workers goldsmiths, farriers and horses. Feast, 1 December.

Eloy was a goldsmith of Limoges who went into the service of King Clotaire II in Paris. The king asked him to make a throne for him, and Eloy was supplied with gold and jewels for the work. After making the throne, there was so much precious metal and so many stones left over that Eloy made a second throne for the king rather than pocket the leftover materials. The king was so pleased with the work and with Eloy's honesty that he took him into his confidence. Clotaire's successor, King Dagobert, made Eloy the Master of the Mint. He cast the dies for the coinage of the realm (13 are known to bear his name). When King Dagobert died, Eloy was made bishop of Noyon.

He was sent to preach in Belgium and, legend says, he went as far as Sweden and Denmark. Before his consecration as bishop, he was tempted by the devil. One day a horse was brought to him to be shod. The animal was possessed by a devil. Eloy cut off the leg of the horse and quietly put on the shoe. When he was done he made the sign of the cross over the leg, and it attached itself to the horse. The greatest oath of Chaucer's Prioress in *The Canterbury Tales* is "By Seint Eloy."

In Christian art St. Eloy of Noyon is portrayed either as a bishop or a smith. In either case he holds his smith's tools, tongs, hammer or bellows. The miracle of the horse is portrayed on the exterior of Or-San-Michele at Florence by Nanni di Banco.

Elves

Elves. In Norse mythology, the English translation of *Alfar*, which also can be translated "dwarfs."

Elysium. In Greek and Roman mythology, the home of blessed dead. In early Greek mythology it was said to be situated in the Islands of the Blessed in some remote part of the earth. In later Greek and Roman mythology the location of the Elysian Fields (another name) was in the underworld. Vergil's *Aeneid* (book 6) tells how the hero Aeneas meets his dead father Anchises in the Elysian fields. Elysium is used in Shakespeare's *Two Gentlemen of Verona* (2.7.37), *Henry VI, Part III* (1.2.30), and *Twelfth Night* (1.2.3); Milton's *Comus* (257), Cowper's *Progress of Error*; Andrew Lang's *The Fortunate Islands*; Schiller's *Elysium*; Shelley's *Ode to Naples* (30); and Swinburne's *Garden of*

Proserpine. The Champs Elysées in Paris is named after the Greek belief.

1083

Emma Ten. In Japanese Buddhist mythology, a god based on the Hindu god of death, Yama, portrayed sometimes as a youth with three eyes, carrying in his right hand a scepter terminating in a small Bodhisattva head. He is one of the Jiu No O, 12 Japanese Buddhist gods and goddesses adopted from Hindu mythology.

1084

Enceladus (hissing). In Greek and Roman mythology, a giant, son of Titan and Gaea. Enceladus fled from Phlegra to Sicily, pursued by Zeus, who hurled a thunderbolt to destroy him. Mount Aetna was then placed above his body. When Enceladus turns over, an earthquake results. When the giant hisses and thrusts out his fiery tongue, Mount Aetna erupts. Vergil's *Aeneid* (book 3) cites the myth. In variant myths he was killed by Heracles or by Athena, who placed Mount Aetna over his body.

1085

Enchanted Horse, The. Tale in *The Thousand and One Nights* (nights 357–371). A Persian inventor constructed a mechanical horse for Sabour, king of the Persians, and as a reward the king offered the old man his daughter. However, the girl did not want to marry the old man and asked her brother to help her. The young prince went to the old man and asked him about the mechanical horse, which could soar into the sky. The inventor, aware of the prince's hatred for him, taught the prince how to mount the horse, and how to let it fly—but he didn't tell him how to get the horse down again.

The young man ascended to the heavens and then realized that he did not know how to get down. After thinking about it for some time and calling upon Allah, he discovered the peg to let the horse down. The prince came to a city where he found a beautiful princess. After many adventures he finally married her and returned home. His father the king then destroyed the magic horse.

1086

Endicott, John. 1589?–1665. In American history and legend, colonial administrator, acting governor of Massachusetts Bay Colony until 1630. An intolerant Puritan, Endicott persecuted the Quakers and high-church Anglicans who did not follow his narrow views of Christianity. Hawthorne's short story "Endicott and the Red Cross," included in *Twice Told Tales*, tells the legend of Endicott's cutting the red cross, symbol of St. George, patron saint of England, from the English flag. Hawthorne has Endicott say:

"Before God and man, I will avouch the deed. . . . Beat the flourish, drummers!—shout, soldiers and people!—in honor of the ensign of New England. Neither Pope nor Tyrant hath part in it now." Longfellow's play *John Endicott*, part of his *New England Tragedies* deals with Endicott's persecution of Quakers in Boston.

1087

Endo Morito. 12th century C.E. In Japanese legend, a hero, a warrior who killed the woman he loved, and later became a monk.

Endo Morito was a captain living in Kyoto who fell in love with Kesa, the wife of a samurai, Watanabe Wataru. When Kesa resisted his advances, Endo Morito vowed to kill her family unless she allowed him to murder her husband and agreed to become his wife. She made an appointment to receive him in her house at night, when he would find her husband asleep alone in a room and could kill him. Endo came and cut off the head of the person he found sleeping in the appointed room, only to discover that it was Kesa herself. Her husband being on a journey, she had dressed herself in some of his clothes and sacrificed herself to save her honor. Endo, was overcome with grief, shaved his head and became a monk, calling himself Mongaku. He retired to the district of Oki and for 21 days remained naked, holding in his teeth the *vajra*-shaped handle of his bell, counting his beads, and praying under a waterfall.

In Japanese art Endo Morito is often portrayed doing his penance.

Variant spellings: Mongaku Shonin, Endo Musha Morito.

1088

Endymion (seduced moon man). In Greek mythology, handsome youth, son of Acthlius or of Zeus and Calyce. Endymion was the king of Elis. In some accounts Zeus gave him the choice of death or immortal sleep. The king chose sleep. Endymion was loved by the moon goddess Selene (or Artemis), who saw him naked. Artemis (or Selene) made love to Endymion while he was asleep and bore him 50 daughters. To preserve his beauty Artemis made him sleep everlastingly. Shakespeare's *The Merchant of Venice* (5.1.109–110) has Portia explain a moonless night by saying, 'the moon sleeps with Endymion,/And would not be awak'd." Endymion appears in Spenser's *Epithalamium* (372 ff.); John Lyly's play *Endymion, the Man in the Moon* (1606), Michael Drayton's *Endymion and Phoebe* (1595), and Keats' narrative poem *Endymion*. Endymion was painted by Tintoretto, Van Dyke and Rubens.

1089

Enkidu. In the Near Eastern epic poem *Gilgamesh*, rival and companion to Gilgamesh. He was molded of clay by Aruru, goddess of creation, in the image of "the essence of Anu," the sky god, and of Ninurta, the war god. Enkidu is a wild or "natural" man in contrast to the sophisticated Gilgamesh. In Babylonian religion he became the patron god of animals because in the poem he is credited with many animal-like qualities.

Variant spellings: Eabani, Endimdu, Engidu, Enkita.

1090

Enlil (storm god). In Near Eastern mythology (Sumero-Akkadian), creator god, storm god, god of earth and air; he was also called father of the gods and king of heaven and earth, as well as the king of all lands, patron god of the city of Nippur, and lord of the underworld. Often Enlil was called Bel (lord) in other Near Eastern mythologies.

In one myth, titled *Enlil and the Creation of the Pickax*, Enlil separates Ansar (the upper heavens) and Kisar (the earth), taking earth as his portion. He then brings up "the seed of the land" from the earth and discovers the pickax, which he teaches man to use. In a variant myth Enlil is responsible for the creation of trees and grains, as well as for appointing the seasons.

Another myth tells how Enlil was banished to the underworld for rape. Before man was created, Enlil lived in the city of Nippur with the goddess Ninlil and her mother Nunbarshegunu. One day the mother told her daughter to bathe in the river so "the bright-eyed Enlil" would see her and then marry her. Enlil saw Ninlil and wanted to have sexual intercourse with her, but the girl said:

"My vagina is too small, it does not know
how to copulate.
My lips are too small, they do not know
how to kiss. . . ."

Enlil paid no attention and raped Ninlil. The gods in anger banished him to the underworld. Ninlil became pregnant and followed Enlil to the underworld, giving birth to the moon god Sin.

Variant spellings: Bel Enlil, Eilil, Illillos.

1091

Ennead (nine). In Egyptian mythology, nine deities whose characteristics symbolize the elemental-primal forces in the universe. The Great Ennead revolved around the mythology of Heliopolis, a suburb of modern Cairo, and consisted of Atum the sole creator, his offspring Shu (air) and Tefnut (water), and their children Geb (earth), Nut (sky), Isis, Osiris, Seth, and Nephthys. As time passed, other cult centers developed their own enneads, and therefore the numbers varied. The ennead at Thebes consisted of 15 deities, and that of Hermopolis consisted of 8. The latter became so famous that it is called the Ogdoad of Hermopolis (the eight deities of that site). They were Nun and Naunet, Huh and Hauhet, Kuk and Kauket, Amen and Amunet. The four male gods were portrayed as frog-headed; the females were shown as snake-headed.

1092

Enoch (dedicated). In the Bible, O.T., father of Methuselah; he "walked with God: and he was not; for God took him"(Gen. 5:24). This is generally understood to mean he did not die but was taken to heaven like the prophet Elijah. In the New Testament the Epistle of Jude (chap. 14) describes Enoch as "the seventh from Adam." In medieval Jewish folklore Aupiel, the tallest angel, is credited with taking Enoch to heaven.

1093

Ephialtes (he who leaps upon). In Greek mythology, a giant, son of Poseidon (or Aloeus and Iphimedeia or Uranus and Gaea), twin brother of Otus. When the war between the Titans (giants) and the gods took place, Ephialtes was nine years old, and had grown nine inches every month. Ephialtes was killed by Apollo, according to some accounts, or by Apollo and Heracles, each of whom shot an arrow into each eye of the giant.

1094

Ephraim ben Sancho and the Parable of the Two Gems. Jewish folktale from *Liber Shebet Yehuda* (The Book of the Rod of Judah) by Solomon ibn Verga, written in the 16th century.

Often Christian kings would invite Jews to debate with Christians the various merits of their faiths. One day Nicholas of Valencia, who hated the Jews, asked Don Pedro, king of Aragon, to bring Ephraim ben Sancho to court to ask him which faith was superior, Judaism or Christianity.

When Ephraim was brought to court he asked the king for three days to come back with an answer. When he returned he had a sad look.

"What is wrong?" asked the king.

"A month ago," replied Ephraim, "a neighbor who is a jeweler went on a journey. Before he left he gave me instructions to keep the peace between his two sons, both of whom he had given precious gems. They came to me asking which gem was the superior of the two. I told them their father was the only man who could answer that and they beat me."

"They have mistreated you," the king replied, "and should be punished."

Erato

"O king," replied Ephraim, "may your ears hear what your mouth has said. The two brothers were Esau and Jacob [the twin sons of Isaac in the Old Testament]. Each received from God a priceless gem. You have asked me which religion is superior. How can I answer; only our Father in heaven can tell us."

When the king heard the wise reply, he rebuked his counselor, Nicholas of Valencia, and praised Ephraim for his wisdom.

1095

Epimenides In Greek mythology, a culture hero and a shepherd of Crete. He wrote poetry, taught the worship of the gods, and built the first temples. One day he fell asleep while searching for lost sheep and slept for 57 years.

1096

Epona (the great mare). In Roman mythology, a Celtic goddess, daughter of a man and a mare; she protected cows, oxen, and horses. Epona was worshiped in Roman Gaul, from Spain to the Balkans and from northern Britain to Italy. In art she was portrayed riding on a horse or seated and surrounded by mares. Juvenal's *Eighth Satire* (157) mentions the goddess.

1097

Erato (passionate). In Greek mythology, one of the nine Muses; Muse of love or erotic poetry, lyrics, and marriage songs; daughter of Zeus and Mnemosyne. Her symbol was a lyre. The Muses are invoked at the beginning of Homer's *Iliad* and *Odyssey*, Spenser's *Teares of the Muses*, and *The Fairie Queen* (Prologue, 2), Shakespeare's *Sonnet XXXVIII*, Gray's *Progress of Poesy* (2.3), Milton's *Paradise Lost* (book 7.1), Byron's *Childe Harold* (1.62), Wordsworth's *Ode* (1816) and Matthew Arnold's *Consolation* and *Empedocles on Etna*.

Erda

1098

Erda (earth). In Germanic mythology, earth goddess, known in Norse mythology as Jord. She appears in Richard Wagner's *Der Ring des Nibelungen*. In his *Das Rhinegold* the goddess warns Wotan (Odin) to give up the ring.

Yield it, Wotan! Yield it!
Flee the ring's dread curse!
Awful
And utter disaster
It will doom thee to

The god does not listen to Erda's plea and as a result eventually brings about the destruction of all of the gods and mankind. During the Middle Ages plows, one of her symbols, were carried in Christian Shrovetide processions to bless the earth, an indiction that the goddess may still have been worshiped. Erda is portrayed by Arthur Rackham in his illustrations for Wagner's Ring Cycle. Erda is also known as Hertha or Aertha.

1099

Eremon. In Celtic mythology, the first Milesian king of Ireland. Eremon was said to be a contemporary of King David of the Bible. He was the elder of two brothers, but after the victory of the Milesians over the Danaans, the original inhabitants of the land, Eber, his brother, refused to obey Eremon. A war ensued in which Eber was killed.

Variant spelling: Herimon.

1100

Ereshkigal (queen of the great below). In Near Eastern mythology (Babylonian-Assyrian), goddess of the underworld, married to the war god Nergal.

Once the gods made a feast and sent a message to Ereshkigal saying that, though they could go down to her realm of the dead, she could not come up to their home, and therefore it would be best if she sent a messenger to fetch the food set aside for her. Ereshkigal sent a messenger. When he arrived, all of the gods stood up to receive him, except for Nergal, who did not show the proper respect.

When the messenger returned to Ereshkigal, he told her what had happened. The goddess then asked that the delinquent be sent to her so that she could kill him. The gods discussed the matter and decided to send the culprit to the vengeful goddess. When Nergal arrived in the underworld, he grabbed Ereshkigal by her hair and dragged her from her throne.

"Do not kill me, my brother," cried the goddess. "Let me speak with you. You shall be my husband and I will be your wife. I will make you to rule the whole earth. I will place the Tablet of Wisdom in your hand. You shall be Lord and I will be Lady."

Nergal kissed the goddess, wiping away her tears.

"Whatever you have asked me in the past will now be yours," Nergal replied. The two were then married.

In many texts Ereshkigal is called Allatu.

1101

Erh-shih-ssu Hsiao (24 examples of filial piety). In Chinese folklore, 24 individuals who exemplify the important virtues. They are:

1. Emperor Shun, 2317–2207 B.C.E. Though mistreated by his father, Shun maintained the proper respect for him. Eventually Emperor Yao chose Shun to succeed him, even passing over his own son. In art Shun is often portrayed plowing a field with the aid of an elephant, which helped him do the work given him by his evil father.

2. Tseng Shen, 505–347 B.C.E., a disciple of Confucius. When he was gathering fuel in the woods, his mother at home, in her anxiety to see him, bit her finger. At once he knew his mother wished to see him because the sympathy between the two was so strong.

3. Emperor Wen, 179–156 B.C.E. He stayed with his mother for three years during her illness, never leaving her room or changing his clothes.

4. Min Sun, sixth century B.C.E., a pupil of Confucius. His father remarried, and the stepmother disliked the boy. When the father discovered this, he wished to divorce his wife, but Min Sun pleaded with his father, saying it would leave her two sons without a mother.

5. Chung Yu, 543–480 B.C.E., a disciple of Confucius. He carried rice bags on his back to support his poor parents. He is said to have been originally the son of the thunder god. He is also called Tze Lu and in Japanese legend is known as Chiuyu.

6. T'ung Yung, second century C.E. He had no money to bury his parents, so he sold himself to raise the money. When he returned home he met a young woman who offered to marry him, releasing him from his bondage. His owner demanded 300 pieces of silk, which the girl wove in a month. She was Chih N'u', the Weaving Damsel, sent by heaven to reward T'ung Yung for his devotion. In Japanese legend he is called Tovei.

7. Yen Tz'u (Chou dynasty?). His parents wanted doe's milk, which he procured by dressing in deer skins and mingling with the herd. In Japanese he is called Enshi.

8. Chiang Ko, 500 C.E. Whenwas captured by robbers, he asked the robber chief permission to take

her away. He then carried her a long distance on his back. *Variant spelling*: Kiang Keh.

9. Lu Hsü, first century C.E. He was released from jail on account of his devotion to his mother. When he was six years old, he was invited to the house of a rich neighbor, Yüan Chou, and was given some oranges to eat. As he was taking leave, his host saw two oranges fall from his dress. Yüan Chou asked the boy why he hadn't eaten the oranges. Lu Hsü replied that his mother was very fond of oranges, and he had not eaten them so he could give them to her. In Japanese legend Lu Hsü is called Rikuzoku. *Variant spelling*: Lu Sü

10. T'ang Fu-jen or Ts'ui Shih, the only woman on the list. She gave milk from her own breasts to her mother-in-law, who had lost her teeth. *Variant spelling*: Ts'ui She.

11. Wu Mêng, fifth century C.E. He allowed himself to be bitten by mosquitoes, rather than brush them off, for fear they might annoy his parents, who were in the same room sleeping. Sometimes Wu Mêng is portrayed crossing a river on a feather fan, which he waves over the boisterous waters. Other times he is shown with a fan in his hand, driving through the heavens in a chariot drawn by two stags. He is credited with slaying a giant snake. In Japanese legend he is called Gomo.

12. Wang Hsiang, 185–269 C.E. To satisfy his stepmother's desire for fish during winter, he lay down naked on the ice pond until a hole melted, out of which jumped two carp. *Variant spelling*: Wang Siang.

13. Kuo Chu, second century C.E. Not having enough food to feed his mother, Kuo Chu proposed that he and his wife kill their son so that there would be enough food to go around, saying that they could have another child but not another mother. When they were about to bury the child alive, they found a bar of gold on which it was written that it was a gift of the gods. Kuo Chu is often portrayed with his wife and son in a garden. *Variant spelling*: Kwoh Ku.

14. Yang Hsiang (Han dynasty). He jumped in front of a tiger to save his father's life, thus losing his own. *Variant spelling*: Yang Hiang.

15. Chu Shou-ch'ang, 1031–1102 C.E. He searched for 50 years to find out the identity of his true mother. When he did, he served her the rest of his life. *Variant spelling*: Cho Show-Chiang.

16. Yu Ch'ien-lou, sixth century C.E.. He left his government post after ten days to take care of his sick father. *Variant spelling*: Yü K'ien-low.

17. Ta'i Shun, first century C.E. He gave his mother ripe berries while he ate only green ones. *Variant spelling*: Tseng Shên.

18. Lao Lai-tsu. At 70 years of age he still dressed as a child to entertain his senile parents. In Japanese legend he is called Roraishi.

19. Huang Hsiang. He lost his mother when he was a child and grieved so much that he became as thin as a skeleton. He devoted the rest of his life to his father, fanning him in the summer, and in winter lying in his father's bed to warm it. *Variant spelling*: Huang Hiang.

20. Chiang Shih (Han dynasty). In conjunction with his wife he devoted himself to waiting on his aged mother. To gratify her he went every day to a pond to draw drinking water and obtain fresh fish for her table. The devotion was rewarded by a miracle. A spring burst forth close by his home, and a pair of carp were daily produced for his mother. *Variant spelling*: Kiang She.

21. Wang P'ou, third century C.E. He sat beside a pine tree, weeping for his dead father so long and devotedly that he caused the tree to rot. *Variant spelling*: Wang Ngai.

22. Ting Lan, first century C.E. After his mother's death he preserved a wooden image of her to which he offered the same respect he had offered her during her life. One day, while he was absent from home, his neighbor Chang Shu came to borrow some household articles. Ting Lan's wife inquired by divining slips whether the image mother would consent to lend the articles. She received a negative reply. The neighbor then struck the image. When Ting Lan returned home, he saw the image of his mother had an expression of displeasure. He then went to beat the neighbor who had insulted his mother.

23. Men Tsung, third century C.E. One cold winter day Men Tsung's mother expressed a craving to eat stewed bamboo shoots. Weeping because such a delicacy could not be gotten so early in the year, Men Tsung still went out to search the snow. He found under the snow a fresh-grown shot of unequaled succulence, which he then brought his mother. In Japanese legend Men Tsung is called Moso or Kobu. *Variant spelling*: Men Sung.

24. Huang T'ing-chien, 1050–1110 C.E. One of the four great scholars of the Sung dynasty, who was deeply devoted to his parents, taking care of his sick mother. *Variant spelling*: Hwang T'ing-kien.

Paul Carus, commenting on the series in his book *Chinese Thought*, wrote: "Some of the stories seem silly to us. . . . Still, it will be wise for us whose habits of life suffer from the opposite extreme . . . to recognize that all of them are pervaded with a noble spirit of respect for parents, which though exaggerated is none the less touching and ought to command our admiration."

1102

Erichthonius (wool on the earth, much earth). In Greek mythology, culture hero, fourth king of Athens, who had serpent's tails for legs. Erichthonius was the son of Hephaestus, the lame god, whose sperm fell on the ground when he attempted to rape Athena. Athena placed Erichthonius in a basket with a serpent and she then gave the basket to the Cecrops daughters, telling them not to look inside. Aglauros, one of the sisters, opened the basket and was punished by Athena, who made her insane or killed her. Erichthonius reigned for 50 years and invented chariots. Athena gave Erichthonius two drops of blood from the Gorgon. One was poisoned, but the other healed. Ovid's *Metamorphoses* (book 2) and Apollodorus' *Bibliotheca* (Library) tell his story.

1103

Erigone (child of strife, plentiful offspring). In Greek mythology, daughter of Icarius of Athens. She was raped by Dionysus, who transformed himself into a grape. When her father was murdered, she hanged herself and was transformed into the constellation Virgo. Ovid's *Metamorphoses* (book 6) tells the tale. A second Erigone was the daughter of Aegisthus and Clytemnestra, sister of Aletes. She had an adulterous affair with Orestes and bore Penthilus and, according to variant accounts, Tisamenus. She killed herself when Orestes was acquitted for the murder of Clytemnestra, their mother.

1104

Erisichthon (wool of the earth, much earth). In Greek mythology, a sacrilegious person, son of Triopas and Hiscilla of Thessaly; brother of Iphimedeia, Messene, and Phorbas; father of Mestra. Mestra could take any beast form; a gift from her lover, Poseidon. Erisichthon would sell Mestra in one form of animal, and she would return in another. When Erisichthon cut down a sacred grove belonging to the goddess Demeter, she cursed him with an insatiable hunger, so he ate his own legs and eventually his whole body. Ovid's *Metamorphoses* (book 8) tells of his fate.

1105

Erlik (man). In Siberian mythology, the devil, also known as Shulman.

Various myths are told of the origin of Erlik. In some he was originally a man who helped the creator god Ulgen make the earth, though later he turned against Ulgen. In a variant myth Erlik is said to have been originally some mud in human form to which Ulgen gave life as it floated on the ocean. Both myths agree that Erlik will be destroyed at the end of the world. In myths told by the Torgot, Erlik is called Shulman. In one, Shulman created three suns in order to burn the earth, which had been newly created by Burkhan-Bakshi, a creator god. But Burkhan, taking the form of the hero Erkho Morgon, shot down the extra two suns, letting them fall into the sea, so that only one remained. In a variant myth Burkhan-Bakshi covered the uninhabited earth with water and destroyed the extra suns. Erlik is also called Erlik-Khan (great man), meaning that he is lord of the dead. He sends out his fellow evil spirits to seize the souls of those who have sinned.

Variant spelling: Irlek.

1106

Erl-King. In Germanic legend, king of the elves or dwarfs. He was believed to be a malevolent goblin of the Black Forest in Germany who lured children to their deaths. He appears in Goethe's literary ballad "Der Erlkönig," which was translated by Sir Walter Scott as "The Erl-King" and set to music in the original German by Schubert. The ballad depicts a father riding with his child. The child sees "the Erl-King with his crown and his shroud" waiting for him. The Erl-King then calls the boy to come with him. The father attempts to save the boy, the Erl-King wins, and the boy is dead in his father's arms. Sir Walter Scott's note says, "To be read by a candle particularly long in the snuff."

1107

Ermine. A weasel having a white winter coat, often used as a symbol of chastity and purity in medieval and Renaissance folklore. It was believed that if the ermine was surrounded by mud it would prefer to be captured rather than dirty its white coat trying to escape. In Christian art St. Mary Magdalen's cloak is sometimes made of ermine to indicate that the former prostitute had reformed her ways. Ermine was often used to line royal garments in the Middle Ages and Renaissance. In some Renaissance art works the Roman goddess of wisdom, Minerva, is portrayed with an ermine to represent virtue.

1108

Eros (erotic love). In Greek mythology, god of love, son of Aphrodite and Ares, or of Chaos with Gaea or Tartarus, or of Aphrodite and Hephaestus; brother of Anteros, Deimos, Enyo, Harmmia, Pallor, and Phobus; married to Psyche; father of Delight; called Cupid by the Romans. *Erotica*, a festival in Eros's honor, was celebrated with sports and games every fifth year by the Thespians. Associated with Eros was his brother Anteros, god of mutual love; Peithos, goddess of persuasion; Himeros, god of desire; Pothos, god of longing; and the Muses and Graces. In art he is often portrayed as a small baby with wings, though he is a youth in the famous

Cupid shooting an arrow

statue in Piccadilly Circus in London. Eros appears in Vergil's *Aeneid* (book 1), Ovid's *Metamorphoses* (book 1), Apuleious' *The Golden Ass*, Keats's *Endymion* and *Ode to Psyche*; Robert Bridges' *Eros and Psyche*.

1109

Erulus. In Roman mythology, a king of Italy, son of Feronia, goddess of the orchard and woods. He had three arms and three lives and had to be killed three times the same day by Evander. Vergil's *Aeneid* (book 8) records his fate.

1110

Eruncha. In Australian mythology, devils who turn people into medicine men. In some accounts, however, the Eruncha are said to eat medicine men.

1111

Erymanthian Boar. In Greek mythology, the boar captured by Heracles as his fourth labor; it lived on Mount Erymanthus in Arcadia. Erymanthus is also the name of a son of Apollo who was blinded by Aphrodite because he had seen the goddess bathing. In retaliation Apollo transformed himself into a boar and killed Admis, the young lover of Aphrodite.

1112

Erytheis (crimson). In Greek mythology, one of the Hesperides who guarded the golden apples in the garden of the Hesperides.

1113

Erzulie. In Haitian voodoo, mother goddess, wife of Agwé, she represents jealousy, vengeance, and discord but also love, perpetual help, goodwill, health, beauty, and fortune. In her demonic role she is called Marinette-Bois Chèche, Erzulie Toho, Erzulie Zandor, and Erzulie Mapiangueh, and in that aspect she causes the people she mounts or possesses to twist in fantastic convulsions. In her beneficent aspect she is called Tsilah Wédo and Ayida. Her symbol is often a heart pierced by swords, the same as that of the Virgin Mary in Christian symbolism.

1114

Esau (hairy). In the Bible, O.T., Isaac's oldest son and twin brother of Jacob. Esau sold his birthright to Jacob for some pottage (lentils) (Gen. 25:24–34). Esau was an ancestor of the Edomites.

1115

Eshu. In African mythology (Yoruba of southwestern Nigeria), trickster who acts as mediator between Olorun, the sky god and the people.

Eshu, who knows all languages, brings down the messages of Olorun to the people and brings up the people's sacrifices to the sky god. He also presides over chance, accidents, and unpredictability, and he lurks in highways, crossroads, and gateways to trick people. Once he had an argument with Shango, the thunder god, over which of them was more powerful. Eshu, who could change shape and size at will, made his penis grow to an enormous size, frightening the other god, who admitted Eshu was the greater of the two. Another time Eshu deliberately brought chaos into the home of a man who was living comfortably with his two wives. Disguising himself as a merchant, Eshu sold a beautiful hat to one of the wives, which made the other very jealous. The second wife bought an even more beautiful hat, until at last rivalry and despair characterized the man's life and household. Eshu is sometimes called Elegbara.

1116

Esmun. In Near Eastern mythology (Syro-Phoenician), sun god of vital force and healing, worshiped at his patron city of Carthage. He was loved by the goddess Astronoe, but when she was about to capture him, he cut off his genitals with an ax. He was then turned into a god of generative heat. Esmun was combined with the goddess Astarte, forming a composite male and female deity, Esmun-Astarte.

Variant spellings: Ashmun, Eshmoun, Eshmun, Esmoun, Esmounos.

Essus (lord). In Celtic mythology, god of vegetation and war, mentioned by ancient Roman writers and identified with Mars or Mercury. Human sacrifices were made to Essus with the victims attached to trees.

Variant spelling: Esus, Hesus.

Esther

Esther (a form of Ishtar, goddess of sexual love). In the Bible, O.T., a Jewish heroine. In Hebrew her name is Hadassah (myrtle). Esther was chosen to replace Queen Vashti, wife of King Ahasuerus (Xerxes) after the queen insulted the king. Esther did not tell the king she was a Jewess. On the advice of her uncle Mordecai she helped destroy Haman, who wished to massacre the Jews. This deliverance is celebrated by Jews today at the Feast of Purim.

The Old Testament Book of Esther never once mentions God. Martin Luther hated the Book of Esther, saying it would have been better if it had been left out of the Old Testament. Jean Racine's *Esther* is based on the Book of Esther in the Vulgate Latin translation of the Bible, which contains passages not found in the King James translation of the Hebrew text. Artemesia Gentileschi painted *Esther before Ahasuerus*, and Rembrandt painted *Haman Begging Esther for Forgiveness*. An epic poem, *Esther* by Jean Desmarets de Saint-Sorlin is based on the biblical tale. Handel's oratorio *Esther* also deals with the heroine.

Estmere. In medieval English legend, a king who defeated a Moorish king and won the daughter of King Adland. The happy-go-lucky Estmere was advised by Adler (either a bosom friend or his brother, depending on which account of the legend is followed) to seek a wife. The two set out for King Adland's palace. He welcomed them after he had determined they were Christians. They asked to see his daughter, and he informed them that a Moor, King Bremor, had wanted his daughter's hand in marriage but he had refused because Bremor was not a Christian. Bremor threatened to return. When the princess was introduced to Estmere, she fell in love with him. When Bremor returned, Estmere defeated him, and King Adland allowed Estmere to marry his daughter. An English ballad tells one version of the tale. It was set to music by Gustav Holst for chorus and orchestra.

Estrildis. In British mythology, the daughter of a German king and mistress to King Humber of Britain. When Humber was drowned in the river that bears his name, Locrine fell in love with Estrildis and would have married her had he not been betrothed already to Guendoloena. However, the two became lovers, and Estrildis bore a daughter named Sabrina.

Estsanatlehi (woman who changes). In North American Indian mythology (Navaho), mother earth, who renews youth with the seasons, brings female rain, and has power over all reproduction on earth. She helped create light for the world through the use of her white shell and turquoise beads and by using a magic crystal. She is also called Whiteshell Woman, Ashonnutli, and Changing Woman.

Etana (strong). In Near Eastern mythology (Babylonian), hero who ascended to the heavens on the back of an eagle only to fall back to earth.

The myth of Etana is found in fragmentary form. It has been pieced together by scholars. One section tells how Etana prayed to the sun god, Shamash, to give a son to his wife by revealing to him the place where the "plant of life" was to be found. How the "plant of life" was found by the hero, however, is missing in the fragment.

Another part of the myth tells of the miraculous journey Etana made to the heavens on the back of an eagle. The eagle kept taking the hero higher and higher, past the abode of the gods Anu, Bel, and Ea, to where the great goddess Ishtar lived. But Etana, not able to bear the journey, fell to the earth, taking the eagle with him.

The character of Etana also appears in the Babylonian epic poem *Gilgamesh*, in which he is said to have founded a kingdom.

Variant spelling: Etanna.

Eteocles and Polynices (true glory and much strife). [1123]
In Greek mythology, sons of Oedipus and Jocasta (or Euryganeia); brothers of Antigone and Ismene. Both sons had insulted their blind father, Oedipus, by giving him a cup that had once belonged to Laius and by giving him a portion of meat not fit for a king. Oedipus cursed both sons. They were to rule jointly after their father's death. Eteocles refused to surrender the throne when his brother's turn came. In the ensuing war both brothers were killed in one-to-one combat. Aeschylus' *Seven against Thebes* and Euripides' *The Phoenician Woman* deal with the tragic tale.

Ethne (little fire). In Celtic mythology, the daughter [1124]
of the god-king Balor, who was informed that his daughter would have a child who would kill him. King Balor therefore imprisoned Ethne in a tower on Tory Island in the charge of 12 matrons who were forbidden to tell her that men existed. Earlier Balor had stolen a magic cow belonging to Kian, who now avenged himself on the king by disguising himself as a woman and entering the tower. From Ethne and Kian's intercourse three children were born, whom Balor ordered drowned. But one, Lugh, was accidentally spared and later killed Balor.

Variant spelling: Ethlinn, Ethna, Eithne, Ethnee, Ethnea, Aithne.

Etna. In Greek and Roman history and mythology, [1125]
volcanic mountain on the eastern coast of Sicily where the forge of Hephaestus, god of fire, was located and where Zeus confined the giants. The volcano is said to be named after Aetna, daughter of Briareus (or Uranus) and mother, by Hephaestus, of the two Palici volcanoes.

Variant spelling: Aetna.

Etzel. Name given in Germanic legend to Attila the [1126]
Hun. In the epic poem the *Nibelungenlied*, Etzel marries Kriemhild, the widow of Siegfried. She is called Gu-

drun in the *Volsunga Saga*, where Attila is given the name Atli.

Eudora (generous). In Greek mythology, one of the [1127]
Nereids, the 50 daughters of Nereus and Doris who attended Poseidon. Homer's *Iliad* (book 18), Hesiod's *Theogony*, and Ovid's *Metamorphoses* all mention the Nereids.

Euhemerus. Fourth century B.C.E. Greek writer on [1128]
mythology whose book, *Sacred History*, theorizes that the gods were originally humans who were later deified.

Eunomia (orderly). In Greek mythology, one of the [1129]
Horae; goddess of order and legislation, daughter of Zeus and Themis. Her sisters were Eirene (peace) and Dice (justice).

Euphrosyne (joy). In Greek mythology, one of the [1130]
three Graces. The others were Aglaia (bright) and Thalia (blood of life). They were all daughters of Zeus and Eurynome.

Eurydice (wide justice). In Greek mythology, a [1131]
dryad, wife of Orpheus, who died of a snakebite as she fled from Aristaeus. Orpheus went to the underworld in search of her. He was given permission to return Eurydice to life if he would not look back before he reached the upper earth. Orpheus did and lost Eurydice forever. The myth is told in Vergil's *Georgics IV*, Ovid's *Metamorphoses* (book 10), Milton's *L'Allegro*, and Landor's *Orpheus and Eurydice*. The many operas on the subject include Monteverdi's *La favola d'Orfeo* (1607), Gluck's *Orfeo ed Euridice*, and Offenbach's comic opera *Orphee aux enfers* (Orpheus in the Underworld) (1858).

Eurytion (full-flowing little one). In Greek myth- [1132]
ology, a centaur who caused the fight at the wedding of Pirithous and Hippodameia. Ovid's *Metamorphoses* (book 12) tells the tale. The same name is born by the herdsman of Geryon, king of Erythia. Both he and his dog Orthus were killed by Heracles during his tenth labor. The name is also held by a companion of Aeneas in Italy who was a great archer.

Eustace, St. (plentiful harvest). Second century C.E. [1133]
In Christian legend, patron saint of hunters. Feast, 20 September. His legend is similar to St. Hubert's, and the two are often confused in legend and art. Eus-

tace's life is found in *The Golden Legend*, a collection of saints' lives written in the 13th century by Jacobus de Voragine.

Eustace, whose Roman name was Placidus, was a Roman soldier under the Emperor Trajan. He had a wife and two sons. One day, while hunting in the forest, he saw a white stag of "marvelous beauty" and pursued it. The stag fled and ascended a high rock. Then Placidus, looking up, beheld, "between the horns of the stag, a cross of radiant light, and on it the image of the crucified Redeemer." He was dazzled by the vision and fell to his knees. A voice cried out: "Placidus? Why dost thou pursue me? I am Christ, whom thou hast hitherto served without knowing me. Dost thou now believe?"

"Lord, I believe," Placidus said.

Placidus went home, converted his wife and sons and in a short time was arrested for being a Christian. The family was asked to sacrifice to the Roman gods. They refused and were placed in a brazen, or bronze, bull and roasted to death.

1134

Evander (good for men). In Roman mythology, culture hero, son of the nymph Carmenta and the god Hermes (or Sarpedon and Laodameia), married Deidamia; father of Pallantia, Pallas, Dyna, Roma, and Sarpedon II. He settled near Rome after the Trojan War. Evander introduced the Greek alphabet and worship of the gods, and he built Pallanteum on the Palatine Hill outside Rome. He was honored by the Romans as a god and worshiped at an altar built on Mount Aventine. Evander appears in Vergil's *Aeneid* (book 8), where he kills Erulus three times in one day.

1135

Evangeline. In American literary folklore, name given to Emmeline Labiche by Henry W. Longfellow in his narrative poem *Evangeline*, in dactylic hexamters. The basis for the legend was told by the Reverend Horace Lorenzo Connolly, an Episcopal priest, to Nathaniel Hawthorne, with the view that the author would use it for a novel; but Hawthorne said, "The story is not in my vein," and offered it to Longfellow. The legend tells how Emmeline Labiche was raised in the French village of St. Gabriel in Acadia, now Nova Scotia. She was to be married to Louis Arceneau, a childhood sweetheart. When the British dispersed the colony, Emmeline and Louis were separated, only to meet years later when he was about to marry another woman. Emmeline went insane and died a few years later. Longfellow took the bare facts and wove them into an American legend. In his poem the lovers are separated, and Gabriel (the name given to Louis) and his father make their way to

Louisiana. Evangeline continues to seek them. After years of wandering she settles in Philadelphia, becoming a Sister of Mercy. There, during a plague, she sees a dying old man. Realizing it is Gabriel, she dies of shock, and the two are buried in a Catholic cemetery. Longfellow's poem, one of the most popular in American literature, was used as the basis for three operas. Statues of the heroine have been erected in Grand Pré, Nova Scotia, and St. Martinville, Louisiana.

1136

Evangelists, The Four (publishers of glad tidings). In Christian tradition, Matthew, Mark, Luke, and John, credited with the authorship of the Four Gospels in the New Testament. During the Middle Ages Matthew was portrayed as a man with an angel nearby, or a winged man; Mark as a lion; Luke as an ox; John as an eagle. St. Jerome set down the generally accepted interpretation of the symbolism. Matthew was given the angel or human semblance because he begins his account with the human generation of Christ; Mark has the lion because he tells the royal dignity of Christ; Luke has an ox because he dwells on the sacrifice of Christ; and John has the eagle because he dwells on the divinity of Christ.

Eve

1137

Eve (the mother of all living?). In the Bible, O.T., first woman, wife of Adam, mother of Cain, Abel, and Seth. (Gen. 3:1–24).

1138

Exaltation of the Holy Cross. Medieval Christian feast, celebrated 14 September, often called Holy Cross Day. The feast commemorates the return to Jerusalem in 630 C.E. of a relic of the true cross. The tale is told in *The Golden Legend* by Jacobus de Voragine. The Emperor Heraclius (c. 575–641) defeated King Chrosröes (Khrosrow II) of the Persians, who

Sir Bedivere casts Excalibur into the lake (A. Beardsley)

had taken a piece of the true cross and used it to make up part of his throne. For his impiety Heraclius had Chroaröes killed and took back the part of the true cross. As he was entering Jerusalem through the gate through which Jesus came, stones fell, barring his entrance. An angel appeared, telling Heraclius that Jesus entered on a donkey, not dressed in royal garb. The king then stripped himself to his shirt and carried in the relic, as the stones miraculously moved out of his way.

1139

Excalibur (to free from the stone?). In Arthurian legend, the sword of King Arthur. The sword was given to Arthur by the Lady of the Lake, according to some accounts. When Arthur lay dying he commanded Sir Bedivere to return Excalibur to the Lady of the Lake. Sir Bedivere threw the sword into the waters, and an arm clothed in white samite appeared to receive it. Arthur's sword is sometimes called Caliburn and Caledwlch.

1140

Exodus (a going out). In the Bible, Greek title of the Old Testament book telling of the escape by the Israelites from their bondage in Egypt. The book is the second part of the Pentateuch, or Torah, giving the account of Moses' birth, the Israelites' departure from Egypt, and their journey to Palestine. The Ten Commandments are found in chapter 20, verses 1–18. Handel's oratorio *Israel in Egypt* uses the book as a basis for its libretto.

1141

Exorcism. The expelling of evil spirits or demons by prayers, incantations, and rites, practiced in all religions that admit the existence of demonic forces in the world.

Pagan, Jewish, Christian, and Islamic religions all believed in demonic possession. Lucian, writing in the second century C.E., tells of a professional exorcist:

> . . . everyone already knows this remarkable man who in the case of people falling down at the sight of the moon, rolling their eyes and foaming at the mouth...sends them home free from their infirmity, for which he charges a large sum each time. When he is with sick persons he asks them how the devil entered into them; the patient remains silent, but the devil replies, in Greek or a barbarian tongue...how he has entered into the man's body.

In the Hebrew Old Testament demons are sent directly by God. When King Saul is tormented (1 Sam. 16:14–16), it is God who is the instigator:

The Cross (Dürer)

> But the Spirit of the Lord departed from Saul, and an evil spirit from the Lord troubled him. And Saul's servants said unto him, "Behold now, an evil spirit from god troubleth thee. Let our lord now command thy servants, which are before thee, to seek out a man, who is a cunning player on an harp: and it shall come to pass, when the evil spirit from God is upon thee, that he shall play with his hand, and thou shalt be well."

King Saul is freed of his evil spirit by David, the future king.

Medieval Jews also believed in demonic possession and exorcism. In a typical example a woman was possessed by the spirit of a drunken Jew "who died without prayer and impenitent." His spirit wandered about for a long time and was allowed to enter the woman's body when she was blaspheming against God. From the moment of possession the woman became a hysteric. A Jewish exorcist was called in. He forced the demon to reveal his true name and then, using the secret name of God, forced the demon out "by the little toe of the possessed."

Christianity is filled with tales of possession, beginning with accounts in the New Testament in which Jesus acts as an exorcist.

Belief in demonic possession can still be found in major Christian churches. The Roman Catholic church has a whole section devoted to exorcism in *The Roman Ritual*, the introduction to which begins "That there is a world of demons is a teaching of revealed religion which is perfectly clear to all who know Sacred Scripture and respect and accept its word as inspired of God. it is part of the whole Christian-Judaeo heritage."

The rite, which consists of prayers and psalms, opens with this passage: "I cast you out, unclean spirit, along with every satanic power of the enemy, every spectre from hell, and all your fell companions; in the name of our Lord Jesus Christ. Begone and stay far from this creature of God."

1142

Ezekiel (may God make the child strong?) Sixth century B.C.E. In the Bible, Hebrew prophet and title of a book in the Old Testament. Ezekiel was taken captive by the Babylonians and moved from Judah to the banks of the Chebar River in Babylonia (Ezek. 1:1). His book, filled with lurid visions, divides as follows: Ezekiel's call (1:1–3:27), prophecies of doom of Jerusalem (4:1–24:27), God's judgment on the nations (25:1–32:32), God's promises (33:1–37:28), prophecy against God (38:1–39:29) and a vision of the future temple and land (40:1–48:35).

In Islamic legend, Hizqil is the name given to Ezekiel. He is believed to be referred to in the Koran (sura 2), although not by name.

The prophet appears in Duccio di Buoninsegna's The Nativity with prophets Ezekiel and Isaiah. He sometimes appears with a scroll in Western art with the Latin form of one of his sayings: *Porta haec clausa erit; non aperietar* (this gate shall be shut, it shall not be opened, and no man shall enter in by it) (Ezek. 44:2) Medieval writers made the text refer to the perpetual virginity of St. Mary the Virgin.

Exodus

Ezra (help). In the Bible, O.T., a Jewish priest who led the Jews back to Jerusalem from their captivity in Babylon about 300 B.C.E. The Book of Ezra, a sequel to Chronicles, tells his story. He is called Esdras in the Apocrypha. In Islamic legend his name is Uzair. He is mentioned in the Koran (sura 9) which says, "The Jews say Uzair is a son of God."

F

Fa. In African cult, a system of divination taken from the Yoruba of southwestern Nigeria and practiced by the Fon of Benin. When God completed the creation of the world, two messengers were sent to the earth to tell man that each person must have his own Fa. Fa can be loosely defined as the knowledge given by God to each man whereby he may come to know how to perform the will of the Creator. It is a system by which one comes to learn the kind of behavior expected of him. One man was selected to contact the oracle by manipulation of nuts from a special palm tree. If the nuts of the palm tree were handled properly, the eyes of Fa would be opened and man would be able to gain a glimpse of the future. This complicated method of divination would permit man to foretell his destiny. A selected group of heavenly messengers were taught how to work the oracle. The nuts of the palm tree were thrown from one hand to the other. A pattern resulted when one counted the number of nuts left over from the throw. Often this pattern was carved on the skin of a calabash, which was placed in a bag so that the secret of one's future could remain hidden from those who might use this information against him.

Fabiola, St. (bean grower). Died 399. C.E. In Christian legend, friend of St. Jerome. Feast, 27 December.

Fabiola had divorced her drunken husband and remarried. After her second husband's death she devoted her life to works of charity, establishing the first Christian hospital in the West. When she told St. Jerome she wished to settle in Bethlehem, he advised her against it, saying she was too lively. Thousands attended her funeral when she died in Rome.

Fafnir. In Norse mythology, a dragon guardian of gold, son of Hreidmar and brother of Regin and Otter. He was slain by the hero Sigurd.

In the *Volsunga Saga* Fafnir, in his lust for gold, slays his father, Hreidmar, and steals the skin of his dead brother, Otter, which contains a gold treasure. To guard his treasure Fafnir transforms himself into a dragon. Sigurd comes to slay the dragon Fafnir and obtain the treasure. He kills Fafnir by a ruse.

According to the *Volsunga Saga*, Fafnir engages in a long discussion with Sigurd to discover who his murderer is, then dies. In *Der Ring des Nibelungen* Richard Wagner makes Fafner (Fafnir) one of the giants who built Valhalla for Wotan (Odin). Fafner and his brother Fasolt accept Alberich's ring in place of the beautiful goddess Freyja, the price originally agreed on. Fafner kills Fasolt and changes himself into a dragon to guard his gold hoard. He is eventually killed by Siegfried (Sigurd). Fafnir is portrayed in Arthur Rackham's illustrations for Wagner's Ring Cycle.

Faith, Hope, and Charity, SS. Second century? C.E. In medieval Christian legend, the three saints were believed to be the children of Saint Sophia (holy wisdom). They were said to have been martyred in Rome under the Emperor Hadrian. In medieval Gothic art St. Faith is often portrayed as a woman holding a cross or chalice. Feast, 1 August. The English Puritans introduced the English words Faith, Hope, and Charity as names in the 16th century.

Falcon and the Owls, The. Moral fable by the Persian Sufi mystic and poet Rumi, in *The Masnavi* (book 2, story 4).

A certain falcon lost his way and found himself in a foul place inhabited by owls. The owls suspected that the falcon had come to seize their nests. They all surrounded him to kill him. The falcon assured them that he had no such design because he lived on the wrist of the king and had no desire to live in their foul place. The owls replied that he was trying to deceive them, since such a strange bird as he was could not possibly be the king's favorite.

"It is true," the falcon replied, "I am not the same as the king, but yet the king's light is reflected in me, the same as water and earth that nourish plants are part of the plant. I am, as it were, the dust beneath the king's feet. If you become like me in this respect, you will be exalted as I am. Copy the outward form you behold in me, and perchance you will reach the real substance of the king."

Fama (talk). In Roman mythology, goddess of fame; equivalent to the Greek goddess Pheme. She was sometimes portrayed blowing a trumpet.

Fan-Wang. In Chinese mythology, a creator god, who hatched the universe from a cosmic egg. Fan-Wang is also found in Chinese Buddhist mythology, not, however, as a creator god (which Buddhism does not have) but as a deity inferior to anyone who is on his way to Buddhahood.

Faran. In African mythology (Songhai of the upper Niger), hero who fought the water spirit Zin-Kibaru. Each night Zin-Kibaru would play his guitar, enticing fish to eat the rice that grew in Faran's pond. Faran was angered, and the two decided to fight. During the battle each one cast a spell on the other, but Faran's spell was stronger. Zin-Kibaru lost, leaving all of his magical instruments and spirit followers to Faran.

Farbauti (cruel striker). In Norse mythology, the father of Loki, the fire-trickster god. Loki's mother was the giantess Laufey, or Nal. Farbauti appears in the *Prose Edda*.

Far Darria. In Irish folklore, a fairy who wears a red cap and coat and spends his time at practical joking, especially of a gruesome kind.

Faridun. In the Persian epic poem *Shah Namah*, by Firdusi, a hero who defeats the evil king Zahhak.

Firdusi's portrait of Faridun is derived from Traetaona, a hero of Persian mythology who had fought with a demon, Azhi Dahaka. In Firdusi's epic Azhi Dahaka is transformed into the evil king, Zahhak, and Traetaona is called Faridun. These changes were made to make the poem acceptable to an Islamic audience that did not want the ancient gods and heroes mentioned in works by Islamic poets. (When Islam conquered Persia, it all but wiped out earlier beliefs.)

One night, according to *Shah Namah*, King Zahhak dreamed that a young man hit him on the head with a mace. When he awoke from his dream, he asked his courtiers what the dream signified, but they refused to give him an answer. When they could no longer avoid answering the king, they said it was an apparition of Faridun, the hero who was "destined to smite" the king on his head.

"But why," demanded the king, "does the youth wish to injure me?"

"Because his father's blood will be spilled by you, and he will have to avenge his father's death," the courtiers replied.

As the courtiers had predicted, Zahhak had Abtin,

Fame eluding her follower

the father of Faridun, killed; but Faranuk, Faridun's mother, and her newborn child escaped. As she fled, she came upon a cow named Pur'maieh, which yielded milk in abundance. Because of the murder of her husband, Faranuk's milk had dried up, and the cow now fed her little son, Faridun. The boy was placed in the care of shepherds by his mother. After some time his hiding place was discovered by King Zahhak, and the shepherds who had protected the lad were killed, but Faridun eluded the slaughterers.

When he was sixteen, his mother told him the story of his father's death at the hands of the evil king, and Faridun resolved to avenge the death. After numerous adventures Faridun succeeded in his task and was made king. His reign is described in *Shah Namah* by an envoy to another court:

> He who has never seen the spring
> Would see it when he looked upon the king.
> A spring of Paradise, 'twas to behold,
> Its dust of amber and its bricks of gold.
> Upon his palace heav'n found resting place
> With Paradise e'er smiling on its face.
> (Alexander Rogers translation)

Faridun had three sons; Silim, Tur, and Irij. Silim continually prodded his brother Tur to have Irij put to death, so that the kingdom would pass to Tur. One day Tur attacked Irij and cut off his head. Irij's murder was later avenged by Minuchihr, who was Faridun's grandson.

Variant spellings: Feridoun, Feridun, Freydun.

Fasces (bundles). In ancient Roman ritual, birch or elm rods held together by a red thong. Fasces were carried by lictors as the symbol of authority of a Roman consul. An ax was added to the fasces to signify that not only whipping but also death was within its power. Italian Fascists adopted the symbol as well as the name for their party.

Fatima. 606?–632 C.E. In Islamic legend, daughter of Muhammad by his first wife, Khadija. Fatima was the wife of Ali, a saint and warrior in Islam. She was one of the four "perfect women." (The others were Khadija; Mary, the mother of Jesus; and Asiyah, wife of the pharaoh drowned in the Red Sea.) In Islamic tradition Fatima is called bright-blooming, which means one who has never menstruated. In actuality, she had three sons by Ali.

In the town of Fátima, near Leiria, Portugal, the Virgin Mary appeared to three children in 1917. The shrine, built in 1944, is called Our Lady of the Rosary of Fátima. Some Roman Catholic writings explain the appearance at the small town as an indication that one day devotion to the Virgin Mary will bring Islam under the banner of Christianity.

Fatima is also the name of a holy woman in the story of Aladdin in *The Thousand and One Nights*. She is slain by the necromancer, brother of the sorcerer. Dressed in Fatima's clothes, he makes his way into Aladdin's house, but Aladdin discovers the disguise and kills the necromancer.

The name is also that of the last wife of Bluebeard in the well-known folktale.

Faunus (he who favors). In Roman mythology, an early Italian god of agriculture, shepherds, woods, and pastures; equivalent of the Greek Pan. In art Faunus was portrayed as a goat-legged half-human creature similar to a Greek satyr. Fauns as the followers of Bacchus appear in Vergil's *Aeneid* (book 7). Debussy's tone poem *Prelude a l'Apres-Midi d'un faune* (Prelude to "The Afternoon of a Faun"), inspired by Mallarmé's poem about Faunus and used as a ballet by Diaghilev's company in 1912, also deals with the god.

Faust (fortunate). 16th century C.E. In European history and legend, Dr. John Faustus, a professional magician in Germany who, according to legend, sold his soul to the devil. The Faust legend is a conglomerate of anonymous folk traditions largely of medieval origin. One of the first books dealing with the legend, *The History of the Damnable Life and Deserved Death of Dr. John Faustus*, has a deep Protestant cast. Mephistopheles, the devil, wears a Franciscan robe, and Faust, with his freethinking and love of the ancients, is condemned for opposing all authority, both state and church. Among the most famous works dealing with the subject are Marlowe's play *Dr. Faustus* and Goethe's epic drama *Faust* (Part 1, 1808; Part 2, 1832), which inspired numerous musical settings, among them Schumann's *Scenes from Goethe's Faust*, Berlioz's *Le Damnation de Faust*, and Gounod's opera *Faust*. Other

Faust

works include Thomas Mann's novel *Dr. Faustus* and Busoni's opera *Doktor Faust*, based on the European puppet plays of Faust.

Fear-Gorta. In Irish folklore, the "man of hunger" who appears as an emaciated phantom going through the land in famine time, begging alms and bringing good luck to the giver.

Feathertop. In American literary folklore, scarecrow given life by the witch Mother Rigby in Hawthorne's short story "Feathertop," included in *Mosses from an Old Manse*. Mother Rigby creates a Lord Ravensbane from a scarecrow to get revenge on her former lover, Justice Merton, but Merton's daughter Rachel falls in love with the mirage. When Feathertop and Rachel look in a glass, however, his true identity is revealed. Fleeing, he returns to Mother Rigby and casts away the magic pipe that made him seem a human and returns to being a scarecrow. Mother Rigby says, "Poor fellow! My poor, dear, pretty Feathertop! There are thousands upon thousands of coxcombs and charlatans in the world, made up of just such a mumble of worn-out, forgotten, and good-for-nothing trash as he was! Yet they live in fair repute, and never see themselves for what they are. And why should my poor puppet be the only one to know himself and perish for it." The tale was dramatized by Percy MacKaye as *The Scarecrow*, which was made into a silent film *Puritan Passions*.

Febold Feboldson. In American folklore, hero of the Great Plains who could influence weather conditions. Once when it was dry, he hypnotized some frogs into croaking, telling them it was raining. When the Indian rain god heard all the croaking, he got a headache and sent down rain to shut up the frogs. Febold Feboldson appears in Paul R. Beath's *Legends of Febold Feboldson*, a pamphlet written for the Federal Writers' Project in Nebraska, and in a later book *Febold Feboldson: Tall Tales from the Great Plains*.

Feng-huang

How much of Feboldson's legend is Beath's invention and how much is folklore is still debated.

Februa. In Roman mythology, god of purification, after whom the month of February is named. The *Feralia* was the Roman All Souls Day (21 February), last of the *dies Parentales* (which began at noon 13 February), when the family made offerings at the graves of their dead. The feast is mentioned in Ovid's *Fasti* (book 2).

Variant spelling: Februus.

Felicitas and Her Seven Sons, St. (lucky). Second century. In Christian legend, martyrs. Invoked by women who want sons. Feast, 10 July. Coming from a rich Roman family, Felicitas was widowed and brought up her seven sons as Christians. She was arrested, and they were killed one by one in front of her. Finally, she was beheaded or placed in a boiling caldron. Medieval art portrays her as a veiled widow with a martyr's palm, surrounded by her seven sons.

Feng-huang. In Chinese mythology, the phoenix; the male, *feng*; the female, *huang*. The phoenix is the emperor of birds as the unicorn is the emperor of quadrupeds. In Chinese belief the unicorn does not prey on living creatures and symbolizes peace and prosperity. The pair of the male and female phoenix is inseparable and symbolizes conjugal fidelity.

In Japanese the phoenix is called Ho-o.

Feng Po. In Chinese mythology, god of winds, often portrayed as an old man with a white beard, yellow cloak, and blue-and-red cap. In his hands he holds a sack that contains the winds.

Fenrir the Wolf

Fenrir (from the swamp). In Norse mythology, a giant wolf, son of the evil fire-trickster god, Loki; brother of Hel. When Fenrir opened his mouth one jaw touched the earth and the other reached to heaven. Fenrir was expected to swallow the god Odin at the day of doom when gods, giants, people and the world would be destroyed. Fenrir appears in the *Poetic Edda*, the *Prose Edda*, and a dramatic poem, *Fenris the Wolf*, by Percy MacKay.

Variant spelling: Fenris.

Ferdinand III of Castile, St. (peace). Died 1252 C.E. In Christian legend, king of Castile when he was 18, Ferdinand spent almost his entire life fighting the Moors. In one battle he was aided by St. James the Apostle, who helped his army kill thousands of Moors. Only one Christian died in the battle. He is buried in the cathedral at Seville, having been canonized in 1668 at the request of Philip IV. Feast, 30 May.

Feronia. In Roman mythology, early Italian goddess of groves, woods, orchards, and fountains; patroness of ex-slaves; mother of Eruius, a king of Italy who had three lives and had to be slain by Evander three times before he died. Feronia had a temple in Feronia near Mount Soracte. A yearly sacrifice was made to her. To wash one's face and hands in her sacred fountain near her temple was one of her rites. Those worshipers whom the goddess filled with her spirit were believed able to walk barefoot over burning coals. Feronia is cited in Vergil's *Aeneid* (book 7).

Fiacre, St. Seventh century C.E. In Christian legend, abbot of Breuil; patron saint of gardeners, florists, trellis makers, box makers, brass beaters, coppersmiths, lead founders, needle makers, hosiers, tile makers, potters, and cab drivers. Invoked against venereal disease, sterility, fistula, colic, tumors, and headache. Protector of field and garden fruits. Feast, 1 September.

Fiacre was born in Ireland and sailed to France to devote himself completely to God. Arriving at Meaux he was given a forest dwelling, called Breuil, by St. Faro, the local bishop. St. Faro offered St. Fiacre as much land as he could turn up in a day. Instead of driving his furrow with a plow, St. Fiacre turned the top of the soil with the point of his staff. He cleared the ground of trees and constructed a cell with a garden. He also made a chapel to the Virgin Mary, and a hospice for travelers later developed near it. Known throughout the area for his healing powers, many faithful often consulted the saint, but he would not allow any women near his hermitage or the chapel. If a woman attempted to break in, she was stopped by some supernatural power. Some died on the spot. After St. Fiacre's death numerous miracles were claimed for his relics at Meaux. Louis XIII was restored to health by invoking the saint, as was Louis XIV.

St. Fiacre is the patron saint of Parisian cab drivers because the first establishment to allow coaches on hire in the 17th century was in the rue Saint-Martin, near the hotel Saint-Fiacre, in Paris. French cabs are called *fiacres*.

1170
Fides (honesty). In Roman mythology, goddess of oaths, honesty, and faith. Numa Pompilius, second king of Rome, was the first to worship Fides. Her feast day was 1 October.

1171
Fierabras, Sir. In the Charlemagne cycle of legends, one of the paladins. He was the son of Balan, king of Spain. Physically he was noted for his stature, breadth of shoulder, and hardness of muscle. He controlled all of Babylon to the Red Sea, and was Seigneur of Russia, lord of Cologne, master of Jerusalem and even of the Holy Sepulcher. He carried away the Crown of Thorns and the balsam used to embalm the body of Jesus, one drop of which would cure any sickness or heal any wound. One of his major feats was the slaying of the "fearful, huge giant that guarded the bridge Mantible." The bridge was noted for its 30 arches of black marble. Fierabras was at first a Saracen knight. He fought with the Christian knight Oliver, and was defeated and converted. He was then accepted by Charlemagne as a paladin. He died "meek as a lamb and humble as a chidden slave."

Variant spelling: Ferumbras.

1172
Fig. A fruit tree. The fig is often cited in European folklore as the fruit eaten by Adam and Eve in the Garden of Eden, as the biblical account in Genesis has the first couple covering "their nakedness" with fig leaves. Thus the fig has come to be connected in Jewish and Christian tradition with lust as well as fertility; but when shown on its tree in art, it signifies peace and plenty. An insulting sexual gesture, called "making a fig," is made by inserting the thumb between the index and middle fingers, indicating the vulva and the penis. Sicilian legend says that Judas hanged himself on a fig tree, and therefore the leaves of the tree house evil spirits. Another Sicilian legend says that if a man rests under a fig tree in the heat of summer a woman dressed as a nun will come and ask whether he will grasp the knife she is holding by the handle or by the blade. If he grasps the blade, the nun will stab him to death. If he grasps the handle, she will help him in all of his endeavors.

In India the god Vishnu is sometimes worshiped in the form of a fig tree, where, it is believed, his spirit hovers. A sacred fig with roots in heaven and branches and fruit on earth is a symbol of the cosmic tree in many mythologies.

The fig is sacred to Buddha because he was seated underneath the bo or pipal tree when he received the perfect knowledge and enlightenment of Nirvana.

1173
Finn. In Celtic mythology, hero who was the son of Cumhal, a king of the Tuatha de Danann, people of the goddess Danu. As a child Finn studied with a magician of the same name, who once caught the Salmon of Knowledge. Touching the Salmon, Finn burned his finger, which he then sucked to ease the pain. As a result he became the possessor of all knowledge.

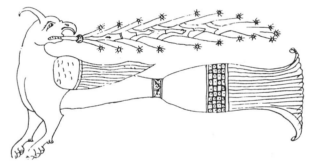

The Firebird

1174
Firebird, The. In Russian folklore, magical bird with golden wings and crystal eyes.

The Firebird appears in many Russian folktales. One of the best known is "Prince Ivan, the Firebird, and the Gray Wolf." One day the Firebird visited the king's garden and plucked golden apples from its magical tree. Ivan, the king's son, was told by his father to capture the Firebird when it returned. After some nights of waiting Ivan caught the bird, but it struggled and escaped. All that remained was a feather from its tail "so wonderful and bright that when carried into a dark chamber it shone as if a great multitude of tapers were lighting the place." Not satisfied, the king sent Ivan and his two brothers, Dmitri and Vassily, to capture the Firebird.

Along the way Ivan met a gray wolf, which aided him in all sorts of difficulties and helped him capture the Firebird. As part of Ivan's adventure's the gray wolf made him fall in love with a beautiful girl, Yelena. On their way home Ivan and Yelena stopped to rest, and Ivan's two brothers attacked the couple. Ivan was killed by Dmitri, and Yelena was taken back with the brothers to the king's palace. Ivan remained dead for some 30 days. After the gray wolf, using *mertvaya voda* (dead water) and *shivaya voda* (living water), restored him to life, Ivan went to his father's palace, claimed his due, and married Yelena. Igor Stravinsky's ballet *L'Oiseau de feu* (The Firebird) uses the well-known folktale, adding to it the evil Kostchei.

1175
Fish. In excavations of ancient Egypt mummified fish have been found. A fish cult existed in the city of Oxyrhynchus, where the mormyrus fish was worshiped. It was believed to have swallowed the phallus of Osiris, god of the dead, when his evil brother Set hacked his body to pieces. In Greek mythology the fish was sacred to Aphrodite, goddess of love, and to Poseidon, god of the sea. In the worship of Adonis a fish was offered to the dead. In Roman mythology the fish was sacred to Venus and to Neptune. In Norse mythology the fish was sacred to Frigga as goddess of love and fertility. In Sumero-Semitic rites the fish was sacrificed to Ishtar, Adapa, Ea, and Thammuz. In Hindu mythology the fish is one of the mounts of Vishnu as savior of the world when he came as a fish to aid Manu. In Christianity the fish is a symbol of Jesus Christ because the first letters of *Iesous Christos Theou Huios Soter* (Jesus Christ, Son of God, Savior) spell *ichthus*, the Greek word for fish. In Buddhist belief a fish is symbolic of the footprint of the Buddha, indicating freedom from desires and attachments.

1176
Flamen Dialis. In Roman ritual, a priest serving Jupiter. A Flamen Dialis could be married only once, could not be divorced, and had to resign his office if his wife died. His person could not touch a horse, flour, dogs, she-goats, beans, or raw meat. He was forbidden to have any knots on his clothing. His headdress was the apex, a conical hat wrapped with a strip of white wool. If the headdress fell off during some ritual, he had to resign office. The Flamen Martialis (Mars) and the Flamen Quirinalis (Quirinus) came from the patrician class; other flamen (of a group of 12 to 15) came from the plebeian class and had fewer restrictions on their persons.

1177
Flaming Angel. In Jewish and Christian mythology, angel often identified with Gabriel, Uriel, or Madiel.

The Flaming or, as he is sometimes called, the Fiery Angel, is mentioned several times in Jewish and Christian literature, His exact identification is not known because the name assigned to him varies

from work to work or is omitted entirely. In the New Testament Book of Revelation (14:18) he is identified as the angel "which had power over fire."

The Russian composer Prokofiev used the demonic aspect of the angel for his opera *The Flaming Angel*, giving the creature the name Madiel.

A painting by Marc Chagall entitled *Descent of the Red Angel* portrays the Flaming Angel descending to earth amid a burst of color.

1178
Flidais. In Celtic mythology, an Irish woodland goddess, wife of Ailill, mother of Fand, connected with hunting and protection of wild animals. Flidau had a magic cow that could produce milk for three hundred men in one night.

Flora

1179

Flora. In Roman mythology, goddess of flowering and blossoming plants; maried to Zephyrus, who gave her perpetual youth; equivalent to the Greek goddess Chloris. Flora's festival, *Floralia*, was held between 28 April and 1 May; it consisted of games and indecent farces. Ovid's *Fasti* (book 5) tells of the goddess, and Robert Herrick's poem *Corinna's Going a-Maying* also cites her.

1180

Florian, St. (flourishing). Fourth century. In Christian legend, one of the patron saints of Austria and Poland; patron of brewers, coopers, chimney sweeps, and soap boilers. Invoked against bad harvests, battles, fires, floods, and storms. Feast, 4 May.

Florian was a Roman soldier who, because he was a Christian, had a millstone tied around his neck and was thrown into the river Enns. One of his many miracles was to put out a large city fire with a single pitcher of water. His image often appears on fountains and pumps in Austria. In medieval Christian art he is portrayed as a young man in armor with a palm in his hand and a burning torch under his feet. Sometimes an eagle is shown near his dead body because legend says such a bird protected his body.

1181

Fly. Any of numerous two-winged insects. In Near Eastern mythology Beelzebub (Matt. 12:24), the Syrian god, was called Lord of the Flies. In Greek mythology Zeus was the god who warded off flies. In Jewish and Christian folklore, the fly is often identified with the devil.

1182

Flying Dutchman, The. Late medieval legend of a ship's captain condemned by God to wander about until the Last Judgment.

According to one account, the Flying Dutchman was a captain who persisted in trying to round the Cape of Good Hope in spite of the violence of a storm and the protests of his passengers and crew. Eventually, a form appeared (some accounts say it was God, others an angel of God) on the deck to warn the captain. Without warning the captain fired on the form and cursed it. As a punishment the Dutchman was condemned to sail and to be the torment of sailors until Judgment Day. Thus, he commands a spectral ship that perpetually rounds the Cape of Good Hope, luring other vessels to their doom. Wagner's opera *Der Fliegende Holländer* uses his own version of the legend.

1183

Fo. In Chinese Buddhism, the name of the Buddha, though it is applied to any person who has attained Buddhahood. Fo is an abbreviated Chinese transliteration of Buddha. In full, Fo-t'o, originally pronounced but-da; in Japan, pronounced *butsu-da*; in Vietnam, *phat*.

1184

Foma Berennikov. In Russian folklore, hero who said he had killed 12 mighty heroes but in actuality had killed 12 gadflies. His boasting and cleverness enabled him to defeat various other heroes. He finally married the daughter of the king of Prussia.

1185

Fomora (under, giant). In Celtic mythology, the gods of the original population in Ireland. They were regarded by the later Celtic inhabitants as hurtful, evil gods, though in reality they seem to have been mainly fertility gods. They were in opposition to the Tuatha de Danann, the gods and the people, or descendants, of the goddess Danu, who represented light and goodness.

1186

Fools, Feast of. In medieval Christianity, festival in honor of the ass on which Jesus made his triumphant entry into Jerusalem of Palm Sunday. The feast was held on 1 January, which is also the day of the feast of the Circumcision of Jesus. The Daily Offices were chanted but in travesty. A procession was formed, and all the town indulged in a fools parade. An ass was part of the feast, and instead of saying "Amen" at the end of prayers the congregation would bray.

Part of the celebration consisted of "fools" being "ordained" as priests and bishops. Dice would be played on the altar, or food eaten, such as puddings, cakes, or sausages. Shoes would be burned as incense, men would often dress as women, and masks would be worn. The Feast of Fools died out by the 16th century under pressure from Protestant Reformers, who disliked any kind of fun, and the Roman church no longer wanted to be identified with it. Scholars have traced the festival to the Roman *Festa Stultorum* and *Saturnalia*.

1187

Fornax (oven). In Roman mythology, goddess who presided over bread baking. Her festivals, called *Fornacalia*, were first instituted by Numa Pompilius, second king of Rome. Ovid's *Fasti* (book 2) tells of the feast, which was held 17 February or earlier.

1188

Forseti (he who sits in the front seat). In Norse mythology, god of justice and conciliation; son of

Baldur and Nanna, whose home was Glitnier. According to the *Prose Edda*, "all disputants at law who bring their cases before him go away perfectly reconciled."

Variant spelling: Forsete.

Fortuna

Fortuna (fortune) In Roman mythology, goddess of fortune, chance, and luck; identified with the Greek goddess Tyche. Originally, Fortuna was an ancient Italian goddess of increase and fertility, but she became goddess of fortune, thus the wheel of fortune. She was invoked by young Roman married women to grant fertility or a safe delivery. Her feast was 11 June according to Ovid's *Fasti* (book 6). The goddess continued to play a prominent role during the Christian Middle Ages, appearing in the 13th-century collection of songs in Latin, German, and French known as *Carmina burana*. Some of the texts

were set by Carl Orff. Fortuna was also known as Fors or Fors fortuna.

Fortunatus. In medieval legend, a hero who possesses an inexhaustible purse and a wishing cap. He is a man on the brink of starvation when Dame Fortune offers to bestow either wisdom, strength, riches, health, beauty, or long life. He chooses riches. She grants his wish, but the gift proves his ruin and that of his sons because of their greed.

Fourteen Holy Helpers, The. In Christian legend, a group of saints honored during the Middle Ages in Germany, Bohemia, Moravia, Hungary, Italy and France. Feast, 8 August.

The names of the 14 Holy Helpers vary, but the most common are the following: *Achatius* (feast, 22 June). *Barbara* (feast, 4 December). Invoked against lightning, fire, explosion, sudden and unprepared death; patron of architects, builders, and fireworks makers. *Blaise* (feast, 3 February). Invoked against throat infections; patron of physicians, wax chandlers, and wool combers. *Catherine of Alexandria* (feast, 25 November). Invoked by philosophers, saddlers, spinsters, students, and rope makers. *Christopher* (feast, 25 July). Invoked against storms and for a safe journey; patron of navigators, sailors, and travelers. *Cyriacus* (feast, 8 August). Invoked against demonic possession. *Denis* (feast, 9 October). Invoked against frenzy, hearabies, and strife. *Erasmus* (feast, 2 June). Invoked against birth pangs, colic, cattle pest, and danger at sea; patron of sailors. *Eustace* (feast, 20 September). Patron of huntsmen. *George* (feast, 23 April). Patron of calvarymen, chivalry, and soldiers. *Giles* (feast, 1 September). Invoked against epilepsy, insanity, and sterility. *Margaret* (feast, Invoked in childbirth and against barrenness or lack of milk; patron of women (virgins), nurses, and peasants. *Pantaleon* (feast, 27 July). Invoked against phthisis. *Vitus* (feast, 15 June). Invoked against epilepsy and St. Vitus dance.

Other saints sometimes included in the list are Dorothy (feast, 6 February), Leonard of Noblac (feast, 6 November), Oswald (feast, 5 August), and Nicholas (feast, 6 December).

The feast of the Fourteen Holy Helpers is still observed in some parts of Germany. A church in Baltimore, Maryland, is dedicated to the group.

Fox. A small wild animal of the dog family; in European mythologies, often a symbol of cunning; in Oriental mythologies women often turn into foxes and are beneficent creatures. Often equated with the devil in Christian symbolism, the fox is noted for his maliciousness, pious fraudulence, revengefulness and thievery. In numerous Aesop fables and fables based on Aesop, the fox is presented as an evil, clever being, out to destroy. In Dante's *Inferno*, part of *The Divine Comedy*, the spirit of Guido de Montefeltro, a famous warrior, says that his deeds were not those of a lion but of a fox. He used crafty, secretive ways to achieve his ends. Machiavelli's *The Prince* advises rulers to imitate two animals: the lion and the fox. The strength of the lion, Machiavelli says, is not sufficient for a ruler; he must also have the deceit of a fox.

Oriental mythologies often take a different approach. Japanese and Chinese tales abound with stories of fox transformations—women turned into foxes or foxes into women. In Oriental tales the appearance of a dog always forces the fox maiden into revealing her true nature. In Japanese folklore a fox maiden can be recognized by a spurt of flame flickering over her human head. The fox also has a strong sexual significance in Chinese and Japanese art and literature. The final panel of a four-panel Japanese screen portrays some merchants engaged in various sexual activities with different women. In the next panel the women have turned into vixens and the men into peasants. Janácek's opera *The Cunning Little Vixen* deals with a Czech legend of a woman turned into a fox.

1193

Fox and the Crow, The. Aesopic fable, probably of Indian origin because some of the *Jatakas, or Birth-Stories of the Former Lives of the Buddha* have the same moral.

A crow who had stolen a piece of cheese was flying toward the top of a tall tree, where he hoped to enjoy his prize, when a fox spied him. "If I plan this right," said the fox to himself, "I shall have cheese for supper."

So, as he sat under the tree, he began to speak in his politest tones: "Good day, Mistress Crow, how well you are looking today! How glossy your wings,

The Fox and the Crow

and your breast is the breast of an eagle. And your claws—I beg pardon—your talons are as are strong as steel. I have not heard your voice, but I am certain that it must surpass that of any other bird just as your beauty does."

The vain crow was pleased by all this flattery. She believed every word of it and waggled her tail and flapped her wings to show her pleasure. She liked especially what friend fox said about her voice, for she had sometimes been told that her caw was a bit rusty. So, chuckling to think how she was going to surprise the fox with her most beautiful caw, she opened her mouth wide.

Down dropped the piece of cheese! The wily fox snatched it before it touched the ground, and as he walked away, licking his chops, he offered these words of advice to the silly crow: "The next time someone praises your beauty be sure to hold your tongue."

Moral: Flatterers are not to be trusted.

There is an English proverb, "The fox praises the

1194

Fox and the Grapes, The. Aesopic fable found in numerous European collections such as Phaedrus, Babrius, and La Fontaine.

Mister Fox was just about famished, and thirsty too, when he stole into a vineyard where the sun-ripened grapes were hanging on a trellis too high for him to reach. He took a run and a jump, snapping at the nearest bunch, but missed. Again and again he jumped, only to miss the luscious prize. At last, worn out with his efforts, he retreated, muttering: "Well, I never really wanted those grapes anyway. I am sure they are sour."

Moral: Any fool can despise what he cannot get.

In La Fontaine's version the fox is something of an aristocrat. He says the grapes were only "fit for meat out of the crow's mouth." The fable is pictured on the Bayeux tapestry, and Thackeray makes use of it in his potpourri of fables in the Prologue to *The Newcomers.*

The Fox and the Grapes

peasants." The expression "sour grapes," used when someone belittles something he or she once wanted but was unable to obtain, is derived from this fable. A modern retelling of the fable, called *The Mookse and the Gripes*, is found in Joyce's *Finnegan's Wake*.

1195

Fox and the Mosquitoes, The. Aesopic fable found in various European collections.

A fox, after crossing a river, got its tail entangled in a bush and could not move. A number of mosquitoes, seeing its plight, settled on it and enjoyed a good meal undisturbed by its tail. A hedgehog strolling by took pity on the fox and went up to him. "You are in a bad way, neighbor," said the hedgehog. "Shall I relieve you by driving off those mosquitoes that are sucking your blood?"

"Thank you, Master Hedgehog," said the fox, "but I would rather not."

"Why, how is that?" asked the hedgehog.

"Well, you see," the fox answered, "these mosquitoes have had their fill; if you drive these away, others will come with fresh appetite and bleed me to death."

Aristotle credits Aesop with the authorship of this fable, and Joseph Jacobs in his edition of *The Fables of Aesop* says it is "the only fable which can be traced with any plausibility to Aesop." Of course, his argument assumes that Aesop was a real person. Roman emperors, Jacobs writes, had a special liking for this fable since they used it to console provincial officials when they were mistreated by proconsuls or procurators.

1196

Francesca da Rimini. 13th century C.E. In medieval history and legend, daughter of Guido da Polenta, lord of Ravenna. She was married to Malatesta, lord of Rimini, but her love for his younger brother, Paolo, was discovered by her husband, and the lovers were murdered by Malatesta in about 1289. In Dante's *The Divine Comedy* (Inferno, canto 5) she appears along with Paolo in Circle 2 of hell, where sins concerned with carnal love are punished. In Dante's work Francesca tells her own sad tale. Dante's poem inspired Tchaikovsky's fantasy for orchestra *Francesca da Rimini*, Rachmaninoff's opera *Francesca da Rimini*, and Zandonai's opera *Francesca da Rimini*.

1197

Francesca Romana, St. (a Frank). 1384–1440. In Christian legend, patron saint of Roman housewives. Feast, 9 March.

Francesca Romana was married to a rich nobleman, Lorenzo Ponziano, but spent most of her time in prayer. After his death she devoted what time was left to more prayer and works of charity.

Once when she was praying she was called away four times at the same verse. The fifth time she found the verse written in golden light on the page of her prayer book by her guardian angel. She is credited with raising a dead child to life, stopping an epidemic by her prayers and multiplying bread to feed the poor. In medieval Christian art she is often portrayed with her deacon (her guardian angel) by her side and holding a book. Sometimes she is portrayed as receiving the Christ Child from the Virgin Mary.

1198

Francis of Assisi, St. (the Frenchman). 1181?– 1226. Patron saint of animals, founder of Fratre Minori, known as the Franciscans, one of the three Mendicant Orders of Friars. Feast, 4 October.

Francis's father, Pietro Bernardone, was a rich merchant. Originally, Francis was named Giovanni, but he was called Francisco (the Frenchman) after his father had him trained in the French language in preparation for a business career. In his early years Francis was known for his passionate nature as well as for his love of all of the pleasures of life. In a quarrel between the people of Assisi and those of Perugia, Francis was taken prisoner and held for a year in the fortress of Perugia. After his release he was ill for many months. During this illness he spent time reflecting on the wasteful life he had led. Soon after his recovery, he met a beggar, whom he recognized as a man who had formerly been rich. Francis exchanged garments with the poor man, giving his rich cloak to the beggar and putting on the man's tattered garments. That night, in a vision, Francis saw himself in a beautiful apartment filled with all kinds of arms, rich jewels, and handsome garments—all of them marked with the sign of the cross. In the midst of the riches stood Jesus, who said to Francis: "These are the riches reserved for my servants and the weapons wherewith I arm those who fight for my cause." Francis took this to mean that he should become a soldier. After the vision Francis went to pray in the half-ruined church of San Damiano. As he knelt to pray a voice a voice said to him, "Francis, repair my church, which falleth to ruin."

Taking the command literally, Francis sold some merchandise and gave the money to the priests of San Damiano to repair the church. His father was so angry that Francis hid in a cave for some days to escape his wrath. When Francis returned to the city, he was so tired and ragged that he wasn't recognized. Believing him insane, Francis's father had him confined, but his mother set him free, begging him at the same time to obey his father and to stop his strange conduct. His father took him to the bishop, and when they were in the presence of the bishop, Francis took off his fine clothes and threw them at his father, saying, "Henceforth I recognize no father but Him who is in heaven." The bishop took a poor man's cloak and covered Francis's naked body. Francis was at that time 25 years of age. He then began taking care of lepers; he begged, wandered about the mountains, and later lived in a cell near the chapel of Santa Maria degli Angeli. Soon he was joined by disciples, who also wished to follow his simple life.

Numerous legends grew about his holy life. One, contained in *Fioretti di San Francisco* (The Little Flowers of St. Francis) tells of a journey to Siena during which he met "three maidens in poor raiment, and exactly resembling each other in age and appearance, who saluted him with the words, 'Welcome, Lady Poverty!' and suddenly disappeared. The brethren not irrationally concluded that this apparition imported some mystery pertaining to St. Francis, and that by the three poor maidens were signified Chastity, Obedience, and Poverty, the beauty and sum of evangelical perfection; all of which shone with equal and consummate luster in the man of God, though he made his chief glory the privilege of Poverty."

In time Francis went to Rome to obtain confirmation of his religious order. At first Pope Innocent III thought Francis was insane, but in a dream the pope saw the Church tottering and kept from falling only by the support of Francis. He immediately sent for Francis and approved his right to preach. Francis's following grew, and missionaries were sent to Muslim countries. Francis even went himself, reaching Damietta, where he was taken before the sultan. The sultan would not let Francis preach but also would not let him be martyred, and he was sent back to Italy. A few years later Pope Honorius confirmed his order. Francis resigned as its head and went to live in a cave on Mount Alverna. There he experienced many visions, the most famous being the one in which he received the Stigmata, the wounds of Jesus, earning him the title of "the Seraphic." Following is the description from *The Little Flowers of St. Francis:*

After having fasted for fifty days in his solitary cell on Mt. Alverna, and passed the time in all the fervor of prayer and ecstatic contemplation, transported almost to heaven by the ardor of his desires; then he beheld as it were a seraph with six shining wings, bearing down upon him from above, and between his wings was the form of a man crucified. By this he understood to be figured a heavenly and immortal intelligence, subject to death and humiliation. And it was manifested to him that he was to be trans-

formed into a resemblance to Christ, not by the martyrdom of the flesh, but by the might and fire of Divine love. When the vision had disappeared and he had recovered a little from its effect, it was seen that in his hands, his feet, and side he carried the wounds of our Savior.

Various legends are associated with Francis's love of animals. He preached to the birds about God's love. The most famous legend is that of the Wolf of Gubbio, who had been ravaging the countryside until Francis spoke to him. He told the wolf that food would be provided by the town, providing that he no longer attacked any of its inhabitants. The wolf obeyed the saint and became a friend of the people. Francis is known as the author of some poetry, among which the *Canticle of the Sun* is best known. His prayer, "Lord make me an instrument of your peace," has now been included in the American Book of Common Prayer of the Episcopal church.

Giotto's frescoes are the best known portrayals of the saint. Other artists who have painted Francis are El Greco, Dürer, and Rubens. Paul Hindemith used episodes from the saint's life for a ballet. In literature, Laurance Houseman's short plays, *Little Plays of St. Francis* (1922) deal with the saint.

1199

Francis Xavier, St. (the Frenchman). 1506–1610 C.E. In Christian legend, missionary. Born of a noble family at his father's castle in the Pyrenees, Francis went to Paris to study theology and there became a friend and associate of St. Ignatius Loyola, the founder of the Jesuits. He joined the community and was sent as a missionary to Goa in India. He spent the rest of his life in the East, and died while on a journey to China.

There are numerous legends of the saint recounted by Cardinal de Monte in his speech before Pope Gregory IX, on the canonization of Francis Xavier. One is the tale of the crab that brought Francis Xavier his crucifix. As Francis was sailing from Ambionum, a city of the Molucca Islands, to Baranula, the ship was overtaken by a storm, which threatened to wreck the vessel. Xavier took his crucifix from his neck and held it in the raging sea in order to still the billows. But suddenly the vessel lurched, and the crucifix dropped into the water. The ship arrived safely the next day at Baranula. When Xavier went ashore, a great crab leaped out of the sea, carrying the crucifix "devoutly, and in an upright direction between its fins." The crab made its way to Francis, delivered the crucifix, and returned to the sea.

The cardinal also told the canonization commission how Francis Xavier had the gift of tongues. As soon as Francis came into any of the strange countries where he preached, he spoke the language of the people instinctively, without any accent.

When Xavier died, his body was laid in a coffin filled with pure lime to consume the flesh. Four months afterward when the coffin was opened, it was found that the grave clothes were entirely intact and his flesh was as fresh as if the body had just died. No stench came from the body, but instead a sweet perfume. The body was put back into the coffin and taken to Malacca, which at the time was suffering from a plague. The moment the coffin arrived the plague ceased. A new coffin was made, but it was too small, and the body had to be forced into it, causing blood to spill out and stain the shroud. The coffin was buried in the churchyard of Our Blessed Lady and was opened again in nine months. Again, the body as fresh and the blood moist on the shroud. The body was now laid in a sumptuous coffin and carried to the Indies. It was received at Goa with great pomp, the viceroy himself taking part in the ceremony. No ointment, spices, or balm had been used, but his body "had a ravishing fragrance" and was laid on the right side of the high altar. Today, however, the body is nearly completely decayed.

Francis Xavier is often shown as a young bearded Jesuit with torch, flame, cross, and lily. Sometimes he is shown with St. Ignatius Loyola, holding a cross.

1200

Frankie and Johnny. American folk ballad, dating to the 19th century and first printed in 1912. It tells how Johnny, a St. Louis black procurer, was killed by his mistress, Frankie, a prostitute, when he went with another woman. There are more than 300 variants of the verses and music. Plays by Mae West and John Huston are based on the ballad, as well as a ballet *Frankie and Johnny*, with music by Jerome Moross. Hollywood's *Frankie and Johnny* (1966) uses the ballad for the tale of a Mississippi riverboat's gambling singer and his mistress, starring Elvis Presley.

1201

Franklin, Benjamin. 1706–1790. In American history and folklore, statesman, printer, scientist and writer, the American self-made man. He was noted in folklore for his great love of women, especially in old age. According to one legend, when he was in France, numerous ladies swarmed around the old man, each asking him if he loved her the most. Franklin's reply was, "Yes, when you are closest to me—because of the force of attraction." Aside from his *Autobiography*, Franklin's most famous work was *Poor Richard's Almanack*, issued from 1732 to 1757. Filled with maxims, some by Franklin but most

based on folk sayings and world literature, the work was extremely popular with the public. Among some of its most famous maxims are: Make haste slowly; God helps them that help themselves; Early to bed and early to rise / Makes a man healthy, wealthy, and wise; Nothing but money is sweeter than honey; Approve not of him who commends all you say.

Franklin was known during his lifetime as Ben the Magician because of his electrical experiments with the lightning rod. He invented the Franklin stove and bifocal spectacles.

1202

Fraus (fraud). In Roman mythology, goddess of treachery, daughter of Orcus (Dis, Hades, Pluto) and Night (Nox).

1203

Fravashis. In Persian mythology, spiritual primeval images of men, preexistent souls. They watch over procreation, do battle, are invoked against danger, and guard the seed of the prophet Zarathustra, which will later be planted in future saviors: Hushedar, Hushedar-man, and Soshyant. The *Zend Avesta*, which is the *Avesta* with a commentary, writes of the Fravashis, "which have existed from of old" and are found in houses, villages, communities, and provinces, that they "hold the heaven in its place apart, and the water, land and cattle, which hold the children in the wombs safely enclosed apart so they do not miscarry."

1204

Freki and Geri (greedy and ravenous). In Norse mythology, two wolves who sit by Odin, chief of the gods, when he feasts. Odin gives them all of the food set before him and only drinks, since food and wine are the same to the god. They appear in the *Poetic Edda* and the *Prose Edda*.

1205

Frenchy Aucion. In American folklore, a lumberman who was turned into a Canada jay after his death, only to be stripped of his feathers and thrown out into the cold night to return to hell.

1206

Frey (lord, master). In Norse mythology, god of fertility, peace, and wealth; son of Njord and patron god of Sweden and Iceland. Frey's wife was Gerda, daughter of mountain-giants Gymir and his wife Aurboda. When Frey first saw Gerda he immediately fell in love with her and sent his messenger Skirnir to her, telling him, "Go, and ask her hand for me, and bring her to me whether her father be willing or not, and I will amply reward you." Skirnir was willing to undertake the mission, provided he was given Frey's wonderful sword, which Frey then gave him. Eventually he returns with Gerda's promise that within nine nights she would come to a place called Barey and there marry Frey. The *Prose Edda* describes Frey as "one of the most celebrated of the gods. He presided over rain and sunshine, and all the fruits of the earth, and should be invoked in order to obtain good harvests and also peace. He moreover, dispenses wealth among men." Among Frey's treasures were Blodighofi (bloody-hoof), his magical horse; Gullinbursti (gold- bristled), a golden boar or a chariot drawn by a boar; and Skidbladnir (wooden-bladed), a magic ship that could be folded up like a tent. Frey's boar reflects the cult of the boar associated with the god. On the eve of the Yule festival a sacrifice called *sónargöltr* (atonement boar) was offered to make Frey favorable to the New Year. The ancient pagan cult still survives in Sweden in the cakes baked at Yule (now Christmastime) in the form of a boar. Frey was sometimes called Ingvi- Frey or Ingunar-Frey (Frey of Ingun) Edward Burne-Jones's painting of Frey portrays him seated with an olive branch and a boar at his feet.

1207

Freyja (the lady). In Norse mythology, one of the Vanir; goddess of youth, beauty, and sexual love; sister of the god Frey; married to Odur. Friday was sacred to the goddess and named after her. In Northern mythology Freyja and Frigga are often confused for the same deity. Freyja, in some accounts, was married to Odur, and their daughter was called Hnossa. But Odur left Freyja in order to travel around the world. Since that time Freyja continually weeps, and her tears are drops of gold. Freyja, according to the *Prose Edda*, rides into battlefields asserting "her right to one-half of the slain, the other half belonging to Odin." Her most famous possession is her necklace, Brising (necklace of the dwarfs?), given her by the dwarfs. One day while Freyja was in the underground kingdom of the dwarfs, she saw them fashion a necklace. She asked the dwarfs to give it to her. They refused at first, but eventually gave it to the goddess on condition she have sexual intercourse with them. Brising was later worn by the god Thor when he impersonated the goddess in order to trick the giants. The necklace was once stolen by the evil god Loki but recovered by Heimdall. Freyja, according to the *Prose Edda*, lends a very favorable ear to those who sue to her for assistance. "She is very fond of love ditties, and all lovers would do well to invoke her." Often in the myths Freyja is accussed of having sexual intercourse with many men and gods. The goddess is called a "she goat" that leaps after goats. The giantess Hyndla taunts the goddess by saying that "many have stolen under thy girdle." Freyja's

home is in Folkvang (field of folks) in which her hall Sessrumnir (rich in feasts) is located. Each day she leaves her mansion in a chariot drawn by two cats. Freyja is also called Mardoll (shining over the sea), Horn, Gefn, Syr, and Vanadjs.

Variant spellings: Frea, Frija, Freya, Foige.

1208

Frigga (lady, mistress, bearer?). In Norse mythology, an Aesir goddess, wife of Odin. She presides over marriage. In the *Prose Edda* she is in the front rank of the goddesses. Her home was Fensalir (sea hall), and she dressed in the plumage of falcons and hawks. Frigga has 11 maidservants: Fulla, Hlin, Gna, Lofn, Vjofn, Syn, Gefjon, Snotra, Eira, Vara, and Vor, who help the goddess preside over marriage and justice. She appears in Richard Wagner's *Der Ring des Nibelungen* as Fricka.

Variant spellings: Frigg, Frija, Fri.

1209

Frithjof's Saga. Thirteenth-century C.E. Icelandic saga believed to have originated in the eighth century C.E. Frithjof (spoiler of the peace) was the son of Thane Thorsten, the friend of King Bele of Norway. He played with the little Princess Ingebjorg and was sent with her to learn wisdom from the sage Hilding. When King Bele and Thorsten died, Princes Helgi and Halfdon assumed the throne. Frithjof inherited from his father a wonder-working sword, Angurvadel, with strange runes that dulled in peace and flamed in war; the arm ring of Wayland the Smith; and *Ellide*, the dragon ship. After the death feast of his father, Frithjof went to the land of Helgi and Halfdon to ask for the hand of Ingebjorg, their sister, in marriage. Helgi sneered at the idea. Another suitor, King Ring, an old widower, was also rejected and returned to make war on Helgi and Halfdon. Ingebjorg was then locked up in Baldur's temple. Frithjof entered the sacred temple, having no fear that he profaned it. He offered to help Ingebjorg's brothers, but they refused his aid. Defaming Baldur's temple was a crime, and on pain of perpetual exile Frithjof was forced to wrest from Yarl Angantyr the tribute due to the sons of King Bele.

Unable to persuade Ingebjorg to go with him, he set sail for an island ruled over by Yarl Angantyr. His dragon ship made a safe voyage even though Helgi caused a storm to be raised by the sea-witches Heyd and Ham. Before reaching the castle he overcame the Viking Atli but spared his life because of Atli's fearlessness; the two became friends. Frithjof was welcomed by Yarl Angantyr, his father's friend, who had given presents, not tribute, to King Bele and had been rewarded with a purse of gold. Remaining with Yarl Angantyr until spring, Frithjof then sailed for seven days to Framnas, only to find that it had been burned and was in ruins. He learned from Hilding that King Ring had married Ingebjorg.

Angry at the turn of events, Frithjof went to the temple of Baldur during a midsummer feast and fought with Helgi in single combat. When he noticed that Ingebjorg's armlet was on the image of the god Baldur, he pulled it off, causing the god's statue to fall into the fire. The temple caught fire, and the surrounding area was set ablaze. Frithjof fled, chased by Helgi with ten warships. Bjorn, however, had bored holes in the ships the previous night, and all aboard were drowned except for Helgi.

Frithjof became a pirate for three years. On his return he dressed as a beggar and appeared at the Yuletide feast of King Ring. When a soldier made fun of Frithjof, he caught him and turned him head over heels. King Ring asked the beggar to take off his disguise but did not seem to recognize Frithjof, though Ingebjorg did. Twice Frithjof had his enemy's life in his hands. But the old king had

recognized him from the first. Finally, King Ring plunged a sword into his own chest. Before Frithjof married Ingebjorg, he went to seek forgiveness from the god Baldur. He made a temple to the god and the wedding took place.

This medieval saga inspired the 19th-century narrative poem *Frithiof-Saga* or *Lay of Frithiof* by Esaias Tegnér, bishop of Vaxjo, Sweden. The work was known to Henry Wadsworth Longfellow, who translated the bishop's narrative poem, ''The Children of the Lord's Supper.''

1210

Frode. In Danish legend, a king who had a magic millstone that ground out gold for him. When he demanded more and more gold, the two giant maidens Frenja and Menja ground out salt. This killed Frode and brought famine to the land.

1211

Frog. A tailless amphibian having long hind legs used for jumping. In Egyptian mythology the frog goddess was Heket and the four male primeval gods

The Frog and the Ox

of the Ogdoad, which formed a group of eight deities who created the world, were portrayed as frog-headed. In Greek and Roman mythology the frog was associated with Aphrodite and Venus, as goddesses of sex and love.

In Christianity the frog is often a symbol of evil. But often the frog and toad are confused in Christian symbolism. Shakespeare's King Richard III is called "this poisonous hunchback'd toad" (1.3) and in Milton's *Paradise Lost* Satan takes the form of a toad to squat at the ear of the sleeping Eve and distill poison into her blood. This recalls the European belief that toads are venomous creatures whose blood, if drunk, would kill instantly. The antidote for toad poison is a jewel found in the toad's head; its existence being a common folk belief.

Some Freudians have viewed the frog as symbolic of the penis. At first the penis is feared by a woman, they contend, but once she experiences sexual contact and pleasure, she realizes that the object of her fear is actually something desirable. This motif is supported in the Grimm folktale *The Frog Prince*. The theory is interesting, but in many variants of the tale the frog turns into a woman.

Frog and the Ox, The. Aesopic fable found in various European collections.

Some frogs had just had a harrowing experience down at the swampy meadow, and they came hopping home to report their adventure.

"Oh, Father," said one of the little frogs, all out of breath, "we have just seen the most terrible monster in all the world. It was enormous, with horns on its head and a long tail and hooves—"

"Why, child, that was no monster. That was only an ox. He isn't so big! If I really put my mind to it, I could make myself as big as an ox. Just watch me!" So the old frog blew himself up. "Was he as big as I am now?" he asked.

"Oh, Father, much bigger," cried the little frogs. Again the father frog blew himself up and asked his children if the ox could be as big as that.

"Bigger, Father, a great deal bigger," chorused the little frogs. "If you blew yourself up until you burst, you could not be as big as the monster we saw in the swampy meadow."

Provoked at being outdone, the old frog made one more attempt. He blew and blew and swelled and swelled until something went *pop*. The old frog had burst.

Moral: Self-conceit leads to self-destruction.

The fable is told by Horace in his *Satires* (book 2), as well as by Thomas Carlyle in his *Miscellanies*, from a German variant. Thackeray uses it in the Prologue to his novel *The Newcomers*.

Froh. In Norse mythology, an ancient god and all-father, whose worship was supplanted by Odin's cult. He appears in Wagner's *Der Ring des Nibelungen*.

Frolka Stay-at-Home. In Russian folklore, a hero who rescued three princesses who had been kidnapped. The first was held by a 5-headed dragon, the second by a 7-headed dragon, and the third by a 12-headed dragon. Frolka, aided by a nameless soldier and a man called Erema, defeated all three monsters.

Fu Daishi. Japanese name for Chinese Buddhist priest credited with the invention of the revolving bookcase, containing the 6,771 sacred books of Buddhism. It is believed that if the bookcase is revolved, three times more merit will be obtained than if one read all of the volumes.

Fuji Hime. In Japanese mythology, Princess Fuji, who inhabits Fuji Yama, the most famous mountain in Japan. Called Ko-no-hana-saku-ya-hime (princess who causes the blossoms of trees to flower), she is portrayed in Japanese art with a large sun hat and a twig of wisteria in her hand.

Fulgora (lightning). In Roman mythology, goddess who protected houses against violent storms.

Furina (thief). In Roman mythology, goddess of robbers, worshiped at a sacred grove in Rome. In some ancient texts she is identified with the Furies. Her festivals were called *Furinelia*.

Fushi Ikazuchi. In Japanese mythology, one of the Ikazuchi, the eight gods of thunder.

Futen. In Japanese Buddhist mythology, god of the winds, derived from the Hindu wind god, Vayu. He is portrayed as an old man, bareheaded, with flowing beard and garments, walking and holding in his left hand a banner blown by the wind. He is one of the Jiu No O, 12 Japanese Buddhist gods and goddesses adopted from Hindu mythology.

Fylgia (follower). In Norwegian folklore, a guardian spirit, or one's double or soul. Often the *fylgia* appears in dreams in animal form. If one sees the *fylgia* when awake, it indicates one's death. When a person dies, the *fylgia* passes on to another member of the family.

G

Gabriel (God is my strength). In Jewish, Christian, and Islamic mythology, archangel. Feast, 18 March in the Western church.

Gabriel plays a prominent role in the Bible as a messenger of God. He first announces to Daniel the return of the Jews from their captivity (Dan. 8:16) and explains the vision of the various nations (Dan. 9:21). In the New Testament Gabriel announces to Zacharias the coming birth of John the Baptist (Luke 1:19) and to the Virgin Mary that she will be the mother of Jesus (Luke 1:26). In Islam the Koran credits Gabriel, who is called Jiburili (Jibril), with dictating from the perfect copy in heaven the earthly copy of the Koran.

Milton, in *Paradise Lost* (book 4:550), calls Gabriel the "Chief of the angelic guards," recalling a Jewish belief. In his musical *Anything Goes* Cole Porter has a brilliant song, "Blow, Gabriel, Blow," which credits the angel with a magnificent trumpet and the task of announcing the end of the world. (The song was introduced by Ethel Merman.)

In Western Christian art Gabriel is usually portrayed as the messenger to the Virgin Mary announcing the coming birth of Jesus. He is often shown kneeling before her, holding a scroll with the words *Ave Maria, gratia plena* (Hail Mary, full of grace). In Greek and Byzantine portrayals Gabriel is usually shown standing, not kneeling.

Gada. In Hindu mythology, the younger brother of Krishna (an incarnation of the god Vishnu).

Gaea (earth). In Greek mythology, Mother Earth; child of air and day of sprung directly form chaos; called Terra or Tellus by the Romans. After the rule of Chaos (one of the infernal deities), Gaea appeared and gave birth to Uranus (the upper regions covering the earth). Then after having sexual intercourse with Uranus, she bore Cronus, Pallas, Oceanus, the Clyclopes, and the Titans. From the spilled blood and semen of Uranus she gave birth to the Erinyes, the giants, the Meliae, and Aurora. From the severed genitals of Uranus she became the mother of Aphrodite. An affair with Hephaestus produced Erichthonius; by Oceanus she bore Ceto, Crius, Eurybia, Nereus, Phorcys, and Thaumas; by Poseidon she bore Ogyges, Charybdis, and Antaeus. She is also the mother of Cecrops, Cranaus, Echo, Palaechthon, Rumor, Arion, and the serpent that guarded the Golden Fleece. Gaea appears in Hesiod's *Theogony* (116 ff.), The Homeric Hymns (not by Homer), and Vergil's *Aeneid*.

Variant spellings: Ge, Gaia.

Gagavitz (hill of fire). In the mythology of the Cakchiquels, a branch of the Mayan Indians, progenitor and culture hero. The myths of Gagavitz are related in *The Annals of the Cakchiquels* (16th century), along with their legendary history. Early in the book, Gagvitz's companion Zactecauh (white mountain, hill of snow) is killed trying to cross a ravine, leaving Gagavitz alone. The hero arrives at Gagxanul (the naked volcano), now called Santa Maria, and is asked by the Indians there to help them capture fire. One Indian, Zakitzunún (white sparrow), offered to help. Gagavitz descended into the volcano while Zakitzunún threw water mixed with green stems of corn into the hole. Gagavitz stayed for some time, and the people were fearful he had been killed; but he emerged, bringing fire. The two were called heroes. Later Gagavitz sent warriors to capture Tolgom, then changed himself into a serpent, and died, leaving two sons, Caynoh and Gaybatz.

Galahad (hawk of battle). In Arthurian legend, the purest and noblest knight, son of Lancelot and Elaine, who seeks the Holy Grail.

When the Round Table was founded, one seat, the Siege Perilous, was left unoccupied and could be used only by the knight who would succeed in the quest for the Holy Grail. All others who had attempted to sit in the seat had been swallowed up by the earth. When Sir Galahad sat in the seat, he was unharmed. Galahad went in search of the Holy Grail, even "took the Lord's body between his hands," and then died. Suddenly, according to one medieval source, "a great multitude of angels did bear his soul up to heaven" and "since then was never no man that could say he had seen the Holy Grail."

Galanthis (weasel). In Greek mythology, Alcmena's maid. She aided her mistress during the birth of Heracles when Hera sent the childbirth goddess, Ilithyia, transformed by the gods into an inexhaustible stream of limpid water, which runs down to the sea to join Galatea. Theocritus' *Idylls* (11) and Ovid's *Metamorphoses* (book 13) tell of the myth, as does Handel's opera *Acis and Galatea* (1721) with a libretto by John Gay. The name Galatea also is given to the statue by Pygmalion that was turned into a live woman by Aphrodite. Pygmalion and Galatea became the parents of Paphos. This myth is told in Ovid's *Metamorphoses* (book 10).

1229

Gama Sennin. In Japanese legend, a deified mortal portrayed holding a frog, sometimes three-legged, in his hand, or with the animal climbing over his clothes or shoulder. Various folktales account for the iconography connected with Gama Sennin. One version tells how Gama Sennin went to bathe and was followed by a man named Bagen, who assumed the form of a frog to observe him. In a variant tale Gama Sennin took the form of a frog whenever he went near the water. In still another, Gama Sennin sold a drug to Bagen that made Bagen live 100 years. This incident is portrayed with Gama Sennin giving the pill to a frog, who is Bagen.

1230

Gandharvas. In Hindu mythology, celestial musicians who sing on mountaintops, under the god Varuna. Sometimes they are dangerous at twilight. Originally, there was only one Gandharva, mentioned in the sacred collection of hymns, the *Rig-Veda*; he guarded the sacred Soma juice. In present-day Hinduism the Gandharvas watch over marriage and protect virgins. One of their homes is in Alaka, located on the sacred mountain Meru. An aerial city, Vismapana (astounding), which appears and disappears, also is said to be one of their homes. It is often called Gandharva-nagana (capital city of the Gandharvas). In post- Vedic Hinduism and in Buddhism, Vismapana is a synonym for a mirage.

1231

Ganelon. In the Charlemagne cycle of legends, a traitor. He was the count of Mayence and one of Charlemagne's paladins. Jealousy of Roland made him betray them all. He planned his evil deed with Marsillus, the Moorish king, and was successful. The Christians were defeated at the battle of Roncesvalles, which forms one of the main episodes of *The Song of Roland*. Ganelon was 6½ feet tall, with large glaring eyes and fiery red hair. He was taciturn and morose. In European legend his name became a byword for a false and faithless friend. He appears in Dante's *The Divine Comedy* (Inferno) and is grouped by Chaucer with Judas, the betrayer of Jesus, in *The Nun's Priest's Tale* in *The Canterbury Tales*.

Sir Galahad

to retard Alcmena's labor with magic incantations. Galanthis fooled Ilithyia by pretending that Alcmena had already delivered. Caught off guard, Ilithyia's spell was broken and Alcmena immediately delivered Heracles. In a fury Ilithyia transformed Galanthis into a weasel. Ovid's *Metamorphoses* (book 9) tells of her transformation.

1228

Galatea (milk-white). In Greek mythology, a Nereid, one of the 50 daughters of Nereus and Doris; sister of Thetis and Amphitrite. Galatea loved the handsome youth Acis, and the Cyclops Polyphemus loved Galatea. When Polyphemus saw Galatea and Acis alone, he killed Acis by hurling a rock at him. The stream of blood from Acis' mangled body was

GANESA.

Ganesha

1232

Ganesha (lord of hosts). In Hindu mythology, the elephant-headed god of wisdom and good fortune.

Ganesha is one of the most popular gods in present-day Hinduism. All sacrifices and religious ceremonies, all literary and musical compositions, all worldly affairs (except funerals) are begun with an invocation to Ganesha. Most Hindu texts open with a ''reverence to Ganesha'' or ''salutation to Ganesha.''

There are a variety of myths accounting for his elephant head and human body. One is that his mother, Parvati, wife of the god Shiva, was so proud of her offspring, that she asked Sani (Saturn) to look at the child. Sani looked on Ganesha and the child's head was immediately burned to ashes. The god Brahma told Parvati to replace the head with the first head she could find—it was an elephant's head.

A variant myth tells how Parvati went to bathe and told her son Ganesha to watch the door so that no one would disturb her. Shiva, her husband, wished to enter. Ganesha tried to stop his father, and Shiva cut the lad's head off. To pacify Parvati, Shiva replaced the head with the first one he could acquire, which was an elephant's head. Another variant tells how Parvati formed Ganesha's head to suit her own desire, and yet another myth tells how Shiva was cursed for slaying Aditya (the sun) and was punished by having his son lose his head. To replace the head Indra used the head from his elephant mount.

Elephant-headed Ganesha, however, has only one tusk. The loss of the other tusk is accounted for in various myths. One says Ganesha used one of his tusks to transcribe the epic poem *The Mahabharata* and then lost it. In another myth his belly burst open from overeating, and the moon laughed at him; so Ganesha broke off his tusk and threw it at the moon, which slowly darkened as a result. In either case Ganesha is called Eka-danta (the single-tusked). Ganesha is leader of the Gana Devatas (troops of lesser gods); who attend his father Shiva.

One Hindu sect, the Ganapatyas, regard Ganesha as the supreme being or god. In the *Ganapati Upanishad* he is thus addressed:

Praise to thee, O Ganesha!
Thou art manifestly the truth; thou art undoubtedly the creator, Preserver, and Destroyer,
the supreme Brahma, the eternal spirit.

In Indian art Ganesha is portrayed as a short fat man with a big belly, four hands, and, of course, his elephant head. In one hand he holds a conch shell, in another a discus, in the third a club or goad, and in the fourth a lotus. Sometimes he is seen riding on a mouse or attended by one, indicating, according to some accounts, his conquest of demonic forces symbolized by the rodent.

Ganesha has many epithets, among them Kari-mikha (elephant-faced), Heramba (boastful), Lamba-karna (long-eared), Lambodara (pendent-bellied), Dwi-deha (double-bodies), Vighna-hara (remover of obstacles), and Dwai-matura (having two mothers), an allusion to another birth myth that he was born from the sweat of his mother Parvati's body.

Variant spellings: Ganesa, Gunesh, Gunputty.

1233

Ganges (going strongly or swiftly). In India, sacred river and goddess whose waters are believed to have the power of cleansing one of past, present, and future sins.

According to Hindu mythology the Viyad-ganga (heavenly Ganges) flowed from the toe of the god Vishnu (some texts say Shiva) and was brought to earth by the prayers of Bhagirathi, a holy man. Bhagirathi called down the river to cleanse the ashes of the 100 sons of King Sagara; they had been burned to death by the sage Kapila after they had accused Kapila of stealing a horse that was to be sacrificed. The sage, having his devotions interrupted "looked upon them for an instant, and they were reduced to ashes by the flames that darted from his person," according to one account. Some texts identify Kapila with the firegod Agni. Though Bhagirathi called the river down to earth, Ganga (who is also a goddess) was caught by the god Shiva on his brow, and her fall was checked by his matted locks. From this action, Shiva gained the epithet Ganga-dhara (upholder or controller of the Ganges). The river descended from Shiva's brow in several streams: four in some accounts, ten in others, seven being the generally accepted number. Another name for the river is Sapta-sindhava (the seven rivers).

Ganymede on Zeus' eagle

1234

Ganymede (rejoicing in virility). In Greek mythology, a beautiful Trojan boy, son of Tros and Callirrhoë; brother of Assaracus, Cleopatra, and Ilus; called Catamitus by the Romans. Zeus, in the form of an eagle, seduced Ganymede and brought him to Olympus to be his cupbearer. Hera, Zeus's wife, hated the boy whom Zeus loved. In an earlier version of the myth Ganymede was the son of King Tros and was carried off by Zeus in exchange for some horses. In the *Hymn to Aphrodite*, one of the hymns attributed to Homer but not by him, Ganymede is carried to heaven by a storm wind; but in Vergil's *Aeneid* (book 5) he was snatched up by an eagle or, according to Ovid's *Metamorphoses* (book 10), by Zeus himself. In some accounts of the myth the eagle was turned into the constellation Aquila and Ganymede into Aquarius. In Greek art Ganymede is portrayed as a beautiful youth. On one fifth-century B.C.E. red-figure mixing bowl he is shown holding a hoop and

cock, favorite gifts from older men to young men. Ganymede's myth is used in Aristophanes' play *Peace*, and Plato uses it in his dialogue *Phaedrus* to explain Socrates' love for his male pupils. During the Christian Middle Ages, Ganymede became a term for a homosexual. Marlowe's play *The Tragedy of Dido, Queen of Carthage* (1594) opens with a scene between Jupiter and Ganymede. Ganymede asks Jupiter a favor and in return Jupiter says, "I will spend my time in thy bright arms." Ganymede has been painted by Corregio, Rubens, and Rembrandt.

1235

Garboncias. In Hungarian folklore, a supernatural being, born with all of his teeth or with extra fingers. The being exercises magical powers when in a trance. It often carries a big black book and begs for milk. Garboncias is similar to Tatlos, another supernatural being with magical powers in Hungarian folklore.

1236

Garden of the Hesperides. In Greek mythology, a garden owned by Atlas that contained a tree with golden apples guarded by the Hesperides and Ladon, a dragon. The tree was a gift to Hera when she married Zeus. Heracles 11th labor was to obtain the apples. He killed the dragon and took the apples, but they could exist only in the magic garden, so they were given to Athena, who returned then. Paris presented one of the golden apples to Aphrodite when he chose her in the Judgment of Paris. Hesiod's *Theogony*, Ovid's *Metamorphoses* (book 4), and Tennyson's *The Hesperides* deal with the myth.

1237

Gareth (gentle). In Arthurian legend, the youngest son of King Lot of Orkney and Margawse, Arthur's half sister. Gareth's mother did not want her son to be at Arthur's court and jestingly said she would consent to his going there only if he concealed his name and went as a scullion for 12 months. Gareth agreed. Sir Kay, the king's steward, named him Beaumains because his hands were extremely large. At the end of a year Gareth was knighted. He aided Lynette by freeing her sister, Liones (Lyonors), who was being held prisoner by Sir Ironside at Castle Perilous. At first Lynette treated Gareth with scorn, calling him a dishwasher and a kitchen boy. After Gareth overthrew five knights and freed her sister, she changed her opinion of him. Tennyson retells the tale in *Gareth and Lynette*, part of his *Idylls of the King*. He changed the medieval legend and has Gareth marry Lynette instead of her sister, Liones.

1238
Gargantua (gullet). In medieval European folklore, a giant famous for his enormous appetite. He appears in Rabelais's *Gargantua and Pantagruel*, in which he is the father of Pantagruel. One of his most famous exploits is to swallow five pilgrims in a salad. Rabelais says that when Gargantua was born he was so large that one of his parents cried out *Que grand tu as!* (how large you are!), which sounds like "Gargantua." In *As You Like It* Shakespeare has a character say: "You must borrow me Gargantua's mouth first: 'tis a word too great for any mouth of this age's size."

1239
Garide Bird. In Siberian mythology, a fantastic bird who defeated the evil giant snakeLosy. He was a form of the creator god Otshirvani and is a variant of the Garuda bird in Hindu mythology.

1240
Garlic. A strong-flavored spice. In European folklore garlic was supposed to keep vampires away and was worn in a small bag around the neck. It is used extensively in folk medicine.

1241
Garm (barking). In Norse mythology, the hound of the underworld, chained in Gnipahellir, the cave at the entrance to Niflheim. Garm will break loose at Ragnarok (the end of the world) and kill the god Tyr and in turn by killed by Tyr. Garm appears in the *Prose Edda* and the *Poetic Edda*.
Variant spelling: Garmr.

Garuda

1242
Garuda (the devourer). In Hindu mythology, a fantastic bird on which the god Vishnu rides.

Garuda is the enemy of all serpents and the king of all birds, having inherited his hatred for serpents from his mother, Vinata, who had quarreled with Kadru, the mother of serpents. When Garuda was born, he was mistaken for Agni, the fire god, because of his brilliance. (He is identified in some texts with fire and the sun.)

Once Garuda stole the Amrita, the water of life, from the gods in order to purchase with it the freedom of his mother Vinata, who was under the control of the evil Kadru. Indra discovered the theft and fought a fierce battle with Garuda, in which the Amrita was recovered but Indra's thunderbolt was smashed.

One myth in the epic poem *The Mahabharata* tells how Garuda's parents gave him permission to eat any evil man but not to touch any priest. Once, however, Garuda swallowed a Brahman and his wife, but the Brahman so burned Garuda's throat that he disgorged both the priest and his wife.

In Indian art Garuda is portrayed as having the head, wings, talons, and back of an eagle and the body and limbs of a man. His face is white, his wings are red, and his body is golden; or he may be green.

Garuda has many epithets, among them Garutman (chief of birds); Pannaga-nasana (destroyer of serpents), Sarparati (enemy of serpents), Taraswin (the swift), and Vishnu-ratha (vehicle of Vishnu), in reference to his being the god's mount. Sometimes Garuda takes the form of Tarkshya, a fantastic figure who appears in some myths as a horse or bird. In variants Tarkshya is called the father of Garuda. Garuda is also called Aksha in some texts.

1243
Gasparilla, José Gaspar. d. 1821. In American history and folklore, king of the pirates who established the kingdom of Gasparilla Island on the Florida Gulf Coast. He would capture a ship, kill all of the men and take all the women into his harem. When he was finally captured by an American ship, he tied a cabin chain around his waist and jumped overboard, drowning himself.

1244
Gasterocheires (bellies with hands). In Greek mythology, the seven Cyclops who built the walls of Tiryns, a city of Argolis in the Peloponwesus, southeast of Argos, founded by Tirynx or Proctus.

1245

Gayomart. In Persian mythology, primeval man and culture hero, created by the good god, Ahura Mazda, and later killed by the evil spirit, Ahriman.

Gayomart appears in the Persian epic poem *Shah Namah*, by Firdusi, as the first king in the world. He lived in the mountains and dressed in animal skins. The animals "assembled round his throne, and did him homage." He had a son, Siyamek, whom he dearly loved, but a demon slew the lad. Later the demon himself was slain by Husheng, the son of Siyamek. Firdusi found Gayomart in Persian mythology, which tells how he was created along with the Celestial Bull. The evil Ahriman, however, "fell . . . upon the Bull and Gayomart: and slew them both." The seed of Gayomart fell to the ground, as did the seed of the Celestial Bull. From Gayomart's seed a rhubarb plant sprung up, which produced the first human couples; from the Celestial Bull's seed all kinds of animals arose.

In Persian art Gayomart often appears dressed in animal skins teaching his people the arts of civilization. Sometimes his robes are more elaborate, with only a hint of the animal-skin origin.

Variant spellings: Gaiumart, Gaya-Maretan, Gayo-Maratan, Gayomard, Gayumarth, Kaiomarts, Kaiumers, Kayumard, Kayumurs.

Geb

1246

Geb (earth). In Egyptian mythology, god who personified the earth's surface; the brother-husband of the sky goddess Nut. According to one myth, Geb was separated from Nut by the god Shu at the request of the sun god Ra, who was angered over their sexual embrace. Thus, the sky above and the earth below were created. The separation, however, left Geb inconsolable, and he cried so fiercely his wailing could be heard day and night, and his tears filled the oceans and seas.

Geb was often portrayed in Egyptian art in grief, lying under the feet of Shu, his head raised on one arm, and one knee bent. He is identified in some myths as the father of Osiris, Isis, Nephthys, Set, and Horus, and as such he was known as "father of the gods" or "chief of the gods." Geb also was portrayed as a man wearing on his head a goose, which is the hieroglyph of his name. The animal was also sacred to him, Geb being called Kenken-ur (the great cackler), referring to the belief expressed in some myths that he laid the egg from which the world sprang. In classical Greek times Geb was identified with Cronus, who was the father of the great Olympian deities.

Variant spellings: Keb, Qeb, Seb.

1247

Geirrod and Agnar (spear thrower). In Norse mythology, sons of King Hrauding; one evil, the other good; watched over by the god Odin and his wife Frigga. One day, when the two boys were eight and ten years old, they went fishing. Suddenly a storm arose, and their boat drifted far out to sea. It was finally stranded on an island inhabited by an old couple, Odin and Frigga in disguise. The boys were warmly welcomed and kindly treated, Odin choosing Geirrod as his favorite and teaching him the use of arms, while Frigga chose Agnar as her favorite. The boys stayed on the island for the winter. When spring came, they left for home on a boat that Odin provided. As the boat neared the shore, Geirrod quickly sprang out and shoved it far into the water, bidding his brother sail away. The wind veered, and Agnar was carried off, while Geirrod hurried home. He was joyfully received by his father, King Hrauding, and in time succeeded him on the throne.

Years later Odin taunted his wife, Frigga, about the outcome of the boys—his favorite had become king, whereas her favorite had married a giantess. Frigga replied that Agnar had a kind heart, but Geirrod was evil and lacked hospitality, mistreating his guests. Odin said he would prove that the charge was not true. Assuming the guise of a wanderer, wearing his cloud-colored cloak and slouch hat and carrying his pilgrim staff, Odin set out. But Frigga, to outwit him, sent Geirrod a secret warning to beware of a man in a wide mantle and broad-brimmed hat, saying he was a wicked enchanter who would destroy Geirrod.

As soon as Odin arrived, he was arrested and chained between two fires, which, however, did not destroy him. Eight days passed and he was given no food, except for some ale that Agnar, who was a menial servant in his brother's palace, gave him. At the end of the eighth day Odin began to sing, first softly, then louder, a prophecy that the king would die by his own sword. As the last notes of the prophecy ended, the chains fell, the flames went out, and Odin appeared in his godlike form. Geirrod drew his sword to kill Odin but tripped and fell on the blade. Agnar then was made king by Odin. In some accounts Agnar is said to have been the son of Geirrod, not his brother.

Variant spelling: Geirroth.

Genius

1248
Genius (guardian spirit). In Roman mythology, a spirit who presided over the birth of a person, a place, or a thing, determining character and destiny. Genius is related to the Greek concept of the Daemon. A person's genius came into being at his birth and accompanied him throughout life, becoming his other living soul after death. Often a personal genius was portrayed as a person, but a genius of a place was portrayed as a serpent. In Shakespeare's *Comedy of Errors* (5.1.332–4) the Duke says of the twins Antipholi and Dromios:

One of these men is genius to the other;
And so of these, which is the natural man
And which the spirit?

Spenser cites genius as a god of generation in both his *Epithalamion* (398–9) and *The Faerie Queene*

(3.6.31–2). Milton's *Ode on the Morning of Christ's Nativity* (184–6) uses the word to refer to departing pagan gods.

1249
George, St. (tiller of the ground). Third century C.E. In Christian legend, patron saint of England, Germany, and Venice; also of soldiers and armorers. Greek Christians gave the title Great Martyr to St. George and venerated him as one of the most important saints in the Eastern church. Feast, 23 April.

In Western Europe St. George's fame was established during the Crusades when Western and Eastern churches came into contact with one another. His cult was brought to England in the 14th century by Edward III, who chose him as patron of England. There are many versions of the saint's life, the most popular being the one in *The Golden Legend* by Jacobus de Voragine. St. George was a knight born in Cappadocia. In one of its cities a dragon molested the population. To appease it, lots were cast for either a young man or a woman to feed to it so that it would not destroy the entire population. One day the lot fell to the daughter of the king. The king tried to stall the event, but the young girl finally had to offer herself to the dragon. Just as the dragon was about the attack the girl, St. George appeared on his horse and "drew out his sword and garnished him with the sign of the cross" and then attacked the dragon, which fell to the ground. George then took the young girl's girdle and placed it around the dragon's neck, and the "dragon followed her as if it had been a meek beast and debonair." St. George is a favorite subject with artists. Among those who painted him are Mantegna, Jan Van Eyck, Rubens, Raphael, Tintoretto, and Dante G. Rossetti. He appears in an old ballad in Percy's *Reliques* and in Spenser's *The Faerie Queen*.

1250
Gerda (fence enclosing tilled land). In Norse mythology, wife of Frey; "the most beautiful of women," according to the *Prose Edda*. She was the daughter of Gymir and the giantess Aurboda and was wooed by the god Frey, whom she at first refused. She finally accepted numerous gifts from the god.

Variant spellings: Gerdr, Gerd.

1251
Germanicus Caesar. 15 B.C.E.–19 C.E. In Roman history and legend, general, nephew, and adopted son of the Emperor Tiberius. According to legend, he was poisoned through black magic by Cnaeus Piso, governor of Syria. Poussin's *The Death of Germanicus* pictures his death.

Geronimo. 1829–1909. In American history and Western folklore, popular name of Goyathlay (one who yawns), an Apache warrior who caused havoc on the Mexico–U.S. border for some 14 years, finally being captured by General George Crook. He appears in numerous Western tales as the symbol of Indian resistance to the white man. At the end of his life he dictated *Geronimo's Story of His Life*. His legend was filmed twice by Hollywood under the title *Geronimo*, in 1939 and in 1962.

Geryon (crane). In Greek mythology, a monster with three heads or three bodies and wings, son of Chrysaor and Callirrhoë, whose flocks were guarded by Orthus, a two-headed dog, and Eurytion, a shepherd. Heracles' tenth labor was to steal the flocks and drive them back to Greece. The hero killed the shepherd, the dog, and Geryon. Dante's *Divine Comedy* (Inferno) uses Geryon as a symbol of fraud. Geryon is the guardian of the Eighth Circle of Hell; he carries Vergil and Dante to its lowest region. William Blake depicted Geryon in his illustrations of Dante's epic.

Gesar Khan. Mongolian epic poem on the life of a fifth- century C.E. hero.

The poem was made available to Europe in a German translation by I. J. Schmidt in 1925 that was based on one printed from woodblocks in Beijing in 1716. In the work Gesar Khan is born with a divine mission: to bring peace and rule the world. As a small boy he is persecuted by his uncle, but in the poem he overcomes not only his uncle but demons, evil kings, and giants, rescues his mother from the underworld, and brings peace to China.

Temples to Gesar Khan are found throughout Tibet, where he is a national hero. In China he is identified with the god of war, Kuan-yu.

Full name: Gesar Ling of Khrom, which is apparently a Tibetan transliteration of "Emperor Caesar of Rome."

Ghoul. In Arabic folklore, demonic being who feeds on human bodies. A ghoul may be either male (ghul) or female (ghulah). Ghouls eat corpses of young children, often taking bodies from graves. If no graveyard is available, they will pursue live victims. Considered the offspring of Iblis, the Islamic Satan, ghouls can appear in various animal forms. Islamic tradition says Muhammad denied that any such beings exist, though some of his followers said he only denied that ghouls could assume various shapes. The term is now applied to certain types of sadists.

Krafft-Ebing in *Psychopathia Sexualis* tells of Sergeant Bertrand, who stole bodies from Paris cemeteries in 1848 and was dubbed a ghoul by the popular press.

Gideon (he that cuts down) 12th century B.C.E. In the Bible, O.T. (Judges), fifth of the judges of Israel. Gideon, a farmer, was threshing corn in a winepress to hide it from the Midianites when an angel appeared to him, telling him he was to deliver Israel (Judg. 6:11–40) from bondage. When Gideon asked the angel for proof of his identity, the angel touched Gideon's bread and meat with his staff and they burst into flames. Convinced that the angel was from God, Gideon prepared to battle the Midianites. He then tested his army of 10,000 men by observing them when they stopped at a stream to drink water. Most of the men bent down and placed their faces in the water, but 300 of the men scooped the water into their hands to drink. Gideon determined that these 300 were his best soldiers because by not putting their faces into the water they remained constantly alert. He dismissed all but the 300 soldiers and staged a surprise attack against the Midianites, convincing the enemy that they were outnumbered by having his men blow trumpets and carry torches concealed in pitchers. When the trumpets were blown and the pitchers broken, revealing the torches, the Midianites fled.

Gideon's attribute in Western art is the broken pitcher (Judg. 7:2– 23). In the New Testament Epistle to the Hebrews Gideon is cited as a great man of faith.

Gidja. In Australian mythology, one of the names of the moon, a male god who created the first woman by castrating Yalungur the Eagle Hawk.

Gikuyu, Masai, and Kamba. In African mythology (Kenya), the three sons of God. Each of the sons became the father of a tribe named after him.

One myth explains how God, who lived on top of Mount Kenya, gave a choice to his sons. They were each to choose one from among three possible gifts. Gikuyu chose the digging stick, and his people became farmers. Kamba chose the bow, and his people became hunters. Masai chose the spear, and his people tended herds. In a variant myth God took Gikuyu to a high place, showing him all that God had made. In the center of creation was a special area selected for Gikuyu, where fig trees grew. God also gave Gikuyu a wife, Moombi, who bore him nine daughters. Gikuyu yearned for sons and went to God, who explained to him what he had to do in order to have sons. Gikuyu did as God told him, and when he returned home, nine young men were waiting there for him. Gikuyu permitted them to marry his daughters after they agreed to live in his household according to matrilineal descent and promised that property would be divided equally among the daughters on their parents' death.

In time, each of the daughters founded a clan that bore her name. Women were permitted to engage in polyandry, i.e., they could each marry several husbands. The men, however, grew tired of sharing their wives with other men and planned a revolt. They agreed to make love to their respective wives at the same time in the hope that the women would become pregnant and therefore less able to put down the insurrection planned by the men. The plan worked, and the group changed its name from Moombi to Gikuyu. Polygamy was instituted, allowing men to have several wives. The women, however, on threat of killing all of the male children, won the right to retain the original female names for the clans.

Variant spelling: Kikuyu.

1259
Giles, St. (young goat). Died c. 712 C.E. In Christian legend, patron of beggars, blacksmiths, and cripples; one of the Fourteen Holy Helpers. Feast, 1 September.

The legend of St. Giles, one of the most popular saints of the Middle Ages, is found in *The Golden Legend* by Jacobus de Voragine, a collection of saints' lives written in the 13th century. Giles was born in Athens of royal blood. He was instructed in Bible studies from his youth. One day, when he was on his way to Mass, he met a sick man who asked him for alms. Giles gave him his cloak. When the cloak was placed on the crippled man, he was restored to health. Some time later Giles' parents died, leaving him heir, and he offered his wealth to the church.

One day, as he was returning from church, he met a man who had been bitten by a serpent. Giles prayed over the man and instantly the poison came out; the man's health was restored. At another time a man who was possessed by a devil was cured by Giles. These miracles, however, did not make Giles proud. Giles's fame reached King Charles (in some accounts said to be Charlemagne), who invited him to court and would often seek his advice. The king told Giles that he suffered from a secret sin that he could not even tell the saint. One Sunday, while Giles was saying Mass, an angel came down with a paper on which was written the king's sin, a prayer for Giles to recite and God's pardon. The paper was shown to the king, who then repented.

St. Giles was widely venerated in Europe. In England alone some 160 churches are dedicated to him. The name Giles is the French form of the Latin Egidius, one of the most common names of the Middle Ages.

1260
Gilgamesh (hero, father). In Near Eastern mythology, hero, king of Uruk in Mesopotamia who appears in a cycle of legends and myths, many incorporated into *The Epic of Gilgamesh*. Some Near Eastern scholars believe Gilgamesh to have been a historical person, the fifth king of Uruk, around whom a group of myths and legends evolved over the centuries. In some ancient accounts not part of the Gilgamesh epic, Gilgamesh's father is said to have been a *lilla*, which may mean an ignorant person or a fool; other accounts say his father was a priest of Kullab; and still others say Gilgamesh was the son of Lugulbanda, a shepherd god, who appears in the epic poem.

The Epic of Gilgamesh, told more than 4,000 years ago, predates the Hebrew scriptures and the Homeric epics. Relating Gilgamesh's quest for immortality, the epic speaks to us today in deeply moving human terms about our mortality. Numerous variant versions of the epic poem emerged throughout ancient Near Eastern history, indicating the extreme popularity of Gilgamesh. The most celebrated version, though incomplete, is preserved on twelve clay tablets from the library at Nineveh of Ashurnasirpal (seventh century B.C.E.). The tablets were discovered in the 19th century and subsequently installed at the British Museum in London as one of its prize possessions. When the gods created Gilgamesh, they endowed him with superhuman gifts and powers. His body was stronger and his courage greater than those of any other man. As a child Gilgamesh had dreamed of a being like himself, strong and handsome. He told his mother, Ninsun, about the dreams and how he longed for a companion equal to himself; but his mother was unable to help him, and he grew up unique and alone. Gilgamesh was proud of his godlike powers and used them to oppress his people with harsh laws, unjust taxes, and forced labor in building Uruk's mighty walls. No man or woman was safe from Gilgamesh. Maidens, wives, and even young men were taken by Gilgamesh to satisfy his lust. After many years of suffering, the people called on the gods to come to their aid. In response the goddess Aruru created Enkidu, a rival for Gilgamesh. Although as strong and courageous as Gilgamesh, Enkidu's body was covered with matted hair like that of a wild animal. The hair on his head was long, like a woman's. Knowing nothing of civilization or the ways of men and women, Enkidu lived among the wild animals and was their companion. One day a young hunter spotted Enkidu freeing a trapped animal. Terrified by Enkidu's primitive appearance, the young man hid. When Enkidu departed, the hunter ran home to tell his father what he had seen. His father advised him to go to Uruk and tell Gilgamesh. When Gilgamesh heard about Enkidu, his proud nature was deeply offended. He told the hunter to go back with a temple prostitute to seduce the wild man. The woman exposed herself and Enkidu became inflamed with sexual desire. The two lay together for six days and seven nights. Having exhausted himself with the woman, Enkidu returned to his animal companions, but they all fled from him. "Enkidu," said the woman, "now you are like a god because you have experienced sexual desire. Come with me to Uruk to meet the great King Gilgamesh."

When the two arrived in the city, they saw the people celebrating a coming marriage. But Gilgamesh came to the assembly hall to take the bride to his bed, as was his right as king. When Enkidu saw Gilgamesh approach the assembly hall, he stepped out of the crowd and blocked the way. The two men grappled with one another like two bulls. After Gilgamesh threw Enkidu to the ground, Gilgamesh's furor ceased. He stared at Enkidu, recognizing the friend and companion of his dreams. "There's not another man like you," Enkidu said to Gilgamesh. "You are favored by the gods, for your strength surpasses that of all men." Gilgamesh bent over and helped Enkidu to his feet. The two then embraced and kissed one another, sealing their friendship. Gilgamesh brought Enkidu to the palace to introduce him to his mother, Ninsun. When Ninsun realized that Enkidu was the man who had appeared in Gilgamesh's dreams, she adopted him as her own son. Because of Enkidu's tender love, Gilgamesh softened toward his people and was no longer oppressive. He established justice and peace in Uruk.

But beyond Uruk's protective walls was a forest inhabited by Humbaba, a fierce monster who guarded the Cedar Tree, sacred to the earth god Enlil. No man ever returned alive from Humbaba's mysterious domain. Gilgamesh and Enkidu went to the cedar forest to battle Humbaba. Both men attacked the monster, and with the aid of Shamash, the god who protected Gilgamesh, the monster was defeated. Enkidu, clutching Gilgamesh's sword, slashed off Humbaba's massive head, which crashed loudly to the ground. Cries from the trees erupted throughout the forest. Even the sacred Cedar Tree cried out, "Why have you done this evil deed?" The two men then cut down the sacred tree.

The goddess Ishtar was so impressed with Gilgamesh's daring that she asked him to become her lover. Gilgamesh refused, however,

remembering how she had destroyed all of her previous lovers. Determined that Gilgamesh should be punished for insulting her, Ishtar appealed to her father, Anu, to create Gudanna, or Alu (the strong), a majestic Bull of Heaven. But Gilgamesh and Enkidu also destroyed the Bull of Heaven. "You'll suffer, Gilgamesh, for scorning me and killing the Bull of Heaven," Ishtar cried out. To add to the insult, Enkidu challenged the goddess by throwing the bull into her face.

A council of the gods was held, and it was decided that Enkidu had to die. Enkidu's body began to waste away. On the twelfth day of his suffering he cried out to Gilgamesh, "The great gods have cursed me. They have no pity. I must die this shameful death, denied the glory of dying heroically in battle." Enkidu then passed into a deep sleep which led to death. "Enkidu, Enkidu, my beloved friend and brother," Gilgamesh cried out in anguish. "Enkidu, I weep for you like a wailing woman. You were the ax by my side, the sword in my belt, the shield before me. And now you've been taken from me by the jealous gods." For seven days and seven nights Gilgamesh cried over his friend's body.

After Enkidu's burial Gilgamesh left Uruk and roamed from place to place. But he could find neither rest nor peace of mind. His thoughts were constantly on Enkidu and on his own mortality: "I'll also die and worms will feast on my flesh. I now fear death and have lost all my courage." Gilgamesh then made the arduous journey to the land of Utnapishtim, the hero of the great flood, to seek the secret of immortal life possessed by Utnapishtim and his wife. Though they told him he could not be immortal, they also gave him the location of a plant that would renew his youth. Gilgamesh found the plant, but when he rested it was stolen by a snake. Sadly Gilgamesh returned to Uruk and Enkidu's spirit appeared to him. When he realized that death was the lot of all, he resigned himself to his mortality.

Near Eastern mythology accorded Gilgamesh the status of a minor god, as it did to his beloved Enkidu. Gilgamesh was invoked as an underworld deity and was associated with Tammuz, another man who descended to the land of the dead. He had control over the souls of heroes, whom he released from their prison house of death for nine days during the months of July and August.

Bohusalav Martinu's cantata for soloists, chorus, and orchestra, *The Epic of Gilgamesh*, is based on R. Campbell Thompson's English version of the poem. Ross Alexander's *Gilgamesh: A Primitive Ritual* tells the epic in dramatic form.

Variant spellings: Gilgamos, Gisdhubar, Gistubar, Izubar.

1261

Gil Morrice. A Scottish ballad, included in Percy's *Reliques*, that tells of a natural son of an earl and the wife of Lord Barnard. He is brought up "in the gude grene wode." Lord Barnard, thinking Gil Morrice to be his wife's lover, killed him with a broadsword, setting his head on a spear.

1262

Ginnungagap (gaping chaos). In Norse mythology, the primeval abyss between Muspell and Niflheim where the primeval giant Ymir was born and where he was slain by the gods Odin, Vili, and Ve. From Ymir's body the earth was formed. The myth appears in the *Prose Edda*.

1263

Ginseng. A root shaped somewhat like a human body, used mainly in folk medicine. In Oriental folk medicine ginseng has long been regarded as a miracle cure; credited with healing epilepsy, insomnia, coughing, mental disorders, and digestive and respiratory illnesses, as well as epidemic illnesses such as cholera, measles, dysentery, malaria, typhoid, influenza, and other diseases. It was also an antidote to impotence and a sexual stimulant.

In Korean legend a 15-year-old boy named Kim lived in a rundown hut with his father, Kang-won-do, who was dying. Kim prayed every day to the mountain spirit. One day he fell asleep during prayer and the mountain spirit appeared and led him to the place where ginseng was growing. Directed by the spirit, he prepared a drink from the root of the ginseng and gave it to his father, who recovered. In another Oriental legend a poor man discovered some ginseng and tried to sell it in his village at an exorbitant price. The man was arrested for greed but managed to hide the ginseng inside his jacket. When the judge demanded the ginseng be presented as evidence, the man took out the root and ate it. The root made him so strong he was able to kill the guards and escape.

1264

Girdle of Venus. In Greek and Roman mythology, the girdle of Aphrodite, a magic girdle that evoked sexual passion in men and gods. Aphrodite used it and often lent it out. Once she lent it to Hera, Zeus's wife, who wanted to beguile the god and take his mind off aiding the Trojans in the war, giving the Greeks, whom Hera favored, a chance in battle.

1265

Gjallar-horn (shrieking horn). In Norse mythology, the horn of the god Heimdall, which will sound to announce the frost giants' attack on the gods when the giants pass the bridge Bifrost at Ragnarok, the end of the world. The *Poetic Edda*, in the poem *Voluspa* (the Sooth Saying of Vala), describes the scene:

> To battle the gods are called
> By the ancient
> Gjallar-horn.
> Loud blows Heimdall,
> His sound is in the air.

Gjallar-horn was either hung on a branch of Yggdrasill, the world tree, or placed in the waters of Mimir's well, where the lost eye of Odin lay.

1266

Glastonbury. In Arthurian legend, the place where Joseph of Arimathea planted his staff. It took root and burst into leaf every Christmas Eve, and the tree is called the Glastonbury Thorn. Glastonbury is a town in Somerset in southwestern England, dating from Roman times. King Arthur's wife, Guinever, is said to have been buried there.

1267

Glaucus (gray-green). In Greek mythology, the name of various men. One was the son of Sisyphus and father of Bellerophon. He refused to let his mares breed, which so angered Aphrodite, goddess of sexual love, that she drove the mares mad. They tore Glaucus to pieces at the funeral games of Pelias. Another Glaucus was the grandson of Bellerophon. He fought on the side of the Trojans, but when he met Diomedes in battle, he laid down his spear and exchanged his gold armor for Diomedes' bronze armor on learning the two had family ties. Glaucus appears in Homer's *Iliad* (book 6) and Vergil's *Aeneid* (book 6). Another Glaucus was an Argonaut and fisherman who wished to live in the ocean. He was transformed into a sea god by Oceanus. His story is in Ovid's *Metamorphoses* (book 13).

1268

Gluskap and Malsum. In North American Indian mythology (Abnaki), twin brothers; Gluskap, a creator god, culture hero, and trickster killed his evil brother Malsum.

Gluskap and Malsum discussed their birth while still in their mother's womb.

"I will be born as others are born," said Gluskap.

But Malsum, being evil, said it was not proper that he should be born as others were. He wished to have an extraordinary birth. Gluskap was born first in the natural manner, but Malsum forced his way out of his mother's armpit, killing her as a result.

The two brothers grew up together. One day Malsum asked Gluskap how he would be killed, since Gluskap, as well as Malsum, possessed a charmed life. Gluskap, remembering how Malsum had caused the death of their mother, told a lie.

"I can be killed by the stroke of an owl's feather," he told Malsum.

"I can die only by a blow from a large fern root," replied Malsum.

One day Malsum decided he would kill his brother. He took his bow and arrow and shot Ko-ko-khas, the owl, and with one of his feathers struck Gluskap while he was asleep. Gluskap awoke suddenly and said it was not by an owl's feather that he would die, but by a blow from a pine root.

The next day Malsum led Gluskap into the deep forest to hunt. After the hunt, while Gluskap slept, Malsum hit him on the head with a pine root. Gluskap awoke and in anger chased Malsum deeper into the woods. Gluskap then came to a brook and said to himself, "Malsum does not know, but only a flowering rush can kill me."

Beaver, who was hidden among the reeds, heard Gluskap, and rushed to Malsum to tell him the secret. In return for the secret Malsum promised to give Beaver whatever he wanted. When Beaver asked for wings like a pigeon, Malsum laughed at him, and Beaver left in anger. Beaver then went to Gluskap and told him what had happened. Gluskap took a large-footed fern and killed Malsum, driving his evil magic below the earth. Malsum then became an evil wolf.

With Malsum out of the way and evil underground, Gluskap created the world from the body of his dead mother. He then took his bow and arrows and shot at ash trees, and people came out of the bark. Gluskap then made all of the animals and taught humankind the arts. But people were not grateful to Gluskap. This saddened him until he could no longer endure it. One day he made a feast by the shore. All of the beasts came to it. When the feast was over he boarded a great canoe and left. The beasts could hear him sing, but his voice grew fainter as the canoe moved on. Then a deep silence fell on the animals. Until then they could all understand one another's language, but from that time they could not, so each fled to his home. One day Gluskap will return to restore the earth and make people and animals live together once more in peace and love.

Variant spellings: Glooscap, Glooska, Gluskabe.

1269

Goat. A hollow-horned ruminant related to the sheep family, the goat was sacred to Hera, wife of Zeus in Greek mythology. Hera was closely identified with the she-goat at Largos, a center of her worship. There youths threw spears at a she-goat during a religious festival in honor of Hera. This rite was supposed to punish the goat for revealing the hiding place of Hera when once she fled to the woods to escape Zeus's anger.

The goat was also associated with Dionysus, a son of Zeus and Semele. To protect his son from Hera, Zeus transformed Dionysus into a black goat, thereby making the animal sacred to Dionysus, who was called "the Kid" or "one of the black goatskin." Dionysus' followers would tear to pieces a live goat and devour its raw flesh. Euripides' *The Bacchae* captures their joy and ecstasy. In one section the god's followers cry out: "Look, he comes. . . . He hunts the wild goat, killing it and tearing its raw flesh for food." Other Greek gods who shared the goat as a symbol are Pan and Silenus, as well as satyrs and fauns.

When one calls a man an "old goat," it still refers to the animal's supposed lecherous nature. In Hebrew mythology a goat was sacrificed to Yahweh and called the scapegoat. Jesus in the New Testament says God will separate the sheep from the goats, meaning the good from the evil, at the last judgment. The Nordic god Thor had his wagon drawn by goats. Late medieval belief often identified the goat with the devil.

1270

God and the Rising Waters. Jewish fable found in the Midrash.

Once the waters on the earth kept rising, reaching almost to God's throne. The Almighty said, "Be still." But the waters cried out: "We are the mightiest of all creation. Let us flood the earth." God became angry, saying, "I will send sand on the earth and it will make a barrier to contain you."

When the waters saw the sand, they laughed. "How can such tiny grains contain us?" the waters said. The sand grains hearing the water, became frightened. "How are we to survive?" they asked.

Their leader said, "Have no fear. True, we are small and each one of us is insignificant. But if we remain united, then the waters will see how strong we are."

When the sand grains heard this, they rose up in mounds, hills and mountains, forming a huge barrier against the waters. When the waters saw how great an army the sand was, they became frightened and retreated.

1271

Godiva, Lady. (gift of God). In English medieval legend, patroness of Coventry. In 1040 Leofric, earl of Mercia and lord of Coventry, imposed certain taxes on his tenants. His wife did not think the taxes were just. Leofric said he would not remove them unless she rode naked through the town at midday. Lady Godiva accepted his challenge and rode through the streets naked. Out of respect, everyone stayed indoors, but a certain tailor peeped through his window to see the lady pass and was struck blind. He was then called "Peeping Tom of Coventry." Leofric removed the taxes as a result of his wife's ride. Tennyson's poem *Godiva, A Tale of Coventry* treats the subject.

Gog and Magog. In medieval British mythology, two giants, the sole survivors of a monstrous brood of children born to the 33 daughters of the evil Roman emperor Diocletian. The women murdered their husbands. Gog and Magog were set adrift on a ship and reached Albion (England), where they became friends of a group of demons. Their children were a race of giants who fought the hero Brut and his companions. All were destroyed except for Gog and Magog, who were brought to London in chains. They were made slaves and forced to act as porters at the royal palace, on the site of the London Guildhall. Statues of them can still be seen in London today. In the Bible Gog and Magog (Rev. 20:8) symbolize all of the future enemies of the Kingdom of God.

Goin. In Australian mythology, an evil spirit in the form of an old man with claws like an eagle hawk and feet like an alligator.

Golden Age. In Greek and Roman mythology, the first of the Four ages of Man, the others being Silver, Bronze, and Iron. The Golden Age first appears in Hesiod's *Work and Days* and was later developed by the Roman poets Horace, Vergil, and Ovid. In Ovid's *Metamorphoses* (book 1) a description that influenced later literature is given of the Four Ages of Man. In English literature, Chaucer, Shakespeare, and Spenser cite the Golden Age. Shelley's poem *Hellas* says: "The world's great age begins anew/ The golden years return. . . ."

Golden Apples of the Hesperides. In Greek mythology, golden apples guarded by the Hesperides, daughters of Atlas and a dragon, Ladon. The golden apples grew on a tree that was a gift to Hera when she married Zeus. Heracles' 11th labor was to fetch the apples. When he did, the apples were given to Athena, who returned them to the Hesperides because they could not survive outside the magic garden. Hesiod's *Theogony*, Ovid's *Metamorphoses* (book 4), and Tennyson's poem, *The Hesperides* recounts the myth.

Golden Bough. In Roman mythology, a bough that the Trojan hero Aeneas obtains as a passport to the underworld. In Vergil's *Aeneid* (book 6) Aeneas is told by the Cumaean Sybil that he cannot enter the underworld until he has found and broken off a golden bough and offered it as a gift to Proserpine, queen of the dead. The bough, identified as the mistletoe, was associated with Diana (a variant form of Proserpine) at Aricia, near Rome. According to some accounts, the golden bough had to be broken off a sacred tree by a slave, who then killed the priest-king guarding the tree and took his place, eventually to be killed in the same manner. This interpretation, given by Servius (fourth century C.E.) in his commentary on Vergil's *Aeneid*, inspired the monumental 12-volume study, *The Golden Bough*, by Sir James Frazer. Frazer opens his work with the ritual surrounding the slaying of the priest-king of Diana in a grove near Memi and then goes on to explain ancient rituals, beliefs, and customs relating to magic, kingship, divinity, tree worship, taboos, totemism, rain, fire, and so on. Frazer's basic assumption is that all peoples have gone through the same cultural development and thus react in the same way. (This aspect of his work is now debated.) Frazer's chapters dealing with the Dying God had great influence on early 20th-century thinking and art. Among classical scholars, Gilbert Murray and Jane Harrison are in his debt. Creative artists such as T. S. Eliot and D. H. Lawrence also were influenced by his ideas, as was Freud in his *Totem and Tabu*. Other works by Frazer are *Totemism and Exogamy, The Belief in Immortality and the Worship of the Dead, Folklore in the Old Testament, The Worship of Nature, Myths of the Origin of Fire* and *The Fear of the Dead in Primitive Religion*.

Golden Cockerel, Tale of the. Literary folk verse tale by Alexander Pushkin, published in 1833.

Pushkin's verse uses the forms of Russian folk poetry to create a satirical folktale. An astrologer gave Czar Dodon a golden cockerel that had the gift of prophecy. When the bird crowed, it was a sign that danger was near. One day the Golden Cockerel crowed as the astrologer came to ask payment for the magical bird. King Dodon, responding to the bird's warning, killed the astrologer. Dodon, however, was then killed by the Golden Cockerel.

Pushkin's satirical verse tale was believed to have been based on a Russian folktale, and numerous anthologies that include the poet's work contain a note to that effect. However, in 1933 the source for Pushkin's tale was found in Washington Irving's well-known book *The Legends of the Alhambra*, which Pushkin read in a French translation published in the same year as the English original. The poet took the tales "The House of the Weathercock" and "The Legend of the Arabian Astrologer" as the bases for his poem. Pushkin's poem was used by the Russian composer Rimsky-Korsakov for his opera *Le coq d'or* (*The Golden Cockerel*).

1278

Golden Fleece. In Greek mythology, the fleece of the winged ram stolen by the hero Jason with the aid of his mistress, Medea. The myth tells how Nephele, wife of King Athamas of Boeotia, convinced the king that his son Phrixus was responsible for a famine and had to be sacrificed to the gods. Phrixus, learning of the plan, fled with his sister Helle on the golden-winged ram. During the flight Helle fell in the water and drowned, but Phrixus reached Colchis. He married Chalciope, daughter of Aetës, and sacrificed the ram. Its fleece was then hung in a sacred grove in Colchis and guarded by a dragon. Jason, with Medea's aid, later stole the Golden Fleece. Apollonius *Argonautica* tells the tale of Jason, Medea, and the quest as does William Morris's *Life and Death of Jason*, a long narrative poem, and Nathaniel Hawthorne's "Golden Fleece" in his children's book *Tanglewood Tales*.

1279

Golden Legend, The (*Legenda Aurea*). In medieval Christianity, collection of saints' lives and stories associated with the Christian year; compiled and written by Jacobus de Voragine, archbishop of Genoa (1230–1298 C.E.). From earliest Christian times the compiling of saints' lives has been one of the main sources of Christian art and legends. The primary works include martyrologies (lists of martyred saints), passions, calendars, biographies, prose and verse compositions, and liturgical texts. One of the first collections of saints' lives was compiled by Eusebius (c. 260–340 C.E.), the church historian. His work, however, was lost. In the tenth century Symeon the Metaphrast rewrote, in elegant and refined Greek, a series of saints' lives based on earlier sources. The most influential work, however, was and still remains *The Golden Legend*. There are more than 500 manuscripts of the work in existence. The first century of printing produced more than 150 editions and translations. William Caxton, the first English printer, produced an English version in the 15th century. The popularity of *The Golden Legend* diminished during the Renaissance and Reformation, because the Humanists disliked its "gutter Latin," and Protestants objected to its acceptance of fantasy.

1280

Golden Stool, The. In African cult, a symbol sacred to the Ashanti of Ghana. During the 18th century

Osei Tutu, one of the rulers of the Ashanti, united his people and formed a powerful nation. Previously, they had been dominated by a neighboring tribe. Anokye, a ruler of that tribe, offended his king and left the country. He came to the Ashanti, saying that the god Onyame had sent him to them so that they would become a great nation. With great fanfare Anokye brought down from the heavens a stool covered with gold, which came to rest on Osei Tutu's knees. The king was so pleased with it that he had four bells made to hang from its corners. Anokye said that the stool was a physical manifestation of the soul of the Ashanti people. A magic potion, made of the hairs and fingernails of members of the Ashanti royalty, was drunk, and what remained was poured over the stool. No one was permitted to sit on the stool, although the king might pretend to and even rest his arm on it. Once a year the stool was carried through the streets under large ceremonial umbrellas in a great procession. Over the years golden items were added to the stool to commemorate very special events.

In 1896 the Ashanti feared that the British, who since 1750 had held a monopoly over the Gold Coast, would destroy the golden stool. When Sir Frederic Hodgon demanded that the stool be brought to him so that he might sit on it, a bloody revolt ensued. The stool disappeared and was not seen again until 1921. While building a road, some men came upon the spot where the stool was hidden, and it was moved to a new location. Thieves discovered it and stole the gold from the stool, but when they tried to sell it, they were caught and jailed. They had to be guarded very carefully lest they be seized and killed. The authorities, recognizing the significance of the stool, restored it to the royal palace in Kumasi.

1281

Goldfinch. A bird with a yellow patch on each wing; in medieval Christian symbolism, the Passion of Christ. According to medieval Christian belief the goldfinch eats thistles and thorns, two symbols of Christ's Passion. In Renaissance paintings one often finds the Christ Child holding a goldfinch, indicating his future suffering and death.

1282

Goldilocks and the Three Bears. Literary folktale by Robert Southey, first appearing in *The Doctor* (1834–1847), a miscellany. A girl, Goldilocks, enters the three bears' house in the woods. She tries three chairs, one is too hard, one too soft, and one just right. She then eats three bowls of porridge and tries out three beds, falling asleep in the smallest. When the bears return, the girl is chased out. Southey may have based his version on a tale in the Grimms' *Schneewittchen.*

1283

Golem (shapeless mass). In medieval Jewish folklore, a robot given life when the mystical name of God was placed upon it. One medieval legend tells how the poet and philosopher Solomon Ibn Gabirol of Valencia created a *golem* maid. When the Christian king heard of the creature, he ordered Solomon killed for practicing black magic. However, the poet-philosopher, proved that the creature was harmless by removing the name of God from it and having it then turn to dust. In a later tale, *The Golem of Chem,* the creature proves too much for its creator, Rabbi Elijah, who removed the magical name of God from the monster when it went on a destructive rampage. In later reworkings of the legends, such as *The Golem of Prague,* the monster becomes a defender of the Jews. In Yiddish, however, the word *golem* is used for a stupid person. The term *golem* appears in the Hebrew Scriptures in Psalm 139:16: The Jewish Publications translation of 1917 renders the term as "unformed substance," and the new Jewish translation of 1985 renders the term as "unformed limbs."

1284

Goliath (an exile). In the Bible, O.T., a Philistine giant who was slain by David. He was nine feet, nine inches tall (1 Sam. 17:4). In Islamic legend Goliath is called Jalut and cited in the Koran (sura 2). In Western art Goliath is often shown decapitated at David's feet or being held by the young David.

1285

Gollveig (gold might). In Norse mythology, a Vanir goddess. She came to the Aesir gods and was mistreated by them, but the exact details are not known. Gollveig was in part responsible for a war between the Vanir and the Aesir deities. In some accounts her name is given as Heid.

1286

González, Conde Fernán. c. 930–970. In medieval Spanish legend, count of Burgos who made Castile independent of the state of León. He is the subject of numerous heroic ballads and the 13th-century narrative poem, *El poema de Fernán González.*

Both González and his wife, Sancha, often appear in Spanish ballads. According to various legends, Sancha rescued the count twice at the risk of her own life. The count had asked her hand in marriage from her father, Garcias, king of Navarre. On his way to join his bride the count was ambushed by men of the queen of León, who was the sister of the king of Navarre and opposed the match. The count was taken to a castle and imprisoned. Then a "pilgrim knight of Normandy," riding through Navarre, came to the castle where the count was imprisoned and later told his intended wife, Sancha, of the deep love the count held for her. In the ballad *The Escape of Count Fernán González* the knight says:

> González loves thee, lady,—he loved the
> long ago,—
> Arise, let love with love be paid, and set
> González free
> (John Gibson Lockhart translation)

Sancha, moved by his words, bribed the jailer and fled with the count to Castile. Many years later, according to another legend, the count was again freed by his wife after he was ambushed by the men of the queen of León. This time Sancha, feigning a pilgrimage to Compostela to visit the tomb of St. James the Greater, passed the night in the castle where her husband was being held prisoner. She exchanged her clothes for his, and he escaped.

El Poema de Fernán González, believed to have been written by a monk of the Castilian monastery of San Pedro de Aslanza in the 13th century, recounts the history of Spain up to the birth of Fernán González and then relates the exploits of the hero.

1287

Go-oh. In North American Indian mythology (Iroquois), the spirit of the winds who lives in the north sky. He controls all four winds; the bear, north wind; the panther, west wind; the moose, east wind; and the fawn, south wind. When the north wind blows, the Iroquois say, "The bear is prowling in the sky." If the west wind is violent, they say, "The panther is whining." When the east wind chills with its rain, they say, "The moose is spreading his breath," and when the south wind wafts soft breezes, they say, "The fawn is returning to its doe."

1288

Goonnear. In Australian mythology, the evil carpet snake. He is the opposite of the wombat snake, Biggarro, who aids man to the spirit land.

1289

Goose. Large web-footed bird, connected with numerous deities in world mythology as a symbol of fertility, watchfulness, war, love, autumn, and the sun. The goose is sacred to various Egyptian deities such as Amun-Ra, Isis, Geb, Osis, Osiris, and Horus. Amun-Ra is sometimes called "The Great Grackler" in reference to his role as creator of the world when he laid the Cosmic Egg. In Greek mythology, the goose is sacred to Hera, as Queen of Heaven, to Apollo as sun god, Ares as war god, and Eros as god of love and sex. According to Roman legend, when

Rome was being invaded, the sacred geese in Juno's temple began to cackle when they spotted the enemy. They were killed by enemy soldiers but not before the Romans had been warned of the invasion. Later a golden goose was carried in procession in honor of the geese. The goose is sacred not only to Juno but to Mars as war god and Priapus as fertility god. In Chinese mythology the goose is the bird of heaven, symbol of Yang, the male principle. In Japanese mythology the goose is a symbol of autumn, associated with the autumn moon. Wild geese are sacred to Brahma in Hindu mythology; he is often shown riding a magnificent gander. In European Christian folklore, the English custom of eating the goose on St. Michael's Day is sometimes said to have originated in the time of Elizabeth I, who on St. Michael's Day received news of the defeat of the Spanish Armada while she was eating goose. But the story is apocryphal because the custom of eating goose can be traced back to the 15th century in England when Edward IV ate the fat goose to augur the termination of the rainy and wintry season. Perhaps the best-known Aesop fable about a goose is "The Goose That Laid the Golden Egg," which has given rise to the saying, "kill the goose that lays the golden egg," whenever people's greed alienates those who are generous to them. Another expression, "cook a person's goose," refers to the European legend of Eric, king of Sweden, who approached an enemy city and found a dead goose hung over one of its walls in derision of his invasion. As he set the town to torch, he is reported to have said, "I'm cooking the goose."

Goose that Laid the Golden Eggs, The. Aesopic fable that appears in many European and Oriental sources, probably originally Indian because it appears in the *Jatakas, or Birth-Stories of the Former Lives of the Buddha.*

1290

A farmer went to the nest of his goose to see whether she had laid an egg. To his surprise he found, instead of an ordinary goose egg, an egg of solid gold. Seizing the golden egg, he rushed to the house in great excitement to show it to his wife.

Every day thereafter the goose laid an egg of pure gold. But as the farmer grew rich, he grew greedy. And thinking that if he killed the goose he could have all of her treasure at once, he cut her open, only to find nothing at all.

Moral: The greedy who want more lose all.

Gorboduc. In British mythology, a king, father of Ferrex and Porrex; he divided his kingdom between them. Ferrex was driven out of the land by his brother; when he attempted to return, he was killed.

1291

Porrex was later murdered by his mother, who had favored Ferrex. *Gorboduc*, written by Thomas Norton and Thomas Sackville, is the first English historical drama.

Gordian Knot. In Greek and Roman legend, a knot tied by a peasant named Gordius, the father of Midas, who became king of Phrygia. The knot was so complex that no one could unravel it nor even find the ends of the cord entwined within the knot. Gordius had dedicated his oxcart or chariot to Zeus, with the yoke tied to the pole in a knot. An oracle decreed that anyone who could unravel it would rule Asia. Alexander the Great cut it with his sword, fulfilling the oracle. Purcell's incidental music to *The Gordian Knot Untied* was written for a play now lost.

1292

Gore (misery). In Slavic folklore, personification of misery and misfortune. Gore is described in one Russian folktale as a "wretched little man, with a miserable face and little thin legs and arms." According to the folktale, a merchant who had lost all his property because of Gore decided to do away with him. He asked Gore if he could make himself small enough to fit into the hub of a wheel. Angry at being challenged, Gore popped into the hole of the hub, and the merchant instantly shut Gore inside. (This kind of trickery is a common motif in folktales.) The merchant then took the wheel to the river and drowned Gore. With Gore's death, the merchant was restored to his former prosperity.

1293

Gorgon

1294

Gorgons (grim ones). In Greek mythology, three women monsters, the Euryae; daughters of Ceto and Phorcys, they are Euryale, Stheno, and Medusa. They had women's bodies, wings, brazen claws, and snakes for hair. They were sisters to the Graeae, three gray-haired old women who acted as their sentries. Euryale and Stheno were immortal and could not die, but Medusa was not and was beheaded by the hero Perseus. Her head was on the aegis or cloak of Zeus and Athena, and the sight of it could turn a person into stone. In Shakespeare's *Macbeth* (2.3.68) at the discovery of Duncan's murder, Macduff says: "Approach the chamber, and destroy your sight/ With a new Gorgon."

Perseus slaying the Gorgon, with Hermes

1295

Gotham, Wise Men of. In British medieval legend, a term for "wise fools." King John, on his way to Lyme Regis, intended to pass through Gotham in Nottinghamshire with his army. To prepare he sent heralds to announce he was coming. The men of Gotham did not want to see the king or his army because it meant that the land would be devastated and they would be forced to provide quarters for the soldiers. They decided to play fools. Some pretended to rake the moon out of a pond, some made a ring to hedge in a bird, and so on. When the king learned of their actions, he abandoned his intention of stopping in the village. One wise man remarked, "We ween there are more fools pass through Gotham than remain in it." A collection of popular tales called *Merie tales of the Mad Men of Gotam* was published during the reign of Henry VIII. Washington Irving gave the name Gotham to New York City in his *Salmagundi Papers.*

1296

Govannon. In Celtic mythology, the British god of smithery, son of Don, brother of Gwydian. Govannon made weapons for the gods and brewed ale. An-

cient Roman writers equated him with their god Vulcan. In later medieval legend he appears as Gobhan Saer, an architect of magic power who is credited with building many towers and churches in Ireland.

1297

Go-vardhana. In Hindu mythology, a sacred mountain on which Krishna (an incarnation of the god Vishnu) ordered the cowherds to worship him instead of Indra, the storm god. This so enraged Indra that he sent a deluge to wash away the mountain as well as the people. Krishna, however, held up the mountain with his little finger for seven days to shelter the people. Indra left baffled and afterward did homage to Krishna, who was called Go-vardhana Dhara (upholder of Go-vardhana).

1298

Gracchi. In Roman mythology, the name given in Vergil's *Aeneid* (book 6) to the spirits or souls of unborn Roman heroes.

1299

Graeae (gray ones). In Greek mythology, daughters of Phorcys and Cero; sisters of the Gorgons. The Graeae were Dino, Enyo, and Pephredo. They had only one tooth and one eye to share among themselves. The eye was stolen by the hero Perseus as they passed it from one to another. He would not give it back to them until they told him where Medusa was hiding.

1300

Grand Bois d'Ilet. In Haitian voodoo, lord of the night and night forests.

1301

Gran Maître. In Haitian voodoo, the creator god, distinct from the loas, who are deified spirits of the dead and looked upon as gods.

1302

Grannos. In Celtic mythology, a god of healing worshiped by the continental Celts. Ancient Roman writers equated Grannos with either Aesculapius, their god of medicine, or Apollo. Several localities in France are named after Grannos, such as Aix-la-Chapelle (Aquae Granni), Graux, and Eaux Graunnes.

1303

Grape. A berry used for making wine. In Greek mythology the grape was associated with Dionysus, whose worship involved sexual rites assisted by wine as an intoxicant. In the Old Testament, Noah is credited with inventing wine and getting drunk (Gen. 9:20– 21). In the New Testament Jesus used wine as part of the ritual around the Holy Eucharist, the other element being bread. Jesus drank wine (Matt. 11:19), and at the marriage feast at Cana (John 2:1–11), his first recorded miracle, he turned water into wine to replenish the supply for the feast. In Christian art the Holy Eucharist is sometimes symbolized by bunches of grapes with ears of wheat.

1304

Grasshopper. Any of numerous insects having hind legs used for leaping. In Egyptian mythology the grasshopper was associated with happiness. In *The Book of the Dead* the deceased is to say: "I have rested in the field of grasshoppers." Another ancient Egyptian text tells how the pharaoh will "arrive in heaven like the grasshopper of Ra," the sun god. In ancient Hebrew belief the grasshopper symbolizes a scourge. In Aesop's fable "The Ant and Grasshopper," the creature is depicted as a fool who does not plan for his life, thus symbolizing irresponsibility. But in Greek belief the creature also symbolized nobility. In Chinese folk belief, abundance, good luck, and numerous sons are symbolized by the grasshopper.

1305

Great Carbuncle. In American folklore, a large, magnificent stone with extraordinary brightness and power. Nathaniel Hawthorne's "The Great Carbuncle," included in *Twice Told Tales* is based on the legend, which the author says is founded on "Indian tradition." In Hawthorne's telling, an alchemist, a merchant, and a cynic go in pursuit of the gem, only to be frustrated. A young couple also go in pursuit of the magnificent stone but come to realize what happiness they have and reject it. When they do, the author says the splendor of the gem waned.

1306

Great Stone Face, The. In American folklore, a mountain that resembles a face, said by the Indians to be that of Manitou, one of their main gods; according to white settlers, the mountain is the face of Daniel Webster. Its power is displayed in Hawthorne's short story, "The Great Stone Face," in *The Snow Image and Other Twice-Told Tales*.

1307

Grede. In Haitian voodoo, god of the dead, who is lord of life as well. In the chamber dedicated to his worship a sculptured phallus lies next to a gravedigger's tools. His symbol is the cross.

1308

Gregory the Great, St. (watchful). Died 604 C.E. In Christian legend, pope, Doctor of the Church. Patron saint of fringe makers, masons, musicians, scholars, singers, students, and teachers. Invoked against gout, plague, and sterility. Feast, 12 March.

St. Gregory

Gregory, the first monk to be made pope, was noted for his learning, kindness, and charity. He sent St. Augustine (not to be confused with the St. Augustine who wrote the *Confessions*) to Canterbury to convert the English. He reformed church music and wrote numerous works on sacred subjects. Gregorian chant, which he was popularly believed to have originated, was named in his honor.

He appears in numerous legends from the Middle Ages. One legend tells how John the Deacon, his secretary and biographer, saw the Holy Ghost in the form of a dove perched on the shoulder of Gregory whenever he dictated his sermons or books. Another legend tells how the Archangel Michael, responding to the prayers of St. Gregory, stopped a plague that was threatening to destroy Rome. The legend of the Supper of St. Gregory tells how 12 poor men came to dine every evening with Gregory. One evening a 13th appeared. After dinner Gregory asked the man who he was. The man replied, "I am the poor man whom thou didst formerly relieve, but my name is Wonderful, and through me thou shall obtain whatever thou shalt ask of God." Gregory then knew that he had been visited by an angel.

The Mass of St. Gregory is the name given to the most famous legend associated with the saint. Once there was a man who doubted that Christ was present at the altar during the Mass. When St. Gregory heard this, he prayed that Christ would make known to the man His real presence at the altar. Suddenly, Christ appeared with the instruments of His Passion on the altar. In another account, when Gregory elevated the sacred Host, it began to bleed, convincing the man that truly this was the Body of Christ.

The miracle of the Brandeum, similar in some ways to the previous miracle, concerns a relic of St. John the Evangelist, the Brandeum, or consecrated cloth. It was sent to the Empress Constantia and rejected by her with contempt. To show her that faith was more important than relics, St. Gregory laid the Brandeum on the altar. After praying, he took up a knife and pierced it, and blood flowed from it as if it were a living body.

Another legend in medieval folklore tells of the prayers of the saint for the soul of the pagan emperor Trajan. As told by Brunetto Latini, the teacher of Dante, the legend maintains that by Gregory's prayers the pagen emperor entered heaven.

In *The Divine Comedy* (Purgatory, canto 10) Dante makes reference to this legend and says that the soul of the emperor was placed in the heaven of Jupiter among the spirits of those who loved and exercised justice.

1309

Gremlins. In American folklore of World War II, imps about 20 inches tall, who wear green breeches, red jackets with ruffles, and top hats and spats and who cause mischief on aircraft. U.S. airmen used the term to account for any mechanical difficulty.

1310

Grettir the Strong. Medieval Icelandic saga, believed to have been written in the 11th century C.E. Grettir was the second son of Asmund and Asdis. His mother favored the boy, but his father took a dislike to him, since he constantly got into trouble. After Grettir slew Skegg in a quarrel about a lost meal bag he was ordered into three years' banishment. He was given a sword by his mother and placed on a boat, *Haflidi*, which was wrecked on the island of Havamsey. Here Grettir remained for some time with its chief, Thorfinn. One evening he saw a fire break out from a mound, and believing that the mound concealed some treasure, he went the next morning to dig. The mound was known as the grave of Old Karr, Thorfinn's father. Working all day and night, he finally came to the treasure and was about to take it when the dead body of Old Karr awoke. A fight began and Grettir cut off Karr's head and made sure it was laid at the thigh of the dead man so that he could not come to life again. He took the treasure and gave all of it except for a short sword to Thorfinn, until he had done some great deed. In a short time he accomplished the deed by killing at Christmas a group of thieves who had come to rob Thorfinn.

After numerous other adventures and murders, Grettir became an outlaw. He was finally killed by a man named Thorbiorn Angle, who found Grettir in a hut asleep after having been wounded by the witch Thurid. Thorbiorn, after a battle with Grettir, seized his short sword and cut off his head. Later Thorbiorn Angle was killed by Grettir's brother, Thorstein Dromond.

1311

Griffin. In European and Near Eastern mythology and folklore, a fantastic animal with the head and wings of an eagle, the body of a lion, and sometimes the tail of a serpent. Griffins drew the chariots of Zeus, called the Hounds of Zeus, and those of Apollo and Nemesis. They guarded the gold and fought with the Arimaspians, a Scythian people who had only one eye. In the Bible, the Cherubim who guard the gate to the Garden of Eden were griffin-like beings as well as those that guarded the Ark of the Covenant. During the Christian Middle Ages numerous legends about griffins concerned the magical properties inherent in their claws. So-called griffin claws, usually antelope horns, were made into drinking cups in the belief that they would change color in the presence of poison. In an Italian medieval bestiary the griffin is symbolic of the devil, but in general the griffin was seen as a symbol of Christ, who was like a lion because he reigned as king and like an eagle because of his Resurrection. Most Dante scholars see the griffin in Dante's *Divine Comedy* (Purgatory, canto 29) as a symbol of Christ.

Variant spelling: Gryphon.

1312

Grimhild (mask). In Norse mythology, wife of Giuki; queen of the Nibelungs, or Burgundians. She used a magic potion to make Sigurd (Siegfried) fall in love with her daughter Gudrun. Grimhild appears in the *Volsunga Saga*, and in Richard Wagner's *Der Ring des Nibelungen* she is the mother of Gunther and Gutrune by King Giuki and mother of Hagen by Alberich, the evil dwarf.

1313

Grimm Brothers (Jacob Ludwig Karl, 1785–1863, and William Karl, 1786–1859). Compilers of *Kinder-und Hausmarchen* (1812–1815), a collection of German folktales, often called "Grimms' Fairy Tales," but also known as *Household Tales*.

Born in Hesse, Jacob and William were librarians by profession, as well as linguists, folklorists, scholars, and teachers. When their land was threatened by a French invasion under Napoleon, they began to collect folklore and folktales around nearby Hessian villages. Their most famous collection is the *Kinder-und Hausmarchen*, which includes such well-known folktales as "The Frog King or Iron Henry," "Faithful John," "Rapunzel," "Hansel and Gretel," "Little Red Riding Hood," "The White Snake," "The Fisherman and His Wife," "Clever Hans," "The Juniper Tree," "Snow White," "Rumpelstiltskin," "The Golden Goose," and "Snow White and Rose Red." Some present-day scholars question the authenticity of the folktales. Many see them as literary rather than as folk products. Most scholars believe them to be fairly accurate renditions of the folktales heard by the brothers. Other works produced by the pair include *German Heroic Tales* (1829), a collection of legends, and *Teutonic Mythology* (1835), a long, four-volume work on German myth and legend.

1314

Grisilda (stone heroine; gray battlemaid). In medieval European legend, a symbol of patience and obedience. Grisilda, the daughter of a charcoal burner, married Walter, marquis of Saluzzo. Her husband spent most of his time testing his wife to see if she would obey him and be faithful. He took away her two children and told her they were murdered. Then he divorced her and sent her home, saying he was about the marry another woman. Finally, he stopped the cruel joking. The tale is told by Chaucer in *The Canterbury Tales* as "The Clerk's Tale." Chaucer based it on Boccaccio's version in *The Decameron*. Boccaccio's source was a French folktale.

1315

Gu. In African mythology (Fon of Benin), god of metal; guardian of hunters, warriors, and blacksmiths. In some accounts Gu is conceived of as a metal weapon wielded by the bisexual creator god, Mawu-Lisa, to clear the earth for humankind.

1316

Guagugiana. In the mythology of the Taino Indians of Cuba at the time of Columbus, a trickster hero. Guagugiana was taught the use of magic amulets by Guabonito, a woman who arose from the sea. Guaguiana's servant, or friend (depending on which way the various accounts are read), was Giadruvava, who was taken up to heaven and transformed into a bird.

Variant spellings: Guaguyona, Vagoniona.

1317

Guallipen. In the folklore of the Araucanian Indians of Chile, a fantastic amphibious animal. It has the head of a calf and the body of a sheep. If a pregnant woman sees, hears, or dreams of a *guallipen* on three successive nights, her child will be born deformed. Often the *guallipen* will rape ewes or cows, though the offspring will occasionally look like the mother, with only the feet or muzzle deformed.

Variant spelling: Huallepen.

1318

Guatavita Lake. In the mythology of the Chibcha Indians of Colombia, site of the temple of a serpent god who received offerings from the people. A certain chief of Guatavita discovered that his favorite wife was unfaithful to him. He had her lover im-paled and then forced his wife to eat her lover's penis and testicles. Overcome with shame, the wife threw herself and her daughter into Guatavita Lake. The chief then asked his magician to bring the two back, as he still loved his wife. The magician went down to the bottom of the lake and found that the wife and child were living in an enchanted kingdom ruled over by a dragon. The chief insisted that they be brought to the surface. The magician again went down and came up with the little girl's dead body, but the dragon had eaten her eyes.

1319

Guayavacuni. In the mythology of the Tehuelcho Indians of the Patagonian pampas in South America, supreme being and beneficent spirit.

Variant spelling: Guayarakunny.

1320

Gucumatz (plumed serpent). In Mayan mythology, hero in the Mayan sacred book *Popol Vuh*, who could transform himself into an eagle, serpent, or tiger, among other animals.

1321

Gudatrigakwitl (old man above). In North American Indian mythology (Wiyot), creator god who brought about his creation by joining his hands and spreading them out.

1322

Gudrun. Name of several different women appearing in Norse and Germanic mythology. In the Norse *Volsunga Saga* Gudrun is the wife of Sigurd. He fell in love with and married her after being given a magic potion. After his death she married Atli but later killed him and his two sons. She appears as Kriemhild in the Germanic epic, the *Nibelungenlied*, and as Gutrune in Wagner's *Der Ring des Nibelungen*.

Gudrun is also the name of the heroine of the Icelandic *Laxdala Saga*, in which she is a selfish woman who marries successively Thorwald, Thord, and Bolli, though she loves Kjartan, whose death she brings about.

A German epic poem of the 13th century is titled *Gudrun*. The first part tells of Hagen, king of Ireland; the second part recounts Hetel's courtship of Hagen's daughter Hilden; and the third part tells of Gudrun, their daughter. Gudrun is engaged to Herwig of Zealand but is stolen by Hartmut of Normandy. She refuses to marry her abductor and for 13 years is forced to do servant's work. At last Herwig, accompanied by Gudrun's brother, rescues her. William Morris's *The Lovers of Gudrun*, part of *The Earthly Paradise*, retells the tale. Gudrun (Gutrune) appears in Arthur Rackham's illustrations for Wagner's Ring Cycle.

Guinever (A. Beardsley)

1323

Guecubu. In the folklore of the Araucanian Indians of Chile, demonic beings capable of assuming animal and human forms. They sow the fields with caterpillars, weaken animals with disease, quake the earth, and devour the fish in rivers and lakes.

Variant spellings: Guecufu, Huecuvu.

1324

Guinechen (master of men?). In mythology of the Araucanian Indians of Chile, supreme god. Guinechen controlled the forces of nature, giving life to people and animals. He was also called Guinemapun, "master of the land," and saved mankind when there was a flood by raising the mountains so that the people could escape the waters.

1325

Guinever (fair and yielding). In Arthurian legend, the wife of King Arthur. Her name in Welsh is Gwenhywvar (the white ghost). According to Malory in *Morte d'Arthur* (he spells her name Guenever), she was the daughter of Leodegraunce, king of the land of Cameliard. She loved Lancelot of the Lake, one of the knights of the Round Table, and had a long love affair with him. When King Arthur went to war against Leo, king of the Romans, Guinever was seduced by Mordred, her husband's nephew (his son in some accounts). Arthur hurried back and Guinever fled. A desperate battle followed between Arthur and Mordred, in which Mordred was slain and Arthur mortally wounded. Guinever then took the nun's veil at Almesbury, where later she died. She was said to be buried at Glastonbury. In Tennyson's *Idylls of the King* she is guilty only of passion for Lancelot and takes no part in Mordred's treachery.

Variant spellings: Ganor, Ganora, Generua, Ginevra, Genievre, Guenever, Guanhumara, Guanhumar, and Guinevere (as Tennyson spells it).

1326

Guirivilo. In folklore of the Araucanian Indians of Chile, a catlike monster. Guirivilo is armed with a claw-pointed tail and lives in the water, coming out to devour people.

Variant spelling: Neguruvilu.

1327

Gula. In Near Eastern mythology (Babylonian), goddess of healing, life-giver, the great physician who preserved the body in health and who removed sickness and disease by the touch of her hand. She was married to Ninib, with whom she shared her powers. She not only did good works but was invoked to bring down punishment on one's enemies. She was also the intermediary between the gods of the living and the gods of the dead.

1328

Gulistan, The (rose garden). A collection of didactic fables in rhymed prose with interspersed verses by the Persian poet Sadi, written in 1258.

The Gulistan is made up of eight chapters or divisions, each one treating a different subject. They are "The Manners of Kings," "The Morals of Dervishes," "On the Excellence of Contentment," "On the Advantages of Silence," "On Love and Youth," "On Weakness and Old Age," "On the Effects of Education," and "On Rules for Conduct of Life."

The fables, which are brilliant gems of terse writing, have short verses interspersed with them to summarize the fables and point out the morals. Often, however, the result is ambiguous. Many of the moral questions brought up by the tales are answered in a Machiavellian manner. One of the English translators of the book in the last century told his readers to skip over these "as some of our queasy clergy do in reading the morning and evening lessons." Yet no less a moralist than Ralph Waldo Emerson wrote that Sadi's *Gulistan* "speaks to all nations, and like Homer, Shakespeare, Cervantes, and Montaigne, is perpetually modern." Emerson found in the book "the universality of moral law."

The first translation of *The Gulistan* into a Western language, Latin, was made in 1651. It soon was a popular book among the 18th-century Enlightenment philosophers such as Voltaire. One of the problems encountered by the book's English translators was Sadi's continual reference to lovemaking among boys, which the poet considered perfectly normal. James Rose, who translated the book in 1823, changed the male gender to the female and decided on "the process of leaving out of the translation a few words of the Persian text." A complete translation, with all of the sexual references, was made by Edward Rehatsek in 1888.

1329

Gunlod (inviter to battle). In Norse mythology, a giantess, daughter of Suttung; mother of the god Bragi. She possessed the mead of inspiration, which was stolen from her by Odin, who seduced her. Gunlod appears in the *Poetic Edda* and the *Prose Edda* .

1330

Guy of Warwick (wit, wide, wood). In medieval British legend, hero whose exploits were first written down by an anonymous Anglo- Norman poet in the 12th century.

Guy, son of Syward of Wallingford, steward of the earl of Warwick, fell in love with Felice la Belle, the earl's daughter. At first Felice rejected Guy's love but later changed her mind and said she would accept him when he became a famous knight.

Knighted by the earl, Guy went to sea, seeking adventures that would make him famous. After a year he returned to England to be honored by King Aethelstan. However, Felice feared that if she married him he would lose all interest in his knighthood. She promised to marry him if he became the most famous knight in the whole world. Still in love, Guy returned to his life of adventure. His greatest achievement was the deliverance of the emperor of Constantinople from the Saracens. His reward for his mighty deeds was half of the emperor's kingdom as well as the emperor's daughter in marriage. At the altar Guy remembered Felice and fainted. The marriage was postponed, and Under a pretext Guy left Constantinople.

Returning through Germany, Guy rescued two lovers, Sir Tirri and Gisel. Back in England, he heard that a dragon was ravaging Northumbria; he hastened there and after a violent battle killed the dragon. When he returned home, he found that his father had died. At Warwick he was welcomed as a hero, and he then married Felice.

After a month of marriage Guy thought of all of the time he had spent winning Felice's love and how little of his life he had given to Jesus. He vowed to expiate his sins by becoming a pilgrim. Felice attempted to stop him, telling him that she was pregnant. Guy told her that when the child was born she should give it to his former master and companion in arms, Sir Haraud of Ardern, to be educated. Felice gave Guy a ring as a parting gift. For many years, through many lands, Guy the Pilgrim "with a glad chere" pursued his way.

Once in the East he put aside his pilgrim's garb to fight the Saracen giant Amourant in behalf of Christian prisoners. Then, returning again to Germany, he helped Sir Tirri once more. Finally, as an old man he returned to England. The land had been invaded by the Danes under Anlaf, and King Aethelstan, directed by angels, begged the pilgrim (he did not know it was Guy) to aid them in their fight against the giant Colbrand. After a desperate fight near Winchester, Guy killed the giant. Leaving Winchester, Guy journeyed to a neighborhood near Warwick and settled in a place where a hermit had once lived. Soon after, Guy fell ill. It was revealed to him in a dream that he would die in a week's time. On the seventh day he found a messenger to carry to Felice the ring that she had given him at parting, so that she might know that he had come back.

The messenger took the ring to Felice, and she begged him for news of Guy. He told her that Guy had been living as a hermit in the woods among wild beasts, eating herbs and roots and that Guy was near death.

Felice mounted her horse and rode to the woods to find Guy. When she entered his cell, Guy raised his eyes and hands toward her, as though asking her pardon for the sorrow he had caused her. She bent and kissed him, and he died.

After his death his body gave forth a sweet spicelike odor. Sick persons were cured of their diseases when they smelled it. It lasted until the day of his burial, which took place in the hermitage, for no man was able to remove the body from the cell, even though 30 knights attempted it. Felice then moved into Guy's cell and died there 40 days later.

1331
Gwain (little hawk). In Arthurian legend, nephew to King Arthur; he appears in the Welsh *Mabinogion* as Gwalchmei. Gwain was known as "the courteous." In the Middle English poem *Sir Gawain and the Green Knight*, Gwain beheads the Green Knight in combat after having promised to meet him for a return stroke 12 months later at the Green Chapel. On the appointed day Gwain and the Green Knight both arrive. Gwain's honor is then tested by the knight's wife, and Gwain proves himself pure. He escapes unharmed.

1332
Gwaten. In Japanese Buddhist mythology, moon goddess, derived from the Hindu god Soma. She is portrayed as a woman holding in her right hand a disk, symbol of the moon. She is one of the Jiu No O, 12 Japanese Buddhist gods and goddesses adopted from Hindu mythology.

1333
Gwydion (to say poetry). In Celtic mythology, a magician, king of the British Celts, son of Don, brother of Amgethon, Gilvaethwy, and Govannon, borther and lover of Arianrhod. Gwydion was noted for the arts of poetry, divination, and prophecy. Many of the myths attached to his name were transferred during the Middle Ages to King Arthur.
Variant spelling: Gwidion.

1334
Gwynn (fair blessed). In Celtic mythology, a god of the underworld, son of Nudd. Gwynn was at first a war god who hunted men's souls, leading them to Annwn, the land of the dead, over which he ruled. In later Welsh legend he is the king of the Tylwyth Teg, the Welsh fairies, and chief of the Ellyllon, a band of elves similar to brownies. Often Gwynn is accompanied by an owl, indicating his earlier role as god of the underworld.
Variant spelling: Gwynwas.

1335

Gyges (earth-born). In Greek mythology, one of the three giants, Hecatoncheires, sons of Uranus and Gaea, the others were Briareus and Cottus. Gyges is also the name of a shepherd (c. 685–657 B.C.E.) who killed the Lydian king and married his widow. He was aided in this feat, according to legend recorded in Plato's *Republic* (book 2), by a magic ring that made him invisible.

H

Habid al-Nadjdjar. In Islamic legend, saint identified with Agabus, a Christian prophet mentioned in the New Testament.

In Acts (11:28) Agabus predicts a famine that is to take place during the reign of the emperor Claudius Caesar. The historian Josephus does mention a famine that depopulated the country of Judea. According to Acts (21:10), Agabus met St. Paul some time after this event.

In the Islamic account Habid al-Nadjdjar (the carpenter) is converted by two Apostles of Jesus and runs to tell the people of the city to follow them. The people are unmoved by his arguments and kill him, telling Habid to "enter into Paradise" (Koran, sura 36). In one legend Habid (who is not directly named in the Koran) was decapitated. He took his head and walked with it for three days, when it cried out: "How gracious Allah hath been to me, and that He hath made me one of His honored ones." This statement is recorded in the Koran (sura 36), although the decapitation is not mentioned. Sura 36 also reports that Allah sent the archangel Gabriel to the people: "And lo! they were extinct." The destruction of the people may stem back to the famine that is part of the Christian legend.

1337

Hacavitz. In Mayan Indian mythology, a mountain god, as well as the mountain where the god was worshiped. The Mayan book *Title of the Lord of Totonicapán* (16th century) says that Hacavitz was the god of Mahucutah, who "went up the height and breadth of Hacavitz itself." Giving the same name to a mountain and a god who dwells on it is quite common in mythology.

1338

Hactcin. In North American Indian mythology (Jicarilla Apache), personification of objects and natural forces, creator of all things.

1339

Haddingjar. In Northern mythology, twin brothers named among the early kings of Norway or Sweden. They are believed by some scholars to have been twin gods.

1340

Hades (unseen, sightless). In Greek and Roman mythology, god of the underworld, son of Cronus

Hades

and Rhea; brother of Demeter, Hera, Hestia, Zeus, and Poseidon. When he was born, Hades was swallowed by his father and later disgorged when Zeus, with the help of Metis, tricked Cronus. When Cronus was defeated by his rebel sons, Zeus, Poseidon, and Hades, the three gods drew lots on which part of the universe each would rule. The underworld fell to Hades. The god fell in love with Persephone, whom he abducted and made his wife, though she never bore him any children. No temples were dedicated to the god. The cypress and narcissus were sacred to him. In ancient art he was portrayed in a manner similiar to his brothers Zeus and Poseidon, bearing a staff, symbol of authority. Sometimes he was accompanied by his wife, Persephone, and the three-headed dog Cerebrus. Among the many names in Greek and Roman mythology borne by the god are Ades, Aides, Aidoneus, Dis, Orcus, Pluto, and Pluton.

1341

Hadith (talk, speech). In Islam, traditional sayings ascribed to Muhammad, which supplement the Koran. They help clarify points of law or ceremonial observance on which the Koran is silent or does not provide enough information. Hadith also deal with the life of Muhammad and the circumstances attending the revelations made to him. Although Muslim authorities have been very strict in the canons laid down for the reception or rejection of these traditions, a great deal of uncertainty exists as to the authenticity of many inclusions in the Hadith. The laws embodied in the traditions are called the *sunnah*. In addition to the Koran and Hadith, the Isma (consensus) of Muslim authorities covers points not explicit in the other works.

1342

Haemus (skillful?). In Greek mythology, king of Thrace; son of Boreas and Orithyia; brother of Calais, Chione, Cleopatra, and Zetes; husband of Rhodope. Haemus and Rhodope were so pleased with themselves that they called themselves Zeus and Hera. For this sacrilege they were transformed into mountains (the Balkans, once called the Haemus range). Ovid's *Metamorphoses* (book 6) tells the tale.

1343

Hafaza. In Islamic mythology, angels who protect people from djinn; two are assigned to a person for the daytime and two for the night. They keep a register of all of one's actions; the one who stands on a man's right keeps a record of his good deeds, and the angel who stands on his left records all of his evil acts. Sometimes the angel on the right tries to persuade his angelic companion not to write down the evil deeds but to give the person at least six or seven hours to repent. The most dangerous time for a person is when the angelic guards are changing shifts, which takes place at the rising and the setting of the sun. The djinn are most active at this time because they know a person's angelic protection is at its weakest.

1344

Hagen. In the *Nibelungenlied* and in Wagner's *Der Ring des Nibelungen*, the slayer of the hero Siegfried. He is called Hagni in the earlier *Volsunga Saga*. Hagen is portrayed in Arthur Rackham's illustrations for Wagner's Ring Cycle.

1345

Hagia Sophia (holy wisdom). In Christianity, Second Person of the Holy Trinity, Jesus Christ. The church dedicated to Hagia Sophia at Constantinople was built by Emperor Justinian between 532 and 537. When the Turks took Constantinople in 1453, the building was turned into a mosque.

The Trinity

1346

Hai K'ang. In Chinese legend, one of the seven Chu-lin Ch'i-Hsien (Seven Immortals). He was a student of the black arts, which he practiced under a willow tree.

In Japanese legend he is called Riurei.

1347

Haitsi-aibed. In African mythology (Hottentot), resurrected hero, born of a cow and the grass it had eaten; patron of hunters.

Haitsi-aibed's most famous battle was with Gaunab (thrower down), a monster who would sit at the edge of a deep pit and dare passersby to hurl a stone at him. The stone always rebounded, hitting the person and causing him to fall into the pit. When Haitsi-aibed accepted the challenge of Gaunab, he made sure to divert the monster, and then he hurled the stone so as to hit him under his ear, causing Gaunab to fall into the pit. In some variant accounts Gaunab falls into the pit three times, escaping twice but dying after the third fall. Other tales tell how Haitsi-aibed died and was resurrected. Even today many caves in South Africa are called Haitsi-aibed graves in reference to the tales.

1348

Halirrhothius (roaring sea). In Greek mythology, son of Poseidon and Euryte. He raped Ares' daughter, Alcippe. Ares in turn killed Halirrhothius and was brought to the Areopagus for trial by Poseidon and acquitted.

Haltia (familiar spirit). In Finno-Ugric mythology, tutelary genius of a person. Each person has his own *haltia*, which goes before him. If the *haltia* is a very potent one, it arrives home before the person does, announcing its presence by a crash. The *haltia* is believed to become a reality three days after birth, and it is considered dangerous for a baby to be alone before that time. The *haltia* is sometimes blamed for a man's poor actions, with people saying, "It was not he, but his *haltia*." Sometimes the terms *saattaja* (guide) and *onni* (fortune) are used in reference to *haltia*.

Halwanli, Hiwanama, and Ourwanama. In the mythology of the Surinam region (formerly Dutch Guiana) in South America, rival brothers. Halwanli was the oldest, the lord of all things inanimate and irrational. Ourwanama, the second brother, was a worker of the fields, a maker of liquor, and the husband of two wives. The youngest brother, Hiwanama, was a hunter.

One day Hiwanama came to the territory of Ourwanama and met his brother's two wives, who got him drunk and then seduced him. When Ourwanama discovered what had happened he exiled his brother. Their mother complained about the loss of her son; as a result the wives were transformed into a bird and a fish, and Ourwanama was drowned in the sea. Halwanli then went in search of Hiwanama and found him among the serpents and other reptiles of the lower world. When he brought him back, Hiwanama became one of the greatest *peaimen*, magician-priests similar to medicine men.

Hamlet (home). In medieval legend, a Danish hero, son of Gerutha and Horvendill.

The legend of Hamlet, or Amleth, was first told by Saxo Grammaticus, a Danish chronicler, in his *Historia Danica*. Hamlet's father Horvendill was killed by his brother Feng, who then married Gerutha, widow of Horvendill. Hamlet, fearful of being killed, pretended to go insane. Feng put him to various tests to see if the madness was real. Among other things he sought to entangle Hamlet with a young girl, his foster sister, but Hamlet's cunning saved him. When Hamlet slew an eavesdropper hidden in his mother's room and then hid all traces of the murder, Feng decided Hamlet was not insane. He sent Hamlet off to England in the company of two attendants, who bore a letter to the king of England, telling him to put Hamlet to death. Hamlet secretly altered the letter, and the two attendants were put to death instead. He also changed the letter to say that the king should allow Hamlet to marry his daughter. After marrying the princess, Hamlet returned to Denmark, taking with him hollow sticks filled with gold. He arrived in time for a funeral feast, held to celebrate his death. During the feast he plied the courtiers with wine and executed his vengeance during their drunken sleep; he covered them with the woolen hangings of the hall, fastened down with sharpened pegs, and then set fire to the palace. With the death of Feng the people proclaimed Hamlet king. He then returned to England for his wife.

Other adventures follow, none of which have left traces on the plays inspired by the legend. The most famous, of course, is Shakespeare's *Hamlet*, which inspired Lizst's symphonic poem *Hamlet*, Tchaikovsky's fantasy overture *Hamlet*, Ambrose Thomas's opera *Hamlet*, and Shostakovich's incidental music to the movie of the play.

Variant spelling: Amleth.

Handaka Sonja. In Japanese Buddhist mythology, one of the perfected disciples, or *arhats* of the Buddha, often portrayed with a bowl from which issues a dragon or a rain cloud (both symbols of water). Handaka Sonja holds the bowl aloft with his left hand and with his right carries the sacred Tama. Sometimes he is portrayed seated on a rock with crouching with a dragon at the side to protect the Tama. In Sanskrit, Handaka Sonja is called Panthaka.

Han Hsiang Tzu

Han Hsiang Tzu. Ninth century C.E. In Chinese Taoist legend, a deified mortal, one of the Pa-Hsien, the

Eight Immortals. He is portrayed playing a flute or floating on a hollow tree trunk. Once he was carried to the top of a magic peach tree growing near a palace. The bough broke and he entered into immortality as he fell. During his lifetime he was credited with magically filling an empty tub with wine, as well as having flowers grow out of an empty pot and having golden poems appear on leaves.

In Japanese legend Han Hsiang Tzu is called Kanshoshi.

1354

Hannya. In Japanese folklore, a female demon who eats children. She often appears in No dramas and is portrayed by a mask with horns, open mouth, and sharp fangs.

1355

Hansel and Gretel. German folktale found in the Grimms' collection of *Household Tales*. Hansel and Gretel are the children of a poor woodcutter, who remarries after the death of his wife. The stepmother hates the children and says there is not enough food for them to eat. The children are abandoned in the forest but find their way home. They are sent out a second time and become lost. They discover the house of a witch, who captures them and prepares to eat them. Each day the witch feeds them and feels their hands and arms to see if they have gained enough weight to make them fit to eat. Instead of putting out his arm, Hansel puts out a bone, and the nearsighted witch keeps postponing the day of doom. Finally, the witch angrily says she is ready to eat Hansel, thin or not. She asks Gretel to go inside the oven to see if it is hot enough. Gretel says she does not know how. The witch demonstrates for her and is pushed into the oven and the door is closed. The two children then fill their pockets with jewels and eventually return home to find their father alive and their stepmother dead. Humperdinck's opera *Hansel und Gretel* is the best-known treatment of the folktale, though it varies the tale somewhat.

1356

Hantu. In Malayan mythology, generic name for demons, ghosts, and spirits.

1357

Hantu Ayer and Hantu Laut. In Malayan mythology, water and sea spirits or demons.

1358

Hantu B'rok. In Malayan mythology, a demon sometimes called the coconut monkey. He is believed to take possession of dancers and enable them to perform wonderful climbing feats.

1359

Hantu Denej. In Malayan mythology, the demon of wild beasts' tracks.

1360

Hantu Kubor. In Malayan mythology, grave demons, who also prey on the living when given the opportunity. With them are the Hantu Orang Mati Di-Bunch, the spirits of murdered men.

1361

Hantu Pemburu (demon hunter). In Malayan mythology, the wild huntsman or specter huntsman who causes havoc for man.

There was a man named Hantu Pemburu, whose wife was pregnant. She was "seized with a violent longing for meat of the *pelandok*, or mouse deer." But it was no ordinary mouse deer the woman wanted. She insisted that it should be a doe, "big with male offspring." Her husband, obedient to his wife's wishes, went into the jungle to seek the *pelandok* taking his weapons and his faithful dogs. Through a misunderstanding, the man hunted the buck *pelandok*, "big with male offspring," of course, an impossible quest.

Hantu Pemburu hunted day and night, slaying one mouse deer after another, which he discarded because he believed they did not fulfill his wife's requirements. He had sworn a solemn oath that he would not return home unless he was successful, and he became a regular denizen of the forest, eating the flesh and drinking the blood of the animals that he slew.

In time he covered the whole earth. "I have hunted the whole earth over without finding what I want," he said to himself. "It is now time to try the firmament." He "holloa'd on his dogs through the sky" while he continued on earth, bending back his neck to watch their progress. After a long time his head became fixed on his back as a result of constantly gazing upward. He was no longer able to look down at the earth. A leaf from the *si limbak* tree fell on his throat and took root, and a shoot grew upward in front of his face. In this state, Hantu Pemburu still hunts through the Malay forest, urging on his dogs as they hunt through the sky, with his gaze always turned upward.

His wife is not forgotten in the myth. She gave birth to two children, a boy and a girl. When the boy was of age, he went in search of his father. On his way he came upon a man who said that the boy's father had borrowed a chisel from him and he wanted it returned. When the son found his father in the forest, he told him about the man.

"I will eat his heart and drink his blood," responded Hantu Pemburu. "So shall he be rewarded."

From that day forth Hantu Pemburu has afflicted mankind.

1362

Hantu Songkei (loosening demon). In Malayan mythology, a demon who sets about untying the knots made by hunters in snares for wildfowl. He is invisible below the waist, and he has a nose of enormous length (a symbol of his penis) and eye sockets stretched sideways to such an extent that he can see all around him.

1363

Hanukkah (dedication). In Judaism, an eight-day festival commemorating the dedication of the second Temple by Judas Maccabeus. The Old Testament Apocrypha book 1 Maccabees (4:59) states, "Moreover Judas and his brethren with the whole congregation of Israel ordained that the days of the dedication of the altar should be kept in their season from year to year by the space of eight days . . . with mirth and gladness." According to one account in the Talmud, the festival lasts eight days because the oil found in the Temple was sufficient for only one day but it burned for eight. The main symbol of Hanukkah is the menorah, an eight-branch candlestick with a socket for a ninth candle. Also called the Feast of Dedication, it falls on the 25th day of the month Kislev (around 10 December).
Variant spelling: Chanukkah.

Hanuman

1364

Hanuman (having large jaws). In the Hindu epic poem *The Ramayana*, a monkey hero.

Hanuman was the son of Vayu, the wind god, by a monkey mother, Vanar. He and his monkey allies assisted Rama in his war against the demon king Ravana. In one episode in *The Ramayana*, Hanuman jumps from India to Lanka (Sri Lanka) in one leap. However, he is caught in the city by Ravana's men and his tail is greased and set on fire. Hanuman jumps around from building to building, burning the entire city. He later helps Rama win back Sita, Rama's wife, from Ravana.

Hanuman is described as "vast as a mountain and as tall as a gigantic tower. His complexion is yellow and glowing like molten gold. His face is as red as the brightest ruby; while his enormous tail spreads out to an interminable length. He stands on a lofty rock and roars like thunder. He leaps into the air and flies among the clouds with a rushing noise, while the ocean waves are roaring and splashing below."

A drama, *Hanuman-nataka*, treating Hanuman's adventures is said to have been written by the monkey hero himself.
Variant spelling: Hanumat.

1365

Haoma. In Persian mythology, sacred healing plant from which an intoxicating drink was made, similar to the Hindu sacred plant Soma.

Thrita, a hero in Persian myth, is called the preparer of Haoma, the third man who prepared the magic drink for the world. He prayed to Ahura Mazda, the good creator god, for a medicine that would withstand the pain, disease, infection, and death that the evil spirits were working against men. In answer to Thrita's prayers Ahura Mazda sent down various healing plants that grew around the Gaokerena tree, a magical tree that had within it the seeds of all plants and trees, among them the sacred Haoma. The Haoma was used in various rites and was believed to make the dead immortal if they tasted it, grant children to women, and give strong men to young girls as their husbands.

1366

Hapi. In Egyptian mythology, god of the Nile, who became identified in some myths with all of the great primeval creative deities and eventually was believed to have been the creator of everything. At a very early period Hapi absorbed the attributes of Nun, the primeval watery mass from which the god Ra emerged on the first day of creation. As a result, Hapi was regarded as the father of all beings. He held a unique position in Egyptian religion, although he was not in any theological system developed by the priests.

The light of Ra brought life to men and animals, but without the waters of Hapi every living thing would perish. Hapi is usually portrayed as a fat man with the breasts of a woman to indicate his powers of fertility. When he represents both the south and north Nile, Hapi holds two plants, the papyrus and the lotus, or two vases, from which he pours out water.

Variant spellings: Hap, Hapy.

Hare

1367

Hare. A rodentlike mammal, related to but larger than the rabbit; the two are often confused in world mythology and folklore. It was believed that the hare was abnormally lustful, and the animal came to be a symbol of lust as portrayed by medieval artists and writers. Most medieval books cite the belief that the hare was capable of changing its sex. The female animal was also believed to be able to conceive without the aid of a male and to retain its virginity. When a hare appears in a painting of the Virgin Mary, it is symbolic of the triumph of chastity. The enemies of Queen Elizabeth I of England called her a hare because her devoted subjects called her the virgin queen. It was a common belief that the appearance of a hare presaged misfortune.

1368

Harimau Kramat. In Malayan mythology, ghost tigers. Once there was a man named Nakhoda Ragam traveling in a boat with his wife, the princess of Malacca. When the princess, for some reason not revealed in the legend, pricked her husband to death with a needle, his blood flooded the boat. Another boat was passing and the master of that vessel asked, "What have you got in your boat?"

"Spinach juice," replied the princess. She then went on her way and landed at the foot of Jurga Hill, where she buried all that remained of her husband—one thigh (she had thrown most of his body overboard). She also took ashore her two cats, which were in the boat with her when she murdered her husband. The cats turned into Harimau Kramat, ghost tigers, and became the guardians of the shrine.

1369

Haris-chandra. In Hindu mythology, a king noted for his suffering.

One day when Haris-chandra was hunting, he heard female voices "from the sciences, who were being mastered by the austerely fervid sage Viswamitra, and were crying out in alarm at his superiority." Haris-chandra, as defender of the distressed, went to the rescue. Viswamitra was so provoked by Haris-chandra's interference that the sciences were destroyed. Haris-chandra was placed under the complete control of Viswamitra. The sage demanded from Haris-chandra a sacrificial gift and Haris-chandra offered Viswamitra whatever he wanted, "gold, his own son, wife, body, life, kingdom, good fortune." Viswamitra stripped Haris-chandra of his wealth and kingdom, leaving him with nothing but a garment of bark and his wife and son.

In this state Haris-chandra left his wife and son, only to have the two also demanded by Viswamitra. With bitter grief the two were sold, and later Haris-chandra, the former king, was carried off "bound, beaten and confused, and afflicted."

The gods finally took pity on his suffering and took him to heaven, but Haris-chandra boasted of his merits and was thrown out. As he was falling, he repented of his foolishness, and his fall was arrested. He now dwells in the aerial city, which can still be seen floating in midair, according to some.

1370

Harmachis (Horus who is on the horizon). In Egyptian mythology, the Greek name for the Egyptian god Rehoarakhty. According to legend, the Pharaoh Tuthmosis IV, while still a prince, was hunting in the deserts near Giza and sought shelter from the noonday sun in the shadow of the great Sphinx. He soon fell asleep and in a dream the Sphinx, as Rehoarakhty, promised him the throne of Egypt if he would clear away the sands that had engulfed the Sphinx. The prince awoke, cleared away the sand, and was later crowned king of Egypt. A stele erected at the site of the Sphinx by Tuthmosis IV records the dream and its consequences.

1371

Harmonia (concord). In Greek mythology, daughter of Ares and Aphrodite, wife of Cadmus, king of Thebes; mother of Agave, Autonoe, Ino, Polydorus, and Semele. When Harmonia was married to Cadmus, Zeus, who arranged the match, gave Harmonia a necklace made by Hephaestus that promised its possessor beauty. In variant accounts, the necklace was given to Cadmus, who gave it to his wife, or the gift was given by Zeus to his mistress Europa or by Aphrodite to Harmonia. Given at the same time to Harmonia was a robe by Athena, who, some variant accounts say, also gave the necklace. Both gifts brought disaster on the family and played an important part in the Seven against Thebes as well as the war of the Epigoni. Finally, to stop the bloodshed, the gifts were placed in the temple of Apollo at Delphi, where they remained until the fourth century B.C.E., when they were stolen. Harmonia and Cadmus were turned into serpents. Ovid's *Metamorphoses* (books 3, 4) tells the story, and Milton's *Paradise Lost* (9.503–506) refers to the transformation.

1372
Haroeris (Horus the elder, Horus the great). In Egyptian mythology, Greek name for Har Wer, who was worshiped at Letopolis. Some texts say he was the son of Geb, the earth god, and Nut, the sky goddess; others that he was the son of Ra, the sun god, and Hathor, the cow goddess. Haroeris was worshiped with his female counterpart, Ta-sent-nefert, and their son, P-neb-taui, forming a trinity. In Egyptian art Haroeris is portrayed as a man with the head of a hawk, wearing the double crown of Upper and Lower Egypt.

1373
Harpies (snatcher). In Greek mythology, winged monsters with women's faces and vulture bodies, daughters of Thaumas and Electra or of Poseidon and Gaea. Some accounts give their names as Aello, Celaeno, and Ocypete. Hesiod's *Theogony* names Aello and Ocypete; Homer names Podarge. In Vergil's *Aeneid* (book 3) they plunder Aeneas' fleet on its way to Italy. In Spenser's *Faerie Queene* (2.12.36) they are "the hellish Harpies, prophets of sad destiny," and in Milton's *Paradise Regained* (book 2.403) the banquet created by Satan vanishes "with sound of Harpies wings, and Talons heard."

1374
Harpokrates (Horus the child, the infant Horus). In Egyptian mythology, Greek name for the Egyptian Heru-p-khart, a form of the god Horus. He was often portrayed with the sidelock of youth and wearing the double crown of Upper and Lower Egypt. His index finger is held to his lips, which the Greeks misinterpreted as a symbol of his discretion. They called Harpokrates the god of silence as a result of this mistake. Sometimes Harpokrates is shown being suckled by his mother, Isis.

1375
Harris, Eliza. In American history and folklore, a black slave woman who fled north with her two chil-

dren. When she reached the Ohio River, it was winter, and the ice was breaking up. Her pursuers, with bloodhounds, were left helpless at the shore as Eliza, leading her children, crossed the river by jumping from one ice floe to another. Harriet Beecher Stowe's antislavery novel *Uncle Tom's Cabin* uses the episode as does the ballet sequence in *The King and I* by Rodgers and Hammerstein.

1376
Harut and Marut. In Islamic mythology, two fallen angels who teach men sorcery and magic. They are the brothers of Iblis, the father of the djinn, who is the best-known fallen angel in Islam.

According to the Koran (sura 2), Harut and Marut teach men "how to cause division between husband and wife." The two can work their evil only by permission of Allah. A number of myths are connected with this passage in the Koran.

In one account, when the angels saw how sinful man was they spoke contemptuously of him to Allah. "If you were in his place," Allah replied, "you would do no better."

The angels did not agree with Allah, and two of them, Harut and Marut, were chosen to fly down to earth for an experiment to test the truth of the matter. Allah told them that they were to abstain from idolatry, whoredom, murder, and drinking of wine (all forbidden to Muslims). When the two came upon a beautiful woman, Zorba (or Zurah), they fell victim to her sexual charms. They were discovered in the act by a man, whom they killed, hoping no one would learn of their deed.

Allah, watching from heaven, saw all that happened. The angels were called to see what Harut and Marut had done. "In truth, Thou wast right," they said to Allah. Harut and Marut were then given the choice of suffering in this world or the next. They chose to suffer on earth and were thrown into a "well in the town of Babylon, where loaded with chains," they took up the business of teaching men magic and sorcery. (In Persian the word *harut* is used for a magician.)

1377
Hatfields and McCoys. In American folklore, two feuding families separated by a few miles of wild mountain and by Tug Fort, a creek that forms a natural boundary between Kentucky and West Virginia. The exact cause of the feud is not known. Some accounts say it had to do with a stolen pig; others, that a Confederate Hatfield discovered that one of the McCoy's was wearing the Union uniform and killed him. In either case, the feud went on for some time, and the death toll ranged from 50 to 200.

Hathor

Hathor's main temple was at Dendera, where she was worshiped with Horus and their son Ihi, or Ahi, who was portrayed as an infant playing the sistrum at her side (the sistrum was believed to drive away evil spirits). Great festivals were celebrated in her temple, the most important being the festival of her birth, held at the new year, which ended with a drunken orgy. Her temple became known as a palace of enjoyment and a house of intoxication and gave rise to her reputation as mistress of merriment and dance, as well as her popularity as a goddess of love, which caused the Greeks to identify her with Aphrodite.

In late Egyptian belief Hathor became the representative of all of the great goddesses in Egypt. Shrines were erected in her honor throughout the land. In her beneficent aspect she was called Nehem Away (the one who takes care of the deprived), referring to those who have been robbed or plundered.

Variant spelling: Athyr, Athor.

1379

Hathsepsut (foremost in nobility). 1501-1447 B.C.E. In Egyptian history and legend, one of the first women to rule in her own right as pharaoh. At the death of Thuthmosis II, Thuthomosis III was too young to rule. The decision was made to name Hathsepsut as regent until the young prince came of age. The beginning of their joint reign was marked by peaceful cooperation. But Hathsepsut soon seized the throne and relegated Thuthmosis III to an insignificant administrative role. She turned her attention to rebuilding Egypt internally and credited her kingship to the god Amun, to whom she built many monuments. The obelisks she erected to Amun in the temples at Karnak were of extraordinary size and were quarried and erected in record time. Her architect, Senemut, erected for her a funerary temple at Dier el Bahari in which the scenes show her famous trading expedition to the legendary land of Punt to obtain incense for Amun's cult. It also shows her divine birth, the episodes of which include the courting of her mother Ahmose by the god Amun. When Hathsepsut died, Thuthmosis III assumed his rightful position as pharaoh. Shortly thereafter, many of the monuments of Hathsepsut were destroyed in an attempt to obliterate her name. Some contend that this destruction was ordered by Thuthmosis III.

1380

Hatim. In a Moroccan Islamic legend, a princess who turned into an almond tree.

Before the advent of Islam, Hatim was a young, generous princess of the Tai tribe. Her father

1378

Hathor (house of Horus). In Egyptian mythology, ancient sky goddess, great mother goddess often portrayed as a cow or with the head of a cow. Hathor, according to one Egyptian myth, stood on the earth as a cow in such a way that her four legs were the pillars holding the sky, and her belly was the firmament. Each evening Horus, as the sun god, flew into Hathor's mouth in his hawk form, and each morning he appeared again, reborn. Consequently, Horus was said to be both her husband and her son.

Hathor was one of the oldest known goddesses of Egypt, considered to be the great mother, or cosmic goddess, who conceived, brought forth, and maintained all life. She not only nourished the living with her milk but was said to supply celestial food for the dead in Duat, the underworld. The goddess also was known for her destructive role. One myth tells how the sun god, who had grown old and wanted to punish mankind for plotting to do away with him, sent Hathor to slay mankind. Hathor enjoyed the slaughter so much that the other deities flooded the fields with an intoxicating brew, causing her to become drunk and cease her slaughter.

objected to her dispensing his wealth as well as her own, so he offered to let her choose exile or death. She chose death but Allah rewarded her for her generous deeds by transforming her into "a tree of great beauty—the almond tree which enhances our orchards."

Even today, as the almond tree, she "continues to distribute gifts; her flowers are the joy of spring; her fruit has a delightful taste; her oil is sweet and clean; she inspires peace and heals the troubled hearts of men."

Hattara Aonja. In Japanese Buddhist mythology, one of the perfected disciples, or *arhats*, of the Buddha, often portrayed with a white tiger crouching at his feet. He holds a *nloi*, a short wand, symbol of power, and is sometimes seated on a rock. In Sanskrit, Hattara Aonja is called Bhadra (auspicious).

Hatto. 10th century. In medieval northern legends, archbishop of Mainz, who was devoured by mice because of his greed.

In 970 there was a famine in Germany. It was known that Hatto had amassed vast stores of wheat in his granaries. When the people asked him for help, he appointed a day for them to receive grain. When the day arrived, the crowd filled the archbishop's barn to capacity. He then locked the door and set the barn on fire, burning all of the people inside to death.

After his murderous act he had a good dinner and a good night's sleep, as usual. The next morning he saw that his portrait had been eaten by rats. As the archbishop was surveying the previous night's destruction, a servant rushed in to tell him rats had also eaten the remainder of the stored wheat. No sooner had the servant told his tale than another appeared to inform the archbishop that rats were converging on the palace. Hatto, looking out the window, could see thousands of the creatures descending on the building.

In terror Hatto fled by boat to a private island, where he had earlier built a tower. His flight, however, was in vain; the rats pursued him, attacked his boat, and landed on the island. The archbishop managed to reach the tower, but the rats caught up with him and ate him alive. Robert Southey in his *Metrical Tales* tells the legend:

They have whetted their teeth against the stones,
And now they pick the Bishop's bones;
They gnaw'd the flesh from every limb,
For they were sent to do judgment on him.

There is a medieval watchtower on the Rhine, near Bingen, called the Mouse Tower, and Hatto's legend is associated with it. The tower, however, was built by Bishop Siegfried some 200 years after Hatto; it was built as a tollhouse for collecting duties on all goods passing through.

Hatuibwari. In Melanesian mythology, a bisexual creator god of the Arosi, sometimes portrayed as a winged serpent with a human head, four eyes, and four breasts to suckle the young. Hatuibwari's symbols are sometimes assigned to another bisexual creator god, Agunus.

Hatyani of Debrecen. 1718–1786. In Finno-Ugric legend, physician and philosopher whose experiments gained him a reputation for black magic. Tales told about him are generally based on literary, not folk, sources.

Haumea. In Polynesian mythology, Hawaiian fertility goddess, mother of Pele, also said to be the first woman. In some myths Haumea is identified with the earth goddess Papa.

Havelok the Dane (of the lake haven). In medieval northern legends, hero, whose exploits are recorded in many 13th-century works, including an English one, *Havelok the Dane*.

When King Aethelwold of England was about to die he committed his only child, Goldborough, to Earl Godrich of Cornwall, who swore to protect the girl and give her in marriage to a strong and handsome man. In Denmark, when King Birkaybeyn was on his deathbed, he entrusted his son Havelok and his two girls to the care of Earl Godard. The evil earl, however, had the two girls killed, and Havelok was given to Grim, a fisherman, who was to kill the boy. But one night in his cottage Grim saw a flame come out of the mouth of the sleeping boy. He looked at the boy and discovered a "king's mark" on his shoulder. Knowing this meant that the boy would one day be a king, he escaped with Havelok and his own family to England.

When Havelok grew up he entered the service of the cook of Earl Godrich of Cornwall. He became known for his strength and kindness. When the earl heard of Havelok he decided the lad should marry Princess Goldborough. Havelok took his wife to Grimsby, but at night Goldborough cried because she had married below her station. Then she saw a bright light come out of the mouth of the sleeping Havelok. She saw a gold cross on his shoulder.

Suddenly an angel's voice said, "Goldborough, do not cry. Havelok is a king's son. He shall be king of England and Denmark, and you shall be his queen."

Happy that she now had a king for a husband, Goldborough sailed with Havelok for Denmark, where because of his magic flame Havelok was made king. Earl Godard was sentenced by the people, flayed, drawn, and hanged. After four years Havelok returned to England, conquered Godrich, and was crowned king of England in London.

1387

Hawk. A bird of prey with a hooked beak and powerful claws. The cult of the hawk or falcon is one of the oldest in Egypt, where the bird was identified with various sky or sun gods, such as the Horus gods and Ra. The bird also was identified with Osiris, the god of the dead. The main center of worship was at Hieraconpolis (hawk city). According to Herodotus' *History* (book 2), the punishment for killing a hawk was death. In Egypt the hawk was also sacred to the Greek god Apollo in his role as diviner. One of the earliest Greek fables, told by Hesiod in his *Works and Days*, is titled "The Hawk and the Nightingale." In it the hawk is portrayed as a greedy, vicious bird.

1388

Hawk and the Nightingale, The. Aesopic fable found in Hesiod's *Work and Days*, written in the eighth century B.C.E. and considered the earliest known example of the Greek fable.

A hawk caught a nightingale and was carrying it high in the sky. The nightingale cried out, but the hawk was unmoved. It said to the poor bird: "What's wrong with you? Why scream? I'm your master and can do with you what I want. If I like I can let you go free, or if I prefer, I can eat you for dinner. He is a fool who fights with someone who is stronger than he—he will not only lose the battle but will also be disgraced."

1389

Haya-griva (horse-necked). In Hindu mythology, a demon who stole the sacred books, the *Vedas*, as they slipped out of the mouth of the god Brahma while he was sleeping. Haya-griva, in one myth, was killed by the god Vishnu. In a variant account Vishnu took the form of Haya-griva, recovering the *Vedas* from two other demons.

1390

Hayk. In Armenian folklore, hero who freed his people from the tyranny of King Bel of Babylonia.

Hayk was a handsome giant with fine limbs, curly hair, bright smiling eyes, and strong arms. The bow and the triangular arrow were his weapons. Hayk freed his people, who lived in the plain of Shinar, from the tyranny of King Bel and brought them to the mountains of Armenia. There, however, he placed the native population in subjugation. The forces of King Bel pursued Hayk, and the hero shot an arrow, piercing the chest of the king and causing his forces to disperse. Hayk's son was Armenak, another Armenian hero.

Hayk is used in Armenian as a term for a giant as well as "great beauty." St. Gregory of Narek called the Virgin Mary "Hayk-like."

1391

Hazel. A small tree of the birch family; in Norse mythology, sacred to Thor, the thunder god, and believed to be the actual embodiment of lightning. Medieval German Christians would place hazel twigs in the form of a cross on windowsills during a storm in the hope of stilling it. During Halloween, sometimes called Nutcrack Night in Europe, hazel nuts are put on the fire to foretell the fate of lovers. This custom is alluded to in Thomas Gray's poem *Elegy in a Country Churchyard*. In European folklore it was the custom for the leader of a wedding party to carry a hazel wand to ensure many offspring for the marriage. One medieval German legend says that Herodias, the wife of King Herod, who killed John the Baptist, was in love with the prophet. When his head was brought to her, she tried to kiss it, but it drew back and blew hard at her. Herodias was whirled up to the top of a hazel tree, where she still sits from midnight to cockcrow, floating in the air the rest of the time.

1392

Head and the Tail, The. Jewish fable found in the Talmud.

Once the tail of a snake said to its head, "How much longer will you lead the way and drag me behind? Let me lead and you follow."

"Very well," the head replied, "you go first."

So the tail led the way and the head followed. Nearing a ditch filled with water, the tail fell in, dragging the head after him. At another place, filled with thorn bushes, the tail and the head became tangled, scratched, and finally wounded.

Is not the head to blame for agreeing to be led by the tail?

1393

Heaven and Hell. Medieval Judaism, Christianity, and Islam all believed in a place of reward for the souls of the just with God and his angels and a place of punishment for the wicked with the devils.

Ancient Hebrew religion, as expressed in the Old Testament, does not have any concept of heaven for the just. All of the dead, both good and evil, are sent to Sheol, the underworld, a dim and hopeless place.

Dives in Hell and Lazarus in Heaven

Thus, King Saul, who was hated by God, and the prophet Samuel, who was loved by God, are both sent to Sheol. Some passages in the Old Testament suggest that God had no control over Sheol; he is concerned only with the living, not the dead. When Judaism came into more contact with pagan religions, such as that of the Persians, the idea of heaven and hell developed. This belief was passed on to the writers of the New Testament and thence to the Christian Middle Ages.

The clearest expression of the concept of heaven is found in *The Divine Comedy* of Dante, in which the poet is given a glimpse of the Divine. Dante based his work on Christian and pagan folklore and religion. Islam also based its descriptions of heaven, or paradise, called *Djanna* (garden), on earlier Jewish, Christian, and pagan folklore and mythology.

Sura 47 of the Koran says of heaven that "therein are rivers of water, which corrupt not; rivers of milk, whose taste changeth not; and rivers of wine,

delicious to those who quaff it; And Rivers of honey clarified: and therein are all kinds of fruit for them from their Lord!" In sura 55, the faithful shall lie "on couches with linings of brocade . . . and the fruit of the two gardens shall be within easy reach. . . . Therein shall be the damsels with retiring glances, whom man nor djinn hath touched before them."

In Islamic mythology Djanna (like Dante's *Paradiso*) consists of various divisions: Gannat al 'Huld, or The Garden of Eternity (sura 25); Dâr as Salâm, or The Abode of Peace (sura 6); Dâr al Qarâr, or The Abode of Rest (sura 40); Gannat Hadn, or The Garden of Eden (sura 9); Gannat al Mâwâ, or The Garden of Resort (sura 32); Gannat al Na'hîm, or The Garden of Pleasure (sura 6); Gannat al Hilliyûn, or The Garden of the Most High (sura 83); Gannat al Pirdaus, or The Garden of Paradise (sura 18).

From the various descriptions in the Koran, heaven is the realization of all that a dweller in a hot, parched, and barren land could desire— shade, water, fruit, rest, pleasant women, young men, and alcohol (denied to the Muslims during their lifetimes).

In later Islamic writings Djanna is represented as a pyramid or cone, consisting of the eight divisions. At the top is the fabulous tree *sidret-el-mounteha*. In *The Ascension of Muhammad*, a work in which Muhammad describes his journey through the various heavens (Muhammad was not the author), he says:

> We attained the *sidret-el-mounteha*. That which is thus called is a large tree, some of whose branches are of emerald, others of pearl, with foliage similar to elephants' ears. Its fruits are of considerable size. From the foot of the tree gush four springs which flow into as many canals. Two of these canals are open to the skies, but the two others are covered. . . . The water of these two rivers is whiter than milk and sweeter than honey. Angels coming toward me, greeted me, and brought three goblets, which they presented to me. In one was milk, in another wine, and in the third was honey.

On the leaves of the tree are the names of all of the people in the world. After sunset on the night of the 15th of Ramadan each year the leaves with the names of those who are to die during the year fall from the tree.

Djanna also contains a fountain, Salsabil (sura 76), signifying water flowing gently down the throat. It may also refer to wine, since it will be lawful to drink wine in paradise, although it is forbidden the Muslims on earth.

The Christian heaven makes no provision for animals, but the Islamic Djanna admits ten animals into its quarters. They are Noah's dove, Abraham's ram, which was sacrificed in place of Isaac; Moses' ox; Balaam's ass; King Solomon's ant; the Queen of Sheba's lapwing Dalkis, Jonah's whale, the Islamic prophet Saleh's she-camel; and Borak, the fabulous animal who took Muhammad to heaven.

Jewish, Christian, and Moslem concepts of hell are quite similar. In *The Divine Comedy* Dante gives an elaborate description of hell in which he is guided by Vergil, the ancient Roman poet who was believed to be a magician during the Middle Ages.

Dante's description of hell was inspired by 1,000 years of Christian myth and legend. In one early nonscriptural Christian work, St. Peter describes hell: "And I saw another place right opposite, rough and being the place of punishment. And those who are punished there and the punishing angels had their robes dark; as the color of the air of the place is also dark; and some people were hung up by their tongues: they were those who had blasphemed the path of righteousness; and underneath them a bright baneful fire was lit."

Hell

Descriptions of hell such as this were the source for the elaborate punishments meted out in Dante's *Inferno*. Another source that may have influenced Dante, since it also had its effects on Christian legend, is found in the *Pistis Sophia*, a third-century work of Christian Gnostics. Gnosticism, which had

many forms, taught the belief that there are two gods, one good God (the father of Jesus) and one evil God (the creator God of the Old Testament). This heresy also held that the Divine Spark, the soul, had to escape from the body, since physical matter was evil because it was controlled by evil spirits. Only through the *gnosis* (knowledge) of the unknown god and the redeemer who comes to earth could one be saved, but this was limited to only a few.

The *Pistis Sophia* reveals all of the elaborate machinery of hell. In one of its sections Mary Magdalene asks Jesus to describe the various regions of hell. Jesus replies: "The outer darkness is a huge dragon, with its tail in its mouth; it is outside the world and surroundeth it completely. There are many regions of punishment therein, for there are in it twelve dungeons of horrible torment. In each dungeon there is a ruler."

These rulers are, according to the *Pistis Sophia*, various demons who are then named and given elaborate descriptions.

The medieval machinery of hell passed on to the Protestant reformers, even though they rejected the doctrine of Purgatory, they accepted the "devil and all his works."

In Islam the name given hell is Jahannam or Djahannam, derived from the Hebrew valley of Hinnom (Josh. 15:8) in the Old Testament. In many translations of the Koran the word is translated as hell or Gehenna.

The Koran frequently mentions Jahannam, although its precise physical image is unclear. Sometimes it appears to be a monster, as when in sura 139 Allah says Jahannam "shall be brought nigh" on the Day of Judgment. According to Islamic tradition Jahannam walks on four legs, each of which is bound by 70,000 rings. On each of them are 70 thousand demons, every one of which is strong enough to destroy mountains. A moving Jahannam makes buzzing, groaning, rattling sounds. Sparks and smoke come out of its mouth. When it is still separated from mortals by 1,000 years, it will break loose from the demons and throw itself on the people assembled for the Last Judgment.

Alongside this image of a monster hell, resembling in many ways the Christian concept of a dragon-mouthed hell popular during the Middle Ages, is the belief that Jahannam has seven gates (sura 39). Islamic tradition has elaborated on the Koranic statement. Accordingly, Jahannam is situated under the pedestal of the world, above the bull Kuyuta and the fish Bahamut (corresponding to the Behemoth and Leviathan in the Bible), who support the earth. Jahannam is composed of seven stories forming a vast crater, where sinners are punished according to the kind and importance of their deeds, as in Dante's *Inferno*. The seven divisions of Jahannam are

Jahannam proper, or Gehenna (sura 19)
Lathâ, or the Flaming Fire (sura 70)
Hutamah, or the Raging Fire that splits everything to pieces (sura 104)
Sa'hîr, or the Blaze (sura 4)
Saqar, or the Scorching Fire (sura 54)
Gahîm, or the Fierce Fire (sura 2)
Hâiyeh, or the Abyss (sura 51)

Above the vast crater of Jahannam is Al-Sirat (or Se-Sirat; Arabic for "the path"), the bridge leading to paradise, the entrance of which is guarded by the angel Ridwan. Al-Sirat is "stretched over the back of Jahannam, sharper than a sword and finer than a hair. The feet of unbelievers slip upon it, by the decrees of Allah, and fall with them into the fire. But the feet of the believers stand firm upon it, by the grace of Allah, and so they pass to Abiding Abode."

At the lowest stage of Jahannam is a tree called Zakkum, which has heads of demons for flowers; a caldron of boiling and stinking pitch; and a well that reaches to the bottom of all things.

The time of punishment allotted to sinners varies with the interpretation of some Koranic texts. Sura 11 says: "The damned shall be cast into the fire . . . they shall dwell there so long as the heavens and the earth shall last, unless Allah wills otherwise." Yet another passage in the Koran (sura 23) reads: "Those who have destroyed themselves in Jahannam . . . shall dwell there forever."

1394
Hebe (youth?). In Greek mythology, cupbearer of the gods, daughter of Zeus and Hera. Hebe was also called Ganymeda. She was replaced in the position by the handsome youth Ganymede, whom Zeus abducted and raped. Hebe is cited in Milton's *L'Allegro* (26–29), Spenser's *Ruines of Time* (384–385) and Keats's *Endymion* (4.415–9). Hebe is sometimes referred to as the wife of Heracles after he was deified.

1395
Hebrus. In Greek mythology, a river in Thrace with sand of gold. Orpheus' head, dismembered body, and lyre were thrown into the Hebrus by the Bacchants after they tore him to pieces. The river received its name from Hebrus, son of Cassandra, and a king of Thrace, who was said to have drowned himself there. Vergil's *Aeneid* (book 4) and Ovid's *Metamorphoses* (book 11) tell of the river.

1396
Hecate (one hundred). In Greek mythology, pre-Hellenic goddess of the underworld, later identified as a form of Artemis. In some accounts she is said to be the daughter of Perses and Asteria or of Zeus and

Heaven and Hell

Demeter. Hecate was worshiped at crossroads and portrayed as a three-headed or three-bodied woman. The heroine in Euripides' *Medea* invokes Hecate, who was noted for her black magic and sorcery. In Shakespeare's *Macbeth* (3.5) Hecate appears as queen of the witches. In *King Lear* (1.1.112) the old king says: "For, by the sacred radiance of the sun, The mysteries of Hecate, and the night." William Blake's watercolor illustrating *Macbeth* also portrays the dark goddess. Hecate's epithets were Enodia (the wayside goddess) and Trioditis (goddess of the meeting of three routes).

1397
Hecatommithi (hundred tales). An Italian collection of tales by Giambattista Giraldi Cinthio (1504–1573) that contains many European folk motifs. The collection influenced the English collection, *Palace of Pleasure* (1566), providing Shakespeare with plots for *Othello* and *Measure for Measure*.

1398

Hector (prop, stay). In Greek mythology, eldest son of King Priam of Troy and Hecuba; brother of Aesaus, Cassandra, Creusa, Deiphobus, Helenus, Paris, Polydorus, Polyxena, and Troilus; married to Andromache; father of Astyanax (Scamandrius). Hector is the Trojan hero of Homer's *Iliad*. He was killed by Achilles and his dead body dragged around the walls of Troy. King Priam asked for his son's body, and Hector's funeral ends Homer's epic. Numerous episodes from his life appear in art and literature; the slaying of Patroclus (Achilles' male lover); Hector's combat with Ajax; his farewell to King Priam and Hecuba; his farewell to his wife, Andromache; his death; and King Priam begging Achilles for his son's body. Hector appears in Homer's *Iliad*, Vergil's *Aeneid* (book 1), Ovid's *Metamorphoses* (books 13, 14), and Shakespeare's bitter play, *Troilus and Cressida*, which ends with "Hector is dead; there is no more to say." (5.10.22)

1399

Hecuba (moving far off). In Greek mythology, second wife of King Priam of Troy, mother of 19 of his 50 sons and 12 of his daughters; daughter of Dymas of Phrygia and Evagora or Glaucippe, of the river god Cisseus, or of the river god Sangarius and Metope; sister of Asius. Among her children are Hector, Paris, Cassandra, Polydorus, and Polyxena.

After the fall of Troy she was taken into captivity by the victorious Greeks. She witnessed the death of her daughter Polyxena and discovered that her son Polydorus had been treacherously murdered by the Thracian king Polymnestor. Insane with sorrow, Hecuba beguiled Polymnestor into a secret place and tore out his eyes. While she was railing at the Greeks, she was transformed into a bitch. Hecuba appears in Euripides' plays *The Trojan Woman* and *Hecabe*, Ovid's *Metamorphoses* (book 13), and is frequently cited by Shakespeare in his plays.

1400

Hegira (the breaking away). Term used in Islam for the migration from Mecca to Yathrib, later Medina, made by Muhammad. The day of his arrival at Medina is not precisely known—16 June in some accounts and 30 September in others. The year usually assigned to it is 622 C.E.. All dates in Islam are reckoned from the Hegira.

Variant spelling: Hijra.

1401

Heidrun (a heath?) In Norse mythology, a she-goat who provides mead for Valhalla. According to the *Prose Edda*, she "feeds on the leaves of a very famous tree called Laerath, and from her teats flows mead in such great abundance that every day a caldron, large

Hector and Ajax (John Flaxman)

The meeting of Hector and Andromache

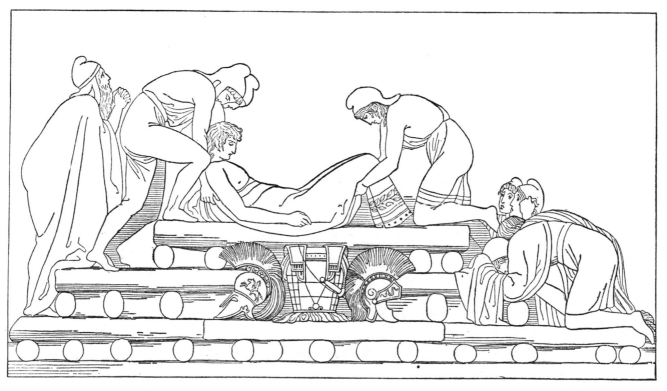

Funeral of Hector (John Flaxman)

enough to hold more than would suffice for all the heroes, is filled with it."

Variant spelling: Heithron.

Heiki-Monogatari (tales of the Heike clan). 13th century C.E. Japanese historical romance telling of the conflict between the Heike (Taira) and the Minamoto (Genji) families.

The work was one of the most popular in medieval Japan, recited by minstrel-priests. It tells how the Heike, an all-powerful family in Japan, are eventually brought low. The novel places heavy emphasis on Buddhist thought, particularly on the evanescence of worldly glory. Toward the close of the work the Cloistered Emperor states: "All these pleasures too were as fleeting as empty dreams of dreams and empty delusions of delusions. All is vanity, as evanescent as the eternal turning of the wheel. Sad are the Five Signs of Decay for celestial beings! How much more so should it be for us, the sentient beings of the world!" (Hiroshi Kitagawa and Bruce Tsuchida translation)

The influence of *Heike-Monogatari* on later Japanese literature was immense. Many of its episodes supplied plots for No plays and later drama. Two other works, the *Gempei Seishuiki* (Records of the Rise and Fall of the Minamoto and Taira Clans) and *Heiji Monogatari* (Tales of Heiji) deal with the same subject.

Heimdall (rainbow). In Norse mythology, one of the Aesir, the god who acts as watchman for the gods; sometimes called Rig. It is his job to announce with his horn, Gjallar-horn, the approach of the frost giants when they come to battle the gods at Ragnarok, the end of the world. Heimdall will be killed by the evil god Loki, who in turn will be killed in battle. The *Prose Edda* describes Heimdall as a "powerful deity" who "requires less sleep than a bird and sees by night as well as by day, a hundred miles around him. So acute is his ear that no sound escapes him, for he can even hear the grass growing on the earth and the wool on a sheep's back." In the *Poetic Edda* the poem *Rigsthula* (The Song of Rig) tells how Heimdall repopulated the earth after some disaster. He fathers serfs, freemen, earls, and kings. Heimdall lives in Himinbjorb (heaven's cliffs) at the end of Bifrost; his horse is called Gulltopp and his sword, Hofund (head).

Heinrich von Aue (home ruler). In medieval northern legends, hero who appears in a 12th-century poem, *Der arme Heinrich*.

Heinrich was a nobleman who was struck with leprosy. He was told that only a virgin who would die in his place could restore his health. He did not believe that any such thing would happen, and he gave away all of his riches to the poor. He went to live with a poor tenant farmer who was one of his vassals. The daughter of the farmer learned of the remedy and offered to die in Heinrich's place. When this was known, Heinrich was cured. Longfellow, in his poetic drama *The Golden Legend* (not to be confused with the medieval collection of saints' lives) used the legend as the basis for his plot. In some medieval accounts Heinrich is called Prince Henry of Hoheneck.

Hel (Johannes Gehrts)

Hel (concealer). In Norse mythology, goddess of death; daughter of the evil god Loki and the giantess Angurboda; sister of Fenris and the serpent Midgard. Hel ruled over Nifelheim, where Odin gave her power over nine worlds or regions. The *Prose Edda* says "all who die through sickness or old age" are

Hel's subjects. Matthew Arnold in his narrative poem *Balder Dead* writes:

> Hela into Niflheim thou threw'st
> And gav'st her nine unlighted worlds to rule,
> A queen, and empire over all the dead.

Hel lived in the palace called Elvidner (misery); her dish was Hunger and her knife, Starvation. She fed on the brains and marrow of people. Hel was believed to leave her home occasionally to roam the earth on her three-legged white horse. In times of pestilence or famine she was said to be using a rake if a part of the population escaped death, and a broom when whole villages and provinces were depopulated, as during the Black Death of the Middle Ages. The English word hell comes from the name of the goddess.

Variant spellings: Hela, Hell.

Invention of the Cross

1406
Helena, St. (bright one). c. 255–330 C.E. In Christian legend, empress, mother of the Emperor Constantine; patron saint of dyers, nailsmiths, and needle makers. Invoked against fire and thunder. Feast, 8 August.

The legend of St. Helena is bound up in the discovery of the true cross. According to the account in *The Golden Legend*, written in the 13th century by Jacobus de Voragine, Helena was probably of British birth, though her parentage and place of birth are still disputed. She married Constantius Cholorus and was the mother of Constantine the Great. Her great desire was to find the actual cross on which Jesus had been crucified. She went to Jerusalem with an army and found three crosses at Calvary. To find out which one of the three was Jesus' cross, she had each cross touch the body of a dead man. When the true cross touched the dead body, the man came back to life. She gave part of the true cross to her son Constantine as well as the nails. Her finding of the true cross was celebrated by a Christian feast observed on 3 May, called Invention of the Cross, from the Latin, *invenire*. The feast was abolished in

1960 by the Roman Catholic church as having no historical foundation. St. Helena is often portrayed holding a large cross. She wears a crown and imperial robes. Paolo Veronese, Agnolo Gaddi, and Piero della Francesca all painted scenes from her life and legend.

St. Helena (Dürer)

1407
Helen of Troy (moon, basket used for offerings to the moon goddess). In Greek mythology, the most beautiful woman in the world; daughter of Zeus and Leda; married to Menelaus; mother of Hermione, Pleisthenes, and Nicostratus.

Zeus, in the form of a swan, seduced Leda, who produced two eggs. From the first hatched Helen and her brother Polydeuces (or Pollux). From the second egg came Clytemnestra and Castor. (The second egg, according to some accounts, was fathered by Tyndareus, the king of Sparta and husband of Leda.) When Helen was a young girl she was abducted by Theseus and Pirithous and rescued by her brothers Castor and Polydeuces, the Dioscuri. In some accounts she was the mother of Iphigenia by Theseus. She was so beautiful that all the available princes in Greece wished to marry her. To calm the intense rivalry Odysseus had all of the suitors swear to support the husband whom Helen would choose and to avenge any wrong to the couple caused by the marriage. After the agreement Helen chose Menelaus, brother of Agamemnon, who was husband of her sister Clytemnestra. Helen and Menelaus seemed to live happily until the day Paris abducted her. (Paris had been promised Helen by Aphrodite as a reward for naming Aphrodite the "fairest" in the Judgment of Paris.) Some accounts say Helen accompanied Paris willingly to Troy; others say she was taken by force. In any event

Menelaus rallied all of Greece to his aid, and the result was the Trojan War.

While in Troy, Helen bore Paris many children, all of whom died in infancy. After Paris' death she was briefly married to Deiphobus. When Troy fell through the trick of the wooden horse, Helen was returned to her husband Menelaus, who took her back as if nothing had happened. She then lived with Menelaus until her death. But some accounts say Helen was hanged by the maids of Argive Polyxo to avenge the death of Tleplemus at Troy.

Some scholars believe Helen was originally a pre-Greek goddess with a tree cult (one in which the goddess was hanged from a tree, which might account for one version of her death) who was worshiped in Laconia and Rhodes. In the Homeric epics, however, Helen is entirely human. Homer's *Iliad* mentions that the Trojans treated her kindly, and in the *Odyssey* she is described as a hospitable wife. A later myth not included in Homer, devised to save her reputation, says that a phantom, not the real Helen, went to Troy. This myth is cited in Plato's *Phaedrus* and is followed in Euripides' *Helen* and Richard Strauss's opera *Die Ägyptische Helena* (The Egyptian Helen) with a libretto by Hofmannsthal. In general, however, most poets take a judgmental view of her behavior, among them Ovid, Seneca, and Vergil. She appears in Euripides' *Helen*, Ovid's *Heroides* (16), Shakespeare's *Troilus and Cressida*, W. B. Yeats's *Leda and the Swan*, Tennyson's *A Dream of Fair Women*; Brooke's *Menelaus and Helen*, and Lang's *Helen of Troy*. Dante's (Hell, Second Circle) places Helen among those driven by lust. Ronsard's *Sonnets pour Hèléne* were written for Hèléne de Surgeres, his last love. In Goethe's *Faust* (Part 2) Faust marries Helen, who symbolizes all that is most beautiful in ancient Greek life. In Marlowe's play *Dr. Faustus* Helen also appears to Faust, and hers is "the face which launched a thousand ships." Homer never describes her features, and she has not frequently appeared in art, though David's *Paris and Helen* portrays the couple, and a work from the school of Fra Angelico portrays *The Rape of Helen*.

1408

Helenus (of the moon). In Greek mythology, a Trojan soothsayer, king of Epirus; son of King Priam and Hecuba; twin of Cassandra, his twin; married to Andromache after both had been given as slaves to Pyrrhus, father of Cestrinus. Helenus said Troy could not be taken by the Greeks unless the sacred Palladium (an image of Athena) was removed from it. He was the only one of Priam's children to survive the war, and he entertained Aeneas on his way from Troy to Italy. He gave Aeneas a plumed helmet. Ho-

Aphrodite presenting Helen to Paris

mer's *Iliad* (book 6), Vergil's *Aeneid* (book 3), and Ovid's *Metamorphoses* (book 13) tell of Helenus.

1409

Heliades. In Greek mythology, Aegiale, Aegle, and Aetheria, sisters of Phaethon and daughters of Apollo (or Helios) and Clymene. They grieved so much over Phaethon's death that they were transformed into poplars. Ovid's *Metamorphoses* (book 2) tell of their fate.

1410

Helios. In Greek mythology, a Titan sun god, son of the Titans Hyperion and Theia; brother of Eos and Selene; married to Perseis (Perse); father of Aëtes, Circe, Phaethon, Pasiphaë, and Perses, as well as of seven sons by Rhode and several daughters by Clymene and Naera. In classical mythology the Greeks identified Helios with Apollo or Hyperion. When Zeus divided the universe, Helios was either away or forgotten and therefore he received no part. To appease him Zeus gave Helios the island of Rhodes, his main cult center, where the Colossus at Rhodes was dedicated to his worship. Helios drove across the sky each day in his quadriga, a four-horse chariot. In Roman mythology he was also called Sol. Among his epithets are Acamas (untiring), Panderces (all-seeing), and Terpimbrotos (he who makes mortals

rejoice.) In his *Laws* Plato advocates a cult of Apollo and Helios, so as to combine ancient ritual and rational thought. Spenser's *Prothalamion* (4) and Robert Herrick's *Corinna's Going a-Maying* cite the god.

1411

Heliotrope. A fragrant, flowered herb of the borage family. In Greek mythology the sun god Apollo and his love, the water nymph Clytie, account for the heliotrope's origin. The nymph fell in love with the god and he with her, but in a short time Apollo grew tired of the girl. She then sat on a riverbank for nine days and nights, taking neither food nor water nor sleep, only watching the chariot of Apollo move across the heavens from sunrise to dusk. The gods, taking pity on her, turned her into a flower, a heliotrope.

1412

Heng-Ê. In Chinese mythology, goddess of the moon, married to the Divine Archer, Hou-I. She stole the drug, or dew, of immortality, fleeing to the moon. In some accounts she is said to have been changed into a frog or toad, though the moon in Chinese mythology is also inhabited by a hare. She is sometimes portrayed as a human figure riding a three-legged frog.

Thetis and Eurynome receiving the infant Hephaestus (John Flaxman)

Hengest and Horsa (stallion and horse). In Anglo-Saxon mythology, two heroes who helped found Kent in England. Their cult was associated with horses.

Henry, St. (home ruler). 972–1024. In Christian legend, Emperor Henry II, husband of St. Cunegund. Feast, 15 July.

Elected Emperor in 1002, Henry fought against the pagans of Poland and Franconia, aided by SS. Lawrence, George, and Adrian. He married Cunegund, and both took vows of chastity. Once the devil convinced Henry that Cunegund had committed adultery with their bishop. Henry commanded his wife "to walk barefoot upon white-hot plowshares a distance of 15 feet." Cunegund called on Christ to vindicate her honor. In anger Henry struck her cheek, but a voice from heaven called out: "The Virgin Mary has delivered Cunegund who also is a virgin." At Henry's death a host of demons arrived to carry off his soul, but St. Lawrence brought a golden bowl and placed it on the balance scales in favor of Henry. The emperor's soul then fled to heaven. A year after his death, Cunegund became a nun.

Henry is portrayed in medieval art in complete armor with his imperial crown, sword, and orb. He is often shown bearing a model of Bamberg cathedral, which he founded.

Hephaestus (he who shines by day?). In Greek mythology, smith-and-fire god, son of Zeus and Hera or possibly of Hera alone; brother of Ares, Arge, Discordia, Eleithyia, and Hebe; married to Aphrodite; father of Eros by Aphrodite, of Camillus by Cabeiro, of Erichthonius by himself or Gaea or Attis, of Olenus and Tullius by Ocrisia, of the two Palici volcanoes by Aetna; also father of Cercyon. Hephaestus was called Vulcan or Mulciber by the Romans. He was born lame and ugly or was made lame by Hera, who was ashamed of his ugliness and threw him out of heaven into the sea, where he landed on the volcanic island of Lemnos. In a variant account Hephaestus' lameness resulted when his father, Zeus, flung him out of heaven for intervening in a fight between Zeus and Hera. After being thrown out of heaven, he lived for nine years with Thetis and Eurynome, water nymphs. He made numerous metal works for them including a metal throne, which was used to trap his mother, Hera. No one could free her except Hephaestus. Dionysus was called on and got Hephaestus drunk and brought him back to Olympus, where he freed his mother from the seat. Hephaestus then was married to Aphrodite, goddess of love. The goddess, however, preferred Ares for her sexual partner. Aphrodite and Ares were discovered by Helios, the Titan sun god, who reported their affair to Hephaestus. Hephaestus placed a net over the bed in which the two deities were making love. Then he called the gods to witness the two in sexual intercourse. Some accounts say Hephaestus created Pandora, the first woman, or that he created mankind. Among Hephaestus' most famous art works are the arms for Achilles, the arms for Aeneas, the shield of Heracles, the necklace (or girdle) of Harmonia, and the scepter of Agamemnon. Hephaestus appears in Homer's *Iliad* and *Odyssey*, Hesiod's *Theogony*, The Homeric Hymns, Vergil's *Aeneid*, and Milton's *Paradise Lost* (book 1.742–46), where the poet captures Hephaestus' fall from heaven. Milton says Hephaestus was the architect of Pandemonium, the council hall of hell. In Greek art Hephaestus is often portrayed helping Zeus give birth to Athena or delivering Achilles' arms to Thetis.

Hera

Hera (lady). In Greek mythology, pre-Hellenic goddess, later said to be the wife of Zeus; sister of Demeter, Hades, Hestia, Poseidon, and Zeus. Her four children by Zeus are Hephaestus, Hebe, Ares, and

Heracles

Ilithyia (Eileithyia). She was the daughter of Cronos and Rhea, according to Hesiod's *Theogony* (454) and was called Juno by the Romans. Hera's main function was as goddess of marriage and the sexual life of women. In many Greek myths she always appears at odds with her wandering husband Zeus, constantly persecuting his numerous mistresses and their children. Like Zeus, she was swallowed at birth by her father, Cronus, and rescued by Zeus, who later, in the form of a cuckoo, seduced her. Hera is portrayed in Greek and Roman art as a large, majestic woman, fully clad, wearing a diadem (in Greek archaic art sometimes a *polos*). Among her attributes are the crow, the cuckoo, the peacock (because she set the 100 eyes of the all-seeing Argus in its tail), and the pomegranate (symbol of fruitfulness). Hera was worshiped throughout Greece. Her most famous temples were at the Heraeum at Nemea in the Argolid, the great temple on the island of Samos, and the temple at Olympia. At her Greek festival, the *Heraia*, a shield was given as the prize in an athletic contest. Her most common Homeric epithet is "ox-eyed," and she is also known as Parthenia, referring to her role as a bride. In Spenser's poem *Epithalamion* he asks for the goddess's blessing on his marriage. Hera also appears in Tennyson's *Oenone*.

1417

Heracles (glory of Hera). In Greek and Roman mythology, hero noted for his immense strength. The Roman spelling of his name, Hercules, is frequently encountered in English literature. He was the son of Zeus and Alcmena. Alcmena had been seduced by Zeus when he assumed the form of her husband, Amphitryon. Heracles was loved by his father, Zeus, but Hera, Zeus's ever-jealous wife, constantly sought Heracles' destruction. She sent two serpents to kill Heracles, but the child strangled them with his bare hands. When he was a youth, Heracles killed the Thespian lion that had been ravaging Amphitryon's flocks. He then wore its skin as a cloak, with the lion's head forming a hood. At one point Hera caused Heracles to go mad, leading him to kill his wife Megara and their children. As penance he had to submit to 12 labors under Eurys-

theus. The first labor was to slay the Nemean lion. He drove it into a cave, strangled it, and then skinned it. The second labor was to slay the Lernaenan Hydra, a many-headed monster that grew a new head to replace each one decapitated. Heracles cut off each head while his charioteer, Iolaus, seared the stump with pitch so that another head could not grow. The third labor was to capture the Erymanthian boar alive. Heracles captured it and returned with it to Eurystheus, who jumped into a jar out of fright at the sight of it. The fourth labor was to capture alive the golden-horned Cerynean hind. He pursued it for a year and finally captured it at a stream as it was drinking. The fifth labor was to drive off the bronze-beaked, arrow-feathered birds infesting the Stymphalian marsh. Athena gave Heracles a bronze rattle that when shaken startled the birds. They rose in flight, and Heracles killed many with arrows. The rest fled to the Black Sea. The sixth labor was to clean, in one day, the dung of 3,000 cattle from the stables of King Augeas of Elis. The hero diverted the rivers Peneus and Alpheus from their regular courses and sent them to clean the stables. When Augeas refused to pay Heracles one-tenth of the herd, Heracles killed him. The seventh labor was to capture the mad Cretan bull. Heracles brought it back to Eurystheus, who let it loose to ravage the land. It was later killed by Theseus. The eighth labor was to kill the man-eating mares of King Diomedes of Thrace. Heracles caught the king and fed him to the mares. The ninth labor was to capture the girdle of the Amazons. Heracles went to Queen Hippolyta, who possessed the girdle and was willing to give it to him. Hera, still jealous, convinced the Amazons that their queen was going to be killed. They attacked Heracles; he defeated them and killed Hippolyta. He took the girdle along with Antiope, sister of Hippolyta, as captive. The girdle was given to Admente, and Antiope was married to Theseus. The tenth labor was to fetch the red cattle of Geryon. The monster Geryon, who had three bodies, lived at Gades. His cattle were guarded by the two-headed dog Orthus and a shepherd, both of whom were slain by Heracles. The eleventh labor was to gather the golden apples of the Hesperides. The golden apples were guarded by a dragon, which Heracles slew, but the apples were later returned by Athena to the garden because they were sacred and could not survive except in the garden. The twelfth labor was to fetch the dog Cerberus from the underworld. Purifying himself at the mysteries of Eleusis, Heracles, guided by Hermes and Athena, descended to Hades and captured the monster, which was later returned to the underworld.

Nemean lion

Other adventures in Heracles' life were his joining of the Argonaut expedition for a short time under Jason, his madness when he killed his male lover Iphitus, and his return to the Oracle at Delphi to seek a cure. When the priestess refused an answer, Heracles seized the sacred tripod, saying he would set up another oracle. Apollo rushed in, and Heracles fought the god, only to be stopped by a thunderbolt hurled by Zeus. The priestess then gave Heracles the oracle he wished. Heracles assisted the gods in their battle against the giants. He married Deianira, Meleager's sister, who bore him five children. Believing it would restore his love for her, she sent her husband a poisoned robe that burned his flesh. While the flames arose, a cloud descended, and Heracles was welcomed in heaven. Hera was then reconciled to the hero, who later married Hebe, goddess of youth and spring. Heracles was popular in Greek cult, where he was a demigod, and among the Romans as a hero who fought against evil. Heracles appears in Sophocles' *Trachinian Women* and *Philoctetes*, Euripides' *Alcestis* and *The Madness of Heracles*, and Seneca's *Hercules Furens*. In the Middle Ages and the Renaissance, Heracles' myth inspired Chaucer's *Monk's Tale* and part of the incomplete *Canterbury Tales*, which gives a summary of his life and deeds. In art perhaps the most famous image of the hero is the

Farnese Heracles, discovered in 1540 in the Baths of Caracalla in Rome. It portrays the hero leaning on a club after his 12 labors, and it is ascribed to the Athenian sculptor Glycon (first century B.C.E.) The myth of the Choice of Heracles, first written down by Xenophon in his *Memoirs of Socrates*, tells how the hero was approached by two beautiful women before his 12 labors. One woman offered Heracles pleasure and a life of ease, and the other offered him a life of duty and labor for humankind. Obviously, the hero chose duty, as portrayed in two cantatas *The Choice of Heracles* one by Bach and one by Handel.

Heracles

1418

Herema. In Greek mythology, a name for Day, a daughter of Erebus and Nox (night). Herema, along with Aether (Light), dethroned their parents and seized control.

1419

Hermaphroditus. In Greek and Roman mythology, son of Hermes and Aphrodite. He was a half-man, half-woman divinity, having been united with the nymph Salmacis to form a hermaphroditic being. Some scholars believe the myth is derived from some ancient marriage rites in which the couples exchanged clothing. The myth is told in Ovid's *Metamorphoses* (book 4). Many ancient statues frequently portrayed Hermaphroditus. Bartholomeus

Spranger's *Hermaphoditus and Salmacis* (c. 1581) portrays the two near the nymph's pool. After the two were united, the pool weakened all who drank from it. Spenser's *Faerie Queene* took the idea of the enfeebling pool from the ancient myth. Hermaphroditus is also called Atlantiades and Atlantius.

Hermes weighing the souls of Achilles and Hector

1420

Hermes (stone pillar). In Greek mythology, messenger of the gods, conductor of the souls of the dead, god of merchants and thieves; son of Zeus and Maia; called Mercury by the Romans. Among Hermes' mistresses (and the offspring produced) are Acacallis (Cydon, possibly); Alcidamea (Bubus); Antianeira (Eurytus, Echion); Aphrodite (Hermaphroditus, Peitho); Carmenta (Evander); Chione (Autolycus); Chthonophyle (Polybus); Clytie (Myrtilus); Eupolemia (Aethalids); Herse (Cephalus, Ceryx); Penelope or Dryope (Pan); and Phylodameia (Pharis). He was also the father of Abderus, Arabus, Chryses, Daphnis, Eurymedon, Hapalycus, Nephalion, Philocaus, and possibly Silenus. Hermes is a complex god, his cult representing various aspects of godly patronage such as death, thievery, commerce, wealth, manual skill, and oratory. After his birth Hermes almost immediately stole Apollo's cattle. He invented the lyre, which he then gave to Apollo, who in turn gave Hermes the caduceus. Hermes appears in *Hymn to Hermes*, (one of the Homeric Hymns ascribed to Homer but not by him) and in Homer's *Odyssey* he is sent by Zeus to tell Odysseus to leave Calypso's island. In Vergil's *Aeneid*, under the name Mercury, he tells the hero Aeneas to leave Dido and continue on his journey. In many ancient art works he was portrayed as an ithyphallic image, which was a stone column with a phallus attached, or sometimes he was portrayed entirely in phallic form. Of ancient art works Praxiteles statue of the nude Hermes holding

the infant Dionysus is among the most famous. Renaissance art works often portrayed Hermes as a graceful, vigorous young man with wings on his sandals and on the crown of his broad-brimmed hat, which came to symbolize his speed. In Roman art the staff came to symbolize the physician as well as the herald. Hermes had many epithets. Among them: Argiphontes (slayer of Argus) Cylleneius, Epimelios (guardian of flocks), Hodios (patron of travelers and wayfarers), Nomios, Oneiropompus (conductor of dreams), Psychopompus (conductor of souls to the underworld).

1421

Hermes Trismegistus (Hermes, three times great or very, very great). In Egyptian mythology, the Greek name for the god Thoth, who was identified by the Greeks with their god Hermes. He was believed to be the first magician and to have left a series of magical books for his followers. Longfellow's poem *Hermes Trismegistus* deals with the deity.

1422

Hermod (courage in battle). In Norse mythology, a son of Odin and Frigga. A handsome god, Hermod was the messenger of the gods. He loved to enter battles and was often called "the valiant in combat." Aside from his helmet and corselet Hermod had a magic wand or staff, Gambantein, which he carried wherever he went.

Once, oppressed by fear of the future, Odin called on Hermod to put on his armor, saddle Sleipnir (the horse Odin alone was allowed to ride), and hasten off to the land of the Finns to see Rossthiof (the horse thief) for an answer to Odin's fear. Hermod hurried off, carrying not his magic wand, Gambantein, but Odin's runic staff. Rossthiof conjured up monsters to hinder Hermod, but Hermod soon mastered Rossthiof, binding him hand and foot and saying he would be set free only when he answered Hermod's questions. Rossthiof, seeing there was no hope of escape, pledged himself to do all Hermod wished. As soon as he was free again, he began to mutter incantations, which made the sun hide behind the clouds, the earth tremble and storm winds rise.

Pointing to the horizon, Rossthiof asked Hermod to look, and the god saw a great stream of blood redden all the ground. While he was gazing at this, a beautiful woman suddenly appeared, and a moment later a boy stood beside her. To Hermod's amazement the child grew to full height in a moment and was carrying a bow and arrows.

Mercury (Laurence Housman)

Rossthiof said the blood portended the murder of one of Odin's sons, but if Odin wooed and won Rinda in the land of the Ruthenes (Russia), she would bear him a son who would attain his full growth in a few hours and avenge his brother's death.

Hermod rushed home to Odin and informed him of what had happened. Odin consoled himself, knowing that when one son died, another would avenge the death. Hermod appears in the *Poetic Edda*, the *Prose Edda*, and Matthew Arnold's narrative poem *Balder Dead*.

1423

Hero and Leander. In Greek mythology, two lovers. Hero was a priestess of Aphrodite at Sestos when Leander fell in love with her. Each night he would swim from his home at Abydos on the opposite side of Hellespont to meet Hero, who guided him with a lit torch in her tower. One stormy night, however, Leander drowned, and Hero killed herself. The myth is told in Vergil's *Georgics* (3) and in Ovid's *Herodides* (18, 19). The most famous treatment in English literature is Marlowe's narrative poem *Hero and Leander* (1598), completed by Chapman. Other English poets who have treated the subject are Byron (who swam the Hellespont), Keats, Tennyson, and Dante Gabriel Rosetti. Mancinelli's opera *Ero e Leandro* (1896) also deals with the myth, as does an 1879 opera by Bottesini.

1424

Heron. A long-legged, long-necked bird having a long bill and large wings. In Egyptian mythology the heron was believed to house the *ba*, or soul. In *The Book of the Dead* there is a spell to help a deceased person effect transformation into a heron.

Hero and Leander

Edition of Hesiod, title page (Hans Holbein)

Hesiod. Eighth century B.C.E. Earliest Greek poet
after Homer. Hesiod is known for his *Works and Days*
and *Theogony*, both of which deal with Greek mythology. Hesiod lived at Ascra in Boeotia, where he
had a small farm on the slopes of Mount Helicon.
According to the poet, the Muses visited him and
gave him the gift of song. In his *Works and Days* he includes the myths of Pandora (he disliked women)
and that of the Golden Age. Included in the work is
the earliest Greek fable, *The Hawk and the Nightingale*.
His other major work, the *Theogony*, is an attempt to
systematize the genealogy of the gods leading to the
kingship of Zeus over his father, Cronus. In this
work he portrays the more sinister aspects of Greek
mythology, such as castration, incest, child-
swallowing, witchcraft, and human sacrifice, which
were minimized or eliminated by Homer and later
Greek and Roman authors. Scholars now believe
that the fragments of a *Shield of Heracles* and a *Catalogue
of Famous Women* once ascribed to the poet, are not by
Hesiod.

1426

Hesione (queen of Asia). In Greek mythology,
daughter of Laomedon, first king of Troy, and
Strymo; sister of Astioche, Cilla, Clytius, Hicetaon,
Lampus, Priam, and Tithonus; married to Telamon;
mother of Teucer. Hesione was rescued from a sea
monster by Heracles. When Heracles demanded
payment, Laomedon refused, and the hero killed
him and all of his sons except Priam. Hesione was

Heracles slaying Ladon (Johannes Schott)

then given by Heracles to his friend Telamon and
she was taken to Greece. Priam sent his son Paris to
fetch her back, but Paris instead abducted Helen.
Ovid's *Metamorphoses* (book 11) tells the tale.

1427

Hesperides (nymphs of the west). In Greek mythology, guardians of the tree of golden apples in the
garden at the world's end in the far west; daughters
of Atlas and Hesperis. The golden apples were protected not only by the Hesperides, but also by a
dragon, Ladon. For his twelfth labor Heracles, aided
by Atlas, had to gather three of the golden apples.
Heracles agreed to hold up the heavens in Atlas's
place while Atlas took the apples. Vergil's *Aeneid*
(book 4), Ovid's *Metamorphoses* (book 4), Milton's
Paradise Lost (book 4), Pope's *Temple of Fame* (81), and
William Morris's *Earthly Paradise* all cite the Apples of
the Hesperides. Robert Herrick's *Hesperides*, a collection of Arcadian lyrics, was so named because it was
written when he was the priest of a parish in the
west of England. Shakespeare's *Love's Labour's Lost*
(4.3.340–41) credits Heracles with gathering the apples: "For valour, is not Love a Hercules,/ Still
climbing trees in the Hesperides?"

1428

Hesperus (evening). In Greek and Roman mythology, the evening star, son of Astraeus and Eos, or
Eos and Cephalius; father of Ceyx and grandfather
of the Hesperides, who guarded the golden apples.
Some Greek and Roman writers make Hesperus the
morning star and use the name for the planet Venus.
Homer's *Iliad* (book 22), Sappho's *Fragments* (95), Milton's *Paradise Lost* (book 4.605; book 9.49) and *Comus*
(980-982), Spenser's *Faerie Queene* (1.2.6), and *Epithalamion* (288) all refer to Hesperus, as well as others
such as Shakespeare, Donne, and Jonson.

The word *vesper* comes from Hesperus via Latin.

1429

Hestia (hearth). In Greek mythology, one of the 12
Olympians; goddess of the hearth and home; firstborn of Cronus and Rhea; sister of Demeter, Hades,
Hera, Poseidon, and Zeus. She was called Vesta by
the Romans, and her shrine in Rome was kept by
vestal virgins. There are no tales of her life, since she
was a virgin who kept her vows.

1430

Hex (six, witch). In American folklore of the Pennsylvania Dutch, a man or woman who can work hex
spells. Symbols and signs often found on Pennsylvania farm buildings are hex spells, which are believed to protect animals from the Evil Eye and other
spells.

daughter. Hiawatha persisted with his crusade and converted the chief Dekanawida (two-river currents flowing together), and together they converted other tribes. Hiawatha then returned and converted Atotarho to the plan. Hiawatha then combed the snakes out of Atotarho's hair, symbolizing his conversion.

Henry Wadsworth Longfellow's narrative poem *The Song of Hiawatha* confused the historical Hiawatha with the god Manabozho, an Algonquian divinity, because his source, *Algic Researches* by H. R. Schoolcraft was in error. Longfellow's poem has inspired many works, including parodies, beginning with Lewis Carroll's *Hiawatha's Photographing*. A series of prints by Currier & Ives deals with the poem. The work has been set to music and has inspired orchestral tone poems, among them ones by Coerne, Delius, and Jong. Samuel Coleridge- Taylor's *Song of Hiawatha* for chorus and orchestra is the best known.

1433

Hidari Jingoro (Jingoro the left-handed). 1584–1634. Japanese sculptor.

According to legend, Jingoro once picked up a mirror that a girl had dropped in the street. On seeing the beautiful girl, he fell so deeply in love with her that he kept the mirror. He carved a wooden statue of her, and when the statue was completed he placed the mirror in a fold of its dress. Suddenly the statue came to life. For some time he was happy, but then his lord's daughter's head was demanded by an enemy of the lord or the enemy would destroy the princedom. Jingoro, an extremely loyal servant, cut off the living head of his statue. When the messenger who delivered the head to the enemy returned, he attacked Jingoro, thinking he had murdered the lord's daughter, and cut off Jingoro's right hand.

1434

Hiisi (dread place). In the Finnish epic poem *The Kalevala*, the devil sometimes called Juutas, from Judas, revealing the Christian influence on the final form of the epic. Hiisi is also used as a general term for demons who haunt Hittola (demon's domain), a dreary region with charred and burned heaths and hills, not far from Pohjola, the Northland.

The Kalevala (runes 13–14) tells of the Hiisi Elk, a magic elk created by Hiisi. The hero Lemminkainen had to subdue it to win the Maiden of Pohjola as his wife. Lemminkainen defeated the Hiisi Elk by the use of magic charms and prayers.

Hiisi originally referred to a sacred or sacrificial grove. In some parts of *The Kalevala* the term is used for dread or haunted places. Paha Mies (evil man) is another designation of the devil in Finnish

Hestia

1431

Hex Chun Chan (the dangerous one). In Mayan mythology, a war god. In present day folklore of the Mayans of Yucatán, he is a demonic spirit, greatly feared.

1432

Hiawatha (he makes rivers). 16th century? In North American Indian history and legend (Iroquois), founder of the League of Five, later Six, Nations: Mohawk, Oneida, Onondaga, Cayuga, Seneca, and Tuscarora, tribes occupying most of upstate New York.

According to Iroquois legend, Hiawatha was an Onondaga chieftain who sought the unity of various Indian tribes. At first he was violently opposed by the magician and war chief, Atotarho, whose head was covered in snakes. Through his magic, Atotarho caused a gigantic white bird to kill Hiawatha's mythology. Paha Mies rules over Paha Valta, another name for hell.

Variant spellings: Hisi, Lempo, Jutas.

Hikuleo. 1435 In Polynesian mythology, Tongan god of the underworld, who lives in Pulotu, the land of the dead, believed to be an unseen island reached by boat.

Hilary of Poitiers, St. 1436 (cheerful). Fourth century. In Christian legend, Doctor of the Church. Patron of retarded children. Invoked against snakes. Feast, 14 January.

Hilary was bishop of Poitiers in France and author of numerous works dealing with Christian theology. One of the most fantastic elements in his legend is the "murder" of his daughter and wife, reported in *Les Petits Bolandistes* (vol. 1). St. Hilary had a daughter named Abra. When she reached marriageable age, the saint prayed that she might die, lest she should be corrupted by the world. His prayer was answered, and she died. His wife, "jealous of her daughter's happiness," asked her husband to pray that she might join her daughter. This he did, and his wife also died. One churchman, defending the saint's "murder" of his wife and daughter, wrote that the miracles were "more extraordinary than raising the dead to life." Brewer, however, in his *Dictionary of Miracles* writes that the saint "deliberately murdered both his victims."

Less gruesome than the death of his daughter and wife is the saint's power to drive serpents away in the manner of St. Patrick and his ability after death to rally forces against Alaric, the Arian king of the Goths, when he attacked Clovis, king of the Franks. The spirit of the saint appeared to Clovis and told him to "delay not, for as captain of the Lord's hosts am I come to thee this day, and the God of battles will deliver the foe into thy hands." The saint's prediction proved true.

Hilda, St. 1437 (battle maid). Seventh century. In Christian legend, abbess of Whitby Abbey. Feast, 17 November. Great granddaughter of King Edwin of Northumbria. Hilda could turn snakes into stone. When she died, her soul ascended to heaven in the company of angels. Medieval art portrays her with a royal crown at her feet or on her head to indicate her royal blood. She also holds a model of Whitby Abbey in her hand.

Hill, Joe. 1438 1879–1915. In American history and folklore, folk hero of radical labor. Born in Sweden, Joel Hagglund came to the United States in 1902, where he first worked at a Bowery saloon in New York City. He became a member of the Industrial Workers of the World, a labor organization, in 1910, and in 1911 he took part in the Mexican Revolution. He was charged with murder of two men in Salt Lake City and later was shot by a firing squad. Some 30,000 people attended his funeral. On May Day of the same year they scattered his ashes in all states except Utah. He is the author of numerous labor songs, among them, "The Union Scab," "The Tramp," and "Scissor Bill." His last telegram before his execution said: "Don't waste any time in mourning. Organize."

Hino. 1439 In North American Indian mythology (Iroquois), the thunderer. Armed with his mighty bow and flaming arrow, Hino slew the great serpent of the waters, who was destroying the earth. Hino's wife is the rainbow, and his assistants are Oshadagea, the great dew eagle who lodges in the western sky and who carries a lake of dew in the hollow of his back, and Keneu, the golden eagle.

Hippogriff

Hippogriff. 1440 In Renaissance mythology, fantastic beast, half horse, half griffin, created by Ariosto in his epic *Orlando Furioso*. The hippogriff was sired by a griffin, and its mother was a mare. The beast had his father's feathers, wings, forelegs, head, and beak, but the rest was horse. Ariosto's imagination was stirred by Vergil's *Aeneid* with its poetic image, to "cross griffins with horses," to signify something impossible.

Griffin

Hippolyte
Hippolyte (of the stampeding horses). In Greek mythology, the queen of the Amazons; daughter of Ares and Otrera; sister of Antiope and Penthesilea. Heracles ninth labor was to obtain Hippolyte's magic girdle. According to one ancient account, Hippolyte was infatuated with Heracles and gave him her girdle, but when she came to deliver it to his ship, her women warriors thought she was being abducted. They attacked, and Heracles killed Hippolyte. Another account says Heracles gave her to Theseus in marriage, and she bore Hippolytus.

1441

Hippolytus (of the stampeding horses). In Greek mythology, son of King Theseus of Athens, and Hippolyte, queen of the Amazons. Hippolytus was dedicated to chastity and worshiped the virgin goddess Artemis. Phaedra, his stepmother, fell madly in love with him, but he refused her advances. She then accused him of attempting to rape her. Theseus, convinced that Phaedra told the truth, prayed to his father, Poseidon, to kill Hippolytus as he drove from

1442

Athens to Troezen. Poseidon sent a sea monster, which frightened Hippolytus' horses, and he was flung from his chariot and dragged to his death. In Roman mythology Hippolytus is restored to life by Diana, the Roman counterpart of Artemis and taken to her sacred grove in Aricia under the name Virbius. Hippolytus is the subject of Euripides' *Hippolytus*, Seneca's *Phaedra*, Racine's *Phèdre*, and Rameau's opera *Hippolyte et Aricie*, in which Hippolytus is restored to life.

1443

Hippolytus, St. (horse destruction). C. Third Century C.E. In Christian legend, patron saint of horses.

Hippolytus was one of the jailers of St. Lawrence but was converted to Christianity by the saint. He helped bury the saint's body and was arrested as a result. The pagan judge "had Hippolytus tied by the feet to the necks of untamed horses, and dragged over thistles and thorns until he breathed his last," according to *The Golden Legend*, a book of saints' lives written in the 13th century by Jacobus de Voragine.

1444

Hippopotamus (river horse). A large mammal with a thick hairless body, found in and near rivers. In Egyptian mythology the hippopotamus had a dual role. Sometimes it was a beneficent being as symbol of the goddess Taurt, who aided women in childbirth. But it could also be a symbol of a demonic being as a form of the evil god Set. A form of Horus, called *Her-tchema* (Horus the piercer), referred to his role in spearing Set, who had assumed the form of a hippopotamus. Among Tutankhamen's treasures is a statue of a man, who may be the young Tut, holding a harpoon or lance pointed at an invisible foe, which may have originally been a figure of a hippopotamus, symbol of Set. In Edfu, a city sacred to Horus, harpooners were maintained whose duty it was to kill the animal. In the Old Testament (Job 40:15-24) the monster Behemoth is sometimes equated with the hippopotamus.

1445

Hiru Ko no Kikoto. In Japanese mythology, eldest son of Izanagi and Izanami, the creator couple. He is sometimes credited with being the first fisherman.
Variant spelling: Hirugo.

1446

Hitomaru. Seventh century C.E. In Japanese legend, deified poet invoked as the god of poetry. He was a foundling, picked up at the foot of a persimmon tree by the warrior Abaye, who adopted him.

Hitopadesha (book of good counsel). Hindu collection of tales and fables, many of which are also found in the more popular collection, *The Panchatantra*.

The setting for the collection of tales-within-a-tale is the court of King Sudarshana. One day the king discovered "that his sons were gaining no wisdom, nor reading the sacred *Vedas*, but were altogether going the wrong way." King Sudarshana decided to set his sons on the right path and chose a sage, Vishnu-Sharman, to instruct them. Vishnu-Sharman decided to enlighten the princes by telling them fables that would point out their duties. The book is divided into four sections: the winning of friends, the parting of friends; war; and peace. In his selection of the fables from the *Hitopadesha* included in *The Fables of India*, Joseph Gaer wrote: "The purpose of the book is to instruct. But the reason it survived through the centuries was not because it was so educational, but because it was so entertaining."

The tales bring out this point. The first, contained in part 1, is "The Jackal, Deer, and Crow."

Once there lived in a forest a deer, a crow, and a jackal. The deer and crow loved each other very much. One day the deer, roaming about, was seen by the jackal.

"Ho," thought the jackal on seeing how fat the deer was, "if I could but get this soft meat for a meal! It might be—if I can only win his confidence."

So the jackal went up to the deer. "Health be to you, dear friend," the jackal said to the deer.

"Who are you?" replied the deer.

"I'm Small-Wit, the jackal," he replied. "I live in the wood here, as the dead do, without a friend. But now that I have met you I feel as if I were beginning life again. Consider me your faithful servant."

"Very well," said the deer, and the two went off to the deer's house. The crow, Sharpe-Sense, spotted the two and called out: "Who is this number two, friend deer?"

"It is the jackal," answered the deer, "that desires our acquaintance."

"You should not become friendly to a stranger without reason," said the crow. "Don't you know?'

To folks by no one known house-room deny:—
The vulture housed the cat, and thence did die."

The second tale, contained in Part 2, is called "The Lion and the Old Hare," another fine example.

Once there was a lion, named Fierce-of-Heart, who made life very difficult for all of the animals because he massacred them all day long. It grew so bad that they all held a public meeting and drew up a respectful remonstrance to the lion.

"Wherefore should Your Majesty make carnage of us all?" they asked. "Let us daily furnish you with a beast for your meal."

"That arrangement is fine with me," the lion replied.

So each day the animals supplied the lion with one of themselves to eat. One day it was the old hare's turn to be eaten. He walked up to the lion at a very leisurely pace. The lion was very hungry and said, "How dare you take so long in coming?"

"Sire," relied the old hare, "I am not to blame. I was detained on the road by another lion, who exacted an oath from me to return when I should have informed Your Majesty."

"Go," replied the lion in a rage. "Show me instantly where this insolent villain of a lion lives." The old hare took the lion to a place where there was a deep well and stopped.

"Let my lord come hither," he said, "and behold the lion."

The lion approached the well and saw his own reflection in the water. He jumped into the well to attack what he believed to be another lion, and so he perished.

Hittola (demon's domain). In Finnish mythology, a dreary region with charred and burned heaths and hills, not far from Pohjola, the Northland. It is filled with demons.

Hkun Ai. In Burmese mythology, a hero who married a Naga, a dragon woman, and fathered a king, Tung Hkam.

Hkun Ai fell in love with a Naga princess and went to live in the kingdom of the Nagas. To make it easier for Hkun Ai, the king of the Nagas ordered all of the dragons to assume human form, which they did. At the time of the Nagas's water festival, however, they had to assume their dragon shapes. After seeing the Nagas sporting in the waters, Hkun Ai became gloomy and wanted to go home to his parents. His wish was granted. The Naga princess, however, said she would lay an egg from which a child would be hatched who could be fed with milk from Hkun Ai's little finger whenever he thought of her.

A child was hatched from the egg and named Tung Hkam, or Golden Dead Leaves. When the boy grew up, he wanted to marry Princess Pappawadi, whose palace was surrounded by water and had to be reached without the use of bridge, boat, or raft. He called on his mother, who appeared and stretched her body from the shore to the palace on the island, and Tung Hkam walked over her to reach the princess, whom he married. Tung Hkam reigned for 72 years and was succeeded by two sons, Hkun Lu and after him Khun Lai.

Hlithskjolf (hill opening, rock opening) In Norse mythology, the high seat of Odin, chief of the gods, in Valaskjalf, from which he could overlook the nine worlds.

Variant spelling: Hlidskjalf.

Hnossa (jewel). In Norse mythology, daughter of the goddess Freyja and Odur. According to the *Prose Edda*, she "is so very handsome that whatever is beautiful and precious is called by her name."

Hodur (war). In Norse mythology, a blind god, son of Odin and Frigga; twin brother of Baldur; tricked by the evil Loki, the fire god, into hurling mistletoe at Baldur, thus killing him. At Ragnarok, the end of the world, Hodur and Baldur will be reconciled when Hodur returns from death after being killed by Vali, and they will return to a new heaven.

Variant spelling: Hod; Hoder.

Hoenir (henlike). In Norse mythology, an Aesir god of silence, brother of Odin, who along with his other brother, Lodur, created Ask and Embla. Hoenir is called Vili (will) in the *Poetic Edda*. After the war between the Aesir and the Vanir, Hoenir went to live with the Vanir as part of an exchange of gods.

Hohodemi and Umi Sachi Hiko. In Japanese mythology, rival brothers. Hohodemi was a great hunter and Umi Sachi Hiko was a great fisher. One day the two exchanged places, but Hohodemi lost the magical fishing hook of Umi Sachi Hiko, who then refused to return his magic bow and arrow. Hohodemi tried to propitiate his brother by making 500 new fishing hooks out of his sword, but Umi Sachi Hiko wanted his original hook. Hohodemi finally went down under the sea to Ryujin, the dragon king, who helped him find the lost hook, which was then returned to Umi Sachi Hiko. Ryujin also gave Hohodemi two jewels, one for the flowing and the other for the ebbing of the tides. With these magical jewels Hohodemi eventually became master of his brother.

Ho Ho Erh-Hsien (the two immortals harmony and togetherness). In Chinese mythology, patron gods of merchants, potters, and lime burners, portrayed as two short, fat, laughing men.

Ho Hsien-Ku

Ho Hsien-Ku (the immortal lady Ho). In Chinese Taoist mythology, one of the Pa-Hsien, the Eight Immortals. She achieved immortality after a course of lonely wandering among the hills, living on powdered mother-of-pearl and moonbeams. When called to court, she disappeared. She is portrayed with the lotus, her emblem, and invoked as the helper and guide to housekeepers.

Holy Grail. In medieval Christian legend, talisman identified as the cup used by Jesus at the Last Supper and the object of a quest in many legends; often called the *Sangreal* (royal blood).

Although not all of the legends mention the origin of the sacred cup, a few trace it back to the creation of the world. They claim that, when Lucifer stood next to God the Father the other angels presented him with a beautiful crown, whose central jewel was a flawless emerald of great size.

When God the Father announced to his heavenly court that he was going to send his Son to earth, a war followed. Lucifer led the revolt against the Son and was cast out of heaven. During his fall to hell, the emerald dropped out of his crown and fell to earth. There it was fashioned into a cup or chalice used by Jesus at the Last Supper. When Jesus was dying on the cross, Joseph of Arimathea caught a few drops of his blood, which flowed from his side into the cup. After the Crucifixion Joseph was locked in prison and was nourished by the Holy Cup, or Grail. He lingered some time in prison until Emperor Vespasian, hearing the tale of Christ, sent messengers to Palestine for relics, hoping to cure his son Titus of leprosy. Titus was cured by the magic handerchief of St. Veronica. Nevertheless, Titus searched out Joseph and freed him from prison. Fearful of being imprisoned again, Joseph embarked with his sister and his brother-in-law, Brons (derived from Bran, the name of the Celtic god), in a vessel bound for Marseilles. During their journey they had all of their needs supplied by the Holy Grail. On landing in France, Joseph was told by a heavenly messenger to construct a round table at which he and his companions could be seated, and the Holy Grail would supply each guest with the food he required. One seat at the table was to remain empty in memory of the traitor Judas. Only a sinless man could occupy the seat. Once a sinner attempted to sit in the seat and was swallowed up by the earth. Joseph was told that the enchanter Merlin would in time make a similar table, at which a descendant of Brons would have the honor of occupying this Siege Perilous.

From Marseilles the group slowly traveled to Glastonbury, England, with the Holy Grail. For some time it was visible to the people but then disappeared because of their sinful lives. It was borne off to Sarras, an island city (presumably located in the Mediterranean), where it was guarded, according to one legend, by King Evelake.

According to another medieval legend, a pilgrim knight laid a golden cross on the Holy Sepulcher, praying for a son. When his prayers were answered he named the boy Titurel and dedicated him to Christ. After Titurel had spent many years in warfare against the Saracens, an angel appeared to him and told him that he had been chosen to guard the Holy Grail, which was about to descend to earth once more and make its home at Montsalvatch. Impelled by this vision and led by a guiding cloud, Titurel set out on a quest for the holy mountain. After ascending the steep mountain, Titurel was given a glimpse of the Holy Grail. He was joined by a number of knights, who had been transported miraculously to the site. The knights, assisted by angels, erected a temple. As soon as it was completed the Holy Grail came down from heaven on a celestial beam of light and stayed in their midst.

Titurel, who was now fisher king and guardian of the sacred object, presided at the round table with the knights, who were miraculously fed by the Holy Grail. From time to time there appeared on the edge of the sacred cup, written in letters of fire, instructions bidding a knight to defend some innocent person or to right some wrong. The group was called the Knights of the Holy Grail. Guided by the Holy Grail, Titurel was told to marry. He chose a Spanish girl, by whom he had a son and daughter. The son, also marrying under divine guidance, had

two sons and three daughters, one of whom became the mother of Perceval (Parzival).

Old and weary of kingship, Titurel resigned his office, first to his son, who was killed in war, and then to his grandson Amfortas. But Amfortas was restless and led a life of pleasure, neglecting his duties as keeper of the Holy Grail. Wounded by a thrust from a poisoned lance (in some accounts it is the same lance that wounded Jesus' side), Amfortas returned to Montsalvatch. His pain was intensified when he thought of his sins. One day he saw words on the rim of the cup that indicated his wound would be healed by a guileless fool.

The guileless fool was Perceval (Parzival), who after many adventures arrived at Montsalvatch. He was led into the banqueting hall and was awed by its splendor. Perceval noticed that his host, Amfortas, was suffering from some illness or wound. Then suddenly the doors opened wide, and a procession entered the hall. It circled the round table and went out again. In the procession were a servant who carried a lance, then some maidens who carried a stand for the Holy Grail, and finally the Holy Grail itself, brought in by Titurel's granddaughter.

After some time the knights were served food from the Holy Grail. When dinner was done, they left Perceval alone to ponder what the entire episode meant. Perceval ate and was taken to a room to sleep. When the next morning came, he found that the castle was deserted. The drawbridge opened as he left and closed after him, and he heard a voice cursing him but saw no one.

Perceval's sin was not asking Amfortas what ailed him. For this failing he had to do severe penance. After completing his penance he again arrived at the castle. Once more he entered the banqueting hall, and once more he beheld the procession. Strengthened by prayer, Perceval then asked the momentous question, whereupon Amfortas's wound was instantly healed, the aged Titurel was released from the pain of living, and Kundrie (the one who had cursed him earlier) was baptized. Perceval was then acclaimed the keeper of the Holy Grail.

Perceval's son Lohengrin, the Knight of the Swan, was another keeper of the Holy Grail as was Galahad, the son of Lancelot and Elaine. After Galahad's death, the Holy Grail returned to Heaven.

Originally, the Holy Grail had nothing to do with Christian legend. Some scholars connect it with the Celtic god Bran, who possessed a magic drinking horn in which "the drink and the food that one asked for, one received in it when one desired." When Christianity denied Bran's godhead, medieval folklore transformed him into an island king who possessed treasures and who sometimes fished from a boat in the river. One of his many treasures, sometimes assigned also to King Rhydderch of Strathclyde who lived in the sixth century, was a platter on which "whatever food one wished thereon was instantly obtained."

1458

Holy Innocents Day. Christian feast, celebrated 28 December, remembering the children of Bethlehem "from two years old and under" who were slaughtered by the order of King Herod in his attempt to kill the infant Jesus (Matt. 2:16–18). In medieval English usage the name given to the day is *Childermass* (child's mass).

1459

Homer (hostage, pledge). Ninth century B.C.E. Traditional author of *The Iliad* and *The Odyssey*.

Scholars still debate whether the poet Homer ever existed at all, many seeing the Homeric poems as composite works, others seeing them as based on traditional myths and legends but welded together by one man. Many "lives" of Homer were told by the ancients, but none have any historical support. Various Greek cities have claimed him as their son, but none can produce any evidence of his existence.

Seven cities claimed the mighty Homer dead,
Through which the living Homer begged his bread.

One tradition says the poet was blind, but others argue that if this were so, how could he possibly have produced such vivid descriptions of people and battle scenes? The only thing that can be said with certainty about the writings are that *The Iliad* and *The Odyssey* are "Homeric poems," among the earliest works of Greek literature that have survived to the present day. The poems of Homer were sung, intoned, or chanted, with instrumental accompaniment of some sort, perhaps a four-stringed instrument. Matthew Arnold, the 19th-century English poet and critic, wrote that "Homer is rapid in his movement, Homer is plain in his words and style, Homer is simple in his ideas, Homer is noble in his manner." Arnold then attempted to capture Homer in English. Here is an example:

So shone forth, in front of Troy, by the bed of the Xanthus,
Between that and the ships, the Trojans' numerous fires.
In the plain there were kindled a thousand fires; by each one
There sat fifty men in the ruddy light of the fire;
By their chariots stood their steeds and champed the white barley

While their master sat by the fire and waited for morning.

Lord Tennyson, a greater poet than Arnold, also attempted to capture Homer, with this example:

As when in heaven the stars about the moon
Look beautiful, when all the winds are laid,
And every height comes out, and jutting peak,
And valley, and the immeasurable heavens
Break open to their highest, and all the stars
Shine, and the shepherd gladdens in his heart:
So many a fire between the ships and stream
Of Xanthus blazed before the towers of Troy,
A thousand on the plain; and close by each
Sat fifty in the blaze of burning fire;
And champing golden grain the horses stood
Hard by their chariots waiting for the dawn.

In Aristotle's *Poetics*, Homer is accorded the greatest praise, and Dante, in *The Divine Comedy*, places him among the greatest poets. Translations into English of the Homeric poems, to name only the most important, are Chapman's, which inspired Keats' poem; Pope's, which Dr. Johnson called a "poetical wonder"; Leaf, Lang, and Myers; Butcher and Lang; William Morris; William Cullen Bryant; T. E. Lawrence; E. V. Rieu; Edward Fitzgerald; and Richmond Lattimore. Homer appears in Raphael's *Parnassus* as well as Ingres's *Apotheosis of Homer*.

1460

Homshuk. In Mayan mythology of the Indians of Veracruz, Mexico, the corn spirit. Homshuk was at first opposed by the god Hurakán, who later accepted and took care of him because corn is necessary to maintain life.

1461

Ho-no-Ikazuchi. In Japanese mythology, one of the Ikazuchi, the eight gods of thunder.

1462

Horae (hours, seasons). In Greek mythology, children of Zeus and Themis; goddesses of the seasons, later of justice. Hesiod's *Theogony* names three: Eunomia (lawfulness), Dice (justice), and Eirene (peace). At Athens, Thallo (bloom), Auxo (growth), and Carpo (fruit) were added to the list. The Horae, along with the Moirae (the Fates), governed all human actions. Ovid's *Metamorphoses* (book 2.118) and Milton's *Comus* (986) cite the Horae. In Italian Renaissance art they are used to represent the four seasons as in the four statues on the S. Trinità bridge in Florence.

1463

Horai. In Japanese mythology, one of the three mountains in the Fortunate Islands of Paradise. It is the home of everlasting life, where live the crane, the tortoise, and the stag and where the plum tree, the pine, the peach, and mushrooms grow in profusion beside a jeweled tree.

Variant spelling: Horaizan.

1464

Horatii. Seventh century B.C.E. In Roman history and legend, three brothers who fought the three Curiatii. According to Livy's *History of Rome* (book 1), two of the Horatii were killed, but the third killed all of the Curiatii on the Alban side. As the victor returned to Rome, he met his sister, who was crying because she was to marry one of the Curiatii who had been killed. Horatius stabbed his sister, was tried for murder by Tullus Hostilius, the third king of Rome, and was acquitted. Corneille's tragedy *Horace* and David's painting *The Oath of the Horatii* deal with the legend.

1465

Horatius Cocles (one-eyed). In Roman history and legend, hero who held the Etruscans at bay on the wooden Sublician bridge. He held the bridge until it was cut down behind him, and then he swam across the Tiber to safety. The legend is told in Livy's *History of Rome*; it inspired Macaulay's poem in the *Lays of Ancient Rome* and a painting by Géricault.

Horus

1466

Horus (that which is above). In Egyptian mythology, the hawk, or falcon, god. Horus is a Latin form of a Greek word for the Egyptian name Heru, or Hor.

Originally, Horus was a local god who was worshiped along the delta region of the Nile. Eventually, his cult spread throughout Egypt and was carried into Roman times, when he was worshiped along with his mother, Isis.

The falcon, or hawk, one of the first animals worshiped in Egypt, was said to be the personification of the god Horus, who made the sky. In predynastic times there arose several hawk deities, among the most important being the falcon god at Hierakonpolis in Upper Egypt, where Horus took on the form of a solar disk with wings. When the kings of the south moved into Lower Egypt, uniting the two lands, Horus became known as the Uniter of the South and North, or Upper and Lower Egypt.

He was sometimes said to be the son of the cow goddess Hathor, whose name literally means "house of Horus." Each evening he would fly into the goddess's mouth, and each morning he would emerge reborn. In the most famous myth associated with him, however, Horus is the son of the god Osiris and the goddess Isis, and he avenges his father's murder by defeating the demonic god Set in a series of battles. Thus Osiris is identified with the dead king and Horus with the living king. Sometimes the living king was said to embody within himself both Horus, the spirit of light, and Set, the spirit of darkness, reflecting the eternal strife that is always present in the universe. In his role as defeater of Set, Horus is variously portrayed as a mounted warrior with the head of a falcon and as a falcon-headed man with a large pointed spear driven into some foe. In one version of the myth, Horus had his left eye, which signified the moon, wounded in his battle with Set, thus giving rise to one explanation for the moon's various phases. The eye was healed by the god Thoth, and the restored eye, known as the *udjat*, became a powerful amulet.

Various "Horus gods" also appear in Egyptian mythology. Originally, many of them were separate deities, but eventually they were all blended into one and were considered various aspects of the same god. Among them are Harpokrates, Harsiesis (Horus the son of Isis), Harmachis (Horus who is on the horizon), Haroeris (Horus the elder), Horus-Behdety (Horus of Behdet), Horus Khenty en Maathyu (Horus at the head of those who see not?, also called blind Horus), Horus Khenty Khat (Horus at the head of the belly?), and Horus Netcher Nedjeitef (Horus the god, he who avenges his father).

Hotai. In Japanese folklore, a being with a monkey's body and a human head with long hair.

Hotaru Hime. In Japanese folklore, daughter of Hi O, king of the fireflies.

Hi O lived in the moat of the castle of Fukui in Echizen. His bright but coquettish daughter, Hotaru Hime, was courted by many lovers, among which were a golden beetle, a black bug, a scarlet dragonfly, and a hawk moth. For each wooer she set a task of bringing her fire. All tried to get it from lamps and were burned to death as a result, except for the hawk moth, which had more cunning and crawled inside the paper wick of a candle. The candle was snuffed out before he reached the flame, but he escaped with his life. Finally, Hi Maro, the firefly prince, heard of the offer and successfully wooed Hotaru Hime. As a result, when dead insects are seen around temple lamps in Japan, there is a saying: "Princess Hotaru must have had many lovers tonight."

Hotots. In Armenian folklore, evil spirits who live in the rivers and swamps. When they appear, they are covered with mire. They entice men with dancing, jesting, and singing, luring them to the swamps, where they drown them. Their companions, the old hags, who have breasts resembling those of ewes, live in pools and swamps. They like to drown children, men, horses, oxen, and buffaloes.

Houri (hour, harlot?). In Islamic mythology, black-eyed damsels who live with the blessed in paradise.

The Koran (sura 55) says that men in paradise will enjoy "damsels with retiring glances, whom no man nor djinn hath touched before them." These houri possess eternal youth and beauty, and their virginity is renewable. Every believer will have 72 of these women to satisfy his sexual needs. The promise of houris in paradise is found almost exclusively in those suras of the Koran written when Muhammad had only one wife, who was 60 years old. Later writings in the Koran speak of the proper wives of the faithful accompanying their husbands into the Garden of Paradise.

Howe's Masquerade. In American history and folklore of the Revolution, a masked ball held by the British general Sir William Howe (1729–1814), commander-in-chief of the British army in the American Revolution, while Boston lay under siege by colonial forces in 1776. To show his contempt for the colonials, Howe asked some of his guests to dress in costumes representing Washington and his generals. But as the party progressed, a funeral dirge was heard outside, and a procession passed through the ballroom. It consisted of figures from the colonial past and last of all a tall man whose face was cloaked. Howe, furious at the interruption of his ball, ran toward the cloaked figure, only to discover it was an caricature of him as the last royal governor. Hawthorne's short story "Howe's Masquerade," included in his *Twice Told Tales*, deals with the legend. According to tradition, the grim procession appears each year.

Hsiao Kung. 13th century C.E. In Chinese legend, a deified mortal worshiped as the god of rivers.

Hsieh p'ing-an. In Chinese folk ritual, a thanksgiving service to the gods for their gifts during the year.

Hsien (immortal). In Chinese mythology, a deified mortal or a deity who has never been mortal. It is similar to the Chinese *shen*, another word for divinity, spirit, god, or deified mortal.

Huaca

Hsi-Shen. In Chinese mythology, the god of joy, portrayed carrying a basket or sieve, in which are planted three arrows made of peach wood. Pictures of the god are used as talismans by brides.

Hsi Wang Mu (queen mother of the west). In Chinese mythology, a goddess whose garden contains a magical peach tree where peaches ripen only once in 3,000 years and bestow immortality.

In Japanese mythology Hsi Wang Mu is called Seiobo.

Huaca. In Inca mythology, a term applied to anything believed to be sacred or possessed of a spirit, such as a totem stone, a grave, the crest of a mountain. One Spanish account, written by Juan de Santa Cruz Pachacuti-Yamqui Salcamayhua, called *Account of the Antiquities of Peru*, says that after the natives were converted to Christianity they "destroyed and pulled down all the huacas and idols" and punished those who consulted them. Today the word is used as a synonym for treasure because of the jewelry and gold objects frequently found near the sites of ancient *huacas*.

Variant spelling: Guaca.

Hua-Kuang Fo. In Chinese Buddhism, the Buddha of Hua-kuang, patron god of goldsmiths and silversmiths and guardian deity of temples.

Huathiacuri. In the mythology of the Huarochiri (Warachiri) Indians of the western side of the coastal Cordillera of Peru, son of the hero god Pariacaca. Huathiacuri learned many arts from his father. He came to a land where a rich Indian pretended he was the creator god. According to Francisco de Ávila, a Roman Catholic priest of San Damian, a parish in the district of the Huarochiri, who wrote *A Narrative of the Error, False Gods, and Other Superstitions and Diabolical Rites . . [of] the Indians* (1608), the rich man's house was roofed with yellow and red birds' feathers, and he had llamas of a great number of colors, so it was unnecessary to dye the wool they produced. This rich man fell ill with a foul disease. As Huathiacuri was traveling toward the sea, he overheard a conversation between two foxes and learned the cause of the great man's illness: his wife had committed adultery, and two serpents were hovering over his house eating his life away while a two-headed toad was hiding under the grinding stone. Huathiacuri caused the wife to confess, the monsters were destroyed, the rich man recovered, and Huathiacuri married the daughter.

Hubert, St. (mind-bright). Eighth century C.E. Bishop of Liège, France; patron saint of huntsmen, metalworkers and mathematicians, and dogs. Feast, 3 November. The legend of St. Hubert is similar to that of St. Eustace, and the two are often confused in art.

Hubert was the son of a nobleman of Aquitaine. On one great church festival all of the faithful went to church, but Hubert decided he wanted to hunt instead. During the hunt a stag of "great beauty" showed itself to Hubert, who was astonished to see a crucifix between its antlers. Then a voice came from the stag, saying: "Hubert, Hubert, how long will you spend your time chasing beasts in the forest and neglecting the things that pertain to your soul? Do you suppose that God sent you into the world to hunt wild beasts, and not rather to know and honor thy Creator?" Hubert was stupefied on hearing these words; he dismounted from his horse, prostrated himself on the ground, and worshiped the cross the stag bore. He vowed to abandon the world and become a hermit.

After studying under St. Lambert, he was ordained a priest and finally became bishop of Liège. Thirteen years after his death his body was disinterred and found entire, even his episcopal robes being without spot or stain from corruption. A century after his death his body was removed from Liège to the Abbey Church of the Benedictines of Ardennes.

Hud. In Islamic legend, a prophet mentioned in the Koran (suras 7, 11, 26, 46) who preached to a pagan tribe, the Ad, who refused to listen to the message of Allah.

There are numerous legends surrounding this mysterious prophet, who is said to have lived some 150 years. The major legend (sura 7) concerns his preaching to the Ad tribe. The tribe refused to listen to the prophet, and as a punishment Allah sent them three years of drought. The tribe then sent Kail Ebn Ithar and Morthed Ebn Saad, with 70 other men, to the temple at Mecca to ask for rain. Mecca was then in the hands of the tribe of Amalek, whose prince was Moâwiyah Ebn Becr. The men were entertained outside the city by Moâwiyah and for a time forgot their mission. Later Moâwiyah told them they could have rain only if they followed the prophet Hud and listened to his preaching.

Kail went into Mecca with some of the others and begged Allah to send rain. Three clouds appeared, a white one, a red one, and a black one. A voice from heaven ordered Kail to choose, and Kail chose the last cloud, thinking it was filled with rain. Suddenly, as the cloud passed over, a terrible storm arose, which destroyed all of them except Hud and his faithful followers.

1482

Huehueteotl. In ancient Mexican mythology, fire god, believed to be the oldest of the gods.

1483

Huemac (strong hand). In Aztec mythology, god of earthquakes, sometimes equated with Quetzalcoatl.

1484

Hueytonantzin (our great ancient mother). In Aztec mythology, Great Mother goddess of the lords of the four directions: Hueytecptl (ancient flint stone), Ixcuin (he who had four faces), Nanactltzatzi (he who speaks when drunk), and Tentmic (lipstone that slays?). Each day the four sons of Hueytonantzin slew their mother and sacrificed her to the sun.

1485

Hugin and Munin (thought and memory). In Norse mythology, two ravens who fly about the world, then sit on Odin's shoulders, telling him what they have seen. They appear in the *Poetic Edda* and the *Prose Edda* .

Variant spellings: Huginn, Muninn.

1486

Huitaca. In the mythology of the Chibcha Indians of Colombia, evil goddess of indulgence, drunkenness, and license. Huitaca came to earth to destroy the good works of the culture hero Nemterequeteba and to teach men evil. In some accounts she is said to be the wife of the chief of the gods, Bochica; in others she is said to be Chibcho, the moon, wife of Zuhe, the sun, who is considered to be a form of Bochica. One myth tells how she was transformed into an owl or into the moon.

1487

Huitzilopochtli (blue hummingbird on the left). In Aztec mythology, a war god associated with the sun. Huitzilopochtli was the brother of Qutezalcoatl. His mother, Coatlicue, one day picked up a ball of bright feathers on her way to the temple of the sun god. She placed them in her bosom, and as a result she became pregnant. When her family discovered her pregnancy they wanted to kill her, but Huitzilopochtli was born fully armed and killed them instead. In a variant myth Huitzilopochtli was a man who was the leader of the Aztecs during their wanderings from home. On his death, or when he returned to heaven, his skull became an oracle and told them

what to do. Bernal Díaz del Castillo, in his *Verdadera historia de la conquista de la Nueva España*, which gives an eyewitness account of the Spanish conquest, describes the shrine of Huitzilopochtli, in which "the walls of the oratory were black and dripping with gouts of blood" and the floor "stank horribly." D. H. Lawrence, in his novel *The Plumed Serpent*, which tells of the reintroduction of Aztec gods to modern Mexico to replace Christ, includes a series of poems in honor of Huitzilopochtli.

1488

Humbaba. In the Babylonian epic poem *Gilgamesh*, demon-spirit, guardian of the sacred Cedar Tree, killed by Gilgamesh and Enkidu. Originally Humbaba may have been a nature divinity who became associated with evil forces. In one ancient prayer he was called the "supporter of evil" and "the merciless demon." In Babylonian art Humbaba is often portrayed with a beard made of the entrails of animals. Demon masks were often hung on doors to ward off evil, in the belief that greater evil—namely, Humbaba—would defeat some minor evil spirit.

Variant spellings: Huwawa. Kumbaba.

1489

Hunab Ku (the only god). In Mayan mythology, incorporeal god, father of Itzamna, the sky and sun god. No images of Hunab Ku were made.

1490

Hunahpú and Xbalanqúe. In Mayan mythology, twin hero gods in the *Popol Vuh*, the sacred book of the ancient Quiché Maya of Guatemala.

One day Hun-Hunahpú, the father of Hunahpú and Xbalanqúe, while playing ball with his brothers, came within the vicinity of Xibalba, the underworld in Mayan mythology. The lords of Xibalba challenged Hun-Hunahpú to a ball game, and eventually he and his brothers were tortured and killed. Hun-Hunahpú's head was placed on a tree, which instantly bore fruit. Some time later, Xquic (little blood or blood of a woman), the daughter of a lord named Cuchumaquic, went to pick the fruit from the tree. She reached up, and some spittle from the skull fell into her palm.

"In my saliva and spittle I have given you my descendants," the tree said to Xquic. The girl then gave birth to Hunahpú and Xbalanqúe. As their father had before them, they encountered the lords of Xibalba. When they arrived in the underworld, they were told to sit down.

"This is not a seat for us; it is only a hot stone," the two told the lords. They then were told to enter the House of Gloom, then the House of Knives, then the House of Jaguars, and the House of Bats, where they encountered the vampire-bat god, Camazotz.

To protect themselves, they hid inside a blowgun. All night bats flew around them but could not touch them. When morning came, Hunahpú went to see if it was light, and Camazotz cut off his head. Hunahpú's head was placed in the ball court by the Xibalbans while a turtle took its place. Eventually, however, his head was restored. The two heroes went on to defeat the lords of Xibalba by using many magic means. They would kill each other and then restore themselves to life. When the lords saw this wonder, they also wanted to be killed and brought back to life. The heroes obliged with the first part but did not bring the lords back to life.

Hunding. In Norse mythology, a king defeated by Helgi. He appears in the *Volsunga Saga* and Richard Wagner's *Die Walküre*, the second opera of *Der Ring des Nibelungen*. Hunding is portrayed in Arthur Rackham's illustrations for Wagner's Ring Cycle.

1491

Hun-tun. In Chinese Taoist mythology, Chaos, from whom emerged the world.

1492

Shû, the god of the Southern Ocean, and Hu, the god of the Northern Ocean, were continually meeting in the land of Hun-tun. He treated them very well. They consulted together how they might repay his kindness.

"Men all have seven orifices for the purpose of seeing, hearing, eating, and breathing," they said, "while Hun-tun, has not one. Let us try and make them." So Shû and Hu placed one orifice in Hun-tun every day for seven days. At the end of the seventh day Hun-tun died.

In Chinese, Shû-hu, the combined names of the two ocean gods, is the word for lightning. This perhaps indicates the belief that lightning was responsible for ordering the mass of Chaos.

In other texts Hun-tun is said to be a large yellow baglike bird; or he is the son of Huang Ti, the Yellow Emperor, who sent his son into exile.

Hurakán (the one-legged). In Mayan mythology, a creator god. In the beginning, according to the *Popol Vuh*, sacred book of the ancient Quiché Maya of Guatemala, there was the god Hurakán hovering in the dense and primeval gloom over a watery waste. Hurakán passed over the surface of the waters as a mighty wind, saying one word, "earth." In response to this utterance a solid mass rose slowly from the deep. The gods (there were many) then took counsel to see what should be done next. Among the gods were Hunahpú, Gucumatz, Xpiyacoc, and Xmucané. After some discussion, it was decided to create animals, which they did. Then the gods carved wooden

1493

manikins and gave them life, but they were too puppetlike. Hurakán sent a great flood to destroy them. All were drowned except for a few handfuls, whose descendants are said to be "the little monkeys that live in the woods." Later Hurakán made four perfect men—Balam-Quitzé, Balam-Agag, Mahucutan, and Iqui-Balam. They are the ancestors of the Quiché.

Variant spelling: Huracán.

Hushedar, Hushedar-mar, and Soshyant. In Persian mythology, three saviors who will announce the end of the world and its rebirth.

1494

Hushedar, the first savior, "will bring the creatures back to their proper state." He will be born of a virgin from the seed of the prophet Zarathustra, which has been preserved in a lake. To prove his mission the sun will stand still at its noontime position for ten days. For three years men will live at peace and see a glimpse of the future happiness; then evil will again assert itself, and the second savior, Hushedar-mar, will come. The sun will then stand still for 20 days, men will no longer eat meat, and they will be even closer to the final victory of good over evil. But evil will again arise in the form of the demon Azhi Dahaka, who will break loose from his bonds in a cave in Mount Demavend. When Azhi Dahaka is killed by the hero Keresaspa, the third and final savior, Soshyant, will arrive; all disease and death will be overcome; and the final judgment will take place.

Variant spellings: Aushedar and Ukhahyadereta, Aushedar-mah and Ukhshyad-nemangh, Soshans, Soshyans; Saoshyant, Saoshyas, Saoshyos.

Husheng. In Persian mythology, king, culture hero, and discoverer of fire, appearing in the epic poem *Shah Namah* by Firdusi.

1495

Husheng began his reign by destroying a demon who had killed his father, King Siyamek. When peace was restored, he went about civilizing the world, spreading justice. Husheng ruled seven regions of the world. He had power not only over men but over demons, who obeyed his commands. The king discovered minerals, separated iron from stone, invented the art of the blacksmith, taught men how to cook food, helped them to irrigate the fields, and most important, discovered fire. Firdusi describes in his epic how the king, passing by a mountain, saw

> Something in aspect terrible—its eyes
> Fountains of blood; its dreadful mouth sent forth
> Volumes of smoke that darkened all the air.
> Fixing his gaze upon the hideous form,
> He seized a stone, and with prodigious force

Hurling it, chanced to strike a jutting rock,
When sparks arose, and presently a fire
O'erspread the plain, in which the monster perished.
(James Atkinson translation)

Husheng reigned for some 40 years and was succeeded by his son Tahumers.
Variant spellings: Hoshang, Hoshyang.

1496
Hyacinth. A large fragrant flower of the lily family. In Greek mythology the hyacinth is associated with the love of the god Apollo for the young boy Hyacinthus, who was killed by a discus sent by the wind, Zephyr, who was also in love with the lad. Hyacinthus' blood was turned into a flower in his honor and Apollo decreed an annual three-day festival, *Hyacinthia*. On the first and third days sacrifices were offered to the dead youth, and his sad fate was recounted in songs. Wearing garlands was forbidden, and no bread could be eaten or songs sung to Apollo. But on the second day joy and amusement reigned; hymns in honor of Apollo were intoned, and citizens kept open house for friends and relatives. According to variant accounts, it was from the blood of the hero Ajax that the flower bloomed, when he lost to Odysseus in a contest for the arms of Achilles. In Christian symbolism the hyacinth stands for prudence, peace of mind, and desire for heaven.

1497
Hyacinthus. In Greek mythology, a young man loved by Apollo; son of Amyclas and Diomede or of Pierus and the Muse Clio. Hyacinthus was killed out of jealousy by Zephyrus, the West Wind, with a discus. Apollo created a flower named in Hyacinthus' honor with Apollo's cries of grief, "Ai, Ai," etched on its petals. Varieties of flowers identified with Hyacinthus are the hyacinth, iris, and gladiolus. The hyacinth has come to stand for mourning. Milton's *Lycidas* (106) calls it "that sanguine flower inscrib'd with woe." Originally, Hyacinthus was a pre-Hellenic god whose worship was absorbed by Apollo's cult. A three-day festival, the *Hyacinthia*, was held at Sparta in honor of the god, who was worshiped at Amyclae in Laconia. On the first day of the festival a sacrifice to the dead was offered at the grave of Hyacinthus, which was under a statue of Apollo in the temple. The following day the people rejoiced. Boys and girls, accompanied by flutes and harps, went to the temple of Apollo, where games, competitions, sacrifices, and entertainments took place. A robe woven by Spartan women was offered to Apollo. Pausanias' *Descriptions of Greece* records a statue of Hyacinthus that portrayed the god with a beard. The myth of Apollo and Hyacinthus is told in Ovid's *Metamorphoses* (book 10). One of Mozart's earliest works, *Apollo et Hyacinthus*, is set to a Latin text.

1498
Hyarekhshaeta, Khorshed, and Mitro. In Persian mythology, three spirits connected with the sun. Hyarekhshaeta is the "brilliant sun" as the eye of the good god, Ahura Mazda, and is drawn in a chariot of swift horses. Khorshed is the "undying, shining, swift-horsed Sun," and Mitro is the angel or spirit of

Heracles killing Hydra

the sun's light, a personification of friendship and good faith. Mitro assists righteous souls in their passage to the other world and punishes those who break promises or are fraudulent.

1499

Hydra (water creature). In Greek mythology, a huge serpent with 7, 9, or 50 heads (accounts vary) in Lake Lerna in Argolis; offspring of Typhon and Echidna. If one head was chopped off, another two would grow in its place. Heracles' second labor was to kill the monster. With the aid of Iolaus he accomplished the feat. The venom of Hydra was poisonous. Arrows dipped in the venom killed Cheiron, Nessus, and Philoctetes. Eventually the poison was used on a garment that killed Heracles. Hesiod's *Theogony*, Vergil's *Aeneid* (book 6), and Ovid's *Metamorphoses* (book 9) all cite the myth.

1500

Hyena. A nocturnal, doglike animal that feeds mainly on carrion. In Greek and Roman folklore it was believed that the hyena changed its sex and that if you caught the animal while it was male and castrated it, you could use its testicles to make a fine powder that would cure cramps. In medieval Christian folklore it was believed that the hyena could imitate the sound of human voices, often fooling men and dogs, who were devoured when they responded to the call. The hyena was also believed to mate with the lion, producing the Crocote, which had no teeth or gums in its mouth; all of its teeth were of one piece, like a box lid. Medieval Christian symbolism saw the hyena as representing the devil, vice, impurity, and hypocrisy.

1501

Hygeia (health.) In Greek mythology, goddess of health, daughter of Asclepius and Epione; sister of Acesis, Aegle, Iaso, Janiscus, Machaon, Panacea, and Podalirius; called Salus by the Romans. She was worshiped along with her father, and her name follows after his in the Hippocratic oath.

1502

Hylas (of the woods). In Greek mythology, an Argonaut, male lover of Heracles; son of Theiodamas, king of the Dryope, and Menodice, a nymph. When Heracles killed Theiodamas (divine tamer) for refusing the gift of a plow ox, he spared his son Hylas, who became his lover. The two went on the voyage of the Argonauts in search of the Golden Fleece. They landed at Cios, and Hylas went to fetch water at a fountain. He was drowned there by a water nymph Pegae, or Dryope, who had fallen in love with the handsome youth. Heracles went in search of Hylas with his sister's son Polyphemus, leaving the Argonauts to go on without him. Failing to find Hylas, Heracles did not leave the island until he had taken hostages from the Mysians. He made them promise to produce Hylas, dead or alive. From that time on, the inhabitants of Cios made a ritual search for Hylas, sacrificed to him every year at the fountain, and called him by name three times. Apollonius Rhodius' short epic *Argonautica* (The Voyage of the Argo) tells the myth.

1503

Hymen (skin). In Greek mythology, god of marriage, son of either Dionysus and Aphrodite or of Apollo and one of the Muses, Urania, Calliope, or Terpichore. According to one account Hymen was an Argive youth who loved a young Athenian girl but could not win the consent of her parents. Disguised as a girl, he followed her to the sacred feast of Demeter at Eleusis, where he and a group of girls were kidnapped. Hymen saved all of them by killing the abductors and became the protector of young women. At Greek weddings the guests would cry out, "Hymen O Hymeneaus!" Eventually, the call came to represent a god of marriage who was seen as a young man holding a marriage torch and wearing a wreath. Spenser's wedding poem, *Epithalamion* (25–29) asks his bride to awake from her sleep for "Hymen is awake." He appears or is cited in numerous English marriage songs and masques of the 17th century. Hymen is also called Hymenaeus.

1504

Hymir (the dark one). In Norse mythology, a sea giant who owned a large caldron, that the gods wanted. Tyr and Thor went off to fetch it from the giant. In one telling of the myth Tyr eventually killed Hymir. In another version Thor knocked Hymir overboard from a ship and he drowned. The myth is told in the poem *Hymigkuitha* in the *Poetic Edda* and in the *Prose Edda* .

1505

Hyperboreans (beyond-the-north-wind men). In Greek mythology, a people who lived in everlasting springtime north of the great river Oceanus, or at the North Pole or in Britain. They were worshipers of Apollo, who, according to their belief, spent the winter months with them when he left his shrine at Delphi. Herodotus' *History* (book 4) says the Hyperboreans sent wheat-straw offerings to Apollo's shrine at Delos. Heracles brought the first olive tree to Olympus from their land, according to some accounts.

1506

Hyperion (moon man on high, the one above). In Greek mythology, a Titan, son of Uranus and Gaea;

husband of his sister Theia; father of the Sun (Helios), the Dawn (Eos), and the Moon (Selene), according to Hesiod's *Theogony* (371 ff). Hyperion is sometimes used as the name of the sun itself. In some accounts Hyperion is said to be a son of Apollo. Keats's unfinished poem *Hyperion* (1818) tells how Hyperion, the last of the Titans, is about to be deposed by Apollo, the Olympian sun god.

1507

Hypermnestra (excessive wooing). In Greek mythology, eldest of the 50 daughters of Danaus, and the only one of the Danaidae who did not murder her husband (Lynceus) on her wedding night. She and Lynceus were the parents of Abas, ancestor of the hero Perseus.

1508

Hypnos. In Greek mythology, god of sleep, son of Nox and Erebus; brother of Thanatos (death), Aether, Cer, Dreams, Hemeia, Momus, Moros, and Nemesis; married to Pasithea; father of Morpheus; called Somnus by the Romans. According to Hesiod's *Theogony* (211,756), Hypnos lived in the underworld, but Homer says he lived in Lemnos. Hypnos had a human figure during the day but was transformed into a bird at night. Vergil's *Aeneid* (book 6) pictures Hypnos as a winged youth who touches the tired with a magical branch. Homer's *Iliad* (book 14), Hesiod's *Theogony*, and Ovid's *Metamorphoses* (book 11) also picture the god.

1509

Hypsipyle (of the high gate). In Greek mythology, queen of Lemnos; daughter of Thoas and Myrina; wife of Jason; mother of Euneus (Evenus), Deipylus, Nebrophonus, and Thoas. Hypsipyle did not kill her father when all of the women on Lemnos killed all of the men. When the Argonauts came to the island, all of the women were raped, and Hypsipyle became the wife of Jason, who abandoned her. Later the women of Lemnos exiled Hypsipyle to Nemea. Ovid's *Heroides* (book 6) and Chaucer's *Legend of Good Women* report her sad fate.

I

Iatiku (bringing to life). In North American Indian mythology (Acoma), creator goddess along with her sister Natsiti. Their children, the Katsinas, have the power to bring rain and food. Some sources give the names of the two goddesses as Utset and Nowutset.

Ibis. A large wading bird related to the heron, with a long, thin, downward-curved bill. In Egyptian mythology the ibis was associated with Thoth. The ancient Greeks believed it was the natural enemy of snakes.

Iblis (slanderer). In Islamic mythology, Satan, originally an angel called Azazil or al-Haris; he is the father of the djinn.

When Allah was forming man, he took clay and after shaping it left it to dry for some 40 days (or 40 years, according to some Islamic versions of the myth). All of the *malaika*, or angels, who were created from rays of light, came to see Allah's new creation. Iblis, one of Allah's most important angels, appeared among them. He looked at the new creation and, knowing that Allah intended to make it more important than any angel, kicked it with his foot until it resounded. Allah then called all of the angels to come and worship Adam. Iblis refused because, as the Koran (sura 2) phrases it, he "was puffed up with pride."

When Allah in anger cast Iblis out of heaven, the angel cried: "Allah, grant me time. Do not banish me to outer darkness yet. Let me tempt Adam and his sons. Then we will see if they have faith!"

"I will give you until the Day of Judgment," Allah replied. "When that day comes, you will regret your evil deeds and pay dearly for them. You will be cast into a dark pit, never again to harm any souls. Now, out! Leave heaven."

Since that day Iblis has been tempting the sons of Adam to sin against Allah. Iblis is the father of Teer (Tir), the demon who brings about calamities, injuries, and losses of various kinds: El-Aawar, who encourages men to live in debauchery; Sot (Sut), who gives men the desire to lie; Dasism, who causes husbands and wives to fight with one another. (Harut and Marut, the Brothers of Iblis, also cause division between husband and wife.) Iblis is also the father of Zeleboor (Zalambur), who hovers over

places of traffic, causing accidents and mischief. Since the invention of the automobile this demon has been kept astonishingly busy. In Western literature Iblis appears in William Beckford's novel *Vathek, an Arabian Tale*.

Ichabod Crane. In American literary folklore, a creation of Washington Irving in "The Legend of Sleepy Hollow," included in *The Sketch Book*. Ichabod looks like "some scarecrow eloped from a corn-field," according to Irving. He is in love with Katrina Van Tassel, daughter of a rich Dutch farmer in Sleepy Hollow on the Hudson in the days before the American Revolution. But his rival, Brom Van Brunt, outwits the Yankee schoolteacher. One night at a party, Ichabod leaves, riding a borrowed plow horse. On his way he is frightened by a headless horseman that rides after him and throws a round object at the terrified schoolmaster. Ichabod leaves the village never to be seen again. The next day the round object is discovered to be a pumpkin. Brunt then marries Katrina. The tale was used as the basis of Max Maretzek's opera *Sleepy Hollow: or, The Headless Horseman*; Douglas Moore's one-act opera *The Headless Horseman: or, A Legend of Sleepy Hollow* with a libretto by Stephen Vincent Benét; and Walt Disney's cartoon feature *Ichabod and Mr. Toad*, in which Irving's legend is narrated by Basil Rathbone.

Ichimokuren (one-eye). In Japanese mythology, one-eyed god invoked to obtain rain during periods of drought.

I Ching (the book of changes). Chinese work ascribed to the legendary Emperor Fu Hsi. It is a book of cosmological hexagrams giving the laws by which things change, used to foretell the future. It is regarded as a practical book and was one of those, along with books on agriculture and medicine, that were not ordered burned by the first emperor of China in his effort to control thought by destroying philosophical books. The book was also regarded as full of wisdom. Confucius said, "If I could study the *I Ching* for many years, I should be faultless." He read his copy so often that the binding twice wore out. He is said to have written some appendices to it. In the

334

Western world it has been regarded as an occult work.

Icon (image). Term used in the Eastern Orthodox church for pictures of Christ, the Virgin Mary, and the saints painted on wooden panels. Icons became popular in the East in the fifth century. In style, icons are hieratic, idealized images. Tradition rather than self-expression is the aim of the artist painting an icon. During the eighth and ninth centuries there was a reaction against icons, called the Iconoclastic Controversy. The triumph of those who defended icons is still celebrated as the Feast of Orthodoxy in the Eastern Church. Icons are kissed, genuflected to and incensed because they are believed to exercise powers such as healing. Numerous icons have had miracles credited to them in legends; for example the Christ of Edessa, which is said "not to have been made with hands" but to have come from heaven. According to another legend, the icon of Our Lady of Iviron was thrown into the sea by iconoclasts at Constantinople and was washed onto the shore of Mount Athos years later. The Russian church commemorates Our Lady of Iviron on 13 October.

Ida. In Hindu mythology, goddess of speech and, in some texts, the earth. In the *Rig-Veda*, an ancient collection of hymns to the gods, she is primarily food, refreshment, or a libation of milk. One myth says she sprang up when the first man performed a sacrifice to obtain children. The two were then married and had children.

Idaten. In Japanese Buddhist mythology, god of peace and contemplation. Portrayed as a young man of martial bearing, he carries a halberd. The loose parts of his garment are kept in place by his feet as a symbol of subdued sexuality. He also is sometimes portrayed with both hands resting on the pommel of his sword.

Idomeneus (knowing one). In Greek mythology, king of Crete; son of Deucalion; brother of Crete; husband of Meda; father of Idamente. Idomeneus went to the Trojan War with 80 ships and achieved great fame as a warrior. On his way home a storm arose, and he vowed to Poseidon that he would sacrifice the first person he encountered on landing if the storm ceased. The sacrificial victim turned out to be his own son Idamante. Leucus, lover of Meda, banished Idomeneus from Italy for the murder. Mozart's opera *Idomeneo re di Creta, Ossia Ilia ed Adamante* (1781) deals with part of the myth.

1520
Iduna (rejuvenation). In Norse mythology, one of the Aesir; goddess of the golden apples of immortal youth, food of the gods; wife of the god Bragi. Loki, the fire-trickster god, was forced by the giant Thjassi to trick the goddess Iduna. He told her that he had found apples growing a short distance from her celestial residence that were of much better quality than her own, and he persuaded her to go and look at them. Deceived by Loki's words, Iduna took her apples and went with him into the forest. When they entered the forest, Thjassi, covered in his eagle plumage, swooped down and took Iduna and her apples into his claws and flew off to Jotunheim, the home of the giants. The gods, deprived of their magic apples, began to wrinkle and turn gray; old age creeping fast upon them. When they discovered that Loki had caused all the trouble they threatened to punish him unless he could get Iduna back. Loki borrowed the goddess Freyja's falcon plumage and flew to Jotunheim. Finding Thjassi out fishing, Loki lost no time in changing Iduna into a sparrow and flying off with her. When Thjassi returned and discovered what had happened, he put on his eagle plumage and gave chase. When the gods saw Loki approaching, holding Iduna transformed into a sparrow between his claws and Thjassi with his outspread eagle wings ready to overtake them, they placed on the wall of Asgard bundles of chips, which they set afire the instant Loki had flown over them. As Thjassi could not stop his flight, the fire caught his plumage; he fell and and was killed by the gods. The myth of Iduna is told in the *Prose Edda*.

Variant spelling: Idunn.

1521
Ifrits. In Islamic mythology, spirits often evil but sometimes good. The Koran (sura 27) makes a brief mention of the "Ifrit, one of the djinn." In Egyptian Islamic folklore an Ifrit means the ghost of a murdered man or one who died a violent death. Yet the female version of the Ifrit, called the Ifriteh, mentioned in *The Thousand and One Nights*, is a benevolent djinn. In one tale, "Second Old Man's Story" (night 2), a pious woman is transformed into an Ifriteh and carries a hero to an island to save his life. In the morning she returns and says: "I have paid thee my debt, for it is I who bore thee up out of the sea and saved thee from death, by permission of Allah. Know that I am of the djinn who believe in Allah and his prophet." Thus, some Ifrits are good spirits, converted to Islam.

Variant spellings: Afrit, Afriteh, Alfrit, Efreet, Ifriteh.

1522
Ignatius Loyola, St. (fiery?). 1491–1556 C.E. In Christian legend, founder of the Society of Jesus, known as the Jesuits. Feast, 31 July.

Born in Spain, Ignatius became a page at the court of King Ferdinand. He entered the army and was severely wounded in 1521. That changed his whole future life. After a period of penance and visions of Christ, he began to study in preparation for a career in preaching. While at Paris he formed a community with five associates, who bound themselves to preach and teach in any part of the world to which they might be sent. After some years the pope confirmed the name of the Society of Jesus. Ignatius became the first general of his order. His most famous work, *The Spiritual Exercises*, describes a retreat of several days during which the soul, removed from all intercourse with the world, is occupied with the "all important business of salvation" of one's soul.

St. Ignatius Loyola is portrayed in one of Rubens's masterpieces, *The Miracles of St. Ignatius Loyola*, in a magnificent cathedral, dramatically imploring God to exorcise demons from the sick and lame. He wears Mass vestments. Sometimes the saint is portrayed with the monogram IHS on his breast.

1523
Ignatius of Antioch, St. (fiery?) c .35–107. In Christian legend, martyr and bishop. Feast, 1 February.

According to numerous early Christian legends, Ignatius was a friend of the early churchman St. Polycarp, both being disciples of St. John the Evangelist. One early tradition says that when Ignatius was a child Christ "set him in the midst" of his disciples. Ignatius took holy orders and was made bishop of Antioch. When the Roman emperor Trajan came to the city, he ordered Ignatius to sacrifice to the Roman gods. Ignatius refused and was sentenced to be eaten by lions. After his death in 107 the name *Jesus* was found written on his heart in golden letters.

1524
Igraine. In Arthurian legend, mother of King Arthur and wife of Gorlois, lord of Tintagel Castle in Cornwall. According to one account, King Uther Pendragon tried to seduce Igraine but failed. As a result Uther and Gorlois fought, and Gorlois was killed. Uther then attacked Tintagel and forced Igraine to become his wife. Nine months later, Uther died and on the same day King Arthur was born. Tennyson calls her Ygerne.

Variant spellings: Igerna, Igerne, Ygerne.

1525
Ikazuchi. In Japanese mythology, the eight gods of thunder. They are O-Ikazuchi, Ho-no-Ikazuchi, Kuro-Ikazuchi, Saku- Ikazuchi, Waki-Ikazuchi, Tschui-Ikazuchi, Naru-Ikazuchi, and Fushi- Ikazuchi.

1526
Ikiryo. In Japanese folklore, the ghost of a living person, his double.

1527
Iktomi. In North American Indian mythology (Dakota and Lakota), trickster who invented human speech.

1528
Iku. In African mythology (Yoruba of Southwestern Nigeria), the death spirit or god.

1529
Ildefonso, St. 657–667. In Christian legend, archbishop of Toledo, Spain, and patron saint of the city; also Doctor of the Church. Feast, 23 January.

Ildefonso was noted for his devotion to the Virgin Mary. She appeared to him one day and said, "You are my chaplain and faithful notary. Receive from me this chasuble which my Son sends you from His treasury." Then the Virgin placed the chasuble on Ildefonso. From that time Ildefonso never sat in the bishop's throne nor wore the holy garment. After his death another bishop attempted to wear the chasuble and died as a result. El Greco painted St. Ildefonso.

1530
Ilé-Ifé (house wide). In African mythology (Yoruba of southwestern Nigeria) the place of creation. One Nigerian myth says that when the earth was created, God sent a chameleon to examine it. He found the earth to be wide enough but not dry enough. The place was called Ifé (wide); later Ilé (house) was added to show that from this "house" all things originated.

1531
Iliad, The (about Ilium). Greek epic poem, ascribed to Homer, written about 900 B.C.E.

The Iliad is about one aspect of the Trojan War, namely, the anger of Achilles. It assumes that the reader has a background knowledge of the various myths and legends to which it alludes. The epic has been divided into 24 books or chapters.

Book 1: After invoking the Muse to aid him, the poet tells us that the theme of the epic is the wrath, or anger, of Achilles. The Greeks, though still unsuccessful in taking Troy, has conquered the neighboring and allied towns. In the division of the spoils a female slave, Chryseis (daughter of Chryses, a priest of Apollo's cult) fell to Agamemnon. But Chryses comes bearing the sacred emblems of his holy office and asks Agamemnon to return his daughter. Agamemnon dismisses the priest, who then calls on Apollo to punish the Greeks if they do not release his child. Apollo sends a plague as a punishment. A Greek council is held, and the blame is placed on Agamemnon for insulting Apollo's priest and withholding Chryseis. Agamemnon, angry that Achilles is leader of this personal attack on him, consents but demands that Achilles should give him his captive slave Briseis in compensation for his loss. Briseis had fallen to Achilles when the spoils were divided. Achilles consents, but he will no longer fight for the Greeks. He withdraws to his tent.

Book 2: That night, while all are asleep, Zeus sends a deceptive dream to Agamemnon, suggesting that the king should attack Troy. At a dawn meeting, matters get out of hand, as various factions present their cases. The disputes are settled by Odysseus, and a feast is held. Attending are Nestor; Idomeneus of Crete; Ajax, the son of Telamon and cousin of Achilles; Ajax the less, son of Oileus; Odysseus; Agamemnon; and Menelaus. Sacrifices are offered to Zeus, but Zeus does not heed them. Finally, a muster of Greek troops by various tribes and by their leaders is decided on, and the army is ready for the fight.

Book 3: Both armies advance, the Trojans uttering shrill outbursts like migratory cranes and the Greeks maintaining silence. Menelaus recognizes Paris, his wife's seducer, and rushes forward to kill him. Paris, terrified, takes refuge among the Trojan army. So cowardly a retreat causes Hector, the great Trojan hero, to say he wished his brother were dead. Paris tells his brother that all men are not the same but says he will fight Menelaus singly if the reward is Helen and her treasures. Both sides accept the offer. The goddess Iris, in the guise of a princess, enters Troy and tells Helen to go quickly to the ramparts to see that the two armies are offering sacrifices to the gods instead of fighting. Putting on a veil and calling her slaves, Helen looks at the scene. All who view her say she is the most beautiful of women. The duel ensues, and Menelaus would have won had not Aphrodite, who loved Paris, saved him from death. Aphrodite takes Paris to Helen's room, where they make love. The Greeks claim victory, but the gods are dissatisfied.

Book 4: All of the gods and goddesses assemble on Mount Olympus and take sides. Aphrodite sides with the Trojans, but Athena and Hera side with the Greeks, not forgetting that Paris awarded Aphrodite the Golden Apple. Zeus tells Athena to go down and have the truce broken. In disguise Athena prompts a Trojan archer to aim a dart at Menelaus, causing a slight wound, and Agamemnon says the treaty is broken. Shortly afterward the Greeks, urged on by

Athena, and the Trojans, urged on by Ares, resume battle. Although the Greeks seem to be the victors, Apollo encourages the Trojans to new efforts of heroism.

Book 5: Various battles between Trojan and Greek heroes make up this book. In one episode Aphrodite saves her son Aeneas but is wounded in the process. She is told by Zeus to stay out of battle and stick to lovemaking and marriage rites.

Book 6: The battle continues. Hector goes to the women of Troy and tells them to pray to Athena; Aeneas rallies the Trojan men. At the Scaean Gate, Hector meets the mothers, wives, the daughters of the men, who at his bidding prepare offerings for Athena's temple. Then Hector goes to find Paris, who is with Helen, and tells him to rejoin the battle. Helen expresses regret that she has caused so much misery for all. At home Hector meets his wife, Andromache, and his son and then leaves to join his brother Paris in the battle.

Book 7: Hector and Paris are greeted by the Trojans on their return to the battlefield. It is decided that Hector will fight any Greek, stipulating that the arms of the vanquished will be the victor's prize but his remains shall receive an honorable burial. Ajax and Hector fight, but neither is a winner. At night the Greeks hold a feast, and the Trojans debate whether to return Helen and her treasures; Paris is opposed. King Priam suggests that they propose an armistice of sufficient time to enable both sides to give proper burial to their dead. Both sides agree and bury their dead.

Book 8: At daybreak Zeus summons the gods and tells them not to take sides during the battle. Then he goes to Mount Ida to watch the battle. But Zeus protects Hector. Terror strikes the Greeks when they realize that Zeus sides with the Trojans. But Hera urges Agamemnon to visit Odysseus and tell him that Achilles must return to battle. At the end of the day the Greeks still possess their tents, but the Trojans are bivouacked on the plain just outside the trench, to prevent their escape.

Book 9: Agamemnon regrets what he did to Achilles and says he will return all to him if the hero will come back to the battle. Achilles refuses the offer. Diomedes says he will prove that the Greeks do not need Achilles to defeat the Trojans.

Book 10: Exhausted by the battle, most Greeks have fallen asleep, but Agamemnon arouses Nestor, Odysseus, and Diomedes to inspect their posts. Odysseus and Diomedes enter the Trojan camp and learn some of their enemies' plans.

Book 11: At daybreak, Zeus sends Discord to awaken the Greeks. Hector, aided by Zeus, battles the Greeks. Agamemnon, Diomedes, and Odysseus are wounded. Patroclus, the lover of Achilles, tells Achilles of the Greek losses.

Book 12: Hector attacks the Greek ramparts, which divide the Greeks and Trojans. With the gates of the Greek camp battered down, the Trojans pour in. Many die on both sides.

Book 13: The Trojans attempt to set fire to the Greek ships, but Poseidon sides with the Greeks to prevent the destruction of the fleet. Hector is beaten back and reviles Paris for all the evil he has brought on the Trojans.

Book 14: Hector and Ajax engage in single combat, and Hector is wounded; but he is rescued by his men, who take him to the river. The cool waters restore Hector's senses.

Book 15: Zeus sends Apollo to heal Hector. He says that the Greeks will continue to lose until Patroclus, wearing Achilles' armor, takes part in the battle. Zeus adds that after Patroclus kills the god's son, Sarpedon, Patroclus will be killed by Hector, who in turn will be killed by Achilles. The Trojans again attempt to burn the Greek fleet.

Book 16: Patroclus puts on the armor of Achilles and enters the battle. He kills Sarpedon and is killed by Hector.

Book 17: A battle ensues for Achilles' armor. Hector abandons the pursuit and is attacked by Menelaus and Ajax. A fierce battle for the body of Patroclus then begins.

Book 18: Hera tells Achilles of the death of Patroclus and says that he must rejoin the battle. His mother, Thetis, is called to get armor for her hero son.

Book 19: Thetis arrives with the armor made by Hephaestus, the smith god. Agamemnon apologizes to Achilles, but the hero, unmoved, jumps into his chariot to enter the battle.

Book 20: Zeus tells the assembled gods that he will not take sides, but they can now enter the battle, provided they remember that Achilles must be the final victor. There are various battles and encounters, one between Achilles and Aeneas, who is saved by the gods. Achilles then seeks out Hector.

Book 21: Fleeing from the Greeks, the Trojans reach the Xanthus river. Achilles plunges in after them, killing hundreds of Trojans. The river god attempts to drown Achilles, but the hero is saved by Poseidon and Athena. The Trojan army flees to the safety of the walls of Troy.

Book 22: Achilles now encounters Hector, who recoils from the fire in Achilles' eyes. The two men circle the citadel. The gods, looking on, know that Hector is fated for death, but they wish him to die gloriously and send Apollo down to urge Hector to continue the fight. In the guise of one of Hector's brothers, Apollo offers to aid him. Hector turns to

Achilles and tries to arrange that the victor will respect the body of the vanquished. Achilles refuses to listen. Athena comes to the aid of Achilles. Hector is finally deserted by Apollo and killed by Achilles. Before he dies, he says that Achilles will be slain by Paris. Achilles then takes Hector's body, ties it to his chariot, and drives off, with the body trailing behind. Andromache hears loud cries and rushes toward the ramparts, only to see her husband's body being dragged by Achilles' chariot.

Book 23: Achilles reaches his tent with Hector's body, which he consigns to a garbage heap. He then has a funeral meal for his lover, Patroclus, who appears to him at night, saying that Achilles soon must die. During the night Hector's body is guarded by Aphrodite.

Book 24: Achilles, still mourning Patroclus, drags Hector's body around Patroclus's tomb, but the body is protected by Aphrodite as well as Apollo. On the 12th day after Patroclus's death, Iris, the messenger of the gods, comes with King Priam to beg for the body of Hector. Achilles is so moved by King Priam that he consents. King Priam takes the body back to Troy, where a funeral pyre is built for Hector. "Such honors Illium to her hero paid / And peaceful slept the might Hector's shade (Pope's translation)."

There are numerous English translations of *The Iliad* in poetry and prose. Among the most famous are George Chapman's (1598), which inspired Keats's "On Looking into Chapman's Homer." Alexander Pope's poem in heroic couplets (1717), considered one of the greatest achievements of 18th-century poetry, William Cullen Bryant's work in blank verse, and modern verse versions by Richmond Lattimore and Robert Fitzgerald. In prose, the pseudo-biblical prose version of Leaf, Lang, and Myers (1882) was very popular but is now replaced by modern prose versions of E. V. Rieu, Robert Graves, and H. D. Rouse.

1532

Ilmarinen (maker of the sky?). In the Finnish epic poem *The Kalevala*, the smith, forger of the magic sampo.

Ilmarinen constructed the magic sampo, a three-sided mill that ground out salt, grain, and money. It was intended for Vainamoinen to give Louhi, the evil mistress of Pohjola, the Northland, to woo her daughter, the Maiden of Pohjola. However, it was Ilmarinen, not Vainamoinen, who won the bride. After the Maiden of Pohjola was murdered, Ilmarinen set out again to Pohjola to woo the sister of his former wife. When the girl refused him, he abducted her. She reviled Ilmarinen, who out of anger turned her into a sea gull.

The hero then constructed a woman of gold and silver to replace his dead wife. All was fine, except there was no life in the creature. At night he lay beside his golden bride and awoke the next morning realizing that his wife was cold. He offered his golden bride to Vainamoinen, who rejected the offer, telling Ilmarinen to melt down his bride for gold.

One of Ilmarinen's last creative acts was to forge a new moon and sun after the evil mistress Louhi had locked up the sun and moon. But, as in the case of the golden bride, the new moon and sun did not shine or have life.

Ilmarinen originally may have been a god, but all traces of his divinity have disappeared from his life as told in *The Kalevala*.

Ilya Muromets (I. Bilibin)

Ilya Muromets. In Russian folklore, hero of super-human strength who appears in the *byliny*, the epic songs, as well as in numerous folktales.

Ilya Muromets was a *bogatyr*, an epic hero, who had been a sickly child and could not move until he was 33 years old. Then two passing pilgrims gave him a "honey draught" that made him powerful. He used his strength to defend Christianity against the "infidels" and invaders from outside Russia. In one of the *byliny* Ilya destroyed "the monstrous pagan idol" that came to the city of Kiev "breathing threats, striving to inspire fear" in the people. Ilya cut the idol in two. The hero's end was sad, for he boasted of his deeds before God and as a result was turned into stone.

Ilya is a combination of various Russian legendary and mythological characters. Some of his attributes, such as his miraculous bow, are similar to those of the pagan Russian god Pyerun. With his bow he could bring down church cupolas and split oaks into thin slivers. There is some evidence that Ilya Muromets actually might have lived in the 12th century. The peasants of Murom, for instance, are noted for their strength and size to this day.

The Russian composer Reinhold Glière used Ilya Muromets legends for his mammoth third symphony, titled *Ilya Muromets*.

Variant spellings: Ilya of Murom, Ilia Murometz, Ilya-Muromyets.

Imana (almighty). In African mythology (Banyar-wanda of Ruanda-Urundi), creator god who tried to save man from Death. Thought of in human form, Imana is believed to be a large person with very long arms. He is a beneficent deity who tried once to stop Death but failed. Imana ordered everyone to stay indoors while he hunted Death. But one woman went out, and Death asked her if he might hide under her skirt. She consented. This angered Imana, who then allowed Death to have its way with humankind. Imana is also credited with creating the first man, Kazikamuntu (root of man), who had many children. Their continual fighting caused them to disperse and that is why mankind is found in every part of the earth.

Imhotep (he who comes in peace). In Egyptian history and legend, a deified sage who lived at the court of King Zoser during the Third Dynasty (2635–2570 B.C.E.). He is said to have designed the step Pyramid. An architect and artist, Imhotep was deified and was invoked by subsequent generations. He was said to be the son of the god Ptah and was worshiped in a triad of gods at Memphis. He is usually portrayed as a priest with a shaved head reading a scroll while seated. The Greeks called him Imuthes or Imouthes.

Imilozi (whistlers). In African mythology (Zulu), ancestral spirits who whistle when they speak to man.

Inanna (lady of heaven). In Near Eastern mythology (Sumerian), Great Mother goddess from whom Ishtar, the great Near Eastern goddess, is derived. Inanna was goddess of fertility. Although associated with many beneficent aspects of nature, she was also believed to be demonic, destroying her numerous male lovers. Her most famous lover was Dumuzi (the true, or faithful, one), a form of Tammuz, who presided over agriculture. Dumuzi was also god of the underworld and was called the shepherd and lord of the sheepfolds. In some myths, even though he was Inanna's husband, she had him destroyed in order to save her life. Most of the myths associated with Inanna were adopted by Ishtar's cult.

1538

Inapertwa. In Australian mythology, two sky gods who formed human beings with stone knives.

1539

Inaras. In Near Eastern mythology (Hittite), goddess who helped slay the evil dragon Illuyankas. She made the dragon drunk with wine, and with the aid of her lover, Hupasiyas, she had the dragon trussed up with a cord and killed by the weather god. As a reward for helping her, Inaras had a house constructed for her lover Hupasiyas but told him never to look out the window or he would see his mortal wife and children. He disobeyed and was killed by Inaras.

1540

Inari. In Japanese mythology, god of rice, often portrayed as a bearded old man sitting on a sack of rice, flanked on either side by a fox. The foxes are his messengers, but often they are confused with the god in popular imagination, Inari is also regarded as the god of prosperity and patron of tradesmen.

1541

Indarapatra. In Philippine mythology, a hero who killed various monsters. His brother was Sulayman, who slew three monsters with his magic ring but was killed by Pah, a huge bird, when he attempted to kill the fourth. Indarapatra killed the fourth monster with the magic water of life. Later he rescued some women and was given one for a wife.

1542

Indigetes (indigenous). In Roman mythology, name given to deified heroes such as Evander, Aeneas, Heracles, and Romulus or to deities worshiped only in particular places.
Variant spelling: Indiges.

1543

Indra. In Hindu mythology, the storm god, who governs the weather and dispenses rain, sending lightning and thunder with his thunderbolt, Vajra.

Indra, whose mother was Nishtigri, is frequently mentioned in the *Rig-Veda*, the ancient collection of hymns to the gods, as being at war with Vritra, the demon of drought and inclement weather. One hymn cites a battle with Vritra (restrainer):

Indra

I will declare the manly deeds of Indra the first that he
    achieved, the thunder- wielder.
He slew Vritra, then disclosed the waters,
And cleft the channels of the mountain torrents. . . .
Footless and handless still, Vritra challenged Indra,
who smote him with his bolt between the shoulders.
Emasculate yet claiming manly vigor, thus
Vritra lay with scattered limbs.

Another hymn in the collection calls Indra:

Highest of Immortals light,
God of gods by lofty might,
He, before whose prowess high
Tremble earth and upper sky,
He is,—mortals, hear my verse,—
Indra, Lord of Universe!

The high position accorded Indra in the *Rig-Veda* is not mentioned in later Hindu mythology, where he is placed in the second rank of the gods. Indra is ruler of the atmosphere and of the east quarter of the compass. He reigns, with his wife, Indrani, in Swarga, Indra's heaven, located on Mount Meru. Sometimes Indra's capital is called Deva- pura (city of the gods) or Pusha-bhasa (sun splendor).

One later myth, recorded in the Hindu epic *The Ramayama*, indicates Indra 's lesser position in the Hindu pantheon. Megha-nada, a demon who had the power of being invisible, used his magic gift to capture Indra and carried off the god to Lanka (Sri Lanka). The gods, headed by Brahma, called the demon Indra-jit (conqueror of Indra). The demon asked for the gift of immortality if the gods wished Indra freed. Brahma refused but finally gave in to the demand. In one version of *The Ramayana*, however, it says that Indra-jit was killed and his head cut off.

In Indian art Indra is portrayed as a man with four arms, holding a lance and thunderbolt; or with two arms and eyes all over his body, giving him the epithet Sahasraksha (the thousand-eyed). Indra is usually shown riding the elephantAiravata, which was produced during the churning of the ocean when the gods and demons fought for the Amrita, the water of life. Indra's horse is Uccaihsravas (neighing loudly, or long-eared).

Indra has many epithets and titles, among them Vritra-hatta (the destroyer of Vritra) and Vajra-pani (of the thunderbolt). His two weapons are the *chakra*, the wheel or discus that cuts off limbs with its sharp edge; and the *svastika* or *vajra* (thunderbolt), which can be a whirling thunderbolt. Other epithets are Megha-vahana (borne upon the clouds), Deva-pati (chief of the gods), Divas-pati (ruler of the atmosphere), Marutwan (lord of the winds), and Swarga-pate (lord of paradise). Indra's chariot is called Vimana; his charioteer, Matali; his bow (the rainbow), Sakradhanus; and his sword, Paran-ja.

1544

Indrani. In Hindu mythology, wife of Indra, the storm god. In the *Rig-Veda*, a collection of hymns to the gods, Indrani is called the most fortunate of females, "for her husband shall never die of old age." Indra chose Indrani as his wife because of her sexual appeal.

1545

Inéz de Castro, Doña. Died 1355. In Portuguese history and legend, murdered mistress of King Pedro I of Portugal. In 1325 Alfonso IV, the Brave, came to the throne. His son, Dom Pedro, was married to Princess Constanza but was in love with her lady-in-waiting Doña Inéz de Castro, who bore Pedro four children. After Constanza's death, King Alfonso feared Doña Inéz's power over his son and had her murdered. Dom Pedro revolted against his father and was made king in 1357, when he issued a general pardon for the murderers. In 1360, however, he had two of them tortured to death. A legend arose that Pedro had the corpse of his beloved Inéz exhumed and crowned queen. Luiz de Camoes' epic poem *The Lusiads* (book 3) tells the legend. Doña Inéz is the subject of Juaquin Serra's ballet *Doña Inéz de Castro* and Thomas Pasatieri's opera *Inés de Castro*.

1546

Inti. In Inca mythology, the sun, from whom the Incas believed they were descended. Married to his sis-ter Mama Quilla, the moon, Inti was portrayed as a human, his face represented by a disk of gold surrounded by rays of flames. Inti was also called Apu-Punchau (the head of day).

1547

Inua. In Eskimo mythology (Unalit peoples at Bering Strait), shade or soul of a person.

1548

Io (moon). In Greek mythology, priestess of Hera and daughter of the river god Inachus and Melia, a priestess of Hera at Argos. Zeus seduced the young virgin Io. Afterward he transformed her into a heifer to protect her from the ever-jealous Hera. Other accounts say Hera transformed her as a punishment for submitting to Zeus. Hera chose Argus, a being with 100 eyes, to watch over Io. Her father, Inachus, looking for his daughter, discovered the heifer, who wrote out her name with her hoof, but Inachus could not help her. At last, Hermes lulled Argus to sleep with songs and stories, then cut off his head. Not giving up, Hera sent a gadfly to punish Io. Io wandered to Egypt where she was restored to human shape and bore Epaphus, a son of Zeus. The Ionian sea, according to some accounts is named after Io, who swam across it after she was changed into a heifer. Ovid's *Metamorphoses* (book 1) tells the myth of Io, and she appears in Aeschylus' *Prometheus Bound*. In Roman art she appears on the frescoes of the house of Livia on the Palatine in Rome. Correggio painted *Io and Jupiter* (Zeus).

1549

Iocauna. In the mythology of the Indians of the Antilles during the time of Columbus, one of the names of their supreme god. Although Iocauna was "one, eternal, omnipotent, and invisible," according to Peter Martyr d'Anghera's account in *De Orbe Novo* (1516), the Indians believed he had a mother, who was known by five names: Attabira (Atabex), Mamon, Guacarapita, Tella, and Guimazoa. Iocauna was also called Guamaonocon or Yochu Vagua Maorocoti.

1550

Ion (moon-man). In Greek mythology, son of Apollo and Creusa; brother of Janus; married to Helice; father of Aegicores, Argades, Gelem, and Hoples. Ion was abandoned by his mother but was rescued by Apollo and sent to Delphi. He became the ancestor of the Ionians. Ion was killed in the Trojan War. Euripides' *Ion* deals with his myth.

1551

Iouskeha and Tawiscaron. In North American Indian mythology (Iroquois), twin gods, one good, the

1553

Iphigenia (mothering a strong race). In Greek mythology, daughter of Agamemnon and Clytemnestra; sister of Electra, Chromythemis, and Orestes. When Agamemnon's ships were stilled at Aulis on their way to the Trojan War, the king sacrificed Iphigenia to placate the virgin goddess Artemis after Agamemnon had killed one of her stags. Knowing that Clytemnestra would never agree to the sacrifice, Agamemnon sent for Iphigenia under the pretext that she was to marry Achilles. In some accounts the sacrifice of Iphigenia was carried out to completion, and she died. Other ancient accounts say that while the sacrifice was being prepared, Artemis swept up Iphigenia and took her off to Tauris, where she became the goddess's priestess. Anyone who was shipwrecked on the island of Tauris was sacrificed to Artemis. Iphigenia's brother Orestes, in search of the sacred image of Artemis, was shipwrecked on the island. After discovering his identify, Iphigenia fled with him, taking the image of Artemis. In Homer's *Iliad* Iphigenia is called Chrysothemis. Aeschylus' *Agamemnon* follows the myth that says she was sacrificed, whereas Euripides' *Iphigenia in Aulis* and *Iphigenia in Tauris* follow the story that says she was saved. Gluck's operas *Iphigénie en Aulide* and *Iphigénie en Tauride* are based on Euripides' version. Racine's *Iphigénie* and Goethe's *Iphigenie auf Tauris* also tell the myth.

other evil. The unborn twins began to quarrel in their mother's womb. After his birth, Tawiscaron killed his mother. But the goddess Ataensic, their grandmother, believed that Iouskeha was evil and Tawiscaron good. The two brothers were constantly in conflict with each other. Iouskeha created fruit trees and pleasant bushes and placed the sun and moon in their sphere of heaven; Tawiscaron created thorns and the Rocky Mountains. In the end, Iouskeha succeeded in imprisoning his evil brother underground.

Variant spelling: Yoskeha and Tawiscara.

1552

Iphicles (famous might). In Greek mythology, twin brother of Heracles, son of Amphitryon and Alcmena. When the two babies were in the cradle, Hera, ever hateful toward Heracles, sent two large snakes to destroy them, but Heracles, only a year old, squeezed the snakes to death. This story is cited in some accounts as evidence that Heracles was fathered by Zeus and Iphicles by Amphitryon. Iphicles was the father of Iolaus, who helped Heracles conquer the Lernean Hydra by cauterizing the place where each head had been cut off.

Iris conducting Aphrodite to Ares (John Flaxman)

1554

Iphimedia (she who strengthens the genitals). In Greek mythology, a daughter of Tropias, married to the giant Aloeus. Iphimedia fled from Aloeus and had two sons, Otus and Ephialtes, by Poseidon. Iphimedia is mentioned in Homer's *Odyssey* (book 11).

Variant spelling: Iphimedeia.

1555

Iphis. In Greek and Roman mythology, daughter of Telethusa of Crete and Ligdus. Iphis was raised secretly as a boy by her mother because her father, Ligdus, wanted only male children and would have killed her had he known she was a girl. When Ianthe, a young girl, fell in love with Iphis, the goddess Isis changed Iphis into a man. Ovid's *Metamorphoses* (book 9) records the myth.

1556

Iris (rainbow). In Greek mythology, goddess of the rainbow and messenger of the gods; daughter of the sea deities Thaumas and Electra. Homer's *Iliad* (books 3, 5, 8) makes her the messenger of Zeus, though in much later mythology she appears as an aide to Hera, wife of Zeus. One of her functions was to cut the thread of life that detained the soul in the body when it was dying. Iris appears in Hesiod's *Theogony*, Ovid's *Metamorphoses* (book 1 et seq.), and Vergil's *Aeneid* (book 4). In English poetry she is cited in Milton's *Paradise Lost* (book 2.244) to describe the vestment of the Archangel Michael with its airy color, like the rainbow. In Greek art she is portrayed as a young woman with wings, carrying a messenger's wand, also used by Hermes. There are two statues of Iris among the Elgin Marbles. Iris survives as the English word for the colored portion of the eye, as well as the name of a family of flowers, including the gladiolus and crocus, which in Christian symbolism is often substituted for the lily in paintings portraying the Virgin Mary.

1557

Iron Crown of Lombardy. In medieval history and legend, crown of the ancient Lombardic kings, said to have been given by Pope Gregory the Great. Charlemagne was crowned with it. It is called the Iron Crown because the inner fillet of iron is said to have been beaten out of a nail from the true cross of Christ, which was given to Emperor Constantine by his mother, St. Helena. The outer circlet is of beaten gold and set with precious stones.

Isaac

Irra. In Near Eastern mythology (Babylonian-Assyrian), god of pestilence, the fearful slaughterer who laid waste the plains, taking delight in destroying both land and humankind.

One poetic myth narrates how Irra determined to destroy Babylon. Ishum, the fire god, is told by Irra:

> In the city whither I send thee,
> Thou shalt fear no one, nor have compassion.
> Kill the young and old alike,
> The tender suckling likewise—spare no one.
> The treasures of Babylon carry off as booty.

After much discussion, Ishum makes Irra settle for some song of praise in the god's honor. Wherever a tablet with the song or incantation was hung or set up, that house would be free from the onslaughts of the god. The text ends:

> He who glorifies my name will rule the world.
> Who proclaims the glory of my power
> Will be without a rival.
> The singer who sings of my deeds will not die through
>   pestilence. . . .
> Let the inhabitants of all places learn to glorify my
>   name.

Variant spellings: Dibbara, Girra, Iea, Ura.

Iruwa. In African mythology (Chaga of Kenya), sun god who forgave a man who attempted to murder him. Once a man decided to destroy the sun for killing his two sons. When the plot was discovered, Iruwa not only forgave the man but gave him more sons and even wealth.

Isaac (laughter). In the Bible, O.T., son of Abraham and Sarah, promised heir of Abraham, half-brother of Ishmael, married to Rebekah, father of Jacob and Esau.

The main events of Isaac's life are told in Genesis. The book tells how Abraham was visited by three men (angels) who predicted the birth of a child to the aged couple, Abraham and Sarah. When Sarah heard this, she laughed.

When Yahweh, the Hebrew god, wished to test Abraham's faith, he ordered him to sacrifice his beloved son Isaac. However, seeing that Abraham was willing to kill his son, Yahweh intervened and stopped the sacrifice. Later Abraham sent a servant to find a wife for Isaac. The first girl who offered the servant water at a well was to be Isaac's wife. It was the daughter of Laban, Rebekah, by whom Isaac had two sons, Esau and Jacob. By a trick Rebekah secured Isaac's deathbed blessing and right of

succession for her favorite, Jacob, by covering his arms and neck with goatskin to impersonate his hairy brother Esau. When Isaac discovered he had been tricked, he could not give Esau back his inheritance, for once a blessing was given it could not be recalled. But Isaac prevented strife between the two brothers, who later buried him in a cave when he died at the age of 108. In Islamic mythology Isaac is called Ishaq. He is mentioned in the Koran (sura 21). Isaac usually appears along with his father, Abraham, in many works titled *The Sacrifice of Isaac*. The scene appears on the Florence Baptistery doors by Lorenzo Ghiberti.

Isaiah (Yahweh is salvation). In the Bible, O.T., one of the Major Prophets, also title of an Old Testament book. Isaiah lived in Judah in the latter part of the eighth century B.C.E. and is believed to have been descended from a royal family. The Book of Isaiah is now considered to be only partly his work: chapters 1 to 39 by Isaiah, chapters 40 to 50 by another hand (referred to as Second Isaiah), and chapters 56 to 66 by a third and unknown author. In the New Testament Jesus often quotes from the Book of Isaiah, citing passages believed to refer to the Messiah. Later Jewish legend, not recorded in the Bible, says that in his old age Isaiah was "sawn asunder in the trunk of a carob tree by order of King Manasseh."

In Christian art Isaiah is often depicted with a scroll inscribed with the Latin words *Ecce virgo concipiet et parium filium* (Behold a virgin shall conceive and bear a son) (Is. 7:15), which is a mistranslation of the Hebrew original. The word *virgin* is not used in the Hebrew, but *young woman*.

In Islamic legend the name given to Isaiah is Sha'ya. He is not mentioned in the Koran, though Islamic as well as Jewish and Christian legend says he was murdered.

Ishana Ten. In Japanese Buddhist mythology, god derived from the Hindu god Shiva, portrayed as a fierce figure with three eyes, holding in his right hand a trident and in his left a shallow vessel containing clotted blood. He is one of the Jiu No O, 12 Japanese Buddhist gods and goddesses adopted from Hindu mythology.

Ishmael (may God hear). In the Bible, O.T., son of Abraham and his concubine Hagar; half-brother to Isaac. Ishamel was cast out of Abraham's house; he married and settled at Paran. The Arabs are said to be descended from his 12 sons. His name has come to mean any outcast and was used by Herman Melville in *Moby Dick* as the name of the narrator.

1564

Ishtar. In Near Eastern mythology, Semitic mother-goddess, in part derived from the Sumerian mother-goddess, Inanna.

Ishtar was both a beneficent goddess, the mother of mankind, and a demonic deity, a warrior goddess "clad in terror," who caused even the gods to tremble. Ishtar thus combined in her person and worship nearly all of the attributes, both good and evil, of many Near Eastern goddesses. As the great mother of the gods and the mother of men, she grieved over people's sorrows, being called in one hymn "she who loveth all men" and in another addressed as the goddess who "lookest mercifully upon a sinner." In this beneficent role Ishtar bestowed life, health, and prosperity with her "life-giving glance." She was the giver of vegetation and the creator of animals, wedlock, maternity, and all earthly blessings and moral laws for humankind.

But, alongside her beneficent role Ishtar was also a demonic goddess. She was the warrior goddess. Part of a votive tablet placed for Hammurabi, the great ruler, reads: "Ishtar has given thee conflict and battle; what more can'st thou hope?" Ishtar was also a storm goddess, "the lofty one who causes the heavens to tremble, the earth to quake . . . who casts down the mountains like dead bodies."

Because Ishtar combined so many attributes of other goddesses, the myths surrounding her are often in conflict. In one account, for example, she is said to be the daughter of the moon god, Sin, and sister of the sun god, Shamash. In another account she is the daughter of Anu, the lord of heaven. Both accounts agree, however, that she is connected with the planet Venus. She is called "lady of resplendent light" in that role and is symbolized by an eight-pointed star, a symbol later associated with the Virgin Mary in Christianity.

Ishtar's most important role, however, was as goddess of sexual love. In this aspect she displayed an extremely despotic attitude. In the Babylonian epic poem *Gilgamesh*, for example, she is at first in love with the shepherd Tammuz, then with a bird, then a lion, then a horse, then a shepherd, then a gardener, and finally with Gilgamesh, the hero king. Gilgamesh, however, rejects Ishtar because she had killed so many of her lovers, which the hero enumerates to the goddess, the prime example being her husband, Tammuz. Their cruel sexual relationship is vividly described in another poem, *Ishtar's Descent into the Underworld.* The poem is known in many different versions in Near Eastern literature, and the name of the goddess is often changed. In one text the name is Inanna.

According to the poem, Ishtar once looked down from her home in heaven to the deep pit of the underworld. She decided she wanted to go down, but she told her minister, Ninshubar, that after she was gone he was to "beat a drum in the holy shrine" for her sake, telling the gods Enlil, Nanna, Eridu, and Enki that she was in the underworld. Ishtar then went down and arrived at the gate of the underworld. Its chief keeper, Neti, asked her what she wanted. She lied, telling him she had come for the burial rites of Gugalanna, husband of Ereshkigal, the queen of the underworld. Ereshkigal was also the sister of Ishtar. Neti then went to Ereshkigal and told her that her sister Ishtar was at the gates and wished to enter. Ereshkigal told Neti that he was to let Ishtar in but to be certain that when each of the seven doors of the underworld was unlocked Ishtar followed the rite connected with passage through the gate.

Ishtar then went from door to door. At each door she was divested of some symbol of her power—her Shugurra, her royal rod, her necklace, two stones that lay on her breast, her golden ring, her pectoral gems, and finally the robe of sovereignty that covered her body.

At the last door Ishtar dropped naked on her knees before her sister, Ereshkigal. The queen, in conjunction with seven judges, pronounced the sentence that Ishtar was to die. Immediately, the goddess died, and her corpse was hung on a pike. Three nights passed. Ninshubar, her faithful follower, then did as the goddess Ishtar had earlier instructed him. He called on the gods for help, but only Enki responded. (In the poem Enki is called Ishtar's father.) He formed two beings, the Kurgarru and the Kalaturru, giving the first the food of life and second the water of life. The two descended to hell asking for Ishtar's body. When they found it, they sprinkled the food and the water on the body, restoring it to life. But one problem remained— another dead body had to be substituted for the restored one of Ishtar. The cruel goddess offered her youthful husband Tammuz, who was then grabbed by seven demons, killed, and taken to hell, where his body replaced that of the resurrected goddess.

A variant poetic version of *Ishtar's Descent into the Underworld* was used by the French composer Vincent d'Indy for his *Istar*, a set of symphonic variations for orchestra. Instead of the main theme coming first, it appears only at the end to indicate the complete nakedness of the goddess before the last gate. In d'Indy's text Ishtar descends to the underworld to find her husband Tammuz. She brings him back to earth because the land is barren without him (he was the spirit, or god, of vegetation).

Ishtar had numerous temples throughout the Near East. The chief seat of her worship was at Erech; others were at Ashur, Babylon, Nineveh, and Ur.

Ishtar was identified with numerous other Near Eastern goddesses, such as Anath, Anunit, Aruru, Ashdar, Asherah, Astarte, Ashtoreth, Athtar, Belit, Innimi, Kilili, Mah, Meni, Nana, Ninharsag, Ninlil, and Nintud; therefore, her symbols were also many. Among them were a dove, an ear of wheat, a forked tree, a lion, a serpent, an ornamented cone, a pillar or tree stem. Sometimes she was portrayed as a woman nursing a child, similar to Egyptian works showing Isis nursing Horus or Christian portrayals of the Virgin Mary nursing the Child Jesus.

Variant spelling: Istar.

1565

Ishvara. In Buddhism, title of the Hindu god Shiva meaning independent existence and used for a transcendent or extramundane god, a personal deity. The Buddha rejected this concept. He said: "If Ishvara be the maker, all living things should have silently to submit to their maker's power. They would be like vessels formed by the potter's hand; and if it were so, how would it be possible to practice virtue? If the world had been made by Ishvara there should be no such thing as sorrow, or calamity, or sin; for both pure and impure deeds must come from him. If not, there would be another cause beside him, and he would not be the self-existent one. Thus, you see, the thought of Ishvara is overthrown." Buddhism teaches the interdependence of all things as at once the causes and effects of everything and does not require an uncaused cause to make the universe.

1566

Isidore of Seville, St. (gift of Isis). Seventh century C.E. In Christian legend, bishop of Seville, Doctor of the Church. Feast, 4 April.

The brother of St. Leander, who preceded him in his bishopric, Isadore was noted for his writings, the most famous being his *Etymologies*, an encyclopedia of information on every subject then known to man. The saint based his work on previous books and did not verify any of the facts or stories. His support of the anti-Semitic canons enacted in Spain against the Jews who did not accept Christianity greatly diminished his reputation.

Numerous miracles are recorded about the saint: Once a man wanted to steal a relic of St. Isidore and hid in the church where the saint was buried. When all was quiet, he broke open the shrine and cut off one of Isidore's fingers. No sooner had he done this than he was turned to stone. He thought it best to return the finger, which, when he could move again, he did, thanking the saint for his mercy in not killing him.

Murillo's painting of St. Isidore and St. Leander portrays each enthroned and robed in white, wearing their bishops' miters.

1567

Isidore the Ploughman, St. (gift of Isis). 12th century. In Christian legend, patron saint of Madrid, Spain.

Isidore was a poor workman who could neither read nor write. One day his master Juan de Vargas went into the fields to see if Isidore was working or, as he had heard from other servants, praying. As Vargas came near the field, he saw two angels guiding the plow while Isidore knelt in prayer. Another legend tells how when Vargas was thirsty Isidore struck a rock with his goad and pure water flowed out. The saint is portrayed dressed as a workman, sometimes with a spade in his hand.

Isis

1568

Isis (seat). In Egyptian mythology, the Greek form of the Egyptian name Ast or Eset, the sister-wife of Osiris and the mother of Horus; a great mother-goddess. Often Isis and the goddess Hathor are commingled because both were great mother goddesses. This merging of religious and cultic beliefs and practices is called syncretism. The term was used by the Greek writer Plutarch for the union of Greek, Roman, and Egyptian cultic deities and beliefs during his day.

Numerous passages in the ancient Pyramid Texts state that Osiris, Isis, Set, and Nephthys were deified members of a family of human beings. Plutarch, in his short book *Isis and Osiris*, writes that when Set killed his brother Osiris and threw his coffin into a river, Isis found the coffin and hid it; but Set discovered the hiding place, cut up Osiris's body, and scattered the pieces throughout Egypt. Isis recovered the dismembered parts, and with the help of the god Thoth restored her brother-husband and had intercourse with him, conceiving a child, who was called Horus. *The Book of the Dead* has many allusions to Isis' loving care of Osiris, but it says little of her devotion to her son Horus, whom she reared so that he would become the avenger of his father.

The Metternich Stele (found in Alexanderia in 1828 and given to Prince Metternich by Mohammed Ali) tells how the goddess in her wanderings and sorrows cried out, "I, even I, am Isis, and I came forth from the house wherein my brother Set has placed me." For Set was not content with murdering his brother Osiris but took further vengeance by shutting Isis up in a prison. While she was confined there, Thoth, the prince of law in both heaven and earth, came to her and gave her advice that would protect her unborn son. With Thoth's help she escaped and later exclaimed, "I came forth from the house at eventide, and there also came forth with me my seven scorpions, who were to accompany me, and to be my helpers. Two scorpions, Tefen and Befen, were behind me, two scorpions, Mestet and Mestetef, were by my side, and three scorpions, Petet, Thetet and Maatet, showed me the way."

The seven scorpion goddesses led Isis to a village near the papyrus swamps. Isis sought shelter from a rich woman, who closed the door in her face (just as Joseph and Mary were not given shelter in the Christian legend). Enraged at the treatment Isis received from the woman, one of the scorpion goddesses, Tefen, made her way under the door of the woman's house, stung her child to death and set the house afire. Isis, taking pity on the woman's grief for her child, restored him to life, and a flood of rain extinguished the fire. Meanwhile a peasant woman invited Isis to her house and the goddess stayed there, while the woman who had rejected Isis suffered agonies of remorse.

Soon after, Isis brought forth her child Horus on a bed of papyrus plants in the swamps. She hid the boy carefully, fearing that he might by stung by some venomous reptile. One day she set out for the city of Am to obtain provisions for her son. When she returned, she found him lying dead, foam on his lips, the ground around him soaked with tears from his eyes. In a moment she realized that Set, in the form of a scorpion, had killed Horus. Her cries brought out the neighbors, but none could help her. Nephthys, her sister, came to her aid, telling her to appeal to the sun god Ra. She cried to the god and the sun stood still in heaven. Thoth (a form of Ra in the myth) descended to earth to comfort Isis, repeating to her a spell that would restore Horus to life.

Isis learned the magic words, and when she uttered them, the poison flowed from her son's body, air entered his lungs, sense and feeling returned to him, and he was restored to life. Thoth ascended to heaven, and the sun resumed his course amid great rejoicing.

When Horus grew up, he fought against Set in a battle that lasted three days and three nights. Horus had gained the advantage when Isis, who was also Set's sister, took pity on her brother and allowed him to escape. Horus, filled with anger at his mother, avenged himself by cutting off her head. However, Thoth intervened and transformed the severed head into the head of a cow and attached it to Isis.

It is evident from a number of passages in various Egyptian texts that Isis possessed great skill in magic. In the *Hymn to Osiris*, Isis' use of magic words helps restore Osiris to life, and in *The Book of the Dead* one entire chapter is devoted to the purpose of bestowing on the deceased some of the magical powers of the goddess.

Isis was worshiped throughout Egypt. She had numerous titles, such as "the divine one," "the greatest of all the gods and goddesses," "the queen of all gods," "the female Ra," "the female Horus," "the lady of the new year," "the maker of sunrise," "the lady of heaven," and "the light giver of heaven." Worship of Isis spread beyond Egypt. From various classical writers we find that she was revered in several places in western Europe, being identified with Persephone, Tethys, and Athena, just as her husband, Osiris, was identified with Hades, Dionysus, and other foreign gods. In her chief temple in Rome the goddess was called Isis Campensis. Apuleius in *The Golden Ass* gives a description of a festival of Isis that was held in Rome in the latter half of the second century C.E. The writer calls the goddess *regina coeli*, or "queen of heaven" (a title later used for the Virgin Mary) and identifies her with Ceres, Venus, and Persephone. The holiest of all her sanctuaries known to the Greeks was at Tithorea. Pausanias, in his *Description of Greece* (chapter

32), writes that a festival was held there in her honor twice a year, in spring and autumn.

Isis was also identified with many local Syrian goddesses, and the early Christians bestowed some of her attributes on the Virgin Mary. Several of the incidents of the wanderings of Mary with the Christ Child in Egypt as recorded in the apocryphal Gospels reflect scenes in the life of Isis as described in the texts found on the Metternich Stele.

Isis is usually portrayed wearing the vulture headdress and holding a papyrus scepter in one hand and the ankh, the symbol of life, in the other. Her most famous symbol is the *thet*, the knot or buckle of Isis, which is indicative of her power to bind and also serves as a symbol of blood and life. Sometimes Isis is portrayed suckling her infant son Horus.

Among the many epithets of the goddess are Khut, as light giver; Usert, as earth goddess; Thenenet, as great goddess of Duat, the underworld; Satis, who spread the life-giving waters of the Nile flood; Anukis, as the embracer of the land and the producer of fertility by her waters; Ankhet, as the producer and giver of life; Kekhet, as the goddess of cultivated land and fields; Renenet, as the goddess of the harvest; Tcheft, as the goddess of food that was offered to the gods; and Ament (hidden goddess), as the great lady of the underworld who assisted in restoring the bodies of the blessed dead to live in the kingdom of Osiris, the lord of the dead.

Jacob

1569

Israel (God fights, God rules?). In the Bible, O.T., name given to Jacob after he had wrestled with the angel (Gen. 32:28) and again by God at Bethel (Gen. 35:10). Israel is also the name given to the region inhabited by the Twelve Tribes fathered by Jacob.

1570

Israfel (serafim; the burning one). Angel in Islamic mythology who will announce the Last Judgment, the end of the world.

Although Israfel is not named directly in the Koran, he appears in Islamic tradition. He is said to be the archangel who for three years was the companion of Muhammad and trained him for his role as the prophet. Gabriel, who is called Jiburili in Islam, then took over the task and dictated the Koran to the prophet from the perfect copy in heaven.

Alexander the Great, an important figure in Islamic legend, met Israfel before arriving in the Land of Darkness. There the angel stood on a hill and blew his trumpet. His trumpet will announce the Day of Resurrection, when he will stand upon the Holy Rock in Jerusalem and give the signal that will bring the dead back to life.

Edgar Allan Poe, fascinated by the sound of the angel's name and his function in Islamic mythology, wrote a poem called *Israfel*. In its preface Poe quotes: "And the angel Israfel, whose heart-strings are a lute, and who has the sweetest voice of all God's creatures.—Koran." Apparently Poe confused a footnote in the Koran with text, as Israfel is not mentioned in the holy book.

In Egypt today it is believed that Israfel's music will refresh the inhabitants of paradise, as he does in Poe's poem, which inspired the title of Harvey Allen's biography of the poet and Edwin Markham's poem in Poe's honor, *Our Israfel*.

1571

Italapas. In North American Indian mythology (Chinook), the name given Coyote, who appears in much Indian mythology. Italapas aided Ikanam, the creator, in forming mankind as well as teaching them the arts. He made the first prairie by pushing the sea back. He elaborated various taboos regarding hunting. His character is different from that of other coyotes in that he is not a mischievous being. In the accounts of the Indians of California, for example, Coyote always attempts to thwart creation.

1572

Itzamná. In Mayan mythology, culture hero and sky god who taught the Indians how to grow corn. Itzamná's most frequent title was Kin-ich-ahau (lord of the sun's face or lord, the eye of day) in his role as the sun's disk. At Itzamal there was a temple dedicated to Itzamná as Kin-ich-kak-mo (the eye of the day, the bird of fire), which people came to in times of pestilence. An offering was placed on the altar at noon and consumed by fire. A temple at Campeche, dedicated to him as Kin-ich-ahau-haban (lord of the sun's face, the hunter), had blood sacrifices; at another temple he was worshiped as Kabil (he of the lucky hand) for cures. In Mayan art Itzamná is portrayed as an old man with toothless jaws and sunken cheeks. Paul Schellhas, when classifying the gods of some Mayan codices, gave Itzamná the letter *D*, and the god is sometimes referred to as God D.

Variant spellings: Yzamana, Zamana.

1573
Ivaldi (the mighty). In Norse mythology, father of the craftsmen dwarfs or elves who constructed the ship *Skithblathnir*; Odin's spear, Gungnir; and the golden hair for Thor's wife, Sif, which had been cut off by the fire-trickster god, Loki, and had to be replaced.

1574
Ivan the Terrible. 1530–1584. In Russian legend, Ivan IV, czar of Muscovy, noted for his extreme cruelty.

In 1564, after the treason of one of his counselors, Ivan organized a personal bodyguard called the Oprichnik, who acted in a manner similar to the Nazi Gestapo. They terrorized the countryside and executed "offenders" against the czar. Ivan's evil reputation made an impact on Russian legend, poetry, and music. Rimsky-Korsakov's opera *Ivan the Terrible*, sometimes called *The Maid of Pskov*, deals with a romantic legend of Ivan's secret daughter, Olga, and her lover, Tutcha, who are killed when defending Pskov against Ivan's lust. Tchaikovsky's opera *The Oprichnik* also has a romantic plot. Anton Rubinstein's opera *The Merchant of Kalashnikov* uses Lermontov's poem *A Song About Tsar Ivan Vasilyevich, the Young Opricknik, and the Merchant Kalashnikov* as the basis for the libretto. Sergei Eisenstein's film *Ivan the Terrible*, in two parts has music by Serge Prokofiev.

1575
Iwa. In Polynesian mythology, Hawaiian trickster and master thief, who stole while he was in his mother's womb. Once he had a contest with other thieves to see who could completely fill up a house with stolen goods in one night. Iwa waited until the thieves had fallen asleep, then he stole all of the goods from their houses and placed them in his house. Possessing a magic paddle, Iwa was capable of rowing from one end of the Hawaiian islands to the other in four strokes.

1576
Ixchel. In Mayan mythology, water goddess who presided over floods, the rainbow, pregnancy, and weaving; believed by some scholars to be the goddess of the moon. Ixchel is a demonic goddess, the personification of the destructive nature of water. In one Mayan art work she is portrayed as an angry old woman destroying the world by flood. Although she is generally demonic, she is married to Itzamná. In Mayan art she is usually portrayed surrounded by the symbols of death and destruction, with a serpent on her head and crossbones on her dress. When classifying the gods in some Mayan codices, Paul Schellhas gave Ixchel the letter *I*, and she is sometimes referred to as Goddess I.

Tantalus, Sisyphus, and Ixion

1577

Ix-huyne. In Mayan mythology, goddess of the moon; though sometimes Ixchel, the water goddess, is given that role.

1578

Ixion (strong moon-man). In Greek mythology, the first murderer; king of the Lapiths in Thessaly; son of Antion and Perimele (or Ares or Phlegyas); married to Dia; father of Perithous and, by a cloud, father of the centaurs and Amycus. Ixion killed his father-in-law and tried to seduce Hera, the wife of Zeus. Ixion was tricked by Zeus, who caused a cloud to appear in the form of Hera. Ixion had sexual intercourse with the cloud, fathering a race of centaurs. Zeus then hurled a thunderbolt at Ixion and had Hermes confine him to the underworld, tied to a fiery wheel that constantly revolved and was lashed by serpents. Ovid's *Metamorphoses* (book 12) tells the story. Ovid's image was passed on to European medieval tradition, which saw Ixion as symbolic of lewdness or sensuality, as it saw Sisyphus as pride and Tantalus as avarice. Ixion appears in Dante's *Divine Comedy* (Hell), Spenser's *Faerie Queene* (1.5.35), Pope's *Rape of the Lock*, and Robert Browning's *Ixion*, in which the English poet has Ixion gain insight through his suffering.

1579

Ixtab. In Mayan mythology, goddess of suicide. According to Mayan belief, a suicide went directly to paradise, as opposed to Christian belief, in which the soul was assigned to hell. In Mayan art Ixtab is portrayed hanging from the sky by a halter around her neck. Her eyes are closed, and signs of decomposition appear on her body.

1580

Ixtlilton (the little black one). In Aztec mythology, god of medicine, whose temple contained jars of water known as *tlital* (black water), used to heal the sick, particularly children. Fray Bernardino de Sahagún, in his *Historia general de las cosas de Nueva España* (1570–1582), writes that when a child was cured, the parents would take into their home a priest who impersonated the god. At the house a feast was held that "consisted of dances and songs." When the priest impersonating the god later left the house, "they gave him rugs or shawls."

Variant spelling: Yxtlilton.

1581

Izanagi and Izanami (the male who invites and the female who invites). In Japanese Shiuto mythology, primeval creator god and goddess, ancestors of many Shinto gods as well as of the principal islands of Japan.

Their myth is told in the *Kojiki* (records of ancient matters), written in 712 C.E. They appeared on the expanse of high heaven before the earth had been created and were chosen by the gods to create the earth. The couple was given a jeweled spear, and standing on the Floating Bridge of Heaven, they pushed down the spear and pulled up brine. They piled up the brine and formed the island of Onogoro.

Izanagi and Izanami then came down to the island of Onogoro but found it deserted. They were lonely, and after looking intently at one another, decided to marry.

"How is thy body formed?" Izanagi asked Izanami.

"My body is completely formed except for one part that is incomplete," she replied.

"My body is completely formed, and there is one part that is superfluous. Suppose that we supplement that which is incomplete in thee with that which is superfluous in me, and thereby procreate lands."

The two slept together. A child was born, but without legs, so they cast it adrift in a reed boat. Their second child was the Island Awa, but they refused it also. Izanagi and Izanami then went up to heaven to ask the gods what the trouble was. They were informed that when they made love Izanami spoke first—which was wrong. The man was to speak first. They again slept together and gave birth to the eight islands that became Japan. Thus, at a Shinto wedding ceremony the groom speaks first.

The couple continued producing islands and gods until Izanami died giving birth to the fire god. Then Izanagi descended to the underworld in search of his wife. He lit a tooth of the comb that held his hair to illuminate his passage. Finding only the decaying corpse of his wife, he fled in horror. Reaching earth again, he hastened to bathe and purify himself in the river. From every garment he threw off and from every part of his body, from his feet to his nose, a fresh god was born, some good and some evil.

1582

Izquitecatl (lord of the place of toasted corn). In Aztec mythology, god included by Fray Diego Durán in his *Historia de las Indias de Nueva España y islas de Tierra Firme* (1580–1581).

1583

Iztaccihuatl (white woman). In Aztec mythology, mountain goddess described by Fray Diego Durán in his *Book of the Gods and Rites* (c. 1576), which deals with Aztec mythology, as a young woman "wearing clipped man's hair on the forehead and hanging down to the shoulders on the sides. Her cheeks were always painted with color." Ixtaci was also the name of a mountain in Mexico some 16,000 feet high which, according to some commentators, resembles a woman lying down in a white shroud.

J

Jack and the Beanstalk (Arthur Rackham)

1584

Jack and the Beanstalk. English folktale popular in the British Isles and the United States. Jack, a rather simple boy, is sent by his mother, a widow, to sell their cow. Jack sells the cow to a butcher for some colored beans. When he returns home, his mother, angry at his stupidity, tosses the beans out a window. The next morning a large beanstalk is seen to have sprouted. Jack climbs the stalk and finds a giant's castle. He hides as he hears the giant sing, "Fee-fi-fo-fum/ I smell the blood of an Englishman/ Be he live or be he dead/ I'll grind his bones to make my bread." Jack sees the giant's wife prepare a big dinner for the giant and watches as a little red hen lays a golden egg. When the giant falls asleep, Jack steals the hen. The next day he climbs the stalk again and this time steals bags of gold. Finally, the third time he steals the giant's harp, which cries out for help. The giant chases Jack down the beanstalk, but Jack cuts down the stalk and the giant is killed.

1585

Jacob (supplanter). In the Bible, O.T., the second son of Isaac and Rebekah, twin brother of Esau. Jacob was later renamed Israel by Yahweh, the Hebrew god.

Jacob's story is found in the Book of Genesis (chaps. 25–50). He was an agriculturalist, and his brother Esau was a hunter. Once when Esau was out hunting, he returned home very hungry and asked Jacob for some food. Jacob, a very wily man, would not give the food unless Esau sold him his birthright, which Esau did for "a pottage of lentils" (Gen. 25:34). In order to claim this birthright Jacob had to obtain a blessing from his father. He knew that his father would give the birthright only to Esau. When his father was old and blind, Jacob, with the help of his mother, Rebekah, disguised himself as Esau by wrapping his arms in goatskin. When his father touched the goatskin, he took Jacob to be Esau, because, as Jacob had said, "Esau my brother is a hairy man, and I am a smooth man" (Gen. 27:11). Isaac became suspicious when he heard Jacob speak. Isaac then said, "The voice is Jacob's voice, but the hands are the hands of Esau" (Gen. 27:22). Nevertheless, he gave his blessing—and Esau's birthright—to Jacob. Esau was so enraged that Jacob fled to his uncle in Haran. On his way Jacob stopped at night and lay down to sleep, using stones (fetish figures of gods) for a pillow. "And he dreamed, and behold a ladder set up on the earth, and the top of it reached to heaven: and behold the angels of God ascending and descending on it. And behold, the Lord [Yahweh] stood above it, and said, 'I am the Lord God of Abraham thy father, and the God of Isaac: the land whereon thou liest, to thee will I give it, and to thy seed.'" When Jacob awoke, he realized that Yahweh had been with him, and he took the stones of his pillow and erected a shrine, pouring oil on it and calling it Bethel (the house of God).

When Jacob arrived at Haran, he met Laban's beautiful daughter Rachel coming to water the sheep. Jacob rolled away the stone from the well, watered the sheep, kissed Rachel, and told her he was her kinsman. He then worked for his uncle for seven years to obtain Rachel, but Laban tricked him and had his daughter Leah slipped into the marriage bed instead of Rachel. When Jacob discovered he had married Leah instead of Rachel, Laban explained to him that it was not possible to give away his youngest daughter before the eldest was married. Jacob then agreed to work another seven years to obtain Rachel as his wife. It was Rachel whom Jacob loved, but it was Leah who bore most of his children, as Rachel was barren until later in life.

After some 20 years, Jacob left with his wives and children for Hebron, the home of his father. Laban pursued him but eventually made peace. Approaching Seir, where Esau lived, Jacob sent many gifts ahead, fearful that his brother would kill him and his family. One night Jacob wrestled with and captured an angel, who begged to be released. Jacob consented on condition that the angel give him a blessing. "And he said, 'Thy name shall be called no more Jacob, but Israel: for as a prince hast thou power with God and with men, and hast prevailed'" (Gen. 32). (Angel is often a term for Yahweh in the Old Testament.) Jacob's most famous son was Joseph. In Islam Jacob is called Ya'qub.

Scenes from his life are frequently found in Western art. Gerbrandt van den Eeckhout's *Isaac Blessing Jacob* is one of the best known.

1586

Jahi. In Persian mythology, demoness of debauchery. Jahi is called a malicious fiend and a harlot in the sacred ancient Persian book *Avesta*.

1587

Jambavat. In the Hindu epic poem *The Ramayana*, the king of the bears, who aids Rama in his invasion of Lanka (Sri Lanka). Jambavat came into possession of a magic gem that protected its owner if he remained good but brought ruin on any evil person who had it. The magic gem came to Jambavat after its owner, Prasena, was killed by a lion for his evil life. The lion was in turn killed by Jambavat, who took the gem. Krishna (an incarnation of the god Vishnu) then came in search of the gem and fought Jambavat for 21 days. At the end of the battle Jambavat not only gave Krishna the gem but also offered his daughter, Jambavati. Later Jambavat joined in the war against the demon Ravana, who had abducted Rama's wife, Sita.

1588

James, Jesse. 1847-1882. In American history and folklore, killer-bandit who, according to legend, stole from the rich to give to the poor.

Born in Clay County, Missouri, the son of a preacher, Jesse and his brother Frank led a band of thieves throughout the 1870s. Popular sentiment was in James's favor, as expressed in the following folktale: One day he and his brother Frank were given a meal by a poor widow who was waiting for her landlord to collect an $800 mortgage. Jesse said the woman reminded him of his mother, and he would lend her the money needed. All she had to do was make sure the landlord gave her a receipt for the amount before he left. Jesse and Frank then left, and the landlord arrived. Taking the widow's money, he gave her the requested receipt and rode off. But he didn't get too far before some masked men held him up and took the $800.

James was later killed by one of his gang, Robert Ford. His brother Frank became a respectable farmer in later life. The American ballad "Jesse James" opens with:

> Jesse James was a lad that killed many a man.
> He robbed the Danville train.
> But that dirty little coward that shot
> Mr. Howard [Jesse]
> He laid poor Jesse in the grave.
> It was Robert Ford, that dirty little coward,
> I wonder how he does feel:
> For he ate of Jesse's bread and slept in Jesse's bed
> And laid poor Jesse in the grave.

Among the Hollywood movies about him are *Jesse James* (1939), *The Return of Frank James* (1940), and *The True Story of Jesse James* (1957); all are more legend than history.

St. James the Greater (Dürer)

1589

James the Greater or Major, St. (Greek form of Jacob, one who takes by the heel, the supplanter) First century C.E. In the Bible, N.T., Apostle; patron of Spain, pilgrims, and furriers. Feast, 25 July.

James, along with Peter and John, was present at the Transfiguration of Christ and the agony in the garden (Mark 5:37; 9:2; 14:33). After Christ's Ascension James was put to death by the sword at the command of Herod Agrippa (Acts 12:2).

The scant information on James in the New Testament was supplemented by medieval Spanish legend in which he was turned into St. Jago or Santiago, the military patron saint of Spain. According to Spanish legend, James was the son of Zebedee, an illustrious baron of Galilee, who, as the proprietor of ships, was accustomed to fish along the shores of a certain lake called Gennesareth solely for good pleasure and recreation. Having James as the son of a well-to-do family, and not a fisherman as in Scripture, accorded more with Spanish concepts of class distinction. In *The Divine Comedy* (Paradise 25:17) Dante calls St. James "the baron," alluding to the medieval belief. According to legend, after Christ's Ascension, James preached the gospel in Judea, then traveled over much of the world, and at last arrived in Spain, where he made few converts. One day, as he stood with his disciples on the banks of the river Ebro, the Virgin Mary appeared to him, seated on the top of a pillar of jasper and surrounded by a choir of angels. James threw himself on his face. The Virgin then commanded him to build on that spot a chapel for her worship, assuring him that all this province of Saragossa, though now pagan, would at a future time be devoted to her. James did as he was told, and the church was called Nuestra Senora del Pillar (Our Lady of the Pillar). James then went back to Judea after a contest with a magician, Hermogenes, who not only renounced his evil ways but became a follower of James, who gave him his staff as the most effective means of defense against demons. James met his death at the command of Herod Agrippa. His body was carried to Joppa and conducted miraculously to Spain, where a church was built in his honor by Queen Lupa after the evil woman had been converted to Christianity by a miracle. When Spain was overrun by the Moors, the shrine of the saint was forgotten, but in 800 C.E. the burial spot was found by a friar. The saint's body was moved to Compostella, where it brought about many miracles. Spanish historians number some 38 apparitions of the saint in which he helped the Spanish defeat their enemies. In one account St. James, mounted on a milk-white charger and waving aloft a white standard, led the Christians against the Moors, leaving some 60,000 Moors dead on the field. The battle cry from that engagement at Clavijo was "Santiago," the war cry of the Spaniards for centuries.

1590
James the Less or Minor, St. (Greek form of Jacob, one who takes by the heel, the supplanter) First century C.E. In the Bible, N.T., Apostle, son of Alphaeus (Matt. 10:3) and of Mary (not to be confused with the Virgin Mary), mentioned in Mark (16:1). He is called "the Less" in the King James Bible and "the Younger" in the Revised Standard Version. Feast, 1 May.

According to early Christian tradition, he was the first bishop of Jerusalem and was martyred when he was flung down from a terrace or parapet of the temple and the mob beat his brains out with a fuller's club (which is his symbol).

1591
Janaka (begetting). In Hindu mythology, the father of Sita, Rama's wife. Janaka was noted for his wisdom as well as for his opposition to the Brahmans. The *Brahmanas*, sacred writings, says: "He refused to submit to the hierarchical pretensions of the Brahmans, and asserted his right of performing sacrifices without the intervention of priests." However, Janaka eventually became a Brahman.

In Hindu mythology Janaka is also the name of the king of Mithila, who was born from the dead body of his father.

1592
Jan-Teng Fo. In Chinese Buddhism, the Lamp Bearing Buddha, or Buddha of Fixed Light. According to one legend, a woman offered a few coins to burn oil before an image on Buddha's altar. The lamp she lit never had to be replenished. It was then prophesied that she would be born as a future Buddha, which, in a later life, she achieved.

1593
Januarius, St. Fourth century? C.E. In Christian legend, bishop of Benevento, Italy; patron saint of goldsmiths. Invoked against eruptions of Mount Vesuvius. Feast, 19 September.

Januarius was beheaded for being a Christian; his body was taken to Naples and buried in the cathedral. Just before his removal, Mount Vesuvius was erupting and threatening to destroy the entire city. No sooner had the body of Januarius entered Naples than the volcano became utterly extinct, "quenched by the merits and patronage of the saint," according to Edward Kinesman's *Lives of the Saints.* When the volcano erupted again in 1631, St. Januarius was invoked, and again the eruption ceased. The most famous feat of the saint, however, concerns the liquefaction of his own blood. The saint's blood is kept in two glass vials in the Church of San Gennaro (Januarius) in Naples. "When either vial, held in the right hand, is presented to the head of the saint," according to Kinesman's account, "the congealed blood first melts, and then goes on apparently to boil." The feat still takes place each year, though scientists give no satisfactory explanation. Each year a major feast is held in Little Italy, in New York City, in honor of San Gennaro. Luca Gordano painted the *Martyrdom of St. Januarius*, and Cosimo Fanzaga did a statue of the saint now in the Duomo, Naples.

1594

Janus (openings, gates, doors). In Roman mythology, ancient Italian god of beginning, opening, doorways, entrances, and endings; husband of the spring nymph Juturna (or Cardea); father of Fontus (Fons). The month of January is named after Janus. In Rome it was the king who sacrificed to Janus, and in later times it was the *rex sacorum*. At each sacrifice Janus was mentioned first in every prayer, even before Jupiter. In early Italian mythology, Janus was connected with the sun as god of light, opening the heavens in the morning and closing them at the end of the day. As god of beginnings, Janus was worshiped at the beginning of the day, the month, and the year. According to Ovid's *Fasti* (book 1), when people greeted one another at the beginning of the year, they were to speak only words of good omen and give gifts of sweetmeats. In private worship Janus was invoked each morning as *pater matutinus*. He was invoked before any important undertaking, such as harvest, marriage, or birth. His most important worship was connected with the Roman Forum. There the hearth fire of the Roman state was kept in the temple of Vesta, and there, symbolically, the people went out to war through the door of the state. The House of Janus (or Arch of Janus) was a small square building of bronze with doors at each end. Between them was a statue of Janus with two faces, facing in two different directions. The building was called *Jani gemini portoe*. This building, according to Vergil's *Aeneid* (book 7), was supposed to be opened with a formal ceremony before a war and was to remain open as long as the army was in the field. Janus's main feast was the *Agonalia* held 9 January.

Janus is cited in Milton's *Paradise Lost* where the cherubim are described as: "Four faces each/ Had, like a double Janus. . . ." (book 2.128–9), and by Shakespeare in *The Merchant of Venice*: "Now, by two-headed Janus,/ Nature hath fram'd strange fellows in her time. . . ." (1.1.50–1). Jonathan Swift's *To Janus on New Year's Day* (1729) opens with "Two-fac'd Janus, God of Time," and W. H. Auden's *New Year Letter* uses, "the Janus of a joke."

Because of his two faces, or double-two, Janus was sometimes known as Bifrons (two-faced) or Quadrifrons (four-faced). The English word *janitor*

comes from one of the meanings of Janus's name, door. In Roman art he was usually represented as a porter, with a staff and key in his hands and with two bearded faces placed back to back and looking in opposite directions. In late Roman art he is portrayed both bearded and unbearded. Instead of a key and staff, the fingers of his right hand exhibit the number 300 (CCC), his left hand the number of the remaining days of the year (LXV).

1595

Jara-sandha. In Hindu mythology, an enemy of Krishna (an incarnation of the god Vishnu). Jara-sandha was born from two mothers who produced half boys; they were united by the demon Jara. He was an ardent worshiper of the god Shiva and opposed Krishna. In the Hindu epic poem *The Mahabharata* he is killed by Bhima.

1596

Jarnvidjur (ironwood). In Norse mythology, the race of witches who lived east of Midgard in a place called Jarnvid.

1597

Jason (healer). In Greek mythology, a hero, son of King Aeson of Thessaly and Alcimede (mighty cunning) or Polymede; brother of Promachus. When Pelias seized Aeson's throne, Jason was hidden and was brought up by the centaur Chiron. Reaching manhood, Jason returned to Thessaly to claim the throne. He arrived wearing only one sandal, having lost the other while helping an old hag (the goddess Hera in disguise). Having been warned of his coming, Pelias said he would gladly give up the throne to Jason, provided he first capture the Golden Fleece of King Aeëtes at Colchis. Gathering men for the journey (which Pelias hoped would end in Jason's death), the hero built the largest (and first) ship, called the *Argo*, and set sail. The Argonauts reached Colchis, and Jason found the Golden Fleece fastened to a sacred oak, guarded by a dragon who never slept. Athena and Aphrodite came to Jason's aid by having Medea, King Aeëtes' daughter, fall in love with him. She helped him capture the fleece by her skill in magic and sorcery. Medea then fled with Jason, taking her young brother Apsyrtus with her. When they were pursued by Aeëtes, she cut up her brother and flung the pieces of his body into the sea, knowing her father would stop to retrieve them. They then arrived at Circe's island (she was aunt to Medea) where they were purified of the murder by pig's blood. When the Colchians caught up with Jason, he quickly married Medea, so they could not take her back to her father. Finally, they reached King Pelias and presented the Golden Fleece, which was hung in Zeus' temple. Pelias murdered Jason's brother, and Medea, again using her witchcraft, killed Pelias by persuading his daughters that he would be restored to youth if they cut up his body and put it into a boiling caldron. Jason did not take the throne but gave it to Pelias' son and returned to Corinth. After ten years of marriage to Medea, he decided to marry Creusa, King Creon's daughter. Seeking revenge for her betrayal, Medea presented Jason's new bride with a beautiful garment that burned her to death when she put it on. Medea then killed her own children, saying to Jason, in the words of Robinson Jeffers's play *Medea*, "because I hated you more than I loved them." She then fled in a chariot to Athens, where she married Aegeus, father of Theseus. Jason died when part of the beached *Argo* fell on him. The myth of Jason inspired Apollonius Rhodius' epic, *Argonautica*, Ovid's *Metamorphoses* (book 7), Euripides' *Medea* and operas based on it. Part of Chaucer's *Legend of Good Women*, Corneille's play, Robinson Jeffers' play, and William Morris's narra-

tive poem *The Life and Death of Jason*, as well as works by Robert Graves and Jean Anouilh, are based on the Euripides version of the myth.

1598
Jataka (birth story). Buddhist fables and folktales of the former lives of the Buddha, collected about 400 C.E. The Pali collection contains 547 tales in which Buddha often appears in animal or human form.

The influence of the Jataka on Buddhist art is immense. In Ajanta, an ancient Buddhist monastery located near Aurangabad in the State of Manarashtra, India, for example, numerous frescoes depicting the episodes from the Jatakas are found. All Buddhist countries have their versions of the tales, which are used for elementary teaching, especially to children.

1599
Javerzaharses and Kaches. In Armenian folklore, patron guardians of marriage and childbirth who

The Jay and the Peacock

love to attend weddings. According to Armenian Christian writers, the Kaches, who are the husbands, are used by God as evil spirits to punish the wicked. This belief stems perhaps from the legend that the wicked Armenian king Edward built a temple to worship the Kaches.

Jay and the Peacock, The. Aesopic fable found in various collections throughout the world.

1600

One day a jay found some feathers a peacock had shed. Sticking them among his own rusty black ones, he began to strut about, ignoring and despising his old friends and companions.

Dressed in his borrowed plumage, he very cockily sought out a flock of peacocks who were walking on the park lawn. Instantly detecting the true identity of the intruder, they stripped him of his finery and, falling on him with their sharp beaks, they drove him away.

The bedraggled jay, sadder but wiser, went to his former companions. He would have been satisfied to associate with them again. But the jays, remembering how obnoxious he had been with his airs and his vanity, drummed him out of their society. One of those whom he had so lately despised offered him the following advice: "Be contented with what nature made you and you will avoid the contempt of your peers and the punishment of your betters."

Moral: Happiness is not to be found in borrowed finery.

Horace, in his *Epistles* (book 1), alludes to the fable when he accuses one writer of borrowing the writings of another and says he will be found out "like the wretched crow when stripped of her stolen hues." Benedict of Oxford, in his Hebrew version of the fables, makes the bird a raven, although most English versions call it a jackdaw. Thackeray included the fable in the Prologue to his novel *The Newcomers*.

Jayanti (conquering). In Hindu mythology, the daughter of Indra, the storm god.

1601

Jemshid. In Persian mythology, a culture hero and proud king, appearing in the epic poem *Shah Namah* by Firdusi.

1602

Jemshid is a later form of the earlier divine hero Yima in Persian mythology. Firdusi took some of the exploits of the earlier mythological personage and used them in his epic. During Jemshid's reign, according to Firdusi, the first manufacture of iron weapons took place, as well as the making of linen

Jephthah and his daughter

and silk clothing, work in precious stones, and the invention of perfume and the art of medicine.

One day Jemshid ordered the demons who were under his power to lift him into the air so that he could see everything and be moved anywhere he wanted to go. All of this power and honor made the king too proud. He said to his learned men and ministers: "Tell me if there exists, or ever existed, in all the world, a king of such magnificence and power as I am?"

"Thou art alone, the mightiest, the most victorious. There is no equal to thee," the frightened ministers replied.

Allah saw how foolish the king was in what he said and punished him by throwing his empire into chaos. Jemshid's reign lasted for some 700 years. He was killed by the evil king, Zahhak, who captured him. Zahhak ordered two planks to be brought and fastened Jemshid down between them. His body was then sawed in two.

Variant spelling: Jamshid.

1603

Jephthah (he sets free). In the Bible, O.T., one of the judges of Israel, whose daughter went out to greet him on his return home from victory over the Ammonites, unaware that her father had vowed to offer up as a sacrifice to Yahweh, the Hebrew god, the first thing he met on returning home. The tale is told in the book of Judges (11:1–12:7). Jephthah's daughter appears in one of the ballads included in Percy's *Reliques*, titled *Jephtah Judge of Israel*, which is quoted by Hamlet (act 1, sc. 2, line 400). She also appears in Alfred Lord Tennyson's poem *Dream of Fair Women*, and Handel's oratorio *Jephthah* deals with the legend.

1604

Jeremiah (whom Yahweh appoints) 627–580 B.C.E.. In the Bible, O.T., one of the Major Prophets and title of an Old Testament book. Jeremiah is sometimes called the "weeping prophet" because he foretold the destruction of Jerusalem. In later Jewish legend, not recorded in the Bible, Jeremiah was taken to Egypt and stoned to death because of his gloomy predictions. Tradition credited him with the authorship of the Book of Lamentations in the Old Testament, though no present day scholar accepts this. Our word *jeremiad* is derived from the prophet's name. Rembrandt's *Jeremiah* is one of the best paintings portraying the prophet.

1605

Jerome, St. (sacred name). c. 342–420 C.E. In Christian legend, one of the Four Latin Doctors of the Church. Translator of the Latin Bible called the Vulgate, which was the Bible of the Middle Ages. Patron of scholars. Feast, 30 September.

Eusebius Hieronymus Sophronius, or Jerome, was born at Strido near Aquileia. After a life of study and

St. Jerome

debate he left for Bethlehem in 385 C.E. to devote his time to retranslating the Latin Bible from the original languages because most of the current translations were flawed. Jerome was helped with his translations from the Hebrew Bible by Jews as well as by a group of women, the most notable being St. Paula.

Jerome was noted for his sharp wit and his bitter attacks on his enemies. He often was at variance with St. Augustine; they wrote polite letters to one another filled with venom. But St. Jerome's most famous letter deals with being a Christian virgin. Its merits for a woman, he writes, are far above marriage; wedlock only gives women "pregnancy, a crying baby, the tortures of jealousy, the cares of household management and the cutting short by death of all its fancied blessings."

The legend most associated with the saint concerns a lion. One day Jerome was reading with some monks when a lion entered the study. Though the lion was lame and limping, the monks were so frightened by the beast that they all ran away. St. Jerome stayed in the room, and the lion came up to him. The lion lifted its paw into the saint's hand, showing how it was bleeding from a thorn. Jerome extracted the thorn and bandaged the paw. When the lion was able to use its paw, Jerome set it to work for the monastery. Each day the lion would fetch food with the help of a donkey. One day the donkey was stolen by some traders, and the lion was accused of eating him, so Jerome forced the lion to do the work of the donkey.

After some time the merchants returned, led by the stolen donkey, who was recognized by the lion. The lion chased the merchants and brought back the donkey.

St. Jerome is often portrayed with a lion nearby. Sometimes a large cat takes its place. He is also shown doing penance in a desert with a lion nearby. Sometimes a cardinal's hat is shown, though there is no historical authority for Jerome having been a cardinal.

Flight into Egypt

1606

Jesus Christ (Greek, Joshua, "Yahweh saves" and anointed One, the Messiah) First century C.E. In Christianity, the Messiah, the Son of God, second person of the Holy Trinity made up of God the Father, God the Son, and God the Holy Spirit.

Details of the life of Jesus are presented in the Four Gospels of the Christian New Testament. In the first three, those of St. Matthew, St. Mark, and St. Luke, many of the same incidents are narrated, earning them the title of the Synoptic Gospels, though they differ in details. The last Gospel, that of St. John, differs radically from the first three. In John's Gospel Jesus speaks in Gnostic terms, stressing the difference between those who have the Light and those who are in Darkness. Most modern scholars agree that it is impossible to reconstruct the "historical Jesus," since all of the documents are written from a Christian bias—the beliefs of the early Christian church—to prove that Jesus was the

Messiah and the Son of God. No record of Jesus' existence is found in other contemporary sources.

Though the character of Jesus varies in the Gospels, the early church began to stress certain aspects of his person. St. Paul, writing in the New Testament, saw Jesus as the mediator between God and man. From Paul's epistles, or letters, it is clear that he does not place Jesus on a plane with God. For Paul, Jesus stopped the righteous anger of God against mankind by his sacrifice on the cross.

Further development in the person of Christ is found in the writings of the Early Church outside of the New Testament. St. Ignatius, bishop of Antioch (first century), writes on the Incarnation (the term used for God being made into man): "There is one physician, fleshly and spiritual, begotten and unbegotten, God in man, true life in death, both of Mary and of God, first passable then impassable, Jesus Christ Our Lord."

When St. Irenaeus (c. 130–c. 200 C.E.) writes on the person of Jesus, we have the belief, also found in St. John's Gospel, but not in the other three, that Jesus existed as God with God before the world began: "We have shown that the Son of God did not then begin to exist. He existed with the Father always; but when he was incarnate and made man, he recapitulated in himself the long line of the human race, procuring for us salvation thus summarily, so that what we had lost in Adam, that is, being in the image and likeness of God, that we should regain in Christ Jesus." However, these statements are those of the church that survived down to the Middle Ages, since the early Christian heresies were wiped out. From them, we have a much different concept of the person of Jesus. Certain heresies stressed that Jesus was only God and assumed human form, but not human nature along with it. Others said only a mirage of Jesus died on the cross. The view that finally dominated was that Jesus was fully man as well as fully God. This is found in the statement of the Council of Chalcedon (act V) held in 451.

Therefore, following the holy fathers, we all with one accord teach men to acknowledge one and the same Son, our Lord Jesus Christ, at once complete in Godhead and complete in manhood, truly God and truly man, consisting also of a reasonable soul and body; of one substance with the Father as regards his Godhead, and at the same time of one substance with us as regards his manhood; like us in all respects, apart from sin; as begotten for us men and for our salvation, of Mary the Virgin, the God-bearer (*Theotokos*); one and the same Christ, Son, Lord, Only-begotten, recognized in two natures without confusion, without change, without division, without separation; the distinction of natures being in no way annulled by the union, but rather the characteristics of each nature preserved and coming together to form one person and substance, not as parted or separated into two persons, but one and the same Son and Only-begotten God the Word, Lord Jesus Christ; even as the prophets from earliest times spoke of him, and our Lord Jesus Christ himself taught us, and the creed of the Fathers has handed down to us.

The main events in the life of Jesus, as recorded in the Gospels are birth of John the Baptist foretold (Luke 1:5–13), Annunciation (Luke 1:26–31, Matt. 1:18–23), birth and naming of John (Luke 1:57–63), birth of Jesus (Luke 2:1–14), circumcision and naming of Jesus (Luke 2:21), presentation in the temple (Luke 2:22), coming of the Magi (Matt. 2:1), flight to and return from Egypt (Matt. 2:13–23), Jesus in the temple (Luke 2:41–50), baptism of Jesus (Matt. 3:13–17, Mark 1:9–11, Luke 3:21–22), temptation of Jesus (Matt. 4:1–11, Mark 1:12, Luke 4:1–13), call of first disciples (Matt. 4:18–22, Mark 1:16–20, Luke 5:1–11, John 1:35–51), Sermon on the Mount (Matt 5–7, Luke 6:17–49), first miracle Cana (John 2:1–11), Nicodemus visits Jesus (John 3:1–21), John the Baptist's death (Matt. 14:1–12, Mark 6:14–29, Luke 9:7–9), the transfiguration (Matt. 17:1–8, Mark 9:2–8, Luke (9:28–36), raising of Lazarus (John 11:1–44), Jesus enters Jerusalem (Matt. 21:1–11, Mark 11:1–11, Luke 19:28–44, John 12–19), cleansing of the temple (Matt. 21:12–16, Mark 11:15–19, Luke 19:45–48), the Last Supper (Matt. 26:20–29, Mark 14:22–25, Luke 22:14–21, John 13:1–12), Jesus washes his disciples' feet (John 13:3–14), Jesus' agony (Matt. 26:36–46, Mark 14:32–42, Luke 22:39–46, John 18:1), betrayal and arrest (Matt. 26:47–56, Mark 14:43–50, Luke 22:47–54, John 18:2), Peter's denials (Matt. 26:69–75, Mark 14:66–72, Luke 22:54–62, John 18:15), Jesus before Pilate (Matt. 27:11–14, Mark 15:1–15, Luke 23:1–25, John 18:28–40), Jesus mocked (Matt. 27:27–31, Mark 15:16–20, John 19:2), crucifixion, death, and burial (Matt. 27:35–66, Mark 15:24–47, Luke 23:33–56, John 19:18–42), resurrection (Matt. 28:1–10, Mark 16:1–14, Luke 24:1–49, John 20:1–23).

The parables recorded in the Gospels are The Builders (Matt 7:24–27, Luke 6:47–49), The Sower (Matt. 13:3–9, Mark 4:1–25, Luke 8:4–15), The Wheat and the Tares (Matt. 13:24–30), The Mustard Seed (Matt. 13:31, Mark 4:30, Luke 13:18), The Leaven (Matt. 13:33, Luke 13:20), The Pearl of Great Price (Matt. 13:45), The Unmerciful Servant (Matt. 18:23–35), The Laborers in the Vineyard (Matt. 20:1–16), The Two Sons (Matt. 21:28–32), The Wicked Husbandmen (Matt. 21:33–56, Luke 20:9–18), The Marriage Feast (Matt. 22:1–14), The Fig Tree (Matt. 24:32), The Ten Virgins (Matt.

25:1–13), The Talents (Matt. 25:14–30), The Good Samaritan (Luke 10:25– 37), The Rich Fool (Luke 12:13–21), The Dishonest Steward (Luke 16:1– 14), The Rich Man and Lazarus (Luke 16:19–31).

Jesus not only appears in the New Testament but also in Islamic legends, in which he is accorded the status of a prophet. The Koran, the sacred book of Islam, calls Jesus: Isa (Jesus), Isa the Maryam (Jesus the son of Mary), Al-Masih (The Messiah), Kalimatu'llah (The Word of Allah), Qaulu 'l-Haqq (The Word of Truth), Ruhum min Allah (A Spirit from Allah), Rasulu 'llah (The messenger of Allah), Abdu'llah (The Servant of Allah), Nabiyu'llah (The Prophet of Allah), Wajihun fi 'd-dunya wa 'l-akhirah (Illustrious in this World and in the Next).

Jesus on the Cross

Episodes from the life of Jesus are found scattered throughout the Koran. Most of them are believed to be derived from early Christian legends and writings, but not the New Testament, since they often contradict the New Testament and agree with various Christian heresies that existed at the time of Muhammad. He may have heard most of the tales orally.

Jesus' birth of a Virgin mother is believed in Islam. The Annunciation to the Virgin and His birth is narrated in Sura 19.

Muhammad believed, as did some heretical Christians, that Jesus was not crucified at all, but that Judas took his place on the cross, or that there was only Jesus' likeness on the cross. Sura 4 of the Koran says: "Yet they slew him not, and they crucified him not, but they had only his likeness. And they who differed about him were in doubt concerning him; No sure knowledge had they about him, but followed only an opinion, and they really did not slay him, but God took him up to Himself. And God is Mighty, Wise."

Though Jesus is highly praised in Islam, the Koran makes it quite clear that he is not God when it states in Sura 19: "Allah could not take to Himself a son." And in Sura 5: "The Messiah, the son of Mary, is only a prophet."

The Christian belief in the Trinity seems to have been misunderstood by Muhammad, who may have thought it consisted of the Father, the Son, and the Virgin Mary.

The Resurrection of Christ

Jezebel (prince, exalted, i.e., Baal). In the Bible, O.T., Phoenician wife of King Ahab of the northern kingdom of Israel in the ninth century B.C.E., symbol of an evil woman. Jezebel was the foe of the prophet Elijah who prophesied her doom saying, "The dogs shall eat Jezebel by the wall of Jezreel" (1 Kings 21:23). Eventually, she was killed when Jehu entered her city and had two eunuchs throw her out of her window. Jehu's horses trampled her body. After he had dined, Jehu ordered his soldiers to bury Jezebel's body, but the dogs had eaten it, leaving the skull, feet, and palms of her hands (2 Kings 9:35).

Jigoku. In Japanese Buddhist mythology, hell located underneath the earth's surface.

Jigoku consists of eight hells of fire and eight of ice. Each of the eight is then divided into sixteen distinct hells. The ruler of Jigoku is Emma-hoo, portrayed with a ferocious expression and dressed as a Chinese judge, wearing a cap. In the paintings and prints of Jigoku that portray Emma-hoo there are heads on either side of him, each on a supporting stand. One is a female head, Miru-me, who can see all sinners' actions and from whom nothing can be hidden. The other head is Kagu-hana (the nose that smells), who can detect the smallest sin. A demon will take a sinner before a magic mirror, where his or her sins are revealed. Prayers by the living, through a Buddhist priest, may eventually save the sinner.

1609

Jim Bludso. In American folklore, a Mississippi steamboat engineer who was burned to death while saving his passengers from fire. He appears in John Hay's *Pike County Ballads*.

1610

Jim Bridger. In American folklore, a frontiersman who passed over a precipice through a petrified mountain in Yellowstone with his horse, saying that gravity itself had become petrified.

1611

Jimmu Tenno. 660–585 B.C.E.? In Japanese Shinto legend, first emperor of Japan, descended from the sun goddess, Amaterasu. The period before the advent of Jimmu Tenno is called *jindai* (the age of the kami) or *taiko* (remote antiquity).

1612

Jina. In Buddhism and Jainism, Sanskrit title meaning conqueror; often used for the Buddha in Buddhism and in Jainism for its leaders.

1613

Jingo Kogo. 170–269 C.E. In Japanese legend, empress who set out to conquer Korea.

The gods twice ordered her husband, the emperor Chuai, to conquer Korea, but the monarch paid no attention to the deities. After his death the empress, under the guidance of the gods, decided to undertake the conquest of Korea. Setting out, she stopped to fish at Matsura Gawa with three grains of rice as bait (the catching of fish was believed to be a lucky omen). She also prayed that if she was to succeed in her venture her hair would part as she was bathing, and this happened. All of the gods are said to have come to her aid, with the exception of Izora, the god of the seashore, who came clad in mud. However, the empress was served by Ryujin, the king of the sea. When a storm arose, large fish came to the surface of the sea to support the boats and prevent them from foundering. Hearing of this, the king of Korea promptly sent 80 boats laden with gold, silver, and cloth as tribute. He repeated the practice each year.

Jingo Kogo had set out while she was pregnant, but she delayed the birth by attaching a heavy stone to her waist. When she returned to Japan, her son Ojin was born. She did not ascend the throne again but served as Ojin's regent for 69 years.

In Japanese art Jingo Kogo is often portrayed writing the words *Koku O* (ruler of state) on a rock. She often is shown with a wide band around her forehead.

1614

Jingu-ji. In Japan, a Buddhist temple within the compound of a Shinto shrine.

1615

Jiten. In Japanese Buddhist mythology, earth goddess, derived from the Hindu goddess Prithivi. She is portrayed as a woman holding in her right hand a basket of peonies. She is one of the Jiu No O, 12 Japanese Buddhist gods and goddesses adopted from Hindu Mythology.

1616

Jiu No O. In Japanese Buddhist mythology, 12 gods and goddesses derived from Hindu mythology. They are Jiten, Gwaten, Bishamon, Futen, Suiten, Rasetsu Ten, Bonten, Nitten, Ishana Ten, Taishaku Ten, Kwaten, and Emma Ten.

Variant: Jiu ni Ten.

1617

Jizo Bosatsu. In Japanese Buddhist mythology, the name of the Sanskrit Bodhisattva, Kshitigarbha (earth womb), consoler of the dead, protector of women and children; called Ti-Tsang in China. As Jizo Bosatsu he is portrayed in the robes of a Buddhist monk, holding a monk's staff in one hand and a precious jewel in the other. This is his most popular form in Japan, though he also appears as Shogun Jizo (Jizo of the victorious armies), a war god mounted on horseback, and as Roku Juzo (the sixth Jizo), referring to his multiplication of himself into six beings to help save the world. The number six refers to the six realms of rebirth; also associated with roads and mountains.

1618

Jo and Uba. In Japanese mythology, two spirits of pine trees. They are portrayed as an old wrinkled couple gathering pine needles: Jo with a rake, Uba with a broom and a fan. The two are usually accompanied by the crane and tortoise, symbols of longevity.

1619

Joan of Arc, St. (form of John, "Yahweh has been gracious"). 1412–1431 C.E. In Christian legend, patron of France. Feast, 30 May.

At 13 years old Joan had visions that she later identified as the voices of St. Michael, St. Catherine, and St. Margaret. When Henry VI of England began the siege of Orleans in 1428, Joan, convinced that God had chosen her to remove the English from French soil, set out. She told the dauphin (later Charles VII) of her mission and, in male dress, led the French troops to victory in May and June of 1429. She stood beside Charles VII at his coronation in July. Not having sufficient numbers of troops to continue her campaign, however, she was taken prisoner in May, 1430, by the Burgundians, who sold her to the English. She was tried on 12 charges of sorcery, wantonness in cutting her hair, and wearing male attire. While she was in jail, an English lord tried to rape her. A physical examination showed that Joan was a virgin, though the results were falsified by Bishop Cauchon, who sat at her trial. At first she gave in and signed a recantation of her claim to have been guided by Divine Providence, but in the following days she resumed her male attire and repudiated her recantation. She said, "If I were to be condemned and saw the fire lit and the wood prepared and the executioner who was to burn me ready to cast me into the fire, still in the fire would I not say anything other than I have said, and I will maintain what I have said until death."

The Trial of Joan of Arc: Being the verbatim report of the proceedings from the Orleans Manuscript, translated by W. S. Scott (1956), recounts that after the sentence was read, the bishop, the inquisitor, and many of the judges went away, leaving Joan on the scaffold. The order to burn her was given by an Englishman. "When Jeanne heard this order given, she began to weep and lament in such a way that all the people present were themselves moved to tears." The fire was lighted and Joan was "martyred tragically," according to the account.

St. Joan was canonized in 1920 and has been a favorite subject of attention in music and literature. In Shakespeare's *Henry VI*, she is called a witch and seen as an impostor. Voltaire in his *La Purcelle* ridiculed Joan, making her visions part of her madness. Schiller, however, in his poetic tragedy *Die Jungfrau von Orleans*, looked at Joan with a romantic and heroic cast of mind. She is not burned at the end of the play but dies in battle. Mark Twain wrote *Personal Recollections of Joan of Arc*, in which he looks with kindly eyes upon the girl, whereas Anatole France's *Life of Joan of Arc* presents a more skeptical approach to the subject. Perhaps the most touching play is G. B. Shaw's *Saint Joan*, in which both sides, Joan's and the church's, are presented in a good light, in contradiction to history. Shaw did not wish to pick sides but merely to depict the clash of different ideologies. Jean Anouilh's *L'Alouette*, translated by Christopher Fry as *The Lark*, presented a different Joan, who was more poetic and less convincing as a human being.

In films the legend of Joan of Arc has been told several times. Geraldine Farrar played her in *Joan the Woman*. Dreyer's *The Passion of Joan of Arc* is considered the classic treatment of the subject on film, though other versions have appeared. Ingrid Bergman's *Joan of Arc* is a very stiff Hollywood treatment of the subject. *Saint Joan*, with Jean Seberg, based on the Shaw play, was a box office failure. Hedy Lamarr made a short appearance as Joan in the *Story of Mankind*, and Robert Bresson did *The Trial of Joan of Arc* with Florence Carrez.

Opera composers also have found Joan of Arc's legend of interest, with more than 25 works devoted to her, though only two are still performed. Verdi composed a *Giovanni d'Arco*, and Tchaikovsky rejected the unhistorical ending of Schiller and instead has Joan die at the stake in his opera *The Maid of Orleans*.

Though Joan of Arc has fared well in literature, movies, and opera, there are few noteworthy paintings of the saint. Ingres' *Joan of Arc at the Coronation of Charles VII* is in the rather stiff, mechanical style that Ingres developed to perfection.

1620

Job (inveterate foe?). In the Bible, O.T., name of a hero and title of a book. The biblical Job is believed to be based on a figure in Near Eastern legend as well as on two Babylonian works, *The Poem of the Righteous Sufferer* and the *Acrostic Dialogue on Theodicy*. The Book of Job is largely in the form of poetry, though parts of it, the introduction and epilogue, are in prose and indicate that the work is based on a folktale. Job was a good man who worshiped God. In return God rewarded Job with many children and with material prosperity. Satan, the Adversary, who was part of God's court, taunted God, saying Job was good only because God took such good care of him. Remove his wealth and Job would curse God, Satan contended. God took up the challange. Job lost his children and his wealth, and finally he was afflicted with a horrible skin disease. Three friends, Bilad, Eliphaz, and Zophar, his "comforters," came to discuss why God had afflicted Job. They contended that Job must have sinned and that god was punishing him for his sin. This belief of reward for good in this life and punishment for evil are central to most Old Testament thought and had a great influence on Puritan and Fundamentalist beliefs. Job, however, would not accept his guilt. He argued with his friends saying that although God was punishing him, he was innocent. Finally, God revealed himself to Job in all of his splendor. The question "Why do the innocent suffer?" is not answered. Instead Job is awed by God and accepts all. The Book of Job concludes with a prose folktale in which Job's goods and health are restored, a contradiction of the main poetic theme of the book.

Some critics consider Job the greatest book in the Bible. Martin Luther called it "magnificent and sublime as no other book of the Scripture," and Alfred Lord Tennyson believed it to be "the greatest poem of ancient and modern times." Major art works inspired by Job include a series of etchings by William Blake and a symphonic score, *Job, a Masque for Dancing*, based on the Book of Job and the Blake etchings, by the English composer Ralph Vaughan Williams. In Islamic legend Job is called Aiyub and is cited in the Koran (sura 21): "And remember Job: When he cried to his Lord."

1621
Jocasta (shining moon). In Greek mythology, both mother and wife of Oedipus, whom she married not knowing he was her son; mother of Eteocles, Polynices, Antigone, and Ismene; daughter of Menoeceus. When Jocasta learned she was Oedipus' mother, she killed herself by hanging. Jocasta appears in Homer's *Odyssey* (book 11), where she is seen in the underworld by Odysseus. Homer calls her Epicaste. Sophocles' *Oedipus Tyrannus*, often called *Oedipus Rex*, and Euripides' *Phoenician Women* also feature Jocasta, as do modern versions of the Oedipus myth by Cocteau and Gide.
Variant spelling: Iocaste.

1622
Joe Baldwin. In American folklore, a train conductor who was decapitated when his train was rammed by another train. His lantern is said to still glow on certain nights, preventing train disasters.

1623
Joe Magarac (jackass?). In American literary folklore, a superhuman steelworker, invented by Owen Francis, who published his Joe Magarac tales in 1931. Joe, born inside an ore mountain, was seven feet tall and made of steel. He worked day and night, only taking time out to eat five meals a day. He ended his life when he melted down his body to make steel for a new mill. He explains his name when he says: "Dat's me. All I do is eatit and workit same lak jackass donkey."

1624
John Barleycorn. In English and Scottish folklore, personification of barley, the grain used to produce liquors.

1625
John Chrysostom, St. (Yahweh is gracious; golden-mouthed). c. 347–407 C.E. In Christian legend, one of the Four Greek Doctors of the Church. Invoked against epilepsy. Feast, 30 March.
Born in Antioch, he was ordained in 363 and soon was recognized for his eloquence, which obtained for him the name Chrysostom or Golden Mouth. In 403 at the Synod of the Oak, John's enemies—and they were many since he was rather violent and provocative in his language—got him banished from his see. He was recalled, but then he angered the Empress Eudoxia and was exiled to Armenia. He was to be moved from there to Pytius in Colchis but died at Comana.
Gibbon in his *Decline and Fall of the Roman Empire* writes that "his relics, thirty years after his death, were transported from their obscure sepulcher to the royal city. The Emperor Theodosius advanced to receive them as far as Chalcedon, and falling prostrate on the coffin, implored, in the name of his guilty parents, Arcadius and Eudoxia, the forgiveness of the injured saint."

1626
John Henry. In American folklore, a black hero, born in Black River Country "where the sun don't never shine." When John Henry was born, he weighed 44 pounds. His mother said he had a "bass voice like a preacher," and his father said "He got shoulders like a cotton- rollin' rousterabout." When John Henry finished his first meal, he went out in search of work. Eventually he found his way to the Chesapeake & Ohio Railroad, which at that time was laying track and driving (digging) tunnels. The major episode in his legend tells of his contest with a steam drill. John Henry drove faster than the steam drill but died "with a hammer in his hand" from the exertion, according to one John Henry ballad. In another account he died during the night from a burst blood vessel. Other accounts say John Henry died on the gallows for murdering a man. He appears in Roark Bradford's novel *John Henry*, as well as in numerous American ballads that were collected by Guy B. Johnson in *John Henry: Tracking Down a Negro Legend*. In some accounts John Henry is said to be white, not black.

1627
Johnny Appleseed. 1774–1847. In American history and folklore, popular name of John Chapman, Massachusetts-born orchardist, who planted fruit trees in Pennsylvania, Ohio, Indiana, and Illinois. He appears in numerous legends, a combination St. Francis and Yankee peddler, going from place to place, unharmed by the Indians, carrying his tools and a Bible. He appears in Vachel Lindsay's free verse poem *In Praise of Johnny Appleseed* and in a pageant *The Return of Johnny Appleseed* by Charles Allen Smart.

1628
John the Baptist, St. (Yahweh is gracious). First century C.E. Patron of farriers and tailors. Forerunner of Christ. Feast, 24 June.
His life is narrated in the New Testament, where he is the son of Elizabeth, a relation of the Virgin Mary. John lived in Judea and preached on

St. John the Baptist

repentance for the forgiveness of sin. Thousands came to be baptized by him, including Jesus. John reproved King Herod for living in adultery with Herodias, his brother Philip's wife. One day Salome (not named in the New Testament), the daughter of Herodias, so pleased the king by her dancing that he vowed he would give her whatever she chose, even half his kingdom. Her mother told her to ask for the head of John the Baptist. The king, unable to take back an oath, sent the executioner to cut off the prophet's head.

St. Jerome writes that the disciples of John the Baptist buried the headless body in Sebaste, in Samaria, where many miracles took place at the tomb of the saint. Julian the Apostate was so annoyed by all of the miracles, according to the *Ecclesiastical History* of Ruffinus, that he had the body disinterred and burned to ashes. Some Christians, however, saved some of the bones.

The head of the saint was buried, according to the same source, by Herodias in the palace of King Herod. It remained hidden until St. John the Baptist appeared to some men and told them where it was hidden. They stole the head and wrapped it in camel's hair. For centuries, however, two churches

vied with each other, each claiming it had the head of the saint.

In Christian art St. John the Baptist is one of the most frequently portrayed saints. Narrations of his life usually include the following incidents culled from the New Testament: the annunciation to Zacharias (Luke 1:5–32) of John's coming birth; the birth and naming of St. John (Luke 1:57–64); St. John in the wilderness (Luke 1:8); baptizing (Matt. 3:5–6); rebuking King Herod for his evil life (Mark 6:17–20); the banquet of Herod at which Salome danced for his head (Mark 6:21–28); beheading, or decollation, and the presentation of the head to Herodias. The burning of the saint's bones by Julian the Apostate sometimes also appears, as in the medieval art of Northern Europe. The saint has been painted by such artists as Tintoretto, Raphael, Titian, Fra Angelico, Da Vinci, and Caravaggio, who in 1595 portrayed the saint playfully embracing a lamb or sheep and again in 1610. In both instances the models seem to have been male favorites of the artist, who was noted for his male lovers.

In the Islamic legend, Yahyu is the name given John the Baptist. He is mentioned three times in the Koran.

1629

John the Bear. In European folktales, hero who is the son of a bear. He is also called Juan el Oso, Juan del Oso, and Ivanko the Bear's Son in various European folktales.

1630

John the Evangelist, St. (Yahweh is gracious). First century C.E. Evangelist and Apostle, credited with the authorship of the Gospel that bears his name and three short general epistles in the New Testament. Christian tradition also credits John with the authorship of the Book of Revelation. Feast, 27 December.

John was the son of Zebedee, a Galilean fisherman, and the brother of James. Their mother, Salome (not to be confused with the woman who danced for the head of John the Baptist), might have been the sister of the Virgin Mary. John was one of the first disciples called by Jesus. Both John and his brother James were called "sons of thunder" or "sons of anger" by Jesus.

From earliest Christian times John has been identified as the "beloved disciple" named in the Gospel. He was present at the Last Supper, where he leaned his head on Jesus' breast. He stood at the cross when Jesus was crucified, and he was the first disciple to reach the tomb on Easter Day.

According to Christian legend, after the death of the Virgin Mary, who had been placed in his care by Jesus when he was on the cross, John preached in Judea with St. Peter. He then traveled to Asia Minor,

St. John the Evangelist

where he founded the Seven Churches and remained principally at Ephesus. During the persecution of the Christians under the Roman emperor Domitian he was sent in chains to Rome and cast into a caldron of boiling oil. He was miraculously preserved and "came out of it as out of a refreshing bath." He was then accused of being a magician and exiled to Patmos in the Aegean, where he wrote the Book of Revelation.

Another legend says that while John was in Rome an attempt was made on his life. A poisoned chalice was given him, but before he could drink, a serpent appeared in the cup, and the hired killer who had poisoned the cup fell down dead at the saint's feet.

In a variant of the tale, the poisoned cup was administered by order of the Emperor Domitian. In still another variant, Aristodemus, the high priest of the goddess Diana at Ephesus defied John to drink from a poisoned cup. John did, and Aristodemus fell dead at his feet.

John is the only Apostle who, according to legend, did not die but fell asleep waiting for the Second Coming of Christ.

1631

Jok (creator). In African mythology (Alur of Uganda and Zaire), creator and rain god who presides over birth as Jok Odudu. Offerings of black goats are made to the god for rainfall.

1632

Jonah (dove). In the Bible, one of the Minor Prophets and title of a book of the Old Testament. Instructed by Yahweh, the Hebrew god, to preach repentance to the great but wicked city of Nineveh, the Hebrew prophet Jonah fled in a ship bound for the Phoenician city of Tarsish. When a storm arose, the sailors cast lots to see who was responsible for their trouble. The lot fell on Jonah, who confessed that Yahweh was displeased with him. Thrown overboard, Jonah was swallowed by "a great fish" (later folklore and the New Testament turn it into a whale) in which he stayed for three days before he was vomited out on dry land. Jonah then went to Nineveh and convinced its king and people that they must repent or be destroyed within 40 days. Yahweh saved the city, but Jonah was angry. Outside the city he built himself a shelter for shade. Yahweh made a gourd grow up to give Jonah additional protection from the burning sun, but at night Yahweh made a worm destroy the plant. Jonah was sorry for the gourd, and Yahweh taught Jonah a lesson, saying: "Thou hast had pity on the gourd, for which thou hast not laboured, neither madest it to grow; which came up in a night, and perished in a night: And should not I spare Nineveh, that great city, wherein are more than sixscore thousand persons that cannot discern between their right hand and their left hand; and also much cattle?" (Jon. 4:10–11).

Christian writers saw the tale of Jonah as foreshadowing certain incidents in the life of Christ. Matthew's Gospel has Jesus say: "For as Jonas [N.T. spelling] was three days and three nights in the whale's body; so shall the Son of Man be three days and three nights in the heart of the earth [tomb]" (Matt. 12:40). Jonah is a symbol of Resurrection, and he frequently appears in early Christian art.

1633

Jonathan (Yahweh has given). In the Bible, O.T. (1 and 2 Samuel), the oldest son of King Saul and male companion to David. He took David's side when David disputed with Jonathan's father, King Saul. When Jonathan and Saul were killed, David lamented his death, saying: "The beauty of Israel is slain upon thy high places: now are the mighty fallen! . . . I am distressed for thee, my brother Jonathan: very pleasant hast thou been unto me: thy love to me was wonderful, passing the love of women" (2 Sam. 1:19, 26). The relationship between David and Jonathan is one of the strongest examples of male bonding in ancient Near Eastern legends, its only rival being Gilgamesh and Enkidu.

1634

Jonathan Moulton. In American New England folklore, a general who sold his soul to the devil in return for a gold coin placed in his boots once a month. Once he put his boots on top of a chimney, and the devil started to drop down the gold coins. Since he had removed the bottom soles, the devil had to fill up the whole fireplace and chimney, but that night the house burned to the ground and no gold was found. At his death his friends opened Moulton's coffin to see if he had taken the gold with him, but they found nothing.

1635

Jones, John Paul. 1747–1792. In American history and folklore of the Revolution, naval hero. Given command of the *Bon Homme Richard* and two other vessels, Jones attacked two British envoy ships *Serapis* and *Countess of Scarborough*. During the battle Jones was asked by the British commander, "Have you struck?" and according to legend, he replied, "Sir, I have not yet begun to fight." After an intense naval battle the *Serapis* surrendered. Jones's earliest biographer, Alexander S. Mackenzie, writing in 1841, said: "No hero ever sounded his own trumpet more unremittingly or with a louder blast." Jones wrote his *Memoirs* and appears in numerous American novels, such as James Fenimore Cooper's *The Pilot*, Herman Melville's *Israel Potter*, and Winston Churchill's *Richard Carvel*. Hollywood took up the hero in *John Paul Jones* (1959), starring Robert Stack as the naval hero and Bette Davis as Catherine the Great of Russia.

1636

Jord (earth). In Norse mythology, primeval earth goddess, first wife of Odin; mother of the god Thor. She was the daughter of Nott (night) and a dwarf. Jord was worshiped on high mountains. In Germanic mythology and in Richard Wagner's *Der Ring des Nibelungen* she is called Erda.

Variant spellings: Jordh, Fyorgyn, Hloldyn, Iord.

1637

Jorkemo (may Yahu establish?). In Jewish folklore, angel of hail. In the Old Testament Book of Daniel tells how King Nebuchadnezzar placed Shadrach, Meshach, and Abednego in a furnace for not worshiping his god. When the king looked into the furnace, he saw the three men and a fourth "like the Son of God" (Dan. 3:25). The three men were left unharmed by the flames. Jewish folklore identifies the fourth as Jorkemo. The angel wanted to quench the flames but lacked the power, so he asked the archangel Gabriel to cool the flames.

Variant spellings: Yrukemi, Yorkami.

1638

Joro Kumo (courtesan spider). In Japanese folklore, a ghost resembling a spider woman, who lures men to their death.

1639

Joseph (may he add, i.e., Yahweh). In the Bible, O.T. (Gen. 37–50), hero, 11th son of Jacob and Rachel; brother of Benjamin, who brought the Hebrews to Egypt. When Joseph was 17 years old, he took care of his father's sheep and goats with his half brothers, sons of the concubines Bilhah and Zilpah. Jacob loved Joseph more than any of his other sons because Joseph was born to him in his old age. Jacob had made for Joseph a robe with long sleeves (inaccurately translated in the King James Version as a coat of many colors). When Joseph's brothers saw his robe, they grew to hate him. He would tell them his dreams, which indicated that he would rule over them. One day while the brothers were at Dothan, they decided to kill Joseph. "Here comes that dreamer. Come on now, let's kill him and throw his body into one of the dry wells. We can say that a wild animal killed him. Then we will see what becomes of his dreams" (Gen. 37:19–20, Today's English Version). But Reuben heard them and tried to save Joseph, saying they should not kill him but just throw him in a dry well. He planned to come back and save Joseph. But Judah instead persuaded his brothers to sell Joseph to a group of Ishmaelites or Midianites (the sources vary in the biblical text). This they did and then told Jacob that Joseph had been killed by a wild animal. The boy was sold in Egypt to Potiphar, one of the pharaoh's officers, who was captain of the palace guard. Joseph prospered with Potiphar, who trusted him with all of his affairs. "Joseph was well built and good looking, and after awhile his master's wife began to desire Joseph and asked him to go to bed with her" (Gen. 39:6–7, Today's English Version). Joseph refused her sexual advances, and Potiphar's wife accused him of attempted rape and Joseph was cast into prison. There he interpreted the dreams of two prisoners; one was the pharaoh's chief baker and the other his wine steward. Joseph told the wine steward he would be free in three days but that the baker would be executed. It happened just as Joseph had predicted, so when the pharaoh had a dream that none of the Egyptian magicians could interpret, the wine steward told him of Joseph the Hebrew who could interpret dreams. Joseph was brought to the court and interpreted the pharaoh's dream as signifying that there would be seven years of plentiful harvest, then seven years of famine. When he heard this, Pharaoh appointed Joseph to take charge of stockpiling grain. Joseph was then called Zaphenath Paneah (revealer of secrets). After the seven years of plenty, the famine was so severe that Joseph's brothers went down to Egypt to get grain so that they would not starve. When Joseph saw them he recognized them, but they did not know him. He put them through various tests to see if they had learned any compassion since the time they attempted to kill him. When he realized they were sorry for what they had done and showed love for Benjamin and Jacob, he revealed himself to them. He then had his father, Jacob, and all of his family settle in Goshen. Before Jacob died, Joseph asked him to bless Joseph's two sons, Manasseh and Ephraim, by Asenath, the daughter of Potiphera, a priest of Heliopolis. Jacob blessed Ephraim, the younger son, but not Manasseh, the older. When Joseph died, he was embalmed and buried in Egypt. At the Exodus his body was taken by the Hebrews. Thomas Mann's novel *Joseph and His Brothers* deals with the legend. Rembrandt's *Joseph and Potiphar's Wife* portrays one episode from the legend, and Handel's oratorio *Joseph and His Brethren* deals with the legend.

1640

Joseph of Arimathea (may he add). First century C.E. In the Bible, N.T., the man who begged for the body of Jesus and laid it in his own tomb (Matt. 27:57–60). Medieval legend says he was imprisoned for years

and kept alive by the Holy Grail, the cup Christ used at the Last Supper. He later brought the Holy Grail to Glastonbury in England.

1641

Joseph, St. (may he add). First century C.E. In the Bible, N.T., husband of the Virgin Mary. Patron of carpenters, confectioners, the dying, engineers, the family, married couples, house hunters, pioneers, and travelers. Invoked in doubt and hesitation. Feast, 19 March.

Little is said of Joseph in the New Testament. He was of the House of David and accepted Jesus as his son when the angel told him "that which is conceived in her womb is of the Holy Ghost" (Matt. 1:20). Joseph died before Jesus began his public ministry.

During the Middle Ages St. Joseph was often referred to as a cuckold by Christians, who neglected his cult in favor of his wife, Mary. But in the 16th century his cult spread throughout the Roman church. According to medieval beliefs, St. Joseph's girdle was kept at Notre Dame, Joinville sur Marne, in the diocese of Langres. His walking stick was preserved in the Monastery of Angels in Florence and another stick and his hammer in the Church of St. Anastasia in Rome. The cloak with which St. Joseph covered Jesus in the stable also was preserved in the church.

Joseph sold into Egypt

1642

Joshua (Yahweh is salvation). In the Bible, O.T., successor of Moses and a leader of the Israelites during the Exodus and the settlement of Canaan. Joshua was the son of Nun, an Ephraimite, and was appointed by Moses as his successor. Three days after Moses' death, Joshua got ready for the invasion of Canaan. He sent out spies and moved camp up to the river Jordan. In one assault after another, he reduced the fortified towns on the opposite banks, the most famous being Jericho. Joshua under the guidance of

Yahweh, the Hebrew god, marched his army around the walls for six days bearing the Ark of the Covenant (which some scholars believe contained a fetish or Hebrew snake god). On the seventh day they circled seven times; the priests blew their trumpets and Joshua ordered the people to shout. As the shouts went up, the walls of Jericho fell down and the Israelites conquered the city (Josh. 6:1–25). In another battle, Joshua ordered the sun to stand still so that his enemies could not escape at night (Josh. 10:13). Most of his legend is told in the Book of Joshua in

Christ on the Cross with three angels (Dürer)

St. Joseph and Jesus

the Old Testament. In Islam Joshua is called Yusha, though he is not named directly in the Koran. Joshua appears in Dante's *The Divine Comedy* (Purgatory, canto 20; Paradise, cantos 9, 18). Handel's oratorio *Joshua* and the folk song *Joshua Fought the Battle of Jericho* tell of how God guided the Hebrews to victory over their enemies.

1643
Jotunheim (home of the devourers). In Norse mythology, the land of the frost giants, located under one of the tree roots of the cosmic or world tree, Yggdrasill, in the far northwest where the ocean joined the world's edge. Its capital was Utgard (outer place).
Variant spellings: Jotunnheim, Jotunheimr.

1644
Jotunn (devourers). In Norse mythology, the giants who ruled before the Aesir gods, among them were the Hrimthursar (frost giants). Most of them were violent and wicked. They had heads of stone and feet of ice. Often they could transform themselves into eagles or wolves. Among the most famous were Kari (tempest) and his three sons: Beli (storm); Thiassi (ice), with his daughter, Skadi (winter); and Thrym (frost). Others were Johul (glacier), Frosti (cold), Snoer (snow), and Orifta (snowdrift). The god Thor married a giantess, Iarnsafa (ironstone), who bore him two sons; Magni (strength) and Modi (courage). It was believed that a battle between the gods and frost giants would bring about Ragnarok, the destruction of the world, and then its renewal.

1645
Joukahainen (genius of ice and snow?). In the Finnish epic poem *The Kalevala*, an evil youth who entered into a contest with Vainamoinen and was defeated.

Hearing that the culture hero Vainamoinen was noted for his magic songs, Joukahainen, against his parents' wishes, challenged him to a singing contest. They questioned one another, asking who was present at the creation of the world. Joukahainen answered that he had been. Vainamoinen replied that Joukahainen was a liar. This so enraged the youth that he challenged Vainamoinen to a fight, but the culture hero sang magic songs that made Joukahainen sink into a swamp. Fearing he would die, Joukahainen offered Vainamoinen his sister Aino as a wife, and the hero released him.

Joukahainen returned home to his farm angry, telling Joukola, his mother, what had happened, but she was pleased that her daughter was to wed Vainamoinen. Joukahainen, however, continued to nurture a hatred against Vainamoinen. Once he lay in wait for him on his journey to Pohjola, the Northland, and shot at him, killing Vainamoinen's horse. Vainamoinen fell into the water and was driven out to sea by a tempest. Joukahainen rejoiced, thinking he at last had overcome Vainamoinen. However, the culture hero was not destroyed.

Joukahainen is often called Jouko, a shortened form of his name.
Variant spelling: Youkahainen.

1646
Jove (sky, in the open air). In Roman mythology, ancient Italian god, identified with the Greek god Zeus; also called Jupiter by the Romans.

1647
Juan Chi. 275–210 B.C.E. In Chinese legend, one of the seven Chu-lin Ch'i-Hsien (Seven Immortals). He is depicted with a boy attendant and his nephew, Juan Hsien, with fan and staff.

In Japanese legend he is called Genshiki.

1648
Judas Iscariot (Judas, man from Kerioth) First century C.E. In the Bible, N.T., one of the Twelve Apostles, who betrayed Jesus to the chief priests in exchange for 30 pieces of silver.

Nothing is said in the New Testament regarding the calling of Judas to be one of Jesus' Twelve Apostles, nor is anything known of his early life. Judas was the Apostles' treasurer and handled the moneybag (John 13:29). When at the Last Supper Jesus announced that one of the Twelve would betray him, all asked, "Is it I?" The motivation for Judas' betrayal may have been more than greed for the 30 pieces of silver. He may have borne a grudge against Jesus after Jesus rebuked him for his criticism of Mary's (the sister of Lazarus) extravagance in using expensive oil from the alabaster box to anoint Jesus. Judas had complained that the oil could be sold and the money used to help the poor. St. John's Gospel (12:6) says of Judas' complaint, "This he said, not that he cared for the poor; but because he was a thief, and had the [money]bag, and bare [carried] what was put therein."

To fulfill his pact with the high priests Judas kissed Jesus in the garden as a signal to the soldiers to arrest Jesus (Mark 14:43–45). After the arrest the traitor Judas tried to give back the blood money (Matt. 27:3–4), but it was refused by the priests, who mocked him saying, "What is that to us?" Judas then went to the Temple area and threw the silver on the floor and later hanged himself (Matt. 27:5). The Acts of the Apostles (1:18), however, gives a different account of Judas' death, saying "this man purchased a field with the reward of iniquity; and falling headlong, he burst asunder in the midst, and all his bowels gushed out." According to Christian tradition the "bursting asunder" was considered a special judgment, in order that his soul should escape from his bowels and not be breathed out through his lips since they had betrayed Jesus with a kiss. Judas appears always as the arch-betrayer. Dante's *The Divine Comedy* (Inferno) has the traitor chewed in the mouth of Satan. In medieval art he is often portrayed with red hair and wearing a yellow garment.

1649

Jude Thaddeus and Simon Zealot, SS. (praise and snub-nosed). First century. In the Bible, N.T., Apostles. Jude is the traditional author of the Epistle that bears his name in the New Testament. He is invoked in desperate situations. Feast for both, 28 October.

Jude may have been one of the brethren (Mark 6:3) of Jesus, being either the son of Mary and Joseph (one tradition held that Jesus had brothers and sisters) or the son of Joseph by a former marriage (another tradition, invoked to protect the virginity of Mary). Both Jude and Simon, according to tradition, preached the gospel in Syria and Mesopotamia and were martyred in Persia. Jude was said to have been killed by a halberd (his symbol) and Simon was sawn asunder (his symbol). Jude is one of the most popular saints in the Roman Catholic church. He is frequently invoked by the faithful who often put ads in local tabloids begging the saints favor.

1650

Judgment of Paris. In Greek mythology, one of the principal myths regarding the origin of the Trojan War. The Judgment involved Paris in a dispute among the goddesses Hera, Athena, and Aphrodite. When Eris, goddess of discord, was not invited to the wedding banquet of Peleus and Thetis, she threw a golden apple marked, "for the fairest" into the gathering. Hera, Athena, and Aphrodite all went after the apple, and each asked Zeus to award her the prize. To avoid making the choice, Zeus told the three goddesses to go to Mount Ida, where a handsome youth, Paris, was tending sheep. They were to ask him to make the judgment. (Paris had become a shepherd because his father, King Priam of Troy, had been warned that the lad would bring disaster upon Troy). Each of the three goddesses sought Paris's favor. Hera offered him power; Athena offered wisdom, and Aphrodite promised him the most beautiful woman in the world, Helen. He chose Helen, and Aphrodite sent Paris to Sparta, where he seduced Helen, wife of King Menelaus, and fled with her to Troy. Menelaus followed with a host of Greeks, and the Trojan War began.

The myth has been frequently retold and painted. The Judgment of Paris is either retold or cited in Vergil's *Aeneid* (book 1); Ovid's *Heroides*, which gives an elaborate description; Lucian, who made the apple golden and magic; the medieval retelling, *The Tale of Troy*; and Tennyson's *Dream of Four Women* and *Oenone*. The subject was painted by, among others, Cranach, Rubens, Watteau, Renoir, and Dali.

Judith giving the head of Holofernes to her servant

Judith (Jewess). In the Bible, O.T. Apocrypha, a heroine who helps save her city of Bethulia by cutting off the head of Holofernes, general of the Assyrian king Nebuchadnezzar. Judith was a young and beautiful widow of Manasseh and strictly followed the Mosaic law. Her city, Bethulia, had its water supply cut off by Holofernes, who wished to destroy the Jews for not aiding his king in the war against Arphaxad, king of the Medes. When the people began to despair and were ready to surrender, Judith told their chief priest Ozias that she would deliver the city. Putting off her widow's garments, she went with her maid to the enemy camp, pretending to have deserted her people. As she had planned, Holofernes fell in love with her and gave a feast in her honor. Holofernes got very drunk at the feast, and when he at last got Judith alone, thinking he was going to sleep with her, she cut off his head with two blows of a sword. She wrapped his head in a bag and left with her maid, pretending to go out to pray. When she returned to her city, she stood on its walls and showed the decapitated head of Holofernes to his army, which fled in terror. She then sang a hymn of praise to the Lord for delivering her people. In the Roman Catholic Breviary her song is a hymn to be sung at Lauds.

Judith's tale inspired numerous paintings, such as those by Matteo di Giovanni and Paolo Veronese (c.1528-1588). Racine's *Judith*, Friedrich Hebbel's *Judith*, and Jean Giraudoux's *Judith* all use the legend, as do Vivaldi and Mozart in oratorios, both titled *Bethulia Liberata*.

1652

Juggernaut (lord of the world). In Hinduism, a sacred image of Krishna, an incarnation of the god Vishnu.

When Krishna was accidentally killed by the hunter Jaras (old age), his body was left to rot under a tree. Some people found the bones and placed them in a box. Vishnu then appeared to Indradyumna, a holy king, and told him to make an image of Krishna called Juggernaut and to place the bones of Krishna inside. Viswakarma, the architect of the gods, undertook the commission on the condition that he be left undisturbed till the work was completed. After 15 days the king was impatient and went to Viswakarma to see how the work was progressing. Viswakarma was angry and left the statue unfinished—it had no hands or feet, only stumps. Indra-dyumna prayed to the god Brahma, who promised the king to make the image of the Juggernaut one of the most sacred in the world. Brahma gave the image eyes and a soul, and acted as high priest at its consecration.

There is, however, a variant account of the origin of the image. A Brahman was once sent to look for a site for a new temple. The Brahman wandered about for many days. He then saw a crow dive into the water. The bird honored the water as if it were some god, and the Brahman chose the site as the one near which the temple should be erected. While the temple was being constructed, King Indra-dyumna was told in a dream: "On a certain day cast thine eyes on the seashore, when there will arise from the water a piece of wood 52 inches long and 18 inches broad; this is the true form of the deity; take it up and keep it hidden in thine house for seven days, and in whatever shape it shall then appear, place it in the temple and worship it."

The image of Juggernaut is located at Puri, a town in the Orissa state of northeast India on the Bay of Bengal. Each summer the images of Juggernaut and his brother and sister are carried on a large cart, dragged by pilgrims to their summer home. Though some worshipers have thrown themselves under the cart, this act is not part of the cult, though it has supplied the English language with the term *Juggernaut* for "customs, institutions, etc., beneath which people are ruthlessly and unnecessarily crushed."

Variant spellings: Jagganth, Jagan-natha, Jagan-nath.

1653

Julana. In Australian mythology, son of Njirana among the Jumu in western Australia, who is in constant pursuit of women with his gigantic penis.

1654

Julian Hospitaller, St. (descended from Jove). In Christian legend, patron of boatmen, ferrymen, innkeepers, musicians, travelers, and wandering singers. Feast, 12 February.

Julian's life is found in *The Golden Legend*, a 13th-century book of the lives of the saints by Jacobus de Voragine. There is no factual information on the saint aside from the legend.

Julian was a young man who, while hunting, came upon a stag that told him he would kill his parents. Horrified at the news, Julian fled to another kingdom, where he became a knight and was given a rich widow as his wife. Meanwhile his parents searched for their son. One day they came to the castle where Julian lived and were received by Julian's wife. When they told their story, she knew that Julian was their son and offered them her own bed to rest the night. When Julian returned to his wife's bed, he saw two figures asleep beneath the blankets. Without a word he drew his sword and killed the couple. Discovering his evil deed, Julian and his wife fled. They lived for years near a shore and ferried people across. One night Julian ferried an aged leper who was so ill that Julian took him home and put him in his own bed. In the morning the leper revealed himself as an angel, saying God had forgiven Julian's murder of his parents. Later he built a hospice.

The legend is illustrated in a series of stained-glass windows in the cathedral of Rouen, presented to the church by some boatmen. Flaubert wrote *The Legend of St. Julian the Hospitaller*, based on the windows.

1655

Jumala (god). In Finnish mythology, a semiabstract term for God. Jumala was sometimes called Kuoja (creator). He was later replaced by Ukko, the Finnish sky god.

1656

Juniper. An evergreen shrub. In European folklore the juniper was regarded as a life-giving tree, as reflected in the *Tale of the Juniper Tree* by the Grimm brothers. The juniper berry is used in folk medicine in America as well as in Germany. The Hopi Indians used the boiled greens of the juniper to relieve sore throat, sour stomach, earache, and constipation. The berries were used to cure snakebite, plague, rheumatism, and venereal disease.

1657

Juno (sky goddess). In Roman mythology, ancient Italian goddess, sister and wife of Jove (Jupiter). The Roman goddess, like her Greek counterpart, Hera, was the queen of heaven, Regina. As such, she was supreme among all of the goddesses and watched over women and marriage. Juno differs from Hera in that she is closely connected with the moon. The Calends were sacred to Juno Lucina, or Lucretia (goddess of childbirth), as the Ides were sacred to her husband, Jupiter. Every woman had her own protecting *juno* whom she worshiped on her birthday, just as every man had his *genius*. As Pronuba Juno, she presided over betrothal. Juno Juga yoked together the husband and wife in marriage. Juno Domiduea was worshiped as the couple was escorted to their new home, and its doorposts were anointed in honor of Juno Unixia. The most important festival of married women was the *Matronalia*, celebrated on 1 March, both at the temple of Juno Lucina and in the home. It was Juno Lucina, as well as Juno Sospita (Juno the savior), who watched over childbirth, protecting mother and child from harm. Juno's main temple was at the Capitol in Rome, close to the temple of Jupiter. In it were kept geese, animals sacred to her because they were prolific and domestic. There was also a temple on the Capitol dedicated to Juno Moneta (the admonisher or goddess of money). The

use of money derived from the goddess and was was coined in the temple of Juno Moneta. One of her other feasts, celebrated on 7 July, was the *Caprotina*. Female slaves took part in the *Caprotina*, reenacting the legend that they once helped save the Romans from defeat. Most references in English use Juno, not only for the Roman goddess but for her Greek counterpart, Hera. Juno appears in or is cited in Shakespeare's *Cymbeline* (5.4.32) as wife, in Spenser's *Faerie Queene* (1.4.17) as Queen of Heaven, and in Milton's *Paradise Lost* (9.18) as a war goddess.

1658

Juno and the Peacock. Aesopic fable found in various European collections.

A peacock once placed a petition before the goddess Juno asking for the voice of a nightingale. Juno refused his request; when the bird persisted and said that he was the goddess's favorite bird, she replied: "Be content with your lot. One cannot be first in everything."

Sean O'Casey's play *Juno and the Paycock* has the antihero, Jack Boyle, called Captain Jack, portrayed as a strutting "paycock." His wife, Juno, however, sees through her husband's poses and defections.

1659

Juok. In African mythology (Shilluk of the Sudan), supreme god who divided the earth with the river Nile. His helper is Nyikang, an ancient king who is the ancestor of the Shilluk and invoked as intermediary between them and Juok.

1660

Jurawadbad. In Australian mythology, snake man, married to a woman who refused to have sexual relations with him. In anger he turned into himself into a snake and hid inside a hollow log. When his wife peered into the log, he bit her and she died.

1661

Jurupari. In mythology of the Uapes Indians of Brazil, chief god, born of a virgin after she drank some *cachari*, a native beer. His cult was associated with male initiation rites from which women were excluded. If by accident a woman witnessed even a part of the rite, she was poisoned as a punishment.

1662

Justa and Rufina, SS. Third century. In Christian legend, patron saints of Seville, Spain. Feast, 19 July.

The two girls sold earthenware in a shop. One day a pagan woman came in to buy some for use in the worship of Venus, the goddess of love. Justa and Rufina refused to sell the goods, so the woman started to wreck the shop. Soon a crowd gathered and the two girls were accused of being Christians.

They were arrested, but before they were taken, they destroyed a statue to Venus. Both were condemned to death. Justa was put on a rack and cooked. Rufina was strangled to death.

1663

Justina of Antioch, St. (just). Fourth century. In Christian legend, virgin martyr. Feast, 26 September.

The saint's life is told in *The Golden Legend*, a collection of saints' lives written in the 13th century by Jacobus de Voragine. Justina was the daughter of a pagan priest. One day as she sat at her window she heard the Gospel read by Proculus, a deacon of the church. She was so moved by his reading that she became a Christian. At night her parents had a vision of Jesus and his angels, and the next day they too became Christians.

Justina, however, was loved by a pagan magician, Cyprian, who had dedicated himself to the devil. He approached the girl with the devil, but the fiend fled when Justina covered her whole body with signs of the cross. Cyprian then invoked another devil, but again his seduction failed. Finally, he invoked the Prince of Demons, who came to Justina's chamber, pounced on her bed, and embraced her. As Justina made the sign of the cross, the demon melted away. Cyprian realized that there was no hope of seducing Justina and converted to Christianity. The two were arrested for being Christians; Justina was put in a boiling caldron and Cyprian was burned to death. Some accounts say they were beheaded.

St. Justina's symbols are a unicorn for virginity and a palm for martyrdom.

1664

Juventas (youth). In Roman mythology, patron goddess of youth; mother of Alexiares and Anticetus by Heracles; equivalent to the Greek goddess Ganymeda (Hebe). Juventas was portrayed as a beautiful woman, dressed in variegated garments.

K

Ka (double). In Egyptian mythology, the double or abstract personality of a person. The *ka* was free to move from place to place and could separate itself from or unite itself to the body at will. The preserving of a dead man's *ka* was necessary if his body was to become everlasting. Funeral offerings, including meats, cakes, wines, and unguents, were made to a person's *ka*, and when food was not available, offerings were painted on the walls and were accompanied by specific prayers. In early Egypt tombs had special chambers where the *ka* was worshiped and received its offerings. The priesthood included a group called "priests of ka," who performed services in its honor. The *ka* is closely associated with the *ba*, the soul; the *ib*, the heart; the *khaibit*, the shadow of a man; and the *khat*, the whole body of a person.

Kaaba (cube). In Islam, a cube-shaped shrine located at Mecca. It contains Al-hajar al-aswad, the Black Stone, which may be a meteorite. The stone was located in the shrine before Muhammad destroyed the idols there when he captured the city. The pagan Arabs used to worship the Black Stone, and Muhammad accommodated them by making it part of the sacred site.

According to some Islamic legends, the site was chosen because of its connection with the prophet Abraham. Abraham was led to Arabia by a stormy wind sent by Allah. The storm was in the shape of two heads (in one account, it had the head of a snake). Allah told Abraham to build a shrine at a site to which the storm would direct him. When the wind reached the site of the Kaaba, it wound itself around and said: "Build on me."

When Abraham was constructing the building, he stood on one of its stones, and his footprint, *Makam Ibrahim*, is shown to pilgrims to this day. The Black Stone in the shrine was once white but, according to Islamic legend, turned black because of the sins of man. It had been brought to the shrine by the archangel Gabriel.

In another, entirely different Islamic legend regarding the foundation of the Kaaba, it was Adam, not Abraham, who was responsible. After the fall Adam went to Mecca. The archangel Gabriel with his massive wings uncovered a foundation. Angels then threw blocks on it from various places until the ground was level. Allah sent from paradise a tent of red jacinth in which Adam was to live. The tent, which was an angel, later became the Black Stone. When Adam made a covenant with men, they signed it on paper, and it was fed to the Black Stone, which ate it up. At the end of the world the Black Stone will sprout a tongue and name all of the good men and all of the sinners.

The Black Stone has been damaged several times. In the 11th century a man was sent by al-Hakim, Fatimid caliph in Egypt, to destroy it but succeeded only in splintering it slightly. The Black Stone is now in a silver casing about ten feet across. The practice of kissing the stone is inherited from pagan times, although Muslims deny that any worship is paid to the stone.

Variant spellings: Ka'ba, Kaabeh, Caaba.

Kabandha. In Hindu mythology, an evil goblin slain by Rama. Originally, Kabandha was a good spirit in the service of the storm god Indra. One day, however, Indra cast a thunderbolt at Kabandha, driving his head and thighs into his body. Kabandha was then "covered with hair, vast as a mountain, without head or neck, having a mouth armed with immense teeth in the middle of his belly, arms a league long, and one enormous eye in his breast." In his new form Kabandha became an evil goblin, who fought against the hero Rama. When Rama defeated Kabandha the goblin asked the hero to have his body burned. When this was done, Kabandha came out of the fire restored to his original shape before Indra's thunderbolt had struck him. He then aided Rama in his war against the demon king Ravana. Kabandha is sometimes called Danu.

Kacha. In the Hindu epic poem *The Mahabharata*, a man who wanted the power to restore the dead to life. Kacha studied with the sage Sukra (Usanas), who had the power of restoring the dead to life. Sukra, however, was a priest in the service of demons and did not wish to pass on his magic powers to Kacha. So instead he killed his student. But each time he was killed, Kacha was restored to life by Sukra, who repented. The third time Kacha was killed, the demons burned his body and mixed the ashes with Sukra's wine. When Devayani, Sukra's daughter, who loved Kacha, asked her father to re-

375

store Kacha to life again, he performed his magic feats but heard the voice of Kacha coming from his own stomach. To save his own life Sukra taught Kacha the charm. He then allowed himself to be ripped open, and Kacha, on coming out, performed the magic rite and restored Sukra to life. Kacha, however, was not in love with Devayani. She therefore cursed him, saying that his magic charms would have no power, and he in turn cursed her, saying she would marry a member of a lower caste instead of a priest.

1669
Kachina. In North American Indian mythology (Hopi and other Pueblo Indians), the spiritual, inner form of reality manifested by masked dancers. The term *kachina* is also used for small painted wooden dolls.

1670
Kadaklan. In Philippine mythology, creator god of the Tinguian Islands. Creator of the earth, sun, moon, and stars, Kadaklan is married to Agemem and has two sons, Adam and Balujen. His dog is Kimat, the lightning. During a storm Kadaklan beats on his drum to amuse himself.

1671
Kae. In Polynesian mythology, an old wicked priest who was killed and eaten.

Tinirau, the sea god, invited Kae to a special ceremony in which his son was to be named. The priest was fed a piece of meat from Tutunui, the pet whale of Tinirau, who still remained alive. Kae so liked the taste of whalemeat that he asked his host if he might ride home on the whale's back. Tinirau agreed, saying Kae had to dismount the whale when they reached shallow water or the animal would die. Kae deliberately let the whale die, took it home, and ate it. The winds carried the scent of the whale meat back to Tinirau, who sent 40 dancing girls to investigate the matter. Kae, they were told, could be identified by his large crooked teeth. The girls started to dance and sing, causing the people to laugh. But Kae kept his mouth shut so as not to reveal his large teeth. Finally, however, he could not restrain himself, and he laughed, revealing his large teeth. Seeing him, the girls cast a spell over the crowd. While Kae slept, they took him back to Tinirau, who had him killed and eaten. The natives say that is why there is cannibalism. In a variant of the myth Kae is married to Hina, a goddess, and their son rides the whale.

1672
Kakebotoke. In Japanese Buddhism, a round copper or wooden plaque on which Buddhist images are carved in relief.

1673
Kakurezator. In Japanese folklore, an evil spirit who carries the souls of sinners to hell. He is portrayed as a blind old man with a knotted staff.

1674
Kala (time). In Hindu mythology, an epithet applied to Yama, god of death, as well as to the creator god, Brahma.

1675
Kalanemi (rim of the wheel of time). In Hindu mythology, an archdemon. Kalanemi took the form of a holy hermit and offered poisoned food to the monkey hero Hanuman. Hanuman, however, refused the food. He went instead to bathe at a nearby pond and was seized by a crocodile. Hanuman dragged it out of the water and killed it. From the crocodile's body arose a beautiful nymph who had earlier been forced by a curse to live in the crocodile's body until Hanuman would free her. The nymph told Hanuman that the holy hermit was the archdemon Kalanemi in disguise. Hearing this, Hanuman went back to Kalanemi, grabbed him by the feet, and hurled him through the air until he landed in Lanka (Sri Lanka) at the feet of the demon king Ravana. Later Krishna (an incarnation of the god Vishnu) killed Kalanemi; but the demon became incarnate again in the evil king Kamsa, the enemy of Krishna, and in Kaliya, a demon snake.

1676
Kalevala, The (the land of heroes). Finnish epic poem compiled by Elias Lönnrot from oral traditions in Karelia, now part of the Soviet Union. The first edition (1835) contained 12,078 lines, the second (1849), 22,795.

The word *Kalevala* is derived from Kaleva, a mythical hero. Kaleva, however, never appears in the epic poem, though his daughter Kalevatoar and his descendant Kalevalainen are mentioned. *The Kalevala* consists of 50 runes (poems or songs, sometimes called cantos; the term appended to each section varies with different English translations) varying in length but all in unrhymed alliterative trochaic tetrameter. Here is an example from W. F. Kirby's translation, which also displays the use of "echo" lines:

Vainamoinen, old and steadfast,
Now resolved upon a journey

To the cold and dreary regions
Of the gloomy land of Pohjola.

The use of a set verse form helps unify the epic, since the sources, from diverse oral traditions, were various folksingers of different ages. *The Kalevala* is the only modern European epic compiled from songs actually existing among the people. Lönnrot visited the most remote regions of the land and with skillful editing produced the epic. He added a prologue of approximately 100 lines as well as some connecting links to unify the epic.

The first part of the epic (runes 1–10) narrates the birth and adventures of one of the main characters in the poem, Vainamoinen, the son of Luonnotar, daughter of the Air. Vainamoinen is a magician, perhaps derived from a shaman in real life, who can work magic through his songs. Shortly after his birth (in the poem he is always portrayed as old) he was challenged to a singing contest by the evil Laplander Joukahainen. The challenge was taken up, and Joukahainen was defeated and plunged into a swamp. To save himself from drowning, Joukahainen promised his sister Aino to Vainamoinen as his wife. Vainamoinen accepted the offer, but Aino did not. She drowned herself to avoid marrying the old culture hero. Not giving up, Vainamoinen went in pursuit of Aino in the river, finding her in the form of a fish. Even in this condition the girl refused and fled back into the water. Vainamoinen then went to Pohjola, the Northland, in search of a wife. While journeying there he was shot at by Joukahainen but escaped with wounds. Vainamoinen reached the land of Pohjola, ruled by the evil mistress Louhi, who told Vainamoinen that she would give him her daughter, the Maiden of Pohjola (the girl's name is never given in the poem), as a wife if he could construct a magic sampo, a mill that produced grain, salt and money.

Unable to construct the sampo by his magic songs alone, Vainamoinen called in the smith Ilmarinen (another hero of the poem) to aid him. Ilmarinen consented and produced the magic sampo. As a result, Ilmarinen was given the Maiden of Pohjola as a wife.

The next section of the epic (runes 11–15) narrates the adventures of Lemminkainen, the Don Juan figure in the epic poem. He married Kyllikki but soon discovered that she was unfaithful to him. He divorced her and went to the land of Pohjola to find a new wife. On his way Lemminkainen was murdered by Markahattu, a partly blind cattle herder whom he had insulted. However, the hero was restored to life by the magic spells of his mother (Lemminkainen's mother remains nameless in the poem).

The next main division (runes 16–25) tells of the marriage of Ilmarinen to the Maiden of Pohjola after performing a series of tasks imposed on him by Louhi, the girl's mother. The next section (runes 26–30) tells of Lemminkainen's coming to the wedding, to which he had not been invited. He entered the castle by force, insulted the guests, killed Louhi's husband, and fled to the island of Sarri. While on the island he slept with all of the women while their husbands were away. Lemminkainen fled the island when the husbands returned. He then set out for Pohjola with his companion-in-arms Kurra (Tiera), but they were defeated in their attempt to destroy the land.

The poem now takes on a tragic cast with the tale of Kullervo (runes 31–36). Kullervo is a tragic hero who raped his sister and then committed suicide. Before he killed himself, however, he murdered the Maiden of Pohjola. The next section (runes 37–49) tells how Vainamoinen, Ilmarinen, and Lemminkainen journeyed to Pohjola to steal the magic sampo. In this adventure the sampo was lost in a lake. A battle then ensued between Louhi's men and the three heroes, in which the final victory was given to Vainamoinen.

The last rune (50) tells how Marjatta, similar to the Virgin Mary, bore a son who became king of Karelia. Vainamoinen then departed the land. The last rune displays a good deal of Christian legendary material, which also is scattered throughout other sections of the poem, though the epic as a whole is certainly not Christian.

The Kalevala had tremendous influence on the national identity of the Finns, coming at a time of political and cultural upheaval against Russian domination. It appeared at one of the high points of European Romanticism, when each national group was seeking heroes in its past history and legend. The two most influential Finnish artists who have been deeply moved by the splendid epic are Jean Sibelius, one of the major composers of the early part of the century, and Akseli Gallen-Kallela, a painter who illustrated many of the scenes of the epic poem. The American poet Longfellow read a German translation of the poem that inspired the verse form of his *Song of Hiawatha*. The American poet not only used the *Kalevala* verse form but also recast some of its episodes, such as the departure of Hiawatha, modeled on the departure of Vainamoinen in the Finnish work.

1677

Kalidasa (Kali's slave). Hindu poet and dramatist of the fifth century.

Numerous legends surround the poet. According to one account, Kalidasa was a Brahman's son. At the age of six months he was left an orphan and was adopted by an ox driver. He grew up without any formal education, but he was remarkably handsome and had graceful manners. Once it happened that the princess of Benares, who rejected one suitor after another because they failed to reach her standard as scholars and poets, rejected a counselor of her father. The counselor planned revenge. He took Kalidasa from the street and gave him the garments of a rich man and a retinue of learned doctors. He then introduced him to the princess, after warning Kalidasa that under no circumstances was he to speak. The princess was struck with Kalidasa's beauty and moved by his silence, which she took to be profound wisdom. She decided to marry him. After the marriage she discovered the trick, but Kalidasa begged her to forgive him. She told her husband to pray to the goddess Kali (a form of the goddess Devi) for wisdom.

The prayer was granted. Knowledge and poetical power descended miraculously upon Kalidasa, who in gratitude assumed the name that means Kali's slave. Feeling he owed this happy change to his wife, he swore that he would treat her only with respect, as his teacher, but without any familiarity (no sexual intercourse). This only angered the princess. She cursed Kalidasa, saying he would meet his death at the hands of a woman. At a later date, the legend continues, the curse was fulfilled. A certain king had written half of a stanza of verse. He offered a large sum of money to any poet who could worthily complete it. Kalidasa completed the stanza, but a woman whom he loved discovered the lines, and greedy for the reward herself, killed Kalidasa and passed off the couplet as hers.

Kalidasa's most important work is the drama *Shukuntala*, based on an episode of the Hindu epic poem *The Mahabharata*.

Kaliya (black). In Hindu mythology, a serpent king subdued by Krishna, an incarnation of the god Vishnu.

Kaliya lived in a pool that he poisoned with venom from his five heads. All the surrounding countryside was being destroyed by his fire and smoke. One day the boy Krishna went to the pool and was trapped by Kaliya in his coils. Kaliya, however, could not hold the boy, whose body miraculously expanded, causing the snake to lose his hold. Krishna then performed a dance of death on the heads of the serpent, causing blood to flow "copiously from his mouths." After this, Kaliya surrendered and worshiped Krishna, who did not kill him but merely sent him to another river to live.

Kaliya is an incarnation of the archdemon Kalanemi, who had been earlier killed by Krishna.

Kalki

Kalki (impure; sinful). In Hindu mythology, the last avatar of the god Vishnu, which has not yet occurred. Vishnu is to appear at the end of the world cycle seated on a white horse, with drawn sword blazing like a comet, for the final destruction of the wicked, the renewal of creation, and the restoration of purity. Gore Vidal's novel *Kalki* uses the Hindu myth.

Kalmasha-pada (spotted feet). In Hindu mythology, a king condemned to eat human flesh.

One day King Kalmasha-pada went out to hunt and found two tigers. He killed one, but as it died it turned into an evil spirit. The other tiger disappeared, threatening vengeance. Kalmasha-pada returned to his palace and celebrated a sacrifice, at which the sage Vashishtha officiated. When the sacrifice was over, Vashishtha went out and the evil spirit of the tiger assumed his form and told Kalmasha-pada to serve the food. The evil spirit then turned into a cook, preparing human flesh and serving it to Vashishtha when he returned. When the sage discovered that the flesh was human, he cursed Kalmasha-pada, saying his appetite should only be excited by similar food. When Vashishtha discovered that it was not Kalmasha-pada's fault, however, he reduced the sentence to 12 years. The angry king, in turn, took water in his hands and was about to cast it at Vashishtha, when Kalmasha-pada's wife dissuaded him. "Unwilling to cast the water on the ground, lest it should wither up the grain, and equally reluctant to throw it up into the air, lest it should blast the clouds and dry up their contents, he threw it on their own feet," and they were scalded by it, becoming spotted black and white.

1681

Kalumba. In African mythology (Luba of Zaire), creator god who attempted to stop Death. One day Kalumba told a goat and dog to watch the roadside because Death and Life were going to pass by. Life was to be allowed to pass, but Death was to be stopped. So the two animals watched, but in a short time they began to argue, and the goat left the dog alone. In no time the dog fell asleep and Death, covered in a grass-cloth, quietly passed by. Next day the goat returned and stationed himself. Life then came by and was attacked by the goat. That is how death came into the world, according to the Luba people.

1682

Kama (desire). In Hindu mythology, the god of love, whose wife is Rati (love play). Kama is lord of the Apsaras, heavenly nymphs. In Indian art he is portrayed armed with a bow and arrow. The bow is of sugar cane, the bowstring a line of bees, and each arrow is tipped with a flower. Kama usually is shown as young and handsome, riding on a parrot and attended by the Apsaras. One of them carries a banner displaying the Makara, a fantastic sea animal, or a fish, on a red ground. From the banner Kama is sometimes called Makara-ketu, and from the flowers, Pushpa-ketana. Other epithets are Kusmayudha (armed with flowers), Pushpa-dhanus (whose bow is flowers), Pushpa-sara (whose arrows are flowers), and Madana (the maddener).

Variant spelling: Kandarpa.

1683

Kambel. In Melanesian mythology, a sky god. According to the beliefs of the Keraki Papuans, Kambel cut down a palm tree and heard sounds issuing from it. Within the tree were people. At night Kambel tried to catch hold of a shining white object that moved upward from the palm tree. It slipped away from him and became the moon.

In another tale Kambel sent several lizards out in search of fire. It was the smallest lizard that succeeded in bringing it back. Kambel cooked the pith of a palm over the fire, and by casting it into the sky, he caused the clouds to be created. It was said that these clouds caused the sky to be pushed up, separating it from the the earth.

Kambel is mentioned in another myth involving the concept of incest. A man became aware of an incestuous relationship occurring between his wife and his son. The father killed his son, and the boy's

dog reproached the man for having committed such an awful act. Kambel put the feather of a cassowary in the dog's mouth to prevent the mother from learning how her son had died. Ever since that event dogs have lost the power of speech.

1684

Kami (above, superior?). In Japanese Shinto mythology, generic term for deities or spirits, used as an honorific title for all that is held sacred, mysterious, powerful, and fearsome, such as wind, thunder, sun, rivers, trees, and rocks, as well as for qualities of growth, fertility, and reproduction.

1685

Kana. In Polynesian mythology, Hawaiian trickster, born in the form of a rope, raised by his grandmother Uli. Once Kana went to rescue a girl who had been abducted and placed on an island hill. Each time he stretched himself to reach the girl, the hill grew taller, moving the girl farther and farther away. He then went to his grandmother Uli to eat because he had grown very thin in stretching himself. Uli fed Kana and told him that the island was really a gigantic turtle whose stretching power lay in its flippers. Kana returned to the island, broke off the turtle flippers, and saved the girl.

1686

Kananesky Amaiyehi. In North American Indian mythology (Cherokee), the water spider who brought back fire to the animals. In the beginning there was no fire, and the entire earth was cold. Using a flash of lightning, the Thunderers put fire into the bottom of a sycamore tree, but no animals were able to go near the tree and get the fire. After many attempts to get the fire, Kananesky Amaiyehi, the water spider, who had downy hair and red stripes on her bottom, volunteered to try. But the problem was, how was she to carry the fire? "I'll manage that," she said as she spun a thread from her body and wove it into a *tusti* bowl, which she fastened on her back. Then she crossed over to the island where the tree was located. She put one little coal of fire into her bowl, and came back with it. Ever since, animals have had fire, and the water spider still keeps her *tusti* bowl.

1687

Kanthaka. In Buddhist legend, the steed of the Buddha.

1688

Kappa. In Japanese folklore, a river demon with the body of a tortoise, the limbs of a frog, and the head of a monkey. His head has a hollow at the top containing a strength-giving fluid. He lives in the water and comes out in the evening to eat. He sucks the

Kappa

blood of horses and cows through their anuses. He also drags humans into the water and sucks out their blood through their anuses. Humans can outwit him by being civil to him and bowing. This act forces Kappa to return the bow; his life fluid spills from his head and he loses his strength.

Karashishi. Stone lions often found in front of Buddhist temples in Japan.

1689

Karasu Tengu (crow Tengu). In Japanese folklore, a trickster spirit.

1690

Karshipta. In Persian mythology, a bird who brought the laws of the creator god, Ahura Mazda, to the underground cavern where Yima, the first man, had stored men and animals to save them from a winter that destroyed the earth. Karshipta recited the sacred *Avesta* in the language of birds.

1691

Karusakahiby and Rairu. In the mythology of the Mundurucu Indians of Brazil, father and son creator gods. Karusakahiby and his son Rairu emerged out of chaos. Rairu stumbled on a bowl-shaped stone, which he picked up, placing it on his head. It began to grow until it formed the heavens. He then knelt

1692

down before his father. The older god was jealous of his son, because he believed Rairu was too clever and therefore might contrive a scheme to overthrow him. When Rairu realized his father wished to kill him, he fled, but Karusakahiby discovered where he was hiding. When Karusakahiby was about to strike his son, Rairu cried out: "Do not hit me, for in the hollow of the earth I have found people, who will come forth and labor for us."

The first people were then brought out from their underground home. They were separated into tribes, the laziest becoming birds, bats, pigs, and butterflies.

Kashyapa (one who swallowed light). In Buddhism, Buddha, the Keeper of Light, who lived on earth for some 20,000 years and converted 20,000 people. His mount is the lion, his right hand is in the pose of "charity," and his left hand holds a monastic garment. In Tibet he is called Hod-srun and in China Chia-yeh. Also the name of a principal disciple of Shakyamuni Buddha.

1693

Kasogonga. In the mythology of the Chaco Indians of central South America, a rain goddess.

1694

Katha Sarit Sagara (the ocean of rivers). Collection of Indian folktales by Somadeva of Kashmir, written in the 12th century C.E. and translated into English by C. H. Tawney in two volumes (1880–1884).

1695

Kaumodaki. In Hindu mythology, the mace of Krishna (an incarnation of the god Vishnu), given to him by Agni, the fire god, when the two battled Indra, the storm god.

1696

Kaundinya. Fifth century B.C.E. In Buddhist legend, the first disciple of the Buddha. According to Buddhist texts, Kaundinya "had thoroughly grasped the doctrine of the Holy One, and the Buddha, looking into his heart said, 'Truly Kaundinya has understood the truth.'" Hence Kaundinya was called Ajnata-Kaundinya (Kaundinya has understood the teaching; Kaundinya has no more to learn).

1697

Kavah. Blacksmith in the Persian epic poem *Shah Namah* by Firdusi who refused to sacrifice his children to the evil king, Zahhak.

1698

Kavah was a strong and brave blacksmith who had a large family. One day the lot fell to two of his sons to be sacrificed to feed the serpents that came out of the neck of King Zahhak. (The serpents had been placed there by the evil spirit, Ahriman.) Kavah went to the king and protested:

Why give the brains of my beloved children
As serpent-food, and talk of doing justice
                    (James Atkinson translation)

Zahhak, taken aback by such boldness, ordered Kavah's sons to be released but placed Kavah's name on the list in their place.

"Are you then men, or what?" cried the blacksmith to the assembled court. "You have made a pact with this devil."

Kavah then tore the register, threw it under his foot, and left the court, taking his two sons with him. After he had left, the nobles complained to the king that such behavior should not be tolerated. Zahhak replied that he did not know what had overcome him in the presence of Kavah. The blacksmith then joined the forces of the hero Faridun, who was fighting against Zahhak and eventually defeated the king.

In the poem Kavah is credited with making the mace used by Faridun in battle. It resembled a cow's head, probably symbolic of fertility and thus strength.

1699

Kelpie (heifer, colt). In Celtic mythology, a Scottish spirit of lakes and rivers who caused travelers to drown. He often appears as a horse who lures victims into mounting him and then rides off, plunging into a river and drowning the rider. Thus, to see a kelpie is a sign of impending death.

Variant spelling: Kelpy.

1700

Kemp Morgan. In American folklore, comic oil-digging hero, who could smell oil underground. He had a tremendous appetite and had a full-time cook, Bull Cook Morrison of Snackover, Oklahoma. Once he dug a well so deep that it came out in Brazil. Another time he dug a well that shot oil up to heaven, causing the clouds to slide. The angels complained, and Kemp put a cap on the well.

1701

Kenelm, St. (brave helmet). Died 819. In Christian legend, saint venerated in Gloucester, Winchcombe, England. Feast, 17 July.

Kenelm was the son of King Kenwulf of Wessex. When he was seven years old he was murdered on orders of his sister. The crime was reported to Rome by a white dove, which alighted on the altar of St. Peter's, bearing the following couplet:

In Clent cow pasture, under a thorn
Of head bereft, lies Kenelm king-born.

1702

Ken-ro-ji-jin. In Japanese mythology, earth god, usually portrayed with a bowl in one hand and a spear in the other.

1703

Kentigern, St. (chief lord?). Sixth or seventh century C.E. In Christian legend, bishop, patron saint of Glasgow, Scotland. Feast, 14 January.

St. Kentigern is credited with the founding of Glasgow Cathedral. The most famous medieval legend associated with the saint deals with Queen Langoureth, who had been unfaithful to her husband, King Roderich. The king had given his wife a ring, and she in turn gave it to her lover. Knowing this, the king stole up on the lover one night and took the ring from his finger without waking him. The next day Roderich asked his wife for the ring. Frightened at what she had done, the queen went to St. Kentigern for help. Kentigern prayed and then went to the Clyde River, where the king had thrown the ring, and caught a salmon. He opened up the fish, extracted the ring, which the fish had swallowed, and gave it to the queen, who showed it to the king. The arms of Glasgow portray a salmon with a ring in its mouth, as well as an oak tree and bell, alluding to the legend that the saint called pagans to worship the Christian God by hanging a bell on an oak tree and ringing it. St. Kentigern is also called St. Mungo (dearest).

1704

Keresaspa. In Persian mythology, hero who will slay the archdemon Azhi Dahaka at the end of the world.

Keresaspa was a beautiful youth. He carried a club with which he slew the golden-heeled monster Gandarewa, and he fought the giant bird, Kamak, which hovered over the earth with its gigantic wings so that no rain could fall. Once Keresaspa fought the horned dragon who ate men and horses. Keresaspa climbed on the monster's back and started to cook lunch, stewing some meat in a kettle. The monster got very hot, began to perspire, and darted forward, causing the hot water and meat to fall. Keresaspa fled in terror.

Though not always successful, Keresaspa will come again at the end of the world and with his club slay the monster Azhi Dahaka when the archdemon escapes from his prison in Mount Demavend to cause havoc in the world.

Variant spellings: Keresasp, Keresaspo, Garshasp.

Keri and Kame. In the mythology of the Bakairi Indians of central Brazil, twin culture heroes. Keri and Kame were the sons of Oka, the jaguar, and his wife, who were originally made of wood. Oka's wife had become pregnant when she swallowed two finger bones. Her mother-in-law, Mero, hated her and murdered her. But before she died, a cesarean operation was performed by the twins' uncle Kuara, and the twin culture heroes were born.

When they grew up, they killed their evil grandmother by setting a forest fire in which she burned to death. During the conflagration Kame also was burned, but Keri blew on him and restored him to life. In the process Keri was burned himself but also was restored to life. In their new forms Keri and Kame chose to take human shapes. They ordered the sun and moon in the heavens, separated the heavens from the earth, created fire from the fox's eye and water from the Great Serpent, and then the brothers went their separate ways.

Kerki. In Finno-Ugric mythology, a spirit who promotes the growth of cattle. His feast was held 1 November, the Feast of All Saints in the Christian calendar. Closely connected with the dead, Kerki was honored by having a feast spread for him as well as by having the bathhouse heated. A straw doll representing Kerki was often set up in the corner near the stove.

Kevin, St. (handsome at birth). Sixth century C.E. In Christian legend, abbot of Glendalough (Wicklow). Also known as St. Coemgen. Feast, 3 June.

One Lent, according to medieval legend, St. Kevin "fled the company of men to a certain solitude." He chose a small hut on an island, where he prayed and read. Every day it was his custom to pray for many hours with his hand outstretched through the window of the hut. Once a blackbird settled on his open hand and began building a nest, then sat in the nest and laid an egg. The saint was so moved by the bird that he did not withdraw his hand until the young birds were hatched. Another legend tells that Kevin would not allow women on his island retreat. One day he was followed to his hut by a woman named Kathleen. In anger the saint hurled Kathleen from a rock. From that day forth her ghost never left the place where St. Kevin lived.

Keyne, St. Fifth century. In Christian legend, a female hermit. Feast, 8 October. St. Keyne was the daughter of King Brycham of Brecknock. When she died, angels came and removed her hairshirt and replaced it with a white robe. Her well, located near Liskeard, Cornwall, is believed to give drinkers of its waters power over their wives or husbands. The trick is to get to the well before one's spouse.

Kezef. In Jewish folklore, an angel of death who fought against Moses in Horeb. Kezef was seized by the high priest Aaron and imprisoned in the Holy Tabernacle. The incidents are not recorded in the Bible, however, but supplied by Jewish nonscriptural writings.

Kezer-Tshingis-Kaira-Khan. In Siberian mythology, the hero of the flood myth as told by the Soyots. He saved his family on a raft when the flood came and re-created everything when the waters subsided. He is credited with the invention of wine, as is Noah in the Old Testament.

Khadau and Mamaldi. In Siberian mythology, the first man and woman in myths told by the Amur. The myths vary: some say Khadau and Mamaldi created the earth or that they were the first parents of the shamans or that they were shamans themselves. Mamaldi created the Asian continent and the Island of Sakhalin and was then murdered by her husband, Khadau. Before she was killed, she gave her husband the souls of future shamans who had been created earlier.

Khadijah. In Islamic history and legend, first wife of the prophet Muhammad. She is one of the four perfect women in Islam, the others being Fatima, the prophet's daughter; Mary, daughter of Imran; and Asia, wife of the pharaoh drowned in the Red Sea.

Khen-Pa. In Tibetan folklore, the Old Man or master of the sky, who is portrayed as an old man with snow-white hair, dressed in white robes, and riding on the white dog of the sky. In his hand he carries a crystal wand.

Scarab

Khepera. In Egyptian mythology, god who represented the rising or morning sun and was closely associated with the scarab, a beetle sacred in ancient Egypt.

Khepera was one of the original creation gods. He was said to have been self-created, born of his own substance. In one myth he copulated with his own shadow and from his semen came Shu, the air, and Tefnut, moisture. From the union of Shu and Tefnut came Geb, the earth, and Nut, the sky; and they in turn bore the great deities Osiris, Isis, Set, and Nephthys. This group of nine deities was worshiped in a cosmological system known as the Ennead or Company of Nine Gods. In another creation myth, the sun god Ra was said to have created himself in primeval time in the form of the god Khepera.

Khepera was portrayed in Egyptian art as a beetle-headed man or as a man with a beetle surmounting his head, or simply as a beetle.

Since it was believed that the beetle was the incarnation of Khepera, beetle amulets were worn to attract the power of the god and secure his protection. In Egyptian funerary practice beetles or beetle amulets, often inscribed with texts from *The Book of the Dead*, were buried with the mummies to help ensure their resurrection. Roman soldiers in battle wore the likeness of the beetle on a ring.

Variant spellings; Khepri, Kheprer, Chepera.

Khnum

Khnum (molder). In Egyptian mythology, a creator god who resided at Elephantine, the region the ancient Egyptians also believed to be the source of the river Nile, personified as the god Hapi. Egyptian views concerning Khnum changed during the course of their long history, but various ancient texts show that Khnum always held an exalted position among the Egyptian deities. He even appears on gnostic gems and papyri for some 200 or 300 years after the birth of Christ. Khnum was believed to have molded on his potter's wheel the great cosmic egg, which contained the sun. He was also known as the potter who fashioned humankind and the gods. As a ram-headed deity, Khnum is often depicted at a potter's wheel fashioning from clay both the *ba* and *ka* of the ruler. The episodes depicting the birth of Hathsepsut at Dier el Bahari contain one vignette in which this scene is portrayed. Among Khnum's epithets are Khnum Nehep (Khnum the creator), Khnum Per-Ankh (Khnum, governor of the house of life), Khnum Khenti-Taui (Khnum, governor of the two lands), Khnum Neb (Khnum, lord), Khnum-Neb-Ta-Ankhtet (Khnum, lord of the land of life), and Khnum Khenti Netchem-Tchem Ankhet (Khnum, lord of the house of the sweet life).

Variant spelling: Khnemu.

Kholumolumo. In African mythology (Sotho of South Africa), a monster who swallowed all of the people and animals except for one pregnant woman. When the woman gave birth she named her son Moshanyana. He later attacked the monster and easily killed it because it could not move. Then Moshanyana opened up its stomach, letting out all of the people and animals. Though most were pleased, some men eventually grew envious of Moshanyana and plotted his death. He escaped three times but was killed on the fourth attempt.

Khon-ma. In Tibetan folklore, the Old Mother, who rides on a ram and is dressed in golden-yellow robes. In her hand she holds a golden noose, and her face contains 80 wrinkles. Her personal attendant is called Sa-thel-nag-po.

Khonsu (navigator, he who crosses the sky in a boat). In Egyptian mythology, a moon god, whose cult center was at Karnak, where he, his father, Amun, and his mother, Mut, formed a holy triad. In this triad Khonsu is represented as an unclad youth with the side lock of hair depicting youth in Egyptian art. On his head are the representations of the full and crescent moon. Khonsu was also a god of healing and aided both women and cattle to become fertile and conceive. One ancient myth tells how he saved a young princess from demonic possession. Once the king of Thebes prayed to a statue of Khonsu on behalf of the daughter of the prince of Bekhten. The god listened to the king's plea, nodded his head (the statue of Khonsu was provided with a movable head, which the priests manipulated), and promised to give his divine power to the statue that was to be sent to the city of the sick princess. The statue arrived in Bekhten, and its magical powers exorcised the princess of the demon that possessed her. The demon then spoke to Khonsu and acknowledged the god's superior power. Khonsu, the demon, and the prince spent a happy day together, after which the demon returned to his own dwelling place, and Khonsu returned to his home in the form of a hawk.

Variant spellings: Chons, Chunsu, Khons.

1719
Khonvum. In African mythology (Pygmy), supreme god, who renews the sun each day by throwing broken pieces of stars at it.

1720
Kibuka. In African mythology (Buganda of Uganda), a war god, brother of the demigod Mukasa.

Kibuka assisted the Buganda army by hovering above the battlefield in the clouds and shooting arrows down at their enemies. During one battle some women were taken prisoners. Despite a warning not to have sexual relations with any of the women, Kibuka brought one of them to his hut. As a result, in the next battle he was mortally wounded on top of a tree and later died.

1721
Kied Kie Jubmel. In Lapland mythology, a stone god worshiped as late as the 17th century. The images of stone gods usually were extremely crude, making it difficult to decipher whether a man or animal or some composite figure was represented. In a ritual connected with Kied Kie Jubmel, a male reindeer was selected for sacrifice. The reindeer's right ear was pierced and a red thread run through it; its blood was then preserved in a barrel. A priest took the blood, some of the fat, the antlers, the bones of the head and neck, and the feet and hooves; he anointed the idol with the fat and blood. The antlers were placed behind the stone image—the right horn with the penis of the animal attached to it, the left horn bearing an amulet of tin and silver worked together with the red thread. The elaborate ritual was performed to guarantee the worshiper good hunting and fishing. Kied Kie Jubmel was called Storjunka

(the great lord) in Swedish. The term is sometimes generically applied to stone gods.

1722
Kikimora (tormenting spirit). In Russian folklore, female house spirit who lives behind the oven, said in some accounts to be the wife of Domovoi, the male house spirit; sometimes said to be a *mora*, a person with two souls.

Kikimora appears in numerous folktales, though no precise image emerges. She looks after poultry and sometimes takes part in household tasks if the wife herself is diligent; if not, she causes havoc by making noises in the night and waking those asleep. Sometimes she causes women to tangle their spinning if they arise from their spinning wheels without making the sign of the cross. Anatol Liadov's symphonic poem *Kikimora* captures the capricious nature of the spirit. Ivan Bilibin's sketch shows a composite animal made up of chicken legs, semihuman hands, furry ears, horns, and a beaked face and wearing a peasant costume.

1723
K'ilin. In Chinese mythology, a unicornlike creature. The male, *k'i*, and the female, *lin*, are combined into a compound word. The k'ilin has the body of a deer, the legs and hooves of a horse; its head is like that of a horse or dragon, its tail like an ox or lion, and its horn is fleshy. Some Chinese works depict the animal as scaly, others as hairy. The k'ilin is a paragon of virtue and filial love. It walks so lightly as to produce no sound and does not hurt anyone. In Chinese legend the birth of Confucius was announced by the appearance of a k'ilin, and so was the philosopher's death.

In Japanese the creature is called a kirin.
Variant spelling: Chi-len.

1724
Kimon (demon gate). In Japan, gate placed on the north side of a garden; through it the spirits of evil are supposed to pass. A Shinto shrine is erected in front of the gate.

1725
King Hal. In American Southern folklore, an escaped slave who ruled a kingdom near the fork of the Alabama and Tombigbee rivers. His kingdom was destroyed when one of his subjects, another runaway slave, went back to his white master and reported where Hal and his subjects lived.

1726
Kinharingan. In the mythology of Borneo, creator of the world and humankind, along with his wife Munsumundok. According to one myth, Kinharingan

and his wife emerged from a rock in the middle of the ocean. They walked on the waters until they came to the house of Bisagit, the spirit of smallpox. He gave them some earth, and the couple proceeded to create land, sun, moon, stars and people. In exchange for the earth, however, Bisagit demanded that half of the people created by Kinharingan would have to die of smallpox. So every 40 years Bisagit comes to claim his due. In a variant myth, Kinharingan and his wife killed one of their children, cut it into small pieces, and planted the pieces in the earth; from it sprang all plants and animals.

1727

Kintu and Nambi. In African mythology (Buganda of Uganda), the first man and woman. Death did not want Kintu and Nambi to leave heaven for earth. Gulu, the sky god and father of Nambi, warned the couple of Death's wish, suggesting that they leave as soon as possible and not return to heaven for any reason. Nambi, however, returned to heaven to ask her father, Gulu, for some grain to feed her fowl. Death, who was Nambi's brother, took this opportunity to follow his sister to earth. Kintu became very angry when his wife came back to earth accompanied by Death, but Nambi told Kintu to wait and see if anything would happen. For a while both Kintu and Nambi lived very happily. They had many children. Eventually, Death came to their home and asked for one of Kintu's children to serve as his cook. After being turned down, Death asked a second time, but still Kintu refused, saying that Gulu would not be pleased to see his grandchild working as Death's cook. Death then threatened to kill the child if Kintu would not agree to give him up. Kintu did not agree, and the child died. In time more of Kintu's children died, so he turned to Gulu to find out what, if anything, could be done to stop Death's rampage. Gulu reminded Kintu of the warning he had given earlier, but nevertheless he sent Kaizuki, brother of Death and Nambi, to aid the couple. Kaizuki fought with Death but could not overcome him. Death went to hide in the ground, and Kaizuki could not get him to come out. Since then Death has lived underground and is always present.

In a variant myth Kintu lived alone with only one cow. Nambi came to visit him one day and fell in love with him. Before long, however, she had to return to her father, Gulu, the sky god. Nambi's relatives disliked Kintu because all he drank was milk, and they objected to her marriage. Gulu then decided to test Kintu and removed his cow, forcing Kintu to eat grass and leaves. Nambi, however, let Kintu know that his cow had been taken to heaven. Various tests were given by Gulu to Kintu, and in each one he succeeded. Finally, Kintu was allowed to marry Nambi. He was asked by Gulu to pick the cow that was his from among three large herds of cows that all looked alike. A bee came and told Kintu not only which cow to pick but which calves had been born to the cow while it was in heaven.

1728

Kirata-n-te-rerei (the most beautiful of men). In Micronesian mythology, ancestor of the people of the Gilbert Islands. The son of Te-ariki-n-tarawa, a hero, and Na Te-reere, a tree goddess, Kirata-n-te-rerei was so handsome that a woman could conceive a child by just looking at his handsome body.

1729

Kisagan-Tengri. In Siberian mythology, a war god worshiped by the Mongols. He protected the army, helped them locate the enemy, and then brought them victory.

1730

Kishimojin. In Japanese mythology, goddess of women in childbirth, prayed to for offspring; protector of the Buddhist world and of children in particular.

Originally, Kishimojin was a cannibal woman in Hindu mythology, mother of 1,000 children. One child, Bingara, was converted by the Buddha, and later Kishimojin also was converted. In one myth she was condemned to give birth to 500 children to pay for her evil deeds, earning for herself the title Mother of Demons. In a variation she was sent to hell and was reborn in the shape of a ghoul to give birth to 500 devils, of whom she was to eat one a day because in life she had sworn to devour all of the children in one village.

She was converted by the Buddha in her second existence.

1731

Kitamba. In African mythology (Mbundu of Angola), a king who ordered all of his subjects to join him in a state of perpetual mourning when his wife died. No one was permitted to speak or make any noise in public. Despite the fact that the lesser chiefs objected strenuously to the king's proclamation, Kitamba continued the mourning. A council of elders appointed a doctor to help resolve the matter. The doctor and his little son dug a grave in the floor of their home in their effort to reach the underworld to see the king's wife. Each day they dug deeper, and at last they succeeded in reaching the king's wife, who explained to them that no one once dead could return to the realm of the living. She gave the doctor her armlet so that Kitamba would know that the doctor had succeeded in reaching her. When

Kitamba saw the armlet, he finally permitted the mourning to end.

Kit Carson. 1809–1869. In American history and folklore, popular name of Christopher Houston, a frontiersman and guide who appears as a hero in many legends. One of Carson's contemporaries said that "Kit Carson's word was as sure as the sun comin' up" and "Kit never cussed more'n was necessary," making Carson a perfect subject for legend. Kit Carson appears in Willa Cather's novel *Death Comes to the Archbishop* and Joaquin Miller's literary ballad, "Kit Carson's Ride," included in his *Songs of the Sierras.*

1732

Kitpusiagana (born by Cesarean operation, taken from guts). In North American Indian mythology (Micmac), culture hero, second in power only to Gluskap.

1733

Kitshi manitou. In North American Indian mythology (Chippewa/Ojibwa), the great spirit, fullness of power.

1734

Kitsune (fox). In Japanese folklore, a character who appears in many folktales and folk beliefs.

1735

Kiyohime. In Japanese legend, a woman who destroyed the monk Anchin when he refused her sexual advances.

1736

Kiyohime was the daughter of an innkeeper at Masago at whose house Anchin, of the monastery of Dojoji, used to stay when on pilgrimage to Kumano. The monk petted the child, giving her a rosary and some charms, never thinking that her childish affection would one day develop into fiery love. However, the young girl's immodest advances soon became the bane of Anchin's life. As a result, her love turned to hatred, and Kiyohime called on the gods of the underworld to aid her in the destruction of Anchin.

Once Kiyohime pursued Anchin into the temple and he fled and hid in the great bell, which was ten feet high and weighed so much that 100 men could not move it. Approaching the bell, Kiyohime lashed herself into a frenzy. As she nearly touched it, the superstructure of the bell suddenly gave way, and the bell fell with a dull sound over the monk, imprisoning him. At the same moment the figure of Kiyohime began to change. Her body became covered with scales, and her legs joined and grew into a dragon's tail. She wrapped herself around the bell, striking it with a T-shaped stick, and emitted flames from all parts of her body. Her blows rained on the bell until it became red hot and finally melted. Kiyohime fell into the molten mass, and only a handful of white ash could be found, the remains of the monk.

The legend is used in a No play.

Knaninja. In Australian mythology, name for totem ancestors who live in the sky as spirits.

1737

Knecht Ruprecht (servant Rupert). In German folklore, the knight or servant of Jesus Christ, or St. Nicholas at Christmastime. In Germany, until the 19th century Knecht Ruprecht was impersonated by a man wearing high boots, a white robe, a yellow wig, and a mask. He would knock at the door on Christmas Eve or St. Nicholas Eve or Day (5 or 6 December) and say he had been sent by Jesus Christ to bring gifts to the children. Parents would then be asked if the children had been good. If the answer was yes, Knecht Ruprecht would give a gift to the children (provided earlier by the parents). If the children had been bad, he would give a whip or rod and tell the parents to use it on their children.

1738

Kohin. In Australian mythology, god dwelling in the Milky Way who sends thunder and lightning. He was once a warrior.

1739

Koi. In Australian mythology, generic name for the spirit of the bush.

1740

Kojiki (records of ancient matters). Book of Japanese Shinto mythology, written in Chinese characters, presented to the Japanese court in 712 C.E.

1741

The *Kojiki* is the oldest Japanese book. It was commissioned by the emperor Temmu (673–686), who wished to preserve native Shinto beliefs under the growing strength of Buddhism, which was taking root in Japan. The book is one of the basic sources for the study of Shinto mythology and belief.

The *Nihongi* or *Nihonshoki* (Chronicles of Japan), completed in 720, is the second most important text for Shinto, being twice the length of the *Kojiki*. It contains many of the myths of the earlier work, often giving variants. Many of the gods appear under different names. It traces myth, legend, and history up to 697.

1742

Kojin. In Japanese Shinto mythology, god of the hearth, sometimes portrayed with three faces and six arms, carrying a bow, arrows, sword, lance, saw, and bell. His shrine is usually located near a fireplace or stove in the kitchen. When his statue is placed in a garden, he is called Ji-Kojin (ground kojin). Sometimes he is portrayed by three thin plates of stone.

1743

Komdei-Mirgan. In Siberian mythology, a hero in a Tartar myth whose head was cut off and restored.

One day Komdei-Mirgan went to hunt the black fox and in doing so broke his leg. He did not know that the black fox was the daughter of Erlik-Khan, the lord of the dead. While Komdei-Mirgan was trying to get up, Yelbegen, a monster with nine heads riding a 40-horned ox, came and cut off his head. Yelbegen then brought the head to the land of the dead. Kubaiko, the sister of Komdei-Mirgan, went in search of the head in the land of the dead. After numerous adventures she succeeded in getting the Water of Life from God, which restored her brother to life.

1744

Kompira. In Japanese mythology, god of sailors and bringer of prosperity. He is portrayed as a fat man sitting down with his legs crossed, a purse in one hand.

1745

Konsei dai-myojin (root of life great shining god). In Japanese Shinto belief, word for natural stones that have phallic shapes. The term also is applied to a stone carved in the shape of a phallus.

1746

Kookinberrook and Berrokborn. In Australian mythology, the first men created, made by the god Pundjel. They married Kunewarra and Kuurook.

1747

Koopoo. In Australian mythology, the red-plain kangaroo responsible for cats having spots. One day Koopoo met Jabbor, the cat who lived in the area Koopoo was traveling through. Jabbor asked Koopoo to divulge to him half of the secret ceremonies of the kangaroos. Koopoo, of course, refused, saying that the corroborees—big dances—belonged only to kangaroos. Jabbor wanted to fight for the secrets, but Koopoo called on other kangaroos, who threw spears at the cat. This act resulted in many cats having spots, for each spot represents a place where a spear entered Jabbor's body. As the cat lay dying, Deert, the moon god, came by and told Jabbor to drink a special kind of water that would permit him to come back to life. The other cats, however, prevented Jabbor from getting to the water. Deert grew angry and declared that because of this act all things would have to die. Only he, Deert, would be able to die and return to life again.

1748

Ko Pala. In Burmese mythology, a king who returned to life as a crab. Ko Pala was chosen king when the ruler of the valley dwellers died with no heir to succeed him. The future king was brought in a basket and placed in the former king's house during the night. The people were so exhausted by the funeral ceremonies for the dead king that they accepted Ko Pala as the new king without any resistance. His reign, however, did not satisfy the people who had put him in the basket, so they placed him on an island and let him starve to death. After many reincarnations he returned as a crab when the entire land was flooded. He stayed until the waters had receded and then went to Loi Pu Kao (hill that the crab entered) and died.

1749

Koran, or **Qur'an, The** (the recitation). Sacred scriptures of Islam, consisting of material given as revelation to Muhammad, the prophet of Islam, during the seventh century C.E., and gathered together for publication by his followers.

Muslims believe that the Koran has existed in heaven from all eternity in a form called *Umm al-kitab*. A copy of this perfect text, which is part of the essence of Allah, was made on paper in heaven, bound in silk, and ornamented with gold and the precious stones of paradise. This sacred text was then given to the archangel Gabriel, who revealed it to Muhammad piecemeal, but he allowed the prophet to see the complete version of the book once a year. The night on which the complete Koran came down to the lowest heaven, where Gabriel could then reveal it to Muhammad, is called *Al Kadr*.

The Koran contains 114 suras or chapters (literally, rows or series), estimated to contain about 6,225 *âyât*, or verses (literally, signs), which in most cases mark a pause in rhythm. The suras are not homogeneous but are unsystematic clusters of fragmented text. Muhammad directed that each fresh revelation that was given to him by the angel Gabriel be "entered into such and such a sura." The final arrangement of the book consists of the longest sura first and proceeds to the shortest last, thus not following the chronology of revelation.

Suras are called either "Meccan" or "Medinan," meaning they belong to the period before or after the Hegira, the immigration of Muhammad from Mecca to Medina (Yathrib) in 622—the year 1 in Islamic reckoning. A sura often contains material from both periods, and scholars have produced various editions and chronological arrangements of the contents of the Koran.

The material of the Koran is highly varied. There are many praises to Allah that equal the majesty of the Old Testament. In many places the heroes of the Hebrew scripture appear in the Koran in legends rendered differently from the accounts in the Old Testament. Jesus and John the Baptist also appear, as well as the Virgin Mary, but here the legends stem not from the New Testament but from many apocryphal writings of the Early Church. Although scholars still debate the question, it is generally believed that Muhammad could not read nor write, so all of his tales that are similar to tales in the Old and New Testaments are thought to have been gathered from oral sources.

The Koran begins with the following sura, in which Allah is entreated as the God of compassion and of mercy (*Rahman*):

> Praise be to Allah, Lord of the worlds!
> The Compassionate, the Merciful!
> King on the day of reckoning!

A modern Muslim, Muhammad Zafrulla Khan, in his edition of *The Quran*, writes that "the Quran is verbal revelation and thus literally the Word of Allah. The reader needs to keep in mind that it is Allah speaking. . . . The Quran is extremely concise and is a masterpiece of condensation. It leaves a great deal to the intelligence of the reader, urges reflection and appeals constantly to the understanding."

Of course, Western commentaries (especially those written prior to the present century) have not necessarily seen the suras of the Koran in the same light. The earliest English translation was made in 1647 by Alexander Ross from a French version. Ross's attitude toward the sacred text can be gleaned from his "needful caveat" addressed to the Christian reader:

> Good Reader, the great Arabian Impostor now at last after a thousand years is by way of France arrived in England, and his *Alcoran* or Gallimaufry of Errors . . . hath learned to speak English.

The translator then goes on to condemn the prophet, who caused "silly people to believe that in his falling sickness . . . he had conference with the angel Gabriel."

Thomas Carlyle, writing in the 19th century, tried to find a *via media* to Muhammad and the religion he preached. Carlyle found the Koran "toilsome reading," yet at the same time he found merit in the "primary character of the Koran . . . its *genuineness* . . . sincerity, in all senses."

Whatever the Western view of the Koran, it continues as perhaps the most widely read book in the world, surpassing the Bible in its readership. Sura 56, speaking of the Koran, says "Only the purified shall touch it." The act of reading the Koran is called *Tadjwid*, and a good Muslim must be ritually pure before embarking on reading or even touching a copy of the sacred text.

There are numerous variant romanized spellings of the Koran, among them Al-Koran, Alcoran, Al-Kur'an, Al-Kuron, the Qur'an. Sometimes the Koran is called Al-Kitab (the book) or Al-Furgân, from the root word "to separate" or "distinguish." The Koran helps separate or distinguish truth from falsehood in religious doctrine.

1750

Korka-Murt and Korka-Kuzo (house man and house ruler). In Russian-Lapland folklore, household spirits who often take the form of the master of the house when they appear. They watch over the family, but if they are angry, they can bring nightmares or tangle the hair of those in the house. Since they are variable in their natures, a child is not left alone in the house because Korka-Murt and Korka-Kuzo might allow it to be kidnapped and replaced by a changeling. Sacrifices of black sheep often were made to the house spirits to appease them when they were angry. Other household spirits are Gid-Kuzo (cattleyard man), a spirit who looks after cattle, protecting them from beasts of prey; Murt's So-Muret (bathhouse ruler), a spirit who lives in a dark corner of the bathhouse and resembles a tall, middle-aged man dressed in a white shirt with wooden shoes. Sometimes he has only one eye. He appears before any great misfortune is about to take place. Obin-Murt is a spirit who protects the barn from fire and storm.

1751

Korobona. In North American Indian mythology (Warrau), heroine, raped by a man-serpent, who gave birth to a boy and girl. Korobona's brothers believed they had killed the boy but years later discovered that their sister had saved him. Angry, they killed the lad, cutting his body into pieces. They allowed their sister to bury the remains, and they returned home. Korobona collected her son's remains and placed leaves and red flowers over them. Then she noticed that the leaves began to move, and suddenly a fully grown man appeared, armed with bow and arrows. He was the first Carib warrior, who later terrorized the Warrau.

1752

Korupira. In the folklore of the Tupi Indians of Brazil, a forest demon. Korupira is often of a mischievous nature, but if he is in a good mood he will help hunters, teaching them the secrets of herbs. However, he does not like hunters to wound an animal, then leave it; each kill must be completed. Two folktales demonstrate the dual character of Korupira. Once, in return for some tobacco, Korupira helped a hunter. His only injunction was that the hunter not tell his wife of the transaction. The wife, sensing something was strange, followed her husband to the forest. As a result, she was killed by Korupira. A second folktale tells how Korupira was killed when a hunter tricked the demon into stabbing himself. After a month the hunter returned to get Korupira's blue teeth. When he struck the teeth, Korupira was restored to life. Not being especially angry, Korupira then gave the hunter a magic bow to hunt with, instructing him not to kill birds. The hunter disobeyed, and as punishment he was torn apart. But out of kindness Korupira replaced his torn flesh with wax, bringing the hunter back to life. Korupira then told the hunter not to eat hot foods. The hunter disobeyed and melted.

Variant spellings: Kurupira, Curupira.

1753

Koshin. In Japanese mythology, god of roads, portrayed with a fierce, scowling face and a third eye. He has either two, four, six, or eight arms. Two hands are folded in prayer. He is also portrayed with the sun and moon riding on clouds. Three monkeys, a cock, and hen are also sometimes included.

1754

Kossuth, Lajos. 1802–1894. In Hungarian history and legend, freedom fighter in the war of independence. He was the minister of finance in the first independent national government and later became governor of Hungary. Following the collapse of the new government he had to flee the country and later died in exile. Hungarian folklore has made him a symbol of freedom. When he appeared, some peasants believed he was a reincarnation of Ferenc Rákóczi, an earlier fighter for Hungarian freedom, who was to come back when the country needed him. Some of the legends attached to Kossuth stem from those assigned to King Mátyás, another popular figure in Hungarian folklore.

1755

Kostchei. In Russian folklore, an evil wizard whose soul is hidden in a duck's egg. Though often called deathless or immortal, Kostchei could die if one could find where the egg that contained his soul was hidden. If the egg was destroyed, Kostchei also would be destroyed. In Stravinksy's ballet *L'Oiseau de feu* (The Firebird) Ivan, the hero, finds the egg in the hollow of a tree and destroys it, causing Kostchei and his evil court to disappear forever. Kostchei appears in James Branch Cabell's novel *Jurgen.*

Variant spellings; Koschey, Katschel.

1756

Koyan. In Australian mythology, a tribal name for the good spirit. He is offered spears in worship.

1757

Kraken. In Western European folklore, a fantastic sea monster or sea snake. Tales about the kraken seem to have originated during the Christian Middle Ages with numerous seamen's accounts of monsters haunting the deep. The kraken was described by Bishop Pontoppidan in his *Natural History of Norway* as being a mile and a half wide with tentacles that could capture ships and bring them down. There is a tale of a bishop returning by sea to his own country, who spotted what he believed to be an island. He went ashore and celebrated Mass. When he returned to his ship, he saw that it was not an island on which he had stood but a kraken afloat. Tennyson's early poem *The Kraken* deals with the fantastic being.

1758

Kralyevich Marko. 1335?–1394. In Serbian legend, a hero believed to have lived for 300 years; he appears in Bulgarian and Rumanian legends as well. He is described as an upright man with a kind heart, even gaining the respect of the enemy Turks. One Serbian heroic ballad tells how he helped a Turkish princess, daughter of the Sultan Bayazeth, and was thereafter called "my foster son" by the sultan, while he called the sultan "my foster father."

1759

Kratti (spirit). A Finno-Ugric guardian spirit who watches the property of the house owner.

1760

Kravyad. In Hindu folklore a flesh-eating goblin or any carnivorous animal. The term comes from *Kravyad,* the fire that consumes bodies on a funeral pyre.

1761

Kriemhild. In the *Nibelungenlied,* sister of Gunther; wife of Siegfried. Siegfried gave her a girdle and the Nibelungs' gold. She later avenged his murder, then was killed herself. In the Norse version of the legend in the *Volsunga Saga* she is called Gudrun, and Siegfried is called Sigurd.

Variant spelling: Krimhild.

1762

Krishna (the dark one). In Hindu mythology, the eighth avatar or incarnation of the god Vishnu.

Krishna

Krishna was sent to earth to rid it of evil spirits who committed "great crimes in the world." His birth accounts vary somewhat in Hindu texts. The major myth tells how Krishna escaped from the slaughter ordered by his evil uncle King Kamsa (brass) of Bhoja. The king heard that his cousin Devaki would have a child who one day would destroy him, so he ordered that Devaki be killed. Devaki, however, convinced Kamsa that she would deliver to him all of her children. Taken in by the promise, Kamsa let Devaki live.

In the meantime in heaven, Vishnu knew what was to happen and went to the subterranean watery hell. He brought back six embryos (which were actually six demons) and placed them in Devaki's womb. He then placed there another embryo, which would be his brother Balarama. (There are variant accounts of the birth of Balarama.) Kamsa killed each of the first six offspring. When it was time for the seventh birth, Devaki seemed to have a miscarriage, though in actuality while she was asleep, the embryo of Balarama was transferred to the womb of Rohini (red, red cow), the wife of the sage Vasudeva. Thus, Balarama was born from Rohini, and Kamsa was no wiser. Devaki, however, thought all seven of her offspring were lost. When she was pregnant for the eighth time, with Krishna, she carefully guarded herself. At the same time Yasoda (conferring fame), also became pregnant.

The two gave birth on the same night; Devaki to Krishna and Yasoda to a girl. The sage Yasudeva, in order to save the boy, switched the children, placing Krishna in Yasoda's crib. When King Kamsa came and saw a girl in Devaki's crib, he was relieved. But he was still filled with anger and took the child "by the foot and whirled her around vigorously and dashed her violently to the stone floor." Miraculously the child "flew to heaven, unbruised."

Krishna's childhood was filled with wonders. Once Krishna and his brother Balarama were playing with some calves. Yasoda, Krishna's foster mother, became angry. To stop Krishna she tied him to a heavy wooden mortar in which corn is threshed and went on with her work. Krishna, trying to free himself, dragged it until it became wedged fast between two trees, which were then uprooted. The trees were two sons of the god of riches, Kubera, who had been trapped into the trees and were now free.

Kamsa, the evil uncle, once sent a demon after Krishna when he was wandering with cattle in the woods. The boy, seeing through the demon's disguise, seized him by the foot, swung him around his head, and dashed him against the ground. The next day another demon, in the form of a crane, attacked Krishna, locking him in its bill. Krishna became so hot that the crane released him, and then Krishna crushed its beak under his foot.

On another occasion Krishna challenged Indra, the storm god. Seeing the cowherds preparing to pray to Indra for rain, Krishna told them to worship the mountain instead because it provided food for their cattle, which in turn supplied them with milk. Acting on Krishna's advice, the cowherds presented to the mountain "curds, milk and flesh." This scheme was really intended to honor Krishna, for upon the summit of the mountain Krishna appeared, saying, "I am the mountain." Indra became so angry that he attempted to drown the people with a rainstorm, but Krishna lifted the mountain and sheltered his worshipers. Indra, defeated, later visited Krishna and praised him for saving the people; and Indrani, wife of Indra, asked Krishna to be a friend of their son, the hero Arjuna, who appears in the Hindu epic poem *The Mahabharata*.

In *The Mahabharata*, Krishna appears as the charioteer of Arjuna, reciting to Arjuna the *Bhagavad-Gita* (which forms part of the epic): "All the Universe has been created by me; all things exist in me." Arjuna addresses Krishna as "the Supreme Universal Spirit, the Supreme Dwelling, the Eternal Person, Divine, prior to all the gods, unborn, omnipresent." In the poem Krishna possesses a weapon, Sata-ghru (slaying hundreds), which is described as a stone set with iron spikes.

Krishna is highly honored as a great lover by the Indians. The love affairs between the *gopis*, girl cowherds, and Krishna are told of in the *Gita-Govinda*, an erotic love poem by Jayadeva, written about 1200. In the poem Krishna is portrayed as an extremely passionate lover of all the *gopis*. His main love, however, is for Radha, a married woman. (In some accounts Radha is said to be an incarnation of Lakshmi, the wife of Narayana, another incarnation of Vishnu.) When Radha's sister-in-law discovered the liaison she rushed to tell her brother Ayanagosha of his wife's infidelity. When Ayanagosha appears, however, Krishna transforms himself into the goddess Kali (a form of the great goddess, Devi) and Ayanagosha thinks his wife is worshiping the goddess. The *Gita-Govinda* in many ways resembles the Hebrew Song of Songs. As with the biblical work, Hindus have given this frankly erotic work a mystical interpretation. An Indian dance, Manipuri, originating in Manipur in northern India, narrates the loves of Krishna and the *gopis*. A ballet, *Radha and Krishna*, by Uday Shan-Kar also tells of the love affair.

On another occasion, when Krishna was dancing with a woman, the demon Arishata appeared in the form of a bull, attacking the party. Krishna seized Arishata by the horns, wrung his neck as if it had been a piece of wet cloth, and at last tore off his horns and beat Arishata to death with them.

Though a god, Krishna met death at the hands of a hunter, Jaraas (old age), who shot him with an arrow in the ankle, his only vulnerable spot. When he died, his spirit went to Goloka, his paradise. Dwaraka (the city of gates), which was holy to Krishna and was one of the seven sacred cities in Hinduism, submerged into the ocean seven days after his death. (The city is sometimes called Abdhi-nagari.)

The concept of Krishna as supreme god is late in Hinduism. Because Krishna is Vishnu, he is also called Hari, a title of Vishnu. The form *Hare* in Hare Krishna is the vocative.

1763

Kriss Kringle (little Christ Child). In Germanic folklore a corruption of the German *Christkindl*, who was said to walk through the streets on Christmas Eve. Children would leave a candle in the window to light the way and hope the Christ Child would bring gifts. Now Kriss Kringle is identified with St. Nicholas or Santa Claus, not the Christ Child.

1764

Krum-ku-dart-boneit. In Australian mythology, evil spirits who wake men at night, take control of their bodies, and force them to hop until they die of exhaustion.

1765

Kshandada-chara (night walkers). In Hindu mythology, evil spirits and ghosts who appear at night.

Kuang Ch'eng-Tzu

1766

Kuang Ch'eng-Tzu. In Chinese legend, a deified sage, credited with the power of controlling evil spirits and giving victory in war. He is portrayed standing with his face turned up and his arms folded, holding a medallion bearing trigrams from the I-Ching.

1767

Kuan Ti. In Chinese legend, a deified general, Chang Sheng, worshiped as a god of war and of literature.

He was a native of Shansi who fled his province after killing an official for sexually abusing someone. He was joined by Chang Fei, a butcher, and Liu Pei, a peddler of straw sandals. Eventually, Kuan Ti was captured and executed. In 1594 the emperor Wan Li conferred on Kuan Ti the title "Supporter of Heaven, Protector of the Realm." Kuan Ti is invoked to avert war, not to encourage it.

1768

Kuan-Yin (regarder of sounds) or **Kuan Shih-Yin** (regarder of the world's sounds). In Chinese and Japanese Buddhism, spirit of mercy, patron of children. Kuan-Yin is a Buddhist entity that manifests itself in whatever form is suitable to rescue human beings from physical and spiritual danger. Some forms are male; some are female. Thirty-three forms are commonly described, but the number is said to be infinite. Kuan-Yin is the Sino-Japanese version of the Bodhisattva Avalokiteshvara (a name of uncertain meaning), who is sometimes worshiped as the chief minister of Amitabha Buddha and sometimes worshiped independently. As the minister of Amitabha, Kuan-Yin is shown as a man, often kneeling toward the worshiper and offering a lotus, in which the worshiper will be reborn in the Western Paradise. As an independent figure, Kuan-Yin is most commonly depicted as a male with 11 heads and 1,000 arms (all-seeing and all-helping) or as a female holding a lotus, symbol of purity, a jar of healing water, or a wishing jewel. She may be accompanied by a child whom she will give to a woman who prays to her for offspring.

According to one Chinese myth, Kuan-Yin was the daughter of an Indian prince. Her name was Miao Shan, and she was a devoted follower of the Buddha. In order to convert her blind father, she visited him disguised as a stranger and informed him that if he swallowed an eyeball of one of his children he would have his sight restored. None of his children, when told, would consent to lose an eye. Miao Shan then miraculously created an eye, which she fed to her father, restoring his sight. She then persuaded her father to become a Buddhist by pointing out the folly of a world where a child would not sacrifice an eye for a parent.

In another myth Kuan-Yin was on her way to enter Nirvana when she paused on its threshold to listen to the cry of the world. She decided to stay in the world to teach mankind compassion and mercy.

An image of Kuan-Yin plays an important part in the plot of the movie *Three Strangers*, in which a sweepstakes ticket is placed under the image of Kuan-Yin to bring good luck. The ticket wins, and each of the three partners attempts to get all of the winnings—one even kills another. In the end no one wins.

In Japanese, Kuan-Yin is known as Kwannon or Kannon, and in various forms is known as Sho (the holy), Juichimen (11-faced), Senju (1,000- handed), bato (horse-headed), and Nyoirin (she of the wishing wheel).

1769

Kubera (ugly body?). In Hindu mythology, god of wealth and guardian of the north; married to Riddhi (prosperity). Kubera was the brother of the demon king Ravana and once possessed Lanka (Sri Lanka). However, his evil brother, Ravana, ousted Kubera and took control. After Kubera had done severe penance, he was given the gift of immortality by Brahma, who appointed him god of wealth. Brahma also gave Kubera a magic aerial car called Pushapaka (that of flowers), which contained within it a city or a palace. It was stolen by Ravana, but recaptured by

the hero Rama and used by him to carry his wife Sita back to their native city, Ayodhya. Later Pushapaka was returned to Kubera. Pushapaka is also known as Ratna-varshuka (that rains jewels).

In Indian art Kubera is portrayed as a white man, having eight teeth, a deformed body, and three legs. His body is covered with various ornaments. He receives no worship in Hinduism but is worshiped in Japanese Buddhism. In Hindu belief Kubera rules over the Yakshas, semidivine beings, sometimes good and sometimes evil, as well as the Guhyakas (hidden beings), minor spirits who are guardians of hidden treasures.

1770

Kuda Sembrani. In Malayan mythology, a magic horse able to swim through water as well as fly through the air.

1771

K'uei Hsing. In Chinese legend, a deified mortal worshiped as a god of literature. He is portrayed as an ugly man with a sea dragon, symbol of wisdom.

1772

Kuinyo. In Australian mythology, an evil death spirit who gives forth a repulsive odor.

1773

Kukulcán (the god of the mighty speech, a serpent adorned with feathers?). In the mythology of the Toltecs, an ancient Nahuatl people of central and southern Mexico whose culture flourished about 1000 C.E., culture hero and god.

One account of Kukulcán's life was written by Las Casas, a Roman Catholic bishop, in his *Historia apologética de las Indias Occidentales*, in an attempt to explain Indian religious belief vis-à-vis Christianity. According to Las Casas, Kukucán was a "great Lord" who arrived at the city of Chichén Itzá from the west with 19 attendants, all bareheaded and wearing long robes and sandals. They ordered the people to "confess and fast," which the people then did ritually on Friday. The bishop seems to be trying to show the similarity between Indian beliefs and Christian ones, and in his work he stresses the superiority of the latter.

In another account of Kukulcán's life, found in an Indian work, the *Books of Chilam Balam*, it is reported that the city of Chichén Itzá was settled by four brothers who came from the four cardinal points. They lived "chastely and righteously" until one left (or died). Two of the brothers then quarreled and were killed by the people, leaving only the last, who was Kukulcán. He calmed the people and helped them build the city. After he finished his work in Chichén Itzá, he founded and named the great city of

Mayapán, which was to become the capital of the confederacy of the Mayas. In that city a temple was built in his honor.

After completing his work Kukulcán journeyed westward to Mexico, or to some other spot where the sun set. The people said he had been taken into the heavens, where he watched over them and from which he answered their prayers. In Mayan art he is portrayed with a serpent's body, a quetzal's plumes, a jaguar's teeth, and a human head in his jaws. He is usually seated on the cross-shaped symbol of the compass.

Variant spellings: Cuculcan, Kukulkan.

1774

Kukumatz and Tochipa. In North American Indian mythology (Mojave), creators, twin brothers. Born of earth (woman) and sky (man), the two needed more room and raised the sky. Then they set the cardinal points and created the first people. In a variant myth, Mustamho, the son of a second generation of earth and sky, created the first people. In a myth told by the Walapai, part of the Yuman group that includes the Mojave, the names of the twins are Hokomata and Tochopa. In their myth the two brothers quarrel. Hokomata, jealous of his brother who brought the arts to humankind, taught men the arts of war. In a rage Hokomata caused a flood that destroyed the earth, saving only his daughter, Pukeheh, in a hollow log, from which she emerged after the flood. She then gave birth to a boy whose father was the sun and to a girl whose father was the waterfall. From these two the earth was repopulated. In the Mojave variant of the myth, Mustamho took some people in his arms and saved them from the flood waters.

1775

Kulhwch and Olwen. Medieval Welsh tale included in *The Mabinogion*. It tells of the hero Kulhwch's love for Olwen, the daughter of the giant Yabaddaden. The giant assigns tasks for Kulhwch to complete before he will consent to give him his daughter in marriage. Kulhwch is aided by King Arthur. The work is one of the first Arthurian romances.

1776

Kullervo (gold, dear one). In the Finnish epic poem *The Kalevala* (runes 31–36), a tragic hero, who unknowingly raped his sister, then in remorse committed suicide.

Kullervo was the son of Kalervo, who had been slain by his brother Untamo. Only one pregnant woman of the Kalervo clan survived, bearing Kullervo at Untamola (Untamo's farm). While he was still in the cradle, Kullervo planned vengeance on his uncle for the slaughter of his father and family. Kullervo grew up strong but stupid. His uncle sent the youth to the smith Ilmarinen, whose wife, the Maiden of Pohjola, immediately took a dislike to him. She gave Kullervo a loaf of bread with a stone in it. In revenge he had her killed by wild beasts.

Escaping from Ilmarinen's farm, Kullervo wandered through the forest, where he met the Old Woman of the Forest, who informed him that his father, mother, brothers and sisters were still living. Following her directions, he found them on the border of Lapland. His mother told him that she had long supposed him dead and that his sister, her eldest daughter, had been lost while gathering berries. The lad then attempted to do different kinds of work for his mother but succeeded only in spoiling everything he touched, so he was sent to pay the land dues. On his way home Kullervo met his sister (he did not, however, know it was she). He dragged her into his sledge and raped her. Afterward, when his sister learned who he was, she threw herself into a torrent. Kullervo rushed home to tell his mother of the tragedy. She dissuaded him from suicide, telling him to retire to a retreat where he could recover from his remorse. But Kullervo resolved to avenge himself on Untamo, who had murdered his father, and prepared for war. He left home to joyous farewells, for no one but his mother was sorry that he was going to his death. He came to Untamola and laid waste the whole district, burning the homestead. On returning home he found his house deserted and no living thing about the place but an old black dog, which accompanied him into the forest where he went to shoot game for food. While traversing the forest, he arrived at the place where he had raped his sister. The memory of his deed came back to him, and he then killed himself.

The tragic legend of Kullervo inspired one of Sibelius' greatest symphonic works, the *Kullervo Symphony*, written when the composer was 27 years old. Scored for soprano, baritone, male chorus and orchestra, it consists of five movements: (1) an orchestral introduction; (2) "Kullervo's Youth"; (3) "Kullervo and His Sister," for chorus, soprano and baritone, portraying the seduction and rape; (4) "Kullervo Goes to Battle," another orchestral section; and (5) "Kullervo's Death," for chorus. The symphony uses the text of *The Kalevala*. It was Sibelius' wish that after 1893 his *Kullervo* Symphony should not be performed. It was not played again until 1958 and first recorded in 1971, taking its place among the most creative and imaginative late Romantic symphonic works.

Kumara-sambhava (Kumara's occasioning). In Hindu mythology, an erotic poem usually translated as *The Birth of the War God*, about the love of the god Shiva and his wife Parvati (a form of the great goddess Devi) and the subsequent birth of their son Kumara. Some sections contain explicit sexual descriptions, and prudish editors have cut them out of their translations.

1778

Kumokums. In North American Indian mythology (Modoc) creator god. One day Kumokums found himself sitting by Tule Lake (in northern California) all alone. There was no land. So Kumokums reached down to the bottom of the lake and pulled up some mud and began to form land and the earth. When he finished that, he created life. Then, growing tired, Kumokums dug a hole and went to sleep inside. But it is believed he will awake one day.

1779

Kumu-honua and Lalo-honua (earth source and earth below). In Polynesian mythology, Hawaiian first man and woman according to some traditions.

1780

Kunapipi. In Australian mythology, the Great Mother goddess who formed the land from her body, produced children, animals, and plants, and taught humankind the gift of language. She is also called Waramurungundju and Imberombera.

1781

Kuninwa-wattalo. In Australian mythology, evil spirits who attack at night, strangling their victims with a cord.

1782

Kuo Tzu-i. Seventh century C.E. In Chinese legend, a deified mortal, worshiped as the god of happiness, often portrayed in blue official robes leading his small son, Kuo-ai, to court.

1783

Kupalo. In Slavic mythology, water god. After the introduction of Christianity, Kupalo's attributes were combined with those of St. John the Baptist, whose festival was celebrated on the same day as the pagan god's, 24 June.

Both water and fire were closely connected with Kupalo's worship, which continued after the coming of Christianity. A straw doll of the god, dressed in a woman's gown and decked out with ribbons and other female ornaments, was carried in elaborate procession to a river, where it was bathed or drowned or in some cases burned. In addition to the god's role as a water deity there were rites

connecting him to the worship of trees, herbs, and flowers. Among the Baltic Slavs, women would cut down a birch tree, remove its lower branches, dress it with garlands and flowers, and then sacrifice a cock to it. No men were allowed to take part in the ritual.

The fire-flower fern was the god's main sacred herb and was believed to control demons, bring good luck, and make one attractive to beautiful women. The only problem was that the fire flower was guarded by demons and could be procured only in the forest at midnight, the hour when the magical flower appeared. When it appeared, it climbed up the stalk and burst into flames. If a person then seized the flower and avoided the demons (who would appear as monsters), the flower would belong to the venturesome person. This all took place on Kupalo's Night, when trees could move from place to place and hold conversations. However, only if one possessed the fire flower could one understand the language of the trees.

1784

Kurra. In the Finnish epic poem *The Kalevala* (rune 30), companion of the hero Lemminkainen.

When Lemminkainen wooed the Maiden of Pohjola, he asked his former comrade-in-arms, Kurra, to join him in an expedition against Pohjola, the Northland. However, Louhi, the evil mistress of Pohjola, sent her son Pakkanen (Jack Frost) to freeze the hero's boat in the lake. The two heroes almost froze to death, but Lemminkainen, with his powerful charms and invocations, overpowered Jack Frost, throwing him into a fire. Lemminkainen and Kurra then walked across the ice to the shore, wandered about in the waste for a long time, and at last made their way home.

Tiera, another name for Kurra in *The Kalevala*, is a Finnish word for snow caked up under a horse's hoof or on a person's shoe.

1785

Kurriwilban. In Australian mythology, a cannibalistic female monster, wife of Yaho. She has an upright horn on each shoulder for piercing her victims, who are always men. Her husband, Yaho, kills women.

1786

Kururumany. In the mythology of the Arawak Indians of the Guianas, a creator god. Kururumany created man and all goodness, while Kulimina created woman.

One day Kururumany came down to earth to view his creation but was displeased to see that mankind had become corrupt and wicked. As punishment he took back the gift of eternal life and gave it to the serpents, lizards, and other vermin. Though Kururumany was a creator god, another deity, Aluberi, was preeminent over him. Aluberi, however, took no interest in the affairs of man.

Kururumany was married to Wurekaddo (she who works in the dark) and Emisiwaddo (she who bored through the earth), a name perhaps suggesting that she was the cushi-ant.

1787

Kvasir (spittle). In Norse mythology, the wisest of men; born from spittle when the Aesir and Vanir gods spit into a caldron. He was killed by the dwarfs Fjalar and Galar, who wanted his magic powers. After Kvasir's death his blood was distilled in the Odhrerir, the magic caldron, and gave wisdom and the art of poetry to any who drank it.

Variant spelling: Kvaser.

1788

Kwannon. In Japanese mythology, the name for the Chinese goddess Kuan-Yin, who in turn is derived from the Mahayana Buddhist being of mercy, Avalokiteshvara.

Variant spelling: Kwanyin.

1789

Kwaten. In Japanese Buddhist mythology, fire god derived from the Hindu god of fire, Agni, portrayed as a bearded old man with four arms. He holds a bamboo twig with a few leaves attached, a water vessel, and a flaming triangle, and he stands on a large flame. Sometimes he is dressed in flowing robes or is clad in a tiger skin. He is one of the Jiu No O, 12 Japanese Buddhist gods and goddesses adopted from Hindu mythology.

1790

Kwoiam. In Melanesian mythology, an ugly child who killed his blind mother when she cursed him for lifting a loop of her hair. He then killed his relatives and numerous other people, taking their skulls and decorating them. Eventually, he grew tired of murder and was turned into stone.

L

1791

Lacedamon (lake demon). In Greek mythology, son of Zeus and Taygeta, the daughter of Atlas; married to Sparta, the daughter of Eruotas, by whom he had Amyclas and Eurydice, the wife of Acrisius. Lacedamon introduced the worship of the Graces in Laconia and built a temple in their honor.

Clotho, Atropos, and Lachesis

1792

Lachesis (measurer). In Greek mythology, one of the three Morae (Fates), the others being Atropos and Clotho. Lachesis measured out the yarn that represented the span of life.

1793

Lado and Lada. In Slavic mythology, husband and wife deities who personified marriage, mirth, pleasure, and happiness. Slavic folklore, under the influence of Christianity, later equated Lada with the Virgin Mary. Lada is also the name for Cinderella in a Slavic version of the folktale, in which she is portrayed as a princess with a golden star on her broom.

1794

Ladon (he who embraces). In Greek mythology, a hundred-headed dragon who guarded the golden apples of the Hesperides; son of Phorcys (or Typhon) and Ceto. Ladon was killed by Heracles when the hero went to fetch the golden apples.

1795

Lady of Shalott, The. In Arthurian legend, a maiden who fell in love with Lancelot of the Lake and died because he did not return the love. Tennyson's poem *The Lady of Shalott* tells the tale.

1796

Lady of the Lake. In Arthurian legend, an enchantress identified with Nimuë or Viviane, the mistress of Merlin. She is responsible for the imprisonment of Merlin in a tree, for giving the magic sword to King Arthur, and for rearing Lancelot as a child. She lived in a castle in the midst of a lake that was impossible to pass. Lancelot was given to her as a child, and she plunged him into the magic lake with her. He was then called Lancelot of the Lake. She appears in Tennyson's *Idylls of the King*, James Branch Cabell's novel *Jurgen*, E. A. Robinson's poem *Lancelot*, and T. H. White's novel *The Once and Future King*.

1797

Laertes (ant). In Greek mythology, the father (or foster father) of Odysseus; king of Ithaca; married to Anticlea, daughter of Autolycus. According to some accounts, Anticlea was pregnant by Sisyphus when she married Laertes. Her son was Odysseus. Eventually, Laertes retired and Odysseus became king. Laertes was still alive when Odysseus returned from his wanderings after the Trojan War. He joyously received his son and aided Odysseus in dealing with the relatives of the slain suitors. Homer's *Odyssey* (book 11) and Ovid's *Metamorphoses* (book 13) feature Laertes.

1798

Laestrygones. In Greek mythology, cannibal giants who sank 11 of Odysseus' 12 ships and ate the men. According to Homer's *Odyssey*, the land where the Laestrygones lived had very short nights; so short that the shepherd driving his flock home would meet another shepherd driving his flock to pasture. The major city was Telepylus, founded by Lamus, and their king was Antiphates. The land has been located in Sicily and at Formiae in central Italy. The land of the Laestrygones is mentioned in Homer's *Odyssey* (books 9, 10), Ovid's *Metamorphoses* (book 14), and Horace's *Odes* (3.16.34) and is portrayed in a series of Roman wall paintings. The eight landscapes were found in 1848 and are now in the Vatican Library .

THE LADY OF THE LAKE
TELLETH ARTHVR OF THE
SWORD EXCALIBVR

Lady of the Lake (A. Beardsley)

La Fontaine, Jean de. 1621–1695. French author of fables, many based on Aesopic sources. The first volume of *Fables* was published in 1668 and added to until 1694. Witty and elegant, La Fontaine's fables are a mainstay of French literature. He was elected to the French Academy in 1683. He also wrote *Contes et novelles* (1664–1674), a collection of bawdy verse tales, based on popular *fabliaux* from France and other parts of Europe.

1800

Lahash (flaming?). In Jewish folklore, demonic angel who attempted to snatch away a prayer of Moses before it could ascend to God. As punishment Lahash and other angels who helped him were cast away from the Divine Presence and bound with fiery chains.

1801

Laindjung. In Australian mythology, ancestral figure, father of Banaidja. He rose out of the sea at Blue Mud Bay, his face foam-stained and his body covered with salt watermarks.

1802

Laius (having cattle?). In Greek mythology, king of Thebes; father of Oedipus; husband of Jocasta; son of Labdacus. An oracle had warned Laius that he would be put to death by his son, so when Oedipus was born, he ordered him killed. A compassionate nurse, unable to kill Oedipus, exposed him instead, and he was rescued and reached manhood. One day Oedipus encountered Laius on the road, not knowing Laius was his father. An altercation ensued over the right-of-way, and Oedipus killed Laius. The king was buried at the crossroads at the foot of Mount Parnassus, the place of his murder, by Damisistratus, king of Plataea.

1803

Lakshamana (endowed with lucky signs). In the Hindu epic poem *The Ramayana*, a half brother of the hero Rama and his constant companion. When Rama was to die, Lakshamana took his place and drowned himself by walking into the waters of the Sarayu River. The gods rained flowers on him and took him to heaven. Lakshamana's twin brother was Satru-ghna (destroyer of foes).

1804

Lakshmi (good fortune). In Hindu mythology, wife of the god Narayana (an incarnation of Vishnu), goddess of good fortune and beauty. Lakshmi is said to have four arms, but, since she is representative of beauty, she is usually portrayed with only two. In one hand she holds a lotus. In the epic poem *The Ramayana*, Lakshmi is called "the mistress of the

Lakshmi

worlds . . . born by her own will, in a beautiful field opened up by the plough." Lakshmi is also known as Jaladhija (ocean born); Lola (the fickle), goddess of fortune and therefore especially worshiped by shopkeepers; and Loka-mata (mother of the world). The heroine in Delibes's opera *Lakmé* is named after the goddess.

1805

Lamb. A young sheep. In the ancient Near East the lamb was often a sacrificial animal, appearing in both the Old and New Testaments as such. Jesus is called the Lamb of God (John 1:29) because he was sacrificed. In early Christian art the Twelve Apostles are sometimes portrayed as twelve lambs. The Book of Revelation (7:9–17) shows the adoration of the lamb. It is somewhat ironic that a church synod of Trullo held in 692 forbade the use of the lamb as a symbol of Christ.

1806

Lamech (wild man). In the Bible, O.T., fifth descendant of Cain; husband of Adah and Ziilah; father of Jabal, Jubal and Tubal-cain, inventors of musical instruments, animal husbandry, and bronze and iron weapons (Gen. 4:19–22).

1807

Lamia (gluttonous, lecherous). In Greek mythology, a fantastic being that sucked blood and ate human flesh; often in the form of a serpent with a woman's head; daughter of Belus and Libya. Lamia was a beautiful woman and a mistress of Zeus, whose children she bore. When Hera, Zeus's wife, discovered this, she killed all the children except for Scylla. In revenge Lamia decided to become a child-killer, and as a result of her evil she became a monster with the ability to remove her eyes at will. Keats's poem *Lamia* is based on a story he found in Burton's *Anatomy of Melancholy*, which in turn came from Philostratus (c. 170–240 B.C.E.) and tells of a young man, Lycius, who falls in love with Lamia. When Lycius discovers she is a serpent, she flees and he dies. Originally, Lamia may have been a Libyan goddess who was debunked by the Achaeans. Closely connected with Lamia, the Empusae had sexual intercourse with young men and sucked their blood while they slept.

1808

Lammas (loaf-mass). In British folklore, Christian feast held 1 August in which loaves made from the first harvest were blessed. The feast became confused with the feast of St. Peter in chains (1 August), when lambs were taken to church to be blessed, many believing that it was a "lamb-mass" not a "loaf-mass." In some parts of Scotland, menstrual blood was sprinkled on cows and on the floors of houses on Lammas Day to protect against evil.

1809

Lancelot of the Lake (lance; weaver's shuttle?). In Arthurian legend, one of the noblest knights of the Round Table, lover of Queen Guinevere. Legends do not agree about Lancelot. In most medieval tales he is the son of King Ban of Benwick and was called Lancelot du Lac (Lancelot of the Lake) because the enchantress Lady of the Lake had plunged him into her magic lake when he was a child. In almost all tales Lancelot is a great champion and the lover of Queen Guinever, the wife of King Arthur. He became the father of Galahad by Elaine, after he had been deceived into thinking he was sleeping with Guinever. When King Arthur discovered his relationship with Guinever their two armies fought. Peace was finally made when Lancelot killed Sir Gwaine. Lancelot came back to court to discover King Arthur dead and Queen Guinever a nun. He then became a monk and died. Lancelot appears in Chrétien de Troyes's *Lancelot*, Malory's *Morte d'Arthur*, Tennyson's *Idylls of the King*, E. A. Robinson's long narrative poem *Lancelot*, and T. H. White's *The Once and Future King*.

1810

Langsuyar. In Malayan mythology, a female demon believed to be the spirit of a woman who died in

Lancelot in combat (Louis Rhead)

childbirth. The original *langsuyar* was a beautiful woman whose child was stillborn. When she was told that the baby had become a *potianak*, or *nati- anak*, a demon in the form of an owl, she clapped her hands and without further warning "flew whinnying away to a tree, upon which she perched."

She is recognized by her green robe, her long tapering nails (considered a sign of beauty), and her long jet-black hair, which she lets hang down to her ankles. She wears her hair long to cover the hole in the back of her neck through which she sucks the blood of children. Her vampirelike proclivities can be successfully stopped if you can cut short her nails and hair and stuff them into the hole in her neck. Then she will become tame and act like an ordinary woman. Some myths report *langsuyars* who have married and had children. But they revert to their ghastly form and fly off at once into the dark forest if they see their children dance at a village festival.

To prevent a dead mother from becoming a *langsuyar*, glass beads are placed in the mouth of the corpse, a hen's egg under each armpit, and needles in the palms. If this is done, the dead woman cannot open her mouth to shriek or wave her arms as wings, or open and shut her hands to assist in her flight from the grave in her night-owl form.

Variant spelling: Langhui.

Lan Ts'ai-ho

1811

Lan Ts'ai-ho. In Chinese Taoist mythology, one of the Pa- Hsien, the Eight Immortals. She often is portrayed in a blue dress with one foot shod and the other bare. She is the patron of flower sellers and sometimes is shown holding a basket of flowers.

1812

Lan-yein and A-mong. In Burmese mythology, a brother and sister who possessed a magic drum. The two were happy for a while until one day Lan-yein, beating the magic drum, got a porcupine and served it for dinner. A-mong was wounded by the quills and believed her brother had intended to kill her. In revenge she destroyed the magic drum. She left for a village, where she married one of the local men. Lan-yein traveled to China, where he became "very powerful and very famous, and in the course of time was chosen Udibwa, or emperor of China."

1813

Laocoön (very perceptive). In Greek and Roman mythology, priest of Apollo and Poseidon at Troy; son of Priam and Hecuba. Laocoön offended Apollo by marrying and profaning the god's image. In the last year of the Trojan War he was chosen priest to appease Poseidon because the Trojans had slain an earlier priest of the god. When the wooden horse was brought into Troy, Laocoön hurled a spear at it, warning the Trojans not to accept the Greek gift. Laocoön said: "I fear the Greeks, especially when they bring gifts." But the Trojans paid no attention to his warning. While Laocoön was sacrificing to Poseidon, Apollo (or Athena) sent a massive serpent that crushed Laocoön and his two sons, Antiphas and Thymbraeus, to death. The Trojans believed it was because he had hurled the spear at the wooden horse, and they therefore accepted it into their city. Vergil's *Aeneid* (book 2) tells the tale. An ancient statue group, carved in Rhodes about 25 B.C.E. and found in the ruins of the Baths of Titus in 1506, was bought by Pope Julius II for the Vatican Museum. The work was admired by Michelangelo, Bernini, Titian, and Rubens. El Greco's *Laocoön* (c. 1601) portrays the scene with a view of Toledo in the background.

1814

Laodameia (tamer of people). In Greek mythology, a heroine; daughter of Acastus and Astydameia; sister of Sthemele, Sterope, and some unnamed brothers; wife of Protesilaus, the first Greek killed immediately on landing at Troy. In her grief Laodameia had a wooden statue made of her husband and slept with it every night. At first it was believed she had a lover, but when the truth was discovered, her father, Iphiculus, had the statue burned, and Laodameia cast herself into the flames and died. Laodameia appears in Homer's *Iliad* (book 2), Vergil's *Aeneid* (book 6), and Ovid's *Heroides* (which influenced Chaucer), where she is the symbol of a faithful lover. Wordsworth's poem *Laodamia* (1814) changes the tale by making her husband Protesilaus rail against his wife's passion and call for "reason," "self-government," and "fortitude."

1815

Laodice (justice of the people). In Greek mythology, daughter of King Priam and Hecuba. Laodice fell in love with Acamas, son of the Greek hero Theseus, when he came to Troy with Diomedes and an embassy to demand the return of Helen. Laodice contrived to meet Acamas at the house of Philebia, wife of the governor of the small town of Troas, which the Greek embassy visited. Laodice had a son by Acamas, whom she called Munitus. Afterward she married Helicaon, son of Antenor and Telephus, king of Mysia. When Troy was being destroyed, she threw herself from the top of a tower, or was swallowed up by the earth. In some ancient accounts her name is given as Astyoche. In Homer's *Iliad* (book 9) Laodice is the name used for Electra, daughter of Agamemnon.

1816

Lao Lang. In Chinese legend, the deified mortal Chuang Taung, worshiped as the god of actors. He is portrayed wearing a dragon crown and dressed in imperial robes. He is worshiped by actors before a performance because his patronage permits them to perform well.

1817

Laomedon (ruler of the people). In Greek mythology, first king of Troy; son of Ilus and Eury-

dice; brother of Themiste; married Rhoeo or Strymo; father of Astyoche, Cilla, Clytius, Hesione, Hicetaon, Lampus, Priam, and Tithonus; also father of Bucolion by Calybe, a nymph. Zeus sent Apollo and Poseidon to build the walls of Troy as a punishment for infringing on his royal rights. They did so but Laomedon refused to pay the gods, so Apollo and Poseidon sent a sea monster to ravage the land. Laomedon then called on Heracles to help save Troy and promised to pay him if he killed the monster. Heracles killed the monster but again Laomedon refused to pay. So Heracles took 18 ships to Troy and destroyed Laomedon and all his sons except Priam. The father and sons were buried in a tomb outside the Scaen gate. It was believed that as long as the tomb remained intact, Troy would not fall. Homer's *Iliad* (book 21), Vergil's *Aeneid* (books, 2, 9), and Ovid's *Metamorphoses* (book 12) all allude to the tale.

1818

Lao Tzu (old boy, master Lao). fl. c. 570 B.C.E. Chinese philosopher, traditionally considered founder of Taoism, the philosophy of the Tao (the way), worshiped as a deity.

Lao Tzu is believed to have been a contemporary of Confucius. He was the son of a high-ranking family, working for some time as an imperial archivist in Lo-Yang, but he left his position to lead a life of solitude. Many legends have grown up around his name. He had no human father, and his mother is said to have carried him in her womb for 72 years

Meeting of Confucius and Lao Tzu

before he emerged from her left armpit, able to talk. Lao Tzu's meeting with Confucius is frequently encountered in Chinese art. After the meeting Confucius was quite bewildered by the mystical Lao Tzu. He said, "I know how the birds fly, how the fishes swim, how animals run. But there is a dragon. I cannot tell how it mounts on the wind through the clouds and flies through the heavens. Today I have seen Lao Tzu, and I can only compare him with the dragon." What most upset Confucius about the Lao Tzu was his remark to repay "injury with kindness." Confucius' reply was that you give good for good, and justice for evil. But Lao Tzu said: "To those who are good to me, I am good, and to those who are not good to me, I am also good. And thus all get to be good. To those who are sincere to me, I am sincere; and to those who are not sincere with me, I am also sincere. And thus all get to be sincere." Lao Tzu is credited with writing the *Tao-Te-ching* (Book of the Tao and Te).

1819

Lapiths (flint chippers). In Greek mythology, a mountain tribe in Thessaly, related to the centaurs through descent from Ixion. The Lapiths came to symbolize civilization; the centaurs, barbarism. Ovid's *Metamorphoses* (book 12) gives a rich description of the battle between the Lapiths under their king, Pirithous, and the centaurs at the marriage feast of Hippodameia. The scene of the battle was featured in the frieze on the metopes (the section between the columns and the roof) of the Parthenon on the west pediment of the temple of Zeus at Olympia, and in the frieze of Apollo's temple at Bassae. Michelangelo did a sculptured relief of the battle, and Piero di Cosimo painted the scene.

Variant spelling: Lapithae.

1820

Lara, Infantes de (princes of Lara). 10th century. In Spanish history and legend, seven brothers who were killed by their uncle Ruy Valásquez in 986. The murder was arranged by Doña Lambra, Ruy's wife; she had the Moors perform the deed. The father of the boys, Gonzalo Gustos, was then invited to the hall of King Almanzor, the Moorish leader, to view his seven dead sons. The Spanish ballad, *The Seven Heads*, relates how the father, seeing the horrible sight, attacks Almanzor and his men and kills 13 of them before being killed himself. Another Spanish ballad, *The Vengeance of Mudara*, tells how Mudara, the son of Gonzalez, the youngest of the seven brothers, avenges the death of his father by slaying Ruy Valásquez and having Doña Lambra stoned to death. Juan de la Cueva's play *Tragedia de los Infantes de Lara*

and Angel de Saavedra's *El Moro Exposito* (the Moor in danger) deal with the legend.

1821

Lares (lords). In Roman mythology, spirits of the dead, worshiped at crossroads and in homes; children of Acca Larentia. Originally, the Romans buried their dead in their own houses, until it was forbidden by the laws of the Twelve Tables. Every house had a *Lar familiaris* who was the tutelary spirit of the family. His chief care was to prevent the family from dying out. The Lares' image, dressed in a toga, was kept in the family. The Romans greeted the Lares with morning prayer and an offering from the table. At the chief meal a portion was left on the fire of the hearth for the family spirits. Regular sacrifices were offered on the calends, nones, and ides of every month and at all important family functions, such as the birthday of the father of the family. On such occasions the Lares were covered with garlands, and cakes and honey were placed before them. Wine, incense, and animals also were offered up to them. Outdoors the Lares were honored as tutelary spirits. At the crossroads (*compita*) there were always two *lares compitales* or *vicorum*, one for each of the intersecting roads. They were honored by a popular festival, called *Compitalia*, held four times a year. The Emperor Augustus added the *Genius Augusti*, and commanded that two feasts be held in honor of these divinities in May and August. In addition, there were the *Lares proestites*, belonging to the whole city. They were invoked with the mother of the Lares and called Lara, Larunda, or Mania. They had an altar and temple in Rome. The Lares were invoked as protectors on a journey, in the country, in war, and on the sea, and they were associated with the Penates, guardians of the household stores. In contrast to the good Lares were the evil spirits, the Lemures.

1822

Latimikaik. In Micronesian mythology, creator goddess who arose from a wave beaten rock along with her husband, Tpereakl.

1823

Latinus (Latin). In Greek and Roman mythology, king of the Latini in Italy; father of Lavinia, the wife of Aeneas; son of Odysseus and Circe, according to Hesiod's *Theogony*, or son of Faunus and Marica, according to Vergil's *Aeneid* (books 7–11). In Vergil's account Latinus takes no part in the war between Aeneas and Turnus, though he arranges for a duel between the two to see who will marry his daughter Lavinia. Latinus also appears in Ovid's *Metamorphoses* (book 13) and Livy's *History of Rome*.

1824

Laurel. An evergreen tree or shrub encompassing many varieties such as sassafras and cinnamon. In Greek mythology the nymph Daphne, who refused Apollo's love, was transformed into a laurel tree. The tree was sacred to Apollo and his priestesses at Delphi; they chewed the leaves to bring on their oracular powers. Champions at the Pythian games, held in honor of Apollo's victory over the monster Python, were crowned with laurel wreaths. In Christianity the laurel is associated with triumph, eternity, and chastity and is a symbol of the Virgin Mary. In English folklore, if two lovers pluck a laurel twig and break it in half, each keeping a piece, they will always be lovers.

1825

Laverna. In Roman mythology, goddess of gain, both just and unjust; her altar was at the gate of Laverna in Rome. She was generally portrayed as a head without a body.

1826

Lavinia. In Roman mythology, second wife of Aeneas; daughter of King Latinus and Amata. She was betrothed to her relative Turnus, but an oracle had said she was to marry a foreign prince. When Aeneas killed Turnus, Lavinia's father gave her to Aeneas. After Aeneas' death, she fled the tyranny of Ascanius, her son-in-law and gave birth to a son, Aeneas Sylvius. Lavinia appears in Vergil's *Aeneid* (books 6, 7) and in Ovid's *Metamorphoses* (book 14). The name is believed to derive from the city of Laviniom.

St. Lawrence (Dürer)

1827

Lawrence, St. (from Laurentium, a city in Latium, a few miles from Rome). Third century C.E. In Christian legend, patron saint of brewers, confectioners, cooks, schoolboys, students, washerwomen, and glaziers; patron of Nuremberg and Genoa. Feast, 10 August.

Lawrence was a deacon of the church who gave away its "treasures" to the poor. He was arrested by the pagan Romans, and when asked where the treasures were, he refused to answer and was "stretched out upon a gridiron . . . burning coals under, and held . . . with forks of iron," according to *The Golden Legend*, a collection of saints' lives written in the 13th century by Jacobus de Voragine. Lawrence is often portrayed dressed in a deacon's vestment, either standing or holding the gridiron, with a censor, palm, or book in the other hand.

1828

Lay of Igor's Army, The. Anonymous Russian epic in rhythmic prose believed to have been written in the 12th century.

The Lay of Igor's Army is considered one of the monuments of early Russian literature and is placed beside such world epics as the German *Nibelungenlied* and the French *Chanson de Roland*, though it is closer in feeling to the Finnish epic poem *The Kalevala*. The 16th-century manuscript of the work was first published in 1800 with a translation into modern Russian, but the manuscript was destroyed in the burning of Moscow during Napoleon's invasion in 1812. Some scholars doubt that the poem is a genuine work of the Middle Ages, assigning it to some clever forger, though the majority of scholars now accept it as genuine. The lay tells of an unsuccessful invasion by Prince Igor against the Polovtzi, or Cumanians, and combines references to both Christian and pagan elements.

Alexander Borodin, one of the "Mighty Five" of Russian music, composed an opera, *Prince Igor*, based on the epic. The famous *Polovtzian Dances*, which are often performed in concert, are from the second act of the opera. They were also used for a ballet, *Prince Igor*, by Michel Fokine. Borodin's score was never completed, and Rimsky-Korsakov and Alexander Glazunov prepared the work for production. Anatol Liadov's symphonic poem *Ballad, In Old Days* was inspired by the epic.

In Russian *The Lay of Igor's Army* is called *Slovo o polku Igoreve* and may be variously translated as The Lay of Igor's Campaign, The Lay of Igor's Host, and The Lay of the Host of Igor. The novelist Vladimir Nabokov published an English translation, *The Song of Igor's Campaign*.

Another Russian medieval work, generally called the *Zadonshchina*, celebrates the 1380 defeat of Russia's Tartar overlords by the armies of Dmitri Donskoy, grand prince of Moscow, and quotes passages from *The Lay of Igor's Army*, implying that Dmitri's victory avenges Igor's earlier defeat.

1829

Lazarus (God my help). In the Bible, N.T., the name of the beggar in the parable of the Rich Man and Lazarus (Luke 16:19–31) and the name of the brother of Mary and Martha of Bethany and a good friend of Jesus. When he died, Jesus brought him back to life (John 11:1–57). In medieval Christian legend Lazarus went with Mary, his sister, to Gaul after the Crucifixion and became the first bishop of Marseilles, where he was later martyred. He is believed by some to have been the first bishop of Kition in Cyprus.

1830

Leah (wild cow). In the Bible, O.T., "tender-eyed" oldest daughter of Laban; sister of Rachel; wife of Jacob; mother of Reuben, Simeon, Levi, Judah, Issachar, and Zebulun. Through deceit by Laban, Leah was substituted in Jacob's marriage bed in place of Rachel, whom Jacob wanted to marry. For justification Laban explained to Jacob that Rachel was younger than Leah and could not be given in marriage before her older sister. Though Jacob loved Rachel best, it was Leah who bore most of his children, Rachel being barren until later in life.

1831

Leanhaun Shee. In Irish folklore, the fairy mistress who seeks the love of mortals. If they refuse, she becomes their slave; if they consent, they are hers and can escape only by finding another to take their place. The Leanhaun Shee leech their captives, and the mortals waste away. Death is no escape from her. According to William Butler Yeats in *Irish Folk Stories and Fairy Tales*, "She is the Gaelic muse, for she gives inspiration to those she persecutes. The Gaelic poets die young, for she is restless, and will not let them remain long on earth—this malignant phantom."

1832

Lear, King (sea). In medieval British mythology, king of Britain, son of Bladud; his legend is told in Geoffrey of Monmouth's *History of the Kings of Britain*. In this version of the legend, Lear was not defeated by his evil daughters and sons-in-law. Instead "Lear led the assembled host together with Aganippus and his daughter [Cordelia] into Britain, fought a battle with his son-in-law, and won the victory, again bringing them all under his own dominions. In the third year thereafter he died, and Aganippus died also, and Cordelia, now mistress of the helm of state in Britain, buried her father in a certain underground chamber." Cordelia ruled the kingdom for some five years and then two sons of her sisters attacked and imprisoned her, and she committed suicide.

Shakespeare's *King Lear* is believed to be based on Holinshed's *Chronicles*, which varies the tale, as does Shakespeare's play.

Variant spellings: Leir, Lir.

1833

Lebe. In African mythology (Dogon of the Republic of Mali), first ancestor to die.

When Amma the creator god finished the creation of the eight basic families, he then turned his attention to the organization of man's existence on earth. Lebe was required to feign death, and orders were given for him to be buried with his head pointing toward the north. The seventh ancestor, taking the form of a snake, swallowed his body and then vomited stones that fell into a pattern representing a human body. This arrangement of stones was believed to determine the nature of social relationships, especially marriages. The stones are regarded as a manifestation of the covenant between Amma and Lebe, who although not truly dead, pretended to be so that man might be given a life force. The shape of the Dogon home is symbolic. The door opens to the north, the direction in which Lebe's head pointed. Various features of the home are fraught with sexual implications: the ceiling, for example, is seen as male and the large central room as female. The flat roof is representative of heaven, and the earthen floor's significance is that Lebe was both buried and restored to life in the earth. The relationship of the ceiling to the floor is symbolic of the original union of god with earth.

1834

Leda (lady). In Greek mythology, an Aetolian princess, daughter of Thestius and Eurythemis; later queen of Sparta; wife of Tyndareus; mother of Clytemnestra, Helen, Castor, and Polydeuces (the Dioscuri). The best-known version of her myth says that Zeus, in the form of a swan, seduced Leda, who hatched Helen and Polydeuces from an egg, Castor and Clytemnestra having been fathered by Tyndareus. Leda and the Swan was a popular motif in both ancient and modern times. Homer's *Odyssey* (book 11), Euripides' *Helen*, Ovid's *Metamorphoses* (book 6), Spenser's *Faerie Queen* (111.11.32) and *Prothalamium* (41), Keats's *Endymion* (1.157), Yeats's *Leda and the Swan*, Aldous Huxley's *Leda*, and Rilke's *Leda* are some of the works that have dealt with the subject. Painters who have treated Leda are Michelangelo, Leonardo da Vinci, Raphael, Tintoretto and Correggio.

1835

Leek. An onionlike vegetable. The ancient Egyptians considered the leek sacred, viewing it as a symbol of the universe, each successive layer or skin of the vegetable corresponding to the layers of heaven and hell. The Hebrews in their exodus from Egypt, mentioned leeks among the foods they missed (Num. 11:5). In Roman belief the leek was a symbol of virtue and sacred to Apollo, whose mother, Latona, longed for leeks. In Welsh legend, St. David, a sixth-century bishop, ordered his men to put leeks on their heads to distinguish themselves from their Saxon enemies during a decisive battle. The Welsh won and credited the victory to the saint's move. In Welsh tradition it was the custom before plowing for the workers to share a common meal in which each had contributed a leek. In Shakespeare's *Henry V* Pistol ridicules the custom and is then forced to "eat the leek," a term that has come to mean to eat one's words.

1836

Le-eyo. In African mythology (Masai of Kenya), ancestor who lost the gift of immortality for humankind. Le-eye was told by God that when a child was being buried he was to repeat: "Man dies but returns to life; the moon dies but does not return to life." This, God told Le-eye, would ensure the rebirth of a person after death. When a child's body was being buried, Le-eye rushed to say the words, but in his confusion he said: "Man dies but does not return to life; the moon dies but returns to life."

1837

Legba. In African mythology (Fon of Benin), trickster of entrances and crossroads, the youngest son of the creator, often portrayed as the cosmic phallus or pictured looking at his genitals.

One myth tells how Legba and God, his father, lived on earth together in the beginning of time. Legba did only what God told him to do, but the people blamed Legba when something bad occurred and credited God for the good things that happened in life. Legba felt that this was an unfair situation. Why should he be blamed for evil? But God said that was how it had to be. One day Legba tricked God by wearing his father's sandals while stealing yams from God's garden. When a search for the thief was conducted, Legba suggested that God must have taken the yams in his sleep. God knew that Legba was trying to deceive him, so he went into the sky, telling Legba to visit him at night and describe what happened each day on earth.

In a variant myth Legba directed an old woman to throw her dirty wash water into the sky. This angered God, who went back to heaven, leaving Legba on earth to report to him the activities of man.

Legba is associated with the oracle of Fa. Each morning Legba climbed into a palm tree and opened Fa's eyes. A system was developed whereby Legba knew if Fa wanted only one or both of his eyes opened. God eventually told Legba to teach men the method of Fa divination so that they could consult the oracle on their own and in this way come to know their destinies.

Worship of Legba is also found in Suriname, Brazil, Trinidad, and Cuba and in the voodoo, or *voudun*, cult in Haiti and New Orleans. In Haitian voodoo mythology Legba is a "principle of life," and his symbol indicates both masculine and feminine attributes, making him a sign of totality. He is the guardian of the sacred gateway, the Grand Chemin, the road leading from the finite world to the spiritual one, and he is often addressed in rites thus: "Papa Legba, open the gate . . . open the gates so that we may pass through." Some sects called the red sects, the voodoo cult representing the demonic forces in the world, believe that Legba was actually Jesus. Legba was hung on a cross, they contend, to serve as an edible human sacrifice—which, they point out, is what is meant by the words used in the Catholic Mass: "This is my Body. . . . This is my Blood." Priests on the island of Haiti, however, use the name Legba as an equivalent for the devil.

Variant spellings: Leba, Legua, Liba.

1838

Leib-olmai. In Lapland mythology, bear spirit worshiped by the Scandinavian Lapps. Leib-olmai protected the bear, who was a holy animal, during the hunt. Only if proper prayers were made to him by the hunters would he allow them to catch the animal.

1839

Leif Ericsson. fl. 1000. In American history and legend, son of Eric the Red, who, according to some accounts, discovered part of North America. According to one account, given in the *Saga of Eric the Red*, Leif Ericsson was blown off his course during a voyage from Norway to Greenland and landed in a place called Vinland. During the 19th century there was a movement among Americans to prove that the saga and other accounts established that the Vikings landed on American soil before Columbus. Many scholars today believe that Leif landed on some part of the North American coast, but there is no agreement as to what part. In 1974 Yale University, owner of the Vinland Map, which indicated that Leif Ericsson discovered America, announced that the map was a fake. Longfellow's literary ballad *The Skeleton in Armor* about a mysterious tower in Touro Park, Newport, Rhode Island, accepts the structure as having been made by the Vikings. This belief is now generally discredited. Edison Marshall's novel *The Viking* is based on Longfellow's ballad. Gerard Tonning's opera *Leif Erikson* is in Norwegian.

Lei Kung

1840
Lei Kung. In Chinese mythology, a thunder god, portrayed as an ugly, black, bat-winged demon with clawed feet, a monkey head, and an eagle beak. He holds a steel chisel in one hand and a hammer in the other.

1841
Leippya. In Burmese mythology, the soul materializing as a butterfly that hovers about the body of the dead. During life, if the soul leaves the body, a person will become sick and die. Sickness is believed to be caused by wandering souls under the control of some evil person or witch. If a mother dies, she may come back as a spirit and attempt to steal the soul of her child. To avoid this, a mirror is placed near the child, and a film of cotton is draped on it. If the film slips down into a kerchief placed below the mirror, it is then laid on the child's breast, and the soul of the child is saved from its evil mother. The soul of King Mindon Min, who died in 1878, lived in a small, flat, heart-shaped piece of gold that was suspended over his body until burial.

1842
Lemminkainen (lover boy). In the Finnish epic poem *The Kalevala*, handsome hero noted for his romantic and heroic exploits.

Lemminkainen's love life forms a good deal of the narrative in *The Kalevala*. One of Lemminkainen's first feats was to find a wife among the women on the island of Saari. At first they mocked him, so Lemminkainen, in anger, carried off Kyllikki to be his wife. She, obviously a woman who liked to have a good time, reproached him for his fighting and he reproached her for her loose life. The two agreed, however, that he would not go to war and she would not go to the village dances. However, Kyllikki forgot her promise. Lemminkainen then left her and went in search of another wife.

Lemminkainen went to the land of Pohjola, the Northland, where he wooed the Maiden of Pohjola. Her mother, Louhi, the evil mistress of Pohjola, set tasks for the hero. He accomplished all of them, except for killing the swan floating on the River of Death. While he was attempting to kill the swan, a partly blind cattle herder, Markahattu, murdered Lemminkainen because earlier the hero had insulted him. Lemminkainen's body was cut into pieces by the son of Tuoni (Death).

Lemminkainen's mother learned of her son's death when his comb began to bleed. She hastened to Pohjola, asking Louhi what had become of her son. Louhi told her the tasks she had set Lemminkainen. Paiva (the sun) then told her how Lemminkainen had died. She went with a long rake in her hand under the cataract in the River of Death and raked the water till she had collected all of the fragments of her son's body. She then joined them together through magic charms and salves.

The Maiden of Pohjola was then given to the smith hero, Ilmarinen, who had forged the magic sampo for Louhi. Enraged at not being invited to the marriage, the resurrected Lemminkainen went to Pohjola and entered the castle by force, killing the husband of Louhi.

When he returned to his home, he discovered his house burned down by raiders from Pohjola, though his mother was still alive. Lemminkainen again went to Pohjola with his companion, Kurra, though they were defeated by the cold. He joined Vainamoinen and Ilmarinen on their adventure to steal the magical sampo, which, however, was lost in the lake, with only fragments coming to the top of the water.

Lemminkainen is often called Lieto (reckless) and Kaukomieli (handsome man with a far-roving mind). He is also called Ahto, the name of the sea god in *The Kalevala*, perhaps indicating that once he was a god.

These adventures appealed to Sibelius, who composed *Four Legends for Orchestra*, based on Lemminkainen's romantic and heroic exploits. The symphonic suite consists of four movements. (1) "Lemminkainen and the Maidens of Saari," dealing with Lemminkainen's seduction of all of the women on the island; (2) "The Swan of Tuonela," which captures the majestic swan floating on the River of Death; (3) "Lemminkainen in Tuonela," the hero's mother restoring her son to life after his murder; and (4) "Lemminkainen's Homeward Journey." Sibelius also composed three piano pieces called *Kyllikki*, evoking the legend of Lemminkainen's marriage to Kyllikki.

1843

Lempi (erotic). In Finnish mythology, personification of erotic love; father of the hero Lemminkainen in the Finnish epic poem *The Kalevala*. In the epic the mythical bay Lemmenlahti (rune 18) is a combination of *Lempi* and *lahti* (bay), suggesting that it was a trysting place for lovers. Lempi's wife, the mother of Lemminkainen, is not named in the epic.

Though Lempi was originally a man's name, it is usually given to women today. The female counterpart of Lempi is Sukkamielli (frenzied love).

1844

Lemures (ghosts). In Roman mythology, evil spirits of the dead who often appeared as skeletons and were known to strike the living with madness. To expel them from the house, expiatory rites were held on 9, 11, and 13 May. This three-day period was called *Lemuria* or *Lemuralia*. According to Roman belief, the feast was first instituted by Romulus to appease the ghost of his murdered brother Remus and was called *Remuria*, later corrupted to *Lemuria*. During the three days of the rites the temples were closed and marriages prohibited. It was the custom for the people to throw black beans on the graves of the dead or to burn the beans, as the smell of the burning beans was believed to make the ghosts flee. Ovid's *Fasti* (book 5) tells of the various customs associated with the feast.

Variant spelling: Larvae

1845

Lentil. Leguminous plant with edible seeds, an ancient food. The Hebrew Book of Genesis (25:29–34) tells how Esau sold his birthright to his brother Jacob for a bowl of lentil pottage. In one of the many versions of *Cinderella*, a folktale found throughout the world, Cinderella is often portrayed as having to pick lentils out of the ashes. In India there is a saying: "Rice is good, but lentils are life."

1846

Leonard, St. (strong as a lion). Sixth century. In Christian legend, patron saint of prisoners, captives, slaves, cattle, and domestic animals. Feast, 6 November.

Popular during the Middle Ages, Leonard's life is told in *The Golden Legend*, a collection of saints' lives written in the 13th century by Jacobus de Voragine. Leonard was a favorite of the king of France. Whenever he visited, he would ask the king to release a prisoner, and the king always complied. Becoming dissatisfied with court life, Leonard went to preach in the forest. One day the king came through the area, accompanied by his pregnant queen. Suddenly the queen began to have labor pains. When Leonard heard her voice, he prayed to God to ease her delivery. The king was so pleased that he offered "many gifts of gold and silver," but Leonard "refused them all, and exhorted the king to give them to the poor." The king then offered him the whole forest, but Leonard chose just enough land to build a monastery on. He called it *Nobiliacum* because it "had been given by a noble king."

It was once believed that any prisoner who invoked the name of Leonard would immediately find himself free.

1847

Leopard. A large, ferocious, spotted carnivore of the cat family, usually having a tawny color with black markings. In Greek and Roman mythology the leopard was associated with Dionysus and Bacchus, the god having his chariot drawn by the animal. In his poem *Ode to a Nightingale* Keats says he prefers to be carried on the "viewless wings of Poesy" rather than be "charioted by Bacchus and his pards." In medieval Christian folklore and symbolism the leopard represented cruelty, sin, lust, luxury, the devil, or Antichrist, depending on the context. In one massive medieval mural of the Last Judgment the leopard is shown devouring the bodies of the damned. Often in Renaissance paintings the leopard is portrayed accompanying the Magi, who have come to honor the Christ Child, as a symbol of the chained devil, eventually destroyed by Christ. In Dante's *The Divine Comedy* (Hell, canto 1) the poet is met by a leopard as he attempts to climb the hill of enlightenment. Most commentators on Dante see the animal as a symbol of his lust or luxury. But the panther, a black leopard, was one symbol of Christ in the Christian Middle Ages because it was believed the animal slept for three days and then emerged from its den with a roar. It was also believed that the panther's breath enticed all animals except the dragon. The dragon would flee to its den and fall asleep. The panther's sweet breath was seen as a symbol of the Holy

Spirit, which came forth from Christ. This gift pleased the whole world except the dragon, who was the devil, and therefore he fled to hell.

1848
Leprechaun (small body?). In Irish folklore, a small roguish elf. The leprechaun is noted for his knowledge of hidden treasure and his work on shoes. William Allingham, in his poem *The Leprecaun, or, Fairy Shoemaker*, tells how he came upon a leprechaun working on a pair of shoes. The leprechaun was:

A wrinkled, wizen'd, and bearded Elf,
Spectacles stuck on his pointed nose,
Silver buckles on his hose,
Leather apron—shoe in his lap—. . .

Just when the poet appears to have captured the leprechaun, the elf offers a pinch from his snuffbox and then flings the dust in the poet's face; the poet sneezes while the leprechaun escapes.
Variant spellings: Leprecaun, Luchorpain.

1849
Leshy (forest spirit). In Slavic folklore, a mischievous forest spirit, who can assume any shape. Said to be the offspring of a demon and a woman, a *leshy* will sometimes seduce a girl and take her to the forest, where he rapes her. Occasionally, a *leshy* will substitute an ugly spirit child for a real one. At the beginning of October the *leshies* disappear, indicating that they have died or gone into some type of hibernation, to reappear the next spring. Some Slavic folktales say the *leshy* marries. His wife is called *Leshachikha* and his children, *keshonki*. Béla Bartók's ballet *The Wooden Prince* uses some of the Slavic beliefs about *leshies* in its plot.
Variant spellings: Lesiy, Lesiye, Lesovik.

1850
Lethe (forgetfulness). In Greek and Roman mythology, river of forgetfulness in Hades (the underworld). In Vergil's *Aeneid* (book 6) the souls of the dead gather there to drink before they are reborn. Ovid's *Metamorphoses* (book 11) mentions Lethe as a river flowing around the Cave of Sleep, where its murmuring induces drowsiness. This passage in Ovid influenced Chaucer in his *Book of the Duchess* as well as Spenser's description of Morpheus in *The Faerie Queene* (book 1). In *The Divine Comedy* Dante says drinking the water of the river frees the souls from remembrance of their past sins. This image is used by Shakespeare in *Henry IV* when the new King Henry says: "May this be wash'd in Lethe and forgotten?" (Part II 5.2.72). Keats twice uses Lethe to mean death of the senses, in *Ode to a Nightingale* and *Ode to Melancholy*.

1851
Leto (stone). In Greek mythology, mother of Apollo and Artemis by Zeus; daughter of the Titans Coeus and Phoebe. Leto was called Latona by the Romans. According to Hesiod's *Theogony* (406), Leto was the "dark-robed and ever mild and gentle" wife of Zeus before he was wedded to Hera. But according to a later account, Leto was the mistress of Zeus after he was married to Hera. The Homeric *Hymn to Apollo* (attributed to Homer but not by him) tells how the goddess was pursued by the hatred of Hera but finally, with the aid of Poseidon, gave birth to her twins, Apollo and Artemis, on the island of Delos, which had been a floating island until that time but was thereafter permanently anchored in honor of the nativity of the twins. When Niobe said her children were more beautiful than Leto's, the goddess had Apollo and Artemis destroy all of Niobe's children. When the giant Tityus attempted to rape Leto, he was cast into the underworld forever. Leto also appears in Homer's *Iliad* (book 21) and Ovid's *Metamorphoses* (book 6).

1852
Lettuce. Salad vegetable with edible leaves; in European folklore, believed to cause sterility. In some parts of England a head of lettuce in the kitchen was thought to render the woman of the house childless. Lettuce also was believed to alleviate lung disease. Its leaf, similar in shape to a lung, was considered beneficial in sympathetic medicine. To eat a head of lettuce before or during a sea voyage would prevent seasickness and ward off storms. In North American Indian belief lettuce tea was given to a woman after childbirth to increase the flow of milk in her breast. Lettuce was eaten by the Egyptian god Set to make him potent; he kept a lettuce garden, from which he ate every day.

1853
Leucippus (white stallion). In Greek mythology, king of Messenia, son of Perieres and Gorgophone. His daughters, Hilaera and Phoebe, called Leueippides, were abducted by Castor and Pollux. Idas and Lycceus, brothers of the two girls, fought to rescue them. Castor was killed, but Polydeuces (Pollux) was allowed by the gods to stand proxy for him in the underworld on alternate days. The myth is told in Pindar's *Nemean Ode 10*. Rubens's painting *The Rape of the Daughters of Leucippus* illustrates the myth. Leucippus is also the name of a son of Oenomaus and Euarete, brother of Hippodameia. He dressed as a woman to get closer to Daphne, whom Apollo loved. Daphne and her followers, on discovering the trick, killed Leucippus with Apollo's darts.

1854

Leucothea (white goddess). In Greek mythology, the sea goddess Ino (she who makes sinewy), daughter of Cadmus and Harmonia, wife of Athamas, sister of Agave, Autonoë, Polydorus, and Semele. When her husband, Athamas, king of Orchomenus, was driven insane by Hera, he thought that Ino was a lioness and that his sons Learchus and Melicertes were whelps. Ino fled with her son Melicertes, jumped into the sea, and was transformed by Zeus into a sea goddess. Melicertes became a minor sea god. Ovid's *Metamorphoses* (book 4) tells her tale. In Homer's *Odyssey* (book 5) Leucothea rises from the sea in the form of a sea mew when Odysseus' ship breaks up. She gives the hero her veil to tie around his waist so that he can swim through the sea to the island of Phaeacia. Milton's *Comus* mentions the goddess in relation to her son Palaemon, a minor sea god.

1855

Leve (the high-up one). In African mythology (Mende of Sierra Leone), the sky god, often called Ngewo. At first Leve gave humankind all of its material desires. But soon Leve realized that greed was a large part of man's nature. "If I continue to give the people all they want, they will never leave me alone," he said. So one day Leve left mankind so that people would be less dependent on his gifts and would have to work to satisfy their needs.

1856

Leza (the one who besets). In African mythology (Central African peoples), sky god, creator of the world and culture hero.

Known to various African peoples, Leza is seen as creator and culture hero of various tribes. In one myth of the Basubiya, a Bantu people, Leza leaves for his sky home by a spider's thread after teaching the people various arts and how to worship him. When the people attempt to follow him by climbing his web, it breaks and they fall back to earth.

In a myth told by the Ila of Zambia, Leza is responsible for death. Once Leza caused the brothers, sisters, and parents of a small girl to die. In time all of the girl's relatives died. Left an orphan, she eventually married, but before long her husband died. After her children gave birth to their children, they also died. Leza then caused the aging woman's grandchildren to die too. To the woman's great surprise, however, each day she seemed to grow younger instead of older. She decided to build a ladder to the sky to ask Leza why he was doing these things. But the ladder crumbled before she could reach the sky, so she tried to find a road that would lead to Leza. She asked everyone she met where the road might be and told her sad story to all of the people along the way. They explained to her that all people were put into the world to suffer and that she was no exception. The woman never found the road to Leza, and like all others she died.

1857

Libanza. In African mythology (Upotos of the Congo), sky god and god of the dead.

Libanza, though chief god, was not the first god. He was born of the union of his father, Lotenge, and Ntsombobelle, his mother. Before Ntsombobelle gave birth to Libanza, she brought forth thousands of serpents, mosquitoes, and other vermin, all of them armed with spears and shields. Libanza roamed the earth after his birth. He married several wives and had one son. He fought many people, killed his brother, and fought his aunt. Sometimes he even restored people to life after he had killed them. His disposition, however, caused his mother and his sister, Ntsongo, to hate him. His mother abandoned him and his sister said to him: "You killed your elder brother and you very nearly killed your own father. Do you imagine that I do not hate you? No, I hate you, and I should be glad to see you die." Earlier, his sister had asked Libanza to pick some palm nuts from a tree. He began to climb the tree, which grew taller and taller, until he reached the heavens, where he found his dead aunt, his murdered brother, and Lombo, king of the air. He fought Lombo and gained complete victory over the sky.

Now Libanza lives in the east, while his sister, Ntsongo, inhabits the west. On the day when he goes to see her in the west, everyone will fall ill and many people will die. The day will come when the sky will collapse and fall on all people. This would have happened already had it not been for the *molimons*, the souls of the dead, who have begged and prayed Libanza not to let the sky fall. The moon is a huge boat that sails across the whole earth, picking up the souls of the dead and bringing them to Libanza. The stars are lit by the souls of the dead, who sleep by day.

Libanza is responsible for death. One day he summoned all the people of the moon and the people of the earth. The people of the moon came promptly and were rewarded by Libanza. He said, "Because you have come at once when I called you, you shall never die. You shall be dead for only two days a month, and that will be to rest; thereafter, you shall return more splendid than before." But when the people of the earth arrived, he said, "Because you did not come at once when I called you, you shall die one day and you shall not return to life except to come to me." This is the reason the moon dies once a month and comes to life after two days, and why men, when they die, do not return, but go to Libanza in the sky.

Libayé. In North American Indian mythology (Mescalero Apache), clown, first of the Gahe, mountain gods, to step forward and sing and dance himself into creation.

Libitina. In Roman mythology, a goddess who presided over death rites. Servius Tullius had a temple built in her honor, where everything needed for a funeral was sold. Lists of the dead were also kept in the temple. Originally, Libitina was an Italian goddess of voluptuous delight and of gardens, vineyards, and vintages. She was also associated with Venus and called Venus Libitina.

Lif and Lifthrasir (life and eager for life?). In Norse mythology, man and woman from whom the new human race will spring after Ragnarok, the destruction of the world, the gods, and the frost giants. The myth is told in the *Prose Edda* .

Siren (C. Corvinus)

Ligeia (shrill). In Greek mythology, one of the three Sirens; daughter of Achelous and Calliope; sister of Leucosia and Parthenope. Her name is used by Edgar Allan Poe as the title of a poem and a short story.

Likho (evil). In Russian folklore, personification of evil, the demonic aspect of Dolya (fate) portrayed as a poorly dressed woman.

In a beneficent mood Dolya protects the family, but if in an evil mood, she is called Likho and brings disaster. According to one Russian folktale, "The One-Eyed Evil," Likho is described as a tall woman, scrawny, crooked, and with one eye. According to the tale, a blacksmith and a tailor went in search of Likho, since they had never seen her. A short time after they arrived at Likho's house she killed the tailor and served him to the blacksmith for dinner. To save himself, the blacksmith told Likho that he could restore her lost eye if only she would let him tie her with some ropes. Likho agreed and was easily tied up, but just as easily she broke her bonds. A stronger rope was brought. She was again tied and this time was held fast as the blacksmith took out her other eye, making her completely blind. The blacksmith escaped by donning a sheepskin. He was nearly caught when his hand stuck to a golden ax in a tree. To free himself he had to cut off his hand because Likho, although blinded, was close behind him. When he arrived at his village, he told everyone what had happened: he had seen Likho, who not only left him with just one hand but also ate his companion.

Lilith (storm goddess). In Jewish, Christian, and Islamic mythology, female demon. In Jewish belief she was the first wife of Adam before Eve but was cast into the air for refusing to obey her husband. It was a medieval custom to place four coins on the Jewish marriage bed, which was to say "Adam and Eve" and "Avaunt thee, Lilith!" In the Old Testament Lilith is referred to as "the screech-owl" in Isaiah (34:14), "the night hag" in the Revised Standard Version. Islamic folklore says she is the wife of Iblis, the devil, and the mother of all evil spirits. She appears in Goethe's *Faust* and Dante Gabriel Rossetti's *Eden Bower*.

Lily. A large funnel-shaped flower. In ancient Egyptian symbolism the lily was sometimes interchangeable with the lotus; it was the symbol for Upper Egypt. In Greek mythology Zeus and Hera used lilies as part of their marriage couch. In Roman mythology Venus was associated with the lily. In European folklore lilies are used as protection against witches. In Christian symbolism the lily is associated with the Virgin Mary and often portrayed in paintings of the Annunciation. St. Joseph, husband of the Virgin Mary, often is portrayed holding a lily as a sign of chastity. The lily of the valley also is assigned to the Virgin Mary in Christian symbolism. This identifica-

Lily (Walter Crane)

tion stems from an interpretation of a verse in the Song of Songs or Song of Solomon (2:1): "I am the rose of Sharon, and the lily of the valleys." In Japanese mythology lilies stand for peace and tiger lilies for war.

1865

Lincoln, Abraham. 1809–1865. In American history and folklore, 16th president of the United States (1861–1865), called Honest Abe, the Rail Splitter, the Great Emancipator, and Great Martyr. He was born in a log cabin in Hardin (now Larue) County, Kentucky. His mother, Nancy Hanks, died in 1818. Lincoln settled in New Salem, Illinois, where he studied law, and worked as a storekeeper, postmaster, and surveyor. Becoming a lawyer in 1836, he served in the state legislature from 1834 to 1841. He fell in love with Ann Rutledge (1816–1835), and their supposed love affair has become part of Lincoln's legend. In 1842 he married Mary Todd. Lincoln served as president during the Civil War and was assassinated on Good Friday, just a week after the conflict had ended. He became for many Americans a Christlike figure. Emerson wrote that Lincoln had "become mythological in a very few years." It is often difficult to separate the historical man from the legendary one. Some of the main legends surrounding Lincoln follow.

He was, from early life, a keen reader, spending hours near the fireside reading. As a store clerk, he was credited with great honesty. One day a woman came into the store and purchased many goods, which Abe totaled at $2.26. Later, he again added the prices and discovered he had made a mistake. He went in search of the woman and returned the difference, earning for himself the name Honest Abe. Being over six feet tall and strong, he was also known as the Rail Splitter. As a young man he was often called on to fight the town bully.

Once Lincoln prayed at the bedside of a young Confederate soldier who was dying. The two repeated the well-known prayer, "Now I lay me down to sleep . . . ." Lincoln's religious faith formed the basis for many legends, but Lincoln was not connected with any religious organization or church. Many Lincoln legends deal with his death. According to some, the president had dreams of his impending death. His ghost is said to inhabit the White House.

Lincoln's life and legend have inspired many works, among them Walt Whitman's *O Captain My Captain* and *When Lilacs Last in the Dooryard Bloom'd*, Robert E. Sherwood's play *Abe Lincoln in Illinois*, Carl Sandburg's six-volume *Abraham Lincoln*, Aaron Copland's work for voice narrator and orchestra, *A Lincoln Portrait*, and various movies, including *Abraham Lincoln* (1925); *Abraham Lincoln* (1930), starring Walter Huston; *Young Mr. Lincoln* (1939), starring Henry Fonda; and *Abe Lincoln in Illinois* (1939), starring Raymond Massey.

1866

Lingam (penis). In Hinduism, the sacred phallus of the god Shiva. Various myths account for the origin of phallus worship in India. According to one myth, after Shiva's wife had immolated herself to prove her love, the god was taunted by a beautiful girl, whom he then raped. Her husband cursed Shiva, saying the god should not be worshiped in his own form but only by the instrument of his violence, the phallus.

In a variant myth, Shiva was wandering naked, and the wives of holy men, excited by his physical appearance, had intercourse with him. The holy men cursed Shiva so that his penis fell off. As it fell to the earth, it grew to an immense size, reaching into the heavens and into the deepest earth. The gods Vishnu and Brahma decided to find out how long Shiva's phallus was. Vishnu descended into the earth and Brahma ascended to the heavens. When the two met, Vishnu said he could not discover the beginning of the phallus, but Brahma lied and said he had touched the top. When Shiva appeared, he called Brahma a liar. In another variant myth, Shiva had intercourse in front of Vishnu and Brahma and, out of shame, cut off his penis.

Lingam worship in India takes many forms. Various metals, stones, and woods are used to construct the phallus. There are even portable *lingam* made of cow dung, butter, sandlewood, grass, and flowers. The *lingam* is normally set in the pan-shaped *yoni* (vagina) to express the union of opposites in Shiva. Members of the Hindu sect called Lingayat, in south India, wear *lingam* around their necks, as a Christian would wear a cross. One of the marriage customs of the Hindus was to have a bride deflowered in Shiva's temple by a carved *lingam* of the deity, thus making the child to be born a son or daughter of the god.

1867

Ling-pai (spirit white). In Chinese folk belief, a white paper or cloth streamer used in rites to call the souls of the dead back from the hells.

1868

Lion. A large and powerful carnivorous cat. In Egyptian mythology the lion or lioness was a symbol of the war goddess Sekhmet. In Greek mythology the lion or lioness was associated with Phoebus, Artemis, Cybele, and Dionysus. In Roman mythology the animal was associated with Juno and Fortuna. In Hindu mythology Narasinha, the fourth avatar of Vishnu, is portrayed as half man, half lion. In Near Eastern mythology the lion or lioness is associated with various manifestations of the great Mother Goddess, as well as the gods Marduk, Ninib, and Nergal. In the Old Testament the lion is a symbol of Judah, and in the New Testament it is a symbol of Jesus Christ "the lion of the tribe of Juda, the Root of David" (Rev. 5:5), as well as a symbol in Christian art for the Gospel According to St. Mark, patron saint of Venice. In medieval Christian symbolism the lion could also stand for the devil (1 Peter 5:8). In the requiem Mass St. Michael was called on to deliver the souls of the faithful "from the mouth of the lion, lest the jaws of the pit swallow them." In medieval folklore it was believed that lion cubs were born dead and given life by their father when he

The Lion and the Mouse

breathed on them. Though the lion was considered king of beasts, medieval folklore said the animal was afraid of creaking wheels, scorpions, fires, snake poison, and most of all, the cock. As a ruler the lion was known for kindness and mercy. Shakespeare in *Troilus and Cressida* (5.3.37–38) has Troilus say:

Brother, you have a vice of mercy in you,
Which better fits a lion than a man.

The lion's kindness is found in such tales as *Androcles and the Lion*, as well as in Aesopic fables.

1869

Lion and the Mouse, The. Aesopic fable found in various collections throughout the world.

A lion was asleep in his den one day when a mouse ran across his outstretched paw and up the royal nose of the king of beasts, awakening him from his nap. The mighty beast clapped his paw on the now thoroughly frightened little creature and would have made an end of him.

"Please," squealed the mouse, "don't kill me. Forgive me this time, O King, and I shall never forget it. A day may come, who knows, when I may do you a good turn to repay your kindness." The lion, smiling at his little prisoner's fright and amused by the thought that so small a creature ever could be of assistance to the king of beasts, let him go.

Not long afterward the lion, while ranging the forest for his prey, was caught in a net hunters had set to catch him. He let out a roar that echoed throughout the forest. Even the mouse heard it and, recognizing the voice of his benefactor, ran to the spot where the lion lay tangled in the net of ropes.

"Well, Your Majesty," said the mouse, "I know you did not believe me once when I said I would return a kindness, but here is my chance." And he set to work to nibble with his sharp little teeth at the ropes that bound the lion. Soon the lion was able to crawl out of the hunter's snare to freedom.

Moral: No act of kindness, no matter how small, is ever wasted.

In the Indian version the lion is replaced by an elephant, as elephants were often tied to trees as a preliminary to taming them. The Greek form of the fable reached Egyptian literature about 200 C.E. The German composer Werner Egk set the fable for narrator, chorus, and orchestra in 1931, for a radio program.

1870

Lion in Love, The. Aesopic fable found in various European collections.

A lion fell in love with the beautiful daughter of a woodman. One day he came to ask the girl's hand in marriage. It was only natural that the woodman was not greatly pleased with the lion's offer and declined the honor of so dangerous an alliance.

Then the lion threatened the parents of the girl with his royal displeasure. The poor father did not know what to do. Finally, he said: "We are greatly flattered by your proposal. But you see, our daughter is a tender child, and her mother and I fear that in expressing your affection for her you may do her an injury. Would Your Majesty consent to have your claws removed and your teeth extracted before becoming a bridegroom?"

So deeply was the lion in love that he permitted the operation to take place. But when he came again to the woodman's home to claim the girl, the father, no longer afraid of the tamed and disarmed king of the beasts, seized a stout club and drove the unhappy suitor from his door.

Moral: Even the wildest can be tamed by love.

The fable was told by Eumenes to warn the Macedonians against the schemes of Antigonus, called the One-Eyed. When the empire of Alexander the Great was divided at his death, Antigonus received Phrygia, Lycia, and Pamphylia. He eventually acquired the whole of Asia Minor. He was defeated and slain at Ipsus by allied forces in 301 B.C.E.

The Lion's Share (Arthur Rackham)

1871

Lion's Share, The. Aesopic fable found in various collections throughout the world.

The lion preferred to hunt alone, but now and then he would invite other beasts to accompany him.

On one such occasion the hunters cornered and killed a fat stag.

Taking a commanding position before the dead stag, the lion roared: "Beasts, it is time to divide the spoils. I demand that it be quartered. The first quarter shall fall to me as king of the beasts. The second is mine as arbiter. A third quarter is due me for my part in the chase. Now, as for the fourth part"—and here the lion gave an ominous growl—"let him take it who dares!"

Moral: Many may share in the labors but not in the spoils.

The companions of the lion in the Greek version of Phaedrus are a cow, a goat, and a sheep. In the medieval versions of Marie de France and Benedict of Oxford (whose tales are in Hebrew) the lion's partners are carnivorous, which seems appropriate to the setting.

1872
Lir (sea). In Celtic mythology, a sea god, one of the Tuatha De Danann, who was deeply devoted to his four children—Fionguala, a daughter; Aed, or Hugh; and Conn and Fiachra, twin boys—by his first wife, Aebh. His second wife, Aeife, became jealous and resolved to destroy the children. She took the children to King Borve the Red, a neighboring ruler, and through magic transformed them into swans. Because of her evil King Borve turned Aeife into a demon of the air. Then Lir and Borve set out to find the children, which they did, but they could not disenchant them. The period of transformation lasted 900 years. When they were finally released from their swan form by a Christian monk, they were old and withered. The monk, seeing that the angel of death would soon claim them, sprinkled each of them with water, baptizing them as they died.

The tale is told in the Irish *Fate of the Children of Lir*. Some believe that Lir is the original for Shakespeare's King Lear. The tale is also cited by James Joyce in his novel *Ulysses*.

Variant spellings: Llyr, Lear, Ler, Leir.

1873
Li T'ien-kuai. 13th century? In Chinese Taoist legend, one of the Pa-Hsien, the Eight Immortals. Li was a very handsome man. One day, as he was going up into the sky in his spirit form (after having mastered the Tao), he told his disciple that if his spirit did not return to his body in seven days, his body should be put in the fire. Six days passed, and the disciple had to go to see his sick mother. He left the body of Li unguarded. When the spirit of Li returned, it could not enter its own body but instead had to go into that of an old beggar. In art Li is portrayed as an old beggar with an ugly face, blowing

Li T'ien-kuai

his spirit into space in the form of a small human figure riding on a staff, horse, or frog.

In Japanese legend Li T'ien-kuai is called Ri-Tekkai.

1874
Little Red Riding Hood. Popular European folktale, found in many collections, among them Perrault's *Petit chaperon rouge* and the Grimms' *Rotkäppchen*. Believed by most scholars to be based on literary sources, the tale tells how Little Red Riding Hood is eaten by a wolf masquerading as her grandmother, or in some accounts, as her mother. Perrault ends his tale with Little Red Riding Hood's death and a short verse warning young girls to avoid wolves. In the Grimms' version a hunter appears who kills the wolf and slits open its belly, which allows the grandmother to reappear. In some variants the hunter kills the wolf before it has eaten Little Red Riding Hood.

1875
Liu Ling. 300–221 B.C.E. In Chinese legend, one of the seven Chu-lin Ch'i-Hsien (Seven Immortals). He was followed by a servant who carried a flask of wine in case he wanted a drink and a shovel in case he fell dead, so he could be buried where he fell. He is portrayed carrying a book.

In Japanese legend he is called Keiko.

1876
Livy. 59 B.C.E.–17 C.E. Titus Livius, Roman historian, whose *History of Rome*, originally in 142 books (of which 35 still exist) tells many Roman legends, such as that of Romulus and Remus. During the Middle Ages Livy's work was highly respected. Dante gave him high praise, and the Renaissance political

thinker Machiavelli wrote a commentary on some of Livy's work.

Lleu Law Gyffes (he of the steady hand?). In Celtic mythology, a culture hero among the British, often identified with the Irish culture hero Lugh, who was also a sun god. Lleu Law Gyffes was worshiped in Gaul and was the mythical founder of Lyons (Lugdunum), where he was known as Lugus.

Loa (laws). In Haitian voodoo, deified spirit of the dead who is looked upon as a god. The voodoo gods, called loas, *mystères*, or *voudoun*, are called forth from their other abode by the Houn'gan or Mam'bo (priest or priestess). They may enter a govi (special jar) or mount (take possession of) a voodoo follower. A loa that takes possession of a person completely controls all of the actions of that person, and the possessed loses all consciousness of self. The possessed person—called the *cheval* (horse) because he or she has been mounted by the loa—may prophesy, dance, and perform magic, none of which is recalled when the possessed awakens. A young girl, for instance, who is mounted by an old loa will become as feeble and practically as speechless as an old woman. Yet if an old man is mounted by a vigorous young loa, he will act like a young man. The sick who normally are unable to walk will dance and leap about. Generally, the entire personality of the mounted person is erased during the loa crisis.

The loas have sensitive feelings and are hurt by disrespect and sometimes cry when they feel neglected by the living. The word *loa* is believed to be derived from the French *lois* (laws), indicating a connection between man and the laws of creation.

Loch Ness monster. A lake monster said to inhabit Loch Ness in Scotland. In April 1933 a motorist driving along the shore of Loch Ness "saw" a fantastic animal some 30 feet long with a long neck and two flippers at about the middle of its body. It was also "seen" and described by others and made newspaper headlines. It is still one of the main attractions to the area. Does the Loch Ness monster really exist? The question still causes debate in Scottish taverns as well as in other English-speaking countries. Reports of the monster would seem to show that under the proper psychological and naturalistic conditions even our science-oriented age can conjure up a monster that can hold its own against fantastic beasts of ancient mythology.

Loco and Ayizan. In Haitian voodoo, two healing loas believed to have been the first houn'gan and mam'bo (priest and priestess). Loco acts as a doctor who heals and repairs the body, and Ayizan protects against malevolent magic.

Lohengrin. In medieval German legend, the Knight of the Swan, son of Perceval (Parzival) and Conduiramour, defender of Else, who was falsely charged with murder. Brought up with the Knights of the Holy Grail, Lohengrin was one day called to defend an innocent victim. He was told he would be conveyed to his destination by a swan. Perceval reminded his son that as a servant of the Holy Grail he must never reveal his name or origin unless asked to do so and that, having once made himself known, he was bound to return without delay. Guided by the swan, Lohengrin arrived as Else, charged with the murder of her brother, was waiting for a champion to defend her in a judicial duel. Lohengrin won the battle against Frederick, who had accused Else. Else then consented to become Lohengrin's wife without knowing his true name. The wedding took place at Antwerp, where the emperor, Henry the Fowler, came to celebrate with them. Lohengrin had cautioned Else that she must never ask him his name. But Else wished to know who her husband really was and finally asked the question. Lohengrin led her into the great hall, where in the presence of the assembled knights he told her that he was Lohengrin, son of Perceval, the guardian of the Holy Grail. Then, embracing her tenderly, he told her that "love cannot live without faith" and that he must now leave her and return to the Holy Mountain. After he had blown his horn three times, the swan boat appeared, and Lohengrin sprang into it and vanished. Some variants of the legend say that Else soon died; others say she lived on. The legend was used by Wagner in his opera *Lohengrin*.

Lokaloka (a world and no world). In Hindu mythology, a belt of mountains bounding the outermost of the seven seas and dividing the visible world from the regions of darkness. Lokaloka is also called Chakra-vada or Chakra-vala.

Lokapalas (world protectors). In Hindu mythology, the four guardians of the quarters of the earth: Yama, Kubera, Varuna, and Indra. Sometimes four other gods are listed: Agni, Vayu, Soma and Surya. They in turn are assisted by the Diggajas (elephants of the directions): Airavata, Pundarika, Vana, Kumuda, Anjana, Pushapadanta, Sarvabhauma, and

Supratika. The Diggajas are also called Dikpala (lord of the directions).

Loki (Aubrey Beardsley)

1884

Loki (fire, flame). In Norse mythology, evil fire-trickster god; son of the giant Farbauti and the giant-ess Laufey, or Nal. Loki's wife was Siguna; Vali and Nari were his children. He became foster brother to the god Odin and was numbered among the Aesir. Loki, or Loptur, is called Loge in Germanic myth-ology and in Richard Wagner's *Der Ring des Nibelungen*.

The *Prose Edda* describes Loki as "the calumniator of the gods, the contriver of all fraud and mischief, and the disgrace of gods and men . . . . Loki is handsome and well made, but of a very fickle mood and most evil disposition. He surpasses all beings in those arts called Cunning and Perfidy. Many a time has he exposed the gods to great perils, and often extricated them again by his artifices." Loki was responsible for the death of the good and fair god Baldur. When the gods discovered Loki's part in Baldur's death, they threatened him with punishment, so he hid himself in the mountains. He built a house with four doors in order to see everything that passed around him. Often he assumed the likeness of a salmon and hid himself

under the waters of a cascade called Franangursfors. One day he took flax and yarn and worked them into a net, but learning that the gods were approaching his dwelling, he threw the net into the fire and fled to the river. When the gods entered Loki's house, Kvasir, who was known for his quickness and knowledge, traced out in the hot embers the vestiges of the burned net and told Odin that it must be an invention to catch fish. The gods then wove another net, following the model that was imprinted in the ashes. They threw the new net into the river in which Loki had hidden himself. Thor held one end of the net, and the rest of the gods held the other, but they failed to catch Loki. The evil god had leaped over the net into the waterfall. The gods divided themselves into two bands: Thor, wading midstream, followed the net, while the others dragged it along toward the sea. Loki knew then that he had only two chances to escape, either to swim out to sea or to leap over the net. He chose the latter, but as he took a tremendous leap, Thor caught him in his hand. Being extremely slippery, Loki would have escaped had not Thor held him fast by the tail, and according to the *Prose Edda*, "this is the reason why salmons have had their tails ever since so fine and thin." The *Prose Edda* continues:

> The gods having thus captured Loki, dragged him without commiseration into a cavern, wherein they placed three sharp-pointed rocks, boring a hole through each of them. Having also seized Loki's children, Vali and Nari, they changed the former into a wolf, and in this likeness he tore his brother to pieces and devoured him. The gods then made cords of his intestines, with which they bound Loki on the points of the rocks, one cord passing under his shoulders, another under his loins, and a third under his hams, and afterwards transformed these cords into thongs of iron. Skadi then suspended a serpent over him in such a manner that the venom should fall on his face, drop by drop. But Siguna, his wife, stands by him and receives the drops as they fall in a cup, which she empties as often as it is filled. But while she is doing this, venom falls upon Loki, which makes him howl with horror, and twist his body about so violently that the whole earth shakes, and this produces what men call earthquakes. There will Loki lie until Ragnarok. (Blackwell translation)

In Wagner's music drama *Die Walküre*, Wotan, who corresponds to Odin, calls on Loge (Loki) to surround Brünnhilde with flames until a hero, Siegfried, frees her. Loki (spelled Lok) also appears in Matthew Arnold's narrative poem *Balder Dead*. Loki (Loge) is portrayed in Arthur Rackham's illustrations for Wagner's Ring Cycle.

1885

Lokman. In Islamic legend, Arabian sage and author of fables. In the Koran (sura 31) Lokman is credited with great wisdom given him by Allah. Muhammad honored him as the author of proverbs, some of which are recorded in the Koran. A few centuries after Muhammad's death Lokman was also credited with the authorship of numerous fables.

The life of Lokman resembles that of Aesop. He was a slave, ugly and deformed, who was offered by Allah the choice of wisdom or prophecy and chose wisdom. In one legend Lokman's master offered him a bitter melon to eat. After Lokman ate the entire fruit, his master asked how he could eat such unpleasant food. Lokman replied that he should take the unpleasant with the pleasant from his master.

The first collection of Lokman's fables appeared in the late 13th century and consisted of some 40 fables. Although derived mainly from a Syriac collection of Sophos, or Aesopus, there is one fable in the collection that has not yet been traced to another source. A thornbush asks a gardener to tend it so that it may delight kings with its flowers and fruits. The gardener waters the bush every day, and it eventually overruns the garden. The fable somewhat resembles the one told by Jotham in Judges (9:7–15) in its depiction of the thornbush's cruel nature.

Some scholars have believed that *Lokman* is a corruption of King Solomon's name.

Variant spellings: Luqman, Lukman.

1886

Longinus, St. First century C.E. In Christian legend, name given to the centurion who pierced the side of Christ when he was on the cross (Matt. 27:54). The lance became a cult object during the Middle Ages, with numerous churches claiming to possess it. Feast, 15 March.

In medieval Christian art St. Longinus is usually portrayed as a knight in full armor, in later Renaissance art as a Roman soldier with a spear or lance.

1887

Long Juju. In African legend, a prophet who lived in Nigeria during the period of the slave trade. Many people believed in his powers and therefore greatly feared him. He would sit at the entrance of a cave while visitors stood in the waters of a small river that ran alongside it and asked him questions, which he answered in a mysterious, nasal tone. He claimed to have the ability to tell which men were guilty of crimes and which were innocent. Those whom he declared guilty were sold into slavery.

1888

Lönnrot, Elias. 1802–1884. Finnish folklorist and compiler of *The Kalevala*, the national Finnish epic poem. The son of a poor country tailor, Lönnrot studied to be a doctor at the University of Helsinki, becoming a district medical officer at Kajaani in eastern Finland. He made extensive collections of traditional oral folk poetry among the Lapps, Estonians, and Finns in Karelia and northwest Russia. He first published *The Kalevala* in 1835 and expanded it in 1849. Aside from this monumental work, Lönnrot edited *Kantelator*, a collection of Finnish folk poetry consisting of 652 poems. Among the ballads are many that show similarity to those of central and western Europe, as well as Finnish versions of Christian legends. Through his efforts for a Finnish national identity, Lönnrot became one of the leaders of the nationalist movement, though more in the nature of a patriarch than a revolutionary.

1889

Lord of Misrule. In medieval European folk custom, a person who directed the festivities of the holiday season during Christmas, from the feast of Christmas to Epiphany, the Twelve Days of Christmas. He was sometimes called the King of the Bean, the Abbas Stultorum, the Boy Bishop, Abbot of Unreason, Abbot of Misrule, or Bon Accord. During his rule he was allowed to tell his "subjects" to do nearly any deed.

1890

Losy. In Siberian mythology, an evil giant snake defeated by the creator god Otshirvani, who took the form of a gigantic bird. In many Central Asian myths, Losy is called Abyrga.

1891

Lotis. In Greek mythology, a nymph, daughter of Poseidon. She fled from Priapus' lust and was transformed into a lotus tree. Ovid's *Metamorphoses* (book 9) tells her tale.

1892

Lot, King (covering). In Arthurian legend, king of Orkney, defeated by King Arthur. In Malory's *Morte d'Arthur* Lot is the father of Gwaine, Agravaine, Gaheris, and Gareth by his wife Margawse, who was also Arthur's sister.

1893

Lotophagi (lotus eaters). In Greek mythology, a fantastic people of coastal Africa who lived on lotus fruit. They were visited by Odysseus on his homeward journey after the Trojan War, according to Homer's *Odyssey* (book 9). Herodotus' *Histories* says the Lotophagi lived in western Libya. The fruit has been identified as the *Cordia myxa* (sour plum) by some writers such as Pliny in his *Natural History*. Whatever the fruit, it produced forgetfulness, making one lose desire for home. Tennyson's *The Lotos-Eaters* deals with the myth.

1894

Lotus. A water flower; in Egyptian mythology, associated with Osiris and his sister-wife Isis as a sign of life and resurrection. One Egyptian work portrays Isis emerging from a lotus flower. Egyptian mummies often held a lotus in their hands as a symbol of new life. In Hindu mythology Vishnu and Brahma are associated with the lotus. Brahma is called "lotus-born" and often portrayed as a giant lotus sprouting from the navel of the god Vishnu, the "lotus-naveled." According to Buddhist legend, whenever the Buddha walked abroad, he left not footprints but the mark of the lotus, the "fairest flower" of the East. In one myth he is said to have first appeared floating on a lotus.

1895

Louhi (witch of the wind?) In the Finnish epic poem *The Kalevala*, evil gap-toothed mistress of Pohjola, the Northland.

Louhi had two daughters, the lovelier being the Maiden of Pohjola, who was wooed by all three heroes in the epic: Vainamoinen, Ilmarinen, and Lemminkainen. Finally, after Ilmarinen forged the magic sampo for Louhi, he was given the bride. The sampo made Pohjola prosperous, and Vainamoinen decided to steal it for his land. He succeeded but was pursued by Louhi and her men. A great battle ensued in which the sampo was lost in the lake, with only a few pieces left floating on the waters. Louhi, angered because her land became barren after the loss of the sampo, sent a plague to Vainamoinen's land, but the hero healed his people by the use of magic. Not satisfied, the evil mistress then sent a great bear to ravish the herds, but Vainamoinen was again victorious. Finally, out of desperation, Louhi stole the sun and moon as well as fire from all of the hearths in Vainamoinen's land; but new fire was kindled by a thunderbolt from Ukko, the sky god. Ilmarinen then forged chains for Louhi, and out of fear Louhi released the sun and moon.

1896

Louis, St. (famous in battle). 1214–1270 C.E. In Christian legend, king of France. Commissioned *La Sainte Chapelle* in honor of relics of the true cross he obtained in the Holy Land. Feast, 25 August.

Louis was born at Poissy and came to the French throne when he was 11 years old. He defeated King Henry III of England in 1242 and twice made trips to the Holy Land. His life was recorded by his personal

St. Louis

friend Jean Joinville (1225–1317) in his *Historie de Saint Louis*. The work deals primarily with the first crusade of St. Louis and Joinville's relationship with the king. When the saint wished to make his second crusade to the Holy Land, Joinville writes that "those who recommended this voyage to the king sinned grievously." He therefore excused himself from the journey. Louis was responsible for the slaughter of many Jews on his way to the Holy Land. Louis died of typhus at Tunis, and his bones and heart were taken back to France and enshrined in the Abbey-church of St. Denis. They were lost during the French Revolution. Another portion of his relics was taken to Palermo and placed in the cathedral of Monreale.

St. Louis is pictured as a king crowned, with fleurs-de-lis on his mantle and scepter. Often a crown of thorns is also shown. El Greco painted the saint with his page (1585–1590).

1897

Lowa. In Micronesian mythology, creator god from whose leg the first man and woman, Wulleb and Limdunanij, emerged. The first couple had two children, one of whom tried to kill his father, Wulleb. Fleeing his murderous son, Wulleb descended to earth, and from his leg two more sons were born, the younger of whom, Edao, became a great magician.

Variant spelling: Loa.

1898

Luchtaine. In Celtic mythology, a woodworker god who made weapons for the Tuatha de Danann (the people of the goddess Danu) when they fought and defeated the Fomors.

1899

Lucifer (light bearer). In Christian mythology, name often given to Satan, though originally it probably referred to the morning star.

In Isaiah (14:4,12) the name Lucifer is figuratively applied to Nebuchadnezzar, "Take up this proverb against the King of Babylon. . . . How art thou fallen from heaven O Lucifer, son of the morning." St. Jerome, writing in the fourth century, as well as other Doctors of the Church, used the name Lucifer for Satan when commenting, "I beheld Satan as lightning fall from heaven" (Luke 10:18). In Christopher Marlowe's play *Doctor Faustus* and Dante's *The Divine Comedy* Lucifer is the king of hell. John Milton, in his epic poem *Paradise Lost*, applies the name to Satan before the Fall. A massive epic play, *Lucifer*, by Joost van den Vondel, the celebrated Dutch poet of the 17th century, has Lucifer as its main protagonist. George Meredith's poem *Lucifer in Starlight* treats Lucifer and his fall in a work tinged with skepticism.

1900

Lucretia. In Roman legend, daughter of Lucretius and wife of the Roman king Tarquinius Collatinus. She was raped by one of Tarquinius' sons, Sextus. Lucretia informed her husband and her father of the deed and then killed herself. Her rape so inflamed the people that they overthrew the monarchy and established a republic. The legend is told in Livy's *History of Rome*, Ovid's *Fasti*, Chaucer's *Legend of Good Women*, and Shakespeare's long poem *The Rape of Lucrece*, which forms the basis for Benjamin Britten's opera *The Rape of Lucretia* (1946). The subject has been painted by Botticelli, Filippino Lippi, Titian, Tintoretto, Cranach, and Veronese.

1901

Lucretius. c. 95–c. 55 B.C.E. Roman poet, Titus Lucretius Carus, author of *De rerum natura* (On the Nature of the Universe), which, in six books, is a Stoic and atheistic approach to the world. Book 1 opens with a magnificent address to Venus as goddess of creation. Parts of *De rerum natura* were translated into English heroic verse by John Dryden. According to a medieval legend first stated by St. Jerome, Lucretius committed suicide after being poisoned by a love philter. Tennyson's *Lucretius* deals with the poet's death.

1902

Lucy of Syracuse, St. (light). Third century C.E. In Christian legend, patron saint of eyes, cutlers, glaziers, notaries, peddlers, saddlers, servant girls, scribes, tailors, and weavers. Invoked against blindness, fire, infection, hemorrhage, and sore throat. Feast, 13 December.

Vowed to chastity, Lucy was arrested for being a Christian and ordered to sacrifice to the pagan gods. She refused and was placed in a whorehouse by the governor Paschasius.

"Here you will lose your chastity," said the governor to the girl. He then ordered some young men to "defoul her, and labor her so much till she be dead," according to *The Golden Legend*, a collection of saints' lives written in the 13th century by Jacobus de Voraghie.

The men tried to rape the saint, but the Holy Spirit made her so "heavy that in no wise might they move her from the place." Paschasius became so enraged that he ordered a servant to pierce her throat with a poniard. She died on the spot.

The legend connecting her with the loss of eyesight is a later medieval legend. A young man fell in love with Lucy because of her beautiful eyes. She plucked them out and sent them to him in a dish. The man became a Christian, and God later restored lucy's eyes.

1903

Lud. In Finno-Ugric ritual, a sacred grove where the spirits of ancient heroes were worshiped. Each family had its own Lud, though children and women were not allowed into the sacred grove. The Lud spirit who lived in the grove usually demanded a blood offering. A foal was generally the victim, but sometimes it was a black sheep. Before beginning the sacrifice the people ascertained whether the Lud spirit would accept the offering by pouring fresh water and twigs over the sacrificial animal as they recited prayers. If the animal shivered, it indicated that the sacrifice was acceptable to the Lud spirit.

1904

Ludd. In Celtic mythology, British sea god, believed equivalent to Nudd (Lludd), a god and king of the Tuatha de Danann. Ludd's temple in London was located near St. Paul's Cathedral, and Ludgate Hill is named after the god. He was called Llawereint (silver handed) because a silver artificial hand replaced one of his hands that had been cut off. In later Celtic mythology, Ludd is the name of a British king, founder of London, buried at Ludgate. The later version is probably a mortal form of the earlier god.

Variant spelling: Lud.

1905

Ludki (little people). In Slavic folklore, dwarfs who originally inhabited Serbia but left when Christianity arrived because they could not stand the sound of church bells. They were small, with large heads and big protruding eyes, and they wore large red hats. They taught mankind how to build homes, and they were fond of music and singing. Gifted with the art of prophecy, they often helped human beings but found it difficult to get along with one another. When one died, his body was burned and his ashes put in a vessel that was buried in the earth. The tears shed at the funeral were collected in small jars and placed in ancient cemeteries. In Poland the dwarfs are called *krasnoludi* or *krasnoludki*; in Hungary, *lutky*.

1906

Lugulbanda. In Near Eastern mythology (Babylonian-Assyrian), shepherd god, who appears as a protector and father of the hero in the epic poem *Gilgamesh*. Some myths say that Lugulbanda slew the monster bird, Zu, who had stolen the tablets of fate from the gods.

St. Luke painting the Madonna

1907

Luke, St. (from Lucama, a district in Southern Italy). First century C.E. Evangelist, author of the Gospel that bears his name and the Acts of the Apostles in the New Testament. Patron saint of artists and physicians. Feast, 18 October.

Luke was the beloved physician (Col. 4:14) of St. Paul in many of his missionary journeys. He accompanied Paul to Rome where he remained with his master and teacher until Paul's martyrdom, according to Christian legend not included in the New Testament. After the death of St. Peter and St. Paul (who were both executed on the same day, according to legend) Luke preached the gospel in Greece and Egypt. There are two traditions regarding his death. In the Greek church he is believed to have died a natural death; in the Western church he is believed to have been crucified at Patras with St. Andrew.

The belief that St. Luke was a painter comes from a Greek legend of the tenth century. A picture of the Virgin Mary was found in the catacombs with an inscription "One of the seven painted by Luca." It was assumed that "Luca" of the inscription was St. Luke. Legend expanded the identification: the Evangelist always carried two portraits with him, one of Christ and another of the Virgin Mary, which he had painted from life.

Numerous medieval European churches displayed "Black Madonnas" that were ascribed to St. Luke because of their age. They are usually black from the smoke of the burning candles that has encrusted the works. Numerous medieval Christian art works portray St. Luke in the process of painting the Madonna and Child. When St. Luke is portrayed as an Evangelist, an ox (winged or unwinged) is often shown with him or made to symbolize the saint.

1908

Luna (the moon). In Roman mythology, ancient Italian mood goddess; identified by the Romans with the Greek goddess Artemis, who was also associated with the moon. Luna had an ancient sanctuary in Rome on the Aventine, in which as goddess ruling the month she received worship on the last day of March, which was the first month of the old Roman year. As Noctiluca (lamps of the night) Luna had a temple on the Palatine that was lit at night.

1909

Lung-rta (wind horse). In Tibetan Buddhism, fantastic horse often found on flags, symbolizing the wind. According to L. Austine Waddell in *The Buddhism of Tibet, or Lamaism*: "The symbol is avowedly a luck-commanding talisman for enhancing the grandeur of the votary."

1910

Lung Wang (dragon king). In Chinese mythology, a general word for a dragon. Dragons control waters and especially rain.

1911

Luonnotar. In Finnish mythology, creator goddess, daughter of air or the heavens in the epic poem *The Kalevala*, who brought about creation.

The opening of *The Kalevala* tells how Luonnotar had spent her life "all alone in the vast emptiness of space." She descended from the heavens, and the waves carried her for 700 years. "The breath of the wind caressed her bosom and the sea made her fertile" as she was tossed by the waves. Then a gull, teal, eagle, or duck (the animal is not exactly identified) came "flying from the horizon," and Luonnotar "lifted her knees from the waves, and on it the bird made her nest and began to hatch her eggs." The girl became excited and felt heat "till she thought her knee was burning" and her "veins were melting." She jerked her knees, and the eggs rolled into the water and were shattered. From the lower fragments of the eggs the solid earth was fashioned, and the cracked eggs' upper fragments became the "lofty arch of heaven." The egg yolks became the sun; the whites, the gleaming moon. The spotted fragments became the stars and the black fragments were the clouds. Luonnotar went on to create capes, bays, seashores, and the depths and shallows of the oceans. Now the water mother, she gave birth to Vainamoinen, the culture hero and demigod in the epic poem.

Sibelius set part of *The Kalevala* text of the creation to music for female soloist and orchestra, calling the work *Luonnotar*.

Variant spelling: Ilnatar.

Lu Pan. In Chinese legend, a deified mortal, worshiped as the god of carpenters and artisans. [1912]

Lupus, St. Seventh century. Bishop of Sens. Feast, 1 September. He could restore sight to the blind and convert heathens by his numerous miracles. Once when he was celebrating Mass, a "precious stone" dropped miraculously into his chalice. It is kept as a relic in the cathedral of Sens treasury. Also kept is Lupus's ring, which was once dropped into a river but was recovered in the belly of a fish. [1913]

Lutin. In Haitian voodoo, the ghost of an unbaptized child, which wanders about never finding rest. [1914]

Lu Tung-pin

Lu Tung-pin. Eighth century C.E. In Chinese Taoist mythology, one of the Pa-Hsien, the Eight Immortals. A scholar and recluse, he attained immortality at the age of 50. He is a patron of barbers, and the sick invoke him. In art he holds a Taoist fly brush and sword, which he uses to fight monsters. He was given the sword after he was tempted ten times and overcame evil. [1915]

Lycaon (deluding wolf). In Greek mythology, a wolfman, king of Arcadia; son of Pelasgus; father of Callisto and 50 sons. Accounts of Lycaon vary. In some myths he appears as impious; in others, as a culture hero. According to one myth, Lycaon's sons were evil, having slain their brother Nyctimus and offering the child in a soup to Zeus (who had disguised himself as a poor laborer). In anger Zeus slew all of the sons with a thunderbolt, restored Nyctimus to life, and transformed Lycaon into a wolf. In a variant account Lycaon himself offered the human flesh to test whether Zeus was really a god. In disgust Zeus sent a flood to destroy the earth; only Deucalion and his wife, Pyrrha, were saved. In yet another variant, Lycaon was a priest of Zeus Lycaeus and was spared death, though his children were killed. Some scholars believe that the myth is related to the cannibalism that was part of the cult of Zeus Lycaeus, in which it was believed that those who ate human flesh were turned into a wolves and wandered in the wild for eight or ten years before being able to return to human form—and then only if they did not eat any more human flesh. Ovid's *Metamorphoses* (book 1) and Vergil's *Georgics* (1.138) deal with the myth. [1916]

Lynx. A wildcat having long limbs, tufted ears, and a short tail. In Egyptian mythology the lynx was called Maftet and regarded as a friend of the dead. In ancient Greek folklore it was believed that the lynx could see through walls or even a mountain. In medieval Christian belief the animal was a symbol of the omniscience and vigilance of Christ because of the belief in its magical sight. But it was also a symbol of avarice. Its urine was believed to harden into precious stones, which the greedy beast buried in the earth so no one could enjoy its treasure. [1917]

M

Maanhaltija. [1918] In Finno-Ugric mythology, the earth spirit who watches over the fruits of the land.

Maat

Maat (truth). [1919] In Egyptian mythology, goddess of truth, daughter of the sun god Ra; her name is represented by an ostrich feather. Her presence is indicated in "The Weighing of the Heart" in *The Book of the Dead*, in which the feather of truth is usually found over the balance scales and also appears as the weight against which the heart is weighed. Egyptian judges in the Plolemaic and Roman periods were often portrayed wearing an amulet of Maat around a cord on their necks as emblems of their office. One

ancient Egyptian text describes the goddess: "Great is Maat, the mighty and unalterable."
Variant spellings: Maa, Maet, Maht, Maut.

Mab (a baby). [1920] In European folklore, queen of the fairies. Shakespeare's *Romeo and Juliet* describes her as the "fairies' midwife," that is, she delivers men's brains to dreams. Berlioz's dramatic symphony *Romeo and Juliet* has a brilliant scherzo depicting Queen Mab.

Mabinogion, The. [1921] Welsh collection of medieval legends and tales translated into English by Lady Charlotte Guest in 1838. It is believed the tales were first written in Welsh in the 14th century, though some may date from the 11th century. Most of the tales deal with Celtic myths and legends.

Mabon (the young). [1922] In Celtic mythology, a Welsh sun god and hero, son of Ruien and Modron, brother of Owain, noted for his hunting, his hound, and his swift horse. In later Arthurian legend Mabon is a mortal released from prison by King Arthur, who needed his help in the chase of the boar Twrch Trwyth.

Machaon (lancet). [1923] In Greek mythology, son of the healing god Asclepius; brother of Acesis, Aegle, Hygieia, Iaso, Janiscus, Panacea, and Podalirius; married Anticleia; father of Alexanor, Gorgasus, and Nichomachus. Machaon was one of the suitors of Helen, and after her abduction he sailed for Troy with Podalirius and 30 ships. He was a doctor, who tended the Greeks during the Trojan War. Some accounts say he was hidden in the wooden horse but others say he was killed before the war began. He was later worshiped as a god. Machaon appears in Homer's *Iliad* (book 2) and Vergil's *Aeneid* (book 2).

Machira, Lake. [1924] In the folklore of the Carib Indians of the Orinoco region of South America, magic lake of the dead. It was believed that most of the souls of the dead were swallowed by great serpents in Lake Machira. The dead were then carried by the serpents to "a land of pleasure in which they entertain themselves with dancing and feasting," according to Fray Ruiz, a 17th-century Christian author who wrote about Indian beliefs in *Conversión en Piritú de Indios Cumuanagotos y Palenques.*

Maconaura and Anuanaitu. In the mythology of the Carib Indian tribes of the Orinoco region of South America, a primeval husband and wife.

After Adaheli, a creator god, had made man and woman, a handsome Indian was born, Maconaura, who lived with his mother. He was a fisherman, and one day he found that his basket net had been broken and his fish stolen. He set out to discover the thief and found that a cayman, a form of South American crocodile, had stolen the fish. Maconaura shot an arrow between the eyes of the cayman, and it disappeared beneath the waters. Then Maconaura heard a noise and found a beautiful Indian girl, Anuanaitu, who was crying. He took her to his home, for she was very young, and they lived with his mother. When she was old enough, he married her. After some time, however, Anuanaitu killed Maconaura and his mother because the cayman, which Maconaura had killed, was her brother.

Macunaima. In Brazilian folklore, hero who appears in the novel *Macunaima*, "the story of a hero without a backbone," by Brazilian novelist Mario de Andrade (1893–1945). Macunaima is described as "jet black," a child of midnight, who would not talk until he was six. When he finally did speak, he said: "Oh, I'm too lazy."

Madderakka. In Finno-Ugric mythology, goddess of birth worshiped by the Lapps, with three goddess daughters, Sarakka, Juksakka, and Uksakka. Madderakka was responsible for making women and cattle fertile and for creating the body of the child in its mother's womb. Her daughter Sarakka helped women in childbirth and also reindeer at the birth of their calves. She was invoked by Lapp women during menstruation. Juksakka, the second daughter, was believed to change the girl child in the womb into a boy child and was also invoked to make boys into good hunters. Uksakka, the last daughter, lived underground, protecting people in their comings and goings. At childbirth she received the new child and watched over its first steps so that it would not injure itself.

Mademoiselle Charlotte. In Haitian voodoo, a loa (deified spirit of the dead) who manifests all the traits of a white European when she mounts or takes possession of a person during voodoo ritual. Thus, when she mounts a black Haitian girl, the girl will then speak eloquent European French. The goddess loves to be shown all the respect due her office and will work only for someone she takes a liking to. Another loa of European background in Haitian voodoo is Dinclinsin, who is believed to have come to Haiti with Mademoiselle Charlotte. Dinclinsin, however, is greatly feared because of his extreme severity.

Madira. In Hindu mythology, goddess of wine and wife of Varuna, god of the ocean. Madira is also called Varuni.

Maev (baby, child). In Celtic mythology, queen of Connaught, an evil war goddess in the cycle of myths around the hero Cuchulain, who is killed by her sorcery. She appears in numerous tales and as a licentious queen. Her appearance deprived soldiers of their strength; she was therefore the goddess who drained men of sexual powers. In later English folklore, Maev became Queen Mab, queen of the fairies, later replaced by Titania.

Variant spellings: Maeve, Medb, Meadhbh.

Magen David (shield of David). Modern symbol of Judaism, the hexagram formed by two equilateral triangles that have the same center and are placed in opposite directions. One of the first appearances of the sign is on a seal in Palestine dated about the 7th century B.C.E. It was used during the Greco-Roman Period on some Synagogues. Sometimes it is called the Star of David, but this is a misnomer.

Magi. In the Bible, N.T., wise men who visited the Christ Child and offered gifts.

The account of the visit is found in Matthew (2:1–12), which tells that when Jesus was born a star appeared in the East. The Magi (or Wise Men in some Bible translations) started from their own country to follow the star. It guided them to Judea. They went to King Herod and asked him where the royal infant was to be found. Herod did not know but asked the Magi to make inquiries and report Christ's whereabouts to him. The Wise Men left, and the star reappeared. They followed it, and it guided them to a shed in Bethlehem where Mary and Joseph had taken temporary lodgings. The Wise Men entered and made their offerings. Warned by an angel not to return to King Herod, they left for their own lands.

In Cologne cathedral in Germany visitors were shown three heads, which they were told were the heads of the three Wise Men. The names given to them are Gaspar (The White One), Melchior (The King of Light), and Balthazar (The Lord of Treasures). The New Testament account does not name the Wise Men nor does it say how many there were. The three gifts signify kingly office (the gold); Godhead (the frankincense); and the coming death of Christ (the myrrh).

Other names are given the three Wise Men: Apellius, Amerus, and Damascus; Magalath, Galgalath, and Sarasin; or Alor, Sator, and Peratoras. Some legendary accounts say they were Shem, Ham, and Japeth of the Old Testament who had fallen asleep and awakened when Christ was born.

1933
Magna Mater (great mother). In Roman mythology, epithet for Cybele and Rhea, both mother goddesses. In Rome the worship of the Magna Mater was introduced in 204 B.C.E. at the command of a Sibylline oracle, to pray for deliverance from Hannibal in Italy. An embassy was sent to fetch a holy stone from Pessinus, and a festival was begun in honor of Magna Mater. Held 4 to 9 April, it was called *Megalesia* (Greek, great mother).

1934
Magnes (magnet). In Greek mythology, a man whose shoe nails became magnetized while he was walking over a mine; thus, our word *magnet*. Magnes was the son of Aeolus and Enarete; father of Dictys and Polydectes by a naiad and father of Eioneas, Hymenaeus, and Pierus. Some accounts say Magnes was a slave of Medea, who transformed him into a magnet.

1935
Magpie. A bird of the crow family with a long tail and black and white plumage, often considered a bird of ill omen in European folklore. In Christian symbolism the magpie represents the devil or vanity. But the bird does possess some good qualities, as in one English rhyme from Lancashire:

One for sorrow
Two for mirth
Three for a wedding
Four for a death

Some variants change the last line to "Four for a birth."

In Oriental folklore, such as Chinese, the magpie is a sign of good luck. A chattering magpie signifies the arrival of guests or some good news. In Nordic mythology the magpie is believed to be a soulbird, one that carries the souls of the dead.

1936
Mah. In Persian mythology, the moon goddess, whose light makes the plants grow.

1937
Mahabharata, The (great war of the Bharatas). Hindu epic poem, longest in the world, consisting of 110,000 couplets. It is divided into 18 *parvans* (sections or books). The original authorship or editing of the work is ascribed to the sage Vyasa, though the entire work was written over subsequent centuries, displaying numerous additions. Dates for the compilation of the epic range from 400 B.C.E. to 200 C.E.

The frame story—the war between two branches of the same family—takes up about one-fourth of the poem; the rest deals with such diverse subjects as mythology, folktales, and cosmology. It also contains philosophical digressions such as the *Bhagavad-Gita*, perhaps the most famous section of the entire work, inserted as episodes and subepisodes.

The following summary gives the main incidents and details connected with the epic proper, that is, the tale of the great war.

There was once a king named Santanu, a descendant of Bharata, who had a son, Bhishma. In his old age King Santanu wished to marry again, but the hereditary rights of his son Bhishma were an obstacle to the king in obtaining a favorable match. Bhishma, in order to assist his father in his quest to marry, gave up his rights to the throne. The king then married Satyavati, who bore him two sons. The eldest, Chitrangada, succeeded to the throne but was killed. He was followed by his brother, Vichitra-virya, who died without any offspring but left two wives, Ambika and Ambalika, daughters of King Kasi. Satyavati then called on Vyasa, the half brother of her husband, to fulfill the law and father children in the name of Vichitra-virya. Vyasa had lived the life of a hermit in the forests and his severe fasts had completely wasted his body, so he was quite ugly. The two widows were so frightened by his appearance that the elder one closed her eyes when making love; she gave birth to a blind son, Dhrita-rashtra. The younger widow turned so pale that her son was called Pandu (the pale).

Satyavati wanted a child without any physical blemish. So instead of sleeping with Vyasa herself she substituted her slave girl, who bore a son, Vidura. The three children, Dhrita-rashtra, Pandu, and Vidura, were brought up by their uncle, Bhishma, who acted as regent. When they came of age the throne was not given to Dhrita-rashtra because he was blind but went instead to Pandu.

Pandu had two wives, Kunti (Pritha) and Madri, but he did not have intercourse with either. Some believe he suffered from leprosy (his name meaning "pale"). Pandu left for the Himalaya Mountains. His two wives, however, had five children, all fathered by different gods. Pandu acknowledged them as his before he died, and they were called the Pandavas. Kunti was the mother of the three oldest sons, Madri the mother of the two younger ones.

Yudhi-shthira (firm in fight) was the son of Yama, god of the dead; Bhima (the terrible) was the son of Vayu, the wind god; Arjuna (white; bright; silvery) was the son of Indra, the storm god. Nakula and Saha-deva, the sons of Madri, were fathered by the Surya, the sun god.

The other branch of the family, that of Dhrita-rashtra, had 100 sons and one daughter, Duh-sala. From their ancestor, Kuru, they were known as the Kauravas.

Thus the two major branches of the family, and the two contending forces in the epic, are the Pandavas and the Kauravas. The Pandava sons were brought up in the court of King Dhrita-rashtra, their uncle, but because he showed them favor over his own sons (he nominated Yudhi-shthira to be his heir apparent), a feud broke out between the two branches. To stop the fight the Pandavas were sent into exile. However, one cousin, Duryodhana, plotted to destroy the Pandavas completely. He had their house set afire. All five sons were thought to be dead, though they escaped into the forest.

While the Pandavas were living in the forest, they heard that King Draupada had proclaimed a *swayamvara*, a tournament in which the daughter of the king would choose her husband from the contenders. The Kauravas also heard of the contest and went to seek the hand of Draupadi, daughter of the king. Being in exile, the Pandavas disguised themselves as Brahmans (priests). At the contest the Pandavas won every feat. After they had thrown off their disguises, the winner of the bride was seen to be Arjuna. The brothers took Draupadi home and told their mother, Kunti, they had made a great acquisition. Kunti, not knowing they meant Draupadi, told them to share it among themselves. A mother's command could not be evaded, and Draupadi became the common wife of all five brothers. Each husband belonged to her for a specific time, during which the others were not to interfere.

Because they had revealed themselves at the *swayamvara* King Dhrita-rashtra called the Pandu brothers back to court and divided his kingdom. Prince Yudhi-shthira was chosen king of the territory given the Pandavas. After having conquered many other countries, King Yudhi-shthira decided he wanted to perform a great horse sacrifice, to set up his claim as universal ruler and king of kings. This move exited the jealousy of the Kauravas, who plotted to destroy the vain king. They persuaded King Yudhi-shthira to gamble with Sakuni, their uncle, who was a cheat. At the end of the gamble Yudhi-shthira lost his entire kingdom, as well as his family. King Dhrita-rashtra forced the Kauravas to restore both to Yudhi-shthira, but he again gambled them away. This time he and his brothers were forced into exile in the forest for 12 years. In the 13th year they joined, in disguise, the service of the king of Virata.

The Pandavas now determined to recover their lost kingdom. The king of Virata became their ally, and preparations were made for war. Krishna (an incarnation of the god Vishnu) and his brother, Balarama, relatives of both the Pandavas and Kauravas, took the side of the Pandavas. Krishna acted as charioteer for his friend Arjuna. It was in this role that Krishna spoke the great *Bhagavad-Gita*, the most famous philosophical part of the epic, while the rival armies were drawn up for battle at Kurukshetra, a plain north of Delhi.

Many battles follow in the epic, the end result being that the Pandavas are the victors. But that is not the end of the epic, for it goes on with the lives of the survivors. Filled with remorse for all of the slaughter he caused, King Yudhi-shthira abdicated his throne, leaving with his brothers for the Himalayas to reach the heaven of Indra, the storm god, located on Mount Meru. The journey was not easy because sins and moral defects proved fatal to the pilgrims. The first to die was Draupadi because "too great was her love for Arjuna." Next was Saha-deva, who "esteemed none equal to himself." Then Nakula; "ever was the thought in his heart, 'There is none equal in beauty to me.'" The great hero Arjuna was next. He said, "In one day I could destroy all my enemies." He died because he boasted and did not fulfill his boast. When Bhima fell, he asked the reason for his death and was told, "When thou last looked on thy foe, thou hast cursed him with thy breath; therefore thou fallest today." Yudhi-shthira went on alone with his faithful dog until he reached the gate of heaven. He was invited by Indra to enter, but he refused unless his brothers and Draupadi could also enter. He was told they were already there, but when he entered he saw all of the Kauravas there instead. He left heaven and was sent to hell, where he heard the voices of his family. He then resolved to stay with them. He was told, however, that this was merely a test, an illusion, for he and his brothers and friends were in Indra's heaven.

The Mahabhratha has been made into a drama by Jean Claude Carriere and directed by Peter Brook.

Mahagir. In Burmese mythology, a *nat*, or supernatural being, in whose honor a coconut is hung on a porch of every Burmese home. Mahagir is portrayed standing on a platform, holding a sword in one hand and a leaf fan in the other. The platform is held up by three demons who are sitting on a kneeling elephant.

Variant spelling: Magaye.

Maharajikas. In Hindu mythology, lesser or inferior gods, whose numbers range from 220 to 236.

Maharishi (great sage). In Hinduism, a term applied to holy men or sages, the term derived from the Prajapatis, the progenitors of the human race in Hindu mythology, who are often called Maharishis.

Mahasthamaprapta (he that has obtained great strength). In Buddhism, an attendant of Amitabha Buddha displaying the *mudra* of worship. In Chinese Buddhism he is called Ta-shih- chih; in Japanese Buddhism, Daiseishi.

Mahavira (great man). Fifth or sixth century B.C.E. In Jainism, a Tirthamkara Mahavira's original name was Vardhamana. His legendary life is found in the *Kalpa Sutra*, a sacred book in Jainism that contains the lives of the Tirthamkara. According to that account, in the night in which Mahavira "took the form of an embryo in the womb" of his mother, Devananda, the wife of a Brahmin, was "on her couch, taking fits of sleep, in a state between sleeping and waking, and having seen the 14 illustrious, beautiful, lucky, blest, suspicious, fortunate great dreams, she woke up. To wit: an elephant, a bull, a lion, the anointing of the goddess Sri, a garland, the moon, the sun, a flag, a vase, a lotus lake, the ocean, a celestial abode, a heap of jewels, and a flame. . . ."

All of these symbols were taken as signs that an important son would be born, one well versed in the learning of the Hindu sages. While this was happening, however, Shakra, the chief of the gods decided to take the embryo from Devananda's womb and place it in the womb of Trisala, a member of the warrior caste. When Mahavira was born, "the gods and goddesses came down from heaven to show their joy."

The boy lived a normal life and later married Yashoda, by whom he had a daughter Riyadarshana, but then decided to leave his worldly life. He gave away his wealth and became an ascetic. When this happened "the gods came down from heaven . . . and did him homage." He continued as an ascetic for 12 years, and then "he sat down near an ancient temple under the sala [teak] tree and remained motionless for two and a half days, fasting and plunged in the deepest meditation. When he arose on the third day enlightenment was complete." After 30 years of preaching he entered Nirvana, and the gods accompanied him. In Oriental art Mahavira is often portrayed enthroned, with a mirror, a vase, a water vessel, a *srivastsa* (said to represent a curl from the god Krishna's breast), and a swastika.

Other Tirthamkara resemble Buddhas but are distinguished from them by being naked, with eyes wide open, lacking a head bump (*usnisa*), and usually having a diamond-shaped mark in the middle of the chest, representing the *jiva* (the indestructible personal life force, or soul).

Mahayana (great way of liberation). A form of Buddhism that is believed to have appeared sometime between the first century B.C.E. and the first century C.E. It holds that the true teaching of Buddhism is of wider appeal, with a great deal of emphasis on the virtue of compassion; in contrast to what it calls the Hinayana school of Buddhism, which it claims places greater emphasis on wisdom. Mahayana Buddhism has produced many myths and legends in comparison to those produced by Hinayana Buddhism. The other major form of Buddhism, Hinayana (small vehicle or vehicle to be abandoned) is a derogatory name for a series of preliminary teachings and practices preserved in fossilized form within Mahayana Buddhism. Hinayana is similar but by no means identical with the living lineage of Theravada. Mahayana is more complex than Theravada, but recent research has illuminated the supposed difference between them as being that Mahayana stands more for "wisdom" and Theravada more for "compassion." Some Mahayana teachers take Hinayana to mean the inner motivation to liberate oneself and not help others, whether or not one is outwardly a follower of Mahayana.

Maheo. In North American Indian mythology (Cheyenne), creator god, the All-Spirit, who created all life by his power.

Mahrach. In Australian mythology, an evil spirit closely connected with death, often called the black ghost. He appears before the death of a person.

Maia (grandmother). In Greek and Roman mythology, mother of Hermes by Zeus; one of the Pleiades; daughter of Pleione and Atlas. Maia is also

Cybele (Maia)

one of the names of the Great Mother goddess Cybele. The Romans identified Maia with an ancient Italian goddess of spring, Maia Maiestas, and with Fauna, Bona Dea, and Ops. She was said to be the wife of Vulcan, to whom the priests of the god sacrificed on 1 May.

Maiden of Pohjola. In the Finnish epic poem *The Kalevala*, elder daughter of Louhi, the evil mistress of Pohjola, the Northland.

Louhi promised her daughter, the Maiden of Pohjola, to Vainamoinen, the culture hero, if he would forge the magic sampo for her. The hero consented, but he commissioned Ilmarinen to forge the sampo for him. When Vainamoinen left Louhi, he was told not to look to the sky or else some evil would befall him. Of course, as he set out, he looked to the heavens and saw the Maiden of Pohjola,

¹⁹⁴⁷

beautifully dressed, spinning. Moved by her beauty, he called to her:

> Come into my sledge, O maiden,
> In the sledge beside me seat thee.

The maiden, however, was not so easily moved by the old man. When he told her she should be married, she replied that wives "are like dogs enchained in kennel." Vainamoinen insisted that women are actually queens when married. The maiden replied she would no longer listen to his wooing unless he completed some tasks she would assign him. The hero accomplished all except the last, fashioning a ship out of her broken spindle. In the attempt Vainamoinen accidentally cut his knee. He was healed only when he sang the magic words of the origin of iron.

Vainamoinen's bad luck with the maiden did not stop Ilmarinen from forging the magic sampo, which entitled him to the beautiful girl. At first she did not want to marry Ilmarinen, but eventually she agreed. Frequently in the epic she is called Ilmarinen's Lady. She was later murdered by Kullervo, a disgruntled servant.

Sibelius used the wooing of the Maiden of Pohjola by Vainamoinen as the basis for his symphonic poem *Pohjola's Daughter*.

Maidere. In Siberian mythology, a savior hero in Tartar myth derived from the Buddhist Maitreya, the living or coming Buddha. Maidere will fight Erlik, the devil, at the end of the world. Ulgen, a creator god, will send down Maidere to teach the love of God and convert mankind. Erlik, however, will then kill Maidere out of envy, but the hero's blood will cover the whole earth and burst into flames that will rise to the heavens. Ulgen will then call the dead to rise, and Erlik and his evil companions will be destroyed.

Maid Marion (rebellion, wished for child?). In British legend, the mistress of Robin Hood. She appears in the late Robin Hood ballads, disguised as a page boy who lived among Robin's men until she was discovered, and she was married to Robin with Christian rites.

Mailkun. In Australian mythology, an evil spirit, wife of Koen. She captures adults in her net and spears children to death. She is also called Tipakalleum.

Maît Carrefour. In Haitian voodoo, a loa (deified spirit of the dead) who is master of the demons of the night and is invoked for protection against them. No one whispers or smiles in the presence of Maît Carrefour. He is also called Kalfu.

Maît Gran Bois. In Haitian voodoo, the loa (deified spirit of the dead) who rules over forests, woods, and plant life.

Maitreya (he whose name is kindness). In Buddhism, name of the Buddha of the Future or the Buddha Who Is to Come. Now he lives in the Tushita heaven. When he comes the world will be renewed. The Buddhists have a legend that tells how Ananda, a disciple of the Buddha, asked his master what would happen after Buddha's death.

"Who shall teach us when thou art gone?" asked Ananda. The Buddha replied: "I am not the first Buddha who came upon earth, nor shall I be the last. I came to teach you the truth, and I have founded on earth the kingdom of truth. Gautama Siddhartha will die, but Buddha will live, for Buddha is the truth, and the truth cannot die. He who believes in truth and lives it is my disciple, and I shall teach him. The truth will be propagated and the kingdom of truth will increase for about five hundred years. Then for a while the clouds of error will darken the light, and in due time another Buddha will arise, and he will reveal to you the selfsame eternal truth which I have taught you." Ananda asked, "How shall we know him?" The Buddha replied: "The Buddha that will come after me will be known as Maitreya."

Often the inscription "Come Maitreya, come" is found carved on rocks in Buddhist Mongolia and Tibet. In Pali the name is rendered Metteyya; in Tibet, Maitreya is called Byams-pa; in China, Mi-lo-fo or Pu-tai Ho-shang; and in Japan, Miroku Bosatsu. Pu-tai was an eccentric monk who was later thought to have been Maitreya. He was also approximated to the god of luck. A fat, jolly figure, he is worshiped for happiness and riches; known as Hotei O-sho in Japan.

Maît Source. In Haitian voodoo, a loa (deified spirit of the dead) who is chosen by a group to watch over streams, lakes, and rivers. Often a cup of water is placed on his altar.

Majestas (majesty). In Roman mythology, goddess of reverence, majesty, and honor; daughter of Honor and Reverentia. Some scholars believe Majestas is a variant name for Bona Dea or Maia, both goddesses.

Makara. In Hindu mythology, a fantastic animal with the head and forelegs of an antelope and the body and tail of a fish. Makara is the mount of the ocean god Varuna, and his figure is shown on the banner of Kama, god of love. He represents the sign of Capricorn in the Hindu zodiac. Makara is also called Jala-rupa (water foam) and Asita-danshtra (black teeth).

Makonaima (one who works in the night?). In the mythology of the Indian tribes of the Orinoco and Guiana regions of South America, a creator god.

"In the beginning," according to the account by W. H. Brett in his book *The Indian Tribes of Guiana*, Makonaima created birds and beasts. They "were all endowed with the gift of speech. Sigu, the son of Makonaima, was placed to rule over them. All lived in harmony together and submitted to his gentle dominion." This ideal paradise did not last. When Sigu uprooted a great tree planted by Makonaima, he found the stump was filled with water, and a great flood ensued. To save the animals, Sigu took some of them to a cave, which he sealed; the others he took to the top of a tree. He dropped large seeds from time to time to test if the waters were receding, until finally the sound of a splash was no longer heard. When the animals came down, however, they had changed somewhat; the arauta howls from his discomfort in the trees, and the trumpeter bird's legs had been chewed by ants, so they are now bony and thin.

Eventually the earth was again populated, but Sigu was persecuted by two evil brothers, who beat him. Each time he was killed he rose again, but finally he ascended a high hill and disappeared into the sky.

In another creation myth about Makonaima, told by Boddam-Whetham in *Roraima and British Guiana*, no mention is made of Sigu. After having created heaven and earth, Makonaima sat down beside a silk-cotton tree by a river, cutting off pieces of its bark. When he cast the bark into the river, fish and birds arose from it. When he cast it on the ground, people and animals arose.

In another myth Makonaima made a "large mould, and out of this fresh, clean clay the white man stepped. After it got a little dirty the Indian was formed, and Spirit [Makonaima] being called away on business for a long period the mould became black and unclean, and out of it walked the Negro."

1951

1952

1953

1954

1955

1956

1957

Variant spellings: Makanaima, Mackonaima, Makunaima, Makaniama.

1958

Malec. In Islamic mythology, principal angel in charge of Djahannam (hell). Malec rules the Zabaniya, who are the guardians of Djahannam according to some accounts; in others, angels who carry the souls of the dead to hell. In the Koran (sura 43) sinners call upon Malec to intercede for them with Allah. Malec, however, remains silent and will not answer the sinners until a thousand years after the Day of Judgment. And when he does answer, he will offer no hope, saying that sinners must remain in Djahannam for eternity.

Variant spelling: Malik.

1959

Malingee. In Australian mythology, the spirit of the night, who during his travels in the dark seeks to find his way home. Malingee's knees knock together as he walks. Both people and beasts fear him, for he kills tribesmen with his stone ax at the slightest provocation. Other animals, such as the eagle hawk, may be killed with the stone knives attached to his elbows. His face is said to be an awful sight, with burning eyes that make him appear to be a devil.

1960

Mama Allpa. In Peruvian Indian mythology, earth goddess invoked for a good harvest; depicted with numerous breasts as a symbol of her fertility.

1961

Mamandabari. In Australian mythology, two culture heroes, either two brothers or father and son. They emerged out of the ground in the north and traveled south, either underground or by flying, teaching men various rituals and customs.

1962

Mama Quilla. In Inca mythology, moon goddess, sister and wife of Inti, the sun, and protector of married women. Many temples were dedicated to her worship, the most famous being the Coricancha at Cuzco, capital of the Inca empire. Cuzco was founded by the first Inca king, Manco Capac, according to some accounts the son of Inti and Mama Quilla.

1963

Mammon (riches). In the Bible, N.T., personification of wealth, money, property, and profit. In Matthew (6:13) Jesus says, "You cannot serve God and mammon." Christian folklore turned the word into the name of a demon of avarice, equating Mammon with Lucifer and Satan. John Milton, in *Paradise Lost* says Mammon was "the last erected spirit that fell" from heaven. He was, according to Milton, "always downward bent," admiring the gold that paved heaven's floor. Mammon is the ambassador of hell to England in De Plancy's *Dictionnaire Infernal*, written in the 19th century.

1964

Manabozho. In North American Indian mythology (Algonquian), trickster, transformer, culture hero, creator of the earth.

Many 19th-century scholars confused Manabozho with the historical figure Hiawatha and the mythical figure Gluskap. Today, most scholars agree that all three are different entities. There are many variant myths relating to Manabozho among the Algonquians. In one, told by the Potawatomi, he was the oldest of four children. The fourth, Flint, killed their mother at his birth. Both Manabozho and the second son had human form, but the third became a white hare and magician. When Manabozho grew up he killed his brother Flint, but the gods became angry and killed the second brother as punishment. Manabozho went on a warpath against them. To stop his wrath the gods initiated him in the Midewiwin, the sacred medicine society. The second brother was brought back to life to preside over the souls of the dead, and Manabozho then initiated the Indians in the Midewiwin.

Variant spellings: Manibozho, Manibozoho, Michabo, Nanabozho, Nanabush.

1965

Managarm (moon's dog). In Norse mythology, an evil giant in the form of a wolf, offspring of a giantess. According to the *Prose Edda*, Managarm "will be filled with the life-blood of men who draw near their end, and will swallow up the moon, and stain the heavens and the earth with blood. Then shall the sun grow dim, and the winds howl tumultuously to and fro," at the end of the world, Ragnarok.

1966

Mananaan (man?). In Celtic mythology, son of the sea god Lir, a Tuatha De Danann, husband of Fand and Uchtdelbh, father of Mongan and Niamh. Mananaan had a ship, *Wave Sweeper*, which was self-propelled, as well as a horse, Splendid Mane. Mananaan was patron god of Irish seamen, protector of the Isle of Man and the Isle of Aran, where his home, Emhain of the Apple Trees, was located. In Welsh mythology he is known as Manawyddan and possessed a magic chariot as well as a cloak of invisibility. In *Ulysses* James Joyce calls the "whitemaned seahorses, champing, bright-windbridled, the steeds of Mananaan."

Variant spelling: Manannan.

1967

Manasseh (making to forget). In the Bible, O.T., name of the 14th king of Judah; son of Hezekiah (2 Kings 21:1– 18), said to have been an evil king. "The Prayer of Manasseh" is not found in the Old Testament but in the Old Testament Apocrypha and is used in some services of *The Book of Common Prayer* (1979 American Version) during times of penitence. Manasseh is also the name of Joseph's first son (Gen. 41:51).

1968

Manco Capac and Mama Oello Huaco. In Inca mythology, first king and queen; they were brother and sister, and children of the sun.

Manco Capac is the culture hero of the Incas. Before he arrived, according to the *Comentarios reales de los Incas* (1609), written by the half-Inca Garcilaso de la Vega, people lived like wild beasts, with "neither order nor religion, neither villages nor houses, neither fields nor clothing." The sun god, pitying the sad plight of mankind, sent his son Manco Capac and his daughter Mama Oello Huaco to earth near Lake Titicaca. He gave them a golden rod that was slightly shorter than a man's arm and about two fingers in thickness.

"Plunge the rod into the earth," the sun god told the two. "The spot where the rod disappears, there you must establish and hold your court."

After some journeying they came to Huanacauri, where the rod sank deep into the earth. Then the couple separated, each taking the good news of the sun god's love to the people. They "taught their subjects everything that had to do with human living."

Some 30 or 40 years after the descent of Manco Capac and Mama Oello Huaco, Manco Capac left his kingdom to his son Sinchi Roca, who became the next Inca King.

Garcilaso's account is but one of many about the first Inca king and the origin of the Incas. In an account by Ramos Gavilan in *Historia del celebre Santuario de Nuestra Señora de Copacabana* (1621), Manco Capac is said to have been merely a human being who dressed in golden robes and fooled the people into believing in his divine origin. This account is prejudiced because the Spanish author wished to destroy the sources of Inca respect for their past.

Another account, given by José de Acosta in *Historia natural y moral de las Indias* (1590), which is earlier than either of of the other two, says that Manco Capac was the founder and chief of the Incas, who came out of "a certain cave by a window, by whom men first began to multiply; and for this reason they call them *Paccari-tambo* [inn of origin]."

Variant spelling: Manko Kapak and Coya Mama.

1969

Mandala (circle). In Hindu and Buddhist ritual, a mystical diagram, usually circular in outline. The purpose is to gather vital spiritual forces together. The mandala is a sacred mountain or house that presents reality ordered in such a way as to liberate those who meditate on or enter into it, according to Buddhist belief. When drawn in two dimensions, the mandala appears as a circle contained in a square. Carl Jung, the Swiss psychologist, discusses the mandala frequently in his works. He sees it as a symbolic representation of the "nuclear atom" of the human psyche, whose essence we do not know. Jung confused quartermites with mandalas: all mandalas are quartermites; some quartermites are mandalas.

1970

Mandrake. A narcotic plant of the nightshade family; in world mythology and folklore, believed to be an aphrodisiac. It appears in Genesis (30:14–24) in the conflict between Rachel and Leah, the wives of Jacob. Leah gets the mandrake root from Rachel's youngest son in order to become pregnant. In English the mandrake is often called love apple. The Arabs call the mandrake the "apples of the djinn," or devil's apples, because they consider the rousing of sexual desire evil. In Machiavelli's play *La Mandragola* the plot hinges on the aphrodisiac qualities of the mandrake. Shakespeare's *Henry VI, Part II* (3.2.310) alludes to some of the folk beliefs about the root, such as that when it is torn from the ground it will utter groans and the person who pulls it will either go mad, die, or both. Juliet, in *Romeo and Juliet* (4.3.47–48), before drinking the sleeping potion lists her fears and apprehensions:

And shrieks like mandrakes' torn out of the earth,
That living mortals, hearing them, run mad.

During the Christian Middle Ages the mandrake was associated with the devil. Witches were said to fashion figures of people out of the plant root as a charm to do harm.

1971

Manes (good). In Roman mythology, good spirits, believed to preside over the burying places and monuments of the dead. Their mother was believed to be the goddess Mania, mother of Lares and Manes, father of Cottys by Callirrhoë. Sacrifices of food were offered to the Manes, and the blood of black sheep, pigs, and oxen were poured over graves during their festival, the *Feralia*, held between 18 and 21 February, during which time the temples were closed. Vergil's *Aeneid* (book 3) cites the Manes. Often *Dis Manibus sacrum* was inscribed on tombstones with the name of the dead person. In some accounts Manes are called Keres.

Mani. 1972 In the mythology of the Indians of Brazil, a culture hero who taught his people various arts. When he was about to die, he predicted that a year after his death the people would find a great treasure—the manioc plant (*manihot esculenta*). One year after Mani's death the plant was found. This myth forms the basis for José Viera Couto de Magalhaes's *O Selvagem*, in which a variant of the story is told.

Manitou. 1973 In North American Indian mythology, a word used in various Algonquian languages for spirit or divine being.

Manjushri. 1974 In Mahayana Buddhism, the personification of the Transcendent Wisdom of the Buddha. In Chinese Buddhist legend he was a Bodhisattva who was told by the Buddha that it was his duty to turn the Wheel of the Dharma and convert the Chinese. He chose a five-peaked mountain in Shan-shi province; one mountain was made of diamonds, the next of sapphires, then emeralds, rubies, and lapis lazuli. On each grew a flower of a special color, and a pagoda was on the summit of each peak.

Manjushri's symbols are the sword of wisdom, a book, and the blue lotus; his *mudra* is turning the Wheel of the Law. A lion supports his throne, or he is shown riding on a lion.

Manman Brigitte. 1975 In Haitian voodoo, a loa (deified spirit of the dead) invoked by people who are constantly embroiled in disputes.

Manman Brigitte does not have her own altar in the Oum'phor (voodoo temple) but is invoked in her favorite tree, the weeping willow or the elm. She is asked to bring disaster on one's enemies, who are assumed to be enemies of the goddess as well. Her principal site of worship was located in the main cemetery of Port-au-Prince, Haiti, but her sacred elm was cut down by government and Catholic authorities because many people were seen praying to Manman Brigitte by placing lighted candles at the foot of her tree. Also known as Mademoiselle Brigitte.

Manta. 1976 In the folklore of the Araucanian Indians of Chile, a cuttlefish that lives in deep lakes. When it cries, it causes the water to boil. If any person enters the water, the Manta rises to the surface, drags him down, and eats him. Sometimes it has intercourse

with other animals and produces monsters. To kill it, one must throw it branches of the quisco, a bush covered with spines that grows in Chile.

A similar monster cuttlefish called Trelquehuecuve, whose tentacles end in hooves, will squeeze to death anything that comes within its reach.

Variant spelling: Huecu.

Manticore

Manticore (man-eater). 1977 Fantastic animal with a lion's body, human head, and scorpion tail. In medieval Christian belief the manticore was a symbol of the devil. Sometimes the animal appears in art works showing the Hebrew prophet Jeremiah.

Manu (man). 1978 In Hindu mythology, a word for the 14 progenitors of the human race, each of whom hold sway for 4,320,000 years. The names of the 14 are Swayam-bhuya (self-created), an epithet of Brahma; Swarochisha; Auttami; Tamasa; Raivata (brilliant); Chakshusha (perceptible by the eye); Vaivaswata or Satya-vrata; Savarna; Daksha (dextrous); Brahma-savarna; Savarna or Rudra-savarna; Rauchya; Bhautya.

Vaivaswata, the seventh Manu, is connected with one version of the myth of the great flood in Hindu mythology. One morning, while Vaivaswata was washing his hands, he caught a fish.

"Take care of me and I will preserve you," the fish told Vaivaswata.

"From what will you preserve me?" Vaivaswata asked.

"A flood will carry away all living beings; I will save you from that," the fish replied.

The fish then told Vaivaswata to keep him alive in an earthen vessel and to put him in a larger container as he grew, eventually placing him in the ocean. The fish grew rapidly and was moved from the smaller container to larger ones and then to the ocean. The fish then told Vaivaswata to construct a ship, or ark, in which Vaivaswata was to go abroad. Vaivaswata did as he was told. The great flood came, and Vaivaswata fastened the cable of the ship to the fish's large magic horn. He passed over the northern mountain and later tied the ship to a tree when the waters receded. Vaivaswata saw that all men and women had been destroyed. Desiring to have children, he prayed and made sacrifice. A woman was produced who came to Vaivaswata, saying she was his daughter. With her he lived "worshiping and toiling in arduous religious rites, desirous of offspring. With her he begat the offspring which is the offspring of Manu."

1979

Maori. In African mythology (Makoni of Zimbabwe), sky and creator god; creator of Mwuetsi, the first man, and Massassi, the first woman.

Maori gave Mwuetsi a horn filled with magic oil and settled him at the bottom of a primeval lake. But Mwuetsi wanted to live on the earth and complained to Maori, who finally consented to his wish. When Mwuetsi was placed on earth he saw it had no plant life; all was waste and desolate. "See," said Maori when Mwuetsi began to cry, "I told you. Now you are set on a path that will only lead to death. But I will give you a companion." So Maori created Massassi, the first woman and gave her the gift of fire-making. Then plant life began on earth. In time Massassi had to die. At her death Mwuetsi was so distraught that Maori created another woman, Morongo, the evening star, to replace her. The couple bore sheep, goats, cattle, chickens, and children. Maori then told Mwuetsi that he was going to die and should no longer have sexual intercourse with Morongo. But the couple continued to sleep together, producing lions, leopards, scorpions, and snakes. One day Mwuetsi tried to force Morongo to have sexual intercourse with him, but a snake, favored by Morongo, bit Mwuetsi. As he weakened from the snake bite, the earth, as well as people and animals, began to die. When Mwuetsi's children learned that only by returning him to the lake could they be saved, they murdered him and placed him back in the lake.

Variant spelling: Mwuetse.

1980

Mara. In Buddhist mythology, the Evil One who attempted to destroy the Buddha but never succeeded.

He appears in numerous Buddhist myths and legends.

Originally Mara was a Hindu demon, Namuchi, often called Vritra, who constantly fought against the storm god Indra. He was a mischievous spirit who prevented rain and produced drought; his name means "not letting go the waters." In many Hindu myths Indra forces Namuchi to send down fertilizing rains and restore the earth.

Mara is also called Papiyan (more wicked; very wicked) and Varshavarti (he who fulfills desires). In this last version his true nature is revealed, fulfilling the desire for existence, the desire for pleasure, and the desire for power. Mara therefore appears in Buddhist mythology as the arch-tempter of the Buddha. *Mara* is also used as a common noun denoting any hindrance to Enlightenment. In Zen, hallucinations are called Makyou (Mara pictures).

1981

Marasta. In Haitian voodoo, a loa (deified spirit of the dead) who represents twins, who are considered sacred.

Marduk

1982

Marduk (bull calf of the sun). In Near Eastern mythology (Babylonian), hero-god who defeated the monster of chaos, Tiamat, and was proclaimed king of the gods. Marduk's myth is told in the Babylonian creation epic poem *Enumu Elish* ("When on high . . ."). Recited at Zag-Muk, the New Year celebration, the poem is believed to have been composed between 1200 and 1000 B.C.E.

"When on high . . ." is the opening of the poem, when the sky was not yet named and "the earth below was nameless." Only Apsu, the abyss, and Tiamat, or chaos, existed. From their mingled waters came forth Mummu, the "tumult of the waves," and the monstrous serpents Lakhmu and Lakhamu. These two in turn gave birth to Anshar and Kishar, two primeval gods. Anshar and Kishar then gave birth to the gods Anu (lofty); Ea, god of sweet waters, earth, and wisdom; Marduk, the hero god; the Igigi, a group of gods who took up their post in the heavens; and the Anunnake, another group of gods who took their position in the underworld.

Shortly, this new creation angered the peace of Apsu, and he complained to his wife.

"During the day I have no rest and I cannot sleep at night," he said to Tiamat.

The married couple then argued about what to do. Their son Ea overheard the argument in which Apsu planned to destroy his offspring. Using magic incantations, Ea seized Apsu and Mummu. Tiamat, angered at this move, gathered a host of gods and gave birth to a group of monsters to fight Ea. Among the monsters were some "with sharp teeth, merciless in slaughter," terrible dragons, storm monsters, savage dogs, scorpion men, fish men, and rams. At the head of her army she appointed Kingu, another monster.

Ea then went to his father, Anshar, to tell of Tiamat's plans to destroy them all. Anshar sent Anu with a message to Tiamat:

Go and step before Tiamat.
May her liver be pacified, her heart softened.

Anu obeyed his father, but as soon as he saw how ugly Tiamat's face was, he took flight. Failing with Anu, Anshar then sent his son Ea, but he was no more courageous. Finally, Anshar decided to send his son Marduk against Tiamat:

Marduk heard the word of his father.
His heart rejoiced and to his father he spoke.

Marduk told his father he was ready to have a contest with Tiamat and would come out the victor. He addressed the assembled gods:

When I shall have become your avenger,
Binding Tiamat and saving your life,
Then come in a body,
In Ubshu-kenna [chamber of fate or destiny], let your-
    selves down joyfully,
My authority instead of yours will assume control,

Unchangeable shall be whatever I do,
Irrevocable and irresistible, be the command of my lips.

The gods, in no position to offer resistance, accepted Marduk's claim to full authority. Marduk then took his weapon, the thunderbolt, mounted his chariot drawn by fiery steeds, and went forth to the enemy camp:

The lord comes nearer with his eye fixed on Tiamat,
Piercing with his glance Kingu her consort.

Kingu, unable to endure the "majestic halo" of Marduk, was killed. Then all of the host of Tiamat left the battlefield except for Tiamat.

"Stand up," cried Marduk. "I and thou, come let us fight."

When Tiamat heard these words of challenge, she "acted as possessed, her senses left her," and she shrieked "wild and loud." All of her rage, however, had no effect on Marduk. The poem describes her undoing:

The lord spread out his net in order to enclose her.
The destructive wind, which was behind him, he sent
    forth into her face.
As Tiamat opened her mouth full wide,
Marduk drove in the destructive wind, so that she
    could not close her lips.
The strong winds inflated her stomach.
Her heart lost its reason, she opened her mouth still
    wider, gasping for breath.
He seized the spear and plunged it into her stomach,
He pierced her entrails, he tore through her heart,
He seized hold of her and put an end to her life.
He threw down her carcass and stepped upon her.
                              (Jastrow translation)

Finished, he then cut her "like one does a flattened fish into two halves." From one half he created a covering for the heavens, from the other, the earth. From the blood of the monster Kingu he created the first man.

In the Old Testament Marduk is often called Bel. Jeremiah (50:2) uses both names when he writes: "Declare ye among the nations, and publish, and set up a standard; publish, and conceal not: say, Babylon is taken, Bel is confounded, Merodach [Marduk] is broken in pieces."

1983

Margaret, St. (pearl). In Christian legend, a female saint who went in the disguise of a man for most of her life. Feast, 20 July.

St. Margaret's life is told in *The Golden Legend*, written in the 13th century by Jacobus de Voragine. She came of a noble family who married her off to a noble youth. On the wedding night, however, she "abstained from the society of her husband, garbed

St. Margaret

herself in the habit of a man" and fled the house. She reached a monastery and passed herself off as Brother Pelagius. She continued in the disguise for years, eventually being made the overseer of the nuns. When one of the nuns became pregnant, Margaret, as Brother Pelagius, was charged, convicted, and locked in a cave, where she was fed bread and water. Years passed. When she was about to die, she wrote a letter to the monastery telling them the true story of her life. In a variant legend, Margaret was swallowed by a dragon, dislodged, and later beheaded at Antioch in Pisidia.

1984
Margawse, Queen. In Arthurian legend, half sister of King Arthur, wife of King Lot and mother of Gwaine, Gareth, Gaheris, and Agravaine. Malory's *Morte d'Arthur* makes her the mother of Mordred by King Arthur. Margawse was killed by her son Gaheris when he discovered her with her lover, Sir Lamorok. Later Gwaine killed Lamorok. Tennyson's *Idylls of the King* uses the name Bellicent for Margawse.

1985
Marindi. In Australian mythology, a dog whose blood turned the rocks red. One day Marindi was passing by the dry bed of a water course when he heard a voice saying "Come out and fight." It was Adno-artina, the gecko lizard, who offered the challenge. Marindi agreed to the fight, but the lizard, seeing Marindi's huge teeth, decided the battle should be put off until the evening, when he would be able to see better. The lizard tied a string around the root of his tail to prevent courage from leaving his body.

As they fought, Adno-artina seized Marindi by the throat. The dog's blood poured out and dyed all of the rocks in the creek red. To this day red ochre, used extensively for decorative purposes, is obtained from the spot where the battle took place.

1986
Marishiten. In Japanese Buddhist mythology, goddess of light. She is portrayed in a martial aspect, mounted on a boar, elephant, tiger, dragon, or snake. Marishiten has three faces; two are gentle, and the left one is fierce. She carries in her eight arms the sun, moon, spear, a bow and arrow, a sword, and a war fan. Warriors worship Marishiten because she has the power to make herself invisible. Sometimes she is called the queen of heaven.

1987
Marjatta (berry). In the Finnish epic poem *The Kalevala* (rune 50), virgin mother of a child who becomes king of Karelia and replaces the culture hero Vainamoinen.

Marjatta, who lived in the Northland, was a virgin, "always pure and holy." One day she asked a cuckoo how long she would remain unmarried and was answered by a berry, who told her to "come and pluck" him. The girl did as she was told and became pregnant. Her family, thinking her a whore, threw her out of the house, and the poor girl sought shelter. She found a stable in a clearing and prayed to the horse in the stable to blow his warm breath on her so that she would not freeze to death. When the horse breathed on her, the whole stable was filled with steam, and she gave birth to a boy. While she was sleeping, however, the child disappeared and was found only with the aid of the sun, who told her the boy was in the swampland or a fen. The boy grew up to be "most beauteous" but had no name. He was called Floweret by his mother and Sluggard by strangers. Marjatta wanted to have the boy baptized, but an old man would not do the ceremony without the father present. Vainamoinen came to investigate the matter and decided the child should be put to death, but the child upbraided Vainamoinen. The boy was then christened and made the king of Karelia, and the angry Vainamoinen left the land.

The 50th rune, which is the last section of the epic, displays a good deal of Christian influence, particularly in the the story of the virgin and her son, and is probably a poetical explanation of the ending of the pagan gods, symbolized by Vainamoinen, and the coming of Christianity. For instance, the Jalo Synty, or Suuri Mies (great birth), referred to in this rune is a title for Jesus Christ, used by the Greek Orthodox Karelians, who view Christ's birth as the birth par excellence.

Variant spelling: Mariatta.

1988

Marko, the Gravedigger. In Russian folk-lore, a monk who restored the dead to life.

Marko was a gravedigger for the Holy Crypt Monastery during the Middle Ages. One day he dug a grave that was not very wide. When the body was brought to the grave, the monks "began to grumble at Marko, for it was neither possible to adjust the dead man's robes nor to anoint him with holy oil." Marko told the monks that he had not felt well when he dug the grave, but they continued to complain until Marko addressed the dead man: "Brother, your grave is so narrow we cannot even anoint you with holy oil. Take the oil and anoint yourself." The dead man rose up slightly, anointed himself with the holy oil, and then lay down and "once more died." Marko performed other such miracles, and when he died was buried in a grave he had dug for himself.

St. Mark

1989

Mark, St. (from Mars, the Roman god of war). First century C.E. In the Bible, N.T., Evangelist, author of the Gospel that bears his name. Patron saint of Venice and of glaziers and notaries. Invoked by captives. Feast, 25 April.

Mark has been identified as the young man who ran away when Jesus was arrested in the garden (Mark 14:51–52) and is believed to be the same "John surnamed Mark" in the Acts of the Apostles (12:12).

According to early Christian legend, Mark preached in Egypt and founded a church at Alexandria, being the first bishop of the city. The pagan population, however, was angry at his miracles and accused him of being a magician. At the feast of the god Serapis the saint was seized, bound, and dragged along the streets until he was dead. At the moment the saint died the police who had arrested him were killed by a bolt of lightning. The Christians at Alexandria buried the mangled remains. Mark's tomb then became a great shrine. About 815 C.E. some Venetian merchants trading in Alexandria stole his relics and brought them to Venice, where they were placed in a church dedicated to the saint. There is a painting by Tintoretto of the finding of the saint's body.

The saint has proved popular in Christian art. When he is represented as one of the four Evangelists, either singly or grouped with the others, he is usually accompanied by a lion, winged or unwinged. Scenes from his legendary life are quite common in Venetian art. There is a painting by Gentile Bellini, based on one of the legends, of Mark preaching at Alexandria.

One day St. Mark saw a poor cobbler, Anianus, who had wounded his hand severely with his awl. The saint healed the wound and Anianus was immediately converted to Christianity. Later, after Mark's death, Anianus became the next bishop of Alexandria.

One of the most popular legends, painted by Giorgione and Paris Bordone, tells how the saint saved Venice from a flood in 1340 by appearing with St. George and St. Nicholas and making the sign of the cross to let the storm demons flee.

Another episode from the saint's life tells how a Christian slave prayed at the shrine of St. Mark even though he was forbidden to do so by his master. As a punishment the man was to be tortured, but St. Mark descended from heaven and the instruments of torture were broken or blunted. There is a painting of this scene by Tintoretto, and a poem, *The Legend of St. Mark*, by John Greenleaf Whittier.

1990

Mars. In Roman mythology, god of war, originally an ancient Italian god who watched over agriculture; identified by the Romans with the Greek war god Ares. Mars was the son of Jupiter and father of Romulus (Quirinus) by Rhea Silvia. March, the first month of the old Roman year, was dedicated to Mars as the fertilizing god of spring. Mars was invoked, along with the goddess Dea Dia, to bless the fields during a festival in May. As god of war Mars was called *Gradivus* (the strider) because of his rapid march in battle. His symbols were the wolf, woodpecker, and lance; his shield was called the Ancile. When war broke out, the cry was *Mars vigila!* (Mars awake!) Numerous sacrifices were offered to Mars and warlike exercises, *Equirria*, were held in his honor on 27 February, 14 March, and 1the last day a horse was sacrificed on his altar in the Campus Martius (field of Mars), a plain lying to the north of Rome, outside the Pomerium, between the Tiber, the Quirinal and the Capitoline Hills. The blood of the horse was collected and preserved in the temple of Vesta and used at the *Palilia* for the purposes of purification. Mar's cult had a special priest, the *flamen martialis*, and a group of *Salci* (dancers). During Mars's feast in March the Salci sang, danced, and beat their shields with staves. Augustus honored Mars as Mars Vitor (avenger of Caesar) in a temple erected in 2 B.C.E. Mars was the patron god of pagan Florence, later replaced by St. John the Baptist, whose church is believed to stand on the spot where Mars's temple originally stood. Dante's *Divine Comedy* (Inferno 13; Paradise 16) cites the legend that the statue of Mars, hidden in the Arno tower, had to be restored before Florence could be rebuilt. Western paintings depicting Mars usually portray his love affair with Venus. Botticelli, Piero di Cosimo, Tintoretto, Veronese, Poussin, and David have all treated the subject.

1991
Marsyas (battler). In Greek mythology, a Phrygian flute player, or satyr, son of Olympus; sometimes called Silenus; follower of the Great Mother goddess Cybele. Marsyas, who took up the flute after it had been discarded by its creator, Athena, challenged Apollo to a contest between his flute and Apollo's lyre. Marsyas lost, and Apollo bound him to a tree and flayed him until he died. All of the spirits and deities of the woods lamented Marsyas' death, and their tears became the river Meander. King Midas, who had taken Marsyas' side in the contest, had his ears turned into those of an ass as punishment. The figure of Marsyas bound to a tree influenced many portrayals of the Crucifixion. In Plato's *Symposium* the great philosopher Socrates is called a Marsyas and a Silenus. Plato's *Republic* mentions the flute as an instrument that evokes the darker Dionysian, unruly passions, as opposed to Apollo's lyre, which represents harmony. Dante's invocation to Apollo in *The Divine Comedy* (Paradise, canto 1) uses the same imagery. Ovid's *Metamorphoses* (book 6) and Matthew Arnold's *Empedocles on Etna* deal with the myth. Raphael, Perugino, Tintoretto, Titian, and Rubens are among the artists who have treated the subject.

1992
Martha, St. (lady). First century C.E. In Christian legend, patron of cooks and housewives. Sister of Mary of Bethany and of Lazarus, whom Christ raised from the dead. Feast, 29 July.

Tertullian and other Early Church Fathers identify Mary of Bethany with Mary Magdalene, though this is not accepted by most biblical scholars today. In Christian art, however, Tertullian's interpretation has made its impact. In *Il Perfetto Legendario* the two sisters are contrasted. "Martha was a chaste and prudent Virgin, and the other publicly contemned for her evil life; notwithstanding which, Martha did not despise her, nor reject her as a sister, but wept for her shame, and admonished her gently and with persuasive words; and reminded her of her noble birth, to which she was a disgrace, and that Lazarus, their brother, being a soldier, would certainly get into trouble on her account. So she prevailed, and conducted her sister to the presence of Christ."

In a Provençal legend Mary Magdalene went to preach in Marseilles, while Martha went to preach in Aix and the surrounding countryside. There was a fearful dragon, called the Tarasque, which St. Martha overcame by sprinkling it with holy water and binding it with her girdle or, in other accounts, her garter. Rubens painted the scene of *Christ in the House of Martha and Mary* which portrays a simple Martha with an apron, while Mary is richly dressed, listening to Christ's words.

St. Martin

1993
Martin of Tours, St. (from Mars, Roman god of war). Fourth century C.E. In Christian legend, patron saint of armorers, beggars, cavalry, coopers, domestic animals, girdlers, glovers, horses and horsemen, millers, innkeepers, tailors, wine merchants, and wool weavers. Invoked against drunkenness, storms and ulcers. Feast, 11 November.

Martin was born in the Roman province of Pannonia during the reign of Constantine. His parents were pagan. He was a tribune in the army and was sent into Gaul on a campaign. The *Dialogues* of Sulpicius Severus gives the well-known legend of St. Martin and the beggar. When he was 18, he was stationed at Amiens during a very severe winter. One bitterly cold day a beggar, naked and shaking, came near his station. Martin, like all the other soldiers, was in armor, but over his steel he had a large military cloak. As none of his companions took notice of the beggar, Martin cut his cloak into two with his sword and gave half of it to the beggar. At night Christ appeared to Martin in a vision. He was dressed in the parted cloak and asked Martin if he recognized the garment, adding, "What is done to the poor in My name is done unto me." Martin then resolved to be baptized. After leaving the army Martin retired to a religious life and was made bishop of Tours in 371. Many other miracles are recorded of him: he raised a widow's son to life, restored a slave of the Proconsul from the possession of the devil, held converse with angels, and quenched fire by prayer.

He is usually pictured on horseback, dividing his cloak with a beggar. There is a well-known painting of this incident by El Greco in which the Saint is portrayed in 16th-century Spanish costume, with a ruff.

1994

Marunogere. In Melanesian mythology, Kiwai Papuan god and culture hero. He created the first pig and coconut tree, built the first house, and instituted sacred ceremonies. Two dogs are his companions.

1995

Maruts (flashing). In Hindu mythology, wind gods who form part of the entourage of Indra, the storm god, or of Rudra (another name for Shiva). Their number varies in different texts, the seven major ones being Vayuvega (wind speed), Vayubala (wind force), Vayuha (wind destroyer), Vayumandala (wind circle), Vayujvala (wind flame), Vayuretas (wind seed), and Vayucakra (wind disk). Maruts are also called Rudras.

1996

Marwe. In an African folktale told by the Chaga of Tanzania, Marwe and her brother were instructed to keep the jungle monkeys from eating the family's beans. After keeping a long watch they grew thirsty and went off to a distant pool to find water. Marwe threw herself into the pool when she learned that in her absence the monkeys had eaten all of the beans. She preferred to die rather than face the anger of her parents. When she reached the bottom of the pool,

she met an old woman who permitted Marwe to live with her.

In time Marwe became homesick and was given the opportunity to return to her parents. First, however, she was asked to choose between hot and cold. Marwe, not knowing what the choice involved, chose cold. She was startled to find her arms and legs covered with expensive bangles. When Marwe appeared by the side of the pool, all of the young men wanted to marry her. She chose Sawoye, whose skin had many blemishes. Soon, however, his skin cleared, and he became a very handsome mate. Marwe and Sawoye prospered, but jealous neighbors killed him. Marwe, however, was able to bring him back to life and hid him in their home. As the neighbors advanced on the home in an effort to take her riches from Marwe, Sawoye suddenly appeared and killed them.

St. Mary Magdalene

1997

Mary Magdalene, St. (rebellion? wished-for child?) First century C.E. In the Bible, N.T., penitent woman. Western art, following Christian legend, makes no distinction between Mary, the sister of Martha and Lazarus, Mary Magdalene, and the "woman which was a sinner," though they appear to have been historically three distinct persons. Feast, 22 July.

In the New Testament Mary Magdalene was a follower of Christ and "ministered" to him. She had been possessed by seven devils, which Christ drove from her. Her courage is illustrated by the fact that she was at the foot of the cross with Mary the mother of Jesus and John, whereas the other disciples fled. Mary was also the first one to see the risen Christ, according to the account in John's Gospel (20:11–17). This episode is called in Latin the *Noli me tangere* (touch me not). It is frequently found in medieval and later Christian art. The New Testament tells us nothing of the later life of the saint, though medieval Christian legend has supplied much. According to legend, Mary Magdalene and her brother Lazarus and sister Martha, accompanied by Maximin and Marcella (later sainted) set out in a ship without sail or oar and came to Marseilles. Here they converted the people, with Lazarus becoming the first bishop of Marseilles.

Despite Mary Magdalene's reformation, the sinful aspect of her life has appealed to both poets and artists, who often portray her as a penitent. Richard Crashaw, the 17th-century English poet, in his *Carmen Deo Nostro* has a poem *St. Mary Magdalene or the Weeper* in which numerous lines are expended on the profusion of tears the saint shed over her sinful life. In paintings St. Mary Magdalene is usually portrayed as a beautiful woman with long fair hair. She has near her a box of ointment, referring to the spices to anoint the dead Jesus. Sometimes, however, she is portrayed as a wasted woman. When she is shown in the desert, praying or reading, the emblems of penance, such as a skull or bones, are nearby. Titian, the great painter of the Italian Renaissance, painted her in this manner.

St. Mary of Egypt

Mary of Egypt, St. (rebellion? wished-for child?)
Fourth century C.E. In Christian legend, prostitute who became a saint. Feast, 2 April.

St. Jerome wrote that in Alexandria there was a woman "whose name was Mary, and who in the infamy of her life far exceeded Mary Magdalene." After having passed 17 years in "every species of vice" one day she spotted a ship that was ready to sail to Jerusalem "to celebrate the feast of the true cross." She was "seized with a sudden desire to accompany them" but had no money, so she paid her way with "every means in her power." When they arrived at Jerusalem, all of the worshipers entered the church except for Mary whose "attempts to pass the threshold were in vain," for a supernatural

power drove "her back in shame, in terror, in despair." Convinced that she should mend her ways, she prayed and renounced her wicked life. She bought three loaves of bread and "wandered forth into the solitude" until she had reached the desert. She lived in the Syrian desert as a female hermit. She was finally discovered by St. Zosimus after 47 years. He was asked to bring the Holy Communion to the saint at the end of the year. When he returned, he was not able to pass over the Jordan, but Mary, "supernaturally assisted," passed over the water and received the Holy Communion. St. Zosimus was to return the next year to give her Communion, but when he arrived he found she had died. He buried her body with the assistance of a lion who helped him dig the grave.

St. Mary of Egypt, though sometimes confused with St. Mary Magdalene, is frequently shown in art as a wasted woman, stripped of her clothes, her long hair covering her body, with three loaves of bread. She is thus portrayed in Quentin Massys's painting *St. Mary of Egypt*, as well as in a painting by Emil Nolde.

Masewi and Oyoyewi. In North American Indian mythology (Acoma), twin war spirits who were sent by their mother to place the sun in the sky in its correct position and to assign clans to the people.

Masnavi, The (couplets). Persian mystical poem in 27,000 couplets, divided into six books, written in the 13th century by Rumi, a Sufi mystic. It embodies fables, folklore, legends from the Koran, and religious and moral teaching.

The Masnavi is considered Rumi's major work, being one of the most important documents of the Sufis, a mystic order related to Islam that employs the language of the senses to express longing for reunion with God. Rumi's text is an attempt to explain the doctrines of Sufism in popular form. Though the Persian poet Omar Khayyam is better known among Westerners because of the 19th-century translation by Edward Fitzgerald, Fitzgerald's teacher, the Reverend Edward B. Cowell, hated the doubting Omar Khayyam but loved *The Masnavi* as one of the most brilliant religious poems in the world.

Variant spellings: Mathnawi, Mathnwi-i-Ma'nawi, Mesnevi.

Mason wasp. One of the most common of African insects, the mason wasp builds its mud nest on almost any type of object. It often creates a nest near a fireplace and for that reason is commonly credited in mythology with having brought fire to earth. According to the Ila people of Zambia, the mason wasp volunteered to go to heaven, along with three birds to ask God for fire so that all of the birds and insects of the world could keep warm during winter. Each of the three birds died en route to heaven, leaving only the mason wasp to petition God for fire. God pitied him and decided to grant his wish. He made him chief of all birds and insects and told him to build his nests near fireplaces.

Mass. In Christianity, common name for the central act of worship, also called the Holy Eucharist, the Liturgy, the Lord's Supper, and Holy Communion. [2002]

Based on Jewish and pagan rituals, the Mass uses bread, which is basic to the human diet, and wine, which is associated with vitality and fellowship, for communion with Christ, the Risen Lord. The earliest account of the ritual is found in St. Paul's first letter to the Corinthians (I Cor. 11:2–26, New Jerusalem Bible):

> For the tradition I received from the Lord and also handed on to you is that on the night he was betrayed, the Lord Jesus took some bread, and after he had given thanks, he broke it, and he said, "This is my body, which is for you; do this in remembrance of me." And in the same way, with the cup after supper, saying, "This cup is the new covenant in my blood. Whenever you drink it, do this as a memorial of me."

For centuries Christians have debated the meaning of the words, sometimes killing one another over their disagreements. Some Christians, such as Roman Catholics, believe that the bread and wine literally become the Body and Blood of Christ, calling it transsubstantiation; Anglicans believe in the real presence, though they don't define it; Lutherans believe in consubstantiation—the bread and wine exist along with the Body and Blood of Christ; and still other Christians hold that the rite is merely symbolic and that the bread and wine remain bread and wine. The ancient mystery cults that existed at the time of the birth of Christianity also had communion meals in which bread and wine were part of the ritual. Worship of Orpheus, Osiris, Mithra, Attis, and Dionysus each had a ritual meal as part of the cult.

The Latin Mass, which was fixed by the Council of Trent in the 16th century, broke down as follows: the Ordinary, with unchanging text, and the Proper, with a changing text, depending on whether the Mass was for a special feast day or a saint's day or

was a Requiem Mass for the dead. Settings of the musical section of the Mass usually were

Kyrie (Lord, have mercy)
Gloria (Glory to God in the highest)
Credo (The Nicene Creed, beginning "I believe in One God")
Sanctus and Benedictus (Holy, Holy, Holy)
Agnus Dei (Lamb of God)

The Mass text has been set by many composers, among them Guillaume de Machaut, Dufay, Ockeghem, Obrecht, Josquin Des Prés, Byrd, Tallis, Palestrina, J. S. Bach, Haydn, Mozart, Beethoven, Cherubini, Schubert, Liszt, Bruckner, Franck, Gounod, Verdi, Villa-Lobos, Poulenc, Stravinsky, and Vaughan Williams. A setting of the Russian liturgy was composed by Tchaikovsky.

Masterson, Bat. d. 1921. In American history and folklore, a sheriff noted for his fine suits, pearl-gray bowler, diamond stickpin, and notched gun. Once a man pestered Masterson to sell him his gun as a souvenir. Not wishing to part with his gun, Masterson went out and purchased a Colt .45 to sell to the gentleman. To make the gun even more interesting he put 22 notches oit. When the collector called for his souvenir, Bat handed him the notched gun. Stunned, the man asked him if he had killed 22 men. According to legenBat replied: "I didn't tell him yes, and I didn't tell him no, and I didn't exactly lie to him. I simply said I hadn't counted either Mexicans or Indians, and he went away tickled to death." Bat Masterson appeared as the subject of a television series. [2003]

Mater Matuta. In Roman mythology, goddess of sea travel, originally an early Italian goddess of birth, dawn (often identified with Aurora), harbors, and the sea, and as such identified with the Greek Leucothea. Her festival, *Matralia* (festival of mothers) was celebrated on 11 June. [2004]

Mati-Syra-Zemlya (moist Mother Earth). In Russian mythology, earth goddess. [2005]

The worship of Mati-Syra-Zemlya continued in Russia up to the eve of World War I, when peasants invoked her protection against the spread of cholera. At midnight the old women of the village would gather, summoning one another without the knowledge of the men. Nine virgins would be chosen to go with the old women to the village outskirts. There they would all undress down to their shifts. The virgins would let down their hair, and the widows would cover their heads with white shawls. A widow would then be hitched to a plow, which was driven by another widow. The nine virgins would take up scythes, and the other women took up such objects as the skulls of animals. They would all march around the village, howling and screaming as they plowed a furrow to allow the spirits of Mati-Syra-Zemlya to emerge and destroy all evil spirits, such as the cholera. If a man happened to see this ceremony, he would be seized and killed.

Some Russian peasants would listen to Mati-Syra-Zemlya by digging the earth with a stick or their fingers. If the digging sounded like a well-stocked sleigh moving over the snow, it meant crops would be good. If it sounded like an empty sleigh, the crops would be bad.

Igor Stravinsky's ballet *Le Sacre du printemps* (The Rite of Spring), deals with the worship of Mother Earth in pagan Russia. The ballet's subtitle is *Pictures of Pagan Russia*. The work was first performed by Diaghilev's Ballets Russes in Paris with choreography by Vaslav Nijinsky, who Stravinsky thought completely misunderstood the ballet. The sets and costumes were by Nicholas Roerich, who was also responsible, with Stravinsky, for the scenario of the ballet. At the ballet's first performance there was a near riot between those who accepted the modern effects of the score and those who violently protested, saying the work violated all known principles of music. Today *Le Sacre du printemps* is recognized as one of the greatest innovations in 20th-century music.

2006

Matowelia. In North American Indian mythology (Mojave), culture hero who led the Mojave Indians from the White Mountains to their home along the Colorado River. At death the spirits of the Indians would return to the White Mountains. If they were not ritually burned, they would become screech owls.

2007

Matronalia (matron, a married woman). In Roman cult, festivals in honor of Mars and Juno, celebrated on 1 march, the anniversary of the foundation of the temple of Juno Lucina on the Esquiline, by married women in commemoration of the rape of the Sabines and of the peace that later ensued. Flowers were offered in the temple of Juno, who was also called Matrona because she presided over marriage and childbirth.

Ma Tsu P'o

Mars

2008

Ma Tsu P'o. In Chinese Taoist mythology, Queen of Heaven and Holy Mother, invoked by sailors to grant good weather and safe sailing. Jesuit missionaries compared Ma Tsu P'o to the Virgin Mary.

2009

Matthew, St. (gift of Yahweh). First century C.E. In the Bible, N.T., Evangelist and Apostle. Author of the Gospel bearing his name. Patron of bankers and tax collectors. Feast, 21 September.

Little is known of his life. The gospels give only the account of his calling by Jesus (Mark 2:14). It is a widely accepted theory that Levi and Matthew are the same person. Jesus is believed to have given Levi the name Matthew. There are two different traditions of the death of St. Matthew. According to Greek legend, he died during the reign of Domitian, but according to Western legend, he was martyred by either a sword or a spear.

In art, aside from his symbol as an angel with a book in his role as evangelist, he is often portrayed at the moment he answered Christ's call, as in Caravaggio's painting.

2010

Mátyás. 1440–1490. In Hungarian legend, a king noted for his just rule. He became popular among the peasants during his lifetime for his humane measures in alleviating the hard life of the serfs. Shortly after his death Mátyás became the subject of numerous legends in the manner of King Arthur or King Solomon. Up to the beginning of the present century Hungarian peasants believed that King Mátyás would reappear again and their lives would then be better. The belief is similar to the English belief that King Arthur will return in a dark time and restore justice. A well-known Hungarian proverb is "King Mátyás is dead; justice has passed with him."

2011

Maui. In Polynesian mythology, great trickster and culture hero who snared the sun and brought fire to mankind but died while attempting to give man immortality.

Maui's father was Tama, the sky, and his mother was Taranga, who gave birth to him prematurely. When he was born, she wrapped him in a tuft of her hair and cast him into the surf, but a jellyfish surrounded the body of the young child, protecting him from any harm. Tama saw the object floating in the ocean and came down to investigate. When he removed the jellyfish he found the baby and took him to his home in the sky, placing the boy on the roof of his house so that he would be warmed by the fire inside. After a short time Maui became restless and decided to go to earth to see his mother and brothers. He entered the assembly hall while his family was attending a dance. Sitting behind his brothers, he waited for his mother, Taranga, to come and count her sons. When she reached Maui, she said he was not one of her children. But when the lad told her his story, she was convinced and said, "You are indeed my last born son." She brought him home

and let him sleep in her bed, which annoyed his brothers.

When Maui's father, Tama, saw his son, he was pleased and decided to perform a naming ceremony, which would make Maui sacred and would cleanse all impurities. After the ceremony it was discovered that some prayers had been omitted and that the gods would punish Maui because of the omission.

Maui is credited with setting the length of the day. Annoyed with the shortness of the day, Maui persuaded his brothers that they should capture the sun in a net and force the sun to slow down.

His brothers at first objected to his plan but later agreed. They made a noose, and Maui took his magic jawbone that he had procured from his grandmother Muri-ranga-whenuam. The brothers then traveled all night to the desert where the sun rises and hid themselves. Maui made a large circle with a length of rope.

Maui said to his brothers, "Keep yourselves hidden, and do not show yourselves to the sun; if you do, you will frighten him. Wait patiently until his head and forelegs are well into the snare, then I will shout. You haul away as hard as you can on both ends of the rope, and I will rush out and beat him until he is nearly dead. And, my brothers, do not let him move you to pity with his shrieks and screams."

When the sun was caught, Maui beat him until he began to move at a slower pace, thus setting the length of the day.

Maui also captured fire for mankind. He went to the underworld and asked Mahu'ike for some fire with which to cook. She (in some accounts a male) gave him one of her fingernails, which contained fire. He later returned to her and said the fire had gone out, and he needed another fingernail, which she gave him. This went on until the goddess was left with only one toenail, and she then realized what Maui was up to. She threw her last toenail to the ground, and it immediately burst into flame. Maui then transformed himself into an eagle in order to escape, but his wings were singed. Mahu'ike saved some of the flames by throwing them into the treetops. To this day men make fire by rubbing two sticks together.

Maui next tried to obtain immortality. He set off with some birds to find Hina-nui-te-po (great goddess of the night), the goddess who ruled the dead. When he arrived in the underworld, he found her asleep.

"My little friends," he said to the birds, "when you see me enter the body of this old chieftainess, be careful not to laugh. If you do, she will awaken and kill me. But when you see me coming out of her mouth, you can laugh, and I will live and Hine-nui-te-po will die."

Maui took off his clothes and entered the goddess through her vagina. When the birds saw his feet sticking out of the goddess's vagina, they almost burst into laughter. One wagtail could not contain himself and let out a laugh, which awoke Hine-nui-te-po, who crushed Maui inside herself. So Maui failed to achieve immortality for humankind.

To this day the Maori recite this proverb: "Men make heirs, but death carries them off."

This account of Maui is based on Sir George Grey's *Polynesian Mythology*. Maui is also known as Amorshashiki, Ma-tshikt-shiki, Mosigsig, and Motikitik.

Variant spelling: Mowee.

2012

Maundy Thursday. In Christian ritual, the Thursday of Holy Week, sometimes called Holy Thursday, Shere, or Chare. The main rite during the day is the washing of the feet of the poor by a priest, based on the command in John's Gospel (13:34) in which Jesus said, "A new commandment I give unto you, love one another as I have loved you." With these words Jesus washed the feet of his disciples. During the Christian Middle Ages it was the custom for a bishop or priest to wash the feet of 12 beggars or a group of pilgrims. St. Oswald, archbishop of York (972–992 C.E.) instructed his clergy to feed 12 poor men and wash their feet every day. English kings also would follow the sacred rite. St. Thomas More tells how King Henry VIII washed the feet of the poor and gave them food and money. Queen Elizabeth I also washed the feet of a pauper, but she first had them washed in herb-scented water by her servants before she performed the rite. The rite of washing the feet is still observed in the Roman and Anglican churches, but was discontinued by Luther, who denounced it. In 1718 12 Lutherans were forced to do public penance for having a duke wash their feet. (The name Maundy is believed to derive from the Latin translation of Jesus' command, *Mandatum novum de vobis*.)

2013

Maurice and the Theban Legion, St. (Moorish, dark-skinned). Died 286 C.E. In Christian legend, Roman captain of the Theban Legion. Patron of armies, armorers, infantry, hatters, and knife grinders. Invoked against demonic possession, enemies of religion, and gout. Venerated at St. Maurice-en-Valois, St. Moritz, and Zofingen. One of the patron saints of Austria. Feast, 22 September.

Among the legions that made up the Roman army at the time of Diocletian and Maximin was one called the Theban Legion because it originated in Thebald. All of the 6,666 soldiers were Christians, and their leader was Maurice or Mauritius. About the year 286 Maximin summoned the legion from the East to reinforce the army about to march into Gaul. After the passage through the Alps, some of the army was sent on to the Rhine while the rest remained on the banks of Lake Geneva, where Emperor Maximin ordered sacrifices to pagan gods, accompanied by games and ceremonies. Maurice and the Christian soldiers retired some three leagues away and made camp at Aganum, now Saint-Maurice. The Emperor demanded that offerings be made to the pagan gods, but Maurice refused.

Some of the Theban Legion were trampled down by the cavalry, some hung on trees and shot with arrows, some killed by the sword. Maurice and some of his officers knelt down and were beheaded.

St. Maurice is usually shown in complete armor; he bears in one hand a standard, in the other a palm. Southern European art often shows him dressed as a Roman soldier, as in El Greco's painting of the saint. German art shows him as a Moorish knight, as in Hans Baldung Grien's painting.

2014

Mauvais. In Haitian voodoo, an evil man or woman who uses the evil eye against a person, often causing death.

2015

Mawu Lisa. In African mythology (Fon of Benin), bisexual god— part male, part female—who became the source of all other gods. Each pair of their children (for all were born as sets of twins) was given an area to rule. Lisa, the male twin, is associated with the sun; Mawu, his female counterpart, is the moon. The first pair was given the earth to rule, and the other six were assigned the sea, weather, hunt, human life span, and similar things to control. Mawu, as the moon, is more inclined to softness, whereas Lisa is forceful and unrelenting. Mawu is the older of the two and is regarded as the embodiment of wisdom; Lisa is the personification of physical strength. At times Mawu is referred to as the Supreme Being without any reference being made to Lisa. Some accounts say Nana Buluka, an androgynous deity, existed before Mawu Lisa and created the god.

2016

Maya. Fifth century B.C.E. In Buddhist legend, mother of the Buddha. She led a pure life, entitling her to be the mother of the coming Buddha. Maya had a dream in which the future Buddha appeared to her as a white elephant and entered her right side. The dream is frequently portrayed in Buddhist art.

2017

Maya (the maker). In Hindu mythology, the architect of the demons. In the epic poem *The Mahabharata* he built a palace for the Pandavas. *Maya* is also the word used to mean the created world as experienced independently by its creator and often is mistakenly translated as "illusion."

2018

Mayan letter gods. System of identifying Mayan deities found in Indian codices or manuscripts. To make it easier to distinguish these nameless gods, the scholar Paul Schellhas published *Representation of Deities of the Maya Manuscripts* (1904), in which he assigned letters *A* through *P* (omitting *J*) to the gods encountered in the manuscripts. They are as follows:

God A. God of death, often identified with Ah Puch, depicted with bells, crossbones, and an owl. He is often portrayed as a skull.

God B. God of rain and thunder, identified with Chac or Kukulcán, portrayed with a long truncated nose and tusks.

God C. God of the North Star, often identified with Xaman Ek (the Venus star), portrayed surrounded by planetary signs.

God D. God of the moon and night sky, often identified with Kukulcán or Itzamná, usually portrayed as an aged man with sunken cheeks, wearing a serpent headdress.

God E. God of corn, often identified with Yum Kaxx; portrayed wearing a leaf of corn as part of his headdress.

God F. God of war and death, often identified with Xipe, the flayed god, portrayed with black lines on his face and body, perhaps signifying death wounds.

God G. God of the sun, Kukulcán in his sun god role, sometimes having a symbol of death nearby because he needed human blood to sustain himself.

God H. Unknown god on whose forehead the scale or skin spot of a serpent appears, perhaps Kukulcán in his serpent aspect.

Goddess I. Goddess of water, often identified with Ixchel, sometimes portrayed wearing a knotted serpent on her head and holding in one hand a vessel from which water is pouring. She is a personification of water in its destructive aspect and is sometimes shown with crossbones, symbols of death.

God K. God of the wind, perhaps Itzamná, related to God B and called by Schellhas the "god of the ornamental nose."

God L. Called the Old Black God by Schellhas because he is portrayed with aged features and toothless gums. One half of his face, sometimes the upper half and other times the lower half, is painted black.

God M. God of traveling merchants, sometimes identified with the god Ex Chuah.

God N. The God of the End of the Year, according to Schellhas, portrayed with the head of an old man and wearing a headdress that includes the sign for the year of 360 days.

Goddess O. Goddess of feminine old age; she appears in only one manuscript, as an old woman with a single tooth in her lower jaw.

God P. The Frog God, according to Schellhas, portrayed with the webbing of a frog and a blue background symbolizing water.

2019

Mayauel. In Aztec mythology, goddess of pulque, the intoxicating drink made from the fermented sap of the agave.

Mayauel was the wife of a farmer. One day she chased a mouse away from the maguey (agave) plantation. She found that the mouse had eaten the heart from one of the plants and had drunk its juice. As a result the mouse swayed unsteadily and was in fact drunk. Mayauel and her husband put some of the juice from the plant in a jar and left it while they went to work in the fields. When they returned, they took a drink. They soon swayed unsteadily and became drunk. The gods, not wanting to miss out on such a discovery, took the spirit of Mayauel and made her into a goddess. In some accounts the pulque god is called Ometochtli (two rabbits). He was killed by Texcatlipoca, the Aztec creator-trickster god.

2020

Mazeppa, Ivan. 1644–1709. In Slavic history and legend, Cossack hero and leader.

Born of a noble family, Mazeppa became a page at the court of the Polish king. He had an affair with the young wife of a nobleman and as a punishment was tied naked to a wild horse, which was then turned loose. Mazeppa was saved by Cossacks, and in time became a hetman, or leader, and Prince of the Ukraine under Peter the Great of Russia. Later, however, Mazeppa betrayed Russia to Charles XII of Sweden, when the king invaded the Ukraine. He appears in Lord Byron's poem *Mazeppa*, Pushkin's poem *Poltava*, and Tchaikovsky's opera *Mazeppa*. Victor Hugo's poem *Mazeppa* tells of the hero's ride while tied to the wild horse; Liszt's tone poem *Mazeppa* and Delacroix's painting deal with the same subject.

2021

Médard of Noyon, St. Died 545. In Christian legend, patron saint of brewers, peasants, and prisoners. Invoked on behalf of idiots and lunatics; also for fruitfulness, both in childbearing and the fields, for rains and vineyards, and against bad weather and tooth-ache. Feast, 8 June.

Once a sudden shower fell, wetting everyone in the town except St. Médard, who remained perfectly dry, for an eagle had spread its wings over him. Ever after he was called *maître de la pluie* (master of the rain), and it was believed that if it rained on Médard's feast day, it would rain for 40 days thereafter. Médard founded the Rose Festival at Salency in which the most virtuous girl in the parish received a crown of roses and a purse of money. De Maupassant's tale "Le Rosier de Madame Husson," which Benjamin Britten used as the basis for his opera *Albert Herring*, describes the festival.

2022

Medea (cunning). In Greek mythology, great sorcer-ess and enchantress, daughter of Aëetes, king of Col-chis, and Eidyia; sister of Absyrtus and half sister of Chalciope; wife of the hero Jason. To assist Jason in his quest for the Golden Fleece, the goddess Aphro-dite caused Medea to fall in love with the handsome hero. Medea aided Jason through her skill in magic and witchcraft. She was a priestess of Hecate, god-dess of night and witchcraft, according to some ac-counts. Medea so loved Jason that she killed her brother Absyrtus when he pursued her as the couple fled. When Medea and Jason arrived at Iolcos, Medea rejuvenated Jason's father Aeson by boiling him with a mixture of magical herbs in a vat. Then, in an evil plan, she encouraged the daughters of Aeson's brother Pelias to do the same for their father. The girls eagerly did as told, and the old man was boiled to death. Again the couple fled, this time to Corinth. Here Jason grew tired of Medea and de-cided to marry Glauce (or Creusa), the king's daugh-ter. Medea destroyed the girl with a poisoned robe and diadem, which caught fire when Glauce put them on. When Glauce's father attempted to save his daughter, he too was destroyed. Not yet satisfied, Medea further punished Jason for his betrayal of her by killing their two sons, Mermerus and Pheres. Leaving Jason desolate, Medea then fled to Athens in a chariot drawn by two dragons. She married Aegeus, king of the city, but later became jealous of his son Theseus and had to flee again. Eventually, she returned to Colchis, where she was believed to be immortal. Medea appears in Euripides' *Medea* and the modern English version by the American poet Robinson Jeffers; Seneca's *Medea*; Ovid's *Heroides* (12) and *Metamorphoses* (book 7); Apollonius Rhodius' short epic poem *Argonautica* (Voyage of the Argo); Gower's *Confessio amantis*; Chaucer's *Legend of Good Women*; Corneille's *Médée*; Cherubini's opera *Medea*; Jean Anouilh's *Médée*; Pasolini's film *Medea*, with Maria Callas, who also sang the role in Cherubini's

opera; Delacroix's painting *Medea*, which portrays her about to kill her children; and Samuel Barber's *Medea's Meditation and Dance of Vengeance* in the ballet "Cave of the Heart" with choreography by Martha Graham.

2023

Mehen. In Egyptian mythology, a great serpent. Me-hen surrounds the sun god in his boat to protect him from the monster serpent Apophis. The sun god is portrayed as a ram-headed deity in his role of cross-ing the heavens at night. He usually wears a solar disk. Around the sun god in this form is a cabin, and Mehen is often portrayed coiling around the cabin as a sign of protection.

Melchizedek

2024

Melchizedek (king of righteousness). In the Bible, O.T., king and high priest of Salem. Abraham met Melchizedek when Abraham was returning from rescuing Lot. Melchizedek blessed Abraham and gave him food and wine (Gen. 14:18). In medieval Christian symbolism, based on the Epistle to the He-brews (5:6) in the New Testament, Melchizedek is seen as a prefiguration of Christ because his offering of food and wine seemed to echo the Christian Eucharist.

2025

Meleager (guinea fowl). In Greek mythology, a hero, an Argonaut son of Ares or Oeneus and Althaea; brother or half brother of Deianeira, Gorge, and Toxeus; husband of Cleopatra, daughter of Idas; fa-ther of Polydora. He was one of the members of the Calydonian boar hunt. In Homer's *Iliad* (book 9) Meleager is cited as a hero who long defended his city and was killed during the Calydonian boar hunt. In Ovid's *Metamorphoses* (book 8) Meleager's life is snuffed out by his mother. She had been told by the

Fates at his birth that as long as a firebrand then in the fireplace did not burn down, Meleager would live. Althaea removed the log and stored it in a chest. When she discovered that Meleager had killed her brothers after the Calydonian boar hunt, she took out the log and cast it into the flames, causing his death. The best-known treatment of the myth in English literature is Swinburne's poetic drama *Atalanta in Calydon*.

2026

Melisenda. In medieval Spanish legends, daughter of Charlemagne and the wife of Gayferos. She was captured by the Moors and held prisoner for seven years. Eventually, she was freed by her husband. Cervantes's *Don Quixote* (Part 2) has the tale acted out by puppets before the Don. This section of the novel was used by Manuel de Falla for his opera *El retablo de maese Pedro*.

2027

Melusina. In European folklore, a being that is half woman, half fish-serpent, who lived some of the time in a well. Melusina was a full woman during most of the week, but on Saturday she had to return to her snake-fish form. In one medieval French tale she married Raymond, nephew of the count of the Poitier, on the condition that she be free on Saturday nights. One day her husband caught Melusina in her snake-fish transformation and she fled. She left two children and is regarded as an ancestor of three noble French families. Occasionally Melusina is depicted in British heraldry as a mermaid with two tails. Mendelssohn's overture *The Fair Melusina* is based on her tale.

2028

Mena (menstruate). In Roman mythology, goddess who presided over women's monthly menstrual periods. Some accounts say young puppies that still suckled their mothers were sacrificed to Mena.

2029

Menelaus (might of the people). In Greek mythology, king of Sparta; son of Atreus and Aerope; younger brother of Agamemnon, Anixibia, and Pleisthenes; husband of Helen. He returned to Sparta with Helen after the Trojan War. His return voyage is described in Homer's *Odyssey* (book 4), and Theocritus' *Idyll 18* is a marriage song for Menelaus and Helen. Menelaus and Helen were worshiped as demigods at Therapne near Sparta. He appears in Homer's *Iliad* and *Odyssey*, Euripides' *Helen*, and Vergil's *Aeneid*.

2030

Menorah (candelabrum). In Judaism, a seven-or eight-branched candlestick. The seven-branched candlestick was used in the Temple and is described in Exodus (37:17–23): "And he [Bezalel] made the candlestick of pure gold: of beaten work made he the candlestick . . . three branches of the candlestick out of the one side thereof, and three branches of the candlestick out of the other side. . . . And he made his seven lamps, and his snuffers, and his snuffdishes, of pure gold."

The Arch of Titus in Rome portrays the menorah of the Second Temple being taken away after the Romans had captured the city. The base consists of squares. Recent research, however, indicates that the menorah of the Second Temple had three legs, not a square base.

The eight-branched menorah is used for the feast of Hanukkah; it has a ninth socket for the candle that lights the other branches. The Kabbalah calls the menorah the Tree of Life. According to one Jewish tradition, the Temple menorah was never extinguished until the destruction of the Temple.

2031

Menthu. In Egyptian mythology, a sun god associated with war, often combined with the god Ra and known as Menthu-Ra. The ancient Greeks equated the Egyptian god with their sun god Apollo.

Variant spellings: Mentu, Mont.

2032

Mephistopheles (he who loves not the light). In Jewish and Christian folklore, either a minion of the devil or the devil himself.

Mephistopheles' most prominent role in folklore is found in the various treatments of the Faust legend, which originated in the late Middle Ages. *The Historie of the Damnable Life, and Deserved Death of Doctor John Faustus*, translated from the German by P. F. in 1592, describes an early appearance of Mephistopheles to Faust, or Faustus. "Suddenly there appeared his Spirit Mephostophiles [sic], in likeness of a fiery man, from whom issued most horrible fiery flames. . . . the Spirit began to blare as in a singing manner. This pretty sport pleased Doctor Faustus well."

Mephistopheles assumes various animal forms to entertain the doctor and then takes on the "apparel" of a friar and offers a document to Faust to sign away his soul. "Faustus being resolute in his damnation, wrote a copy thereof, and gave the Devil the one, and kept in store the other." In this account Mephistopheles is himself the devil. In Marlowe's play *The Tragical History of Doctor Faustus*, Mephistopheles is the leading demonic character, though Lucifer and Beelzebub also appear. When

As long as on earth he shall survive,
So long you'll meet no prohibition
Man errs as long as he doth strive.
(George M. Priest translation)

In Goethe's play Faust is saved; in Marlowe's work he is lost.

Mephistopheles is the main character in Arrigo Boïto's opera *Mefistofele*, based on Goethe's work and on Ferruccio Busoni's *Doktor Faust*, another opera based on Goethe. In Franz Liszt's *Faust Symphony* the last movement depicts the character of Mephistopheles in grotesque variations because according to the philosopher Hegel, he "represents the negative principle." Perhaps the best graphic representation of Mephistopheles is in the series of lithographs by Eugene Delacroix published in 1828 to illustrate Goethe's *Faust*; though a series done by Harry Clarke in a Beardsleyesque style capture better some of the grotesque qualities of the demon.

2033

Mera (glistening). In Greek mythology, a faithful dog who was transformed into the Lesser Dog Star, Canis (or Sirius). Mera showed Erigone, Icarius' daughter, where her murdered father had been thrown. Immediately after the discovery, Erigone hanged herself, and the Mera dog pined away. The myth is found in Ovid's *Metamorphoses* (book 7). The name Mera is also borne by a priest of Aphrodite.

Mephistopheles

Faustus asks Mephistopheles how he is "out of hell," the demon replies:

Why, this is hell, nor am I out of it:
Thinkest thou that I, who saw the face of God,
And tasted th' eternal joys of heaven,
Am not tormented with ten thousand hells,
In being depriv'd of everlasting bliss?

In Goethe's working of the Faust legend in his mammoth drama *Faust*, Mephistopheles makes a wager with God, much as Satan does in the book of Job in the Old Testament, about how faithful Faust is to God. Mephistopheles says:

What will you wager? Him you yet shall lose,
If you will give me your permission
To lead him gently on the path I choose.

The Lord answers:

2034

Mercurius, St. (Mercury [Roman god]). Died 250. In Christian legend, warrior saint who murdered Julian the Apostate. Venerated in the Eastern Orthodox church. Feast, 25 November.

According to legend, Julian sold his soul to the devil when he renounced Christianity. On the night he was to go to battle against the Persians, St. Basil the Great had a vision of the Virgin Mary seated on a throne and around her a great multitude of angels. She commanded one of them, saying, "Go forthwith, and awaken Mercurius [who had been killed by Julian for being a Christian], who sleepeth in the sepulchre, that he may slay Julian the Apostate, that proud blasphemer against me and my son!"

When St. Basil awoke, he went to the tomb of Mercurius and saw that the body was missing. He returned the next day and found the body back in place, dressed in full armor, with the lance stained with blood. One medieval account says: "For on the day of battle, when the wicked emperor was at the head of his army, an unknown warrior, bareheaded, and of a pale and ghastly countenance, was seen mounted on a white charger, which he spurred forward, and, brandishing his lance, he pierced

Julian through the body and then vanished suddenly as he had appeared."

Julian was then taken to his tent. Taking a handful of the blood that flowed from his wound, he flung it into the air, saying, "Thou hast conquered, Galilean! Thou has conquered!" The devils then came and took his body to hell.

This fanciful Christian version of history has no basis in fact. Julian was killed by a javelin flung by an unknown hand.

2035

Mercury (merchant). In Roman mythology, ancient Italian god of merchants and traders; son of Jupiter and Maia; the Romans equated Mercury with the Greek god Hermes. Mercury was protector of the corn trade, especially in Sicily. He was honored in Rome by a temple near the Circus Maximus. Here, a merchants' guild, known as *Mercuriales*, established by the state presided over Mercury's worship. At the yearly festival of the temple and guild on 15 May the merchants sacrificed to Mercury and his mother, Maia. At the Porta Capena they sprinkled themselves and their merchandise with holy water. Mercury is cited or appears in Vergil's *Aeneid* (book 4); Ovid's *Fasti* (5); Chaucer's "Knight's Tale", part of *The Canterbury Tales*; Shakespeare's *Troilus and Cressida* (2.2.45), *Hamlet* (3.4.58), *King Henry IV, Part I* (4.1.106), *Anthony and Cleopatra* (4.15.36); Milton's *Paradise Lost* (4.717–5.285) and *Comus* (637). The element mercury,

Merlin (A. Beardsley)

also called quicksilver, was named after the god known for his swiftness. His attributes are the winged hat, winged shoes, and caduceus. An American automobile produced by the Ford Motor Company is also named after Mercury.

2036
Merlin (sparrow hawk). In Arthurian legend, the great enchanter, or magician. Some scholars believe that a person named Merlin lived in the fifth century C.E. and served under the British chiefs Aurelius Ambrosius and King Arthur. Legend says he lost his mind after the battle of Solway Firth, broke his sword, and retired into the forest, where he was later found dead beside a riverbank. This thread of Merlin's story was greatly amplified during the Middle Ages.

According to various medieval sources, King Constans, who drove the Jute Hengist from England, was the father of three sons, Constantine, Aurelius Ambrosius, and Uther Pendragon. The dying Constans left the throne to his eldest son, Constantine, who chose Vortigern as his prime minister. Shortly after Constantine's accession, Hengist again invaded England. Constantine was deserted by Vortigern and was treacherously killed. In reward for his defection Vortigern was offered the crown, which he accepted. But Constans's other two sons (who, according to a variant account, were called Uther and Pendragon) were still alive and sought vengeance.

To defend himself against any army that might attempt to deprive him of his throne, Vortigern built a great fortress on Salisbury Plain. But although the masons worked diligently by day, building high, thick walls, they always found them overturned the next morning. Astrologers were consulted, and they said the walls would not stand until the ground had been watered with the blood of a child who could claim no human father.

Five years prior to this prediction, the demons, seeing that so many souls escaped hell owing to a Divine Child (Jesus Christ), had decided to have the devil father a child by a human virgin. A beautiful girl was chosen for the purpose. As she daily went to confession to a priest named Blaise, he soon discovered the evil plot of the demons and resolved to frustrate it.

On Blaise's advice the girl, instead of being immediately put to death for intercourse with the devil, was locked up in a tower, where she gave birth to a son. As soon as he heard the child's cries, Blaise ran in and baptized him, giving him the name Merlin. The Christian rite annulled the evil purpose of the demons, but nevertheless the child was gifted with strange and marvelous powers. When he was

five years old, he defended his mother from charges of witchcraft and proved her innocent.

His fame grew, and he came to the court of Vortigern. When asked why the walls of Salisbury would not stand, Merlin replied that two dragons— one red and one white—fought underground each night. A search was made, the dragons were discovered, and a battle was fought between the two. The white dragon won and then disappeared. Work on the walls then continued. Vortigern, however, was very uneasy because Merlin foresaw the coming conflict with Constans's sons and Vortigern's ultimate defeat. Merlin's prediction was soon fulfilled. Uther and his brother Pendragon landed in Britain with an army, and Vortigern was burned to death in his castle.

Shortly after the victory a war arose between the Britons, under Uther and Pendragon, and the Saxons, under Hengist. Merlin, who aided Uther and Pendragon, said they would be victorious but only one would survive. Pendragon was killed, and Uther added his brother's name to his own, becoming Uther Pendragon. His first care was to bury his brother, and he asked Merlin to erect a suitable monument to Pendragon's memory. Merlin conveyed great stones from Ireland to England in the course of a single night and then set them up at Stonehenge.

Merlin then went to Carduel (Carlisle) and through magic constructed a beautiful castle and established a round table for Uther Pendragon. Merlin also aided Uther Pendragon in a deception that enabled him to sleep with Igraine in the guise of her husband. From their union King Arthur was born.

When Arthur was made king, Merlin became his advisor. As Merlin could assume any shape he pleased, Arthur often used him as a messenger. Once he went to Rome in the guise of a stag to bear Arthur's challenge to Julius Caesar (not the conqueror of Gaul but the mythical father of Oberon) to single combat.

Merlin was said to have made many magic objects, among which was a cup that would reveal whether the drinker had led a pure life. It always overflowed when touched by "polluted lips." He was also the artificer of King Arthur's armor and of a magic mirror in which one could see whatever one wished. But Merlin had a fatal weakness, women. Viviane, the Lady of the Lake, sometimes called Nimuë, beguiled him and learned all of his magic secrets. Then she went with him to the magic forest of Broceliande in Brittany. Wishing to rid herself of her aged lover, she cast a magic spell over him, enclosing him in a hawthorn tree, where he would dwell forever. There are, however, other legends

Merlin (A. Beardsley)

accounting for Merlin's end. According to one, Merlin, having grown old, once sat down at the Siege Perilous (the seat at the Round Table commemorating Judas's betrayal), forgetting that only a sinless man could sit upon it. He was immediately swallowed up by the earth. Another version says Viviane imprisoned Merlin in an underground palace, where she alone could visit him. There he dwells, unchanged by time, and daily increases his store of knowledge. He appears in all retellings of the Arthurian legends. Tennyson's "Merlin and Vivien," part of *Idylls of the King*, and E. A. Robinson's *Merlin* include him. Ernest Chausson's symphonic poem *Viviane* deals with Merlin's seduction and end as does Burne-Jones's painting *The Beguiling of Merlin*, in which Viviane is casting her magic spell over the old magician.

Variant spellings: Merddin, Myrddin.

2037
Mermaid. In European folklore, fantastic beings, half fish, half woman, with gold or green hair. Mermaids can be spotted on moonlit evenings, looking in a mirror as they comb their hair. Often they lure sailors to their death and are credited with knowing the future. In 16th-century English the word *mermaid* was often used for a courtesan, as in Shakespeare's *Comedy of Errors* (3.2, etc.). Hollywood's *Mr. Peabody and the Mermaid* tells of a very respectable businessman who falls in love with one of the beautiful creatures. The male version of the creature is called a merman. He appears in Matthew Arnold's poem "The Forsaken Merman", which tells of a merman deserted by his human wife.

2038
Mermerus and Pheres (care-laden and bearer). In Greek mythology, children of Medea and Jason. When Jason betrayed Medea, she killed the children to punish him.

2039
Meru. In Hindu mythology, a fantastic golden mountain, the *axis mundi*, situated in the navel of the earth; on it is Swarga, Indra's heaven. It contains the cities of the gods and the homes of celestial spirits.

2040
Mesede. In Melanesian mythology, the great marksman, whose bow ignites when it is drawn. Once Mesede rescued Abere's son from a crocodile, but he took Abere's daughters as a prize. Mesede's wife was angry at this and had the girls killed. The head of the youngest was cast into the sea, where it turned into a log. When it was washed ashore, flies hollowed it out. Morave, another hero, covered one end with skin, creating the Dibiri drum that is symbolic of a human body and is used in various rituals.

Metamorphoses, The (transformation). Latin narrative poem by Ovid, in 15 books, narrating some 250 myths and legends from Greek, Roman, and Near Eastern sources; one of the main sources for the stories in Western art, music, and literature.

The main tales narrated in *The Metamorphoses* are the following:

Book 1: Invocation. Chaos and Creation. Ages of Gold, Silver, Bronze, and Iron. The Great Flood. Deucalion and Pyrrha. The New Creation. Apollo and Daphne. Io and Jove. Pan. Io.

Book 2: Phaethon's Ride. Jove and the Arcadian Nymph. The Raven. Ocyrhoe. Mercury and Battus. Mercury and Herse. Jove and Europa.

Book 3: Cadmus. Actaeon. Semele. Tiresias. Echo and Narcissus. Pentheus and Bacchus.

Book 4: Pyramus and Thisbe. Mars and Venus. The Sun and Leucothea. Salmacis and Hermaphroditus. Ino and Athamas. Transformation of Cadmus. Perseus.

Book 5: Battles of Perseus. Pallas Athena and the Muses. Death and Proserpine. Arethus. Triptolemus. Transformation of the Pierides.

Book 6: Arachne. Niobe and Latona. Marysas. Pelops. Tereus, Procne, and Philomela. Boreas and Orithyia.

Book 7: Jason and Medea. Minos. The Myrmidons. Cephalus and Procis.

Book 8: Minos, Nessus, and Scylla. Daedalus and Icarus. Meleager and the Boar. Althaea and Meleager. Achelous. Baucis and Philemon. Erysicthon.

Book 9: Achelous and Hercules. Hercules, Nessus, and Deianira. Birth of Hercules. Dryope. Prophecy of Themis. Byblis and Caunus. Iphis and Ianthe.

Book 10: Orpheus and Eurydice. Cyparissus. Ganymede. Apollo and Hyacinthus. Pygmalion. Cinyras and Myrrha. Venus and Adonis. Atalanta. Transformation of Adonis.

Book 11: Orpheus's Death. Midas. Building of Troy. Thetis and Peleus. Daedalion. Cattle of Peleus. Journeys of Ceyx. Sleep. Transformation of Alcyone. Aesacus and Hesperia.

Book 12: Beginning of the Trojan War. Caenis. Nestor's Tale of the Centaurs. Achilles' Death.

Book 13: Dispute over Achilles' Armor. The Fall of Troy. Polyxena's Sacrifice. Hecuba. Memnon. Aeneas. Galatea and Polyphemus. Glaucus.

Book 14: Circe, Glaucus, and Scylla. Aeneas at Cumae. Achaemides and Polyphemus. Circe. Picus and Canens. Conquests of Aeneas. Kings of Alba. Pomona and Vertumnus. Iphis and Anaxarete. Kings of Italia.

Book 15: Numa. Story of Myscelos. The Philosopher. Death of Numa. Hippolytus. Cipus. Aesculapius. Caesar. Epilogue.

Ovid's narrative style is brilliant, elegant and sometimes deeply moving. Its influence on European literature is tremendous. The poem was known during the Middle Ages and was one of the main sources for Greek and Roman mythology. During the Renaissance the poem inspired many paintings. In English literature the best-known version, believed to have been used by Shakespeare, was a translation by Arthur Golding in 1567. Ezra Pound called the translation "the most beautiful book in the language." Others who have translated parts of the poem are Addison, Congreve, Dryden, Gay, and Pope. Scenes from the poem are found on the borders of the bronze doors of St. Peter's in Rome and in decorations at Fontainebleu and Sans Souci. Rubens often drew upon the poem, as did Poussin, who frequently painted scenes from it. In 1931 Picasso did a series of 30 illustrations for an edition of *The Metamorphoses.*

2042

Metatron (one who occupies the throne next to the divine throne?). In Jewish folklore, angel who led the children of Israel through the wilderness after the Exodus from Egypt. In the biblical account (Exod. 12:5), however, the Israelites are guided by Yahweh, the Hebrew god himself. In some Jewish legends Metatron is said to have been the patriarch Enoch, transformed into an angel after his death. Genesis (5:24) records that Enoch did not die but was taken bodily to heaven by God. Metatron is sometimes called Lad (tender age).

Variant spellings: Metratton, Mittron, Metaraon, Merraton.

2043

Methuselah (man of the dart). In the Bible, O.T., son of Enoch and grandfather of Noah; he lived 969 years (Gen. 5:27). In Gershwin's opera *Porgy and Bess* he is cited for his old age in one of the songs. Methuselah is a common epithet for a very old man.

2044

Metis (counsel). In Greek mythology, a Titaness, daughter of Oceanus and Tethys; first wife of Zeus, according to Hesiod's *Theogony* (886 ff). When Zeus was told by Heaven and Earth that his wife was to bear a child who would overthrow him, he swallowed Metis through trickery. Athena was born fully armed from Zeus's head, which was split open by Hephaestus' ax, or by Prometheus. In Greek religion Metis was a personification of counsel, prudence, and insight.

2045

Metsanneitsyt (forest virgin). In Finnish mythology, a spirit who lures men to make love to her. She is beautiful in front, but her back is hollow, like a tree stump or trough.

2046

Metztli. In Aztec mythology, moon goddess. In order to make a light for the daytime Metztli sacrificed herself and Nanahuatl the Leper in a fire. When she disappeared into the flames, the sun was created. The male form of the moon was called Tecciztecatl. He was portrayed as an old man with a large seashell on his back.

Variant spelling: Metzli.

2047

Mezuzah (doorpost). In Judaism, small parchment talisman that contains the Jewish *Shema* or creed (Deut. 6:4): "Hear, O Israel: The Lord our God is one Lord." The command to the Jewish people to attach mezuzahs to their doorposts is found in Deuteronomy (6:8–9). It was commanded: "And thou shalt bind them for a sign upon thine hand, and they shall be as frontlets between thine eyes. And thou shalt write them upon the posts of thy house, and on thy gates." The parchment is placed so that the word *Shaddai* (Almighty) is visible through an opening. It is placed at head height beside the door because it is a Jewish custom to kiss the mezuzah on entering or leaving a house.

2048

Mice in Council, or Belling the Cat, The. Aesopic fable, probably originally from India, found in numerous European collections.

For many years the mice had been living in constant dread of their enemy, the cat. It was decided to call a meeting to determine the best means of handling the situation. Many plans were discussed and rejected.

At last a young mouse got up. "I propose," said he, looking very important, "that a bell be hung around the cat's neck. Then whenever the cat approaches, we always shall have notice of her presence and so be able to escape."

The young mouse sat down to tremendous applause. The suggestion was put to a motion and passed almost unanimously.

But just then an old mouse, who had sat silent all the while, rose to his feet and said: "My friends, it takes a young mouse to think of a plan so ingenious and yet so simple. With a bell about the cat's neck to warn us we shall all be safe. I have but one brief question to put to the supporters of the plan—which of you is going to bell the cat?"

Moral: It is one thing to propose, another to execute.

The fable is told in the Prologue to *Piers Plowman* by Langland, where the cat is the symbol of John of Gaunt. Archibald Douglas, fifth earl of Angus (d. 1514), was called Archibald Bell-the-Cat because he killed some of the male favorites of James III who had been created earls. When the Scottish nobles held a council in the church of Lauder for the purpose of putting down the favorites of the king, Lord Gray asked, "Who will bell the cat?" "That will I," said Douglas, who then, in the king's presence, proceeded to kill the young men.

Michael

2049
Michael (who is like unto God). In Jewish, Christian, and Islamic mythology, archangel leader of the Jews and Prince of the Church Militant, guardian of redeemed souls against the devil. Feast, 29 September in the Western church.

In the Old Testament Book of Daniel (12:1) the archangel Michael is "the great prince which standeth for the children of thy people." Thus, Michael is considered the guardian of the Hebrew people. In the New Testament (Rev. 12:7–9) Michael fights the devil. "And there was war in heaven: Michael and his angels fought against the dragon; and the dragon fought his angels, and prevailed not; neither was their place any more in heaven. And the great dragon was cast out, that old serpent, called the Devil, and Satan, which deceiveth the whole world: he was cast out into the earth, and his angels were cast out with him."

In the Epistle of Jude (verse 9) the myth that Michael fought the devil for the body of Moses is alluded to: "Yet Michael the archangel, when contending with the devil he disputed about the body of Moses, durst not bring against him a railing accusation, but said, the Lord rebuke thee." The myth is found in later Jewish and Christian writings. The Koran (sura 2) says that "who so is an enemy to God or his angels . . . or to Mikail (Michael) shall have God as his enemy: for verily God is an enemy of Infidels."

Michael owes his popularity in Western Christianity to three legendary apparitions. In the first, which occurred during the fifth century C.E., Michael descended to Mount Galgano in Italy and ordered a church to be erected and sanctified there in his honor. When the people entered the cavern at the foot of the mountain, they found three altars already erected, one of them covered with a rich altar cloth of crimson and gold. A stream of limpid water springing from the rock healed all diseases. The church was built, and it attracted many pilgrims.

The second apparition of Michael was in the sixth century, when he healed a pestilence at Rome. St. Gregory the Great dedicated the tomb of Hadrian to the saint and called it Castel Sant' Angelo. The third apparition was to Aubert, bishop of Avranches (706) in the Gulf of Avranches in Normandy. St. Michael appeared to the bishop and ordered that a church be erected in his honor. The legend is in many ways similar to that of Mount Galgano.

Both Dante and Milton mention Michael in their works, as does Longfellow in his poetic drama *The Golden Legend*, (not to be confused with the medieval book of saints' lives) and Yeats in his poem *The Rose of Peace*, in which Michael is called "leader of God's host." Michael is often portrayed in medieval armor, standing over the devil, whom he has defeated.

2050
Mictlantecuhtli. In Aztec mythology, death god, lord of the land of the dead, who with his wife, Mictlantecihuatl, cared for the dead who came to

Mictlantecuhtli

their kingdom, Mictlan (Mictlancalco), the place of the dead. Mictlantecuhtli was portrayed as an open-mouthed monster ready to devour the souls of the dead. Sometimes he was portrayed as an owl, with skull and bones. He was associated with the north, and his color was red. Mictlantecuhtli is regarded in some texts as an aspect of the god Tezcatlipoca (mirror that smokes), the Aztec creator-trickster god. Mictlantecuhtli was also known as Tzontemoc (he of the falling hair), perhaps indicative of his role as death god.

Variant spelling: Mictlanteculi.

2051

Midas (seed). In Greek mythology, king of Phrygia; son of the goddess Cybele and a satyr. Midas helped Silenus, a follower of Dionysus (Bacchus), to find his way back to his god, and Dionysus rewarded Midas by granting him any wish. He wished that whatever he touched would turn to gold. Eventually he had to ask that the gift be revoked, because even his food turned to gold and he was unable to eat. To rid himself of his gift Midas had to wash in the Pactolus river, whose sands then became gold. Because he favored Marsyas in his contest with Apollo, Midas was punished by having his ears turned into those of an ass. Ovid's *Metamorphoses* (book 11), John Lyly's *Midas*, Shakespeare's *Merchant of Venice* (3.2.101), Pope's *Dunciad* (3.324), Swift's *Fable of Midas*, Shelley's *Hymn of Pan*, and W. S. Landor's *Silenus* all deal with Midas or cite him. Poussin's *Midas and Bacchus* portrays Midas with Silenus,

2052

Midgard (middle world). In Norse mythology, the world of people, midway between the home of the gods, Asgard, and the home of the frost giants, Jotunheim. Midgard was formed from the giant Ymir's body. His blood or sweat became the oceans; his bones, the mountains; his teeth, the cliffs; and his hair, the trees and other plant life. Ymir's skull

formed the vaulted heavens, held up by four dwarfs—Nordi, Sudi, Austri, and Westri. Midgard appears in the *Poetic Edda*, the *Prose Edda*, and Matthew Arnold's narrative poem *Balder Dead*. Midgard is also called Mana-heim.

2053

Midgard Serpent (middle world serpent). In Norse mythology, a venomous monster, fathered by the fire-trickster god, Loki. Odin cast Midgard into the sea, where its movements caused storms. Midgard's body encircled the whole earth, and it bit its own tail. The god Thor took on the monster in battle. The *Prose Edda* tells how Thor "launched his mallet at him, and there are some who say that it struck off the monster's head at the bottom of the sea, but one may assert with more certainty that he still lives and lies in the ocean." Another name for the Midgard Serpent is Jormungand (wolf-serpent).

2054

Midrash (to examine). In Judaism, genre of rabbinic literature, consisting of verse by verse interpretation of the Hebrew Scriptures, using homily (sometimes parables and folktales) and exegesis.

2055

Mihr. In Armenian mythology, the fire god, derived in part from the Persian god Mithras. His worship was added to that of Vahagn, who was a sun, lightning, and fire god native to Armenia.

2056

Mikula. In Russian folklore, hero with superhuman strength, who appears in the *byliny*, the epic songs, as well as in folktales. Mikula is a *bogatyr*, an epic hero, whose little wooden plow was so heavy that a whole troop of men could not lift it, though Mikula could, with one hand. Part of Mikula's power came from Mati-Syra-Zemlya (moist Mother Earth), since he was her lover.

2057

Milarepa (Mila the cotton clad). 1038–1122. Tibetan Buddhist poet and saint, author of numerous songs. In his early life he was a black magician but later converted. He is portrayed with his right hand to his ear, listening to the many hymns he composed, or listening to the "sound" of emptiness, which his songs embody.

2058

Milkmaid and Her Pail, The. Aesopic fable, probably derived from the Indian collection *The Panchatantra*.

A milkmaid was on her way to market, carrying a pail of milk on the top of her head. As she walked along the road in the early morning she began to turn over in her mind what she would do with the money she would receive for the milk.

"I shall buy some hens from a neighbor," said she to herself, "and they will lay eggs every day which I shall sell to the pastor's wife. And with the egg money I'll buy myself a new frock and ribbon. Green they shall be, for green becomes my complexion best. And in this lovely green gown I will go to the fair. All the young men will strive to have me for a partner. I shall pretend that I do not see them. When they become too insistent I shall disdainfully toss my head—like this."

As the milkmaid spoke she tossed her head back, and down came the pail of milk, spilling all over the ground. And so all of her imaginary happiness vanished, and nothing was left but an empty pail and the promise of a scolding when she returned home.

Moral: Do not count your chickens before they are hatched.

La Fontaine's version of the fable is perhaps the best known. The Frenchman derived the work from Bonaventure des Periers's *Contes et Nouvelles*, which in turn derived it from other sources.

2059

Milomaki. In Brazilian Indian folklore, culture hero, from whose ashes grew the paxiuba palm. Long ago a little boy was sent from the great waterhouse, the home of the sun, to earth. He sang so beautifully that the people came to hear him. When he was finished, they returned home and ate their fish, after which they fell down dead. Their relatives then seized Milomaki, blaming him for the deaths, and burned him. As he went to his death, Milomaki sang even as the flames flickered around his body. When his body was ready to burst from the heat, he sang: "Now bursts my body! Now I am dead!" Though his body was destroyed, his soul went to heaven.

The same day a long green blade sprang from his ashes. It grew into the first paxiuba palm.

2060

Mimir (pondering). In Norse mythology, a giant noted for his wisdom; uncle of Odin. Mimir was at one time the keeper of a magic caldron, Odhrerir, or a magic well at the roots of the world tree, Yggdrasill. Mimir drank from the caldron or well and knew all things—past, present, and future. He once allowed Odin to drink, but the god had to give one of his eyes as the price. Thus, Odin is often portrayed as one-eyed, the socket being covered by his broad-brimmed hat or a lock of hair. In other accounts Odin, after having tasted the well, never smiled again. Mimir lived among the gods even though he was of the giants' race. He was sent as a

hostage to the Vanir, another group of gods, who beheaded him. Odin got back Mimir's head, breathed life into it, and consulted it on very important matters. The myth is told in the *Prose Edda*.

Min

2061

Min. In Egyptian mythology, god of fertility, rain, and crops. Min was honored in harvest festivals, during which the first-cut sheaf of the harvest was offered to him by the king. According to some texts, he was also worshiped as a god of roads and travelers and was evoked by caravan leaders before setting out through the desert.

Min is portrayed as a man with an erect phallus, holding a whip in his right hand. On his head he wears a crown surmounted by two tall plumes, with a streamer descending from its back. In later times the Egyptians identified him with Amun-Ra, and the Greeks with Pan. He was also closely associated with Horus, who was in some texts addressed as Min-Horus.

Minawara and Multultu. In Australian mythology, kangaroo men of the Nambutji tribe in central Australia; created after a great flood, they instituted sacred rites for the men of the tribe.

2062

Mindi. In Australian mythology, the great evil snake who sends diseases such as smallpox, which is called Mindi's dust.

2063

Minerva. In Roman mythology, ancient Italian goddess of wisdom and the arts and sciences; the Romans equated Minerva with the Greek goddess Athena. Minerva had a temple on the Capitoline Hill, her chief seat of worship, along with Jupiter and Juno. Her main festival in Rome, the *Quinquatria* or *Quinquatrus* (fifth day), began on 18 or 19 March and lastSacrifices and oblations were made on the first day, but no blood was shed. On the second, third, and fourth days, gladiators performed, and on the fifth day there was a solemn procession through the streets of the city. During the festival scholars were on holiday and prayed to the goddess for wisdom. Most of the Greek myths attached to Athena were adopted by the Romans for Minerva. Minerva appears in Mantegna's painting *Triumph of Wisdom Over Vice*, where she is seen routing the sex goddess Venus. Minerva also appears in Perugino's painting *Combat of Love and Chastity*, in which she aids Diana, goddess of virgins. In English poetry she appears in Lord Byron's *The Curse of Minerva*, in which he attacks Lord Elgin for removing the famous marbles from the Parthenon to the British Museum. The goddess also appears in Poe's poem *Raven*, in which a bird of ill omen perches on a bust of Pallas, another name for Minerva.

2064

Minos (the moon's creature). In Greek mythology, one of the judges of the dead, once a king of Crete, son of Zeus and Europa; brother of Rhadamanthys and Sarpedon; married to Pasiphae; father of Acacallis, Androgeus, Ariadne, Catreus, Deucalion, Euryale, Giaucus, Lycastus, Phaedra, and Xenodice. In some accounts Minos is a wise king; in others a tyrant who was killed by Daedalaus, whom Minos had imprisoned. He was made a judge of the dead along with Rhadamanthys and Aeacus or Sarpedon. Dante's *Divine Comedy* (Inferno) makes Minos the king of hell. Rodin's statue of *The Thinker*, part of his *Gates of Hell*, has been identified by some art scholars as Minos.

2065

Minotaur (Minos bull). In Greek mythology, a monster, half man and half bull, born of Pasiphaë, a wife of King Minos, and the Cretan (or Marathonian) bull. The Minotaur, also called Asterius, was kept in the labyrinth built by Daedalus and was fed young boys and girls, one of each once a year. The monster was killed by the hero Theseus. In Dante's *Divine Comedy*, the Minotaur, called *l'infamia di Creti* (the infamy of Crete) guards the Seventh Circle of Hell. The Minotaur appears in L. Cottrell's *The Bull of Minos*, Mary Renault's novel, *The King Must Die* (1958), and André Gide's *Thésée* and is pictured in Picasso's 15 plates in his Vollard Suite (1930–1937).

2066

Minuchihr. A hero king appearing in the Persian epic poem *Shah Namah* by Firdusi.

Minuchihr killed his two evil uncles, Silim and Tur, who were responsible for the death of his father, Irij. When the great hero Faridun, his grandfather, died, Minuchihr came to the throne and was deeply loved by the people. He reigned for 120 years. One day his astrologers told him that his death was close at hand.

"The time approaches when thou must die," they told the beloved king. "Before you are placed in the damp earth, prepare for a successor."

Minuchihr called his son Nauder to his side and instructed him. He then closed his eyes and died.

2067

Miriam

Miriam (rebellion). In the Bible, O.T., sister of Moses and Aaron, who watched over the infant Moses when he was in the ark of bulrushes in the river Nile (Exod. 2:1–10). After the Exodus from Egypt she was known as a prophetess and assisted Moses and Aaron, but she complained, as did Aaron, when Moses married a Cushite (Ethiopian) woman

2068

(Num. 12:1–16). For this rebellion she was stricken with leprosy. She died and was buried in the Wilderness of Wandering.

2069

Miroku Bosatsu. In Japanese Buddhist mythology, the name given to Maitreya (friendly; benevolent). According to Buddhist legend, before the Buddha was born as a human he lived in the Tushita heaven. Before leaving, he commissioned Maitreya as his successor. Some Buddhist traditions say Maitreya has already appeared in the form of a fat, jolly, eccentric monk, Hotei (Pu-tai), the so-called Laughing Buddha.

2070

Mister Dooley. In American literary folklore, Irish American who runs a small saloon on Archey Road in Chicago, created by Peter Finley Dunne (1867–1936) in newspapers and later collected into books. Martin Dooley usually comments on political situations. One of his most famous remarks was "Whether th' Constitution follows th' flag or not, th' Supreme Court follows th' illiction return." A collection, *Mr. Dooley at His Best*, edited by Elmer Ellis, has an introduction by Dunne. Mr. Dooley's remarks were read by Henry Adams and Henry James, who took delight in them.

2071

Mistletoe. A parasitic plant found growing in various deciduous trees; in European mythologies, a sacred plant and symbol of fertility and immortality. The Druids called mistletoe "all healer." In Norse mythology the mistletoe was sacred to Baldur, and in Roman mythology the magical Golden Bough plucked by the hero Aeneas has been identified as the mistletoe. The early Italians collected mistletoe on the first day after the full moon; a common European practice until recently was to gather mistletoe on Midsummer's Eve or Day.

2072

Mithras. In Persian mythology, god of life, heat, fertility, a mediator between the gods and men, and chief aide to the good god, Ahura Mazda, in his war against the evil spirit, Ahriman.

Between 1400 B.C.E. and 400 C.E. Persians, Indians, Romans, and Greeks all worshiped the god Mithras, who originally may have been the sun god, Mitra, mentioned in the Indian *Rig-Veda*. During Roman times the worship of Mithras was converted into a mystery religion. The god was worshiped by the soldiers and imperial officials of Rome.

Rudyard Kipling's poem *A Song to Mithras* captures the mood of the Roman belief in the god's powers:

Mithras, God of the Morning, our trumpets waken the Wall!
Now as the names are answered, and the guards are marched away,
Mithras, also a soldier, give us strength for the day!
Mithras, God of the Midnight, here where the great Bull dies,
Look on Thy Children in darkness. Oh, take our sacrifice!
Many roads Thou hast fashioned—all of them lead to Light!
Mithras, also a soldier, teach us to die aright!

Part of Kipling's poem refers to the repeated reliefs or statues that portray Mithras slaying a bull. The scene portrays a young man wearing a Phrygian cap slaying a massive bull while a dog licks the blood, a serpent crawls nearby, and a scorpion seems to be removing the bull's testicles. On either side of the scene is a young man, one with a torch uplifted, the other with the torch facing downward.

What exactly this scene symbolizes has puzzled scholars and thinkers. Carl Jung, picking up the similarity between the mysteries of Mithras and of Christianity, sees the slaying of the bull as "essentially a self-sacrifice, since the bull is a world bull which was originally identical with Mithras himself. . . . The representations of the sacrificial act, the tauroctony [bull slaying], recall the crucifixion between two thieves, one of whom is raised up to paradise while the other goes down to hell."

Jung, however, was not the first to recognize the similarities. Tertullian, the Early Church writer, seeing that the pagan cult contained baptism and the use of bread, water, and wine consecrated by priests, called fathers, wrote that the similarities of the Mithraic cult to Christianity were inspired by the devil, who wished to mock the Christian sacraments in order to lead the faithful to hell. The French author Ernest Renan, in the skeptical 19th-century tradition, wrote: "If Christianity had been arrested in its growth . . . the world would have been Mithraist."

The religion of Mithras was suppressed by Emperor Constantine when he established Christianity as the state religion in the Roman Empire. Present-day Zoroastrians, however, still worship Mithras as a god.

Variant spelling: Mithra.

2073

Mitokht. In Persian mythology, demon of falsehood; son of the evil spirit, Ahriman.

2074

Mixcoatl (cloud serpent). In Aztec mythology, god of hunting, lord of the chase, often identified with the god Tezcatlipoca, the Aztec creator-trickster god worshiped by warriors and magicians. The Spanish cleric Fray Diego Durán, in his *Book of the Gods and Rites* (c. 1576), says that Mixcoatl was the "inventor of the ways and manners of hunting." The god was portrayed as a man with long hair and black eyes. He wore a crown of plumes on his head, and his nose was pierced with a berry pit. In one hand he held a basket containing food, in the other a bow and arrow. His body was covered with white stripes from the top to the bottom. Human sacrifices were made to him. Mixcoatl was also known as *Iztac Mixcoatl* (the white cloud serpent). He was a progenitor, father of seven sons who were the founders of the seven cities speaking the Nahuatl language. His first wife was Ilamatechtli, a form of Coatlicue, and his second wife was Chimalmatl (green shield).

Variant spellings: Yemaxtli, Yoamaxtli.

2075

Mnevis bull. In Egyptian mythology, Greek name for the Egyptian sacred bull Wer-mer, who was worshiped at Heliopolis. Mnevis was said to be an incarnation of the sun. He was portrayed as a bull with a disk and the uraeus between his horns. Some art works portray him as a bull-headed man.

2076

Moccus. In Celtic mythology, a swine god, worshiped in Britain and on the Continent. Ancient Roman writers equated Moccus with their god Mercury.

Variant spelling: Mocco.

2077

Mokoi (evil spirit). In Australian mythology, evil spirit invoked by sorcerers among the Murngin of northern Australia.

2078

Mokos. In Slavic mythology, a goddess who appears in many folktales as Mokusa. During Lent she wanders about at night disguised as a woman, visiting houses, worrying wool spinners, guarding and fleecing sheep herself. At night strands of fleece are laid beside stoves to appease her anger.

2079

Mole. Burrowing mammal with a pointed nose, small eyes, and tiny teeth. In Egyptian mythology the mole was a symbol of blindness because it was believed the animal neither heard nor saw. In medieval Christianity the mole was seen as symbolic of the earth and avariciousness. In medieval folk belief, if a man ate the heart of a mole when it had just been removed from the dead animal, he could foretell the future.

2080

Molimons. In African mythology (Upotos of the Congo), the souls of the dead, who begged the sky god Libanza not to let the sky fall.

2081

Molly Pitcher. 1754–1832. In American history and folklore of the Revolution, the popular name of Mary L. Hays McCauley, who took her husband's place manning a cannon after he was killed in battle. Legend says a cannon ball shot through her legs, taking off her petticoat. Whittier's poem "Molly Pitcher" deals with the legend. It is believed, however, that a Margaret Corbin (1751–1800) was the woman who performed the heroic act. On Molly Pitcher's grave there is a cannon and a flag.

2082

Moly. In Greek mythology, plant with a black root and white flower that saved Odysseus from Circe's enchantments on her island, Aeaea, where he was detained for a year. The plant was given to Odysseus by Hermes. Moly is cited in Homer's *Odyssey* (book 10), Spenser's *Faerie Queene*, Milton's *Comus*, Arnold's *The Strayed Reveller*, and D. G. Rosetti's *The Wine of Circe*.

2083

Momotaro. In Japanese folktales, a hero who emerged from a peach and defeated the demon Akandoji.

One day the wife of a poor woodcutter went to the river to wash some clothes. As she was about to return she saw a large object floating in the water. She pulled it close to land and saw that it was a large peach, larger than any she had ever seen. She took it home, washed it, and handed it to her husband to open. As the man cut it, a boy emerged from the kernel; they adopted him as a present from the gods to comfort them in their old age. They called the boy Momotaro (the elder son of the peach). He grew up big and strong, surpassing other boys his age. One day Momotaro decided to leave his foster parents and go to Onigashima, the Island of Devils, to seek his fortune. The foster parents gave him some dumplings to take with him. He soon met a dog that asked him for a dumpling and promised to accompany him. Then a monkey and a pheasant came with similar requests. With the three companions he reached the Devil's Fortress. They made their way in and had a terrible battle with the demons, but the animals helped Momotaro. Finally, they reached the inner part of the fortress, where the chief devil, Akandoji, was waiting for them with an iron war club. He was thrown down by Momotaro, who bound him with ropes and made him disclose the secret of his treasures. Then Momotaro helped himself to Akandoji's treasures and left with his three companions for home, where he became a rich and honored member of the community.

Momus. In Greek mythology, a son of Nox (night) and Erebus; brother of Aether, Cer, Dreams, Hemera, Hypnos, Moros, Nemesis, Thantatos and Charon. Momus was god of criticism, ridicule, or faultfinding, according to Hesiod's *Theogony* (214). He was thrown out of heaven by the gods when he criticized Zeus for placing a bull's horns on its head rather than on its shoulders, which were stronger, and for ridiculing the feet or shoes of Aphrodite, though he did not complain about her naked body. Momus is now used as a term for someone who makes fun or carps at things, though George Meredith's poem *Ode to the Comic Spirit* uses the god as a symbol of healthy criticism. In Greek art Momus is often portrayed raising a mask from his face and holding a small figure in his hand.

Variant spelling: Momos

Monan (ancient one). In the mythology of the Tupi Indians of Brazil, creator god. Though creator, Monan also twice destroyed the earth, once with fire and once by flood. He was followed by Maire- Monan, the transformer, who changed people and animals into other forms and punished them for their sins.

Monica, St. (alone?, to advise?). 332–387 C.E. In Christian legend, patron of married women and mother of St. Augustine. Feast, 4 May.

Her story is found in her son's autobiography, *The Confessions.* Although she was a Christian, her son Augustine was not brought up in the faith. She prayed continually for his conversion. One day she had a dream. Augustine writes, "She saw herself standing on a certain wooden rule, and a bright youth advancing towards her, joyous and smiling on her, whilst she was grieving and bowed down with sorrow. But he having inquired of her the cause of her sorrow and daily weeping . . . and she answering that it was my perdition she was lamenting, he bade her rest contented, and told her to behold and see where she was, there was I also." Eventually the prayers of Monica were answered, and her son was converted. She died at Ostia on the way back to Africa with Augustine after they had been to Italy. In Christian art she is often portrayed with her son, wearing either a black or a gray habit of a nun.

Montezuma II (sad or angry lord). 1480–1520. In Aztec history and legend, last ruler, who ascended the throne when he was 23 and engaged in a campaign to extend his empire. He was noted for his martial prowess, having taken part in nine battles and being a member of the Quachichin, the highest military order of his nation. According to W. H. Prescott in *The History of the Conquest of Mexico* (1843), Montezuma II's court was lavish with pomp and "forms of courtly etiquette unknown to his ruder predecessors. He was, in short, most attentive to all that concerned the exterior and pomp of royalty." He "received the Spaniards as being predicted by his oracles. The anxious dread, with which he had evaded their proffered visit, was founded on the same feeling which led him blindly to resign himself to them on their approach."

Roger Sessions composed the opera *Montezuma,* with a libretto by Giuseppe Borgese.

Variant spellings: Monteczoma, Motechuzoma, Moctezuma, Montecuzomatzin.

Moo-roo-bul. In Australian mythology, an evil water spirit who drags his victims to the bottom of a river.

Morgan le Fay (Howard Pyle)

2089

Mora (tormenting spirit). In Slavic folkore, a person possessing two souls. A *mora* could assume any shape, animal or vegetable, though frequently it could be identified by its bushy black eyebrows growing together above the nose. Kikimora of Russian folktales is sometimes said to be a *mora*.

2090

Morgan le Fay (bright, great fairy). In Arthurian legend, a witch, the sister or half sister of King Arthur, who continually plots his downfall. In Malory's *Morte d'Arthur* she steals the sword Excalibur and gives it to her lover so that he can kill Arthur. Though the rest of Arthur's enemies are defeated at the end of the work, Morgan le Fay is not. She appears in Ariosto's *Orlando Furioso* and Boiardo's *Orlando Innamorato*. She is also called Fata Morgana, which is the name Longfellow uses in his poem about her.

2091

Morgante (sea dweller?). In the Charlemagne cycle of legends, a giant who appears in *Il Morgante Maggiore*, a comic epic poem by Luigi Pulci published in 1483. Morgante aids Orlando (Roland) and other paladins of Charlemagne in their various adventures. Byron translated the first canto of the poem into English in 1822.

2092

Morkul-kua-luan. In Australian mythology, the spirit of the long grass, portrayed with a beaklike nose and half-closed eyelids that protect him as he glides through the fields of wild grain containing prickling grass seeds.

2093

Morpheus (fashioner). In Greek mythology, god of dreams; one of the sons of Hypnos (Somnus), who was god of sleep. His brother Icelus created dreams in animals, and his brother Phantastus created dreams in inanimate objects. Ovid's *Metamorphoses* (book 11) describes the Cave of Sleep. Chaucer's *Book of the Duchess* (137) calls Morpheus "the god of sleep." The word *morphine* is derived from the god's name.

2094

Morrigu, The. In Celtic mythology, a major war goddess, the great queen associated with other war goddesses such as Badhbh and Nemhain, or Macha. It is believed all of those goddesses are merely different manifestations of the Morrigu. She was portrayed as a woman with red eyebrows, wearing a blood-stained garment, fully armed, and drawn in a chariot by red horses. In Arthurian legends she appears as Morgan le Fay, sister of King Arthur. She appears in William Butler Yeats's play *The Death of*

Cuchulain as "a woman with a crow's head," referring to her role as a death goddess.

Moses

2095

Moses (a son). In the Bible, O.T., leader of the Israelite departure from Egyptian bondage. Moses was a prophet and lawgiver whose legend is told in the first books of the Hebrew Bible; Exodus, Leviticus, Numbers, and Deuteronomy. It was once believed that Moses was the author of these works, but scholars now agree that he was not.

Moses was born in Egypt to Hebrew parents, Amram, a Levite, and Jochebed. When Pharaoh ordered that all newborn Hebrew male children be put to death, Moses' mother hid him in a basket among the reeds by a stream. Pharaoh's daughter, coming to bathe, found the babe and raised him as her own, giving him the name Moses, which is Egyptian. Moses' wet-nurse was his own mother, though the Egyptians were not aware of this (Exod. 2:1–10).

As a young man Moses saw an Egyptian strike a Hebrew. In anger, he killed the Egyptian and fled the royal court and lived with Midian shepherds. He served the shepherd-priest Jethro for many years and married Jethro's daughter Zipporah, by whom he had a son, Gershom (Exod. 2:11–22).

While tending sheep on a mountainside in the Sinai Peninsula, Moses heard the voice of Yahweh, the Hebrew cult god, commanding him to lead the children of Israel out of Egypt. He knew it was Yahweh because God appeared "unto him in a flame of fire out of the midst of a bush: and he looked, and, behold, the bush burned with fire, and the bush was not consumed" (Exod. 3:2).

Moses appeared before Pharaoh with his brother Aaron, asking that the people be freed. Pharaoh refused until Yahweh produced a series of plagues, the last one bringing about the death of the male firstborn among the Egyptians. To appease Yahweh, Pharaoh then let the Israelites go.

After the Israelites left, Pharaoh changed his mind, and the Egyptian army pursued them. When they overtook the Israelites on the shores of the Red Sea, "Moses stretched out his hand over the sea; and the Lord caused the sea to go back by a strong east wind all that night, and made the sea dry land, and the waters were divided" (Exod. 14:21).

The Israelites crossed safely, but the Egyptians were all drowned as the waters closed over them. Moses and his people then wandered 40 years in the desert. In lean times Moses sustained the people with manna, a wild sweet edible, and with quail. Once he brought water from a rock by striking it with his rod (Exod. 17:6).

After three months of wandering Moses went up on a high peak of Mount Sinai and received from Yahweh, who was originally a storm and thunder god, the Ten Commandments (Exod. 20:1–17). When Moses came down from the mountain he found that his brother Aaron had made a golden calf to be worshiped by the people. Moses was so angry that he broke the tablets and destroyed the golden calf.

Moses died at Mount Pisgah, and leadership passed to Joshua. Moses was not allowed to enter the Promised Land because he had earlier defied Yahweh by striking the rock to obtain water before commanded to do so by Yahweh.

In art Moses is often portrayed with two blunt lumps resembling horns because of a mistranslation in the Vulgate Bible by St. Jerome, in which he mistook the Hebrew word for "rays" as the word for "horns," which it closely resembles (Vulgate Exod. 34:29). The horns can be seen on Michelangelo's statue of Moses in San Pietro in Vincoli, Rome.

Various legends about Moses not included in the Bible are found in other Jewish writings. One tells of Moses as a child sitting on Pharaoh's lap. The child threw a crown, decorated with an Egyptian god, to the ground. The wise men of the court said this indicated that Moses would overthrow the throne and suggested that the child be killed. To test the child, two platters were put before him; one was heaped with hot coals and the other with cherries. Moses reached for the coals, then, screaming, put his burned hand into his mouth, a sign that he should be allowed to live. His burned mouth caused him speech difficulties throughout his life. The biblical narrative relates that Moses was slow of speech and Aaron often spoke for him. Numerous paintings exist of Moses, among them *The Finding of Moses* by Sebastian Bourdon and *Moses Before the Burning Bush* by Dierc Bouts. In music, Rossini's *Moses in Egitto* (Moses in Egypt) and Arnold Schoenberg's *Moses und Aron*

deal with the Hebrew hero. In Islamic legend Moses is called Musa.

Manna

2096

Mot (death, sterility). In Near Eastern mythology (Phoenician), god of death, produced from the primeval egg, a child of air and chaos. Mot was the father of the sun, moon, and stars.

2097

Mother Goose. Popular title for a traditional collection of children's rhymes, jingles, riddles, tongue twisters, and tales. Numerous editions have been published since the 18th century, ranging from 50 to 700 entries. The first American edition was published by Isaiah Thomas in Worcester, Massachusetts, and titled *Mother Goose's Melody: or, Sonnets for the Cradle* (1785). It contained 52 nursery rhymes. The author of the collection is not known, but it is sometimes credited in legend to an Elizabeth Goose (Vergoose or Verboose) from Boston. In England "Mother Goose" was published by John Newbery (1713–1767), a publisher of children's books. One of his workers was Oliver Goldsmith, who may have written "Goody Two Shoes" for the collection. Scholars still debate the exact origin of the collection.

2098

Mountain in Labor, The. Aesopic fable found in various European collections.

One day the people of a certain country heard a mighty rumbling in the nearby mountain. Smoke was pouring from the summit. The earth was trembling, and great rocks came hurtling down into the valley. The mountain seemed to be in labor, and all of the people rushed to a vantage point where they could see what terrible thing was about to happen.

They waited and waited, while the sky grew dark and the rumblings and thunderings increased. Finally, as the people watched, there was one earthquake more violent than all of the others. Suddenly, a huge fissure appeared in the side of the mountain. The people threw themselves down on their knees. Some of them fainted. The rest waited with bated breath to see what would happen next.

The thundering stopped. A deep silence fell. And out of the gap in the side of the mountain popped a mouse!

Moral: Magnificent promises often end in paltry performances.

The fable is referred to both by Lucian in his *True History* and by Horace in his *Art of Poetry*. When Horace is giving instructions on how to write, he says: "Begin not as did the cyclic writer of old: 'Of Prima's fate and farfame war I'll sing.' What will this braggart produce worthy of so bombastic a boast? Mountains are in labor; to the birth comes a most absurd mouse."

2099

Moyna. In African mythology (Dogon of the Republic of Mali), hero who discovered the principle of the bull-roarer, a flat object made of wood or metal that creates a peculiar sound when whirled at the end of a rope. Many people are frightened by its sound, and it is often used in African secret societies. According to Dogon mythology, Moyna discovered the bull-roarer by tying a piece of metal to a string and whirling it about. At a masked dance, which women were not allowed to view but often did, Moyna began to whirl the bull-roarer. All of the women ran away in fright. Moyna explained to them later that the sound they heard was the voice of the Great Mask and that women and children must remain indoors when it sounded or they would be destroyed by it. Moyna passed the secret of the bull-roarer on to his sons, telling them to use it at the death of an important person because its irregular sounds are like the voices of the spirits of the dead.

2100

Mrarts. In Australian mythology, evil spirits of the dead, often found around burial grounds.

2101

Mrs. O'Leary's Cow. In American history and folklore, the cow of Mrs. Patrick O'Leary; it supposedly started the Great Chicago Fire in 1871 when it kicked over a lighted lantern while it was being milked. The fire killed several hundred people and destroyed nearly $200 million worth of property.

2102

Mudgegong. In Australian mythology, an evil spirit created by Baiame. Mudgegong destroyed all of Baiame's children, who were turned into wild animals.

2103

Mudra. In Oriental art, ritual gesture of the hands, fingers and arms, signifying powers and special actions. Among the most common forms are the following:

Abhaya mudra, symbol of protection or reassurance. The right arm is raised and slightly bent. The palm is open and held outward, the fingers extended and directed upward; the hand is level with the shoulders.

Anjali mudra, symbol of offering or salutation. Both arms may be raised fully upward above the head, the palms turned up and fingers extended. The joined palms can be held downwards, straight in front, in front of the face, or over the head, depending on the degree of honor being offered.

Bhumisparsa mudra, symbol of witness, the Buddha's earth-touching gesture. The right arm is pendant over the right knee. The hand has all fingers stretched downward, touching the earth, with the palm inward.

Dharmachakra mudra, symbol of the preaching of the Wheel of the Dharma in Buddhism. The hands are held against the chest, the left hand covering the right hand.

Dhyana mudra, symbol of meditation. Hands lie in lap, one on the other, palms upward and fingers extended. Figure seated with legs crossed.

Vara mudra, symbol of giving or bestowing. The arm is pendant, the hand palm outward with fingers fully extended.

Vitarka mudra, symbol of discussion. The hand is held up, palm outward, with the index finger or ring finger touching the thumb.

Vyakhyana mudra, symbol of exposition. The right arm is raised and slightly bent, with the thumb and forefinger touching.

2104

Muhammad (praised one). The Apostle of Allah; the Seal of the Prophets (570–632 C.E.).

Muhammad was born in the Year of the Elephants into an impoverished family of the Koreish (Quraish) tribe. After the death of his mother and father, Abdallah and Amina, he was affectionately cared for by his grandfather, Abd Al Muttalib. When the grandfather died, the boy was left to the guardianship of his son, Muhammad's uncle Abu Talib. Muhammad tended sheep and goats, an occupation that to the present day is considered by the Bedouin as degrading to the male. At the age of

24, Muhammad was employed by a rich widow named Khadija (also Hadigah, Hadija) to drive the caravans of camels with which she carried on an extensive trade. He did so well that she offered him her hand in marriage, although she was 40 years old and he barely 25. Long after her death his love for Khadija remained fresh in his heart, and he never let an opportunity pass to extol her virtues. He would often kill a sheep and distribute its flesh to the poor in honor of her memory.

While married to Khadija, Muhammad would spend time on Mount Hirâ, a wild and lonely mountain near Mecca. An angel, identified as Gabriel, appeared to him and said: "Recite!"

"I am no reader!" Muhammad replied, whereupon the angel shook him violently and again told him to read. This was repeated three times. Then the angel uttered the fives lines of sura 96 of the Koran:

> Read! in the name of thy Lord, who did create—
> Who did create man from congealed blood.
> Read! for thy Lord is the most generous,
> Who has taught the use of the pen,—
> Has taught man what he did not know.

Terribly frightened, Muhammad hastened home to his wife. Not certain of his calling, he had thoughts of suicide. On a few occasions he climbed the steep slopes of Mount Hirâ with the intention of killing himself. At last a glorious angel appeared, and Muhammad in terror ran to his wife, Khadija, and cried: "*Daththiruni*" (Wrap me up). He lay down entirely wrapped in his cloak. The angel spoke to him: "O thou covered! Rise up and warn! and thy Lord magnify! and thy garments purify; and abomination shun! and grant not favors to gain increase; and for thy Lord await!" (sura 74). After this the revelations came in rapid succession, and Muhammad no longer doubted the urgency of his inspiration.

At first his only convert was his wife, who was afterward called Umm el Mu'minin, "the mother of believers." Next were his daughters, then his cousin Ali, Abu Talib's youngest son, whom Muhammad had adopted. Then came Zaid (Zayo), his freedman and favorite companion, and then Abu-Bakr who because of his reputation was called El Ziddiq, "the true."

Muhammad's other converts were among the women and slaves at first, and then some influential men of the community became believers. The majority of the citizens of Mecca threw insults and even injured the prophet when he attempted to deliver his message. In time Muhammad made his migration from Mecca to Yathrib, later Medina. This historic act, called the Hegira or Hijra (the breaking away) is the starting point of the Islamic era. The date of the arrival at Medina is not precisely known, set on 16 June in some accounts and 30 September in others. The year usually assigned is 622 C.E. Once Muhammad was established at Medina, he proceeded to set out the rites and ceremonies of Islam, and he built a mosque to serve as a place of prayer and hall of general assembly. He appointed Bilal, his Abyssinian slave, as crier to call the faithful to prayer five times a day.

Soon afterward he turned his attention to his native Mecca. Feeling sufficiently strong to take the offensive, he began to preach the Holy War to convert the infidel. After some petty raids on the enemies' caravans, a fierce encounter took place between the Muslims and the Meccans. During the first part of the battle the Muslims, by Muhammad's order, stood firm at their posts while he encouraged them by promising the immediate reward of paradise to those who should fall martyred in the cause. A strong winter windstorm suddenly arose in the faces of the enemy. Muhammad called the storm the work of the archangel Gabriel, whose thousands of angels were now fighting for Islam. Muhammad took a handful of dirt and threw it toward the Meccans. "May their faces be covered with shame!" he cried. "Muslims, to the attack!" The Meccans were completely routed. Of the captives six were executed by Muhammad's order; others embraced Islam. Mecca was conquered in 630 and theeventually became devoted followers of the Prophet.

In March 632, Muhammad made his last pilgrimage to Mecca, the "farewell pilgrimage." Standing on Mount Arafat he addressed the people, more than 40,000, telling them to stand firm in the faith he had taught them, and he called Allah to witness that he had delivered His message and fulfilled His mission. In June he fell sick and died that month in the arms of Ayesha, his wife and the daughter of Abu-Bakr.

Numerous legends have arisen around Muhammad that are part of the folklore of the Islamic cultures. It is said in one Swahili legend that Allah created the seeds of the prophets out of a handful of his light. There were 25 sparks. The first was given to Adam and the last was placed in the loins of Abdullah, the father of Muhammad. His mother Amina was visited by an angel at night and told that Allah had filled her womb with the light of paradise. The angel said to her: "You will become the mother of the lord of all the Arabs, of the last prophet God will send to earth before Judgment. When he is born, call him Muhammad, the praised one, for that is his earthly name." As soon as Muhammad was born, "he made all the movements of the ritual prayer." An angel came and carried him to the four corners of the earth, to show him his future kingdoms and acquaint him with all of the peoples and spirits of the world.

When Muhammad was a boy of 12, he was examined by a hermit who found "between the boy's shoulder blades" the seal of prophecy in the form of a star, with the words: "There is no god but Allah and Muhammad is his Prophet."

The most famous legend associated with Muhammad concerns his Ascension or Assumption into heaven. Muhammad said he saw himself transported to heaven and brought face to face with God. The Ascension is referred to in the Koran (sura 17): "Celebrated be the praises of Him who took His servant a journey by night from the Sacred Mosque to the Remote Mosque, the precinct of which we have blessed, to show him our signs!" This passage and a few others in the Koran form the basis of a fantastic legendary voyage through the heavens. In the *Ascension of Muhammad*, the journey is described in elaborate detail as it is in *The Life of Muhammad* by Ibn Ishaq, which survives in parts of the biography compiled by Ibn Hisham.

In the biography Muhammad tells how the angel Gabriel kicked him to awaken him and then placed him on Burak, the fabulous animal that transported Muhammad to Jerusalem, where "he found Abraham and Moses and other prophets." Muhammad then describes the prophets. Moses was a "tall, dark, lively man with curled hair and a long nose"; Jesus was "neither tall nor short, with flowing hair, and a countenance shining as if he had just come out of a bath"; and Abraham looked just like Muhammad.

Several miracles are traditionally ascribed to Muhammad. One of the best known concerns the moon. Habid the Wise asked Muhammad to prove his mission by cleaving the moon in two. Muhammad raised his hands toward the heavens and commanded the moon to do Habid's bidding. Accordingly, it descended to the top of the Kaaba, made seven circuits, and, coming to the Prophet, entered his right sleeve and came out of his left. It then entered the collar of his robe, descended to the skirt, and clove itself into two plaits, one of which appeared in the east of the sky and the other in the west. The two parts ultimately reunited.

To Western readers, the best-known legend concerns Mount Safa. Muhammad was again asked for proof of his mission. He commanded Mount Safa to come to him, but it did not move. He said: "Allah is merciful. Had it obeyed my words, it would have fallen on us to our destruction. I will therefore go to the mountain, and thank Allah that He has had mercy on a stiff-necked generation."

Muhammad is the spelling of the Prophet's name preferred by Muslim scholars writing in English, although there are many variants: Mohammad, Mohammed, Mahomet.

2105

Mujaji II. In African mythology (Lovedu, a Bantu tribe of the Transvaal), the name of the rain queen, who is believed to live forever. Mujaji II was the daughter of an incestuous union of a daughter and father. Her mother's name was also Mujaji, and both ruled for a time over the people. The two were often confused with one another. Mujaji I lived in seclusion and was called "white-faced" and "radiant as the sun." The tale of the two influenced H. Rider Haggard's novel *She*, which tells of a land ruled by an ageless queen and of the magic fire that enabled her to live thousands of years. The novel was filmed in 1935 and again in 1965.

2106

Mukasa. In African mythology (Buganda of Uganda), a demigod. As a child, Mukasa would not eat the food his parents prepared for him. He left home to live by himself, under a tree on an island. A man discovered him there and took the child with him to his garden. At the man's home Mukasa would not eat anything until an ox was killed. He then asked for its heart, liver, and blood. From that time on the people of the village came to regard Mukasa as a god. (Asking for these special things to eat was an indication to them of his divinity.) Mukasa married and lived very well among these people, but one day he disappeared. In time mediums claimed to be able to receive messages from Mukasa. The female mediums would smoke tobacco in a hut in front of Mukasa's cone-shaped house. Once having served as mediums, the women had to live the rest of their lives removed from men.

2107

Mu Kung (Duke Good). In Chinese mythology, the spirit of wood, who made himself clothes of hawthorn leaves. He is one of the Wu Lao, spirits of the five natural forces.

2108

Mulberry. A tree used in silkworm culture. In Greek mythology it was a symbol of tragic love, having been formed from the blood of the lovers Pyramus and Thisbe. The Romans dedicated the mulberry to Minerva, their counterpart of the Greek Athena. In Hebrew mythology and legend King David consults a mulberry tree to learn when to attack the Philistines. God tells him: "And let it be, when thou hearest the sound of a going in the tops of the mulberry trees, that then thou shalt bestir thyself; for then shall the Lord go out before thee, to smite the host of the Philistines" (2 Sam. 5:24). David does as Yahweh commanded and defeats the Philistines. "Balsam" is substituted for "mulberry" in the Revised Standard Version of the text. In China the mulberry is sacred to the goddess San Ku Fu Jén. But in Chinese folklore the mulberry is never planted in front of a house, as it might bring sorrow or disaster. If a Chinese woman carries a mulberry staff, this indicates that she is in mourning for a child.

2109

Mullion. In Australian mythology, an eagle hawk who built his nest on the top of an enormous tree that reached almost to the sky. From this location he would swoop down, catch solitary victims, and bring them back to his eaglets for food. In an effort to bring an end to this practice, two headmen decided to climb the great tree. Their plan was to set fire to the nest at the top. First Koomba tried, but he could not reach the top. Then Murriwunda climbed up. He came back down exhausted, saying that he too had been unable to reach the top. Actually, he had instructed the fire not to burn until after he and the other headmen had left the site of Mullion's tree. When they were a safe distance away, a blaze broke out that lit the evening sky. It completely burned the tree, even its roots. Today it is said that hollows can be traced in the ground where the roots once grew.

2110

Mullo (mule). In Celtic mythology, a tutelary god of mule drivers, worshiped by the continental Celts. Ancient Roman writers equated Mullo with their god Mars.

2111

Mulungu. In African mythology (Nyamwezi of Tanzania), supreme being equated by African Christians, who make up over 40 percent of the population, with God. Most Christian translations of the Bible in various African languages have adopted Mulungu for the word god.

2112

Mummy (bituminized thing). The body of a human being or animal that has been intentionally preserved. The Egyptians evolved the ritual and practices of mummification over the course of several centuries, and the methods used varied widely throughout the course of time. In general, the soft tissues of the body were removed through the nose and via an incision in the flank of the torso. Those internal organs deemed worthy of preservation were entrusted to the care of the canopic jars. The body was then treated with natron, a drying agent, and in the better examples was bathed in unguents and

ointments and anointed with oils as it was wrapped in strips of linen. Throughout the wrapping process various amulets used to ensure certain protections and prerogatives of the deceased in his journey to the underworld were wrapped within those bandages. It is thought that the embalming process in its most elaborate form took up to 70 days. One description of the process is found in Herodotus' *History* (book 2). Mummies, or parts of mummies, were used as medicine for centuries in Christian Europe. In Scotland, for example, in 1612 a mummy cost eight shillings a pound. When genuine Egyptian mummies were not available, the bodies of criminals were used instead. The 17th-century English author Sir Thomas Browne wrote that "Mummy is become merchandise." Interest in mummies increased with the discovery of Tutankhamen's tomb in 1922. Various Hollywood films deal with them, the most famous starring Boris Karloff in 1932, titled *The Mummy*.

2113

Mu-monto. In Siberian mythology, hero in a Buriat myth who visited the land of the dead.

Once Mu-monto went to the land of the dead to demand the return of a horse he had sacrificed at his father's funeral. To reach the land of the dead, Mu-monto went due north and found a rock, which he lifted. He said, "Come here." Suddenly a black fox appeared from under the rock and led him the rest of the way. When he arrived in the land of the dead, he saw all types of punishments meted out to those who had led evil lives. Thieves were bound, liars had their lips sewn up, and adulterous wives were tied to thorn bushes. Mu-monto also saw the reward for the good. There was a poor woman who now lived a life of luxury and an evil rich woman who lived in rags. (The myth does not tell if Mu-monto recovered his horse.)

2114

Mungan-Ngana. In Australian mythology, culture hero who taught the people crafts and gave them names. His son was Tundun, who taught men initiation ceremonies. However, the ceremonies were then revealed to women, and as a result Mungan-Ngana sent fire between heaven and earth, killing all life except for Tundun and his wife, who were turned into porpoises and later founded the Kurnai tribe.

2115

Munkar and Nakir. In Islamic mythology, two angels who command the dead to sit upright in their tombs when they are to be examined on the Day of Judgment.

Both the faithful and sinners are questioned on the role of Muhammad. If the correct answer is given (that he is the Prophet, or Apostle, of Allah), the body will receive air from paradise. If no answer or an incorrect one is given, the sinner is beaten, then feels pressure from the earth, and is finally gnawed or stung by dragonlike beasts until the Day of Resurrection, when faithful and sinners alike will have to answer to Allah.

In the *Fikh Akbar*, a collection of laws for Islam written through the centuries, it is stated that "the interrogation of the dead in the tomb by Munkar and Nakir is a reality and the reunion of the body with the spirit in the tomb is a reality." It goes on to say that the pressure and punishment felt by the body are also "a reality."

According to other Islamic traditions, however, the angel Ruman will deliver the dead person over to punishment. At the sound of his voice the tomb will contract, almost crushing the body within it, until the first Friday of Rajab, the seventh month of the Muslim calendar. If a man is lucky enough to die on Friday (a sacred day of the week) he is not questioned.

2116

Mura. In Hindu mythology, a demon slain by Krishna (an incarnation of the god Vishnu). Krishna not only killed Mura but "burnt his seven thousand sons like moths with the flame of the edge of his discus."

Variant spelling: Muru.

2117

Murile. In African mythology (Chaga of Tanzania), culture hero who brought fire. One day a young boy named Murile was being scolded by his mother for his misbehavior. He took his father's stool and commanded it to go into the air. First it went up into a tree and then into the sky. Murile then set out to find the home of the moon- chief, asking people he met for directions. After he had worked for some of these people for a period of time, they told him the way. When he arrived at the moon-chief's village, he saw people eating uncooked food. The moon-chief explained that they knew nothing of fire and so obviously could not cook their food. Murile was promised animals as gifts if he would show them how to make fire. He did so, and in time prospered greatly among these people. By and by, however, he wished to return to his own home and sent a mockingbird back to his people as a messenger. His family did not believe the bird, thinking that their son, who had been gone so long, must be dead. So Murile set off on the journey home with all of his herds, but gradually he grew very tired. A bull promised to carry him if Murile agreed never to eat his flesh. Murile agreed and directed his parents to spare the bull. His father,

however, disregarded Murile's command and killed the bull. Not realizing it, Murile ate some food prepared by his mother with fat that had come from the animal. As he sank into the ground, he called out to his mother, saying that she had disobeyed him.

Clio

2118

Muses (mountain goddesses). In Greek and Roman mythology, the nine daughters of Zeus and Mnemosyne (memory), according to Hesiod's *Theogony*. They were called Camenae by the Romans. They were born at the foot of Mount Olympus in Pieria. Mount Helicon in Boeotia was sacred to them. The nine Muses are Calliope, Muse of epic poetry, mother of Orpheus by Apollo; Clio, Muse of history, whose attribute is a laurel and scroll; Erato, Muse of lyric poetry, love poetry, and marriage songs, whose attribute is a lyre (Erato was invoked by lovers in April); Euterpe, Muse of music and lyric poetry, whose attribute is a flute; Melpomene, Muse of tragedy, whose attribute is the tragic mask and *cothurnus* (buskin); Polyhymnia (Polymnia), Muse of sacred song, oratory, lyric, singing, and rhetoric, whose attribute is a veil; Terpsichore, Muse of dancing, whose attribute is a crown of laurel and a musical instrument in her hand; Thalia, Muse of comedy, whose attribute was the comic mask and the "sock," a shoe worn by comic actors; and Urania, Muse of astronomy, whose attribute is a glove and a pair of compasses. Urania was the mother of Linus by Apollo and of Hymenaeus by Dionysus. In Renaissance poetry she is often said to be the Muse of poetry.

Erato

2119
Mushroom. An edible fungus. In ancient Egypt the pharaohs forbade any commoner to touch mushrooms because they were sacred. The Hebrews had a general taboo against fungus eating. The Romans, however, loved mushrooms, though the philosopher-poet Seneca called them "voluptuous poison." Certain types of fungi grow in the form of fairy rings, small circles within which fairies are believed to dance at night. Shakespeare's *The Tempest* (5:1) has Prospero invoke the fairies.

Euterpe

2120
Muspellsheim (home of destruction). In Norse mythology, the realm of fire, the heat from which helped in the creation of the world. Surt guards Muspellsheim with a flaming sword. He will destroy the gods and the world by fire at Ragnarok, the end of the world.

2121
Mustard Seed, The. Buddhist parable about the reality of death, found in various collections. Krisha Gautami, a young orphan girl, had only one child. One day the child died, and Krisha was heartbroken. She carried the dead child to all of her neighbors, asking them for medicine to restore the child to life. Finally, she met a man who said to her, "I cannot

give you medicine for your dead child, but I know a physician who can." The man sent Krisha to the Buddha. When she arrived she asked, "Lord and Master, give me the medicine that will restore my son to life." The Buddha replied, "I want a handful of mustard seeds taken from a house where no one has lost a child, husband, parent, or friend." Krisha went from house to house. "Here is mustard seed. Take it," they would say. But when she asked, "Did a son or daughter, a father or mother die in your family?" They answered her, "Yes, the living are few, but the dead are many." She then realized that death is common to all humankind. She buried her son and returned to the Buddha, taking comfort in his teaching.

Mut

2122

Mut (mother). In Egyptian mythology, a great mother-goddess, believed to possess both male and female reproductive organs. Her temple at Thebes had a horseshoe-shaped Sacred Lake. Her sanctuary there was in use for 2,000 years. Mut is usually portrayed in Egyptian art as a woman wearing on her head the united crowns of Upper and Lower Egypt and holding in her hands the papyrus scepter and the ankh, sign of life. Sometimes she is portrayed standing upright, with her large winged arms stretched out full length. At her feet is the feather of Maat, or Truth, and on her head is the vulture headdress. Sometimes, however, this versatile deity is portrayed with the head of a man or a vulture and with a phallus and lion claws. The Greeks identified Mut with Hera, the wife of Zeus.

2123

Muta (silence). In Roman mythology, goddess of silence and quiet. Ovid's *Fasti* (book 2) cites the goddess.

2124

Mwambu and Sela. In African mythology (Luyia of Kenya), the first man and woman. Wele, the creator god, made the sun shine for them and gave them water from heaven to drink. This water eventually made all of the lakes and rivers of the earth. Mwambu and Sela were told which kinds of meat to eat and which to refrain from eating, which types of food were permitted and which were not. Wele gave them young calves, male and female, so that they might prosper. The children of Mwambu and Sela came down from their parents' home, which was built on posts, and learned to live on the ground.

2125

Myo-o (kings of wisdom). In Japanese Buddhist mythology, the five fierce or terrible manifestations of the Buddha; their fierce appearance destroys ignorance, the major hindrance to enlightenment. They are Dai-itoku-Myo-o, Fudo-Myo-o, Gonzanze, Kongo-yasha-Myo-o, and Aizen-Myo-o. The most important is Aizen-Myo-o, who is equated in Japanese folklore with the god of love. He is portrayed with a ferocious face, having three eyes, one of which is in the middle of his forehead, placed vertically between his eyebrows. On his head is a lion headdress. He usually has six arms and carries a metal bell, a quiver and bow, a wheel, a thunderbolt, a man's head or hook, and a lotus flower. Various Buddhist texts explain some of the symbolism of his iconography. If his body is painted red, it symbolizes his compassion, which issues from every pore of his body like drops of blood. His three eyes allow him to behold heaven, earth, and hell. He wears a lion's headdress because he is like a lion. The bell awakens enlightenment; the thunderbolt symbolizes a pure heart or is a means to strike down the wicked. The bow and arrow drive away forgetfulness, and the lotus calms the agitation of guilt.

2126

Myrimidons (ants). In Greek mythology, ants who were turned into soldiers to accompany Achilles during the Trojan War. King Aeacus of Aegina, a son of Zeus, prayed to his father to replenish the population of his kingdom, which had been destroyed by a plague sent by Hera to punish one of the women whom her husband, Zeus, had loved. A variant account says there were no people to begin with. Zeus answered the prayer of Aeacus by transforming ants into warriors, who later joined Achilles in the Trojan War. Today the term Myrimidons is used for warriors "who execute an order, especially a military command, with ruthless indifference to its baseness or inhumanity" (Bergen Evans). Homer's *Iliad* (book 2) and Ovid's *Metamorphoses* (book 7) tell of the Myrimidons.

2127

Myrrh. A tree resin used for incense, associated in Greek mythology with a tale recounted by Ovid in his *Metamorphoses* (book 10) about a princess, Myrrha, in love with her father, Cinyras, king of Cyprus. In remorse for her incestuous feelings she attempted suicide but was rescued by her nurse, who then promised to help her. She told the king that a very beautiful girl longed to sleep with him and arranged an assignation. Drunk with wine, the king did not recognize Myrrha when she came to him, but after several encounters he discovered that his mistress was his own daughter. Horrified to discover his incest, he tried to kill her; but she fled to the land of Sabaea, where she bore a son, Adonis, and afterward she turned into a tree, the myrrh. Her tears became the fragrant resin of the tree. Adonis was worshiped with burning of myrrh at his festival.

Variant spelling: Smyrna.

2128

Myrtle. An evergreen shrub; in European mythology and folklore, often associated with birth and resurrection. Greek colonists carried myrtle boughs to their new countries to symbolize the end of one life and the beginning of another. The myrtle was associated with Aphrodite, Greek goddess of sex, love, and fecundity, as well as with her Roman counterpart, Venus. Among Romans the myrtle was a symbol of marriage, a rite over which both Venus and Juno presided. Its blossoms were worn by brides, and bridegrooms wore myrtle sprigs. Yet the Romans also saw an evil side to the myrtle: it was identified with unlawful and incestuous love and was not allowed to be displayed at some public functions. In the Old Testament the myrtle is a token of the goodness of Yahweh, for He promised to plant a myrtle in the wilderness for the children of Israel (Isa. 41:19).

2129

Mystère. In Haitian voodoo, the sun, one of the main symbols in voodoo worship; also a loa (deified spirit of the dead).

N

Na Atibu. In Micronesian mythology, a creator god of the Gilbert Islands. Earth and people were formed from Na Atibu's body. From his spine the sacred tree Kai-n-tiku-abu (tree of many branches) sprang, with people as its fruit. But one day a man named Koura-abi got angry when some excrement fell on him from the tree. He attacked the tree, breaking its branches and scattering the people throughout the world.

Nabu (announcer). In Near Eastern mythology (Babylonian), god of wisdom, speech, and writing; son of Marduk. Nabu appears in the Old Testament (Is. 46.1) as Nebo where he is ridiculed, along with the god Bel, for his helplessness.

Naenia (dirge). In Roman mythology, goddess who presided over funerals. Her temple was outside the city gate in Rome.

Naga (snake). In Hindu and Buddhist mythology, fantastic beings with the head of a man or woman and the body of a snake, ruled over by Shesha, the serpent king. The Nagas guard various treasures, especially pearls. Sometimes Nagas' upper bodies are human and their lower bodies serpentine. They are said to inhabit Nagaloka, Niraya, or Patala. Often the Buddha is shown surrounded by Nagas in complete serpentine form.
Variant spellings: Naia, Naja, Naje.

Naglfar (conveyance made of nails). In Norse mythology, the ship of the giants, made of dead men's nails. Naglfar will carry the giants to their final battle, Ragnarok, against the gods. It was an ancient Nordic custom to cut short the nails of deceased persons to delay the coming of Ragnarok. Thus, the size of Naglfar depends on how many people are buried with long fingernails that were not cut. At Ragnarok, the end of the world, Naglfar will bring the Jotunn giants to fight the Aesir gods. Naglfar appears in the *Prose Edda*. Naglfar is also the name of a giant who was the first husband of Nott.

Nain Rouge (red dwarf). In American folklore, a ghost of a red-faced creature who is believed to be responsible for the burning of Detroit in 1805. To avoid its evil spell some citizens paint the sign of the cross on their homes.

Nairyo-sangha. In Persian mythology, messenger of the good god, Ahura Mazda. He lives in the navel of kings and is a companion of the god Mithra. Nairyo-sangha is worshiped along with Sraosha, one of the seven Amesha Spentas, who will help judge the world.

Najara. In Australian mythology, a spirit who lures young boys away from their tribes and makes them forget their language. Najara was a tribesman of the Djauan country. One day he went off to spear an emu. He sat down at the base of a palm tree and saw some dingoes—wild dogs—come along smelling the ground. They killed Najara and ripped his body to pieces. The moon god, Deert, found Najara's body and buried it. At the end of three days Najara returned to life and rose from his grave. Deert asked him how he was able to accomplish this. Najara answered that the moon god did not need his "cleverness." Najara knew that Deert too had the secret of returning from the dead.

Najara went off into the desert. When he came upon a boy from his tribe, he whistled to him. The boy came over, and the two camped together for several months. When they were at last sighted by other members of the tribe, the boy fled. Eventually he was caught and brought back to the tribal camp. Najara, on the other hand, showed no fear. He suddenly disappeared and was never seen again. It was a long time before the boy would eat the food of his tribe or speak their language. To this day it is believed that when the spirit of Najara whistles in the grass, boys will be lured away and forget their tribe's language.

Nakaa. In Micronesian mythology, the guardian of a primordial tree. According to a Gilbert Island myth, it was Nakaa who watched over a tree given to women at the beginning of time. Men, who were made to lie apart from women, were innocent and were forbidden to touch the tree. The men were given a fish trap that supplied them with plentiful fish. They were also given a tree of their own, which bore a single nut. Each time the nut was picked, another would grow in its place. One day when Nakaa was away, the men disobeyed him and touched the women's tree. When Nakaa returned, he found some of the men's hairs on it and knew they had been there. He grew very angry and permitted death to enter the world.

Nakaa sat down by the entrance to the spirit world and wove a net, which he used to capture the spirits of the wrongdoers as they attempted to seek rest for their souls. The spirits of the good people were free to enter the realm of the afterlife, but the spirits of the violators could not. Depending on which tribe is telling the myth, the souls of the blessed go either to an island, somewhere underground, or to a place in the sky.

2139

Nakk. In Finno-Ugric mythology, evil water spirit living in the deepest spot in the water. Nakk could appear in many different shapes, both human and animal, though the Estonians usually imagined him as a gray old man who swallowed everything in the water that came his way. Sometimes he seated himself on the shore to watch people or bewitched them with his songs, which forced men and animals to dance until they fell into the sea and were drowned. The female counterpart of Nakk was Nakineiu (Nakk's maid), a beautiful girl who sat on the surface of the water, on a stone on the shore, or in the shadow of a tree growing near the river, combing her long golden-yellow hair. Sometimes she appeared naked with a half-human and half-fish body. Like her male counterpart she too sang.

2140

Nalul. In Australian mythology, a man of unknown origin who one day came out of the desert to a lovely green place of fig trees, palms, and flowers. He heard the sound of laughing girls and, ever so gradually crept up to them. Unseen by them, he parted the reeds and saw a beautiful girl with long hair. Nalul caught her by the hair, but she fought him. Finally, he threw sand into her eyes and while she was blinded, he tied her to a tree. In time he brought her some honey to eat, but she seemed not to know what it was and apparently did not understand his language. Only after he rubbed the sweat of his body across her mouth, ears, and eyes could she understand him. He then heated some bark and placed it by the girl's ears so she could hear the sound of water. When he had finished, Nalul called her Nyal-Warrai-Warrai, the girl from the water. Now she

freely went with him and no longer had to be tied. When they passed the country where her sisters lived, they called to her. Although she did not want to, she felt compelled to go back to the water whence she had come. She was never seen by Nalul again. It is said that she went to be with her father, the rainbow snake.

2141

Nama. In Siberian mythology, hero of the flood myth as told by the Altaics.

Nama was commanded by the creator god Ulgen to construct an ark. Because Nama was partly blind, he asked the assistance of his three sons, Sozun-uul, Sar-uul, and Balyka. When the ark was finished Nama, his wife, his sons, some other people, and animals were placed aboard. When the flood came, all were saved. After many years, when Nama had grown old and was near death, his wife asked him to kill all of the people and animals he had originally saved so he could be lord of the dead in the next world. However, his son, Sozun-uul, convinced his father that this was wrong, so instead the old man killed his wife by cutting her in two. When Nama died, he took his son Sozun-uul to heaven with him, where he was later transformed into a constellation of five stars.

In later mythology Nama became lord of the dead and is called Jaik-Khan (the flood prince). He is invoked as an intermediary between God and man, living in the Third Heaven, that of the Kudai, seven spirits who watch over men's destinies. When Nama sends the life force to each child born into the world, he is called Jujutshi.

2142

Namuchi (not releasing the heavenly waters). In Hindu mythology, a demon slain by Indra, the storm god. When Indra conquered the demons, Namuchi alone resisted so strongly that he overpowered Indra, making him a prisoner. Namuchi offered to let Indra go if Indra promised not to kill him by day or night, wet or dry. Indra promised and was released. Later, however, the god cut off Namuchi's head at twilight, between day and night, and with water foam, which was neither wet nor dry. In the Hindu epic poem *The Mahabharata*, the severed head of Namuchi follows Indra, crying out: "O wicked slayer of thy friend." The same myth is recounted with Narasinha, an incarnation of Vishnu, as the slayer.

2143

Nana. In African mythology (Yoruba of southwest Nigeria and Fon of Benin), earth goddess; married to Obaluwaye, the earth god; mother of Omolu, another earth god. Nana, Obaluwaye, and Omolu also appear in African cults of Brazil and Cuba.

Nanda. In Buddhist legend, a woman who gave rice pudding or, in other versions of the legend, very rich cream (the cream of the cream of the milk from 100 cows) to the Buddha after he had given up mortifications, which he found useless to Enlightenment.

Nandin (the happy one). In Hindu mythology, the bull-vehicle of Shiva, who watches the lingam outside the temple. He has one leg crooked, ready to stand up and go as needed. Nandin is also called Viraka (little hero).

Nane. In Armenian mythology, goddess, daughter of the supreme god, Aramazd. She may have been derived from the Sumerian goddess Nana, though in Hellenistic times Nane was often identified with the Greek goddess Athena as a wise and warlike goddess.

Variant spelling: Hanea.

Nanimulap. In Micronesian mythology, god of fertility in the Caroline Islands. His sacred animal is the turtle, which may be eaten only by chiefs.

Nanna (mother of the brave). In Norse mythology, the wife of Baldur and mother of Forseti. After Baldur's death Nanna died of anguish at his funeral fire and was burned along with him. Nanna appears in the *Prose Edda* and in Matthew Arnold's narrative poem *Balder Dead*.

Naomi Wise. American ballad of the 19th century that tells how Naomi was murdered by her lover. The ballad is believed by some to be based on the murder of Naomi Wise by Jonathan Lewis in 1808.

Napi (old man, dawn-light-color man). In North American Indian mythology (Blackfoot), creator god, culture hero, and trickster. Napi created the first people out of clay. He then appeared to his creatures near a river. A woman asked him if people were to live forever. He replied that he had not thought of that question. "We must decide what shall happen. I will toss a piece of wood into the river. If it floats, when people die they will return to life in four days. But if the wood sinks, death will be forever." The wood was cast into the river, and it floated. Then the first woman picked up a stone and said, "If it floats, we will live forever; but if it sinks, we will die." The stone was cast into the river and immediately sank. "You have chosen," replied the god. Some accounts say that Napi left after the creation and went to live in the mountains, promising to return one day.

Narcissus

Narcissus (benumbing, narcotic). In Greek mythology, son of Cephisus and Lirope. Narcissus scorned the love of Echo, a nymph (or according to another account, a male lover). As punishment, the gods made Narcissus fall in love with his own reflection in a pool. Because he received no answer from his image, the youth killed himself and was transformed into a flower. In another variation Narcissus had a twin sister who died. When he looked into the pool, he thought he saw her image, not his own. Narcissus has been cited in English literature by many poets, among them, Spenser in *The Faerie Queene* (3.6.45): Christopher Marlowe in *Hero and Leander* (1.74–6), Keats in *I Stood Tip-toe upon a Little Hill* (163); and Shelley in *The Sensitive Plant* (1.18– 20). Narcissus was painted by Caravaggio, Tintoretto, Claude, Poussin, and Turner.

Nareau (spider lord). In Micronesian mythology, two creator gods, Ancient Spider and Young Spider.

According to some accounts, Ancient Spider is a preexistent being, living in either darkness, a void, endless space, or the sea. Other accounts say he was born when Te Bo Ma (darkness) and Te Maki (the cleaving together) had sexual intercourse, producing Void, Night, Daylight, Thunder, Lightning, Ancient

Spider, and Younger Spider. In the account of the Gilbert Islands, Ancient Spider made heaven and earth from a shell. He commanded the sand and water to have sexual intercourse. Their children included Nakika, the octopus; Riiki, the eel; and a son whose name was also Nareau, or Young Spider. Young Nareau's task was to transform fools and mutes into normal human beings. He loosened their tongues and limbs and opened their eyes and ears. Then he commanded them to lift the sky, but they could not. So he called on Riiki and Nakika to assist him. While Young Spider chanted, Riiki raised the sky and the earth sank. Young Spider pulled the sides of the sky down to meet the edge of the horizon, leaving the fools and deaf mutes in the middle of the sea. Four women were placed in position to support the heavens. Exhausted with his labors, Riiki died and became the Milky Way. Ancient Spider became the sun and moon; his brains became the stars, trees, and rocks, and humans sprang from the remainder of his body.

Variant spellings: Naareau, Narleau, Na-areau, Areop-enap.

2153
Narguns. In Australian mythology, evil beings, half human and half animal, made of stone. They cannot be killed.

2154
Nari. In Norse mythology, son of the fire-trickster god, Loki, and his wife, Siguna. Nari appears in the *Prose Edda*.

Variant spelling: Narvi.

2155
Nasnas. In Persian-Islamic folklore, a demon who appears in the shape of a feeble old man. Nasnas usually sits on the bank of a river, and when a traveler approaches, Nasnas asks for help in crossing. If the traveler consents, Nasnas mounts his shoulders. When they reach midstream, he wraps his legs around his victim and drowns him.

2156
Nasu. In Persian mythology, corpse demon, the personification of corruption, decomposition, contagion, and impurity. Nasu often appears in the form of a fly that hovers above rotting bodies. He is driven away by the glance of a dog in the rite called sag-did (dog-sight). In some texts Nasu is regarded as a demoness.

Variant spellings: Nas; Nasus, Nasrust, Druj Nasa.

2157
Natigay. In Siberian mythology, the earth god worshiped by the Tartars to protect children, cattle, and grain. Marco Polo, in his *Travels* (book 1), has a description of the images of Natigay he encountered on his journeys. They were "covered with felt or cloth," and one was placed in each dwelling. At mealtimes the images of Natigay and of his wife and children, were "fed" by having grease from the meal rubbed on their mouths. Natigay is probably a corruption of Otukhan, a pagan Turkish god adopted by the Tartars.

Variant spelling: Natigai.

2158
Nation, Carry. 1846–1911. In American history and folklore, fanatic temperance leader, who hatcheted her way to fame. She believed that God had given her a divine mission to destroy saloons and the drinking of hard liquor. She lectured extensively on her divine call and told her story in a book, *The Use and the Need of the Life of Carry A. Nation*. She appears as the lead in Douglas Moore's opera *Carry Nation*, as well as in limericks and tales.

2159
Natos. In North American Indian mythology (Blackfoot), the sun, whose wife is Kokomikeis, the moon. All of their children were destroyed by pelicans, except Apisuahts, the morning star.

2160
Nats. In Burmese mythology, generic name for supernatural beings, both good and evil, who inhabit air, land, and sea. In some accounts they are believed to be the spirits of the dead who have to be placated by offerings. The most famous group appears in the work *Maha Gita Medani*, a handbook in verse that contains short biographical sketches. Verses from the book are recited at festivals by a *nat-kadaw* or female medium, who is believed to be under the possession of a *nat*. The most famous *nat* is Thagya Min, whose yearly descent to earth marks the beginning of the Burmese new year. In Burmese art Thagya Min is portrayed standing on a lotus, which in turn rests on three elephants.

2161
Natty Bumppo. In American literary folklore, hero of James Fenimore Cooper's *Leatherstocking* Tales, a series of novels deriving its name from Natty Bumppo's long deerskin leggings. Natty Bumppo is called Bumppo or Deerslayer in *The Deerslayer*, Hawkeye in *The Last of the Mohicans*, Pathfinder in *The Pathfinder*, Natty Bumppo or Leatherstocking in *The Pioneers*, and the trapper in *The Prairie*. Natty Bumppo, whose character is based in part on Daniel Boone, is the ideal outdoorsman; kind, strong, honest, and resourceful. He appears in Hollywood's movie *The Last of the Mohicans* (1936), starring Randolph Scott.

Nausicaa (burner of ships). In Greek mythology, daughter of Alcinous, king of Phaeacia, and Arete. In Homer's *Odyssey* (book 6) Nausicaa befriended Odysseus, bringing him to the home of her father before the hero was sent on his way back to his wife. In later tradition Nausicaa married Telemachus, the son of Odysseus, and was the mother of Perseptolis or Poliporthus. Samuel Butler, the English novelist, who translated both *The Iliad* and *The Odyssey* into English prose, also wrote a book in which he argued that Nausicaa, not Homer, was the real author of *The Odyssey*.

2163

Ndauthina. In Melanesian mythology, Fijian trickster god of fire and of fishermen. He protects fishermen but causes trouble for others.

2164

Ndengei. In Melanesian mythology, Fijian creator god in serpent form whose movements cause earthquakes. Offerings of pigs and first fruits are made to the god. Ndengei's son, Rokomautu, who is sometimes called a creator god, gave fire to humankind.

2165

Nebuchadnezzar (Nebo protect the landmark). In the Bible, O.T., king of Assyria who reigned from 604 to 561 B.C.E. He rebuilt Babylon, restored the temple of the god Bel, and may be responsible for the Hanging Gardens. He appears in many legends. He supposedly went mad at the height of his achievements, as described in Daniel (4:33) when he "did eat grass as oxen . . . his hairs were grown like eagles' feathers, and his nails like birds' claws." William Blake painted the ruler in this state, and a 15th-century Umbrian panel from a cassone (marriage trunk) portrays scenes from the life of Nebuchadnezzar.

2166

Nectar. In Greek mythology, the magical drink of the gods that conferred immortality. It was given to the gods in golden cups by Hebe or Ganymede. Ambrosia was the food of the gods.

2167

Nefer. In ancient Egyptian cult, an amulet of the windpipe and stomach, often made of a semiprecious stone. It is the sign for the concept of "good" and is the plural for "beauty."

2168

Nefertiti (the beautiful one has come). fl. 1372–1350 B.C.E. Egyptian queen, wife of Akhenaten, who worked with her husband in establishing the worship of Aten. The famous head of Nefertiti in the Egyptian Museum of West Berlin is but one of many fine portraits of the ruler.

2169

Neith. In Egyptian mythology, goddess of the city of Saïs, which served as Egypt's capital during the Twenty-Sixth Dynasty. When Saïs became the major city, Neith's importance increased considerably. A great festival, called the Feast of Lamps, was held in her honor. During the festival, according to Herodotus' *History* (book 2), devotees burned a multitude of lights in her honor all night in the open air. Neith became associated with creation myths, similar to those surrounding Hathor. As a goddess of weaving and the domestic arts, Neith was said to have woven the world with her shuttle. She was sometimes called the first birthgiver, the mother who bore the sun before anything else existed. On her temple wall was inscribed: "I am all that has been, that is, and that will be." In Egyptian art Neith was usually depicted as a woman wearing the crown of Lower Egypt, holding a scepter in one hand and the ankh, sign of life, in the other. The Greeks identified Neith with their goddess Athena.

Variant spellings: Neit, Net, Nit.

2170

Nei Tituaabine. In Micronesian mythology, Gilbert Island tree goddess. She was once a mortal who fell in love with a chief, Auriaria, but died when she bore no offspring. From her body sprouted various trees and fruits.

2171

Nekhebet. In Egyptian mythology, the vulture goddess of Upper Egypt, a patron of childbirth. She was called "the father of fathers, the mother of mothers" in some texts. Often she was portrayed as a vulture, though she also appeared in Egyptian art as a woman wearing the vulture headdress surmounted by the white crown of Upper Egypt. The Greeks identified her with their goddess Eileithyia.

Variant spelling: Nechbet.

2172

Nemesis (due enactment, divine vengeance). In Greek mythology, goddess of vengeance or personification of the righteous anger of the gods; daughter of Erebus and Nox; sister of Cer, Aether, Dreams, Hemera, Hypnos, Momus, Thanatos, and Charon. She was seduced by Zeus, and some accounts say she was the mother of Helen. Nemesis was the daughter of Nyx and Erebus. Nemesis punishes *hubris* (presumption or pride) as when she pursued Agamemnon for his pride in victory. Dürer made a woodcut of the goddess. Byron's dramatic poem *Manfred* has Nemesis as a servant of Arimanes, the devil.

Nemterequeteba. In the mythology of the Chibcha Indians of Colombia, a culture hero, often identified with the chief of the gods, Bochica. Nemterequeteba organized a cult, appointed a high priest, and taught chastity, sobriety, social order, and the arts of spinning, weaving, and textile painting. When his task was finished, he disappeared.

In Chibcha art he is portrayed as an old man with long hair and a beard down to his girdle. Nemterequeteba is also called Chimizapagua, the messenger of Chiminigagua (the creator god) and Sugumonxe or Sugunsua, the person who disappears.

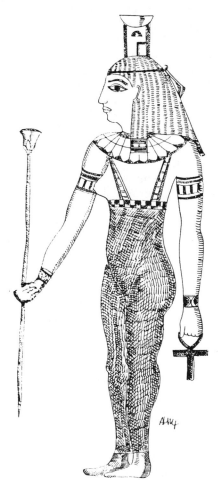

Nephthys

Nephthys. In Egyptian mythology, Greek name form of Nebthet; sister of Osiris, Set and Isis; often associated with darkness, decay, and death. In early Egyptian mythology Nephthys was usually regarded as the female counterpart of the evil god Set. According to one myth, Nephthys abandoned Set, with whom she had remained barren, for her other brother, Osiris, and then tricked Osiris, whose wife was Isis, into copulating with her. She then conceived Anubis, the jackal-headed god. Later, however, she became the faithful friend of Isis and helped her sister collect the scattered limbs of Osiris, who had been dismembered by Set, and reassemble his body. In the Pyramid Texts she is considered the friend of the dead, and the same role is attributed to her in *The Book of the Dead*.

Although Nephthys was a goddess of death, she was also the female counterpart of the ithyphallic god Mim, who symbolized virility, reproduction, and regeneration.

Nephthys was also skilled in magic and "words of power," and as a healing deity she was, with Isis and Osiris, one of the great deities of Mendes in the delta region. She often appeared with Isis on the walls of coffins, with winged arms outstretched in a gesture of protection. Among her many titles were "mistress of the gods," "great goddess, lady of life," "sister of the god," and "lady of heaven, mistress of two lands."

Egyptian art portrays Nephthys as a woman wearing on her head a pair of horns and a disk surmounted by the hieroglyph of her name.

Neptune

2175

Neptune. In Roman mythology, the early Italian sea god, possibly called Nethunus by the Etruscans; called Poseidon by the Greeks; husband of Salacia.

Generally, in English literature Neptune is seen as a personification of the ocean. Shakespeare's *Macbeth* says: "Will all great Neptune's ocean wash this blood/ Clean from my hand? (2.2.60– 61). Neptune

Neptune riding on a dolphin into Venice harbor (Jacopo de Barberi)

also was seen as the god who watched over England, and he is cited in Shakespeare's *Cymbeline* (3.2.19–20) as such. He also is cited or appears in Milton's *Comus*, and his epic *Paradise Lost*, Ben Jonson's *Neptune's Triumph*, and the opening masque in Beaumont and Fletcher's *The Maid's Tragedy*. The most famous image of the god is probably that by Bernini in the Trevi Fountain in Rome. The artist also did a *Neptune and Triton*. Neptune's attributes are the trident, a weapon favored by Mediterranean fishermen, and the whip, reminding his worshiper that he was also a god of horses. Neptune's festival date was 23 July.

Nereids (the wet ones). In Greek mythology, sea nymphs or mermaids, the 50 or 100 daughters of Nersus, a sea god, and Doris. Among them were Actaee, Agave, Amatheia, Amphinome, Amphithoe, Amphitrite, Apseudes, Callianassa, Callianeira, Clymene, Creusa, Cymodoce, Cymothoe, Dexamene, Doris, Doto, Dynamene, Erato, Eudora, Galatea, Glauce, Halie, Iaera, Ianassa, Ianeira, Limnoreia, Maera, Melite, Nemertes, Nesaera, Oreithyia, Panope, Pasithea, Pherusa, Proto, Psamanthe, Speio, Thalia, Thetis, and Thoe. The Nereids were attendants on Poseidon. The most famous are Amphitrite, wife of Poseidon, and Thetis, mother of Achilles. Images of Nereids were often carved on Roman sarcophagi indicating the passage of the soul to the other world.

Nergal (lord of the great city). In Near Eastern mythology (Babylonian-Assyrian), war god, lord of the underworld, husband of Ereshkigal, goddess of the underworld. In some accounts he is said to be the son of Bel. He was addressed as "the hero of the gods, who marches in front of them" to battle, and among his names (when identified with the planet Mars) are those of Allamu and Almu. Assyrian kings regarded Nergal as the patron god of hunting. Nergal was portrayed wearing a crown and was waited on by 14 attendants. His sacred city of the dead was Cutha.

Nero, Claudius Caesar. 54–68 C.E. In Roman history and legend, emperor who "fiddled while Rome burned" and then blamed the Christians for the fire. The fiddling is legend and has no historical basis. Nero's mother, Agrippina, was suspected of killing the Emperor Claudius, her uncle, so that Nero would succeed instead of Britannicus, Claudius' own son. Nero later had his mother killed. He was tutored by Seneca, the author and philosopher. Poppaea Sabina, his mistress from 58 C.E. and then his wife from 62 until her death in 65, was believed responsible for the death of Nero's mother and his divorce from Octavia for sterility. When Nero's armies revolted on the Rhine, the emperor killed himself, but for some time rumors circulated that he had not really died. His dying words were "what an artist dies in me."

Thetis ordering the Nereids into the sea (John Flaxman)

After the fire in Rome he built the *domus aurea* (golden house) in a park overlooking an artificial lake. In front stood a massive statue of the emperor as the sun god. Monteverdi's opera *Poppaea* deals with Nero and his mistress and wife. Nero's life is given in Suetonius' *Lives of the Twelve Caesars*.

2179

Nerthus (earth). In Germanic mythology, mother earth, fertility goddess of tribes. The Roman writer Tacitus in his *Germania* (40) calls her Terra Mater. Processions in Nerthus' honor, in which she was worshiped as goddess of fertility, peace, and plenty, were elaborate. A statue of the goddess was drawn every spring to promote fertility. Slaves dedicated to the goddess were drowned in her honor.

Variant spelling: Nertha, Hertha.

2180

Nessus (young bird or animal). In Greek mythology, a centaur, son of Ixion and a cloud, who attempted to rape Deianira, wife of Heracles. Nessus was killed by Heracles with an arrow poisoned with the blood of the Lernean Hydra. Some of the blood spilled on Nessus' shirt, which later was given to Heracles by Deianira in the belief that it would reclaim Heracles's love for her. In fact, the shirt caused Heracles's death. The expression "shirt of Nessus" is used to indicate a fatal gift. Ovid's *Metamorphoses* (book 4) tells the tale, and it is alluded to in Shakespeare's *All's Well That Ends Well* (4.3.283) and *Anthony and Cleopatra* (4.12.93). In *The Divine Comedy* (Inferno, cantos 12, 13) Vergil points out Nessus to Dante. Later Nessus is sent by Chiron to escort Vergil and Dante and to show them the ford across the river Phlegethon.

2181

Nestor (newly speaking). In Greek mythology, a wise man, son of Neleus and Chloris, noted for his eloquence during the Trojan War. Homer's *Iliad* (book 1) identifies Nestor as king of Pylos. His wife was Eurydice, according to Homer, but other sources name Anaxibia. He had two daughters and seven sons. According to late accounts, Nestor lived to be 300 years old, having been blessed by Apollo, who added the years to compensate for the god's murder of the sons of Niobe and Amphion, Nestor's uncles. Nestor also appears in Homer's *Odyssey* (book 3), where he entertains Telemachus, the son of Odysseus. Nestor's tale is told in Ovid's *Metamorphoses* (book 12). He also appears in Shakespeare's *Troilus and Cressida*.

2182

Net-net. In Australian mythology, small, hairy, mischievous people who have claws instead of fingernails and toenails.

2183

Neulam-kurrk. In Australian mythology, an evil female spirit who kidnaps children and eats them.

2184

Ngalalbal. In Australian mythology, wife of the gigantic old god Baiame and mother of the creator god Daramulum.

2185

Ngallenyook. In Australian mythology, an evil spirit who sends sickness and whom medicine men cannot destroy.

2186

Ngarangs. In Australian mythology, evil beings who resemble men, with long, flowing hair and beards. They live at the roots of old gum trees, coming out at night to capture victims, whom they eat.

2187

Ngunung-ngunnut. In Australian mythology, the bat who created the first woman, to remedy the imbalance in nature in which only men existed.

2188

Ngunza. In African mythology (Mbundu of Angola), a hero who captured Death. Ngunza was one of two brothers. While he was on a trip away from home, he dreamed that his brother had died. When he returned, his mother explained that Death had taken his brother. So Ngunza set a large trap to capture Death. When Death was caught, he begged to be set free, arguing that he was not responsible for killing people. Death said that it was invariably the fault of some human being, often the person himself. Death and Ngunza set off together to visit the land of the dead so that Ngunza could see this for himself. Ngunza found his brother living well, better than he had lived when he was on earth. Ngunza returned home and was given the seeds of all of the significant plants that grow in Angola. In time Death came looking for him. Ngunza resented the persistent way in which he was pursued by Death. Finally, however, Death threw an ax at Ngunza, who quickly died and turned into a spirit.

2189

Nhangs. In Armenian mythology, evil spirits, often in the form of mermaids, who lured people to their death. One Armenian commentary on the Bible calls Salome, the girl who danced for the head of St. John the Baptist, more bloodthirsty than "the Nhangs of the sea," referring to the belief that Nhangs, vampirelike, sometimes sucked the blood from their victims.

Siegfried and Kriemhild

Nibelungenlied (lay of the Nibelungs). Thirteenth-century C.E. epic poem of 2,327 stanzas by an unknown Austrian. The work is divided into 39 adventures or chapters.

First Adventure. Three Burgundian princes, or Nibelungs, live at Worms on the Rhine. Their sister Kriemhild has a vision in which she sees two eagles pursue a falcon and tear it to pieces when it seeks refuge on her breast. Knowing her mother is skilled at interpreting dreams, Kriemhild asks her what the dream means. She is told that her future husband will be attacked.

Second Adventure. At Xantan on the Rhine, King Siegmund and his wife hold a tournament for the coming of age of their only son Siegfried, who distinguishes himself greatly at the feast. His mother lavishes great gifts upon him.

Third Adventure. Siegfried hears of Kriemhild's beauty and goes to woo her, taking with him only 11 men. He arrives at Worms. Hagen, a cousin of King Gunther, Kriemhild's brother, tells the king that Siegfried once killed a dragon and now is the owner of the Nibelungen hoard (the dwarfs' gold). The hoard had belonged to two brothers, who asked Siegfried to divide it between them. He undertook the task in exchange for a sword, Balmung, which lay on top of the heap of gold. But no sooner had he made the division than the brothers killed one another, leaving Siegfried with the treasure.

On hearing that Siegfried has come to challenge Gunther to a duel, the Burgundians are very upset. They persuade Siegfried to disarm and stay as a guest for a year. Kriemhild watches Siegfried from a window and falls in love with him.

Fourth Adventure. Siegfried aids Gunther by defeating the kings of Saxony and Denmark. He defeats the enemy with only 1,000 men against their 4,000. When the messenger comes to announce Siegfried's victory, Kriemhild flushes with pleasure.

Fifth Adventure. A tournament is held at Worms in honor of the victory. Siegfried and Kriemhild meet face to face and fall in love. Siegfried then asks Gunther for Kriemhild's hand.

Sixth Adventure. Gunther bargains with Siegfried, asking that before he claims Kriemhild he should go with Gunther to Isenland and help him win Brunhild. Gunther needs Siegfried's help in wooing because Brunhild has vowed to marry only a man who can throw a spear and a stone farther than she can and surpass her in jumping. Siegfried, failing to dissuade Gunther, decides to accompany him on his quest and suggests that Hagen and another knight join them. Kriemhild provides them with handmade garments, and they reach Isenland 12 days later. As their ship nears the land, Siegfried asks his companions to tell everyone that he is Gunther's vassal, and he behaves as if that were his true station.

Seventh Adventure. Brunhild sees the ship arriving and believes Siegfried, who had come to her realm once before, has come to woo her. When she realizes that it is Gunther who wishes to win her, she warns him that if he fails to hurl the spear and stone further than she, he and his men must die. When Gunther sees Brunhild's spear, which took 12 men to lift, he loses heart. Siegfried whispers in his ear not to fear but to go through the motions. Siegfried, concealed by his Tarnkappe, a cloak of invisibility, will accomplish the tasks. Siegfried does so, and Gunther wins Brunhild, though she is upset by the outcome.

Eighth Adventure. Brunhild summons to her castle a large number of warriors in the hope of not having to marry Gunther. Siegfried sails off to the land of the Nibelungs, forces them to recognize him as their lord, and brings 1,000 back with him to Isenland. When Brunhild sees his force she does not resist.

Ninth Adventure. The bride, escorted by all of the men, sails across the sea and up the Rhine. As they near Burgundy, Gunther decides to send word of their arrival. He persuades Siegfried to act as his messenger, assuring him that he will earn Kriemhild's gratitude.

Tenth Adventure. Siegfried marries Kriemhild, and the two couples sit side by side at an evening meal. When Gunther goes to their bedroom with Brunhild, she picks him up and hangs him on a peg and leaves him there all night, taking him down in the morning. The next day all notice that Siegfried is radiant but Gunther is not at all happy. Gunther then tells Siegfried what happened. Siegfried says he will help by putting on his magic cloak in the evening and teaching Brunhild how to treat her husband. That night Siegfried, unseen, follows Gunther and Brunhild into their room. When the lights are put out, he wrestles with Brunhild until she acknowledges herself beaten. She believes she is yielding to Gunther, but it is Siegfried who snatches her girdle and ring, before leaving Gunther alone with her. Once Brunhild has submitted to a man, she loses all of her miraculous power. Siegfried returns to Kriemhild and tells her all that happened and gives her the girdle and ring.

Eleventh Adventure. Siegfried returns to Xantan with Kriemhild, and his parents relinquish the throne to them. They have a son.

Twelfth Adventure. Ten years pass, and Brunhild asks Gunther why Siegfried and Kriemhild have not visited them. Gunther invites the couple to visit.

Thirteenth Adventure. Siegfried and Kriemhild arrive with Siegmund, Siegfried's father. A feast is held, at which Brunhild curtly informs Kriemhild that Siegfried can scarcely be as great as Kriemhild pretends, since he is one of Gunther's vassals.

Fourteenth Adventure. Kriemhild denies this. Brunhild insists and declares she will prove her point at church when the two attend mass. Both women, angry, arrive simultaneously at mass, escorted by imposing trains. Seeing Kriemhild make a motion to enter first, Brunhild bids her pause. The two get into a verbal duel. In the heat of the argument Kriemhild insinuates that Brunhild granted Siegfried sexual favors. She then shows her the girdle and ring. The men enter; Siegfried denies taking advantage of Brunhild. Brunhild refuses to listen, and Gunther refuses to avenge her. She finally persuades Hagen, her kinsman, to take up her quarrel. Believing Brunhild had been wronged by Siegfried, Hagen urges Gunther to kill Siegfried.

Fifteenth Adventure. Hagen devises a plan to kill Siegfried. He discovers that Siegfried is invulnerable, having bathed in the blood of a dragon, except for one spot between his shoulders, where a linden leaf, sticking fast, prevented the blood from touching. Hagen tells Kriemhild to embroider a cross on her husband's garment over the spot to protect Siegfried. They then go off hunting in the Odenwald.

Sixteenth Adventure. The three, Gunther, Hagen, and Siegfried, race to a neighboring spring to drink. When Siegfried stoops over the spring to drink, Hagen runs a spear through the mark of the cross. Mortally wounded, Siegfried turns, grasps his shield, and hurls it at Hagen with such force that he dashes it to pieces. As he dies, he asks Gunther to take care of Kriemhild.

Seventeenth Adventure. The funeral train arrives at Worms. Hagen tells the bearers to lay Siegfried's body at Kriemhild's door. Kriemhild comes out in the morning to attend mass and falls over the body. Realizing it is her husband, she faints. The Nibelung knights arrive to carry the body to the minster, where Kriemhild insists that all those who took part in the hunt shall file past the body. It was believed that a dead man's wounds would bleed whenever his murderer drew near. Siegfried's wounds drop blood at Hagen's touch. Kriemhild publicly denounces him as the murderer, but he says he did his duty.

Eighteenth Adventure. Siegmund, the father of Siegfried, asks that Kriemhild come home to Xantan with him. Throughout it all, Brunhild shows no pity.

Nineteenth Adventure. Three years pass before Hagen suggests to Gunther that Kriemhild send for the Nibelung hoard, which was given her in marriage. Kriemhild consents, and the treasure arrives. It is so large that Hagen fears it will cause Kriemhild to become too independent, so he has it buried and tells no one its location but his masters.

Twentieth Adventure. Kriemhild is wooed by Rudiger for Etzel, king of Hungary. She accepts when Rudiger tells her Etzel will aid her in avenging Siegfried's death. Then, escorted by her faithful Ekkewart and carrying off with her the small portion of the Nibelungen treasure that still remains to her, she starts off for Hungary.

Twenty-first Adventure. Kriemhild proceeds on her way and is met on all sides by ovations of her future subjects.

Twenty-second Adventure. Kriemhild meets Etzel and other heroes, such as Dietrich of Bern. Under his escort they proceed to Vienna for the marriage festivities, which last 17 days.

Twenty-third Adventure. Seven years pass. Kriemhild has a son by Etzel, but she still grieves for Siegfried. One day she suggests that King Etzel invite her kinsmen to Hungary. When he consents, she gives special instructions to make sure that Hagen accompanies her brothers.

Twenty-fourth Adventure. Hagen is invited and comes fully armed, with an escort of 1,000 men.

Twenty-fifth Adventure. The Burgundians leave Brunhild and her son in the care of a steward and set out. As they are now the possessors of the Nibelung hoard, the poem terms them Nibelungs in the remainder of the work. Under the guidance of Hagen, who alone knows the way, the party reaches the banks of the Danube. They find no vessels to ferry them across, so Hagen asks them to wait until he can provide means of transportation. Walking down to the river, he surprises three swan maidens bathing. He captures their garments and forces them to tell the future. Although one promises him sexual pleasures, her companions, having recovered their garments, warn Hagen that none of his party but a priest will return safely to Burgundy. They inform him that he can secure a boat by telling the ferryman on the opposite bank that his (Hagen's) name is Amalung. Hagen induces the ferryman to cross the river and springs into his boat before the man, discovering the trick, attacks him with his oar. Forced to defend himself, Hagen kills the man. He then proceeds to convey relays of the Burgundian army across the river. Casting off for the last crossing, Hagen notices the priest on board and, wishing to prove the swan maidens wrong, casts the cleric overboard. When the priest swims back to shore, Hagen realizes that none of the rest will return.

Twenty-sixth Adventure. The Burgundians continue their journey, and though warned by Ekkewart, they go on to visit Bishop Pilgrin and Rudiger.

Twenty-seventh Adventure. At Hagen's suggestion a marriage is arranged between Giseler, the youngest Burgundian prince and Rudiger's daughter. Rudiger then guides the Burgundians to Etzel's court, where Kriemhild rejoices.

Twenty-eighth Adventure. Kriemhild meets the guests and asks Hagen for her gold. He says it will stay at the bottom of the Rhine until the Last Judgment. Hagen's men spend the next three days armed, fearing what is to come.

Twenty-ninth Adventure. Kriemhild asks her men to kill Hagen. She points him out and accuses him, but they are fearful of him and flee. Hagen then joins Etzel, who is portrayed as an old, inoffensive man.

Thirtieth Adventure. A night attack is made on Hagen, but again he frightens the Hungarians by his menacing glance.

Thirty-first Adventure. A tournament is held, at which the Huns and Burgundians argue. To calm them, Etzel invites the Burgundians to a banquet. They arrive fully armed.

Thirty-second Adventure. While the banquet is on, the Huns attack the Burgundians, who are outside.

Thirty-third Adventure. Hagen, hearing what has happened outside the banquet hall, takes out his sword and cuts off the head of Etzel and Kriemhild's

child, which bounces into Kriemhild's lap. The king and queen are saved by Dietrich of Berne.

Thirty-fourth Adventure. The Burgundians pause after the slaughter but are again attacked by the Huns. Kriemhild cries that she will reward with gold anyone who will bring her Hagen's head.

Thirty-fifth Adventure. Attempts are made to kill Hagen, but all fail.

Thirty-sixth Adventure. Kriemhild orders the hall where the Burgundians are holding out to be set afire. It is built of stone and they quench the fire with the blood of the dead, and they even drink the blood.

Thirty-seventh Adventure. Rudiger, in obedience to Kriemhild, enters the hall. Gernot, one of Kriemhild's brothers, and Rudiger slay each other.

Thirty-eighth Adventure. More battle ensues, and of the Burgundians only Hagen and Gunther remain alive.

Thirty-ninth Adventure. Dietrich enters the hall and attacks Hagen. He captures him and brings him to Kriemhild.

While Dietrich is securing Gunther, Kriemhild, left alone with Hagen, again demands her treasures. Hagen answers that, having promised never to reveal its hiding place as long as his lords live, he cannot reveal the secret to her. Kriemhild, who now is insane, orders the death of her brother Gunther. She carries his head to Hagen as proof that there is no reason to keep the secret. Hagen still will not tell her, so she cuts off his head with Siegfried's sword. Neither Etzel nor the hero Hildebrand is quick enough to stop Kriemhild when her fierceness overpowers them. Hildebrand then kills Kriemhild.

This epic was very popular with German Romantic poets and dramatists. In 1810 Friedrich Heinrich Karl La Motte-Fouqué wrote a Nibelungen trilogy titled *The Hero of the North.* It consisted of *Sigurd the Dragon Slayer, Sigurd's Revenge,* and *Aslauga.* Ernst Raupach wrote a five-act drama with a prologue called *The Nibelungen Hoard,* and Emanuel Geibel's drama *Brunhild* dealt with the love of Brunhild and Siegfried. Christian Friedrich Hebbel's trilogy *The Nibelungen* was followed by *Sigfrid and Chriemhilde* by Wegener and later by *Sigfrid Sage,* the first part of Wilhelm Jordan's epic poem entitled *Die Nibelunge;* the second part, *Hildebrant's Homecoming,* appeared in 1874. Richard Wagner's great *Der Ring des Nibelungen,* although using many of the names from the *Nibelungenlied,* actually follows the plot of the *Volsunga Saga.*

2191

Nibelungs. In Norse mythology, the dwarfs or elves who possessed a hoard of gold. In the Norse *Volsunga Saga* Nibelung is the son of Hogni and grandson of

Giuki. In later Norse myth the name Nibelungs is used for the followers of Sigurd (Siegfried), since he possessed the gold ring crafted by the dwarfs. It is also used in the Germanic epic *Nibelungenlied* for the Burgundians under King Gunther. In *Der Ring des Nibelungen* Richard Wagner uses Nibelungs for the gnomes, dwarfs, or elves, such as Alberich and Mime. They are portrayed in Arthur Rackham's illustrations for Wagner's Ring Cycle.

St. Nicholas (Dürer)

2192

Nicholas, St. (victory people, prevailing among the people). Died 350 C.E. In Christian legend, bishop of Myra; as Santa Claus, patron saint of children, patron of bankers, captives, pawnbrokers, and sailors. Feast, 6 December.

According to legend, Nicholas was born of Christian parents in their old age. As soon as he was born he arose in his bath and joined his hands, praising God that he had been brought into the world. From that day on he would only nurse at his mother's breast on Wednesdays and Fridays. When he was still young, his parents died and left all of their wealth to Nicholas. The saint devised means to get rid of the money. *The Golden Legend*, a collection of saints' lives written in the 13th century by Jacobus de Voragine, tells how the saint gave gold to save three girls who would have to become whores if they did not have dowries.

After this episode, the see of the bishop of Myra was vacant and the Church assembled to choose a successor. One bishop had a dream that the first man who should come through the church doors should

be consecrated bishop. Nicholas walked through the doors and was therefore chosen.

St. Nicholas's role as patron of sailors is related to the legend that when a ship was about to be destroyed, the sailors called on St. Nicholas, who appeared to them and stilled the storm.

At the Reformation his feast day was abolished in many Protestant countries; but when the Dutch Protestants came to establish the colony of New Amsterdam they still celebrated the old "visit of St. Nicholas" the night before 6 December. When the English took over New Amsterdam and renamed it New York, the custom stayed, and the visitor was called Sinter Klaas. Since he appeared as a bishop and many English Protestants disliked the idea of a bishop, St. Nicholas was stripped of his ecclesiastical robes and turned into a figure that combined the old saint with that of the Germanic god Thor. The feast day was then moved to Christmas. The final development of the legend was the poem *A Visit from St. Nicholas* by Clement Clarke Moore, which became the standard version of the legend.

St. Nicholas was removed from the calendar of saints of the Roman Catholic church in 1969.

2193

Nicodemus (conqueror of the people). First century C.E. In the Bible, N.T., a Pharisee and member of the Sanhedrin, or Jewish governing body, who followed Jesus but in secret. Nicodemus assisted at the burial of Jesus and brought a mixture of myrrh and aloes to anoint Jesus' body (John 19:39). In paintings of the Eastern Church he is often shown in portrayals of the descent from the cross and the entombment of Christ. In some paintings he is shown bending down, extracting one or more nails from Jesus' feet and placing them in a basket, the so-called Basket of Nicodemus.

2194

Nidaba. In Near Eastern mythology (Sumerian), grain goddess who brought the arts of civilization to humankind.

2195

Nidhogg (hateful). In Norse mythology, the dragon in Nifelheim at the foot of the cosmic tree, Yggdrasill; he gnaws at its roots. The squirrel Ratatosk "runs up and down the ash," according to the *Prose Edda*, "and seeks to cause strife between the eagle and Nidhogg." In some accounts Nidhogg is described as a flying dragon that eats corpses.

Variant spellings: Nithogg, Niohoggr.

2196

Nidra (sleep). In Hindu mythology, a personification of sleep, sometimes said to be a female form of the god Brahma. Other accounts say Nidra was produced at the churning of the ocean, when the gods and demons sought the Amrita, or water of life.

Nifelheim (world of fog). In Norse mythology, the land of dark, cold, and mist; distinguished from Hel, the land of the dead. In the midst of Nifelheim was Hvergelmir (bubbling caldron), the fountain from which and to which all waters found their way. From Hvergelmir flowed the river Elivagar (rivers whipped by passing showers). Nifelheim was located at the foot of the world tree, Yggdrasill, and was the home of Nidhogg the dragon and of the Fenrir wolf. Nifelheim appears in the *Prose Edda*.

2197

Nightingale. A small migratory thrush noted for its song, which is a warning to all other male nightingales to stay out of the singer's territory, as well as being an invitation to the females to join the male. In Greek mythology Philomila was transformed into a nightingale. The nightingale is often associated with death as in Keats's *Ode to a Nightingale*. Hans Christian Andersen's tale *The Nightingale* has the bird bargain with death to save the Chinese Emperor's life. Stravinsky's opera *The Nightingale* is based on Andersen's tale.

2198

Nihongi (Chronicles of Japan). Japanese Shinto book completed in 720. It is longer than the earlier *Kojiki*, the original authoritative work on Japanese Shinto, but contains many of the same myths, often giving variant accounts. Many of the gods appear under different names or are rendered in Chinese characters. The *Nihongi* traces myth, legend, and history up to 697 C.E..

Variant spelling: Nihonshoki.

2199

Nijuhachi Bushu. General term in Japanese mythology for the 28 gods who symbolize the constellations. The group is generally made up of the following: Basosennin, Daibenzaiten, Naraen, Misshakukongo, Daibonten, Teishakuten, Makeshura, Tohoten, Konshiki-kujaku, Zochoten, Bishamon-ten, Mawaraten, Mansenshao, Shimmoten, Gobujo, Nadaryu-o, Karura- o, Kinnara-o, Magora-o, Ashira-o, Konda-o, Kendatsuba, Shakara-o, Kompira- o, Mansen-o, Sanshi-taisho, Hibakara-o.

2200

Nike (victory). In Greek mythology, winged goddess of victory called Victoria by the Romans. In Hesiod's *Theogony* (383) Nike is said to be the daughter of the Titan Pallas and Styx; and sister of Zelos (eager ri-

2201

valry), Kratos (strength) and Bia (force). There are numerous references to Nike in Greek literature because she was closely associated with Athena. Sometimes Athena was worshiped as Athena Nike. Whereas Athena was the goddess of wisdom, Nike was the embodiment of victory in athletic and musical contests, as well as in battle. In one ancient Greek work, the Bacchylides *Fragment XI*, her role is clearly stated: "Nike, dispenser of sweet gifts, standing beside Zeus on Olympus, bright with gold, allots to mortals and the immortals the prize of valor." The most famous statue of the goddess is the Nike of Samothrace, now in the Louvre. Roman art often portrayed the goddess as the symbol over death, and these statues may have influenced early Christian art.

Nikkal. In Near Eastern mythology (Canaanite), goddess of the fruits of the earth; daughter of Hiribi, god of summer; and wife of Yarikh, the moon god. Her marriage to Yarikh is celebrated in an ancient poem in which the Kathirat, wise goddesses, act to settle the marriage affair, and Hiribi acts as an intermediary for the bridal payment.

2202

Nine Worlds. In Norse mythology, the worlds that made up the cosmos, watched over by Odin. They are Asgard, the home of the Aesir gods; Vanaheim, the home of the Vanir gods; Midgard, the home of humankind; Alfheim, the home of the light dwarfs or elves; Jotunheim, the home of giants; Svartalfaheim, the home of the dark elves; Nifelheim, the land of dark, cold, and mist; the ninth is unknown, though some accounts say it is Nithavellir, the land of the dwarfs.

2203

Nine Worthies, The. In medieval European folk belief, a series of nine ideal types of people, taken from the Bible, the Greek and Roman world, and the Middle Ages. The nine worthies usually listed are Joshua, David, Judas Maccabaeus, all from the Bible; Hector, Alexander the Great, and Julius Caesar from the Greek and Roman world; and King Arthur, Charlemagne, and Godfrey of Bouillon from the Middle Ages. They are portrayed in tapestries in the Cloisters museum in New York City.

2204

Ninib. In Near Eastern mythology (Babylonian), god of the summer sun who opposes Marduk, the hero god and god of the spring sun and vegetation.

Variant spellings: Nerig, Nineb, Nin-ip, Nirig.

2205

2206

Ninurta. In Near Eastern mythology (Sumero-Akkadian), war god and patron of hunting, son of Enlil or Bel and Innini. He was called "The arrow, the mighty hero." Some scholars believe that Nimrod in the Old Testament (Gen. 10:9) is a variant for Ninurta. Ninurta's symbol was an eagle with outstretched wings.

Variant spelling: Ningirsu, Nimurta, Nimurash.

2207

Ni-o (kings of compassion). In Japanese Buddhist mythology, fierce warrior gods at the gates of temples, whose duty is to prevent evil spirits from entering. They stem from Hindu mythology, being representations of the gods Indra and Brahma.

2208

Niobe (snowy). In Greek mythology, daughter of Tantalus and Dione; wife of Amphion; mother of ten sons and ten daughters (some accounts say six or seven). Niobe taunted Leto, mother of Apollo and Artemis, for having only two children. As punishment all of Niobe's children except Chloris, wife of Neleus and mother of Nestor, were killed by Apollo and Artemis. The Olympians buried the children, and Niobe was transformed into stone, still dripping tears on Mount Sipylus in Lydia. Niobe's myth appears in Homer's *Iliad* (book 24), Hesiod's *Theogony*, and Ovid's *Metamorphoses* (book 6). In Dante's *Divine Comedy* (Purgatory, canto 12) Niobe figures among the examples of defeated Pride, one of the Seven Deadly Sins in Christianity. Shakespeare's *Hamlet* has the hero say of his mother, "Like Niobe, all tears," referring to Gertrude's tears over her dead husband. Byron's *Childe Harold's Pilgrimage* calls Rome "the Niobe of Nations." Ancient Greek and Roman statues often portray Niobe's vain attempt to save her children from the deities' wrath. David, the French classical artist, painted the death of the children.

2209

Nirvana (gone out [as a flame]; extinction [of passion]; cooled; rolled up or away; blowing away or extinguishing). In Buddhism, the state of enlightenment and liberation, often confused by some Western writers with a sort of Christianlike heaven. D. T. Suzuki writes in his study *Outlines of Mahayana Buddhism* that Nirvana "is the annihilation of the notion of ego-substance and of all desire that arises from this erroneous conception. But this represents the negative side of the doctrine, and its positive side consists in universal love or sympathy (*karuna*) for all beings. These two aspects of Nirvana (i.e., negatively, the destruction of evil passions, and positively, the practice of sympathy) are comple-

mentary to each other; and when we have one we have the other."

In Jain mythology Nirvana is the place of liberated souls at "the ceiling of the universe where they live in unconscious, eternal bliss." Nirvana is described negatively as the destruction of the passions and positively as the attainment of selfless bliss. Death after Nirvana is called pari-nirvana (final Nirvana) and is not followed by rebirth. In Pali it is called Nibbana.

2210

Nithavellir (the dark fields). In Norse mythology, the home of the dwarfs, according to some accounts. Some scholars believe the term should be Nitafjoll (the dark crags).

2211

Nitten. In Japanese Buddhist mythology, sun goddess, derived from the Hindu god Surya. She is portrayed holding a lotus, on the calyx of which reposes a sphere, symbol of the sun. She is one of the Jiu No O, 12 Japanese Buddhist gods and goddesses adopted from Hindu mythology.

2212

Nivata-Kavachas. In Hindu mythology, sea giants "clothed in impenetrable armor" who lived in the depths of the sea. According to the epic poem *The Mahabharata*, there were some 30 million of them.

2213

Nixie. In Germanic folklore, a watery being who is often unfriendly to humans, causing them to drown. They are capable of assuming various forms, and they sometimes marry humans. In some parts of Germany it is considered bad luck to save a drowning person because the person has been fated as an offering to the nixies, who must have at least one human sacrifice per year.

2214

Njinyi (he who is everywhere). In African mythology (Bamum of Cameroon), creator god who allowed death to take human life. Njinyi created humans healthy and strong but discovered that in time they died. So he went to Death and asked him if he were responsible for killing people. Death said people really wanted to die, and he would prove it to Njinyi. They went to a roadside, and Njinyi hid behind a tree while Death sat underneath it. Soon an old slave passed by, mumbling to himself, "I wish I had never been born. It's better to be dead." No sooner had the words left his mouth than he fell down dead. Next came an old woman, complaining of her sad lot and wishing she were dead. As soon as she uttered the words, she fell down dead. "Look," said Death to Njinyi, "people want to die. They call me." So Njinyi left, sad that humankind choose death instead of life.

Njord (humid). In Norse mythology, one of the Vanir; god of winds, sea, fire, and wealth; husband of his sister Nerthus; father of Frey and Freyja. When Njord went to Asgard, he married Skadi, but she preferred living in her father's home Thrymheim, but Njord loved to reside at his home, Noatun (ships' heaven). According to the *Prose Edda*, "They at last agreed that they should pass together nine nights in Thrymheim, and then three in Noatun." The *Prose Edda* says that Njord "is so wealthy that he can give possessions and treasures to those who call on him for them." A sponge is called Njord's glove in Norse mythology.
Variant spellings: Niord; Njordhr.

No. Stylized Japanese drama, using masks, that had its beginnings in the 14th century.
Many No plays are Buddhist or Shinto texts, which contain numerous myths and legends, though some are based on secular works, such as the *Tales of the Heike Clan*. One of the most famous No plays is *Aoi-no-ue* by Zeami Motokiyo, written in the 14th century, about a "revengeful ghost." In it Lady Aoi is freed from a sinister incubus, while the ghost of Princess Rokujo, her dead rival in love for Prince Genji, is delivered from the evil spirit haunting her, and allowed to enter into the Buddhist paradise. Another play by Zeami Motokiyo, *Takasago*, tells of two pine trees inhabited by gods.
Sotoba Kimachi (Komachi and the Gravestone) by Kan'nami Kiyotsugo (1333–1384) tells of an old woman who sits on a *stupa*, a sacred shrine of Buddha. She is accused by a Buddhist priest of sacrilege but tells him all things are sacred—both she

Noah's Ark

and the old *stupa*. Suddenly she goes insane, seeing her old lover, but recovers in time to know she will die and enter the Buddhist paradise.
Variant spelling: Noh.

Noah (rest). In the Bible, O.T. (Gen. 6–9), the son of Lamech; a tenth- generation descendant of Adam, who saved himself and his family during the great Flood. God entrusted Noah with the construction of an ark or houseboat. Noah took his family and various animals aboard as God sent the floods to destroy all life. When the waters finally began to subside, the ark rested on Mount Ararat, and Noah sent a raven and a dove to determine the degree the waters had receded. The dove returned with a bit of an olive branch, which showed that the waters had abated. God directed Noah to disembark with everything in the ark. Noah erected an altar and made sacrifice, and God blessed him and his sons. Noah was also the first to make wine and is often portrayed as drunken. Various scenes from his life popular with artists are the building of the ark, the Flood, the sacrifice of Noah, and the drunkenness of Noah. Benjamin Britten's cantata *Noyes Fludde* is based on a medieval English play. In Islam Noah is called Nuh, and his story is told in the Koran (sura 2).

No-no-Kami. In Japanese mythology, god of the fields and plant life in general.

Norns

Norns (pronouncers). In Norse mythology, the fates, women who determine the fate of each person. Three—Urd (past), Verdandi (present), and Skuld (future)—live near a fountain under the massive ash, Yggdrasill, the world tree. "These maidens fix the lifetime of all men," according to the *Prose Edda*. "But there are, indeed, many other Norns, for, when a man is born, there is a Norn to determine his fate. Some are known to be of heavenly origin, but others belong to the races of elves and dwarfs." They appear in the *Poetic Edda*, the *Prose Edda*, and Richard Wagner's *Götterdämmerung*, the last music drama of

Der Ring des Nibelungen. They also appear in Thomas Gray's poem, *The Fatal Sisters: An Ode.* In Germanic folklore they appear as fairy godmothers or three spinners.

2220

Nott (night). In Norse mythology, a giantess whose first husband was Naglfar and her second husband, Annar, a dwarf. She became the mother of Jord (the earth) and Dagr (day) by her second husband. Nott's horse was Hrimfaxi (frost-maned).

2221

Nox (night). In Greek mythology, daughter of Chaos and Darkness; wife of her brother Erebus (the covered pot, often identified with Hades) whose children were the three Fates, Thanatos, Sleep, Dreams, Care, Momus, the Hesperides, Nemesis, Discord, Fraud, Eris, and others. Nox is mentioned in Vergil's *Aeneid* (book 6), which deals with Aeneas' visit to the underworld. Nox is also mentioned in Hesiod's *Theogony.*
Variant spelling: Nyx.

2222

Nudd. In Celtic mythology, a sea god and king of the Tuatha de Danann (people of the goddess Danu). Nudd lost one hand in battle, thus losing his throne because a maimed king could not rule. His hand was replaced by a silver artificial one, regaining his throne for him and earning him the title *Argetlam* (the silver handed). Some scholars believe that Ludd, the British sea god, is an equivalent of Nudd, who also lost one hand, had it replaced by a silver artificial one, and was called Llawereint (silver handed). Ludd's temple in London was located near St. Paul's Cathedral and Ludgate Hill is named after the god. Sometimes Ludd was known as Nudd in Britain.

2223

Nuga. In Melanesian mythology, the crocodile father of the Kiwaians. Nuga was originally carved from wood by a man named Ipila. While carving a wooden human figure, Ipila put some sago milk on its face, and the figure came to life. The first sound it made was that of a crocodile. Nuga asked Ipila to make three other men for him so that he would not be lonely. The men he made wanted more than sago for food, so they began killing animals. Soon they became half crocodile, and no one wanted anything to do with the crocodile men. They tried to reproduce, but only male children were born to them. From these beings descended those who claim the crocodile as ancestor. Ipila was displeased with his creations and forced Nuga to hold the earth on his shoulders forever.
Variant spellings: Nugu, Nugi.

2224

Nules-murt. In Finno-Ugric folklore, a forest spirit appearing in human form, with one eye. Nules-murt can lengthen and shorten his body at will, though he usually prefers to be as tall as a tree. He lives in the forest with his vast treasures of gold, silver, and cattle. Offerings are made to him by the people. Other spirits of the forest are Pales-murt (half man), who has half the body of a man; Yskal-pydo-murt (cow-footed man), an evil spirit; Surali, a hairy spirit; Cheremiss Kozla-ia, another forest spirit; and Ovda, an evil forest spirit who lives in the chasm in the rocks and ruins of old buildings.
Nules-murt is also called Unt-Tongk and Miskhun.

2225

Numbakulla. In Australian mythology, self-created sky gods who created humans from amorphous creatures.

2226

Nummo. In African mythology (Dogon of the Republic of Mali), twins, one male and one female, produced when Amma, or God, united with the Earth.

Amma, male, was lonely and came close to the female Earth for intercourse. The union was at first blocked by a red termite hill, which had to be removed. The resultant act was therefore imperfect, and a jackal was born instead of twins, which would have been the proper outcome. Amma and Earth united again. This time they produced twins, one male and one female, called Nummo; they were green, hairy, waterlike creatures. Their top halves were human and their bottom halves snakelike. They had forked tongues and red eyes. The Nummo went to Amma, their father, for instructions. He told them they were the essence of water. From heaven they saw that Earth was in need of help, so they came with heavenly plants, the fibers of which were used later by man to make clothing. Earth developed the basis of a language, but she was raped by her son, the jackal, who was jealous of his mother's possession of language. Amma then wanted to create things without the help of Earth, but the Nummo spirits drew a male and a female outline on the ground to be sure that twin births would continue. As a result, all human beings have two souls at birth and are bisexual. At circumcision the female spirit is removed from the male, and at excision the male spirit is removed from the female.

In heaven the Nummo spirits served as blacksmiths. Once an ancestor stole some of the sun from their smithy, and as he was escaping, the Nummo threw a thunderbolt at him. The ancestor slid down a rainbow to earth so fast that he broke both his arms and his legs. Since then men have joints at both elbows and knees. This first ancestor was a blacksmith, but with time others learned to develop other occupations.

Variant spelling: Nommo.

2227
Nunyunuwi (dressed in stone). In North American Indian mythology (Cherokee), cannibal monster whose body was covered with a skin of solid stone. Nunyunuwi loved to kill and eat hunters, but he could not bear the sight of menstruating women. In one myth, he came upon seven such women, and when he saw the last one, "blood poured from his mouth, and he fell down on the trail." The medicine men then drove seven sourwood stakes through his body and placed logs underneath him, which they ignited. As the fire burned, Nunyunuwi spoke and "told them the medicine for all kinds of sickness." When the fire had burned down, some red paint and a magic stone was left. The medicine man took the stone for himself, but the red paint he used to paint the faces and chests of the people. The red paint granted its wearer hunting success, skill, or a long life.

Nut

2228
Nure Onna (wet woman). In Japanese folklore, a female ghost having long hair and a flickering tongue to taste the wind. For many Japanese she is the personification of all evil.

2229
Nut (sky). In Egyptian mythology, goddess who personified the sky. Nut was the wife of Geb, the earth god. Nut was also Geb's twin sister and copulated with him against the wishes of Ra. In revenge Ra had the couple separated by Shu, who held up the sky, and said that Nut could not bear any children during any month of the year. Thoth, the god of wisdom as well as scribe of the gods, took pity on Nut and constructed five new days not part of the curse. On these days Nut gave birth to Osiris, Horus, Set, Isis, and Nephthys, according to some texts. The sycamore was sacred to Nut. Each morning the sun god Ra passed between the goddess's two turquoise-colored sycamores at Heliopolis when he began his journey across the sky.

In Egyptian art Nut was usually portrayed as a woman bearing a vase of water on her head. She sometimes wears a headdress of horns and the disk of the goddess Hathor and holds a papyrus scepter in one hand and the ankh, symbol of life, in the other.

2230
Nut. Fruit of numerous trees; in European mythologies and folklores, often a symbol of fertility because of its resemblance to testicles. At weddings in ancient Rome the bridegroom would scatter nuts as he led his bride to the temple. This signified that the husband was giving up his childhood habits and sports. Catullus' *Carmen Nuptialis* says: "Give nuts to the slaves, boy; / your time is past. / You have played with nuts long enough." The nut's connection with childhood is symbolized in Jewish custom in a game children traditionally play at Passover in which nuts are the stakes. In Russian folklore peasants would carry nuts in their purses as a charm to make money. In English folklore the discovery of a double nut indicated that good fortune was on the way. To make sure of the good luck the finder had to eat one nut and throw the other over his or her shoulder.

2231
Nyame (shining one). In African mythology (Ashanti of Ghana), creator god, often symbolized by the moon or as Nyankopon, the sun. Lightning, Nyame's thunderbolts, is called God's axes. Stone axes are placed in sacred forked posts standing by doorways, and pots with special offerings are also made for the god.

2232

Nymphs (young unmarried women). In Greek mythology, lesser female spirits of nature, often cited as daughters of Zeus. Among the various nymphs were the oreads (mountain nymphs), dryads and hamadryads (tree nymphs), naiads (spirits of fountains and rivers), oceanides (spirits of the great stream Oceanus), and Nereids (50 daughters of Nereus who watched the Mediterranean). Though nymphs lived long, they were not immortal and often would fall in love with mortals. Among some of the most important nymphs were Echo, Arethusa, Oenone, Dryope, Calypso, Thetis, Amphitrite, and Panope. Nymphs were cited in Spenser's *Epithalamion* (37–39), Pope's *Rape of the Lock* (2.19–20), T. S. Eliot's *Waste Land* (178–183), Milton's *Lycidas* (50–51, 98–102) and his masque *Comus* in which he invents a nymph he calls Sabrina.

2233

Nzambi. In African mythology (Bakongo of Angola), bisexual creator god, identified with the sky and Mother Earth. Nyambe, Njambi, and Nzame are names by which the deity is known among other African tribes.

O

Oak (Arthur Rackham)

Oak. A hardwood tree, sacred to the Greek sky god
Zeus and his Roman counterpart, Jupiter or Jove.
The oracle of Zeus at Dodona was located in an oak
grove, where the priestess pronounced oracles after
listening to the rustling of the oak leaves. In both
Greek and Roman mythology the first food of mankind was the acorn, seed of the oak. North American
Indians, who ate acorns, believed the oak was a gift
from Wy-ot, the firstborn of the sky and earth.

In Germany, when St. Boniface wanted to convert
the populace, one of his first acts was to destroy an
oak tree sacred to the Druids. The oak was thought
to be the home of demons, dragons, and dwarfs. In
some northern areas the punishment for injuring an
oak was to have one's navel cut out and nailed to the
wound in the tree, then to have one's intestines
wound around the tree.

In England Royal Oak Day, 29 May,
commemorates the restoration of King Charles II; it
is named for the oak that sheltered him in its thick
branches when he was fleeing Cromwell's troops.

Oakley, Annie. 1860–1926. In American history and
folklore, stage name of Phoebe Anna Oakley Mozee,
markswoman, a member of Buffalo Bill's Original
Wild West Show. She is reported to have shot the
ashes off a cigarette held in the lips of Germany's
Kaiser Wilhelm II. Irving Berlin's *Annie Get Your Gun*
starred Ethel Merman as Annie. The Hollywood film
Annie Oakley starred Barbara Stanwyck. Annie Oak-
leys are free passes to a theatrical performance, so-
called because they usually have holes punched into
them.

Obatala (king of the white cloth). In African mythology (Yoruba of southwestern Nigeria), second son
of Olorun, the sky god, who helped create land on
the water. He is said to have founded the first
Yoruba city, Ifé.

Oberon (elf king). In medieval European folklore,
king of the elves or dwarfs, believed by some schol-
ars to be derived from Alberich in Norse mythology.
Oberon appears in the medieval French romance
Huon of Bordeaux, in which he is said to be the son of
Julius Caesar and Morgan le Fay, the sister of King
Arthur. Shakespeare uses him in *Midsummer Night's
Dream*, and he is the subject of Karl Maria von We-
ber's opera *Oberon*.

Obumo. In African mythology (Ibibios of southern
Nigeria), the thunder god, usually regarded as the
principal deity and the creator of all things. His
home is in the sky. Being too far away to trouble
about the petty affairs of men, he leaves these in the
hands of lesser powers, reserving to himself the ordering of the great events of the years, such as the
succession of the seasons. At the beginning of the
rainy season Obumo descends in the form of a fish
hawk to woo his terrestrial wife, Eka Abassi.

2239

Oceanus (of the swift queen). In Greek mythology, an early sea god, eldest son of Uranus and Gaea; married to his Titan sister Tethys; father by Tethys of the 3,000 sea nymphs, Oceanides, and other sea gods. Among them are Doris, Eidyia, Electra, Callirrhoë, Perseis, Proteus, Pleione, Styx, Inachus, Melia, Meliboea, Arethusa, and Fortuna. Homer cites Oceanus as the river that encircles the entire earth. Oceanus appears in Aeschylus' *Prometheus Bound*, and his 3,000 sea-nymph daughters inspired Jean Sibelius' tone poem *Oceanides* (1914).

2240

Odhrerir (heart stirrer). In Norse mythology, a magic caldron containing a magic potion, the mead of poets. It was prepared by the dwarfs Fjalar and Galar from honey mingled with the blood of Kvasir, the wisest of men, who had been created from the spittle of the Aesir and Vanir gods. (The treaty of peace between the two groups had been sealed by each side spitting into a vessel.) The drink conferred wisdom and knowledge of runes and magic charms, as well as poetic facility. Odin, the chief Aesir god, was aware of its power, and transformed himself into a snake to capture the mead. It was under the control of the giant Suttung, whose daughter Gunlod guarded it. In his snake form Odin bored his way through a rock to where Gunlod sat on her golden stool. She let the snake drink as it lay in her arms for three days. Having drained the caldron dry, Odin flew away in the form of an eagle. When he arrived in Asgard, he spit the drink into a vessel. Odhrerir was also known as Eldhrimir.

Variant spellings: Odherir, Odhroerir, Odrorir.

Odin (W. G. Collingwood)

2241

Odin (wild, ecstasy, furious?). In Norse mythology, one-eyed chief of the Aesir gods; god of wisdom and war; son of Bor and the giantess Bestla; brother of Vili and Ve (or Hoenir and Lodur); married to Frigga; father of Thor (Tyr). Odin was called Voden, Woden, Wotan, Wuotan, or Votan in Germanic and Anglo-Saxon mythologies. The *Prose Edda* describes Odin as the god who "governs all things."

Odin was the wisest of the gods, and all the other deities came to him for advice. He drew his wisdom from the well of the giant Mimir. Odin gave up one of his eyes to Mimir as a pawn to gain wisdom and was sometimes portrayed as a one-eyed old man. Occasionally, however, he appears as a heroic man with a spear and shield. In Valhalla and Vingolf Odin gave elaborate banquets, but he only drank wine, which was all he needed to sustain himself. The meat served to the god was given to his wolves, Geri and Freki (the greedy one). Odin had two ravens called Hugin (thought) and Munin (memory) that perched on his shoulders. Every day they flew forth throughout the universe and brought news home to the god. Odin was often called God of Ravens. From his throne Lidskjalf in Valaskkalf, the god could see everything pass before him. His horse was Sleipnir, an eight-footed animal; his spear was called Gungnir and could hit anything aimed at; and on his arm he wore a precious ring, Draupner, from which dropped eight other rings every nine nights.

Part of Odin's worship consisted of human sacrifices. It was believed that the god once hung on a gallows, wounded with the thrust of a spear, and thus gained wisdom. Some of his worshipers were hung on gallows in the same manner. Odin was called God of Hanged Men or Lord of the Gallows because of this. He would tell one of his ravens to fly to the hanged man, or he would go himself to talk to the man. An 11th- century account by Adam of Bremen tells of a sacrificial grove near a temple at Uppsala where human bodies hung from the branches of the sacred trees.

Among the many epithets of the god are Ygg (the awful), Gagnrad (he who determines victories), Herjan (god of battles), Veratyr (lord of men), Har (the high one), Jafnhar (even as high), Thridi (third), Bileyg (one with evasive eyes), Baleyg (one with flaming eyes), Bolverk (the worker of misfortune, applied to Odin's role in granting or not granting victory to his followers), Sigfather (the father of battle or of victory), Gaut (the creator), and Tveggi (the twofold). Odin appears as Wotan in Wagner's *Der Ring des Nibelungen* and is portrayed in Arthur Rackham's illustrations for Richard Wagner's Ring Cycle.

Variant spelling: Othin.

2242

Odysseus (angry). In Greek mythology, a hero, king of Ithaca, son of Laertes or Sisyphus and Anticleia;

Odysseus offering the cyclops wine

married to Penelope; father of Telemachus. Noted for his cleverness and strength, he appears in Homer's *Iliad* and *Odyssey*. The Latin name form Ulysses (or Ulixes) was used by by the Romans. Odysseus began to demonstrate his heroic strength at an early age. Once when his grandparents came to visit him, Odysseus saved them from a wild boar attack. He killed the boar, but not before he had been wounded on the knee, which left a permanent scar. He received his mighty bow from Heracles' friend Iphitus, whose father, Eurytus, had given it to him. Only Odysseus with his massive strength could string the bow. When he reached manhood, his father, Laertes, gave up the throne, and Odysseus became king. He tried to win Helen's hand, failed, and later married Penelope, who bore him a son, Telemachus. While Telemachus was still a baby, the Trojan War broke out, and Odysseus, not wishing to honor his vow to fight, pretended to be insane. He yoked a horse and cow together and pretended to plow when the officials came to call him to the war. To test if he were really mad, the officials placed the infant Telemachus in the way of the plow, and Odysseus immediately stopped plowing, so he was judged sane and recruited. His mission was to convince Achilles to join the war. During the Trojan War Odysseus mediated the quarreling between Agamemnon and Achilles, rescued the body of Achilles and was awarded his armor. When the Trojan prophet Helenus was captured and asked what the Greeks must do to win the war, he named three things: enlist Neoptolemus, the son of Achilles, to fight; capture the bow and arrows of Heracles, and capture the Palladium, the sacred statue of Athena that protected Troy. Odysseus suc-

ceeded in all three tasks. Finally, prompted by Athena, he proposed the trick of the wooden horse, which destroyed Troy.

After Troy fell, the Greeks set out for home. Odysseus, who had offended the sea god Poseidon, was not allowed to return home for ten years. His adventures from that point form the basis of Homer's *Odyssey*. A later myth, not recorded in Homer, tells how Odysseus grew tired of simple home life and set out again, seeking adventure, and how he later died at sea. Dante's *Divine Comedy* (Inferno, canto 26), using the Latin name form, places Ulysses among the Fraudulent Counselors because of the wooden horse. Dante has Ulysses tell how he and a few companions set out beyond the Pillars of Heracles to gain experience of the world and see human goodness and evil, telling his men: "You were not made to live like beasts, but to follow virtue and knowledge." The crew reached the Mount of Purgatory, where a storm destroyed the ship and Ulysses died. In medieval literature Odysseus is generally seen as a dishonest rogue. He appears as such in the *Tale of Troy*, a medieval reworking of the Greek legends, and in Gower's *Confessio Amantis* he appears as a magician who was taught his skills by Calypso and Circe, two enchantresses. Tennyson's *Ulysses* is a poem treating the Dante myth. The major modern work dealing with the character is James Joyce's novel *Ulysses*, in which Leopold Bloom is a modern-day Ulysses. Nikos Kazantzakis' epic, *The Odyssey: A Modern Sequel*, takes up where Homer's *Odyssey* leaves off. Other works that treat Odysseus are Shakespeare's *Troilus and Cressida*, Monteverdi's opera *Il ritorno d'Ulisse in patria* (The Return of Ulysses to his country), Giraudoux's *Tiger at the Gates*, and Gide's *Philoctète*.

2243

Odyssey, The. Greek epic poem ascribed to Homer, telling of the homeward journey of Odysseus, believed to date from about 900 B.C.E.

The second epic ascribed to Homer deals with Odysseus (called Ulysses in Latin) and his homeward journey to his kingdom in Ithaca after the fall of Troy. The work is divided into 24 books, or chapters.

Book 1: After an invocation to the Muse, the poet begins his narrative. It is nearly ten years since the taking of Troy by the Greeks. The Olympian gods look down and see the sole survivor of his troops, Odysseus, stranded on an island with Calypso, an enchantress. Zeus orders that Odysseus return to his home in Ithaca. During Odysseus' absence various suitors have been besieging his wife, Penelope. Claiming that Odysseus is dead, the suitors are clamoring to marry Penelope. In obedience to Zeus's decree, Athena puts on golden sandals to enable her to fly over land and sea. She goes to Ithaca to see Telemachus, the son of Odysseus. She tells the youth to visit Nestor and Menelaus, the husband of Helen, to find out if Odysseus is alive or dead.

Book 2: Telemachus rises at dawn, goes to the marketplace, and complains in a public council about the suitors' waste of his father's estate. He tells them he is going in quest of his father. The suitors cry that Penelope has tricked them by saying she would make a decision when she had finished weaving a winding sheet for her father-in-law, Laertes. But, they contend, instead of completing her task as soon as possible, she unraveled at night the work she had completed during the day. They say that Telemachus should send Penelope back to her father, but the youth refuses. When the council closes, Telemachus prays for vengeance. Athena, in the guise of Telemachus' tutor, helps the youth arrange for his departure. Telemachus then returns to the palace, where the suitors are holding another feast. Refusing to join them, he finds his old nurse, Eurycleia, and tells her to provide for his journey. In the meantime Athena, in the form of Telemachus, searches the town and gathers a group of men to join him on his quest. Then, to make sure that Telemachus' departure is not known, the goddess sends the suitors into a deep sleep.

Book 3: Telemachus reaches Pylos, the home of Nestor, and is informed of what has happened to the various Greeks after the Trojan War. Agamemnon was murdered by his wife, Clytemnestra, and her lover, Aegisthus; Odysseus was lost. Telemachus spends the night at Nestor's palace and the next day leaves for Sparta to question Menelaus.

Book 4: After a time Menelaus and Helen recognize Telemachus as Odysseus's son, and Menelaus tells the youth that he knows his father was detained on the island controlled by Calypso. In the meantime the suitors discover that Telemachus has left; they decide to guard the port and kill him on his return. When Penelope discovers the plot to kill her son, she is distraught but is finally calmed by a vision that assures her that Telemachus will soon be restored to her.

Book 5: Zeus assembles the gods on Mount Olympus, and Athena pleads that Odysseus be allowed to return home. Hermes is sent to Calypso's island to tell the enchantress that she must let Odysseus go. A raft is built, and Odysseus, given provisions by Calypso, sets out on his homeward journey. When Poseidon sees that Odysseus is on his way home, he causes a storm because he hates Odysseus more than any other Greek. The craft is wrecked, but Odysseus is saved by the sea nymph Leucothea, who helps him to the shore. There he falls down exhausted.

Book 6: Odysseus sleeps while Athena, in a dream, inspires Nausicaa, daughter of Alcinous, king of Phaeacia, with a desire to wash her garments to be ready for her wedding. The young girl leaves the palace and departs with her slaves to the shore where the clothes are washed. Later the girls play ball, and the noise wakes Odysseus, who appears before them, covering his nakedness. Nausicaa believes the story he tells of being shipwrecked and tells him to follow her into the city.

Book 7: With Athena's aid, Odysseus is presented to the court of the king and queen, who promise to protect him.

Book 8: The next day festivities and games are held, at which Odysseus shows his immense power. Songs are sung about the Trojan War, and Odysseus begins to weep. He is asked if he had lost some relative in the war and eventually is questioned about himself.

Book 9: Odysseus narrates some of his adventures on his homeward journey. Driven by contrary winds to Ismarus, his crew sacks the town, only to be ambushed later by some of its inhabitants. With the remaining crew Odysseus then goes to the land of the Lotus-Eaters, a people who live on narcotic plants. He had to drag some of his men back to the ship after they had tasted the plants. Next they went to the land of the giant Cyclopes. Here the men are caught by Polyphemus, but Odysseus tricks the giant, boring out his one eye, thus saving those of his men who had not been eaten by the Cyclopes. Escaping from Polyphemus' cave, they head for their ship. Polyphemus hurls a large rock after them and promises that his father, Poseidon, will avenge his blindness.

Book 10: Odysseus next arrives at the cave of Aeolus, king of the winds, who gives the hero a bag containing all contrary winds so that his journey home will be safe. Odysseus' men, however, believe the bag contains jewels and open it. As a result the ship is tossed in the wrong direction, back to Aeolus, who now casts them out. They then arrive at the harbor of the Laestrygonians, cannibal giants, who eat many of the crew; and finally they land on Circe's island. Circe is an enchantress who drugs men and then turns them into animals. Some of Odysseus' men are turned into pigs. With the aid of Hermes, who provides a magic herb to annul the effect of Circe, Odysseus forces her to free his men. But they stay on the island for a year, and Odysseus becomes the lover of Circe. When the year is up, Circe helps Odysseus depart, but the hero must visit the underworld before he can return home.

Book 11: Odysseus describes his visit to the underworld, where he meets the ghosts of

Agamemnon, Achilles, and Ajax. Achilles says he would rather be a slave in the upper world than king of the dead, and Ajax refuses to speak to Odysseus because he had won the armor of Achilles. Odysseus also speaks with his mother, who describes the state of the soul at death, and he sees the judges of the dead.

Book 12: Once again aided by Circe, Odysseus departs. He is warned to beware of the Sirens, the threatening rocks, the monster Scylla and the whirlpool Charybdis on either side of the Messenian Strait, and the cattle of Trinacia. The hero successfully passes each test, but in the land of Trinacia his men steal the Cattle of the Sun and are punished for eating some of them. All of the men die in a storm, and only Odysseus is saved.

Book 13: Having ended his narrative, Odysseus sets out. He is reassured by Athena that Penelope has been faithful to him, though he in no way has been faithful to her.

Book 14: Transformed by Athena into a ragged beggar, Odysseus visits his swineherd, who puts him up for the night. Odysseus tells the man that his master will soon return.

Book 15: Athena tells Telemachus to leave Sparta, and she sets him on his way to the swineherd's hut.

Book 16: Telemachus arrives at the swineherd's house and meets Odysseus, who shortly is transformed into his strong, handsome, younger self. The two plot how to undo the suitors.

Book 17: At daybreak Telemachus hurries back to the palace; Odysseus is to arrive later. The suitors are having another feast when Odysseus arrives, and he is mistreated by Antinous, who flings a stool at him. Such a violation of the rights of hospitality causes some commotion in the palace. Penelope expresses her desire to speak to the beggar to see if he may perhaps know of her long-lost husband.

Book 18: In the meantime Athena restores youthful beauty to Penelope. She tells the suitors that she will soon choose and that they all should give her gifts so that she can choose which one will eventually be her husband. When she says she believes Odysseus is surely dead, the suitors are overjoyed.

Book 19: Odysseus and Telemachus remove all arms from the hall. Penelope then arrives and asks the beggar to relate when and how he met Odysseus. This time the stranger gives such an accurate description of Odysseus that Penelope summons the old nurse to bathe the man's feet. While Penelope dozes, the old nurse recognizes her master by the scar on his leg but is told by Odysseus not to reveal his identify.

Book 20: Again the suitors return and mistreat Odysseus as an old beggar and insult Telemachus, who pays them no heed.

Book 21: Meanwhile Athena prompts Penelope to propose to the suitors that they string Odysseus' bow and shoot an arrow through 12 rings. None of the suitors can, but Odysseus accomplishes the feat. Afterward he is aided by his faithful servants and Telemachus in securing the doors of the palace, ready for the fight.

Book 22: Casting aside his beggar garments, Odysseus now reveals himself to the suitors, who attempt to save themselves but are slain. The maids who had been faithless are forced to remove the corpses before they are hanged.

Book 23: In the meantime the old nurse tells the faithful staff and Penelope that Odysseus has returned and slain the suitors. Penelope is not convinced that the beggar is her long-lost husband. Only when he tells her who cut down the tree that formed one of the posts for her bed—known only to Penelope, the maker of the bed, and Odysseus—does she believe.

Book 24: Hermes, conductor of the souls of the dead, enters the palace and conveys the souls of the suitors to the underworld. Odysseus then meets his father, Laertes. Allies of the slain suitors wish to avenge their deaths, but Athena and Zeus make Odysseus and the attacking party conclude a peace treaty.

Among the most famous versions of *The Odyssey* in English are those of Chapman, Pope, William Cullen Bryant, William Morris, and Richmond Lattimore in verse; and those of Butcher and Lang, E. V. Rieu, T. E. Lawrence, and Walter Shewring in prose. James Joyce's novel *Ulysses* uses the plot structure of Homer, and Nikos Kazantzakis's *The Odyssey: A Modern Sequel* (1958) employs the theme. Monteverdi's opera *Il ritorno d'Ulisse in patria* (1641) also deals with the poem.

Oedipus and the Sphinx

Oedipus (swollen foot, child of swollen foot). In Greek mythology, son of Jocasta and King Laius of Thebes; he unknowingly killed his father and married his mother. An oracle had informed Laius and Jocasta that their son would bring about the death of Laius, his father. When Oedipus was born, Laius had the boy exposed to die on the slopes of Mount Cithaeron, his ankles pierced by a long pin. The baby was rescued by a shepherd, who took him to King Polybus of Corinth, who brought the boy up as his own son. Hearing rumors that Polybus was not his natural father, Oedipus went to Delphi to ask the oracle of Apollo his true parentage. The oracle informed him that he would cause the death of his father and marry his mother but did not reveal that Laius and Jocasta were his natural parents. Oedipus then left Corinth and became a wanderer. One day on a narrow road in the mountains, Oedipus met Laius, who was himself returning from the oracle at Delphi. Oedipus blocked the narrow road, not letting Laius or his servants pass. A confrontation ensued, and one of Laius' servants killed one of Oedipus' horses. In a rage the young man killed not only the servant but King Laius as well. Thus, the first part of the oracle was fulfilled, although Oedipus was completely unaware of the fact. He then arrived in Thebes where he discovered that the city was being ravaged by the Sphinx, a winged monster with the body of a lion and the head and breasts of a woman. The Sphinx would ask travelers a riddle, then cast them from a high rock when they did not answer correctly. The Sphinx asked Oedipus the riddle: "What animal in the morning goes on four feet, at noon on two, and in the evening on three?" Oedipus replied that it was man who went on all fours when a child, on two feet as a man, and on three (two feet plus a staff) as an old man. The Sphinx was so infuriated at being outwitted that she threw herself off the rock and was killed. The people of Thebes, unaware that Oedipus was the killer of Laius, offered him the throne and Jocasta, Laius' widow, as a reward for saving Thebes from the Sphinx. Oedipus and Jocasta had two daughters, Antigone and Ismene, and two sons, Eteocles and Polynices. When a famine struck the land, the blind prophet Tiresias was called to determine what must be done. Tiresias said that the murderer of Laius must be found and punished. Oedipus agreed, and in a short time it was discovered that it was he who was responsible for Laius' death and that Laius had been Oedipus' father. Jocasta was horrified at the discovery and committed suicide. In despair Oedipus blinded himself and was led into exile by Antigone, his daughter. He reached Colonus in Attica after years of wandering and was given the protection of Theseus of Athens. Oedipus' sons then fought to regain his throne in an expedition known as the Seven against Thebes. Both sons knew from an oracle that whoever had Oedipus' blessing would be victorious. His son Polynices went to Attica to ask Oedipus' blessing but was cursed instead. Eteocles sent Creon to bring Oedipus back for his side, but Theseus prevented his going, and Oedipus cursed Eteocles as well. The sons then killed each other. Oedipus died (or disappeared) in a grove sacred to the Eumenides at Colonus, not far from Athens. Oedipus' body was not allowed to be buried at Thebes and Colonus and finally found a resting place at Eteonos at a shrine named Oedipodion, sacred to Demeter.

Sophocles' *King Oedipus*, also known as *Oedipus Rex* or *Oedipus Tyrannus*, as well as his *Oedipus at Colonus*, deal with the major myth. The *King Oedipus* play served as the basis for Cocteau's Latin version, *Oedipus-Rex*, with music by Stravinsky. It was also the basis for Cocteau's play *The Infernal Machine*. The Sophocles' play was translated into English by W. B. Yeats. Other treatments are by Gide in his *Oedipe* and *Théséa* and by Pasolini in his film *Oedipus Rex*. Ingres painted *Oedipus and the Sphinx*. Homer's version in the *Odyssey* tells us that Oedipus, the son of Laius, accidentally killed his father and later married his mother. When the truth came out, Jocasta hanged herself, but Oedipus continued to reign. Homer's *Iliad* adds that Oedipus was buried with full honors after he was killed in battle. Statius' epic poem the *Thebais*, in 12 books, part of which was translated by Alexander Pope, tells the story of Oedipus' curse on his sons and the fight between Polynices and Eteocles. Freud coined the term Oedipus complex to refer to men with unresolved sexual conflicts concerning their relationship with their mothers.

Oenone warning Paris

2245

Oenone (queen of wine). In Greek mythology, a nymph of Phrygian Mount Ida, daughter of Cebren, a river god; mother of Corythus and Daphnis; a wife of Paris. Oenone knew Paris would leave her for Helen and bring destruction on Troy. When Paris was fatally wounded, Oenone, unable to forgive him, refused him help. One of Ovid's *Heroides* (5) tells her tale, as do Tennyson's *Oenone* and *The Death of Oenone* and William Morris's poetic tale in his collection, *The Earthly Paradise.*

2246

Ogier the Dane (wealth-spear). In the Charlemagne cycle of legends, one of the paladins who lives in Avalon.

Charlemagne made war against the king of Denmark and took his son Ogier as hostage. The young Danish prince was favored by the fairies from the time of his birth. Six of them appeared to him. Five promised him every earthly joy, and the sixth, Morgan le Fay, foretold that he would never die, but would dwell with her in Avalon, the land where King Arthur also lives forever. While in prison Ogier fell in love with and secretly married the governor's daughter, Bellissande. When Charlemagne was about to depart for war, he freed Ogier to aid him because Ogier was known for his heroic nature. Ogier returned to France after the war and learned that Bellissande had borne him a son and that his father had died. He was now the rightful king of Denmark.

Charlemagne gave him permission to return home, where he ruled for some years, and then he returned to France. His son, now grown up, had a dispute with Prince Charlot over a game of chess. The dispute became so bitter that the prince used the chessboard as a weapon and killed Ogier's son. Outraged at the murder of his son and unable to achieve any satisfaction from Charlemagne, Ogier insulted the emperor and fled to Didier (Desiderius), king of Lombardy, with whom Charlemagne was at war.

Charlemagne attacked Didier, but Ogier escaped from the besieged castle. Shortly after, however, when asleep near a fountain, Ogier was taken by Turpin, the archbishop and friend of Charlemagne. Ogier was led before the emperor and refused all offers of reconciliation. He insisted that Charlot be killed for the death of his son. Then an angel from heaven appeared, telling Ogier not to demand the death of Charlot. Ogier consented and was fully reinstated.

He attacked a Saracen giant, defeated him, and earned the hand of Clarice, princess of England. He was then made king of England but soon grew weary of ruling and journeyed to the East, where he besieged Acre, Babylon, and Jerusalem. On his way back to france, his ship was attracted by a magic lodestone, and all his companions perished. Ogier alone escaped to land. He then came to an adamantine castle, invisible by day but radiant at night, where he was welcomed by Papillon, a magic horse. The next day, while wandering across a flowery meadow, Ogier met Morgan le Fay, who gave him a magic ring. Although Ogier was now 100 years old, as soon as he put on the ring, he became a young man again. Then, putting on the crown of oblivion, he forgot his home and joined King Arthur, Oberon, Tristram, and Lancelot in Avalon, where he spent 200 years.

At the end of that time his crown accidentally dropped off, and Ogier remembered the past. He returned to France, riding Papillon. He reached the court during the reign of one of the Capetian kings. Ogier was amazed at the changes in court life. One day he had his magic ring playfully taken from his finger and placed on that of the countess of Senlis. When she realized that it made her young again, she wanted the ring for herself. She sent 30 knights to take it from Ogier, who defeated them all. The king having died, Ogier next married the widowed queen. But Morgan Le Fay, jealous of his love for the queen, spirited Ogier away in the midst of the marriage ceremony and bore him to the Isle of Avalon, from which, like King Arthur, he will return only when his country needs him. Longfellow, in one of his *Tales of a Wayside Inn*, tells the legend of Ogier and Didier (Desiderius).

2247

Ogma. In Celtic mythology, the Irish god of literature, eloquence, fertility, healing, poetry, prophecy, and war; son of Dagda; husband of Etain; father of Cairbe, MacCecht, MacCool, MacGreiné, and Tuirenn. Ancient Roman writers identified Ogma with both Hercules and Mercury. On the Continent he was worshiped under the name Ogmios.

Variant spelling: Ogham.

2248

Ogoun. In Haitian voodoo, god of war and fire, who is known as a healer and shows concern for the welfare of children. As a god of fire, red is Ogoun's sacred color, and rum is poured out as an offering to him, then set afire.

2249

Ogun Onire (Ogun, owner of the town of Ife). In African mythology (Yoruba of southwestern Nigeria), god of iron and war; married to Yemoja, the female spirit of the Ogun River; patron of blacksmiths and hunters.

Ogun Onire once descended to earth by a spider's web with his iron ax in hand. He wanted to go hunting. Olorun, the sky god, asked him if he could borrow his iron ax because Olorun had only a bronze one that would not cut down trees. Ogun Onire consented after he was offered the gift of a crown. At first he was pleased, but then decided he just wanted to go hunting and live away from the other gods. Because of his love of hunting the other gods avoided him. Human sacrifices were offered to Ogun Onire in past centuries, and blacksmiths in Yoruba sacrifice dogs to him every two weeks. Once a year the people hold a three-day feast in Ogun Onire's honor at which they dance and eat dogs.

O-Ikazuchi. In Japanese mythology, one of the Ikazuchi, the eight gods of thunder.

O Kiku. In Japanese legend, the spirit of a girl who was thrown into a well.

O Kiku was the maid of a great man, Aoyama. He was given ten precious plates, which he entrusted to O Kiku's keeping. He constantly told O Kiku that he loved her, but she refused all of his offers. In anger Aoyama hid one of the plates and then asked O Kiku to produce the whole set. A hundred times she counted the pieces, but each time only nine came up. Aoyama then suggested that if she became his mistress he would overlook the loss. O Kiku refused and was killed by Aoyama, who threw her body into an old well. Since then her ghost has visited the place of the murder, counting one, two, three . . . up to nine.

In a variant of the legend, O Kiku is said to have actually broken a plate. She was imprisoned by Aoyama but escaped, eventually drowning herself. O Kiku is portrayed in Hokusai's *Manga* (Ten Thousand Sketches).

Okonorote. In the mythology of the Warau Indians of the Guianas, a young hunter who discovered a hole in the sky and descended to the earth.

In the beginning the Warau had lived in the sky. One day Okonorote, a young hunter, shot an arrow and missed his target. Searching for the arrow, he found it had fallen through a hole in the sky. Okonorote looked down and saw the earth below, covered with forests and pampas. Using a cotton rope, he climbed down to look around. When he came back up, he told the Warau what he had seen and persuaded them to go down also. One fat woman could not get through the hole and was stuck, which prevented the Warau from returning to the sky after they had descended to earth.

Olaf, St. (forefather). c. 995–1030 C.E. In Christian legend, King Olaf II Haraldson of Norway. Feast, 29 July

As a young man Olaf fought in England for King Ethelred against the Danes. He became a Christian, tried forcibly to convert the Norwegians to the new faith, and was murdered. Soon after his death numerous miracles were reported.

Snorri Sturlason's *Heimsktringla* contains a long section on the life and death of St. Olaf. He writes that the king's body was found complete, with no decay. A bishop then trimmed the beard and hair of the dead king, saying the hair was sacred. This was doubted by some, so the bishop set the hair on fire but "it was not consumed." When a spring arose at the site of Olaf's murder, it became a cult site, "infirmities were cured by its waters."

Henry W. Longfellow, in his *Tales of a Wayside Inn* has The "Saga of King Olaf" which captures some of the vigor and style of the old Nordic poems. Tooley, a street in London, is believed to be a corruption of St. Olaf's name. Formerly it was a colony of Scandinavians in the Southwark district.

Old John. In American folklore, a tramp printer who could make type fall into place simultaneously with one sweep of his left hand. At death Old John was believed to have gone to a printer's shop in heaven where everything was clean.

Old Man and Death, The. Aesopic fable found in various collections throughout the world.

An old laborer, bent double with age and toil, was gathering sticks in a forest. At last he grew so tired and hopeless that he threw down the bundle of sticks. "I cannot bear this life any longer," he cried out. "Ah, I wish death would only come and take me!"

As he spoke, death, a grisly skeleton, appeared and said to him: "I heard you call me."

"Please, sir," replied the woodcutter, "would you kindly help me to lift this faggot of sticks onto my shoulder?"

Moral: We would often be sorry if our wishes were gratified.

This fable forms part of the collections of Lôqman, La Fontaine, and L'Estrange. There is a similar fable from India, called *The Messengers of Death*.

Olelbis. In North American Indian mythology (Wintun), creator god. Before Olelbis created humankind, he sent two buzzards, called Hus, to the earth to build a stone ladder from it to the sky. Half-way up the ladder they were to place a pool to drink from and a place to rest. At the top were to be two springs, one to drink from and the other for ritual bathing. "When a man or woman grows old," Olelbis said, "let him or her climb to Olelpanti (heaven), bathe and drink, and their youth will be restored." So the two buzzards left and began to build the ladder. Coyote, called Sedit in this myth, said to the two: "I am wise. Let us reason about this matter. Suppose an old woman and an old man go up, go alone, one after the other, and come back alone, young. They will be alone as before, and will grow old a second time, and go up again and come back young, but they will be alone, just the same as the first time. They will have nothing on earth to rejoice about. They will never have any friends, any children. They will never have any pleasure in the world. They will never have anything to do but to go up this road old and come back down young again. Joy at birth and grief for the dead is better, for these mean love." The two buzzards agreed, but one said to Coyote, "You too shall die and lie in the ground." Realizing what he had done to himself, Coyote tried to fly to heaven with wings made of sunflowers, but he fell back to earth and was dashed to pieces. "It is his own fault," Olelbis said. "He was killed by his own words. From now on all people will fall and die."

Olifat. In Micronesian mythology, trickster and culture hero, son of a mortal woman and the sky god Luk (Lukelong).

Olifat was born from his mother's head when she pulled a twist of coconut leaf rib that was tied around a lock of her hair. He was no sooner born than he began to run about. Luk told his wife that the boy was never to drink from a coconut with a hole bored at its top. But one day Olifat did just that. As he tipped back his head to get the last drop of juice, he saw his father in the sky. Immediately, he decided to visit his father's home. Riding on a column of smoke that rose from a fire of coconut shells, he arrived to see that workmen were building a Farmal, or house, for the spirits of the dead. Though his father recognized him, he did not let the workmen know who the boy was. The workmen decided to sacrifice Olifat to ensure the foundations of the house. They had planned to put him in a hole and then jam the house post on top of him. But Olifat knew their plans. While the hole was being dug, he made a hollow to one side of it at the bottom. When the men threw him in, he climbed into the side hole as the post was pushed down. With the help of some termites, Olifat made his way to the top of the pole and shouted, almost frightening the

men to death. After that he went on various adventures, many of which concerned seducing relatives' wives. Once he turned himself into a mosquito so that he could be swallowed by his brother's wife in her drinking water in order to father a son with her. In a more beneficent role Olifat sent a bird down to earth with fire in its beak. The fire was placed in different trees so that men might learn to obtain fire from rubbing sticks together.

Variant spelling: Olofat.

Oliver (olive tree). In the Charlemagne cycle of legends, one of Charlemagne's paladins and close friend of Roland (Orlando). He appears in the *Chanson de Roland*, which describes his death, as well as in Pulci's *Il Morgante Maggiore*, Boiardo's *Orlando Innamorato*, and Ariosto's *Orlando Furioso*.

Olokun (owner of the sea). In African mythology (Yoruba of southwestern Nigeria), sea goddess or god. Beliefs vary as to the sex of Olokun, indicating that perhaps at first Olokun was a bisexual deity.

In one myth Olokun is a male god in conflict with Olorun, the sky god. Once Olokun asked Olorun to appear dressed in his finest clothing. Olokun agreed to do the same so that the people would be able to decide which of the two gods was the greatest. But Olorun sent the chameleon, dressed in clothing exactly like Olokun's. Olokun then put on ever more splendid robes to outdo this display; but each time he changed his robes to surpass the raiment of the chameleon, the chameleon was able to match him. This frustrated Olokun, who came to accept the fact that Olorun's power was greater than his own if his messenger, the chameleon, could outdo him. From that day on Olokun has taken second place to Olorun. In African art Olokun is portrayed with a royal coral dress and mudfish legs. Both of his hands hold lizards.

Olorun (owner of the sky). In African mythology (Yoruba of southwestern Nigeria), sky god, who is not interested in man's affairs but lives in the heavens. He delegated his creative power to Obatala or Oshala, who fashioned human children in the mother's womb. Obatala is wedded to Odudua. Obatala and Odudua had Aganju, lord of the soil, and Yemaja, the goddess of water. The two in turn got married and had Orungan, the god of the upper air. But the lustful Orungan raped his mother, Yemaja, and from the incestuous union a whole brood of gods was born at a single birth, including Orun, the sun god; Oahu, the moon god; Shango, the storm god; Dada, god of vegetation; Orisha Oko, god of agriculture; Oshosi, god of hunting; Ogun, god of iron; and Shankpana, god of smallpox.

Olorun is also known as Oba-Orun (king of the sky), Ododumare (owner of endless space), Eleda (creator), Oluwa (lord), and Orisha-Oke (sky god).

2261

Olympian Gods. In Greek mythology, the 12 (sometimes 13) major gods (with Roman names in parentheses): Zeus (Jupiter), Hera (Juno), Poseidon (Neptune), Demeter (Ceres), Apollo (Apollo), Artemis (Diana), Hephaestus (Vulcan), Pallas Athena (Minerva), Ares (Mars), Aphrodite (Venus), Hermes (Mercury), Hestia (Vesta), and Pluto or Hades (Orcus or Dis). The Romans called the Olympian gods *dii majorum gentium*. They lived on Mount Olympus, the highest mountain, 2,980 meters, in Greece, on the borders of Macedonia in northern Greece.

Ceres (Demeter)

2262

Om. In Hinduism, a sacred sound used in prayer and meditation. It is a single syllable formed by the combination of all other syllables. It signifies creation–maintenance–destruction of a cosmic cycle. One Hindu text, *The Mandukya Upanishad*, says: "Om. This syllable is all. Its interpretation is that which has been, that which is, and that which is to be. All is Om, and only Om, and whatever is beyond trinal time is Om, and only Om." According to one myth, only Agni, the fire god, possessed immortality; the other gods did not. Fearing that death would destroy them all, the gods took refuge in the sound of Om, which was given the epithet "slayer of death."

2263

Omacatl (two reeds). In Aztec mythology, god of joy, festivity, and happiness; worshiped by the rich, who held banquets in his honor. According to Fray Bernardino de Sahagún in *Historia general de las cosas de Nueva España* (1570–1582), the god would sometimes appear at festivals for him. If for any reason he was not satisfied, he would say: "Wicked men, for what reason has thou omitted to honor me with respect? I will henceforth abandon thee, and thou wilt pay dearly for the injury thou has put upon me." Then many of the guests would become ill, suffering dizziness and headache.

Omacatl is regarded in some texts as an aspect of Tezcatlipoca, the Aztec creator-trickster god.

2264

Ometecuhtli (the dual lord, lord of duality). In Aztec mythology, supreme being, who was outside of space and time and was the source of all life. C. A. Burland in *The Gods of Mexico* (1967) writes that the Mexicans "were quite sure that in everything there was a unity of opposing factors, of male and female, of light and dark, of movement and stillness, of order and disorder. This opposition and duality was an essential of everything, and they felt that it was through this principle that life came into being. Hence, this god was a revelation of something very deep but so unknowable that he was the only god with no material temple."

Variant spelling: Ometecutli.

2265

Omphale (navel). In Greek mythology, a Lydian queen, daughter of Iardanus and married to Tinolus, who bought Heracles as a slave and kept him three years in her service. Omphale became his mistress and mother of several of his children, Agelaos, Alceus, and Lamus. During Heracles' stay he dressed as a woman. Saint-Saëns tone poem, *Omphale's Spinning Wheel* (1871) is, according to the composer, about "feminine seduction, the victorious struggle of weakness against strength."

2266

Oni. In Japanese folklore, word for ogres or devils. Usually an oni has claws, a square head with two horns, sharp teeth, and evil eyes surmounted by big eyebrows. Occasionally he wears trousers made of tiger's skin. Sometimes, however, he takes on another form, such as that of a begging monk or a woman. In some Japanese tales an oni is converted to Buddhism and becomes a monk, first having his horns sawed off. Often in Japanese art priests are shown sawing off the horns of oni, who then become temple guardians who beat gongs and perform other menial ceremonies. Oni occasionally march at night in groups of 100 in imitation of religious ceremonies. When they are thus aligned they are called Hiakku no Yako. At the beginning of the year, a ceremony called *oni-yarai* is held, during which beans are cast around a house to rid it of any oni that might be lingering in corners.

2267

Onion. A pungent edible bulb, related to the leek. Plutarch writes in *Isis and Osiris* that Egyptian priests "kept themselves clear of the onion, because it is the only plant that thrives in the waning of the moon. It is suitable neither for fasting nor festival, because in the one case it causes thirst, and in the other tears for those who partake of it."

In Poland a folk custom says that childbearing is eased if the expectant mother sits over a pail of boiling onions. On the other hand, a 12th-century Egyptian-Jewish physician, Ibn al-Jamil, recommended rubbing onion juice on the penis as a contraceptive.

2268

Onyankopon (the great one). In African mythology (Ashanti of Ghana), sky god who became disgusted with humankind and returned to his sky home.

When Onyankopon lived on the earth, there was a very old woman who pounded her yams so hard with her pestle that she knocked against Onyankopon. "Why do you always do that?" he asked the old woman. "If you continue, I will leave for my home in the sky." Taking no heed of Onyankopon, the old woman continued, and Onyankopon kept his word and left for his home in the sky. Then the old woman told her children to use mortars piled one on top of another to reach Onyankopon's home in the sky. They piled one on the other and almost reached the top, but they needed one more mortar. The old woman told them to remove the one from the bottom of the pile. When

they did, all of the mortars crashed to the ground, killing the children and many onlookers.

Onyankopon is also called Otumfoo (the powerful one), Ananse Kokroko (the great wise spider), and Otomankoma (the eternal one).

2269

Opochtli (the left-handed). In Aztec mythology, god of fishing and bird snaring, who invented the fishing rod and harpoon. Opochtli was portrayed as a naked man painted black, his head decked with plumes from wild birds and a coronet in the shape of a rose. He was portrayed surrounded by green paper and wore white sandals. In his left hand he held a red shield, and a white flower of four petals was placed crosswise on it. In his right hand he held a cup.

2270

Ops (abundance). In Roman mythology, goddess of fertility; wife of Saturn; she was either the same as Rhea-Cybele or a seperate deity. As goddess of plenty, human growth, and birth, Ops was invoked by touching the earth. Her major festivals were the *Opalia* (19 December), the *Opiconsivia* (25 August), and the *Volcanalia* (23 August).

Orange

2271

Orange. A citrus fruit, sometimes identified in European folklore as the fruit eaten by Adam and Eve; the exact fruit is not named in the Genesis text. It also was associated with the Virgin Mary as a symbol of purity, chastity, and generosity. Both Italian and English witches traditionally used the orange to represent the victim's heart. The name of the victim was written on a paper and pinned to the fruit, which was then placed in a chimney to rot until the victim died.

2272

Oranyan. In African mythology (Yoruba of southwestern Nigeria), hero king, son of Oduduwa.

Oduduwa, the father of Oranyan, was the brother of God and helped create the earth when God grew tired of his work. Because of this Oduduwa felt that he should become owner of the land. The Yoruba regard him as their founder and say that Oduduwa was their first king. Oranyan, his son, was a great hunter who, as he grew older, spent most of his time in a grove. He came out only to help his people when they were attacked by enemies. One day during a celebration a drunken man called out that the village was being attacked. The aging Oranyan came out on horseback and randomly began killing his own people. The people cried out to him to stop. Oranyan did, promising never to fight again, and he thrust his staff into the ground. Then, according to some accounts, both he and his wife were turned to stone. Pieces of his staff have been carefully placed together at the sacred city of Ifé, forming what is called the staff of Oranyan. The 20-foot staff has many nails driven into it, though its exact symbolism is not known.

2273

Orcus (boar). In Roman mythology, one of the names of the god of the underworld, identified by the Romans with the Greek god Hades, who had a temple in Rome. Orcus also was often used as a name for the underworld. In Vergil's *Aeneid* (book 6) the hero Aeneas passes through the Gate of Orcus, where Harpies, Gorgons, and other monsters dwell. Orcus was the god who brought death rather than a king of the dead. He had a store chamber in which he gathered his harvest, for Orcus was often pictured as a reaper cutting the ripened grain. In some accounts Orcus is believed to be a form of Dis Pater, a Roman god of the dead to whom sacrifices of black animals were made.

2274

Orehu. In mythology of the Arawak Indians of the Guianas, a water spirit, somewhat resembling a mermaid. One day an Arawak was walking beside the water when he saw an orehu arise from the stream, bearing a branch in her hand. She told him to plant the branch, which he did. Its fruit was the calabash, until then unknown among the Arawaks. The orehu appeared a second time with small white pebbles. She told the Indian to enclose them in the gourd so as to make a magic rattle, which was then used by the Semecihi, the medicine men of the Arawaks, to ward off the Yauhau, demon spirits.

2275

Orestes (mountaineer). In Greek mythology, son of Agamemnon and Clytemnestra, brother of Electra, Iphigenia, and Chrysosthemis. Orestes killed his mother and her lover, Aegisthus, in revenge for the

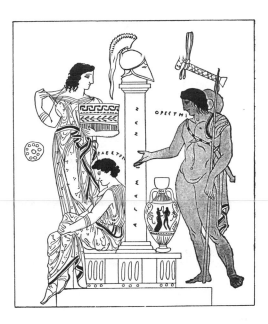

Orestes and Electra at the tomb of Agamemnon

murder of Agamemnon. When Agamemnon returned from the Trojan War, his wife and her lover, Aegisthus, killed him and seized his throne. Orestes, Agamemnon's son, was taken by his sister Electra to the court of Strophius, the king of Phocis, then Electra returned to her mother. After seven years the oracle of Apollo at Delphi ordered Orestes to avenge his father's murder. Orestes and his male lover, Pylades, son of King Strophius, went to Argos, where, with Electra, they planned the killing of Clytemnestra and Aegisthus. Orestes and Pylades went to the palace disguised as messengers, ostensibly to announce the death of Orestes. Eager to hear the news, Aegisthus was caught off guard and was the first killed. The two then turned to Clytemnestra, who protested that a son would not kill his mother. Orestes almost relented, until Pylades reminded him of the oracle, and they then killed Clytemnestra. Guilt for his deed followed Orestes in the form of the Erinyes (Furies). Eventually, Athena calmed the Erinyes, changing them into the Eumenides (kindly ones), and forgave Orestes. Aeschylus' trilogy, the *Oresteia*, made up of *Agamemnon*, *The Choephoroe*, and *The Eumenides*, deals with the myth. Sophocles' *Electra* and Euripides' *Andromache*, *Iphigenia in Tauris*, and *Orestes*, also deal with Orestes myth but make the Furies imagined fantasies of Orestes' guilt-ridden mind. Others who deal with or cite the myth are Homer, Herodotus, Ovid, Pausanias, and Vergil among the ancient authors and Alfieri, Goethe, Giraudoux, O'Neill, and Sartre in modern times. Strauss's *Electra*, with a libretto by Hofmannsthal, and Darius Milhaud's *Choephoroe* treat the subject musically.

2276

Orion (moon-man of the mountains). In Greek mythology, handsome hunter-hero, son of Poseidon, Zeus, or Hermes and Euryale; husband of Side (pomegranate), who was cast into the underworld for boasting she was more beautiful than the goddess Hera. Orion then fell in love with Merope, daughter of King Oenopion of the island of Chios. While wooing Merope, Orion cleared the island of wild beasts. King Oenopion, however, tried various schemes to prevent the marriage. One day Orion got drunk and raped Merope and was blinded by Oenopion as a punishment. Learning that he could regain his sight from the rays of the rising sun, Orion persuaded an attendant to the smith god Hephaestus to guide him to the island of Lemnos, where the sun restored his sight. In another myth he was a follower of Artemis and was accidentally slain by the goddess or was killed when he attempted to rape her. In another variant Orion was in the service of Artemis when he was seen by Eos, dawn goddess, who fell in love with him and carried him away. Artemis killed him out of jealousy according to some accounts, by having a scorpion bite him. Both the scorpion and Orion were then made into a heavenly constellation. Vergil's *Aeneid* (book 1) and Ovid's *Metamorphoses* (book 12) tell of Orion. Spenser's *The Faerie Queene* (1.3.31) tells the myth of his death; Milton's Latin poem *Ad Patream* deals with Orion; Keat's *Endymion* (2.198) has the line "blind Orion hungry for the dawn," and Longfellow's *Occultation of Orion* also uses the myth. Nicholas Poussin's painting *Blind Orion Seeking the Rising Sun* is one of his greatest works.

2277

Orisha. In African mythology (Yoruba of southwestern Nigeria), the name of a god, demigod, or deified ancestor.

2278

Oro. In Polynesian mythology, Tahitian war god, son of Hina-tu-a-uta (Hina of the land) and Ta'aroa, the creator god. Celebrations in Oro's honor, involving singing and dancing, were arranged by hereditary priests. Oro had three daughters; To'i-mata (ax with eyes), 'Ai-tupuai (eater of summit), and Mahu-fatu-rau (frog of many owners). Hoa-tapu (sworn friend) was his only son. Sometimes Oro was called Oro-i-tea-moe (Oro of the laid down spear), making him a god of peacetime.

2279

Orokeet. In Australian mythology, a name given to both a male and a female evil spirit.

2280

Orpheus (of the river bank?). In Greek mythology, poet and musician, son of Apollo and Calliope (or Oeagrus and Cleio); who could enchant gods, people, animals, trees, and rocks with the sound of his magic lyre, given him by Apollo; married to the Dryad (or nymph) Eurydice. Orpheus sailed with the crew of the Argonauts in their quest for the Golden Fleece. He helped them through the magic of his music when he played his lyre as they passed through the Clashing Rocks and the region of the Sirens. On his return from the adventure he married Eurydice, but according to Vergil's account in *Georgics* (4), she died when the beekeeper Aristaeus tried to rape her. As Eurydice ran from her attacker, she stepped on a poisonous snake, which bit and killed her. Distraught by his wife's death, Orpheus went to the underworld to bring her back. Orpheus' music so charmed Pluto and Persephone, king and queen of the dead, that either one or both agreed that he could take Eurydice back to the upper world. Orpheus was told, however, that he must not look at Eurydice until they reached the upper world. Orpheus could not resist the temptation to look at Eurydice and lost her. This version of the myth is told by Vergil, Ovid, and Seneca, but in a variant Orpheus was told he could have Eurydice for only one day; then Hermes, as guide for the dead, would come to bring her back to the underworld. After losing Eurydice, Orpheus wandered about Thrace. He died on Mount Rhodope, either killed by the Maenads, followers of Dionysus, because he failed to honor their god or torn to pieces by women jealous of his love for Eurydice. The pieces of his torn body were gathered up by the Muses. His head, still singing, and his lyre floated on the river Hebrus to the island of Lesbos, where they were dedicated to Apollo. Orphism, discussed by Plato and Vergil, is a mystical religion that taught death and resurrection and that one could become purified only when the soul was separated from the body.

Ovid's *Metamorphoses* (book 10) formed the basis for Politian's *Orfeo*, the first Italian drama on a classical subject; Monteverdi's opera *Orfeo*; Gluck's *Orfeo ed Euridice*, in which Eurydice is restored to Orpheus; Stravinsky's ballet *Orpheus*; Jean Anouilh's play *Eurydice*; Marcel Camus' film *Black Orpheus*; two plays by Cocteau plus some art work; and Rilke's *Sonnets to Orpheus*. Orpheus is cited in numerous English poems and plays, among them Spenser's *Amoretti* (44); Shakespeare's *The Merchant of Venice* (5.1.79–82) and *Henry VIII* (3.1.3–8); Milton's *Il Peneroso* (107–8), *L'Allegro* (149–50), *Lycides* (58–63) and *Paradise Lost* (book 7.26–27, 32–39); William Morris's *Life and Death of Jason* and Browning's *Eurydice to*

Orpheus. Moreau, Redon, and Lord Leighton used Orpheus as a subject for paintings.

Orunmila (the sky knows who will prosper). In African mythology (Yoruba of southwestern Nigeria), god of divination; eldest son of Olorun, the sky god. As god of divination Orunmila is called Ifa, a word that means divining. As Ifa, the god came to improve the health of his people and assist in supernatural matters. Ifa visited many villages but finally made his home in the sacred city of Ilé-Ifé. Ifa could speak all of the languages known to humankind. Because of his gifts he is seen as an intermediary between his father, Olorun, and the people.

Osa. In African mythology (Edo of Benin), sky god, supreme being who lives in heaven. Osa created the world, while his evil counterpart, Osanoha (Osa of the bush), made a house in which diseases live. When men and women on their way from heaven to earth came near the house, rain fell and drove them to it for shelter; thus sickness came to the earth. And because the wicked Osanoha created animals, man became their enemy and hunted them. In a variant myth Osa and Osanoha agreed to reckon up and compare their riches. Osa had more children than Osanoha, and the two have been enemies ever since.

Osa's emblem is a long pole with a white cloth attached. In some villages Osa is represented by a pot; in others, by a tree with a white cloth tied to it.

Osawa. In African mythology (Ekoi of Nigeria), sky god who sent two messages to man, one of life and one of death. Osawa sent a frog with the message that death ends all things. Then he sent a duck with a message that said that the dead will come back to life. The frog arrived with his message, but the duck stopped on the way and never delivered his message.

Oshossi. In African mythology (Yoruba of southwestern Nigeria), god of the forest and hunt, whose worship is found today in Cuba and Brazil. His followers dance to him carrying a small bow, his symbol.

Oshun. In African mythology (Yoruba of southwestern Nigeria), goddess of the Oshun river and fresh water; wife of Shango, the thunder god. Her worshipers wear amber beads, and her cult is found in Africa, Cuba, and Trinidad.

Oshunmare. In African mythology (Yoruba of Nigeria), the rainbow serpent, whose worship is found in parts of Brazil.

Osiris

Osiris. In Egyptian mythology, Greek name form of the Egyptian Asar, Ausar, or Ser; god of death and resurrection; the brother-husband of Isis; father of Horus; brother of Set and Nephthys.

The main source for the connected narrative of the myth of Osiris is Plutarch's work *Isis and Osiris*, which deals with Egyptian beliefs. In some cases Plutarch was mistaken about Egyptian beliefs, though his narrative has left its mark on Greek and Roman sources.

When Osiris was born, a voice was heard to say that the lord of creation was born. In the course of time Osiris became the king of Egypt and devoted himself to civilizing his subjects and teaching them the craft of husbandry. He established a code of laws and taught people to worship the gods. Having made Egypt peaceful and flourishing, he set out to teach other nations of the world. During his absence his sister-wife, Isis, ruled the state. When Osiris returned, his evil brother Set (identified by Plutarch with Typhon) plotted with 72 others, including Aso, the queen of Ethiopia, to slay Osiris. The conspirators built a chest to the measurements of Osiris's body. The box was brought into Osiris's banqueting hall while he was eating, and by a ruse he was induced to lie down in the chest, whereupon Set and his cohort closed the box and took it immediately to the mouth of the Nile, where they set it afloat.

These events happened on the 17th day of the month of Hathor, when Osiris was in the 28th year of his reign. This day was subsequently marked on the calendar as triply unlucky because it was the day Isis and Nephthys began their great lamentation for Osiris.

When the report of the treachery reached Isis, she cut off a lock of her hair, a sign of mourning, and set out to find her husband's body. In the course of her wanderings she discovered that Osiris had slept with their sister Nephthys and that the offspring of the union was the jackal- headed god Anubis, whom Isis found and brought up to guard her. Actually, Osiris had not lusted after Nephthys, who was in love with him, but had been unwittingly tricked by his sister into sleeping with her.

Isis learned that the chest had been carried by the waves to the coast of Byblos and there lodged in the branches of a bush, which quickly shot up into a large and beautiful tree, enclosing the chest on every side so that it could not be seen. The king of Byblos was attracted by the tree's unusual size and had it cut down to make a pillar for one of the rooms of his palace. Isis learned of this and went to Byblos, where she was taken to the palace to become nurse to one of the queen's sons. The goddess would transform herself into a swallow at every opportunity and hover around the pillar, bemoaning her sad fate. Each night she placed the queen's son in a special fire to consume his mortal parts, until the queen finally discovered her son in the flames and cried out. Isis revealed her story and begged for the pillar that supported the room. The queen took pity and ordered that the pillar be cut open and the chest containing Osiris's body be removed. When Isis saw the body of her dead husband, she cried out with such a fierceness that one of the queen's children died of fright.

Isis set sail for Egypt, where she again embraced the corpse and wept bitterly. She hid Osiris's body in a secluded spot. The evil Set stumbled on the chest when he was out hunting one night, realized what it contained and proceeded to cut Osiris's body into 14 pieces, which he dispersed all over Egypt.

When Isis heard of this, she took a boat made of papyrus, a plant abhorred by the crocodile, and sailed about collecting the fragments of Osiris's body. Wherever she found a part of her husband, she built a tomb. It is said that that is why there are so many tombs of the god scattered throughout Egypt. Isis collected all of the pieces of her husband but one, the penis, which had been devoured by the lepidotus, the phagrus, and the oxyrhynchus, fish that the Egyptians thereafter especially avoided. Isis then constructed a phallus to take the place of her husband's penis, and a festival was held in its honor.

After some time Osiris's spirit returned from the dead and appeared to his son Horus, encouraging Horus to avenge his father's death. Horus and Set engaged in a great battle that lasted for three days. Horus was the victor, but Isis, taking pity on her brother, let him go free. Then Horus, enraged, cut off his mother's head, which the god Thoth replaced with a cow's head. (The goddess sometimes appears cow-headed.) Set appeared before the gods and accused Horus of being a bastard, but Thoth defended Horus. Thereupon two more battles ensued between the two combatant gods, and Horus again proved victorious.

This is the general outline of the Osirian myth as written by Plutarch . Osiris was the man-god (he was first human and later deified) who had conquered death, and so, the Egyptians believed, would his followers. In every funeral inscription from the Pyramid Texts to the Roman period, rituals performed for Osiris were also done for the deceased, the deceased being identified with Osiris.

Osiris absorbed the characteristics of so many gods that he became both the god of the dead and the god of the living. Originally, he was the personification of the flooding of the Nile. He also may have represented the sun after it had set, and as such symbolized the motionless dead. Some later texts identify him with the moon. The Egyptians said that Osiris was the father of the gods who had given birth to him, as he was the father of the past, the present and the future (immortality).

In Egyptian art Osiris is usually portrayed as a mummy with a beard, wearing the white crown of Lower Egypt on his head and the *menat*, an amulet, around his neck. Sometimes he appears as the Tet pillar, symbol of strength and stability in life and renewed power after death, and is called Osiris Tet. Other composite forms of Osiris frequently appear:

Osiris-Seker—the god as a hawk-headed mummy, sometimes standing upright sometimes sitting. When seated, he holds in his hands the whip, scepter, and crook. This composite god signifies that Osiris became overlord of Duat, the underworld, and absorbed the death god Seker into himself.

Osiris-Neper—combination in which Osiris was coupled with one of the oldest grain gods of Egypt, Nepra.

Osiris Aah (Osiris as the moon god)—He appears with a crescent moon and full moon on his head. In his hands he holds the signs of life, stability, serenity, power, and dominion.

Osiris-Sah or *Osiris-Orion*—as such his female counterpart was Isis-Sept, or Isis-Sothis.

Osiris-Horus—Osiris coupled with his son; together they become a form of the rising sun.

Osiris-Ra—composite god in which Osiris represented the day and night suns.

Osiris-Neb-Heu (Osiris, lord of eternity)—the god in the form of a mummy with the head of the benu, or phoenix.

Osiris-Seb—Osiris fused with the ancient creation god, who produced the world from the Cosmic Egg.

Asar-Hep or *Serapis*—Osiris coupled with the old bull god Apis.

Osiris is also called Unnefer (he who is continually happy), referring to his role in defeating death.

2288

Ossian (little dear). Third century C.E.? Legendary Celtic poet whose "works" were published by James Macpherson as *Fragments of Ancient Poetry Collected in the Highlands of Scotland, and Translated from the Gaelic or Erse Language*; *Fingal, an Ancient Epic Poem in Six Books*; and *Temora*. The books claimed to be translations of ancient poems, but Dr. Johnson remarked that he considered the poems "to be as gross an imposition as ever the world was troubled with." In fact, the poems were mainly the work of Macpherson's vivid imagination and not of the poet as claimed. Nevertheless, Europe was taken by storm with the poems. German Romantics placed Ossian on a level with Homer. In Goethe's novel *Werther* the hero and Charlotte weep over the poems. The French artist Ingres painted *Ossian's Dream*, and James Joyce cites the bard in his novel *Ulysses*.

Variant spelling: Oisin.

2289

Oswald, St. (god power) c. 605–642. In Christian legend, king of Northumbria. Feast, 5 August.

Oswald defeated the Welsh king Caedwalla near Hexham in 634 and was made king of Northumbria. He was baptized at Iona and with the aid of St. Aidan tried to convert his people to Christianity.

One medieval legend records his charity. At a dinner he was told that there were some beggars outside his door. He had before him a silver plate filled with meat. Oswald told his servant to give the food and the plate to the beggars. St. Aidan, who was present, held the king's right hand, saying, "May this hand never wither."

When Oswald was killed in battle at Masefield fighting against pagans and their Welsh Christian allies, his right hand, which had been amputated, remained whole and "free from decay." His head was taken to a church at Lindisfarne and buried between the arms of St. Cuthbert. His right hand was carried to Bamborough Castle.

"May God have mercy on their souls, as Oswald said when he fell," was a common proverb for many years in England.

2290

Otoroshi. In Japanese folklore, a fantastic animal that protects temples and shrines from impious people. If an impious person enters the grounds, the otoroshi will pounce on the person and tear him or her to shreds.

2291

Otshirvani. In Siberian mythology, a creator god who defeated the evil giant snakeLosy.

In a Mongolian myth Losy lived in the water and spent his time spitting out venom over the earth, trying to kill people and animals. God decided to have the monster killed and asked Otshirvani to battle him. Otshirvani took on the beast but was losing the battle until he fled to Sumer, the world mountain, where he was changed into the Garide bird. As this fantastic bird, he seized Losy by his head and dragged him three times around Mount Sumer, finally smashing the monster's head against a rock. Losy, however, was so large that his body wrapped around the mountain three times, and his tail was still in the ocean. Otshirvani appears in some Siberian myths with the creator god Chagan-Shukuty.

2292

Otter. An aquatic, fur-bearing mammal having webbed feet and a long, slightly flattened tail. In medieval Christian belief the otter symbolized Christ because it was believed that the otter killed the crocodile (the devil) by entering its mouth and devouring its bowels before reappearing. This was seen as symbolic of Christ's descent into hell (the devil's mouth) to free Adam and Eve and all of the Old Testament holy men and women. But in contrast the medieval symbolists also saw the animal as the devil because it insinuated itself into a person's heart in order to bring about its destruction. In the Norse *Volsunga Saga*, Otter, son of a human father, is killed by the trickster god Loki, and to appease Otter's father the gods agree to pay him enough gold to cover Otter's body inside and out. Fafnir, a brother of Otter, kills his father to obtain the gold. Fafnir then turns himself into a dragon to guard the gold and is in the end killed by the hero Sigurd.

2293

Oum'phor. In Haitian voodoo, temple resembling Moses's design for the ark of the covenant and the tabernacle (Exod. 25–27).

The Oum'phor consists of a large area, usually covered, with a center post called poteau-mitan, which recalls the staff of Moses in the Bible. All important voodoo rituals are conducted around the poteau-mitan, the top of which is believed to be the center of the sky, and the bottom the center of hell.

The poteau-mitan is usually square and set in a circular pedestal made of masonry. Around the pedestal are triangular niches. The pedestal itself is a form of altar on which are placed various ritualistic implements. These include the jars called pot-de-tête, containing spirits of the people who worship at the Oum'phor, and govis, jars that receive the voodoo loas (deified spirits of the dead) when they are called down by the houn'gan and mam'bo, the priest and priestess of the cult. The large area is the Oum'phor proper, a square house resembling the Holy of Holies of the Bible.

According to voodoo legend, Moses was taught voodoo by Jethro, called Ra-Gu-El Pethro in voodoo belief. Zipporah, the daughter of Jethro, was Moses's wife and bore the prophet two mulatto sons, which so upset Aaron and Miriam, the brother and sister of Moses, that Moses eventually divorced Zipporah. The voodoo loas were so angry at this that they caused Miriam to turn white with leprosy. The voodoo version of the biblical account is of course at variance with the explanations offered in the Hebrew narrative (Num. 12:1-15).

Variant spellings: Hounfor, Hunfor.

Ouroboros

2294
Ouroboros. In world folk belief, a serpent or dragon devouring its own tail; often a symbol of eternity.

2295
Ovid. 43 B.C.–?18 C.E. Publius Ovidius Naso, Roman poet best known for his great poem *The Metamorphoses*, in 15 books that tell Greek, Roman and some near Eastern myths from the creation of the world to the deification of Julius Caesar. In 8 C.E. Ovid, who had held minor official posts, was exiled by the Emperor Augustus to Tomi (Costanza), a town on the Danube near the Black Sea. The exact cause of the exile is not known, though some scholars believe it is related to a scandal concerning Augustus' granddaughter Julia, who was also exiled. While in exile, Ovid continued to write his *Tristia* (Elegies) and *Epistulae ex Ponto* (Letters from Exile). Earlier he had written *Ars Amatoria* (The Art of Love), which Augustus did not like because of its frankness about sexual matters; *Remedius Amoris* (Remedy for Love), a series of short love poems; *Amores* (Loves); and the *Heroides*, verse letters from women of myth and history. Aside from these, he left the *Fasti*, a calendar of the Roman year; but it was incomplete, covering only the first six months of the calendar. Ovid's fame, however, rests on his masterpiece, *The Metamorphoses*, which inspired many poets and writers, among them, Dante, Chaucer, Gower, Wordsworth, Pope, Dryden, Goethe, Marlowe, Spenser, and Shakespeare. In *The Divine Comedy* Dante places Ovid with Homer as one of the greatest poets.

Owl

In art *The Metamorphoses* influenced most major European artists, especially Rubens, Poussin, and Picasso. Delacroix's *Ovid among the Scythians* portrays the poet in exile.

2296

Owl. A nocturnal bird of prey with large eyes and a broad head. The Egyptian hieroglyph for owl symbolized death, night, cold, and passivity and was also used to indicate the sun below the horizon when it crossed the sea of darkness in its daily journey. In Aztec mythology Techolotl, god of the underworld, was symbolized by a night owl. In North American Indian mythology (Pimas) the owl was a symbol of the souls of the dead. If an owl happened to be hooting at the time of death, it was certain that the owl was waiting for the soul of the dying person. Owl feathers were always given to a dying person to help him or her in the next world. If a family had no owl feathers, they would obtain them from a medicine man, who traditionally kept a stock of them. In Greek and Roman mythology the owl was sacred to the goddess of wisdom, Athena, and her Roman counterpart, Minerva. The city of Athens had so many owls that the proverb "taking owls to Athens" was an ancient equivalent of "coals to Newcastle." On the other hand, the Romans ritually purified Rome if an owl accidentally strayed into the capital city, considering it an ill omen. In medieval Christian folklore the owl was seen as a demonic bird.

One British folktale tells how Jesus changed a girl into an owl for being stingy. One day Jesus, in disguise, went into a baker's shop and begged for some bread. The mistress of the shop immediately put some dough in the oven. "That is too much," cried the woman's daughter. The girl went to the oven and reduced the amount to half. Not satisfied with that, she went back to the oven and reduced the dough again. But the dough began to rise and rise in the oven, pushing open the doors and falling across the floor. "Heugh, heugh, heugh," cried the girl, owl-like, and at that moment Jesus turned her into an owl. Shakespeare was familiar with the legend, since he has Ophelia say in *Hamlet* (4:5): "They say the owl was a baker's daughter."

To Shakespeare and many of his contemporaries the owl was a demonic bird. It was the "vile owl" in the poet's *Troilus and Cressida* (2.1) and the "obscure bird" in *Macbeth* (2.3). The poet inherited the medieval bias that identified the bird with Jews, who "lived in darkness." In Jewish folklore Lilith, the first wife of Adam before Eve, flew about as a night owl, making off with children. Although the Old Testament does not contain the Lilith myth, the prophet Isaiah (34:11–15) chooses the owl as one of the demonic birds that will haunt the land of Edom.

2297

Ozymandias. Greek name for the Egyptian Rameses; used by the Greek historian Diodorus Siculus when he translated an inscription at the foot of a gigantic statue of Rameses II. It ran: "My name is Ozymandias, king of kings: if any would know how great I am and where I lie, let him surpass me in any of my works." The English poet Shelley, who hated all despots, used the quotation with a twist in his poem *Ozymandias*. Shelley's poem concludes:

"My name is Ozymandias, King of Kings:
Look on my works, ye Mighty, and despair!"
Nothing beside remains. Round the decay
Of that colossal wreck, boundless and bare
The lone and level sands stretch far away.

P

Pabid. In the mythology of the Tupi Indians of Brazil, spirit of the dead.

When a person died, it was believed that the eyes left the body, which changed into a *pabid*; then the *pabid* would pass over two great crocodiles and two giant snakes into the land of the dead. Once there the *pabid* would be greeted by two fat worms, which would bore a hole in the belly, removing all of the intestines. When they had finished their meal, they would present the *pabid* to Patobkia, the head magician, who would sprinkle pepper juice into the eye sockets, restoring the lost sight.

In the land of the dead a male *pabid* had to have intercourse with Vaugh'en, the ancient giantess. Female spirits had to have intercourse with Mpokalero. After this one sexual experience, no further sexual acts took place—men had merely to place leaves on the backs of women, who then bore children. When *pabids* wished to sleep, they would lean against the poles in their huts, cover their eyes, and sleep standing up.

While the *pabid* lived in the land of the dead, the heart of the dead person would sprout after three days a *ki-agpga-pod*, a little man who grew bigger and bigger until it burst the heart. A magician then called up the spirit, which assumed a visible form and was sent up into the air.

Pachacamac (earthquaker, he who sustains or gives life to the universe). In the mythology of the ancient coastal people of Peru, supreme god, often identified with the god Virachocha, supreme god and creator of the Incas.

Pachacamac created man and woman but failed to provide them with food. When the first man died of starvation, the sun aided the woman by giving her a son. This child taught her how to live on wild fruits. His action angered Pachacamac, who killed the young man. From his buried body, however, maize and other cultivated plants arose. The sun then gave the woman another son, Wichama. Angered again, Pachacamac killed the woman. In revenge Wichama pursued Pachacamac, driving him into the sea. Wichama then burned up the lands and turned men into stone.

In another myth Pachacamac is the son of the moon and sun. In this version, Con, who may have been an earlier supreme god, filled the land with men and women he had created, giving them all of the necessities of life. When some of the people annoyed the god, he turned the fertile land into barren wastes. He left the people only the rivers so that they might support themselves by irrigation and hard work. Pachacamac came and drove out Con, changing his men into monkeys. He then created the men and women whose descendants exist today.

The chief center of the worship of Pachacamac was a temple built on a small hill in the fertile coastal valley of the same name south of present-day Lima, Peru. His cult included priests and sacrifices, and he was consulted as an oracle.

Pachamama (mother earth). In Inca mythology, earth goddess still worshiped in some parts of Bolivia, Ecuador, Peru, and northwestern Argentina. Her festivals take place at the beginning and end of the various agricultural cycles. Among Christian Indians her cult has been absorbed into that of the Virgin Mary.

Padmasambhava (lotus-born). Eighth century C.E. Indian Buddhist worshiped in Tibet as founder of Buddhism in that country. He is said to have been born from a lotus in the north Indian pilgrimage town of Ujjain (Tibetan: Odiyan), where the elbow of the dismembered goddess fell to earth. At the request of King Thi-Sron Detsan, Padmasambhava came to Tibet, remaining for 50 years and teaching the doctrine of Tantra-Yogacara. He destroyed all of the evil gods of the country and converted those remaining to Buddhism. After 50 years Padmasambhava miraculously disappeared. Legend says he entered the body of a demon king, Me-wal, where he reigned.

He is often called Guru Rinpoche (precious master) and is portrayed in art seated on a lotus with his legs locked, his right hand holding the *vajra*, the thunderbolt, and the left hand lying in his lap holding a bowl made from a human skull. A trident with three heads—peaceful, sorrowful, and a skull, symbolizing the Hinayana, Mahayana, and Vajrayana—is supported against his left side by his elbow. His garments are usually red. He has eight forms:

Guru Pädma Jungnä (born of a lotus), for the happiness of the three worlds, the central figure in the plate.

Guru Pädma-sambhava (savior by the religious doctrine).

Guru Pädma Gyélpo (the king of the three collections of scriptures).

Guru Dŏrje Dŏlö (the Dorje, or diamond comforter of all).

Guru Ñima Od-zer (the enlightening sun of darkness).

Guru S'akya Sen-ge (the second Sakya—the lion), who does the work of eight sages.

Guru Seng-ge da dok (the propagator of religion in the six worlds, with the roaring lion's voice).

Guru Lŏ-ten Ch'og-Se (the conveyer of knowledge to all worlds).

Pa-Hsien (eight immortals). In Chinese Taoist mythology, eight beings who as mortals followed the Tao (the way) and achieved the status of enlightened spirits. They are Chung-li Ch'üan, Chang Kuo-lao, Lu Tung-pin, Ts'ao Kuo-chu, Li T'ien-kuai, Han hsiang Tzu, Lan Ts'ai-ho, and Ho Hsien-ku.

Pahuanuiapitasitera'i (the great one that opens the sky). In Polynesian mythology, Tahitian sea spirit, feared by sailors along with other sea spirits, such as Arematapopoto (short wave), Aremataroroa (long wave) and Puatutahi (coral rock standing alone).

Pairikas. In Persian mythology, evil beings who act as enchantresses, aiding the evil spirit, Ahriman. One of the group, the demoness Pairika, symbolizes idolatry. She is put to flight by the proper prayers and rites.

Paiva and Kuu. In the Finnish epic poem *The Kalevala*, the sun and moon.

Both Paiva and Kuu attempted to woo the beautiful Kyllikki, the "flower of the islands," to become the wife of their respective sons. Kyllikki refused the offer of Paiva. She did not want to live at Paivala, the sun's abode, because it was too hot. She also refused Kuu's offer because she did not want to live in Kuutola, the moon's abode. Eventually, Kyllikki was abducted by the hero Lemminkainen, but he later left her for being unfaithful.

Sibelius composed *Terve Kuu,* for chorus, on rune 49 of *The Kalevala,* in which Vainamoinen calls on Kuu, the moon, in a mystic invocation.

The sun spirit is called Paivatar or Paivan Tytar (sun's daughter); Kuutar is the moon spirit or daughter in the poem.

Pajana. In Siberian mythology, a creator god of the Black Tartars.

Pajana formed creatures from the earth, but seeing that they lacked life, he went to the Kudai (seven spirits who watch over men's destinies) to obtain from them life-giving spirits to instill in his new creatures. Pajana left a naked dog to guard them while he was away. Erlik, the devil came and said he would cover the dog with golden hair if the dog would give him the soulless bodies. The dog agreed, and Erlik then spat on the bodies. When Pajana returned and saw what had happened, he turned the bodies inside out; that is why man's insides are filled with the devil's dirt.

Pajanvaki (smithy folk). In Finno-Ugric folklore, spirits who preside over metals.

Paladins, The Twelve (courtier). In the Charlemagne cycle of legends, 12 knights devoted to Charlemagne's service. The number 12 is derived from the 12 Apostles surrounding Jesus. The usual 12 are Roland (Orlando), nephew of Charlemagne; Rinaldo (Renault), of Montalban, Roland's cousin; Namo (Nami), duke of Favaria; Salomon (Solomon), king of Brittany; Astolpho of England; Archbishop Turpin; Florismart; Malagigi (Maugis), the magician; Ganelon (Gan), the traitor; Ogier the Dane; Fierambras (Ferumbras), the Saracen; and Oliver. Other names given in various legends are Ivon, Ivory, Otton, Berengier, Anseis, Gerin, Gerier, Engelier, Samson, and Gerard.

Palden Lhamo. In Tibetan Buddhism, a goddess, portrayed with eye teeth four inches long, with three eyes, sitting on a chestnut-colored mule. Her clothes consist of a girdle made of the skin of a recently flayed man. Her mule, with girth and cropper made of living snakes, tramples underfoot the mangled remains of a human body. The goddess drinks human blood out of a skull.

Pales. In Roman mythology, one of the Numina; a goddess of herds and shepherds, invoked for fertility, worshiped at Rome. Pales' festival, *Palilia,* was celebrated on 21 April, the date Romulus laid the foundations of the city of Rome. Vergil's *Georgics* (3) and Ovid's *Fasti* (book 4) mention the goddess.

2311

Palinurus. In Roman mythology, the helmsman of Aeneas who guided the ship through a storm past Scylla and Charybdis after the defeated Trojans left Carthage. Tempted by the god of sleep, Palinurus closed his eyes and fell overboard. He was found by local tribesmen, who killed him. In Vergil's *Aeneid* (book 6) Palinurus describes his fate when the Trojan hero Aeneas visits the underworld. Because his body had been left on the seashore without proper burial rites, Palinurus was unable to cross the Styx, the river of death. The Sibyl who accompanied Aeneas on his underworld journey then promised Palinurus that, even though denied burial, a shrine (Capo Palinuro in Lucania) would be erected in his honor.

2312

Palis (foot licker). In Persian-Islamic mythology, a demon who attacks those who fall asleep in the desert. Palis kills his victim by licking the soles of the feet until he has sucked out all of the blood. Once two camel drivers found a way to ward off attacks from Palis. They lay down foot-to-foot on the ground and covered themselves with their clothes. The demon arrived and began to go around the sleepers trying to find their feet but found nothing but their two heads. In despair the demon gave up, crying out: "I have traveled a thousand valleys and thirty-three but never met a man with two heads."

2313

Palladium (shield of Pallas). In Greek and Roman mythology, a fetish of Athena that was believed to protect the city of Troy. When it was stolen by the clever Odysseus and Diomedes, it signified that Troy would fall to the enemy. It was believed by the Trojans that the statue or image was sent down from heaven by Zeus to Dardanus, Troy's founder, to ensure Troy's protection. In a variant myth, the Trojan Aeneas rescued the Palladium from Troy and eventually brought the image to Rome. On several occasions it helped save the city. Homer's *Iliad* (book 10), Vergil's *Aeneid* (book 2), and Ovid's *Metamorphoses* (book 13) all tell of the sacred image. The *London Palladium* derives its name from the mistaken idea that the Palladium was a circus. In English usage the word is figuratively applied to anything on which the safety of a country or people is believed to depend.

2314

Pallas (maiden, shield, youth). In Greek and Roman mythology, epithet often given to Athena in post-classical times. Botticelli's *Pallas and the Centaur* and Edgar Allan Poe's poem *The Raven* both use the title for Athena. Some scholars believe the name Pallas derives from one of the Titans whom Athena flayed and whose skin she then used as a covering. Pallas is also a common name in Greek and Roman mythology. One of the best known is a son of Evander who fought with Aeneas in Italy, killing many of the Rutuli. That Pallas was killed by Turnus, king of the Rutulians, according to Vergil's *Aeneid* (books 8–10). Others include a giant son of Uranus and Gaea; a brother of Aegeus, king of Athens and uncle of Theseus, who tried to usurp his brother's kingdom; and a Titan who was the son of Crius and Eurybea, married to Styx and father of Nike, goddess of victory.

2315

Pallian. In Australian mythology, brother of Pundjel, a creator god.

2316

Pallor and Pavor (paleness and bright). In Roman mythology, companions of the war god Mars. On Roman coins Pallor is portrayed as a boy with dishevelled hair and Pavor as man with bristling hair and an expression of horror.

2317

Palm. A tropical evergreen tree; in Near Eastern mythology, associated with the Tree of Life. In the Old Testament the palm is sometimes a symbol of the ruler of Israel (Isa. 19:15 RSV). In the New Testament the blessed are clothed in white and have "palms in their hands" (Rev. 7:9) as tokens of their martyrdom. In the Christian rite of Ash Wednesday the ashes are made from the palms used the previous year on Palm Sunday. In Sicily the palms blessed on Palm Sunday are not only used to remember Christ's triumphant entry into Jerusalem but are hung in homes to induce rain and plentiful harvests.

Pan

Pan (pasture). In Greek mythology, an Arcadian god of flocks, fertility, shepherds, forests, and wild life; son of Hermes and Dryope or Penelope, or of Zeus and Hybris; called Faunus by the Romans. Pan was often portrayed with an erect phallus, though later Greek and Roman art portrayed him as a horned man with a beard and the lower part of a goat (which Christianity later identified with Satan). Pan invented the seven-reed flute, calling it Syrinx after the nymph Syrinx who, when he tried to rape her, was transformed into a reed, which Pan used for his first flute pipe. The English word *panic* derives from the fear inspired by Pan, though in some accounts, Panic is the son of Ares, the war god, and the brother of Eris (discord), Phobos (alarm), Metus (fear), Demios (dread), and Pallor (paleness). One of the Homeric Hymns (attributed to Homer but not by him) deals with Pan, as does the poet Pindar. Other literary works about Pan are Shelley's *Hymn to Pan* and E. M. Forster's *Story of Panic*. Elizabeth Browning's poem *The Dead Pan* (1844) deals with the myth that when Christ died on the Cross, the cry "Great Pan is dead" swept across the world, telling all that the pagan gods were no more. One of the most famous paintings of the god, Luca Signorelli's *The Realm of Pan*, was destroyed in World War II.

2318

Panacea (heal-all). In Roman mythology, goddess of health, daughter of Aesculapius and sister of Hygeia, Machaon, and Podalirius. The word *panacea* comes from the name of the goddess.

2319

Panathenea. In ancient Greek ritual, the summer festival in honor of Athena's birthday. As part of the rite the people presented a *peplus*, a woman's garment, large, broad, hanging in folds and richly embroided, to the goddess in a long procession along the Sacred Way to the Parthenon. This scene is depicted on one of the temple friezes of the Elgin Marbles.

2320

Panchajana. In Hindu mythology, a demon who lived in the sea in the form of a conch shell. Panchajana was killed by Krishna (an incarnation of the god Vishnu), who then used the conch shell for a horn. Later the conch shell became one of the symbols of Krishna and Vishnu.

2321

Panchatantra, The (five books). Hindu collection of fables and tales within a narrative framework; some

2322

were composed about 200 B.C.E., although the standard text dates from 1199 C.E.

There once lived a king called Immortal Power who had three sons, Rich Power, Fierce Power, and Endless Power. All three sons "were supreme blockheads," and the king therefore called his wise men to see what could be done to educate his sons and prepare them for their duties. He chose a wise Brahman (priest), Vishnusharman, who promised to render the king's sons wise and intelligent in six months, or else, he told the king, "His Majesty is at liberty to show me His Majestic bare bottom."

Vishnusharman took the three princes home and assigned them to learn "by heart five books" of fables that he had composed, as follows:

The Loss of Friends, telling of the broken friendship between a lion, Rusty, and a bull, Lively. There are more than 30 tales in this section, told by two jackals, Victor and Cheek;

The Winning of Friends, which has as its framing story the tale of the friendship of the crow, the mouse, the turtle, and the deer, who are called, respectively, Swift, Gold, Slow, and Spot.

Crows and Owls, telling of the war between the crows and owls.

Loss of Gains, containing some 12 tales, one of which is the well-known *The Ass in the Tiger Skin*, which is found in many Aesopic collections as *The Ass and the Lion*.

Ill-Considered Action, containing 11 tales relating to that subject.

In the various tales in *The Panchatantra* the actors are animals that conform to most folkloric beliefs: the lion is strong but dull-witted; the jackal, crafty; the heron, stupid; the cat, a hypocrite; and so on.

In his translation of *The Panchatantra* Arthur W. Ryder writes that it "contains the most widely known stories in the world. If it were further declared that the *Panchatantra* is the best collection of stories in the world, the assertion could hardly be disproved, and would probably command the assent of those possessing the knowledge for a judgment."

By the 17th century *The Panchatantra* had been translated into all major European languages. One of its most important influences was on various Aesopic collections of fables. One tale in the collection influenced Hans Christian Andersen, whose *The Princess and the Pea* was inspired by one of the Indian fables.

2323

Pancras, St. Fourth century? In Christian legend, martyr. Invoked against cramp, false witness, headache, and perjury. Feast, 12 May.

Pancras was martyred at 14 after he told Emperor Diocletian that if the ruler's servants behaved as the

Roman gods did he would "haste to put them to death." The emperor did not like the quick wit of the boy and had him beheaded. According to St. Gregory of Tours, whenever a "perjurer nears the tomb of St. Pancras, either he falls dead on the flagstones, or else, a demon seizes him and sets him writhing in a fit." Formerly, French kings confirmed treaties in the name of St. Pancras, feeling that either party swearing falsely would drop dead immediately. One legend recorded in *The Golden Legend*, written in the 13th century by Jacobus de Voragine, tells how two men were on trial and "the judge knew which of them was the culprit," but he let them swear their innocence before the altar of St. Peter. When they both remained unharmed he said, "Old Saint Peter is too merciful! Let us consult the young Saint Pancras." They did, and the liar "fell dead in a moment."

2324

Pandarus (he who flays all). In Greek and Roman mythology, the go-between of the lovers Troilus and Cressida. Pandarus was killed by Diomedes during the Trojan War. Pandarus appears in Homer's *Iliad* (book 2), Vergil's *Aeneid* (book 5), Boccaccio's *Filostrato*, Chaucer's *Troilus and Criseyde* and Shakespeare's *Troilus and Cressida*. The word *pander*, meaning procurer, comes from Pandarus.

2325

Pandora (all gifts). In Greek mythology, the first woman. After Prometheus had created man, Pandora was made of clay by Hephaestus at Zeus's command, in order to punish men. Pandora was given a jar (or box) that contained all of the evils of the world and was told not to open it. She did open it and let loose all evils. All that remained in the box was Elpis (Hope). The expression "Pandora's box" comes from the myth, which is cited by Apollodorus *Bibliotheca* (Library) and Hyginus' *Fables* It inspired Milton's lines in *Paradise Lost* (book 4.714) that described the fatal beauty of Eve. Pandora also is the subject of Spenser's *Sonnet XXIV*, Dante Gabriel Rossetti's poem *Pandora*, and Longfellow's *Masque of Pandora*.

2326

P'ang Chu, P'ang Ch'ê, and P'ang Chiao. In Chinese mythology, three goddesses of the corpse, portrayed as Buddhist nuns, one dressed in green, one in white, and one in red. The three live in the body. When they leave the body they tell the gods of the sins committed by the dead.

2327

Panis (misers). In Hindu mythology, a race of demons who stole cows and hid them in caverns. In the sacred collection of hymns, the *Rig-Veda*, they are called "the senseless, false, evil-speaking, unbelieving, unpraising, unworshiping Panis." Some scholars believe them to be the native inhabitants of India, who were enemies of the invading Aryans.

2328

P'an-ku. In Chinese mythology, primeval being, creator of mankind.

In some texts P'an-ku emerged from the cosmic hen's egg, which was all that existed before heaven and earth were created. The contents of the egg then divided, producing the Yin and Yang. The heavy elements descended, bringing forth the earth, while the lighter elements produced the sky. For 18,000 years P'an-ku grew at the rate of ten feet a day between heaven and earth, filling the space between the two. When he died, his body became the natural elements making up the earth. In a variant myth P'an-ku made the world, plants, and animals while he was alive. Realizing that there were no people, he made figures out of clay. When they were dry, they were to be impregnated with the vital forces of Yin and Yang. Before full life came to them, however, a storm arose and P'an-ku brought into his house all of the figurines that were out baking in the sun. Some of them were damaged, and that is why some people are born lame or sick.

In Chinese art P'an-ku, though a giant, is portrayed as a dwarf, dressed either in a bearskin or in leaves. Sometimes he holds the symbol for Yin and Yang.

Variant spelling: Phan-ku.

2329

Parameshthin (who stands in the highest place). In Hindu mythology, a title often applied to the gods or to distinguished mortals.

2330

Paran-ja. In Hindu mythology, the sword of the storm god, Indra.

2331

Pariacaca. In the mythology of the Huarochiri (Warachiri) Indians on the western side of the coastal Cordillera of Peru, a hero-god. The myth of Pariacaca is told by Francisco de Ávila, a Roman Catholic priest of San Damian, a parish in the district of the Huarochiri, in *A Narrative of the Errors, False Gods, and Other Superstitions and Diabolical Rites . . . [of] the Indians* (1608).

There was a great flood and five eggs were deposited on Mount Condorcoto. From the eggs were born five falcons who turned into men, Pariacaca and his brothers. They went about doing many marvelous things.

Pariacaca decided to try his strength against the rival god, Hulallallo Caruincho, and went in search of him. Pariacaca's strength lay in wind, rain, and flood, Caruincho's, in fire. Passing through a village called Huagaihusa in the guise of a poor man, he was not well received except by one young woman, who brought him chicha to drink. He destroyed the place by rain and flood, having first warned the woman and her family so that they could escape. He defeated Hulallallo Caruincho and caused him to flee toward the Amazonian forest.

But Caruincho only pretended to enter the forest. He turned himself into a bird and hid on a cliff on Mount Tacilluka. This time the five sons of Pariacaca swept the mountain with thunderbolts and a storm, and Caruincho had to flee again; but he left behind an enormous serpent with two heads that was changed to stone by Pariacaca. Closely pursued, Caruincho took refuge in the jungle. The sons of Pariacaca went to Mount Llamallaku, where they called together all of the peoples and established the cult of Pariacaca. Long afterward when the Inca came to power, they took over this cult.

Pariacaca is believed by some scholars to be a god of the waters or a deified mountain that gives both rain and irrigating streams.

Paris (wallet). In Greek mythology, abductor of Helen, second son of King Priam of Troy and Queen Hecuba; brother of Aesacus, Cassandra, Creusa, Deiphobus, Hector, Helenus, Polyxena, and Troilus; married to Oenone; father of Corythus and Daphnis. Before Paris was born, Hecuba dreamed she would deliver a firebrand that would destroy Troy. Priam, therefore, had Paris, also called Alexander (champion), exposed at birth on Mount Ida. But the child was suckled by a she-bear for five days and then raised by a shepherd, Agelaus, as his own son. While a youth, Paris married the nymph Oenone, whom he later deserted. To settle an argument among the goddesses about who would receive a golden apple and have the honor of being called the fairest, Zeus, who did not wish to make a choice, sent his messenger god Hermes to Paris to ask him to make the choice. The three goddesses, Aphrodite, Artemis, and Hera, appeared before the youth in what has come to be known as the Judgment of Paris. Hera, wife of Zeus, promised Paris royal power, Athena promised victory in war, and Aphrodite promised him the most beautiful woman in the world. Paris chose Aphrodite as the fairest and gave her the golden apple. Of course, he made enemies of the other goddesses by his decision. His prize, the most beautiful woman in

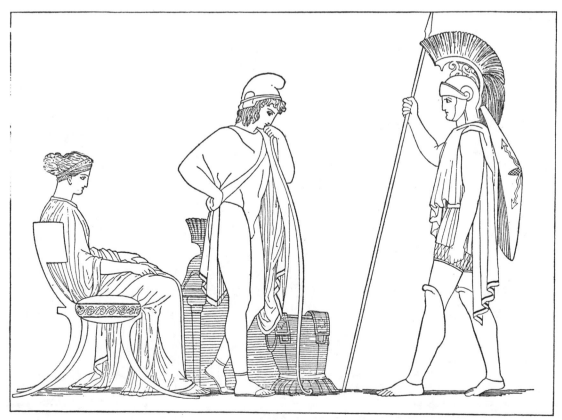

Hector chiding Paris (John Flaxman)

the world, was Helen, wife of King Menelaus of Sparta and mother of Hermione. Keeping her word, the goddess Aphrodite led Paris to Sparta, where he was entertained by Menelaus and Helen as a guest. While Menelaus was away, Aphrodite made Helen fall in love with Paris, and the two fled. Eventually this rash act led to the Trojan War when the Greek forces under Agamemnon sought to return Helen to Menelaus.

During the Trojan War, Paris' reputation was that of a coward because he was apt to run away from the fight and go home to have sexual intercourse with Helen. After ten years of war Paris and Menelaus met one to one on the battlefield. It was believed that the war would end when the duel was over. Paris threw his spear at Menelaus, but Menelaus turned the spear aside with his shield. Then Menelaus cast his spear, which only ripped Paris' tunic. The two men then drew their swords. Menelaus' sword broke during the first exchange, but he was so angry he grabbed Paris by his helmet and dragged him toward the Greek camp by his helmet's chin strap. Aphrodite, fearful that her favorite would die, cut the strap, covered Paris in a cloud, and took him to Helen's bedroom to make love. Homer's *Iliad* does not tell us of the end of Paris, but later Greek myth says he killed Achilles with a poisoned arrow in the

hero's vulnerable heel and was then killed by a poisoned arrow of Philoctetes. Paris asked his men to take him to Oenone, the nymph he had deserted. She refused to save his life, but when he died she killed herself. Paris appears in Homer's *Iliad*; Vergil's *Aeneid* (books 1, 7); Ovid's *Metamorphoses* (book 12) and *Heroides* (16, 17); William Morris's *Death of Paris* in *The Earthly Paradise*; W. S. Landor's *Death of Paris and Oenone*; Tennyson's *Dream of Fair Women, Oenone,* and *Death of Oenone*; and in David's painting *Paris and Helen.*

2333

Parnassus (scattered?). In Greek history and mythology, mountain of Phoas near Delphi, northwest of Athens, consecrated to Apollo, the Muses, and Dionysus. Its slopes contained the famous oracle of Apollo. The boat of Deucalion came to rest on the mountain's slopes after the flood. The theme of Apollo and the Muses was painted by Raphael, Mantegna, Poussin, and Domenichino, all using images from Ovid's *Metamorphoses*. The name of the culture center in Paris, Montparnasse, is derived from Parnassus. Between 1860 and 1876 a group of young artsts published a periodical *Le Parnasse contemporain* (The Modern Parnassus) in which they showed their love for Greek and Roman art and cultue.

The Judgment of Paris (John Flaxman)

2334

Parsley. An herb in ancient Greek and Roman ritual, associated with death and resurrection. The Greeks and Romans often decked their tombs with parsley wreaths. The ancient Greek expression "to be in need of parsley" was a way of saying someone was close to death. According to Greek mythology, the parsley herb sprang up from the blood of the hero Achemorus when he was slain by a great serpent. The Nemean Games were held in Achemorus' honor, with foot, horse, and chariot races, boxing, and wrestling. Wreaths of parsley crowned the winners. In Homer's *Odyssey* Calypso's magic island is covered with parsley, which connects the herb with sexual love. In English folklore it was believed that babies were found in parsley beds.

2335

Parthenope (maiden face). In Greek mythology, one of the Sirens, daughter of Achelous and Calliope; sister of Ligeia and Leucosia. She drowned herself after she failed to lure Odysseus to his death. Homer's *Odyssey* (book 12) tells of her fate.

2336

Parthenos (virgin). In Greek cult, title frequently applied to Athena as virgin goddess but also used for other female deities. The Parthenon, on the highest part of the Acropolis in Athens, was dedicated to Athena Parthenos. Begun in 447 B.C.E., the temple was dedicated in 438; it was designed by Callicrates and Ictinus and contained what are now called the Elgin Marbles as well as the statue of the goddess Athena by Phidias (c. 490–415 B.C.E.). The temple became a Christian church dedicated to the Virgin Mary; later it was converted into a mosque.

2337

Partridge. Fowl-like bird with a short beak, short legs, and a short tail. In Greek mythology the partridge, symbolic of fecundity and fertility, is sacred to both Aphrodite and Zeus. In ancient Hebrew folk belief the female partridge was believed to steal the eggs of other birds (Jer. 17:11). An early Christian work, *The Acts of John*, sees the bird as a symbol of the soul, but St. Ambrose, writing later, sees it as the devil. Ambrose's concept is reflected in a 12th-century Latin bestiary that cites the bird for its "evil sexual habits": a male partridge coupled with another male.

2338

Paruksti (the wonderful). In North American Indian mythology (Pawnee), storm and thunder personified as all of the life-giving and self-renewing powers of the earth.

2339

Pasiphaë (she who shines for all). In Greek mythology, daughter of the Titan sun god Helios and Perseis (Perse); sister of Aeetes, Circe, and Perses; married to King Minos of Crete; mother of Acacallis, Androgeus, Ariadne, Catreus, Deucalion, Euryale, Glaucus, Lycastus, Phaedra, and Xenodice. She was also mother of the Minotaur by the white bull. Minos had requested from the sea god Poseidon a magnificent bull for sacrifice. The god sent a white bull, but Minos substituted another. In revenge, Poseidon had Pasiphaë fall in love with the bull. Daedalus built a wooden cow for Pasiphaë to hide in while having sexual intercourse with the white bull. Their offspring was the Minotaur, half bull and half man. The monster, which fed on human flesh, was hidden in a labyrinth constructed by Daedalus. Pasiphaë bewitched Minos so that all of his mistresses died after having sexual intercourse with him. Pasiphaë appears in Boccaccio's *Genealogy of the Gods* in which she is a symbol of the soul, while her husband is human. She also appears in Henri de Montherlant's *Pasiphaé* with illustrations by Henri Matisse in 1944 and Jean Cocteau in 1948.

Passover

2340

Passover (Pesah). In Judaism, feast beginning on the 15th of Nisan (March–April) commemorating the Exodus of the Hebrews from bondage in Egypt; it is one of the three seasonal festivals, the others being Shavouth (Pentecost), also called the Feast of Weeks, and Sukkoth, or Feast of Booths. The narrative and ritual of the feast is told in the Book of Exodus (chaps. 12–15). Originally, according to some biblical scholars, at the first full moon in the first month of spring it was the custom for a lamb or goat to be slaughtered at twilight, then eaten at a common meal in the middle of the night along with unleavened bread and bitter herbs. This was to be done in haste.

Whatever portion remained uneaten was to be burned before daybreak. As soon as the slaughtering had been done, a bunch of hyssop was dipped into the lamb's or goat's blood and used to sprinkle a few drops on the lintels and doorposts of each house. This ritual was known as *pesah*. It was followed by a Feast of Unleavened Bread, during which no fermented food was allowed to be eaten. It is believed that the Exodus from Egypt coincided with the traditional *pesah* ceremony and was later incorporated into the Hebrew feast. It is now believed by most biblical scholars that not all of the tribes of Israel went down to Egypt nor came out of it at the Exodus.

The main ceremony of Passover is the *Seder* (order of service or formal procedure), in which various foods are eaten and the narrative, called *Haggadah* (recital) of the Exodus recalled. Some of the foods eaten are *matzah* (unleavened bread), bitter herbs (e.g., horseradish), and *haroseth* (a mixture of chopped apples, raisins, nuts, and cinnamon), recalling the mortar used to build the cities of Pithol and Rameses by the Hebrews for their Egyptian masters. Wine, at least four cups, is also drunk during the ceremony. At the conclusion of the meal an extra cup of wine is filled for Elijah the prophet, who will come, it is believed, on Passover night to herald the final redemption of Israel. The door of the house is flung open to allow the prophet to enter. Some biblical scholars believe that Jesus was celebrating the Passover at the Last Supper, though many others believe it was a simple Jewish meal. In the liturgy of the Holy Eucharist in *The Book of Common Prayer* (1929 American), the priest says "Christ, our Passover is sacrificed for us," and the people answer with "Therefore let us keep the feast." This is based on Paul's writing in 1 Corinthians (5:7–8).

2341
Patala. In Hindu mythology, collective name for the lowest region of the underworld, which consists of Atala, Sutala, Vitala, Tatala, Mahatala, Rastala, and Patala. In contrast to most underworlds Patala is a place filled with sensual gratification, not punishment.

2342
Patrick, St. (noble man). c. 385–461 C.E. In Christian legend, Apostle of Ireland. Feast, 17 March.

Part of the biography of St. Patrick is supplied by the saint himself in *The Confession of Saint Patrick*, which is considered authentic by most scholars. In the *Confession* Patrick tells us that his father's name was Calpurnius and that he collected taxes for the Romans. Patrick lived with his family on a farm that was raided by pirates when he was 16. He was captured and carried off to Ireland where he was sold as a slave. He eventually escaped and returned to his parents in Britain. Some time later he left to study for the priesthood in Gaul. He rose to the rank of bishop and was sent to convert the Irish.

The legends surrounding the saint's activities in Ireland are numerous. The most famous legend is that he drove all of the snakes out of Ireland. When St. Patrick ordered the snakes into the sea, one of the older reptiles refused to obey. St. Patrick made a box and invited the serpent to enter, pretending it was a place for the creature to rest. The serpent said the box was too small, but St. Patrick said it was large enough. The serpent kept insisting it was too small, while St. Patrick said it was just right. Eventually the serpent entered the box to prove his point and Patrick closed the lid and threw the box into the sea.

A tale recorded in *The Golden Legend*, written in the 13th century, tells how Patrick "traced a wide circle with his staff, and a very deep pit opened within it. And it was revealed to Patrick that the pit was the opening to a purgatory, and that those who chose to go down in it could expiate their sins, and would be spared their purgatory after death."

In actuality, St. Patrick's purgatory was a small cave on the island of Lough Derg, a lake near Pettigoe in Donegal. St. Patrick had the walls painted with various scenes of torment to instill fear in those who visited the cave. The cave became a place of pilgrimage for those who wanted to experience the pains of purgatory and hell in this life, to avoid them in the next. Pilgrims would spend nine days fasting as part of the ritual. Henry of Saltrey tells how Sir Owain visited it. The hero Fortunatus also was supposed to have been to the place. The cave was blocked on St. Patrick's day in 1497 by orders of the pope. Calderón's play, *El Purgatorio de San Patricio* deals with the legend.

2343
Patroclus (glory of the father). In Greek mythology, male lover of Achilles; son of Menoetius and Periopis or Sthenele. Patroclus was killed by the Trojan

St. Patrick

hero Hector, who in turn was killed by Achilles in revenge. Twelve Trojan nobles were sacrificed on Patroclus' funeral pyre. In later Greek mythology, it was said that his ashes were mixed with those of Achilles. Both were worshiped on the White Island as semideities. The funeral games of Patroclus form book 23 of Homer's *Iliad*. Patroclus also appears in Ovid's *Metamorpheses* (book 13) and and Shakespeare's *Triolus and Cressida*.

2344

Paul Bunyan. In American folklore, giant lumberjack of the Great Lakes and the Pacific Northwest.

Various places claim Paul Bunyan as their own: Maine, Michigan, Minnesota, and the Canadian woods. As a child Paul grew so fast that his father could not keep making cradles to fit him. At one month Paul was 20 feet tall and still growing. Tired his parents' arguing, he took his cradle and left home to begin a life of adventure. He invented a huge hotcake griddle that had to be greased by men skating on it with strips of bacon attached to their feet. Among Paul's companions are Babe the Blue Ox; Hot Biscuit Slim, a cook; Febold Febold, a Swede, who looked after Paul's tools; Little Merry, who got the food; Johnny Inslinger, who kept the books; Shanty Boy, who could sing any song; and Galloping Kid, who gave up being a cowboy to be with Paul.

Scholars question whether Paul Bunyan is true folklore or is an invention of W. B. Laughead, who wrote *Paul Bunyan and His Big Blue Ox*, a pamphlet for the Red River Lumber Company, originally located in Minnesota. Laughead wrote: "The student of folklore will easily distinguish the material derived from original sources from that written for the purpose of this book. It should be stated that the names of the supporting characters, including the animals, are inventions by the writer of this version. The oral chroniclers did not, in his hearing, which goes back to 1901, call any of the characters by name except Paul Bunyan himself." Both Douglas Malloch's narrative poem "The Round River Drive," which appeared in *The American Lumberman*, and Carl Sandburg's "Who Made Paul Bunyan?" in *The People, Yes* deal with Paul's legend, as did Virginia Tunvey, Father Shepard, James Stevens, Glen Rounds, Dell J. McCormick, and Louis Untermeyer. Robert Frost's poem "Paul's Wife" deals with the hero's wife.

2345

Paul, St. (small, little). First century C.E. In the Bible, N.T., Apostle to the Gentiles. Patron of tent-makers, weavers, saddlers, basket weavers, theologians, workmen's associations. Invoked in stormy weather on the ocean and as protection against snakebite. Patron of many countries and cities such as London,

Patroclus' funeral pyre

The conversion of St. Paul

Rome, Malta, Frankfurt, and Berlin. Feast, 29 June.

Nearly all of the original materials for the life of St. Paul are contained in the Acts of the Apostles and in his epistles or letters in the New Testament. Added to these biblical works is the apocryphal *Acts of St. Paul*, written in the latter half of the second century, which gives legends not contained in the biblical works (though it also covers those with a romantic interpretation) and *The Golden Legend*, written in the 13th century, which incorporates the earlier works.

Paul was born in Tarsus, a city in Cilicia, Asia Minor, about 1 B.C.E. His Jewish name was Saul, and his Latin name, to which as a Roman citizen he was entitled, was Paul. The latter was used exclusively after he became the Apostle to the Gentiles. Of his parents we know nothing, except that his father was of the tribe of Benjamin (Phil. 3:5), and a Pharisee (Acts 23:6). Paul dictated his letters in Greek. He was sent to Jerusalem for his education "at the feet of Gamaliel," one of the most eminent of all Doctors of the Law. As was the custom with rabbis, Paul also learned a trade, tent making. Saul was yet a "young man" (Acts 7:58) when St. Stephen was stoned to death. Among those who disputed with Stephen were some "of them of Cilicia." Paul held the cloaks of those who stoned Stephen while he was witnessing the act of murder. St. Augustine believed that when Paul saw St. Stephen pray for his enemies the seeds of his conversion to Christ were planted. At first, however, Paul wished to pursue this new group of Christians and punish them by reporting them to the Jewish high priest. On a mission to Damascus to arrest some Christians and bring them to Jerusalem for trial, the decisive event in his life occurred. His conversion is told three times in the Acts of the Apostles (9:1–10; 22:5–16; and 26:12–18). According to these accounts Paul saw a great light and heard the words, "Saul, Saul, why persecutest thou Me?" In reply to the question, "Who art thou, Lord?" Paul heard, "I am Jesus, Whom thou persecutest." Paul was then blinded for some time.

Soon afterward he received Baptism and the imposition of hands from Ananias (Acts 9:17) and then left for Arabia (Gal. 1:17). He then went on three important missionary journeys and returned to Jerusalem. He was met by a hostile mob, who accused him of transgression of the law of Moses. He was beaten by the mob and rescued by Roman soldiers, who put him in protective custody (Acts 21:27–36). After a time he was sent to Rome for trial (he was a Roman citizen). On the way he was shipwrecked on Malta, where he miraculously escaped being bitten by a poisonous snake. The Acts of the Apostles ends with the statement that St. Paul remained in captivity in Rome for two years. The rest of his life is not told us. Christian legend, however, has supplied the remainder.

According to *The Golden Legend*, "When Paul came to Rome, Nero's reign had not as yet been confirmed. When Nero heard that Paul and the Jews were quarreling about Jewish law and Christian faith, he paid so little attention to Paul that the saint was free and could go "wherever he wished and could preach without obstacles." Paul became well known as a preacher. One day "Nero's cup-bearer," and one of his favorites, named Patroclus, climbed up onto a window ledge so he could hear Paul preach. He fell asleep, fell out of the window, and was killed. Paul thought Nero would grieve for him, so he asked that the body of the young man be brought to him. "When the corpse was lying in front of Paul he awakened him and sent him to the Emperor." Nero, however, was very upset that his old lover returned and had him, along with others who now professed belief in Christ, imprisoned. He also had Paul handcuffed and brought before him. Paul was freed, however, after the Roman mob threatened Nero, but he was brought again before the emperor, who accused Paul of being a magician. "Behead this deceiver. Make an end to this criminal," Nero cried. Paul was beheaded. "When his head was severed from his body . . . there flowed a stream of milk" from his neck. Paul's ghost then appeared to Nero, who became so terrified that "he became mad and no longer knew what to do."

The scene in St. Paul's life that is most usually painted is the Conversion of St. Paul. Among the most famous works are those of Peter Brueghel, painted in 1567, Caravaggio, and Jacopo Tintoretto's fantastic canvas in the National Gallery of Art, Washington, DC. Rembrandt painted *Paul in Prison* in 1627, and Giotto painted *The Beheading of St. Paul* about 1311. In many paintings and sculptures St. Paul is shown with a sword. If placed downward it symbolizes his death; if placed upward, his preaching. Often he carries a book, the symbol of the epistles in the New Testament. His physical features were described in the *Acts of Paul* by a man named Titus, who had personally seen the saint. He was "small, bald, had bowlegs but a strong body, with eyebrows meeting and with a slightly bent but graceful nose, and at times he looked like a human being and then again he had the face of an angel."

Sholem Asch's novel about St. Paul, entitled *The Apostle*, has a major portion devoted to Paul's Jewish background. Mendelssohn's Oratorio *St. Paul* also deals with the saint.

2346

Pausanias. Second century C.E. Greek travel author of the *Description of Greece*, which covers topography, legends, myths, rituals, and histories of various places. It is an invaluable source for many myths and lost art works. The ten books are (1) Attica and Megara; (2) Argolis, and others; (3) Laconia; (4) Messenia; (5–6) Elis and Olympia; (7) Achaia; (8) Arcadia; (9) Boeotia; and (10) Phocis and Delphi. James G. Frazer, the author of *The Golden Bough*, translated the work, with numerous notes, in six volumes.

2347

Pawang (wizard). In the Malay Peninsula, wizard, medicine man, or magician. The office is usually hereditary, or the appointment is practically confined to the members of one family. The *pawang* or *bomor* is the intermediary between man and the supernatural. He attends new projects and important rites, such as those connected with birth, marriage, and death. He also acts as a spirit medium and pronounces oracles while in a trance; he possesses considerable political influence; occasionally practices austerities; and observes some sexual taboos. A related term, *pantang*, is used for anything that is forbidden or taboo in the culture.

2348

Pawang Pukat. In Malayan mythology, a wizard who was turned into a porpoise. Once there was a Pawang Pukat who had bad luck all of the time. He resolved to use magic to change his fortune. One day, having caught nothing, he asked his friends to collect an immense quantity of mangrove leaves in their boat. He carried the leaves out to the fishing ground, scattered them on the surface of the water, together with a few handfuls of parched and saffron-stained rice, and repeated a series of spells over them as he did so.

The next time he went fishing, the leaves had been transformed into fish of all shapes and sizes, and an immense haul was the result. The fishing wizard gave directions to have all the proceeds divided among his family and debtors. Then, without warning, he plunged into the sea, reappearing as a porpoise.

2349

Pax (peace). In Roman mythology, goddess of peace; equivalent to the Greek goddess Eirene; also called Salus and Concordia by the Romans. Her cult became popular during the reign of Augustus Caesar, and her most famous monument was the Ara Pacis, a large altar dedicated on 30 January 9 B.C.E. by the Roman Senate to commemorate Augustus' safe return from Gaul and Spain. The feast of Pax was held 3 January.

2350

Paynal (he who hastens). In an Aztec rite, name given to the man who played the part of the war god Huitzilopochtli. According to Fray Bernardino de Sahagún in *Historia general de las cosas de Nueva España* (1570–1582), this deputy god "had to go personally to summon men so that they might go forthwith to fight the enemy." When Paynal died he was honored by the people.

Variant spelling: Paynalton.

2351

Peach. A fruit tree. In China the peach stands for immortality and springtime. The Chinese god of longevity is often portrayed emerging from a peach. In European Christian tradition the peach is a sign of salvation, often appearing in paintings of the Virgin and Child.

2352

Peacock. The male peafowl, having long, spotted, iridescent tail feathers that can be spread out like a fan. In world mythology and folklore the peacock is sometimes a symbol of pride and vanity. In *Henry VI, Part I* (3.3) Shakespeare writes:

Let frantic Talbot triumph for a while
And like a peacock sweep along his tail;
We'll pull his plumes and take away his train.

Shakespeare knew the Greek myth of the origin of the peacock's colorful tail feathers. Hera, the wife of Zeus, sent the hundred-eyed giant Argos to watch Io, a mistress of Zeus who had been transformed into a heifer. Zeus, in the guise of a woodpecker, led the god Hermes to slay the giant. Hera, unable to take revenge on either Hermes or Zeus, contented herself with taking the giant's eyes and placing them in the tail of her favorite bird, the peacock, which made the bird quite proud.

In Buddhist mythology the peacock is a symbol of vanity but also a symbol of compassion and watchfulness. In Chinese mythology and folklore the peacock is a symbol of rank, beauty, and dignity and was an emblem of the Ming Dynasty. In Hindu mythology the peacock is the mount of Brahma, Kama, and Skanda and emblem of Sarasvati.

In Christian symbolism the peacock's tail was sometimes used as the All-Seeing Eye of the Church. It also symbolized immortality of the soul since it was believed that the peacock's flesh did not decay. St. Augustine wrote in *The City of God*: "Who except God, the Creator of all things, endowed the flesh of the dead peacock with the power of never decaying." Christian legend says the saint experimented with a dead peacock and found this to be true. In early Christian art two peacocks facing each other was symbolic of the souls of the faithful drinking from the Fountain of Life.

In Islamic folklore the peacock was the original guardian of the Gates of Paradise, but it ate the devil, who then, inside the bird, entered Paradise and worked the fall of Adam and Eve. In Persian mythology two peacocks facing on either side of the Tree of Life symbolize man's dual nature of good and evil.

2353

Pecos Bill. In American folklore, a tough Western hero who was the subject of many adventures. After he had killed "all the Indians and bad men," as one tale says," he headed West. First, he encountered a 12-foot snake, which he killed, and then a big mountain lion, which he used as his riding mount to replace his wounded horse. When he arrived at a cowboy campsite, he grabbed a handful of beans and crammed them into his mouth, then he grabbed the coffeepot to wash them down. He said, "Who in the hell is boss around here, anyway?" "I was," said a big fellow about seven feet tall, "but you are now, stranger." Other legends tell how he first invented roping. He had a rope that reached from the Rio Grande to the Big Bow, and he would amuse himself by throwing a loop up in the sky and catching buzzards and eagles. He could also rope bears, wolves, and panthers. The first time he saw a train he thought it was some varmint, and he threw his rope around it and brought it to a halt. There are at least two accounts of his death. One tale says he died laughing when he saw a Boston man dressed up in "a

mail-order cowboy outfit," and another tale says he "died of solemncholy" when he heard a country lawyer talk about keeping "inviolate the sacred traditions of the old west."

2354

Pedro the Cruel. 1334–1369. In medieval history and legend, king of Castile and León, who appears in numerous Spanish ballads. Don Pedro was popular with the people but hated by the nobles. Legend credits him with the death of his wife, Queen Blanche, and the murder of her three brothers. When Pedro died in battle, his head was cut off and his remains buried. Later they were disinterred by his daughter, the wife of the English John of Gaunt, and deposited in Seville.

Pegasus

2355

Pegasus (of the wells). In Greek mythology, a winged horse who sprang from the blood of the slain Gorgon Medusa when her head was cut off by the hero Perseus. Bellerophon, another Greek hero, captured the winged horse with the aid of a golden bridle given him by Athena when she encountered Pegasus drinking from the Pierian spring. With Pegasus' aid Bellerophon killed the monster Chimera. When Pegasus' hoof touched the earth, the magical spring Hippocrene gushed forth. Bellerophon, becoming overly ambitious, tried to reach Mount Olympus on Pegasus, but Pegasus knew better and threw his rider. Finally, Zeus gave Pegasus a home on Mount Olympus. Homer's *Iliad* (book 6), Ovid's *Metamorphoses* (book 4), Horace's *Odes IV* (11.27), Spenser's *Faerie Queene* (1.9.21), Shakespeare's *King Henry Part I* (4.1.109), Milton's *Paradise Lost* (book 7.4), Pope's *Essay on Criticism* (1.150), and Schiller's *Pegasus im Joche* all deal with the mythical animal.

2356
Peklo. In Slavic mythology, a name for the underworld, the land of the dead.

2357
Peko. In Finno-Ugric mythology, a barley god worshiped by the Estonians. Peko's image, made of wax, was the common property of the community, with each farm having the privilege of hosting the god's image for a year. For Peko's feast (which was held at Whitsuntide) a special beer was brewed, and prayers were offered to the god, calling on "Peko, our god, shepherd our herds," to "look after our horses, protect also our corn from snow, from hail!" The image of the god was then left at the feast, and a wrestling contest took place outside. The person who was first bruised was then chosen the guardian of the god for the next year.
Variant spelling: Pekko.

2358
Pele. In Polynesian mythology, Hawaiian volcanic goddess who lives in the crater of Kilauea on Hawaii.

In some myths Pele is said to have come to Hawaii from Tahiti, fleeing from her sister, whose husband she had seduced. In another account she is said to have fled from a flood, and a third version says she simply liked to travel. A sister, Hi'iaka, is Pele's constant companion. When Pele settled at Kilauea she fell in love with a young chief, Lohiau, from Kana'i. She told him she would send someone to fetch him in three days. Back at her volcano home, she instructed her sister Hi'iaka to fetch her husband. When Hi'iaka arrived she discovered that Lohiau had died of a broken heart, but she caught his fleeing spirit, placed it back in his body, and brought him to her sister.

However, during this delay Pele had become so jealous of her sister that she caused a lava stream to destroy Hopoe, her sister's close friend. Finally, the two sisters played a game of kilu (similar to quoits) to determine who would have the love of Lohiau. Hi'iaka won, but Pele was not happy and tried to kill the couple. Hi'iaka's magic protected her from Pele's flames, but Lohiau was destroyed, only to be restored once again to life by Hi'iaka's magic.

2359
Peleus (muddy). In Greek mythology, king of the Myrmidons and an Argonaut; son of Aeacus, king of Aegina and Endeis; husband of the sea nymph Thetis; father of Achilles. In Catullus' poem *Peleus and Thetis*, it was at Peleus' marriage feast that Eris (discord) threw an apple with the inscription "for the fairest" into the gathering and caused a dispute among the goddesses for possession of the apple. That dispute led to the Judgment of Paris and the Trojan War. Homer's *Iliad* (book 9), Euripides' *Andromache*, Apollodorus' *Bibliotheca* (Library), and Ovid's *Metamorphoses* (book 11) all refer to Peleus or tell his tale.

Pelican

Pelican. A large web-footed, fish-eating bird having a large bill with a distensible pouch. In medieval Christian belief the pelican was a symbol of a pious, self-sacrificing creature identified with Christ. St. Jerome writes that the pelican was known to restore life to its dead young by shedding its own blood after the offspring had been killed by a serpent. The saint then explained that the serpent was the devil; the offspring, mankind trapped in sin; and the pelican, Christ, who shed his blood to save mankind. Dante's *The Divine Comedy* calls Christ *nostro pelicano* (our pelican).

Pelops (muddy face). In Greek mythology, a hero, son of Tantalus and Atlas's daughter, Dione; brother of Niobe; father of Atreus and Thyestes. When he was a child, his father killed him, cooked him, and served him at a feast of the gods to test whether a god would recognize human flesh. Only Demeter, mourning the loss of Persephone, ate part of Pelops' shoulder bone. Hermes reconstructed Pelops' body, and Demeter gave him an ivory shoulder to replace the one she had eaten. As a man, Pelops fell in love with Hippodameia. To win her hand, he had to enter a chariot race against her father, Oenomaus. He won by bribing Oenomaus' charioteer, Myrtilus, to remove the axle pin of Oenomaus' chariot just before the race. After his victory Pelops killed Myrtilus, either to avoid paying him or perhaps to silence the only witness to his crime, by casting him in the ocean afterward called Myrtoan, Myrtilus, or Oenomaus. His tale appears in Pindar, Appollonius, Hyginus, and Ovid's *Metamorphoses* (book 6). The preparations for the chariot race appear on the east pediment of the Temple of Zeus at Olympia.

Penanngga Lan. In Malayan mythology, a vampire woman, often a woman who has died in childbirth, returning to torment small children with her horrible face and her entrails hanging out.

Penates (inner chamber, storehouse). In Roman mythology, household gods, originally spirits of the dead. Their images were generally made of wax, ivory, silver, or earth; and offerings of wine, incense, fruits, and sometimes lambs, sheep, or goats were made to them. When a family moved from one house to another or from one place to another, it was customary for the head of the family to remove his Penates and establish them in the new house even before he thought of his family's comfort. Vergil's *Aeneid* (book 2) tells how Aeneas, before fleeing burning Troy, placed the Penates and Lares on his

father's back and then carried his father on his back. Raphael painted the scene of the flight.

Penelope and Telemachus

Penelope (with a web over her face, striped duck). In Greek mythology, the faithful wife of Odysseus, daughter of Icarius and Periboea or Asterodia. Penelope was mother of Telemachus. When Odysseus sailed for the Trojan War, Penelope was left to manage the household affairs in Ithaca. In a short time she was hounded by local suitors to remarry. She kept them at bay by saying she first had to finish weaving a shroud for her father-in-law, Laertes. Each day she would weave, but at night she would undo the work. Finally, after three years, she was betrayed by one of her maids and forced to finish the piece. Athena, who protected Penelope and her husband, told her to offer herself to the suitor who could string the great bow of Odysseus and shoot through a row of double-headed axes. By this time Odysseus, who had been gone some 20 years, had returned and was disguised as a beggar in the hall. He not only strung the bow but also killed the suitors. The couple were then reunited. In Homer's *Odyssey* (books 16, 17) Penelope is characterized as a model of feminine virtue and chastity, being called "wise" and "prudent." In later, post-Homeric legend, she maintained that characterization, except in Pelopponesus where it was believed she had committed adultery. There was a cult to Penelope associated with a duck or other species of bird in eastern Arcadia, supposedly the site of her death. Ovid's *Heroides* (1) and *Ars Amatoria* (3.15) deal with her love for Odysseus.

Shakespeare's *Coriolanus* (1.3.92), Spenser's *Sonnet XXIII*, and W. S. Landor's *Penelope and Pheido* all cite or deal with Penelope. In opera the myth of Penelope has been treated by Cimarosa, Fauré, Galuppi, Piccinni, Jommelli, and Libermann.

2365

Penthesilea (forcing men to mourn). In Greek mythology, an Amazon, daughter of Ares and Otrera, who fought for the Trojans during the Trojan War after Achilles had killed Hector. Penthesilea was killed by Achilles' spear. When he saw her great beauty, Achilles fell in love with her and returned her body to King Priam for proper funeral honors. Achilles' display of sentimentality made Thersites ridicule him, and Achilles killed him. The myth is told in Vergil's *Aeneid* (book 1), Ovid's *Metamorphoses* (book 12), and the *Aethiopia*, an anonymous epic poem that continues Homer's *Iliad*, written about 775 B.C.E. Hugo Wolf's symphonic poem, *Penthesilea*, is based on Heinrich von Kleist's poetic tragedy *Penthesilea*. Penthesilea's death is often portrayed in ancient Greek art. It was one of the subjects painted by Panaenus around Phidias' statue of Zeus.

2366

Pentheus (grief). In Greek mythology, king of Thebes, son of Echion and Agave. Pentheus refused to worship Dionysus and was killed when the god inspired a frenzy in his worshipers, the Bacchae. Believing Pentheus to be a wild boar, they tore him to pieces. The first to attack was Agave (highborn), his mother, followed by Pentheus' two sisters, Ino and Autonoe. Euripides' *The Bacchae*, Vergil's *Aeneid* (book 4), and Ovid's *Metamorphoses* (book 3) tell the tale.

2367

Perahera. In Buddhism, a torchlight procession held every August at Kandy, where the Tooth Relic of the Buddha is carried around the city on the back of an elephant.

2368

Perceval (pierce valley). In Arthurian legend, a knight of the Holy Grail. Medieval versions of his legend vary greatly in detail, but all tell of a boy brought up in the forest ignorant of knights and courtly manners. He goes to the court of King Arthur, eventually becomes a knight of the Round Table, and goes in quest of the Holy Grail. He is allowed to view the Grail because he is pure. Perceval makes his first appearance in medieval legend in Chrétien de Troyes's *Perceval, le conte del Graal*. He then appears in "Peredur, Son of Efrawg," a tale in *The Mabinogion*. His legend is also told in Wolfram von Eschenbach's long poem *Parzival* and Malory's *Morte d'Arthur*. Wagner took most of his material from Wolfram von Eschenbach's telling for his opera *Parsifal*.

    Variant spellings: Percival, Percivale, Parsifal, Parzival.

2369

Perdix (partridge). In Greek mythology, culture hero, Athenian inventor of the saw, compass, and potter's wheel; son of Perdix, the sister of Daedalus. He was murdered by Daedalus and transformed into a partridge. The story is in Ovid's *Metamorphoses* (book 8).

2370

Persephone (bringer of destruction). In Greek mythology, goddess of the underworld; a pre-Greek goddess, also called Kore (maiden) and later Proserpina by the Romans; daughter of Demeter and Zeus. Pluto (Hades or Dis), god of the underworld, wished to marry Persephone, but his offer was refused by her parents. One day while Persephone was out gathering flowers, Pluto came in a chariot drawn by four black horses and abducted Persephone, taking

Perceval (Louis Rhead)

Rape of Persephone

her to his underground kingdom. Her mother, Demeter, was wild with madness and withdrew all plant life from the earth. Zeus, fearful that all life would die without Demeter's help, sent Hermes to the underworld to retrieve Persephone, but she had eaten pomegranates (fruit of the underworld) and was compelled to stay in Pluto's kingdom for as many months as the number of fruits she had eaten. When Persephone returned to her mother, the earth's vegetation was restored. Thus, Persephone became a goddess of fertility, of the birth and death of vegetation. Under the name Kore she was worshiped, along with Demeter and Dionysus, at the Eleusinian Mysteries. Ancient Greek art portrayed Persephone as a beautiful maiden. Her attributes were a horn of plenty, a sheaf of wheat, a cock (the rising sun), a torch, and a pomegranate (rebirth after death). Homer's *Odyssey* (book 11), Hesiod's *Theogony*, The Homeric Hymns (not by Homer), Vergil's *Aeneid* (books 4, 6,), Ovid's *Metamorphoses* (book 5), Shelley's *Song of Proserpine, While Gathering Flowers on the Plain of Enna*, Tennyson's *Demeter and Persephone*, Swinburne's *Hymn to Proserpine* and *The Garden of Proserpine*, George Meredith's *The Appeasement of Demeter*, and Stravinsky's *Perséphone* (1934) with libretto by André Gide all have dealt with the myth.

2371
Perseus (destroyer). In Greek mythology, hero, son of Zeus and Danaë. When Perseus was a baby, his grandfather, Acrisius, was warned by an oracle that Perseus would kill him when he grew up. Fearful, he placed Danaë and Perseus in a wooden box and had them thrown into the sea. They were cast ashore and found by Dictys, a fisherman on the island of Seriphus. Dictys brought up Perseus and took care of Danaë. After some time, when Perseus was a young man, King Polydectes fell in love with Danaë and wanted to marry her. She refused, and Polydectes believed it was because of Perseus, so he sent him on a quest to retrieve the head of Medusa, the snakehaired Gorgon. Polydectes hoped Perseus would die in the quest. But Hermes, messenger of the gods,

Perseus carrying the head of Medusa

helped Perseus, and the hero returned with Medusa's head. When the giant Atlas refused Perseus shelter, Perseus showed him the Gorgon's head, and Atlas turned to stone. As he flew home on the winged sandals given him by Hermes, he saw Andromeda chained to a rock by the sea, waiting to be devoured by a sea monster. Perseus slew the monster from the air with one blow and then married Andromeda. At the wedding feast a former suitor of Andromeda appeared and wished to fight the hero. Perseus exposed Medusa's head to him, and the suitor and all of the guests were turned to stone. Returning to his mother with his bride, he found Danaë had hidden herself from Polydectes' sexual advances. Again he exposed Medusa's head at a feast held by Polydectes and turned the king and his guests to stone. Perseus put Dictys on the throne, and gave Medusa's head to Athena for her shield, the Aegis.

At Argos, while attending funeral games, Perseus accidentally killed his grandfather, Acrisius, fulfilling the oracle. He was killed by Megapenthes. Cellini's *Perseus* and Antonio Canova's statue *Perseus with the Head of Medusa* are among the best representations of the myth. Perseus' myth is found in Apollordorus' *Bibliotheca* (Library); Ovid's *Metamorphoses* (book 4); William Morris's *Doom of King Acrisius*, part of *The Earthly Paradise*; Charles Kinglsey's *Heroes*; Nathaniel Hawthorne's *Wonder Book*; as well as works by Tennyson, Browning, Hopkins, and Auden.

Peter, Martyr, St. (stone, rock). 1205–1253. In Christian legend, patron saint of inquisitors and midwives. Venerated in Verona, Italy. Feast, 29 April.

Peter was a noted Dominican preacher who hounded heretics and Jews and was finally murdered by a group of hired assassins in the forest on his way from Como to Milan. One of the assassins struck him on the head with an ax and then went in pursuit of Peter's companion. When the assassin returned, he found Peter had written the Apostles Creed with his own blood on the ground, or according to another account, was reciting the Creed aloud. In either case the murderer pierced Peter with a sword.

Peter Rugg. In American folklore, a man who cannot die and spends his years in constant wanderings. He does not age but rides around in his buggy on New England roads around Boston. William Austin's tale *Peter Rugg, The Missing Man* narrates the legend.

Christ giving the Keys to St. Peter

Peter, St. (stone, rock). First century C.E. In the Bible, N.T., Apostle. Patron of bakers, bridge builders, butchers, carpenters, clockmakers, fishermen, fishmongers, glaziers, masons, net makers, potters, stationers, and shipwrights. Invoked against fever, foot troubles, frenzy, snakebite, wolves, and for a long life. Feast, 29 June.

Peter's original name was Simon (snub-nosed). He was the son of a man named Jonas or John, who was a fisherman. Peter and brother Andrew followed their father's profession. They were partners with John and James, the sons of Zebedee. Both Peter and Andrew were followers of John the Baptist, but when Jesus said, "Follow me, and I will make you fishers of men" (Matt. 4:19), Peter immediately joined him. He was always regarded as the first of the Apostles and is so listed in every account given in the New Testament as well as in legendary sources. Peter appears in the most important happenings in the life of Christ. He is present at the raising of Jairus's daughter (Luke 8:41–51), the Transfiguration (Matt. 17:1–2), the Last Supper (Luke 22:8ff.), the Agony in the Garden (Matt. 26:37–40), and the Resurrection (John 24:12). It is Peter who catches the fish with the coin in its mouth needed to pay the tribute when Christ says, "Render therefore unto Caesar the things that are Caesar's; and unto God the things that are God's (Matt. 22:21)."

The high position of Peter among the Apostles both during Christ's life and later are summed up in the words Christ addresses to him. "Thou art Peter [rock], and upon this rock I will build my church: and the gates of hell shall not prevail against it. And I will give unto thee the keys of the kingdom of heaven: and whatsoever thou shalt bind on earth, shall be bound in heaven: and whatsoever thou shalt loose on earth shall be loosed in heaven (Matt. 16:18–19)."

Yet in his high position (differently interpreted by Catholics and Protestants from the text) Peter is also weak and sometimes blind to Christ's mission. He rejects the idea that Jesus must suffer. Jesus is so angered by this that he tells Peter, "Get thee behind me, Satan: thou art an offence unto me: for thou savourest not the things that be of God, but those that be of men (Matt. 16:23)." Toward the close of Christ's ministry Peter's role becomes very prominent. At the Last Supper he asks the reason Jesus is washing his disciples' feet. He also says he would never deny Christ, which he does. He is reminded by the cock crowing.

Peter's story is continued in The Acts of the Apostles in the New Testament. In the first part of the work Peter is clearly the leader of the Apostles. Accompanied by his wife, he travels to various cities, bringing the gospel. We are not told, however, how he died, nor are we told about a journey to Rome, where he and St. Paul, according to legend, were martyred on the same day. Christian legend, however, has supplied what was lacking in the biblical accounts. The most important legend concerns the magician Simon Magus. The miracles of Peter were so superior to any done by Simon Magus that the magician fled to Rome. St. Peter followed him there. Many years passed, and Simon Magus became a favorite of the Emperor Nero. According to

The Golden Legend, written in the 13th century, Simon said he was the Son of God, who, if his head were to be cut off, would rise again on the third day. "Nero ordered the executioner to cut off his head; but Simon, by his magic art, caused the executioner to behead a ram, thinking the while that he was beheading Simon himself." The magician then hid for three days, made his appearance, and the emperor eventually put up a statue to "the holy god Simon." After some time Peter and Simon came into a contest before the emperor. The final feat was Simon's journey to heaven, "since the earth was no longer worthy of him." On the set day he climbed to the top of a high tower and began his flight with a laurel crown on his head. Nero called out to Peter to look at the flight of Simon Magus. But Peter called out, "Angels of Satan, who hold this man up in the air, in the name of my master Jesus Christ, I command you to hold him up no longer." Simon was then dashed to the earth, "his skull was split, and he died."

When Rome was burning the Christians asked Peter to flee for his safety because the Christians were being blamed for the deed. As he went along the Appian way, he met Christ, walking toward Rome. He said, "Lord, whither goest thou?" And Christ replied, "I go to Rome to be crucified anew." "To be crucified anew?" asked Peter. "Yes," said Christ. "Then, Lord, I too return to Rome, to be crucified with thee."

Peter, not being a Roman citizen like St. Paul, was "condemned to die on the cross." He asked that he be crucified with his "head toward the earth" and his feet pointing to heaven. For he said, "I am not worthy to die as my master died."

In Christian art, Peter is usually shown holding the keys of heaven, sometimes a fish or a cock. The number of art works dealing with him is staggering. Among the most noteworthy are those of Giotto, Crivelli, Caravaggio, Raphael, Michelangelo, Masaccio, Giovanni Bellini, Quentin Massys, Hans Holbein, Rubens, Francisco de Zurbaran, Murillo, Fra Bartolommeo, and El Greco.

Petro Simbi. In Haitian voodoo, a loa (deified spirit of the dead) of rain; patron of magicians. Petro Simbi is both benevolent and aggressive. Symbolized by a glowing iron rod stuck upright in a charcoal fire, his color is red. Sacrifices of goats and pigs are made to him.

                                                                        2375

                                                                        2376
Phaedra (bright one). In Greek mythology, daughter of Minos and Pasiphae; sister of Acacallis, Androgeus, Ariadne, Catreus, Deucalion, Euryale,

Glaucus, Lycastus, and Xenodice; wife of Theseus; mother of Acamas and Demophon; in love with Hippolytus, her stepson. Phaedra married Theseus after the death of Antiope, his previous wife. Being much younger than Theseus, Phaedra fell in love with her stepson Hippolytus; but the youth rejected Phaedra's advances. In retaliation for the rejection Phaedra accused Hippolytus of attempting to rape her and then hanged herself. Theseus banished Hippolytus and prayed for vengeance on him, and Hippolytus was then killed by Poseidon. Phaedra appears in Euripides' *Hippolytus*, Seneca's *Phaedra*, and Ovid's *Heroides* (4). Racine's *Phèdre* was used as the basis for the Jean Cocteau ballet with music of Georges Auric. Others works using Racine's text were Ildebrando Pizetti's opera *Phaedra* (1915) and a modern movie version of the plot, *Phaedra* (1961) staring Melina Mercouri.

The fall of Phaethon

                                                                        2377
Phaethon (shining). In Greek mythology, son of Apollo or Helios, both sun gods, and the nymph Clymene. Phaethon was laughed at by his companions when he said he was the son of Apollo. He went to Apollo and begged to be allowed to drive Apollo's sun chariot across the heavens. Reluctantly consenting, Apollo gave Phaethon his horses and chariot. After a time Phaethon could not control the chariot. It plunged to the earth and parched Libya. Zeus, in response, killed the boy with a thunderbolt. Phaethon fell into the Eridanus or Po River and was transformed into a swan. There his sisters, the Heliades, mourning him, were transformed into willow trees and their tears into drops of amber. Ovid's *Metamorphoses* (books 1, 2) tell the myth in detail. Spenser's *Tears of the Muses* calls Phaethon "Phoebus foolish sonne." In Shakespeare's *Two Gentlemen of Verona* (3.1.154–5) the Duke compares Valentine to Phaethon when he plans to elope with Silvia: "Wilt thou aspire to guide the heavenly car/ And with thy daring folly burn the world?" Shakespeare also cites the image of the falling Phaethon in *Richard II* (3.3.178–79). The Heliades appear in Andrew Mar-

vell's poem *The Nymph Complaining for the Death of Her Faun* (99–100). In music Lully's opera *Phaëton* (1683) and Saint-Saëns' tone poem *Phaëton* (1873) deal with the myth. In art Hans Rottenhammer's *Fall of Phaeton* portrays the ride.

Phaon. In Greek legend, a boatman of the Mytilene in Lesbos, loved by the poet Sappho. Phaon rejected Sappho's love, and as a result she killed herself by leaping off a cliff on the island of Leucas. Originally Phaon was old and ugly, but he received from Aphrodite a small box containing an ointment that made him young and handsome. Sappho was a Lesbian, and the legend evolved to avoid this delicate issue. Ovid's *Heroides* (15) has a letter from Sappho to Phaon. David's painting of Sappho also pictures Phaon.

Pharaoh

2379

Pharaoh (great house). In ancient Egypt, title for the kings, who were believed to be incarnations of Horus, the son of Osiris. When a pharaoh died he became Osiris, one with the god of the dead. In the Bible the word *pharaoh* is used as if it were a proper name. We have no evidence in the Bible as to which

pharaoh is referred to in the story of the Exodus from Egypt by the Hebrews.

2380

Philip, St. (lover of horses). First century. In the Bible, N.T., Apostle. Patron of hatters, pastry cooks, Brabant, and Luxemborg. Feast, 1 May.

Born at Bethsaida, Philip was one of the first men called by Jesus early in his ministry at Bethany, beyond the Jordan where John was baptizing (John 1:28). He was present with the faithful disciples when they prayed in the upper room in Jerusalem after Christ's Ascension (Acts 1:12–14).

According to legend, Philip went to preach in Scythia, where he worked for some 20 years. Then, according to the account in *The Golden Legend*, written in the 13th century, but based on earlier sources, he was taken by the pagans.

> . . . which would constrain him to make sacrifice to an idol which was called Mars, their God, and anon under the idol issued out a right great dragon, which forthwith slew the bishop's [king's] son that appointed the fire for to make the sacrifice, and the two provost also, whose servants held St. Philip in iron bonds; and the dragon corrupted the people with his breath that they were all sick, and St. Philip said: "Believe ye me and break this idol and set in his place the cross of Jesu Christ and after, worship ye it, and they that be here dead shall revive, and all the sick people shall be made whole." And anon St. Philip commanded the dragon that he should go in to desert without grieving or doing any harm to any person, and anon he departed. (Caxton translation)

The pagan priests were upset by Philip's power, so they bound him on a cross and stoned him to death, "and his body was worshipfully buried there, and his two daughters died long after him and were also buried, that one on the right side, and the other on the left side of the body of their father."

When St. Philip is shown in art, alone or in a series of apostles, he is generally a man in the prime of life, with a small beard and a benign countenance. His attribute is a cross, sometimes a small one carried in his hand, a high cross in the form of a T, or a tall staff with a Latin cross at top. The cross symbol, according to Jameson in *Sacred and Legendary Art*, may "allude to his martyrdom; or to his conquest over the idols through the power of the cross; or, when placed on the top of the pilgrim's staff, it may allude to his mission among the barbarians as preacher of the cross of salvation."

2381

Philoctetes (love of possessions). In Greek mythology, an Argonaut, male lover of Heracles, great archer, son of Poeas and Demonassa. Philoctetes joined the expedition against Troy. On the way to the city he and his companions landed on a small island to offer sacrifice to a local goddess. In one account he was bitten by a snake; in another he was scratched by one of his own poisoned arrows. In either case, the wound festered and his companions left him on the island of Lemnos, where he lived for ten years. Near the close of the Trojan War the Greeks captured the Trojan prophet Helenus, who informed them that only if the bows and arrows of Heracles were obtained could they be victorious. The bow and arrows were in the possession of Philoctetes, who had obtained them when he lit Heracles' funeral pyre on Mount Oeta. Odysseus and Neoptolemus (or Diomedes) were sent to Philoctetes to obtain the bow and arrow. Only when Heracles appeared, risen from the dead, did Philoctetes give up the bow and arrows. Machaon, a son of Asclepius, the god of healing, cured Philoctetes' wound. Philoctetes later founded two cities in Italy. Homer's *Iliad* (book 2), Sophocles' *Philoctetes* and Ovid's *Metamorphoses* (books 9, 13) all deal with Philoctetes.

Philomela (sweet melody). In Greek mythology, sister of Procne; daughter of King Pandion of Athens and Zeuxippe. Procne's husband Tereus, king of Thrace, raped Philomela and then cut out her tongue so she could not speak. However, the girl wove her sad tale on a tapestry and sent it to her sister Procne. As revenge, the two sisters killed Itylus, the five-year-old son of Tereus, and served the boy to the father at dinner. During the dinner, Philomela threw Itylus' head on the table. The gods then transformed Philomela into a nightingale, Tereus into a hawk (or hoopoe), Procne into a swallow, and Itylus into a pheasant (or sandpiper). Ovid's *Metamorphoses* (book 6) and Chaucer's *Legend of Good Women* narrate the myth. Other works that have dealt with or referred to the myth are Sir Philip Sidney's *The Nightingale*; Edmund Spenser's *Virgils Gnat* (401–3); Shakespeare's *Titus Andronicus*, in which part of the plot is similar to the myth; Milton's *Il Penseroso* (56–62); Matthew Arnold's *Philomela*; Swinburne's *Itylus*; Oscar Wilde's *The Burden of Itylus*; T. S. Eliot's *Sweeney among the Nightingales* and *The Waste Land*.

Phlegethon (blazing). In Greek mythology, one of the five rivers of Hades, the underworld in which those who have committed violence against their families are cast until they are forgiven. Homer's *Odyssey* (book 10) and Ovid's *Metamorphoses* (book 15) mention the river. In Dante's *Divine Comedy* (Inferno) it is one of the three rivers of Hell (the others being

Acheron and Styx); sinners who have shed blood are cast forever into this river of boiling blood. In Plato's dialogue *Phaedo*, the river is called Pyriphlegethon (river of fire).

Phlegyas (fiery). In Greek mythology, king of Lapithae and son of Ares and Chryse. Phlegyas burned Apollo's temple at Delphi when he discovered that the god had raped Coronis, Phlegyas' daughter and the mother of Asclepius. Apollo killed Phlegyas and placed him in the underworld with a massive stone above his head, which constantly threatened to fall on him. Vergil's *Aeneid* (book 6), which narrates Aeneas' visit to the underworld, tells of Phlegyas' fate.

Phocas, St. Third century C.E. In Christian legend of the Eastern Church, patron saint of gardeners. Feast, 3 July.

Phocas lived outside the gate of Sinope, in Pontus, where he cultivated a garden and gave the produce to the poor. One night as he was at supper, some strangers came in, and as he kept open house, he invited them to stay. They said they had come to find a certain Phocas, whom they were hired to kill. Phocas said nothing. He gave them a night's lodging and while they were asleep he went out and dug a grave in his garden among the flowers. In the morning he told his guests that Phocas was found and "insisted on their beheading him at the grave, and they buried him there."

In Byzantine art St. Phocas is presented as an aged man holding a spade.

Phoenix

2386

Phoenix. In world mythology, fantastic bird who is reborn from its own ashes. The standard ancient account of the phoenix is found in Herodotus' *History* in which he says he never saw the creature but was told that it lived for 500 years, and upon its death was reborn from its own ashes, which were lit in the Temple of the Sun in Heliopolis, Egypt. In Christian symbolism the phoenix became a sign of the Resurrection of Christ. St. Clement, a convert of St. Paul, refers to the phoenix in one of his letters to attest to the truth of Christ's Resurrection. A 12th-century Latin bestiary also cites the phoenix as proof of Christ's Resurrection. "If the phoenix has the power to die and rise again, why silly man are you scandalized at the word of God . . . . who offered himself on the Altar of the cross to suffer for us and on the third day rise again?" (T. H. White translation)

2387

Phyllis (leafy). In Greek mythology, daughter of King Lycurgus (or Phyleus or Sithon, all kings of Thrace); sister of Dryas. She married Demophon, son of the hero Theseus but was loved by his brother Acamas, by whom she had a son, Munitus. Phyllis killed herself and was turned into an almond tree when Demophon did not return to her after a month's absence. One of Ovid's *Heroides* (2) and Chaucer's *Legend of Good Women* tell her tragic tale.

2388

Picus (woodpecker). In Roman mythology, son of Saturn; father of Faunus and husband of Canens. Picus also loved Pomona. When the enchantress Circe fell in love with Picus, he rejected her advances, so she turned him into a purple woodpecker. Ovid's *Metamorphoses* (book 14) and Vergil's *Aeneid* (book 7) tell of the transformation.

2389

Pied Piper of Hamelin. In medieval German legend, a magician who rid Hamelin of a rat plague in 1284. The Pied Piper appeared dressed in multicolored clothes and offered to rid the city of the rats for a fee. The town fathers agreed, and the Pied Piper began playing his pipe. Rats came swarming out of their holes and began to follow the magician to the Weser River, where they were drowned. When he tried to collect his fee, the town fathers refused to pay it, so the Pied Piper began to play his pipe again. This time children came out and followed him to Koppenberg Hill, where they vanished. The legend was used by Robert Browning in *The Pied Piper of Hamelin*.

2390

Pien ch'eng. In Chinese mythology, ruler of the sixth hell of Ti Yü, the underworld.

2391

Pien Ch'iao. Sixth century B.C.E. In Chinese legend, a deified innkeeper, honored as a god of medicine. Pien Ch'iao was the first man to dissect the human body. He had a transparent abdomen and could not only follow the course of his blood but also watch the action of drugs. He is usually portrayed as a handsome man in fine clothes, whereas his spirit teacher, Ch'ang Sang-chün, is shown nude, ugly, and unkempt.

In Japanese legend Pien Ch'iao is called Henjaku.

2392

Pietas (piety). In Roman mythology, goddess of piety, respect, and duty toward the gods, parents, and country. A temple in her honor was erected in Rome on the reputed spot where a woman had fed with her own milk her aged father, who had been imprisoned by the Roman senate and deprived of food. In Roman art Pietas was portrayed as a woman, often with a stork, a symbol of piety. Aeneas, the greatest Roman hero, was often called "pious Aeneas," referring to his high religious, social, and patriotic ideals.

2393

Pikoi. In Polynesian mythology, Hawaiian hero called the rat shooter. Once he strung 40 rats by their whiskers with one arrow.

Pilate washing his hands (Dürer)

2394

Pilate, Pontius. First century C.E. In the Bible, N.T., Roman procurator in Judea, about 26–36 C.E., who plays a prominent part in the Passion of Christ. Although Pilate was convinced of Jesus' innocence, according to the Gospel accounts, he still allowed Jesus to be crucified. He "absolved" himself from the act by washing his hands. In Christian art Pontius Pilate is portrayed publicly washing his hands, saying, "I am innocent of the blood of this just person" (Matt. 27:24). Pilate was finally brought to Rome for slaughtering Samaritans and either was executed or killed himself. Ironically, in some calendars of the Eastern Church he is placed among the saints, alluding to a Christian legend that he became converted to Christ by his wife Claudia Procla, who had asked him not to condemn Jesus. The Gospels try to downplay Pilate's responsibility because they did not want the Romans blamed for Jesus' death; instead they place the blame on the Jews, who were not responsible at all.

2395

Pilwiz. In Germanic folklore, a spirit with a sickle on his big toe. He was generally of an evil temper but offerings made to him helped to appease his spirit.
Variant spelling: Bilwis.

2396

Pine. A cone-bearing evergreen tree; in Near Eastern mythology, associated with the worship of the Great Mother goddess Cybele and her lover-consort Attis. On 22 March a pine tree was felled and brought into the goddess's sanctuary. Its trunk was swathed like a corpse in woolen blankets and decorated with wreaths of violets, said to have sprung from the blood of Attis when he was castrated by a wild boar and transformed into a pine tree. On 24 March, the Day of Blood, the high priest drew blood from his arms and presented it to the goddess. His offering was followed by those of other men, some of whom castrated themselves on the altar. They then would run through the city carrying their genitals. When a man threw his genitals into a particular house, that house was considered honored and had to furnish him with female attire and ornaments, which he would wear the rest of his life. In Greek mythology the pine was associated with Dionysus, and in Greek art a wand tipped with a pine cone often is carried by the god or his worshipers. For the Romans the pine cone was a symbol of virginity. In Japan the pine is a symbol of longevity, constancy, and marital faithfulness under the spirits of Jo and Uba.

2397

P'ing-Teng. In Chinese mythology, ruler of the eighth hell of Ti Yü, the underworld.

2398

Piper, The. Aesopic fable found in various European collections.

There was a piper who was walking by the seaside when he saw some fish. He began to pipe, thinking they would come out of the water onto the land. After some time he realized that his music did not charm them, so he got a net and cast it into the sea. A great draft of fishes was drawn up. They began to leap and dance. The piper said, "Cease your dancing now, as you did not dance when I piped for you."

The fable was told by Cyrus of Sardis to a group of Ionian and Aeolian Greeks who had come to plead with the conqueror. Cyrus had earlier urged them to revolt against Croesus––whom he had since defeated—but they had refused. "It was in anger, therefore, that he made them this reply," according to Herodotus in his *History of the Persian Wars* (book 1). There is an English proverb, "Fish are not to be caught with a bird call," which may stem from this fable.

2399

Pisachas (flesh eaters). In Hindu mythology, demons created by the god Brahma from stray drops of water that fell from the water used to create gods and men.

2400

Pleiades (sailing ones, flock of doves). In Greek mythology, seven daughters of Atlas and Pleione: Alcyone (winter storm), Celaeno (darkness), Electra (amber), Maia (fertility), Merope (mortality), Sterope (Asterope), and Taygeta (nymph of the mountain in Lacedaemon). They were born in Arcadia on Mount Cyllene. They were pursued by the giant Orion and transformed into the heavenly constellation Pleiades, or they wept at the suffering of the father, Atlas, and were transformed into stars. One of the Pleiades is invisible. Some accounts say it is Merope, who married a mortal and hides out of shame; other accounts say it is Electra, who hides from grief for the destruction of Troy. Ovid's *Metamorphoses* (book 13) tells the myth. Lord Byron's *Beppo* (14) refers to "the lost Pleiad." The term is frequently given to groups of seven illustrious persons, such as the 16th-century French poets La Pléiade. Their leader was Ronsard.

2401

Pluto (rich one or wealth giver). In Greek and Roman mythology, a cult name for Hades, god of the dead and the underworld; also called Ades, Aides, Aidoneus, Pluton, Dis; married to Persephone, whom he raped to obtain. No temples or offerings were made to Pluto. Shakespeare's *Henry IV, Part II* (2.4.109) refers to "Pluto's damned lake by this hand, to the infernal deep,/ With Erebus and tortures vile also," describing the realm of the underworld.

2402

Plutus (wealth). In Greek mythology, god of wealth, son of Demeter and the Titan Iasion. Plutus was originally connected with agricultural prosperity but later became the god of riches. He was believed to be blind because wealth was given indiscriminately to good and bad alike. In Thebes and Athens the god was portrayed as a child on the arm of Tyche, goddess of fortune and of Eirene, goddess of peace. Hesiod's *Theogony* cites the god, as do Aristophanes' comedy *Plutus*, in which his sight is restored so that he can give wealth to the deserving, and Dante's *Divine Comedy* (Hell), where he appears as Pluto, the Italian form of Plutus (not to be confused with Pluto, the god of the underworld).

2403

Pocahontas (playful one). c. 1595–1617. In American history and folklore, popular name of Matoaka, daughter of the Indian chief Powhatan. In legend as recorded in Captain John Smith's *Generall Historie*, she saved the life of John Smith when Powhatan was about "to beate out his brains." Pocahontas intervened, placing Smith's "head in her armes, and laid her owne upon his to save him from death" (book III, chapter 2). Pocahontas later became a Christian, married John Rolfe in 1614, went to England and died there. Pocahontas is mentioned in Ben Jonson's *Staple of News*, and Thomas Fuller's *Worthies of England*, as well as various novels, poems, and plays, among them, John Davis's *The Indian Princess, or La Belle Sauvage*, John Esten Cooke's *My Lady Pokahontas*, Vachel Lindsay's poem *Pocahontas, Our Mother*, and Hart Crane's poem *The Bridge*. Though most historians have rejected Smith's account, Bradford Smith (*Captain John Smith, His Life and Legend*) believes there may be some truth in the tale.

2404

Poetic Edda. Collection of poems on Norse mythological and legendary themes, believed to date from the eighth or ninth century C.E., sometimes called the *Elder Edda* or *Saemund's Edda*.

The title *Saemund's Edda* was given by Icelandic scholars in the 17th century in the erroneous belief that the poems were written or collected by Saemund the Learned. Actually, the poems were first written down from oral tradition in the 12th or 13th century. The oldest part of the *Poetic Edda* deals with myths of the Norse gods in the form of dialogues between Odin and another—either a giant, human being, or another deity. The most important poem of the group is the *Voluspa* (the Wise Woman's Prophecy), which deals with a visit by Odin to the oracle and gives an account of the origins of the world, its present state, Ragnarok (the end of the world), and the new world that will emerge after Ragnarok. The other poems are *Hovamol* (the Lay of the High One), *Vafthruthnismol* (the Lay of Vafthruthnir, "the Mighty in Riddles"), *Grimnismol* (the Lay of Grimmer), *Skirnismol* (the Lay of Skirnir), *Harbarthsljoth* (the Lay of Harbarth, "Gray-Beard," i.e., Odin.), *Hymiskvitha* (the Lay of Hymir), *Lokasenna* (Loki's mocking), *Thrymskvitha* (the Lay of Thrym), *Alvissmol* (the Lay of Alvis, "All-Knowing"), *Baldrs Draumar* (Baldur's Dream), *Rigsthula* (the Lay of Rig), *Hyndluljoth* (the Lay of Hyndla, "She-Dog"), *Svipdagsmol* (the Lay of Svipdog, "Swift-Day").

Aside from poems dealing with Norse gods, other poems or lays deal with heroes of the Northlands, such as *Helgakvioa Hjorvarossonar* (the Lay of Helgi the Son of Hjorvaror), which tells of the wooing of Svava by King Helgi. Some of the poems of the *Poetic Edda* were translated into English by William Morris in the 19th century. Earlier, the English poet Thomas Gray used the *Vegtamskvioa* (the Lay of the Wayfarer), which is a supplement to the *Voluspa*, in writing his poem "The Descent of Odin, an Ode."

2405

Polednice (the noonday witch). In Slavic folklore, a noonday witch. She appears in Karel Jaromir Erben's literary folk ballad in his *Kytice* (The Garland). It tells of a mother who threatens her unruly child with a visit from Polednice if the child does not behave. At noonday a "little shriveled spectral woman leaning on a crooked stick" arrives and kills the child. This gruesome ballad was used by Dvořák in his symphonic poem *Polednice*. The Czech title is sometimes translated *The Midday Witch* or *The Noonday Witch*.

Polevik (I. Bilibin)

Polevik (field spirit). In Slavic folklore, spirit of the field, whose nature is variable. Sometimes he is mischievous, causing people to lose their way, or even worse, he sometimes strangles them, particularly if they are drunk. If a worker fell asleep in a field at noontime or before sunset, the *polevik* would ride over him with his horse or send some disease. To earn the *polevik's* good will, two eggs must be placed in a ditch with an elderly cock that can no longer crow. The performer of this rite must complete it before being seen by anyone, or it will have no power. When the *polevik* appears, he is often dressed in full white. He often has a black body, and each eye is a different color. In northern Russia the *poludnitsa*, a female field spirit, will sometimes lure children away. She is a tall creature and wears white.

Variant spellings: polevoy, polevoi.

Polong. In Malayan mythology, a demon about as big as the first joint of a little finger. It will fly through the air wherever it is told to go; but it is always preceded by its pet or plaything, the *pelesit*, which is a species of house cricket.

To create a *polong*, the blood of a murdered man is placed in a bottle with a wide bottom and a long, narrow neck. Prayers are recited over the bottle for 7 or 14 days (depending on which account of the ritual is followed) until a sound like the chirping of young birds is heard from the bottle. The creator then cuts one finger and inserts it into the bottle so that the *polong* can suck the blood. If the creator is a man, he is called its father, if a woman, its mother. Every day the parent feeds the *polong* with his or her blood to keep the demon under its control so that the *polong* will afflict whomever it is directed to. Sometimes the *polong* is rented out for a fee by its creator.

A person attacked by a *polong* cries out and loses consciousness, tears off clothing, bites and strikes, and is blind and deaf to everything. To effect a cure, formulas are chanted by a medicine man over the head of the afflicted, his or her thumb is pinched, and medicines are applied. When the remedy is successful, the sick person cries out: "Let me go, I want to go home." The medicine man then replies, "I will not let you go if you do not make known who it is that has sent you here, and why you have come, and who are your father and mother."

Sometimes the *polong* will not answer or confess, but at other times it will give all of the particulars, though it is also capable of lying and accusing the wrong persons of the evil deed. If it tells the truth, the sick person will recover; if not, the victim shrieks and yells in anger and dies in a day or two. After the

death, blood pours forth bubbling from the mouth and the whole body is blue with bruises.

Polycrates. Sixth century B.C.E. In Greek history and legend, tyrant of Samos; son of Aeacus; known for his wealth and as a patron of the arts. According to a legend recorded in Herodotus' *History* (book 3), Polycrates was told he could avoid an evil fate if he would throw away his most precious possession. He therefore cast his favorite ring into the sea, only to have it returned to him in the belly of a fish. The ring was said to have been kept in the temple of Concord in Rome. Polycrates was crucified by Oroetes, a Persian govenor who was envious of his good fortune.

Polydamna. In Greek mythology, wife of Thonis, king of Egypt. She entertained Helen of Troy, giving her a magic drug to help banish melancholy and care. The myth is a late one that says Helen never went to Troy, only her shadow; the true Helen was in Egypt. This version forms the basis for Richard Strauss's opera *Die aegyptische Helena* (1928) with a libretto by Hugo von Hofmannsthal.

Polyphemus (famous). In Greek mythology, the one-eyed Cyclops from Sicily in the *Odyssey* (book 9), blinded by Odysseus; son of Poseidon and Thoosa. Polyphemus had earlier killed Acis, whom Galatea loved. Vergil's *Aeneid* (book 3), Ovid's *Metamorphoses* (book 13), Euripides' *The Cyclops*, where he appears as a comic character, and Turner's painting *Ulysses Deriding Polyphemus* all deal with Polyphemus. Handel's *Acis and Galatea* also features the Cyclops.

Polyxena (many guests). In Greek mythology, a daughter of King Priam of Troy and Hecuba; sister of Aesaus, Cassandra, Creusa, Deiphobus, Hector, Helenus, Paris, and Troilus; she was loved by Achilles. Polyxena does not appear in Homer, but later Greek mythology says she was sacrificed to the ghost of Achilles by his son Neoptolemus as the Greeks were leaving Troy. A variant account says she killed herself. Euripides' tragedy *Hecuba* deals with her tale, as does W. S. Landor's *The Espousal of Polyxena*.

Pomegranate. Semitropical fruit-bearing tree, often cited in both Jewish and Christian folklore as the fruit eaten by Adam and Eve, though the account in Genesis does not say which fruit was eaten. In Greek mythology the pomegranate is associated with Persephone and the underworld. In Mesopotamia the pomegranate was believed to increase sexual potency. According to one myth, the god Attis was conceived when his mother Nana, a virgin, put a pomegranate on her bosom. Variants of the myth cite the almond. In European folklore a dream about pomegranates means love is on the way.

Pomona

2413

Pomona (tree fruits). In Roman mythology, goddess of fruit trees. She married Vertumnus, who, disguised as an old woman, successfully prevailed on her to break her vow of celibacy. Her other suitors were Pan, Picus, Priapus, and Silonus. Ovid's *Metamorphoses* (book 14) tells how Vertumnus fell in love with Pomona.

2414

Pope Elhanan. In medieval Jewish legend, a Jew who became pope. In some accounts Elhanan left the papacy and, according to one medieval legend, "became a Jew greatly respected in the eyes of all the people." Elhanan's legend is placed by some scholars in the 13th century. Anacletus II, who was pope from 1130 to 1138, was of Jewish descent and was called *Judaeo-pontifex* (the Jewish pope); he may have inspired the legend.

2415

Pope Joan (Yahweh has been gracious). In medieval legend, a woman who disguised herself as a man and was elected pope as John VIII. Joan was English by birth. She disguised herself as a man when she went to Athens to study. She then went on to Rome where, according to Bartolomeo Plantina in his *Lives of the Popes*, "she met with few that could equal, much less go beyond her, even in the knowledge of Holy Scriptures; and by her learned and ingenious readings and disputations, she acquired so great a respect and authority that upon the death of Leo . . . by common consent she was chosen pope in his place." As she was going to the Lateran Church for a service, labor pains came upon her, and she died after having been pope for a little over two years. The legend inspired Emmanuel Royidis's novel *Pope Joan*, translated into English by Lawrence Durrell.

2416

Popol Vuh (book of the community?). Sacred book of the ancient Quiché Maya Indians of Guatemala.

The *Popol Vuh* was first written down in the Quiché language, but in Latin characters, sometime in the middle of the 16th century by an unknown Mayan convert to Christianity. The now-lost manuscript was copied at the end of the 17th century by Father Francisco Ximénez, a parish priest of the village of Santo Tomás Chichicastenango in the highlands of Guatemala. The work was rediscovered by the Austrian scholar Carl Scherzer in 1857. The *Popol Vuh* is divided into four parts. The first deals with the creation of the world. The second and third books are concerned with the heroes of the Indians, such as Hunahpú and Xbalanqué. The last section gives myths of cult origins, accounts of tribal wars, and records of historic rulers. Tales from the *Popol Vuh* were used by Charles Finger in his *Tales from Silver Lands*.

2417

Poro. In African cult (Mende of Sierra Leone), a group of secret societies. They serve a variety of functions, including the initiation of youths into manhood during puberty rituals and the perpetuation of old customs. The society is arranged in a hierarchy controlled by the elders of the community. Women may join, but rarely become leaders. The members meet at a secret location that they refer to as a "sacred bush," located near the spot where the founder of their group is buried. The masked spirit of the society is the Gbeni, which may be viewed only by fellow members. A society similar to this one, used for the initiation of girls, is the Sande.

2418

Po' Sandy. In American folklore, a runaway slave who was transformed into a tree in order to escape capture. Charles W. Chesnutt's *Po' Sandy* narrates the tale.

2419

Poseidon (he who gives drink from wooded mountain). In Greek mythology, one of the 12 Olympian gods, god of the sea, earthquakes, and horses; son of Cronus and Rhea; brother of Zeus, Demeter, Hades, Hera, and Hestia; identified by the Romans with their god Neptune. Poseidon ruled the Mediterranean and the Black Sea; rivers not navigated by the Greeks were ruled by Oceanus and Pontus, the latter also a Titan god as old as Oceanus. Poseidon and his wife, Amphitrite, a daughter of Nereus, lived in a palace of gold at the bottom of the sea. When the god appeared in his golden chariot, drawn by horses with brass hooves and golden manes, the waters grew calm, though he could raise sudden storms or cause shipwrecks. Black bulls were sacrificed to him. Poseidon and Athena had a contest to determine who would rule Athens. It was agreed that the deity who could create the most useful gift for humankind should rule Athens. Poseidon, striking a stone with his trident, produced the horse. Athena, however, invented the olive tree, and the city was awarded to her patronage because the olive branch was a symbol of peace and the horse a symbol of war. Poseidon also lost in his attempt to win Argos from Hera and Corinth from the sun god Helios. During the Trojan War Poseidon sided with the Greeks. Before the war Poseidon and Apollo had to build the walls of Troy as a punishment for offending Zeus. When the walls were completed, Laomedon, the ruler, refused to pay the gods. In revenge Poseidon sent a monster to kill the Trojans. To appease the angry god, Laomedon offered his daughter Hesione as a sacrifice, but Heracles saved the girl. Never forgetting the wrong done him, Poseidon aided the Greeks in the Trojan War until Troy was burned to the ground. Like his brother Zeus, Poseidon loved to have numerous mistresses, among them Gaea, Demeter, Aphrodite, the Gorgon Medusa and many nymphs. Among his numerous offspring were Amyous, Antaeus, Arion, Pegasus, Polyphemus, and Triton. Poseidon appears or is cited in Homer's *Iliad* and *Odyssey*; Hesiod's *Theogony*; Vergil's *Aeneid*; Ovid's *Metamorphoses*; Spenser's *Faerie Queene*; Shakespeare's *Coriolanus* (3.1.256), *The Tempest* (5.1.35), and *Cymbeline* (3.1.20); and Pope's *Rape of the Lock* (5.50), as well as works by Milton, Jonson, Beaumont and Fletcher; and W. B. Yeats among others. Most of these cite him under his Latin name form, Neptune. In ancient Greek and Roman art Poseidon is portrayed as a strong older man with thick, curly hair and beard, holding a trident (three-pronged fork) and with a dolphin nearby, often with his wife, Amphitrite, and sometimes with Triton, one of his many sons. His contest with Athena for Athens is featured on the west pediment of the Parthenon. One of his most famous temples is on the

Poseidon rising from the sea (John Flaxman)

promontory of Sunium in Attica, dating from the fifth century B.C.E.

Poseidon (Neptune) riding on a Hippocampus

2420

Potato. An edible tuber of the nightshade family, at one time condemned by 18th-century Scots because it was not mentioned in the Bible and therefore was considered unholy. It was once believed to be poisonous, and in Elizabethan England it was believed to restore sexual potency. In Shakespeare's *Troilus and Cressida* (5:2) Diomedes says to Cressida, "How the devil luxury, with his fat rump and potato-finger, tickles these together! Fry, lechery, fry!" In this context potato-finger means penis.

2421

Pothos. In Greek mythology, personification of longing and desire; companion of Aphrodite.

2422

Potkoorok. In Australian mythology, mischievous spirits who play tricks on fishermen.

2423

Potok-Mikhailo-Ivanovich. In Russian folklore, a *bogatyr* or epic hero with superhuman strength, who appears in the *byliny*, the epic songs, as well as in many folktales.

When Potok-Mikhailo-Ivanovich's wife died, he went to her grave with his horse and sat there all night. At midnight a great serpent appeared, all aflame. Potok-Mikhailo-Ivanovich killed the monster with his sharp saber and cut off its head. He then took the head and anointed the body of his wife with its blood, and she immediately was restored to life. The two were allowed by the priest "to live as formerly." When Potok-Mikhailo-Ivanovich died, his wife "was buried alive with him in the dank earth."

2424

Potoyan. In Australian mythology, a tribal name for the evil spirit. He can be driven away by fire because he is afraid of it.

2425

Pradyumna. In Hindu mythology, a son of Krishna (an incarnation of the god Vishnu). Pradyumna, when he was six days old, was stolen by the demon Sambara and thrown into the ocean, where he was swallowed by a fish. When the fish was later caught, Pradyumna was released. He was brought up by Maya-devi (Maya-vati), a mistress of the demon Sambara. Later, when Pradyumna grew up, he challenged Sambara and killed him. Pradyumna himself was killed in the presence of his father, Krishna, during a drunken brawl.

In a variant myth Pradyumna is said to be a form of the god of love, Kama, while in the epic poem *The Mahabharata* Pradyumna is said to be the son of the god Brahma.

2426

Prajapati (lord of creatures). In Hindu mythology, an epithet of the god Brahma or an epithet applied to sages who were the progenitors of the human race. Their number varies from 7 to 21 in different accounts. In the Hindu epic poem *The Mahabharata*, for example, there are 21 Prajapatis, whereas in the *Vedas* the term is also applied to Indra, the storm god, and to the 10 mind-born sons of Brahma. The term, therefore, is fluid in its uses. The major Prajapatis are Angiras, Atri (an eater), Atharvan, Bhrigu, Daksha, Kasshhyapa, Kratu, Marichi, Narada (bringing to man?), Pulaha, Pulastya, Pracetas, Vasishtha (most wealthy), Viswamitra (friend of all), Viraj (ruling afar), and Virana (heroic).

2427

Prakriti. In Buddhist legend, a woman of low caste who fell in love with Ananda, a disciple of the Buddha. She followed Ananda and met the Buddha, who converted her to his doctrine.

2428

Prana (breath of life). In Hinduism, a name for the supreme spirit. The sacred Atharva-Veda calls for

"Reverence to Prana, to whom all this universe is subject, who has become lord of the all, on whom the all is supported."

2429
Pratyeka-Buddha (isolated enlightened one). In Buddhism, a Buddha who obtains Enlightenment without a teacher and cannot proclaim his Enlightenment. Sometimes the term Silent Buddha is used. In Pali it is called Pacceka-Buddha.

2430
Prayer Wheel (precious Dharma wheel). In Tibetan Buddhism, a wheel containing either passages from sacred writings or a series of mantras, such as the *Om Mani Padme Hum*, an untranslatable formula representing the entire Buddhist teaching, learned in childhood and repeated constantly up to one's death. Prayer wheels can be small enough to be held in one's hand or taller than a man's head; they can be made from any material, including wood, ivory, copper, and silver. A prayer wheel is a means of disseminating the spiritual power of a mantra, which is a sound or sequence of sounds that sacramentally effect what it signifies. Thus, the mantra *Om-Ah-Hum* signifies the entry of Buddha-nature into the manifest work and effects the manifestation when it is recited or otherwise disseminated. The power of the mantra is made available whenever a prayer wheel is rotated, but its fullest effect is felt by those who through faith open themselves to its power.

2431
Prester John. In medieval legend, a Christian king and priest who ruled over a country in Asia or Africa. In the 12th century letters purportedly written by Prester John circulated in Europe. He describes his country, writing that "our land streams with honey, and is overflowing with milk." Prester John also appears in medieval Jewish legend. Joshua Lorki, a Jewish physician to Pope Benedict XIII, wrote that some people "live in a place under the yoke of a strange people . . . governed by a Christian chief, Preste-Cuan [Prester John]." Benjamin of Tudela, another Jew, traveled in the East between 1159 and 1173 and wrote that Prester John was a Jewish king who ruled with great splendor over a realm inhabited by the Jews. According to the later account of Sir John Mandeville in his *Travels*, Prester John was a lineal descendant of Ogier the Dane, who reached the North of India with 15 of his barons.

Iris advising Priam to obtain Hector's body (John Flaxman)

Marco Polo, in his *Travels*, says Genghis Khan "fought against Prester John, and, after a desperate fight, overcame and slew him."

Preta (ghosts). In Hindu mythology, a ghost or evil spirit animating a dead body and haunting cemeteries.

Priam (redeemed). In Greek mythology, king of Troy; son of Laomedon and Strymo (or Placid); husband of Hecuba; father of 50 sons and 50 daughters, among whom were Hector, Paris, Troilus, Cassandra, and Creusa. When Heracles took the city of Troy, Priam was one of the prisoners. His sister Hesione redeemed him, and he changed his original name, Podarces, to Priam (redeemed). Heracles later placed him on the throne of Troy. Priam had earlier married Arisba but divorced her to marry Hecuba. He then wished to recover his sister Hesione, whom Heracles had carried to Greece and married to his friend Telamon. To carry out his plan, Priam manned a fleet and gave his son Paris command of it. But Paris returned with Helen, wife of Menelaus, as a prize for choosing Aphrodite to receive the golden apple in the incident of the Judgment of Paris, and thus the seeds of the Trojan War were sown. In Homer's *Iliad* Priam is portrayed as an old man. When his son Hector is killed by Achilles, Priam goes to the Greek hero and begs the body of his dead son. According to post-Homeric accounts, Priam was killed at the altar of Zeus by Neopotolemus. Among ancient authors Priam appears in Homer's *Iliad*, Vergil's *Aeneid* (book 2), and Ovid's *Metamorphoses* (books 12, 13). In English literature references to Priam are found in the works of Chaucer, Spenser, Shakespeare, Milton, Dryden, Pope, Byron, Wordsworth, Tennyson, Keats, William Morris, D. G. Rossetti, Robert Bridges, and John Masefield. Priam appears in a series of wall frescoes in Pompeii. Berlioz's *The Trojans* and Tippets' *King Priam* are operas that feature the tragic king.

Priam visiting Achilles

Priapus (pruner of the pear tree). In Greek and Roman mythology, god of sexual generation in animals and humans; son of Dionysus and Aphrodite. Priapus also was called Lutinus and Mutinus by the Romans. Originally a god from the Hellespont region, his cult spread to Greece, Alexandria, and Italy. Donkeys, symbols of lust, were sacrificed to him. Horace, Tibullus, and Martial wrote of him, and he appears in Petronius' novel *Satyricon*, in which the hero Encolpius' inability to have an erection is a punishment of Priapus. Priapus was portrayed with an erection, and statues of him were placed in gardens. He is mentioned in Chaucer's *Parliament of Fowls*, Shelley's *Witch of Atlas*, Swinburne's *Dolores*, D. H. Lawrence's *Hymn to Priapus*, and T. S. Eliot's *Mr. Apollinax*. Poussin's *Dance in Honor of Priapus* portrays the god as a *Herm*, a square pillar supporting a bust of Hermes and having erect male genitals. Herms often stood at the crossroads in Greek cities as a protection. A sculpture series was designed by Poussin for the gardens at Versailles in which Pan, Faunus, Heracles, Flora, Pomona, and Venus are portrayed.

Princess on the Pea. Literary folktale by Hans Christian Andersen about a prince who wants to marry.

A young woman stops at a castle and asks for lodging for the night. She claims to be a princess, and the prince falls in love with her and wants to marry her. The prince's mother, fearing she might be an impostor, devises a test to see if she has the true sensitivity of a princess. The old queen has the guest's bed prepared with 20 mattresses and 20 eiderdowns. Underneath the bottom mattress she places a pea, saying that if the girl is a true princess she will be able to detect it. The next morning the princess complains that she was unable to sleep because there was something hard underneath the mattress. She is proclaimed a true princess and marries the prince.

The Grimms' *Die Erbensprobe* also has a version of the tale, and there are variants of it in Hungary, Greece, Rumania, Arabia, and India. The tale furnished the plot for the musical comedy *Once upon a Mattress*, starring Carol Burnett, in which the pea under the mattress was supplemented with pots and pans by the prince's partisans, who were determined to see him marry.

Priya-vrata. In Hindu mythology, a son of the god Brahma. Priya-vrata was unhappy about the fact that only half the earth at a time was lit by the sun. One day he "followed the sun seven times round the earth in his own flaming car of equal velocity, like another celestial orb, resolved to turn night into day," according to the *Bhagavata Purana*. Before his father, Brahma, stopped him, "the ruts which were formed by the motion of his chariot wheels were the seven oceans. In this way the seven continents of the earth were formed."

Procrustes (stretcher-out). In Greek mythology, robber, tyrant of Attica; son of Poseidon; also called Damastes or Polypemon. He tied travelers to his iron bed, cutting off their legs to make them fit if they were too long or stretching them if too short. He was killed by the hero Theseus, who forced Procrustes to lie in his own bed. "Procrustean" has come to symbolize tyranny and enforced labor. Apollodorus' *Bibliotheca* (Library), Ovid's *Metamorphoses* (book 7), and *Heroides* (book 2) all deal with Procrustes. His son Sinis, by Sylea, was also a murderer. He would tie victims between two bent pines on the ground. When he released the trees the victim was torn apart. He was called Pityocamptes (pine-bender) and was also killed by Theseus.

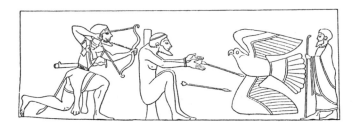

Prometheus bound by Zeus

2438

Prometheus (forethought). In Greek mythology, Titan culture hero who gave mankind fire; invented architecture, astronomy, medicine, navigation, metalworking, and writing; son of the Titan Iapetos and either the goddess Themis (later married to Zeus) or Clymene (Asia), an Oceanide; brother of Atlas Epimetheus (afterthought), and Menoetlus (defying fate or ruined strength), married to Hesione; father of Deucalion by Hesione or Pronoea.

After the gods had defeated the Titans in the battle to rule the universe, the gods negotiated with man about the honor man was to pay to the gods. Since Prometheus, though a Titan, had sided with the gods, he was chosen to decide how sacrificial victims were to be offered. Prometheus cut up an ox and divided it into two parts. He wrapped the choice cuts in the skin of the ox and placed the stomach on top of it to make it look unappetizing. The remainder of the animal, which was made up of bones, Prometheus covered with fat to make it look

desirable. Zeus had to make the choice of which portion was to be set aside for the gods. Zeus knew that Prometheus had set up a trick but still chose the heap of bones and fat. Then, as a punishment to mankind, Zeus deprived them of the gift of fire, leaving them in darkness and cold.

That did not stop Prometheus, who, according to Hesiod's *Theogony*, "cheated him, and stole the far seen splendor of untiring fire in a hollow fennelstalk" and gave it to man. Zeus, angered that man now had fire, called on the smith god Hephaestus to make a beautiful woman of clay, whom Zeus called Pandora. Until that time man had lived alone. Zeus called on the goddess Athena, who, according to Hesiod, "girded and arrayed Pandora in silver-white raiment (and) placed around her head lovely garlands freshbudding with meadow-flowers." Hermes, the messenger of the gods, then carried to Pandora a jar (or box) as her dowry. In the jar was every evil that was to come into the world. Pandora was brought before Epimetheus. Though Prometheus had warned his brother not to accept any gifts from Zeus, Epimetheus was so moved by Pandora's beauty that he married her. Pandora removed the lid from the jar and out flew all the evils, troubles, and diseases that were unknown to man until that time. Only Hope remained in the jar when Pandora closed it again. The misogynist Hesiod wrote: "Just so to mortal men high-thundering Zeus gave woman as an evil." But Zeus was not satisfied with punishing man; he now turned on Prometheus and had him bound in adamantine chains to a pillar, with an eagle (or vulture) who ate Prometheus' liver each day. The liver was restored at night only to be eaten again the next day.

Epimetheus accepts Pandora from Mercury

In a variant myth recorded in Ovid's *Metamorphoses* (book 1), Prometheus is made the actual creator of humankind: "Prometheus tempere'd into paste,/ And, mix't with living streams, the godlike image cast" (John Dryden translation). Goethe used this image in his poem *Prometheus*, which was set to music by Franz Schubert and Hugo Wolf. The combination of defiance of omnipresent authority and godly powers of creation have made Prometheus one of the most popular subjects in Western art, music, and literature. Among the most important works is Aeschylus' *Prometheus Bound*, part of a trilogy. The other two plays in the trilogy, *Prometheus the Firebringer* and *Prometheus Released* have been lost. Other works include Shelley's *Prometheus Unbound*, Beethoven's *Die Geschöpfe des Prometheus* (The Creatures of Prometheus) (1801); Alexander Scriabin's *Prometheus, Poem of Fire*; Franz Liszt's symphonic poem *Prometheus* (1850); as well as his setting of texts of the German Romantic poet Herder, who wrote a play *Prometheus*; and André Gide's *Le Prométhée mal Enchaîné*, in which the eagle or vulture is kept as a pet by Prometheus. Others who have treated the theme are Lord Byron, Henry Wadsworth Longfellow, Robert Bridges, James Russell Lowell, and Robert Graves. Artists using Prometheus as a subject include Piero di Cosimo, Rubens, Jordaens, and Jacob Epstein. The best-known modern sculpture is in Rockefeller Center in New York City and portrays Prometheus giving the gift of fire to mankind.

2439

Prose Edda. Handbook of Norse mythology for poets, written by Snorri Sturluson (1179–1241 C.E.). The work is sometimes called the *Younger Edda* to distinguish it from the *Poetic Edda* or *Elder Edda*.

The *Prose Edda* was designed as a handbook for poets who wished to compose in the style of the scalds of the Viking ages. It consists of three parts. The first part, "Gylfaginning" (the deluding of Gylfi), tells the myths of the Norse gods. It is often our major source for the tales. The second part,

Prose Edda (W.G. Collingwood)

"Skaldskaparmal" (poetic diction), consists mainly of a catalog of kennings (figurative expressions of various kinds), whose use in ancient Viking poetry is illustrated by numerous examples from old poems. It also contains some mythological and legendary tales. The third part, "Hattatal" (account of meters), is a

Prometheus forming man out of clay

poem Snorri composed about King Haakon and Earl (later Duke) Skuli Baroarson, between 1221 and 1223. This is made up of some 100 stanzas and is accompanied by a prose commentary on the variations of meter and style exemplified by each verse.

The major interest of the *Prose Edda* today is the first part, which deals with tales of the deities of Norse mythology. The *Prose Edda* had a major influence on Matthew Arnold's narrative poem *Balder Dead*.

2440
Proteus (first man). In Greek mythology, sea god; the old man of the sea; son of Oceanus and Tethys. He had the gift of prophecy and the ability to change his shape until caught and held firmly down. Homer's *Odyssey* (book 4) and Ovid's *Metamorphoses* (book 8) deal with Proteus. In Spenser's *Faerie Queene* (book 1) the great deceiver Archimago can take "As many formes and shapes in seeming wise/ As ever Proteus to himselfe could make." Milton's *Comus* calls Proteus "the Carpathian wizard," referring to Vergil's comment in the *Fourth Georgic* that the sea god lived most of the time in the Carpathian Sea between Crete and Rhodes. Other poets who have used Proteus are Pope in *The Dunciad*, Archibald MacLeish in *Men of My Century Loved Mozart*; Rolfe Humphries in *Proteus, or the Shapes of Conscience*; and Wordsworth in *The World is Too Much with Us*.

2441
Pryderi (anxiety). In Celtic mythology, hero who was the son of Pwyll, the god of Arawn, the underworld, and Rhiannon, the "great queen." As a child Pryderi was stolen by Teyrnon Twry Bliant, a ruler of part of Wales lying between the Wye and the Usk. He was given the name Gwri (he of the golden hair), but when he was returned to his parents he was named Pryderi. Later in life Pryderi exchanged some valuable swine for illusory horses and hounds offered by Gwydion, the British king and magician. A fight ensued, and Pryderi was killed.
Variant spelling: Phyderi.

2442
Psyche (soul). In Greek and Roman mythology, a girl loved by Eros (Cupid), who was god of love; mother of Voluptas, who was goddess of pleasure. Psyche was a beautiful girl, so admired by many young men that they neglected the worship of Aphrodite, goddess of love. Angry, Aphrodite sent her son Eros to cause Psyche to fall in love with an ugly monster, but instead Eros fell in love with Psyche. He had her sent to a secret palace and made love to her each night under cover of darkness, telling her she must not look upon him in the light.

Curious about her lover, Psyche, carrying a lamp, came into the chamber when Eros was asleep and dropped hot oil on him, causing him to flee. Psyche went in search of him, but Aphrodite thwarted her with a series of mishaps. In the end the two lovers were reunited and married. Apuleius' novel *The Golden Ass*; William Morris's *Cupid and Psyche*, part of *The Earthly Paradise*; and Keats's *Ode to Psyche* all deal with the subject. Numerous paintings and sculptures have portrayed Psyche and Eros, including a Hellenistic marble group called *Invention of the Kiss*, Raphael's frescoes for the Loggia di Psyche in the Farnese Palace in Rome; sculptures by Canova and Rodin, and a painting by Edward Burne-Jones called *Psyche in Her Chamber*. César Franck wrote a symphonic poem called *Psyché*.

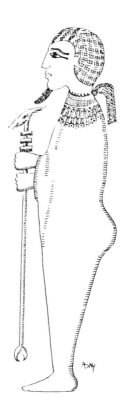

Ptah

2443
Ptah. In Egyptian mythology, chief god of Memphis; the craft god, protector of artisans; his wife was Sakhmet; his son, Nefertem. Ptah was identified by the Greeks with their god Hephaestus and by the Romans with their god Vulcan.

Ptah filled many roles in Egyptian belief. He was the master craftsman who brought forth everything, according to one myth. He fashioned the gods, made the cities, founded the *nomes* (provinces), installed the gods in their shrines, and established offerings for them and made likenesses of them to their satisfaction. In Egyptian art Ptah was portrayed as a bearded man with a tight-fitting cap and a tight-fitting garment from which his hands extended. In Verdi's *Aïda* the priests call upon Ptah in the last scene of the opera.

2444

P'u Hsien. In Chinese Buddhism, a Bodhisattva who becomes patron god of Mount O-mei in Szechuan, portrayed with a greenish face, wearing a yellow robe with a red collar, and riding on an elephant. At one time the elephant was a man who battled and was defeated by P'u Hsien. P'u Hsien is derived from the Sanskrit name A Samantabhadra, the Bodhisattva of the protection of worldly activity or of religious practice.

2445

Puloman. In Hindu mythology, a demon killed by Indra, the storm god, when he cursed Indra for raping his daughter Sachi.

2446

Pundjel. In Australian mythology, a creator god who first created man. He made the first couple, two men, from clay on pieces of bark. The black creature was called Kookinberrook, the lighter-colored creature, Berrokborn. Pundjel breathed on them and danced them to life. Then Pallian, the brother of Pundjel, discovered two female forms gradually emerging head first from muddy waters. One was Kunewarra; the other was Kuurook. They became the wives of the first two men. The men were given spears; the women, digging sticks. In time children were born, and the earth was inhabited, but Pundjel and Pallian found the children to be evil and cut them into pieces. A great wind then came and scattered the pieces, and they were turned into whole people.

2447

Puntan. In Micronesian mythology, preexistent creator god. When Puntan was about to die, he ordered his sister to create from his body a place for humans to live. His breast and back became the earth and sky; his eyes, the sun and moon; and his eyebrows, the rainbow.

2448

Purah (fire?). In Jewish folklore, angel associated with the close of the Sabbath. Purah appears in Isaac Bashevis Singer's short story "Jachid and Jechidah."
Variant spellings: Puta, Poteh.

2449

Puranas (ancient). Popular Hindu texts, later than the epics, in which the myths of the gods are given.

There are 18 commonly accepted Puranas, of varying length and content. Usually a purana is devoted to the praise of one god. The Puranas reflect popular folk beliefs and the various cults that arose in India over the centuries. They are as follows:

Vishnu Purana, in which Vishnu is praised as the creator, sustainer, and controller of the world.

Narada Purana (Naradiya), in which the sage Narada describes the duties of man in society.

Bhagavata Purana or *Srimad Bhagavatam*, which narrates the life of Krishna (an incarnation of the god Vishnu).

Garuda Purana, named after the fantastic bird Garuda, which carries Vishnu; it deals with death rites.

Padma Purana, which describes the creation of the world when it was a golden *padma* (lotus) and describes Patala, the lowest part of the underworld.

Varaha Purana, a revelation of Vishnu as the boar incarnation, Varaha.

Matsya Purana, a revelation of Vishnu as the Matysa (fish) incarnation.

Kurma

Kurma Purana, a revelation of Vishnu as the Kurma (tortoise) incarnation.

Lingam Purana, which explains the worship of the lingam (phallus) of the god Shiva.

Vayu Purana, devoted to the god Shiva.

Skanda Purana, devoted to Skanda, god of war and a son of Shiva.

Agni Purana, a mixture of various matters told by the fire god, Agni, to the sage Vasishtha.

Brahma Purana, devoted to the sun god Surya.

Brahamanda Purana, devoted to the *anda* (egg) of the god Brahma.

Brahma-Vaivasvata Purana, devoted to the worship of Krishna and his mistress Radha.

Markandeya Purana, which tells how birds recite the sacred *Vedas* as well as the myth of Shakti, as mother goddess, who saved the earth from demons.

Bhavishya Purana, a handbook of rites.

Vamana Purana, a revelation of Vishnu as the dwarf incarnation, Vamana.

2450

Purusha (man). In Hindu mythology, the primeval male, according to some accounts. The title is sometimes applied to the god Brahma, and Purushottama (best of men) is used for the god Vishnu or for any deity regarded as supreme.

2451

Pushan (nourisher). In Hindu mythology, a sun god, keeper of herds and bringer of prosperity. Pushan protects and multiplies cattle, is a guide on roads and journeys, and is patron god of conjurers, especially those who discover stolen goods. He is also connected with marriage and is invoked to bless the bride. Pushan is toothless because the god Shiva knocked out his teeth. As a result he eats gruel and is known as Karambhad (pap). In Indian art Pushan is often portrayed carrying an ox goad in a chariot drawn by goats.

2452

Pushpa-danta. In Hindu mythology, one of the eight elephants that protect the eight points of the compass. Pushpa-danta is also an attendant of Shiva, condemned to be reborn as a man for recounting a private conversation between Shiva and his wife Parvati.

2453

Puss in Boots. Popular world folktale, best known in Perrault's version, *Chat botté* (1697), in which a cat aids his master by devising ruses for his enemies. In most Western European versions the cat is the animal helper, but a fox appears in Eastern European variants, a jackal in Indian tales, and a monkey in Philippine versions.

2454

Pu-tai Ho-shang (hemp bag master). In Chinese Buddhism, an eccentric monk regarded as a manifestation of Maitreya, the Buddha of the Future, por-

trayed as a fat man with the upper part of his body exposed. Called the Laughing Buddha, he is often shown with a bundle of papers and a pilgrim's staff or a fly-whisk. He is also shown carrying a hemp bag and surrounded by children. The hemp bag is said to contain junk he picked up. He called it "The Bag of Wonderful Things," and the children would crowd around as he drew mysterious objects out of it and gave them away. In Japanese mythology he is called Hotei o-sho.

2455

Putana (stinking). In Hindu mythology, a demoness who attempted to kill the infant Krishna (an incarnation of the god Vishnu) by suckling him to death. Her breasts were filled with poison, but Krishna suckled and dried them up, and she died. In Hindu folklore Putana is regarded as a demoness who causes disease in children.

Four-handed Avalokiteshvara

2456

Pyan-ras-gsigs. In Tibetan Buddhism, name of Avalokiteshvara, the Bodhisattva of Perfect Compassion, one of the five Dhyani-Bodhisattvas, who is known as Kuan-Yin in China and Kwannon in Japan; also an independent entity. In Pure Land Buddhist iconography he is, together with Mahasthemaprapta, one of the two Bodhisattvas attendant on Amitabha Buddha. He is recognized by the small figure of Amitabha in his crown and is often shown holding a lotus, in which the devotee is reborn into the Pure Land.

2457

Pyerun (to strike, i.e., thunder). In Slavic mythology, god of thunder and war. He had a golden beard and rode a flaming chariot across the sky, piercing the clouds with his miraculous bow. The oak was his sacred tree.

The idol of Pyerun was erected under the open sky in Kiev, Russia, and served by the *kniaz* (a prince), the military chief of the city. It is believed, therefore, that his cult was in many ways a warrior cult. When Prince Vladimir of Kiev (who was later sainted by the Russian church) was converted to Byzantine orthodoxy in 988, he ordered the image of Pyerun to be cut down and thrown into the river. The god's attributes were transferred to other figures in Russian folklore and mythology.

In White Russian mythology Pyerun lost his chariot but still roamed the sky with his bow. The folk hero Ilya Muromets, though a Christian, possessed some of the attributes of Pyerun, and the prophet Elijah from the Old Testament also was identified with the god because he ascended to heaven in a fiery chariot (2 Kings 2:11). (In the Russian church Elijah is called Iliya the Prophet, and his feast day is 20 July.)

Variants of Pyerun's name among Slavic peoples are Perkunas, the Lithuanian god who created the universe from the warmth of his body; Perkons, the Lettish god of thunder and lightning; Piorun among the Poles; Peranu among the Bohemians and Peroon among the Serbians.

Variant spellings: Perun, Peruw.

2458

Pygmalion (shaggy fist). In Greek mythology, a king (or sculptor) of Cyprus, who made a statue of a woman and fell in love with it. Pygmalion prayed to Aphrodite, goddess of love, to help him, and she turned the statue into a living woman, called Galatea. Galatea bore Pygmalion's son, Paphus. The story is told in Ovid's *Metamorphoses* (book 10), which in part inspired the final scene of the living statue in Shakespeare's *Winter's Tale*. A one-act opera by Rameau also treats the tale. William Morris's *Earthly Paradise* recounts the myth, and George Bernard Shaw's *Pygmalion* also uses it. Shaw's play was the basis for the musical play *My Fair Lady*. The movie *One Touch of Venus*, with a score by Kurt Weill and starring Ava Gardner, also uses the story, but in the movie it is a statue of Venus that comes alive in a department store.

2459

Pyramid Texts. Ancient Egyptian texts found in the pyramid of King Unas of the Fifth Dynasty, as well as in other pyramids of the Sixth Dynasty. The texts, engraved on the walls, consist of prayers, magic formulas, and various rubrics to help the deceased in his journey to the other world.

2460

Pyramus and Thisbe. In Greek and Roman mythology, two lovers. Pyramus and Thisbe lived in adjoining houses in Babylon. They were forbidden to see or speak to each other by their feuding families. They managed, however, to whisper through a chink in the wall separating the two properties. One day they agreed to meet at night in a wooded spot outside the city. Thisbe, arriving first, was frightened by a lion and fled, dropping her scarf. Pyramus, reaching the spot later, found the lion's footprints and the torn scarf. Believing Thisbe dead, he killed himself by falling on his sword. Thisbe returned, found Pyramus' body, and killed herself. From their blood the mulberry tree grew blood-red fruit. The tale is told in Ovid's *Metamorphoses* (book 4) and is played out by Bottom the weaver and his friends in Shakespeare's *A Midsummer Night's Dream*. Pyramus and Thisbe are also reminiscent of Shakespeare's *Romeo and Juliet*. The tale is also told by Chaucer in his *Legend of Good Women* and by Gower in *Confessio Amantis*. Poussin painted a canvas called *Pyramus and Thisbe*.

2461

Pythia. In Greek ritual, priestess of Apollo at Delphi, who delivered oracles called the Pythia. Her name is derived, according to some accounts, from Python (serpent), a giant snake that was produced by Gaea, goddess of earth, and haunted Mount Parnassus. The monster was slain in the cave at Delphi by Apollo with his first arrow. A sacred rite, called the Pythian Games, was enacted in ancient Greece to commemorate the event. A bronze column in the form of a three-headed snake supporting a gold tripod was placed at the site. The myth is told in the Homeric Hymn to Pythian Apollo (attributed to Homer but not by him) and Ovid's *Metamorphoses* (book 1). Keats's *Hymn to Apollo* and Byron's *Childe Harold* (III, 81) make reference to Pythia.

Q

Qat. [2462] In Melanesian mythology, hero, trickster, and creator god, whose companion is Marawa, a spider.

Qat, according to some accounts, made the first humans by shaping wood into men and women and beguiling them into life. His companion, Marawa, did the same. But when Marawa's figures began to move, he buried them in a pit. Seven days later Marawa dug them up and found only rotting corpses. That is why there is death in the world. In other accounts Marawa is a wood sprite who aids Qat in various adventures. Once he saves him from his evil brothers, who try to crush him to death. Another myth tells how Qat brought night into the world. His brothers complained because the sun always shone and they could not rest. So Qat went to Oong (night) for help. He then told his brothers how to fall asleep. When the cock crowed, he took a red flint stone and cut Oong, causing the dawn. In other sections of Melanesia, Qat's adventures are credited to Tangaro.

Questing Beast. [2463] In Arthurian legend, a monster called Glatisaunt, which had the head of a serpent, the buttocks of a lion, the body of a leopard, and the feet of a deer. It made "the noise of 30 couple of hounds questing [baying]," according to Malory's *Morte d'Arthur*. The Questing Beast was hunted by King Pellinore, who was later killed by Sir Gawaine to avenge the death of Gawaine's father, King Lot.

Quetzalcoatl [2464] (feathered serpent, precious serpent, precious twin). In Toltec mythology, wind god. Another Quetzalcoatl was a culture hero. In his purely mythical form the god Quetzalcoatl was one of four brothers born in the 13th heaven. Of the four, one was called the black and one the red Texcatlipoca, and the fourth was Huitzilopochtli. Texcatlipoca (the black and red are combined) was the wisest. He knew all thoughts and could see into the future. At a certain time the four gathered together and consulted concerning creation. The work was left to Quetzalcoatl and Huitzilopochtli. First they made fire, then half a sun, the heavens, the waters, and a great fish called Cipactli; and from Cipactli's flesh they made the solid earth.

The first people were Cipactonal, a man, and Oxomuco, a woman. They had a son, but there was no wife for him to marry, so the four gods made one out of the hair taken from the head of their divine mother, Zochiquetzal.

The half sun created by Quetzalcoatl and Huitzilopochtli was a poor light for the world, and the four brothers came together to find a means of adding another half to the sun. Not waiting for their decision, Tezcatlipoca transformed himself into a sun. The other brothers then filled the world with giants, who tore up the trees with their hands. After some time Quetzalcoatl took a stick and "with a blow of it knocked Tezcatlipoca from the sky into the waters." He then made himself the sun. Tezcatlipoca transformed himself into a tiger and emerged from the waves, attacking and devouring the giants; then, passing to the nocturnal heavens, he became the constellation of the Great Bear.

As the sun, Quetzalcoatl made the earth flourish, but Tezcatlipoca was merely biding his time. When the right moment came, Tezcatlipoca appeared in his tiger form and gave Quetzalcoatl such a blow with his paw that it hurled him from the skies. Quetzalcoatl then swept the earth with a violent tornado that destroyed all of the inhabitants except for a few "who were changed into monkeys." Then, when Tezcatlipoca placed Tlaloc, the rain god, as the sun in the heavens, Quetzalcoatl "poured a flood of fire upon the earth, drove Tlaloc from the sky, and placed in his stead, as sun, the goddess Chalchiutlicue, the Emerald Skirted, wife of Tlaloc." When she ruled as sun, the earth was flooded, and all humans were drowned again except for those who were changed into fishes. As a result, "the heavens themselves fell, and the sun and stars were alike quenched."

The two then realized that their struggle had to end, so they united "their efforts and raised again the sky, resting it on two mighty trees, the Tree of the Mirror (*tezcaquahuitl*) and the Beautiful Great Rose Tree (*quetzalveixochitl*) on which the concave heavens have ever since securely rested."

The earth still had no sun to light it, and the four brothers met again. They decided to make a sun, one that would "eat the hearts and drink the blood of victims, and there must be wars upon the earth, that these victims could be obtained for the sacrifice." Quetzalcoatl then built a great fire and took his son, born of his own flesh without any mother, and cast him into the flames, "whence he rose into the sky as the sun which lights the world." Tlaloc then threw his son into the flames, creating the moon.

The Quetzalcoatl of that myth is a god. Another Quetzalcoatl is a culture hero, a high priest of the city of Tula. He was the teacher of arts, the wise lawgiver, the virtuous prince, the master builder, and the merciful judge. He lived a life of fasting and prayer.

The hero (not the god) Quetzalcoatl either came as a stranger to the Aztecs from an unknown land or was born in Tula, where he reigned as priest-king. For many years he ruled the city and at last began to build a very great temple. While it was being constructed Texcatlipoca (who in other myths is a creator-trickster god but here is a demonic force, or sorcerer) came to Quetzalcoatl one day and told him that toward Honduras, in a place called Tlapallan, a house was ready for him. He should leave Tula and go to live and die in the new home.

Quetzalcoatl said that the heavens and the stars had already warned him that after four years he must leave, and he would therefore obey. He left with all of the inhabitants of Tula. Some he left in Cholula and others in Cempoal. At last he reached Tlapallan, and on the day he arrived he fell sick and died.

There is another, better-known account in the *Annals of Cuauhtitlan*. When those opposed to Quetzalcoatl did not succeed in their designs to rid themselves of his presence, they summoned Tezcatlipoca. He said: "We will give him a drink to dull his reason, and we will show him his own face in a mirror, and surely he will be lost."

Then Tezcatlipoca brewed an intoxicating drink, the pulque, and taking a mirror he wrapped it in a rabbit skin and went to Quetzalcoatl's house.

"Go tell your master," he said to the servants, "that I have come to show him his own flesh."

"What is this?" asked Quetzalcoatl when the message was delivered. "What does he call my own flesh? Go and ask him." But Tezcatlipoca said he would speak only with Quetzalcoatl. He was then admitted into the presence of Quetzalcoatl.

"Welcome, youth. You have troubled yourself much. Whence come you? What is this, my flesh, that you would show me?"

"My lord and priest," replied Tezcatlipoca, "I come from the mountainside of Nonoalco. Look now at your flesh; know yourself; see yourself as you are seen by others." And with that he handed him the mirror.

As soon as Quetzalcoatl saw his face in the mirror, he said: "How is it possible my subjects can look on me without affright? Well might they flee from me. How can a man remain among them filled as I am with foul sores, his face wrinkled and his aspect loathsome? I shall be seen no more: I shall no longer frighten my people."

But Texcatlipoca said he could conceal the defects on Quetzalcoatl's face. He painted the ruler's cheeks green and dyed his lips red. The forehead he colored yellow and, taking the feathers of the quetzal bird, he made a beard. Quetzalcoatl looked at himself in the mirror and was pleased with the artifice.

Then Tezcatlipoca took the strong pulque he had brewed and gave some to Quetzalcoatl, who became drunk. He called his attendants and asked that his sister Quetzalpetlatl come to him. She instantly obeyed and, drinking some of the pulque, also became drunk.

It is not clear whether Quetzalcoatl slept with his sister in the myth, but the next morning he said, "I have sinned, the stain on my name can never be erased. I am not fit to rule this people. Let them build for me a habitation deep underground; let them bury my bright treasures in the earth; let them throw the gleaming gold and shining stone into the holy fountain where I take my daily bath."

He then journeyed eastward to a place where the sky, land, and water met. There his attendants built a funeral pyre, and he threw himself into the flames. As his body burned his heart rose to heaven, and after four days he became the planet Venus, the Morning Star.

In a variant of the end of the legend, Quetzalcoatl departed on a raft toward the east, saying he would one day return. When Spanish conquistador Hernando Cortéz arrived in the 16th century, the Aztecs believed that their hero had returned to them as he had promised—a belief that helped seal their doom. The conflict between the two cultures is told in W. H. Prescott's *The History of The Conquest of Mexico*, the novels *The Fair God* by Lew Wallace and *Captain from Castile* by Samuel Shellabarger, which was made into a film.

2465

Quiracus, St. Third century. In Christian legend, bishop of Ostia, who was stabbed in the back and beheaded. His dog retrieved and returned his head, and he appears in medieval art holding his head in his hands. Feast, 23 August.

R

Ra

Ra (creator, creative power?). In Egyptian mythology, the major sun god, often merged with the god Amun, forming the composite god Amun-Ra.

2466

One of the first acts of creation in Egyptian mythology was the appearance of Ra's sun disk above the waters of Nun (chaos). Time was said to have begun with the first rising of Ra. Because the Egyptians believed that the sun was made of fire and could not have risen directly out of the waters of chaos without some means of conveyance, it was assumed that Ra made his journey over the waters in a boat. The morning boat was called Matet (becoming strong) and the evening boat, Semktet (becoming weak). The course of Ra was said to have been mapped out by the goddess Maat, who was the personification of physical and moral law. In the evening after the sun had set in the west, Ra entered Duat, the underworld. With the help of the gods there he successfully passed through that region in a boat and appeared in the sky the next morning. As he passed through Duat he gave air, light, and food to those who were condemned to live there. Two fishes, Abtu and Ant, swam before Ra's boat and acted as pilots.

Each morning just before he left Duat and was about to enter the sky, Ra engaged in a battle with Apophis, a giant serpent and night demon. Apophis' attacks failed because Ra cast a spell on him, making the monster incapable of moving. Then the supporters of the sun god bound Apophis in chains and hacked him to pieces, after which he was destroyed by the flames of Ra—symbolic of the sun destroying the vapors and dampness of the night. In the *Books of the Overthrowing of Apophis* a ritual is prescribed to be recited daily in the temple of Amun-Ra at Thebes. It cataloged in great detail the destruction that was to befall Apophis and his monstrous helpers, Sebau and Nak.

All of the kings of Egypt in the early empire believed themselves to be the sons of Ra. It was said that whenever the divine blood of the kings needed replenishing, the god took the form of the reigning king of Egypt and visited the queen in her chamber, becoming then the true father of the child born to her. When the child was born, it was regarded as the god incarnate. In due time it was presented to the sun god in his temple. This gave the priests of Ra great power in Egypt.

One myth, however, tells how Ra was almost destroyed by the goddess Isis, who sought his true name. The ancients believed that to possess the true name of a god enabled one to have power over him. Many gods had more than one name—one by which the god was generally known and another that might be called his real name, which he kept secret lest it come into the hands of his enemies, who would use it against him. Isis once wished to make Ra reveal to her his greatest and most secret name. "Cannot I by means of the sacred name of God make myself mistress of the earth and become a goddess of like rank and power to Ra in heaven and upon earth?" she asked. Using her magic skill, she made a venomous reptile out of dust mixed with Ra's spittle, and by uttering certain words of power over the reptile she made it sting Ra as he passed through the heavens. The sun god, finding himself on the point of death, was forced to reveal his hidden name. Having achieved her goal, Isis spoke an incantation that drained the poison from Ra's limbs, and the god recovered.

In the Fifth Dynasty, when the cult of the man-god Osiris spread over the delta region from Busiris (the northern center of the cult) and throughout Upper Egypt from Abydos (the southern center), the priests of the sun god fought to maintain Ra's authority. However, before the end of the Sixth Dynasty the cult of Osiris prevailed, and Ra was relegated to an inferior position, with the greatest of his attributes ascribed to Osiris. From the Twelfth

Dynasty onward all of the attributes of Ra were absorbed by Amun, who was the dominant god of Upper Egypt. During the 19th and 20th dynasties 75 forms of Ra were known, comprising part of a litany to Ra, which is believed to have been sung during services in the temples. The litany was painted on the walls of several tombs, such as those of Seti I and Rameses IV.

Ra was connected at a very early period with the hawk god Horus, who personified the height of heaven, and in Egyptian art Ra is usually portrayed as a hawk-headed man and sometimes simply in the form of a hawk. On his head he wears the disk of the sun encircled by a serpent. When he appears in human form, he holds the ankh, sign of life, in his right hand and a scepter in his left. Mau, the great cat, is sometimes equated with Ra. In this form he cuts off the head of the evil monster serpent Apophis.

Variant spellings: Re, Phra.

Eye of Ra

2467

Rabbi Eliezer. Jewish folktale found in the Talmud.

Rabbi Eliezer, who was as much distinguished by the greatness of his mind as by the extraordinary size of his body, once paid a visit to Rabbi Simon. The learned Simon received him most cordially and, filling a cup with wine, handed it to him. Eliezer took it and drank it off in one gulp. Another cup was poured, and it went just as quickly.

"Brother Eliezer," said Simon jestingly, "remember what the wise men have said on this subject of drinking?"

"I well remember," answered the corpulent Eliezer, "the saying of our instructors—that people ought not to take a cup at one draught; but," he added, "the wise men have not so defined their rule to admit of no exceptions. And in this instance, friend Simon, there are no less than three: the cup is small, the receiver large, and your wine delicious!"

2468

Rabi'a al-'Adawiya. 714–801 C.E. In Islamic legend, saint and mystic; born in a poor home, she was kidnapped and sold into slavery. She gained her freedom, however, and gathered around her a group of followers. Her life was one of extreme asceticism and

otherworldliness; she was noted especially for her sayings.

She is credited with many miracles, such as feeding a crowd on very little food. One legend tells of a camel that she restored to life after it had died during a pilgrimage. When she was dying she asked that all of her friends leave so that the messengers of Allah would have free access to her. Her friends could then hear her reciting the end of sura 89 of the Koran: "O thou my soul which art at rest, return unto thy Lord, well pleased with thy reward, and well pleasing unto Allah; enter among my servants; and enter my paradise."

She appeared in a vision after her death and told how she answered the angels Munkar and Nakir when they questioned her: "I said, return and tell your Lord, 'Notwithstanding the thousands and thousands and thousands of Thy creatures, Thou hast not forgotten a weak old woman. I, who had only Thee in all the world, have never forgotten Thee, that Thou shouldst ask, Who is thy Lord?'"

The tradition that angels appear to the soul immediately after death to impose a minor judgment before the final major judgment at the end of the world is a late Islamic belief.

2469

Rabican. In the Charlemagne cycle of legends, a horse that fed on air and was unsurpassed for swiftness. He appears in Ariosto's *Orlando Furioso*.

2470

Rachel (ewe, sheep). In the Bible, O.T., the younger daughter of Laban. Rachel was one of Jacob's wives and was the mother of Joseph and Benjamin. Jacob served his uncle Laban in Maran "twice seven" years in exchange for Rachel's hand. Rachel's marriage to Jacob was initially thwarted by her father, who wanted to marry off his elder daughter Leah. He tricked Jacob into marrying Leah, then had Jacob work a second seven-year period to obtain Rachel. After the marriage Rachel remained barren while Leah bore Jacob six sons and a daughter. In jealous desperation Rachel sent her handmaiden Billah to sleep with Jacob, and Billah bore two sons. Then Leah sent her handmaiden to Jacob, who also bore two sons. Finally, Yahweh blessed Jacob, and Rachel gave birth to Joseph. Rachel died at Eprath giving birth to a second son, Benjamin. Jacob erected a pillar over her grave, "the pillar of Rachel's grave unto this day" (Gen. 35:20). Rachel and Leah appear in Dante's *The Divine Comedy* (Purgatory, canto 27), where they are seen as types of the contemplative and active life.

2471

Radish. A small, potent, edible root. During the Jewish feast of Passover radishes are a part of the traditional meal. In today's celebrations of the rite the radish is symbolic of spring and a sign of "the perpetual renewal of life and ever-sustaining hope of human redemption."

2472

Ragnarok (destruction of the powers). In Norse mythology, the final battle between the gods and the giants that will bring about the end of the world. The battle will take place at Vigrith (field of battle). The destruction, however, will not be the complete end. The *Prose Edda* gives an account of a new "earth most lovely and verdant, and with pleasant fields where the grain shall grow unsown." Some of the gods will return, such as Baldur and Hodur from Hel, the underworld, and a new couple, Lifthrasir and Lif (life), will repeople the land "and their descendants shall soon spread over the whole earth." The *Poetic Edda* contains a description of the end in the poem *Voluspa*. Wagner's last music drama in the cycle *Der Ring des Nibelungen*, titled *Götterdämmerung*, deals with the destruction of the gods.

2473

Rahu (the seizer). In Hindu mythology, a demon who seizes the sun and moon, causing eclipses. Rahu has four arms, and his body ends in a dragon's tail. When the gods and demons were fighting for the Amrita, the water of life, at the churning of the ocean, Rahu disguised himself and drank some of the Amrita. When the sun and moon saw what he had done, they told the god Vishnu, who then cut off Rahu's head and two of his arms. Rahu, however, had gained immortality by drinking the Amrita, and his body was placed in the heavens. The upper part, represented by a dragon's head, is the ascending node, and the lower part, the descending node. The *Vishnu Purana*, one of the 18 Puranas, tells how "eight black horses draw the dusky chariot of Rahu, and once harnessed are attached to it for ever. . . . Rahu directs his course from the sun to the moon, and back again from the moon to the sun."

Rahu is also called Abhra-pisacha (the demon of the sky) and Kabandha (the headless).

2474

Raiden. In Japanese mythology, thunder god, portrayed with the features of a demon: horns on his head, a tusk, and a wide mouth. Sometimes he carries a circle of 12 round, flat drums, which he beats with sticks; or he is portrayed caught by Uzume, goddess of mirth, who is shown in her bath. Raiden likes to eat navels; thus, children are dressed to cover their abdomens.

Variant spellings;: Raijin, Kaminarisan.

2475

Railroad Bill. In American folklore, a black man from Escambia County, Alabama, who could transform himself into an animal when pursued by the law.

2476

Rainbow Snake. In Australian mythology, name of the gigantic snake whose body arches across the sky as the rainbow.

Known as Taipan among the Wikmunkan people, he is associated with the gift of blood to humankind, controlling the circulation of the blood as well as the menstrual cycle of women. Looked on as a great healer, Taipan demands that his sexual laws and customs be followed. His anger at breaking any of them is expressed by thunder and lightning. Medicine men and rain makers invoke Taipan by using quartz crystal and seashells in their rituals. Called Julunggul among the people of the eastern Arnhem Land, the Rainbow Snake is believed to swallow young boys and later vomit them up. This is symbolic of their rebirth, or the transition from youth to manhood. Known as Kunmanggur in a myth told by the Murinbata of the Northern Territory to W. Stanner, the Rainbow Snake is either bisexual or a woman. Sometimes he is described as a male but is portrayed with female breasts. Other names by which the Rainbow Snake is known in Australia are Galeru, Ungur, Wonungur, Worombi, Wonambi, Wollunqua, Yurlunggur, Langal, Muit, and Yero.

2477

Rais, Gilles de. 1404–1440 C.E. In medieval history and legend, marshal of France who fought with St. Joan of Arc against the English invaders. He was accused of sorcery, as was Joan, and was executed for heresy and the rape and murder of children. It is believed by some scholars that the legend of Bluebeard is based on his life.

2478

Raji. In Hindu mythology, a man who usurped the throne of the storm god Indra. When there was a war between the gods and demons, the god Brahma declared that the victory should be given to the side that Raji joined. The demons sought Raji's aid but would not make him king as he requested. However, the gods promised Raji that if he sided with them he would be made king of the gods, and Indra, the king of the gods, would worship him. After the demons were defeated, Raji was made king of the gods as promised. Later, when he returned to his own city, he left Indra as his deputy in heaven. On Raji's death

Indra refused to acknowledge the succession of his sons (he had 500 sons) and retained the title for himself.

2479

Rákóczi, Ferenc. 1675–1735. In Hungarian legend, prince who led a revolt against Austrian oppression. According to some tales, he did not die but is resting, waiting for the time to come to Hungary's aid. Rákóczi has given his name to a well-known Hungarian marching tune used by Hector Berlioz in his cantata *The Damnation of Faust* and also by Franz Liszt in Hungarian Rhapsody No. 15, written in the 1840s.

2480

Rakshasas (to be guarded against). In Hindu mythology, a class of demons under the leadership of the demon king Ravana. In the Hindu epic poem *The Ramayana*, when the monkey chief Hanuman enters the Lanka (Sri Lanka), Ravana's capital, he sees "the Rakshasas sleeping in the houses were of every shape and form. Some of them disgusted the eye, while some were beautiful to look upon. Some had long arms and frightful shapes; some were very fat and some were very lean; some were mere dwarfs and some were very tall. Some had only one eye and others only one ear. Some had monstrous bellies, hanging breasts, long protruding teeth, and crooked thighs, while others were exceedingly beautiful to behold and clothed in great splendor. Some had two legs, some three legs, and some four legs. Some had the heads of serpents, some the heads of donkeys, some the heads of horses, and some the heads of elephants."

Variant spelling: Raksasas.

2481

Ram. A male sheep. In Egyptian mythology the ram was sacred to the god Khnemu, who was portrayed as a ram-headed god. A ram was sacrificed to the god Amun-Ra once a year. It was skinned and the skin placed over the image of the god, recalling the time when Amun-Ra was incarnated in the form of a ram. In ancient Hebrew belief the ram was sacrificed instead of Isaac when Isaac's father, Abraham, was commanded by Yahweh god to sacrifice his son (Gen. 22:13). In later Jewish folklore the ram had been trapped in a thicket since the sixth day of creation, waiting for Abraham's sacrifice. From the bones of that sacrificed ram the foundations of the Holy of Holies of the Temple were built; the ram's veins became the strings for King David's harp, and its skin was made into the prophet Elijah's belt and girdle; its left horn made the shofar used by Moses on Mount Sinai; and its right horn the shofar that the prophet Elijah will blow on Mount Moriah to announce the coming of the Messiah. In Islamic belief

Abraham's ram was admitted into heaven. In Hindu mythology the ram is the steed or mount of the fire god Agni.

2482

Ram. In Persian mythology, spirit of the air, or angel, who receives the good soul on its way to the other world after death.

2483

Rama (charming). In Hindu mythology, a hero, chief character in the epic poem by Valmiki, *The Ramayana*. In some Hindu texts, such as Tulasi Das's vernacular version of the Sanskrit *Ramayana*, titled *Ramacheritamanasa* (the holy lake of the acts of Rama), Rama is regarded as an incarnation of the god Vishnu. As such, Rama, along with his wife Sita, is worshiped in many parts of India. One line in Tulasi Das's epic captures the love of the people for their hero god: "Rama knows the hearts of all; in him dwell meekness, love, and mercy. Comfort your heart with this assurance, and come, take rest." Rama appears in Bhavabhuti's plays *The Acts of Rama* and *Later Acts of Rama*. Gandhi's dying words were "Long live Rama," not "O God!" as recorded in the movie *Gandhi*.

2484

Ramadan. In Islam, ninth month of the lunar year; the time of an annual fast. It is the only month mentioned in the Koran (sura 2), which says that the Koran "was sent down" from heaven in that month.

During Ramadan the believer is commanded to fast the whole month every day, from the first appearance of daybreak until sunset. He must abstain from eating, drinking, smoking, smelling perfumes, and every unnecessary indulgence or pleasure of a worldly nature, even from knowingly swallowing his spittle. When Ramadan falls in summer (since the year is lunar, each month retrogrades through all of the seasons in the course of about every 33½ years), the fast is very severe. Therefore, persons who are sick or on a journey and soldiers in time of war are not obliged to fast. But if they do not fast during Ramadan, they should fast an equal number of days at another time. Fasting is also dispensed with for nurses and pregnant women.

'Id al-Fitr, commonly called *al-'id al-saghir*, or the lesser festival, is a feast for the breaking of the fast when Ramadan is ended. Alms are dispensed, people give gifts, and there is general celebration. In *Moby Dick* Melville titled chapter 17 "The Ramadan," which refers to Queequeg's "fasting and humiliation."

Ramayana, The (the tale of Rama). Hindu epic poem of 24,000 *Shlokas* (48,000 lines), attributed to the sage Valmiki in the third century C.E. It is divided into seven *kandas*, books of unequal length.

Bala-Kanda (book 1). King Dasa-ratha ruled over Ayodhya, a beautiful city. His one complaint, however, was that he had no children. He therefore performed a great sacrifice in the hope of obtaining offspring. The gods accepted his sacrifice, and Dasa-ratha received the promise of four sons. At the request of the god Brahma, the god Vishnu agreed to become incarnate in the body of Rama, one of the four sons to be born, and the other sons, Bharata and the twins Lakshmana and Satru-ghna, also shared some of Vishnu's godhead.

While King Dasa-ratha was performing the sacrifice, Vishnu appeared to him in full glory from out of the sacrificial fire. Vishnu gave the king a pot of nectar for his wives to drink. Dasa-ratha gave half of the magic drink to Kausalya, who became the mother of Rama; a quarter to his wife Kaikeyi, who became the mother of Bharata; and a fourth to his wife Su-mitra, who became the mother of the twins Lakshmana and Satru-ghna.

The four brothers grew up together at Ayodhya. While they were still young, the sage Viswamitra sought Rama's help in protecting him from demons who had been tormenting him. Though unwilling to have his sons leave his court, Dasa-ratha consented, and Rama and Lakshmana went to the hermitage of Viswamitra. There Rama killed the demoness Taraka. Viswamitra had earlier supplied Rama with magic arms that aided the hero in his conquest of Taraka. After the defeat of the demoness, Viswamitra took Rama and Lakshmana to the court of Janaka, king of Videha. At the court was Sita, daughter of the king, who was offered in marriage to anyone who could bend the bow that had belonged to the god Shiva. Rama not only bent the bow but broke it, winning the hand of Sita. Rama's brothers were also married. Urmila, Sita's sister, became the wife of Lakshmana; Mandavi and Sruta-kriti, cousins of Sita, became the wives of Bharata and Satru-ghna.

Ayodhya-Kanda (book 2). When the four couples returned to Ayodhya, the king decided to name Rama, his eldest, heir to the throne. The announcement angered the king's wife Kaikeyi, the mother of Bharata. She reminded the king that he had once promised her any two wishes she asked. The angered king, realizing what she wanted, swore to keep his word. The queen then asked that Rama be banished for 14 years and that her son, Bharata, be appointed viceroy in his place.

Rama, being a dutiful son, left with his wife Sita and his brother Lakshmana for the Dandaka forest. Soon after his departure King Dasa-ratha died, and Bharata was called on to be king. Bharata declined, leaving for the forest to bring back Rama. When the two brothers met there was a long discussion, Rama refusing to return until the 14 years had been completed. It was agreed, however, that Bharata should return and act as regent for Rama. As a sign that Rama was king, Bharata brought back a pair of Rama's shoes, placing them on the throne.

Aranya-Kanda (book 3). Rama passed his years of banishment moving from one hermitage to another. At last he arrived at the hermitage of Argastya, a sage, near the Vidhya Mountains. Argastya told Rama to live at Panchavati on the river Godavari. Rama's party went to live at Panchavati, but the area was found to be infested with demons. One of them, Surpa-nakha, a sister of the demon king Ravana, fell in love with Rama. When Rama rejected her advances, the demoness attacked Sita. Lakshmana then cut off Surpa-nakha's ears and nose. Calling on her demon friends, Surpa-nakha tried to avenge the wrong, but all of the demons were destroyed. Surpa-nakha then went to her brother Ravana. He became so excited by the physical description of Sita's beauty that he decided to abduct her. Ravana took his magic cart and kidnapped Sita while Rama was lured away from home by Maricha, a demoness who took the form of a deer.

Kishkindha-Kanda (book 4). Rama and Lakshmana go in pursuit of Ravana. On their way they killed Kabandha, a headless monster, whose disembodied spirit told Rama to seek the aid of the king of the monkeys, Sugriva. The two brothers went to Sugriva and formed an alliance. They also obtained the aid of the monkey leader Hanuman, son of the wind god Vayu.

Sundara-Kanda (book 5). With Hanuman's extraordinary powers of leaping and flying, the monkey armies were transported over *Rama-setu* (Rama's bridge), and entered Lanka, Ravana's country.

Yuddha-Kanda (book 6). After a series of battles, Lanka was conquered and Ravana killed by Rama. Sita, to prove she had been faithful to Rama, then underwent an ordeal of fire. Sita entered the flames in the presence of men and gods. Agni, the fire god, led her and placed her in Rama's arms unhurt after the ordeal. Rama then returned to his kingdom with his brothers.

Uttara-Kanda (book 7). Rama, however, could not rest, still having doubts of Sita's faithfulness, especially since the populace doubted that she had remained faithful. In order to please the public Rama sent Sita away to spend the rest of her life at the hermitage of the sage Valmiki (the supposed author of the poem). There Sita had twin sons, Kusa and Lava. When they were about 15 years old, they wandered accidentally into Ayodhya and were recognized by Rama as his children. Rama then called Sita back. She declared in public that she had been faithful to Rama, calling on the earth to verify her words. The ground opened, receiving "the daughter of the furrow." Unable to live without Sita, Rama asked the gods to release him. He was told by Time in the form of an ascetic, that he must stay on earth or ascend to the heavens. Lakshmana tried to save his brother from Time, but as a result was sentenced to death and sent bodily to the storm god Indra's heaven. Rama then went to the Sarayu River. Walking into the water, he heard the voice of the god Brahma, and he entered into heaven. In a variant ending to the epic, Rama and Sita live happily together, and she is not swallowed by the earth.

The story of Rama and Sita is acted every autumn in many parts of India during a 10-day celebration. At the end of the festival Ravana and his demon hordes are burned in effigy. A suite for orchestra, *Ramayana*, by the American composer Bertram Shapleigh is based on the epic poem.

2486

Ran (robbery). In Norse mythology, wife of the sea god Aegir. She caught the dead at sea in her net and took them to her underworld. Human sacrifices were made to Ran by pre-Christian Scandinavian sailors before embarking on a voyage. In Northern folklore, when she lost her status as goddess, she became a siren who was often seen reclining on the shores, combing her hair. In Sweden the spirit Sjöran is believed to be derived from Ran.

2487

Rangda (witch). In Balinese folklore, a witch; she appears together with Barong, the dragon, in a folk play, *Tjalon Arang*, symbolizing male and female sexual aspects.

2488

Ranieri, St. c. 1100–1161. In Christian legend, patron saint of Pisa, Italy. Called St. Ranieri dell Agua, or St. Ranieri of Water. Feast, 17 June.

St. Ranieri's life was written by Canon Benincasa, a personal friend, shortly after the saint's death. Ranieri spent his youth in pleasure, but one day while he was playing on a lyre amid his mistresses, a holy man passed by and looked at him with pity. Struck with sudden feelings of guilt for his past, Ranieri followed the man. Shortly afterward he left for Jerusalem, where he took off his rich garments and wore a *schiavina*, or slave shirt, a tunic of coarse wool with short sleeves. While doing penances in the desert he had a vision of a silver and gold vase set with jewels but filled with pitch, oil, and sulfur. The contents were set on fire, and the vase burned. A ewer full of water was put near Ranieri. He placed his hands in it and put two or three drops of water on the flames, and they were extinguished. According to Jameson in *Sacred and Legendary Art*, "The vase signified his human frame . . . the pitch and sulphur burning within it were the appetites and passions . . . the water was the water of temperance. Thenceforward Ranieri lived wholly on coarse bread and water."

Another legend tells of Ranieri and an innkeeper in Messina who diluted his wine, which was then sold to his customers. St. Ranieri revealed the fraud when he unmasked the devil, seated on one of the wine casks in the shape of a huge cat with batlike wings.

St. Ranieri's life was painted by Simone Memmi and Antonio Veneziano in Pisa in 1356.

2489

Raphael (God has healed). In the Bible, archangel in Jewish and Christian mythology, patron of humanity. Feast, 21 September in the Western church.

The most prominent role given to Raphael is in the Book of Tobit in the Old Testament Apocrypha. He acts as a companion and guide to Tobit's son Tobias and helps him rid Sara, the intended wife of Tobias, from her demon-lover Asmodeus, who had slain her seven previous husbands.

In Tobit (12:15) Raphael describes himself as "one of the seven holy angels, which present the prayers of the saints, and which go in and out before the glory of the Holy One." According to Rabbi Abba in *The Zohar I*, Raphael is "charged to heal the earth, and through him . . . the earth furnishes an abode for man, whom also he heals of his maladies." Raphael appears in Milton's *Paradise Lost*. He is often pictured accompanying Tobias and shown holding a pilgrim's staff and a fish (which was used as the charm to rid Sara of her demon-lover). Tobias, often shown as a mere youth, walks close to the angel with his dog nearby.

2490

Rapithwin. In Persian mythology, god of the noonday heat and the summer. When the good god, Ahura Mazda, performed the sacrifice that created the world, it was at the time of day belonging to Rapithwin. When Rapithwin returns at springtime, it is a foreshadowing of the final victory over evil by good, an event at which he will be present.

Rasetsu Ten. In Japanese Buddhist mythology, king of demons, portrayed bearded and with upright hair. He holds a sword in his right hand, and his left hand is raised in a sign of fearlessness. He is one of the Jiu No O, 12 Japanese Buddhist gods and goddesses adopted from Hindu mythology.

2491

Rashnu. In Persian mythology, angel of justice, who weighs the good works and sins in his golden scales when the soul's account is balanced in the third night after his death. Rashnu is assisted in his work by the angel Astad.

2492

Rat. In Egyptian mythology, wife of the sun god Ra. She was called "mother of the gods," as Ra was called "father of the gods." However, she was really a late development in the cult of Ra and amounts to little more than Ra's name feminized. The sun god was said to have sired the first divine couple without recourse to a female. Rat was portrayed in Egyptian art as a woman wearing on her head a disk with horns and the uraeus. Sometimes there were two feathers on the disk.

2493

Country mouse and city mouse

Rat and Mouse. A rat is a long-tailed rodent resembling a mouse but much larger. The two rodents are often confused in world mythology and folklore. In Greek mythology the mouse was sacred to Apollo in his role as sender of plague. Apollo was appealed to as "O Smintheus" (O mouse) when he was invoked in his role as plague sender. Many ancient peoples realized that there was a connection between mice and plague, though the scientific explanation was unknown to them. The mouse or rat, therefore, often became a symbol of death.

2494

The pagan Germans worshiped a goddess called Nehalennia or Hludana, whose symbol was a rat and whose function was to accompany the souls of the dead. St. Gertrude, a 12th-century saint, was also credited with helping the souls of the dead and was nearly always portrayed with a rat as her companion. One German medieval tale tells how Bishop Hatto was destroyed by mice and rats after he had his flock burned to death in a barn where they had gathered after he had promised them grain.

In America Walt Disney's cartoon character Mickey Mouse, who first appeared in *Steamboat Willie*, has since sung his way to fortune, minus his demonic character and genitals.

Ratatosk (swift-tusked). In Norse mythology, the squirrel that runs up and down the cosmic or world tree, Yggdrasill, carrying abusive language from the dragon Nidhogg at the bottom of the tree to the eagle at the top, and vice versa. Ratatosk appears in the *Poetic Edda* and the *Prose Edda* .

2495

Rati (love play). In Hindu mythology, goddess of love, wife of Kama, the god of love. Rati is also called Kama-priya (beloved of Kama); Raga-lata (vine of love); Mayavati (deceiver); Kelikila (wanton); and Subhangi (fair-limbed).

2496

Ratnapani (jewel in hand). In Mahayana Buddhism, one of the five Dhyani-Bodhisattvas, whose symbol is a magic jewel.

2497

Ratu-mai-mbulu. In Melanesian mythology, Fijian serpent god of the dead, who lives in a cave. A beneficent being, he causes trees and crops to grow. One month of the year is dedicated to him. During that month no singing or dancing is allowed so as not to disturb the god.

2498

Rausch, Bruder (Brother Rush). In Germanic folklore, a house spirit who made people drunk. He appears in English folklore as Friar Rush, and his tale is told in a prose *History of Friar Rush*.

2499

Ravana (screaming). In Hindu mythology, the demon king of Lanka (Sri Lanka), leader of the Rakshasas, demons and evil spirits.

Ravana overthrew his brother Kubera (later made god of wealth) and set himself up as king of Lanka. Ravana was made invulnerable against gods and demons by the god Brahma or Shiva because of his penance and devotion to the god. The only way

2500

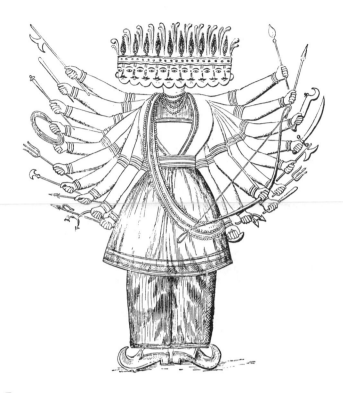

Ravana

Ravana could meet death was through a woman, though in actuality he was killed by the hero Rama for having abducted Rama's wife, Sita. In a sense, then, Ravana was killed through a woman. In the Hindu epic poem *The Ramayana*, Ravana is described as having "ten heads, twenty arms, and copper-colored eyes, and bright teeth like the moon. His form was as a thick cloud or a mountain, or the god of death with open mouth. He had all the marks of royalty, but his body bore the impress of wounds inflicted by all the divine arms in his warfare with the gods. It was scarred by the thunderbolt of Indra, by the tusks of Indra's elephant Airavata, and by the discus of Vishnu. His strength was so great that he could agitate the seas and split the tops of mountains. He was a breaker of all laws and a ravisher of other men's wives. . . . Tall as a mountain peak, he stopped with his arms the sun and the moon in their course, and prevented their rising."

Ravana's deeds cried to heaven. Vishnu came to earth in the form of Rama to destroy the demon king. Rama cut off one of Ravana's heads with his sharp arrow, "but no sooner did the head fall on the ground than another sprang up in its place." Rama then took an arrow that had been given to him by the god Brahma. He shot it at Ravana's chest and it came out of the demon's back, went into the ocean, and then returned clean to Rama's quiver. "Ravana fell to the ground and died, and the gods sounded the celestial music in the heavens, and assembled in the sky and praised Rama."

One sect in south India, however, assigns the victory to Ravana and celebrates the demons' victory over Rama.

Ravana was not alone in his evil works. He was helped by the Naikasheyas, carnivorous imps descended from Nikasha, mother of Ravana. Sometimes his demon aides are called Pistasanas or Nikashatmajas.

2501

Raven. A large black bird of the crow family having a loud, harsh call. In Greek mythology, the raven was once believed to have been white but was transformed into a black bird by Apollo for informing the god of the infidelity of Coronis, a beautiful maiden loved by the god. The bird was associated with Apollo as god of prophecy.

In Norse mythology two ravens, Hugin and Munin, brought news to Odin of each day's happenings. As a result Odin was sometimes called God of Ravens. The ominous character of the raven is cited in Shakespeare's *Julius Caesar* (5.1); Cassius tells how the ravens "Fly o'er our heads and downward look on us / As we were sickly prey" reflecting the belief that the bird would "smell death" and was therefore a dreaded visitor. But in a Roman legend the raven is a symbol of good. It alighted on the helmet of Valerius, a soldier, when he was about to fight a Gallic warrior. Valerius took this as a good sign and prayed to the gods to aid him in battle. They did, sending the raven to pluck out the eyes of the Gallic warrior. In Arthurian legend King Arthur still lives in the guise of a raven, and therefore the birds are never killed. In Eskimo mythology the Great Raven is the creator of animals and women. Poe's *The Raven* is the best-known poem on the raven.

2502

Raymond Nonnato, St. (counsel-protection). d.1240. In Christian legend, patron saint of children, domestic animals, innocent persons falsely accused, and nurses. Invoked during childbirth and fever. Venerated in Spain. Feast, 31 August.

St. Raymond was a member of the Order of Mercy or Mercedarians, who worked to free captive Christians from the Moors. *Les Petits Bollandistes* (vol. 10), a collection of saints' lives, gives the legend of St. Raymond speaking when his lips were locked.

Raymond went to Algiers to redeem Christian captives but was captured by the Moors and imprisoned. Though a captive he still preached the gospel, which upset the ruling pasha Setim, who ordered him to be whipped, naked, at every street corner. Then a red-hot iron padlock was fastened through his lips. The key was kept by the jailer and the lock was opened only when he was given food. Yet one day when the jailer came in, he found Raymond reciting one of the Psalms. The jailer, convinced he was a sorcerer, kicked him and left without feeding him.

Eventually, Raymond made it back to Christian lands and was made a cardinal and general of the Order of Mercy. Both Pope Gregory IX and King James of Aragon attended his funeral.

St. Raymond is shown as a Mercedarian with a white badge on his breast and a chain and padlock on his lips. Sometimes he is shown surrounded by Moors and captives.

Raymond of Pennaforte, St. (counsel-protection). 2503
13th century. In Christian legend, patron saint of canon lawyers, venerated in Spain and Majorca. Feast, 23 January.

Raymond was born of a noble Spanish family. He joined the Dominican Order and through his preaching was partly responsible for the expulsion of the Moors from Spain. His miracles, which are numerous, fill some 16 pages of *Les Petits Bollandistes*, a collection of saints' lives. One legend, included in Leandre Alberti's *Life of St. Raymund*, tells how St. Raymond sailed some 160 miles on his cloak.

King James was living in adultery with a lady of the court. St. Raymond reprimanded him, but the king ignored him. St. Raymond then said he could no longer live in a court where sin was tolerated. The king strictly forbade any shipper, under pain of death, to convey St. Raymond across the water. St. Raymond spread his cloak on the water, jumped on it, held up on his staff a corner of the cloak to make a sail, and sailed all the way to Barcelona. On reaching shore he drew his cloak up and threw it across his shoulders—and it was dry. When the king heard of the miracle, he abandoned his mistress and became an ideal king. The same legend of using a cloak as a sail is also told of St. Bernardino in the 15th century, St. Isidore's wife, and Elijah, who in 2 Kings (2:8) took his mantle and, wrapping it together, "smote the waters, and they were divided hither and thither, so that they two went over Jordan as dry land."

St. Raymond is shown in the Dominican habit, kneeling on his magic mantle.

Raziel (secret of God). In Jewish mythology, angel 2504
entrusted with guarding or transmitting the "mysteries" or "secrets" of God. Raziel is credited with authorship of *The Book of the Angel Raziel*, a medieval Jewish work popular in Eastern Europe, where a copy of the book was believed to keep a house safe from fire. The book says that the "secrets" contained in it were given by the Angel Raziel to Adam after he was cast out of the Garden of Eden, then passed on to Noah before he entered the Ark, and finally came into the possession of King Solomon, who is credited in both Jewish and Islamic folklore with being a great magician.

Razin, Stenka. d. 1671. In Russian legend, a Cossack 2505
leader. Numerous tales grew up around his character; one, which influenced the Russian composer Alexander Glazunov, relates to Razin's death. Stenka Razin was on his magnificent boat with a captive Persian princess when she told him a dream she had had. She had seen her own death as well as the destruction of Stenka Razin and his followers. Fearful of what she said, Stenka Razin killed her, offered her as a sacrifice to the Volga River, and went out to fight the czar's troops—who defeated him. He was executed in 1671. Glazunov's symphonic poem *Stenka Razin* which uses as a main theme the traditional song of the Volga boatman; Shostakovich's *The Execution of Stepan Razin*, for bass, chorus, and orchestra, based on a poem by Yevgeny Yevtushenko; and a group sculpture *Stepan Razin and His Troops* by Sergei Konenkov, all deal with the hero.

Rebekah (ensnarer). In the Bible, O.T., a daughter of 2506
Bethuel and the wife of Isaac; mother of Jacob and Esau. The story of her marriage is told in Genesis (chap. 24). When Abraham, Isaac's father, was old, he wanted to be sure that his son was married. He sent his trusted servant Eliezar back to Chaldea, his native land, to choose a wife for Isaac. Near the city of Nahor the servant prayed for Yahweh's guidance. He asked that when he should stop by the public well with his animals whichever maiden drawing

Ruth and Boaz (Holbein)

water there would first offer to draw water for him would be his choice for Isaac's wife. The prayer was answered when Rebekah offered to draw the water. A scene frequently painted is Rebekah at the Well, such as the painting by Murillio.

2507

Regin. In Norse mythology, youngest son of Hreidmer and brother of Fafnir and Otter. Exiled by his brother Fafnir over possession of the Nibelung gold, Regin became the great teacher of all craft to mankind. He educated Sigurd, made him promise to avenge the wrongs done him by Fafnir, and forged Sigurd's magic sword. Regin appears in the *Volsunga Saga*.

2508

Regulus, St. Third century. In Christian legend, first bishop of Senlis, France, as well as its patron saint. Feast, 30 March. One day St. Regulus encountered a man possessed by a devil. "If you cast me out of the man," said the devil, "let me go into the nearby ass." The saint agreed, but the ass made the sign of the cross with its forefoot, and the devil fled. Another legend tells how the saint, when preaching, told some frogs to stop croaking. They complied. One chapel dedicated to the saint contains images of frogs.

2509

Rémy, St. 438–533. In Christian legend, bishop of Rheims, France; converted and baptized Clovis, the king of the Franks, in 496. Feast, 1 October.

Rémy was made bishop of Rheims when he was 22 because of his brilliance and great learning. After the conversion of Clovis the king helped him in his great project of bringing Christianity to the Franks.

There are numerous legends connected with his life. One tells how St. Rémy stopped a fire from destroying Rheims by making the sign of the cross before it. The fire kept moving back as the saint walked toward it until it reached the city gates "when it rolled itself into a ball" and disappeared in the fields. Another legend tells that when St. Rémy was an old man he had a dream that there would be years of plenty followed by years of dearth. So he stored corn in Celtum against the years of famine. The villagers, supposing he was going to market the corn to their loss, set fire to his granaries. As the fire was raging, the old saint appeared and said, "Be sure of this, that God will not forget to punish those who have done this mischief." Immediately the persons who had set the fire became hunchbacks."

The most famous painting of the saint is by the Master of St. Giles and is called *The Baptism of Clovis*.

2510

Renpet (rising goddess?). In Egyptian mythology, goddess of the year's duration. She was particularly associated with springtime and youth. In Egyptian art she was portrayed as a woman wearing above her head a long palm shoot curved at the end, which was the ideogram of her name.

Variant spellings: Renenutet, Rannut, Remute, Ernuted.

2511

Reshpu (fiery bolt?). In Near Eastern mythology (Syrian), god of lightning and the thunderbolt, the "Great God, Lord of Eternity, Prince of Everlastingness, Lord of Twofold Strength among the Company of the Gods." Reshpu was worshiped in ancient Egypt, where he was depicted as a warrior with a shield and spear in his left hand and a club in his right hand.

Variant spelling: Resheph, Reshef, Reshep, Reshiph-Mical.

2512

Revati. In Hindu mythology, wife of the hero Balarama, brother of Krishna (an incarnation of the god Vishnu). Revati was given to Balarama by the god Brahma, but the hero thought Revati was too tall for him and "shortened her with the end of a ploughshare, and she became his wife." The couple had two sons.

2513

Revere, Paul. 1735–1818. In American history and folklore, patriot, craftsman, and political cartoonist. A skilled silversmith, Revere also did portraits and produced false teeth. When the conflict between the colonies and Great Britain broke out, Revere issued crude cartoons attacking the British. He is noted in American legend for his famous midnight ride from Boston to Lexington on 18–19 April 1775 to warn the colonists of the Redcoats' approach. Longfellow's literary ballad "The Midnight Ride of Paul Revere," included in his collection *Tales of a Wayside Inn*, tells how Revere waited for a signal in the Old North Church tower before he began his famous ride. Longfellow's ballad, however, is more legend than fact. Paul Revere did not make the whole ride. A young Dr. Prescott carried the news to Concord, and Revere went to Lexington.

2514

Reynard the Fox (hard counsel). In medieval folklore, a clever fox who outwits other animals. His tale begins with all of the animals complaining about Reynard, who has robbed them. Noble, the lion king, decides to send Bruin, the bear, to arrest Reynard. Bruin, however, is outwitted, as is Tybert, the cat. Finally, Grymbart, the badger, brings in Reynard for trial. He is found guilty and sentenced to be hanged. The clever fox, however, convinces Noble, who is judge, that he has hidden treasure. In hope of obtaining the treasure, Noble unties Reynard, who escapes and continues stealing and raping his neighbors. Arrested for the second time on charges of raping the wife of Isengrin, the wolf, Reynard not only kills Isengrin in a duel, but is made second in command by Noble. William Caxton translated a Flemish version of the tale into English in 1481. Goethe's long narrative poem *Reynard the Fox* and Stravinsky's *Renard the Fox*, for soloists and orchestra, also treat the legend.

2515

Rhadamanthus (he who divines with a wand). In Greek mythology, son of Zeus and Europa; brother of Minos and Sarpedon; married to Alcmene; father of Erythus and Gortys. He was born on Crete and ruled over the Cyclades and later was made one of the three judges of the underworld along with Minos and Sarpedon (or Aeacus). He is cited in Homer's *Iliad* (book 4), Vergil's *Aeneid* (book 6) and Ovid's *Metamorphoses* (book 9).

2516

Rhampsinitus, Treasure of. Ancient Egyptian literary folktale told by Herodotus in his *History* (book 2). Herodotus claimed that it had been told to him by Egyptian priests. In the tale a rogue tricks everyone—even the pharaoh, who exclaims at the end: "The Egyptians excelled all the rest of the world in wisdom, and this man excelled all other Egyptians."

2517

Rhesus (breaker). In Greek mythology, king of Thrace, ally of Priam; son of Strymon (or Eioneus) and Calliope (or Euterpe); married Arganthoe. His horses protected Troy. Homer's *Iliad* (book 10) tells how Rhesus was killed by Odysseus and Diomedes in a night raid in which his magnificent white horses were taken. Euripides' *Rhesus*, Vergil's *Aeneid* (book 1), and Ovid's *Metamorphoses* (book 13) also tell the tale.

2518

Rhoecus. In Greek mythology, a handsome young man who propped up a fallen oak tree, thus saving the life of the nymph or dryad who lived in the tree. As a reward, Rhoecus asked that the nymph love him. She said she would send a messenger to tell him when to meet her. When the bee messenger arrived, Rhoecus had already forgotten the incident and waved the bee away. In punishment, the nymph blinded Rhoecus. Rhoecus is also the name of a centaur killed by Dionysus at the wedding of Pirithous

and Hippodameia, according to Ovid's *Metamorphoses* (book 12), as well as a name of a Titan killed by Dionysus in the war between the gods and the Titans.

2519

Ribhus (clever, skilful). In Hindu mythology, mortals who were raised to divine status after they fashioned the storm god Indra's chariot and horses. They live in the solar atmosphere and are supporters of the sky.

2520

Rice. A cereal grain. In some parts of Java, just before rice is to bloom, farmers bring their wives into the rice field and have sexual intercourse to ensure a successful crop. The Kayans of Central Borneo precede the sowing of rice by an elaborate dance, in which dancers wear masks with gogglelike eyes, large teeth and ears, and beards made of goat hair, dressing themselves in banana leaves to look like walking plants. With a hook they ceremonially catch the soul of the rice, which otherwise might wander away, causing crop failure.

2521

Richard the Lion-Hearted. 1157–1199. In English history and legend, king of England, also called Richard Coeur de Lion, who took part in the Crusades, though he never reached Jerusalem. He became a prisoner of the Emperor Henry VI in 1193 but was ransomed by his English subjects. He died while besieging a castle. His character appealed to Walter Scott, who at the tournament in *Ivanhoe* introduced him disguised as the Black Knight. Scott's *The Talisman* portrays Richard crusading in the Holy Land, both the friend and the enemy of Saladin.

2522

Rig-Veda (Veda of praise). In Hinduism, the most ancient and sacred part of the *Vedas* (knowledge), consisting of more than 1,000 hymns to the gods and various natural phenomena, composed between 1400 and 1000 B.C.E.

The *Rig-Veda* is divided into 10 *mandalas* (circles), or books, consisting of hymns by various *rishis* (sages).

In some versions the name of the *rishi* who is reputed to be the teller or reciter is prefixed to each hymn becasue the hymns are believed to have been "breathed out" by the god Brahma. They were transmitted orally from generation to generation until, according to tradition, they were collected by Krishna Dwaipayna (the arranger).

The greatest impact of the *Rig-Veda* on Western music is contained in *Choral Hymns* by Gustav Holst. Early in his career he had written for baritone an *Invocation to Dawn*, based on his own translation of some of the *Rig-Veda*. Later Holst set four groups of hymns to various texts he had translated. In the first group, for mixed voices and orchestra, are *Battle Hymn*, *Hymn to the Unknown God*, and *Funeral Hymn*. The second group, for female voices and orchestra, contains *To Varuna*, *To Agni*, and *Funeral Chant*. The third group, for female voices and harp, includes *Hymn to Dawn*, *Hymn to the Waters*, *Hymn to Vena*, and *Hymn to the Travellers*. The last group is *Hymn to Agni*, *Hymn to Soma*, *Hymn to Manas*, and *Hymn to Indra*. The American composer Bertram Shapleigh composed *Vedic Hymn* on a text from the *Rig-Veda*.

Variant spelling: Rg-Veda.

2523

Rimmon (the thunderer). In Near Eastern mythology (Babylonian-Assyrian), the storm god, often called Adad.

In the biblical book 2 Kings (5:1–18), Naaman, the commander of the Syrian army, worshiped Rimmon; but when he was cured of his leprosy by the prophet Elisha, he said he would worship the Hebrew god, Yahweh, instead. In the Babylonian version of the flood myth, before the great flood "the whirlwind of Adad [Rimmon] mounted up into the heavens, and all light was turned into darkness." Rimmon was portrayed holding lightning rods in his left hand and an ax in his right. His sacred animal was the bull; his sacred tree, the cypress. His wife was Shala, which may simply mean "woman." Rimmon was also called Martu (the Amorite) and Kur-Ga (great mountain) in Canaan. He was called Hadad by the Syrians and Teshub by the Hittites.

Variant spellings: Ramman, Rammanu.

2524

Rinaldo. In the Charlemagne cycle of legends, Charlemagne's nephew and one of his 12 paladins. Rinaldo is the rival of his cousin Orlando for the love of Angelica in Ariosto's *Orlando Furioso*. He also appears in Tasso's *Jerusalem Delivered*. Rinaldo is also called Renault.

2525

Rinda (crust of the earth?). In Norse mythology, a goddess, a mistress of Odin, and mother of Vali. Odin used various disguises and magic to have sexual intercourse with Rinda.

2526

Ring des Nibelungen, Der (The Ring of the Nibelung). A stage-festival-play to be performed over a three-day period and a preliminary evening; words and music by Richard Wagner. First complete performance, Bayreuth, 13–17 August 1876. The work consists of *Das Rheingold*, *Die Walküre*, *Siegfried*, and *Götterdämmerung*.

Alberich

Wagner wrote the text for his music dramas in reverse order. In 1848 he wrote *Siegfrieds Tod*, which dealt with the death of Siegfried. Realizing that he had to explain more, he wrote *Der Junge Siegfried* (The Young Siegfried). He then felt he needed even more text. *Siegfrieds Tod* became the last work *Götterdämmerung*, and *Das Rheingold*, the first part, was written last. The texts for all of the dramas were published in 1854. The music, however, was written in the order of presentation.

Wagner used the names found in the *Nibelungenlied*, the medieval German epic, but he used the related plot of the *Volsunga Saga* as the basis for his work. He changed characters and text to suit his artistic purposes, and thus created a "mythology" of his own.

The first drama, *Das Rheingold* (The Rhinegold), had its premiere 22 September 1869 at Munich. Three Rhine maidens guard the precious Rhinegold, which if stolen and forged into a ring will give its owner great powers. But anyone who possesses the gold must renounce love. Alberich, the dwarf, unable to win the Rhine maidens' love, renounces love and carries off the gold to Niebelheim, the land of fog.

As a reward for building Walhalla, Wotan, king of the gods, has promised to give Freia, goddess of youth and love, to the giants Fafner and Fasolt. The other gods refuse to permit this, and Wotan has nothing to offer the giants instead. Loge, the fire god, is called and suggests as a substitute the Rhinegold, of which Alberich is the possessor. The two giants agree. Wotan and Loge set off to steal it.

Wotan and Loge enter Niebelheim. Alberich shows them the treasure, as well as a helmet by which the wearer is able to assume any form. Loge persuades Alberich to transform himself into a toad. When Alberich does this, he is overpowered, and Wotan takes the treasure. However, Alberich puts a curse on the ring so that it will bring disaster on all who possess it.

The gold and the fatal ring are given to the giants, who then release Freia to the gods. They joyfully enter their palace over a rainbow bridge, but during the last scene the giant Fasolt is killed by Fafner. The curse of Alberich begins to work.

Wotan, knowing of the death of Fasolt, fears that the curse of the ring will fall on the gods. To defend Walhalla against this and the attacks of the Nibelungs, he fathers with Erda, the earth goddess, nine daughters (the Walkyries, chief of whom is Brünnhilde). One of their functions is to ride through the air bearing to Walhalla the bodies of dead heroes, who will be revived and will aid the gods in the coming battle.

To break the curse, it is also necessary to restore the ring to the Rhine maidens, but this task has to be done by a human. Wotan, in the guise of Walse, begets with a woman two Walsung twins, Siegmund and Sieglinde. Wotan hopes Siegmund will be the hero to slay Fafner and return the ring to its rightful owners. To prepare Siegmund for the task, Wotan sets various hardships for him. Sieglinde is made to marry the robber Hunding.

The second music drama is *Die Walküre* (The Valkyries), first performed 26 June 1870 in Munich. Siegmund staggers storm-driven into Hunding's empty hut. Sieglinde enters and finds the stranger—they are unknown to one another, though brother and sister—and they love each other at first sight. Hunding enters, and, enraged at what he finds, he challenges Siegmund to a fight the next day. Sieglinde gives Hunding a sleeping potion, and after a passionate duet the two lovers flee into the night.

Fricka, Wotan's wife, also the protector of the marriage vow, demands that Siegmund, who has sinned by sleeping with his sister, shall die in the coming combat with Hunding. Wotan reluctantly yields and commissions Brünnhilde to bring about Siegmund's defeat. Brünnhilde, however, sympathizes with the lovers and protects Siegmund in the battle. But she is foiled when Wotan enters and allows Hunding to kill Siegmund. Wotan thereupon slays Hunding. Brünnhilde comforts the bereaved Sieglinde, but because of her disobedience Brünnhilde is deprived of her divinity and is put to sleep by Wotan on a fire-encompassed rock. She can

be awakened only by a fearless hero, who can then claim her as his bride.

The third music drama, *Siegfried*, had its premiere 16 August 1876. Siegfried is the son of Sieglinde, born after the death of his father, Siegmund. Mime, Alberich's deformed brother, has reared Siegfried in his home in the forest. He hopes that someday Siegfried will slay Fafner, who changed himself into a dragon to guard the treasure. The act ends with Siegfried successfully forging a magic sword.

Siegfried slays Fafner. Mime offers a sleeping potion to Siegfried, who discovers his evil purpose and kills him. Having by chance put his finger, stained with the dragon's blood, to his lips, Siegfried is enabled to understand a bird as it sings. The bird tells of the sleeping Brünnhilde, and Siegfried goes to find her.

On his way Siegfried meets Wotan, who opposes him with his spear, but the spear is shattered by Siegfried's magic sword. Siegfried reaches the fire rock, rushes through the flames, and claims Brünnhilde as his bride.

The fourth and last music drama, *Götterdämmerung* (The Twilight of the Gods), had its premiere 17 August 1876 at Bayreuth. The opera opens in the Hall of the Gibichungs on the Rhine, where Siegfried has arrived, having left Brünnhilde behind. Here he is drugged with a magic love potion by Gutrune, who wants to marry him. The drug causes him to forget his love for Brünnhilde, and he falls in love with Gutrune. Gunther, Gutrune's brother, plots to marry Brünnhilde but knows he lacks the power to overcome her. Siegfried goes with Gunther to capture Brünnhilde. Disguised as Gunther, Siegfried overcomes Brünnhilde and hands her over to the Gibichungs. Siegfried, still under the spell of the drug, becomes Gutrune's lover, and Gunther becomes the lover of Brünnhilde.

Hagen stabs Siegfried, who in his last moments recovers his memory. Brünnhilde finds Siegfried dead and she realizes that he was under a spell. She still loves him. Logs are heaped up for a pyre, and the dead hero is placed on it but not before Brünnhilde has taken the fatal ring from his finger and cast it into the Rhine. The Rhine maidens appear singing. The sky darkens; the flames rise. Brünnhilde on her horse leaps into the flames. The Rhine rises, and Walhalla is seen to burst into flames.

In 1848 Wagner wrote a "sketch" for the four dramas. His early sketch is important in shedding light on those elements that he kept in the telling of the myth and those which he left out of the final version of the dramas. Numerous books have been written to explain Wagner's *Ring*. Among the best known is George Bernard Shaw's *The Perfect Wagnerite: A Commentary of the Niblung's Ring*. Arthur Rackham illustrated the English translation of the *Ring* by Margaret Armour, which was published in 1910.

Ripheus. In Greek and Roman mythology, a Trojan who joined Aeneas the night Troy was destroyed; he was slain after killing many Greeks. Ripheus is cited for his love of justice and equity in Vergil's *Aeneid* (book 2) and Dante's *Divine Comedy* (Paradise, canto 20). Ripheus is also the name of one of the centaurs killed by Theseus at the marriage of Pirithous and Hippodameia, as told in Ovid's *Metamorphoses* (book 12).

2528

Rip Van Winkle. In American literary folklore, creation of Washington Irving in *The Sketch Book*. Rip, who lives with a shrewish wife, one day goes hunting in the Catskills with his dog. There he meets dwarflike beings and drinks some liquor they give him. He falls asleep and awakens 20 years later, an old man, who discovers that his wife has died and the American Revolution has taken place. He goes to live with his grown daughter and makes new friends.

2529

Rival Schools of Thought. Jewish moral tale found in the Talmud. For more than two years two rival schools in the study of the Talmud, that of Shammai and that of Hillel, debated whether it would have been better if men had not been created. The followers of Shammai said it would have been better if God had not created man, but the school of Hillel said it was good that man had been created.

Finally, they concluded their arguments by a compromise: It would have been far better if man had not been created, but since he has been placed on earth, it is his duty to do the best he can to live a righteous life.

2530

Robert, St. (fame-bright). 11th century. In Christian legend, abbot, founder of the Monastery of Chaise-Dieu in the Auvergne. Feast, 17 April. As a child, Robert would nurse only at the breasts of good women, not "irreligious ones." When Robert became an abbot, the cook one day informed him that there wasn't enough food. As Robert was celebrating Mass, an eagle flew into the church and dropped an enormous fish, large enough to feed all the monks. When Robert died his soul ascended to heaven as a globe of fire.

2531

Robigo (mildew). In Roman mythology, goddess invoked to preserve grain from mildew. Her festival, *Robigalia*, was celebrated on 25 April with offerings of incense and entrails of a sheep and a dog. Ovid's *Fasti* (book 4) describes the feast.

2532

Robin. Any of several small birds having reddish breasts. A medieval Christian legend accounts for the red breast.

The night of Jesus' birth Mary and Joseph sought shelter in a cave inhabited by a small brown bird. When the angels came to praise the baby Jesus the little brown bird was awakened by the light glowing from the angels and by the heavenly singing. Moved by the beautiful song, the bird joined in and became the first nightingale.

Outside the cave another small bird saw shepherds leave their campfire and approach the cave. The bird flew to the fire and fanned it with its wing. The flames soared high into the air and colored the breast of the bird with yellow-red light. The bird became the first robin.

In the legend the nightingale is identified as male and the robin as female. Oscar Wilde in *The Nightingale and the Rose* identifies the bird as female.

2533

Robin Hood (fame-bright). 12th or 13th century. In medieval British legend, outlaw who stole from the rich to give to the poor. He was believed to be Robert Fitzooth, the outlawed earl of Huntingdon. He had 100 "tall men," all good archers. He took spoils, but according to an account of 1386, "he suffered no women to be oppressed, violated or otherwise molested; poor men's goods he spared, abundantly relieving them with that which by theft he got from abbeys and houses of rich men." Robin Hood's companions in Sherwood Forest and Barnesdale, Yorkshire, were Little John, Friar Tuck, Will Scarlet, Allan-a-Dale, George-a-Greene, and Maid Marion. According to one legend Robin Hood was treacherously slain by a nun at the command of his kinsman the prior of Kirkless, in Nottinghamshire. Another tradition says he died with Little John at the Battle of Evesham. Various operas on the subject of Robin Hood have been written, the most famous being Reginald De Koven's operetta *Robin Hood* (1890). Hollywood made several Robin Hood movies, one of the earliest starring Douglas Fairbanks in 1922.

2534

Roch, St. (repose). 14th century C.E. In Christian legend, patron saint of prisoners, the sick in hospitals and victims of plague. Feast, 6 August.

Roch was the son of the governor of Montpellier, France, who died when the saint was 20 years old. The lad then went to Rome, where a plague was raging and took care of the sick. He went from city to city in Italy helping the plague-stricken. Then, according to the account in Jameson's *Sacred and Legendary Art*, "One night, being in a hospital, he sank down to the ground, overpowered by fatigue and went to sleep. On waking, he found himself plague-stricken; a fever burned in every limb, and a horrible ulcer had broken out in his left thigh."

Fearful that he would disturb the other patients, Roch left for the woods, where he intended to die. However, his dog and an angel took care of him by tending his sore and bringing him bread every day. When he arrived home at Montpellier, he was so changed and wasted by his illness that no one recognized him. He was arrested as a spy and his uncle, who was the judge, had him locked in prison. After five years the jailor entered his cell one day and was dazzled by a bright light. He found Roch dead and near him a paper with these words: "All those who are stricken by the plague, and who pray through the merits and intercession of Roch, the servant of God, shall be healed."

Roch was then buried with honor at Montpellier, but Italian merchants stole his remains (in the Middle Ages it was quite common for saints' bodies or body parts to be removed or stolen from one shrine and placed in another) and brought them to Venice where they lie in the Church of San Rocco.

St. Roch's attributes are his dog and the physical markings of the plague. He often appears in paintings, as in Parmigianino's work, exposing his groin with its buboes (lymphatic swellings) or pointing to a purpuric spot on his leg. A statue of the saint using this iconography was carried in Constance in 1414 when a plague had broken out, and legend has it that the invocation of St. Roch stilled the plague. A more sedate episode from the saint's life was chosen by Julius Schnoor von Carolsfeld in his *St. Roch Distributing Alms*. The painting, done in sharp outline with clear colors, attempts to capture for the 19th century the religious art of early Italian and German masters.

Roderick, Don (fame-rule). Eighth century. In medieval Spanish history and legend, last Visigoth king of Spain, appearing in many Spanish ballads. He was defeated by the Moors in July 711, disappearing on the battlefield. He either was killed, drowned, or escaped. Some legends say he is alive and will return to Spain in its time of need.

Rodomont. In the Charlemagne cycle of legends, a Saracen hero who was killed by Ruggiero when he accused Ruggiero of turning traitor by becoming a Christian. Rodomont appears in Ariosto's *Orlando Furioso* and is mentioned by Cervantes in *Don Quixote*: "Who more brave than Rodomont?"

Rokola. In Melanesian mythology, Fijian god of carpenters who taught the people how to navigate.

Roland (fame; land). In the Charlemagne cycle of legends, one of the 12 paladins, called Orlando in Italian legends.

Roland was the count of Mans and knight of Blaives. He was the son of Duke Milo of Aigland and Bertha, the sister of Charlemagne. Medieval legend describes him as eight feet tall, brave, loyal, and somewhat simple-minded.

The most famous work on Roland is the 11th-century French poem *Chanson de Roland* (Song of Roland). When Charlemagne had been in Spain for six years, he sent Ganelon on an embassy to Marsilius, the Saracen king of Saragossa. Out of jealousy Ganelon told Marsilius the route that the Christian army was to take on its way home. Marsilius arrived at Roncesvalles just as Roland was going through the pass with a rearguard of 20,000 men. Roland fought until 100,000 Saracens were slain and only 50 of his own men were left alive. But another Saracen army of some 50,000 now poured in from the mountains. Roland blew his ivory horn, Olivant, which he had won from the giant Jutmundus. The third blast cracked the horn in two, birds fell dead from the sky, and the Saracen army fled, panic-stricken. Charlemagne heard the horn and rushed to the rescue, but it was too late. Roland had died of wounds from the battle.

Roland's sword, Durindana, or Durandal, had once belonged to the Trojan hero Hector. It had on its hilt a thread from the Virgin Mary's cloak, a tooth of St. Peter, one of St. Denis's hairs and a drop of St. Basil's blood. To prevent Durindana from falling into the hands of the Saracens, Roland hurled it into a poisoned stream.

Roland appears as Orlando in Italian works such as Boiardo's *Orlando Innamorato* (Orlando in Love) and Ariosto's *Orlando Furioso*. Ariosto's poem tells how Orlando goes mad when he is rejected by Angelica, daughter of the king of Cathay. She runs away with a Moor named Medoro. Orlando's wits are then deposited on the moon. Astolpho goes in search of them, using Elijah's chariot. St. John, who lives on the moon, gives Astolpho an urn containing Orlando's wits. On reaching earth again, Astolpho holds the urn to Orlando's nose and he is cured.

Roma (Rome). Capital of the Roman Empire, founded, according to Roman mythology, by Romu-

The goddess Roma

lus on 21 April 753 B.C.E. The city was built on seven hills: Palatium, Cermalus, Velia, Oppius, Cispius, Fagutal, and Sucusa. Roma or Dea Roma, the goddess of the city, was portrayed with a crown, sometimes in the form of Minerva or as an Amazon. On Roman coins she appears with a winged helmet. The Emperor Hadrian erected a temple in honor of Roma and Venus as ancestresses of the Roman people. Bizet's symphonic suite *Roma* and Respighi's three tone poems *The Pines of Rome, The Fountains of Rome*, and *Roman Festivals* try to capture the city in music.

2540

Romanus, St. Seventh century. In Christian legend, archbishop of Rouen, France; patron saint of merchants. Invoked against drowning, madness, poison and demonic possession. Feast, 23 October.

Romanus is best known in medieval legend for his destruction of the dragon Gargonille, which was eating the Christians in the area. His only helper in capturing the dragon was a murderer. After making the sign of the cross, Romanus walked into the dragon's den and threw a net over its head. The murderer then dragged the monster through the town to a large bonfire, where it was burned alive. In reward, the murderer was set free. From that day on it was a custom of the Chapter of Rouen to pardon a criminal condemned to death. The custom lasted until the French Revolution. The life of St. Romanus is found on the stained-glass windows of the cathedral of Rouen.

Romulus and Remus

2541

Romulus and Remus (? and oar). In Roman mythology, twin sons of Mars and Rhea Silvia, who was the daughter of Numitor (Numa), king of Alba Longa. Numitor's brother Amulius deposed Numitor and forced Rhea Silvia to become a vestal virgin.

When the twins Romulus and Remus were born, Amulius had Rhea Silvia placed in prison and the twins cast into the Tiber. The boys were discovered and rescued by Faustulus, a shepherd, who found a she-wolf to nurse them. When the boys grew up, they restored their grandfather Numitor to his rightful throne. The two then established a new city on the Palatine Hill, but in an argument about the exact site Romulus killed Remus and later became king. To populate his new city Romulus took fugitives for citizens and helped find them wives by encouraging them to rape the Sabine women. He ruled Rome for about 40 years. Romulus then mysteriously vanished in a whirlwind on the Campus Martius and was later worshiped by the Romans as Quirinus (the lance), a Sabine god, on the Quirinal Hill. His feast, *Quirinalia*, was celebrated on 13 March, the calends. The tale of Romulus and Remus is told or cited in Plutarch's *Life of Romulus*, Livy's *History of Rome*, Ovid's *Fasti* (book 2) and *Metamorphoses* (book 14), and Vergil's *Aeneid* (book 6). Livy's narrative was used as the basis for Macaulay's *Lays of Ancient Rome*. Machiavelli's *The Prince* singles out Romulus as a hero who helped raise his people out of chaos. The best-known artistic representation of Romulus and Remus is the bronze she-wolf nursing the two babies, which is now in the Capitoline Museum in Rome. The statue of the she-wolf outside the Palazzo Pubblico at Siena, by Giovanni di Turnio (1459), is that city's arms. Rubens also painted the she-wolf and the twins.

2542

Roraima, Mount. In Brazilian folklore, magic mountain guarded by demons in Roraima, Brazil. One traveler, Boddham-Whetham, in his *Roraima and British Guiana* (1879), tells how he and his party traveled up the mountain. They were met by an "unpleasant-looking Indian," who told them not to go any farther because the demon spirit that possessed the Indian had so ordered it. The mountain, he said, was guarded by an enormous serpentlike creature that could entwine 100 people in its folds. The Indians believed the mountain to be inhabited by white jaguars, white eagles, and didis (half-man, half-monkey creatures). When Boddham-Whetham returned, the Indians rejoiced to see him, "as they had not expected that the mountain-demons would allow us to return," he wrote.

2543

Rosalia, St. (rose garden). 12th century. In Christian legend, patron saint of Palermo, Sicily. Invoked against plague. Feast, 4 September. Rosalia left home at 16 and went to live in a cave, where she eventually died. In time her body was covered with stalactites.

When a plague broke out in Palermo in 1624, the people took her body and carried it in procession. The plague then stopped. In gratitude the people constructed a chapel in the cave. The saint is usually portrayed reclining in her cave with a bright light around her. Angels crown her with roses, and she holds a crucifix on her breast. She wears a brown tunic, sometimes ragged, and her hair is loose.

2544

Rosamund (fame). Sixth century. In medieval legend, daughter of King Cunimond of the Gepidae. She was forced to marry Alboin, king of the Lombards, after he killed her father. Later he made her drink from the skull of her dead father. In revenge, she had Perideus, the secretary of Helmechis, her lover, murder Alboin. She then married Helmechis and fled to Ravenna, but later planned his death so that she could marry Longines. Helmechis, knowing of the plot, forced Rosamund to drink from a poisoned cup, and she died. Swinburne's play *Rosamund, Queen of the Lombards* deals with the murderess.

Rose (Walter Crane)

2545

Rose. A thorny shrub with fragrant flowers; in world mythology and folklore, often associated with death and resurrection. The ancient Romans sometimes decked their tombs with roses, and Roman wills frequently specified that roses be planted on the grave. In Switzerland cemeteries still are known as rosegardens. In Christian symbolism the rose is associated with the Virgin Mary. For Arabs the rose is a symbol of masculine beauty.

Rose and the Butterfly, The. Turkish fable. A rose and a butterfly were debating who was the better. The rose said: "Poor creature, how short your life is! You are here today and gone tomorrow. But I remain on my stalk, spread my leaves in the sun, and scatter scent on the air without change."

"You are a prisoner," the butterfly replied, "while I have the power of going into many gardens. Besides, your life is also short. A storm may throw you to the ground at any moment." The rose replied that she, at least, was beautiful—the butterfly was a worm with wings!

As they argued, a woman came and plucked the rose, and a bird swooped down and carried off the butterfly. *Moral*: Pride and vanity often make people fancy themselves superior to others, though they are really of no importance, being subject to the same conditions of decay and death.

Rosebush and the Apple Tree, The. Jewish fable found in the Talmud.

A rosebush and an apple tree were having a debate.

"Who can compare with me?" the rosebush asked. "My flowers are beautiful and sweet to smell. True, you are larger, but what pleasure do you give to mankind?"

"Even though you are more beautiful than I," replied the apple, "you are not as good as I am."

"What do you mean?" replied the rosebush. "How are you better than I?"

"You do not give your flowers to man unless you first wound him with your thorns. But I give my fruit to all, even those who throw stones at me."

Rosemary. A pungent herb in European folklore, often associated with rejuvenation and love. According to English folklore, it could make one young again. It also was believed that if a girl took rosemary blended with thyme on St. Agnes's Eve (20 January), she would be sent a vision of her lover-to-be.

Rose of Lima, St. (fame, kind). 1568–1617 C.E. In Christian legend, patron of South America and the Philippines. Feast, 30 August.

Born Isabel de Flores y de Oliva, but known as Rose, the saint came of a poor family in Lima, Peru. She was noted for her beauty. Many men asked for her hand in marriage, but she refused. She went so far as to disfigure her face with a compound of pepper and quicklime. When her mother asked her to wear a wreath of roses around her head, they turned into a crown of thorns. St. Rose joined the Dominican Order, where her reputation for ecstasy and mystical transports caused a scandal as well as a church investigation. St. Rose bore it all with patience and spent her time taking care of Indians enslaved by the Spaniards.

When Pope Clement X was asked to canonize in 1671, her he refused, saying, "Indian and a saint! That is as likely as roses raining from heaven." Instantly a shower of roses fell on the Vatican until the pope acknowledged his error. The saint was painted by Murillo wearing a thorny crown, holding in her hand the figure of the Infant Christ. She was also the subject of a painting by Fernando Botero.

Rosetta stone. Popular name given to a slab of black basalt containing inscriptions in hieroglyphics, demotic, and Greek. It allowed Jean François Champollion (1790–1832) to decipher the meaning of the hieroglyphics—until that time unknown to the modern world—because the Rosetta stone had the Greek translation for each hieroglyphic alongside it. The Rosetta stone came into the possession of the British Museum after the French were defeated by the English in 1801.

Rosh Ha-Shanah (beginning of the year). In Judaism, feast of the New Year, celebrated the first and second days of Tishri (September–October). The feast may originally have been a commemoration of the dead, because it was a common belief of ancient peoples that the dead rejoined the living at the beginning of the year; but as the feast developed, the commemoration of the dead was pushed into the background, and Rosh Ha-Shanah now begings a time of prayer, penitence, and charity that leads to Yom Kippur, the greatest Jewish feast. One of the main features of the feast is the blowing of the *shofar*, a ram's horn, recalling the trumpets and thunders heard on Mount Sinai by Moses and the people (Exod. 19:19). It also recalls the belief that Yahweh, the Hebrew god, could dispel the powers of evil (Zech. 9:14–15).

As part of the synagogue service the poem *U-netanneh Tokeph* (Let us rehearse the grandeur) is recited, telling of the Day of Judgment when God will judge all people. The poem, according to medieval Jewish legend, was written by Ammon of Mayence (tenth century C.E.). He was called by the archbishop of Mayence to renounce his Jewish faith. When he did not respond, the archbishop had him arrested and his toes and fingers were cut off. Dying, he was brought to the synagogue. As the cantor was about to intone the Sanctification (Holy, holy, holy is the Lord of Hosts), Ammon said, "Pause, that I may sanctify the most holy Name." He began to recite but died when he reached "Yet Thy glories cover us, For Thy name is over us." On Rosh Ha-Shanah Jewish legend says God opens three books. The first book contains the names of pious and virtuous people who will be blessed for the coming 12 months. The second book contains the names of the wicked who are inscribed for death. In the third book, which is the largest, are the names of those who are between, neither very pious nor very evil. These people are given a chance to make a final choice before the record is sealed on Yom Kippur. One ceremony associated with the holiday is called *Tashlich* (Thou wilt cast), in which it is customary to cast or shake crumbs from one's pocket into the water, symbolizing the casting away of sins. The custom stems from ancient pagan practice in which sops were cast to the spirits of rivers on important days of the year. The Romans, for example, cast straw puppets into the Tiber on the Ides of May. In European folkways offerings used to be cast into the Danube, Rhine, Rhone, Elbe and Neckar on New Year's Eve.

2552

Rosie the Riveter. In American folklore of World War II, name given to a fictional woman who symbolized women's contributions to the war effort. Norman Rockwell's painting *Rosie the Riveter* is modeled on Michelangelo's fresco of the prophet Isaiah in the Sistine Chapel.

2553

Ross, Betsy. 1752–1836. In American history and folklore, creator of the first Stars and StripesAmerican flag. According to an account read before the Historical Society of Pennsylvania on 29 May 1870 by William Canby, Betsy Ross's grandson, the first flag was made in June 1776 at the request of a committee made up of George Washington, Robert Morris, and George Ross; but no evidence exists to support this. In 1781 Francis Hopkinson, who had designed a naval flag, asked Congress to reimburse him for the design of the original Stars and Stripes. Congress declined.

2554

Round Table. In Arthurian legend, the table made by Merlin at Carduel for Uther Pendragon, the father of King Arthur. Uther Pendragon gave the table to King Leodegraunce of Cameliard, who gave it to King Arthur when Arthur married Guinever, Leodegraunce's daughter.

Its circular design eliminated the usual head and foot and therefore assured equality of the knights and prevented jealousy. According to Malory's *Morte d'Arthur*, there were 150 knights who had "sieges," or seats, at the Round Table. King Leodegraunce brought 100 men to the wedding of King Arthur and Guinever. Merlin filled up 28 of the vacant seats, and King Arthur elected Gwaine and Tor. The remaining seats were left to those who might prove worthy of the honor. Always 12 knights, the number of Apostles of Jesus, were associated with the Round Table, though their names vary in different sources. The most frequent names were Lancelot, Tristram, Lamora, Tor, Galahad, Gwaine, Gareth, Plaomides, Kay, Mark, Mordred, Accolon, Ballamore, Beleobus, Belvoure, Bersunt, Bors, Ector de Maris, Ywaine, Floll, Gaheris, Galohalt, Grislet, Lionell, Marhaus, Paginet, Pelles, Perceval, Sagris, Superabilis, and Turquine.

2555

Rowan (red). A small tree sometimes known as the mountain ash. In medieval Christian belief the rowan, which had been associated with the pagan Druids, was believed to be potent against witchcraft. In Scotland suspected witches touched with a rowan branch were believed to be then carried away by the devil. Crosses of rowan branches were placed in strategic places, such as over doorways, as protection against evil.

In one legend the wood of the True Cross of Christ is rowan, only one of many trees so credited. Another belief was that rowans growing in graveyards kept the dead in their graves until Judgment Day.

2556

Rubezhal (turnip counter). In Germanic folklore, the turnip-counter spirit. He once abducted a princess who desired turnips. He planted them for her, and she asked him to count the seeds. While Rubezhal was counting, she escaped.

2557

Rudra (howler, ruddy one). In Hindu mythology, a storm god, later identified with Shiva; father of the Rudras or Maruts, wind gods.

In the *Rig-Veda*, the sacred collection of hymns to the gods, Rudra is portrayed as both beneficent and demonic. He is the god who heals both men and cattle, as in one hymn:

We implore Rudra,
the lord of songs,
the lord of animal sacrifices,
for health, wealth, and his favor.

In his demonic role he is addressed in another hymn:

> May the weapon of Rudra avoid us,
> may the great anger of the flaring one pass us by....
> O tawny and manly god, showing thyself,
> so as neither to be angry nor to kill,
> be mindful of our invocations,
> and rich in brave sons,
> we shall magnify thee in the congregation.

In some texts Rudra is said to have been born a boy from the forehead of Brahma. In another account he is said to have later divided into male and female, then multiplied, producing the Maruts, or Rudras.

2558
Rue. An aromatic evergreen, called by Shakespeare the "sour herbs of grace." It appears in English folklore and literature as a symbol of pity, mercy, and forgiveness, but it also symbolizes grief, repentance, bitterness, and disdain. An early English meaning still current is sorrow or regret. In the Middle Ages witches' brew contained rue because it was a potent force in the working of evil—but it was also an antidote to witchcraft. In Italy rue warded off spells cast by the evil eye. Dipped in holy water, rue branches were used to sprinkle bedrooms to counter demons that were upsetting a couple's sexual relations.

2559
Ruggiero. In the Charlemagne cycle of legends, a Saracen hero, also called Roger. He was nursed by a lioness and brought up by Atlantes, a magician, who gave him a dazzling magic shield. He threw it into a well because he thought it unfair to fight with it. Ruggiero deserted the Moorish army for Charlemagne's, becoming a Christian. He married Bradamant, Charlemagne's niece, and later killed Rodomont, another Saracen hero, who at his wedding accused him of being a traitor. Ruggiero appears in Ariosto's *Orlando Furioso* and Tasso's *Jerusalem Delivered*.

2560
Ruh (breath). In Islamic mythology, angel often identified with Gabriel. Ruh's duty is to bring motion to heavenly spheres, as well as to living beings. With the permission of Allah, Ruh can also stop the heavenly spheres. In the Koran (sura 16) the term *ruh* is used for spirit, as when Allah sends "down angels with the spirit" on "whomsoever He will." In early Arabic poetry, *ruh* meant breath or wind, but in later literature it was used not only for the angel but also for the human spirit and sometimes even to mean the djinn or demons.

2561
Ruhanga (creator). In African mythology (Ankore and Banyoro of Uganda), creator god who first allowed humans to return to life after death. All the people had to do was express happiness at the return of the dead. One day a woman refused to put on her best clothes and rejoice when one of the dead returned. This so angered Ruhanga that he decided that men and women should die just as the animals do and not return to life. Ruhanga is also known as Kazooba (sun) in his role as sun god; Mukameiguru (he who reigns in the sky) as sky god; and Rugaba (giver) as the giver of life to man, animals, and plants.

2562
Ruidoso. In American Western folklore, a big maverick steer that brought destruction on all who came in contact with it. At its death it turned into the ghost steer of the Pecos. Its agressive roar, that of a bull ready to charge, can still be heard at night.

2563
Rumina (teat). In Roman mythology, goddess of suckling infants and animals, consort of Ruminus, her male counterpart. In Rome a sanctuary to both deities stood at the foot of the Palatine Hill in the neighborhood of the Lupercal. In the same place stood the Ruminal fig tree, believed by some scholars to be an early emblem or symbol of Rumina and said to be the one under which Romulus and Remus were suckled by the she-wolf. It is mentioned in Ovid's *Fasti* (book 2).

Rumpelstiltskin

2564
Rumpelstiltskin. Popular European folktale, best known in the Grimms' version. Rumpelstiltskin is a dwarf who promises to help a maiden spin flax into gold if she will give him her firstborn child. In desperation she agrees, but when the child is born, she begs Rumpelstiltskin to let her keep him. He agrees to let her keep the child if she can guess his name within three days. She dispatches all of her servants

in an effort to learn his name. One overhears Rumpelstiltskin say his name while reciting a rhyme and dancing in the forest. At the end of three days he returns, and the girl is ready for him and speaks his name. He is so angry that he drives himself into the ground by stamping his foot and tears himself in half trying to extricate himself. In some European versions the dwarf is called Tit-Tot, Titeliture, Riodin-Riodon, and Dancing Vargaluska.

2565

Rusalka (female water spirit). In Slavic folklore, female water spirit who lives part of the year in water and part in the forest.

Two types of *rusalkai* are found in Slavic folktales. The northern type is a demonic being, somewhat pale, who entices men with her songs and then drowns them, much like Sirens in Greek mythology. The southern variant is an attractive girl, who also entices men but truly loves them. When a man dies in her arms, it is considered a blessing. Among the Bulgarians, the *rusalkai* are called *samovily* and are believed to be the spirits of unbaptized dead girls. The Slovaks believe them to be the souls of brides who died after their marriage night. Poles believe them to be beautiful girls punished for leading wicked lives. The Polish variety are good to those who were kind to them in life and punish those

Rustum fighting the White Demon

where were unkind. The Russian composer Alexander Dargomizhsky composed an opera *Rusalka*, as did the Czech composer Antonin Dvořák. Dvořák's *Rusalka* is based on a story by Alexander Pushkin.

2566

Rustum. In the Persian epic poem *Shah Namah*, by Firdusi, great hero and father of Sohrab.

While yet a child, Rustum displayed great courage and strength. He ate as much as five men could eat in a day and was nursed by ten women. When Rustum grew up, King Kai-Kaus appointed him captain-general of his army. One day the king decided he wanted to invade Mazinderan, a beautiful and rich city. The idea was planted in the king's mind by a demon who wished the venture to bring about the monarch's destruction. When the king of Mazinderan heard that Kai-Kaus was on his way to invade his kingdom, he called on the White Demon for help. Meanwhile, Kai-Kaus, full of anticipation of victory, was camped on a plain near the city, but hailstorms poured down in the night, destroying most of the army. For seven days the king lamented the loss of his army. Then he heard the voice of the White Demon, which said to him:

O king, thou art the willow-tree, all barren,
With neither fruit, nor flower. What could induce
The dream of conquering Mazinderan?
(James Atkinson translation)

The White Demon seized the king, but the king managed to send a message asking for help. Rustum started on his journey to free the king. In one day he came to a forest full of wild asses. Hungry, he caught one and cooked it for dinner. While he was asleep a wild lion attacked him, but Rustum was saved by his faithful horse, Ruksh. The next day the two continued on their journey. Coming to a desert, Rustum prayed for some water, which was granted him. After drinking, Rustum addressed his faithful horse:

Beware, my steed, of future strife.
Again, thou must not risk thy life;
Encounter not with lion fell,
Nor demon still more terrible;
But should an enemy appear,
Ring loud the warning in my ear.
(James Atkinson translation)

After delivering his speech, Rustum lay down to sleep, leaving Ruksh unbridled and at liberty to graze close by. At midnight a monstrous dragon, eight yards long, appeared. Ruksh awoke his master, who attacked the monster. Ruksh helped his master by biting and tearing the monster's scaly hide while Rustum severed its head.

After killing the dragon Rustum resumed his journey, coming to a beautiful green spot where he settled for the night. He found a ready-roasted deer, some bread, and salt. He sat down to eat when suddenly the food disappeared; a flask of wine and a tambourine took its place. Rustum played the instrument, and a beautiful woman appeared. Not knowing she was a demoness, Rustum placed in her hands a cup of wine, calling upon the name of Allah. Suddenly she turned into a Black Demon. Seeing this, Rustum took his sword and cut her in two.

Next the hero encountered Aulad, who ruled part of the land. The two fought and Aulad lost. Rustum then asked Aulad to give him information as to where King Kai-Kaus was being held prisoner. Rustum promised to make Aulad the next king of Mazinderan if Aulad gave the correct information. Aulad told him where the demons were located, and Rustum went to their hiding place and defeated the demon Arzend. Then the two, Rustum and Aulad, went to the city of Mazinderan. Ruksh, Rustum's horse, neighed so loudly that the sound of it reached the imprisoned king.

Before Rustum could free the king, however, he had to fight the White Demon at Halt-koh (seven mountains). He went to the mountain and found 400 demons. He asked Aulad when to attack and was told that the best time was when the sun was at its hottest because the demons always liked to take a nap during the heat. When the sun was at its height and the demons napping, Rustum dismembered them. A few, however, escaped to tell the White Demon.

Advancing to the White Demon's cave, Rustum looked down and saw that the cave was as dark as hell itself.

"Are you tired of life," the White Demon cried out, "that you invade my kingdom? Tell me your name, since I do not want to destroy a nameless thing."

Rustum then told the White Demon his name and the battle began. The hero pierced the White Demon's thigh, lopping off a limb. The two fought furiously until at last Rustum grabbed the White Demon, lifted him in the air, and dashed him to the ground. He then tore out the demon's heart, and demons came out of his body as he bled. Rustum then took the heart of the White Demon and restored the sight of King Kai-Kaus, who had earlier been blinded by the demons.

In Persian art Rustum is often portrayed wearing armor and a helmet, with the skin of a leopard as part of his outfit.

Variant spellings: Rostastahm, Rustem.

Ruth (friendship). In the Bible, O.T., a Moabite heroine and name of an Old Testament book. She was
an ancestress of King David and Jesus. During the
days of the Judges, Elimelech and Naomi, with their
two sons, went to Moab to escape a famine in their
native Bethlehem. The sons, Mahlon and Chilion
married Moabite women, Orpah and Ruth. Then all
of the men died. Naomi, hearing that there was again
bread in her native land, decided to return, and her
two daughters-in-law wished to go with her. Naomi
told them to return to their own families. Orpah
agreed, but Ruth said to Naomi, "Intreat me not to
leave thee, or to return from following after thee . . .
thy people shall be my people, and thy God my
God" (Ruth 1:16). In Bethlehem Ruth gleaned in the
field of Boaz, a kinsman of Elimelech and "a mighty
man of wealth," and she found favor in his eyes.
Recognizing her kinship and its customary rights,
Boaz protected her by marriage, and from this union
King David descended. In Christian art the Tree of
Jesse, the father of King David, sometimes portrays
Boaz on one of its branches.

S

Sab-dag. In Tibetan folklore, the house-god, devil or spirit, who must be appeased or else he will cause harm. To make sure he is in a good mood, once a year the Lamas propitiate him by doing "the water sacrifice for the eight injurers."

Sadhyas (to be attained). In Hindu mythology, a group of spirits who inhabit the region between the earth and one sun. Their number varies from 12 to 17.

Sadi. c. 1184–1263. Assumed name of the Persian poet Sheikh Muslih Addin, whose major works are *The Gulistan* and *The Bustan*, didactic works in prose and verse containing numerous fables.

A descendant of Ali, Muhammad's son-in-law, Sadi studied at Baghdad and, according to some accounts, was made a prisoner by the Christian Crusaders, then ransomed. His major works, *The Gulistan* and *The Bustan*, have been known in the West for centuries, even though his predilection for homosexual liaisons was often masked in translations of his works.

Ralph Waldo Emerson so admired Sadi that he often used Sadi's name as a pseudonym for his poems. One of Emerson's major poems, titled *Saadi*, contains Emerson's summation of the man whom he considered a great poet and moralist.

Sadko. In Russian folklore, a merchant *bogatyr*, an epic hero. He appears in the *byliny*, the epic songs, as well as in folktales.

Sadko was a rich merchant who sailed the sea but never paid tribute to the czar of the sea. One day he descended to the watery depths, met the czar and played for him on his *qusli*, a stringed instrument. The czar of the sea was so moved that he began to dance, causing a storm that wrecked many ships. When Sadko came to the water's surface again, he sailed on the River Volga for some 12 years. Wishing to return to his city of Novgorod, he cut a slice of bread, put some salt on it, and placed it on the waves of the Volga. The river thanked Sadko for his kindness and told him to see its brother, the lake of Ilmen. In reward for his kindness the lake told Sadko to cast his nets into the waters. They were at once filled with fish, which then were miraculously transformed into silver.

Nikolai Rimsky-Korsakov used some of the legends for his opera *Sadko*.

Saehrimnir (blackened). In Norse mythology, the magic boar that was partaken of by the gods and heroes in Valhalla. It was killed daily, cooked and eaten, and returned to life the next day, so the ritual could be repeated. Saehrimnir was prepared by Andhrimnir (sooty-faced), the cook of the gods, who boiled the boar in the magic caldron, Eldhrimir. In the *Lay of Grimnir*, one of the poems in the *Poetic Edda*, Saehrimnir is said to be "the best of flesh."

Sage. A shrub of the mint family, used as an herb in cooking, also an all-purpose remedy in Greek and Roman folk medicine. It was dedicated to the Greek god Zeus and the Roman Jupiter. In Christian folk medicine sage was used to freshen the blood, cure nervous stomach, and relieve epilepsy, palsy, fever, and the plague. An English folk rhyme says: "He that would live for aye, / Must eat sage in May."

Sage was planted on graves in medieval England.

Saints. Holy ones in Christianity, also holy ones in Islamic and Judaic folklore and legend.

During the Middle Ages the cult of the saints among Christians was one of the main aspects of religion. Many shrines and relics of the saints were honored, and numerous churches built in their honor. The most important saint was the Virgin Mary, whose cult was the most popular, but thousands of other saints were also honored because it was believed that the saints in heaven could plead with God for the people still on earth. St. Thomas Aquinas had written: "A propitious predestination can be helped by the prayers of the saints." From the ninth century on, the legends of the saints abound in medieval thought.

Saints were invoked to cure diseases and ills; for example, St. Christopher to protect against bad dreams or St. Thomas à Becket to prevent or cure blindness. St. Agatha was invoked to protect against fire, but St. Florian should be invoked if the fire had already started. Those with toothache called on St. Appolonia because she had all her teeth pulled out at her martyrdom. Saints also were patrons of cities, churches, and countries. St. George protected England, St. Peter protected Flanders, and St. Ursula protected Cologne.

Saints were invoked by children, wives, idiots, students; every aspect of medieval life had a patron saint to watch over it. Archers had St. Sebastian, who had been shot at with arrows. Bakers prayed to St. Winifred because he was also a baker. Captives looked to St. Barbara since she had been locked in a tower. The insane, if they could pray, invoked St. Dymphna.

The thousands of saints during the Middle Ages did not receive formal recognition from the Church. Most of the cult grew up under popular support. The first historically attested canonization of a saint took place in 993 C.E. when Pope John XV sainted Ulrich of Augsburg. Sometimes a bishop would saint a person in the hope that revenue would come into his diocese from the saint's relics, which would then be encased in an elaborate shrine for the faithful.

A reaction against the cult of saints came at the close of the Middle Ages. At the Reformation the practice was attacked by Calvinists and Zwinglians on the grounds that the Bible did not sanction such practice. The Church of England in the Thirty-Nine Articles held: "The Romish Doctrine concerning . . . Images as Relics, and also Invocation of Saints, is a fond thing, vainly invented, and grounded upon no warranty of Scripture, but rather repugnant to the Word of God." (Article 22)

The Protestant attack on the saints was countered by the Roman Catholics. The Council of Trent (1563) stated: "The saints, who reign together with Christ, offer up their own prayers to God for men. . . . it is good and useful suppliantly to invoke them, and to have recourse to their prayers, aid, and help for obtaining the benefits of God."

The Catholic–Protestant battle of the saints continues into the present century. Some Protestant groups have relaxed their attack, and the Roman church has softened its cry for the saints. Secular writers have entered the field. William James, in *The Varieties of Religious Experience*, wrote: "In the life of the saints, technically so called, the spiritual faculties are strong, but what gives the impression of extravagance proves usually on examination to be a relative deficiency of intellect." Mussolini was not so subtle in his attack. In a speech given in 1904 he said, "The history of the saints is mainly the history of insane people." A comic note was struck by Ambrose Bierce in *The Devil's Dictionary* in which saint is defined as "a dead sinner revised and edited."

2575

Sakatimuna. In Islamic mythology, enormous serpent killed by the archangel Gabriel. Allah sent Gabriel saying: "Take down for me the iron staff of the 'creed' which dangles at the gate of heaven, and kill the serpent Sakatimuna." Gabriel did as God had commanded and the serpent was broken apart, the head and forepart shooting up above the heavens and the tail penetrating downward beneath the earth. Some commentators believe this tale is to be taken as an explanation of an eclipse.

2576

Sakhar. In Jewish and Islamic legend, a demon who impersonated King Solomon.

King Solomon, having defeated Sidon, slew the king of that city and brought away the king's daughter, Jerada, to be one of his mistresses. The young girl continually cried over the death of her father. To calm her, Solomon ordered the djinn to make an image of the dead king. When it was finished, it was placed in Jerada's chamber, where she and her maids worshiped it every day. Solomon learned from his vizier Asaf that the women were committing idolatry, and he ordered the image destroyed. To atone for his mistake Solomon then went into the desert to ask God for forgiveness. But God wanted more than a plea from Solomon.

It was the king's custom when he washed or "eased himself" to remove his magic ring and hand it to the concubine Amina. One day, when she had the ring in her custody, the demon Sakhar appeared in the shape of Solomon and took the ring. With it Sakhar had complete control of the entire kingdom. Solomon in the meantime had changed in appearance and was not recognized by his subjects. He wandered about for 40 days (the same length of time the image had been worshiped); then Sakhar flew away, casting the magic ring into the sea. The king later recovered it from inside a fish. Solomon eventually captured Sakhar and tied a great stone to his neck and threw him into the Lake of Tiberias.

2577

Sakhmet (the powerful one). In Egyptian mythology, the lion goddess, honored as goddess of war; called Sakhmis by the Greeks. She was the consort of the god Ptah, and together with their son Nefertem they formed the divine triad of gods worshiped at Memphis. In Egyptian art Sakhmet is often depicted as a woman with the head of a lioness, which is surmounted by the solar disk encircled by a uraeus. The numerous images of the lioness goddess in hardstone that are often found in museums throughout the world represent Sakhmet and were all originally found in the precinct of the goddess Mut in southern Karnak. It is assumed by scholars that there were two images of Sakhmet for each day of the year to which prayers were addressed to gain her favor.

Variant spellings: Sekhmet, Sechmet, Sekhait, Sekhauit, Skhautet, Sekhem.

2578

Sakradhanus. In Hindu mythology, the bow (rainbow) of the storm god, Indra.

2579

Saku-Ikazuchi. In Japanese mythology, one of the Ikazuchi, the eight gods of thunder.

2580

Salacia. In Roman mythology, goddess of spring water; wife of Neptune. She was identified by the Romans with the Greek Amphitrite.

2581

Saladin. 1137–1193. In medieval history and legend, sultan over Syria and Egypt. He was the enemy, as well as the friend, of Richard the Lion-Hearted. Saladin appears as Sultan Aladine in Tasso's epic of the First Crusade, *Jerusalem Delivered*. Walter Scott introduces him in his novel *The Talisman*, first disguised as Sheerkohf, emir of Kurdistan, and later as Adonbeck el Hakim, the physician.

2582

Salamander. A small amphibian, similar to a lizard, with smooth, moist skin.

In world mythology and folklore, the salamander was believed to be poisonous. The antidote for its poison was a drink made by brewing stinging nettle in a tortoise broth. In Greek folklore, according to Pliny, the salamander "seeks the hottest fire to breed in, but quenches it with the extreme frigidity of its body." Christians, echoing this belief, adopted the salamander as a symbol of the Christian struggle against the desires of hot, sinful flesh. Francis I of France, seeking an appropriate symbol for his absolute dictatorial powers, chose a salamander surrounded by flames above the inscription: "I nourish and extinguish."

2583

Saleh. In Islamic legend, prophet who preached to the Thamudites. They insisted that Saleh perform a miracle if he wished them to believe in Allah. They suggested that he come to their festival, where they would ask their gods for help and he would ask Allah. They called upon their idols and received no response. Then Jonda Ebn Amru, their leader, pointed to a rock and told Saleh that if he could make a pregnant she-camel come out of the rock he would believe. Saleh called upon Allah, the rock went into labor, and a she-camel appeared and gave birth to a young camel. Seeing this miracle, Jonda believed, although the majority of people did not. Allah then destroyed the unbelievers. The Koran (sura 7) mentions the "she-camel of Allah" but does not give the legend, which was supplied by Islamic commentaries on the sacred text.

2584

Salman al-Parisi. Seventh century. In Islamic legend, saint, patron of all corporations. A companion of Muhammad, who spoke highly of him, Salman ran away as a boy to follow a Christian monk but eventually was convinced that Muhammad was the prophet sent to restore the faith of Abraham of the Old Testament. Salman is considered one of the founders of Sufism, the mystical sect of Islam. Its name is believed to be derived from the Arabic word *suf*, wool, because of the coarse woolen garments worn by ascetics. Other possible sources of the term are the Arabic word for purity and the Greek word *sophia*, wisdom. The early Sufis dedicated their lives to devotion and seclusion. There are references to them in the *Rubaiyat* of Omar Khayyam, such as the ironic number 87:

Whereat some one of the loquacious Lot—
I think a Súfi pipkin—waxing hot—
"All this of Pot and Potter—Tell me then,
Who is the Potter, pray, and who the Pot?

2585

Salmon of Knowledge. In Celtic mythology, a magic fish fed by nuts dropped from the nine hazel trees on the edge of the river Boyne.

2586

Salome (peaceful). In the Bible, N.T., the wife of Zebedee and the mother of James and John. She witnessed the Crucifixion and was at the tomb on Easter (Mark 15:40). The name is also given to the daughter of Herodias and Herod Philip in Jewish and Christian tradition, though the the girl is not named in the Bible. Her tale is told in Matthew (14:6–8): "But when Herod's birthday was kept, the daughter of Herodias danced before them, and pleased Herod. Whereupon he promised with an oath to give her whatsoever she would ask. And she, being before instructed by her mother, said, 'Give me here John Baptist's head in a charger.'" An executioner then beheaded the prophet. Medieval legend said that Herodias had been in love with John the Baptist and Herod in love with Salome. Hermann Sudermann's tragedy *The Fires of St. John* and Oscar Wilde's *Salome*, illustrated by Aubrey Beardsley, are the best-known versions of the legend. Richard Strauss's opera *Salome* uses the Wilde play in a German translation. Flaubert's *Herodias* also uses the legend.

Salome (Beardsley)

Saluka-Jataka. Buddhist folktale, number 286 of the *Jatakas*, or *Birth-Stories of the Former Lives of the Buddha*.

When Brahmadatta ruled as king of Benares, the future Buddha was born as an ox named Big Redcoat. He had a younger brother called Little Redcoat. Both of them worked for a family in a small village. When one of the girls in the family came of age, she was asked for in marriage by a neighboring family for their son. In the girl's family there was a pig, called Celery, who was being fatted to serve as the main meal on the coming wedding day. "Brother," said Little Redcoat one day to Big Redcoat, "we work for this family and help them earn a living. Yet they only give us grass and straw, while they feed Celery, the pig, with rice porridge, and he sleeps comfortably on a platform under the eaves. What can he do for them that we can't?"

"Don't be envious of Celery's porridge," said Big Redcoat. "They want to make him fat for the wedding feast of the young lady of the house. That's

why they are feeding him. Wait a few days and you'll see him dragged out, killed, chopped to pieces, and eaten up by the wedding guests."

A few days later, the wedding guests came, and Celery was killed and eaten. Both oxen, seeing what happened, were now quite pleased with their ration.

"In this tale of my former life," said the Buddha, "Ananda, my disciple, was Little Redcoat and I was Big Redcoat."

Samantabhadra. In Mahayana Buddhism, one of the five Dhyani-Bodhisattvas, representing universal kindness. His symbols are a magic jewel and a scroll; his mount is an elephant. In some Tibetan traditions he is a Buddha, sky blue in color, without clothing or ornaments.

Samaritan, Good. In the Bible, N.T., a parable told by Jesus (Luke 10:29–37), in answer to: "Who is my neighbor?" It tells of a man left half dead by robbers on the road from Jerusalem to Jericho. A priest and Levite pass him by in turn, but a Samaritan—a group despised by the Jews—took care of him and paid for his lodgings. Jesus ends the parable by saying, "Which of these three, thinkest thou, was neighbor unto him that fell among the thieves? And he said, He that shewed mercy on him. Then said Jesus unto him, Go, do thou likewise" (Luke 10:36–37). The scene has been painted numerous times in Western art.

Samba. In Hindu mythology, a son of Krishna (an incarnation of the god Vishnu) by Jambavati; he scoffed at sacred things. Once he dressed up as a pregnant woman and went to three holy men, asking whether he would give birth to a girl or a boy. They answered, "This is not a woman, but the son of Krishna, and he shall bring forth an iron club which shall destroy the whole race of Yadu . . . and you and all your people shall destroy the race by the club." Samba then gave birth to an iron club, which later formed part of the tip of an arrow that killed Krishna when Jaras (old age) shot at him. In later life Samba became a leper, but the sun god, Surya, cured him through fasting and penance. Later Samba built a temple to worship the sun.

Sambiki Saru. In Japanese mythology, three apes: Mizaru (not seeing) with hands over his eyes, who sees no evil; Kikazaru (not hearing) covering his ears, who listens to no evil; and Iwarazaru (not speaking) with his hands on his mouth, who speaks no evil. They attend either Saruta Hito no Mikoto, the long-nosed Shinto god whose nasal appendage is said to be some seven cubits long, or the god Koshin.

Sam Hart of Woburn. In American folklore of New England, a horseman who once entered into a race with the devil. The devil appeared to Sam in the form of a country parson riding a black horse and challenged Sam to a race. Both set off at once, but Sam soon realized that the horse and its rider were none other than the devil. He headed for church land, which he knew the devil could not traverse. When he reached the sacred site, the devil's black horse went down on its haunches and threw the devil. Realizing he had lost, the devil said: "You've cheated one whose business is cheating, and I'm a decent enough fellow to own up when I'm beaten. Here's your money. Catch it, for you know I can't cross holy ground, you rascal. And here's my horse. He'll be tractable enough after I've gone home and as safe as your mare. Good luck to you." A whiff of sulfur smoke burst up from the road, and the devil disappeared. But Sam's neighbors never trusted his black horse. One day, they said, it would carry its owner to hell to meet the devil.

Samiasa (the name Azza). In Jewish folklore, a fallen angel who hangs suspended between heaven and earth, with his nose pierced, as punishment for having had sexual intercourse with a mortal woman. Samiasa is responsible for the worship of the sun, moon, and stars because he has the power to move them when men pray to him. The English Romantic poet Lord Byron has Samiasa as one of the principal characters in his poetic drama *Heaven and Earth*. This drama deals with the biblical myth of the marriage between the Sons of God, or angels, and the daughters of men (Gen. 6:12).

Variant spellings: Azza, Semiaza, Shemhazai, Shamazya, Amezzyarak, Uzza.

Sammael (poison angel). In medieval Jewish folklore, principal angel of death, regarded as both beneficent and demonic.

Sammael appears in many Jewish folktales as a dispenser of death, under the control of God. One tells how he was outwitted by two clever foxes. Sammael asks God for permission to kill two of every creature since as yet no one had died in the world. God grants the request with the proviso that nothing be killed before its allotted time. Sammael agreed and then proceeded to break his promise. Coming upon two young foxes, he is about to murder them when they cry out that he has already killed their parents.

"Look into the water," they say to Sammael.

The angel looks down and sees the reflection of the two young foxes. Thinking the reflection to be foxes he already drowned, he allows the young foxes to go free.

Sammael is mentioned in Longfellow's poetic drama *Christus: A Mystery* as "full of eyes," holding a "sword, from which doth fall . . . a drop of gall" into the mouth of the dying, thus causing death. One scene in the drama deals with the young Judas Iscariot, the betrayer of Jesus. Judas is being taught by a rabbi who asks the boy why dogs howl at night. Judas replies that "dogs howl, when the icy breath" of the "Great Sammael, the Angel of Death," is taking flight "through the town."

Variant spellings: Satanil, Samil, Seir, Salmail.

Sampo (prop of life?). In the Finnish epic poem *The Kalevala*, magic object forged by the smith Ilmarinen for Louhi, the evil mistress of Pohjola, the Northland, as part payment for the hand of her daughter, the Maiden of Pohjola.

Louhi set up the magic sampo in a hillside cave, where it took root, producing prosperity for her land. Vainamoinen, the culture hero, determined to steal the sampo from Louhi. He constructed a ship, and the smith Ilmarinen forged a sword for him. Both then set off for Pohjola. On the way the hero Lemminkainen called to them from the shore, asking to accompany them. They took him along, but during the voyage their boat was struck by a giant pike. Vainamoinen killed the pike and made a harp with which he lulled all of the people of Pohjola to sleep. With the help of an ox, the three heroes stole the sampo and started home. However, Louhi awoke and sent fog and wind after the three, causing Vainamoinen's harp to fall overboard. Louhi and her men pursued them in a boat and caught up with them. A battle ensued in which the sampo fell into the lake and was broken to pieces. Only a few pieces floated to the shore. Vainamoinen then planted them for good luck.

In *The Kalevala* the sampo is pictured as a three-sided mill, one side or face grinding out grain, one salt, and one money all in unlimited amounts. Its *kirjokansai* (lid) is described as being of "many colors." Yet scholars are not at all sure what the sampo actually represents. Some see it as a magic mill, others as a symbol of the North Star, and yet others as a dragon.

Sam Slick. In American literary folklore, a Yankee peddler, shrewd, ruthless, and full of wise sayings; created by Thomas Chandler Haliburton. Sam Slick appears in a series of Haliburton's books, the first being *The Clockmaker, or, The Sayings and Doings of Samuel Slick of Slickville*. Some of Slick's sayings are "Time is like a woman and pigs; the more you want it to go, the more it won't;" "Politics make a man as crooked as a pack does a peddler; not that they are so awful heavy either, but it teaches a man to stoop in the long run." Born in Nova Scotia, Haliburton left for England in 1856 and was elected to the House of Commons.

2597

Samson (sunny or sun-hero). In the Bible, O.T., a hero, one of the Judges, whose tale is told in the Book of Judges (chaps. 13–16). After many childless years Manoah and his wife were told by an angel that she would bear a son, Samson. He later became a leader of the Israelites in their struggle against the Philistines. Brought up as a Nazarene, his hair had never been cut, and he had great strength. On one occasion he caught 300 foxes, tied firebrands to their tails and set them loose in the Philistine field (Judg. 15:4–6). Three thousand of his compatriots, afraid that the Philistines would punish them for Samson's bravery, tied him up and delivered him to the Philistines. Breaking his bonds, he picked up from a dead carcass the jawbone of an ass and killed 1,000 Philis-

tines (Judg. 15:10–15). After a night in Gaza with a whore he still had enough strength to tear up and carry away the city gates (Judg. 16:1–3). He then fell in love with Delilah, a Philistine woman, who seduced him into telling her the source of his strength—his hair. While he slept, she had his hair cut off, and his strength was gone. The Philistines then bound him and put out his eyes. During a feast in the temple of Dagon, the Philistine god, the blind and now weakened Samson was paraded before the guests. Feeling his way, he found the pillars supporting the building and pulled down the temple, killing himself and thousands of Philistines (Judg. 16:4–31).

Rembrandt's dramatic *Blinding of Samson*, Milton's dramatic poem *Samson Agonistes*, Saint-Saëns' opera *Samson et Delilah*, and Handel's oratorio *Samson* all deal with the legend, as does a Hollywood film, *Samson and Delilah*, directed by Cecil B. DeMille.

2598

Samuel (name of God) 11th century B.C.E. In the Bible, O.T., Prophet, son of Elkanah and Hannah. His legend is told in 1 and 2 Samuel. At his birth he was consecrated to temple service by his mother, Hannah. When still a child, he heard the voice of Yahweh, the Hebrew god, in the night. He continued the work of Moses by reuniting the people. After a

Samuel anoints Saul as king

Samson and Delilah

long life as priest and leader, he yielded to the people's demand for a king and anointed Saul as Israel's first king. He also anointed David after Saul had been rejected by Yahweh. He appears in Barent Fabritius' painting *Consecration of Young Samuel by the Priest Eli*. In Islamic legend his name is Shamwil and sometimes Ishmawil. He is referred to in the Koran (sura 2).

2599
Sanaka (the ancient). In Hindu mythology, one of the four mind-born sons of Brahma.

2600
Sananda (joyous). In Hindu mythology, one of the four mind- born sons of Brahma.

2601
Sanatana (eternal). In Hindu mythology, one of the four mind-born sons of Brahma.

2602
Sanatkumara (eternally a youth). In Hindu mythology, one of the four mind-born sons of Brahma.

2603
Sancus. In ancient Italian mythology, god of oaths, marriage, treaties, and hospitality, identified by the Romans with Apollo or Jupiter. He was also called Semo Sancus or Semo Sancus Dius Fidius.

2604
Sandalphon (co-brother). In Jewish folklore, angel who stands on earth with his head reaching to the door of heaven. The American poet Henry Wadsworth Longfellow, in his poem *Sandalphon*, based on his reading of *The Traditions of the Jews* by J. P. Stehelin, writes of how Sandalphon "gathers the prayers" of the faithful and turns them into flower "garlands of purple and red" and presents them to God. In the poem Sandalphon is described as "the Angel of Glory" and "the Angel of Prayer."

Variant spellings: Sandolphon; Sandolfon.

2605
Sand Man. In European folklore, the man who puts children to sleep by sprinkling sand or dust in their eyes.

2606
Sang Gala Raja (black king of the djinn). In Islamic mythology, the mightiest djinn; in Malay belief, a combination of the Hindu god Shiva in his destructive role and an Islamic djinn. One account says Sang Gala Raja was formed from drops of blood that shot up to heaven when Habil and Kabil (analogous to the biblical Abel and Cain) bit their thumbs. Another account says Sang Gala Raja was formed from parts of Sakatimuna, the monster serpent, when he was slain by the archangel Gabriel. Sang Gala Raja is believed to live in the heart of the jungle with his wife Sang Gadin and his seven children.

2607
Sangha (assembly). In Buddhism, term used for the community of Buddha's disciples. It is divided into four classes: monks, nuns, laymen, laywomen. Monks and nuns are of two sorts: novices, those who have taken *pabbajja* (going forth), and the fully professed, those who have *upasampada* (completion). Sometimes the term is used exclusively to refer to the monks and sometimes it is used to distinguish Buddhists according to a scheme of spiritual achievement without regard to their ecclesiastical status.

2608
San Hsien Shan (the three mountains of the immortals). In Chinese mythology, the three isles of the blessed, which are P'eng- lai, Fang-chang, and Ying-chou, said to be located in the Eastern Sea. Once an expedition was sent to procure from them the plant of immortality. The expedition failed.

2609
Sanjna (conscience). In Hindu mythology, the wife of Surya, the sun god. Sanjna is also called Dyumayi (the brilliant) and Maha- virya (the very powerful).

2610
Sansenjin. In Japanese mythology, the three gods of war, portrayed as a man with three heads and six arms riding on a boar.

2611
Santaramet. In Armenian mythology, goddess of the underworld, or a term for the underworld. Santaramet is derived from the Persian guardian of the earth, Armaiti, one of the seven Amesha Spentas.

2612
Santes of Monte Fabri, St. 14th century. In Christian legend, Franciscan lay brother. Feast, 6 September. Medieval legend tells how the saint saw the walls of a church open up. One day, being prevented by his duties from attending Mass, St. Santes fell on his knees when he heard the bell announce the elevation of the Host during Mass. Immediately the four walls of the church opened so that he might see the altar and the Host, which was radiant with light. When the Mass was over, the walls of the church closed.

2613
San-yu. In Chinese folklore, three friends—plum, pine, and bamboo—all symbols of longevity, winter, and the traits associated with a gentleman. The three are also symbols of the three religions of China: Taoism, Confucianism, and Buddhism.

2614
Sarah (princess). In the Bible, O.T., the wife and half sister of Abraham, married to him before they left Ur. Her legend is told in Genesis (chaps. 12–23). Sarah was childless for many years until Yahweh, the Hebrew god, gave her Isaac in her old age. After his birth Sarah became jealous of Abraham's concubine Hagar and drove her and her son Ishmael into the desert.

2615
Sarka (warrior maiden?). 14th century C.E. In Czech legend, a warrior maiden who, with her followers, killed a troop of male warriors.

Sarka swore vengeance on all men when she discovered that her lover, Ctirad, had been unfaithful to her. When Ctirad was heard approaching the forest with a group of his men, the maidens tied one of their group to a tree, and she then feigned crying. Seeing her, Ctirad fell in love with her and freed her. Using a potion, she made his men drunk, and they fell into a deep sleep. She blew the hunting horn, and the other maidens, hidden nearby, rushed out to kill the men.

This legend inspired Bedrich Smetana's *Sarka*, part of his cycle of six symphonic poems included in *Má*

Vlast (My Country); an opera by Zdenko Fibich, *Sarka*; and one of the earliest operas by Leos Janacek, *Sarka*.

2616
Sarpanitum (silvery bright one). In Near Eastern mythology (Babylonian-Assyrian), goddess who presided over the sweet waters, earth, and wisdom. She was the wife of the hero god Marduk and daughter of the god Ea. Often she was merged with Erua, who also was regarded as the wife of Marduk. The goddess Eria is believed to be identical with Erua.

2617
Sarpedon (rejoicing in a wooden ark). In Greek mythology, hero, son of Zeus and Laodamia; or Europa; grandson of Bellerophon. Sarpedon was the commander of the Lycian contingent of King Priam's allies during the Trojan War. At the storming of the Greek camp he and Glaucus, his cousin, were the first upon the enemy walls. Sarpedon, however, was killed by Patroculus. A battle then arose over the possession of Sarpedon's body. Apollo, commanded by Zeus, rescued the disfigured corpse from the Greeks. After washing and anointing it with ambrosia, Apollo had Sleep and Death carry the body through the air to Lycia for burial. He was worshiped as a demi-god in Lycia. Sarpedon appears in Homer's *Iliad* (books 2, 12, 16).

2618
Satan (adversary). In the Bible, O.T., part of the heavenly court of God (Job 1:6–7) and in the N.T. (Rev. 12:7–9), the devil.

The concept of Satan as the devil is not found in the Old Testament, since his role is merely as the "adversary" to Job. The Bible makes it clear that Satan is part of God's scheme. God grants Satan the power to be Job's adversary. His power, however, is only over the physical aspects of Job, not the spiritual. But as Judaism developed and came into contact with the dualism of the Persians—in which the conflict between the good god, Ahura-Mazda, and Ahriman, the spirit of evil, was emphasized—Satan took on the characteristics of the evil god of the Persians. By the time of the New Testament Satan was generally regarded as an evil demon or the ruler of demons (Matt. 12:24–30). He not only controls the body but also has power over spiritual nature. Since early Christians could not account for God creating something inherently evil, they concluded that Satan was a fallen angel, "prince of the world" (John 12:31) and even "god of this world" (2 Cor. 4:4). In *Paradise Lost* Milton, following late Jewish sources, makes Satan the monarch of hell, who rules all of the fallen angels. His chief lords, all derived from Near Eastern mythology, are Beelzebub, Chemos, Thammuz, Dagon, Rimmon, and Belial. Satan's character, as portrayed by Milton, is one of daring and ambition and has inspired some critics to say that Satan is the hero of *Paradise Lost*.

In one medieval tale, however, Satan is less proud or heroic. A man named Theophilus gives to Satan a sealed parchment in which he promises to renounce God, the Virgin Mary, and all of the Church in exchange for gold. Satan accepts the offer and Theophilus becomes rich. Then, realizing what a terrible bargain he has made with Satan, Theophilus runs to a statue of the Virgin and begs her to intercede for him. The Virgin steps down from the pedestal and places the baby Jesus on the floor. She then asks Jesus to help the man, but the child remains mute. Finally, Jesus says, "Why, Mother dear, do you beg so much for this stinking body of a man?" The Virgin insists, however, and Satan is called up from hell to restore the sealed parchment. The Virgin then gives the letter to Theophilus and returns to her pedestal. William Blake's portrayal of Satan in his illustrations for Milton's *Paradise Lost* and the biblical Book of Job are well known. In music, Ralph Vaughan Williams's ballet *Job*, inspired by Blake's illustrations, portrays Satan.

2619

Sati (the good woman). In Hindu mythology, a form of the great goddess, Devi. *Sati* is also the word used to refer to a widow who, in a practice now outlawed, throws herself on her husband's funeral pyre.

Variant spelling: **Suttee.**

2620

Saturn (the seed-sower). In Roman mythology, ancient Italian god of harvest and seedtime; husband of Rhea; father of Jupiter; identified by the Romans with the Greek Cronus. Saturn's reign was regarded as the Golden Age. His temple, consecrated in 497 B.C.E. foot of the Capitoline Hill in Rome, and under it was the Roman treasury. Throughout the year, except for his festival, his statue had woolen ribbons wound around its feet. People offered sacrifices to Saturn, especially during the *Saturnalia* (December 17–23), which was a festival of great mirth and which eventually was replaced by Christmas. During the festival, people exchanged presents, in particular wax tapers and dolls. They played many games, one of the most popular being a game for nuts—symbol of fruitfulness. In English literature, Chaucer, Shakespeare, Spenser, and Keats all write about Saturn. Gustav Holst's symphonic suite *The Planets* also pictures Saturn.

Variant spelling: **Saturnus.**

2621

Satyrs. In Greek mythology, creatures of the hills and woods, half-men, half-animal; followers of Dionysus and Pan. Noted for their love of wine, women, and nymphs, they were called by the moralistic Hesiod "good for nothing." In Roman art they appear with goat legs and horns, and were later identified by the Christians with the devil because of their noted sexual appetites. Satyrs appear in Euripides' *Cyclops*, Ovid's *Fasti* (book 3), and Spenser's *Faerie Queene* (I.vi.18). In art Rubens painted a *Nymphs and Satyrs*, while satyrs appear in Botticelli's *Venus and Mars* and Michelangelo's statue *Bacchus*.

Saul

2622

Saul (desired) 11th century B.C.E. In the Bible, O.T., the first king of Israel, anointed by Samuel when the people demanded a king. His legend is told in 1 Samuel (9–31). Saul was the son of Kish, a Benjamite. He was chosen by Samuel because "from his shoulders and upward he was higher than any of the people." He proved himself in battle against the invading Ammonites and Philistines, but he fell out with Samuel, usurping Samuel's priestly functions and acting as priest-king. Samuel then secretly anointed David to be Saul's successor. Saul became melancholy because Yahweh, the Hebrew god, sent him an evil spirit to torment him. Saul turned against David when he heard people saying that "Saul hath slain his thousands, and David his ten thousands." Open hostilities broke out between David and Saul during the war with the Philistines. Jonathan, Saul's son, sided with David in the dispute. The night before the last battle, Saul consulted the Witch of Endor, calling up the spirit of the dead Samuel, who told him he would die the next day in battle. The Philistines beheaded him and his sons, nailing their bodies to the walls of the temple of Ashtaroth. William Blake's *The Witch of Endor Summoning the Shade of Samuel* *for Saul*, Handel's oratorio *Saul*, and Robert Browning's dramatic monologue *Saul* all deal with the legend. Rembrandt's *Saul* portrays Saul grasping a javelin while the young David plays a harp to assuage Saul's melancholy. Saul was also the name of St. Paul before his conversion to Christianity. In Islam Saul is called Talut.

Savitri (descended from the sun). In Hindu mythology, a name given to a heroine who brought back her husband from the dead; also a name for the sun and for the daughter and wife of Brahma, as well as an alternate name for Gayatri, the sacred verse used daily by devout Brahmans.

The legend of Savitri is told in the epic poem *The Mahabharata*. It was popularized among English-speaking peoples in the last century by Edwin Arnold's verse translation of the episode *Savitri, or Love and Death*. Savitri was the daughter of King Aswa-pati and was in love with Satyavan, whom she wanted to marry. She was told by a holy man, however, that when she married her husband would die within the year. Nevertheless, she married Satyavan. One day when Satyavan went out to cut wood, she followed him and saw him fall. Standing nearby was Yama, the god of death. Yama told Savitri he had come to take her husband to the land of the dead. Savitri pleaded with Yama, and the god relented, restoring Satyavan to Savitri. The tale was used as the basis for a chamber opera, *Savitri*, by Gustav Holst.

Scaevola, Gaius Mucius (an amulet worn by Roman children, wrongly connected with *scaeva*, the left hand). In Roman history and legend, head of the Mucius family in Rome. Livy's *History of Rome* tells of how he went to the camp of Lars Porsenna, an Etruscan chieftain, and, after failing to kill him, laid his right hand on a burning altar to show his strength and fortitude. The scene was painted by Tiepolo and Mantegna.

Schildburg. In Germanic folklore, a city that acquired a reputation for wisdom. Its inhabitants were forced to pretend to be fools in order to be left in peace. One tale tells how they built a house without windows and tried to carry the sunlight in. Their legend is told in a 16th-century work, *The History of the Schildburgers*.

Scipio Africanus Major, Publius Cornelius. 236–184 B.C.E. In Roman history and legend, hero of the Second Punic War against Hannibal, whom he defeated at the battle of Zama in 202 B.C.E. Livy's *History of Rome* (book 26) tells the legend of Scipio being offered a beautiful captive woman as a slave and refusing her, restoring her to the young man she had been pledged to marry. This legend has often been painted under the title *Continence of Scipio*. Giulio Romano did a series of tapestries with that title. Poussin's and Mantegna's paintings of the subject are called *Triumph of Scipio*. Scipio Africanus also appears in Cicero's *Republic* (book 6) in the famous *Somnium Scipionis* (Scipio's Dream) episode. In the dream the hero appears to his grandson and explains the nature of the universe, including Pythagoras' theories of the transmigration of souls and of immortality. The dream influenced *Consolation of Philosophy* by Boethius; the medieval author of the *Roman de la Rose*; Chaucer's *Parliament of Fowls*; Shakespeare's *Troilus and Cressida* and one of Lorenzo's speeches in *The Merchant of Venice*, beginning "There's not the smallest orb which thou behold'st/ But in his motion like an angel sings," and Milton's *Hymn on the Morning of Christ's Nativity*.

Scorpion. An arachnid with a long, narrow tail that ends in a venomous sting. In Egyptian mythology, the scorpion was an attribute of the evil god Set but was also a protector of the dead. Seven scorpions accompanied Isis on her search for her dead husband, Osiris. In one Egyptian myth Set, in the form of a scorpion, attempts to kill Horus, the son of Isis and Osiris, but the gods restore Horus to life.

In European folklore the scorpion is a symbol of evil and treachery. Jesus (Luke 10:19) gives his disciples authority and power over scorpions, which symbolized all that opposed God's rule and kingdom. Medieval symbolism chose the creature, therefore, as a sign of both Judas, the archbetrayer of Jesus, and the Jews, whom medieval Christians persecuted.

Scylla and Charybdis (she who rends and sucker down). In Greek mythology, sea monsters. Scylla, according to most accounts, was a daughter of Phorcys and Ceto and Charybdis, a daughter of Poseidon and Gaea. Originally Scylla was a beautiful nymph loved by Glaucus, a man who was transformed into a god. Scylla, however, rejected his love and went to Circe for a magic drug to get rid of Glaucus's romantic attachment. Instead Circe fell in love with Glaucus, who rejected her. So Circe poisoned the water in which Scylla bathed and the nymph was transformed into a sea monster that devoured ships and men. Opposite Scylla, who was located in the straits of Messina, between Sicily and Italy, was Charybdis.

She also once had another form, that of a woman, but she had a tremendous appetite. Zeus transformed her into a monster who swallowed as much water as she could hold, then spewed it out. Sailors passing between the two monsters had to avoid being eaten by the six ravenous dogs' heads of Scylla or drowning in the whirlpool of Charybdis. The expression, "between Scylla and Charybdis" has come to mean that in avoiding one evil, we fall upon an even greater one. Homer's *Odyssey* (book 11), Vergil's *Aeneid* (book 3), Ovid's *Metamorphoses* (book 13), and Spenser's *Faerie Queene* (2.12.9) cite Scylla and Charybdis.

2629

Sebald, St. Eighth century. In Christian legend, patron of Nuremberg, Germany. Invoked against cold weather. Feast, 19 August.

Sebald was the son of a Danish king. He left England with St. Boniface to convert the Germans. He traveled through the north of Germany, preaching as a missionary, and settled at last in Nuremberg. Living in a cell not far from the city, he would go there daily to teach the poor, and he was in the habit of stopping on his way at a hut owned by a cartwright.

One day when it was very cold he found the family nearly frozen to death in the hut because they had no fuel. Sebald told them to bring him the icicles that hung from the roof, and he used them as fuel for the fire as if they were pieces of wood.

Another day Sebald wanted a fish to eat (it was a meatless day), and he sent the same cartwright to buy one in the city. The lord of Nuremberg had an edict that no one was to buy fish until his castle storehouse was supplied. As punishment for having broken the edict, the cartwright was blinded by the soldiers of the lord. St. Sebald restored his sight.

His church, the Sebaldskirche in Nuremberg, was begun in 1508 and finished in 1523; it contains a statue of the saint by Peter Vischer that shows St. Sebald as an elderly pilgrim warming his feet at a fire made of icicles. Usually, as in the woodcuts of Albrecht Dürer, he is shown holding the Sebaldskirche, his church with two towers.

Variant spellings: Seward, Siward, Sigward.

2630

Sebastian, Don. 1554–1578. In Portuguese history and legend, king killed in the battle of Alcazar who, according to legend, was not killed but was spirited away to safety and will return to help Portugal in time of need. After his death various pretenders to the throne appeared. John Dryden's tragedy *Don Sebastian, King of Portugal* takes up the legend.

2631

Sebastian, St. (man from Sebastia, a city in Asia Minor). Third century C.E. In Christian legend, patron of armorers, bookbinders, burial societies, arrowsmiths, corn chandlers, gardeners, ironmongers, lead founders, needle makers, potters, racquetmakers, stonemasons. Invoked against cattle pest, epilepsy, enemies of religion, plague, and by the dying. Feast, 20 January.

The legend of St. Sebastian dates from the first centuries of Christianity. He was descended from a noble family and, as commander of a company of the Praetorian Guards, was very close to the Emperor Diocletian. When it was discovered that Sebastian was a Christian, the emperor asked him to renounce his faith, but Sebastian refused. Then, as *The Golden Legend*, written in the 13th century, tells the tale:

> Diocletian was much angry and wroth, and commanded him to be led to the field and there to be bounden to a stake for to be shot at. And the archers shot at him till he was full of arrows as an urchin is full of pricks, and thus left him there for dead. The night after came a Christian woman [St. Irene] for to take his body and to bury it, but she found him alive and brought him to her house, and took charge of him till he was all whole.

With his health restored Sebastian "stood upon a step where the emperor should pass by" and told him to renounce his gods, but Diocletian had him arrested again, "brought into prison into his palace," and stoned to death.

St. Sebastian's association with arrows and pestilence betrays him as being a Christian variation of the Greek god Apollo, who was also invoked against plague, which he sent by arrows, as shown in Homer's *Iliad*. In art St. Sebastian is always portrayed as a young man, which gave artists an opportunity to display the naked form without the Church banning the picture as obscene. St. Sebastian is a favorite subject, therefore, with Italian Renaissance painters such as Botticelli, Lotto, Caravaggio, and Mantegna. Perhaps one of the most moving works, however, is by the French artist Georges de la Tour, showing St. Irene tending the wounded body with two female attendants.

2632

Sebek. In Egyptian mythology, the crocodile god, called Suchos by the Greeks. In Egyptian art Sebek is portrayed as a crocodile-headed man, wearing either a solar disk encircled by a uraeus or a pair of ram's horns surmounted by a disk and a pair of plumes. Frequently, however, the god appears simply as a crocodile. Sometimes Sebek is combined with the sun god Ra to form the composite god Sebek-Ra.

Variant spellings: Sebeq, Suchos, Sobek, Sebak.

Sebek

Sedna. In Eskimo mythology, great goddess, queen 2633
of Adlivun (those beneath us), the land of the dead
under the sea; she is also called Avilayoq, Nuliajuk,
Nerrivik, and Arnarquagssaq.

In one myth Sedna was once a beautiful girl who
was wooed by many suitors, but she rejected all of
them. Once a fulmar flew over the ice and sang to
her: "Come to me, come into the land of the birds,
where there is never hunger, where my tent is made
of the most beautiful skins. You shall rest on soft
bearskins. My fellows, the fulmars, shall bring you
all your heart desires; their feathers shall clothe you;
your lamp shall always be filled with oil, your pot
with meat."

Sedna listened to the fulmar and decided to
become his wife. She discovered, however, that he
had lied to her and did not possess all of the things
he claimed. In a year her father came to visit her, and
she told him she wanted to go home. Angry that his
daughter had been mistreated, he killed the fulmar
and took Sedna away in his boat. The fulmars,
companions of the murdered bird, followed the
fleeing couple. A storm arose, threatening to kill
both of them. Sedna's father decided to offer Sedna
to the birds as a sacrifice. He flung her overboard, but
she clung to the boat. The cruel father then cut off
the first joints of her fingers. Falling into the sea, the
finger joints were transformed into whales, the nails

turning into whalebones. The second finger joints
fell on the sharp knife and swam away as seals.
When the father cut off the stumps of her fingers
they became ground seals.

In the meantime the storm subsided and the
fulmars believed Sedna had been drowned. The
father then allowed her to come back into the boat.
But Sedna now hated her father. One night she
called her dogs and had them gnaw off his feet and
hands while he slept. When he awoke he cursed
himself, Sedna, and the dogs. Suddenly, the earth
opened and swallowed the hut, father, Sedna, and
the dogs. Ever since, Sedna has reigned as queen of
Adlivun, the land of the dead in the sea and has been
hostile to humans.

In a variant myth Sedna refused all suitors except
a dog or a bird. Her enraged parents cast Sedna,
fingerless, into the sea, where she now reigns as
queen of the dead. Another variant says Sedna was a
girl who ate so much that her parents were in
despair. Once she even started to eat their arms and
legs. They awoke and threw her into the sea, first
cutting off her fingers.

As goddess of sea creatures, Sedna is invoked for
success in hunting. When taboos are broken, the
shaman is called and goes into a trance, during which
it is believed that his spirit flies to Sedna's land,
where he attempts to appease the goddess's anger.

When the Danish explorer Knud Rasmussen
asked one Eskimo about the goddess he was told:
"We do not believe, we only fear. And most of all we
fear Nuliajuk [Sedna] . . . Nuliajuk is the name we
give to the Mother of Beasts. All the game we have
comes from her; from her comes all the caribou, all
the foxes, the birds and fishes."

Seker. In Egyptian mythology, death god of the ne- 2634
cropolis of Memphis. Originally, Seker may have
been a vegetation god. Later he was combined with
Osiris, the god of the dead. The two were also combined with the craft god Ptah to form the god Ptah-
Seker-Osiris. Ptah provided new bodies in which the
souls of the righteous were to live, thus symbolizing
the addition of creative power (Ptah) to death (Seker
and Osiris). Egyptian art usually portrayed Seker as
a hawk-headed mummy.

Variant spellings: Sacharis, Seger, Sokar, Solare,
Sokaris.

Sekhet-Aaru (field of the reeds). In Egyptian myth- 2635
ology, a paradise, the name originally given to the island of the delta where the blessed souls of the dead
lived and saw the sun god Ra each day. The land was

filled with wheat as high as five cubits and barley as high as seven.

2636

Selene (moon). In Greek mythology, ancient moon goddess; daughter of the Titan Hyperion and Theia; sister of Helios and Eos. Selene was a beautiful woman with long wings and a golden diadem that shed a mild light. She rode in a chariot drawn by two white horses. In later Greek and Roman mythology Selene was identified with Artemis, Luna, Hecate, and Persephone. Selene was also known by her epithet, Phoebe (bright moon). She appears riding in her chariot on the east pediment of the Parthenon.

2637

Semargl (family/barley). In Slavic mythology, god of the family and of barley; worshiped among the Russians. He appears in *The Lay of Igor's Army*, and some scholars believe him to have been invented by the author of that work. There is some disagreement as to whether Semargl is one god or two (known as Sem and Rgl).

2638

Semele (moon). In Greek mythology, daughter of Cadmus, king of Thebes; and Harmonia, mother of Dionysus by Zeus. Zeus fell in love with Semele and often visited her. Hera, ever jealous of her husband's escapades, took the form of Semele's nurse, Beroe, and convinced the girl to ask Zeus to show himself to her in all his godlike splendor. Zeus agreed to Semele's wish and appeared amid thunder and lightning. Semele was consumed by flames. Before she died she gave birth to a six month's child, Dionysus, whom Zeus saved from the flames and hid in his thigh until it was time for the child to be born. When Dionysus was born he raised his dead mother and placed her in the heavens under the name Thyone. Semele is believed to be a form of Selene or Zemelo, a Phrygian earth goddess. She is cited in Homer's *Iliad* (book 14), Euripides *The Bacchae*, and Ovid's *Metamorphoses* (book 3) and appears in Handel's secular oratorio *Semele* (1744). *Jupiter and Semele* was painted by Tintoretto.

2639

Semiramis. In Near Eastern mythology, queen of Assyria; daughter of the goddess Derceto. Semiramis is known chiefly as the murderer of her second husband, King Ninus of Assyria, as well as the builder of many great cities. As a murderess she appears in Rossini's opera *Semiramide* (1823).

2640

Semones (to sow?). In Roman mythology, a name for lesser gods and goddesses, such as Pan, Janus and Priapus, as well as deified heroes.

2641

Seng-don-ma. In Tibetan Buddhism, a woman, often portrayed with the face of a lion, who stamps out human ignorance.

2642

Sennacherib (Sin, the mood god, has compensated me for [the loss of my] brothers). 704–681 B.C.E. In Near Eastern history and legend, king of Assyria who captured and destroyed Babylon. He conquered Jerusalem during the days of Hezekiah, but at night, according to the Old Testament (2 Kings 19:35), "the angel of the Lord went out, and smote in the camp the Assyrians an hundred four-score and five thousand." Lord Byron's poem *The Destruction of Sennacherib* was set for chorus and orchestra by Modest Mussorgsky.

2643

Sennadius, Dream of. In Christian legend, a dream recorded by St. Augustine in one of his epistles to prove that man has two natures.

Sennadius was a physician who did not believe in the duality of man's nature and consequently in a future life. One night an angel appeared to him in a dream and asked him to follow. The angel took Sennadius to the confines of a city, where he was "ravished with celestial music" that the angel told him came from the voices of perfect spirits. Sennadius thought no more about the dream when he awoke. Sometime afterward the angel appeared to him again, recalled to him the memory of the former visit, and then asked him if the vision had occurred while Sennadius was awake or during sleep. Sennadius replied, "During sleep." "Just so," said the angel. "What you saw and heard was not by your bodily senses then, for your eyes and ears were closed in sleep." "True," said the physician. "Then," continued the angel, "with what eyes did you see, and with what ears did your hear?" Sennadius could not answer. The angel said, "It must be evident, if you see when your bodily eyes are shut and hear when your bodily ears are closed in sleep, that you must have other eyes and ears beside those of your material body. When, therefore, your body sleeps, that other something may be awake. When your body dies, that other something may live on."

2644

Seraphim (burning, glowing). In the Bible, O.T., an order of angels, stemming from demonic spirits in Babylonian mythology.

When the prophet Isaiah (Isa. 6:2–3) describes the throne of Yahweh, the Hebrew god, he says that above it "stood the seraphims: each one had six wings; with twain he covered his face, and with twain he covered his feet, and with twain he did fly. And one cried unto another and said, Holy, holy, holy is the Lord of hosts: the whole earth is full of his glory." Isaiah's seraphim, from the root "to burn," are believed to come from the "fiery serpents" mentioned in Numbers (21:6). From early Christian times, however, the seraphim were made into a category of angels and are mentioned in the Preface to the Roman Mass as well as in the great hymn *Te Deum*, composed by Niceta of Remesiana, where they repeat the phrase from Isaiah.

2645

Serapion the Sinonite, St. (ardent?) Fourth century. In Christian legend, a saint known for his generosity not only in giving away his goods to the poor but in

selling himself several times for the benefit of the poor. Feast, 2 March.

The first time, according to Alban Butler's account in his *Lives of the Saints*, he sold himself to a comedian for 20 pieces of silver. The comedian was a pagan, but Serapion converted him to Christianity and also persuaded him to leave the stage (considered an evil profession by the Early Church). The comedian freed Serapion and offered him 20 pieces of silver, which the saint refused. Next he sold himself to relieve a poor widow. After having stayed with his master for the allotted time he was again given his liberty as well as a cloak, a tunic, an under garment, and a copy of the Gospels. He had "scarce gone from the door, when he gave his cloak to one poor man, and his tunic to another." A stranger came up and asked him why he was out in the cold without a cloak. Had he been robbed? Who caused his condition? "This book," replied Serapion, showing the stranger the Gospels. The rest of his life was

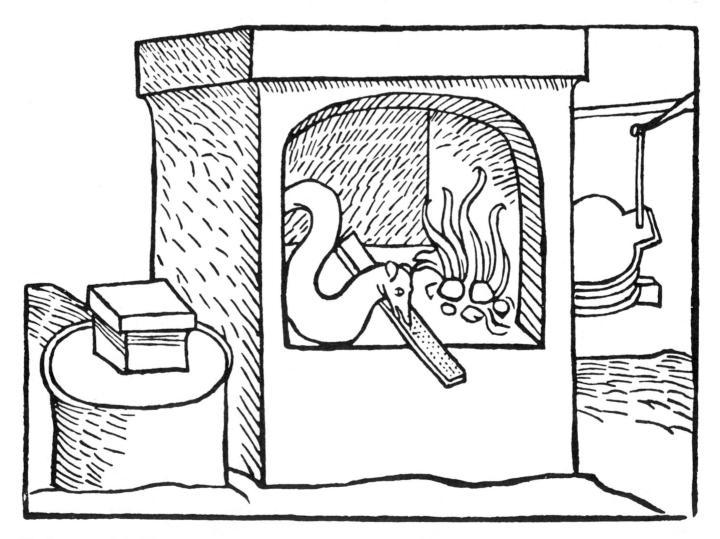

The Serpent and the File

devoted to selling himself to help the poor. Serapion "at length died in Egypt, in a desert, at the age of sixty years."

2646

Serapis. In Egyptian mythology, Greek name for the composite god made up of the god Osiris, called Ser in Egyptian, and the sacred bull of Memphis, Apis. The date of the introduction of the cult of Serapis is disputed by scholars. Some believe it was the artificial creation of either Ptolemy I or Ptolemy II, who used the cult of Serapis in an attempt to blend the existing Egyptian concepts with those of the Greeks who settled in Egypt after the conquest by Alexander the Great. It was an attempt to give both segments of the population a common religious heritage. Serapis was worshiped by Greeks, Romans, and Egyptians at a common shrine. In the Roman Empire his worship, along with that of Isis, rivaled all other Mediterranean cults. In art Serapis was portrayed as a bull-headed man wearing a solar disk and the uraeus between his horns and holding symbols associated with Osiris.

2647

Serpent and the File, The. Aesopic fable found in various collections throughout the world.

In the course of its wanderings a serpent came into an armorer's shop. As he glided over the floor, he felt his skin pricked by a file lying there. In a rage he turned on it and tried to dart his fangs into it. However, he could do no harm to the heavy iron and gave up his anger.

Moral: It's useless to attack the insensible.

The fable is told in the Arabic fables of Lôqman. In his version, however, the snake's part is taken by a cat. R. L. Stevenson quotes the fable in his novel *The Master of Ballantrae.*

2648

Serqet. In Egyptian mythology, scorpion goddess. Serqet was associated with the dead and was often seen on the walls of tombs with winged arms outstretched in a protective gesture. She was believed to have special province over the entrails of the deceased. Serqet was a companion of the goddess Isis in her wanderings, and it was said that those who worshiped Isis were never stung by a scorpion. Egyptian art portrays Serqet as a woman with a scorpion on her head or as a scorpion with the head of a woman.

Variant spellings: Selket, Selqet, Selquet.

2649

Set. In Egyptian mythology, the evil god; brother of Osiris, Isis, and Nephthys; called Typhon by the

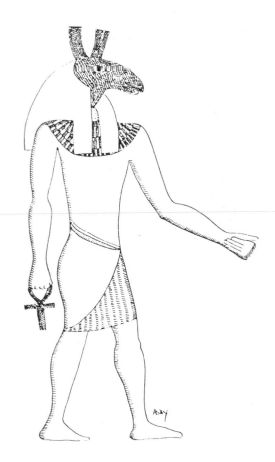

Set

Greeks. He murdered his brother, Osiris, who was avenged by Horus, the son of Osiris.

The worship of Set was one of the oldest cults of Egypt. Originally, he was a beneficent god of Upper Egypt, whose realm was the abode of the blessed dead, where he performed friendly offices for the deceased. When the followers of Horus (the elder), the supreme god of Lower Egypt, conquered the followers of Set, Set's place in the Egyptian pantheon of gods fell into disrepute, and eventually the priests of Horus declared Set a god of the unclean, an enemy of all other gods, and ordered all of his images destroyed.

Set was the archenemy of the sun god, and almost all allusions and myths pertaining to him reflect the battles he waged against the sun. In the earliest and simplest form of the myth Set represented the cosmic opposition of darkness and light. In a later form of the myth, Set is the antagonist of the sun god Ra and seeks, in the form of the monstrous serpent Apophis, to prevent him from appearing in the east daily. The result was always the same. Apophis would be annihilated by the burning heat of Ra, and Set, who could renew himself daily, would collect his noxious cohort and ready himself for the next night's battle against the sunrise.

In the most famous and complex version of the myth, Set is the murderer and dismemberer of his brother, Osiris, who was sometimes called his twin brother. He pursued and persecuted Osiris's widow, Isis, who was also his own sister. He also persecuted Isis' and Osiris's child Horus. Later Horus was called on to avenge his father's death, and in a series of battles he defeated Set and would have destroyed him if it had not been for the interference of Isis, who took pity on her brother and spared him.

The Egyptians viewed the battle between Set and Horus as the ultimate victory of good over evil. Yet according to some interpretations, in the sphere of the eternal, where there is no duality, Set and Horus are one; that is, death and life, darkness and light are one. In Egyptian religion this has been referred to as "the secret of the two partners," reflecting the hidden understanding of the two combatant gods. Set, representing strife, is perennially subdued but never destroyed by Horus, representing peace. In the end there is reconciliation. The pharaoh who was sometimes known as the Two Lords was identified with both of these gods as an inseparable pair.

As the great antagonist of light, Set was frequently symbolized by the black boar, whose emblem was the primeval knife, the instrument of dismemberment and death. His female counterpart was his sister Nephthys, who was herself a goddess of darkness and decay.

In Egyptian art Set is usually portrayed as a man with the head of a fantastic beast with pointed muzzle and high, square ears. This unidentifiable beast has been commonly called the Typhonian animal, Typhon being the god with whom the Greeks identified Set. Sometimes Set is portrayed with horns, which made him the ideal image for the devil in Egyptian Christianity. Other animals associated with Set were the antelope, the crocodile, and the ass.

Set was sometimes said to have a mane of red hair, and Plutarch writes in *Isis and Osiris* that an ass was thrown down a precipice because the animal bore a resemblance to Set in its redness. Persons who had red complexions were often treated ignominiously.

Variant spellings: Seth, Sethi, Sit, Sut, Sutekh.

2650

Seven Kings of Rome. In Roman history and legend, they are Romulus, Numa Pompilius, Tullus Hostillus, Ancus Martius, Tarquinius Priscus, Servius Tullius, and Tarquinius Superbus.

2651

Seven Sages of Greece. In Greek history and legend, seven men noted for their wisdom. They are Thales of Miletus (seventh century B.C.E.), who believed the material basis for the world was water and was noted for his absentmindedness, as when he fell down a well while not paying attention; Solon of Athens (c. 640–c. 560 B.C.E.), a lawmaker noted for his remark to Croesus, whom he met in Lydia, that no man could be said to have lived a happy life until he was dead; Bias of Priene (sixth century B.C.E.); Chilon of Sparta (sixth century B.C.E.), who brought back the bones of Orestes; Cleobulus of Rhodes (sixth century B.C.E.); Periander of Corinth (c. 625–585 B.C.E.), patron of the arts who dedicated the Chest of Cypselus at Olympia, which was decorated with gold and ivory reliefs of scenes from Greek mythology, his court being the setting of Plutarch's *Symposium of the Seven Sages*; and Pittacus of Mytilene (c. 650–570 B.C.E.), a moderate democratic reformer.

2652

Seven Sleepers of Ephesus, The. Legend in both Christian and Islamic folklore. In Islamic folklore the seven are called *Ashab al-Kahf* (the people of the cave). They are seven youths who fled to a cave to hide persecution for being Christian. They fell asleep and awoke some 200 years later and died.

St. Gregory of Tours, writing in *De Gloria Martyrum* in the sixth century, gives one Christian version of the legend. According to his account, seven noble youths in the household of the Emperor Decian fled the court when the Emperor began to persecute Christians. They entered a cave and fell asleep. Some 230 years later the cave was opened and the youths awoke, but they died soon afterward. Their bodies were buried in a large coffin in St. Victor's Church in Marseilles. Their names were Constantine, Dionysius, John, Maximian, Malchus, Martinian, and Serapion.

The Islamic account is found in the Koran (Sura 18) and differs from the Christian account. In it a dog, Katmir, not directly named in the sacred text, "lay . . . with paws outstretched" outside the entry to the cave. (Katmir is one of the ten animals admitted to Paradise in Islamic belief.) After 309 years the sleepers awoke and sent one of their number into the town to buy bread. As to what happened later the Koran is silent, though various other Islamic accounts fill in the gaps in the tale.

Goethe's poem *The Seven Sleepers of Ephesus* combines both Christian and Islamic accounts, ending with the eight of them (Goethe counts the dog):

Thenceforth from the world were sundered.
The most blessed Angel Gabriel
By the will of God Almighty,
Walling up the cave for ever,
Led them unto Paradise.

The Koranic account of the legend was used by Taufig al-Hakim in his play *Ashab al-Kahf*.

The legend seems to have arisen from taking the expression "fell asleep in the Lord" literally, and not as was meant, having died. Though many Christian writers through the ages have dismissed the legend, the feast of the Seven Sleepers is celebrated on 27 July.

Seven Wonders of the World. In the ancient 2653 Greco-Roman world they were the Pyramids of Egypt, the Hanging Gardens of Babylon, the Tomb of Mausolus, the Temple of Diana of Ephesus, the Colossus of Rhodes, the Statue of Zeus by Phidias and the Tower of Pharos at Alexandria. During the Christian Middle Ages another seven were added. They were the Coliseum (amphitheater) of Rome, the Catacombs of Alexandria, the Great Wall of China, Stonehenge, the Leaning Tower of Pisa, the Porcelain Tower of Nankin, and the Mosque of St. Sophia at Constantinople.

Shahapet. In Armenian mythology, serpent spirit 2654 that appeared as both a man and a serpent. Generally, the Shahapet, who often inhabited vine stocks and olive trees, was a beneficent spirit unless angered. Agathangelos, the Christian historian of Armenia in ancient times, calls Christ the Shahapet of the graveyards.

Shah Namah (book of kings). Persian epic poem by 2655 Firdusi, completed in 1010 C.E., narrating the mythical and legendary history of Iran from the days of Gayomart, its first king, to the fall of the Sassanian dynasty in 641 C.E. under the impact of Islam. The epic consists of more than 50,000 couplets, divided into 50 chapters.

Firdusi based his poem on various collections of Persian history and lore. Yezdjird, the last Sassanian king, had collected all of the histories and traditions connected with Persia and had them bound into a book known as *Bustan-Namah*. After the Islamic conquest of Persia, additional material was added to the book, bringing it up to the death of Yezdjird. Mahmud of Ghazna, the king of Persia, wished the prose chronicle to be turned into a verse epic. From it he selected seven tales, which he distributed among seven poets of the court, so that he might pick which was to complete the massive work.

Dagiqi, a poet, was given the tale of Rustum and Sohrab, two of the main heroes in the work. The king was so pleased with the poet's treatment of the tale that Dagiqi was commissioned to complete the work. In the meantime Dagiqi had introduced another poet, Abu'l-Qasim Mansur, to the court, and he so captivated the king that the king changed the poet's name to Firdusi (paradise). The legend relates that the king said, "You have made my court as resplendent as *firdusi*."

Dagiqi died in 980 and the task of completing the epic was given to Firdusi. He was promised 1,000 gold pieces for every 1,000 couplets of the work. Firdusi refused payment until the work was completed. When it was completed, the king's prime minister, Hasan Meymendi, a conceited favorite of the king who hated the poet, had silver substituted for the gold. According to legend, Firdusi gave away one-third of the silver payment to the slave who brought it.

"The sultan shall know," he said, "that I did not bestow the labor of 30 years on a work to be rewarded by silver."

In his anger the poet wrote an insulting poem against the king and then, thinking it best to move, fled his city. He finally died in Tus.

Again according to legend, when the king ultimately discovered what his prime minister had done, changing the gold payment for a silver one, he had the gold sent, but it was too late; the poet had died. The money was finally used by the family to build a stone embankment in the city of Firdusi, a dream he had held all his life.

Among the heroes treated in the epic are Bahram Gur, the hero king and the "great hunter"; Jemshid, a culture hero and proud king; Faridun, the hero who defeats the evil king Zahhak; Gayomart, the first king and primeval man; Husheng, a king, culture hero, and discoverer of fire; Kavah, a blacksmith who refused to sacrifice his children to the evil Zahhak; Minuchihr, a hero king who came to the throne on the death of the great hero Faridun; Mirtas, the good king who was the father of Zahhak, the evil king; Rustum, the great hero of the poem, father of Sohrab, whom he accidentally killed in battle; Tahumers, a king who was a slayer of demons; and Zal.

Shaitans. In Islamic mythology, evil spirits more 2656 dangerous than the djinn. Allah created Al-Shaitan, perhaps another name for Iblis, the devil, who then produced eggs from which other demons were hatched. In a variant myth Allah not only created Al-Shaitan but a wife for him, who then produced three eggs as their offspring. The children are all ugly, having hoofed feet. Shaitans are even more ugly in their eating habits. They like excrement and other dirt and waste and prefer the shade to sunlight. It is believed that every person has a personal shaitan or demon, just as he has a personal guardian angel.

Sometimes the shaitan is considered the muse of poetic inspiration.

Variant spelling: sayatin.

Shakuntala (bird protected). In Hindu mythology, a
heroine in love with King Dushyanta.

2657

Shakuntala was born in a forest and lived there on
the food supplied to her by birds until she was found
by the sage Kanwa. The sage brought her up in his
hermitage as his daughter. One day she was seen by
King Dushyanta, who immediately fell in love with
her. He wooed her and she accepted him, not in a
marriage but in a simple declaration of mutual love.
On leaving her to return to his city, he gave her a
ring as a pledge of their love.

When later the sage Dur-vasas came to visit
Kanwa, Shakuntala was so absorbed in thoughts
about King Dushyanta that she paid little attention
to the guest. Dur-vasas became so angry that he
cursed Shakuntala, saying she would be forgotten by
Dushyanta. Relenting later from the harshness of his
curse, Dur-vasas said the curse would be removed as
soon as King Dushyanta saw the ring he had given
Shakuntala as a token of love. Pregnant, Shakuntala
set off to see King Dushyanta. Before leaving she
bathed and lost the ring. When she reached the
palace, Dushyanta did not recognize her, fulfilling
the curse. She was taken back to the forest, where a
son, Bharata, was born. Later the ring was found in a
fish by a fisherman and brought to the king. He
recognized it and then accepted Shakuntala and his
son.

Shakuntala forms the basis for the best-known
play by the Indian playwright Kalidasa, titled after
the heroine. The work was made known to the
English-speaking world through a translation by Sir
William Jones in 1789. The great German poet
Goethe wrote of the drama:

> Wouldst thou the young year's blossoms and the fruits
>   of its decline,
> And all by which the soul is charmed, enraptured,
>   fasted, fed?
> Wouldst thou the earth and heaven itself in one sole
>   name combine?
> I name thee, O Shakuntala, and all at once is said.
>   (Eastwich translation)

Variant spellings: Sakuntala, Sakoontala.

Shamash. In Near Eastern mythology (Babylonian-
Assyrian), sun god, god of justice and healing, his
consort was the goddess Aa, and his attendants were
Kittu (truth) and Mesharu (righteousness). He appears in the epic poem *Gilgamesh* as a friend of the

2658

hero. He is portrayed in the relief atop the stele of
Hammurabi in the Louvre in Paris as the divine
source and justification for the laws that were codified under Hammurabi and given to his subjects to
obey. Among his epithets were Babbar (shiner) and
Ma-banda-anna (sky ship).

Shamba. In African legend, the 93rd chief of the
Bakongo of Zaire. It is not at all clear what the rulers
before him were like, but he is said to have been a
very wise, peaceful, and innovative man. From
childhood he had a great desire to travel. He felt that
travel was the best teacher, and over the years he
visited many countries. From each place he learned
about new things, including embroidery, tobacco,
weaving, and a game called Mankala. He forbade the
use of lethal weapons, rarely killed anyone, and under all conditions spared the lives of women and
children. As a judge he showed great wisdom in both
criminal and civil cases. Shamba once rebuked a person for offering hearsay evidence at court, saying
that only those who have actually seen something
with their own eyes have the right to speak.

2659

Shango. In African mythology (Yoruba of southwestern Nigeria), thunder god; husband of Oya,
goddess of the Niger River, and Oshun, goddess of
the Oshun River.

2660

Shango was once a mortal; he served as fourth
king of his people. A powerful ruler, he was feared
because of his ability to breathe fire from his mouth.
But two of his political aides challenged his
authority. Shango tried to have the two men fight
with each other, thus diverting their anger from him.
He succeeded in having one kill the other, but the
victor then turned on Shango, trying to kill him.
Shango was forced to flee, along with his wife and
faithful followers. They wandered about until they
arrived at Koso, where Shango hanged himself from
a tree. Shango's enemies made fun of his remaining
followers, but they continued to honor their dead
ruler, praying that fire would consume Shango's
enemies. Then their prayers seemed to be answered
for numerous fires began to spread and destroy
many houses. Fear gripped Shango's enemies, who
now believed he had not died but had disappeared
into the woods and later ascended to the sky. A
temple was erected in Shango's honor at Koso.
Today the ram is sacred to the Yoruba for its bellow,
which is said to be the noise of Shango's thunder.
Shango is also known as Jakuta (stone thrower) and
Oba Koso (the king does not hang), in reference to
his death and rebirth.

Shang-Ti (the emperor above). In Chinese mythology, a sky god, also worshiped as T'ien (sky or heavenly god). When the Jesuits came to China in the 17th century, they created the term T'ien Chu (heavenly or sky lord) to designate the Christian God.

2661

Shan T'ao. 283–205 B.C.E. In Chinese legend, one of the seven Chu-lin Ch'i-Hsien (Seven Immortals). He is the patron of rising talent, portrayed as an old man with a staff.

In Japanese legend he is called Santo.

2662

Shatarupa (Sarasvati)

Shatarupa (the hundred-formed). In Hindu mythology, daughter and wife of the god Brahma, goddess of wisdom and science, mother of the sacred *Vedas*. In Indian art Shatarupa is often portrayed seated on a lotus, playing a type of banjo, or with four arms, holding a book of palm leaves representing learning; a string of pearls called Sivamala (Shiva's garland), which serves as a rosary; and a rose, which she presents to her husband, Brahma. Shatarupa is also known as Savitri (descended from the sun); Sarasvati (flowing), referring to her earlier role as river goddess; Vach (speech), as goddess of speech; Brahami, as wife of Brahma; and Gayatri (song), the sacred verse recited daily by Brahmans.

2663

Shayast la-Shavast (the proper and improper). A ritual text in Zoroastrian belief, written in Pahlavi, a southwestern dialect of Middle Persian; it deals with sin and impurity and gives details on ceremonies. It

2664

often quotes from the sacred book, the *Avesta*, as does the *Denkard*, of which large sections summarize the contents of the *Avesta*.

Shen (divine, spirit, god). In Chinese mythology, a shen refers to a divinity, spirit, god, or deified mortal. The Japanese word *Kami* is written with the Chinese character *shen*.

2665

Shen Nung (divine farmer). In Chinese mythology, a culture hero, the ox-headed divine farmer, second of the Five Sovereigns. He taught men the art of agriculture as well as the use of healing drugs, being honored as the god of medicine. Shen Nung is also the god of burning wind. During his reign the people were saved by the intervention of Ch'ih Sung-tzu (red-pine sow), the lord of rain.

2666

Sheol (to ask?). In the Bible, O.T., the place of the dead, under the earth, translated as hell in the King James Version of the Bible. The Revised Standard Version often uses Sheol or Hades. It is place of punishment. All of the dead, good and bad, reside there as shadows.

2667

Shesha (remainder). In Hindu mythology, a serpent king of the Nagas. Shesha serves as the couch of Vishnu when the god sleeps during the intervals of creation. At the end of each age Shesha vomits fire, which destroys all creation. He is the son of Kadru, who mothered a thousand powerful many-headed serpents, and brother of Manasa-devi, who has special power in counteracting poison. Shesha is also called Mahoraga (great serpent) or Ananta (endless) as a symbol of eternity. He is sometimes identified with the serpent king Vasuki.

2668

Shichi Fukujin. In Japanese Shinto mythology, the seven gods of good luck and fortune. They are Ebisu, the god of daily food; Daikoku, god of wealth; Bishamon, war god and god of riches; Benten, goddess of love, beauty, music, and other arts; Hotei, the so-called "Laughing Buddha;" Jorojin, the god of longevity and wisdom; and Fuku-roku-ju, the god of fortune. All of these gods are borrowed from Chinese mythology.

2669

Shitenno. In Japanese Buddhist mythology, four heavenly guarding kings who live on the slopes of the cosmic mountain, Sumeru, guarding the four corners of the earth. They are Jikoku, Zocho, Komoku, and Bishamon. The Shitenno are Hindu

2670

deities believed to have been converted to Buddhism by the Buddha. According to one Buddhist text, *Golden Light Sutra*, they will protect the territories of Buddhist kings; thus temples were built for them by the Japanese emperors.

Shiva

2671

Shiva (auspicious). In Hinduism, sometimes regarded as the supreme god and sometimes the third god of the Hindu triad made up of Brahma, the creator; Vishnu, the preserver; and Shiva, the destroyer. Shiva is often identified with the earlier god Rudra mentioned in the *Rig-Veda*.

Shiva is the god of cosmic destruction. In Hindu mythology, however, the term *destroyer* is understood as meaning that Shiva causes beings to assume new forms of existence. He is, therefore, a re-creator, who is perpetually restoring that which has been destroyed. In this role he is worshiped by his symbol, the *lingam* (phallus) or by the *lingam* and the *yoni* (womb) of his wife Devi, who in some texts is regarded as his *shakti*, or female energy.

In Indian art Shiva is often portrayed as a handsome man with five faces and four arms. He is often seated in yogic posture and has a third eye in the middle of his forehead, contained in or surmounted by a crescent moon. In his role as god of the ascetics his matted locks are often gathered up in

a coil that bears the symbol of the Ganges, which he caught as the goddess of the river fell from heaven to earth. He wears a *munda-mala*, necklace of skulls, and serpents twine about his neck in a collar called a *naga-kundala*. Shiva's neck is blue from drinking the deadly poison that would have destroyed the world. In one hand he holds the *trishula* (trident), called Pinaka. He is frequently naked but may wear the skin of a tiger, a deer, or an elephant. The god is often accompanied by his sacred bull, Nandin, chief of Shiva's personal attendants, who carries a staff of office. Nandin is also the guardian of all four quarters of the earth. He is portrayed milky white and is often seen at entrances to temples dedicated to Shiva. Other accessories of Shiva are a bow, Ajagava; a drum, Khatwanga, in the shape of an hour glass; and a club with a skull at the end and a cord for binding offenders.

The great German poet Goethe, in his poem *The God and the Bayadere*, writes of one of Shiva's appearances on earth:

> Mahadeva (Shiva), Lord of earth,
> For the sixth time comes below
> As a man of mortal birth,—
> Like him, feeling joy and woe.
> Hither loves he to repair,
> And his power behind to leave;
> If to punish or to spare,
> Men as man he'd fain perceive. . . .

Shiva sees and falls in love with a *bayadere* (dancing girl) and she with him. One night she falls asleep,

> And she finds the much-loved guest
> On her bosom, lying dead. . . .

When they bury the body of Shiva, the *bayadere* jumps onto the funeral pyre:

> But the youth divine outsprings
> From the flame with heavenly grace,
> And on high his flight he wings,
> While his arms his love embrace. . . .
>   (Bowring translation)

Among the many titles by which Shiva is invoked are Aghora (horrible); Bhagavat (blessed); Ardhanari (half man), a form in which Shiva is shown as half male and half female, typifying the male and female energies in the universe; Chandra-sekhara (moon-crested); Ganga dhara (controller of the Ganges); Girisa (mountain lord); Hara (seizer); Isana (ruler); Jala-murti (whose form is water); Jata-dhara (wearing matted hair); Kala (time); Kalanjara (wearing a garland of skulls); Mahesha (great lord); Mrityunjaya (vanquisher of death); Pashu-pati (lord of animals); Sthanu (the firm); Tryambaka (three-eyed); Ugra (fierce); Virupaksha (of misformed eyes); and Viswanatha (lord of all). Maha-kala (great time), the form in which Shiva is portrayed on the cave at Elephanta, shows him with eight arms. In one hand he holds a human figure; in another, a sword or sacrificial ax; in the third, a basin of blood; in the fourth, the sacrificial bell. With two other hands he is drawing behind him the veil that extinguishes the sin. The other two arms of the sculpture found at Elephanta have been destroyed.

Vira-bhadra (gracious to heroes) is considered in some texts to be a son of Shiva; in others, an emanation of Shiva. In one text, *Vayu Purana*, he is described as having "a thousand heads, a thousand eyes, a thousand feet, wielding a thousand clubs, a thousand shafts; holding the shell, the discus, the mace, and bearing the blazing bow and battle ax; fierce and terrible, shining with dreadful splendor, and decorated with the crescent moon; clothed in a tiger's skin, dripping with blood, having a capacious stomach and a vast mouth armed with formidable tusks."

Variant spellings: Seeva, Siva.

Shou Hsing

2672

Shou Hsing (longevity star). In Chinese legend, the deified sage Tung Fang So, worshiped as the god of longevity.

One day Emperor Wu Ti saw a green sparrow and asked Tung Fang So whether it was an omen. Tung Fang So replied that it showed that Hsi Wang Mu, the goddess of peaches, was coming to visit the emperor with seven peaches from the magic peach tree that grew in her sacred garden. Each magic fruit, *p'an-t'ao*, conferred on the person who ate it 3,000 years of life. As the sage had predicted, the goddess Hsi Wang Mu appeared to the emperor. As the goddess was eating one of the peaches with the emperor she noticed that Tung Fang So was peeping at her through a window.

"This man stole and ate three of my peaches," she said to the emperor, "and now he is to live for thousands of years."

Shou Hsing is portrayed as an old man carrying one, two, or three peaches, accompanied by a deer or issuing from a peach.

In Japanese legend, Shou Hsing is called Tobosaku.

2673

Shri (prosperity; luck). In Hindu mythology, goddess of prosperity and luck, often identified with Lakshmi, another goddess of good fortune. Shri is also associated with fertility. One of her epithets is Karisin (abounding in dung), referring to her role with food and soil.

Shiva and Parvati

Shu (he who holds up?). In Egyptian mythology, god of the air. He and his twin sister, Tefnut, comprised the first couple of the Ennead, which was a system of gods worshiped in Egypt. According to one myth, the sun god conceived Shu and Tefnut without benefit of a partner and then spewed them forth from his mouth. Others say that Shu was the first son of the sun god Ra and the sky goddess Hathor. At the request of Ra, Shu was said to have separated the sky (Nut) from the earth (Geb) and maintained the division with his upraised arms. As a result, light and space were created as well as heaven above and earth below. Shu is often compared to Atlas in Greek mythology, who supported the heavens with his head and hands. In Egyptian art Shu was almost always portrayed in human form, wearing a feather or feathers on his head, and holding a scepter in his hand. Sometimes he was pictured with his arms upraised and the four pillars of heaven near his head.

2675

Shuddhodana. Fifth century B.C.E. In Buddhist legend, father of Gautama, the Buddha. He was the chieftain of the North Indian Shakya tribe. In some accounts he is said to have been a king. Told by soothsayers that his son would be either a universal monarch or a Buddha, an Enlightened One, he tried to prevent him from becoming a Buddha but failed.

2676

Shui Ching-tzu (son of water essence, water spirit). In Chinese mythology, the spirit of water, who made himself clothes of ebony bark. He is one of the Wu Lao, the five spirits of natural forces.

2677

Shvod. In Armenian folklore, guardian house spirit, who is often cited as an ogre and used to frighten children.

2678

Sibu. In the mythology of the Indians of the Isthmus of Panama, the supreme god. Sibu entrusted a basket containing the seeds of all life to Sura, a lesser god, but demonic powers were continually after the basket. The evil god Jaburu stole it and ate the seeds. When Sura returned, Jaburu killed him. From Sura's grave a cacao tree and a calabash tree rose. Sibu forced Jaburu to drink a mixture made from the cacao tree served in a drinking vessel made of the calabash. Jaburu liked the chocolate taste and drank until his stomach began to swell. When it blew up, Sibu picked up the seeds that came out of Jaburu's body. "Let Sura wake up again!" Sibu declared. He

again gave Sura the basket containing the seeds of all life.

In another creation myth Sibu and Jaburu threw cacao pods at one another. Sibu used green pods, and Jaburu used ripe pods. At the third throw the pod broke in Jaburu's hand and mankind was born.

2679

Sibyls (the will of God?). In Greek and Roman cult, name given to women endowed with prophetic gifts, under the god Apollo. Their number varied from one to ten to twelve, and various sites were chosen for their abode. The most famous Sibyl was that of Cumae in Campania, Italy. This Sibyl leads Aeneas in the Underworld after has broken off the Golden Bough. According to some accounts the Cumanean Sibyl was once the mistress of Apollo. She tells Aeneas that she has lived seven generations already because Apollo granted her wish that she have as many years as their were grains in a handful of dust. The Sibyl, however, forgot to ask the god for perpetual youth and thus aged and shrank. In Petronius' novel *Satyricon* the Sibyl has shrunk to a tiny being, all shriveled up, who is kept in a cage and asks only to die. In another myth associated with the Sibyl, she offered King Tarquinius Priscus nine books of sibylline oracles. The king, however, refused to buy them at the price she set, so she burned three and again offered the remaining six. Again, he refused, and she burned three more, still asking the full price. Realizing that all of the books would be destroyed, Tarquinius agreed to buy the remaining three for the price of the original nine. The sacred books were kept under the charge of Roman priests and could only be consulted by order of the Senate. In 83 B.C.E. they were destroyed by fire and another set was produced. Eventually the Christians and Jews began producing sets of sibylline books, and 14 such books appeared that are still extant. During the Middle Ages the Sibyls along with the Hebrew Prophets were said to have predicted the coming of Christ. In the *Dies Irae*, the great medieval hymn for the dead, the Sibyl is cited along with King David. Michelangelo painted five Sibyls on the ceiling of the Sistine Chapel, and Raphael, Mantegna, Rembrandt, and Turner also painted Sibyls. The Sibyl's most famous role is in Vergil's *Aeneid* (book 6).

2680

Sick Lion, The. Aesopic fable found in various European collections.

The lion allowed word to get around that he was on his deathbed and wished all of the animals of his kingdom to come to his cave to hear his last will and testament.

The fox did not wish to be the first to enter the cave. So he lingered near the entrance while the goat and the sheep and the calf went in to receive the last wishes of the king of beasts.

After a time, the lion seemed to make a remarkable recovery and came to the mouth of the cave. Seeing the fox a safe distance away, he bellowed: "Why do you not come in to pay your respects to me, Friend Fox?"

"Please pardon me, Your Majesty," replied the fox, "but I did not wish to crowd you. I noticed the tracks of many of your subjects going into your cave, but so far I have seen none coming out. Until some of them come out and there is more room in the cave, I think I'll stay out here in the open air."

Moral: Don't believe all you hear.

The fable is alluded to by Horace in his *Satires* (book 1).

In a variation of the fable, *The Ailing Lion and His Visitors*, included in Juan Ruiz's *El Libro de Buen Amor* (The Book of Good Love), the lion is actually sick. When he is visited by the other animals they offer themselves for his supper. The lion chooses a bull for dinner, and the wolf is chosen to do the honors of carving. Thinking to get the better of the lion, the wolf gives him the entrails, saying they will be better for his health. However, the lion raises his paw and tears away the skin and an ear from the wolf's head. The fox is then ordered to do the honors of serving. Fearful and clever at the same time, she gives the whole trunk of the bull to the lion and the entrails to the rest of the party.

"Who taught you, dear madam, to carve so well, so judiciously, so properly?" asked the lion.

"I studied the wolf's head and learned from it," the fox replied.

2681
Sido. In Melanesian mythology, trickster of New Guinea. Sido fell in love with a beautiful woman named Sagaru, only to lose her to a more powerful magician. Battling the magician to try to win her back cost Sido his life. But his spirit was not allowed to enter Adiri, the land of the dead. So he went about seducing women and children. After wandering for some time he entered Adiri and planted a garden to feed the dead. Transforming himself into a pig, he cut out his backbone to form the roof of a house for the dead. The Kiwaians on New Guinea commemorate this event by fastening parts of a pig to the framework of their homes. Sido is also known as Hido and Iko.

2682
Siegfried (victory peace). In the *Nibelungenlied*, a hero; called Sigurd in the *Volsunga Saga*, an earlier version of the legend.

2683
Sif (kinship). In Norse mythology, grain goddess, the second wife of Thor and mother of Ull, Thor's stepson. The fire-trickster god, Loki, stole Sif's hair and was forced to replace it with golden hair made by the dwarfs.

2684
Siggeir. In Norse mythology, king of the Goths and husband of Signy. He took over the Volsung kingdom, slaying Volsung and setting wild beasts to devour Volsung's ten sons; only Sigmund survived. He was finally killed by being burned alive in a palace set on fire by Sigmund and Sinfiotli. Siggeir appears in the *Volsunga Saga*.

2685
Sigi. In Norse mythology, a son of Odin; a murderer and an outlaw. Before he was killed he became the father of Rerir, who was the father of Volsung.

2686
Sigmund (victory shield). In Norse mythology, son of Volsung and Ljod. Sigmund was father (by his sister Signy) of Sinfiotli, co-avenger of Volsung's death, and father (by Hjordis) of the great hero Sigurd. Sigmund was killed by the will of the gods for having had sexual intercourse with his sister. He appears in the *Volsunga Saga* and Richard Wagner's *Der Ring des Nibelungen*. Sigmund is portrayed by Arthur Rackham in his illustrations for Wagner's Ring Cycle.

2687
Signy. In Norse mythology, daughter of Volsung and Ljod; sister of Sigmund, and mother by him of Sinfiotli. Signy was forced to become the wife of King Siggeir. She contrived to save one of her brothers, Sigmund, from death by wild beasts. She then deceived him, disguised as a gypsy, and bore him Sinfiotli, who became Sigmund's companion in avenging Volsung's death. She died when Siggeir's palace was set on fire. She appears in the *Volsunga Saga* and as Sieglinde in Richard Wagner's *Der Ring des Nibelungen*.

2688
Siguna (victory giver). In Norse mythology, the wife of Loki, the fire-trickster god. She tended him when he was finally bound under the earth.
Variant spelling: Sigyn.

Sigurd (Willy Pogany)

2689

Sigurd. In Norse mythology, a hero; in Germanic mythology called Siegfried. Sigurd was the son of Sigmund and Hjordis; husband of Gudrun; and father of Sigmund, Swanhild, and Awlaug (by Brynhild). He appears in the *Volsunga Saga*, in William Morris's *Sigurd the Volsung and the Fall of the Niblungs*, a four-book epic in anapestic couplets, and Richard Wagner's *Der Ring des Nibelungen* as Siegfried. He is portrayed in Arthur Rackham's illustrations for Wagner's Ring Cycle.

2690

Sileni (moon men). In Greek mythology, creatures of the hills and woods, often confused with satyrs, having horse's ears, flattened noses, horse's tails or legs, or both. The most famous of the group was Silenus, teacher of Dionysus, who was made drunk by King Midas. The Greeks compared Socrates with Silenus, not only because he was a teacher, but because he was also ugly, as was Silenus. Vergil's *Sixth Ecologue*, Ovid's *Metamorphoses* (book 11), Pope's *Dunciad* (III,324), Swift's *The Fable of Midas*, Shelley's *Hymn to Pan*, and W.S. Landor's *Silenus*, also cite or tell of Silenus. Silenus appears in paintings of Titian, Piero di Cosimo, Rubens, and Géricault.

2691

Silvanus (woods, forest). In Roman mythology, god of agriculture, watching over hunters, shepherds, and boundaries; patron god of houses and flocks. Under the Empire Silvanus was credited with protecting parks and gardens. In Roman art he was portrayed as a strong woodsman. Vergil's *Aeneid* (book 8) describes a grove near Caere, dedicated to Silvanus, which served as the boundary between Latium and Ethruria.

2692

Simeon Stylites, St. (hearing-high pillar). 390–459 C.E. In Christian legend, first pillar saint. Patron of

shepherds. Feast, Roman church and 1 September in the Eastern Orthodox church.

St. Simeon wanted to mortify his body, so according to a fifth-century account in Theodoret's *Ecclesiastical History*, he "elevated himself on a pillar . . . of forty cubits in height, and there stood he for 37 years with a chain around his neck, a spectacle to men and to angels." The account goes on to tell that St. Simeon sometimes made as many as 1,244 "inclinations of the body in one day." He also "stood one whole year on one foot." He died on his pillar. Tennyson's poem *St. Simeon Stylites* deals with the mad saint.

2693

Simon Magus (Simon the magician). First century C.E. In the Bible, N.T., a magician rebuked by St. Peter because he attempted to buy the power of the Holy Spirit (Acts 8:9–13). The word *simony*, the buying of ecclesiastical power, derives from his name. Christian tradition not included in the New Testament says that Simon was a constant foe of Peter, even following him to Rome. One account says Simon requested that he be buried alive, certain he would rise up on the third day. Another account says he tried to fly from a tower and was killed when he fell.

Simurugh

2694

Simurgh (thirty). In Persian mythology, a gigantic bird whose wings were as large as clouds.

The Simurgh sat on the magical tree, Gaokerena, which produced the seeds of all plant life. When he moved, a thousand branches and twigs of the tree fell in all directions. They were then gathered by another bird, the Camrosh, which took them to the rain god, Tishtrya, who fertilized them.

The Persian mystic poet Farid Al-Din Attar (fl. c. 1180–1220) used the Simurgh as a symbol of the godhead in his poem *Nantiq-al- Tayr* (The Conference of the Birds). The work is an elaborate allegory in which 30 birds (Persian, *si murgh*) set out in search of the Simurgh, only to realize in the end that they are the Simurgh.

Variant spellings: Saena, Semuru, Senmury, Simorg, Simurg.

2695

Sin (moon). In Near Eastern mythology (Sumerian), moon god of Ur and son of Enlil, the storm god. Abraham, the Hebrew patriarch in the Old Testament, came from Ur by way of Harran, both cities being devoted to the moon god Sin. Mount Sinai is also believed to have been originally dedicated to Sin.

2696

Sinbad the Sailor. Hero in the tale of "Sinbad the Sailor and Sinbad the Porter" in *The Thousand and One Nights* (nights 536–566), which contains the seven voyages of Sinbad the Sailor. Sinbad was a merchant in Baghdad who acquired great wealth by making seven voyages, which he narrated to Sinbad the Porter, a poor man.

First Voyage (nights 538–541): Sinbad, a wealthy youth, squanders all of his money and, attempting to recoup his loss, buys some merchandise and sails away. The ship stops in the Indian Ocean, and he and others of the ship visit what they think is an island but which is actually a large sleeping whale. They light a fire on the whale's back, and the heat wakes the monster, which instantly dives into the ocean. Sinbad is rescued by some merchants and returns home.

Second Voyage (nights 543–546): Bored with life on land, Sinbad takes another journey by ship. He falls asleep on an island where the ship has stopped for water, and he is left behind. He discovers a roc's egg, about 50 feet in diameter. When the monstrous roc appears, Sinbad grabs hold of one of its feet and is flown away to the Valley of Diamonds. Here merchants on the cliffs above, unable to reach the valley, throw down meat to the birds in the valley. The diamonds strewn on the valley's bottom stick to the meat, which the birds carry up and deposit in their cliffside nests. The men then come and steal the diamonds. Sinbad attaches himself to a piece of meat and is lifted to an eagle's nest. Later he is rescued by the jewel collectors and returns home to Baghdad a rich man.

Third Voyage (nights 546–550): Sinbad's ship is captured by some savage dwarfs and is taken to an island where a giant one-eyed ogre (similar to the Cyclops of Greek mythology) begins eating the crew one by one. Sinbad heats two iron spits and rams them into the monster's eye. The ogre summons two other monsters and most of the men are killed. But Sinbad and two others escape, only to be lured to an island by a serpent that attempts to swallow Sinbad. He builds a wooden enclosure around himself that makes it impossible for the serpent to reach him. Sinbad is saved by a ship that sails from island to island, and while on it Sinbad sees a fish like a cow, fish like asses, and a bird born from a seashell.

Fourth Voyage (nights 550–555): Sinbad is shipwrecked and cast ashore with his companions on an island inhabited by cannibals, who imprison and fatten them for better eating, though Sinbad eats little so as to remain thin. He eventually escapes and reaches a kingdom where bridles and stirrups are unknown. Sinbad makes himself rich by "inventing" them, and the king gives his daughter as wife to Sinbad. When she dies, he is buried alive with her body according to the custom of the land. Sinbad escapes, however, and returns to Baghdad, rich from rifling the bodies of the dead on his way out of the catacombs.

Fifth Voyage (nights 556–559): Sinbad's ship is destroyed by two rocs whose offspring has been eaten by merchants. Seizing a floating piece of wreckage, Sinbad is washed ashore on a beautiful island. He comes upon an old man who appears "weak and infirm" sitting on the bank of a stream. Thinking to help the old man, Sinbad carries him on his back, but the man "clasped his legs nimbly" around Sinbad's neck, making it difficult to walk. Eventually Sinbad makes a liquor to get the old man drunk and then dashes "his head to pieces." After being rescued, Sinbad learns the man was the Old Man of the Sea, and Sinbad is "the first who ever escaped strangling by his malicious tricks."

Sixth Voyage (nights 560–562): Sinbad's ship is driven ashore and breaks up on a barren island. Here he finds many precious stones and also an underground river, on which he rides a raft to the city of Serendib, where the king welcomes Sinbad; he is sent home with great wealth plus a present for Caliph Harun al-Rashid.

Seventh Voyage (nights 563–566): Caliph Harun al-Rashid sends Sinbad back to Serendib with gifts for the king. On his way, Sinbad is captured by pirates and sold as a slave to a merchant who makes him an elephant hunter. He is so successful that he learns of the burial ground of the elephants, where a huge store of ivory is located. He is rewarded with his freedom and given a stock of ivory, with which he returns home.

The romantic adventures of Sinbad appeal to writers of adventure fiction, particularly children's stories, and Hollywood has produced films of many versions of the legends.

2697
Sindri (cinder). In Norse mythology, a worker in gold among the dwarfs; brother of Brok. Sindri created Odin's arm ring, Draupnir; Frey's golden boar; and Thor's hammer, Mjolmir.

2698
Sinon (plunderer). In Greek mythology, a young Greek soldier, a relative of Odysseus, who pretended to desert to Troy and convinced the Trojans to bring in the wooden horse. When night came, Sinon let the Greeks out of the wooden horse, and Troy was sacked. Vergil's *Aeneid* (book 2) and Dante's *Divine Comedy* (Inferno, canto 30) cite him as an example of treachery. In the latter he is among the falsifiers of words, called *il falso Sinon greco* (the false Greek Sinon).

2699
Sinuhe. Hero in the ancient Egyptian "Tale of Sinuhe," found in various Egyptian manuscripts. The tale was used by the scribes and students of the 12th and 13th dynasties, who copied it on ostraca (limestone flakes) as part of their studies. The tale is of a man who has to flee Egypt but always wishes to return to his beloved land. Eventually, he is called back. The short tale inspired Mika Waltari's novel *The Egyptian*, which was made into a popular Hollywood film.

2700
Sirens (those who bind with a cord, or those who wither). In Greek mythology, three water nymphs, Ligeia, Leucosia and Parthenope, who with their singing, lured seamen to watery graves. They lived on an island between Circe's isle and Scylla, where they sat in a flowery bed surrounded by the rotting bodies of the shipwrecked men. When Odysseus sailed past them, he had the ears of his men stopped up with wax so they could not hear the Sirens' song. He, however, wanted to hear the song so he had his men tie him to the mast. When the Argonauts took the same watery route, they were saved by the song of Orpheus, which defeated the songs of the Sirens. Either Odysseus or Orpheus is responsible for their deaths. The three cast themselves into the sea when they failed to lure Odysseus or Orpheus. They were transformed into sunken rocks. Generally, early Greek art portrayed the Sirens as great birds with the heads of women, or with the upper part of the body like that of a woman, with the legs of a bird, with or

without wings. In later Greek art the Sirens were portrayed as beautiful women. They are sometimes associated with the cult of the dead and were believed to guide souls to the Underworld. As such they appear on various Greek tombs. Sirens appear in Homer's *Odyssey* (book 12), Apollonius of Rhodes's *The Argonautica*, Dante's *The Divine Comedy*, where they are symbols of sensual pleasure, William Morris's *The Life and Death of Jason*, and E.M. Forster's *Story of the Siren*. Debussy's last section of his *Nocturnes* (1898) for orchestra, "Sirènes," captures the song of the Sirens with a women's wordless chorus.

2701
Sir Patrick Spens. Late medieval English ballad that tells of a ship sent in wintertime to Norway. On its journey home, Sir Patrick's ship is wrecked, and everyone on board is lost.

2702
Sisyphus (shrewd or wise). In Greek mythology, first king of Corinth, a trickster noted for shrewdness and cleverness; son of Aeolus, king of Thessaly, and Enarete. When Zeus raped the nymph Aegina, daughter of the river god Asopus, Sisyphus promised to tell Asopus what had happened, but only on the condition that Asopus would give Corinth a spring on top of the Acrocorinth, its acropolis. Zeus was so angry at what happened that he sent Thanatos, Death, to kill Sisyphus, only to have Thanatos bound by Sisyphus so that no one could die. Zeus then sent Ares, the war god, to free Thanatos. As soon as Thanatos was free, he killed Sisyphus, but before Sisyphus died he asked his wife, Merope, not to perform the prescribed funeral rites for his burial. This angered both Hades and his wife, Persephone, deities of the Underworld, who sent Sisyphus back to earth to have the burial sacrifices offered. Sisyphus promised to return to the Underworld afterwards, but he lived to a very old age before he died again. Zeus, angered, devised a punishment for Sisyphus when he did return to the Underworld. He was required to roll a boulder up a hill, but whenever it reached the top, it rolled back down—and had to be rolled up the hill again, over and over. Thus "Sisyphean" came to mean a fruitless, endless task. Sisyphus appears or is cited in Ovid's *Metamorphoses* (book 4); Spenser's *Faerie Queene* (I.v.35); Pope's *Ode for the Music on St. Cecilia's Day* and supplies the title for Camus' collection of existential essays, *The Myth of Sisyphus* (1942), in which Camus explores the absurdity of life. Titian painted a *Sisyphus*.

2703
Sivamala (Shiva's garland). In Hindu mythology, a rosary that the goddess of wisdom, Shatarupa, gave to Brahma, her husband and father.

2704

Sjoran. In Swedish folklore, a spirit of the sea, derived, according to some scholars, from the Norse goddess Ran, wife of the sea god Aegir.

2705

Skadi (damage). In Norse mythology, a giantess, wife of the sea god Njord and daughter of the giant Thjassi. When her father was slain for stealing Iduna's magic apples, Skadi demanded satisfaction for the deed. She was allowed to choose a husband from among the gods on the condition that she make her choice by seeing only their feet from behind a curtain. She thought she had chosen the handsome god Baldur but instead received Njord. She lived part of the time at her father's home, Thrymheim, and part at her husband's, Noatun. According to the *Prose Edda* , she liked to spend "her time in the chase of savage beasts, and is called the Ondur goddess, or Ondurdis."

Variant spelling: Skade.

Karttikeya (Skanda)

2706

Skanda. In Hindu mythology, the six-headed war god, son of Shiva. In some texts Skanda is said to have no mother at all; Shiva cast his semen into fire, and Skanda arose. In other texts Skanda, called Karttikeya (son of the razors), is said to have as his mothers the seven Kritikas (the Pleiades). Sometimes represented as a razor, Skanda is also called Guha (reared in a secret place) and Kumara (the youth). The last epithet is sometimes also applied to Agni, the fire god.

2707

Skinfaxi (shining mane). In Norse mythology, horse of Dagr (the day). From Skinfaxi's mane, light was shed over the earth and the heavens. Skinfaxi appears in the *Prose Edda*.

2708

Skipper Ireson's Ride. American literary ballad by John Greenleaf Whittier, written in 1857. It tells how Skipper Floyd Ireson deserted his ship, causing the death of his companions. Whittier said that his ballad "was founded solely on a fragment of rhyme which I heard from one of my early schoolmates, a native of Marblehead." The refrain:

Poor Floyd Ireson, for his hard heart,
Tarred and feathered and carried in a cart
By the women of Marblehead.

In the 1888 edition of his poems Whittier says the poem was "pure fancy." In reality the incident took place in 1808 and Benjamin Ireson, not Floyd, was accused of deserting his men, though in fact the crew was responsible for the wreck. In Samuel Roads's *History of Marblehead* the victim, contrary to the legend and ballad, was carried in a dory, not a cart, and men, not women, were the principal avengers.

2709

Skirnir (he who makes things shine). In Norse mythology, the favorite servant of the god Frey. He acted as a go-between for Frey when he sought Gerda's love.

2710

Skoll and Hati (to stick to). In Norse mythology, two wolves that pursue the sun and moon. The *Prose Edda* describes them as finally devouring the sun and moon at Ragnarok, the end of the world.

2711

Skritek. In Slavic folklore, a household spirit, often in the form of a small boy, who lives behind the oven or in the stable. He protects the family, which in turn leaves portions of their meals for his consumption, especially on Thursdays and Christmas. If for some reason the *skritek* is offended, he causes havoc in the house. His statue, made of wood, portrays him with his arms crossed and wearing a crown. The statue is placed on the table to guard the hearth when the family is away. In Polish folklore the *skritek* appears as a drenched chicken, dragging its wings and tail.

2712

Skuld (future). In Norse mythology, one of the three named Norns; the others being Urd and Verdandi. Skuld is portrayed veiled, facing the future with a scroll in her hands.

2713

Slave and the Master, The. Moral fable by the Persian poet Sadi, in *The Gulistan* (chapter 5, story 2).

A gentleman possessed a slave of exquisite beauty, whom he regarded with love and affection. One day he said to a friend, "Would that this slave of mine, with all the beauty and good qualities he possesses, had not a long and uncivil tongue."

"Brother," his friend replied, "do not expect service after professing friendship, because when relations between lover and beloved come in, the relations between master and servant are superseded."

Sleeping Beauty (Walter Crane)

2714

Sleeping Beauty, The. European folktale, the most popular versions being Perrault's *La Belle au bois dormant* and the Grimms' *Little Briar Rose*.

After many prayers a childless king and queen were rewarded with the birth of a baby girl. The king and queen invited all of the people in the kingdom to her christening, and in addition they invited 12 of the 13 Wise Women (supernatural beings). They omitted asking the 13th because they had only enough gold goblets to serve 12 of them. At the christening each of the Wise Women bestowed a gift on the child. Before the end of the ceremony the uninvited Wise Woman appeared, and in retribution for not being invited, she cursed the baby, saying she would prick her finger on a spindle and die. It happened that one of the 12 Wise Women had not yet bestowed her gift, so she was able to temper the curse with her gift, though not revoke it. For her gift she declared that the princess would not die but would sleep for 100 years when she pricked her finger and could then be awakened by the kiss of a prince.

In an effort to forestall the curse the king ordered all spindles in the kingdom be destroyed. However, the 13th Wise Woman disguised herself as an old woman and hid a spinning wheel in a remote tower of the castle, where she sat spinning until the child's 15th birthday. On that day the Princess wandered into the remote tower and found the old woman and the spinning wheel. Offering to let her try her hand at spinning, the old woman made sure the girl pricked her finger. The girl began to get sleepy and went to her room to lie down. Sleep then overcame everyone in the castle, and eventually vines grew up over every portal and window, completely covering the structure.

The story of the sleeping princess spread throughout the land, and many princes attempted to scale the fortress to reach her and revive her, but all failed. Then when 100 years had passed, a young prince made an attempt to reach the princess and succeeded. His kiss awakened her, and then the entire castle awoke. The prince and princess then married. Perrault's version was used by Tchaikovsky for his ballet *The Sleeping Beauty*. Walt Disney's feature-length cartoon *Sleeping Beauty* deals with the folktale in a sentimental manner.

2715

Slith (the dark fields). In Norse mythology, a river that flowed in the land of the giants. In the *Voluspa*, the first poem in the *Poetic Edda*, which narrates the creation and destruction of the world, the river is said to come from the east "through poisoned vales with swords and daggers," i.e., icy cold.

2716

Snake. A legless reptile. In world mythology and folklore the snake, or serpent, is sometimes a symbol of a beneficent being, sometimes a demonic one. In Jewish and Christian belief the snake is often equated with evil or the devil. In Genesis (3:1) the serpent is described as "more subtil than any beast of the field which the Lord had made." The text does not identify the serpent with the devil, but the writers of the New Testament did. According to the Book of Numbers (21:5–9), Moses erected a brass serpent in the desert when the Hebrews were in danger of being wiped out by a snake plague. All of the people who looked upon the brass snake would recover from the poisonous snakebites. The image erected by Moses was similar to the one dedicated to the life-giving god Nin-gis-zida in ancient Sumerian ritual. The brass serpent seems to have been in use for some time, for we are told that it was venerated during the reign of Hezekiah (717–686 B.C.E.) and destroyed by that king because "the children of Israel did burn incense to it: and he called it Nehusthan" (2 Kings 18:14). Jesus uses the image of the brass serpent when he says: "And as Moses lifted up the serpent in the wilderness, even so must the Son of Man be lifted up: That whosoever believeth in him should not perish, but have eternal life" (John 3:1–15).

In ancient Egyptian mythology the monster-serpent Apophis, enemy of the gods Horus, Amen, Ra, and Osiris always tried to prevent the sun god Amun-Ra from rising every day. But the clever priests of Amun-Ra devised a magic ceremony to guarantee that the sun would rise. They made a snake out of wax, inscribed it with the name of Apophis, and while reciting spells and incantations cast it into the fire. The magic worked, for every day the sun did rise over the land of Egypt. But the same Egyptians saw the snake as a symbol of resurrection because it shed its skin. One ancient Egyptian text, devised to help the dead achieve resurrection, puts the following lines into the mouth of the deceased:

I am the serpent Sata whose years are many,
I die and I am born again each day . . . .
I renew myself,
And I grow young each day.

The Greeks also used the snake or serpent as a symbol of rebirth and healing. Asklepius, god of medicine, was often shown with the caduceus, a wand with two entwined serpents surmounted by small wings or a winged helmet, both indicating quick movement. In Aztec mythology Quetzalcoatl (green-feathered serpent) was portrayed in serpent form. In Persian mythology the serpent or snake is believed to bring disease and death. Ahirman, the evil spirit, once transformed himself into a serpent, entering human beings and producing lust, greed, falsehood, slander, and revenge.

Numerous goddesses in world mythology are also identified with the snake or serpent, such as the Sumerian goddess Inanna, Queen of Heaven, who is often portrayed holding snakes in her hands, symbolic of her control of the phallus. The Minoan Mother Goddess, who was "the master of men," was also pictured with snakes on her person in Hindu mythology. The serpent is associated with Vishnu, who sleeps on a coiled serpent on the primordial waters.

2717
Snegurotchka (the snow maiden). In Russian mythology, lovely daughter of King Frost and Fairy Spring.

Snegurotchka was brought up in the cold forest because sunlight would destroy her. As long as she knew nothing of love, she was safe from the sun god's fatal caress. But one day she heard the song of a shepherd's son, Lel, and asked her father to let her join humanity. She was so overjoyed at sharing in human emotions that she asked Fairy Spring to give her the power to love. The wish was granted and she fell in love with Prince Mizgyr, who left his betrothed, Kupava, for Snegurotchka. But when the two declared their love for each other, the sun's rays touched Snegurotchka and she melted. Mizgyr cursed the gods and drowned himself in a lake.

The tale of Snegurotchka was used by Alexander Ostrovsky in his play *Snegurotchka*; Tchaikovsky wrote incidental music for the first performance. Rimsky-Korsakov used Ostrovsky's play as the basis for his opera *Snegurotchka*.

Sodom and Gomorrah

2718

Sodom and Gomorrah (burning and submersion). In the Bible, O.T., two cities of the plain of the River Jordan, destroyed by fire and brimstone by Yahweh, the Hebrew god. The legend, told in Genesis (19:1–29) tells how the patriarch Abraham asked Yahweh to spare Sodom if ten righteous men could be found (women did not count). But none were found. Yahweh sent three angels to the city, and the angels encountered Lot as they entered through the gates. Lot offered them lodging and brought them to his house. Some men of the city knocked at Lot's door and demanded that Lot send the three strangers outside "that we may know [have sexual intercourse with] them" (Gen. 19:5). Lot refused, offering instead to send out his virgin daughters to be abused sexually. The angels intervened and told Lot to prepare his family to flee the city because it was to be destroyed by God. While Abraham and his family and Lot and his family fled, the city was destroyed. Lot's wife looked back on the destruction and was turned into a pillar of salt (Gen. 19:26). The city was punished, according to some biblical commentators, because of its homosexual practices, but the biblical text makes it clear that the crime was inhospitality to strangers, since Lot was willing to offer his daughters to the men of the city for sexual intercourse rather than have his guests violated. But the incorrect popular interpretation has stuck, and the word *sodomy* is used to refer to homosexual activity. In Marcel Proust's *Remembrance of Things Past*, the novel *Sodome et Gomorrhe*, translated into English as *Cities of the Plain*, deals in part with the narrator discovering that Baron Charlus is a homosexual.

2719

Sohrab. In the Persian epic poem *Shah Namah*, by Firdusi, son of the hero Rustum; he is killed by his father in battle.

The story of Sohrab and Rustum, that of the combat between a father and a son who did not know one another, forms part of the narrative in Firdusi's epic. Rustum, one of the greatest warriors of the Persians, in the course of his wanderings married the daughter of the king of Ader-baijan but soon left his wife in pursuit of more adventure. She bore him a son named Sohrab, but fearing that Rustum would take the boy and turn him into a soldier, she sent a message saying she had given birth to a girl. Sohrab grew to manhood and, longing to find his warrior father, went into the service of the Tartars. A battle then ensued between the Persians and the Tartars, with Sohrab on the side of the Tartars and Rustum on the side of the Persians. When Sohrab first saw Rustum, he had an intuition who his antagonist was and eagerly inquired if he

was Rustum. But Rustum, ignorant of Sohrab's intuition, refused to reveal his identity and challenged Sohrab to combat. In their first encounter, after an exchange of spears Sohrab evaded his opponent's club, but because of the weight of the club Rustum lost his balance and fell. Sohrab, however, refused to take advantage and offered a truce. Rustum, enraged at his downfall, renewed the struggle. Rustum then called out his own name, and Sohrab, bewildered by the fact that the man he thought was his father seemed to be calling for Rustum, ceased to fight and was fatally pierced by his father's spear. Unsure of the identity of his slayer, he declared that Rustum, his father, would avenge his death. Finally, the truth came out: each discovered the identity of the other, but it was too late; Sohrab was dead.

This pathetic episode from *Shah Namah* inspired an essay by the French writer Sainte-Beuve, which was read by the English poet Matthew Arnold, who in turn used the essay to form the basis for his blank verse narrative poem *Sohrab and Rustum*. Arnold also consulted an account of the episode he found in Sir John Malcolm's *History of Persia*.

The poem was characterized by English poet Coventry Patmore, writing in the *North British Review*, as a "vivid reproduction of Homer's manner and spirit" but not "a new and independent creation." This criticism was echoed by Douglas Bush in *Mythology and the Romantic Tradition in English Poetry*. He writes that the poem is "academic" and has all of "the defects of a poem written to illustrate a theory."

Variant spelling: Suhrab.

2720

Sol(sun). In Norse mythology, the sun, believed to be the daughter of Mundilfari. Sol's brother was Mani, the moon.

2721

Solbon. In Siberian mythology, god of horses, worshiped by the Buriat; he rides through the sky with a lasso in his hand.

Solbon has three wives, one of them a former Buriat girl whom he abducted from her wedding feast. She bore him a son; his two other wives are childless. In one myth Solbon left his horses in the care of his groom, Dogedoi, while he traveled in the western sky (Solbon is identified with the planet Venus). Dogedoi, however, left the horses unattended for three days and went out for a walk with Buto, his dog. When he returned, he found that wolves had scattered some of the horses and eaten the others. When Solbon returned, Dogedoi was severely punished.

Some horses are dedicated to Solbon by the Buriat and are thereby removed from any secular service in the community. During the spring the manes and tails of the horses are cut in preparation for a sacrifice to Solbon. Meats, cream porridge, and wines are also prepared for the god. The wine is thrown into the air in Solbon's honor, and the food is burned.

Variant spellings: Sulbundu, Tscholbon.

2722

Solomon (peaceful) c. 971–931 B.C.E. In the Bible, O.T., third king of Israel, son of King David and Bathsheba, noted for his wisdom, though this is often in conflict in the various accounts in the Bible regarding the king and his extensive wealth. Two episodes from his life are most often encountered in art and music: the visit of the Queen of Sheba (1 Kings 10) and the Judgment of Solomon. The rich and beautiful Queen of Sheba arrived at Solomon's court in Jerusalem with a great entourage. She had heard reports of the king's greatness and wisdom. Sheba tested Solomon by asking him many difficult questions, which he answered correctly. When she left Jerusalem, the Queen gave him many gifts. The second episode deals with the king choosing the genuine mother between two whores, each of whom claimed to be the mother of a certain baby (1 Kings 3:16–28). The women lived in the same house, each had borne a child, and one of the two children died at night. Both women claimed the surviving child as her own. The dispute was brought before Solomon, who called for a sword to divide the living child in two, saying he would give half to each. The real mother cried out, "O my lord, give her the living child, and in no wise slay it." But the other woman said, "Let it be neither mine nor thine, but divide it" (1 Kings 3:26). Solomon then gave the child to the first woman, because a true mother would rather lose her child than see it die. Aside from the numerous paintings depicting the subjects, Handel wrote an oratorio *Solomon*. In Islam Solomon is called Sulaiman. Solomon is credited in the Bible with the authorship of the Song of Songs, the Proverbs, Ecclesiastes, and the O.T. Apocrypha Wisdom of Solomon. However, no serious biblical scholar accepts his authorship of these works even though tradition assigns them to him.

2723

Sovi. In Slavic folklore, a hero responsible for originating cremation of the dead. The tale is found in a 13th-century Russian work that may have been derived from a Finnish source.

When Sovi's son died, Sovi buried him in the ground. The next day he asked his son if he had rested well. But the son groaned: "Oh! Worms and reptiles have eaten me!" Sovi then gave his son supper and put the body in the hollow of a tree for the night. The next day he asked the same question, and the boy replied: "Countless bees and mosquitoes have stung me. Oh, I have slept badly." So the following day Sovi made a huge funeral pyre and threw the body of his son into it. The next day when he asked the same question the boy replied: "I slept as peacefully as an infant in the cradle."

The custom of cremation was common in earlier times in Slavic countries. In Lithuania, when Great Duke Algirdas (or Oligerd) was burned in 1377, some 18 saddle horses also were included in the funeral pyre. The body was dressed in a robe of rich purple brocade, a mantle studded with pearls and precious stones, and a belt of gold and silver.

2724

Spes (expectation). In Roman mythology, goddess of hope, invoked at births, marriages and for a good harvest. She had several temples in Rome. Portrayed as a young woman, she held a bud, either closed or just about to open, in her right hand.

2725

Sphinx (Throttler). In Greek mythology, a monster, half-woman, half-beast; daughter of Echidna and Orthus or Typhon. The Sphinx had the head of a woman and the body of a lion. She was sent by Hera or Apollo to punish King Laius of Thebes. She would sit on a rock and ask the following riddle: "What is it which, though it has one voice, becomes four-footed and two- footed and three-footed." If those questioned could not answer the riddle the Sphinx hurled them from her rock, or else she ate them. When Oedipus passed by the Sphinx he was asked the riddle and replied that the answer was man, for as an infant he is four-footed, creeping on hands and feet; in his prime he is two-footed; and in old age he uses a cane as a third foot. When the Sphinx heard the correct answer, she threw herself over the cliff and died. Pausanias, to rationalize the myth, wrote in his *Description of Greece* that the Sphinx was a woman bandit who waylaid travelers, her headquarters being on Mount Phicium. Carl Jung, giving a psychological account, says that the Sphinx represents the Great Mother Goddess who is destroyed by the stronger masculine force represented by Oedipus. In the Egyptian version of the Sphinx, however, it is always a male and often symbolizes royal strength and dignity. The Great Sphinx at Gizeh represents the god Horus trying to catch sight of his father Ra, the rising sun, as he journeys across the valley. Ingres and Moreau both painted the Sphinx and Oedipus.

2726

Spider. An arachnid that spins webs that trap prey and serve as nests. In Egyptian mythology the spider is an attribute of the goddess Neith as weaver of the world. In Greek mythology it is associated with Athene, Harmonia, the Fates, the Moirai, and Persephone. Athene transformed Arachne into a spider for challenging the goddess to a weaving contest. The spider is also associated with Holda and the Norns in Norse mythology and Ishtar and Atagatis in Near Eastern mythology. In Christianity the spider is a symbol of evil or the devil. The Chibcha Indians, a North Andean tribe of Colombia, believe that the dead cross the lake of death on boats made of spiderwebs. They therefore hold the spider in awe and will not kill it. Some South American Indian mythologies believe the spiderweb to be the means of climbing from the "lower world" to the "upper world." In African mythology, Yiyi, a spider man, brings fire from heaven to help humankind. Yiyi's web is used by the handmaidens of the sun to come down to earth to draw water and then reascend to heaven. According to the Nauru Island natives of the South Pacific, the world was created by Areop-Enap (ancient spider).

2727

Springfield Mountain. American ballad, believed to be the oldest original American ballad still in circulation. It tells of the death by snakebite of Timothy Myrick at Wilberham (then Springfield Mountain), Massachusetts, on 7 August 1761.

2728

Sreca (fate). In Serbian folklore, female personification of fate, often portrayed as a beautiful maiden spinning thread. If in a beneficent mood, she protected the family. When in an evil mood, she was called Nesreca and portrayed as an old woman with bloodshot eyes who paid no attention to the welfare of the family. With the proper spells the evil Nesreca could be dismissed, but Sreca, a person's fate, was his for his entire life.

2729

Stacker Lee. In American folklore, a black man who sold his soul to the devil for a magic hat that enabled him to transform himself into various forms. Eventually, the devil took back his magic hat and sent Stacker Lee to hell for killing Billy Lyon (Lion, Galion).

2730

Stag. An adult male deer. In Greek mythology the goddess Artemis (Diana in Roman mythology) punished Actaeon for spying on her nudity by turning him into a stag, which was then devoured by mad dogs. When Agamemnon and his fleet were about to set sail for Troy, the Greeks asked their priest how to placate the goddess. Agamemnon was told to sacrifice his daughter Iphigenia. When the sacrifice was about to take place, Artemis (according to one account) substituted a stag for Iphigenia and took the maiden away to Tauris, where she became a priestess of the goddess. In Christian medieval folklore it was believed that when the stag reached the age of 50 years it would search for a snake, kill and eat it, and then make a mad dash to the nearest pool and drink as much water as possible to renew its antlers for another 50 years. If, however, the animal did not get to the water within three days after eating the snake, it would die. For Christians the stag became a symbol of the soul thirsting after God.

2731

Standish, Miles. c. 1584–1656. In American history and folklore, military leader of the Pilgrims. He appears in Longfellow's long narrative poem *The Courtship of Miles Standish*, which is pure legend. Miles was not in love with Priscilla and never sent John Alden to woo the girl in his name. According to Longfellow's poem, Priscilla's reply when Alden asked her to marry Standish was, "Why don't you speak for yourself, John?" In reality Standish was married twice. He believed in religious tolerance, in contrast to his Puritan contemporaries. He also appears in John Lothrop Motley's *Marry-Mount*, and Helen Carlisle's *We Begin*, both works of fiction. Aside from Longfellow's legend, James Russel Lowell's poem *Interview with Miles Standish* is also legend. Longfellow's poem was made into operas by seven different composers, but none is still performed.

2732

Stanislaus of Cracow, St. (camp glory?) 1030–1079. In Christian legend, martyr bishop of Cracow. Invoked by soldiers in battle. Feast, 7 May. Stanislaus was appointed bishop of Cracow in 1072. Because of the oppressive rule of Prince Boleslaus II, the bishop excommunicated him. In revenge Boleslaus murdered the bishop with his own hands at the altar. The body was then hacked to pieces; parts were placed in goblets and flung out of doors to be eaten by carrion birds. However, four eagles watched over the remains of the saint. Then suddenly, the bones came together, sinew to sinew, limb to limb, and the whole body was restored.

2733

Star of Bethlehem. A flowered plant of the lily family. In medieval Christian legend, it was blessed by the Child Jesus as he lay in his manger because it served as his pillow. At Christmastime in Italy the manger is decked with star of Bethlehem.

Stata Mater. In Roman mythology, ancient Italian goddess associated with protection from fire. In some accounts she is identified with Vesta, goddess of the hearth and domestic life.

St. Stephen

Stephen, St. (crown). First century C.E. In the Bible, N.T., proto- or first Christian martyr, who was stoned to death. Feast, 26 December. His legend is told in the Acts of the Apostles (6,7). Medieval legend deals with the recovery of the saint's body, which had been missing for some 400 years after his death. Lucian, a priest of Carsagamala in Palestine, was visited in a dream by Gamaliel, the Jewish doctor of the law who had taught St. Paul. Gamaliel revealed to Lucian that after the death of Stephen he had carried away the body and buried it in his own tomb. Gamaliel had also placed near St. Stephen's body those of Nicodemus and other saints. Lucian had the dream of Gamaliel three times. He went to his bishop, told the dream, and a crew went out to dig at the spot indicated in the dream. The crew discovered the remains of St. Stephen as well as those of some other saints. The relics were first placed in Jerusalem, then later taken to Constantinople, and finally to Rome, where they were placed in a tomb with the body of St. Lawrence. One medieval legend relates that when they opened the tomb and lowered St. Stephen's body, St. Lawrence's body moved on its side, giving place of honor on the right to St. Stephen. From the legend, the Romans called St. Lawrence *Il cortese Spagnuolo* (the courteous Spaniard).

Stonehenge. A prehistoric circle of very large stones on Salisbury Plain in England. The medieval historian Geoffrey of Monmouth in his *History of the Kings of Britain* says that Stonehenge was erected by Merlin to perpetuate the memory of the teacher of Hengist the Jute, who killed King Vortigern and 400 of his attendants, while pretending peace. Merlin was asked by Auralius Ambrosius to devise a memento to this cruel event. By magic Merlin transported the Giant's Dance, stones that had been brought by a race of giants to Killaraus in Ireland from Africa. The stones were said to possess magic properties. Legend also associates Stonehenge with the Druids.

Stone of Scone. In British legend, believed to be the stone on which Jacob rested his head at Bethel, as recorded in the Old Testament. Medieval legend said that it was carried to Egypt, Spain, Ireland, and finally to Scotland, where it was placed in the monastery of Scone. Scottish kings were crowned on the sacred stone. The English coronation chair, made for King Edward I, was designed to enclose the Stone of Scone, which he seized from the Scots in 1297. The chair, made of oak, was painted with birds, foliage, and animals on a gilt ground. Since 1308 every English sovereign, except Edward V and Edward VIII, has been crowned on it.

Stork. A large wading bird having long legs and a long neck and bill. In Western European folklore the stork is believed to bring babies. Many Germans believed that if a stork flew over a house it meant a child was on the way. This reflects the early belief that children were brought up out of the water or found in rocky caves. In Greek mythology the stork was sacred to the goddess Hera and in Roman mythology, to Juno, Hera's counterpart. In Christian symbolism the stork represents chastity, purity, and piety and is a harbinger of spring. Aristotle wrote that "it is a common story of the stork that the old birds are fed by their grateful progeny." It was believed in the Middle Ages, partly based on Aristotle, that when a stork grew old its children would surround it, provide it with food, and aid it when it flew by supporting it gently on each side with their wings.

Strap Buckner. In American Western folklore, a giant of a man who could drink any of his companions under the table. He had a red beard and rode a swift gray horse. One day he was challenged at cards by the devil and lost when the demon grew to nearly 200 feet tall and some 80 feet in girth. Strap Buckner's spirit is still seen astride his gray horse, riding through the night.

Strawberry. A small bush producing sweet berries. In Norse mythology the strawberry is associated with the love goddess Frigga; in Christian symbolism it is associated with the Virgin Mary.

2741

Stribog. In Slavic mythology, god of winds. In the Russian epic *The Lay of Igor's Army*, the winds are called the grandsons of Stribog. Other Slavic wind gods are Varpulis, who caused the noise of a storm; Erisvorsh, god of the "holy tempest"; and Vikhor, god of whirlwinds.

2742

Stupa (mound). A mound of earth covered with masonry, containing at its center a relic, usually of the Buddha or Jina, or a portion of scripture. According to Buddhist legend, when the Buddha was about to die, he was asked by a disciple what would happen to his remains after death. The Buddha answered that a *stupa* should be built to contain them. Ashoka, the Buddhist king, built *stupas* at sites associated with the birth, life, and death of the Buddha. In Ceylon *stupa* is called *thupa*. Various architectural terms developed from the term stupa: in Burma, *asgopa*; in China and Japan, *pagoda*; and in Tibet, *chörten*. Some older accounts call a *stupa* a *tope*. A *chaitya* is a hall containing a *stupa* or an image of Buddha. The *stupa* provides a physical focus for worship so that the mind may ascend to contemplation of spiritual realities.

2743

Stymphalian Birds (Priapic member?). In Greek mythology, bronze-beaked, man-eating, fantastic birdlike beings, expelled from Lake Stymphalus in Arcadia as Heracles sixth labor. The hero frightened the birds with bronze castanets given him by the goddess Athena. Heracles then shot at them; some escaped and flew to the Black Sea, later to threaten the Argonauts. They were believed to be associated with Artemis' cult. Images of them were carved on the metopes of Zeus' temple at Olympia. Pausanias' *Description of Greece* (book 8) tells of the birds. Dürer's *Hercules Killing the Stymphalian Birds* shows the hero drawing his bow to kill them.

2744

Styx (hated). In Greek mythology, one of the five rivers of Hades, the Underworld, over which Charon ferried the spirits of the dead. It was named after Styx, the eldest daughter of Oceanus and Tethys and mother of Zelus (zeal), Nike (victory), Kratos (power), and Bia (strength) by the Titan Pallas. In the battle between the gods and the Titans Styx sided with the gods and was rewarded for her service and made ruler of the river named after her. The gods swore by the sacred Styx, and if they violated their oath, they would be punished by nine years of banishment from the council of the gods and would

spend one year speechless and breathless. Though its waters were believed to be poisoned, Thetis immersed her son Achilles in its water to make him invulnerable. The Styx appears or is cited in Homer's *Odyssey* (book 10), Hesiod's *Theogony*, Vergil's *Aeneid* (book 6), Ovid's *Metamorphoses* (book 3), Dante's *Divine Comedy* (Hell, cantos 7, 9, 14), Shakespeare's *Troilus and Cressida* (V.4), *Titus Andronicus* (1.11), Milton's *L'Allegro* and *Paradise Lost* (Book 2), and Pope's *Dunciad* (2.338). In art Joachim Patinir's *Charon Crossing the Styx* and Delacroix's *Dante and Virgil Crossing the Styx* are best known.

2745

Su-bhadra. In Hindu mythology, sister of Krishna (an incarnation of the god Vishnu) and a wife of the hero Arjuna. According to some accounts Su-bhadra had an incestuous relationship with her brother Krishna.

2746

Sucellos. In Celtic mythology, a thunder god, portrayed as an elderly, benign fat man, associated with the underworld.

2747

Suiten (water god). In Japanese Buddhist mythology, water god, derived from the Hindu god Varuna, portrayed as an old man seated on a *makara*, a mythical animal with the body and tail of a fish and an antelope head and legs. In some representations Suiten is shown as a young man holding a sword in his right hand and in his left hand a snake coiled like a question mark, with five snakes issuing from his hair. Suiten is one of the Jiu No O, 12 Japanese Buddhist gods and goddesses adopted from Hindu mythology.

2748

Sukkoth (booths). In Judaism, feast of Booths, or Tabernacles, celebrated from the 15th to the 22nd of Tishri (September–October). Originally it was called the Feast of Ingathering, when the summer crops and fruits were gathered. Parts of the feast, according to the Old Testament (Deut. 16:9–12, Exod. 34:22, Lev. 23:15– 21, Num. 29:12–40), were reaping of the crops and fruits, special rituals to induce rain, and dwelling in *sukkoth* (booths), actually trellis-roofed cabins made of plaited twigs of carob and oleander and roofed with palm leaves. Leviticus (23:42–43) says: "All the people of Israel shall live in shelters for seven days, so that your descendants may know that the Lord made the people of Israel live in simple shelters when he led them out of Egypt. He is the Lord your God" (Today's English Version). Of course, this is a later interpretation, because when the Israelites wandered through the desert they lived in tents, not booths; wood and green leaves were unavailable to them. Sukkoth is a joyous festival and includes a blessing of the sun. Originally, it was based on a pagan magic rite to rekindle the decadent sun at the time of the autumnal equinox and to hail it when it rose at dawn. This folk custom is still found in the Islamic "*Ashura*, New Year, where children and unmarried men leap over flames as did the ancient Romans who leaped over fires and ran through the fields with blazing torches." Bonfires in European folklore are part of the ritual, especially at Halloween, which was the eve of the ancient New Year as celebrated in Europe.

2749

Sukusendal. In Finnish mythology, a nightmare spirit who has sexual intercourse with people while they sleep, appearing as a person of the opposite sex. Sometimes it replaces rightful children with changelings. To protect children, mothers placed a pair of scissors or some iron object in the cradle; this made the spirit unable to do evil. If a person went to the bathhouse late at night, however, he or she might be killed by the Sukusendal.

2750

Sul. In Celtic mythology, a goddess of the sun and hot springs, whose temple at Bath, England, had perpetual fires burning in her honor. Some ancient Roman writers equated her with their goddess Minerva as well as with the Italian goddess Salus, who presided over health and prosperity.

2751

Sumangat. In Malayan mythology, the human soul, believed to be a spirit copy of the human form, which leaves the body during sleep and at death.

2752

Summanus. In Roman mythology, ancient Italian god associated with evening lightning. He had a temple near the Circus Maximus where on 20 June sacrifices were offered to him.

2753

Sumsumara-Jataka. Buddhist folktale, number 208 of the *Jatakas*, or *Birth-Stories of the Former Lives of the Buddha*.

When Brahmadatta ruled as king of Benares, the future Buddha was born a monkey at the foot of the Himalayas. He grew strong and sturdy, with a big, muscular frame. He lived near a bend in the Ganges River close to the forest.

At the same time a crocodile also lived nearby in the Ganges. The crocodile's wife one day saw the monkey, and impressed by his massive size, thought how nice it would be to eat his big heart. She said to her husband, "I want to eat the heart of that big monkey that lives nearby."

"Good wife," said the crocodile, "I live in the water and he lives on the dry land. How can we catch him?"

"By hook or by crook," she replied, "but catch him we must. If I don't get him, I'll die."

"All right," said the crocodile, consoling his wife. "I have a plan. I will give you his heart to eat."

One day while the monkey was sitting on the bank of the Ganges, after taking a drink of water, the crocodile drew near.

"Sir Monkey," said the crocodile, "why do you live on rotten fruits in this part of the forest? On the other side of the river there is no end of mango trees and all sorts of delicious fruits, some as sweet as honey. Why don't you let me carry you over to the other side of the river."

The monkey trusted the crocodile and climbed onto his back. After the crocodile had swum well into the center of the river, he plunged deep into the water, and the monkey began to flay about in the water.

"Good friend," cried the monkey, "I will drown."

"What, do you think I agreed to carry you across the river out of the goodness of my heart?" the crocodile answered. "Not a bit. My wife wants to eat your heart, and I promised her that I would get it for her."

"Friend," said the monkey, "that's nice of you to tell me. But I don't have my heart with me. Why, if my heart were inside me when I jump among the trees, it would be all broken to pieces."

"Well, then," said the angry crocodile, "where do you keep your heart?"

The monkey pointed to a fruit-laden fig tree in the distance on the shore. "See," he said, "there is my heart, hanging on the fig tree with the fruit."

"If you show me your heart," the crocodile replied, "then I won't kill you."

"Take me to the shore, then" said the monkey, "and I'll point it out to you hanging right in front of your eyes."

The crocodile took the monkey across the river and brought him to the fig tree. The monkey leaped off his back, climbed the fig tree, and sat on one of its branches.

"You stupid crocodile," he cried from the safety of the tree branch, "you thought that I kept my heart in a tree. You are a fool. I have outsmarted you. You may keep the fruit for yourself. You may have a strong body, but you have no common sense."

The crocodile, feeling miserably foolish, went back home.

"In this tale of a former life," said the Buddha, "the crocodile was Devadatta, my life-long enemy, the lady Cinca was his wife, and I was the monkey."

2754

Sung-ti wang. In Chinese mythology, the ruler of the third hell of Ti Yü, the underworld.

2755

Sun Snarer. In North American Indian mythology (Northern, Plateau, California, Great Basin, Plains), a boy who captures the sun. Because he felt mistreated, a boy lay down, and the sun burned his robe. Taking pubic hair from his sister, the boy made a noose and captured the sun in a snare. Darkness then covered the earth, and the sun nearly died of strangulation. Various animals attempted to gnaw through the noose, and one animal succeeded, thus saving the earth.

2756

Supratika. In Hindu mythology, one of the eight elephants who protect the eight points of the compass. The group is called Diggajas.

2757

Surt (black). In Norse mythology, a fire giant who is to enkindle the universe at Ragnarok, the end of the world, when the gods and giants will be destroyed. He rules Muspellsheim. Surt appears in the *Prose Edda.*

Surya

2758

Surya (to shine?). In Hindu mythology, the sun god, whose chariot is drawn by the Harits (green), seven mares, or by one seven-headed horse, Etasha. His wife is Sanjna (conscience), who is also called Dyumayi (the brilliant) and Maha-virya (the very powerful).

Sanjna was unable to bear the intense love of Surya so she gave him Chhaya (shade) as his mistress. Surya, not noticing that there had been a substitution, had three children by Chhaya: Sani, the planet Saturn; the Manu Savarna; and a daughter, the Tapati (heating) River. Sanjna then became jealous of Surya's love for these children by his mistress and fled, but Surya went in search of her and brought her back. Their child was Yama, god of the dead. In Indian art Surya is portrayed drawn by the Harits, or by Etasha, surrounded by rays. His charioteer is Vivaswat (the bright one), also another name for the sun, who is credited with being the father of the Aswins, twin gods who precede the dawn. Closely connected with Surya are Suras, lesser gods or spirits who are part of his heavenly court. An earlier Vedic god, Arusha, representing the morning or rising sun, is considered in some texts to be another form of Surya.

Among Surya's many epithets are Dinakara (the maker of day); Bhaskara (the creator of light); Mihira (he who waters the earth), referring to Surya's drawing the moisture up from the seas so that clouds are formed; Grahapati (the lord of the stars); and Karmasakshi (the witness of men's deeds).

2759

Susano (swift-impetuous male, the impetuous god). In Japanese Shinto mythology, storm god, brother of the sun goddess Amaterasu. He was born from the nose of the primeval creator god Izanagi.

Susano is both good and evil in Japanese mythology, often displaying the traits of a trickster. After he had driven his sister Amaterasu to hide in a cave, thereby plunging the world into darkness, he was exiled by the gods from the Plain of Heaven to earth. In the *Kojiki* (records of ancient matters) his subsequent fate is told. He arrived at the river Hi in Izumo, where he saw some chopsticks floating down the stream. He thought, therefore, that there must be people above. Proceeding upstream in search of them, he discovered an old man and woman with a young girl between them. They were crying. He asked who they were.

"I am an earth spirit," the old man said, "and my name is Foot-Stroking Elder. My wife's name is Hand-stroking Elder. And this is our daughter whose name is Mistress Head Comb."

Susano then asked, "And what is the cause of the weeping?"

"Once we had eight daughters," the old man said, "but there is an eight-forked serpent that comes each year and eats one. His time has come round again. That is why we weep."

"What is the serpent's form?" Susano asked.

"Its eyes are as red as the winter cherry. It has one body with eight heads and tails. On that body moss grows, and conifers. Its length extends over eight valleys and eight hills, and if one looks at the belly, it is constantly bloody and inflamed."

Then, looking at the girl, Susano asked, "Your daughter, will you give her to me?"

The old man replied, "With reverence. However, I do not know your name."

"I am the elder brother of the goddess Amaterasu, and I descended here from heaven."

"That being so, with reverence, she is yours," the old man replied.

Susano took the girl at once, changed her into a multitudinously close-toothed comb and placed it in his hair.

"Distill a brew of eightfold refined liquor," he told the old couple. "Also, make a fence round about, and in that fence let there be eight gates; at each gate let there be eight platforms and on each platform a liquor vat; into each of which pour some eightfold liquor and wait."

They did as they were told. The eight-forked serpent came at the appointed time and dipped a head into each vat. Then, as the dragon became drunk, every one of its heads lay down to sleep. Susano drew his sword and cut the monster into pieces.

2760

Sutra (thread or row). A short verse or aphorism, a collection of such sayings, or a work giving the essence of teachings. In Hinduism, sutras may explain the Vedas or the teachings of a philosophical school; they also may be concerned with secular matters such as Sanskrit grammar and courtly love. In Buddhism a sutra is a sermon of the Buddha on a topic of general interest. In Pali, *sutta*.

2761

Suttung (heavy with broth). In Norse mythology, a giant who possessed Odhrerir, a magic caldron containing a potion that conferred wisdom and the gift of poetry. The god Odin seduced Gunlod, the daughter of Suttung, and obtained the potion from her.

2762

Svadilfare (slippery ice?) In Norse mythology, a horse belonging to the giants; father of Sleipnir,

Odin's horse. Svadilfare worked in the building of a structure for the gods. The animal was lured away from his task for sexual intercourse by the fire-trickster god, Loki, disguised as a mare, and the gods therefore did not pay the giants because the work was not completed on time. The myth is told in the *Prose Edda*.

2763

Svantovit (strong lord?). In Slavic mythology, war god; in some accounts the father of Dazhbog, the sun god, and Svarogich, the fire god.

Portrayed as a four-faced man wearing a hat, he held in one hand a bull's horn containing wine. Once a year the high priest would examine the contents of the bull's horn to see if any wine remained. If some did, it was a good omen, meaning the year would be fruitful and happy. If the wine had diminished considerably, poor crops and trouble were to be expected. Each year a captive Christian was chosen by lottery and sacrificed to the god. When the Christian Danish king Valdemar conquered Arkona in 1168, he destroyed Svantovit's temple and dragged the god's image out to humiliate it. Svantovit's followers waited for their god to destroy the Christians, but instead the Christians hacked the idol to pieces and burned it. A black animal was seen to emerge from the god's burning image and flee the Christian warriors, who said it was the devil.

Closely connected with Svantovit were other gods, who may have been variants of him, such as Triglav, portrayed with three heads, his eyes and lips covered by a golden veil; Rugevit, a warrior god who was armed with eight swords, seven hanging from his girdle and the eighth held in his right hand; Yarovit, portrayed with a golden shield. Radigast, also a war god, held a double-edged ax. On his chest he wore a bull's head, and on his curly head was a swan with outstretched wings.

2764

Svarogich (son of Svarog). In Slavic mythology, god of fire, son of Svarog (heaven), the sky god, and brother of Dazhbog, the sun god. Svarogich was portrayed wearing a birdlike helmet on his head and the image of a black bison's head on his breast; his left hand held a double-edged sword. Svarogich was called on for his prophetic powers, and human beings were sacrificed to him. After John, bishop of Mecklenburg, was captured in battle in 1066, his head was offered to the god.

Variant spelling: Svarazic.

2765

Svyatogor. In Russian folklore, a *bogatyr*, or epic hero, with superhuman strength, who appears in the *byliny*, the epic songs, as well as in folklore.

Svyatogor once boasted that if he could find the place where all of the earth was concentrated, he could lift it. He found a small bag on a steppe and touched it with his staff, but it did not move. Nor did it move when he touched it with his finger. Without getting off his horse he grabbed the bag in his hand, but again it would not move. He then got off his horse and took the bag with both hands and lifted it above his knees, but as he did he sank deep into the earth. The poem ends: "Svyatogor had indeed found the weight of the earth, but God punished him for his pride."

2766

Swallow. A small bird noted for its swift and graceful movement. In Egyptian mythology the swallow was sacred to Isis as the Great Mother. In Greek mythology the bird was sacred to Aphrodite and in Roman mythology, to Venus, her counterpart. It is also associated with the Sumero-Semitic goddess Nina. In medieval Christian belief the swallow became a symbol of the Incarnation and Resurrection of Christ because the bird disappears in winter and reappears in spring. Many paintings of the Nativity depict a swallow nesting under the eaves, and some Christian art works portraying the Crucifixion have a swallow hovering above the cross offering Jesus consolation, hence the name "bird of consolation" for the swallow. In Jewish folklore the swallow is said to have convinced God through a trick that the best food in the world for the snake would be a frog, not a man. When the snake found out what the swallow did, it leaped up and caught some of its tail. That is why some swallows have forked tails.

2767

Swamp Fox. In American history and folklore, popular name of Francis Marion of South Carolina, who fought on the side of the Patriots during the American Revolution. One legend tells how he entertained a British officer during an exchange of prisoners. When the officer saw the Americans poorly clad and eating bark, he returned to his post and later resigned his commission, feeling he could never again fight against such dedicated men. G. W. Mark's primitive painting, *Marion Feasting the British Officer*, illustrates the tale. Marion earned his name Swamp Fox, according to one legend, because he used the cry of a swamp fox as a signal, although no such animal exists.

2768

Swan. A large aquatic bird with a long slender neck and often white plumage. In Greek mythology swans were sacred to the muses, who were associated with the god Apollo. The best-known

Greek myth relating to the swan concerns Zeus and Leda. Zeus, in the form of a swan, seduced Leda beside the river Eurotas. Later Leda laid an egg, which produced Helen, Castor, and Polydeuces. Swans were honored in Sparta as symbols of the goddess Aphrodite. In a late Greek myth Helen is united with the hero Achilles on a spirit isle in northern Pontus, where they are served by swans. In medieval legend Lohengrin is called the Knight of the Swan and appears in a boat drawn by a silver swan. The legend was used by Wagner for his opera *Lohengrin*. In Hindu mythology the god Brahma often rides a swan. In Celtic mythology the swan is a solar symbol and beneficent. In many European tales girls are turned into swans. This motif is used in Tchaikovsky's great ballet *Swan Lake*.

2769

Swine. The boar, sow, and pig frequently appear in world mythology and folklore; sometimes one is confused with another. A boar is the uncastrated male swine; a pig is a young swine, and the sow is an adult female swine. The boar is often a phallic symbol and associated with Attis, Adonis, Osiris, Set, Vishnu, Ares, Mars, Tammuz, Odin, and Woden, all male deities. It is also sacred to various goddesses in mythology, such as Aphrodite, Demeter, and Freya, as well as the Greek heroine Atalanta. Norse mythology has the gods and heroes of Valhalla continually feasting on Saehrimir, a magic boar who is constantly replenished after he is eaten. Freya, the Norse goddess, had a lover, Ottar, who was a golden boar. In Northern cult a boar was sacrificed to the god Frey at the winter solstice. Part of that custom continues today in the form of roast pig at Christmas feasts. In Egyptian mythology the goddess Nut was sometimes portrayed as a sow with her piglets. It was believed that each morning Nut ate the piglets; that is, the stars were eaten by the sky goddess. The Greek goddess Demeter was often portrayed with a sow at her feet or in her arms, and the Tibetan goddess Vajravareh was also identified with the sow. The ancient Hebrews regarded swine as unclean animals, forbidding the eating of pork, although some Jews did keep swine. In medieval Christian belief the pig was a symbol of lust and sensuality. In Buddhist belief the pig is also an unclean animal and symbol of lust. In Chinese folklore the pig is a symbol of the wealth of the forest, and the Japanese use parts of the boar as a talisman against snakes.

2770

Swithen, St. Ninth century C.E. In Christian legend, bishop of Winchester, chaplain and counselor to King Egbert of the West Saxons. Feast, 15 July.

The most famous legend connected with the saint says that if it rains on his feast day, it will rain for another 40 days. According to one explanation of the origin of the legend, St. Swithen asked that his body be buried with the poor people, outside the church, "under the feet of passersby, and exposed to the droppings of the eaves from above." This was done, but 100 years later it was decided to move the saint's body inside the church because a workman said he had a vision of the saint requesting that his body be moved. When they attempted to move the remains, however, it began to rain and continued for some 40 days, which held up the removal. During the reign of William the Conqueror, Walkelin, bishop of Winchester, laid the foundation for a new cathedral church, and on 15 July 1093, the shrine of St. Swithen was removed, or translated, from the old to the new church. The shrine became very famous. Henry VIII, however, destroyed it along with numerous others but found that its gold and jewels were fakes. A new shrine was dedicated in 1962.

Other saints having legends of rain continuing for some time after their feast days are SS. Gervase and Protase, St. Médard in France, St. Cewydd in Wales, and St. Godelième in Flanders. An old English couplet captures the folk belief:

St. Swithin's day, gif ye do rain, for forty day it will remain;
St. Swithin's day, an ye be fair, for forty days twill rain nae mair.

Variant spellings: Swithin, Swithun, and Swithunus.

2771

Syaha (hail). In Hinduism, the exclamation spoken when an offering is made to the gods. Syaha is also the name of the wife of the fire god, Agni, where offerings are made over fire.

T

Tagaro. In Melanesian mythology, trickster and culture hero often in conflict with his brother Suce-mutua.

One account tells how Tagaro creates edible fruits for humankind while his evil brother Suce-mutua creates useless ones. Variants give the name of the evil brother as Meragubutto. In one tale Tagaro devises a plot to destroy Meragubutto through a clever trick. He tells his brother that he wishes to gain more magic power, but to do so he must be burned alive in his own house. Meragubutto is only too pleased to set a torch to his brother's house and agrees to help. Tagaro goes into his house and enters a deep pit that he had dug earlier. Meragubutto lights the fire and the house goes up in flames. When the fire dies down, Tagaro reappears. Impressed and believing that Tagaro's magic has been increased by the fire, he resolves to do the same. He enters his house, which is then set afire by Tagaro, and is burned to death.

Tag-Mar. In Tibetan Buddhism, the Red-Tiger Devil, portrayed with the head of a tiger and the body of a man.

Tahumers. In Persian mythology, a king, culture hero, and slayer of demons, appearing in the epic poem *Shah Namah* by Firdusi.

Tahumers succeeded his father, King Husheng, and continued his father's role as teacher of the arts of civilization: spinning wool, weaving carpets, training wild animals, and hunting. In Firdusi's epic, Tahumers is often called Diw-bund (binder of demons) because of his power over the demonic underworld.

One day the evil spirit, Ahriman, attempted to destroy Tahumers, but the king "bound Ahriman by his magic spells and rode him like a swift steed. He saddled Ahriman and without respite made him carry him on a tour of the world." While the king was away, however, other demons attempted to take control of his kingdom. Tahumers returned "girded with majesty and master of the world. On his shoulder he bore a massive club."

The demon army was poised against Tahumers and his army, but Tahumers "bound up two-thirds of them by magic and struck down the others with his heavy club." The demons were tied together to be executed.

"Do not kill us," they cried out, "and thou shalt learn from us a new art."

Interested in their offer, the king spared them. The demons immediately brought a pen, ink, and a book and taught Tahumers how to read and write. His mind "with learning was illuminated. The world was blest / with quiet and repose...." Tahumers reigned for some 30 years more and was succeeded by his son, the hero Jemshid.

Variant spellings: Tahuras, Takhmoruw, Takhmorup, Takhma-Urupa, Tahmuraf, Tatmurath.

Taikó-mol (solitude walker). In North American Indian mythology (Yuki), creator god who appeared on the foam of the primeval water wearing an eagle headdress. After he had created the earth, by using four *lilkae* (stone crooks), he went up into the sky.

Taillefer. Died 1066. In medieval history and legend, Norman warrior and minstrel. Before the Battle of Hastings he sang songs in praise of Charlemagne and Roland. His singing encouraged the troops of William the Conqueror. Taillefer struck the first blow in the battle and was the first Norman casualty.

Taiowa. In North American Indian mythology (Hopi), creative void, force, mindful presence. Taiowa's first creation was Sotuknang, who undertook creation of people with the aid of Kohyangwuti, the spider woman.

Taishaku Ten. In Japanese Buddhist mythology, a god, derived from the Hindu god Indra, portrayed with three eyes, holding in his right hand a thunderbolt trident, called Dokko, and in his left hand a cup. Taishaku Ten is one of the Jiu No O, 12 Japanese Buddhist gods and goddesses adopted from Hindu mythology.

T'ai-shan kun wang. In Chinese mythology, ruler of the seventh hell of Ti Yü, the underworld.

2780

Talassio. In Roman mythology, god of marriage; equated by the Romans with the Greek god Hymen. He is associated with the myth of the Rape of the Sabine Women. Livy's *History of Rome* (book 1) tells of Talassio and his name was invoked at weddings..

2781

Tale of Bygone Years, The. Medieval Russian chronicle compiled from about 1040 to 1118 by various hands, though traditionally ascribed to Friar Nestor (1056–1114). The work comprises a history of Russia from the creation of the world through the eventual overthrow of the old Slavic gods and the coming of Christianity under Prince Vladimir, who was later canonized by the Russian Orthodox church. Rich in legends, folktales, and myths, *The Tale of Bygone Years* is also a main source for early Russian history. It is sometimes called *The Primary Chronicle*.

2782

Taliesin (radiant brow). Sixth century. In medieval Welsh legend, bard who appears in *The Mabinogion*, in which he is credited with supernatural powers.

2783

Talmud (study or learning). In Judaism, books of civil and religious law written between 500 B.C.E. and 500 C.E.. There are two collections, the Babylonian and the Jerusalem Talmuds. Part of the Talmud contains *Haggadah* (narration) consisting of myths, legends, and fables to explain various beliefs, rites, and parts of Scripture.

2784

Talonhaltija (guardian spirit). In Finno-Ugric mythology, spirit believed to be the ghost of the first person to die in a house, or else the ghost of the first person who kindled a fire in the house. The *talonhaltija* is beneficent, looking after the welfare of the family.

2785

Talus (brass or sufferer?). In Greek mythology, a man created from brass by the smith-god Hephaestus. Talus was given to King Minos of Crete to protect the island. Every time a stranger appeared Talus would greet the visitor, becoming red hot and embracing the person to death. When the Argonauts arrived he threw rocks at them. Eventually he was killed by Poeas, an Argonaut. Another person named Talus was a nephew of Daedalus and credited with the invention of the saw and the compass. Daedalus, however, was quite jealous of Talus's gifts and killed him by hurling him down the Acropolis of Athens. *Variant spelling*: Talos.

2786

Tamar (palm tree). In the Bible, O.T., Absalom's sister, daughter of King David; she was raped by Amnon, another of King David's sons. Amnon was killed by Absalom (2 Sam. 1:32). Robinson Jeffers's *Tamar, and Other Poems* is based on the biblical tale but deals with a modern Tamar who lives on the Monterey coast. She seduces her brother and brings destruction to her whole family.

2787

Tambora. In Australian mythology, headless female beings who dragged men to their dark caves.

2788

Tamburlaine the Great (Timur the Lame). d. 1405. In medieval history and legend, despot, who ruled by terror over various parts of Asia and India. He appears in Marlowe's *Tamburlaine the Great* (1587), an epic play in two parts, written in blank verse.

2789

Tam-Din. In Tibetan Buddhism, a "wrathful entity," often portrayed with a horse's head; derived from the Hindu god Hayagriva.

2790

Tammuz (true son?). In Near Eastern mythology god of corn and vegetation; he died each winter and was resurrected each spring; originally a Sumerian deity, Dumuzi.

Tammuz was originally a sun god, the son of Ea and the goddess Siduri, and the lover or husband of the great goddess Ishtar. His love affair and death are told in the ancient poem *Ishtar's Descent into the Underworld*, known in various versions throughout the Near East, in which the goddess offers her youthful lover to be killed in place of herself. In Canaan Tammuz was called Adonai (my lord), and a great festival, celebrating his death and resurrection, was observed in various Near Eastern cities. Gebal was the chief seat of the spring festival in Phoenicia. "Gardens of Adonis" were planted—pots filled with earth and cut herbs (which soon withered away) in which wooden figures of the god had been placed. Wailing women tore their hair and lacerated their breasts during the seven days of the festival. The Hebrew prophet Ezekiel saw women in the north gate of the temple "weeping for Tammuz" (Ezekiel 8:14).

2791

Tancred (thought, advice). 1076–1112. In medieval history and legend, one of the chief heroes of the First Crusade. Tancred appears in Tasso's epic poem *Jerusalem Delivered*. He was the son of Eudes (Otho) and Emma, sister of Robert Guiscard. Boemond

(Bohemond) was his uncle. In *Jerusalem Delivered* he was the greatest of Christian warriors except for Rinaldo. His one "fault" was his passion for Clorinda, a pagan. He accidentally killed her in a night attack and lamented his loss. When he was wounded, he was nursed by Erminia, who was in love with him. Tancred appears in Tasso's *Jerusalem Delivered*, Rossini's opera *Tancredi*, and the earlier Monteverdi work *Il combattimento di Tancredi e Clorinda*.

2793

Tane (male). In Polynesian mythology, creator god, lord of the forest, son of Atea and Papa, father and husband of the goddess Hina.

According to some accounts, Tane tried to have sexual intercourse with his mother, but she rejected his advances. He then left home in search of a wife. He had sexual intercourse with various beings, producing such offspring as rocks, streams, trees, and reptiles. Not satisfied with any of his children because they did not have his human shape, he formed a woman out of soft red sand and breathed life into her. He called her Hina and married her. She is regarded as the first woman in Polynesian mythology and is associated with the moon and with fertility, and she guards the entrance to the land of the dead. In some accounts she is married to Tiki, the first man, and founded a royal line. Hina was portrayed with two faces. Tane's sexual organ was also called Tiki. Tiki appears in some legends as the creator of the first woman.

In Hawaiian mythology Tane is called Kane and is known as a major god who possessed a gigantic penis. In many myths his enemy is Kanaloa, the squid god. Kane's home is Kane-huna-moku (hidden land of Kane).

2794

Tangaloa. In Polynesian mythology, creator god, who is also known as Ta'aroa, Tangaroa, and Kanaloa.

According to one Samoan myth, Tangaloa lived alone in a limitless, formless void, in which there was neither light nor motion. One day he cast down a rock, which became Manu's Groves, the main island in the Samoan group. Next he made the remaining islands. Tangaloa's bird, Tuli, flying over the island in search of rest, pointed out to the god that the land lacked shade. Tangaloa gave Tuli a creeping vine for shade. When the vine withered and decomposed, maggots formed, eventually becoming the first man and woman.

According to a Tahitian account, Tangaloa created himself, having no mother or father, and lived in a

shell called Rumia (upset). After a time he became bored and slipped out of the shell, only to find a totally dark void, so he found a new shell in which to hide. For thousands of eons he remained in the shell in deep contemplation. Then, using the new shell for the foundation and the old shell for the dome, he formed the sky. Calling himself Te Tumu (the source), he created various gods, whom he decked out with red and yellow feathers. When the feathers fell to the ground, they turned into trees and plants. Tangaloa then commissioned some artisan gods to fashion "a good-looking boy," though some variants say he first created woman.

Another tradition says Tangaloa and the god Akea Wakea had a dispute about which one was the father of a child born to the goddess Papa. To settle the argument, Papa cut the child in half, giving a half to each god. Akea Wakea threw his half into the sky, and it became the sun. Tangaloa held his half until it decomposed. He then threw it into the sky, and it became the moon.

2795

Tanner of Tamworth, The. In medieval legend, English hero who mistook Edward IV for a highwayman. After an altercation they changed horses, the king giving his hunter for the Tanner's cob, worth about four shillings. As soon as the tanner mounted the king's horse, it threw him, and the tanner gladly paid a sum of money to get back his old mount. King Edward then blew the hunting horn, and his courtiers gathered round. "I expect I shall be hanged for this," cried Tanner. King Edward, however, gave him the manor of Plumpton Park, with an income of 300 marks a year.

2796

Tannhäuser (dweller in the house of Tann, a name for Venus). 13th century. In medieval German history and legend, a knight who fell in love with the pagan goddess Venus. His tale is told in many ballads.

Tannhäuser was a minnesinger. One day he wandered near Hörselberg in Thuringia and heard the alluring song of Venus. He entered the Venusberg, her home, through a subterranean cave. He stayed with he goddess, "yielding to Venus's witching spells." After a while, however, his sexual appetite was dulled, and he fled the goddess.

Wishing to return to his betrothed, he felt guilty because of his passion for Venus. He decided to go to Rome and ask the pope for forgiveness.

"No," said Pope Urban, "you can no more hope for mercy than this dry staff can be expected to bud again."

Distraught, the knight left. On the third day after the pope had dismissed him, the papal staff bloomed. Realizing his error, the pope sent to find Tannhäuser, but the knight had returned to Venus.

Wagner's opera *Tannhäuser* is based on the medieval legend. The composer has the hero return from the Venusberg to the court of the landgrave of Thuringia, where Elizabeth, his betrothed, has remained true to Tannhäuser. At a great singing tournament, Tannhäuser's friend Wolfram von Eschenbach sings of spiritual love, and Tannhäuser sings of erotic love. Wolfram then mentions the name of Elizabeth, and Tannhäuser rejects Venus, who appears briefly on the mountain, singing seductively. A funeral procession then approaches. On the bier is Elizabeth. When Tannhäuser sees her, he dies. The next morning, pilgrims arrive from Rome bearing the pope's staff, which has miraculously bloomed.

2797

Tano. In African mythology (Togoland), the river god.

God had two sons, Tano and Bia. The older, Bia, was more obedient, and God wanted to give him the fertile lands to control. Tano was to receive the barren lands. A goat told Tano of God's plan. So

The return of Tannhäuser to Venusberg

Tano disguised himself as Bia and arrived at God's house before Bia had a chance to get there. God mistakenly gave the fertile lands to Tano and could not later revoke what he had given.

In another myth, a hunter, after trying for many days, failed to catch anything. He finally hit an antelope, which was transformed into the god Tano. Tano quelled the hunter's fears, offering to protect him. As they traveled together, they came upon Death. Death opposed Tano's traveling with the hunter. Tano resented Death's interference in the matter. The two then started singing songs to one another in a contest. Neither one, however, would agree that the other was better. At last they agreed that when a man became ill, the outcome of that illness would depend on which of the two got to him first. If Tano arrived first, the man would live, but if it were Death, the man would die.

2798

Tantalus (lurching or most wretched). In Greek mythology, king of Sipylos in Lydia; son of Zeus; father of Pelops and Niobe; grandfather of Atreus and Thyestes; punished by the gods for the murder of his son. At first the gods loved Tantalus, inviting him to their numerous feasts. This honor went to his head, and he decided to test the gods' knowledge. He killed his son Pelops and served him at a banquet, hoping to prove that the gods could not tell the difference between human and animal flesh. None of the gods ate the food, except for Demeter, who absent-mindedly consumed part of the boy's shoulder. Later Pelops was restored to life and his missing shoulder blade replaced by an ivory one. But, Tantalus was sent to Tartarus, the lowest section of Hades, the Underworld, to be punished. Homer's *Odyssey* (book 11) described Tantalus as being in water up to his neck but unable to quench his thirst because as he reaches' for the water, it recedes. Also, close by, is a fruit-laden tree, but when he tries to eat, the fruits vanish. According to Pindar, Tantalus is suspended in the air, while above his head hangs a massive rock, ready to fall and crush him at any moment. Euripides uses elements from both versions. Some accounts say that Tantalus was punished for revealing a secret of Zeus, or stealing the nectar and ambrosia of the gods, or taking a dog of Zeus. The word "tantalize" comes from the myth.

2799

Tanuki Bozu. In Japanese folklore, badger disguised as a Buddhist monk. He is believed to bring luck and wealth and is often enshrined in Japanese stores, though he may also take on various forms to waylay, deceive, or annoy travelers.

2800

T'ao t'ieh (ravenous). In Chinese folk art, an ogre mask of an animal having feline characteristics. Some scholars believe it depicts a stylized tiger because the tiger was the guardian of graves in ancient China and fought off evil spirits. Others see it as symbolic of the dualistic concepts of life and death, light and darkness. It also has been interpreted as symbolic of death, which swallows up all things in its gluttonous mouth.

2801

Tapio (worker in Traps, i.e., hunting). In Finnish mythology, forest god. His wife, Meilikki, his son Nyyrikki, and his daughter, the wind spirit Tuulikki, were all spirits of the forest. Tapio's realm was called Tapiola, which is used in the Finnish epic poem *The Kalevala* for the forest in general and is almost synonymous with *Metsola* (woodland). Sometimes Tapio aided the wanderer in the forest, but if he was in a mischievous mood, he would tickle or smother the person to death. His mysterious spirit and nature inspired Sibelius' last major symphonic composition, *Tapiola*, which was first performed in New York under the conductor Walter Damrosch.

Another name for Tapiola is Kuippana (king of the forest), who was a minor tutelary genius.

2802

Tara (she who carries across [to Nirvana]). In Tibetan Buddhism, a female entity, especially one of two deified wives of King Sron Tsan Gampo, known as the White Tara and the Green Tara; sometimes called Dölma (mother).

One wife, Princess Wen-ch'eng, deified as the White Tara, is portrayed as an Indian woman with a white complexion, seated and holding in her left hand a long-stemmed lotus flower. She has seven eyes—the eye of foreknowledge in the forehead, two others on the face, and one in each palm and each sole. She is called the Seven-Eyed White Tara and uses her eyes to see and aid the suffering. She is worshiped by the Mongols.

The second wife, a Nepalese, was deified as the Green Tara and portrayed as a beautiful Indian woman with uncovered head and a green complexion, seated on a lotus, with her left leg pendant and holding in her left hand a long-stemmed lotus flower.

The following injunction is included in her worship: "If we worship this sublime and pure-souled goddess when we retire at night and arise in the morning, then all our fears and worldly anxieties will disappear and our sins will be forgiven. She—the conqueror of myriad hosts—will strengthen us. She will do more than this! She will convey us directly to the end of our transmigration—Buddha and Nirvana."

Green Tara is regarded as being born from a teardrop of Avalokiteshvara, the Bodhisattva of Infinite Compassion. Aside from these two Taras the Tibetans have a list of 21 others.

2803

Tara (star). In Hindu mythology, wife of Brihaspati, raped by the moon god Soma. As a result of the rape a war broke out between the gods and demons. It was ended by the intervention of the god Brahma. Tara was given back to her husband, but she bore a son, Budha (he who knows), whose father was Soma.

2804

Taranis. In Celtic mythology, a thunder god, mentioned by ancient Roman writers and equated with their god Jupiter. Human sacrifices were offered to the god, who originally may have been a goddess of death. Taranis's symbol was a wheel.

2805

Tarchon. In Roman mythology, ancestor of the Etruscan Tarquins, leader of the emigrants from Lydia and founder of Tarquinii and other Etruscan cities. In Vergil's *Aeneid* (book 8) he joined the Trojan hero Aeneas as an ally.

2806

Tarkshya. In Hindu mythology, a fantastic animal, sometimes bird or horse, often equated with the fantastic bird Garuda. In some myths Tarkshya is called the father of Garuda.

2807

Tarnkappe (camouflage cloak). In Norse mythology, German name for the magic cap or cloak that rendered its wearer invisible or unrecognizable by transformation into another form. Sigurd in the Norse *Volsunga Saga* and Siegfried, his German counterpart in the *Nibelungenlied*, both have such caps. In Richard Wagner's *Der Ring des Nibelungen* it is called *tarnhelm* and is at first the possession of the dwarf Alberich, but it is stolen from him by Loge (Loki) and Wotan (Odin).

2808

Tarpeia. In Roman history and legend, a vestal virgin, betrayer of the Romans; daughter of Spurius Tarpeius, Roman commander of the garrison stationed at the Capitol at the time of the Sabine Wars. Meeting Tatius, leader of the Sabines, Tarpeia was either bribed or volunteered to open the gates of the city's citadel if Tatius would give her what his men "wore on their shield-arms," according to Livy's *History of Rome* (book 1). Expecting rich gold bracelets,

Tarpeia was not only given the bracelets but had the shields thrown at her, knocking her to the ground. Then other soldiers crushed her to death with their shields. The Tarpeian Rock, from which convicted criminals were flung to their death, is said to be named after Tarpeia. Ovid's *Metamorphoses* (book 14) tells one version of the myth.

2809

Tarquin. In Arthurian legend, a "recreant knight" who held some knights of the Round Table prisoner. Sir Lancelot met a lady who asked him to free the knights from Tarquin's power. Coming to a river, Lancelot saw a copper basin suspended from a tree. He struck it so hard that it broke. This brought out Tarquin. A battle ensued in which Lancelot killed Tarquin. Then some "threescore knights and four, all of the Table Round," were freed.

2810

Tarquinius Priscus. Reigning 616–579 B.C.E. In Roman history and legend, fifth king of Rome, who built temples on the Capitol and started the city's drainage system, using Etruscan workmen. He is said to have brought the Sibylline Books, collections of prophecy, to Rome.

2811

Tartarus (far west?). In Greek mythology, the lowest section of the Underworld, where the most evil were punished. Among its inhabitants were the rebellious Titans, Ixion, Sisyphus, Tantalus and Tityus. The region is described in Homer's *Odyssey* (book 11), Hesiod's *Theogony*, Vergil's *Aeneid* (book 6), Ovid's *Metamorphoses* (book 4), and Dante's *Divine Comedy* (Hell).

2812

Tathagata (thus come; thus gone?). Title of the Buddha used by himself and his followers. It may mean, "He who has come and gone as former Buddhas," that is, teaching the same truths, following the same paths to the same goal. Another interpretation is "one who has attained full realization of Suchness," that is, one who has realized that things are such-as-they-are, so that he neither comes from anywhere nor does he go anywhere.

2813

Taui'goad (wounded knee). In African mythology (Hottentot), rain god, creator, who "died" on several occasions but continues to return to life. One day Taui'goad had a battle with Gaunab, a great Hottentot chief. Gaunab won each battle, but Taui'goad kept growing stronger until he finally killed his opponent. Just before he died Gaunab hit Taui'goad's knee, and the god has been known as Taui'goad (wounded knee) ever since.

2814
Taurt (the fat one). In Egyptian mythology, hippopotamus goddess. She was a patron of childbirth and maternity, often identified with the goddess Hathor. The Greeks rendered her name Thoueris. She was both a beneficent deity, as when she protected the dead, or an avenging deity, when she was the female counterpart of the evil god Set.

Egyptian art portrays her as a female hippopotamus with distended teats, standing upright on her back legs. Taurt's front foot rests on the *sa*, a sign of protection represented by a stylized life preserver, made of papyrus, worn by river travelers.

Variant spellings: Taueret, Rert, Rertu, Apet, Opet.

2815
Tawiskaron (flint). In North American Indian mythology (Mohawk), an evil being who attempts to build a bridge to allow wild animals to travel so that they can prey on humans. He is foiled in his evil design by Sapling, who sends a bluejay with a cricket's hind legs stuck in its mouth to frighten Tawiskaron. When Tawiskaron sees the sight, he believes it is human legs; he flees, and his bridge disappears.

2816
Tchue. In African mythology (Bushman), culture hero who gave people the gift of fire. He is capable of transforming himself into various animals and forms such as a fly, lizard, elephant, bird, or water hole.

2817
Tcoxoltcwedin. In North American Indian mythology (Hupa), creator god who sprang from the earth. When he was born, there was a ringing noise like the striking together of metals. Before he was born, smoke was seen, which settled on a mountainside. When pieces of rotten wood fell into his hands, fire was created.

2818
Tefnut (the spitter?). In Egyptian mythology, goddess of moisture. She and her twin brother, Shu, comprised the first couple of the Ennead, which was a system of gods worshiped in Egypt.

According to one myth, the primeval sun god created Tefnut and Shu by an act of masturbation or, according to another account, from the spittle of his mouth. Then, with Shu, Tefnut conceived the sky goddess, Nut, and the earth god, Geb, and they in turn bore the great gods Osiris, Isis, Nephthys, and Set, thus completing the great Ennead. Together with Shu, Tefnut helped support the sky and each day received the new sun as it rose in the east. Sometimes she represented the power of sunlight.

Tefnut, however, could also be ferocious. Her original home was said to be the Nubian deserts, where she roamed drenched in the blood of her enemies. When Thoth, the god of wisdom, upbraided her for abandoning Egypt and leaving the country desolate, Tefnut wept great tears; but her tears soon turned to wrath, and she changed into a bloodthirsty lioness whose mane smoked with fire and whose face glowed like the sun.

Egyptian art portrays Tefnut as a woman with the head of a lioness surmounted by a disk or the uraeus or both.

Variant spelling: Tefenet.

2819
Telegonus (last born). In Greek mythology, son of Odysseus and Circe; brother of Ardea and Agrius; half-brother of Latinus. Telegonus does not appear in Homer, but in Ovid and Plutarch, who narrate that Telegonus accidentally killed his father, Odysseus. Telegonus was either shipwrecked or landed in Ithaca in search of his father. When he landed he began to plunder the land. Odysseus and his son Telemachus came out to defend the land, and in the ensuing fight, Telegonus killed Odysseus with a lance given him by his mother, Circe. He then discovered that the man he killed was his father. Odysseus's body was taken then by Telegonus, Penelope, and Telemachus and buried on Aeaea. Athena then commanded Telegonus to wed Penelope. Their son was named Italus, after which Italy is named. Telegonus and Penelope eventually went to the Blessed Isles where they were said to live forever.

2820
Telemachus (decisive battle). In Greek mythology, son of Odysseus and Penelope, who went in search of his father and aided him in the slaughter of Penelope's suitors. His story appears in Homer's *Odyssey*. In post-Homeric myth, he married either Nausicaa, Circe, or Cassiphone, a daughter of Circe, and had a son, Latinus. Some accounts say he murdered Circe and fled to Italy. Telemachus appears in Fénelon's novel *Télémaque* and inspired the portrait of Stephen Dadalus in James Joyce's novel *Ulysses*.

2821
Telephus (suckles by a doe). In Greek mythology, king of Mysia, son of Heracles and Auge. Abandoned by his mother, Telephus was raised on Mount Parthenius by a doe or goat and later adopted by King Teuthras. Telephus was wounded by Achilles' lance and could only be healed by the same lance. He promised to lead the Greeks to Troy if Achilles cured

him, which he did, but he refused to take part in the battle because his wife, Astyoche, was a sister of Troy's King Priam.

Telepinus. In Near Eastern mythology (Hittite), god of agriculture who left the earth in anger, causing it to dry up and all life to cease reproduction. His father, the storm god, cried out: "Telepinus has flown into a rage and taken every good thing with him." The gods sent an eagle to search for Telepinus, but he could not be found, so Hannahanna, the Great Mother goddess, asked the weather god himself to search for his son. When the weather god had no success, Hannahanna sent a bee to find Telepinus. The bee found Telepinus and stung him to wake him up, but that merely made Telepinus angrier. Kamrusepas, the goddess of magic and healing, finally pacified Telepinus with her medicine. The god returned home, and life was restored to the land and people.

Telesphorus (he who brings to an end). In Greek mythology, an attendant of Asclepius, the god of medicine, who gave strength to recovering patients.

Tem. In Egyptian mythology, a primeval, creator god; one of the most ancient deities worshiped in Egypt.

The priests of Anu, or Heliopolis, made Tem the head of their company of gods, identifying him with a form of the sun god. Tem appears in *The Book of the Dead* as the evening or setting sun (Khepera is the morning sun and Ra the noonday sun). In the Theban recension of the book, Tem is identified with Osiris as being one of the gods whose flesh never saw physical corruption. Many of the attributes of Tem were absorbed by Khepera, who was also a creator god. In later times the Egyptians named a female counterpart of Tem, calling her Temt or Temit. According to one myth, Tem was responsible for the primeval flood, which covered the entire earth and destroyed all of mankind except those in Tem's boat.

Egyptian art portrays Tem as a man, sometimes a king, wearing the crowns of Upper and Lower Egypt. Like many other gods, he carries in his hands the scepter and ankh, emblem of life.

Variant spellings: Tum, Temu, Atem, Atum, Atmu.

Tembo. In African legend, a king of the Buganda of Uganda. Tembo was the father of two children, a son and a daughter. Two rivers were supposed to have sprung from the bodies of these children. Tembo's son eventually married his sister.

Tengri (god, heaven). In Siberian mythology, the sky god, and a general term for God among the Mongolians. There are two aspects to the Mongolian sky god: Blue Tengri, who represents the power of the various phenomena of the sky that brings fruitfulness to the earth, and Eternal Tengri, who rules over the fate of mankind. The two terms are often used interchangeably.

Variant spellings: Tangara, Tengeri, Tura.

Tengu

Tengu (long-nose). In Japanese folklore, trickster spirits whose bodies are half human and half bird, with wings and claws and frequently a large beak or elongated nose. The long-nosed variety are called *kohola tengu*; the beaked version, *karasu tengu* (crow tengu). According to legend they are born from eggs, from which they are often seen emerging, and live in the mountains on the upper branches of trees.

Tennin. In Japanese-Chinese Buddhist mythology, beautiful winged maidens, inhabitants of a Buddhist paradise. They soar into the air, usually clasping lotus flowers or playing instruments. In Chinese tradition they wear feather robes of five colors. In Japanese folklore Hagoromo (feathery robe) was a tennin who left her feather robe on earth. One day she came down to the forest of Mio, near Okitsu. She admired the view and then, after hanging her feather robe on a pine tree, started to dance on the sandy beach. A fisherman, Hakurio, happened to pass by and thought her a beautiful woman. His looks, however, frightened Hagoromo, who fled, minus her robe, which is still preserved in a nearby temple. Her tale is the subject of a *No* play.

Tenten and Caicai. In the mythology of the Araucanian Indians of Chile, two serpents who fought, causing a flood that covered the earth. The people sought shelter on two mountains, which were raised by Tenten as the evil Caicai raised the water level. The people on one of the mountains were turned into animals, fish, and birds.

In a variant of this flood myth, the waters came about by the evil work of the Guecubus demons. This time the people fled to two mountains, called Tenten and Caicai (the names of the serpents in the other myth). The god Guinechen raised the mountains to save the people from the ever-rising waters.

Teresa of Avila, St. (summer, harvest?). 1515–1582 C.E. In Christian legend, Spanish mystical writer and founder of the discalced, or barefoot, Carmelites. Patron of lacemakers and second patron saint of Spain by order of King Philip II. Invoked by those in need of grace. Feast, 15 October.

Born of a part Jewish family, St. Teresa's father was Don Alphonzo Sanchez de Cepeda. Her mother's name was Beatrix. Her father was of a serious nature, but her mother tended to be of a romantic frame of mind. The young girl inherited both aspects in her personality and vacillated between the two. As a young girl of nine she decided she wanted to die a martyr. She set out for the "land of the Moors" but was caught by her family. Eventually her father thought it best to send her to a convent, but she did not like the religious life and would often become ill, sometimes near death.

The writings of St. Jerome, who wrote numerous letters on how women were to behave, caught her imagination. She writes in her great *Life*, or *Autobiography*, that for 20 years she did not find the repose for which she had hoped. But she adds, "At

length God took pity on me. I read the *Confessions of St. Augustine*. I saw how he had been tempted, how he had been tried, and how he had at length conquered."

About 1561, against great opposition that lasted the remainder of her life, she set about reforming the Carmelite order, which had fallen into slack ways. The first convent of the new, reformed rule had eight nuns. By the end of her life there were some 30 convents established according to her rule. Toward the end of her life she was frequently ill. She died in her own convent of St. Joseph. In her last moments she repeated a verse from the psalm *Miserere*, "A broken and contrite heart, O Lord, thou wilt not despise."

The most famous representation of the saint is the *Ecstasy of St. Teresa* by Bernini. In her *Life* she tells how an angel plunged into her breast a golden spear, symbolizing Divine Love. When the spear was withdrawn, she was "utterly consumed by the great love of God." As depicted by Bernini in the Cornaro Chapel, Santa Maria della Vittoria in Rome, the greatest baroque sculptor, the saint ecstatically sinks back onto a cloud, her eyes nearly closed, her lips parted in a soft moan, evocative of repose after orgasm. Rubens painted *St. Teresa Delivering Bernadin de Mendoza from Purgatory*, in which a rather full-faced saint is confronted by a half-clad Christ, while sinners at the bottom of the painting are enveloped in flames.

Terminus (limit). In Roman mythology, god of boundaries. Stones, which marked boundaries, were under the protection of Terminus. Any person removing a stone could legally be killed. His festival, *Terminalia*, was 23 February, with sacrifices around the boundary stones. Terminalis was an epithet of Jupiter and the god Terminus may be another form of Jupiter. Erasmus, the great Renaissance humanist, used a figure of Terminus for his emblem to signify readiness for death.

Terpsichore (rejoicing in the dance). In Greek mythology, one of the nine Muses, the Muse of Dance; daughter of Zeus and Mnemosyne. Some accounts say she was the mother of the Sirens by Achelous. Her symbols were a laurel crown and a lyre.

Terra or **Tellus Mater** (mother earth). In Roman mythology, ancient Italian mother goddess, invoked during birth, marriage and earthquakes. Her feast, *Fordicidia*, was 15 April. Sacrifices to her were made 13 December, when the dead returned to Mother Earth. Her temple in Rome was dedicated in 268 B.C.E.

Tezcatlipoca (mirror that smokes). In Toltec mythology, creator trickster god worshiped by warriors and magicians, opposed to Quetzalcoatl.

Tezcatlipoca formed the thin air and darkness, presiding over darkness and night. Dreams and the phantoms of gloom were sent by this god. His sacred animals were those associated with night, such as the skunk and the coyote. This demonic nature is commented on by Fray Bernardino de Sahagún in his *Historia general de las cosas de Nueva España* (1570–1582). He says that Tezcatlipoca "caused wars, enmities and discords." Sahagún then gives some of the numerous titles applied to the god: Titlacauan (we are slaves); Telpochtli (the youth), because he never aged; Moyocoyatzin (the determined doer), a name Sahagún says was given to the god because he could do what he pleased on earth or in heaven; Monenequi (he who demands prayers); Teyocoyani (creator of men); and Teimatini (disposer of men). Because Tezcatlipoca was a jealous god who brought plagues and famines, he was also called Yaotzin (the arch enemy); Yaotl Necoc (the enemy of both sides); Moquequeloa (the mocker); and Yoalliehecatl (the night wind).

Thais, St. Fourth century C.E. In Christian legend, penitent, saint, patron of fallen women or courtesans. Feast, 8 October.

The Golden Legend, written in the 13th century, tells the story of the saint from various earlier sources, such as the *Lives of the Fathers*. Thais was a courtesan who through her charms "reduced to the direst poverty" the men who paid for her affections. However, she met Abbot Paphnutius, who not only convinced her of her guilt but "shut her up in a little cell" and "sealed the door with lead." When Thais asked what she was to do with her "natural issue of water," the abbot replied to her to leave it in the cell as "thou deservest!" After three years Thais came out, reformed, and died 15 days later.

The edifying life of the reformed whore inspired the novel *Thaïs* by the cynic Anatole France. In it Paphnutius, a young rake turned monk, lives in the desert and dreams of the courtesan Thaïs. He interprets the dream as a call to reform the woman, which he does. The problem, however, is that Paphnutius still has lustful dreams of the girl even though she is now living the saintly life of a hermit. In an attempt to rid himself of his lust he tries all manner of mortifications until he realizes that he really wants her. He tries to persuade her to flee the convent with him. As she dies (it was too much for her sensitive soul to bear), the abbess sends Paphnutius away when she sees the lust written on

his face. Jules Massenet wrote an operatic version of France's novel.

Thalia (blood of life). In Greek mythology, one of the three Graces. The others were Euphrosyne (joy) and Aglaia (bright). They were all daughters of Zeus and Eurynome.

Thalia (festive). In Greek mythology, a name of three different beings: one, the Muse of Comedy, daughter of Zeus and Mnemosyne, whose symbol was the mask used by comedians; the second, one of the graces, daughter of Zeus and Eurynome, sister of Aglaca, Pasithea and Euphrosyne, mother of the Palici by Zeus; and the third, one of the Nereids. A famous movie house in New York City devoted to old and classic movies is named for Thalia.

Thallo (sprouting). In Greek mythology, the spring, one of the seasons; daughter of Zeus and Themis; sister of Carpo and Auxo.

Thamar (date palm). In Russian Georgian legend, an evil queen who feasted with lovers then threw them into a river the next day.

Queen Thamar's castle was located near the mighty Terek River. From her window at night came the sound of her "enchanting voice, whose song lured traveler, merchant, warrior or peasant to see her within the castle." When the gates to the castle were opened and the wanderer entered, he would find himself in a luxurious room, where Thamar, "richly bedecked in brocade and jewels, reclined voluptuously on a couch." She would feast with the man, locking him in "passionate embraces," but the next morning "the waters of the Terek River would bear away his corpse." From her window could be heard the whispered "farewell."

Thamar's legend was used by the Russian poet Mikhail Lermontov in his short narrative poem *Thamar*, which in turn was used as the story basis for Mili Balakirev's symphonic poem *Thamar*. Balakirev's score was later used for the ballet *Thamar* by Michel Fokine, with scenery and costumes by Léon Bakst.

Lermontov also used the character Thamar in his long narrative poem *The Demon*. It tells of a former angel who rebels against God. He sees the beautiful Thamar and falls in love with her, thinking it will reconcile him to God, "In Paradise again I'd shine, like a new angel in new splendor." Thamar cannot resist the demon and they kiss, but she dies and her soul goes to heaven. The demon, however, is left alone. Anton Rubinstein used the poem for *The Demon*, his most popular opera during his lifetime. Boris Pasternak wrote a poem, *In Memory of The Demon*, in praise of Lermontov's poem.

2840

Thamyris (thick-set). In Greek mythology, a Thracian musician, son of Philammon and Argiope, who challenged the Muses to a contest of musical skill. Thamyris lost and was blinded, his voice destroyed, and his lyre broken as punishment. He was said to be the lover of Hyacinthus. Homer's *Iliad* (book 2) and Milton's *Paradise Lost* (Book 3:35) cite the musician.

2841

Thanatos (death). In Greek mythology, death, son of Nyx and Erebus; twin brother of Hypnos; brother of Aether, Cer, Dreams, Hemera, Chron, Momus, Moros and Nemesis; and called Mors by the Romans. William Cullen Bryant's poem *Thanatopsis* deals with the theme of death.

2842

Than ka (colored picture). In Buddhism, any icon that is colored. Its function is to open the consciousness of the beholder to the spiritual world. Woodcuts of similar design but without color are used by poorer people.

2843

Thecla, St. (god-famed). First century. In Christian legend, first female Christian martyr. Patron of Este and Milan, Italy. Feast, 23 September. St. Thecla was one of the most honored female saints in the Early Church because of a book called *The Acts of Paul and Thecla*, which said she was a follower of St. Paul. According to the legend, her reputation for holiness and the cures she effected aroused the hatred of local physicians in Iconium. They claimed she was a priestess of Diana. "It is by her chastity she does these cures," they cried. "If we could destroy that, her power would be overthrown." So they sent a delegation to rape Thecla. The saint ran from them, praying all the time, and then she "saw a rock opened to as large a degree as that a man might enter . . . and she went into the rock, which instantly so closed, that there was not any crack visible where it had opened." All the mob found was her veil, lost where she entered the rock.

Though she did not die a martyr's death, the Eastern church so honors her. In the medieval Roman church, St. Martin of Tours advocated her cult.

2844

Themis (order). In Greek mythology, a Titaness, later a goddess who presided over hospitality, law, order, justice, and prophecy. Themis was the wife of the Titan Iapetus, but later married Zeus after Metis was swallowed. She was the mother of the Horae (seasons), the three Moerae (Fates), and Astraea, and some accounts say Themis was also the mother of Prometheus. When Themis was no longer Zeus's wife she became his trusted advisor, representing divine justice. She was the protector of the oppressed and was called *Soteira* (saving goddess) in her role as protector. Before Apollo's oracle at Delphi, Themis had a shrine in the same location. In Greek art Themis is portrayed as a woman holding a pair of scales and a cornucopia, symbol of the blessing of order which the goddess gives her people.

2845

Thersites (son of courage). In Greek mythology, ugly, hated Greek, son of Agrius. He laughed at Achilles for the hero's lamenting the death of Penthesilea, the queen of the Amazons. Achilles, in anger, killed Thersites. He appears in Shakespeare's *Troilus and Cressida* as a mean-spirited commentator on the play's characters.

2846

Theseus (he who lies down). In Greek mythology, hero, son of Aethra and Aegeus or Poseidon; husband of Hippolyte, father of Hippolytus; husband of Ariadne, father of Oenopion and Staphylus; and husband of Phaedra, father of Acamas and Demophon.

There are two accounts of the birth of Theseus. In one, his father is King Aegeus and he was raised by Pittheus, his grandfather. In a variant account, Theseus's father is the sea god Poseidon. According to this variant account, Theseus was challenged by King Minos of Crete to prove that Poseidon was his father. The king cast a ring into the sea, asking that Theseus recover it. Not only did Theseus recover the ring, but he also was given a golden wreath by the sea goddess Amphitrite to prove Poseidon was his father.

Six labors are usually assigned to Theseus, all of them performed on his way from Troezen to Athens. In each he kills some monster or giant. The six monsters are: Periphetes, Sinis, the Crommyonian sow, Sceiron, Cercym, and Procrustes. For these killings, Theseus was purified near Athens, and then he entered the city a hero. Theseus's father, King Aegeus was now married to Medea, the former mistress of Jason and a witch. When Medea saw the handsome Theseus she realized that her control over Aegeus would be lessened, so she prepared a poisoned cup for Theseus. Her plot to kill him failed and Medea fled in a winged chariot. At this time the Athenians were paying a yearly tribute of seven young boys and girls to King Minos of Crete who offered them as sacrifices to the monster Minotaur, dwelling in the labyrinth of Crete. King Minos demanded the tribute as punishment for Aegeus, who sent Androgeus, the son of Minos, against the Marathonian bull, which had killed the boy. Theseus told his father he would slay the Minotaur and return with all the youths. He set sail in a ship with black sails and promised, when he returned, to change the sails to white if he defeated the monster. Aphrodite, goddess of love, was on Theseus' side and when he arrived in Crete, she made Ariadne, daughter of Minos, fall in love the Theseus. Ariadne aided Theseus by means of a ball of magic thread, which she gave him, telling him to fasten one end of it to the lintel of the labyrinth as he entered and unwind it until he came to the Minotaur. In order to escape, he would simply rewind the thread. Theseus killed the Minotaur, then offered it as a sacrifice to Poseidon. He then fled with Ariadne, coming to the isle of Naxos where, while she was asleep, he abandoned her. Either she died of grief or was later made the mistress of the god Dionysus.

Returning home to Athens, Theseus forgot to change the black sails to white as he had promised. When Aegeus saw the black sails he believed that Theseus was dead and committed suicide. Theseus was then made king of Athens. He entered into battle with the Amazons, capturing their queen, Antiope, or as some variant accounts say, winning her love. But as in the case of Ariadne, he grew tired of Antiope and was ready to cast her off. Antiope tried to kill Theseus, but failed, and she in turn was killed by Heracles. Theseus then married Phaedra, sister of Ariadne. His new wife, however, fell in love with her stepson Hippolytus and tried to seduce him. When she failed, she killed herself, leaving a note for Theseus saying that Hippolytus had tried to rape her. Furious, Theseus prayed to Poseidon to destroy his son. Theseus' relations with women were failures. Theseus planned with his friend Pirithous, king of the Lapiths, to abduct Persephone, queen of the Underworld. They failed and Hades chained both men to rocks. Heracles, who had come to the Underworld to capture Cerberus as one of his labors, freed Theseus, but failed to free Pirithous.

Returning to Athens, he found another ruler on the throne, and the people rejected Theseus, who was now old. He went to King Lycomedes on the island of Scyrus, where he owned some land. Lycomedes pretended to be pleased with Theseus's visit, but plotted his death. He took Theseus to a cliff overlooking his vast lands and pushed the hero to his death. In later belief, an image of the ghost of Theseus appeared in full armor, rallying the Athenians against the Persians, in the Battle of Marathon (490 B.C.E.).

Theseus appears in works by Apollodorus, Herodotus, Homer, Hyginus, Ovid, Pausanias, Statius, and Vergil and in English literature in Chaucer, Shakespeare, Christina Rossetti, W. H. Auden, and T.S. Eliot. Mary Renault's novels *The King Must Die* (1958) and *The Bull from the Sea* (1962) also feature Theseus.

2847

Thespis. (sixth century B.C.E.) In Greek history and legend, an Attic poet who is believed to be the first actor to appear on stage separate from the chorus. He introduced the prologue and set speeches for himself, removing them from the chorus, which previously had narrated the entire drama. The use of masks in Greek tragic drama as a device to develop character is also credited to him.

2848

Thespius (divinely sounding?). In Greek mythology, king of Boeotia, who gave his 50, 51, or 52 daughters to sleep with Heracles. Accounts vary. Some say Heracles slept with each one, 51 in all, for 51 nights. Another account says he had sexual intercourse with all 51 on the same night. In either case, only one girl refused, and she was forced to remain a virgin for life. Heracles fathered 51 sons, who later colonized the island of Sardinia.

2849

Thethys (disposer or the nourisher?). In Greek mythology, Titaness; daughter of Uranus and Gaea; wife of her brother, Oceanus; mother of Asia, Callirrhoe, Clymene, Clytia, Doris, Eruopa, Eidyia, Electra, Inachus, Meliboea, Perseis, Pleione, Proteus, Styx, the rivers and the 3,000 Oceanides. Milton's *Comus* refers to the deity's "grave majestic pace."

2850

Thetis (disposer). In Greek mythology, sea goddess, daughter of Nereus and Doris; sister of the Nereids; wife of Peleus, mother of Achilles. Both Zeus and Poseidon pursued Thetis, but she avoided both. They gave up their quest when they were told that the son Thetis would bear would be greater than his father. To make it safe for both, the two gods forced Thetis to marry Peleus, king of the Myrmidons in Thessaly. She tried to avoid the unwanted union, transforming herself into various shapes, but eventually she was forced to marry him. Their son was Achilles. At their wedding, Eris, the goddess of discord, threw a golden apple inscribed "For the fairest" into the throng, and all the goddesses tried to claim it. Zeus picked Paris to choose the fairest, and his choice of Aphrodite won him Helen, which eventually led to the Trojan War. Thetis, wishing to make her son Achilles invulnerable, dipped him in the waters of the Styx. She held him by his heel, thus leaving one vulnerable part that did not touch the water. Later in the Trojan War it was this heel that Paris shot, killing Achilles. Thetis appears in Homer's *Iliad* and *Odyssey*, Ovid's *Metamorphoses* (book 11), and in Ingres painting, *Jupiter and Thetis*, which portrays the goddess asking Jupiter (Zeus) to aid her son.

Thinan-malkia. 2851 In Australian mythology, evil spirits who capture victims with nets that entangle their feet.

Thistle. 2852 A prickly plant, emblem of Scotland. During the reign of Malcolm I (935–958 C.E.) a party of invading Norsemen or Danes, attempting to surprise Scottish forces, approached the camp under cover of darkness. One of them accidentally stepped on a thistle and cried out, thus rousing the Scots, who defeated the invaders. However, there is no record of the thistle as the Scottish symbol until the reign of James VI, better known as James I of England. On some coins issued at his coronation half of a thistle is combined with half of a rose, apparently joining the two sides of his family, the Scottish Thistle and the Tudor Rose.

Thomas à Becket, St. 2853 (twin). 1118–1170 C.E. In Christian legend, archbishop of Canterbury and martyr whose shrine at Canterbury was a famous goal of pilgrims during the Middle Ages.

Thomas was born in London of Norman background. In 1154, after filling various posts, he was ordained a deacon and nominated archdeacon of Canterbury. In the following year he was made lord chancellor by his close friend King Henry II. Though Thomas was known for his hot temper and worldliness, his life seemed to change. He opposed the king in his demands on the liberties of the clergy. Thomas described himself as "a proud vain man, a feeder of birds and follower of hounds," who was now "a shepherd of sheep."

The disputes between the king and the archbishop continued for seven years, with Thomas spending some time in exile in France. He returned to England on 1 December 1170. King Henry was reported to have said then, "Of the cowards that eat my bread, is there none that will rid me of this upstart priest." Four Norman knights then bound themselves with an oath to kill Thomas. They went to Canterbury, at first unarmed, but after meeting with Thomas, who defied their demand, they returned with swords. Thomas then ordered the cross of Canterbury to be borne before him as he passed through the cloister into the church. His followers closed the gates behind him, but he commanded them to be reopened, saying, "God's house should never be fortified as a place of defense."

As Thomas ascended the steps of the choir, the four knights with twelve attendants, all armed, burst into the church.

"Where is the traitor?" one asked.

All were silent.

"Where is the archbishop?" asked Reginald Fitzurse.

"Here I am," replied Thomas, "the archbishop and no traitor, Reginald; I have granted thee many favors. What is thy object now? If thou seekest my life, let that suffice. I command thee, in the name of God, not to touch my people."

Thomas was then told he must absolve the archbishop of York and the bishop of Salisbury, whom he had excommunicated.

"Till they make satisfaction, I will not absolve them," he firmly replied.

"Then die," said Tracy, one of the four knights.

The first blow aimed at his head was broken in its force by Thomas' cross-bearer so that the archbishop was only slightly wounded. Feeling the blood on his face, he bowed his head, saying, "In the name of Christ and for the defense of His Church I am ready to die."

The murderers then attempted to remove him from the church because they did not wish to kill him in a sacred place. But Thomas could not be moved.

"I will not stir," he said. Again they struck him.

He was so beaten by the four knights that his brains were strewn on the pavement before the altar. The monks of the cathedral then bore Thomas's body on a bier and placed it in the choir of the cathedral. The people collected the blood and remains that were left on the pavement. It was not long before stories of miracles in connection with his relics spread. Eventually, a shrine to the saint was erected in the cathedral, and it became one of the most famous pilgrim sites in medieval Europe. Chaucer's Canterbury pilgrims followed routes from London; others took the Pilgrim Way across the North Downs from Winchester. Other pilgrims came from the continent.

In 1538 King Henry VIII issued a proclamation to the effect that "from henceforth the said Thomas Becket shall not be esteemed, named, reputed, nor called a Saint, but Bishop Becket, and that his images and pictures through the whole realm shall be put down and avoided out of all churches, chapels and all other places: and that henceforth the days used to be as festival in his name shall not be observed, nor the service, office, antiphons, collects and prayers in his name read, but erased and put out of all books."

As a result of Henry's order no trace can now be found of Thomas's body, since it, along with his famous shrine, were destroyed and the gold and jewels given to the Royal Treasury of Henry.

Thomas's legend, however, continued to fascinate the Middle Ages. After his murder friends and enemies vied with each other in praise of the saint. Within a few years of his murder no fewer than nine Latin and one French lives of the saint were in circulation. Three of the Latin lives were the work of men who said they were present at the events.

Aside from providing a framework for Chaucer's *The Canterbury Tales*, the legend has been used by Alfred Tennyson in his play *Becket*, and by T. S. Eliot in his verse drama *Murder in the Cathedral*, which was made into an opera as *Assassinio nella catterdrale* by Pizzetti. A French play by Jean Anouilh, *Becket*, was made into a film.

St. Thomas Aquinas

2854

Thomas Aquinas, St. (twin). c. 1225–1274 C.E. In Christian legend, Doctor Angelicus (angelic doctor) of the Roman church. Patron of booksellers, Catholic universities, pencil makers, scholars, and students. Invoked for chastity and learning and against storms and lightning. Feast, 28 January.

Though called the Dumb Ox, because of his slowness, St. Thomas became one of the greatest thinkers of the Roman church during the Middle Ages. He produced the *Summa Theologiae*, the culmination of scholastic philosophy, faith, and reason. He was also noted for some hymns, particularly *Adoro Te*, which was translated into English by the baroque poet Richard Crashaw in the 17th century.

Thomas was probably born at Roccasecca, near Aquino in Campania, Italy. He was educated at Monte Cassino and then the University of Naples. While he was an undergraduate, he decided to become a Dominican. The order was not quite 30 years old and Thomas's family, of noble blood, thought it shocking that he should waste himself becoming a mendicant friar. The family kidnapped him and shut him up in the family castle, but the Dominicans of Naples went in disguise to the castle and, with the help of Thomas's sister, let him down from the castle by lowering a basket. This episode is similar to St. Paul's escape in Acts (9:25).

St. Thomas spent the remainder of his life reading and writing. He died in the Cistercian abbey at Fossa Nova.

Numerous legends circulated during the Middle Ages about the saint. One relates that as he knelt before a crucifix it spoke to him, asking him what he most desired. Thomas replied, "Thyself only, O Lord." Another medieval legend tells that at his birth there were three bright stars in the heavens—one for him, one for St. Ambrose of Siena and one for St. James of Menavia—all born on the same day.

Toward the end of his life St. Thomas was more and more disengaged from everyday matters. His eyes were often fixed on other horizons. His ecstasies were said to be quite frequent and to last for a long time. After each one he is reported to have said, "Oh, who will deliver me from this body of death?"

Though St. Thomas is recognized by the Roman church as one of its greatest theologians, there was a time when his writings were condemned by various church councils. The Franciscans, a rival order to the Dominicans, for some time forbade their members to read any of the saint's works.

St. Thomas is portrayed in medieval art wearing the Dominican habit, with a book or pen, or a Host (he defended the Roman Catholic doctrine of Transubstantiation), and with a sun or human eye on his breast. Often a star is seen overhead, referring to one of his legends.

2855

Thomas More, St. (twin). 1478–1535 C.E. In Christian legend, martyr and lord chancellor of England under Henry VIII. Feast, 6 July.

His son-in-law William Roper wrote a life of Thomas More and described More's last day when he was led "towards the place of execution, where, going up the scaffold, which was so weak that it was ready to fall, he said to Mr. Lieutenant, 'I pray you, I pray you, Mr. Lieutenant, see me safe up, and for my coming down let me shift for myself.'" He then turned to the executioner "and with a cheerful countenance spoke to him. 'Pluck up thy spirits, man, and be not afraid to do thine office. My neck is very short. Take heed therefore thou strike not awry for saving of thine honor.'"

The famous painting of Thomas More by Hans Holbein, the court painter to Henry VIII, is in the Frick collection in New York City. The artist also made sketches of the saint and his family. There is a picture of the saint by Antoine Caron in the Museum at Blois, in which he is shown as an old man with a long beard, surrounded by what seem to be Roman soldiers, being embraced by his daughter on his way to execution. More forms the subject for a play by Robert Bolt, *A Man for All Seasons*, which has on its opening page a quotation from Samuel Johnson that More "was the person of the greatest virtue these islands ever produced."

2856

Thomas, St. (twin). First century C.E. In the Bible, N.T., one of the Twelve Apostles of Jesus. Patron saint of architects, builders, carpenters, masons, geometricians, and theologians, and of Portugal and Parma. Feast, 21 December.

Thomas is named in the Gospels of Matthew, Mark, and Luke, but he is called Didymus (twin) in John's account (11:16). Thomas refused to believe that Christ had risen until he touched Jesus' wounds with his fingers (John 20:24–29), thus the expression "doubting Thomas."

According to *The Golden Legend*, a 13th-century account of the lives of saints, Thomas traveled to the East and founded a church in India, where he met the three Magi whom he baptized. While in Caesarea, Thomas had a vision in which Christ appeared and told him that Gondolforus, king of the Indies, needed an architect to build him a palace. Thomas went, and Gondolforus gave him money to build the palace; then he left for two years. When the king returned, he found that Thomas had given all the money to the poor and sick. The king, in anger, put Thomas in prison, but a few days later the king's brother died and "there was made for him a rich sepulchre, and the fourth day he that had been dead arose from death to life, and all men were abashed and fled. And he said to his brother; 'This man that thou intendest to slay and burn is the friend of God, and the angels of God serve him, and they brought me in to paradise, and have showed me a palace of gold and silver. . . . And when I marveled of the great beauty thereof, they said to me: "This is the palace that Thomas hath made for thy brother."'

After hearing about the dream, the king freed Thomas. According to another legend, the Portuguese found at Meliapore an inscription saying Thomas had been pierced with a lance at the foot of a cross that he had erected in that city, and his body had been moved to Goa in 1523.

The legend of *La Madonna della Cintola* (Our Lady of the Girdle) says that when the Virgin Mary ascended to heaven, St. Thomas was not present with the other Apostles. Three days later, when he returned, he could not believe their account and wished to see her tomb. The tomb was opened and the Virgin dropped her girdle from heaven for Thomas.

When St. Thomas is portrayed as an Apostle, he holds a builder's rule or square; when he is shown as a martyr he holds a lance. Two scenes from his life are most often portrayed: The Incredulity of Thomas, when he puts his finger in the side of Christ, and La Madonna della Cintola.

Thor (W. G. Collingwood)

2857

Thor (thunderer). In Norse mythology, the sky god; son of Odin and Fjorgyn (earth); husband of Sif; associated with thunder and lightning. One of Thor's main epithets is Vingnir (the hurler); he appears in Richard Wagner's *Der Ring des Nibelungen* as Donner. The *Prose Edda* describes Thor as "the strongest of the gods and men." His realm is called Thrudvang; his mansion of 540 rooms, Bilskirnir (lightning). His chariot is drawn by two goats, Tanngniost and Tanngrisnir. Among his possessions are a magic hammer, Mjolnir (thunderbolt), forged by the dwarf Sindri. When Thor threw Mjolnir, the hammer would return to him of its own power. The evil fire-trickster god, Loki, disguised as a fly, tried to interfere with the forging by flying around Sindri. As a result, the hammer had a short handle. A blow from Mjolnir brought instant death, but it could also restore life. Thor used Mjolnir to bless weddings on

Thursday (Thor's day). The giant Thrym (noise) once stole Thor's hammer and demanded the goddess Freyja as payment for its return. Thor, disguised as Freyja, had Thrym lay the hammer in his lap and then slew Thrym and all of his giant companions with it. Thor also possessed a magic belt, Megingjardir, which doubled his strength when he wore it.

His worship continued into the Christian Middle Ages. Thor's temples and images, like Odin's, were made of wood, and the majority were destroyed in the 11th century by King Olaf II, who was later sainted by the church. According to some accounts, the saintly king often forced his subjects to reject Thor's worship in favor of Christ's. Olaf was especially angry at the inhabitants of one province who worshiped a primitive image of Thor which they decked with golden ornaments. Every evening they set food before the image, and the next morning it was gone—they believed Thor had eaten it. When the people were called by Olaf in to renounce Thor's worship in favor of the One, True God, Christ, they asked for a miracle. They would believe if it were cloudy the next day; it was cloudy. Then they asked that if they were to believe in the Christian god, the following day should be filled with sunshine. Olaf spent the night in prayer, but at dawn the sky was overcast. Nevertheless, determined to win the people for Christ, he assembled them near Thor's image. Suddenly, while they all were listening to him, Olaf pointed to the horizon, where the sun was slowly breaking through the clouds. "Behold our God!" he cried. While the people looked at the sun coming through the clouds, Olaf's guards destroyed Thor's image. Mice and other vermin came out of the wrecked image. Seeing that the food had been eaten by animals, and not by their god, the people accepted the worship of Christ. Thor appears in the *Poetic Edda*, the *Prose Edda*, and Henry W. Longfellow's "The Saga of King Olaf" (part of his *Tales of a Wayside Inn*) in which the "Challenge of Thor" opens:

I am the God Thor,
I am the War God,
I am the Thunderer!
Here in my Northland,
My fastness and fortress,
Reign I forever!

Thor appears as Donner in Arthur Rackham's illustrations for Wagner's Ring Cycle.
Variant spellings: Thur, Thunar, Thunaer.

2858
Thoth. In Egyptian mythology, ibis-headed moon god, also patron of wisdom, arts, speech; inventor of

Thoth

hieroglyphics and science; he was believed to be the author of *The Book of the Dead*.

Thoth was regarded as both the heart and tongue of the great sun god Ra. When Thoth spoke, the wishes of Ra were fulfilled, as when the heavens and the earth were created and when Isis was given the words by which to revive the dead body of her son Horus. In the judgment scene in *The Book of the Dead*, Thoth, after weighing the words of the deceased, gives to the gods the final verdict as to whether a soul is to be blessed or punished.

Thoth was also called Tehuti (the measurer). In this capacity he had the power to grant life for millions of years to the deceased. When the great battle took place between Horus and Set, Thoth acted as the judge, being called Wep-rehewy (judge of the two opponent gods). During the struggle he gave Isis a cow's head in place of her own, which had been severed by Horus in anger when Isis befriended Set.

The Greeks identified Thoth with their god Hermes. They described him as the inventor of astronomy and astrology, the science of numbers and mathematics, geometry, land surveying, medicine, and botany. They said he was the first to organize religion and government, establishing the rules concerning worship of the gods. He was said to have composed hymns, prayers, and liturgical works and to have invented numbers, hieroglyphics, reading, writing, and oratory. In short, he was the author of every branch of knowledge, both human and divine.

In Egyptian art Thoth usually appears in human form with the head of an ibis, although sometimes he appears as the ibis alone. The bird was sacred to him and was associated with the moon, as was Thoth as the measurer of time. Sometimes he is portrayed as a seated baboon wearing the crescent moon on his head. This image reflects the belief that Thoth, as the moon god, took the place of Ra, the sun god, while Ra made his nightly journey through the underworld. When Thoth is portrayed in human form, he holds a scepter and ankh, sign of life, properties common to all of the gods. His headdress, however, varies according to the particular aspect of the god the artist wished to depict. As the reckoner of time and the seasons, Thoth wears on his head the crescent moon. Sometimes he wears the Atef crown and sometimes the united crowns of Upper and Lower Egypt. In *The Book of the Dead* he appears as the "scribe of Maat," or justice, holding the writing reed and palette. His close connection with the god Ra is sometimes indicated by his carrying the *utchat*, which symbolized the strength of the eye of Ra.

Variant spellings: Tahuti, Techa, Thout, Dhouti, Zhouti.

2859

Thousand and One Nights, The, or **The Arabian Nights.** English translation of the Arabic collection of tales *Alf Laylah wa-laylah*, which is based on a Persian collection, *Hazar Afsana*, A Thousand Tales.

The tales are arranged within a narrative framework. The Persian monarch Shahriyar had little trust in women's fidelity, so he adopted the habit of taking a new wife each night and killing her the next morning. However, the clever Shahrazad, or Sheherazade, kept the monarch amused each night by telling a tale that always carried over to the next night so that, as it says at the end of the massive collection, "the Sultan of the Indies could not fail to admire the prodigious store of interesting stories with which the sultana had whiled away the time through one thousand and one nights." He decided not to kill her and the two lived happily together and "their names were loved and respected throughout the wide territory of the Empire of the Indies."

The collection contains 264 tales of varying length, from short anecdotes of a few lines to novellas of several hundred pages.

The first translation of the tales into a European tongue was done by a French Orientalist, Antone Galland (1647–1715), who adapted many of the tales to the taste of his age with elaborate fictional detail. This version's influence on European literature was immense. Direct imitation of the collection is found in such works as Beckford's *Vathek* and Marryat's *The Pasha of Many Tales*; the form of the work inspired Robert Louis Stevenson's *New Arabian Nights* and *More Arabian Nights*. Among other writers Goethe, in his *Westostlicher Diwan*; Platen, in *Die Abbassiden*; and Victor Hugo, in *Orientales*, demonstrate the influence of the Arabic work.

In general the English reaction to the work was one of approval. Tennyson's *Recollections of the Arabian Nights* was, according to the poet, based on two tales in Galland's translation. Thomas Carlyle, however, would not allow the book in his house because it was filled with "downright lies." His puritanical attitude is similar to the general one of orthodox Muslims, as reflected by one 10th-century historian, Ali Aboulhusn el Mesoudi, who said the collection was "indeed vulgar."

The Thousand and One Nights has influenced other European arts in addition to literature. In music Rimsky-Korsakov's symphonic suite *Scheherezade* attempts, in its four movements, to evoke the mood of the tales. The suite was used by Michel Fokine for

The Thousand and One Nights (Thomas Henry)

a ballet of the same title with fantastical costumes by Léon Bakst. In 1898 Maurice Ravel began an opera to be titled *Shéhérazade* but completed only an overture. He did compose a set of songs to words by Tristan Klingsor, called *Shéhérazade*. One of the most popular operas of the last century, *The Barber of Bagdad* by Peter Cornelius, was based on the collection; and Ernest Reyer's *La Statue*, Issai Obrowen's *A Thousand and One Nights*, and Henri Raboud's *Mârouf* also are based on this source. Other works in the 20th century include British composer Benno Bardi's *Fatme* and Victor de Sabata's *Mille e una notte*.

Filmmakers have been fascinated by the Oriental background of the collection and have produced numerous film epics drawn from the tales. Typical is *Arabian Nights*, starring Maria Montez, Jon Hall, and Sabu.

2860

Thunderbird. In North American Indian mythology (North Pacific Coast, in the Plateau, and the Pomo of California), a giant bird, symbol of thunder, who not only causes thunder but brings war and blessings. Lightning is the flashing of his eyes; thunder, the sound of his wings flapping.

2861

Ti-Albert. In Haitian voodoo, a loa (deified spirit of the dead) symbolized by a dwarf with one leg. He aids priests and priestesses in driving people insane for wrongdoing. He is offered fruit, eggs, and olive or peanut oil. When he possesses a person, he makes that person a better sex partner.

2862

Tiberinus. In Roman mythology, a king of Italy; son of Janus and Camasena; he drowned in the Albula river, which was renamed Tiber. Some accounts say Tiberinus and the river god Volturnus were combined to form one god, Tiber. In a variant tale Tiberinus, not Helenus as in Vergil, appears to Aeneas, telling him where to found the new city, Rome. His festival was 8 December.

2863

T'ien Hou (heavenly empress). In Chinese mythology, a deified mortal, worshiped as goddess of the sea. In life she was able to calm a storm by closing her eyes. She also is called Ch'uan Hou (river empress) and portrayed as a princess in elaborate court costume.

2864

Tiger. A large animal of the cat family having a tawny coat with narrow black stripes; in Chinese mythology, king of the beasts, taking the place of the lion of Western folklore. In Chinese Buddhist mythology it symbolizes anger, one of the Three Senseless Creatures, the others being the monkey as greed and the deer as lovesickness. In Hindu mythology the tiger is the mount of the goddess Durga, as destroyer, and of Shiva, who sometimes wears a tiger skin. In the West, T. S. Eliot's poem *Gerontion* depicts Christ as a tiger, recalling the terror, strength, and awe the beast conjures up in humankind, as does William Blake's *The Tyger*.

2865

Tigranes. In Armenian folklore, a dragon slayer and king. Azadhak, king of Media, had a dream in which a fair-eyed woman gave birth to a dragon slayer who attacked the king and destroyed his idols. When Azadhak awoke, he asked his wise men what the dream signified. They told him that the famous dragon slayer Tigranes was on his way to the kingdom. Wishing to save himself, the king offered to marry Tigranes' sister Tigranuhi, but he told her he planned to kill her brother. The faithful sister so informed her brother. Tigranes came to the king and plunged his triangular spearhead into Azadhak's chest. Azadhak's family was forced to move to Armenia and settle around Massis. They became the children of the dragon, since the first queen of Azadhak was Anush, the mother of dragons. Azadhak is a variation of the Persian demon Azhi Dahaka, who in Persian mythology appears as King Zahhak in the epic poem of Firdusi, *The Shah Namah*.

2866

Ti-Jean-Pied-Sec. In Haitian voodoo, an evil loa (deified spirit of the dead) who makes people commit rape. He is one-legged and eats raw meat.

2867

Tiki (image). In Polynesian mythology, the first man created by the god Tane from red clay. In a variant myth, Tiki is the name of a creator god who forms a man, Tiki-ahua, who resembles the god's form.

2868

Tilaka (mole). In Hinduism, the mark on the forehead and/or arms and/or chest made with red, yellow, or white pigment during the morning devotions at the home altar. Sometimes the term *Tika* (spot) is used.

2869

Till Eulenspiegel (owl glass). In medieval German legend, a trickster. He was a native of Brunswick who died in 1350 after a life in which he was noted for often brutal tricks and practical jokes, played mostly on tradespeople and innkeepers. His adventures were put into book form by Thomas Murner, a Franciscan monk of Strasbourg. In English he was called Tyll Owlyglass or Tyll Owleglass. Richard Strauss's tone poem *Till Eulenspiegel's Merry Pranks* is a rondo for orchestra based on the trickster.

Tilottama. In Hindu mythology, a nymph loved by the god Shiva. He became so enamored of Tilottama's looks that he took on four faces so that he could gaze at her beauty at all times.

Timon of Athens. Fifth century B.C.E. In Greek legend, a misanthrope who came to the conclusion that life was a fraud. Timon appears in Plutarch's *Life of Anthony*, which inspired Shakespeare's play *Timon of Athens*.

Tinirau. In Polynesian mythology, sea god who had two forms, one divine, and the other human. As a human being he was handsome and pleasant, having a liaison with the goddess Hina. In animal form he appeared as a man-of-war bird, hovering above the waters and striking without warning, destroying both men and their boats. Tinirau is also referred to as Sinilau, Kinilau, Timirau, and Tinilau.

Tintagel (stronghold of the resplendent mighty god). In Arthurian legend, a castle on the coast of Cornwall where various episodes from Arthurian legends took place. Arnold Bax's symphonic poem *Tintagel* captures the feeling of the area.

Tipitaka (three baskets). Three collections of sacred books in Buddhism, the *Vinaya Pitaka*, the *Sutta Pitaka*, and the *Abhidhamma Pitaka*, converted from the oral to the written tradition sometime in the first century C.E. The first book, the *Vinaya*, contains rules for the monks and nuns; the second, *Sutta*, is a series of sermons on general topics; and the last, Abhidhamma, is a collection of material on advanced topics concerning the nature of consciousness. In Sanskrit; Tripitaka.

Tirawahat. In North American Indian mythology (Pawnee), supreme god, creator of the heavenly bodies. Thunder, lightning, winds, and rain are his messengers.

Tiresias (he who delights in signs). In Greek mythology, blind prophet; son of Everes and Chariclo; father of Chloris and Manto.

There are variant accounts of why Tiresias became blind. In one version, he saw two snakes mating, killed the female, and immediate was transformed into a woman. After seven years he again saw two snakes mating, but this time he killed the male and was transformed back into a man. When an argument arose between Zeus and Hera as to who had more pleasure during sexual intercourse, man or woman, they consulted Tiresias as the one best able to speak from experience. He answered that women received more pleasure during the sex act. This so angered Hera, that she blinded Tiresias as a punishment for telling the truth. Zeus, who could not withdraw the blindness, gifted Tiresias with prophetic powers and a very long life. In a variant account Tiresias was punished for having seen Athena bathe in the fountain of Hippocrene. In another account he was blinded because when he was seven years old he revealed secrets. Tiresias died when he drank from the icy waters of the fountain of Telphusa. He appears or is cited in Homer, Aeschylus, Apollodorus, Diodorus, Hyginus, Pausanias, Pindar, and Sophocles in ancient literature. In English literature both Tennyson and Swinburne have poems called *Tiresias*. He also appears in T.S. Eliot's *The Waste Land*.

Variant spelling: Teiresias.

Tirthamkara (one who makes a ford). In Jainism, title applied to 24 teachers who have been liberated from continual rebirths, having attained Nirvana. Because they have complete liberation from the world, they are transcendent, omniscient, actionless, and absolutely at peace. This concept, however, is mitigated in Jain practice, in which they are objects of worship.

Tishtrya. In Persian mythology, rain god, primeval producer of rain, seas, and lakes, often called the bright and glorious star and identified with Sirius, to whom sacrifices were made to bring purification to the soul.

As rain god, Tishtrya was in continual battle against the demons of drought, particularly Apaosha. One day, Tishtrya, in the form of a beautiful white horse, went down to the ocean's depths and met Apaosha, who was in the form of a black horse. The two battled for three days and three nights. Apaosha was gaining the upper hand when Tishtrya called upon the good god, Ahura Mazda, for aid. Ahura Mazda then made sacrifices to Tishtrya to renew his strength. With this newly gained energy Tishtrya defeated the demon Apaosha.

Variant spellings: Tistar, Tistrya.

2879

Titans (lords, rulers). In Greek mythology, primeval gigantic beings; children of Uranus and Gaea. Their number varies, though 12 are generally named, coinciding with the 12 Olympian gods who replace the Titans as rulers. They are Oceanus, Tethys, Hyperion, Thia, Crius, Mnemosyne (Eurybia), Coeus, Phoebe, Cronus, Rhea, Iapetus, and Themis. Added to the list sometimes are Briareus, Cottus, Gyges, Enceladus, Porphyrion, and Rhoetus, though some accounts say they were just giants, not Titans. Also called Titans are Prometheus, Epimetheus, and Atlas. Cronus, their leader, overthrew his father Uranus and castrated him. Cronus, in turn, was overthrown by his son Zeus. In the ensuing war Iapetus and all the 12 Titans, except Oceanus, sided with their brother Cronus against Zeus. The war continued for ten years until Zeus, advised by Gaea, released from Tartarus, the lowest section of the Underworld, the Cyclopes and the Hecatonchires, who sided with Zeus and helped him defeat the Titans, who were then cast into Tartarus. Prometheus also sided with zeus in the battle and was rewarded. The Titans appear in Hesiod's *Theogony*, Hyginus's *Fables*, and Apollodorus's *Biblioteca* (Library). Keats's unfinished epic, *The Fall of Hyperion*, deals with the sun god of the Titans. Mahler's Symphony No. 1 in D is subtitled "Titan."

2880

Titha Jumma. In Burmese mythology, a disciple of the Buddha. Titha Jumma and his brother Zaya Kumma were hatched from eggs left by a dragon woman. They were brought up by two hermit brothers. Titha Jumma died when he was ten but was reborn when the Buddha appeared in his country, and he became a disciple of the Buddha.

2881

Tithonus (partner of the Queen of Day). In Greek mythology, handsome young man; son of Laomedon, king of Troy and Leucippe. Aurora, the dawn, fell in love with the handsome youth and granted him immortality at his request. Tithonus, however, forgot to ask for perpetual youth. As he grew older and older he begged the goddess to kill him. Aurora eventually changed him into a grasshopper. Tennyson's *Tithonus*, a dramatic monologue, deals with his tragic fate.

2882

Ti Tsang. In Chinese Buddhism, a Bodhisattva, god of the underworld and instructor of the regions of darkness, who travels unceasingly throughout the nether world to succor the dead.

Ti Tsang is the Chinese form of the Sanskrit Kshitigarbha. As a young man Ti Tsang was a young Brahman who, being converted to the Buddha of that time, took a vow to become a Buddha, but not before he had saved all beings sunk in ignorance and brought them over the river of Samsara to the Happy Land. During his numerous reincarnations he sacrificed himself to fulfill this vow.

He is especially concerned with dead children. Mothers who have lost a child pray to him and place a child's bib around the neck of his image. He is portrayed as a monk. In Japanese he is called Jizo.

2883

Titurel. In medieval legends associated with the Holy Grail, a knight who was the first guardian of the Grail. He was succeeded by his son Frimutel and later by Amfortas.

2884

Tiur. In Armenian mythology, scribe of the supreme god, Aramazd; Tiur kept a record of the good and evil deeds of men for future judgment. He also wrote down the decrees that were issued from Aramazd concerning human events. Some scholars believe Tiur was also the god who conducted the souls to the underworld. The common Armenian expression "May Tiur carry him off!" refers to the god in his possible role as conductor of the dead.

Variant spelling: Tir.

2885

Ti Yü (the earth prison). In Chinese mythology, the underworld or hell, made up of ten sections, governed by the Shih-Tien Yen Wang (the Yama kings of the ten hills). Each king rules over one of the hells. The are Ch'in-kuang wang, Ch'u-kuang wang, Sung-ti wang, Wu-kuan wang, Yen-mo wang, Pien ch'eng, T'ai-shan kun wang, P'ing-Teng, Tu-shi, and Chuan-lun wang.

2886

Tjinimin the Bat. In Australian mythology, the trickster bat, son of Kunmanggur, the Rainbow Snake. He raped his sisters and eventually killed his father with a spear.

2887

Tlaloc (path under the earth, wine of earth, long cave?). In Aztec mythology, god of rain, thunder, and lightning. He controlled mountain springs and weather.

Tlaloc lived in a luxurious paradise, Tlalocan, peopled by those who had drowned or had been killed by lightning. One mural from Tepantitla (first to sixth century C.E.) in Teotinuácan portrays the god in his heaven, where there are flowers and butterflies. He is attended by priests, water flows from his hands, and aquatic creatures play at his feet.

The souls of those who live in his paradise are portrayed in the lower half of the work and seem to be extremely happy. However, during Tlaloc's feast, called Etzalqualiztli (13 May), children and virgins were sacrificed to him. His offspring by his wife Chalchihuitlicue were the Tlalocs, or clouds.

Variant spellings: Tecutli, Tlaloque.

2888
Tlazolteotl (lady of dirt). In Aztec mythology, sex goddess who produced lust and then forgave the sinner. According to Fray Bernardino do Sahagún in *Historia general de las cosas de Nueva España* (1570–1582), the goddess was also known as Ixcuina (two- faced) and had four aspects: the goddesses Tiacapán, Teicu, Tlacotl, and Xocutzin. All four "had the power to produce lust" and "could provoke carnal intercourse and favored illicit love affairs." These four aspects of the goddess are believed by C. A. Burland in *The Gods of Mexico* (1967) to be "the four phases of the moon" and associate the goddess with witchcraft.

Variant spelling: Tlaculteutl.

Return of Tobias

2889
Tobit (God is good). In the Bible, O.T. Apocrypha, hero, along with his son Tobias. The tale is included in the Latin Vulgate as part of sacred scripture and was so accepted by the church until the Protestant Reformation. Even Martin Luther, who rejected many books from the standard canon, admired the work, saying he preferred it to Esther, a book that he intensely disliked.

Tobit, a devout and charitable Jew living in exile in Nineveh, became blind. He sent his son Tobias with his faithful dog (in the Bible the dog is always looked on as dirty and unclean, except in this tale) to a distant city to collect a debt. The boy met a companion, a young man who was the angel Raphael in disguise. Tobias, with the help of

Raphael, succeeded in collecting the money. Tobias then met a woman, Sarah, who was afflicted with a demon who had killed each of her seven husbands on their wedding nights. With Raphael's aid, Tobias exorcised the demon, married Sarah, returned home with her and cured his father's blindness. At the end of the tale Raphael reveals himself to them.

Christian art has often portrayed Tobias with the angel and a fish. On Tobias's journey Raphael saved him from being eaten by a great fish. He instructed Tobias to catch the fish, roast it, and eat it but to save the heart, liver, and gall. The first two were used to exorcise the evil spirit haunting Sarah, and the gall was used to cure Tobit's blindness. One of the most famous paintings portraying this legend is *Tobias and the Angel* from the school of Andrea del Verrocchio. Franz Joseph Haydn composed an oratorio *Tobit*.

2890
Toci (our grandmother). In Aztec mythology, goddess. Fray Diego Durán, in his *Book of the Gods and Rites* (c. 1576), calls Toci the "Mother of the Gods and Heart of the Earth." According to C. A. Burland, in *The Gods of Mexico* (1967), Toci was a "life-giving spirit" who "cleansed sins and cared for her little grandchildren." She presided over the sweat bath. Her image was placed above the doorway.

Variant spellings: Tozi, Temazcalteci.

2891
To-Kabinana and To-Karvuvu. In Melanesian mythology, the first two men created by a nameless creator god.

One day the creator god drew two male figures on the ground and sprinkled them with his blood, giving them life. To-Kabinana was regarded as the creator of good things, and his brother To-Karvuvu was responsible for all of the trouble in the world. Beautiful women were created by To-Kabinana when he dropped two coconuts on the ground. When his brother repeated the act, women with flat noses emerged because the coconuts fell in the wrong position. In another myth To-Kabinana created fish from a wooden image. When his brother repeated the act, he created the shark.

2892
Tomato. A fruit-bearing plant in the nightshade family, introduced in Europe in the 16th century by Spaniards returning from Mexico. In European folklore the tomato was sometimes identified as the fruit eaten by Adam and Eve in the Garden of Eden, though it is not named in the account in Genesis. The Germans call the tomato *Paradies Apfel* (paradise apple). In French folklore the tomato was believed to be poisonous, but in small amounts it was believed

to be an aphrodisiac. The French call it *pomme d'amour* (love apple).

Tom Quick. In American folklore, "Indian Slayer" or "The Avenger of the Delaware." According to one legend, Tom avenged himself on various Indians for the murder of his father by Mushwink, an Indian, whom Tom later met and killed. One legend tells how he tricked the Indians. As he was splitting a log, he found himself surrounded by Indians. They were ready to take him back to camp and torture him, but Tom asked them if they would help him split the log first. The Indians pulled at the log, but instead of driving the wedge in farther, Tom knocked it out and slaughtered the Indians with the ax.

Tonacatecutli (lord of our existence). In Aztec mythology, bisexual god who was infinite and intangible. Tonacatecutli was also known as Tzinteotl (god of the beginning), Tonaca Cihuatl (queen of our existence), Xochiquetzal (beautiful rose), Citlallicue (the star- skirted, or the milky way), Citlaltonac (the star that warms, or the morning), Chicomecoatl (the seven serpents), and Chicomexochit (seven flames).
Variant spelling: Tonacateotle.

Tonapa. In Bolivian Indian folklore, culture hero. Tonapa was a blue-eyed man who came from the north with five disciples. He preached against war, drunkenness, and polygamy. Makuri, a cruel tyrant, roused the people against Tonapa's preaching, and they set his house on fire while he was sleeping. He escaped but was later caught by Makuri, who martyred the disciples and left Tonapa for dead.

According to Ramos Gavilan, writing in 1621, Tonapa's body was placed in a boat that "sailed away with such speed that those who had tried so cruelly to kill him were left behind in terror and astonishment for they knew the lake had no current."

Tonapa was identified with St. Bartholomew in some Christian-Indian legends because he carried a cross on his back as he went to see Makuri, and St. Bartholomew was martyred on a cross. Scholars believe Tonapa to be a version of Tupan (Toupan) the thunder god of the Botocudo Indians of Brazil.
Variant spellings: Thunupa, Taapac.

Tonatiuh. In Aztec mythology, a sun god, fourth in a series of sun gods. Tonatiuh gave strength to warriors, receiving them along with women who died in childbirth, into his paradise, which was identical with Tollan (place of the seed), the Aztec paradise

where crops grew in abundance. Offerings of human hearts and blood were made to the god. In some Aztec accounts he was thought of as an eagle who flew near the sun with the souls of the heroic dead.

Tontuu. In Finno-Ugric mythology, spirit of a somewhat capricious nature who watches over the welfare of a household, rewarding its members with corn and money.

Tony Beaver. In American folklore, comic hero of the West Virginia lumberjacks whose antics often take place in the Cumberland Mountains. In one tale he built a wagon cart that covered ten acres of land to carry watermelons. When the wagon broke, causing melons to fall into the Eel River, his friends each straddled a seed and rowed away. Tony is credited with inventing peanut brittle. Once when a river was overflowing, Tony took some molasses and peanuts, throwing them into the river to stop it up. Tony Beaver's tales are told in Margaret Prescott Montague's *Up Eel River*.

Too-Roo-Dun. In Australian mythology, an evil water spirit who seizes his victims and eats them.

Torongoi and Edji. In Siberian mythology, the first man and woman.

Both Torongoi and Edji were created with fur on their bodies to keep them warm. They were told they could eat fruit from branches that pointed toward the sunrise but were not allowed to eat from branches that pointed to the sunset. To help the couple, God set a dog and a snake to bite the devil if he came. When God returned to heaven, the devil came and crept into the skin of the sleeping serpent and tempted the woman with the forbidden fruit. She persuaded her husband to eat it too. They both became so frightened afterward that the fur fell off their bodies. When God came down from heaven, Torongoi and Edji hid. God asked them what happened. Torongoi said Edji made him eat the fruit; Edji said the snake made her eat the fruit; the snake said the devil was inside him; and the dog said he had seen nothing.

Tortoise and the Birds, The. Aesopic fable found in various collections throughout the world.

A tortoise became dissatisfied with his lowly life when he beheld so many of his neighbors the birds in the clouds, and he thought that if he could but once get up into the air, he could soar with the best of them. One day he called on an eagle and offered him all of the treasures of the ocean if he would only teach him to fly.

The eagle tried to decline the task, assuring him that the thing was not only absurd but impossible; but being further pressed by the entreaties and promises of the tortoise, he at length consented to do the best he could. He took the tortoise up to a great height and loosed his hold on him. "Now, then!" cried the eagle. But before the tortoise could answer a word, he fell on a rock and was dashed to pieces.

The legend that the Greek dramatist Aeschylus was killed when a tortoise was dropped on his bald head by an eagle is believed to have derived from this fable. The fable appears in the Indian collection the *Kacchapa Jataka*, in which a tortoise, holding a stick in its mouth, is carried by two birds. It falls when it opens its mouth to rebuke the birds that are scoffing at it. Buddha cites it as a lesson to a talkative king.

2902

Totem. In world religion and mythology, a North American Indian (Ojibwa) word for a plant, animal, or other natural object that is revered by a group because of its relationship to the group, which often believes it is descended from the totem. People of the same totem are forbidden to marry, and the totem animal or plant is not to be eaten except at certain ritual times. Some tribes tattoo the totem on their bodies, make masks, or carve totem poles. Frazer's *Totemism and Exogamy* (1910; 4 volumes) and Freud's *Totem and Taboo* (1918), which is based in part on Frazer, offer elaborate theories on the origin of religion and various cultic practices.

2903

Tou Mu. In Chinese mythology, goddess of the North Star, who is portrayed on a lotus. She is accompanied by two attendants, Yu Pi and Tao Fu. Sometimes she is seen with the star gods of longevity and affluence.

2904

Town Mouse and the Country Mouse, The. Aesopic fable found in various European collections.

A country mouse who had a friend in town invited him, for old acquaintance sake, to pay him a visit in the country. Though plain and rough and somewhat frugal in his nature, the country mouse opened his heart and store in honor of an old friend. There was not a carefully stored-up morsel that he did not produce from his larder—peas and barley, cheese parings and nuts—to please the palate of his city-bred guest.

The town mouse, however, turned up his long nose at the rough country fare. "How is it, my friend," he exclaimed, "that you can endure the boredom of living like a toad in a hole? You can't really prefer these solitary rocks and woods to the excitement of the city. You are wasting your time out here in the wilderness. A mouse, you know, does not live forever; one must make the most of life while it lasts. So come with me and I'll show you life and the town."

In the end the country mouse allowed himself to be persuaded, and the two friends set out together on their journey to town. It was late in the evening when they crept stealthily into the city, and midnight before they reached the great house where the town mouse lived.

On the table of the splendid banquet room were the remains of a lavish feast. It was now the turn of the city mouse to play host. He ran to and fro to supply all of his guest's wants. He pressed dish after dish and dainty after dainty on his friend, as though he were waiting on a king. The country mouse, for his part, pretended to feel quite at home and blessed the good fortune that had wrought such a change in his way of life.

But in the midst of his enjoyment, just as he was beginning to feel contempt for his frugal life in the country, the sound of barking and growling could be heard outside the door.

"What is that?" said the country mouse.

"Oh, that is only the master's dogs," replied the town mouse.

"Only!" replied the visitor in dismay. "I can't say that I like music with my dinner."

At that moment the door flew open and a party of revelers, together with two huge dogs, burst into the room. The frightened friends jumped from the table and concealed themselves in a far corner of the room. Finally, when things seemed quiet, the country mouse stole out from his hiding place and, bidding his friend good-bye, whispered in his ear: "This fine way of living may do for those who like it. But give me my barley bread in the security of my country home in preference to your dainty fare partaken with fear and trembling."

Moral: A crust eaten in peace is better than a banquet partaken in anxiety.

Horace, in his *Satires* (book 2), tells the fable to point out that wealth brings along with it many problems, though one wonders if his readers were convinced. La Fontaine also tells the tale in his collection of fables, though he substitutes rats for mice.

2905

Tree and the Reed, The. Aesopic fable found in various collections throughout the world.

"Well, little one," said a tree to a reed, "why do you not plant your feet deeply in the ground, and raise your head boldly in the air as I do?"

"I am contented with my lot," said the reed. "I may not be so grand as you, but I think I am safer."

"Safe!" sneered the tree. "Who shall pluck me up by the roots or bow my head to the ground?"

That night a hurricane arose and tore the tree from its roots and cast it to the ground, a useless log. The reed, however, bent with the force of the wind during the hurricane and stood upright again when the storm was over.

Moral: Obscurity often brings safety.

In the great Indian epic poem *The Mahabharata*, a similar fable is told in which the sea complains that the rivers bring down to it oaks, but not reeds. Shakespeare, in *Cymbeline* (4:2), seems to refer to the fable in the dirge: "To thee the reed is as the oak," and Wordsworth's poem *The Oak and the Broom* develops the subject in his typical moralistic manner, ending with the oak being "whirled" far away while

The little careless broom was left
To live for many a day.

2906

Tree of Jesse. In Christian lore, tree or root of Jesse, an Old Testament ancestor of Christ. This is frequently seen in medieval art, particularly in stained-glass windows. According to the genealogy in the Gospel of Matthew (1:6), Jesse, father of King David, started the royal line that ended in Christ, the Messiah. Representation of the tree of Jesse in medieval art (usually shown sprouting from the loins of a reclining Jesse) is based on the prophecy of Isaiah (11:1–2): "And there shall come forth a rod out of the stem of Jesse, and a Branch shall grow out of his roots: And the Spirit of the Lord shall rest upon him."

Saint Ambrose interprets the passage thus: "The root is the family of the Jews, the stem Mary, the flower of Mary is Christ."

2907

Trickster. In world mythology and folklore, an amoral, bisexual being—human, animal, or a combination—who is both a creator-hero and a destroyer; knowing neither good nor evil, yet often being responsible for both in the world. The trickster lacks a moral consciousness and may represent one of humankind's earliest attempts to deal with the problem of good and evil. The trickster often suffers from his own pranks and is punished in various myths, perhaps because a morally conscious mankind must resolve the problem of unpunished crime. In North American Indian mythology, for example, Coyote is a trickster, whereas Spider is the trickster in certain regions of West Africa; and in Dahomey, Legba, youngest son of the creator god, is a trickster. In Greek mythology Prometheus is a trickster, fooling Zeus, then paying a price for his misdeed. In Norse mythology, Loki is the trickster, often persuading both gods and people to behave in a manner in direct opposition to their best interests.

In general, the character of the trickster is erotic (in one North American Indian myth he extends his penis across a river to rape a girl on the other side), greedy, imitative, stupid, clever, pretentious, and deceitful. In one North American Indian myth he casts the vote that people must die, and then, seeing his own son die, is incapable of bringing him back to life. Often the trickster dies in the tale but is alive in the next story or is brought back to life. In movie cartoons Bugs Bunny and Daffy Duck are the two best modern examples of the trickster. They are blown up in explosions, run over by trains, and catapulted into outer space, but they emerge unscathed and victorious.

2908

Tri-loka (three worlds). In Hinduism, the three divisions of the universe. An early division was Dyu-loka (bright realm, the sky), Antar-loka (middle realm, the atmosphere) and Bhur-loka (beings realm, the earth). The notion of separate heavens and hells does not occur before the sixth century B.C.E. at the earliest. The three principal gods over the three realms were Surya, Indra, and Agni.

2909

Trimurti (having three forms). In Hinduism, a triad of gods made up of Brahma, Vishnu, and Shiva. The concept, however, is not typical of everyday Hinduism.

2910

Tri-ratna (triple jewel). In Buddhism, the Buddha, the Dharma, and the Sangha. In Buddhist art the Tri-ratna is sometimes portrayed as three large egg-shaped gems, with the narrow ends directed downward and the central member placed slightly above the other two. The whole composition is surrounded by flames. Buddhist services commonly begin by taking refuge in the Tri-ratna.

2911

Trisiras (three-headed). In Hindu mythology, a demon killed by the storm god Indra; he symbolizes heat, cold, and sweating. Trisiras is also used as a name for Kubera, god of wealth.

2912

Tristram and Iseult (sad, tumult). In medieval legend, two lovers whose romance became associated

Tristram and Iseult (A. Beardsley)

with the Arthurian cycle of legends. Tristram's legend is found in nearly all medieval European languages. He was the son of Blanchefleur, sister of King Mark of Cornwall, and Meliadus. The father died in battle at the hands of Morgan when Tristram was born. In another account his mother died in childbirth. Kurvenal (Rohand, Rual), a faithful friend of Blanchefleur, took the child and reared him as his own. Tristram grew up without knowing who his real parents were. He became a knight, a hunter, and a harp player. One day he boarded a Norwegian vessel and eventually landed in Cornwall. He found his way to King Mark's court, and the king informed him of his parents and their fate. After hearing the story of his father's death at the hands of Morgan in battle, he determined to avenge it. He immediately set out, slew Morgan, and recovered his father's lands at Lyonesse, which he entrusted to Kurvenal. When he returned to Cornwall, he found that King Mark had to pay Morold, brother of the King of Ireland, a tribute of 300 pounds of silver and tin and 300 youths to be handed over to slavery. Tristram challenged Morold to combat. Morold, who was a giant and had a poisoned sword, accepted. Morold's sword pierced Tristram's side. Morold told Tristram that if he surrendered he would help him obtain balsam from Iseult (Isolde, Ysolde) to cure him. Tristram would not yield but, in a burst of energy, attacked and slew Morold. He cut through Morold's helmet and pierced the giant's skull, which was so hard that a fragment of his sword remained embedded within the wound.

The people of Cornwall were delighted, and King Mark, who had no son, proclaimed Tristram his heir. Tristram's wound, however, would not heal. He decided to seek Iseult's aid. Knowing that she would not help him if she knew his identity, he arrived in Ireland calling himself Tantris, a minstrel. Iseult, charmed by his music, cured him of his wound. Tristram remained at the Irish court for some time, spending many hours with Iseult. After some months had passed, Tristram returned to Cornwall, where he related to King Mark the story of his cure. He also told of the beauty of the young Iseult, and King Mark expressed a desire to marry her. On the advice of the courtiers, who were jealous of Tristram and hoped he would fail in the mission, the young hero was sent to Ireland to ask for Iseult's hand and to escort her safely to Cornwall.

When Tristram arrived in Dublin, the people were being threatened by a dragon, and he realized that the best way to win Iseult for King Mark would be to kill the dragon. After a fierce battle he slew the monster, cut out the dragon's tongue, and placed it in his pocket. He had gone only a few steps when he fell down exhausted. A few moments later another knight, seeing the dead dragon and the body of a knight nearby, cut off the dragon's head and went back to the palace claiming he had killed the dragon. However, Iseult and her mother did not believe the knight and went to the scene. They found Tristram with the dragon's tongue in his pocket.

They took him to the palace to nurse him back to health. While the young Iseult sat beside her sleeping patient, she idly drew his sword from its scabbard. Suddenly her eye caught the broken blade, a piece of which had been found in her Uncle Morold's skull. She was about to kill Tristram when her mother stopped her, saying Tristram atoned for the deed by saving them from the dragon. When Tristram had recovered, he challenged the lying knight, won, and then asked for the hand of Iseult for King Mark. Iseult was stunned because she had believed Tristram had come for her hand for himself. But she obeyed her father and prepared to leave. To help save her daughter, her mother brewed a magic love potion, which was put in a golden cup and entrusted to Brangwaine, Iseult's attendant. The potion was to be given to Iseult and King Mark on their wedding day. On the journey Tristram entertained Iseult with songs. One day, after singing, he asked for a drink. She went to the cupboard and took the magic potion, not knowing what it was. The two drank from the cup, and the potion aroused in them a passionate love for each other. Still, they resolved to hide their love and continue as planned. Iseult landed in Cornwall and married King Mark. Brangwaine, who knew all that had happened, tried to shield her mistress.

In time the love of the two was known, and Meliadus, a knight who hated Tristram, told King Mark. The queen was publicly accused and compelled to prove her innocence by undergoing the ordeal of fire or by taking a public oath that she had shown favor to none but King Mark. On her way to where the ordeal was to take place, Iseult was carried across a stream by Tristram disguised as a beggar and, at his request, kissed him in reward for his service.

When Iseult was called on to take the oath before the judges, she could swear that, with the exception of a beggar, no other man than the king had received her favor. Tristram, however, went mad. When he recovered, he went to the court of King Arthur, but he was again wounded, this time by a poisoned arrow. Again, he could not be cured. Afraid to go again to Iseult for balsam, Tristram went to Brittany, where another Iseult—Iseult of the White Hands—equally skilled in medicine, nursed him back to health. Iseult of the White Hands believed that Tristram loved her as much as she loved him because she heard him sing of Iseult and did not know another existed with the same name. Tristram married Iseult of the White Hands, but he did not love her or show any signs of affection. He could not forget Iseult of Cornwall. When his brother-in- law Ganhardin discovered the truth, he forgave Tristram and asked him to take him to Cornwall, for Ganhardin had fallen in love with a portrait of Brangwaine. On their way the two knights aided King Arthur in freeing himself from the Lady of the Lake. They also carried off Iseult of Cornwall to Lancelot's castle of Joyeuse Garde. There Iseult of Cornwall remained with Guinever.

Once again Tristram was wounded. This time Iseult of the White Hands could not cure him, and Iseult of Cornwall was called on. Kurvenal, who went to fetch Iseult of Cornwall, said he would change the black sails of the vessel for white if his mission was successful. Tristram now watched impatiently for the returning sail but died just as it came in sight. When Iseult of Cornwall arrived and saw his body, she too died. Both bodies were carried to Cornwall, where they were buried in separate

graves by order of King Mark. But a vine grew from Tristram's grave to Iseult's. It was cut down three times but always grew back.

Tristram's legend has inspired numerous poems, such as *Tristan und Isolde* by Gottfried von Strassburg, *Tristram and Iseult* by Matthew Arnold, *Tristram of Lyonesse* by Swinburne, part of *Idylls of the King* by Tennyson, and *Tristram* by Edwin Arlington Robinson. The most important musical work about Tristram, having a great effect on all 19th-century musical development, is Wagner's *Tristan und Isolde*.

Variant spellings: Tristran, Trystan, Ysolde, Ysonde, Yseult, Isold, Isolte, Yseulte, Isot, Izot.

2913

Triton (being in her third day). In Greek mythology, merman, half-man, half-fish; son of Poseidon and Amphitrite; brother of Albion, Charybdis, Benthesicyme and Rhode. Triton appears in Vergil's *Aeneid* (book 6), in which she drowns Misenus, a human, for daring to challenge him to a musical contest on conchs. Ovid's *Metamorphoses* (book 2) has him ap-

Iseult (A. Beardsley)

pear in the story of Deucalion, the Flood myth, in which he blows his horn or conch shell to summon the waters to retreat. In European art Triton appears in Bernini's Trevi Fountain, and Triton Fountain in the Piazza Barberini in Rome. Wordsworth cites Triton in his *Sonnet* (1807), in which he wishes to "hear old Triton blow his wreathed horn."

2914

Troilus and Cressida. In medieval legend, two lovers; he was faithful, but she was not.

The medieval tale developed out of Greco-Roman mythology. Troilus was the son of King Priam of Troy. In Vergil's *Aeneid* (book 1) Troilus is said to have thrown down his arms during a battle and to have fled in his chariot. He was transfixed with a spear thrown by Achilles. In medieval legend he had a love affair with Cressida, an older Trojan woman. Chaucer's long narrative poem *Troilus and Criseyde* is partly based on the *Filostrato* of Boccaccio. Troilus, a prince of the royal house of Troy, scoffs at love and lovers until one day he sees the beautiful Criseyde, a young widow, at the temple of the Palladium. He falls madly in love with her. Pandarus, her uncle and Troilus's friend, coaxes his secret from the timid youth and promises to help him with his niece. Pandarus finds Criseyde sitting with the women, poring over tales of knights and chivalry. Pandarus tells Criseyde that Troilus is madly in love with her. After he leaves, a ballad sung by Antigone sets Criseyde to daydreaming. At this moment, Troilus rides by her window, returning from a battle with the Greeks, amid the shouts of the people. The next day Pandarus returns with a letter, which Criseyde at first refuses to receive but at last consents to answer. Pandarus persuades his niece to go to the palace on a plausible pretext and so contrives to have the lovers meet. He next invites Criseyde to supper at his home, telling her that Troilus is away and cannot be there. Criseyde is induced to spend the night at her uncle's house because of a storm. Pandarus comes to her room with the news of Troilus's unexpected arrival. She consents to see him, and later the two make love.

Criseyde's father is a traitor in the Greek camp. He sends for his daughter in an exchange of prisoners. The lovers are heartbroken at the parting, but Criseyde, with vows that "shake the throned gods," swears to return in ten days. She soon discovers that no pretext for return will avail because her father, a priest, has foreknowledge that Troy is destined to be destroyed by the Greeks. Diomede, a young Greek, pays court to Criseyde and wins her, though she grieves for Troilus. But, there is no need for her to repent; she will make amends by being true to her new lover. When Troilus can no

longer continue to believe Criseyde is faithful, he seeks death in battle and is slain by Achilles.

In English the name Criseyde became a byword for faithlessness in love. Shakespeare took up the story in his play *Troilus and Cressida*, with licentiousness as his main theme. William Walton's opera *Troilus and Cressida* is based on Chaucer's work.

2915

Trojanu. In Slavic mythology, a spirit of darkness who possessed wax wings. He was believed to be the spirit of the Roman emperor Trajan, who conquered the Dacians in the first century C.E. Often in mythology a feared enemy was worshiped as a demon god in the hope of appeasing his anger. Trojanu is cited in *The Lay of Igor's Army*.

Variant spelling: Troiaw.

2916

Troll (to tread, giant, monster). In Scandinavian folklore, a dwarf who lives in caves and hills. Originally, trolls were giants. In general they are skillful craftsmen but are not smart.

2917

Trophonius (increaser of sales). In Greek mythology, underworld god; son of Apollo, whose oracle at Lebadeia in Boeotia, between Athens and Delphi, was associated with the deities of the underworld. Pausanias' *Description of Greece* (book 9) tells of the elaborate ritual associated with the god. After ritual preparation worshipers were sent down into a hole and swept along by an underground river. When they came out at the end they were in a daze, having heard mysterious voices. A short period of rest was required for them to regain their senses. Trophonius also is the name of a brother of Agamedes, son of Apollo, who built temples at Delphi. Apollo rewarded them with a peaceful death. Some accounts say both the hero and god are one and the same, the god being a deified mortal.

2918

Troy. Ancient Phrygian city, main site of the Trojan War, also called Ilion (Latin, Ilium); believed to be located near present day Hissarlik, in north-west Turkey, some four miles from the Dardanelles. In Greek mythology the city was originally founded by Dardanus, who called it Dardania. He was succeeded by his son Erichthonius, who was succeeded by Tros, who had three sons. One son, Ilus, renamed the city Ilion, and later it was called Troy. In the city was the sacred Palladium, a cult wooden image of the goddess Athena. As long as the city retained the image, no harm could come to it. The image was taken by the Greeks during the Trojan War when they invaded the city and destroyed it. For centuries it was believed that Troy was the invention of Homer in his *Iliad* and never actually existed. Heinrich Schliemann, however, believed in Homer's account and went in search of the city. Between 1870 and 1873 he discovered what he believed, and present-day scholars agree, to be the site of Troy as represented in Homer.

Ts'ai Shen, god of riches

2919

Ts'ai Shen. In Chinese legend, the deified sage Pi Kan, worshiped as the god of wealth.

Pi Kan, who is believed to have lived in the 12th century B.C.E., was noted for his profound wisdom. His relative, the emperor Chou, was reproved by the sage for his wickedness. The emperor became so angry that he ordered Pi Kan's heart to be torn out. He had always heard that the heart of a wise man had seven orifices, and he wished to know how wise Pi Kan actually was.

Ts'ai Shen is worshiped throughout China, where there are numerous home shrines and temples dedicated to him. In art there are two forms of Ts'ai Shen, a civil form and a military form.

2920

Tsao Kuo-chiu. 930–999 C.E. In Chinese Taoist mythology, one of the Pa-Hsien, the Eight Immortals. Of noble birth, he is portrayed in court dress, holding a pair of castanets in one hand.

2921

Tsao Shen. In Chinese legend, a deified mortal, worshiped as the god of the hearth or kitchen. In homes,

Pi Kan

pictures of Tsao Shen are placed near the stove. He is worshiped with offerings of meat, fruit, and wine in an annual ceremony. After the ceremony is finished, the picture is taken down and burned, together with paper money presented to the god. Then a new picture of the god is placed on the wall for the coming year. Tsao Shen is portrayed in court costume.

2922

Ts'ien K'eng. In Chinese legend, a deified mortal, who lived chiefly on mother-of-pearl. He is said to have been the orphan son or grandson of the em-

Tsao Kuo-chiu

Tsao Shen

peror, being 767 years old at the end of the Yin dynasty1123 B.C.E. He is portrayed as an old man reclining on the waves because he could sleep in the water for a day at a time. He also could lie motionless for a year until covered with dust an inch thick. After living 150 years he looked no more than 20 years old.

2923

Tu (erect, to stand). In Polynesian mythology, war god, called Ku in Hawaii, to whom human sacrifices were made. A whole family of gods called Ku existed in Hawaii.

2924

Tuan Mac Carell. Sixth century C.E. In Celtic mythology, Irish chief who went through a series of metamorphoses. Tuan Mac Carell's legend is told in the *Book of the Dun Cow*, a manuscript dating from about the 11th century. He tells some Christian monks that he has lived hundreds of years, being a descendant of the first man to set foot in Ireland, Partholan. In his various transformations he was a deer, a boar, an eagle, and a salmon. In his last form he was eaten by Queen Carell and was born again as a man.
Variant spelling: Tuan Mac Cairill.

2925

Tuatha de Danann (people of the goddess Dana). In Celtic mythology, the gods and the people or descendants of the goddess Danu, who was a mother goddess and culture heroine. The Tuatha de Danann invaded Ireland from a magic cloud, giving battle to

the earlier inhabitants, the Firbolgs. They pushed the Firbolgs back, taking the best part of the country for themselves. Then the Tuatha de Danann battled and defeated the Fomoro, who had replaced the Firbolgs, but they in turn were defeated by the incoming Milesians, who deified, worshiped, and enshrined the Tuatha de Danann in underground kingdoms.

2926

Tuesco. In Germanic mythology, a primeval god who issued from the earth, according to the Roman writer Tacitus in his *Germania*.

2927

Tulugal. In Australian mythology, man's shadow, which is cared for by the creator god Daramulum.

2928

Tu-lu'kau-guk. In Eskimo mythology (Unalit peoples at Bering Strait), raven father, creator of everything.

2929

Tumudurere. In Melanesian mythology, god of the dead in New Guinea; he rules Hiyoyoa, which lies under the ocean near Maivara on Milne Bay.

2930

Tunghat. In Eskimo mythology (Unalit peoples at Bering Strait), supernatural beings whose spirit power is controlled by shamans.

2931

Tuonetar. In the epic poem *The Kalevala* (rune 16), daughter of Tuoni (Death).

Once the culture hero Vainamoinen constructed a magic boat but discovered he could not complete the work without the proper magic words. He went in search of them in Tuonela, the land of the dead. When he came to the River of Death, he saw "Death's stumpy daughter," Tuonetar, washing clothes. She asked him how he expected to cross the river without dying. He offered her various lies, which she detected, and finally told her the truth. She then helped ferry him across the River of Death, but he did not find the magic words. He was informed, however, that the primeval giant Antero Vipunen possessed them. He then went in search of the giant and eventually obtained the magic words.

Tuonetar is also known as Tuonen Tytto (death's maiden) as well as Loviatar (half-blind daughter of Tuoni).

2932

Tuoni (death). In Finnish mythology, god of death who rules over Tuonela, the land of the dead, sometimes called Manala or Ulappala (wasteland).

The land of the dead was reached by crossing a black bridge that spanned black water. In the river were *kynsikoski* (rapids), that made the way treacherous. On the black water glided a majestic swan. In his *Four Legends for Orchestra* Sibelius has two movements that deal with Tuonela. "The Swan of Tuonela" evokes, with English horn, the majestic swan, and "Lemminkainen in Tuonela" portrays the death of Lemminkainen at the hands of a herdsman after the hero attempted to kill the swan. Lemminkainen is murdered and his body borne on the icy waters to Tuonela.

Tuoni is also called Mana or Kalma (grave).

2933
Turong. In Australian mythology, mischievous spirits who play tricks on hunters.

2934
Tursas (giant). In the Finnish epic poem *The Kalevala* (rune 2), a water spirit who aided the culture hero Vainamoinen in sowing the earth.

At one time Vainamoinen found that although all of the seeds he planted made a rich forest, there was no oak, the "tree of heaven." The reason was that the oak was asleep inside the acorn. The culture hero wondered how he could magically conjure it out of its hiding place. After Vainamoinen consulted five water maidens, the water spirit Tursas arose out of the waves. He burned hay that the water maidens had raked together and planted the acorn in the ashes of the hay. Quickly a tree arose that was so large it blotted out the sun. Terrified at what had happened, Vainamoinen wanted to destroy the oak. He called on his mother, Luonnotar, who sent a pygmy, armed with copper, who transformed himself into a giant and cut down the tree, scattering its trunk to the east, its top to the west, its leaves to the south, and its branches to the north. The chips from the fallen oak were later used to make magic arrows.

2935
Turtle and Tortoise. In world folklore, the turtle and tortoise are often confused. In Chinese mythology the tortoise represents the watery element, the Yin principle, and is called the Black Warrior. In medieval Christian symbolism it represents modesty. In Japanese mythology the tortoise or turtle represents longevity and good luck. In Greek mythology the tortoise was sacred to Aphrodite and Hermes, and in Roman mythology to Venus and Mercury. The well-known fable *The Hare and the Tortoise* is best known for its moral tag: "Slow and steady wins the race."

2936
Tutankhamen (the living image of Amun). 1361–1352 B.C.E. Egyptian pharaoh whose tomb was discovered in 1922 by Howard Carter and Lord Carnarvon in the Valley of the Kings in Egypt.

Tutankhamen was the successor of Akhenaten. The young pharaoh was Akhenaten's son-in-law, or possibly his son, brother or close relation. Originally, the pharaoh was called Tutankhaten (gracious of life is Aten), which indicated that he was a follower of the cult of Aten, the sun disk. He changed his name to Tutankhamen when he came to power because the Theban priests had restored the worship of Amun-Ra, which had been rejected by Aknenaten, who worshiped Aten. The wife of Tutankhamen, following her husband's move, changed her name, Ankhensen-paaten, to Ankhesenamen, indicating her allegiance to the god Amun-Ra. The young pharaoh was probably murdered. He was succeeded by a minister, Ay. Treasures from his tomb have been displayed throughout the world.

2937
Tutugals. In Australian mythology, spirits who punish children for being evil.

2938
Tuulikki (wind). In Finnish mythology, the wind spirit, daughter of Tapio, the forest god, and his wife, Meilikki.
Variant spelling: Tellervo.

2939
Twashtri (architect). In Hindu mythology, artisan of the gods. Twashtri carries a great iron ax, forging thunderbolts for the storm god, Indra. He is invoked to bestow offspring and forms husband and wife for each other while still in the womb. He also develops the seminal germ in the womb and is the former or shaper of all human and animal life.
Variant spelling: Tvastr.

2940
Twe. In African mythology, a spirit god who inhabits Lake Bosomtive in Ghana. This lake occasionally loses all of its water under the drying rays of the sun. Twe emerged from the lake one day and wished to make love to an old woman. The woman at first refused him, saying that it would be difficult for her to find water and food for a child if she were to become pregnant. Twe assured her that all she had to do was bang on the edge of the lake and fish would come to her. Hearing this, she agreed to their union and bore Twe a son named Twe Adodo. Twe's son was to become the founder of a clan that believes the

sprirt of Twe, his father, helps them whenever they go fishing.

Two Brothers, Tale of

Two Brothers, Tale of. Egyptian literary folktale, also known as "Anpu and Bata," written about 1225 B.C.E.

Anpu and Bata were brothers. Anpu, the older, was married; Bata, the younger, worked for him in the field, becoming so proficient at his labor that it was said the spirit of God was in him. Bata was so good at his work, in fact, that even the cattle spoke to him, and he understood them. One day while the two brothers were working in the field, Anpu sent Bata back to the farm to get some grain. Bata did as he was told, but before he could return Anpu's wife tried to seduce him. When he rejected her advances, she told her husband that Bata had tried to rape her. Anpu became enraged and set out to kill his younger brother, but Bata escaped with the help of the sun god Ra. The two brothers later met, and to prove his innocence Bata swore an oath and cut off a piece of his flesh and cast it into the water. After numerous adventures Bata died and was reborn again as the pharaoh, and Anpu became heir to the throne, thus reversing the order of primogeniture.

The attempted seduction of a virtuous youth by an older woman is found in numerous mythologies. Among the most famous examples are those of Potiphar's wife in Genesis (39:7–20), who attempted to seduce Joseph, and Hippolytus and Phaedra in Greek mythology. According to some scholars, the "Tale of Two Brothers" is based on a myth of two gods— Anubis (Anpu) and Bet (Bata). Anubis was the well-known jackal god of Egypt, and Bet was a pastoral god, whose cult image was a mummified ram or bull. There is little agreement as to what the tale actually signifies, although most scholars agree that it served for entertainment rather than for religious or moral purposes.

Two Pots, The

Two Pots, The. Aesopic fable found in various collections throughout the world.

Two pots, one of brass and one of earthenware, had been left on the bank of a river. When the tide rose they both floated off down the stream. The earthenware pot tried its best to keep aloof from the brass one, which cried out: "Fear nothing, friend, I will not strike you."

"But I may come in contact with you," said the other, "if I come too close; and whether I hit you or you hit me, I shall suffer for it."

Moral: The strong and the weak cannot keep company.

An allusion to the fable occurs in the Old Testament Apocrypha, "Have no fellowship with one that is mightier and richer than thyself: for how agree the kettle and earthen pot together?" (Eccles 13:2). There is a Talmudic proverb: "If a jug fall on a stone, woe to the jug; if a stone fall on a jug, woe to the jug."

Two-Toe Tom

Two-Toe Tom. In American folklore, a 14-foot alligator, in Alabama marsh country near Montgomery, who ate people and animals. When his pond was dynamited by Pap Haines, the monster escaped by an underground route and later ate Haines's 12-year-old daughter.

Typhon

Typhon (hurricane, hot wind, smoke). In Greek mythology, a monster, son of Gaea and Tartarus, with a hundred snake heads that spit out fire. He attacked Zeus, who now was the ruler after he had defeated Cronus, his father. Zeus hurled thunderbolts at Typhon and hurled him down to the Underworld. Typhon was said to be buried under Mount Etna, according to some accounts. Before he was imprisoned, however, he fathered with Echidna a host of monsters, including Cerberus, Orthus, the Nemean Lion, the Sphinx, the Chimera, and the Lernean Hydra. Typhon appears in or is cited in Hesiod's *Theogony*, Homer's *Iliad* (book 2), Aeschylus's *Prometheus Bound* and *Seven Against Thebes*, Vergil's *Aeneid*, (book 9), and Ovid's *Metamorphoses* (book 5).

Tyr

Tyr (god shining). In Norse mythology, a war god son of Odin and Firgga. He lost one hand when he placed it in the mouth of the Fenrir wolf. Tyr was the patron of the sword and athletic sports. The *Prose Edda* describes Tyr as "the most daring and intrepid of all the gods. 'Tis he who dispenses valour in war, hence warriors do well to invoke him . . . . He is not regarded as a peacemaker among men." Tuesday was named after the god. In Anglo-Saxon mythology, Tyr is called Tiw, Tiv, or Ziv, or identified with their god Saxnot. During the Roman period Tyr was called Mars Thingsus and associated with an assembly hall where men met to settle disputes. Tyr's name is also given as Tîwaz.

Tzitsimine

Tzitsimine. In Aztec mythology, spirits of women who died in childbirth and who returned to plague the living. They appeared skull-faced and brought children sickness and injury, as well as contagious diseases. Sometimes a Tzitsimine would appear sitting on a lonely rock, weeping. When a passerby would ask what was wrong, she would display her skull face, frightening the person almost to death.

U

Ubshukinna (chamber of destinies). In Near Eastern mythology (Babylonian), heavenly council hall of the gods. It was reproduced in the earthly temple complex, where the Zag-Muk, the great New Year celebration, was held. The ceremony honored the hero god Marduk, who on that day told the destiny of men for the coming year from the tablets of fate. *Variant spellings*: Ubshukenna; Upshukkinaku.

2948

Uccaihsravas (neighing loudly, long-eared). In Hindu mythology, the horse of the storm god, Indra.

2949

Ueuecoyotl (the old, old coyote). In Aztec mythology, god associated with sex, useless expenditure on ornament, and unexpected pleasures—all three condemned by the puritanical Aztecs.

2950

Ugolino, Count. 13th century. In Italian history and legend, a leader of the Guelphs in Pisa. Ugolino was raised to the highest honors, but Archbishop Ruggieri incited the Pisans against his rule. His castle was attacked, two of his grandsons were killed, and the count and his two sons and two surviving grandsons were imprisoned in a tower; its keys were then flung into the Arno River. All food was withheld from the group. On the fourth day, Ugolino's son Gaddo died, and by the sixth day his son Anselm and the two grandchildren died. Last of all the count died. The prison cell has since been called "The Tower of Famine." Dante's *Divine Comedy* (Inferno) portrays Ugolino as devouring the head of Archbishop Ruggieri while frozen in the lake of ice in hell. In *The Canterbury Tales* Chaucer has the monk briefly tell the story of *Hugeline of Pise.*

2951

Uguku and Tskili. In North American Indian mythology (Cherokee), the hoot owl and the horned owl, who went down to the hollow of a tree where the first fire burned. It burned so fiercely that the smoke nearly blinded Uguku and Tskili, and the wind carried the smoke, making white rings around their eyes.

2952

Uixtocihuatl. In Aztec mythology, salt goddess whose festival Tecuilhuitontli, was held on 2 June. A woman was sacrificed in her honor at the pyramid of the rain god, Tlaloc.

2953

Ujigami. In Japanese Shinto mythology, tutelary or special guarding deity of a clan or locality.

2954

Ukko (old man). In Finnish mythology, sky god, often used for God. Ukko replaced the earlier Jumala, a semiabstract term for God, who was sometimes addressed as Kuoja (creator). Ukko is sometimes called Pauanne (thunder), indicating that his role is similar to that of Zeus in Greek and Thor in Norse mythology. He is the most frequently evoked god in the Finnish epic poem *The Kalevala*. He restored fire when Louhi, the evil mistress of Pohjola, the Northland, stole the sun, moon, and fire. Seeing the land plunged into darkness, Ukko struck lightning and sent it down to earth, where it was swallowed by a pike in Lake Alue. Burning inside, the pike swam about madly until it was swallowed by a larger fish which in turn was caught by the culture hero Vainamoinen, who restored the fire to his people.

Ukko was worshiped in a ceremony called Ukko's Wedding or Ukko's Chest, at which birchbark chests containing sacrifices such as sheep were placed on a holy mountain to be eaten by the god. Ukko ate his share at night, and the people ate the rest the next day. One festival of the god was described by the Christian bishop Agricola in the 16th century. He found that "many shameful things were done" in honor of the great god. The bishop was obviously referring to a sexual orgy that took place after the people had drunk "to excess." Eventually, Ukko's ceremonies were absorbed into Christian ones, and Christ and St. John were evoked instead of Ukko.

Jean Sibelius' *The Origin of Fire* or *Ukko the Firemaker*, based on rune 47 of *The Kalevala*, depicts the re-creation of fire. Scored for baritone, male chorus, and orchestra, the work is, according to music critic Cecil Gray, of "epic power and grandeur."

2955

Ukuhi. In North American Indian mythology (Cherokee), the black racer snake. Ukuhi went to search for fire, but when he found it, he was scorched black, and ever since he has the habit of darting and doubling back on his tracks as if trying to escape fire.

Ulfius. In Arthurian legend, a knight of the Round Table. Ulfius accompanied Uther Pendragon, King Arthur's father, when Uther went to Tintagel. Afterward Ulfius aided King Arthur in his battle against the 11 kings. Ulfius was usually accompanied by Sir Brastias.

Ulgen (rich?). In Siberian mythology, a creator god. Various myths are told of Ulgen's role in creation. According to the Altaics, Ulgen came down from heaven to the waters with the desire to create the earth, though he did not know how to do it. Suddenly Erlik (man) appeared and told him he knew how it could be accomplished. With Ulgen's approval, Erlik dived down to the water's depths and brought up a piece of dirt. He gave part of it to Ulgen and kept part for himself. Ulgen created the earth with his part, and Erlik's piece formed the swamps and bogs of the earth.

A variant tells how Ulgen saw some mud with humanlike features floating on the water. He gave it life and the name Erlik. At first Erlik was Ulgen's friend and brother but later became his enemy and the devil.

In another myth Ulgen created the earth on the waters with three great fish to support it. One fish was placed in the center and one at each end, and all were tied to the pillars of heaven. If one fish nods, the earth becomes flooded. To prevent this, Mandishire (adopted from Buddhist mythology's Bodhisattva of Miraculous Birth, Manjursi) controls the ropes so that he can raise and lower the earth. If the fish shakes, however, there are earthquakes.

Uli-tarra. In Australian mythology, the first man, who is said to have come from the east. At the beginning of time there was no sea, only the water from a hole that Uli-tarra dug. Uli-tarra was the leader of an aboriginal tribe who left one day to fight a tribe on the other side of the mountain. They painted themselves white and red. On the way to the battle the men came upon two women whom Uli-tarra had once beaten for misbehavior. These two women found two straight sticks and pounded them against the ground, then they departed. The beating of the sticks caused the ocean to form, as well as all other bodies of water, both large and small. As the men returned from their journey they found that the ocean, which had not been there before, blocked their passage. They took the entrails of a deer and blew into them, creating a bridge over the water. One man tried to eat the rope the bridge was made of but was stopped, and the men were able to return to their homes safely.

Ull (the shaggy one). In Norse mythology, stepson of Thor and son of Sif, Thor's wife. He lived at Ydalir (yew valley). He is associated with winter and is known as an archer.

Variant spellings: Ullur, Ullr.

Ulrich, St. (wolf-powerful). 890–973. In Christian legend, bishop of Augsburg and patron of weavers. Invoked for a happy birth and a peaceful death; against birth pangs, fever, frenzy, mice, moles, and faintness. Feast, 4 July.

Though of delicate health, Ulrich rose to be the bishop of Augsburg in 923 after the land had been laid waste by the invading Magyars. He was a model bishop according to all accounts of his life. In a biography written by Gerhard, a contemporary of the saint, the legend of Ulrich as the "fish-bishop" is explained. One Thursday Ulrich and his friend Bishop Wolfgang were having a goose for dinner. They talked into the late hours of the night and early morning. Friday arrived (a meatless day), and the messenger of the emperor arrived and saw the two men seated at a table with a goose. Ulrich broke off one of its legs and handed it to the messenger, who put it into his pouch. He hurried away to show the emperor that the two were guilty of eating meat on a Friday. When he arrived at court, he put his hand into the pouch and drew out a fish instead.

Numerous miracles were recorded at the tomb of St. Ulrich, and he was the first saint canonized by Pope John XV in 993—the first solemn canonization by a pope of a saint. Before that local bishops or clergy and laity would proclaim a saint, or legends would grow around a person who would then be venerated as a saint.

In art St. Ulrich is usually portrayed holding a fish. Sometimes he is shown with his co-patron of Augsburg, St. Afra.

Ulysses (wounded in the thigh). Latin name of the Greek hero Odysseus. In English translations of Homer's *Iliad* and *Odyssey* as far back as Alexander Pope's, Ulysses is the usual translation of the name. In *The Divine Comedy* Dante places Ulysses and Diomedes among the counselors of evil in the Eighth Circle of Hell. The two are enveloped in a single flame divided at the top. In reply to a request Vergil (Dante cannot speak Greek, so he cannot question Ulysses), Ulysses relates how, after spending more than a year with Circe, he was impelled to go forth and see "the untravelled world." He set forth with one ship and a few faithful companions and at last came to the narrow strait at the Pillars of Heracles, the limit of the habitable world. He inspired his comrades to go forward with him into the unknown sea and sailed westward for five months, until they sighted a lofty mountain in the dim distance. In the midst of their rejoicing at the sight a storm broke from the distant land, striking their ship, which whirled around three times and then plunged, bow foremost, into the depths of the sea. Medieval tradition said Ulysses was a great liar. Later Shakespeare called him "sly Ulysses" in his poem *The Rape of Lucrece*.

Tennyson's poem *Ulysses* (1842) presents an entirely different aspect of the hero from that provided by Dante. He had read H. F. Cary's translation of Dante, published in 1805. Tennyson's poem was written soon after the death of his close friend Arthur Hallam. The poem ends:

Though much is taken, much abides; and though
We are not now that strength which in old days
Moved earth and heaven; that which we are, we are;
One equal temper of heroic hearts,
Made weak by time and fate, but strong in will
To strive, to seek, to find, and not to yield.

James Joyce's novel *Ulysses* (1922) deals with the events of one day in Dublin in June 1904. Its chapters roughly correspond to the episodes in Homer's *Odyssey*.

2962

Uma (light). In Hindu mythology, a form of the great goddess, Devi, wife of the god Shiva.

2963

Umai-hulhlya-wit. In North American Indian mythology (Diegueño), giant serpent. He lived in the ocean but was called to a ceremony after Chakopá and Chakomát had created the earth, sun, moon, and stars. The people built a large enclosure of brush for Umai-hulhlya-wit to stay in. He came and coiled himself but could not fit inside. On the third day, when he had coiled as much of his body as possible into the structure, the people set it aflame and burned him. When his body exploded, all knowledge, songs, magic secrets, languages, ceremonies, and customs were scattered over the land.

2964

Unas. In Egyptian mythology, a deified pharaoh of the Fifth Dynasty. Unas was said to have been the son of the god Tem and to have eaten the flesh of gods to become strong. He then journeyed through the heavens and became Orion.

Variant spellings: Unus, Unis, Onnos.

2965

Uncle Remus. In American literary folklore, black house slave, creation of Joel Chandler Harris. Uncle Remus narrates tales of Br'er Rabbit, Br'er Fox, Br'er Wolf, and others, collected in *Uncle Remus: His Songs and Sayings*. His character is based on several blacks whom Harris knew, including George Terrell. Uncle Remus appears in Walt Disney's movie *Song of the South* (1947), which combines live actors and cartoon animation.

2966

Uncle Sam. In American folklore, personification of the United States, portrayed as a tall, lean Yankee with long white hair, chin whiskers, striped pants, swallow-tail coat, and star-spangled plug hat. Originally a derogatory nickname used by New England opponents of the federal government's policies during the War of 1812, its exact origin is not fully known. According to some accounts, Uncle Sam is based on Samuel Wilson (1766–1854), known as Uncle Sam, a meat inspector in Troy, New York, who worked for Elbert Anderson. When the initials "E.A.—U.S." were stamped on meat carts, the initials were explained as meaning "Uncle Sam" had inspected the meat. Other accounts say the Uncle Sam is merely an extension of U.S., the initials of the United States. The first reported book to name the character of Uncle Sam was written by a "Frederick Augustus Fidfaddy" and called *The Adventures of Uncle Sam*. The character of Uncle Sam eventually replaced that of Brother Jonathan, a nickname once used for New Englanders and for Americans in general. Legend says that George Washington always relied on the advice of Jonathan Trumbull (1710–1785), colonial governor of Connecticut. In one tale Washington held a meeting with his officers about the shortage of ammunition, and when no answer was forthcoming, Washington remarked, "We must consult Brother Jonathan." Brother Jonathan appears in Royall Tyler's play *The Contrast*.

2967

Undine. In European folklore, a water sprite who could be mortal if she married a human being. An undine was created without a soul but had the privilege of obtaining one if she married a mortal and bore him a child. She had to suffer all of the pains of being a human. The creature appears in La Motte-Fouqué's *Undine*, Giraudoux's *Ondine*, and Tchaikovsky's *Undine*, an early stage work by the composer, later destroyed, though some parts were used in the ballet *Swan Lake*.

2968

Unicorn. In world mythology and folklore, a fantastic animal usually portrayed as a small horselike creature with a single horn protruding from its head.

In European mythologies the unicorn is usually viewed as a beneficent being. A medieval description

Unicorn

of the fantastic animal is found in *Le Bestiaire Divin de Guillaume Clerc de Normandie.*

> The Unicorn has but one horn in the middle of its forehead. It is the only animal that ventures to attack the elephant; and so sharp is the nail of its foot, that with one blow it can rip the belly out of that beast. Hunters can catch the unicorn only by placing a young virgin in his haunts. No sooner does he see the damsel, than he runs towards her, and lies down at her feet, and so suffers himself to be captured by the hunters. The unicorn represents Jesus Christ, who took on Him our nature in the Virgin's womb. . . . Its one horn signifies the Gospel of Truth.

The European belief in unicorns stems in part from ancient pagan Greek sources as well as the Septuagint versions of the Hebrew Scripture. When the Hebrew Bible was translated into Greek, the Hebrew word *reem*, which might mean a wild ox, was translated *monokeros* (one-horned). This rendering was followed in later Latin versions of the Bible, which in turn influenced English translations such as the King James Version. The Book of Numbers (23:22) says: "God brought them out of Egypt; he hath as it were the strength of an unicorn." The Revised Standard Version of the Bible in its translation of the verse substitutes "wild ox" for unicorn. One medieval Jewish folktale said the unicorn had perished in Noah's flood because it was too large to enter the ark. Another Jewish folktale argued that God never destroys his own creation; if the unicorn was too large to get into the ark, then God would have let it swim behind the ark.

Along with the unicorn as a beneficent symbol, such as Jesus Christ, the animal was also identified with evil and death. In *The Golden Legend*, a series of

saints' lives by Jacobus de Voragine, written in the 13th century, the "unicorn is the figure of Death, which continually followeth man and desireth to seize him." Death rides a unicorn in some late medieval Books of Hours. In the *Ancrene Riwle*, a 12-century book of rules for nuns, the unicorn appears as a symbol of wrath, along with the lion for pride, the serpent for envy, and the bear for sloth. The Church Fathers at the Council of Trent, held in the 16th century, forbade the use of the unicorn as a symbol of Christ. One legend they cited was from Leonardo da Vinci's *Bestiary* in which the artist made the unicorn a symbol of lust.

The unicorn's horn was thought to have magic curative powers; many late medieval monasteries and cathedrals were believed to possess them, and they appear in inventories of Queen Elizabeth I and other monarchs of the period. Powders purporting to be made from crushed unicorn horns were sold by apothecaries.

As late as the French Revolution the unicorn was believed to exist, and a "unicorn's" horn was used to detect poison in food fed to royalty.

In Chinese mythology the unicorn was one of the four animals of good omen, the others being the phoenix, the dragon, and the tortoise. According to one story, when Confucius was born, a unicorn spit out a piece of jade with the inscription announcing the event: "Son of the essence of water, kingdoms shall pass away, but you will be a king, though without a throne."

2969

Unktomi. In North American Indian mythology (Oglala Dakota), spider, the trickster, both culture hero and creator. Variants of his name among the tribes are Iktomé, Ikto, Ictcinike, and Ictinike.

2970

Unkulunkulu (chief). In African mythology (Zulu), sky god who instituted marriage. Unkulunkulu sent a chameleon with the message of life and a lizard with the message of death. On the way the chameleon stopped to eat, and the lizard arrived with his death message, which he delivered. To compensate humankind for the loss of immortality, Unkulunkulu instituted marriage so that people's lives were carried on through their children.

2971

Unquiet Grave. English ballad, collected in F. J. Child's *English and Scottish Popular Ballads* (1882–1885). In the ballad the dead sweetheart begs the surviving lover to stop mourning over the grave because it disturbs the dead.

Unsinkable Molly Brown. In American history and folklore, Molly Brown, wife of a Colorado millionaire; she was on the Titanic when it struck an iceberg in 1912. Molly stripped down to her corset and bloomers, had her pistol strapped to her side, and covered a child with her chinchilla coat. She took command of one lifeboat, saying, "Keep rowing, you sons of bitches, or I'll toss you all overboard." When she was asked why she had been saved when so many others died, she replied, "I'm unsinkable." A musical comedy *The Unsinkable Molly Brown*, and a film in 1964 deal with her life and legend.

Untsaiyi (brass). In North American Indian mythology (Cherokee), trickster who loved to gamble. Untsaiyi had always won, but once he was fooled by a young boy who beat him at every game. In the end Untsaiyi wagered his life and lost. Untsaiyi's hands and feet were tied by the boy, and a long stake was driven through his chest. He was then placed far out in deep water. But Untsaiyi did not die, and according to the myth, "cannot die until the end of the world." He lies in the water with his face up. Sometimes he struggles to get free. Sometimes the beavers, his friends, come to gnaw at the ropes to release him, but two crows sitting atop the stake cry out, "ka, ka, ka," and scare the beavers away.

Upanishads (Sanskrit, from *upa,* "additional," and *ni-sad,* "to sit down at the feet of a teacher"). In Hinduism, a collection of philosophical writings composed over a period of time, the most important being about 500 B.C.E. The German philosopher Schopenhauer kept a Latin translation of the *Upanishads* on his table and read it before he went to bed. He wrote of it: "From every sentence, deep, original and sublime thoughts arise, and the whole is pervaded by a high and holy and earnest spirit. . . . They are the products of the highest wisdom. They are destined sooner or later to become the faith of the people."

Upirikutsu (great star). In North American Indian mythology (Pawnee), Morning Star, who overcame Evening Star in her realm of darkness. From their union the first human was created. A memorial sacrifice of a captive, often a female, was offered to Morning Star until 1838.

Urania (heavenly). In Greek mythology, one of the nine Muses, the Muse of astronomy and celestial forces; daughter of Zeus and Mnemosyne. Among the ancients Urania was one of the most important of the nine Muses and was considered the arbiter of fate. Some myths say she was the mother of Linus by Apollo and the mother of Hymenaeus by Dionysus. However, in *Paradise Lose* (book 7.1) Milton calls on Urania as the Muse of poetry. Her symbol is a globe.

Uranus (heaven, king of the mountain). In Greek mythology, the sky; son and husband of Gaea, the earth; called Coelus by the Romans. Gaea bore him the Titans, the Cyclopes, and the Hecatonchires. He did not allow any of his children to see the light of day but pushed them into Tartarus, a gloomy place in the underworld. Gaea persuaded her Titan sons to attack their father. Led by Cronus, the youngest of the seven, they surprised Uranus as he slept and castrated him with a flint sickle given them by their mother. From the blood dropping upon the earth, Gaea bore the three Erinyes, the Furies, and the Melic nymphs. Some accounts say Aphrodite was born from the sea foam stirred up when Uranus' genitals fell into the sea. Cronus, son of Uranus, became king. Before he died, Uranus prophesied that Cronus also would be dethroned by a son. Eventually, Zeus dethroned his father, Cronus. Ouranos (overhanging heavens) was another name for Uranus. Hesiod's *Theogony* (133-87, 616-23) tells of Uranus' fate.

Urd (the past). In Norse mythology, one of the three named Norns; the others being Verdandi and Skuld. Urd is the oldest of the Norns and looks to the past.
Variant spelling: Urdhr.

Uriel (the light of God). In Jewish and Christian mythology, archangel. His name is found on Jewish amulets as a charm to ward off evil.

Unlike the archangels Michael, Gabriel, and Raphael, all of whom are mentioned in the Bible, Uriel appears to be less important since he is not mentioned there, though he is found in the Old Testament Apocrypha Book of Second Esdras (4:1). Uriel also appears in the *Book of Enoch*, a pseudepigraphic Jewish–Christian work in which he is the watcher over the world and over Tartarus, the lowest part of hell. He serves as the principal guide to Enoch in his various visions.

According to one Christian legend, Uriel, not Christ, appeared to the disciples on the way to Emmaus, though the New Testament text does not support this contention. In Jewish literature Uriel is often called the "one who brings light to Israel." In *Paradise Lost* (book 3:690) Milton, recalling the Jewish belief, calls Uriel the "Regent of the Sun" and "sharpest-sighted spirit" of all in heaven. Dryden, in his poetic play *The State of Innocence*, based on Milton's *Paradise Lost*, pictures Uriel descending from heaven in a chariot drawn by white horses. Less dramatic is Longfellow's Uriel in *The Golden Legend*, in which Uriel is one of the seven angels of the seven planets bearing the star of Bethlehem.

Uriel is rarely portrayed in Christian art. When he is, he is shown holding a book or scroll, symbolic of his role as interpreter of visions and prophecies as in the cases of Enoch and Esdras. Burne-Jones's painting of Uriel portrays the angel in the traditional pose. Uriel is also known as Nuriel and is sometimes identified with the Flaming Angel.

2980
Urim and Thummin (lights and perfection?). In the Bible, O.T. (Exod. 28:30), two cult objects used to determine the will of Yahweh, the Hebrew god. Scholars are not quite sure what they were but believe their markings made them resemble dice. They were carried in the breastplate of the high priest.

2981
Urna (wool). In Oriental art, the jewel or small protuberance between the eyes, or circle of hair or eye, seen on gods and Buddhas, representing the third eye for spiritual vision or foreknowledge. The Urna seems to be a circle of hair in the earliest texts. It then becomes an eye and is represented as an eye, a bump, or a jewel. Its symbolism is variously interpreted, but basically it is just a very strong eye that illuminates all universes at once. Eyes are believed to emit light.

2982
Urre. In Arthurian legend, one of the knights of the Round Table. When Urre was wounded, King Arthur tried to heal him with his touch but failed. Then Sir Lancelot tried, and Urre was healed.

2983
Ursula, St. (bean). Fifth century? C.E. In Christian legend, virgin martyr. Patron saint of maidens, drapers, and teachers. Invoked for chastity and holy wedlock and against plague. Feast, 21 October.

There are various medieval versions of St. Ursula's life. In one version she is the daughter of Dianotus, a British king, and was sought in marriage by Holofernes, a pagan prince. Dianotus consented to the alliance, but Ursula said she would marry the prince only if he was baptized and she was given three years to travel with her 11 maidens, accompanied by 1,000 companions. The conditions were accepted, and all of the women set sail. They went to Cologne, then to Rome, where they visited the tombs of various saints. When they returned to Cologne, they were all seized by Attila the Hun. All of the women except Ursula were killed.

"Weep not, for though thou hast lost thy companions," said Attila, "I will be thy husband, and thou shalt be the greatest queen in Germany." Ursula screamed back at Attila, causing his anger to flare up "and bending his bow, which he had in his hand, he, with three arrows, transfixed her pure breast, so that she fell dead, and her spirit ascended into Heaven, with all the glorious sisterhood of martyrs."

Another medieval version makes the legend of St. Ursula a Christian parallel to the rape of the Sabine women in Roman history. This tale is told by Geoffrey of Monmouth in his *History of the Kings of Britain*. Maximian, the British king, having conquered Armonica (now called Brittany), gave it to Conan Meriadoc, his nephew. His country being almost depopulated by war, Conan wished to find wives for himself and his men. He asked for the assistance of Dianotus, brother and successor of Caradoc, king of Cornwall. Dianotus had a daughter named Ursula, whom he promised to Conan as his wife. Dianotus then summoned all of the chief men of his kingdom and also collected 11,000 maidens, whom he shipped to Conan together with his daughter. When on the seas, contrary winds arose, causing the fleet to go off course. It was found in the Rhine by Huns who attacked the ships and killed all of the women.

2984
Urvasi. In Hindu mythology, a nymph loved by the sage Puru-ravas; she bore him several children.

Urvasi agreed to live with Puru-ravas on certain conditions. "I have two rams," she said, "which I love as children. They must be kept near my bedside and never allowed to be carried away. You must take care never to see me when you are undressed and clarified butter alone must be my food."

Urvasi came from the storm god Indra's heaven, and its inhabitants were anxious for her return, so they told the Gandharvas, heavenly musicians, to steal the rams. Puru-ravas was undressed when it happened and so at first he did not pursue the thieves. Urvasi cried, however, impelling him to take his sword and rush after them. The Gandharvas then produced a flash of lightning, which showed Puru-ravas naked, thus breaking the compact. Urvasi disappeared and Puru-ravas went in search of her. He eventually found her and she told him she was pregnant and would bring him the child at the end of the year. At the end of the year he met Urvasi, who gave him the son, Ayus. She bore him five or eight more sons.

Ushnisha (head-band; turban). In Buddhist art, the protuberance on the top of the head of a Buddha, variously interpreted. In some Buddhist works the form is that of a flame, representing enlightenment. It is one of the major bodily characteristics of a *maha-pursusha* (hero)—either of an emperor (*cakravartin*) or Buddha.

2986

Utchat. Ancient Egyptian amulet of the eye of the sun god Ra.

In the Pyramid Texts the *utchat* is identified with the uraeus cobra, which spat venom and fire against the enemies of the sun god. It appeared on the crown of the pharaoh, the living sun god, who would also defeat his enemies.

According to one myth, the eye of Ra (Tefnut in this version) was separated from her father, Ra, and went to live in the Nubian desert as a bloodthirsty lion. Ra, wanting her back, sent the god Thoth, who persuaded her to return; when she did, she became the goddess Hathor, the great deity who represented the sky. (In Egyptian mythology the gods often change from one form to another.) In a variant of the myth, Tefnut was a cat, a form of the goddess Bast, who became a lion when she was angry. When the eye of Ra was removed from the god (the symbol was also given to other sun gods), it was said that a disturbance occurred in the natural order of the universe, and that when it was returned, the natural order was restored.

The twin *utchats* represent the eye of the sun and the eye of the moon. One myth tells how the powers of evil succeeded in blinding the eye of Ra, the sun god, during an eclipse or prolonged storm. Thoth came to the god and healed his eye. In another myth Thoth healed the eye of the god Horus when it was injured in his battle with the demonic god Set. The restored eye became known as the *utchat*, and its powers as an amulet were thought to be extensive. *The Book of the Dead* contains a spell that will cause Thoth to bring the *utchat* to the deceased during his journey to the kingdom of Osiris.

Variant spelling: Udjat.

2987

Utgard (outer place). In Norse mythology, chief city of Jotunheim, the land of the giants. Its ruler was Skrymir, who was called Utgard-Loki (Magus of Utgard) when he encountered Thor. Utgard appears in the *Poetic Edda* and the *Prose Edda*. In some medieval literature Utgard and Loki are combined to form the name of a devil in Christian folklore.

2988

Uther Ben (wonderful head). In Celtic mythology, the head of the god Bran, unearthed by King Arthur.

Uther Pendragon (Howard Pyle)

2989

Uther Pendragon (chief leader in war). In Arthurian legend, father of King Arthur by Igraine, wife of the duke of Tintagel. Uther killed the duke and later married Igraine after he had earlier disguised himself as her husband and made love to her.

2990

Utnapishtim (he who saw light? I have found life?). In Near Eastern mythology, Babylonian hero of the flood myth who was granted immortal life by the gods.

In the epic *Gilgamesh*, Utnapishtim tells his story to the hero of the poem, who came to him seeking immortality.

"I will tell you, Gilgamesh, the marvelous story," said Utnapishtim, "of the decision of the gods. The city of Shurippak was corrupt, so the gods decided to destroy it by bringing a rainstorm upon it. The god Ea, however, warned me, telling me to build a ship, to save my self from the coming deluge."

After the ship, or ark, was completed, Utnapishtim loaded it with gold and silver, and "living creatures of all kinds." He then took his family aboard the ark. When the time came, he entered the ark, closed the door, and entrusted Puzar-Shadurabu, the sailor, with guiding the vessel. When the dawn came, dark clouds arose from the horizon, all of the light was changed to darkness, and a storm began that lasted for seven days. Everything was destroyed; men were turned back to clay, from which they had originally been made. In place of dams constructed by men, marshes were everywhere. Water was over the whole earth.

After "twelve double hours" the waters began to abate and on the seventh day Utnapishtim sent out a dove, but it found no resting place. Then he sent a swallow, which also returned. Finally he sent a raven, which did not return, indicating that dry land had now appeared. Utnapishtim then left the ship and offered sacrifices to the gods, who had relented—even the great god Bel, who was determined to destroy all life. The god came upon the ship, lifted up Utnapishtim, brought up his wife, and made her kneel by her husband's side. The god then blessed the couple, saying: "Hitherto Utnapishtim was mortal, but now Utnapishtim and his wife shall be gods like us."

Utnapishtim was then placed "at the confluence of the streams," where he and his wife were to live forever.

Variant spelling: Parnapishtim.

2991
Utukku. In Near Eastern mythology, generic name for demons among the Babylonians and Assyrians.

The Babylonians believed that evil spirits resided everywhere, lying in wait to attack people. Each demon was given a name, often describing his or her function. Thus, Lilu (night spirit) and Lilitu, the female form, indicated demonic spirits that worked their evil at nighttime. Eki mmu (seizer) was a shadowy demon that hovered around graves waiting to attack any passersby. Rabisu (the one that lies in wait) and Labartu (the oppressor) were the demons who gave nightmares to the sleeping. Ardat Lili (maid of the night) was a demoness who approached men, aroused their sexual passions, and then did not permit them to have orgasms. Other demons were Akhakhazu (the capturer), Namtar (the demon of plague), Ashakku (the demon of wasting disease), and Namataru, the spirit of fate and son of the great god Bel, who executed instructions given him concerning the destiny of mankind.

To protect themselves against these various demons the Babylonians and Assyrians evolved an elaborate series of incantations to ward off evils. They also pictured the demons as monstrous beings, made of animal heads and bodies resembling human shape. With gaping mouths and armed with weapons, the *utukku* stood ready to attack their next victim. Assyrian kings acknowledged the power of the *utukku* by having statues of them placed at the approaches, entrances, and divisions of their temples and palaces. This was done in the hope of securing their protection instead of their vengeance. The great bulls and lions with human heads often seen on various monuments are part of the same concept. These colossal statues were known as Shedu, another term for demon. Even though the demons assumed animal forms they could also make themselves invisible.

Because there were so many demonic beings, incantations often would number them, such as the famous text *Seven Are They*:

> Seven are they, they are seven,
> In the subterranean deep, they are seven,
> Perched in the sky, they are seven,
> In a section of the subterranean deep they were reared.
> They are neither male nor are they female,
> They are destructive whirlwinds,
> They have no wife, nor do they beget offspring.

This ancient text was set to music by the Russian composer Sergei Prokofiev for tenor, chorus, and orchestra as *Seven Are They*. The seven evil spirits are elsewhere compared to various monstrous animals with the power to bewitch even the gods. The eclipse of the moon, for example, was attributed to them. The number seven is not to be taken literally; it means, as in many other mythologies, a miscellaneous group.

2992
Uwolowu. In African mythology (Akposso of Togo), sky god. Uwolowu created everything, including the lesser gods. He bestows on men the blessings of offspring and harvest, of rain and sunshine. He has also given man fire. He is almighty and can impart all good things.

Various myths are told of Uwolowu. In one he had two wives. One of them was a frog, and the other was a bird called Itanco. Uwolowu loved his frog wife more than his bird wife; he gave his frog wife all sorts of pretty things but gave nothing to his bird wife. One day he said he would put their love to the test. He gave each of them seven pots and made believe he was dead. His widows were to weep for him and let the tears fall into the seven pots. The frog wife began to weep, but as fast as her tears fell they were licked up by ants. Then the bird wife wept, and her tears filled the seven pots. Uwolowu said, "She whom I did not love has filled seven pots with the tears which she wept for me, and she whom I loved has wept very little." With these words the god lunged out with his foot and kicked his frog wife into the slime, where she has wallowed ever since.

But as for his bird wife, Uwolowu set her free to roam forever in the air.

Another myth tells of the origin of death. Once upon a time men sent a dog with a message to Uwolowu to say that when they died they would like to come to life again. Off the dog trotted to deliver the message. But on the way the dog felt hungry and went into a house where a man was boiling magic herbs. The dog sat down and thought to himself, "He is cooking food." In the meantime a frog had set out to tell Uwolowu that when men died they would rather not come to life again. Nobody had asked the frog to take that message: he had made up the lie.

The dog, who still sat hopefully watching the man cook, saw the frog racing by but said to himself, "When I have had a snack, I'll catch up with froggy." However, the frog came in first and said to Uwolowu, "When men die, they would rather not come to life again." After the frog delivered his message, the dog entered and said, "When men die, they would like to come to life again." Uwolowu was puzzled and said to the dog: "I really don't understand these two messages. As I heard the frog's message first, I will heed his and not yours."

That is the reason death is in the world.

V

2993

Vacub-Caquix (seven macaws). In Mayan mythology, an evil giant mentioned in the *Popol Vuh*, the sacred book of the ancient Quiché Maya of Guatemala.

Vacub-Caquix was a being "who was very proud of himself," thinking he was the sun and the moon. He was married to Chimalmat and had two sons: Zipacna, a giant who carried mountains on his back and who ate flesh and crabs, and Cabraca (double giant, or earthquake). Vacub-Caquix and his sons boasted that they had created the earth and were the sun, so the gods decided to destroy them. Two youths, the hero gods Hunahpú and Xbalanqué, were dispatched to kill the giant and his sons.

Vacub-Caquix had a beautiful tropical tree that produced a very aromatic fruit. He ate the fruit of the tree each day, climbing into its branches. One day Hunahpú and Xbalanqué "lay in ambush at the foot of the tree." As soon as Vacub-Caquix appeared they shot with a blowgun and "struck him squarely in the jaw," breaking some of his teeth, and the giant fell from the tree. Hunahpú ran over to the giant to give the coup-de-grâce, but Vacub-Caquix tore off Hunahpú's arm and took it home with him. Hunahpú and Xbalanqué then spoke with Azqui-Nim-Ac (great white wild boar) and his wife, Zaqui-Nim-Tziis (great white coat). These two are the creator man and woman in the *Popol Vuh*. They appear in different guises throughout the book.

The couple and the two heroes then went to Vacub-Caquix's house. When they arrived they heard the giant "screaming because his tooth pained him." Not realizing that the two youths were the ones who had attacked him and thinking they were the sons or grandsons of the couple, Vacub-Caquix asked if they knew how to cure his toothache. Pretending to help him, the two heroes pulled out all of his teeth, blinded him, and "took all his riches," leaving the giant to die. His wife, Chimalmat, also died soon after, though we are not told how. Later Hunahpú's arm was restored.

The giant's two sons, Zipacna and Cabraca, were undone by Hunahpú and Xbalanqué later on. Zipacna was turned into stone and Cabraca was fed a bird coated with chalk, which made him weak so that he was easy prey for the two heroes, who threw him to the ground and buried him alive.

2994

Vacuna. In Roman mythology, a Sabine goddess of agriculture, later known as goddess of leisure. She is identified in some ancient accounts with the goddesses Victoria, Venus, Minerva, Bellona, and Diana. Horace's *Epistles* (1.10.49) cites the goddess.

2995

Vahagn. In Armenian mythology, sun, lightning, and fire god, invoked for courage because he battled dragons. Vahagn was the son of heaven, earth, and the sea. One old poem describes him as having "hair of fire," and a "beard of flame," and says "his eyes were suns." Some scholars believe Vahagn also may have been the patron of game and hunting because his Christian replacement in Armenian folklore, St. Athenogenes, a bishop and martyr of the early fourth century (Feast, 16 July), is patron of both. Vahagn survives also in modern folklore as Dsovean (sea-born), who with Dsovinar, an angry female storm spirit, rules over the seas.

2996

Vainamoinen (river's mouth?). In the Finnish epic poem *The Kalevala*, a culture hero son of Luonnotar, daughter of the air, who brought about creation.

Vainamoinen was the inventor of the harp, "forger of the runes" or poems, and a great magician. In Finnish mythology the heavenly sign Orion is called the scythe of Vainamoinen; the Pleiades, the sword of Vainamoinen. Vainamoinen's home was called Vainola.

The hero's birth forms part of the opening (rune 1) of *The Kalevala*, which tells how the hero "rested in his mother's body" for the space of thirty years as she tossed on the waves. The hero finally reached the shore, where the evil Laplander Joukahainen challenged him to a singing contest and lost, whereupon Vainamoinen plunged him into a swamp. In order to save his life, Joukahainen pledged his sister Aino in marriage to Vainamoinen. However, the girl did not want to marry an old man. Vainamoinen is always portrayed as old in *The Kalevala*, being called "old and steadfast."

Joukahainen again attempted to kill Vainamoinen, but the hero escaped on an eagle, which brought him to Pohjola, the Northland, ruled by the evil mistress Louhi. She promised her daughter to Vainamoinen if he could forge the sampo, which magically made corn, salt, and coins.

However, the Maiden of Pohjola, Louhi's daughter, set additional tasks for Vainamoinen, not all of which he could complete, and she eventually married Ilmarinen, who did forge the sampo.

Vainamoinen is portrayed by the Finnish painter Akseli Gallen-Kallela as an old man with a white beard and rather robust or muscular body. Sibelius' tone poem *Pohjola's Daughter* portrays Vainamoinen's wooing of the Maiden of Pohjola. Vainamoinen's departure at the end of the epic when a new king of Karelia is crowned (the king represents Jesus Christ, and Vainamoinen symbolizes the old pagan gods), was used by Longfellow for his description of the departure of Hiawatha in his poem. Sibelius set *The Song of Vaino* for mixed chorus and orchestra, using rune 43, in which Vainamoinen calls on God to protect Finland "from the designs of men" and "the plots of women," while destroying the wicked and laying low the "water wizards."

Vaino is a shortened form of Vainamoinen and is a common name in Finland today.

Variant spellings: Vainanoinen; Wainamoinen.

Vairocana (intensity shining). In Tibetan Buddhism, one of the five Dhyani-Buddhas, the illuminator. In Japanese Shingon Buddhism, he is supreme. He is portrayed in Tibetan art on a blue lotus with the Wheel of Dharma and also mounted on a lion. His *mudra* pose is that of teaching.

In Tibetan Buddhism, Vairocana is subsidiary to the Adi Buddha (Vajradhara or some other Buddha).

In Shingon he is the Adi-Buddha and appears at the center of the Two Great Mandalas. In the static mandala his *mudra* is *dhyani-mudra* and in the ninefold dynamic mandala his *mudra* is *vairocana-mudra* (fingers of the right hand enclosing the index finger of the left hand, held upright before the chest). In the Daibutsu of the Todai temple at Nara, he displays *abhaya* and *varada* mudras. In Japanese, he is called Dainichi Butsu.

Vajra (thunderbolt). In Buddhism , thunderbolt, symbol of the penis.

Vajra-Dhara (Vajra holder). In Tibetan Buddhism, the name for the Adi-Buddha. He holds a *vajra* (thunderbolt) in each hand, which he crosses before his chest.

Vajrapani (wielder of the thunderbolt). In Tantric Buddhism, a Dhyani-Bodhisattva; god of rain, a form of the Hindu god Indra, and the spiritual son of the second celestial Buddha, Akshobhya. He is often portrayed in a fierce form, black or dark blue, wielding his thunderbolt in his uplifted right hand. In his left hand he holds a bell, snare, or other implement, according to which title he holds, there are some 15. He is called Chana Dorje in Tibetan Buddhism.

Vajravarahi (adamantine sow). In Mahayana Buddhism, goddess of light. According to one myth, a certain Buddhist abbess had an excrescence behind her ear shaped like a sow's head. A Mongol warrior wanted the abbess to show her mark, but when the warrior and his men broke into the monastery, they found only sows and pigs led by a sow bigger than the rest. The warrior was so startled by the sight that he stopped his men from pillaging the place. When they left, the sows and pigs were transformed into monks and nuns, and the large sow into the abbess.

Vajravarahi is usually portrayed riding a chariot drawn by a team of swine. She is shown with three faces, one in the shape of a sow's head, and eight arms. Her hands hold various weapons, including an ax and snare. In Tibetan Buddhism, she is called Marici.

Variant spelling: Varahi.

Vaks-oza. In Finno-Ugric mythology, mill-ruler spirit appearing as a man or woman. It lived in the mill under the floor or behind the waterwheel. Usually, the *vaks-oza* was friendly to the miller, but if it was not on friendly terms, it had to be appeased by an offering of porridge with a pat of butter on a spoon.

Valedjád. In the mythology of the Tupi Indians of Brazil, the first man, an evil magician. At first there was no heaven or earth, only a big block of rock, smooth and beautiful. This rock was a woman. One day it split open amid streams of blood, producing the first man, Valedjád. Later, where the earth was peopled, the magician Arkoanyó hid in a tree and poured liquid wax on Valedjád as he passed by, sealing up his eyes, nostrils, and fingers so he could no longer do evil. To ensure that Valedjád would not free himself, a large bird flew away with him to the cold north country.

Valentine and Orson (to be strong; bean). In medieval French legend, twin brothers; sons of Bellisant, sister of King Pepin and wife of Alexander, emperor of Constantinople. The twins were born in a forest near Orléans. While Bellisant went in search of Orson, who had been carried off by a bear, Pepin accidentally found Valentine and took the child with him. Valentine later married Clerimond, niece of the Green Knight. Orson was suckled by a bear. When he grew up, he became a wild man and was called the Wild Man of the Forest. His brother Valentine brought him back to civilization.

Valentine, St. (to be strong). Third century C.E. In Christian legend, patron saint of beekeepers, engaged couples, travelers, and young people. Invoked against epilepsy, fainting, and plague and for a happy marriage. Feast, 14 February.

3005

Valentine was a Roman priest who is believed to have suffered martyrdom during the persecution of Claudius the Goth. The custom of sending valentines on the feast day of the saint is believed to have originated from the popular belief that birds begin to pair on St. Valentine's Day. Chaucer makes mention of the fact in his *Parliament of Fowls*. However, 15 February was the festival of Februta Juno (Juno the fructifier), and the medieval church may have substituted St. Valentine for the heathen Roman goddess. An early reference to St. Valentine's Day as a day for lovers is found in the *Paston Letters* in which Elizabeth Drews wrote to her daughter's prospective bridegroom in February 1477: "And, Cousin, upon Friday is St. Valentine's Day and every bird chooseth him a mate, and if it like you to come on Thursday at night . . , I trust to God that you shall speak to my husband, and I shall pray that we shall bring the matter to a conclusion."

It was a custom in England to draw lots for lovers on St. Valentine's Day. The person drawn was the drawer's valentine and was given a present, such as a pair of gloves. Chapman, in *Monsieur d'Olive*, written in 1605, refers to the custom when he says, "If I stood affected that way [i.e. to marriage] I would choose my wife as men do valentines— blindfold or draw cuts for them; for so I shall not be deceived in the choosing."

Valhalla (hall of the slain). In Norse mythology, the home of slain heroes. Its outer gate is *Valgrind* (the death's gate) and it is surrounded by a river, *Thund* (swollen or roaring). All of the slain heroes are kept at Valhalla waiting for the day when they will join the gods to fight the giants at Ragnarok, the end of the world. They are fed on Saehrimnir, a boar whose flesh is restored every night after being slaughtered and cooked. The cook is called Andhrimnir and the kettle, Eldhrimnir. While they wait for the last day, the heroes pass the time, according to the *Prose Edda*, by riding out into the fields and fighting "until they cut each other to pieces. This is their pastime, but when meal-time approaches they remount their

3006

steeds and return to drink in Valhalla." Valhalla appears in the *Poetic Edda*, the *Prose Edda*, Matthew Arnold's narrative poem *Balder Dead*, and as Walhalla in Wagner's *Der Ring des Nibelungen*.

Vali (terrible). In Norse mythology, son of Odin and the giantess Rinda. He grew to full stature in one day and avenged the death of Baldur by killing blind Hodur.

3007

Valkyries (choosers of the slain). In Norse mythology, the fierce daughters of Odin, the chief of the gods. They daily chose those who were to fall in battle, bringing them to Valhalla, the hall of the slain. They often rode horses but could transform themselves into ravens or wolves. Their names vary in different sources. Those listed in the *Poetic Edda* in the poem *Grimismol* are Hrist (shaker), Mist (mist), Skeggjold (ax time), Skogul (raging?), Hild (warrior), Thruth (might), Hlok (shrieking), Herfjotur (host fetter), Gol (screaming), Geironul (spear bearer), Randgrith (shield bearer), and Rathgrith (plan destroyer?). Richard Wagner's "Ride of the Valkyries," which appears in his music drama *Die Walküre*, part of *Der Ring des Nibelungen*, is one of the most stirring works in 19th-century orchestral repertory. Arthur Rackham portrays the Valkyries in his illustrations for Wagner's the Ring Cycle. In Old English, the word *Waelcyrge* is used for the chooser of the slain.
Variant spelling: Valkyrjr.

3008

Vanir (friendly). In Norse mythology, a race of gods and goddesses who lived in Vanaheim, originally fertility deities. At first the Vanir fought the Aesir, another race of gods, but later they made a truce so that they could fight the giants. Njord and his children, Frey and Freya, went to live with the Aesir gods and goddesses at Asgard in exchange for the Aesir deities Hoenir and Mimir, who went to live with the Vanir.
Variant spellings: Vanas, Vanis, Van.

3009

Van-xuong. In Indo-Chinese mythology, god of literature, who now lives in the Great Bear in heaven. He is portrayed as a man standing, holding a pen in one hand.

3010

Var (truth or promise). In Norse mythology, a goddess of the vows of love, one of the deities that surround Frigga.

3011

Varuna (all-enveloping). In Hindu mythology, god of the waters, who rides on a fantastic animal, the

3012

Varuna

called Vasava (of the Vasus); later they attended Vishnu. They are Ap (waters), Dhruva (pole star), Soma (moon), Dhara (earth), Anila (wind), Anala (fire), Prabhasa (dawn), and Pratyusha (light).

Sometimes the following are called Vasus: the Aswins, the twin brothers who preceded the dawn; the gods Vishnu, Shiva, and Kubera; and the eight Adityas, children of the goddess Aditi.

Vayu

Makara. Varuna is married to the goddess Varuni, who sprang up at the churning of the ocean, when the gods and demons sought the Amrita, or water of life. Varuna's son is called Agasti.

3013

Vasavadatta. In Buddhist legend, a courtesan who fell in love with Upagupta, one of the Buddha's disciples. Vasavadatta sent a message to Upagupta to come to her, but he replied: "The time has not yet arrived when Upagupta will visit Vasavadatta." Astonished at his reply, she told him she did not want any money, just his love. But again he made the same reply. Later, after Vasavadatta had been punished for the murder of one of her lovers by having her ears, nose, and feet cut off, Upagupta came to see her. "Once this body was fragrant like the lotus, and I offered you my love. In those days I was covered with pearls and fine muslin. Now I am mangled by the executioner and covered with filth and blood." "Sister," Upagupta replied, "it is not for my pleasure that I approach you. It is to restore to you a nobler beauty than the charms which you have lost." He then told her of the teachings of the Buddha and converted her so that she died in peace.

3014

Vasus. In Hindu mythology, eight gods originally attendant on Indra, the storm god, who is sometimes

3015

Vayu (air, wind). In Hindu mythology, the wind and the wind god. Vayu rides with Indra, the storm god, in a golden chariot. Vayu married the nymph Ghritachi and had 100 daughters. Vayu wished his daughters to accompany him to the sky, but they all refused. Vayu then cursed them, turning them into deformed creatures. In some texts Vayu is made head of the Gandharvas, the heavenly musicians, and rules over the Anilas, 49 wind gods who are associated with him.

3016

Vedanta (end of the Veda). In Hinduism, an interpretation of the Vedas in which everything consists of or is reducible to one substance. This interpretation influenced such Western writers and thinkers as Schopenhauer, Emerson, and Mary Baker Eddy, whose Christian Science is a kind of Western Vedanta.

3017

Vedas (the knowledge). In Hinduism, sacred texts regarded as divine truth breathed out by the god Brahma. They are the *Rig-Veda, Yajur-Veda, Sama-Veda,* and *Atharva-Veda.* The first three are called the triple Veda and are liturgical and public; the last is nonliturgical and private.

Velo Men (living). In African mythology (the
Malagasy of Madagascar), little clay people. They
were created by Earth, the daughter of God, and
given life when God breathed into them. They
worked for Earth and made her very rich. Since they
did not die, it was obvious that Earth would continue to prosper. God, seeing this, demanded half of
the wealth they produced, but Earth refused to give
up her enormous profits. God then took the breath
that he had given to the Velo Men, and since then
they grow old and die like ordinary people.

Vena. In Hindu mythology, a proud king who was
punished by the priests and then saved. When Vena
became king he issued a proclamation that said:
"Men must not sacrifice or give gifts or present offerings. Who else but myself is the priest of sacrifices? I
am forever the lord of offerings." The Brahmans
(priests), angry that the king had usurped their
power, killed the king. They realized after his death,
however, that there was no heir to the throne. The
priests then rubbed Vena's thigh or right arm (depending on which text is consulted) and from the
corpse came Prithu, "resplendent in body, glowing
like the fire god Agni." (Prithu is sometimes called
Prithi-vainya, "Prithi, son of Vena.")

   With the birth of Prithu, Vena was freed from his
sin. In some accounts the king is not killed by the
priests but only beaten, so he is then able to retire to
a hermitage and do penance. Later the god Vishnu

gives Vena the gift of becoming one with himself.
Gustav Holst wrote a *Hymn to Vena* for female voices
and harp, using his own translation of a Sanskrit
text.

Venus. In Roman mythology, ancient Italian goddess of love, wife of Vulcan and mistress of Mars;
the mother of Cupid; identified with the Greek
Aphrodite. Originally, Venus was an Italian goddess
who watched over market gardens and was the protector of vegetation. The day on which her temple
was founded in Rome was observed as a holiday by
the vegetable sellers. Yet it was not as goddess of
vegetation that Venus became one of the most important deities in Roman mythology. Instead, she
was identified with the Greek goddess Aphrodite.
Her role in Roman religion is found in Lucretius'
work *On the Nature of Things* which opens with an invocation to the goddess as the great moving force in
life.

   At Rome Venus was worshiped as the goddess of
erotic love. *Vinalia* was the festival of Venus and
Jupiter. As the mother of Aeneas and the ancestor of
the Roman people, she was given special honors.
Julius Caesar built a temple to Venus Genetrix, the
mother of the Julian family, and established games
in her honor. Venus also was the protector of the
family as Venus Verticordia. It was this aspect of
Venus whose image was bathed and adorned with
flowers each spring by women of the upper classes.
In the second century C.E. Emperor Hadrian wished
to restore the worship of Venus to its rightful place.
A poem, the *Pervigilium Veneris* (The Virgil of Venus),
believed to be of the same century, deals with
Venus's role. It opens: "Let those love now, who
never loved before;/ And those who always loved,
now love the more." The work, in English
translation, was set to music by the American
composer Virgil Thomson.

   Numerous references to Venus are found in
literature, since the Roman name for Aphrodite was
used more frequently than the Greek. She appears in
Ovid's *Metamorphoses*; Chaucer's *The Knightes Tale*, part
of *The Canterbury Tales*; Spenser's *Epithalamium*, and in
Shakespeare's *The Tempest* and his long narrative
poem *Venus and Adonis*, in which she appears as
goddess of lust. Milton, less erotic than Shakespeare,
writes in *Comus*, "Venus now wakes, and wakens
love."

   Venus appears in the medieval Christian legend of
Tannhäuser. The legend inspired Swinburne's poem
Laus Veneris and Wagner's opera *Tannhäuser*. She also
appears in Dante Gabriel Rossetti's poem *Venus
Victrix* as the conquering force of love and in W. H.
Auden's poem, *Venus Will Now Say a Few Words.*

VENUS.

Venus

Among the attributes of Venus are a pair of doves or swans, sometimes drawing her chariot; the scallop shell and dolphins, relating to her birth from the sea; her magic girdle or belt, which induced love; a flaming torch that kindled love; and the myrtle, which was evergreen as love. The first day of April was sacred to Venus. She, along with Fortuna Virilis, the goddess of prosperity in the intercourse of men and women, was worshiped by women. With Concordia, Venus was worshiped as Verticordia, the goddess who turns the hearts of women to chastity and modesty. Other holidays in April honored her as the goddess of prostitution.

The Uranian Venus was the title given to Venus for her role as goddess of chastity to distinguish that role from Venus Pandemos, the Venus of erotic love. Tennyson, in his poem *The Princess* (1830), writes:

> The seal was Cupid bent above a scroll,
> And o'er his head Uranian Venus hang
> And raised the blinding bandage from his eyes.

Matthew Arnold's poem *Urania* (1869) is about a cold woman.

In Western European art Venus appears in many forms. Sometimes the word *Venus*, with no mythological significance, was used to mean "the female form." The best-known ancient representation of the goddess is the Venus di Milo, a Greek statue now in the Louvre in Paris. It was found on the island of Melos in 1829. (Sometimes it is called Venus of Melos.) A common form of the goddess is the Venus Pudica (Venus of modesty), in which she appears with one arm slightly flexed, one hand covering the pubic area while the other covers the breasts. This form is found in Botticelli's painting *The Birth of Venus*. Other great works portraying the goddess are Veronese's *Venus and Mars*, Titian's *Venus and Adonis*, and Boucher's *Venus and Vulcan*.

Common art motifs portraying the goddess are the Toilet of Venus, in which the goddess is shown reclining, with Cupid holding a mirror. The best-known version of this motif is Velázquez's *Venus at Her Mirror*, painted about 1650.

Another common motif portraying the goddess is that of Sacred and Profane Love. In this, two kinds of love—erotic and Platonic—are portrayed by two Venuses. The Venus Vulgaris is the erotic or common Venus, and the Venus Coelestis is the more spiritual one. The erotic Venus is portrayed in rich garments, and the spiritual Venus is portrayed naked. One of the examples of this type is Titian's *Sacred and Profane Love*.

The Triumph of Venus, another popular motif in art, portrays the goddess enthroned on her triumphal chariot drawn by doves or swans. An unknown American artist of the early 19th century painted *Venus Drawn by Doves* in watercolor. In the work the doves are larger than the goddess, and the landscape is American.

Venusberg (mountain of Venus). In medieval German legend, the mound or hill of Venus, the pagan Roman goddess. Here the Christian knight Tannhäuser stayed. Wagner's opera *Tannhäuser* has elaborate music depicting the erotic delights of the mountain.

Verdandi (present). In Norse mythology, one of the three named Norns, personifying the present; the other two are Urd and Skuld.

Verethraghna. In Persian mythology, war god noted for his ten incarnations, which are enumerated in the sacred *Avesta*. They are (1) a "strong, beautiful wind"; (2) "a beautiful bull, with yellow ears and golden horns"; (3) "a white, beautiful horse"; (4) "a burden-bearing camel, sharp-toothed, swift"; (5) "a sharp-toothed he-boar"; (6) "a beautiful youth of fifteen, shining, clear-eyed, thin-heeled"; (7) "a raven... the swiftest of birds"; (8) "a wild, beautiful ram, with horns bent round"; (9) "a beautiful fighting buck, with sharp horns"; (10) "a man, bright and beautiful," holding "a sword with a golden blade, inlaid with all sorts of ornaments."

Of the ten incarnations the most popular with the soldiers who worshiped Verethraghna were those of the raven and the boar. The raven was believed to make a man inviolable during battle, and the boar was an ages-old symbol of war gods.

St. Veronica (Dürer)

Veritas (truth). In Roman mythology, daughter of Saturn and mother of Virtue. She was portrayed as a young virgin dressed in white. Because she was so difficult to find, it was believed that she hid herself at the bottom of a well.

3025

Veronica, St. (true image). First century C.E. In Christian legend, patron saint of linen-drapers and washerwomen. Feast, 4 February.

An early Christian legend says that as Christ was bearing his cross to Calvary, a woman, seeing the drops of blood flow from his brow, wiped them off with her veil or handkerchief. When she looked at the cloth, she found the image of Christ impressed on it. The veil was later called the Vera Icon (true image) by Pope Gregory I. According to the same tradition, the name of the woman was Seraphina, but due to a misunderstanding in the transmission of the legend through the ages, the Vera Icon was turned into a proper name for a woman, and she was called St. Veronica.

That legend is the one generally circulated during the Middle Ages, though there is another account of the origin of the Vera Icon. It tells of a woman's being healed by touching Christ's garment. She then asked St. Luke to paint a picture of Christ on a piece of cloth. When she next saw Christ, she realized that he had changed and that the likeness on the cloth painted by St. Luke was not correct. Then Christ said to her, "Unless I come to your help, all Luke's art is in vain. My face is known only to Him who sent me." He then told her to prepare a meal for him, which she did. After the meal he wiped his face with a cloth and left his image on it. "This is like me," he said, "and will do great things."

Various Christian legends credit the Vera Icon with healing. One tells how it healed a Roman Emperor (either Vespasian or Tiberius) who was suffering from "worms in the head" or a "wasp's nest in the nose." As a result of seeing the image of Christ, the emperor ransacked Jerusalem and destroyed the Jews, selling them for 30 pieces of silver each. The anti-Semite legend was an attempt to blame the Jews for the death of Christ and to free the Romans from the actual guilt for the deed. (The Romans, not the Jews, killed Jesus.)

St. Brigit, who lived in the sixth century, complained of those who doubted that the face on the Vera Icon was that of Christ. Dante mentions the Vera Icon in *The Divine Comedy*. A statue of St. Veronica, or Seraphina portraying her holding the Vera Icon, is in St. Peter's Basilica in Rome. Numerous artists have portrayed the subject.

Vertumnus

3026

Vertumnus (the turner or changer). In Roman mythology, Italian god of fruits, who presided over the changing year. He had the power to assume any shape or form and used this power when he fell in love with Pomona, the Roman goddess of fruit trees. But the girl refused his advances. None of the various forms assumed by the god pleased Pomona. He appeared as an old woman and pleaded his case. Finally, he transformed himself into his natural shape, a handsome young man. Pomona then accepted him and became his wife. Milton, in *Paradise Lost* (book 9.394–95), describes the innocence of Eve before the Fall, writing: "Likeliest she seemed, Pomona when she fled/ Vertumnus. . . ." The tale is told in Ovid's *Metamorphoses* (book 14). A bronze statue of Vertumnus was located in the Tuscan business quarter in Rome, where he was regarded as the protector of business and exchange. His feast was 13 August, at which time sacrifices were made to him in his chapel on the Aventine.

Variant spellings: Vortumnus, Virtumnus.

3027

Vesper (evening). In Roman mythology, the planet Venus as the evening star. The Greek form, Hesperus, is often used in English literature. *Vesper* has come to be the name for evening services in the Christian church in Western Europe and America.

3028

Vesta. In Roman mythology, the goddess of the hearth, equivalent of the Greek Hestia.

Vesta's cult was introduced by Numa Pompilius from Lavinium, where Aeneas, according to Roman myth, had brought the Penates (gods of the store chamber) and the sacred fire from Troy. Roman consuls and dictators, on taking up and laying down their office, sacrificed in the temple of Vesta at Lavinium. It was customary in Italy, as in Greece, for the colonies to kindle the fire of their own Vesta at the hearth of the mother city. The ancient round temple of Vesta, which served as the central point of the city, was built by Numa Pompilius. In its neighborhood was the Atrium of Vesta, the home of the virgin priestesses of the goddess. Here the goddess was worshiped not in the form of a statue but under the symbol of eternal fire. It was the chief duty of the vestal virgins to keep the flame alive, and every 1 March it was renewed. If it went out, the guilty vestal was scourged by the pontifex. The fire could be rekindled only by a burning glass or by the friction of boring a piece of wood from a fruit tree. A daily sacrifice of food in a clay vessel was made. The daily purifications could be made only with flowing water, which the vestal virgins carried in pitchers on their heads from the fountain of Egeria or from the fountain of the Muses. During the day anyone could enter the temple, except for that part in which the *palladium* and other sacred objects were kept. At night men were not allowed in.

Vesta was the goddess of every sacrificial fire, whether in the home or the temple. She was worshiped along with Janus. His praise opened the service, and Vesta's closed it. Vesta's festival, the *Vestalia*, was held on 9 June. The matrons of the city walked barefoot in procession to her temple and asked the goddess to protect their households. Millers and bakers also kept the feast. The asses who worked the mills were decked out with garlands, with loaves suspended about their necks. Vesta's worship continued into the Christian era. It was abolished in the fourth century C.E. Although there was no image of the goddess in her temples, statues of Vesta were not uncommon in Rome. She was portrayed clothed and veiled, with chalice, torch, scepter and palladium. Vergil's *Aeneid* (book 2), Ovid's *Metamorphoses* (book 15) and *Fasti* (book 6), and Macaulay's poem *Battle of Lake Regillus* tell of Vesta.

3029

Vestal Virgins. In Roman cult, the priestesses of the goddess Vesta. To be called as a vestal virgin, girls had to be not younger than six and not older than ten years of age. They had to be without personal blemish and of free, respectable families. Their parents had to be living in Italy. The choice was made by casting lots from nominations made by the pontifex. The virgin accepted for the priestly office immediately left her father's authority and entered that of the goddess Vesta. After the rites of entrance the girl was taken into the Atrium of Vesta, her future home; she was ceremonially dressed, and her head was shorn. The time of service was 30 years—ten for learning, ten for performing the rites, and ten for teaching the duties. At the end of this time set by law the women were allowed to go and marry. They seldom did.

The vestal virgins were under the complete control of the pontifex. In the name of the goddess he exercised paternal authority over them. He administered corporal punishment if they neglected their duties. If they broke their vow of chastity, they were carried out on a bier to the *campus sceleratus* (the field of transgression) near the Colline Gate, beaten with rods, and buried alive. The guilty man was then scourged to death. No man was allowed to enter their quarters. Their service consisted of maintaining and keeping the eternal flame in the temple of Vesta, watching the sacred shrines, performing sacrifices, and offering prayers for the welfare of the nation. They took part in the feasts of Vesta, Tellus, and Bona Dea.

The vestal virgins dressed entirely in white, with a coronet-shaped headband, ornamented with ribbons suspended from it. When they sacrificed, they covered it with a white veil, a hood made of a piece of white woolen cloth with a purple border, rectangular in shape. It was folded over the head and fastened in front below the throat. The chief part in the sacrifices was taken by the eldest, the *virgo vestalis maxima*.

Various privileges were accorded the vestal virgins. When they went out, they were accompanied by a lictor (guard). At public games they were given the place of honor. When they gave evidence, they did not have to take the oath. They were entrusted with wills and public treaties. If anyone injured a vestal virgin, the penalty was death. If anyone, on the way to punishment, chanced to meet a vestal virgin in the street, the punishment was revoked. They had the honor of being buried in the Forum.

Shakespeare, in *Romeo and Juliet* (3.3.38), speaks of the "pure and vestal modesty" of Juliet's lips, and Alexander Pope in *Eliosa to Abelard* uses the term "the blameless vestal" for a Christian nun. Spontini's opera *La Vestale* (1807) deals with the vestal virgins.

Vetala. In Hindu mythology, demon in human form who haunts graveyards. His hand and feet are turned backwards.

3030

Vibhishana (terrifying). In Hindu mythology, brother of the demon-king Ravana, though in opposition to his brother. He left Lanka (Sri Lanka), Ravana's capital, and sided with the hero Rama in his fight to regain his throne. When Ravana died, Vibhishana was placed on the throne of Lanka.
Variant spelling: Vibhisana

3031

Victor de Plancy, St. (conqueror). Sixth century. In Christian legend, hermit saint. Feast, 26 February.

According to medieval legend as told by St. Bernard, St. Victor was very good at exorcism. One day St. Victor sent some workers to sow wheat. One of them, however, stole two bushels of seed. Instantly, the thief was possessed by the devil, who made smoke and fire issue from his mouth. St. Victor took pity on the man and made the sign of the cross. The devil fled, and the man confessed his guilt. In another legend St. Victor turned water into wine. One day the king of France, Chilperic, paid a visit to Victor. The saint greeted the king and offered him some water to drink. "O Lord," said Victor, "bless this water and fill the vessel which holds it with heavenly dew." The water was turned into wine.

3032

Victoria (victory). In Roman mythology, goddess of victory, daughter of Pallas and Styx, equated with the Greek goddess Nike. In Rome she had a temple, and festivals were held in her honor. Victoria was portrayed with wings, crowned with laurel, and holding a branch of palm in her hand. A gold statue of the goddess, weighing some 320 pounds, was given to the Romans by Hiero, king of Syracuse, and placed in the temple of Jupiter on the Capitoline Hill.

3033

Victor of Marseilles, St. (conqueror). Fourth century. In Christian legend, Roman soldier martyred under the emperor Diocletian. Patron of millers. Invoked against lightning and on behalf of weak or sick children. Feast, 21 July.

Victor was asked to sacrifice to the Roman god Jupiter. He not only refused; he destroyed the statue of the god. For his crime he was crushed with a millstone and finally beheaded. Three companions who had looked on his suffering became converted to Christianity. At the moment of Victor's death angels were heard singing, "Victory, Victory."

3034

St. Victor of Marseilles is portrayed in medieval Christian art with a millstone or dressed in full chain armor with shield and spurs.

Vidar (ruler of large territories). In Norse mythology, son of Odin and the giantess Grid. Known as the silent god, he is the one who will avenge Odin's death by slaying the Fenrir wolf at Ragnarok, the end of the world, and then will rule the new world.

3035

Vila (perish). In Slavic folklore, a female spirit, often the ghost of a girl who died before her wedding day, or was a suicide, or died unbaptized. A *vila* appears at night, enticing men to their doom by inviting them to her grave. This motif is used in Adolphe Charles Adam's ballet *Giselle, ou les Wilis*. It also supplied the subject for Giacomo Puccini's first opera, *Le Villi*.

3036

Vilacha. In Inca ritual, a ceremony performed after the sacrifice of a child; it consisted of smearing the sacrificer and other celebrants with the blood of the dead child. The child was laid on an altar, face upward, and strangled, garroted, or cut open with a knife. Another name for the ceremony is Pipano.

3037

Vili. In Norse mythology, one of Odin's brothers, along with Ve; sons of Borr and the giantess Bestla.

3038

Vimalakirti (stainless fame). In Buddhism, a man visited by Manjushri, the personification of wisdom, and thousands of disciples of the Buddha as well as goblins and deities, who all convened in one small square room. A long dialogue ensued, forming a work that has been translated into English as *The Holy Teaching of Vimalakirti*.

3039

Vimani. In Hindu mythology, the chariot of the storm god, Indra. The charioteer is Matali.

3040

Vincent de Paul, St. (to conquer). 1576–1660 C.E. In Christian legend, founder of Sisters of Charity; also Congregation Missions, or Priests of the Mission. Patron of all charitable societies, hospitals, lazarhouses (hospices for those afflicted with disease), and prisoners. Invoked to find lost articles and for spiritual help. Feast, 14 July.

St. Vincent de Paul is usually portrayed in a clerical cassock with a newborn infant in his arms. Sometimes a Sister of Charity is kneeling before him, or he extends his hand to a beggar.

3041

Vincent, St. (to conquer). Died 304. In Christian legend, deacon and Christian martyr. Patron of bakers, roofmakers, sailors, schoolgirls, and vine dressers. Patron saint of Lisbon, Valencia, and Saragossa. Feast, 22 January.

Vincent was born in Saragossa, Spain. During the persecution of the Emperor Diocletian he was about 20 and a deacon in the church. The proconsul Dacian rounded up all of the Christians of Saragossa, promised them immunity, then ordered them massacred. Vincent was brought before the tribunal along with Bishop Valerius. When they were accused, Valerius answered, but his reply was not heard because he had a speech impediment.

"Can you not speak loudly and defy this pagan dog?" Vincent asked the bishop. "Speak that the world may hear, or allow me, thy servant, to speak in your stead."

Vincent then spoke of the joys of being a Christian. Dacian was unmoved and ordered Vincent tortured. He was torn with iron forks and thrown into a dungeon. Nearly dead, he was miraculously sustained by angels. Dacian then tried to destroy Vincent by other means. He gave the saint every comfort, including a bed of roses. Finally, the saint died. Dacian, however, was still not satisfied. He had the dead body thrown into a garbage ditch. There it was left unburied, to be eaten by wild beasts and birds of prey. However, God sent a raven to watch over the body and to ward off wolves. On being told of this, Dacian had the body wrapped in oxhide, heavily weighted with stones, and cast into the sea. The body was carried out to sea but later appeared on the beach and was buried in the sand. Not long afterward the saint appeared to a widow and told her where he was buried. The widow went to the spot, found the body, and carried it to Valencia.

When the Christians in Valencia were fleeing the Moors in the eighth century, they took the body of the saint with them. Their ship was driven onto a promontory on the coast of Portugal. There they buried the body of the saint, naming the place Cape Saint Vincent, and two ravens guarded the remains. Part of the cape is called "El Monte de las Cuervas" in memory of the event. In 1147 King Alonzo I removed the saint's remains to Lisbon. This time two crows accompanied the vessel, one at the prow and one at the stern. The crows multiplied at such a rate in Lisbon that taxes were collected to support them.

In medieval Christian art St. Vincent is portrayed as a deacon with a raven nearby. An old missal printed in 1504 contains this proverb for the feast day of the saint:

If St. Vincent's Day be fine
'Twill be a famous year for wine.

Vindheim (home of the winds). In Norse mythology, the sky.

Vindsval (the wind cold). In Norse mythology, father of winter, sometimes called Vindloni (the wind man). In the *Prose Edda* he is described as having an "icy breath, and is of a grim and gloomy aspect."

Violet. An herb with a purple flower. In Near Eastern mythology the violet grew from the blood of the slain Attis, killed by a wild boar. He was consort to the Great Mother goddess Cybele. In Greek mythology the violet is sacred to Ares and Io, and in Christian symbolism white violets are associated with the Virgin Mary. In European folklore the flower also is associated with mourning, suffering, and death and was believed to spring from the graves of virgins.

Viracocha (lake of fat, foam of the water). In Inca mythology, supreme god and creator, lord of the generation of all life.

Viracocha made and molded the sun, endowing it with a portion of his own divinity. He placed the moon to guard and watch over the waters and winds, over the queens of the earth and the parturition of woman. He also created Chasca, the planet Venus. Viracocha was invisible and incorporeal, as were his messengers, called *huaminca* (faithful soldiers) and *hayhuaypanti* (shining ones). These, according to the *Relación anonyma de los costumbres antiquos de los naturales del Piru* (1615), carried Viracocha's message to every part of the world.

The writer says that when the Indians worshiped a river, spring, mountain, or grove, "it was not that they believed that some particular divinity was there, or that it was a living thing, but because they believed that the great god Illa Ticci (another name for Viracocha) had created and placed it there and impressed upon it some mark of distinction, beyond other objects of its class, that it might thus be designated as an appropriate spot whereat to worship the maker of all things; and this is manifest from the prayers they uttered when engaged in adoration, because they are not addressed to that mountain, or river, or cave, but to the great Illa Ticci Viracocha, who, they believed, lived in the heavens, and yet was invisibly present in that sacred object."

Viracocha was invoked in prayers for the dead to protect the body so that it would not undergo corruption or be lost in the earth. He conducted the soul to a heaven of contentment.

One of the more cruel aspects of Viracocha's cult was the sacrifice of children in his temple. The children, brought by their mothers, who considered it a great honor, were either drugged or, if very young, suckled shortly before the sacrifice. The child was laid on an altar, face toward the sun, and was strangled, garroted, or cut open with a knife. With their blood Vilacha, or Pipano, was performed, which consisted of smearing the sacrificer and other celebrants with the blood. Then a prayer was offered: "Oh Lord, we offer thee this child, in order that thou wilt maintain us in comfort, and give us victory in war, and keep to our Lord, the Inca, his greatness and his state, and grant him wisdom that he may govern us righteously."

The *Relación anonyma* says that the great temple at Cuzco, which was afterward the site of a Christian cathedral, was dedicated to Viracocha. It contained only one altar, and on it was a marble statue of the god, which is described as "both as to the hair, complexion, features, raiment and sandals, just as painters represent the Apostle, Saint Bartholomew."

Virgin and Child (Dürer)

Viracocha was known by several names, among them Usapu (he who accomplishes all that he undertakes or he who is successful in all things); Pachayachachi (teacher of the world); Caylla (the ever-present one); Taripaca (to sit in judgment), used for the god as the final arbiter of the actions and destinies of men; Tukupay (he who finishes); and Zapala (the one or the only one).

Variant spelling: Huracocha.

3047

Virgin Mary. First century C.E. In the Bible, N.T., the mother of Jesus. Her cult during the Middle Ages was the most influential in the development in Christian art and theology.

The Virgin Mary receives small notice in the New Testament. The accounts of Jesus' birth and early years do stress the Virgin, but she is in the background in most of the narratives. She appears at the foot of the cross and receives the Holy Spirit, as do the Apostles. No details are given of her birth or death.

One of the earliest beliefs was that Mary gave birth to Jesus, the Son of God (Luke 1:31–33), without losing her virginity. This doctrine is called the Virgin Birth. By the fourth century she was called *Theotokos* (God bearer,) and her cult began to spread throughout Christendom. Her cult, however, was based on earlier cults of various pagan goddesses, such as Isis, Diana, Ceres, and Rhea, whose marks of devotion were transferred to the Virgin. Their statues sometimes were used to portray the Virgin and Child. Isis, the great Egyptian goddess, for example, was often portrayed with the infant Horus. The switch from Isis and Horus to the Virgin and Child was therefore easy. Mary inherited not only the statues of pagan goddesses but the cults associated with them. She was called the Queen of Heaven, as were the goddesses, and was often identified with the moon. In France during the Middle Ages the peasants of the Perche district called the moon *Notre Dame* (Our Lady). In Portugal the people called the moon the Mother of God, and in Sicily Christ and the Virgin were identified with the sun and moon. An eclipse was explained as the outcome of a quarrel between Mother and Son.

Aside from the ancient influences, the medieval cult of the Virgin Mary was in part a reflection of the social background of the Middle Ages themselves. Much that was feudal and chivalrous in concept was applied to her cult. The Court of Heaven was very much like a medieval feudal court. Mary was the queen; the saints were her barons. This belief is expressed in one 14th-century tale written by a Franciscan. "We ought," he wrote, "to imitate the man who has incurred the king's anger. What does he do? He goes secretly to the queen and promises a present, then to the earls and barons and does the same, then to the freemen of the household and lastly to the footmen. So when we have offended Christ we should first go to the Queen of Heaven and offer Mary, instead of a present, prayers, fasting, vigils and alms; then she, like a mother, will come between thee and Christ, the father who wished to beat us, and she will throw the cloak of her mercy between the rod of punishment and us and soften the king's anger against us."

The Virgin Mary not only pleaded for sinners, she could even joust like a knight. Once the knight Walter of Birback was on his way to a tournament. He turned aside to pray to the Virgin Mary in a chapel and became so lost in prayer that he missed all of the jousting. When he finally arrived at the tournament, he was met with shouts of applause from the other knights and learned that he had performed marvelous feats and taken all of the prizes and prisoners. He knew then that it was the Virgin Mary, lance in hand, who had taken his place in the lists.

Mary also appears in a tale associated with St. Thomas à Becket. While a young man in Paris, among a company of fellow students, he boasted that he had a mistress "whom I call sweetheart . . . for there is no woman in all France to compare with her in beauty and loving kindness." He was referring to the Virgin Mary, but the students laughed at him because they knew he had no mistress. Thomas left and asked pardon of the Virgin for his deception. Suddenly she appeared to him and gave him a golden casket containing a chasuble and blade to show to his companions in token of the troth between them.

In her role as mistress the Virgin Mary could be as jealous as any woman. One of many tales is that of a young clerk in minor orders who was deeply devoted to the Virgin Mary, but one day he decided to leave his order and marry. In the midst of the wedding feast the Virgin Mary appeared.

"Tell me," she said, "you that once loved me with all your heart, why now you have cast me aside? Tell me, tell me, where is she who is kindlier and fairer than I? Why this miserable, misled, deceived wretch, which you have chosen instead of me, instead of the Queen of Heaven? What an exchange! You have left me for a strange woman, I that have loved you with true love. Even now in Heaven I have dressed for you a rich bed in my chamber, whereon to rest your soul in great bliss. If you do not quickly change your mind, your bed will be unmade in Heaven and made up in the flames of Hell instead."

At midnight the clerk climbed out of his bridal chamber and returned to his hermitage.

Sometimes a person could threaten the Virgin Mary to achieve an end. Once there was a woman who honored the Virgin by placing flowers before her shrine daily. One day the woman's son was taken prisoner. Weeping, the mother went to the shrine of the Virgin and Child and begged the image to return her son.

"O Blessed Virgin Mary, often have I asked thee for the deliverance of my son and thou hast not heard me. Therefore, as my son was taken from me, so will I take away thine, and will put him in durance as hostage for mine."

The woman then took the image of the Christ Child from the bosom of the Virgin, went home, wrapped up the image in a clean cloth, and shut it up carefully in a chest. The following night the Virgin appeared to the woman's captive son and said, "Tell your mother to give me my Son." The young boy was then miraculously freed. He came to his mother and told her that the Virgin Mary had freed him from prison. Thankful, the woman took the image of the Christ Child and placed it back in the bosom of the Virgin.

From the many tales that emerged during the Middle Ages regarding the Virgin, a very well defined picture of her character was presented. She loved soldiers, for example, and was often seen on the battlefield defending the Christians. She accompanied the Christian Crusaders when they went to the Holy Land to fight the Moslems. Joinville, the medieval historian, in his *Life of St. Louis*, tells how a man in Syria possessed by the devil was taken to a shrine of the Virgin Mary to be cured. The devil inside the man said when he arrived, "Our Lady is not here; she is in Egypt, helping the king of France and the other Christians who will come to this land this day, they on foot against the pagans all ahorse."

It is interesting to remember that the Virgin Mary also holds an honored place in the religion of Islam. In the Koran, the birth of Mary, her upbringing in the temple, the Annunciation and the birth of Jesus "under a palm tree" (Suras 3 and 19) are narrated. The incidents do not come from the New Testament, but from the apocryphal writings of the early Christian church. In the Koranic account the angel of the Annunciation, who is understood as the Spirit of God, says to Mary: "God has chosen you over all women" (Sura 3:37). Islam accepts the doctrine that Mary remained a virgin. One saying, attributed to Muhammad, is: "Every child is stung by Satan, except Mary and her Son." Islam, however, stops short of looking upon her as a female substitute for the Deity. Sura 5 of the Koran accuses Christians of worshiping Mary as a "third god." Of course, Islam rejects the doctrine that Jesus is God's son by saying, "It is not for Allah to take to Himself any offspring." (Sura 19). Prayer to the Virgin Mary is also forbidden in Sura 39 of the Koran.

The Islamic rejection of the excessive medieval Christian cult of the Virgin Mary was echoed by the Protestant Reformers, who also rejected the medieval excess. Eventually, Roman Catholics began to temper the excessive devotion of the Mary cult. Peter Canisus, a Jesuit theologian in the 16th century wrote: "We recognize that things have crept into the cult of Mary which disfigures it, and they may do so again. . . . There are some fanatics who have grown crazy enough to practice superstition and idolatry instead of the true cult."

John Donne, the great English poet, wrote in a sermon preached in 1624, "They hurt Religion as much, that ascribe too little to the Blessed Virgin, as they who ascribe too much." Donne thus stated the Anglican middle view of the Virgin's place in Christian theology. In one poem, *A Thanksgiving for the Virgin's Part in the Scheme of Redemption* he wrote:

> For that fair blessed Mother-maid,
> Whose flesh redeem'd us; That she-Cherubin,
> Which unlock'd Paradise, and made
> One claim for innocence, and disseiz'd sin,
> Whose womb was a strange heav'n, for there
> God cloath'd Himself, and grew,
> Our zealous thanks we pour. All her deeds were
> Our helps, so are her prayers; nor can she sue
> In vain, who hath such title unto you.

Will Durant in *The Age of Faith*, which is a study of the Middle Ages, wrote concerning the cult of the Virgin: "The worship of Mary transformed Catholicism from a religion of terror—perhaps necessary in the Dark Ages—into a religion of mercy and love."

The six principle feasts of the Virgin Mary observed in the Western church are those of the Immaculate Conception (8 December), sometimes simply called her Conception to avoid the doctrine of the Immaculate Conception, which is that Mary was born without Original Sin; her Nativity (8 September), the Purification (2 February), the Visitation (2 July) and the Assumption (15 August), sometimes called the Dormation of the Virgin to avoid the Roman Catholic doctrine that the Virgin was taken to heaven body and soul.

3048

Virgo (virgin). One of the constellations and the sixth sign of the Zodiac. The sun enters it about 23 August. In Greek mythology Erigone, who hanged herself after finding the murdered body of her father, Icarius of Athens, was transformed into the constellation Virgo. Virgo is portrayed as a robed woman holding a sheaf of grain in her left hand.

3049

Viriplaca. In Roman mythology, goddess who presided over the peace of families. If a couple quarreled, they went to the temple of Viriplaca, which was located on the Palatine Hill, and were supposed to be reconciled there.

Variant spelling: Veraplaca.

3050

Virtus (manliness, bravery, virtue). In Roman mythology, the virtues deified. There were two temples to Virtus erected in Rome, one to Virtue and the other to Honor. They were constructed so that to see the temple of Honor it was necessary to pass through the temple of Virtue. The main virtues were Prudence, portrayed as a woman holding a ruler pointing to a globe at her feet; Temperance with a bridle; Justice with an equal balance; Fortitude, leaning against her sword; Honesty, dressed in a transparent veil; Modesty; veiled; Clemency wearing an olive branch; Devotion, throwing incense on an altar; Tranquillity, leaning on a column; Health, portrayed with a serpent; Liberty, with a cap; and Gaiety, with a myrtle.

Vishnu

3051

Vis and Ramin. In Persian legend, two lovers who were "joined as bride and groom" after their deaths. The tale of the lovers is told in a narrative poem, *Vis O Ramin*, by the Persian poet Fakhr Ud-Din Gurgani.

3052

Vishakha. Fifth century B.C.E. In Buddhist legend, a wealthy woman disciple of the Buddha. She was the first to become the leader of the lay sisters.

3053

Vishnu (to pervade; to enter). In Hinduism, the supreme deity or the second god of the triad made up of Brahma, the creator; Vishnu, the preserver; and Shiva, the destroyer.

Vishnu, along with Shiva and Devi, is among the most popular deities in present-day Hinduism. In the ancient collection of hymns, the *Rig-Veda*, he is not of the first rank, but in later works, such as *The Mahabharata* and the *Puranas*, he is the embodiment of Sattwa-guna, the quality of mercy and goodness that displays itself as the preserving power, the self-existent, all-pervading spirit. Some worshipers of Vishnu called Varshnavas recognize him as the supreme being from whom all things originate.

Vishnu's preserving and restoring power has been manifested in the world in various avatars (descents), commonly called incarnations, in which a portion or all of his divine nature is wholly or partially in a human or animal form, either constantly or occasionally. All of the avatars were sent to correct some evil in the world. Ten is the number most commonly accepted, though some texts say 22, and others say they are numberless. The most popular are Rama, the seventh, and Krishna, the eighth.

The ten avatars are as follows:

Matsya (a fish). Vishnu took the form of a fish and saved Manu, one of the progenitors of the human race, from the great flood that destroyed the world. Manu found a small fish that asked him for protection. The fish grew rapidly, and Manu recognized it as Vishnu incarnate. When the great flood came, Vishnu, as Matsya, led the ark over the waters and saved Manu and the seeds of all living things. There are various accounts of this myth, with Vishnu appearing only in the later ones.

Kurma (the tortoise; turtle). The god took the form of Kurma to recover valuable objects lost in the great flood. During the churning of the ocean, when the gods and demons struggled to obtain the Amrita, the water of life, Vishnu also appeared as Kurma, helping the gods.

Varaha (the boar). Vishnu became Varaha to rid the world of the demon giant Hiranyaksha (golden eye). The demon had dragged the earth to the depth of the ocean. Vishnu fought the demon for 1,000

Matsya

years before he slew him. The epic poem *The Ramayana*, however, says that the god "Brahma became a boar and raised up the earth." The feat was only later ascribed to Vishnu by his worshipers.

Nara-sinha (man lion). Vishnu became Nara-sinha to rid the world of the demon Hiranya-kasipu (golden dress), who had control over the three worlds—sky, atmosphere, and earth—for a million years. The demon had obtained the control from either Brahma or Shiva (accounts vary). He had also obtained the boon of being invulnerable to man or beast, by night or day, on sea or land, and to any solid or liquid weapon. (This boon is sometimes ascribed to other deities.) The demon's son, Prahlada, however, worshiped Vishnu, which naturally upset his father. Hiranya-kasipu then tried to kill his son, but the boy was protected by Vishnu. In a scornful tone Hiranya-kasipu asked his son if Vishnu was in a pillar supporting the hall of his palace. The boy said, "Yes." Then the demon said, "I will kill him." He then struck the pillar. Vishnu stepped out of the pillar as Nara-sinha and tore Hiranya-kasipu to shreds.

Vamana (the dwarf). Bali (offering), a king, through his devotions and severe austerities, acquired control over the three worlds. He so humbled all of the gods that they asked Vishnu to protect them from Bali's power. Vishnu then took the form of Vamana and came to earth. He asked

Bali to be allowed to make three steps (the three strides of Vishnu, mentioned in the *Rig-Veda*). As much land as Vamana could cover in three steps would then belong to him. Because Vamana was a dwarf, Bali consented. Then Vishnu took two gigantic steps, striding over the heaven and earth, but out of respect for Bali he stopped short of the underworld, leaving that domain for the king. There are numerous variants of the three steps taken by the god. In Hindu texts Bali is sometimes called Mahabali (great Bali).

Parashu-rama

Parashu-rama (Rama with the ax). Parashu-rama came to earth to deliver the Brahmans (priests) from the control of the Kshatriyas (the warrior caste). He is said to have cleared the earth of the Kshatriyas 21 times. In his early life Parashu-rama was under the protection of the god Shiva, who taught him the use of arms and gave him the *parashu* (ax), from which he took his name. The first act told of him in the Hindu epic poem *The Mahabharata* relates to his mortal father, Jamadagni (fire-eating). Jamadagni was a king who ordered his sons to kill their mother, Runuka, because she was defiled by unworthy

thoughts. Four of Jamadagni's sons would not do so, and as a result the king cursed them, turning them into idiots. The fifth son, Parashu-rama, struck off his mother's head with an ax. Jamadagni then asked Parashu-rama what gift or request he wished. Parashu-rama begged his father to restore his mother to life and his brothers to sanity. The request was granted.

Rama-chandra (Rama the charming; beautiful-charming). Rama is regarded by his followers as a full incarnation of Vishnu, whereas the other avatars are only partial ones. Rama's tale is told in many Hindu works, the most famous being the *Ramayana*, which is found in numerous retellings.

Krishna (the dark one). Vishnu came to save the world from evil spirits who committed great crimes. Among the most famous was the demon-king Kamsa.

The Buddha (enlightened). The Buddha rejected the revealed character of the *Vedas* and the immortality of the deities. His religion became very popular throughout India but largely died out by about 1000 C.E. passing to the rest of Asia, until it was revived in modern times. The Brahmans claimed that the Buddha was an incarnation of Vishnu, who had come either to defeat the *asuras* (who had gained great power by worshiping the *Vedas*) by telling them the *Vedas* were not divine, or to draw people away from the worship of the *Vedas* and thus ensure the decline of the world cycle according to cosmic law.

Kalki (impure; sinful). This avatar has not yet occurred. Vishnu is to appear at the end of the world cycle, seated on a white horse, with drawn sword blazing like a comet, for the final destruction of the wicked, the renewal of creation, and the restoration of purity.

Among Vishnu's many titles are Achyuta (unfallen); Ananta (the endless); Ananta-sayana (who sleeps on the waters); Janarddana (whom men worship); Kesava (the hairy, the radiant); Kiritin (wearing a tiara); Lakshmipati (lord of Lakshmi), in reference to his wife, Lakshmi, in his incarnation as Narayana; Madhusudana (destroyer of Madhu); Mukunda (deliverer); Murari (the foe of Mura); Nara (the man); Narayana (who moves in the waters); Panchayudha (armed with five weapons); Padmanabha (lotus navel); Pitam-bara (clothed in yellow garments); Purusha (the man, the spirit); Purushottama (the highest of men, the supreme spirit); Sarngin (carrying the bow Sarnga); Vaikuntha-natha (lord of Vaikuntha), which is his paradise; and Yajneswara (lord of sacrifice).

Variant spellings: Visnu, Vishnoo.

Vishvakarman (all-maker). In Hindu mythology, a god said to have created man from speech. In the *Rig-Veda*, the sacred collection of ancient hymns to the gods, Vishvakarman is called the "all-seeing god, who has on every side eyes, faces, arms, and feet, who when producing the heavens and earth, blows them forth with his arms and wings; the father, generator, disposer, who knows all worlds, gives the gods their names, and is beyond the comprehension of mortals." The term was sometimes used for a Prajapati, a progenitor of the human race, and later for Twashtri, the architect and artisan of the gods.

3055

Vishvapani. In Mahayana Buddhism, one of the five Dhyani-Bodhisattvas, the wielder of the double thunderbolt, which is his symbol.

3056

Viswamitra (friend of all). In Hindu mythology, a Prajapati, born a member of the warrior class. Through his intense austerities Viswamitra became a Brahman. He appears in both epics, *The Mahabharata* and *The Ramayana*, where he is the adviser of Rama's father and Rama's own guru. Both epics tell of Viswamitra's love for the nymph Menaka. His austerities so alarmed the gods that they sent Menaka to seduce him. She succeeded, and the result was a child, Shakuntala.

3057

Vitalis, St. (vital). First century. In Christian legend, martyr and patron saint of Ravenna, Italy. Feast, 22 September.

St. Vitalis was one of the converts of St. Peter. He was the father of SS. Gervasius and Protasius. He served in the army of Nero and suffered martyrdom for burying the body of a Christian who had been martyred. After being tortured by a club set with spikes, Vitalis was buried alive.

The church at Ravenna that was dedicated to St. Vitalis during the reign of Emperor Justinian is considered one of the best examples of Byzantine architecture in Italy. The building was erected over the spot where the saint was supposedly buried alive. The Greek mosaics in the vault of the church portray Christ seated on the globe of the universe, and with his right hand St. Vitalis offers Christ his crown of martyrdom.

3058

Vitus, St. Died c. 300. In Christian legend, patron saint of dogs, domestic animals, young people, dancers, coppersmiths, actors, and mummers. Invoked against epilepsy, lightning, St. Vitus' dance, sleep-lessness, and snakebite. Patron of Prague, Saxony, and Sicily. Feast, 15 June.

Vitus was the son of noble Sicilian parents who were pagans. The boy, however, was a Christian, having been taught the faith by his nurse Cresentia and his foster father, Modestus. When Vitus' real father heard his son, now 12, was a Christian, he had him locked in a room or dungeon. When he looked through the keyhole to see what was happening, he saw his son dancing with seven angels. The sight so dazzled him that the man went blind. The boy cured his father, but his father still was against him, so Vitus and his nurse, Modestus, left by boat for Italy. An angel guided the boat safely to Jucania, where they remained for some time preaching to the people and being fed by an eagle sent by God. They then went to Rome where St. Vitus cured the Emperor Diocletian of his evil spirit, but the emperor still wanted Vitus to sacrifice to the pagan gods. Vitus refused and was cast into a caldron filled with molten lead, pitch, and resin. He came out safely. He was then exposed to a lion, but the animal did not touch him. Then Modestus, Crescentia, and Vitus were racked on an iron horse until their limbs were dislocated. At this point a great storm arose that destroyed their persecutors as well as their temples. An angel then came down from heaven and set the three free and brought them to Lucania, where they died in peace.

Vitus is often shown with a cock beside him, as in the statue to the saint in the cathedral of Prague. The cock symbol was used for an earlier pagan god and was given to the saint in popular lore. Offering a cock to the saint was practiced in Prague well into the 18th century.

3059

Vitzilopuchtl (sorcerer). In Aztec mythology, a war god, who could change himself into any shape. According to various Spanish accounts, Vitzilopuchtl was originally a sorcerer of the black arts who was noted for his strength in battle. When he died, he was deified and slaves were sacrificed to him. A dragonlike creature was his symbol.

3060

Viviane (living, alive?). In Arthurian legend, the enchantress who was loved by Merlin but later betrayed him. Viviane, called Nimuë in Malory's *Morte d'Arthur*, was a beautiful woman whom Merlin, in his old age, fell madly in love with. Viviane asked Merlin to teach her all of his magic art. After many years, when she had learned all of his magic and had grown tired of him, she asked him to show her how a person could be imprisoned by enchantment without wall, towers, or chains. After Merlin had complied she lulled him into a deep sleep under a white-

Viviane (Louis Rhead)

thorn laded with flowers. While he slept, she made a ring around the bush with her wimple and performed the magic Merlin had taught her. When Merlin awoke he found himself a prisoner. He never freed himself. Tennyson's "Vivien," part of the *Idylls of the King* and Ernest Chausson's symphonic poem *Vivian* treat the legend of Merlin and Viviane. Viviane is identified as the Lady of the Lake in many Arthurian legends.

3061

Vladimir of Kiev, St. c. 957–1015 C.E. In Christian legend, Apostle of Russia; responsible for that country's conversion to Orthodox Christianity. Feast, 15 July.

Vladimir was the great prince of Kiev, the "God-protected mother of Russian Cities," during the last quarter of the tenth century. He was brought up a pagan and, according to the *Chronicle of Nestor*, his "desire for women was too much for him." He had five wives and numerous female slaves. His conversion to Christianity is shrouded in mystery. He was faced with the need to choose a religion for his people and vacillated between Islam, Judaism, the Christianity of the West, and the Christianity of the East , or Byzantium. He sent ambassadors to witness the ceremonies of each religion, and they came back with the report that the Byzantine form of worship was the most beautiful and therefore must be for the true God. St. Vladimir therefore accepted the Byzantine form of Christianity. After his conversion he forced Orthodox Christianity on his subjects, imposing severe penalties on those who refused baptism.

"The Devil was overcome by fools and madmen," says the *Chronicle of Nestor*, stressing the fact that St. Vladimir received grace from God to overcome his evil earlier life. He put away his former wives and mistresses and married Anne, sister of the Greek emperor Basil II, which helped him politically. His bouts with his past life, however, continued. "When he had in a moment of passion fallen into sin he at once sought to make up for it by penitence and almsgiving," the *Chronicle of Nestor* says in support of the saint's varying moods.

3062

Vlkodlak. In Slavic folklore, a wolfman. If a child is born feet first and with teeth, it will become a *vlkodlak*; but one might also be transformed into a *vlkodlak* through witchcraft, in which case only the person who cast the spell can remove it. A *vlkodlak* also can appear as a hen, horse, cow, dog, or cat. The only remedy against the *vlkodlak* is the *kresnik*, a good spirit who will battle it.

Variant spellings: vukodlak, vrkolak, volkun.

3063

Vodyanik (water grandfather). In Slavic folklore, water spirit, the male counterpart of the female water spirit, Rusalka. Assuming many forms, Vodyanik can appear as an old man with a fat belly, wearing a cap of reeds and a belt of rushes. When he appears in a village, he assumes he can be spotted by the water oozing from the left side of his coat. Often he stays in the water, where he makes his home, appearing at night to comb his green hair. His nature varies and is either good or bad, depending on his mood at the time. If in a good mood he helps fishermen, but in a bad frame of mind he causes floods, overturns boats, and drowns men.

Variants of Vodyanik in Slavic folklore are Deduska Vodyancy (water grandfather) among the

Russians; Vodeni Moz (water man) among the Slovenians; Topielec (drowner) among the Poles; and Vodnik (water goblin) among the Czechs. Dvořák's symphonic poem *Vodník*, often called *The Water Goblin* or *The Water Sprite* in English, is based on a literary folk ballad by Karel Jaromir Erben in his collection *Kytice*.

3064

Volkh (sorcerer). In Russian folklore, hero of super-human strength who appears in the *byliny*, the epic songs, as well as in folktales. Volkh is a *bogatyr*, an epic hero, who could turn himself into a falcon, a gray wolf, a white bull with golden horns, or a small ant.

Variant spelling: Volga.

3065

Volos (ox?). In Slavic mythology, god of beasts and flocks, worshiped in some sections of Russia into the 19th century.

The demonic aspects of Volos were applied to demons, but his beneficent aspects were attached to St. Blaise (third century), patron saint of physicians, wax chandlers, and wool combers. In Russian Blaise is called Vlas or Vlassy. On his feast day a prayer is addressed to him that resembles an ancient prayer to Volos: "Saint Vlas, give us good luck, so that our heifers shall be sleek and our oxen fat." The rite of "curling Volos' hair" was still practiced in the 19th century, when peasants tied the last sheaf of grain into a knot at harvest time.

The Russian artist Tcheko Potocka portrayed a sacrifice to Volos that shows peasants slaughtering a horse at the feet of a massive statue of the god. In Lithuania, Volos is called Ganyklos.

Variant spellings: Veles, Vyelyes.

3066

Volsunga Saga. Scandinavian prose epic, believed to have been written in the 12th century C.E., telling of the hero Sigurd, who appears in Germanic myth as Siegfried.

Volsung, a lineal descendant of the god Odin, built his home around the trunk of the Branstock oak, whose branches overshadowed all that surrounded it. When Signy, Volsung's only daughter, was married against her will to Siggeir, king of the Goths, a one-eyed stranger (Odin in disguise) appeared among the wedding guests. He thrust a sword, Balmung, deep into the oak. Before leaving he said that the weapon should belong to the man who pulled it out. He then promised that Balmung would assure its owner of victory in every fight.

Although conscious that Odin had been among them, Volsung courteously invited the bridegroom,

Siggeir, to try his luck first. Siggeir did not succeed, nor did Volsung nor any of his ten sons—except for Sigmund, the youngest.

Siggeir offered to purchase the sword, but Sigmund refused. Angry at his refusal, Siggeir left the next day. Although Signy warned her kinsmen that her husband Siggeir was plotting revenge, the Volsungs accepted Siggeir's invitation to visit them.

When Volsung and his ten sons arrived in Gothland, Signy again warned them. The Volsungs were drawn into an ambush and bound fast to a fallen tree in the forest. Each night a wild beast (wolf) devoured one of the boys. Closely watched by her cruel husband, Signy could not aid her family. Only Sigmund, the youngest, was left alive. Signy told a slave to cover Sigmund's face with honey. A wild beast, attracted by the sweet odor, licked Sigmund's face. This enabled Sigmund to catch the animal's tongue between his teeth and struggle free.

When Siggeir went to investigate the next day, his messenger reported that no prisoners were left bound to the tree and that only a heap of bones was visible. Convinced that all of his enemies were dead, Siggeir ceased to watch Signy. She then stole out into the forest to bury the remains of her father and brothers, and there she discovered Sigmund. They both promised to seek revenge. Later Signy sent her two sons to Sigmund to be trained as avengers, but both proved deficient in courage. Signy came to the conclusion that only a pureblood Volsung would prove capable of the task. She disguised herself as a gypsy to visit Sigmund's hut and had a child by him, Sinfiotli. When Sinfiotli grew up, Signy sent him to Sigmund, who did not know it was his sister with whom he had slept.

With Sinfiotli as his helper Sigmund went to the cellar of the palace to capture Siggeir. But warned by two of his young children that murderers were hiding behind the casks, Siggeir had Sigmund and Sinfiotli seized and cast into separate cells. He ordered that they should be starved to death. But before the prison was closed, Signy cast into it a bundle of straw in which she had concealed Balmung, the magic sword.

With the sword the two freed themselves and set Siggeir's palace afire. Siggeir and his men were killed. Sigmund went to save Signy, who merely stepped out of the palace long enough to tell Sigmund that Sinfiotli was his son and then plunged back into the flames.

Sigmund returned home. In his old age he was killed in battle. Before he died, however, he had fathered a son, Sigurd, upon his young wife, Hjordis. In one version the mother died in childbirth, and Sigurd was raised by Mimer, a magician as well as a blacksmith. In a variant version of the saga a Viking discovered the young wife mourning over Sigmund's dead body and carried her off. She consented to become the Viking's wife if he would promise to be a good foster father to Sigmund's child. In his home Sigurd was educated by the wisest of men, Regin, who taught the hero all he needed to know. He advised Sigurd on the choice of a wonderful steed, Grane or Greyfell.

Seeing that the lad was ready for adventure, Regin told him of the gods Odin, Hoenir, and Loki, and how they had killed Otter and had to pay the price for the deed with gold; this gold was now guarded by Fafnir, who had transformed himself into a dragon. Sigurd, with the fragments of his father's sword, forged a new blade and went out to kill Fafnir. A one-eyed ferryman (Odin in disguise) conveyed him to where the dragon was and explained how best to kill the monster.

After Sigurd killed Fafnir, Regin joined him. Regin asked Sigurd to cut out the dragon's heart and roast it for him. Sigurd did as he was told, but while he was cooking the heart, he burned his finger. As he licked the burn, the taste of Fafnir's heart blood gave Sigurd the power to understand the language of birds. One bird nearby told him that Regin was coming up behind to kill him with his own sword. Enraged, Sigurd slew Regin. After piling up most of the treasure in a cave, where it continued to be guarded by the dead body of the dragon, Sigurd rode away, taking with him his sword, a magic helmet, and the ring.

Guided by the birds, he came to a place in the forest that was surrounded by flames. He rode through them and came upon Brynhild, asleep. The two fell in love. Brynhild told Sigurd she was a daughter of the god Odin. She had been placed there as punishment for saving a man whom Odin had doomed to death. As a result she was condemned to marry any mortal who could claim her. Sigurd gave Brynhild the ring.

Shortly after, he left and went to Burgundy, the land of the Nibelungs. Their ruler, Giuki, had a beautiful daughter, Gudrun, who fell in love with Sigurd and gave him a love potion, which made him forget Brynhild and fall in love with Gudrun. Sigurd asked for her hand in marriage. The marriage was agreed to if Sigurd would help Gunnar, a brother of Gudrun, to gain Brynhild as his wife.

Taking on Gunnar's form by use of the magic helmet, Sigurd went through the flames again, fought with Brynhild, and took back the ring. Not knowing it was Sigurd, she was forced to marry her "hero" and thus was made Gunnar's bride. When she reached the court, Sigurd did not know her because of the love potion. Brynhild became very bitter.

Brynhild would not have sexual intercourse with her husband, and Gunnar again sought Sigurd for help. The hero, once again using his magic helmet, fought with Brynhild one night and took her girdle and ring, which he carried off and gave to his wife Gudrun. Brynhild believed it was Gunnar who had conquered her.

However, Brynhild's resentment still smoldered. When Gudrun and Brynhild had an argument over who was to be first at bathing in the river, Gudrun showed Brynhild the magic ring and girdle, saying her Sigurd had wooed and won Gunnar's bride. Hogni, a kinsman of the Nibelungs, took Brynhild's side and told her he would help her avenge the insult. In one version Hogni killed Sigurd in bed by discovering his one vulnerable spot. In a variation, Sigurd was killed by Hogni while hunting in the forest.

By order of Gudrun, Sigurd's corpse was placed on a pyre which consumed his weapons and horse. Just as the flames were rising, Brynhild plunged into them and also died. A variant version records that she stabbed herself and asked to be burned beside Sigurd, his naked sword lying between them and the magic ring on her finger.

Atli of the Huns, Brynhild's brother, sought revenge for his sister's death. However, he accepted Gudrun as his wife. Gudrun agreed to the marriage because she was given a magic potion. When it wore off, however, she hated her husband. The end was a battle of Gunnar's and Hogni's men against Atli's forces. When Gunnar and Hogni were caught by Atli, he attempted to force them to tell him the hiding place of the treasure. Gunnar said he would not reveal it as long as Hogni lived because he had given Hogni his word. Atli then had Hogni's heart brought to Gunnar to show him he was dead. Gunnar still refused to tell and was killed. Atli then ordered a festival, but he was killed by Gudrun, who either stabbed him to death with Sigurd's sword or set fire to the palace and perished with the Huns. A third variation recounts that Gudrun was cast adrift and landed in Denmark, where she married the king and bore him three sons. These youths, in an attempt to avenge the death of their stepsister Swanhild, were stoned to death. Gudrun finally committed suicide by casting herself into the flames of a huge funeral pyre.

The *Volsunga Saga* was translated into English in the 19th century by the poet William Morris. He also tells the story in his long narrative poem, *Sigurd the Volsung and the Fall of the Niblungs*, an epic in four books.

3067

Volturnus. In Roman mythology, a god of the Tiber River. He was identified in later Roman belief with

Tiberinus, a legendary king for whom the Tiber was named after he drowned there. His feast was 27 August.

3068

Volva (carrier of a magic staff). In Norse mythology, the sibyl who recited the *Voluspa*, the first poem of the *Poetic Edda*, which narrates the creation and destruction of the world.

3069

Vortigern. In medieval British mythology, a monk who killed King Constans and usurped his throne. He built a tower, to which he fled when his land was invaded by Ambrosius Aurelius, and he was burned to death.

3070

Votan (the breast, the heart?). In Mayan mythology, a culture hero and god. At some time in the past Votan had come from Valum Votan (the land of Votan) in the far east. He was sent by God to divide out and assign to the different races their portion of the earth and to give each its own language.

His message was brought to the Tzentals (Tzendals), a Mayan tribe living in Mexico. According to Daniel G. Brinton in *American Hero-Myths* (1882), "Previous to his arrival they were ignorant, barbarous, and without fixed habitations. He collected them into villages, taught them how to cultivate the maize and cotton, and invented the hieroglyphic signs, which they learned to carve on the walls of their temples. It was even said that he wrote his own history in them."

Votan also instituted civil laws and reformed religious worship, earning the title "master of the sacred drum" because of its use in ritual dances. He also invented the calendar and founded the cities of Palenque, Nachan, and Huehuetlán. In Heuhuetlán he built an underground temple "by merely blowing with his breath. In this gloomy mansion he deposited his treasures and appointed a priestess to guard it, for whose assistance he created the tapirs."

When it was time for him to depart, after he had civilized the Indians, he "penetrated through a cave into the underground, and found his way to the root of heaven."

Variant spelling: Voton.

3071

Vourukasha. In Persian mythology, sea god or the sea. Also the name of the heavenly lake in which grows the tree of life.

3072

Vretil. In medieval Jewish folklore, angel identified with the "man clothed with linen" carrying "a writer's inkhorn by his side," described by the prophet Ezekiel (9:2). Vretil wears linen since it is ritually clean, whereas wool, coming from an animal, is not. The "man clothed with linen" in Ezekiel (9:1) is to go "through the midst of Jerusalem and set a mark upon the foreheads of the men that sigh and that cry for all the abominations that be done in the midst thereof."

3073

Vritra (restrainer). In Hindu mythology, the demon of drought, constantly at war with Indra, the storm god. Vritra is sometimes called Vritrasura or Ahi, though in some texts Ahi is a distinct personality.

Hephaestus (Vulcan)

3074

Vulcan (volcano). In Roman mythology, the ancient Italian fire god, god of forging and smelting, equivalent of the Greek god Hephaestus.

As smith (or god) of the forge, Vulcan was called Mulciber (the softener or smelter). As a beneficent god of nature who ripens the fruit with his warmth, he was the husband of Maia (or Maiesta), the Italian goddess of spring. Both Vulcan and Hephaestus had sacrifices offered to them by the *flamen Volcanalis* priests after Vulcan became identified with the Greek fire god Hephaestus. When the Roman Venus was identified with the Greek goddess Aphrodite, Vulcan was regarded as her husband. Chaucer, in *The Knightes Tale*, writes, "Venus . . . spouse to Vulcanus." Vulcan's best-known shrine in Rome was the Volcanal, a level space raised above the surface of the Comitium and serving as the hearth of the spot where the citizens' assemblies were held. Vulcan's chief festival was the *Vulcanalia*, observed 23 August, when certain fish were thrown into the fire on the hearth and races were held in the Circus Flaminius. Sacrifices were offered to Vulcan as god of metalworking on 23 May, the day appointed for a cleansing of the trumpets used in worship. As Lord of Fire, Vulcan was also god of conflagrations. His temple in Rome was situated in the Campus Martius. Juturna and Stata Mater, goddesses who caused fires to be quenched, were worshiped along with him at the festival of *Vulcanalia*.

Shakespeare, in *Hamlet*, has Hamlet speak to Horatio, making reference to Vulcan:

> . . . if his occulted guilt
> Do not itself unkennel in one speech,
> It is a damned ghost that we have seen,
> And my imaginations are as foul
> As Vulcan's smithy. (3.2.85–89)

The references are to Hamlet's own imagination as well as to his plot to discover the guilt of Claudius.

There is a 17th-century copy of Breughel the Elder's *Venus at the Forge of Vulcan* as well as a brilliant *Forge of Vulcan* by Velázquez, painted in 1630.

In English our word *volcanoes* comes from Vulcan, as does the verb *vulcanize*, the chemical process for treating crude rubber.

Variant spellings: Vulcanus, Volcanus.

3075

Vulture. A large bird that feeds on dead animals. The ancient Egyptian cult of the vulture dates from predynastic times, when the pharaoh was called Nekhebet (lord of the city of the vulture), referring to the vulture goddess Nekhebet. The bird was also associated with Mut and Neith. Vultures were believed to follow men into battle, hover over those who would die, and later eat their flesh. Thus the bird was sacred to the Greek war god Ares and his Roman counterpart, Mars. All vultures were believed to be female and to be impregnated by turning their backs to the south or southwest wind while flying. They were believed to bring forth their young in three years.

W

Wabosso (white hare or maker of white). In North American mythology (Algonquian), brother of Nanabozho, culture hero and trickster.

Wade. In Northern mythology, giant father of Wayland the Smith, who appears in Anglo-Saxon and Danish tales.

Wahan Tanka. In North American Indian mythology (Oglala Lakota), Great Spirit, who appears as Wanbli Galeshka, the spotted eagle.

Waki-Ikazuchi. In Japanese mythology, one of the Ikazuchi, the eight gods of thunder.

Wakinyan-Tanka. In North American Indian mythology (Oglala Lakota), great thunderbird of the west, protector of the sacred pipe.

Wakonda. In North American Indian mythology (Omaha), creator god, in whose mind all things existed until they found a place for bodily existence.

Walangada (belonging to the sky). In Australian mythology, a primal being of unidentified form who ascended to the sky to become the Milky Way.

Walpurga, St. Died 779 C.E. In Christian legend, abbess of Heidenheim. Invoked against coughs, rabies, frenzy, and plague and for a good harvest. One of her feast days, 1 May, is preceded by the *Walpurgisnacht* in Germany, which, according to folklore and legend, is the night when witches gather together on the Brocken—also called Blocks-berg, the highest peak of the Harz Mountains—and revel and carouse with demons.

The name *Walpurgishnacht* derives from the English saint, Walpurga, who was the niece of St. Boniface. She spent some 27 years of her life at the monastery in Winburn, in Dorset, England, before she went on a missionary journey with ten other nuns to Germany. She was made the first abbess of a Benedictine nunnery at Heidenheim, between Munich and Nuremburg. During her lifetime she was noted for her skill in medicine, and her tomb was credited with healing powers. Since the earlier pagan festival marked the beginning of spring, the saint's feast became confused with the pagan one, and the witches' sabbath was named after the nun.

The *Walpurgisnacht* appealed particularly to the 19th-century German artists. Goethe twice treated the theme: once in a poem he called a "dramatic-ballad," *Die erste Walpurgisnacht* (The First Walpurgis Night) and in *Faust* (parts 1 and 2). Mendelssohn set Goethe's text for soloists, chorus, and orchestra as *Die erste Walpurgisnacht*, Opus 60, in 1832.

Thomas Mann's novel *The Magic Mountain* has a chapter entitled "Walpurgis-Night," dealing with the Shrovetide festival. Mann, in recalling the name that was used by Goethe, wished to stress the similarity of his theme with that of Goethe's *Faust*.

In art St. Walpurga is usually portrayed as a royal abbess with a small flask of oil on a book. Sometimes she is shown with three ears of corn in her hand (bringing in the symbolism of the pagan festival). Her main festival is now observed on 25 February.

Variant spellings: Walpurgis, Walburga, Bugga.

Walwalag Sisters. In Australian mythology, two sisters who were eaten and regurgitated by the Rainbow Snake. Their story is reenacted in various fertility rites of the tribes.

Wambeen. In Australian mythology, an evil being who sends lightning and fire. When he comes down to earth, he kills travelers. He is recognized by an evil odor.

Wandering Jew. In medieval anti-Semitic legend, a Jew who was said to have cursed Jesus on his way to be crucified and was punished by having to wait for Christ's Second Coming. The earliest mention of the legend is in the 13th-century Chronicles of the Abbey of St. Albans. According to that account, when Jesus was on his way out of Pilate's hall, a porter, called Cartaphilus, "impiously struck him on the back with his hand and said in mockery, 'Go quicker, Jesus, go quicker; why do you loiter?' And Jesus, looking back on him with severe countenance, said to him, 'I am going, and you will wait till I return.'"

The chronicle goes on to say that Cartaphilus was 30 at the time. He later became a Christian and, according to the account, is still alive, waiting for the Second Coming of Christ. Though the name Cartaphilus is given in the earliest account, other names have been given to the Wandering Jew. In Latin versions he is called Johannes Buttadeus (John the God Smiter). In German versions he is called Ahasuerus. The medieval legend has inspired Goethe's *Der ewige Jude*, Edgar Quinet's prose drama *Ahasvérus*, George Groly's *Salathiel*, and Eugene Sue's long novel *The Wandering Jew*.

3087

Wanga. In Haitian voodoo, an evil spell that causes death in seven days.

3088

Wang Jung. 305–234 B.C.E. In Chinese legend, one of the seven Chu-lin Ch'i-Hsien (Seven Immortals). He was once a court minister but left his position for a life of pleasure. Once he sold a plum tree cut from his estate only after removing the plums so it could not be grown elsewhere.

In Japanese legend he is called Oju.

3089

Wang Mu (Mother Wang, Queen Mother). In Chinese mythology, the spirit of metal, who was born with a tiger's teeth. She is one of the five spirits of natural forces, the Wu Lao.

3090

Washington, George (1732-1799). In American history and folklore, first president of the United States, father of his country. The best- known Washington legend was invented by Parson Mason Weems in *The Life of George Washington . . . . .* According to Weems, when Washington was about six years old his father gave him a hatchet. "One day, in the garden, he unluckily tried the edge of his hatchet on the body of a beautiful English cherry tree, which he barked terribly." When his father discovered that the tree had been chopped down, he asked who might be responsible. "George," said his father, "do you know who killed that beautiful little cherry tree yonder in the garden?" "I can't tell a lie, Pa; you know I can't. I did cut it with my hatchet." The father then called George into his loving arms. This moral tale, which turns George into an American saint, was painted by Grant Wood. Nathaniel Hawthorne, the great American novelist, commented that George Washington "had no nakedness but was born with his clothes on and his hair powdered."

Though there is no history in the cherry tree tale, there is history in the legend of the crossing of the Delaware in December 1776, as well as in the Valley Forge story. In each case greater drama has been added by folklore. In Emmanuel Leutze's famous painting of the crossing of the Delaware, for example, the flag portrayed was not in use until 1777. Another example of the sainting of Washington portrays him kneeling in a lonely clearing near Valley Forge. According to legend, a man told his wife, "I am greatly deceived if God do not, through Washington, work out a great salvation for America." George Washington was far from being a believer in established religion. In fact, he almost had to be dragged to church. The cult of Washington found its greatest growth during the 19th century. Americans compared him to Moses, Jesus, and various saints. He was often portrayed as a Roman nobleman or a knight. One 19th century Chinese painting portrays Washington ascending to heaven with an angel.

3091

Watauineiwa (the most ancient one). In the mythology of the Yahgan Indians of Tierra del Fuego, supreme being. He is a beneficent god with no body, and he lives in the heavens. Though not the creator, Watauineiwa sustains life and is believed to be the upholder of moral order.

3092

Water of Life. In world folklore, magic water that restores the dead to life, cures all illness, or bestows immortality. Ponce de León's quest for the Fountain of Youth contains the motif of a water of life, as does Hawthorne's tale *Dr. Heidigger's Experiment*.

3093

Wave maidens. In Norse mythology, the nine daughters of the sea god Aegir and his sister-wife Ran, mother of Heimdall. They are Gialp (yelper), Greip (gripper), Egia (foamer), Augeia (sand strewer), Ulfrun (she-wolf), Aurgiafa (sorrow-whelmer), Sindur (dusk), Atla (fury), Aiarnsaxa (iron sword). They appear in the *Poetic Edda* in *The Lay of Hyndla*.

3094

Wayland the Smith (artful smith). In medieval English legend, the wonder-working smith, sometimes called simply Wayland or Smith and in Norse, Volund the Smith.

Wayland was the son of a sailor and a mermaid. He was king of the elves and a maker of magic articles, such as a feather boat, a garment with wings, a solid gold arm ring, and magic swords. His brothers married Valkyries. Despite his cleverness, Wayland was made a prisoner by Nidudr, the evil king of Sweden, who had his feet mutilated. Eventually, Wayland killed two sons of Nidudr and raped his daughter Bodhilda. He set the skulls of the slain boys in gold and gave them to Nidudr. He gave their mother jewelry fashioned from their eyes. Their teeth were made into a breast pin for their sister. After he had given his gifts and told Nidudr what they were, he flew away to Valhalla on his magic wings.

Sir Walter Scott mentions Wayland in his novel *Kenilworth*, which says that he lived in a cave near Lambourn, Berkshire, since called Wayland Smith's Cave. It was believed that if a traveler tied up his horse there, left sixpence for a fee, and hid from sight, he would find his horse shod when he returned.

3095

Weasel. A small carnivorous mammal with a long slender body. For the ancient Greeks the weasel was a symbol of evil. If one appeared at a meeting, the group would disperse. In Apuleius's *Golden Ass* witches transform themselves into weasels. It was believed by medieval Christians that the weasel conceived through the ear. For the medieval Christian it became a symbol of unfaithfulness, though there was also a medieval belief that the Virgin Mary was impregnated through the ear. The saying was "God spoke through the angel and the Virgin was impregnated through the ear." The *Gesta Romanorum* uses the weasel as a symbol of St. John or Christ himself because the weasel was an enemy of the basilisk, or serpent—the devil. In the 1840s popular song *Pop Goes the Weasel*, the weasel may stand for a whore.

3096

Webster, Daniel. 1782–1852. In American history and folklore, lawyer, public official, statesman, and orator. He appears in Stephen Vincent Benét's short story *The Devil and Daniel Webster*. In it Jabez Stone, a New Hampshire farmer, sells his soul to Mr. Scratch, the devil. When Mr. Scratch comes to collect, Daniel Webster defends Stone before a jury of depraved characters and wins the case. Benét dramatized the tale, and Douglas Moore wrote the music for the opera *The Devil and Daniel Webster*. A Hollywood film of the tale was made, titled *All That Money Can Buy* (1941), starring Walter Huston as Mr. Scratch.

3097

Wei T'o. In Chinese Buddhism, a god who protects the Buddhist religion. His image is placed in the first hall of a Buddhist monastery. He is portrayed in complete armor and holding a scepter-shaped weapon of assault.

3098

Wele (high one). In African mythology (Abaluyia of Kenya), creator sky god who sent death as a punishment for man's cruelty. Once Wele observed how a farmer refused food to a hungry chameleon. Angered, the chameleon cursed the farmer, saying the farmer would die. The chameleon left and was later fed by a snake. Wele then decided that humans should die for their evil natures, but the kind snake should be rewarded with renewed life by shedding his skin.

3099

Wenceslaus and Ludmilla, SS. Tenth century C.E. In Christian legend, Wenceslaus is the patron saint of Bohemia. Wenceslaus' feast day is 28 September, and Ludmilla's is 16 September.

Wenceslaus was brought up a Christian by his grandmother, Ludmilla. Drahomia, his mother, and her son Boleslaus were pagans and opposed the conversion of Bohemia to Christianity by Wenceslaus and Ludmilla. Drahomia and Boleslaus had Ludmilla killed by hired assassins who strangled her to death with a veil or a rope. Wenceslaus, however, made peace with his mother and brother. After Wenceslaus married, Boleslaus realized he would not be made king. He therefore arranged for the murder of Wenceslaus. He invited the king to celebrate the feast of Sts. Cosmos and Damien. On his way to Mass, Wenceslaus was killed by his brother and some hired henchmen. The people immediately claimed the king as a martyr.

The English carol *Good King Wenceslaus*, written in the 19th century by J. M. Neale, is about the sainted king. Antonin Dvořák's oratorio *St. Ludmilla* is based on the medieval legend.

Wen Chang Ti-chun

In medieval Christian art St. Wenceslaus is portrayed as a king with an eagle on his banner or shield. St. Ludmilla is shown with a veil or rope, symbols of her martyrdom. Wenceslaus is the English form of the Czech name Vaclav.

Wen Chang Ti-chun. Fourth century C.E.? In Chinese Taoist mythology, the deified mortal Chang Ya-Tzu, worshiped as the principal god of literature. In Chinese art he is often portrayed holding a pen and a book on which is written: "Heaven decides literary success." Sometimes he is portrayed as a handsome young man in a sitting position.

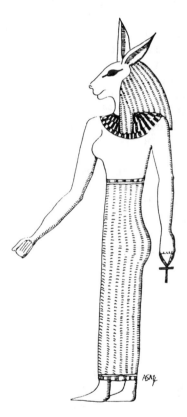

Wenenut

Wenenut. In Egyptian mythology, goddess portrayed as a woman with the head of a hare or rabbit. Wenenut usually holds a knife in each hand, identifying her with the destructive goddess Sekhet. But in her more benevolent aspect Wenenut holds a scepter in one hand and the ankh, sign of life, in the other. Her male counterpart was the hare godWonenu, who was considered a form of Osiris, the god of resurrection.

Were (father of grace). In African mythology (Luo of Kenya), creator god, cause of life and death, who punishes evildoers with his thunderbolts. Sacrifices and offerings to Were are made in the morning under large trees.

Wesak. In Theravada Buddhism, the combined feast of the Buddha's birth, enlightenment, and *parimbbana* (death and Nirvana), observed at the May full moon. *Variant spelling*: Vesak.

Whale. A large air-breathing marine mammal with a fishlike body. In Christian folklore the whale has often been equated with the devil or demonic forces. One medieval Christian belief was that a whale would lure fish by its sweet breath and then eat them, just as the devil would lure a person to sin. One tale found in the Jewish Talmud tells how sailors could mistake a whale for an island and board the monster. After they made a fire, the whale would begin to descend, taking the crew to their watery death. The tale was also told in medieval Europe. Milton's *Paradise Lost* gives a variant of the tale and identifies the whale with Leviathan, the primeval dragon in the Old Testament (Psalm 74:14) that Yahweh, the Hebrew God, subdued. In the biblical Book of Jonah the prophet fled the Lord by boarding a ship so that he would not have to preach. A storm arose; the sailors blamed Jonah and cast him into the sea. "Now the Lord has prepared a great fish to swallow Jonah, and Jonah was in the belly of the fish three days and three nights" (Jonah 1:17). The author of the Gospel According to St. Matthew, not satisfied with "great fish," writes that Jonah "was three days and three nights in the whale's belly" (Matt. 12:40). The symbolism was to suggest that Christ would be three days and three nights in the tomb before he would arise. The most famous use of the whale in modern literature is Herman Melville's novel *Moby Dick, or The White Whale*, in which scholars see the whale as a symbol of the devil, God, a combination of both, or man.

Wheat. Cereal grasses cultivated for their grain, often called corn in English literature. Wheat was sacred to the Greek goddess Demeter, who gave it as a gift to humankind. In Roman mythology wheat was sacred to Ceres, goddess of the harvest. In Christian ritual wheat, which makes bread, forms part of the Holy Eucharist. In French Christian folklore the Virgin Mary is sometimes addressed as *Notre-Dame Penetière* (Our Lady the Bread Giver).

Whitsunday. In Christian ritual, English name for the feast of Pentecost, ranking in importance with Christmas and Easter. Whitsunday commemorates the descent of the Holy Spirit on the Apostles and disciples, the founding of the Church, the gifts of the Holy Spirit, and the mission to bring the Christian faith to all peoples throughout the world. The name Pentecost comes from the Greek word for 50 and refers to the 50 days after the Jewish Passover, which the ancient Jews celebrated as Shavuoth, a festival of thanksgiving for the year's harvest (Exodus 23:16). The Jewish feast also commemorated the giving of the Law of Moses. The entire time from Passover to Pentecost was also called Pentecost, and thus the disciples were gathered together, as described in Acts 2:1ff, at the end of the 50 days. The Early Church adopted the Greek name from the Jewish feast. When the feast is called Whitsunday, as in *The Book of Common Prayer*, it refers to the custom in Northern European countries of conferring baptism during the time. The candidates for baptism were dressed in white, thus White-Sunday, or Whitsunday. Since it was too cold in many Northern European countries to baptize during the great Easter vigil, many of the customs were transferred to Pentecost.

As part of the great feast the hymn *Veni Sancte Spiritus* (Come Holy Spirit) is sung during the Eucharist. The hymn is attributed to Stephen Langton, archbishop of Canterbury in the early 12th century. In England during the Middle Ages Pentecost was the time when people would contribute to the upkeep of the church building, as well as give money to the cathedral if their house had a chimney. The offering to the cathedral was called Whitsun-farthing or smoke-farthing. Local churches also sold church ale, often called Whitsun ale. Other European Christians would let loose doves from the church rafters or send down hot or lighted coals (or Tongues of Fire) to recapture the descent of the Holy Spirit on the apostles. The doves were released when the priest intoned the *Veni Sancte Spiritus*, and the people made loud noises with drums, whistles, and other noisemakers to symbolize the sound "as of a violent wind blowing," as described in Acts 2:2. In some countries in Europe on the night before Pentecost people still walk barefoot on the grass to obtain its healing power, while others collect the dew of the eve of Pentecost on cakes or bread and serve it to the animals to protect them from illness. The Maypole, so hated by the English Puritans, was also one of the symbols connected with Pentecost.

Whittington, Dick. 15th century. In English history and legend, a poor orphaned country boy who becomes the lord mayor of London.

Dick heard that London was "paved with gold" and went there to earn a living. At the point of near starvation Dick found work with a kind merchant's family as a cook's helper. The cook, however, mistreated Dick, and the boy ran away. Resting by a roadside, he heard the Bow bells ring, and they seemed to say to him: "Turn again, Whittington, thrice Lord Mayor of London." So Dick returned to his master. In time his master made Dick an offer to go on a ship bound for Morocco. Dick had nothing but a cat, which accompanied him. When he arrived in Morocco, he discovered that the king of Morocco was having trouble with mice, and Whittington's cat eliminated them. This so pleased the king that he bought the cat from Whittington at a fantastic price. Dick invested the money, married his master's daughter, was knighted, and was thrice elected lord mayor of London.

An epitaph destroyed in the Great Fire of London said:

Beneath this stone lies Whittington,
Sir Richard rightly named,
Who three times Lord Mayor served in London,
In which he ne'er was blamed.
He rose from indigence to wealth
By industry and that,
For lo! he scorned to gain by stealth
What he got by a cat.

Wi-haru (the place where the wise words of those who have gone before us are resting). In North American Indian mythology (Pawnee), an invisible but sacred spot in a traditional Pawnee home, between the buffalo altar at the rear of the lodge and the central fireplace, all of these on a line from the entrance.

Wihio. In North American Indian mythology (Cheyenne), the trickster. In one myth Wihio persuades a coyote to dress as a baby, while he dresses as a woman, so that they can get some food from a man who stores tongue. The man gives the tongue to Wihio, who proceeds to eat it all. "Give me some too; I'm also hungry," the coyote cries out. But Wihio just continues to eat the tongue and dips his fingers in the soup for the coyote to lick. When the coyote threatens to reveal the deception to the man who gave them food, Wihio takes him out and throws him into the lake.

William of Norwich, St. Died 1137? In Christian anti-Semite legend, child saint said to have been "ritually murdered" by the Jews. The accusation was quite common during the Middle Ages and was used by secular and religious authorities in their attempt to destroy the Jews. Feast, 9 April.

Thomas de Monmouth in his *History of the Martyrdom of William of Norwich*, a contemporary account, writes that the 12-year-old William, who was apprenticed to a tanner at Norwich, England, was killed on Good Friday, 9 April 1137, by Jews. The lurid account describes how the boy was taken, gagged, and crucified. After he was dead, his body was placed in a sack and carried to the city gates of Thorpe Wood, where it was to be burned. The murderers were surprised and left the body hanging near a tree. A chapel was afterward erected on the spot and dedicated to St. William in the Wood. In 1144 the body was removed to the churchyard of the cathedral of the Holy Trinity.

Numerous other child saints with similar tales abound in medieval Christian legend. Among them are Hugh of Lincoln, St. Janot of Cologne, St. Richard of Pontoise, St. Michael of Sappendelf, St. Simon of Trent, St. Vernier, St. Werner or Garnier.

William of Orange (will-helmet). In the Charlemagne cycle of legends, a hero who appears in numerous French epics. All we know of the historical William is that he was a contemporary of Charlemagne, whom he served as a military leader and administrator. In legend, he is a devoted protector of Louis, Charlemagne's son, as well as a defender of the Christian faith against the Moslems of Spain. Seven French epics describe his life. Dante's *The Divine Comedy* places him in Paradise in the sphere of Crusaders, beside Charlemagne and Godfrey of Boulogne. He also appears in medieval Norse, Italian, and Latin legends. In some accounts he is credited with being a saint, because he spent his last years in a monastery.

William of Palermo (will-helmet). In medieval legend, a hero, son of King Apulia of Palermo. As heir to the throne, William's life was in danger, so he was carried away by Alphonse, a werewolf prince of Spain who had been transformed by his evil stepmother. Alphonse brought the child to Rome, where William was adopted by a shepherd. When the boy grew up, he became a page to the Roman emperor's daughter, Melior. The two fell in love and after many adventures were married. Alphonse, the werewolf, was finally disenchanted. William appears in the English poem *William of Palerne*, based on a French metrical romance.

William of York, St. (will-helmet). Died 1154. In Christian legend, William Fitzherbert, archbishop of York. Feast, 8 June.

William's appointment as archbishop was opposed by the Cistercians. St. Bernard, also a Cistercian, described William as a "man rotten from the soles of his feet to the crown of his head." After taking the case to Rome and much arguing back and forth, William finally took his office in 1154. Less than a year later he was dead. He had been seized by violent pains while celebrating Mass on Trinity Sunday. Officially, it was said he died a natural death, though he is listed as a martyr in some medieval church calendars.

In medieval English Christian art William is often portrayed in his episcopal robes. Sometimes he is shown as a tonsured monk praying in the wilderness with a dove nearby. His shield had eight lozenges.

William Tell (will-helmet). 14th century. In Swiss history and legend, national hero who fought against the Austrians. William, according to legend, refused to salute the Austrian governor, Gessler. As punishment for the insult he was sentenced to shoot an apple off the head of his own son with his bow and arrow. William succeeded, but in his agitation dropped a second arrow from his coat. Gessler insolently demanded what the second arrow was for. William replied: "To shoot you had I failed in the task imposed upon me." Gessler then ordered William to be bound and locked in Küssnacht Castle. Later William was freed by the people and led his country in a war against Austrian domination. He also shot Gessler. His legend and life form the subject of Schiller's verse play *Wilhelm Tell* as well as Rossini's opera *Guillaume Tell*, based on Schiller's play.

William the Conqueror (will-helmet). c. 1027–1087. In English history and legend, king of England and duke of Normandy after the Norman Conquest in 1066. At the Battle of Hastings between the Norman and Saxons, King Harold of the Saxons was killed. William at once marched on to London and was crowned on Christmas Day at Westminster. Many of the people believed that Harold was the rightful king, not William, even though the church supported William's claims. William died after a horseback accident. At his funeral, according to legend, his body burst open, and a foul odor was emitted, forcing the mourners to flee the church. The conquered people said it was God's judgment on the

Norman for killing Harold, the last of the Saxon kings. The conflict of William and Harold is the subject of Tennyson's verse play *Harold* and Hope Muntz's novel *The Golden Warrior: The Story of Harold and William.*

3116

Willow. A tree; in Near Eastern mythology, sacred to the Great Mother goddess. Called Artemis Lygodesma, she was portrayed as a mother suckling a child decked with branches of the *lygos*, a member of the willow family. In Greek mythology the willow was sacred to Hera, Circe, Hecate, and Persephone, all forms of the Great Mother goddess and associated with life and death. In Jewish folklore the willow is associated with mourning, sadness, and death, as reflected in Psalm 137:1. In Christian symbolism the willow is one of the trees associated with the Virgin Mary, and in Chinese mythology it is associated with the goddess of mercy, Kuan Yin. Shakespeare combines the image of the willow's sadness with that of death in Desdemona's "Willow Song" before she is murdered on her marriage bed by Othello. In *The Merchant of Venice* (5:1) Lorenzo refers to Dido, Queen of Carthage, as holding a "willow in her hand" the night she killed herself for love of Aeneas, who deserted her.

3117

Windigo. In North American Indian mythology (Chippewa/Ojibwa), cannibal ice monster, threat to all who practice evil medicine.

3118

Windingo. In American folklore, a ghost about 15 feet tall who frightened the citizens of Roseau, Minnesota, for generations. Each time the ghost was seen, a person died.

3119

Winefred, St. (blessed reconciliation). Died 650. In Christian legend, saint venerated at Holywell, Wales. Feast, 3 November.

According to medieval Christian legend, one day Cradorus (Caradoc), the son of King Alan of North Wales, found Winefred alone in her father's house and tried to rape her. She fled, pursued by Cradorus, who cut off her head. When the head of Winefred hit the ground, a fountain sprang up, later called Winefred's Well or Holywell. Her spiritual teacher, St. Beno (Beuno), came upon her head and set it back on her torso, and the girl returned home in one piece.

In medieval Christian art St. Winefred is portrayed with a sword, a fountain at her feet, and a red ring around her neck to indicate that her head had been cut off.

Variant spellings: Winefride, Wenefrida, Gwenfrewi, Guinevra.

3120

Wisdom to Fools. Jewish fable found in the Midrash.

One day a woman asked Rabbi Yose bar Halaftah, "Why is it written in the Book of Daniel that God gives wisdom to the wise? Would it not be better if he gave wisdom to fools, who need it?"

The rabbi said he would explain the answer by a parable. "Imagine two people who wish to borrow money from you. One is rich and one is poor. To which of the two would you lend your money?" "The rich man," replied the woman. "Why?" the rabbi asked.

"Because if he loses his money, he'll find some means to repay me. But where will a poor man get money to repay me?"

"Well," replied Rabbi Yose, "if God gave wisdom to fools, what would they do with it? They would waste it. That's why he gives wisdom to the wise to use in study."

3121

Witch of Endor. In the Bible, O.T., a medium consulted by King Saul on the eve of the battle in which Saul was killed, in which she raised the dead prophet Samuel. Samuel told Saul that he would be dead the next day and would join him in the land of the dead (1 Sam. 28:7-25). Handel's oratorio *Saul* contains a magnificent scene for the Witch of Endor.

3122

Witch of Wellfleet. In American folklore of New England, a 17th-century witch, believed to be Goody Hallett, who always wore scarlet shoes. Hallett was 15 years old when she was seduced by a pirate named Samuel "Black" Bellamy. When she was found with child, she was arrested and whipped by the townspeople. While she was in prison, the devil, dressed as a handsome French dandy, appeared, and she signed away her soul to get revenge on Bellamy, whose ship was then sunk by the devil. She appeared in many guises over the years, often causing storms to drown seamen. When a storm arose, people said, "Thar be pore Goody, dancin with the lost souls." Her exact end is not known, though some say she was strangled to death by the devil when she beat him at dice. Others say she married an Indian.

3123

Wiwonderrer. In Australian mythology, stone animals who kill human beings. They can be destroyed only if speared in the eyes or the mouth.

Woden. The Anglo-Saxon name of the Norse god Odin. Wednesday (Woden's day) is derived from his name. In Richard Wagner's *Der Ring des Nibelungen* he is called Wotan.

Variant spellings: Voden, Votan, Wootan.

Wolf and the Crane, The. Aesopic fable found in various collections throughout the world.

A wolf, in gorging himself on some poor animal he had killed, got a small bone stuck in his throat. The pain was terrible, and he ran up and down beseeching every animal he met to relieve him. None of the animals, however, felt very sorry for the wolf, for, as one of them put it, "That bone which is stuck in the wolf's throat might just as well be one of mine."

Finally the suffering wolf met the crane. "I'll give you anything," he whined, "if you will help take this bone out of my throat."

The crane, moved by his entreaties and promises of reward, ventured her long neck down the wolf's throat and drew out the bone. She then modestly asked for the promised reward.

"Reward?" barked the wolf, showing his teeth. "Of all the ungrateful creatures! I have permitted you to live to tell your grandchildren that you put your head in a wolf's mouth without having it bitten off, and then you ask for a reward! Get out of here before I change my mind!"

Moral: Those who live on expectation are sure to be disappointed.

The fable probably originated in India, where in one account the Buddha tells the story of a lion and a crane to illustrate the ingratitude of the wicked. The fable ends: "The master, having given the lesson, summed up the moral: 'At the time the lion was Devaddatta [the Buddhist Judas] and the crane was myself.'"

The Buddhistic form of the fable first became known to Europe in 1691 in De la Loubere's *Description of Siam*. One version, which uses the lion instead of the wolf, was used by Rabbi Jochanan ben Saccai (c. 120 C.E.) to persuade the Jews not to revolt against the Romans. The account is found in *Bereshith*

The Wolf and the Lamb

Rabba, a commentary on Genesis. The fable is pictured on the Bayeux tapestry.

3126

Wolf and the Lamb, The. Aesopic fable found in various collections throughout the world.

As a wolf was lapping at the head of a running brook he spied a lamb daintily paddling his feet some distance down the stream.

"There's my supper," thought the wolf. "But I'll have to find some excuse for attacking such a harmless creature."

So he shouted down at the lamb: "How dare you foul my stream."

"But you must be mistaken," bleated the lamb. "How can I be spoiling your water, since it runs from you to me and not from me to you?"

"Don't argue," snapped the wolf. "I know you. You are the one who was saying those ugly things about me behind my back a year ago."

"Oh, sir," replied the lamb, trembling, "a year ago I was not even born."

"Well," snarled the wolf, "if it was not you, then it was your father." Without another word he fell on the helpless lamb and tore her to pieces.

Moral: Any excuse will serve a tyrant.

The fable appears in Tibet and in Madagascar. In the *Jatakas, or Birth-Stories of the Former Lives of the Buddha*, a panther meets a kid and complains that his tail has been stepped on. The kid gently points out that the panther's face was toward him, so how could he have stepped on his tail?

The panther says: "My tail covers the earth."

The kid replies: "But I came through the air."

The panther says: "I saw you frightening the beasts by coming through the air. You prevented my getting any prey."

3127

Wolfgang, St. (wolf-strife). Died 994. In Christian legend, bishop who once forced the devil to hold the Gospel book while he read aloud from it. He is the patron saint of carpenters, shepherds, and woodsmen and is invoked against gout, hemorrhage, lameness, stomach troubles, and wolves. Feast, 31 October.

3128

Wolf in Sheep's Clothing, The. Aesopic fable, though it does not occur in any early collections attributed to Aesop. It is derived from the New Testament (Matt. 7:15) by an Italian fabulist, Abstemius, of the 15th century.

A wolf had been lurking near a flock of sheep for several days. But the shepherd had been so vigilant in guarding his animals that the wolf was becoming desperate.

Then one day the wolf found a sheepskin that had been thrown away. Quickly, he slipped it on over his own hide and made his way among the flock of grazing sheep. Even the shepherd was deceived by the ruse. When night came the wolf in his disguise was shut up with the sheep in the fold.

But that evening the shepherd, wanting something for his supper, went down to the fold and, reaching in, seized the first animal he came to. Mistaking the wolf for a sheep, the shepherd killed him on the spot.

Moral: Appearances often are deceiving.

Thackeray makes use of the fable in the Prologue to his novel *The Newcomers*.

3129

Wollonqua. In Australian mythology, the great snake of the Warramunga, who rose out of the Thapauerlu, a vast water hole in the Murchinson Ranges. Wollonqua is said to be so gigantic that even though he traveled many miles from his water hole, his tail was still in it. Wollonqua's human male companion, Mumumanugara, tried to force the great snake back into his hole, but instead the snake coiled itself around him. In Warramunga ritual the journeys of Wollonqua are acted out by the men. They draw various designs on the ground portraying the adventures of the great snake, who is portrayed covered with red down.

3130

Wondjina. In Australian mythology, primal beings who appear in various myths that take place during Ungud (dreamtime). Most Wondjina transform themselves into rock paintings while their spirits inhabit some sacred water hole. The natives frequently retouch these sacred paintings to promote rains or to stimulate fertility. When a person dies his body is painted with red ochre and placed in the cave where his clan's Wondjina resides; the dead man's spirit descends to a nearby pool to await rebirth. Paintings of the Wondjina range from a few feet to 16 feet. Painted againsta white ground, the head is outlined in red or yellow. The first nonaborigine to see and comment on them was Sir George Grey in 1838. He interpreted them as priests with halos. The eyes and nose of the Wondjina are linked. No mouth is portrayed because it is believed that would cause it to rain all of the time. The figures are painted with white stripes symbolizing the rain.

3131

Wooden Horse or **Trojan Horse**. In Greek and Roman mythology, a large wooden horse in which Greek soldiers hid in order to sack Troy. The horse was designed by Epeius, son of Panopeus. When the horse was taken into Troy, the Greeks came out of hiding at night and destroyed the city.

No mention is made in Homer's *Iliad* of the wooden horse, but in the *Odyssey* (book 11) Odysseus tells the ghost of Achilles in the underworld that his son Neoptolemus had been one of those chosen to go into the device, which was invented by Odysseus. Vergil's *Aeneid* (book 2) gives details of the wooden horse and the fall of Troy.

Sinon, a Greek, pretended that he had been an intended victim of a sacrifice to assure a safe retreat by the Greeks but had escaped as the Greeks sailed away from Troy. He convinced the Trojans that the wooden horse had been built as a tribute to Athena and had been abandoned on the beach when the Greeks decided to retreat. On hearing this, the Trojans decided to bring the horse into the city. Both Cassandra, the king's daughter, and Laocoön, a priest, warned the Trojans not to trust the Greeks. Laocoön hurled his spear into the horse's side and uttered a warning: *Timeo Danaos et dona ferentes* (I fear the Greeks even when they bring gifts). Shortly after that Laocoön was destroyed by a sea monster, and the Trojans took that as a favorable sign for bringing in the wooden horse. During the night, after the horse was safely inside the city walls, the Greeks emerged from it and opened the city gates to their waiting troops. The city fell.

The event was painted by Giovanni Battista Tiepolo in a work titled *The Building of the Trojan Horse* (c. 1760). There is an early Roman wall painting from Pompeii depicting *The Wooden Horse Brought into Troy* (second half of the first century C.E.) and a late 15th-century Franco-Flemish tapestry that shows the Trojan horse within the walls of Troy.

3132
Woodman and the Serpent, The. Aesopic fable found in various collections throughout the world.

One winter's day as a woodman was homeward bound from market he found a snakelying half dead with cold by the roadside. Taking compassion on the frozen creature, he placed it under his coat to warm it. Then he hastened home and put the serpent down on the hearth where a cheery fire was blazing.

The children watched it with great interest and rejoiced to see it slowly come to life again. But as one of them knelt down to stroke the reviving snake, it raised its head and darted out its fangs and would have stung the child to death. Quickly the woodman seized his matlock and with one stroke cut the serpent in two.

Moral: No gratitude is to be expected from the wicked.

The fable occurs in the great Indian epic poem *The Mahabharata*. Versions vary as to the threatened

victim. In some it is the woodman himself, in others, it is one of his children after he arrives home. In one medieval version a woman finds and nourishes the snake.

3133
Woodpecker. Bird with strong, straight, pointed beak, long tongue with barbs at the tip, and tail feathers that are stiff and pointed at the tip. In Greek mythology the woodpecker was a prophetic bird with great magical power and sacred to Zeus, the sky god, and Ares, the war god. In Roman mythology both Jupiter and Mars, the Latin counterparts of Zeus and Ares, also were associated with the bird. In Hindu mythology the sky god Indra transformed himself into a woodpecker for some of his sexual exploits, as did Zeus in Greek mythology and Mars in Roman mythology. Partly because of the woodpecker's association with Greek and Roman beliefs, the early Christians identified the bird with the devil. In animated cartoons the character of Woody Woodpecker captures the trickster nature ascribed to so many animals in world mythology and folklore.

3134
Wotan. In Germanic mythology, the name given to the Norse god Odin. It is used by Richard Wagner in his *Der Ring des Nibelungen*.
Variant spellings: Woden, Wuotan, Voden, Votan.

3135
Wreck of the Hesperus, The. American literary ballad by Henry W. Longfellow, published in 1841, about the wreck of a schooner named *Hesperus*. Longfellow's ballad was influenced by the old Scottish ballad *Sir Patrick Spens*.

3136
Wu-fu (the five happinesses). In Chinese folk belief, the five blessings: long life; riches; tranquillity; a love of virtue, and a good end to one's life. The five characters often appear on chopsticks.

3137
Wu-kuan wang. In Chinese mythology, ruler of the fourth hell of Ti Yü, the underworld.

3138
Wu Lao (five odd ones). In Chinese mythology, spirits of the five natural forces. They are Wang Mu (metal), Mu Kung (wood), Shui Ching-tzu (water), Ch'ih Ching-tzu (fire), and Huang Lao (earth).

3139
Wulfilaic, St (wolf rule). Died 595. In Christian legend, one of the pillar saints of the Western church.

Wulfilaic was a native of Lombardy who spent part of his life in severe austerities on a mountain in the valley of Chiers in Belgium. St. Gregory of Tours went to see him and wrote down the following account of the saint in his *History of the Franks* (book 8). Wulfilaic tells his own story:

> I came to this mountain because here was erected the gigantic statue of Diana, which the inhabitants worshiped as a god. Beside this idol I built a pillar, on the top of which I placed myself barefooted, and my sufferings defy description. In winter the cold froze my feet and all the nails of my toes. . . . The rain which saturated my beard turned to ice, which glistened like candles. . . . My only food was a little bread and a few vegetables and my only drink was water. Though my sufferings were so great, yet I felt satisfaction in my austerities. When I saw the people come to my pillar I preached to them, and told them Diana was no goddess, and the songs which they sang in her honor ought to be addressed to the Creator of heaven and earth. Often did I pray that God would overturn the idol, and snatch the people from the error of their ways. The people listened to my words, the Savior lent an ear to my prayers, and the people were converted. I appealed to some of my converts to assist me in overthrowing the statue of Diana. . . . but it resisted all our efforts. I now went to church, prostrated myself on the earth, prayed earnestly, wept, and groaned in spirit, imploring Christ to destroy by His almighty power that which the power of man could not move. My prayer being ended I went to rejoin the workmen. We seized the ropes, and with a vigorous pull succeeded in overthrowing the gigantic image. I broke it to pieces and reduced it to powder with a huge sledge hammer.

That night, the devil covered Wulfilaic "with pustules," but the saint anointed himself "from head to foot with some oil" from St. Martin's tomb and was cured. Later the archbishop of Tréves asked that Wulfilaic come down from his pillar and enter a monastery. The saint obeyed.

3140

Wulfram, St. 647–720. In Christian legend, saint venerated at Fontenelle, Frisia, and Sens. Feast, 20 March.

Wulfram succeeded Lambert as archbishop of Sens but left his office to become a missionary among the Frisians, taking with him monks from Fontenelle. Numerous medieval legends are told of the saint. One tells of his ability to make a silver paten float on the sea. As St. Wulfram was sailing from Caudebec to Frisia, Mass was being celebrated on board. St. Vando, who was the celebrant, dropped the paten into the sea while wiping it. St. Wulfram told Vando to put his hand into the sea. Immediately, the silver paten was buoyed up into his hand.

Another medieval legend tells how St. Wulfram put an end to human sacrifices. The Frisians used to offer human sacrifices to their pagan gods. These sacrifices were sometimes made by strangulation, the sword, fire, or water. One day the lot fell on two children of one mother, children five and seven years old. St. Wulfram asked King (or Duke) Radbod to prohibit such cruelty, but the king replied he could not violate the laws of his gods. The children were taken to the sacrifice site near where two rivers flowed into the sea. Wulfram prayed to God to save the children, and suddenly the waters of the two rivers stood like a wall around them. Walking on the water, Wulfram took the children and gave them to their mother. The people were amazed and many became Christians, including King Radbod.

St. Wulfram is often portrayed in medieval Christian art as a bishop baptizing a young king or arriving by ship with monks and then baptizing the king.

3141

Wu ta chia (five big families). In Chinese folklore, the five animals—fox, weasel, hedgehog, snake, and rat—that are feared because they are believed to bewitch people.

3142

Wu-yuan kuei (unrelated ghosts). In Chinese folklore, a ghost who has no descendants to provide him with food offerings.

X

Xaman Ek. In Mayan mythology, god of the North Star, the guide of merchants. Incense was offered to him at roadside altars by his faithful followers. In Mayan art he is portrayed with a snub nose and black markings on his head. Paul Schellhas, classifying the gods in some Mayan codices, gave Xaman Ek the letter *C*, and he is sometimes known as God C.

Xanthus (yellow). In Greek mythology, the name given to the river god of the Scamander River in the Troas, the territory surrounding Troy in N.W. Mysia, Asia Minor. In Homer's *Iliad* (book 20), when Zeus allowed the gods to choose either side in the Trojan War, Xanthus flooded the banks of the Scamander to stop the slaughter of the Trojans by Achilles because their blood was polluting the river. To help Achilles, Hera asked the fire god Hephaestus to set the river aflame. Xanthus surrendered before the holocaust and promised not to reenter the battle. Xanthus is also the name of the immortal horse of Achilles; son of Boreas (or Zephyrus) and Podarge; brother of Balius (piebald). The goddess Hera gave Xanthus the power of speech. He forewarned Achilles of his coming death. Xanthus wept at the death of Patroclus.

Xilonen. In Aztec mythology, goddess of the growing corn, whose festival, Uei Tecuilhuitl (22 June), was celebrated with corn tortillas wrapped around pieces of spiced vegetables and baked. Some scholars regard Xilonen as an aspect of the great goddess Coatlicue.

Xipe Totec (the flayed one). In Aztec mythology, god of vegetation, newly planted seeds, penitential torture, and the west. Xipe Totec gave himself as food to the world by having himself skinned alive.

Xiuhtecuhtli. In Aztec mythology, fire god worshiped as the center of all things and the spindle of the universe. The god determined the time of death of each individual.
Variant spelling: Xiuhtecutli.

Xochiquetzal (lady precious flower, beautiful rose?). In Aztec mythology, goddess of sexual love and courtesans, patroness of painters, embroiderers, weavers, silversmiths, sculptors, and all whose profession was to imitate nature in crafts and drawings. On the Day of the Dead the goddess was offered marigolds by her faithful followers. She is the female form of the bisexual god Tonacatocutli.

Xolas. In the mythology of the Alacaluf Indians of Tierra del Fuego, supreme being. Xolas puts the soul into each new child. When a man or woman dies, the soul is reabsorbed by Xolas.

Xolotl Huetzi (servant?). In Aztec mythology, lord of the evening star, twin brother of the god Quetzalcoatl. Though credited with animallike demonic qualities, Xolotl was also responsible for repeopling the earth after it had been depopulated. He went to the underworld and brought back a bone of a previous man. As he was leaving, he was pursued by the god of the underworld (who was not at all pleased with his action), and he fell with the bone. It broke into unequal parts, but Xolotl took what he could of it and sprinkled it with his own blood. After four days a boy was born and after seven days a girl. He then raised the two on the milk of the thistle, and they became the first parents of mankind. Xolotl sometimes appeared as a dwarf or as a dog.

Xpiyacoc and Xmucané. In Mayan mythology, creator deities, the "old man" and "old woman," who were involved with the creation of material objects. The Mayans believed their gods to be sorcerers, and through magic Xpiyacoc and Xmucané aided the creator god Hurakán in forming man through various magic rites.

Y

Yabons. In Australian mythology, friendly spirits who aid men, often warning them of danger. ^{3152}

Yacatecutli (lord of travelers, he who leads). In Aztec mythology, god of merchants, whose symbol was a staff, often sprinkled with blood by his worshipers. Slaves also were sacrificed to the god after they had been made sufficiently fat and pleasing because they were to be eaten later at a cannibalistic feast. ^{3153}

Yaho. In Australian mythology, a cannibalistic male monster who lives in the mountains. He kills and roasts his victims, who are always women. His evil wife is Kurriwilban. He is also known as Koyorowen. ^{3154}

Yahweh (he causes to be, he brings into existence?). In the Bible, O.T., the personal name of the god of Israel, preserved only in its four consonants or the tetragrammaton YHWH. By the third century B.C.E. the Jews had either forgotten the correct pronunciation or had omitted spelling out the entire name out of reverence because in ancient belief to know a god's name was to have power over the god. The Jews substituted the word *Adonai* (Lord or my Lords) for YHWH. The vowels of the word *Adonai* were later added to the consonants YHWH, creating the hybrid form Jehovah, a name never used by the ancient Hebrews. According to one account in the Old Testament, the name Yahweh was revealed to Moses. God spoke to Moses and said, "I am Yahweh. To Abraham and Isaac and Jacob I appeared as El Shaddai; I did not make myself known to them by my name Yahweh" (Exod. 6:2–3, Jerusalem Bible). But the name Yahweh appears in biblical narratives before Moses. In most English Bible translations, including the King James Version, Yahweh is not used; LORD is used in its place. The ancient praise-shout *Hallelujah* (praise the god Yah) contains the name of the god. Yahweh is used in the Jerusalem Bible, but the Revised Standard Version and the New English Bible use LORD. ^{3155}

Yakushi Nyorai (master physician Buddha). In Japanese mythology, god of healing, derived from the *hongji*, the universal Buddhist principle; portrayed holding a small flask that contains medicine. He is often shown with Gakko (moonlight) and Nikko (sunlight) on either side. ^{3156}

Yalahau. In Mayan mythology, god of water, darkness, night, and blackness. Yalahau was a fearsome warrior, cruel to his people when he came to earth. In some accounts he is said to be the brother of the culture hero and god Votan, to whom he is an antagonist. ^{3157}

Yama

Yama (the binder, twin, curb, bridle). In Hindu mythology, the god of death, king of hell. ^{3158}

Variant accounts are given for the origin of Yama. In some texts he is said to have been the son of Surya, the sun, and married to Saranya. Yami, his twin sister, suggested that the two sleep together and people the earth, but Yama refused the offer. In another text Yama was the first mortal to die. He discovered the way to the underworld, earning for himself the title of god of the dead. In the ancient collection of hymns, the *Rig-Veda*, Yama is god of the dead, though he does not punish the wicked, as he does in later Hindu mythology. One hymn in the *Rig-Veda* sums up his role:

To the great King Yama homage pay,
Who was the first of men that died,
That crossed the mighty gulf and spied
For mortals out the heavenward way.

Yama has two dogs, each with four eyes and wide nostrils, that guard the road to his kingdom. His scribe is Chitra-gupta, who records the sins and virtues of the dead. The dead are told to hurry past them. The dogs go about as messengers of Yama, calling people to his kingdom. In his kingdom some are allowed sensual pleasures.

In Indian art Yama is portrayed as a green man, dressed in red, crowned with a flower in his hair. He is armed with a club and often rides a buffalo. Among his numerous titles are Antaka (the ender, death), Kritanta (the finisher), Samana (the settler), Dandi or Danda-dhara (the rod bearer), Bhimasasana (of terrible decrees), Pasi (the noose carrier), Pitri-pati (lord of the manes), Preta-raja (king of the ghosts), Sraddha-deva (god of the faithful offerings), and Dharma-raja (just king).

3159
Yama-otoko (mountain men). In Japanese folklore, wild men who have human-headed she-wolves as companions. They are considered insane and often dangerous.

3160
Yama-uba. In Japanese folklore, female mountain spirits, sometimes seen as terrifying creatures and at other times as beneficent ones. In the demonic form one often appears as a woman with a mouth on top of her head under her hair, the locks of which transform themselves into serpents, catching small children, on whom she feeds.

3161
Yankee Doodle. Popular North American ballad, sung during the American Revolution. Believed to have been written in 1775 by Richard Shuckburth, a British army doctor, to ridicule the Continental army, the tune and verse were adopted by the Americans to poke fun at the British. The American version was sung by the Americans when Cornwallis surrendered at Yorktown in 1781. The Hollywood film *Yankee Doodle Dandy* (1942), starring James Cagney, is about the entertainer George M. Cohan.

3162
Yao. 2000 B.C.E.? In Chinese legend, culture hero, emperor of the Golden Age, who was born with eyebrows of eight different colors. With the help of Yi, the Divine Archer, he subdued the winds, and with the help of K'un he attempted to quell the floodwaters of the Yellow River. When he wished to pass his throne on to Shun, rather than to his own

Emperor Yao

sons, the earth was nearly destroyed by the appearance of ten suns, which scorched it. Yi stopped the suns by shooting down nine of them.

3163
Yao-Shih Fo. In Chinese Buddhism, the Healing Buddha, who received his powers from the historical Buddha. He gives spiritual medicine to the sick when they touch part of his image, which is usually made of bronze, though when painted it must be blue. He is known as Yakushi Butsu in Japan, where many early temples are dedicated to him. In Sanskrit he is called Bhaisajyaguru.

3164
Yara. In the mythology of the Amazonian Indians of Brazil, a siren.

The Brazilian journalist and historian, Alfonso Arinhos de Melo Franco (1868–1916) tells a tale, *The Yara*, of how a *yara* seduced a youth. Jaguarari is depicted as a handsome hunter loved by all of the villagers. One day he discovered a *yara* at Taruman Point, and from then on he was completely under her spell. He told his mother of the vision, and she warned him never to go back to the enchanted spot. Jaguarari, however, could not resist. He was seen in his canoe "rushing straight toward the sun, as though it would hurl itself into a flaming disk. And beside the young warrior, clasping him like a vine, stood a white figure, of a beautiful form, in a halo of silvery light that contrasted with the ruddy gleam of the setting sun, and crowned the long loose golden tresses."

3165

Yarilo (ardent, passionate). In Slavic mythology, god of springtime and fecundity, who was worshiped in some Slavic countries as late as the 19th century with various rites to ensure crop fertility. In legends from White Russia, Yarilo is pictured as young and handsome, riding a white horse and dressed in a white cloak. On his head he wears a crown of wild flowers, and he holds a bunch of wheat ears in his hand. His feet are always bare. In one of his rites, White Russian peasants dressed the most beautiful maiden in Yarilo's costume and put her on a white horse while they sang:

> Where he sets his foot,
> The corn grows in mountains;
> Wherever he glances,
> The grain flourishes.

Yarilo's death was celebrated in summer by lamentations and sexual excess. His straw idol was carried in procession and buried, after which the peasants would again begin feasting and drinking. These rites were condemned by the Russian Orthodox church.

3166

Yarrow. A pungent herb. In Chinese folk belief yarrow sticks, also called milfoil, are used in the *I Ching* as a form of divination. In European folklore yarrow is associated with sexual love. Sometimes called the herb of Venus, it was used in the 17th century as a cure for gonorrhea. In English folklore yarrow was used by lovesick maidens to determine who their future lovers would be. They would pluck the flower from a young man's grave, repeating at the same time:

> Yarrow, sweet yarrow, the first that I have found,
> In the name of Jesus Christ I pluck it from the ground
> As Jesus loved sweet Mary and took her for His dear,
> So in a dream this night I hope my true love to appear

The chant was supposed to give the yarrow power to bring a vision of the future. But, if one dreamed of yarrow, it meant losing the object of one's affection. If one was married and dreamed of the plant, it signified death in the family. Yarrow is often found on gravesites and thus is often associated with death. It also was used against witchcraft during the Christian Middle Ages.

3167

Yashodhara. Fifth century B.C.E. In Buddhist legend, wife of Gautama, the Buddha, and mother of Rahula. Gautama won the hand of Yashodhara in a contest of arms when he was 16. When he left her and his young son to seek enlightenment, she went into despair. When they met years later she still showed her deep love for her husband. Their son Rahula became a Buddhist monk. Many of the *Jataka*, folktales of the Former Lives of the Buddha, are addressed to Rahula. He is said to have died before his father. Some texts give the name Gopa as the wife of the Buddha.

3168

Yatawm and Yatai. In Indo-Chinese mythology, two creator beings, neither spirits nor humans, who were responsible for the creation of animals and people.

Hkun Hsang Long, the creator spirit, or god, looked down from his heavenly home, Mong Hsang, and saw Yatawm and Yatai. He dropped down to them two *hwe-sampi*, or gourds. The two ate the gourds and planted the seeds, which grew to gourds as large as hills, containing animals and people. Yatawm was then called Ta-hsang Kahsi (great all-powerful) and Yatai was called Ya-hsang Ka-hsi (great mother all-powerful).

The myth is not clear as to whether Hkun Hsang Long wanted the two to eat the gourds, because when they ate them, death and sexual passion came into the world. However, the myth may have Christian overtones from missionaries who first recorded it for Western readers.

3169

Yayati. In Hindu mythology, a king who exchanged his old age for the youth of his son Puru.

Yayati, fifth king of the Chandra (lunar) race, was invited by Indra, the storm god, to visit heaven. Matali, the charioteer of Indra, came to fetch Yayati. On their way they held a philosophical discussion that made a deep impression on Yayati. When he returned to earth he administered his kingdom with such virtue that his subjects were exempt from decay and death. Yama, the god of the dead, complained to Indra. Then Indra sent Kama, god of love, and his daughter, Asruvindumati, to arouse passion in

Yayati. The king fell in love with Asruvindumati, but he was too old for the young girl. Yayati asked his son Puru, after his other four sons had refused, to exchange his youth for Yayati's old age. Puru agreed. After a while Asruvindumati persuaded Yayati to return to heaven. Before the king left, however, he returned the youth to his son Puru.

In a variant account found in some texts Yayati was given a celestial chariot by Indra. With the chariot Yayati conquered the earth and even subdued the gods. The chariot then passed on to his successors but was finally lost. In the variant tale, Yayati, after restoring his youth to Puru, retired to the forest with his wife and gave himself up to mortification. Abstaining from food, Yayati died and ascended to heaven. He and his five sons are called Rajarshis.

3170

Yazatas. In Persian mythology, the "adorable" or "worpshipful ones," ranking after the good god, Ahura Mazda, and the Amesha Spentas, the seven "immortal bounteous ones." The Yazatas are innumerable and guard the sun, moon, and stars; they also are personifications of abstract ideas such as blessing, truth, or peace.

3171

Yedo Go Nin Otoko. In Japanese legend, five men who stole from the rich and gave to the poor. They all dressed alike, and though mischievous, they gained the support of people because of their aid. They usually are portrayed with flutes and big tobacco pouches, either talking to one another or competing in a physical contest.

Variant spelling: Edo Go Nin Otoko.

3172

Yeh Ching (karmic mirror). In Chinese mythology, a magic mirror that shows the dead the form into which they are to be reborn.

3173

Yen Kung (Duke Yen). In Chinese mythology, a deified mortal, worshiped as the god of sailors.

3174

Yen-Mo wang. In Chinese mythology, ruler of the fifth hell of Ti Yü, the underworld.

3175

Yesod (foundation). In Jewish folklore, angel invoked by Moses to bring death to the firstborn males in Egypt. In the biblical account (Exod. 12:29), however, it says Yahweh "smote all the firstborn in the land of Egypt." In Jewish folklore naming an angel or other spirit as a substitute for Yahweh, God himself,

in earthly affairs is quite common; it is done to maintain God's distance from humankind.

Variant spelling: Yasodiel.

3176

Yew. An evergreen tree; in European folklore, planted in graveyards to prevent witches from destroying churches and gravestones and sometimes buried with the dead to ward off demons.

Because the yew is poisonous, hunting bows made from the tree are said to be doubly fatal, killing both with its poison and as a weapon. Shakespeare's *Hamlet* speaks of the juice of the cursed hebona, believed to be the yew. Christopher Marlowe, in his play *The Jew of Malta*, calls the yew the "juice of hebon."

3177

Yggdrasill (the horse of the terrible one, i.e., Odin's steed). In Norse mythology, the great cosmic ash tree, also known as the world tree. The *Prose Edda* describes Yggdrasill as "the greatest and best of all trees. Its branches spread over the whole world, and even reach above heaven. It has three roots very wide asunder. One of them extends to the Aesir (the gods), another to the Frost-giants in that very place where was formerly Ginnungagap (the primeval abyss), and the third stands over Nifelheim (the land of dark, cold and mist), and under this root, which is constantly gnawed by Nidhogg (the dragon), is Hvergelmir." On top of the Yggdrasill an eagle perches. Between its eyes sits a hawk called Vedurfolnir. The squirrel named Ratatosk runs up and down Yggdrasill, trying to cause strife between the eagle and Nidhogg. Four harts—Dainn, Dvalinn, Duneyr, and Durathor—run across its branches and bite its buds. The Norns sit under the Urdar-fount, which is located at the third root of the tree. Here also the gods sit in judgment. Every day they ride up on horseback over Bifrost. Every day the Norns draw water from the Urdar-fount and sprinkle the ash, so its branches may not rot or wither. This water is so holy that everything placed in the Urdar-fount becomes as white as the film within an eggshell. The dew that falls from it is honey-dew. Two fowls are fed in the Urdar- fount. They are called swans, and from them are descended all of the birds of this species.

Variant spellings: Igdrasil.

3178

Yima. In Persian mythology, divine hero, who in some texts is considered the first man, the first king, and the founder of civilization. As the first man he is also the first of the dead, over whom he rules in a region of bliss. Yima becomes the culture hero Jemshid in the Persian epic poem *Shah Namah* by Firdusi.

In the sacred book *Avesta* two myths, somewhat contradictory, are told of Yima. Once Ahura Mazda, the good creator god, asked Yima to receive his law from him and bring it to men as a prophet. "I was not born, I was not taught to be the preacher and the bearer of thy law," Yima told Ahura Mazda.

Then the god said to Yima: "Since thou wantest not to be a preacher and the bearer of my law, then make thou my worlds thrive, make my worlds increase: undertake thou to nourish, to rule, and to watch over my world."

Yima did as Ahura Mazda asked, and the world thrived, "six hundred winters passed away, and the earth was replenished with flocks and herds, with men and dogs and birds and with red blazing fires, and there was no more room for the flocks, herds, and men." Then Yima made the "earth grow larger by two-thirds" to accommodate the new inhabitants.

The second myth narrated in the *Avesta* tells how Ahura Mazda told Yima that a winter was to come that would destroy every living creature. Yima built a *vara*, an underground cavern, and like Noah in the biblical tale, brought "the seeds of men and women, of the greatest, best and finest on this earth" to inhabit his kingdom. Again, the people and animals prospered.

The end of Yima is not exactly known. He was condemned by the gods, though the reason is not clear, and killed either by his brother, Spityura, who cut him in two, or by the demon Azhi Dahaka, in the form of a tyrant king, Zahhak, the evil king of Babylon in the Persian epic *Shah Namah* by Firdusi.

Variant spelling: Yam.

3179
Yin and Yang (dark side and sunny side of a hill). In Chinese mythology and philosophy, a symbol expressing conflict and resolution. Yin represents the female and Yang the male.

3180
Ymir (a confused noise). In Norse mythology, primeval giant formed from fire and ice, slain by the Aesir gods Odin, Vili, and Ve. From Ymir's body these three gods formed the earth, according to the *Prose Edda*: "From Ymir's blood they made the seas and waters; from his flesh the land; from his bones the mountains; and his teeth and jaws, together with some bits of broken bones, served them to make the stones and pebbles." Ymir's skull formed the heavens that the gods placed over the earth, with a dwarf at each corner to hold it up. Ymir's brains were tossed in the air to form the clouds.

3181
Yoga (yoking; harnessing; union). In Hinduism, various methods of mental and physical self-control or discipline, used for various ends. In the *Bhaguad Gita*, part of the Hindu epic poem *The Mahabharata*, the term is widely used to mean a method or discipline leading to salvation.

3182
Yoni (womb; source). In Hinduism, the female organ of generation, connected with the great goddess Devi. The *yoni* is worshiped along with the *lingam*, the phallus of the god Shiva, who is the husband of Devi.

3183
Yryn-Ajy-Tojon. In Siberian mythology, white creator god worshiped by the Yakuts.

When Yryn-Ajy-Tojon saw a bladder floating on the waters, he asked what it was. The bladder replied that it was Satan, who lived on the earth under the water. "If there is really earth under the water, then bring me a piece of it," Yryn-Ajy-Tojon said to Satan, who then dived under the water and returned with a piece of earth. It was blessed by Yryn-Ajy-Tojon and placed on the waters, where he sat on it. Angry, Satan tried to drown Yryn-Ajy-Tojon by stretching out the earth; but the more he pulled, the larger it got, until it covered the waters.

In addition to containing elements found in other Siberian myths relating to the origin of the earth and the devil, this myth, by its use of Satan as the name of the devil, suggests that it is a Christian reworking of a pagan myth.

3184
Yua. In Eskimo mythology (Unalit peoples at Bering Strait), spirit of elements, places, and things.

3185
Yuga (age). In Hindu mythology, an age of the world, of which there are commonly said to be four:

Krita Yuga, the first age, when men were righteous and in harmony with life. It lasted for a period of 1,728,000 years.

Treta, the second age, when people began to decline in righteousness.

Dvapar, the third age, when more evil came into the world.

Kali, the present age, which began in 3102 B.C.E. and is to last 430,000 years. It will see hunger, fear, and calamities increase.

Each Yuga is shorter than the one before it, and all four make a Maha-Yuga. A thousand Maha-Yugas make a Kalpa, which is a day and night for the Hindu god Brahma, or 4,320,000,000 human years. The term *Mahy-pralaya* means total destruction of the world and universe, when men and gods are annihilated. Other terms for the age of the world are Jahanaka, Kahita, and Sanhara.

Yü Huang, the Jade Emperor

3186
Yü Huang. In Chinese Taoist mythology, the Jade Emperor, supreme god; symbol of jade, or absolute purity, who lives in the highest heaven, Ta-lo. He replaced the earlier god, Yüan-Shih T'ien-Tsun, the "heavenly honored one of origin and beginning," who now lives on Yü Shan (the Jade Mountain).

3187
Yuki Onna (snow woman). In Japanese folklore, a female ghost who appears in snowstorms, causing travelers to fall asleep and freeze to death.

3188
Yule (wheel). A pre-Christian Norse feast held anywhere from mid-November to mid-January, in which sacrifices were made to the Aesir gods. Some Yule customs became absorbed into Christmas customs in the Northern countries when the people were converted to Christianity. The most familiar custom was the Yule log burned during the Middle Ages, recalling the pagan custom of lighting a log in honor of Thor with a fragment of the previous year's log. Christians believed that the preservation of the last year's Yule log was effective in preventing fire in the house. Yule is now a term sometimes used for Christmas.

3189
Yul-lha (rural deity). In Tibetan mythology, lesser gods and demons of the countryside. They are ranked as follows:

Lha. Gods, all male, white in color, and generally genial.

Tsan. Goblins or ghosts, all male, red in color. These are vindictive ghosts of lamas, discontented priests, and they haunt temples.

bDub. Devils, all male, black in color. They are the ghosts of the persecutors of Lamaism and cannot be appeased without the sacrifice of a pig.

gZah. Planets, piebald in color.

dMu. Bloated fiends, dark purple in color.

Srin-po. Cannibal fiends, raw-flesh colored and bloodthirsty.

rGyal-po. King fiends, the wealth-masters, white in color, the spirits of apotheosized heroes.

Ma-mo. Mother she-devils, black colored, the disease mistresses. They are sometimes the wives of the demons.

3190
Yü Shih (rain master). In Chinese mythology, the rain god, portrayed in yellow scale armor and wearing a blue hat, standing on a cloud and pouring rain onto the earth from a watering can.

3191
Yves, St. (archer). 1253–1303 C.E. In Christian legend, patron of lawyers, judges, and notaries. Feast, 19 May.

Yves was born near Treguier in Brittany and became an ecclesiastical and civil lawyer. As an official of the diocese of Rennes he was noted for his protection of orphans, his defense of the poor, and his impartiality in the administration of justice. Dom Lobineau, in his *Lives of the Saints of Britain*, recounts the legend of St. Yves, the widow and two swindlers.

Two swindlers deposited with a widow a valise they said contained 200 gold pistoles. They told her not to give the valise to anyone unless both of them were present. After six days one of the men came for the bag and carried it off. The other swindler then brought the widow before a judge and demanded either the bag or the 200 pistoles. The widow was about to lose the case when St. Yves interfered and said his client could not produce the valise unless *both* of the claimants were present. The plaintiff, therefore, must bring his fellow into court before the valise could be given up. The judge at once saw the justice of this and ordered the plaintiff to produce his companion. He did not and confessed that it was a hoax to get money out of the woman.

Another legend, from the same source, tells how St. Yves multiplied trees. The lord of Rosternen gave St. Yves permission to fell some oak trees in a forest for building the cathedral of Treguier. The steward complained that St. Yves had made "too great havoc with the trees." When the lord was taken to see the "devastation," he found two oaks growing for every one that had been felled.

Still another legend from the same source tells of St. Yves saying Mass, when a dove, all shining, lighted on his head, then flew to the high altar and almost immediately disappeared. Another day, as the saint was dining with a large number of the poor, a dove entered the room, fluttered around him, then lighted on his head. It did not fly away until St. Yves gave it a blessing.

St. Yves is often shown surrounded by supplicants, holding parchment and pointing upward. Sometimes he is shown in a lawyer's gown, holding a book.

Variant spellings: Ives, Ivo, Ybus, Helory.

Z

Za'afiel (wrath of God). In Jewish and Christian mythology, angel in control of hurricanes and storms. In some accounts he is a good angel; in others, an evil one.

3192

Zacchaeus (pure). First century. In the Bible, N.T., the rich publican at Jericho who was visited by Jesus. According to medieval French legend, he arrived in Gaul to preach the gospel. His feast in the Coptic church is 20 April.

3193

Zacharias (Yahweh remembers). In the Bible, name of two biblical characters: one in the New Testament, the father of John the Baptist (Luke 1:15); the other, the Old Testament prophet Zechariah, spelled Zacharias in Greek. In the Koran (sura 6) he is called Zakariya, the father of John the Baptist, and is reckoned, along with John, Jesus, and Elias, among the righteous.

In the New Testament (Luke 1:5–25) Zacharias is a priest married to Elisabeth, who was a kinswoman of the Virgin Mary. While he was performing his priestly duties in the temple, he had a vision in which the archangel Gabriel promised him and his barren wife a son. When old Zacharias doubted the angel's word, he was made speechless. Eight days after the child was born Zacharias went to the Temple to have the child circumcised. After making a sign that the boy was to be called John, not Zacharias, his speech was restored. In Islamic legend, after John the Baptist's death Zakariya escapes into a tree that opens for him. The hem of his garment remains outside the tree and is spotted by the demon, Iblis, who betrays him. The tree is sawn down and with it Zakariya. Jesus in the Gospels refers to "Zacharias son of Barachias" in Matthew (23:35) as having been slain "between the temple and the altar." Some biblical commentators on the text think Jesus is referring to the father of John the Baptist, but the majority believe Jesus is referring to the Old Testament prophet, Zechariah, though Jewish tradition says the prophet died a natural death. The Jewish, Christian and Islamic legends evidence influence from one another.

3194

Zacharias, St. (Yahweh remembers). Second century. In Christian legend, second bishop of Vienne, a disciple of St. Peter, according to Christian tradition. A medieval legend says he brought to Vienne the tablecloth on which Jesus instituted the Last Supper. Feast, 26 May.

3195

Zadkiel (the righteousness of God). In Jewish and Christian mythology, archangel who held back the knife when Abraham was about to sacrifice his son Isaac (Gen. 22:11–19), though he is not named directly in the biblical text. In another Jewish tale Zadkiel is credited with leading the Israelites out of Egypt. The name Zadkiel was adopted as a pseudonym by the astrologer Richard James Morrison, a naval lieutenant and author of the *Prophetic Almanac*, which was commonly called Zadkiel's Almanac.

Variant spellings: Zidekiel, Zadakiel, Zedekiel, Tzadkie.

3196

Zadok (just). In the Bible, O.T., a descendant of Aaron and a high priest of Israel in the time of King David and Solomon. He served as high priest jointly with Abiathar during most of David's reign (1 Chron. 24:3; 2 Sam. 15:24–29; 1 Kings 1:38–39). Handel's choral work *Zadok the Priest*, in praise of the king, is sung at English coronations.

3197

Zag-Muk. Babylonian New Year festival held in spring in honor of the great hero god Marduk, who on that day decided the fate of men for the coming year. One of the rites associated with the festival was the "visit" paid by the god Nabu, a son of Marduk, to his father. An image of Nabu was carried in a ship to the temple of Marduk and then returned to its own shrine.

Variant spelling: Zagmuku.

3198

Zagzagel (divine splendor). In Jewish mythology, angel who assisted God, along with Michael and Gabriel, in burying Moses. He is not mentioned in the Old Testament, but arises from Jewish folklore.

3199

Zahhak. In the Persian epic poem *Shah Namah*, by Firdusi, an evil king who is defeated by the hero Faridun.

3200

Azhi Dahaka as King Zahhak

King Zahhak was an evil king who had dedicated his life to Iblis, the devil. Out of the king's head came two serpents that had to be fed by human flesh. Human sacrifices of young men and women were made to satisfy the serpents. The hero Faridun challenged the king but was stopped from killing him by a supernatural voice that said:

> Slay him not now—his time is not yet come,
> His punishment must be prolonged awhile;
> And as he cannot now survive the wound,
> Bind him with heavy chains—convey him straight
> Upon the mountain, there within a cave,
> Deep, dark, and horrible—with none to sooth
> His sufferings, let the murderer lingering die.
>
> (James Atkinson translation)

The character of Zahhak is based on the archdemon in Persian mythology, Azhi Dahaka, who was defeated by the hero Traetaona and also imprisoned in a mountain.

Variant spellings: Zohak, Zuhak, Dahhak.

Zaka. In Haitian voodoo, a good loa (deified spirit of the dead), guardian of farmers and the destitute. Offerings of corn, rum, and oil-soaked bread are made to him. He is symbolized by an ear of corn with a hat on it and a pin stuck in it.

3201

Zakiqoxol (he who strikes from flint). In the mythology of the Cakchiquels, a branch of the Mayan Indians, demon spirit of fire and the forest. When the

3202

heroes Gagavitz and Zactecauh met Zakiqoxol, as told in *The Annals of the Cakchiquels* (16th century), they at first wanted to kill the demon. But instead they gave him a breastplate and sandals, all blood-colored, as a gift, and "he departed and descended to the foot of the mountain." In Cakchiquel folklore the demon is called "the little man of the woods."

Variant spelling: Zaquicoxol.

3203

Zal. In the Persian epic poem *Shah Namah*, by Firdusi, father of the hero Rustum.

When Zal was born, he was perfect in all aspects except one: he had white hair. When Sam, his father, was told that his child possessed this defect, he exposed the babe on a distant mountain. The mysterious and magical bird Simurgh heard the cries of the child and took him to his nest. A voice came from heaven telling Simurgh:

> To thee this mortal I resign,
> Protected by the power divine.
> Let him thy fostering kindness share,
> Nourish him with paternal care.
>
> (James Atkinson translation)

Warned in a dream, Sam repented what he had done to his infant son and went in search of Zal. When he finally found Zal, who had now grown to early manhood, he confessed his crime and asked for forgiveness. Zal then forgave his father.

One of the most interesting episodes in *Shah Namah* relating to Zal is his wooing of Rudabeh (Rudaba, Raduvah), who eventually became his wife and the mother of the great hero of the epic, Rustum.

One day while journeying through his father's domains Zal came to Kabul, where he stayed with Mihrab, who paid Sam an annual tribute to secure the safety of his state. On the arrival of Zal, Mihrab went out of the city to greet him. The young hero entertained Mihrab and soon discovered that Mihrab had a beautiful daughter:

> Her name was Rudabeh; screen from public view
> Her countenance is brilliant as the sun;
> From head to foot her lovely form is fair
> As polished ivory. . . .
>
> (James Atkinson translation)

After some tribulations Rudabeh and Zal were married. The astrologers consulted about the marriage replied that "this virtuous couple will have a son like unto a war-elephant, a stoutly girded son who will submit all man to the might of his sword and raise the king's throne above the clouds. . . ."

The name of the son was Rustum, the great hero of the epic poem.

Zamzam (abundant water). In Islam, sacred well at Mecca, also called Ishmael's Well. According to Islamic tradition the archangel Gabriel opened the well to Hagar when her Ishmael was dying of thirst in the desert. Before leaving Mecca, pilgrims often dip their burial clothes in the well.

3204

Zao Gongen. In Japanese mythology, patron god of Mount Kimpu in Japan and special guardian of the Buddhist Shugendo sect, a group of wandering mountain ascetics, whose adherents are called *yamabushi* (those who sleep on mountains).

3205

Zarathustra. Sixth century B.C.E. Prophet, mystic, and reformer of Persian religion; also known as Zoroaster, the Greek rendering of his name.

3206

Numerous legends surround the life of the historical Zarathustra. According to them, his birth, as with other saviors in world mythology, was foretold. His mother, only 15, bore him after having contact with the sacred Haoma plant. As soon as the child was born, he could converse and spoke with the good god, Ahura Mazda. At the age of 30 Zarathustra had his first vision. After his religious experience he began to teach the Good Religion (one of the names given by his followers to his doctrine). It is also called Mazdaism in some texts. At first no one would accept his teachings. He taught that Ahura Mazda, the good god who had created the world, was in conflict with Ahriman, the evil spirit. In the end, however, the forces of Ahura Mazda would be victorious and evil destroyed. Zarathustra brought his doctrine to the court of King Vishtaspa, who, though impressed by the prophet, still let his own priests jail Zarathustra on charges of being a necromancer.

One day the king's favorite black horse drew up all of its legs into its body so that it could not move. Zarathustra offered to heal the animal if four conditions were granted him: first, that the king should accept his teaching; second, that the great warlike prince, Isfandiyar, fight to spread Zarathustra's doctrine; third, that the queen also accept his doctrine; and fourth, the names of the men who plotted against him should be revealed. As each condition was fulfilled, one of the horse's legs was restored, and it could walk again.

Tradition records that Zarathustra was murdered while he knelt praying. After his death his doctrine was modified by the magi (priests of his religion), who restored some of the earlier beliefs in the old gods and spirits. This form of Zoroastrianism, as it is called, became the faith of Persia and lasted until the Islamic conquest of the country in the seventh century C.E. There are few remaining believers—those called Guebers (Ghebers) by the Islamics, meaning "unbelievers" in the faith of Islam, and some in India called Paris (Parsees) from the ancient name of Persia. The doctrine of Zarathustra, however, had a great impact on Judaism, Mithraism, Gnosticism, Manichaeism, and Christianity.

For the ancient Greeks, Zarathustra was a great magician and philosopher. Plato is said to have wanted to be able to study with the magi. Socrates is believed to have been taught by one. The magi who visited the infant Christ as the "three wise men" of tradition are perhaps the most celebrated.

The English poet Wordsworth, in the fourth book of his long narrative poem *The Excursion*, wrote on the ancient Persian religion:

> . . . the Persian,—zealous to reject
> Altar and Image, and the inclusive walls
> And roofs of temples built by human hands,—
> The loftiest heights ascending, from their tops,
> With myrtle-wreathed Tiara on his brows,
> Presented sacrifice to Moon and Stars,
> And to the winds and mother Elements,
> And the whole circle of the Heavens, for him
> A sensitive existence and a God.

Lord Byron, in the third book of his melancholic poem *Childe Harold's Pilgrimage*, wrote also of the Persian belief:

> Not vainly did the early Persian make
> His altar the high places and the peak
> Of earth-o'er-gazing mountains, and thus take
> A fit and unwalled temple, there to seek
> The Spirit, in whose honour shrines are weak,
> Upreared of human hands. Come and compare
> Columns and idol-dwellings, Goth or Greek,
> With Nature's realms of worship, earth and air,
> Nor fix on fond abodes to circumscribe thy prayer.

A lesser poet than Wordsworth and Byron, the Anglo-Irish Thomas Moore, in his metrical tale *The Fire-Worshippers*, part of his longer *Lalia Rookh*, has a Gueber chief say to an Islamic:

> "Yes, I am of that impious race,
> Those slaves of Fire, that morn and even
> Hail their creator's dwelling place
> Among the living lights of heaven;
> Yes! I am of that outcast crew
> To Iran and to Vengeance true,
> Who curse the hour your Arabs came
> To desecrate our shrines of flame,

And swear before God's burning eye
To break our country's chains or die."

A brilliant and more interesting description is
found in Shelley's poetic drama *Prometheus Unbound*:

. . . Ere Babylon was dust,
The Magus Zoroaster, my dead child,
Met his own image walking in the garden.
That apparition, sole of men, he saw.
For know there are two worlds of life and death:
One that which thou beholdest; but the other
Is underneath the grave, where do inhabit
The shadows of all forms that think and live,
Till death unite them and they part no more.

This theme was referred to and expanded by
Charles Williams in his novel *Descent into Hell*.

The Frenchman Voltaire, however, was not at all
enthusiastic about Zarathustra. He says in his
Ignorant Philosopher that Zarathustra "established
ridiculous superstitions" though the prophet's
"morals prove him not corrupt."

In Nietzsche's *Thus Spake Zarathustra* the poet uses
Zarathustra for his own mouthpiece. Nietzsche
stresses in the complex work that life is the will to
power. A man must overcome the beliefs and
conventions of common men. He must become an
"overman," or as it is usually translated,
"superman." In one section of the work Zarathustra
reaches a town where a group of people are watching
a tightrope walker. He says to them: "I teach you the
overman. Man is something that shall be overcome."
He then proceeds to explain that salvation is found in
this world and not the next world. His teachings
are rejected. Since he cannot teach the masses, he
decides to gather together some few disciples.
Nietzsche's work is the basis for the long orchestral
work *Also Sprach Zarathustra* by Richard Strauss.

Variant spellings: Zardusht, Zartust, Zoroaster.

3207

Zaremaya. In Persian mythology, spring that produced oil or butter to feed the souls in paradise.

3208

Zatik. In Armenian mythology, a vegetation god.
The Armenian translation of the Bible calls the Jewish passover "the festival of Zatik," and Armenian
Christians call Easter the Festival of Zatik. This has
led some scholars to believe that Zatik was a vegetation god, whose resurrection began at the winter solstice and was completed in the spring. Similarly, St.
Bede derives the English name for the feast of the
Resurrection from a pagan spring goddess, Eostre.

3209

Zduh (soul). In Slavic mythology, a term for the soul
of either a person or an animal. The *zduh* could leave
the body during sleep and engage in a battle with
other souls. If it lost the battle, the sleeper would die.
Aside from the *zduhs* of people and animals, there
were *zduhs* of the land, which caused drought, and a
zduh of the sea, which caused rain and storms.
Another term for the soul in Slavic mythology is
vjedogonja.

Variant spelling: Zduhacz.

3210

Zemi. In the mythology of the Indians of the Antilles at the time of Columbus, cult images of animals
or humans, worshiped as gods. They were invoked
to "send rain or sunshine," according to Peter Martyr d'Anghera in his book *De Orbe Nova* (1516), describing customs and beliefs of the Indians.

3211

Zenobio, St. (force of Zeus). Fourth century C.E. In
Christian legend, bishop of Florence; invoked
against headache. Feast, 25 May.

The legendary life of the saint is found in several
short biographies, all written after the 11th century
and included in the *Acta Sanctorum*, a collection of
saints' lives.

According to the accounts, Zenobio was born of a
noble family. His father, Lucian, and his mother,
Sophia, were both pagans. The boy, however, was
converted to Christianity and eventually succeeded
in converting his parents to the new faith. He lived
in Rome as a deacon and was also secretary to Pope
Damascus I. He was sent to Florence when two
factions, the Catholics and the Arians (a rival
Christian group), were fighting to have one of their
sect chosen bishop of the city. When Zenobio
arrived, both sides agreed that he should be the
bishop and elected him to the office. He led a life of
poverty and self-denial, keeping the two religious
factions at peace.

Many legends centered around the saint. Once he
made a journey to a city in the Apennines to
consecrate a church. On the occasion his friend, St.
Ambrose, sent messengers to him with gifts of
precious relics. But it happened that the chief of the
messengers, in passing through the gorge in the
mountains, fell with his mule down a steep precipice
and was crushed to death. His companions brought
his mutilated body and laid it at the feet of St.
Zenobio. The bishop prayed over the corpse, and the
man was restored to life.

Another legend says a Frenchwoman, while on a
pilgrimage to Rome, stopped off at Florence and left
her son in the care of the saint. The boy died the day
the woman returned, but when the child was laid at

the feet of St. Zenobio, the prayers of the saint restored the child to life. The saint placed him in the arms of his mother.

Still another medieval legend tells how a little child, straying from his mother in the streets of Florence, was run over and trampled by two oxen. Again, the good bishop prayed over the body of the dead child, and the child was restored to life.

Miracles were performed by Zenobio not only while he lived but even after his death. When the remains of St. Zenobio were carried through the city to be deposited under the high altar of the cathedral, the people crowded around to kiss him and touch his garments. In passing through the Piazza del Duomo the body of the saint was thrown against the trunk of a withered elm standing near the spot. Suddenly the tree, which had been dead for years, burst into fresh leaves.

St. Zenobio's life has been a favorite subject for Christian artists. Lorenzo Ghiberti designed a bronze sarcophagus to house the relics of the saint. The bas-reliefs portray the miracle of the restoration of the son of the Frenchwoman, the restoration of the messenger, and the story of the trampled child. Botticelli painted *The Three Miracles of Saint Zenobio.* Masaccio also painted the raising of the dead child.

The legendary connection of invoking St. Zenobio against headaches, however, is lost.

3212

Zeno, St. Died 371. In Christian legend, bishop of Verona, invoked for children learning to speak and walk. Feast, 12 April.

The bishop is noted for his kindness to children. *The Life of St. Zeno, Bishop of Verona* by Peter and Jerome Ballerini tells how the daughter of Emperor Gallianus was grievously tormented by the devil and was healed by the saint. One day, when she was nearly suffocating she cried out, "I can never be relieved of this torture but by Zeno." The devil added, "And I will never quit my abode here unless compelled to do so by Zeno." The emperor sent for the saint, who arrived quickly and entered the room where the young girl lay. As soon as he entered the devil cried out, "Zeno, you are come to drive me out, for here I cannot abide in the presence of thy holiness." The saint replied, "In the name of the Lord Jesus Christ I command thee to quit the body of this young maiden." The devil came out and said as he left, "Good-bye, Zeno, I am off to Verona, and there you will find me on your return."

St. Gregory the Great, in his *Dialogues*, explains Zeno's connection with the Adige River. One day, when the clergy and people of Verona were assembled to celebrate the festival of St. Zeno (he was now dead and sainted), the river Adige overflowed its banks, but though the doors of the church "were wide open, the waters were afraid to enter." Instead they formed a wall around the church.

Zeno's symbol is usually a fish, stemming from his legend.

3213

Zephyrus. In Greek mythology, the West Wind, son of Astraeus and Eos; married to Chloris; father of Carpus, god of fruit; also father of Balius and Xanthus, immortal horses of Achilles, by Podarge; called Favonius by the Romans and also known as Caurus. Zephyrus also loved Hyacinthus, a young male, but Hyacinthus loved Apollo. The angry West Wind caused Hyacinthus' death by blowing the quoit of Apollo against Hyacinthus' head. Frequent use is made of Zephyrus in literature. Ovid's *Heroides* (14.39) cites the wind, and Chaucer, in the Prologue to *The Canterbury Tales*, opens with

When Zephirus eek with his swete breeth
Enspired hath in every holt and heeth
The tendre croppes . . .

In *The Bard* Thomas Gray writes:

Zeus

Fair laughs the Morn and soft the Zephyr blows,
While proudly riding o'er the azure realm
In gallant rim the gilded vessel goes;
Youth on the prow, and Pleasure at the helm

Zephyrus appears in Botticelli's paintings, breathing life into Flora in *Primavera* and wafting Venus to the shore in *The Birth of Venus*. In ancient art Zephyrus is often portrayed as partly unclothed, carrying flowers in the folds of his robe.

3214

Zetes (searcher). In Greek mythology, son of Boreas and Orithyia winged twin of Calais; brother of Chione and Cleopatra; son of Thracian king Boreas and Orithyia. Zetes and his brother Calais took part in the Argonaut expedition and fought the Harpies in Bithynia. Eventually the two were killed by Heracles.

3215

Zeus (bright sky). In Greek mythology, sky god, the chief of the 12 Olympian gods; son of Cronus and Rhea; brother of Hades, Hestia, Demeter, Hera, and Poseidon; married to Hera; called Jupiter or Jove by the Romans.

Cronus had been told by an oracle of Gaea that he would be overthrown by one of his children, even as he had overthrown his father Uranus. To prevent this, Cronus swallowed his children as soon as they were born. When the time came for Zeus's birth, Rhea was determined to save her child. She went to Mount Lycaeus in Arcadia to a place called Cretea and gave birth to Zeus. When Cronus asked Rhea for the child so that he could swallow him, she gave her husband a stone wrapped in swaddling clothes. The god swallowed the stone at once. Rhea then washed the real Zeus in the Neda River and entrusted him to Gaea to be given to the nymphs of Crete to be raised.

Zeus

Zeus was raised by the nymphs Adrastea and Ida, daughters of Melisseus. The infant god was fed on milk and honey by the goat Amalthea. To drown out the infant's cries and prevent them from reaching the ears of Cronus, the Curetes (people of Crete) crashed their shields.

When Zeus grew up, he went to see Metis, who, some accounts say, was his first wife. Metis was a female Titan who advised Zeus how to force Cronus to disgorge Zeus's brothers and sisters. Metis gave Zeus a potion to give to Cronus. Zeus disguised himself as a cupbearer and gave the drink to his father. Hestia, Demeter, Hera, Hades, Poseidon, and the stone were vomited out. The stone was later set up at Delphi as the *Omphalos* (navel), or center of the earth.

Cronus and Rhea, father and mother of Zeus

Zeus, with his brothers Hades and Poseidon, then made war on his father and the Titans. The war, however, dragged on for ten years with no end in sight. Then Zeus was told by Gaea that if he released the Cyclopes and the Hecatonchires from their prison in Tartarus, he would defeat Cronus. Zeus descended to Tartarus, killed the woman jailer Campe, and freed the Cyclopes and Hecatonchires. The Cyclopes forged a thunderbolt for Zeus, a magic cap that made Hades invisible, and a trident for Poseidon. The gods, thus armed, defeated Cronus and the Titans. All of the defeated except Atlas were sent to Tartarus to be guarded by the Hecatonchires. Zeus, Hades, and Poseidon then cast lots into a helmet to decide what sections of the universe each god was to rule. Zeus drew the heavens, Hades the

underworld, and Poseidon the sea. The earth and Olympus were the common property of all three. Zeus was chosen head.

The marriages of Zeus in Greek mythology are numerous. As the husband of Mnemosyne (memory) he was the father of the Muses; Themis (justice) bore him the Horae, the seasons of the year; and Eurynome (far ruler) was the mother of the Charities or Graces. Zeus is the only Greek god who is the father of other Olympian gods. On Mount Cyllene Zeus was honored as the husband of Maia and the father of Hermes. At Dodona his wife was Dione, but in time his sister Hera was recognized as his legitimate wife and queen. Aside from numerous wives, Zeus also had many love affairs with both women and men. Robert Herrick, the English poet, using the Latin name Jove for Zeus, wrote in *To the Maids to Walk Abroad*:

> But fables we'll relate, how Jove
> Put on all shapes to get a love,
> As now a satyr, then a swan,
> A bull then, and now a man.

Zeus had many roles in Greek mythology, he was the sky god, the god of storms and rain, the mighty thunderer, master of the lightning. The mountains were his seat. As the god of storms, Zeus was also the god of battles, being the father of Ares and Athena, both war deities. The decision about which side would win in battle was believed to reside with Zeus. The statue of the Olympian Zeus by Phidias carried the Nike (victory) in its right hand. Though the Greeks made the children of Zeus war deities, Zeus was honored as the patron of physical contests. The olive branch of Zeus was awarded to the swift, the strong and skillful at Olympia. In many places in Greece, games were celebrated in honor of Zeus or found expression in the worship of his sons Apollo, Hermes, and Heracles.

As the sky god Zeus revealed his will with signs in the heavens. Prophecy and inspiration belonged to Zeus and his son Apollo. In Aeschylus' *Prometheus Bound*, Prometheus is made to say:

> . . . tokens by the way
> And flight of taloned birds I clearly marked
> Those on the right propitious to mankind,
> And those sinister,–and what form of life
> They each maintain, and what their enmities
> Each with the other, and their loves and friendships
> (Translated by Plumptre)

The priest Calchas saw a serpent devouring a sparrow with nine young and knew it was a sign from Zeus that Troy would fall. At Dodona, one of

Zeus's great shrines, doves or priestesses made the will of Zeus known. A lofty oak, sacred to Zeus, who sent rain for the farmers, was the home of these doves. The rustling of its leaves revealed the presence of the god. In Athens a spatter of rain or a thunderbolt was a sign that the gods were not looking down with favor, so public assemblies were at once adjourned. Spenser, in the *Faerie Queene* (book 1), using the Latin name Jove for Zeus wrote: "And angry Jove an hideous storme of raine/ Did poure . . ." Pope, in *The Rape of the lock*, also using Zeus' Latin name Jove, wrote: "Jove's thunder roars, heaven trembles all around."

Aside from his role in the heavens, Zeus was also worshiped as a patron of agriculture. Offerings of fruit were brought to Zeus Polieus, the guardian of the city on the Acropolis. In the variable weather of spring, both public and secret rites were performed to render Zeus propitious. In summer, when heat and drought threatened the crops, the Athenians again joined in the worship of Zeus.

The concept of Zeus changed over the many centuries during which the god was worshiped. In Homer's *Iliad* and *Odyssey* the rule of Zeus over gods and men is set forth. Zeus was always the protector of the state. On the Acropolis at Athens was an altar to Zeus, the protector of the city. The earliest altar of the state was the altar in the king's palace, the altar on which the king sacrificed in behalf of his people. Two kings of Sparta claimed descent from Zeus. At Athens sacrifices were offered to him as the god of phratry, or clan, when children were enrolled in its lists. Though he was not faithful to his wife, he was regarded as the god of the family. He was one of the gods who presided over marriage, along with his wife, Hera.

Zeus was invoked in oaths. The oath breaker feared the vengeance of Zeus. Earlier Zeus had declared that oaths of the gods must be sworn by the waters of the Styx because the Styx and her children had come to his aid in the war against his father and the Titans.

An elevated concept of Zeus's divine role is found in the *Agamemnon* of Aeschylus. The chorus gives an account of the god's nature:

Zeus–it to The Unknown
That name of many names seem good—
Zeus, upon Thee I call.
thro' the mind's every road
I passed, but vain are all,
Save that which names thee Zeus, the Highest One,
Were it but mine to cast away the load,
The weary load, that weighs my spirit down.
He that was Lord of old,
In full-blown pride of place and valor bold,
Hath fallen and is gone, even as an old tale told!

And he that next held sway,
By stronger grasp o'erthrown
Hath pass'd away!
And whoso now shall bid the triumph-chant arise
To Zeus, and Zeus alone,
He shall be found the truly wise.
'Tis Zeus alone who shows the perfect way
Of knowledge: He hath ruled,
Men shall learn wisdom, by affliction schooled.
(Translation by Morshead)

The eagle and the oak were sacred to Zeus. The eagle, together with the scepter and the lightning, is one of his most frequently encountered attributes. The most famous statue of Zeus in the ancient world was the one Phidias executed for the temple of Olympia. About 40 feet high, it was made of gold and ivory and portrayed the god seated. The bearded head was ornamented with olive leaves, and the upper part of the statue's body was made of ivory; the lower part was wrapped in a golden mantle falling from the hips to the feet, which wore golden sandals and rested on a footstool. Lying beside Zeus were golden lions. Zeus's right hand bore Nike; the left hand bore the scepter, surmounted by an eagle.

Zeus had many epithets, among them Cronides (son of Cronus); Coccygius (cuckoo), the bird whose form he assumed when he raped Hera; Aegichus (aegis bearing); Anchesmius (of Anchesmus); Apesantius (of Apesas); Aphesius (releaser); Capotas (reliever); Catharsius (purifier); Chthonius (of the underworld); Clarius (of lots); Ctesius (grain god); Eleutherius (god of freedom); Herceius (of the courtyard); Homagyrius (assembler); Lecheates (in childbed); Leucaeus (of the white poplar); Lycaeus (wolfish); Mechaneus (contriver); Megistus (almighty); Meilichius (gracious); Moeragetes (guide of Fate); Hypaistus (most high); Panhellenius (god of the Greeks); Patrous (paternal); Philius (friendly); Phyxius (god of flight); Semaleus (sign-giving); Soter (savior); Sthenius (strong); Teleius (full grown),Tropaean (he who turns to flight), and Terminalis (protector of boundaries).

3216

Ziggurat (pinnacle). Mesopotamian stepped pyramid usually built of brick and forming part of any temple complex. Because Babylonians believed that the gods lived on mountains, they designed the ziggurat in imitation of a natural mountain. The great ziggurat at Babylon was called Etemenaki (the house of the foundation of heaven and earth), and the ziggurat at Nippur was called house of oracle. The tower of Babel in the Bible (Gen. 11:1–9), as well as Jacob's dream (Gen. 28:11–19), probably stem from the ziggurat; it was the link between heaven and earth, as the tower and Jacob's ladder were in the Hebrew legends.

Variant spellings: zikkurat, ziqqurat.

Zin. In African mythology (Songhai of the upper Niger), water spirits. One day a zin, in the form of a snake, sat by its lake sunning itself. When a lovely girl passed by, he immediately fell in love with her. As dowry, her parents asked the zin for possession of the lake. He agreed but on occasion visited his palace at the bottom of the lake. When he grew old and died, his son became the guardian of the lake. It angers the zin when people enter the lake with weapons made of iron.

Zita, St. (to seek). 13th century. In Christian legend, patron saint of domestic servants; venerated at Lucca, Italy. Feast, 27 April.

Zita became a servant at the age of 12 and continued to be employed by the same family for some 48 years. One saying ascribed to the saint is "A servant is not good if she is not industrious: Work-shy piety in people of our position is sham piety." However, the traditional saying seems to have been invented by her masters.

One legend of the saint in the *Vita Sanctorum*, a collection of saints' lives, tells how Zita stayed too long at church and did not have time to make breakfast for her master. Zita rushed home and found to her joy that an angel had done the work for her. The bread was baked and ready to eat.

Another legend tells how Zita, touched with pity for the half-starved who came to her master's house during a severe famine, gave them the beans from her master's granary without asking his permission. Not long afterward the master, Pagano, was taking stock and went to measure the beans. Zita was frightened and hid herself behind her mistress. The master found the measure correct. Zita thanked God for restoring what had been taken.

Zita is portrayed in Christian art as a serving maid.

Variant spellings: Sitha, Citha.

Ziusudra. In Near Eastern mythology (Sumerian), hero of the flood myth, which is fragmentary and has in part been reconstructed. Told of a coming deluge, Ziusudra wrote down the history and traditions of his people and placed the tablets at Sippar, the city of the sun god. Then, taking his wife, daughter, and a pilot, he embarked in an ark, which eventually landed on the top of a mountain as the waters of the flood receded. When the four disembarked from the ark, they offered sacrifices to the gods. The gods Anu and Enlil gave Ziusudra "breath eternal like that of a god" as a reward for his faithfulness. Many of the incidents in the Sumerian version of the flood myth are also found in the Hebrew narrative of the flood in the Old Testament (Gen. 6–9).

Variant spellings: Sisouthros, Ziudsuddu.

Zoa. In African mythology (Songhai of the upper Niger), primal ancestor, wise man, and protector.

Word was passed to Zoa that if a pregnant woman was fed sheep's liver, it was actually the unborn child who ate it. He opened the stomach of a pregnant slave and found this to be true. Zoa performed many other astonishing acts, such as tending a wounded lioness and then going hunting with her. He predicted that a particular bird would suddenly die and be cooked on a fire that would light by itself. All things happened just as Zoa said they would. His son was greatly saddened when the bird died, and so Zoa commanded the earth to open, predicting that his son would become the next chief. Zoa told the people what offerings should be brought to him in times of trouble and which people were unworthy to visit his shrine. Then he entered the hole in the earth that he had previously ordered to open, and the ground closed around him. Four trees grew from that spot. They are taken to represent the four points of the compass.

Zodiac (circle of animals or relating to animals). Imaginary zone (or belt) in the heavens, extending about eight degrees to each side of the ecliptic, which the sun traverses every year. The signs of the Zodiac were named after deities and animals whose shape or outline could be seen in the heavens. The names are derived from Greek and Roman mythology. The 12 signs of the Zodiac were often combined in the Middle Ages, in psalters and books of hours, with the 12 months, or labors of the month.

The signs with their attributes and the date when the sun enters their path are

1. Aries, the Ram (Golden Fleece), 21 March
2. Taurus, the Bull (Europa's mount), 20 April
3. Gemini, the Twins (Castor and Pollux), 21 May
4. Cancer, the Crab (Heracles' tormentor), 22 June
5. Leo, the Lion (Nemean Lion), 23 July
6. Virgo, the Virgin, 23 August
7. Libra, the Scales, 23 September
8. Scorpio, the Scorpion (Orion's torturer), 24 October
9. Sagittarius, the Archer (Chiron), 22 November
10. Capricorn, the Goat (Amalthea), 22 December
11. Aquarius, the Water Bearer (Ganymede), 20 January

12. Pisces, the Fish (Aphrodite and Eros), 19 February

Frequent references are made to the Zodiac in European literature throughout the ages. Chaucer wrote a treatise on the *Astrolabe*, which describes the workings of a mechanical device for indicating the movement of the planets. In the prologue to *The Canterbury Tales*, he makes reference to the fact that "the younge sonne/ Hath in the Rame his halve cours yronne." In *The Faerie Queene* Spenser gives an elaborate description of the months with figures from the Zodiac. Milton also makes use of the Zodiac in *Paradise Lost* (book 10).

3222

Zohar, The (splendor). Medieval Jewish kabalistic work, written partly in Hebrew, partly in Aramaic. It is credited to Moses de León, a 13th-century Castilian cabalist, who died in 1305. It deals with the divine names of God, the soul, the Torah, the Messiah, and other Jewish topics in a mystical way, incorporating many mythical motifs. Its basic belief is that there is a correspondence between the upper world and the lower world—that is, what happens in heaven can affect earth and vice versa.

3223

Zombie. In Haitian voodoo, a person who has been "murdered" by poison and brought back to life by a *bocor*, a voodoo witch doctor.

In Haiti a zombie is one of the most feared of beings, and his or her existence is not doubted. Haiti's criminal code says: "Also shall be qualified as attempted murder the employment . . . against any person of substances, which, without causing actual death, produces a lethargic coma more or less prolonged. If, after the administering of such substances, the person has been buried, the act shall be considered murder no matter what result follows."

Recent research, reported in *Time* magazine (17 October 1983) quoted Harvard botanist E. Wade Davis, who has made a study of zombies: "Zombism exists and is a societal phenomenon that can be explained logically." The toxin used to poison victims was found to be coma-inducing. The effect of the poison depends on the dosage. Too much will actually kill. The zombie must be exhumed about eight hours after burial or he or she will suffocate. When the victim is awakened, he or she is fed a paste made of sweet potato and datura, a hallucinogenic plant. Often the victim is then used for slave labor.

Zombies are found not only in Haiti but also in movies. Victor Halperin's *White Zombie* was the first sound film on the subject. The term *zombie* was also applied to a strong rum drink said to leave the drinker apparently lifeless with intoxication. In a Ritz Brothers film the three comedians walk up to a bartender and order "Three zombies." "I can see that," the bartender replies, "but what'll you have to drink?"

3224

Zophiel (the beauty of God). In Jewish and Christian mythology, archangel who drove Adam and Eve from the Garden of Eden.

The account in Genesis (3:23–24), however, nowhere mentions an angel but "the Lord God" himself as responsible for casting the two out of the garden. In Genesis cherubim and "a flaming sword which turned every way" guarded the way to the Tree of Life. Cherubim were griffinlike monsters from Near Eastern mythology who were later made into angels in Jewish and Christian mythology. In *Paradise Lost* (book 6:535) Milton calls Zophiel "of cherubim the swiftest wing," and the angel's name forms part of a book-length poem, *Zophiel, or, The Bride of Seven* by the American Maria Gowen Brooks. The poem was quite influential in England, though not as popular in America. Charles Lamb, impressed by the work, could not believe "a woman capable of anything so great!"

Variant spellings: Jophiel, Iophiel, Iofiel, Jofiel.

3225

Zotz. In the mythology of the Zotzil Indians who live in the Chiapas, a bat god. One Mayan carving in Copan portrays the hero god Kukulcán battling the Zotz. The term *zotz* also was used by the Mayans for a 20-day period of their calendar.

3226

Zu. In Near Eastern mythology (Babylonian), storm god in the form of a massive bird who stole the tablets of fate.

In his greed for power and dominion Zu determined to steal from the great god Bel (variant: Enlil) the tablets of fate, or destiny. The tablets gave their possessor supreme power over men and gods.

"I will possess the tablets," Zu said to himself, "and all things will be under my power and subject to me. The spirits of heaven will bow before me and the oracles of the gods will be under my command. I shall wear the crown, symbol of sovereignty, and the robe, symbol of godhead. I shall rule over men and gods."

Zu entered the great hall of Bel, where he awaited the coming of the day. As Bel was making the day appear, Zu snatched the tablets from Bel's hands and flew off. He then hid himself in his mountain. Zu's act caused consternation among the gods. Anu, the sky god, called an assembly of the gods to find a means of capturing Zu. As he calls on one of the gods to come forth, the text of the myth breaks off. Scholars suggest the gods Shamash, Rimmon, Marduk, or Lugulbanda as possible heroes in the end of the myth.

3227

Zupay. In Spanish South American mythology, a forest demon who often seduces women. A *zupay* can take the form of a handsome young man or a satyr. He appears in Ricardo Rojas's short story "The Incubus."

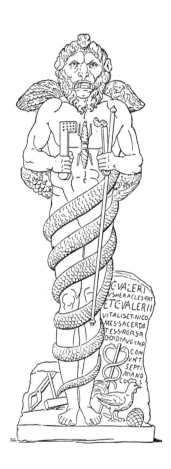

Zurvan

3228

Zurvan. In Persian mythology, god of time-space, father of the good god, Ahura Mazda, and his evil brother, Ahriman. Zurvan appears as the main god in Zurvanism, an offshoot of Zoroastrian belief. One of the main beliefs of Zurvanism was that the universe was not an act of God but an evolutionary development of formless primeval matter, infinite time and space, or Zurvan. This is opposed to Zoroastrian belief in a good creator god, Ahura Mazda, a life after death, and a moral order in which there is reward and punishment.

In one Zoroastrian book, the *Bundahishn*, Zurvan is called Zarman, "the demon who makes decrepit, whom they call old age."

Zurvan also appears as a god in Mithraism, where the image of the lion-headed figure with signs of the zodiac on his body is believed to represent the god. Some scholars, however, identify the statue as that of Ahriman.

Variant spellings: Akarana, Zarvan, Zervan, Zrvan.

Annotated Bibliography

It would require another volume to list all of the sources consulted in writing the Encyclopedia. This Annotated Bibliography, therefore, makes no pretense to completeness, but it does list major works, both of original sources available in English and books dealing with various mythologies. It is hoped the reader will wish to explore many of the books on the list. Some of the books cited are available in different editions or have been reprinted various times, sometimes with a title change. The works are grouped according to category, beginning with general references and proceeding to more specialized groupings according to geographical, cultural, and ethnic divisions.

General Reference Works on Mythology, Folklore, and Religion

Ballou, Robert, ed., *The Bible of the World*; The Viking Press, New York, 1939. Excellent anthology, though some of the translations are stilted, of the major religious texts that form so much a part of world mythology. Notes. Index.

Barber, Richard, *A Companion to World Mythology*; Delacorte Press, New York, 1979. An A-to-Z listing, with illustrations by Pauline Baynes on every page. Contains maps, Index of Topics, and Index of Places.

Brandon, S. G. F., ed., *Dictionary of Comparative Religion*; Charles Scribner's Sons, New York, 1970. Unbalanced work, difficult to use, often with anti-Christian bias, though entries of Buddhist and Hindu mythology and religion are very good. Synoptic index. General index.

Bulfinch, Thomas, "Bulfinch's Mythology"; Thomas Y. Crowell, New York, 1970. An edition containing *The Age of Fable* (1855), about Greek and Roman mythology, mainly based on Ovid and Vergil, *The Age of Chivalry* (1858), dealing with medieval legends, and *Legends of Charlemagne* (1863). One of the most popular 19th-century retellings of mythology, leaving out any reference to sexual matters. This particular edition has a helpful dictionary and index. Numerous other editions of "Bulfinch's Mythology" are offered by other publishers.

Campbell, Joseph, *The Hero with a Thousand Faces*; Pantheon Books, New York, 1949. Now classic study of the subject. Index.

Canney, Maurice A., *An Encyclopedia of Religions*; G. Routledge & Sons, Ltd., London, 1921. Reissued by Gale Research Company, Detroit, 1970. A one-volume work mainly concerned with Christianity, though some of the entries on other religions are of use. No index.

Cavendish, Richard, ed., *Legends of the World*; Orbis Publishing, London, 1982. Dictionary, divided into group sections, such as Hindu, etc., written by various authors. Comparative Survey of World Legends. Bibliography.

———, *Man, Myth, & Magic: An Illustrated Encyclopedia of the Supernatural*. Marshall Cavendish Corp. New York, 1970. A fully illustrated encyclopedia in 24 thin volumes with some excellent articles on mythology. The major problem with the work is its emphasis on occult matters that have little bearing on mythology or folklore. Bibliography. Index.

Cooper, J. C., *An Illustrated Encyclopedia of Traditional Symbols*; Thames and Hudson, London, 1978. A heavily illustrated guide covering a wide spectrum of symbols. Bibliography.

Cotterell, Arthur, *A Dictionary of World Mythology*; Perigee Books, published by G. P. Putnam's Sons, New York, 1979. A short, well-written, illustrated dictionary, done in group sections. Selected Reading list and good index.

Daniel, Howard, *Encyclopedia of Themes and Subjects in Painting*; Harry N. Abrams, Inc., New York, 1971. An A-to-Z listing covering mythological (Greek and Roman), biblical (Christian), historical, allegorical, and topical subjects in Western Art.

Frazer, James George, *The Golden Bough: A Study in Magic and Religion*: Macmillan & Co. Ltd., London, 1912. A massive, 13-volume work, which is fascinating reading on many levels. Though some of it is dated, it still forms a good basis for the study of mythology and legend. The author published a one-volume abridgment in 1922, also issued by Macmillan. Good index.

Gaskell, G. A. *Dictionary of All Scriptures and Myths*; The Julian Press, Inc., New York, 1960. A muddled, misleading dictionary with a very strong occult bias but valuable for its numerous quotations within entries.

Gaster, Theodor H., *The New Golden Bough: A New Abridgment of the Classic Work by Sir James George Frazer*; Criterion Books, New York, 1959. A present-day scholar takes Frazer's work and adds notes to bring it up to date. One of the most valuable editions of Frazer available. Notes. Index.

Hall, James, *Dictionary of Subjects & Symbols in Art*; Harper & Row, New York, 1974. Good, well written and researched, with an introduction by Kenneth Clark. Useful for Greek, Roman, and Christian mythology.

Hastings, James, *Encyclopedia of Religion and Ethics*; Charles Scribner's Sons, New York, 1911. A 13-volume reference work, obviously dated in outlook and prejudiced in favor of Christianity in many articles but filled with much information that is useful for mythology and folklore. One-volume index.

Hinnells, John R., ed., *The Facts On File Dictionary of Religions*; Facts On File, New York, 1984. An A-to-Z listing. Good bibliography. Index. Helpful for quick reference.

Ions, Veronica, *The World's Mythology in Colour*; Hamlyn, London, 1974. Richly illustrated in color, with an introduction by Jacquetta Hawkes, the book makes a quick survey of its subject. Further Reading List. Index.

Jobes, Gertrude, *Dictionary of Mythology, Folklore and Symbols*; The Scarecrow Press, Inc., New York, 1962. A three-volume work, often unreliable in its entries, particularly on interpretations, which tend to be of the 19th-century Solar School of Max Müller that saw the sun and moon in all mythology. Index in third volume based on "mythic" themes.

Leach, Maria, ed., *Standard Dictionary of Folklore, Mythology and Legend*; Funk & Wagnalls, New York, 1972. An extensive, one-volume work, written by various hands. Very wide coverage of folklore but lacking in religion and mythology.

MacCulloch, John Arnott (general editor), *The Mythology of All Races*; Marshall Jones Co., 1916. Reissued by Cooper Square Publisher, Inc., New York, 1964. A 13-volume work dealing with Greek, Roman (1), Eddic (2), Celtic, Slavic (3), Finno-Ugric, Siberian (4), Semitic (5), Indian, Iranian (6), Armenian, African (7), Chinese, Japanese (8), Oceanic (9), North American (10), American, Latin (11), Egypt, Far East (12), Index (13). Usefulness varies from volume to volume depending on the author. Extensive bibliographies in each volume.

Mercatante, Anthony S., *Good and Evil: Mythology and Folklore*; Harper & Row, New York, 1978. A short world study, dealing with the myths, legends, and beliefs surrounding Good and Evil. Annotated Bibliography. Index.

New Larousse Encyclopedia of Mythology; Prometheus Press, London, 1959. Does not list an editor, though the work contains an introduction by Robert Graves and various articles by scholars. Some are excellent. Further Reading List. Index.

Parrinder, Geoffrey, *A Dictionary of Non-Christian Religions*; The Westminster Press, Philadelphia, 1971. A good one-volume guide for basic entries on religion, many of which deal with mythology, and sacred books.

————, ed., *Religions of the World: From Primitive Beliefs to Modern Faiths*; Grosset & Dunlap, New York, 1971. Written by a variety of scholars, the book varies in quality but on the whole is worth reading. Heavily illustrated. Bibliography. Good index.

Radford, E. and M. A., *Encyclopedia of Superstitions*; Hutchinson, London, 1948. Excellent one-volume work, dealing mainly with English beliefs, customs, and folklore.

Rosenberg, Donna, *World Mythology: An Anthology of the Great Myths and Epics*; Passport Books, Lincolnwood, Ill., 1986. Retellings of the major myths by often condensing the texts. Selected Bibliography. Index.

Walker, Barbara G., *The Woman's Encyclopedia of Myths and Secrets*; Harper & Row, San Francisco, 1983. One-volume encyclopedia with some very interesting entries with a very strong bias toward the women's movement. Bibliography.

Whittlesey, E. S., *Symbols and Legends in Western Art*; Charles Scribner's Sons, New York, 1972. An A- to Z illustrated guide. Helpful for Greek, Roman, and Christian mythology and legend.

World Folktale Collections

Clarkson, Atelia, and Gilbert B. Cross, eds., *World Folktales*; Charles Scribner's Sons, New York, 1980. A selection of folktales with comments. Good introduction. Appendixes covering various aspects of the folktale. Select bibliography.

Cole, Joanna, ed., *Best-Loved Folktales of the World*; Doubleday and Company, Inc., Garden City, N.Y., 1982. A popular collection of tales arranged according to country. Introduction. Index of categories of tales.

Foster, James R., ed., *The World's Great Folktales*; Harper & Brothers, New York, 1953. A collection arranged according to types of tales. Introduction. Notes.

Lee, F. H., ed., *Folk Tales of All Nations*; Tudor Publishing Co., New York, 1930. A very rich collection from around the world arranged according to country.

Rugoff, Milton, ed., *A Harvest of World Folk Tales*; The Viking Press, New York, 1949. A collection, based on literary sources, of a wide range of tales with comments. Introduction.

Sideman, Belle Becker, ed., *The World's Best Fairy Tales*; The Reader's Digest Association, Pleasantville, N. Y., 1967. A collection of some of the world's best known folktales from a variety of sources.

Thompson, Stith, *The Folktale*; Holt, Rinehart and Winston, New York, 1946. The now classic study of the folktale throughout the world. Introduction. In Appendix B: Principal Collections of Folktales. Index.

Fable Collections

Aesop, Fables from; translated by Ennis Rees; Oxford University Press, New York, 1966. Verse versions of many of the favorite fables derived from a variety of sources. Introduction. Index of titles.

Aesop, The Fables of; edited by Joseph Jacobs; Schocken Books, New York, 1966; reissue of 1894 edition. The fables retold by Jacobs. Notes on sources. Index.

Aesop, Fables of; translated by S. A. Handford; Penguin Books, New York, 1954. An excellent collection, except the translator insists on using titles not at all familiar to the reader. Introduction. Notes.

Bidpai, *Kalila and Dimna: Selected Fables;* retold by Ramsay Wood; Alfred A. Knopf, New York, 1980. Retelling of classic fables, many of which appear in later Aesopic fables. Based on Sanskrit versions. Introduction by Doris Lessing.

Barius, Valerius, *Aesop's Fables;* translated by Denison B. Hull; The University of Chicago Press, Chicago, 1960. A verse translation of one of the most famous ancient versions of Aesop. Notes. Index.

Jacobs, Joseph, ed., *The Fables of Aesop as First Printed by William Caxton in 1484;* Burt Franklin, New York, 1970; reprint of 1889 edition. A study of the history of the Aesopic fable. Introduction. Synopsis of Parallels. Index.

Kennerly, Karen, ed., *Hesitant Wolf & Scrupulous Fox: Fables Selected from World Literature;* Random House, New York, 1973. A varied collection of fables from around the world. Biographical notes on the fabulists. Index.

Komroff, Manuel, ed., *The Great Fables;* Tudor Publishing Co., New York, 1928. A massive collection of Aesopic fables ranging the entire world. No index.

La Fontaine, *The Fables;* translated by Elizur Wright; G. Bell and Sons, Ltd., London, 1917; reissue of 1841 edition. A complete edition of all of the fables. Introduction. Brief notes.

———, *The Fables;* translated by Marianne Moore; The Viking Press, New York, 1952. A translation by a major American poet that is often quite good.

———, *Selected Fables;* translated by James Michie; The Viking Press, New York, 1971. A selection of some of the best-known fables in verse. Introduction by Geoffrey Grigson.

The Panchatantra; translated by Arthur W. Ryder; The University of Chicago Press, Chicago, 1925. A classic English translation of a classic Sanskrit text of animal fables.

Perry, Ben Edwin, ed. and trans., *Babrius and Phaedrus: Fables;* The Loeb Classical Library, 1965. A collection of fables in Greek by Babrius and in Latin by Phaedrus with English translation. Introduction. Notes.

Shapiro, Norman R., trans.,*Fables from Old French: Aesop's Beasts and Bumpkins;* Wesleyan University Press, Middletown, Conn., 1982. A collection of Aesopic fables by Marie de France, Isopet I, Isopet II de Paris, and Isopet de Chartres. Notes. Selected bibliography.

Ballad Collections

Child, Francis James, ed., *The English and Scottish Popular Ballads;* Houghton, Mifflin and Company, New York, 1884–1898. Reissued by Dover Publications, Inc., New York, 1965. The classic five-volume work with the ballads, variants, notes, etc. A standard text.

Kinsley, James, ed., *The Oxford Book of Ballads;* Oxford at the Clarendon Press, Oxford, 1969. A collection with the music. Introduction. Notes.

Leach, MacEdward, ed., *The Ballad Book* Harper & Brothers, New York, 1955. Excellent selection with English, Scottish, and American ballads. Good introduction. Notes. Index.

Lockhart, J. G., ed. and trans., *The Spanish Ballads;* The Century Co., New York, 1907. An edition with notes of one of the most popular 19th-century translations.

Olrik, Axel, ed., *A Book of Danish Ballads;* translated by E. M. Smith-Dampier; Princeton University Press, Princeton, N. J., 1939. A selection of ballads in a wide range. Long, good introduction.

Percy, Thomas, ed., *Reliques of Ancient English Poetry;* edited by J. V. Prichard; Thomas Y. Crowell and Co., New York, 1875. An edition of the classic collection. Introduction. Notes. Glossary.

Wimberly, Lowry C., *Folklore in the English and Scottish Ballads;* Frederick Ungar Publishing Co., New York, 1928. Study of the customs and beliefs in English and Scottish ballads relating to religion and magic. Bibliography. Index.

Animals in Mythology and Folklore

Gubernatis, Angelo de, *Zoological Mythology, or The Legends of Animals;* Trubner & Co., London, 1872. Reissued by Singing Tree Press, Detroit, 1968. The work contains a wealth of information as well as summaries of myths, fables, and legends relating to animals. But a major drawback is that the author ascribes nearly every incident in each tale to a natural phenomenon such as Dawn, Sunset, Wind, Storm, and others. Index.

Ingersoll, Ernest, *Birds in Legend, Fable and Folklore;* Longmans, Green and Company, New York, 1923. Reissued by Singing Tree Press, Detroit, 1968. A good study of birds in mythology and folklore. Index.

Lum, Peter, *Fabulous Beasts;* Pantheon Books, New York, 1951. A popular study of fantastic and mythical animals. Index.

Mercatante, Anthony S., *Zoo of the Gods: Animals in Myth, Legend, and Fable;* Harper & Row, New York, 1974. A comparative study of world myth and legend relating to various animals. Illustrated. Annotated bibliography. Index.

White, T. H., ed. and trans., *The Bestiary;* Capricorn Books, G. P. Putnam's Sons, New York, 1960. A translation of a medieval bestiary of the 12th century. Wonderful reading. Illustrated. Introduction.

Mercatante, Anthony S., *The Magic Garden: The Myth and Folklore of Flowers, Plants, Trees, and Herbs;* Harper & Row, New York, 1976. A coverage that explores world folklore. Introduction. Illustrations. Annotated bibliography. Index.

Porteous, Alexander, *Forest Folklore, Mythology, and Romance*; George Allen & Unwin, Ltd., London, 1928. A general survey of the topic. Index.

Thiselton-Dyer, T. F., *The Folklore of Plants*; Chatto & Windus, London, 1889. Reissued by Singing Tree Press, Detroit, 1968. Basically a coverage of English folklore regarding the plant world. Index.

English Bibles, Apocryphal Books, Biblical Legends, Commentaries, Dictionaries, and Encyclopedias

The Apocryphal New Testament, edited and translated by Montague Rhodes James, Oxford University Press, 1924. An excellent selection but a stiff translation of the various apocryphal gospels, acts, epistles, and apocalypses not included in the New Testament. Index of subjects.

Apocryphal Gospels, Acts and Revelations, edited and translated by Alexander Walker; T. & T. Clark, Edinburgh, 1890. An excellent selection of the tales and legends not included in the New Testament. Index.

Charlesworth, James H., ed., *The Old Testament Pseudepigrapha*; Doubleday & Company, Inc., Garden City, N. Y., 1985. A massive, two-volume work, containing all of the material not included in the Old Testament but rich in folklore. Notes. Index.

Frazer, James George, *Folklore in the Old Testament*; The Macmillan Company, London, 1918. A three-volume study of the subject. There is also a one-volume abridged edition by Frazer published in 1923.

Gaer, Joseph, *The Lore of the New Testament*; Little, Brown and Co., Boston, 1952. An excellent collection built around the figures of the New Testament. Notes on sources.

————, *The Lore of the Old Testament*; Little, Brown and Co., Boston, 1951. An excellent collection of legends built around Bible stories. Notes on sources.

Gaster, Theodor H., *Myth, Legend, and Custom in the Old Testament: A Comparative Study with Chapters from Sir James G. Frazer's Folklore in the Old Testament*; Harper & Row, New York, 1969. An edition of Frazer updated with much new material. A must for biblical mythology and legend. Introduction. Notes.

Hastings, James, ed., *A Dictionary of the Bible*; Charles Scribner's Sons, New York, 1898. A four-volume work dealing with every aspect of the Bible. An additional volume was included in 1904, bringing it up to that date.

The Holy Bible: A Translation from the Latin Vulgate in the Light of the Hebrew and Greek Originals; translated by Ronald Knox; Sheed & Ward, Inc., New York, 1944. An important translation because it is from the Latin Bible, which was the one used during the Middle Ages and had the greatest influence on art.

The Interpreter's Bible; Abingdon Press, New York/Nashville, 1952. A 12-volume work with the King James Version and Revised Standard Version as texts. Numerous general articles. Indexes.

The Interpreter's Dictionary of the Bible: An Illustrated Encyclopedia; Abingdon Press, Nashville, Tenn., 1964. A four-volume reference work that is a must.

The Jerome Biblical Commentary, edited by R. E. Brown, J. A. Fitzmyer, and R. E. Murphy; Prentice-Hall, Inc., Englewood Cliffs, N. J., 1968. A good one-volume Catholic commentary. Index.

Sanmel, Samuel, gen. ed., *The New English Bible with the Apocrypha*; Oxford Study Edition. Contemporary British translation of the Bible. Introductions. Annotations. Cross-references. Indexes.

The New Jerusalem Bible; Doubleday & Company, Inc., Garden City, N. Y., 1985. A revision of the earlier 1966 version, which is very popular. Must be used with caution. Numerous misprints. Very Roman catholic notes.

The Oxford Annotated Bible with the Apocrypha; Revised Standard Version, edited by H. G. May and B. M. Metzger, Oxford University Press, New York, 1965. A handy one-volume annotated RSV Bible. Charts. Tables. Indexes.

Peake's Commentary on the Bible, edited by M. Black and H. H. Rowley; Thomas Nelson and Sons, Ltd., London, 1962. A good one-volume commentary on the Bible. Index.

Tanakh: A New Translation of The Holy Scriptures According to the Traditional Hebrew Text; The Jewish Publication Society, Philadelphia, 1985. A new English translation of the Hebrew Scriptures. Reading it against standard Christian translations of the Old Testament is very enlightening. Notes.

Ancient Near East

Gilgamesh, The Epic of; Penguin Book, Baltimore, 1960. A prose version of the epic by N. K. Sandars, pulling together various ancient versions. Contains a long introduction giving background. Glossary.

Gray, John, *Near Eastern Mythology: Mesopotamia, Syria, Palestine*; Hamlyn Publishing Group, Ltd., London, 1969. A very useful, short, illustrated study of a very complex subject. Reading list. Index.

Heidel, Alexander, *The Gilgamesh Epic and Old Testament Parallels*; The University of Chicago Press, Chicago, 1946. A translation and interpretation of the ancient epic poem, with other myths and legends relating to it. No index.

Jastrow, Morris, *The Religion of Babylonia and Assyria*; Ginn & Company, Boston, 1898. Classic, 19th-century study by a well-known scholar. Bibliography. Index.

Pritchard, James B., ed., *The Ancient Near East: An Anthology of Texts and Pictures*; Princeton University Press, Princeton, N. J., 1958. A collection of important Near Eastern texts, many relating to mythology, such as Gilgamesh. Illustrations. Notes. Glossary. Index.

Pritchard, James B., *Ancient Near Eastern Texts Relating to the Old Testament;* Princeton University Press, Princeton, N. J., 1955. An important collection of texts, many of which are original sources for myths and legends relating to the Near East. The work is fully annotated. Some of the translations, however, are very stiff and awkward. Index of biblical names.

Sandars, N. K., ed., *Poems of Heaven and Hell from Ancient Mesopotamia;* Penguin Books, Baltimore. An excellent collection of texts. Notes. Glossary.

Spence, Lewis, *Myths & Legends of Babylonia and Assyria;* Harrap & Co., London, 1916. Reissued by Gale Research Company, Detroit, 1975. A popular study of these fascinating myths but often confusing. Glossary. Index.

Egyptian

Aldred, Cyril, *Akhenaten: Pharaoh of Egypt—A New Study;* McGraw-Hill, New York, 1968. Deromanticizes Akhenaten as a religious revolutionary. One of the few books to mention Akhenaten's homosexuality. Chronology. Notes. Select Bibliography. Index.

The Book of the Dead: The Hieroglyphic Transcript of the Papyrus of Ani; translated by E. A. Wallis Budge; Medici Society Edition, 1913. Reissued by University Books, New Hyde Park, N. Y., 1960. Based on various editions published by Budge, 1890, 1894, and 1913. A major source book but very difficult to read. It contains rubrics and rituals and alludes to mythology. It is similar to trying to reconstruct Christian mythology from a hymnal.

Budge, E. A. Wallis, *Egyptian Religion: Egyptian Ideas of the Future Life;* reissued by Bell Publishing Company, New York, 1969. Original edition, London, 1900. A short study of the cult of Osiris, the major god of death and resurrection in ancient Egypt. No index.

———, *The Gods of the Egyptians, or Studies in Egyptian Mythology;* The Open Court Publishing Company, Chicago, 1904. Reissued by Dover Publications, New York, 1969. Classic study with quotes from many ancient Egyptian texts, but it is poorly arranged and often contradicts itself from one section to another. Illustrations. Index.

Erman, Aldolf, *The Ancient Egyptians: A Sourcebook of Their Writings;* translated by Aylward M. Blackman; Harper Torchbooks, New York, 1966. An interesting anthology, though many of the translations are very stiff and awkward. The Harper Torchbook edition is a republication of *The Literature of the Ancient Egyptians* (1927 English translation).

Frankfort, Henri, *Ancient Egyptian Religion;* Columbia University Press, New York, 1948. Reissued by Harper Torchbooks, New York, 1961. A short survey of Egyptian gods and goddesses, way of life, art, and literature. Index.

Ions, Veronica, *Egyptian Mythology;* Hamlyn, London, 1965. A fully illustrated study of the gods and goddesses of ancient Egypt. Index.

James, T. G. H., *Myths and Legends of Ancient Egypt;* Grosset & Dunlap, New York, 1971. Popular retellings of various Egyptian myths with contemporary illustrations. Index.

Maspero, Gaston C. C., *Popular Stories of Ancient Egypt;* translated by A. S. Johns; reissued by University Books, New Hyde Park, N. Y., 1969. Original edition in English, 1915. Contains 17 complete Egyptian stories and six fragments. Many of the tales are classics in world folklore.

Mercatante, Anthony S., *Who's Who in Egyptian Mythology;* Clarkson N. Potter, Inc., New York, 1978. An A-to-Z dictionary of Egyptian mythology, illustrated by the author. Numerous cross-references. Introduction by Dr. Robert S. Bianchi of the Department of Egyptian and Classical Art, The Brooklyn Museum. Bibliography.

Simpson, William Kelly, *The Literature of Ancient Egypt: An Anthology of Stories, Instructions and Poetry;* Yale University Press, New Haven, Conn., and London, 1972. An excellent anthology. Translations vary in merit. Introduction.

Persian Mythology and Folklore

Christensen, Arthur, ed., *Persian Folktales;* translated by Alfred Kurti; G. Bell & Sons Ltd., London, 1971. Good selection of folktales. Notes and Sources.

Fardusi, *The Shah-Namah;* translated by Alexander Rogers; reissued by Heritage Publishers, Delhi, India, 1973. Original edition, 1907. An abridged translation of the massive epic poem in both prose and verse.

Hinnells, John R., *Persian Mythology;* Hamlyn Publishing Group, Ltd., London, 1973. Excellent, illustrated short study. Bibliography. Index.

Hebrew and Jewish Mythology and Folklore

Ausubel, Nathan, *A Treasury of Jewish Folklore;* Crown Publishers, New York, 1948. An excellent anthology, covering stories, traditions, legends, humor, wisdom, and folk song. Glossary. Index.

Bin Gorion, Micha Joseph bin, collector, *Mimekor Yisrael: Classical Jewish Folktales;* translated by Dan Ben-Amos; Indiana University Press, Bloomington, Ind., and London, 1976. A three-volume collection made up of religious tales, national tales, folktales, and oriental tales. Sources and References.

Gaster, Theodor H., *Customs and Folkways of Jewish Life;* William Sloane Associates Publishers, New York, 1955. A reissue of *The Holy and the Profane,* covering various aspects of Jewish beliefs and rituals in relation to world folklore. Bibliography. Index.

————, *Festivals of the Jewish Year*; William Sloane Associates, New York, 1952. Excellent study with rich folklore background. Notes. No index.

Ginzberg, Louis, *The Legends of the Jews*; translated by Henrietta Szold; The Jewish Publication Society of America, Philadelphia, 1900. A seven-volume collection of Jewish legends built around biblical themes. Sources. Index.

Noy, Dove, and Baharav, Gene, eds. and trans., *Folktales of Israel*; The University of Chicago Press, Chicago, 1963. Excellent collection with scholarly notes. Glossary. Bibliography. Index of Motifs and Index of Tale Types. General Index.

Talmud, The, Selections; translated by H. Polano; Frederick Warne & Co., Ltd., London, reprinted 1965. Good selection of various biblical themes and stories built around them. No index.

Christian Mythology, Legend and Folklore

Ballou, Robert O., *The Other Jesus*; Doubleday & Co., Garden City, N. Y., 1972. A narrative based on the apocryphal stories of Jesus not included in the canon of the New Testament but very much a part of Christian legend. Sources.

Brewer, E. Cobham, *A Dictionary of Miracles*; J. B. Lippincott Co., Philadelphia, 1884. Reissued by Gale Research Co., Detroit, 1966. Absolutely fascinating reading about the saints and miracles.

Butler, Alban, *The Lives of the Saints*; edited by Herbert Thurston and Donald Attwater; P. J. Kennedy & Sons, New York, 1965. A four-volume set, based on Butler but drastically rewritten. Florid prose. Major source book for lives of the saints. Arranged according to the Christian calendar.

Cross, F. L., ed., *The Oxford Dictionary of the Christian Church*; Oxford University Press, London, 1957. The best one-volume guide to the Christian Church, its saints, and customs.

Jameson, Mrs. *The History of Our Lord*; Longmans, Green, and Co., London, 1872. The classic two-volume study of the life of Jesus as portrayed in works of art. Gives numerous legends. Index.

———— *Legends of the Madonna*; Longmans, Green, and Co., London, 1879. The classic study of the Virgin Mary in works of art. Gives numerous legends. Index.

————, *Legends of the Monastic Orders*; Longmans, Green, and Co., London, 1880. A study of saints connected with monastic orders and their portrayal in art. Numerous legends. Index.

————, *Sacred and legendary Art*; Longmans, Green, and Co., London, 1879. Longmans, Green, and Co., London, 1879. A two-volume set covering angels, archangels, evangelists, apostles, doctors of the church, and Mary Magdalene, as portrayed in art. Numerous legends. Index.

Metford, J. C. J., *Dictionary of Christian Lore and Legend*; Thames and Hudson, Ltd., London, 1983. Excellent one-volume, illustrated guide to Christian lore and legend.

Voragine, Jacobus, *The Golden Legend*; translated and adapted by Granger Ryan and Helmut Ripperger, Longmans, Green and Co., New York, 1941. A shortened version that often omits the best parts of the legends because they might seem outlandish to present-day Roman Catholics. Index.

————, *The Golden Legend or Lives of the Saints*; translated by William Caxton; J. M. Dent and Co., London, 1900. An edition of Caxton's English version, with modern spelling, in seven volumes.

Armenian Mythology and Folklore

Ananikian, Mardiros H., *Armenian Mythology*; Marshall Jones Company, Boston, 1925. Volume 7, *The Mythology of All Races*; reissued by Cooper Square Publishers, Inc., New York, 1964. Notes. Bibliography. No index, except in final volume of full set.

Arnot, Robert, ed., *Armenian Literature*; The Colonial Press, New York, 1901. An anthology containing poetry, drama, and folklore.

Islamic Mythology, Legend and Folklore

Arabian Nights' Entertainments, or The Thousand and One Nights; translated by Edward William Lane; Tudor Publishing Co., New York, 1946. A contemporary edition of the famous Lane translation, published in 1838 and 1840. Extensive notes.

The Book of the Thousand Nights and One Night; rendered into English from the literal and complete French translation of Dr. J. C. Mardrus by Powys Mathers; St. Martin's Press, New York, 1972. A four-volume edition of the classic work in a very readable English form.

Gibb, H. A. R., and Kramers, J. H., eds., *Shorter Encyclopedia of Islam*; E. J. Brill, Leiden, 1961. A very scholarly one-volume edition on Islam. Helpful for background. Various entries on legendary persons, heaven and hell. Register of subjects.

Jeffery, Arthur, ed., *Islam: Muhammad and His Religion*; The Liberal Arts Press, New York, 1958. Anthology covering varying aspects of Islam, some of which deals with folklore. Glossary.

The Koran; translated by J. M. Rodwell; J. M. Dent & Sons, Ltd., London, 1909. An edition of the classic English translation. Notes.

Hughes, Thomas Patrick, *Dictionary of Islam*; Cosmo Publications, New Delhi, India, 1977. Reprint of 1885 edition. A one-volume dictionary with some entries on mythology and folklore in Islam. Index.

The Qur'an; translated by Richard Bell; T. & T. Clark, Edinburgh, 1937. A two-volume edition of the Qur'an (The Koran) with a rearrangement of the suras. Notes.

The Quran: The Eternal Revelation Vouchsafed to Muhammad, The Seal of the Prophets; translated by Muhammad Zafrulla Khan; Curzon Press, 1971. An English translation with Arabic text facing; it presents the book in English by a believer. Index.

Greek and Roman Mythology and Legend (Classical)

Apollodorus, *The Library;* translated by James George Frazer; Loeb Classical Library, New York, 1921. A two-volume edition of one of the basic sources for Greek mythology. Introduction. Notes. Appendix comparing Greek myth with world myth. Index.

Apollonius of Rhodes, *The Voyage of the Argo: The Argonautica;* translated by E. V. Rieu; Penguin Books, Baltimore, 1959. A prose translation of the short epic. Introduction. Glossary.

Duckworth, George E., ed., *The Complete Roman Drama;* Random House, New York, 1943. All of the plays in a variety of English translations.

Gayley, Charles Mills, *The Classic Myths in English Literature and in Art;* Ginn & Co., Boston, 1883. Popular study based on Bulfinch's *Age of Fable* (1855). Commentary. Notes. Index.

Gilbert, John, *Myths and Legends of Ancient Rome;* Hamlyn, London, 1970. A short collection of myths and legends.

Godolphin, F. R. B., ed., *Great Classical Myths;* The Modern Library, New York, 1964. A collection of myths from a variety of sources in a variety of translations. Introduction. Glossary. Index.

Grant, Michael, *Myths of the Greeks and Romans;* World Publishing Company, Cleveland, Ohio, 1962. A study with numerous references to art, music, and literature. Bibliography. Index.

Graves, Robert, *The Greek Myths;* George Braziller, Inc., New York, 1955. Excellent retellings of the myths based on the ancient sources. Complete notes. One may disagree with Graves's interpretations, but the stories are very well told. Index.

Greene, David, and Richmond Lattimore, eds., *The Complete Greek Tragedies;* The University of Chicago Press, Chicago, 1959. A four-volume set of the complete works of the Greek dramatists in contemporary English poetic translations. Introductions.

Hendricks, Rhoda A., ed. and trans., *Classical Gods and Heroes; Myths as Told by Ancient Authors;* Frederick Ungar Publishing Co., New York, 1972. Modern translations of original sources for many myths. Introduction. Glossary.

Hesiod, *Theogony, Works and Days;* translated by Dorothea Wender; Penguin Books, Baltimore, 1973. A prose translation of the important texts. Introduction. Notes.

———, *Works and Days;* translated by Hugh G. Evelyn-White; Loeb Classical Library, 1914. A Greek text with English prose translation. Book also includes the Homeric Hymns and other Homerica. Introduction. Index.

———, *The Works and Days, Theogony, The Shield of Herakles;* translated by Richmond Lattimore; The University of Michigan Press, Ann Arbor, Mich., 1959. A poetic translation of some basic texts on Greek mythology. Introduction.

Homer, *The Iliad;* translated by Richmond Lattimore; The University of Chicago Press, Chicago, 1951. A modern verse translation of the epic. Introduction. Glossary.

———, *The Iliad;* translated by Alexander Pope; edited by Reuben A. Brower and W. H. Bond; The Macmillan Co., New York, 1965. The most famous translation into English. Introduction. Textual notes.

———, *The Iliad, The Odyssey and The Lesser Homerica;* edited by Allardyce Nicoll; Princeton University Press, Princeton, N. J., 1967. An edition in two volumes of the classic Chapman's translations. Introduction. Notes. Commentary.

———, *The Odyssey;* translated by E. V. Rieu; Penguin Books, Baltimore, 1946. A simple prose version of the epic poem. Introduction.

Kravitz, David, *Who's Who in Greek and Roman Mythology;* Clarkson N. Potter, Inc., New York, 1975. An A-to-Z listing, important in that it gives all of the relationships—mother, father, husband, wife, offspring, etc.

Lempriere's Classical Dictionary of Proper names Mentioned in Ancient Authors; edited by F. A. Wright; E. P. Dutton & Co., Inc., New York, 1955. An edition of a classic dictionary, used by Keats and other Romantic poets. The names, however, are listed under their Roman forms.

Mayerson, Philip, *Classical Mythology in Literature, Art and Music;* Xerox College Publishing, Lexington, Mass., 1971. Excellent illustrated coverage of Greek and Roman mythology in relation to the arts. Introduction. Index.

Melas, Evi, *Temples and Sanctuaries of Ancient Greece;* translated by F. Maxwell Brownjohn; Thames and Hudson, London, 1970. A rich study of Greek temples and the cults surrounding them. Illustrated. Index.

Norton, Dan S., and Peters Rushton, *Classical Myths in English Literature;* Rinehard & Company, Inc., 1952. A very thorough coverage of the myths and how they are used in English literature, arranged A to Z.

Ovid, *Heroides and Amores;* translated by Grant Showerman; Loeb Classical Library, New York, 1921. Latin with English prose translation on facing page.

———, *The Metamorphoses;* translated by Horace Gregory; The Viking Press, New York, 1958. A major poetic translation of the poem. Introduction. Glossary.

———, *The Metamorphoses;* translated by Rolfe Humphries; Indiana University Press, Bloomington, Ind., 1964. A spirited blank-verse translation of one of the major sources of Greek and Roman mythology. Glossary. Index.

————, *The Metamorphoses*; translated by Mary M. Innes; Penguin Books, Baltimore, 1955. A modern, somewhat stiff prose translation of the brilliant poem. Introduction.

————, *The Metamorphoses*; translated by Frank Justus Miller; Loeb Classical Library, New York, 1916. A two-volume prose translation with Latin on facing pages.

Ovid's Metamorphoses: The Arthur Golding Translation (1567); edited by John Frederick Nims; The Macmillan Co., New York, 1965. A modern edition of the classic English translation read by Shakespeare. Notes. Glossary.

Ovid's Works; translated into English prose by Henry T. Riley; G. Bell & Sons, Ltd., London, 1912. A three-volume set containing all of the works, translated into a very dull English but useful because of its completeness.

Perowne, Stewart, *Roman Mythology*; Paul Hamlyn, London, 1969. Excellent, fully illustrated study. Introduction. Further reading list. Index.

Rose, H. J., *A Handbook of Greek Mythology*; Methuen & Co., Ltd., London, 1928. Interesting study. Notes. Bibliography. Indexes.

Scherer, Margaret R., *The Legends of Troy in Art and Literature*; Phaidon Press, New York and London, 1963. A study, with illustrations, of the rich art works and books produced from the Troy legend. Contains a list of works of literature and music dealing with the Trojan War. Index.

Seyefert, Oskar S., *A Dictionary of Classical Antiquities, Mythology, Religion, Literature and Art*; William Glaisher, Ltd., London, 1891. An excellent dictionary compiled in the 19th century.

Vergil, *The Aeneid*; translated by Patrick Dickinson; The New American Library, New York, 1961. A poetic translation of the classic.

————, *The Aeneid*; translated by John Dryden; edited by Robert Fitzgerald; The Macmillan Co., New York, 1965. The most famous English translation in heroic couplets. Introduction. Notes.

————, *The Aeneid*; translated by Robert Fitzgerald; Random House, New York, 1981. A new poetic translation by an important poet.

————, *The Aeneid*; translated by William Morris; Longmans, Green, and Co., London, 1900. A very interesting translation by the 19th-century English designer and poet.

Zimmerman, J. E., *Dictionary of Classical Mythology*; Harper & Row, New York, 1964. A concise dictionary with references to literature. Introduction.

Medieval Legends (General)

Gesta Romanorum; translated by Charles Swan; Bohn Library Edition, 1876. Reissued by Dover Publications, New York, 1959. The classic medieval collection of tales from a variety of sources.

Guerber, H. A., *Legends of the Middle Ages*; American Book Co., New York, 1896. A popular retelling of many medieval legends, connecting them to literature. Glossary. Index.

Guido dele Colonne, *Historia Destructionis Troiae*; translated by Mary Elizabeth Meek; Indiana University Press, Bloomington, Ind., 1974. The medieval version of the destruction of Troy, which had a great influence on the legends in Europe. Introduction. Notes.

Jones, Charles W., ed., *Medieval Literature in Translation*; Longmans, Green and Co., New York, 1950. An excellent anthology with a variety of literature, including much legendary material. Introduction. Bibliography.

Medieval Epics; The Modern Library, New York, 1963. An anthology, no listing of an editor, of *Beowulf*, translated by William Alfred (1963), *The Song of Roland*, translated by W. S. Merwin (1959), *The Nibelungenlied*, translated by Helen M. Mustard (1963), and *The Poem of the Cid*, translated by W. S. Merwin, 1959.

Schlauch, Margaret, trans., *Medieval Narrative: A Book of Translations*; Gordian Press, New York, 1928. A varied collection, including Icelandic sagas, chansons de geste, the Tristan legend, the legend of the Holy Grail, the Nibelung cycle, the tale of Troy, the legend of Alexander the Great, saints' lives, and *fabliaux*.

Spence, Lewis, *A Dictionary of Medieval Romance and Romance Writers*; Routledge & Kegan Paul Ltd., London, 1913. Reissued by Humanities Press, Inc., New York, 1962. A dictionary of much medieval legend but somewhat difficult to follow.

Arthurian Legends

The High History of the Holy Graal; translated by Sebastian Evans; J. M. Dent & Sons, Ltd., London, 1898. A classic translation of the legend surrounding the Holy Grail.

Jenkins, Elizabeth, *The Mystery of King Arthur*; Coward, McCann & Geohegan, Inc., New York, 1975. A study of the legends, with numerous illustrations.

Malory, Sir Thomas, *Le Morte D'Arthur*; edited by A. W. Pollard; University Books, New Hyde Park, N. Y., 1961. An edition of the classic Arthurian account in English. Glossary.

————, *Le Morte D'Arthur*; edited by Edward Stachey; Macmillan and Co., Ltd., London, 1868. An edition of Caxton's text. Introduction. Notes. Glossary.

Steinbeck, John, *The Acts of King Arthur and His Noble Knights*; edited by Chase Horton; Farrar, Straus and Giroux, New York, 1976. An edition of Malory from the

Winchester manuscript. A reworking of the Arthurian legends by a modern novelist.

British and Welsh Mythology and Legend

Beowulf; translated by Burton Raffel; The New American Library, New York, 1963. A poetic translation. Afterword by Robert P. Creed. Glossary of names.

Beowulf; translated by Chauncey Brewster Tinker; Newson & Company, New York, 1902. A prose translation of the great epic. Notes. Index of proper names.

Briggs, Katharine M., ed., *A Dictionary of British Folk-Tales*; Indiana University Press, Bloomington, Ind., 1971. The most complete collection to date. Introduction. Notes.

Ebbutt, M. I., *The British: Myths and Legends Series*; George G. Harrap & Co., London, 1910. Reissued by Avenel Books, New York, 1986. Popular retellings of the major myths and legends from Beowulf to Robin Hood. Glossary and Index.

Geoffrey of Monmouth, *Histories of the Kings of Britain*; translated by Sebastian Evans; J. M. Dent and Co., London. A translation of one of the major sources of British mythology.

———, *The History of the Kings of Britain*; translated by Lewis Thorpe; Penguin Books Ltd., 1966. A modern translation. Excellent introduction.

The Mabinogion; translated by Charlotte Guest; Bernard Quaritch, London, 1877. Reissued by Academy Press Ltd., Chicago, 1978. A classic translation of the tales that made them popular with English-speaking peoples. Introduction Notes.

The Mabinogion; translated by Gwyn Jones and Thomas Jones; Everyman's Library, New York, 1949. A more exact translation of the text than that of Guest. Introduction. Notes.

Spaeth, J. Duncan, trans., *Old English Poetry*; Gordian Press, New York, 1967; reprint of 1921 edition. A collection, translated into verse, ranging from Beowulf to legends of the saints. Introduction. Notes.

Weston, Jessie L., ed. and trans., *The Chief Middle English Poets: Selected Poems*. Phaeton Press, New York, 1968. Reprint of 1914 edition. A collection in verse ranging from Layamon to romances, such as Havelok the Dane. Bibliography. Index.

Celtic Mythology and Folklore

Colum, Padraic, ed., *A Treasury of Irish Folklore*; Crown Publishers, Inc., New York, 1954. A collection of stories, traditions, legends, humor, wisdom, ballads, and songs. Index.

Cross, Tom Pette, and Chark Harris Slover, eds., *Ancient Irish Tales*; Barnes & Noble, Inc., New York, 1936. Very good collection of myths. Introduction. Bibliography. Glossary.

Curtin, Jeremiah, *Myths and Folk-Lore of Ireland*; Little, Brown and Co., Boston, 1890. Reissued by Singing Tree Press, Detroit, 1968. Selection of folktales. Glossary.

Graves, Alfred Perceval, *The Irish Fairy Book*; Crescent Books, New York, 1987. A reissued volume of a collection made by the father of the poet Robert Graves.

Jacobs, Joseph, ed., *Celtic Fairy Tales*; World Publishing Co., New York, 1971. A volume that combines Jacobs' *Celtic Fairy Tales* (1891) and *More Celtic Fairy Tales* (1894), both published by David Nutt, London. Notes and References.

Joyce, P. W., *Old Celtic Romances: Tales from Irish Mythology*; David Nutt, London, 1879. Reissued by Devin-Adair Co., New York, 1962. Well-known 19th-century collection of tales. Introduction. Notes. List of proper names.

Lover, Samuel, and Thomas Crofton Crokes, *Legends and Tales of Ireland*; Crescent Books, New York, 1987. A volume that reprints in one volume Samuel Lover's *Legends and Tales of Ireland* and Thomas Crofton Croker's *Fairy Legends of the South of Ireland*, both works written in the last century.

MacCana, Proinsias, *Celtic Mythology*; Hamlyn, London, 1970. An excellent study of a very involved and complex subject. Illustrated. Bibliography. Index.

McGarry, Mary, ed., *Great Folktales of Old Ireland*; Bell Publishing Company, New York, 1972. A collection of 17 stories, myths, legends from a variety of sources.

Squire, Charles, *Celtic Myth and Legend*; Newcastle Publishing Co., Inc., Hollywood, Calif., 1975. Originally published as *The Mythology of the British Isles* (1905) in London. Index.

Italian

Ariosto, Ludovico, *Orlando Furioso*; translated by Guido Walkman; Oxford University Press, London, 1974. A prose translation of the entire work, which is based on medieval legend and lore. Introduction.

———, *Orlando Furioso*; translated by Sir John Harington; edited by R. Gottfried; Indiana University Press, Bloomington, Ind., and London, 1963. The classic Elizabethan translation of one of the most popular European works based on medieval legend.

Boccaccio, *The Decameron*; anonymous translation, published in 1620; The Heritage Press, New York, 1940. The great collection of tales, many of which are part of European folklore.

Calvino, Italo, *Italian Folktales*; translated by George Martin; Pantheon Books, New York, 1956. A wonderful collection, but in many cases there is more Calvino than Italian folklore in the tales.

Crane, Thomas Frederick, *Italian Popular Tales*; Houghton, Mifflin, Boston, 1885. Reissued by Singing Tree Press, Detroit, 1968. Good selection with many variants of the tales. Notes. Sources.

Dante Alighieri, *The Comedy of Dante Alighieri*; translated by Dorothy L. Sayers; Basic Books, Inc., New York,

1963. A three-volume poetic translation with copious notes. Long introduction. Excellent version.

————, *The Divine Comedy*; translated by John Ciardi, The Franklin Library, Franklin Center, Pennsylvania, 1977. A poetic translation with notes. One of the best contemporary versions available.

————, *The Divine Comedy*; translated by Charles S. Singleton; Princeton University Press, Princeton, N. J., 1970. A six-volume set with original text, prose translation. Introduction. Notes.

Tasso, Torquato, *Jerusalem Delivered*; translated by Joseph Tusiani; Fairleigh Dickinson Press, Rutherford, N. J., 1970. A contemporary poetic translation of the Renaissance epic based on medieval legends. Introduction.

Toynbee, Paget, *Concise Dictionary of Proper Names and Notable Matters in the Works of Dante*; Phaeton Press, New York, 1968. Reprint of the 1914 edition. Extremely helpful in locating legendary and mythological references, but you must know the spelling in Dante's Italian text.

Spanish

Don Juan Manuel, *Count Lucanor; or the Fifty Pleasant Stories of Patronio*; translated by James York; Gibbings & Company, Ltd., London, 1899. An edition of the work originally published in 1868. Preface. Notes.

The Lay of the Cid; translated by Leonard Bacon and Selden Rose; University of California Press, Berkeley, Calif., 1919. A poetic translation of the Spanish epic poem.

Ruiz, Juan, *The Book of True Love*; translated by Saralyn R. Daly; The Pennsylvania State University Press, University Park, Pa., and London, 1978. A bilingual edition of the text with an English verse translation. Introduction. Notes. Reader's Guide.

Spence, Lewis, *Spain: Myths and Legends*; George C. Harrap & Co., London, 1920. Reissued by Avenel Books, New York, 1986. A popular retelling of Spanish myths and legends, including those of the Cid and Amadis de Gaul, and the ballads.

French

Delarue, Paul, ed., *The Borzoi Book of French Folk Tales*; translated by Austin E. Fife; Alfred A. Knopf, New York, 1956. An excellent collection of French tales. Sources and Commentary.

Marie de France, Lays of; translated by Eugene Mason; J. M. Dent & Sons, Ltd., London, 1911. The book not only includes tales ascribed to Marie de France but other French legends.

Massignon, Genevieve, ed., *Folktales of France*; translated by Jacqueline Hyland. University of Chicago Press, Chicago, 1968. An anthology, part of *The Folktales of the World* series edited by Richard M. Dorson. Extensive notes.

Morris, William, trans., *Old French Romances*; Charles Scribner's Sons, New York, 1896. A classic translation of the French medieval tales and legends.

Perrault, Charles, *Fairy Tales*; translated by A. E. Johnson and others; Dodd, Mead & Co., New York, 1961. All of the classic tales are included in this edition, such as 'Blue Beard" and 'Cinderella."

The Song of Roland; translated by Charles Scott Moncrieff; The Heritage Press, New York, 1938. An English poetic version that tries to capture the beauty of the original.

Norse, Germanic Mythology, Legend and Folklore

Craigie, William A., ed. and trans., *Scandinavian Folk-Lore*; Alexander Gardner, London, 1896. Reissued by Singing Tree Press, Detroit, 1970. A collection of documents relating to Scandinavian folk beliefs. Notes. Index.

Dasent, George Webbe, compiler, *Popular Tales from the Norse*; David Douglas, Edinburgh, 1888. Reissued by Grand River Books, Detroit, 1971. A translation of 59 Norwegian folktales from the *Norske Folke-eventyr* published by Peter Christen Asbjornsen and Jorgen Moe in 1843 and 1844 and expanded in 1852. The collection was also republished by Dover Publications in 1970 as *East o' the Sun and West o' the Moon*.

Davidson, H. R. Ellis, *Gods and Myths of Northern Europe*; Penguin Books, Baltimore, 1964. One of the best current studies on the subject. Index.

————, *Scandinavian Mythology*; Paul Hamlyn, London, 1969. A well-written, concise, illustrated study. Bibliography. Index.

The Poetic Edda, translated by Henry Adams Bellows; American-Scandinavian Foundation, New York, 1923. Reissued by Biblo and Tannen, New York, 1969. A complete translation. Introduction. Notes. Index.

The Elder Edda: A Selection, translated by W. H. Auden and Paul B. Taylor; Random House, New York, 1967. A poetic translation by one of the great poets of the century. Introduction. Notes. Glossary.

The Elder Edda and the Younger Edda, translated by Benjamin Thorpe and L. A. Blackwell; Norroena Society, London, 1907. *The Elder (or Poetic) Edda*, translated into stiff prose by Thorpe, and *The Younger (or Prose) Edda*, translated by Blackwell. Glossary.

Grimm, Brothers, *Grimm's Household Tales*, translated by Margaret Hunt; George Bell and Sons, London, 1884. Reissued by Singing Tree Press, Detroit, 1968. A two-volume edition of the famous folktales. Good introduction by Andrew Lang. Notes.

Grimm, Jacob, *Teutonic Mythology*; George Bell and Sons, London, 1883. Reissued by Dover Publications, New York, 1966. A four-volume complex study of Germanic mythology. Not at all as interesting as the folktale collection but filled with information. Index.

Guerber, H. A., *Myths of Northern Lands*; American Book Co., New York, 1895. A popular retelling of various myths and legends associated with the North countries. Constant references to art. Glossary. Index.

Jones, Gwynn, *Scandinavian Legends and Folk-Tales*; Oxford University Press, London, 1956. Popular retellings of various myths and legends from a variety of sources.

Mackenzie, Donald A., *Teutonic Myth and Legend*; The Gresham Publishing Co., London, n. d. A popular retelling of various Norse and Germanic myths. Numerous editions available. Index.

Munch, Peter Andreas, *Norse Mythology: Legends of Gods and Heroes*, translated by Sigurd Bernhard Hustvedt; The American-Scandinavian Foundation, New York, 1927. Classic 19th-century study. Notes. Index.

Palmer, Philip Mason, and Robert Pattison More, *The Sources of the Faust Tradition*; Oxford University Press, Ltd., London, 1936. Reissued by Octagon Books, New York, 1969. A collection of documents on the Faust legend serving as background for Goethe's *Faust*. Good source book. Index.

Ranke, Kurt, ed., *Folktales of Germany*, translated by Lotte Baumann; The University of Chicago Press, Chicago, 1966. Good selection. Part of the series *Folktales of the World*, under the editorship of Richard M. Dorson. Notes. Sources. Index.

Sturluson, Snorr, *The Prose Edda: Tales from Norse Mythology*, translated by Jean I. Young; University of California, Berkeley, Calif., 1964. A contemporary translation. Introduction. Notes. Index.

Finnish Mythology and Folklore

Holmberg, Uno, *Finno-Ugric and Siberian Mythology*, Vol. 4 in *The Mythology of All Races*; Marshall Jones Co., 1916. Reissued by Cooper Square Publishers, Inc., New York, 1964. A long, dull, and confused account containing a vast amount of information that has to be sorted out by the reader. No index in volume; index of complete set in last volume. Bibliography.

The Kalevala: The Epic Poem of Finland, translated by John Martin Crawford; The Robert Clarke Company, Cincinnati, 1904. A two-volume edition of the epic, done in the original meter, but using spellings of the major names different from those used in other translations.

Kalevala: The Land of Heroes, translated by W. F. Kirby, introduction by J. B. C. Grundy; J. M Dent & Sons, Ltd., London, 1907. A two-volume edition of the epic done in the original meter. Often quite good, though the metrical scheme becomes somewhat tiring to read at length.

The Kalevala, or Poems of the Kaleva District, compiled by Elias Lönnrot, translated by Francis Peabody Magoun, Jr.; Harvard University Press, Cambridge, Mass., 1963.
A prose translation. The best edition of the work available in English. Introduction. Glossary.

The Old Kalevala and Certain Antecedents, compiled by Elias Lönnrot, translated by Francis Peabody Magoun, Jr.; Harvard University Press, Cambridge, Mass., 1969. An earlier edition of *The Kalevala* compiled in 1835, translated into prose. A perfect companion to Magoun's translations of the 1849 *Kalevala*. Introduction. Glossary.

Slavic Mythology and Folklore

Afanasiev, compiler, *Russian Fairy Tales*, translated by Norbert Guterman; Pantheon Books, Inc., New York, 1945. The best one-volume edition of Russian folktales in English. Index.

Curcija-Prodanovic, Nada, *Heroes of Serbia*; Oxford University Press, London, 1963. Folk ballads retold by the author in prose.

Curtin, Jeremiah, ed., *Myths and Folktales of the Russians, Western Slavs and Magyars*; Little, Brown and Co., Boston, 1890. Interesting collection of folktales. Notes. Good introduction.

Guerney, Bernard Guilbert, ed., *A Treasury of Russian Literature*; Vanguard Press, New York, 1943. Excellent anthology, containing a complete version of the epic *The Lay of Igor's Army* as well as excerpts from the Ilya Muromets legends.

Krylov, Ivan, *Fables*, translated by Bernard Pares; Harcourt, Brace and Co., New York, n. d. A complete edition of one of the best writers of Aesopic fables. Introduction. No index.

Machal, Jan, *Slavic Mythology*; Vol. 3 in *The Mythology of All Races*; The Marshall Jones Co., Boston, 1918. Reissued by Cooper Square Publishers, Inc., New York, 1964. Useful for much information. Bibliography. No index, except in last volume of complete set.

Mijatovies, Csedomille, ed., and trans., *Serbian Folklore*; Benjamin Bloom, Inc., New York, 1968; reissue of 1874 edition. A collection of folktales.

Obolensky, Dimitri, ed., *The Penguin Book of Russian Verse*; Penguin Books, England, 1962. Russian texts and prose translations at the bottom of the page. Contains *The Lay of Igor's Army*, some *Byliny*, and a selection of Ivan Krylov's fables.

Petrovitch, Woislav M., *Hero Tales and Legends of the Serbians*; George G. Harrap & Co., Ltd., London, 1914. A collection of tales, prose ballads, and folklore. Glossary. Index.

Ransome, Arthur, ed., *Old Peter's Russian Tales*; T. C. and E. C. Jack, Ltd., London, 1916. Reissued by Dover Publications, Inc., New York, 1969. Many of the tales are from Afanasiev's collections, but the editor has often softened them or changed the endings.

Zenkovsky, Serge A., ed., *Medieval Russia's Epics, Chronicles and Tales*; A Dutton Paperback, E. P. Dutton, Inc., New York, 1974. A massive collection of hard-to-find material in English translation. Includes a generous selection from *The Tale of Bygone Years* and a complete version of *The Lay of Igor's Army*. Good introduction. Notes.

Hindu Mythology and Folklore

Atharva-Veda, Hymns of the, translated by Maurice Bloomfield; Volume 42 of the *Sacred Books of the East*; Oxford University Press, 1897. Reprinted by Motilal Banarsidass, India, 1964. The hymns, plus extracts from the ritual books and commentaries. The translation is somewhat awkward. Introduction. Notes.

Bhagavadgita, The Sanatsugatiya and the Anugita, translated by Kashinath Trimbak Telang; Volume 8 of the *Sacred Books of the East*; Oxford University Press, 1882. Reprinted by Motilal Banarsidass, India. 1965. Three important texts; the most important being the *Bhagavadgita*.

Bhagavad-Gita: The Song Celestial, translated by Edwin Arnold from the Sanskrit text into English verse; The Heritage Press, New York, 1965. A modern edition of the classic 19th-century translation in blank verse. Introduction by Shri Sri Prakasa.

Dandin's Dasha-Kumara-Charita: The Ten Princes, translated by Arthur W. Ryder from the Sanskrit; The University of Chicago Press, Chicago, 1927. A modern translation of a classic Indian collection of tales.

Das, Tulasi, *The Holy Lake of the Acts of Rama*, translated by W. Douglas; Oxford University Press, London, 1952. A classic Hindu retelling of the epic of Rama. Appendix listing the main characters in the epic.

Dimmitt, Cornelia, and J. A. B. van Buitenen, *Classical Hindu Mythology: A Reader in the Sanskrit Puranas*; Temple University Press, Philadelphia, 1978. Excellent collection of myths. Glossary. Notes on Sources. Bibliography of Sanskrit Puranas. Index.

Dowson, John, *A Classical Dictionary of Hindu Mythology and Religion, Geography, History and Literature*; Turbner's Oriental Series, Routledge & Kegan, London, 1878. Reissued. Excellent A-to-Z guide to Hindu mythology and legend.

Gaer, Joseph, *The Fables of India*; Little, Brown and Co., Boston, 1955. An excellent collection of tales from *The Panchatantra, The Hitopadesa, The Jatakas*. Good introduction. Annotated bibliography.

Hindu Scriptures, translated by R. C. Zaehner; Everyman's Library, London, 1966. A selection of hymns from the *Rig-Veda*, the *Atharva-Veda*, the *Upanishads*, and the complete *Bhagavad-Gita*. Difficult reading, and a rather heavy translation of the texts. Zaehner's edition replaces the earlier Hindu Scriptures edited by Nicol Macnicol (1938), which had a different emphasis.

Institutes of Vishnu, translated by Julius Jolly; Volume 7 of the *Sacred Books of the East*; Oxford University Press, 1880. Reprinted by Motilal Banarsidass, India, 1965.

The *Vishnu-smriti*, or *Vaishnava Dharmasastra*, is a collection of ancient aphorisms on the sacred laws of India. Part 1 contains a discussion between the god Vishnu and the earth goddess. Difficult reading.

Ions, Veronica, *Indian Mythology*; Paul Hamlyn, London, 1967. A concise, well-illustrated book on Hindu mythology. In addition to Hindu mythology, there is a section on Buddhist mythology and Jain mythology.

Jacobs, Joseph, ed., *Indian Fairy Tales*; David Nutt, London, 1892. Reissued by Dover Publications, Inc., New York, 1969. Popular collection of folktales. Notes and references at back of volume to show relationship to similar folk tales throughout the world.

The Laws of Manu, translated by G. Bühler; Volume 25 of the *Sacred Books of the East*; Oxford University Press, 1886. Reprinted by Motilal Banarsidass, India, 1964. An important book of Hindu thought with a long introduction. Aside from the *Manu* text, it contains extracts from seven commentaries.

The Mahabharata, edited by Chakravarthi V. Narasimhan; Columbia University Press, New York, 1965. An English-language version based on selected verses. Introduction. Genealogical tables. Glossary. Index of verses on which the English prose version is based.

The Mahabharata of Krishna-Dwaipayana Vyasa, translated by Pratap Chandra Roy; reissued by Munshiram Manoharlal Publishers, India, 1974. Complete translation in 12 volumes done in the last century.

O'Flaherty, Wendy Doniger, ed., and trans., *Hindu Myths: A Sourcebook Translated from the Sanskrit*; Penguin Books, Baltimore, 1975. Excellent collection of Hindu myths with a very good introduction. Selected bibliography. Notes. Glossary. Index of Proper Names.

The Ramayan of Valmiki, translated into English verse by Ralph T. H. Griffith; The Chowkhamba Sanskrit Series Office, India, 1963. A reprint of the complete translation published between 1870 and 1875. The poetics of the translation often have leave much to be desired. Introduction. Notes.

The Ramayana of Valmiki, edited and translated by Hari Prasad Shastri; Shantisadan, London, 1962. Complete prose translation of the epic in three volumes. The best English edition available. Appendixes and glossaries.

Rigveda, The Hymns of the, edited and translated by Ralph T. H. Griffith; 1896. Reissued by Motilal Banarsidass, Delhi, India, 1973. A reissue, edited by J. L. Shastri, of a complete translation (with notes) of the hymns of the *Rig-Veda*. Appendixes. Index of hymns according to deities and subjects. Index.

The Upanishads, translated by F. Max Müller; Volumes 1 and 15 of the *Sacred Books of the East*; Oxford University Press, 1879 and 1884. Reprinted by Motilal Banarsidass, India, 1965. A long introduction and 12 Upanishads in a stiff, awkward translation.

Vedanta-Sutras, translated by George Thibaut; Volumes 34, 38, and 48 in the *Sacred Books of the East*; Oxford University Press, 1904. Reprinted by Motilal Banarsidass, India, 1962. The *Vedanta-Sutras* with commentary by Sankaracarya and a book-length introduction in volumes 34 and 38. Volume 48 contains the *Vedanta-Sutras* with the commentary by Ramanuja. Myth and legend scattered throughout but very difficult reading.

Vedic Hymns, translated by Max Müller and Hermann Oldenberg, Volumes 32 and 46 in the *Sacred Books of the East*; Oxford University Press, 1891. Reprinted by Motilal Banarsidass, India, 1964. Volume 32, with a long introduction and copious notes by Max Müller, contains hymns to the Maruts, Rudra, Vayu, and Vata. Volume 46 contains hymns to Agni. The translations in both cases are stiff and awkward.

Weber, Max, *The Religion of India*; The Free Press, New York, 1958. A study of the sociology of Hinduism and Buddhism. Notes. Index.

Wilkins, W. J., *Hindu Mythology: Vedic and Puranic*; Curzon Press, London, and Rowman & Littlefield, Totowa, N. J., 1973. Reissue of 1892 edition. Popular retelling of Hindu mythology and legend. Illustrated. Index.

Wilson, Epiphanius, ed., *Hindu Literature*; The Colonial Press, New York, 1900. An anthology containing *The Book of Good Counsels*, the 'Nala and Damayanti'' episode from the epic *Mahabharata*, the drama *Sakoontala*, and a shortened version of the epic poem, *The Ramayana*.

Buddhist Mythology and Folklore

Burtt, E. A., ed., *The Teachings of the Compassionate Buddha*; New American Library, Mentor Books, New York, 1966. Excellent collection of original texts in English translation with a commentary. Introduction.

Carus, Paul, *The Gospel of Buddha; Compiled from Ancient Records*; The Open Court Publishing Co., LaSalle, Ill., 1894 (numerous reprints). A classic retelling of the life and teaching of the Buddha, strung together, and written in a pseudo-biblical style. Contains many of the important legends associated with Buddha's life. Glossary of Names and Terms.

Conze, Edward, ed. and trans., *Buddhist Scriptures*; Penguin Books, Baltimore, 1959. An excellent collection and translation of important Buddhist texts. Introduction. Sources. Glossary.

————, *Buddhist Texts Through the Ages*; Bruno Cassier, Oxford, 1954; reissued by Harper Torchbooks, New York, 1964. A collection of various Buddhist texts from a variety of sources. Introduction. Bibliography. Glossary.

Coomaraswamy, Ananada, *Buddha and the Gospel of Buddhism*; University Books, New Hyde Park, N. Y., 1964; reissue of 1916 volume. A popular, classic study of the entire realm of Buddhism. Bibliography. Glossary. Index.

Cowell, E. B., ed. and trans., *Buddhist Mahayana Texts*; Volume 49 of the *Sacred Books of the East*; Oxford University Press, 1894. Reissued by Motilal Banarsidass, India, 1965. A collection of various original texts in English translation. Notes. Introduction.

The Dhammapada; translated by P. Lal; Farrar, Straus & Giroux, New York, 1967. A translation from the Pali text. Excellent introduction. Select bibliography.

Getty, Alice, *The Gods of Northern Buddhism*; Oxford University Press, 1928; reissued by Charles E. Tuttle Co., Rutland, Vt., 1962. A fully illustrated study of the history, iconography, and development of various Buddhist deities, with explanations of various Sanskrit words used in the text. Index.

Humphreys, Christmas, *Buddhism*; Penguin Books, Middlesex, England, 1951. A short, popular study of the vast subject with illustrations. Bibliography. Glossary. Index.

The Jataka, or Stories of the Buddha's Former Births; edited by E. B. Cowell; reissued by Cosmo Publications, India, 1973 of 1895 edition. A six-volume set, translated by different hands, of all of the fables relating to the Buddha's former lives. A must for the folklore of Buddhism. Index in volume 6 of the entire set.

Ling, Trevor, *The Buddha: Buddhist Civilization in India and Ceylon*; Charles Scribner's Sons, New York, 1973. A modern life of the Buddha that attempts, not too successfully, to interpret the social and religious background of the time. Notes. Index.

Rhys, T. W., ed. and trans., *Buddhist Suttas*; Volume 11 of the *Sacred Books of the East*; Oxford University Press, 1881. Reissued by Motilal Banarsidass, India, 1965. A collection of short texts, originally in Pali. Introduction. Notes. Index.

The Tibetan Book of the Dead; edited by W. Y. Evans-Wentz; Oxford University Press, London, 1960. Popular edition of one of the standard texts on dying and Buddhism.

Waddell, L. Austin, *The Buddhism of Tibet, or Lamaism*; W. H. Allen & Co., London, 1895. Reissued by Dover Books, New York, 1971, under the title *Tibetan Buddhism*. An illustrated, turn-of-the-century study of the 'mystic cults, symbolism and mythology'' of Tibetan Buddhism. Index.

Warren, Henry Clarke, ed. and trans., *Buddhism in Translation*; Harvard University Press, Cambridge, Mass., 1896. Reissued by Atheneum, New York, 1972. An excellent translation of original sources in Pali. No index.

Chinese Mythology and Folklore

Chai, Ch'u, and Winbert Chi, eds. and trans., *The Sacred Books of Confucius and Other Confucian Classics*; Bantam Books, Inc., New York, 1965. Contemporary and useful translation of some of the major texts. A help in understanding the background of much Chinese belief.

Christie, Anthony, *Chinese Mythology*; Paul Hamlyn, London, 1968. Excellent study with numerous illustrations. Bibliography. Index.

Dennys, N. B., *The Folk-Lore of China and its Affinities with That of the Aryan and Semitic Races*; Trubner and Co., London, 1876. Reissued by Tower Books, Detroit, 1971. An interesting work dealing with such subjects as birth, marriage, and death as well as superstitions, ghosts, witchcraft, and demonology. Index.

Eberhard, Wolfram, ed., *Folktales of China*; translated by Desmond Parsons; University of Chicago Press, Chicago, 1965. One of the volumes in the series *Folktales of the World* under the editorship of Richard M. Dorson. Many of the tales in this collection originally appeared in *Chinese Fairy and Folk Tales*. The present collection contains extensive notes. Index of Motifs. Bibliography. General index.

Ferguson, John C., *Chinese Mythology*; Volume 8 in the *Mythology of All Races*; Marshall Jones Co., Boston, 1928. Reissued by Cooper Square Publishers, New York, 1964. A short study, with numerous illustrations, giving a general view of Chinese mythology. Bibliography. Index only in last volume of the complete set.

Legge, James, ed., and trans., *The Sacred Books of China*; Clarendon Press, Oxford, 1891. Reissued by Motilal Banarsidass, Delhi, India, 1966. These six volumes contain translations of the texts of Confucianism and Taoism. The Confucian texts are the *Shu King* the *Religious Portions of the Shi King*, the *Hsiao King*, the *Yi King*, and the *Ki Ki*. The Taoist texts are the *Tao Teh king*, the writings of *Kwang-Tze* (Chuang-Tsu), and *Thai-Shang Tractate of Actions and Their Retributions*. Extensive notes. Introduction. Various indexes.

Roberts, Moss, ed. and trans., *Chinese Fairy Tales and Fantasies*; Pantheon Books, New York, 1979. A popular collection of various types of tales found in China. Introduction. Sources.

Smith, D. Howard, *Chinese Religions from 1000 B. C. to the Present*; Holt, Rinehart and Winston, New York, 1968. General overview of a complex subject. Glossary. Index.

Weber, Max, *The Religion of China*; The Free Press, New York, 1951. A sociological study of Confucianism and Taoism. Notes. Index.

Werner, E. T. C., *A Dictionary of Chinese Mythology*; Kelley and Walsh, Ltd., Shanghai, 1932. Reissued by The Julian Press, New York, 1961. A standard work in the field, but one that must be used with extreme caution because it contains numerous mistakes. Bibliography.

————, *Myths and Legends of China*; Arno Press, A New York Times Company, 1976 reissue of the 1922 edition.

Chinese myths and legends in a popular style for the general reader. Introduction. Index.

Williams, C. A. S., *Outlines of Chinese Symbolism and Art Motives*; Kelly and Walsh, Ltd., Shanghai, 1941. Reissued by Charles E. Tuttle Co., Rutland, Vt./Tokyo, Japan, 1974. This popular study, illustrated with line drawings from various sources, is an alphabetical listing of various legends, gods, customs, etc. Index.

Wilhelm, Richard, ed., *Chinese Folktales*; translated by Ewald Osers; G. Bell & Sons, London, 1971. Good selection of tales. Notes.

Wilson, Epiphanius, ed., *Chinese Literature*; The Colonial Press, New York, 1900. An anthology containing *The Analects of Confucius*, *The Sayings of Mencius*, *The Shi-King*, *The Travels of Fa-Hien* in 19th-century translations.

Wu Ch'eng-en, *Monkey*; translated by Arthur Waley; The John Day Co., New York, 1943. The classic English translation, shortened from the original, of the classic Chinese novel that contains so much folklore and mythology.

Japanese Mythology and Folklore

Anesaki, Masaharu, *History of Japanese Religion*; Kegan Paul, Trench, Trübner & Co., London, 1930. Reissued by Charles E. Tuttle Co., Vermont/Tokyo, 1963. A classic study of Japanese religious beliefs with emphasis on Shinto practices.

Czaja, Michael, *Gods of Myth and Stone: Phallicism in Japanese Folk Religion*; Weatherhill, Tokyo/New York, 1974. A very thorough study of various Shinto deities worshiped in Japan. Illustrations. Notes. Bibliography.

Hearn, Lafcadio, *Kwaidan: Stories and Studies of Strange Things*; The Shimbi Shoin, Ltd., Tokyo, 1932 (for the Limited Editions Club). Reissued by Dover Publications, New York, 1968. A classic collection of Japanese ghost tales with an introduction by Oscar Lewis and illustrations by Yasumasa Fujita.

Joly, Henri L., *Legend in Japanese Art*; John Lane The Bodley Head, London, 1908. Reissued by Charles E. Tuttle Co., Vermont/Tokyo, 1967. An A-to-Z listing of over a 1,000 figures, etc., from myth, legend, and folklore in Japan, with 700 illustrations. Generally an invaluable guide, though weak in entries on mythology.

Kiej'e, Nikolas, compiler, *Japanese Grotesqueries*; Charles E. Tuttle Co., Rutland, Vt./Tokyo, Japan, 1973. A collection of Japanese prints of various demons and spirits, with short comments. Helpful introduction by Terence Barrow.

Kojiki; edited and translated by Donald L. Philippi; Princeton University Press, University of Tokyo Press, 1969. A modern, up-to-date translation of a classic text on Japanese mythology. Long introduction. Glossary of over 200 pages. A must for any study of Japanese mythology.

Ko-Ji-Ki: Records of Ancient Matters, edited and translated by Basil H. Chamberlain; Lane, Crawford & Co., Kelly & Co., Yokohama, 1883. One of the main original sources for Japanese mythology in a rather stiff translation that avoids the 'obscene" passages of the work.

McAlpine, Helen and Wiliam, *Japanese Tales and Legends*; Oxford University Press, Oxford, 1958. A collection of epic and legends retold, including *Tales of the Heike*. Glossary.

Nibongi: Chronicles of Japan from the Earliest Times to AD 697, edited and translated by W. G. Aston; Kegan Paul, Trench, Trübner & Co., London, 1896. Reissued by Allen and Unwin, London, 1956. An original source book of Japanese mythology, forming with the *Kojiki* the main source for the study of Japanese mythology.

Ozaki, Yei Theodora, compiler, *The Japanese Fairy Book*; Archibald Constable & Co., Ltd., 1903. Reissued by Dover Publications, New York, 1967. An excellent collection of Japanese folktales compiled at the suggestion of the folklorist Andrew Lang, the great compiler of folktales in 19th-century England.

Piggott, Juliet, *Japanese Mythology*; Paul Hamlyn, London, 1969. A fully illustrated study of Japanese mythology and legend. Bibliography. Index.

Redesdale, Lord, ed., *Tales of Old Japan*; Macmillan and Co., Ltd., London, 1908 edition. A popular collection of Japanese tales from various sources.

Ury, Marian, trans., *Tales of Times Now Past: Sixty-Two Stories from a Medieval Japanese Collection*; University of California Press, Berkeley, Calif., 1979. An interesting collection of tales, chosen from over 1,000 in the collection. Good introduction.

American Indian Mythologies

Alvarado, de Pedro, *An Account of the Conquest of Guatemala in 1524*, translated by Sedley J. Mackie; The Cortes Society, New York, 1924. A classic Spanish study of the encounter of Christianity with native American beliefs. Notes. Bibliography.

Burland, C. A., *The Gods of Mexico*; Eyre & Spottiswoode, London, 1967. A concise and informative treatment of a very complex subject. Short annotated bibliography. Index.

Burland, Cottie, *North American Indian Mythology*; Hamlyn Publishing Corp., London, 1965. An excellent short, illustrated volume on the subject. Bibliography. Index.

Burr, Hartley, *North American Indian Mythology*; Volume 10 of *The Mythology of All Races*; Marshall Jones Company, Boston, 1916. Reissued by Cooper Square Publishers, New York, 1964. A discussion of North American Indian mythology by area, such as the Far North, etc. Introduction. Notes. Bibliography.

Clark, Cora, and Texa Bowen Williams, eds., *Pomo Indian Myths and Some of Their Sacred Meanings*; Vantage Press, Inc., New York, 1954. A diverse collection of myths and legends as well as some native Indian explanations of their meanings.

Curtin, Jeremiah, ed., *Myths of the Modocs: Indian Legends of the Northwest*; Benjamin Blom, Inc., New York, 1971; reissue of 1912 edition. An early collection of tales by a famous collector. Notes.

Durán, Fray Diego, *Book of the Gods and Rites* and *The Ancient Calendar*; translated by Fernando Horcasitas and Doris Heyden; University of Oklahoma Press, Norman, 1971. A must. A Christian view of the ancient rites, but filled with rich information. Glossary. Bibliography. Index.

———, *The History of the Indies of New Spain*; translated by Doris Heyden and Fernando Horcasitas; Orion Press, New York, 1964. Eyewitness account by a Spanish priest who attempts to understand native American religious beliefs and rites. Bibliography. Index.

Leland, Charles G., ed., *The Algonquin Legends of New England, or Myths and Folk Lore of the Micmac, Passamaquoddy, and Penobscot Tribes*; Houghton, Mifflin and Co., Boston, 1884. Reissued by Singing Tree Press, Detroit, 1968. Classic retellings done in the 19th century in a stilted and unnatural English.

Macfarlan, Allan A., ed., *American Indian Legends*; The Heritage Press, New York, 1968. A varied collection, mainly from literary sources but valuable. Introduction. Sources.

Marriott, Alice, and Carol K. Rachlin, eds., *American Indian Mythology*; Thomas Y. Crowell Co., New York, 1968. An excellent collection, mainly derived from oral sources. Introduction. Bibliography.

Popul Vuh: The Sacred Book of the Ancient Quiché Maya, edited and translated by Delia Goetz and Sylvanus G. Morley; University of Oklahoma Press, 1950. An English version by the editors based on the Spanish translation of Andrián Recinos. The book is one of the most important documents for the mythology of the Maya. This edition contains a long introduction. Notes. Index.

Radin, Paul, *The Trickster: A Study in American Indian Mythology*; Philosophical Library, New York, 1956. A very useful study of the role of the Trickster in North American Indian as well as other cultures. Commentaries by Karl Kerényi and C. G. Jung included.

Schoolcraft, Henry R., ed., *The Myth of Hiawatha and Other Oral Legends, Mythologic and Allegoric of the North American Indian*; J. B. Lippincott & Co., Philadelphia, 1856. Reissued by Kraus Reprint Co., New York, 1971. One of the first collections in English of North American Indian myths and legends. However, Schoolcraft made the mistake of identifying Hiawa-

tha, the historical personage, with the god Manabozho, calling them both Hiawatha.

Thompson, Stith, ed., *Tales of the North American Indians*; Indiana University Press, Bloomington, Ind., 1929. A
collection of tales including mythological stories,
mythical incidents, trickster tales, hero tales, journeys to the other world, animal wives and husbands,
miscellaneous tales, tales borrowed from Europeans,
and tales based on Bible stories. One of the best collections. Introduction. Notes. Bibliography.

Toor, Frances, *Mexican Folkways*; Crown Publishers, New
York, 1947. Excellent collection of customs, myths,
folklore, traditions, etc. Introduction. Glossary. Index.

Turner, Frederick W., ed., *The Portable North American Reader*;
The Viking Press, New York, 1973. An excellent an-
thology with more than 200 pages devoted to North
American Indian myths and legends. Introduction.

Wherry, Joseph H., *Indian Masks and Myths of the West*; Funk
& Wagnalls, New York, 1969. An interesting, helpful, and understanding account. Illustrations. Bibliography. Index of mythical beings. Index.

North American Folklore and Legend

Botkin, B. A., ed., *A Civil War Treasury of Tales, Legends and
Folklore*; Random House, New York, 1960. A collection from a variety of sources. Introduction. Index.

————, *A Treasury of American Folklore*; Crown Publishers,
New York, 1944. An excellent anthology from a variety of sources. Index.

————, *A Treasury of Mississippi River Folklore*; Bonanza
Books, New York, 1978 reprint. Stories, ballads, traditions, folkways, relating to the great river. Introduction. Indexes.

————, *A Treasury of Southern Folklore*; Crown Publishers,
New York, 1949. A collection of stories, ballads, traditions, and folkways. Indexes.

————, *A Treasury of Western Folklore*; Crown Publishers,
Inc., New York, 1951. A very varied collection, from
a variety of sources, including tales, songs, ballads.
Indexes.

Brewer, J. Mason, ed., *American Negro Folklore*; Quadrangle/
The New york Times Book Co., New York, 1968. A
collection of tales, songs, superstitions, etc. Index.

Clough, Ben C., ed., *The American Imagination at Work: Tall
Tales and Folk Tales*; Alfred A. Knopf, New York, 1947.
Rich, excellent collection from a variety of sources.
Introduction. Bibliography.

Coffin, Tristram Potter, and Hennig Cohen, eds., *The Parade
of Heroes: Legendary Figures in American Lore*; Anchor
Press, Doubleday, Garden City, N. Y., 1978. A selection from the journals and archives of American
folklore and culture. Notes. Index.

Flanagan, John T., and Arthur Palmer Hudson, eds., *The
American Folklore Reader: Folklore in American Literature*; A.
S. Barnes & Co., New York, 1958. A collection of

works by American writers on folklore themes,
ranging from the American Indian to devil tales,
witchcraft, literary ballads, heroes, Yankees, Negro
tales, and folk songs and ballads. Bibliographical
notes. Bibliography. Index of authors and titles.

Lamar, Howard R., ed., *The Reader's Encyclopedia of the American West*; Thomas Y. Crowell Co., New York, 1977.
An excellent, one-volume encyclopedia, filled with
fascinating information, much regarding American
legend.

Editors of *Life, The Life Treasury of American Folklore*; Time,
Inc., New York, 1961. A heavily illustrated, popular
guide to the subject. Index.

Reader's Digest, *American Folklore and Legend*; The Reader's
Digest Association, Inc., Pleasantville, N. Y., 1978. A
popular, illustrated collection from a variety of
sources. Index.

Voodoo

Deren, Maya, *Divine Horsemen: Voodoo Gods of Haiti*; Chelsea
House Publishers, New York, 1970. Often interesting, though one may disagree with many of its theories.

Pelton, Robert W., *Voodoo Secrets from A to Z*; A. S. Barnes and
Co., South Brunswick, N. J., 1973. A short A-to-Z
listing of Voodoo terms. Helpful for quick reference.

Rigaud, Milo, *Secrets of Voodoo*; translated by Robert B.
Cross; Arco, New York, 1969. A sympathetic study
of the subject. Book lacks an index, making it difficult for reference.

Oceanic Mythology and Legend

Alpers, Anthony, *Legends of the South Seas: The World of the
Polynesians Seen through Their Myths and Legends, Poetry
and Art*; Thomas Y. Crowell Co., New York, 1970.
Excellent collection of myths, relating to creation,
heroes, etc. References. Glossary. Index.

Dixon, R. B., *Oceanic*; Vol. 9, *The Mythology of All Races*; Marshall Jones Publishing Corp., Boston, 1916. Reissued
by Cooper Square Publishing, Inc., New York, 1964.
A study, rather stiff, of a very rich subject. Bibliography.

Grey, George, *Polynesian Mythology*; edited by W. W. Bird;
Taplinger Publishing Co., New York, n. d. A slightly
reedited version of Grey's 1855 book. Index.

Massola, Aldo, *Bunjil's Cave: Myths, Legends and Superstitions of
the Aborigines of Southeast Australia*. Lansdowne Press,
Melbourne, 1968. Myths, legends, and folk beliefs.
Introduction. Glossary.

Parker, K. Langloah, collector, *Australian Legendary Tales*;
Bodley Head Ltd., London, 1978. A volume that
combines two collections made by Parker, one in
1896 and the other in 1898, published by David Nutt
in London.

Poignant, Roslyn, *Myths and Legends of the South Seas*; Hamlyn, London, 1970. An excellent little book covering
Melanesia, Micronesia, Polynesia. Index.

————, *Oceanic Mythology*; Paul Hamlyn, London, 1967. A fully illustrated volume covering Polynesia, Micronesia, Melanesia, and Australia. Reading list. Index.

Reed, A. W., *Myths and Legends of Australia*; Taplinger Publishing Co., New York, 1965. A selection of myths and legends, creation myths, myths of the sun, moon, stars, animals, etc. Introduction. Glossary.

African Mythologies and Folklores

Carey, Margaret, *Myths and Legends of Africa*; Paul Hamlyn, London, 1970. An excellent retelling of some African folktales. Good introduction.

Courlander, Harold, *Tales of Yoruba Gods and Heroes*; Fawcett Publications, Inc., New York, 1974. Intelligent collection of Yoruba folklore and customs.

Dorson, Richard, ed., *African Folklore*; Doubleday, Garden City, N. Y., 1972. Scholarly treatment of folklore concepts applied to oral traditions of Africa. Introduction.

Herskovits, Melville J. and Frances, *Dahomean Narrative: A Cross-Cultural Analysis*; Northwestern University Press, Evanston, 1958. A collection of folktales with a very long introduction of over 100 pages.

Feya, Abayomi, *Fourteen Hundred Cowries and Other African Tales*; Washington Square Press, New York, 1971. Detailed retellings of the Yoruba people's West African tales.

Parrinder, Geoffrey, *African Mythology*; Paul Hamlyn Group, Ltd., London, 1967. Valuable book for those not familiar with the vast scope of African mythology. Bibliography. Index.

Key to Variant Spellings

A

A: Aa
Ab: Av
Abdal: Badal
Abe no Yasunari: Abe no Seimei
Absu: Apsu
Adon: Aten
Adramelech: Adrammelech
Adramelek: Adrammelech
Aeshm: Aeshma
Aetna: Etna
Afanasyeff: Afanasiev
Afanasyeu: Afanasiev
Afrit: Ifrits
Afriteh: Ifrits
Agoue: Agwe
Agoueh R Oyo: Agwe
Aguet: Agwe
Ah-Puchah: Ah Puch
Ahal Puh: Ah Puch
Aharman: Ahriman
Ahpuch: Ah Puch
Ahshur: Ashur
Ahura Mazdah: Ahura Mazda
Aithne: Ethne
Akarana: Zurvan
Al Arg: Al Aaraaf
Al Jassaca: Al Jassasa
Al-Khidr: Al-Khadir
Alaeddin: Aladdin
Alfrit: Ifrits
Allen-a-Dale: Allan-a-Dale
Allin-a-Dale: Allan-a-Dale
Ama-no-uki-hasi: Ama-no-hashidate
Ama-no-yase-kawa: Ama-no-Kawa
Aman: Amun
Amaryu: Amario
Ame-no-iha-fune: Ama-no-hashidate
Ame-no-yasu-no-kawa: Ama-no-kawa
Amen: Amun
Ameshospends: Amesha Spentas
Amezzyarak: Samiasa
Amleth: Hamlet
Ammon: Amun
Amon: Amun
Amphiorax: Amphiaraus
Amshaspands: Amesha Spentas
An: Anu
Ana: Anu
Anaitis: Anahita
Anat: Anath
Anata: Anath

And Kamba
Angra Mainyu: Ahriman
Angus: Aengus
Anos: Anu
Anra Mainyu: Ahriman
Antarah: Antar
Anunit: Aa
Anunna: Anunnaki
Anunnake: Anunnaki
Apason: Apsu
Apet: Taurt
Apsu-Rishtu: Apsu
Arallu: Aralu
Aredvi sura Anahita: Anahita
Aricoute: Aroteh and Tovapod
Arinniti: Arinna
Ashir: Ashur
Ashmun: Esmun
Ashoka: Asoka
Ashwin: Ashwins
Asi Dahak: Azhi Dahaka
Asir: Ashur
Asklepios: Asclepius
Asshur: Ashur
Assors: Anshar
Asur: Ashur
Atarate: Atargatis
Atargat: Atargatis
Ataro: Atar
Athene: Athena
Atherate: Atagatis
Athor: Hathor
Athyr: Hathor
Aton: Aten
Attes: Attis
Atys: Attis
Audhumbla: Audhumla
Audumla: Audhumla
Auga: Auge
Augea: Auge
Auhar Mazd: Ahura Mazda
Avfruvva: Akkruva
Aya: Aa
Az-i Dahak: Azhi Dahaka
Azza: Samiasa

B

Ba'al: Baal
Ba-neb-Tatau: Ba-neb-djet
Ba-neb-Tet: Ba-neb-djet
Babako: Baka
Bacis: Bucephalus
Badjang: Bajang
Bahram Gor: Bahram Gur

Bahramgor: Bahram Gur
Balder: Baldur
Baldr: Baldur
Ball: Baal
Balldr: Baldur
Baltein: Beltaine
Bastet: Bast
Bealtuinn: Beltaine
Beltan: Beltaine
Beltane: Beltaine
Ben Enlil: Enlil
Benedbdetet: Ba-neb-djet
Bensaiten: Benten
Benten Sama: Benten
Berezisauanh: Bahram fire
Bergelmer: Bergelmir
Bif-raust: Bifrost
Bilrost: Bifrost
Bilwis: Pilwiz
Bkha: Bucephalus
Blathine: Blathnat
Bostan: Bustan
Bouto: Buto
Brid: Brigit
Bride: Brigit
Bridget: Brigit
Brigid: Brigit
Brigindo: Brigit
Brokk: Brok
Brunhild: Brynhild
Brunhilda: Brynhild
Brunnhilde: Brynhild
Bugga: Walpurga
Burkhan-Bakshi: Burkhan
Byelbog: Byelobog and Chernobog

C

Caaba: Kaaba
Camael: Chamuel
Camalotz: Camazotz
Camial: Chamuel
Camniel: Chamuel
Cancel: Chamuel
Cassibellawn: Caswallawn
Cassiope: Cassiopea
Cassiopeia: Cassiopea
Cassipea: Cassiopea
Cassivelaonus: Caswallawn
Cauke: Damkina
Cephalon: Caphaurus
Cernobog: Byelobog and Chernobog
Cerridwen: Ceridwen
Chalchiucihuatl: Chalchihuitlicue

Chalchiuhtlicue: Chalchihuitlicue
Chamael: Chamuel
Chang Liang: Chung-li Ch'uan
Chanukkah: Hanukkah
Chepera: Khepera
Chi-len: K'ilin
Chicchechum: Chicachum
Chimizigagua: Chiminigagua
Chlchiuhtliycue: Chalchihuitlicue
Chons: Khonsu
Chunsu: Khonsu
Ciauapipiltin: Ciuateteo
Cihuacoatl: Coatlicue
Citha: Zita
Ciuacoatl: Coatlicue
Civocoatl: Coatlicue
Coatlantona: Coatlicue
Cocagne: Cockaigne
Cockayne: Cockaigne
Con: Cun
Conteotl: Coatlicue
Cuculcan: Kukulcan
Curupira: Korupira

D

Dadghda: Dagda
Dadhica: Dadhyanch
Dadhicha: Dadhyanch
Dahhak: Azhi Dahaka
Dahkma: Dakhma
Dai Bensaiten: Benten
Damballa: Danbhalah Houe-Do
Damballah: Danbhalah Houe-Do
Dan-Gbe: Danbhalah Houe-Do
Dana: Anu
Danu: Anu
Dawkina: Damkina
Dazbog: Dazhbog
Dazdbog: Dazhbog
Deidra: Deirdre
Deidre: Deirdre
Deidrie: Deirdre
Dhouti: Thoth
Dierdrie: Deirdre
Dimas: Dismas
Domocik: Domovoi
Domoule: Domovoi
Domovou: Domovoi
Domovov: Domovoi
Douma: Dumah
Druj Nasa: Nasu
Dysmas: Dismas

E

Eabani: Enkidu
Edo Go Nin Otoko: Yedo Go Nin
  Otoko
Efreet: Ifrits
Eilil: Enlil
Eithne: Ethne

Ekako: Ekkekko
Ekeko: Ekkekko
El Khizr: Al-Khadir
Endimdu: Enkidu
Endo Musha Morita: Endo Morito
Engidu: Enkidu
Enkita: Enkidu
Ennuki: Anunnaki
Eq'eq'o: Ekkekko
Equabalam: Ek Balam
Ernuted: Renpet
Eshmoun: Esmun
Eshmun: Esmun
Esmoun: Esmun
Esmounos: Esmun
Esus: Essus
Etanna: Etana
Ethlinn: Ethne
Ethna: Ethne
Ethnea: Ethne
Ethnee: Ethne
Eton: Aten

F

Fenris: Fenrir
Feridoun: Faridun
Feridun: Faridun
Ferumbras: Fierabras
Freydun: Faridun
Fri: Frigga
Frigg: Frigga
Frija: Frigga
Fyorgyn: Jord

G

Gaiumart: Gayomart
Ganesa: Ganesha
Ganor: Guinever
Ganora: Guinever
Garmr: Garm
Gaya-Maretan: Gayomart
Gayo-Maratan: Gayomart
Gayomard: Gayomart
Gayumarth: Gayomart
Ge: Gaea
Geirroth: Geirrod and Agnar
Generua: Guinever
Genievre: Guinever
Gerd: Gerda
Gerdr: Gerda
Gilgamos: Gilgamesh
Ginevra: Guinever
Gisdhubar: Gilgamesh
Gistubar: Gilgamesh
Glooscap: Gluskap and Malsum
Glooska: Gluskap and Malsum
Gluskabe: Gluskap and Malsum
Gryphon: Griffin
Guaca: Huaca
Guaguyona: Guagugiana

Guanhumar: Guinever
Guanhumare: Guinever
Guayarakunny: Guayavacuni
Guecufu: Guecubu
Guenever: Guinever
Guinevere: Guinever
Guinevra: Winefred
Gunesh: Ganeshaea
Gunputty: Ganesha
Gwenfrewi: Winefred
Gwidion: Gwydion
Gwynwas: Gwynn

H

Hamiel: Anael
Hammon: Amun
Hanata: Anath
Hanea: Nane
Haniel: Anael
Hanumat: Hanuman
Hap: Hapi
Hapy: Hapi
Havfru: Akkruva
Hea: Ea
Heithron: Heidrun
Hela: Hel
Hell: Hel
Helory: Yves
Herimon: Eremon
Hertha: Nerthus
Hesus: Essus
Hijra: Hegira
Hlidskjalf: Hlithskjolf
Hloldyn: Jord
Hoa: Ea
Hod: Hodur
Hoder: Hodur
Horaizan: Harai
Hounfor: Oum'phor
Huallepen: Guallipen
Huecuvu: Guecubu
Huginn: Hugin and Munin
Hunfor: Oum'phor
Huracan: Hurakan
Huracocha: Viracocha
Huwawa: Humbaba

I

Iebak: Sebek
Ifriteh: Ifrits
Igdrasil: Yggdrasill
Igerna: Igraine
Igerne: Igraine
Ikhnaton: Akhenaton
Ilia Murometz: Ilya Muromets
Illillos: Enlil
Ilntar: Luonnotar
Ilya of Murom: Ilya Muromets
Ilya-Muromyets: Ilya Muromets
Indiges: Indigetes

Iocaste: Jocasta
Iofiel: Zophiel
Iophiel: Zophiel
Iord: Jord
Iphimedeia: Iphimedia
Irkalla: Aralu
Irlek: Erlik
Istar: Ishtar
Ives: Yves
Ivo: Yves
Izrail: Azrael
Izuber: Gilgamesh

J

Jagan-nath: Juggernaut
Jagan-natha: Juggernaut
Jagganth: Juggernaut
Jamshid: Jemshid
Jiu ni Ten: Jiu No O
Jofiel: Zophiel
Jophiel: Zophiel
Jordh: Jord
Jotunheimr: Jotunheim
Jotunnheim: Jotunheim

K

Ka'ba: Kaaba
Kaabeh: Kaaba
Kaiomarts: Gayomart
Kaiumers: Gayomart
Kaminarisan: Raiden
Kamo Hogon: Abe no Seimei
Kamo Yasunari: Abe no Seimei
Kandarpa: Kama
Katschel: Kossuth
Kayumard: Gayomart
Kayumurs: Gayomart
Keb: Geb
Kelpy: Kelpie
Kemuel: Chamuel
Keridwen: Ceridwen
Khamael: Chamuel
Kheprer: Khepera
Khepri: Khepera
Khnum: Khnemu
Khons: Khonsu
Kiang Keh: Erh-shih-ssu Hsiao
Kiang She: Erh-shih-ssu Hsiao
Kikuya: Gikuya
Koschey: Kossuth
Krimhild: Kriemhild
Kukulkan: Kukulcan
Kumbaba: Humbaba
Kurupira: Korupira
Kvaser: Kvasir
Kwanyin: Kwannon

L

Lapithae: Lapiths
Leba: Legba
Legua: Legba
Leir: Lear
Lesiy: Leshy
Lesiye: Leshy
Lesovik: Leshy
Liba: Legba
Lir: Lear
Lud: Ludd
Lukman: Lokman
Luqman: Lokman

M

Maa: Maat
Madb: Maev
Maet: Maat
Maeve: Maev
Magaye: Mahagir
Maht: Maat
Malik: Makonaima
Manannan: Mananaan
Manibazho: Manabozho
Manibozoho: Manabozho
Manko Kapak and Coya Mama:
    Manco Capac
Mariatta: Marjatta
Mathnawi: Masnavi
Mathnwi-i-Ma'nawe: Masnavi
Maut: Maat
Meadhbh: Maev
Merddin: Merlin
Mesnevi: Masnavi
Michabo: Manabozho
Mictlanteculi: Mictlantecuhtli
Mocco: Moccus
Monctezuma: Montezuma II
Mongako Shonin: Endo Morito
Mongaku: Endo Morito
Montecuzomatizin: Montezuma II
Monteczoma: Montezuma II
Motechuzoma: Montezuma II
Mowee: Maui
Muninn: Hugin and Munin
Muru: Mura
Mwetse: Maori
Myrddin: Merlin

N

Nanabozho: Manabozho
Nanabush: Manabozho
Nanu: Anu
Narvi: Nari
Nas: Nasu
Nasrust: Nasu
Nasus: Nasu
Natigai: Natigay
Nechbet: Nekhebet

Neguruvilu: Guirivilo
Neit: Neith
Nertha: Nerthus
Net: Neith
Nihonshoki: Nihongi
Nimurash: Ninurta
Nimurta: Ninurta
Ningirsu: Ninurta
Niohoggr: Nidhogg
Niord: Njord
Nit: Neith
Nithbogg: Nidhogg
Njordhr: Njord
Noh: No
Nommo: Nummo
Nugi: Nuga
Nugu: Nuga
Nyx: Nox

O

Odherir: Odhrerir
Odhroerir: Odhrerir
Odrorir: Odhrerir
Oengus: Aengus
Ogham: Ogma
Oisin: Ossian
Olofat: Olifat
Ometecutli: Ometecuhtli
Onnos: Umai-hulhlya-wit
Onoel: Anael
Opet: Taurt
Othin: Odin

P

Parnapishtim: Utnapishtim
Parsifal: Perceval
Parzival: Perceval
Pasht: Bast
Paynalton: Paynal
Pekko: Peko
Percival: Perceval
Percivale: Perceval
Perun: Pyerun
Peruw: Pyerun
Phan-ku: P'an-ku
Phra: Ra
Phyderi: Pryderi
Polevoi: Polevik
Polevoy: Polevik
Poteh: Purah
Puta: Purah

Q

Qeb: Geb

R

Raijin: Raiden
Raksasas: Rakshasas
Rannut: Renpet
Re: Ra
Remute: Renpet
Renenutet: Renpet
Rephaim: Anakims
Rert: Taurt
Rertu: Taurt
Reshef: Reshpu
Reshep: Reshpu
Resheph: Reshpu
Reshiph-Mical: Reshpu
Rg-Veda: Rig-Veda
Rostastahm: Rustum
Rustem: Rustum

S

Sacharis: Seker
Saena: Simurugh
Sakoontala: Shakuntala
Sakuntala: Shakuntala
Salmail: Sammael
Samil: Sammael
Sandofon: Sandalphon
Sandolphon: Sandalphon
Sarazic: Syarogich
Satanil: Sammael
Sayatin: Shaitans
Seb: Geb
Sebeq: Sebek
Sechmet: Sakhmet
Seeva: Shiva
Seger: Seker
Segward: Sebald
Seir: Sammael
Sekhait: Sakhmet
Sekhauit: Sakhmet
Sekhem: Sakhmet
Sekhmet: Sakhmet
Selket: Serqet
Selqet: Serqet
Selquet: Serqet
Semiaza: Samiasa
Semuru: Simurugh
Senmury: Simurugh
Seth: Set
Sethi: Set
Seward: Sebald
Shamazya: Samiasa
Shar: Anshar
Shemhazai: Samiasa
Sigyn: Siguna
Simorg: Simurugh
Sirona: Dirona
Sisouthros: Ziusudra
Sit: Set
Sitha: Zita
Siva: Shiva
Siward: Sebald
Skade: Skadi

Skhautet: Sakhmet
Sobek: Sebek
Sokar: Seker
Sokaris: Seker
Solare: Seker
Suchos: Sebek
Suhrab: Sohrab
Sulbundu: Solbon
Supai: Cupay
Supay: Cupay
Sut: Set
Sutekh: Set
Suttee: Sati
Swithin: Swithen
Swithun: Swithen
Swithunus: Swithen

T

Taapac: Tonapa
Tahmuraf: Tahumers
Tahuras: Tahumers
Tahuti: Thoth
Takhma-Urupa: Tahumers
Takhmorup: Tahumers
Takhmoruw: Tahumers
Tamazcalteci: Toci
Tangara: Tengri
Tatmurath: Tahumers
Taueret: Taurt
Techa: Thoth
Tefenet: Tefnut
Tellervo: Tuulikki
Tengeri: Tengri
Thout: Thoth
Thunaer: Thor
Thunar: Thor
Thunupa: Tonapa
Thur: Thor
Timondonar: Aroteh and Tovapod
Tistar: Tishtya
Tistrya: Tishtrya
Tjuringa: Churinga
Tlaculteutl: Tlazolteotl
Tozi: Toci
Troiaw: Trojanu
Tuan Mac Cairill: Tuan Mac Carell
Tuat: Duat
Tura: Tengri
Tvastr: Twashtri
Tzadkie: Zadkiel

U

Ubshukenna: Ubshukinna
Udjat: Utchat
Ullr: Ull
Ullur: Ull
Unis: Umai-hulhlya-wit
Unus: Umai-hulhlya-wit
Upshukkinaku: Ubshukinna
Urdhr: Urd

Uzza: Samiasa

V

Vagonioa: Guagugiana
Vainanoinen: Vainamoinen
Valkyrjr: Valkyries
Van: Vanir
Vanas: Vanir
Vanis: Vanir
Varahi: Vajravarahi
Veles: Volos
Veraplaca: Viriplaca
Vesak: Wesak
Vibhisana: Vibhishana
Virtumnus: Vertumnus
Vishnoo: Vishnu
Visnu: Vishnu
Voden: Woden
Voden: Wotan
Volga: Volkh
Volkun: Vlkodlak
Vortumnus: Vertumnus
Votan: Woden
Votan: Wotan
Vrkolak: Vlkodlak
Vukodlak: Vlkodlak
Vyelyes: Volos

W

Wainamoinen: Vainamoinen
Walburga: Walpurga
Walpurgis: Walpurga
Wedo: Danbhalah Houe-Do
Wenefrida: Winefred
Winefride: Winefred
Wipunen: Antero Vipunen
Woden: Wotan
Wootan: Woden
Woutan: Wotan

X

Xiutecutli: Xiutecuhtli

Y

Yam: Yima
Yasodiel: Yesod
Yasu: Ama-no-Kawa
Ybus: Yves
Ygerne: Igraine
Yorkami: Jorkemo
Yoskeha and Tawiscara: Iouskeha
    and Tawisc
Youkahainen: Joukahainen
Yrukemi: Jorkemo
Yxtilton: Ixtilton

Z

Cultural and Ethnic Index

A

Aesopic
Aesopic fables, 0084
Ant and the Grasshopper, The, 0264
Ass in the Lion's Skin, The, 0364
Ass's Brains, 0365
Avaricious and Envious, The, 0419
Belly and Its Members, The, 0535
Cat Maiden, The, 0745
Cock and the Pearl, The, 0841
Dog and His Shadow, The, 0994
Eagle and the Arrow, The, 1043
Fox and the Crow, The, 1193
Fox and the Grapes, The, 1194
Fox and the Mosquitoes, The, 1195
Frog and the Ox, The, 1212
Goose that Laid the Golden Eggs, The, 1290
Hawk and the Nightingale, The, 1388
Jay and the Peacock, The, 1600
Juno and the Peacock, 1658
Lion and the Mouse, The, 1869
Lion in Love, The, 1870
Lion's Share, The, 1871
Mice in Council, or Belling the Cat, The, 2048
Milkmaid and Her Pail, The, 2058
Mountain in Labor, The, 2098
Old Man and Death, The, 2255
Piper, The, 2398
Serpent and the File, The, 2647
Sick Lion, The, 2680
Tortoise and the Birds, The, 2901
Town Mouse and the Country Mouse, The, 2904
Tree and the Reed, The, 2905
Two Pots, The, 2942
Wolf and the Crane, The, 3125
Wolf and the Lamb, The, 3126
Wolf in Sheep's Clothing, The, 3128
Woodman and the Serpent, The, 3132

African
Abuk and Garang, 0024
Adu Ogyinae, 0062
Aiwel, 0126
Ala, 0137
Anansi, 0232
Atai, 0377
Bomazi, 0606
Bumba, 0659
Cagn, 0686
Da, 0884
Deng, 0945
Efé, 1053
Eka Abassi, 1059
Eshu, 1115
Fa, 1144
Faran, 1151
Gikuyu, Masai, and Kamba, 1258
Golden Stool, The, 1280
Gu, 1315
Haitsi-aibed, 1347
Iku, 1528
Ilé-Ifé (house wide), 1530
Imana, 1534
Imilozi, 1536
Iruwa, 1559
Jok, 1631
Juok, 1659
Kalumba, 1681
Kholumolumo, 1716
Khonvum, 1719
Kibuka, 1720
Kintu and Nambi, 1727
Kitamba, 1731
Lebe, 1833
Le-eyo, 1836
Legba, 1837
Leve, 1855
Leza, 1856
Libanza, 1857
Long Juju, 1887
Maori, 1979
Marwe, 1996
Mason wasp, 2001
Mawu Lisa, 2015
Molimons, 2080
Moyna, 2099
Mujaji II, 2105
Mukasa, 2106
Mulungu, 2111
Murile, 2117
Mwambu and Sela, 2124
Nana, 2143
Ngunza, 2188
Njinyi, 2214
Nummo, 2226
Nyame, 2231
Nzambi, 2233
Obatala, 2236
Obumo, 2238
Ogun Onire, 2249
Olokun, 2259
Olorun, 2260
Onyankopon, 2268
Oranyan, 2272
Orisha, 2277
Orunmila, 2281
Osa, 2282
Osawa, 2283
Oshossi, 2284
Oshun, 2285
Oshunmare, 2286
Poro, 2417
Ruhanga, 2561
Shamba, 2659
Shango, 2660
Tano, 2797
Taui'goad, 2813
Tchue, 2816
Tembo, 2825
Twe, 2940
Unkulunkulu, 2970
Uwolowu, 2992
Velo Men, 3018
Wele, 3098
Were, 3102
Zin, 3217
Zoa, 3220

American
Allen, Ethan, 0178
Allison, Clay, 0179
Angel of Hadley, 0250
Annie Christmas, 0259
Appomattox Apple Tree, 0297
Army of the Dead, 0335
Babe, the Blue Ox, 0439
Baca, Elfego, 0442
Banjo, 0476
Barada, Antoine, 0483
Barbara Frietchie, 0485
Barnum, Phineas Taylor, 0491
Bass, Sam, 0498
Bean, Judge Roy, 0511
Belle Starr, 0533
Big Harpe, 0573
Big Owl, 0574
Billy Potts, 0578
Billy the Kid, 0579
Black Bart, 0587
Blackbeard, 0588
Boone, Daniel, 0612
Borden, Lizzie, 0615
Boyde, Rebel Belle, 0621
Br'er Fox, 0629
Br'er Rabbit, 0630

Ngallenyook, 2185
Ngarangs, 2186
Ngunung-ngunnut, 2187
Numbakulla, 2225
Orokeet, 2279
Pallian, 2315
Potkoorok, 2422
Potoyan, 2424
Pundjel, 2446
Rainbow Snake, 2476
Tambora, 2787
Thinan-malkia, 2851
Tjinimin the Bat, 2886
Too-Roo-Dun, 2899
Tulugal, 2927
Turong, 2933
Tutugals, 2937
Uli-tarra, 2958
Walangada, 3082
Walwalag Sisters, 3084
Wambeen, 3085
Wiwonderrer, 3123
Wollonqua, 3129
Wondjina, 3130
Yabons, 3152
Yaho, 3154

Aztec
Apizteotl, 0286
Atlacamanc, 0390
Atlatonan, 0394
Atlaua, 0395
Chachalmeca, 0765
Chalchihuitlicue, 0768
Chalmecaciuatl, 0769
Chiconquiahuitl, 0796
Ciuateteo, 0828
Coatlicue, 0838
Coyolxauhqui, 0858
Ehecatl, 1056
Huemac, 1483
Hueytonantzin, 1484
Huitzilopochtli, 1487
Ixtlilton, 1580
Izquitecatl, 1582
Iztaccihuatl, 1583
Mayauel, 2019
Metztli, 2046
Mictlantecuhtli, 2050
Mixcoatl, 2074
Montezuma II, 2087
Omacatl, 2263
Ometecuhtli, 2264
Opochtli, 2269
Paynal, 2350
Tlaloc, 2887
Tlazolteotl, 2888
Toci, 2890
Tonacatecutli, 2894
Tonatiuh, 2896
Tzitsimine, 2946
Ueuecoyotl, 2949
Uixtocihuatl, 2952
Vitzilopuchtli, 3059
Xilonen, 3145

Xipe Totec, 3146
Xiuhtecuhtli, 3147
Xochiquetzal, 3148
Xolotl Huetzi, 3150
Yacatecutli, 3153

B

Babylonian
Adapa, 0047
Allallu, 0176
Anunnake, 0279
Apsu, 0299
Aralu, 0305
Av, 0415
Bau, 0505
Bel, 0525
Benini, 0540
Enkidu, 1089
Etana, 1122
Gula, 1327
Humbaba, 1488
Marduk, 1982
Nabu, 2131
Ninib, 2205
Tammuz, 2790
Ubshukinna, 2947
Zag-Muk, 3198
Zu, 0097

Babylonian-Assyrian
Aa, 0001
Aruru, 0341
Belit, 0531
Damkina, 0908
Ereshkigal, 1100
Irra, 1558
Lugulbanda, 1906
Nergal, 2177
Rimmon, 2523
Sarpanitum, 2616
Shamash, 2658

Balinese
Rangda, 2487

Borneo
Kinharingan, 1726

British (including Arthurian)
Accolon of Gaul, 0031
Acheflour, 0034
Adam Bell, 0046
Addanc of the Lake, 0049
Agaran, 0091
Agretes, 0105
Albania, 0143
Albion, 0146
Aldinger, Sir, 0157
Aleine, 0160
Alfasem, 0166
Alisaunder, 0171
Allan-a-Dale, 0177
Amangons, 0198
Amant, Sir, 0202
Amfortas, 0214

Angarad of the Golden Hand, 0247
Aroundight, 0338
Arthur, 0340
Astolat, 0369
Avalon, 0417
Babes in the Wood, 0438
Bacon, Roger, 0447
Bailiff's Daughter of Islington, 0456
Balan and Balin, 0462
Bedivere, Sir, 0518
Belin, 0527
Beowulf, 0545
Bevis of Hampton, 0557
Billy Blin, 0577
Bladud, 0589
Blunderbore, 0596
Boadicea, 0598
Bogy, 0605
Brut, 0647
Camelot, 0704
Captain Kidd, 0718
Caractacus, 0720
Carausius, 0721
Cavall, 0751
Clem of the Clouth, 0831
Clootie, 0832
Constans, 0848
Conwenna, 0850
Cophetua, 0851
Cradlemont, 0861
Cradock, 0862
Curtana, 0876
Cymbeline, 0882
Dagonet, 0895
Dun Cow, 1023
Edmund, St, 1051
Edyrn, 1052
Elaine, 1064
Elfthryth, 1070
Elidure, 1072
Estmere, 1119
Estrildis, 1120
Excalibur, 1139
Galahad, 1226
Gareth, 1237
Gil Morrice, 1261
Glastonbury, 1266
Godiva, Lady, 1271
Gog and Magog, 1272
Gorboduc, 1291
Gotham, Wise Men of, 1295
Guinever, 1325
Guy of Warwick, 1330
Gwain, 1331
Igraine, 1524
Jack and the Beanstalk, 1584
John Barleycorn, 1624
Kulhwch and Olwen, 1775
Lady of Shalott, The, 1795
Lady of the Lake, 1796
Lancelot of the Lake, 1809
Lear, King, 1832

Buddhism

Buddhist

Burmese

C

Canaanite

Asherah, 0349
Dagon, 0894
Nikkal, 2202
Celtic
Aengus, 0077
Albiorix, 0147
Amaethon, 0196
Anu, 0276
Arianrod, 0323
Avalon, 0418
Aynia, 0427
Balor, 0469
Banba, 0474
Banshee, 0478
Belinus, 0528
Belisama, 0529
Beltaine, 0537
Bith and Birren, 0585
Blathnat, 0594
Boann, 0599
Borvo, 0620
Bran, 0625
Branwen, 0626
Bress, 0631
Brian, 0633
Brigit, 0635
Brownie, 0643
Bussumarus, 0664
Camulos, 0709
Caswallawn, 0740
Cenn Cruaich, 0758
Ceridwen, 0760
Cernunnos, 0761
Cessair, 0762
Cluricane, 0835
Credne, 0864
Cuchulain, 0870
Cyhiraeth, 0881
Dagda, 0893
Danu, 0918
Deirdre, 0936
Diancecht, 0970
Dirona, 0981
Domnu, 0997
Druids, 1015
Dwyvan and Dwyvach, 1033
Dylan, 1036
Eremon, 1099
Essus, 1117
Ethne, 1124
Far Darria, 1153
Fear-Gorta, 1159
Finn, 1173
Flidais, 1178
Fomora, 1185
Govannon, 1296
Grannos, 1302
Gwydion, 1333
Gwynn, 1334
Kelpie, 1699
Leanhaun Shee, 1831
Leprechaun, 1848
Lir, 1872
Lleu Law Gyffes, 1877

Luchtaine, 1898
Ludd, 1904
Mabon, 1922
Maev, 1930
Mananaan, 1966
Moccus, 2076
Morrigu, The, 2094
Mullo, 2110
Nudd, 2222
Ogma, 2247
Ossian, 2288
Pryderi, 2441
Salmon of Knowledge, 2585
Sucellos, 2746
Sul, 2750
Taranis, 2804
Tuan Mac Carell, 2924
Tuatha de Danann, 2925
Uther Ben, 2988
Chinese
Chang Chiu, 0773
Chang Hsien, 0774
Chang Kuo-lao, 0775
Cheng San-kung, 0786
Ch'en Nan, 0787
Ch'ih Ching-tzu, 0797
Chih Nu, 0798
Ch'i Ku-tzu, 0799
Ching Tu, 0803
Ch'in-kuang wang, 0804
Chiu-t'ien Lei Kung, 0807
Chuang Tzu, 0813
Chu Jung, 0814
Chu-ko Liang, 0815
Chu-lin Chi'i-Hsien, 0816
Chung-li Ch'üan, 0818
Chun T'i, 0819
Confucius, 0846
Erh-shih-ssu Hsiao, 1101
Fan-Wang, 1150
Feng-huang, 1164
Feng Po, 1165
Hai K'ang, 1346
Han Hsiang Tzu, 1353
Heng-Ê, 1412
Ho Ho Erh-Hsien, 1455
Ho Hsien-Ku, 1456
Hsiao Kung, 1472
Hsieh p'ing-an, 1473
Hsien, 1474
Hsi-Shen, 1475
Hsi Wang Mu, 1476
Hun-tun, 1492
Juan Chi, 1647
K'ilin, 1723
Kuang Ch'eng-Tzu, 1766
Kuan Ti, 1767
K'uei Hsing, 1771
Kuo Tzu-i, 1782
Lan Ts'ai-ho, 1811
Lao Lang, 1816
Lao Tzu, 1818
Lei Kung, 1840
Ling-pai, 1867

Li T'ien-kuai, 1873
Liu Ling, 1875
Lung Wang, 1910
Lu Pan, 1912
Lu Tung-pin, 1915
Ma Tsu P'o, 2008
Mu Kung, 2107
Pa-Hsien, 2302
P'ang Chu, P'ang Ch'ê, and
   P'ang Chiao, 2326
P'an-ku, 2328
Pien ch'eng, 2390
Pien Ch'iao, 2391
P'ing-Teng, 2397
San Hsien Shan, 2608
San-yu, 2613
Shang-Ti, 2661
Shan T'ao, 2662
Shen, 2665
Shen Nung, 2666
Shou Hsing, 2672
Shui Ching-tzu, 2676
Sung-ti wang, 2754
T'ai-shan kun wang, 2779
T'ao t'ieh, 2800
T'ien Hou, 2863
Ti Yü, 2885
Tou Mu, 2903
Ts'ai Shen, 2919
Tsao Kuo-chiu, 2920
Tsao Shen, 2921
Ts'ien K'eng, 2922
Wang Jung, 3088
Wang Mu, 3089
Wen Chang Ti-chun, 3100
Wu-fu, 3136
Wu-kuan wang, 3137
Wu Lao, 3138
Wu ta chia, 3141
Wu-yuan kuei, 3142
Yao, 3162
Yeh Ching, 3172
Yen Kung, 3173
Yen-Mo wang, 3174
Yin and Yang, 3179
Yü Huang, 3186
Yü Shih, 3190
Christian (also New Testament)
Abgar, 0013
Abomination of Desolation,
   0017
Adam and Eve, 0044
Adrian, St., 0061
Advent, 0063
Afra, St., 0088
Agatha, St., 0093
Agnes of Montepulciano, St.,
   0098
Agnes, St., 0099
Alban, St., 0144
Albertus Magnus, St., 0145
All Saints' Day, 0180
All Souls' Day, 0181
Alphege, St., 0187

Ambrose, St., 0209
Andrew, St., 0240
Anna, 0257
Anthony of Padua, St., 0270
Anthony the Abbot, St., 0271
Apollonia, St., 0291
Apollyon, 0292
Apostle, 0294
Ash Wednesday, 0354
Aspen, 0361
Athanasius, St., 0387
Augustine of Canterbury, St.,
    0405
Augustine, St., 0406
Baphomet, 0479
Baptism, 0481
Barbara, St., 0486
Barlaam and Josaphat, 0489
Barnabas, St., 0490
Bartholomew, St., 0495
Basil the Great, St., 0497
Bavon, St., 0508
Bede the Venerable, St., 0517
Befana, 0521
Benedict, St., 0539
Bernardino of Siena, St., 0548
Bernard of Clairvaux, St., 0550
Blaise, St., 0591
Bonaventura, St., 0608
Boniface, St., 0609
Boris and Gleb, SS., 0618
Brendan, St., 0628
Bridget of Sweden, St., 0634
Brigit, St., 0636
Bruno, St., 0646
Cain and Abel, 0689
Candlemas Day, 0712
Casilda, St., 0734
Casimir of Poland, St., 0735
Catherine of Alexandria, St.,
    0743
Catherine of Siena, St., 0744
Cecilia, St., 0752
Chad, St., 0766
Cheron, St., 0790
Christina the Astonishing, St.,
    0809
Christmas, 0810
Christopher, St., 0811
Clare, St., 0829
Clement, St., 0830
Clotilda, St., 0833
Columba, St., 0845
Constantine the Great, 0849
Corpus Christi, 0854
Cosmas and Damian, SS., 0856
Crispin and Crispinian, SS., 0865
Cross, 0868
Cuthbert, St., 0878
Cuthman, St., 0879
Cyril and Methodius, SS., 0883
David, St., 0927
Denis of France, St., 0946
Diego d'Alcalá, St., 0972

Dismas, 0982
Dives, 0985
Doctors of the Church, 0991
Domitilla, Nereus, and
    Achilleus, SS., 0996
Donato of Arezzo, St., 0999
Dorothy, St., 1003
Drithelm, St., 1012
Duns Scotus, Joannes, 1024
Dunstan, St., 1025
Durán, Fray Diego, 1027
Easter, 1045
Ebba of Codingham, St., 1046
Edith of Wilton, St., 1050
Elizabeth of Portugal, St., 1076
Elizabeth, St., 1077
Eloy of Noyon, St., 1080
Eustace, St., 1133
Evangelists, The Four, 1136
Exaltation of the Holy Cross,
    1138
Fabiola, St., 1145
Faith, Hope, and Charity, SS.,
    1147
Felicitas and Her Seven Sons,
    St., 1163
Ferdinand III of Castile, St.,
    1167
Fiacre, St., 1169
Florian, St., 1180
Fools, Feast of, 1186
Fourteen Holy Helpers, The,
    1191
Francesca Romana, St., 1197
Francis of Assisi, St., 1198
Francis Xavier, St., 1199
George, St., 1249
Giles, St., 1259
Golden Legend, The, 1279
Gregory the Great, St., 1308
Hagia Sophia, 1345
Helena, St., 1406
Henry, St., 1414
Hilary of Poitiers, St., 1436
Hilda, St., 1437
Hippolytus, St., 1443
Holy Innocents Day, 1458
Hubert, St., 1480
Icon, 1516
Ignatius Loyola, St., 1522
Ignatius of Antioch, St., 1523
Ildefonso, St., 1529
Isidore of Seville, St., 1566
Isidore the Ploughman, St., 1567
James the Greater or Major, St.,
    1589
James the Less or Minor, St.,
    1590
Januarius, St., 1593
Jerome, St., 1605
Jesus Christ, 1606
Joachin, 0257
Joan of Arc, St., 1619
John Chrysostom, St., 1625

John the Baptist, St., 1628
John the Evangelist, St., 1630
Joseph of Arimathea, 1640
Joseph, St., 1641
Judas Iscariot, 1648
Jude Thaddeus and Simon
    Zealot, SS., 1649
Julian Hospitaller, St., 1654
Justa and Rufina, SS., 1662
Justina of Antioch, St., 1663
Kenelm, St., 1701
Kentigern, St., 1703
Kevin, St., 1707
Keyne, St., 1708
Kriss Kringle, 1763
Lammas, 1808
Lawrence, St., 1827
Lazarus, 1829
Leonard, St., 1846
Longinus, St., 1886
Lord of Misrule, 1889
Louis, St., 1896
Lucifer, 1899
Lucy of Syracuse, St., 1902
Luke, St., 1907
Magi, 1932
Mammon, 1963
Margaret, St., 1983
Mark, St., 1989
Martha, St., 1992
Martin of Tours, St., 1993
Mary Magdalene, St., 1997
Mary of Egypt, St., 1998
Mass, 2002
Matthew, St., 2009
Maundy Thursday, 2012
Maurice and the Theban Legion,
    St., 2013
Médard of Noyon, St., 2021
Mercurius, St., 2034
Monica, St., 2086
Nicholas, St., 2192
Nicodemus, 2193
Olaf, St., 2253
Oswald, St., 2289
Pancras, St., 2323
Patrick, St., 2342
Paul, St., 2345
Peter, Martyr, St., 2372
Peter, St., 2374
Philip, St., 2380
Phocas, St., 2385
Pilate, Pontius, 2394
Quiracus, St., 2465
Rais, Gilles de, 2477
Ranieri, St., 2488
Raymond Nonnato, St., 2502
Raymond of Pennaforte, St.,
    2503
Regulus, St., 2508
Rémy, St., 2509
Robert, St., 2530
Roch, St., 2534
Romanus, St., 2540

Louhi, 1895
Luonnotar, 1911
Maiden of Pohjola, 1947
Marjatta, 1987
Metsanneitsyt, 2045
Paiva and Kuu, 2305
Sampo, 2595
Sukusendal, 2749
Tapio, 2801
Tuonetar, 2931
Tuoni, 2932
Tursas, 2934
Tuulikki, 2938
Ukko, 2954
Vainamoinen, 2996

Finno-Ugric
Akkruva, 0132
Haltia, 1349
Hatyani of Debrecen, 1384
Kerki, 1706
Kratti, 1759
Lud, 1903
Maanhaltija, 1918
Madderakka, 1927
Nakk, 2139
Nules-murt, 2224
Pajanvaki, 2307
Peko, 2357
Talonhaltija, 2784
Tontuu, 2897
Vaks-oza, 3002

French
Agramante, 0103
Alcina, 0150
Angelica, 0249
Armida, 0333
Astarotte, 0366
Astolpho, 0370
Atlantes, 0391
Aymon, The Four Sons of, 0426
Bayard, 0509
Bicorn and Chichevache, 0569
Blanchefleur, 0592
Chanson de geste, 0777
Charlemagne, 0779
Drac, 1007
Fierabras, Sir, 1171
Ganelon, 1231
La Fontaine, Jean de, 1799
Morgante, 2091
Ogier the Dane, 2246
Oliver, 2258
Paladins, The Twelve, 2308
Rabican, 2469
Rinaldo, 2524
Rodomont, 2536
Roland, 2538
Ruggiero, 2559
Taillefer, 2776
Valentine and Orson, 3004
William of Orange, 3111

G
German
Hansel and Gretel, 1355
Knecht Ruprecht, 1738
Lohengrin, 1881
Nixie, 2213
Pied Piper of Hamelin, 2389
Tannhäuser, 2796
Till Eulenspiegel, 2869
Venusberg, 3021

Germanic
Bertha, 0552
Egil, 1055
Erda, 1098
Erl-King, 1106
Etzel, 1126
Gudrun, 1322
Hagen, 1344
Kriemhild, 1761
Nerthus, 2179
Nibelungenlied, 2190
Pilwiz, 2395
Rausch, Bruder, 2499
Rubezhal, 2556
Schildburg, 2625
Siegfried, 2682
Tuesco, 2926
Wotan, 3134

Greek
Abaris, 0004
Abderus, 0005
Absyrtus, 0023
Acamas, 0025
Acantha, 0026
Acarnan and Amphoterus, 0028
Acastus, 0029
Acestes, 0032
Achelous, 0035
Acheron, 0036
Achilles, 0037
Acidalia, 0038
Acontius of Cea, 0039
Acrisius, 0040
Actaeus, 0041
Actis, 0042
Adamanthaea, 0045
Admetus, 0056
Adrasteia, 0059
Adrastus, 0060
Aeacus, 0064
Aeaea, 0065
Aëdon, 0066
Aegeus, 0067
Aegialeia, 0068
Aeginetan Sculptures, 0069
Aegis, 0071
Aegisthus, 0072
Aegle, 0073
Aegyptus, 0074
Aeneas, 0075
Aeolus, 0078
Aerope, 0080

Aesacus, 0081
Aethra, 0085
Agamemnon, 0090
Agathodaemon, 0094
Agenor, 0095
Aglaia, 0096
Ajax, 0127
Alastor, 0142
Alcathous, 0148
Alcestis, 0149
Alcinous, 0151
Alcithoe, 0152
Alcmaeon, 0153
Alcmene, 0154
Alcyone, 0155
Alcyoneus, 0156
Alecto, 0158
Alectryon, 0159
Alexander the Great, 0162
Aloadae, 0183
Alope, 0185
Alphesiboea, 0188
Altis, 0191
Amalthea, 0197
Amazons, 0207
Ambrosia, 0210
Amphiaraus, 0219
Amphilochus, 0220
Amphion and Zethus, 0221
Amphitrite, 0223
Amphitryon, 0224
Amycus, 0227
Anchises, 0235
Androgeos, 0242
Andromache, 0243
Andromeda, 0244
Anius, 0255
Antaeus, 0263
Antenor, 0267
Anteros, 0268
Antigone, 0272
Antilochus, 0273
Antiope, 0275
Aphrodite, 0283
Apis, 0285
Apollo, 0289
Apollodorus, 0290
Apple of Discord, 0296
Arachne, 0303
Arcadia, 0308
Arcas, 0309
Ares, 0312
Arethusa, 0313
Aretos, 0314
Arge, 0315
Argeia, 0316
Argives, 0317
Argo, 0318
Argonauts, 0319
Argus, 0320
Ariadne, 0322
Arimaspi, 0325
Aristaeus, 0328
Aristotle, 0329

H
Hindu

Inti, 1546
Mama Quilla, 1962
Manco Capac and Mama Oello
   Huaco, 1968
Pachamama, 2300
Vilacha, 3037
Viracocha, 3046
Indo-Chinese
   Van-xuong, 3010
   Yatawm and Yatai, 3168
Islamic
   Adam and Eve, 0044
   Ahl-at-tral, 0109
   Ahmad, 0110
   Al Aaraaf, 0139
   Ali, 0168
   Al Jassasa, 0172
   Al-Khadir, 0174
   Allah, 0175
   Ayesha, 0424
   Azrael, 0433
   Badal, 0448
   Barsisa, 0493
   Borak, 0614
   Cain and Abel, 0689
   Djokhrane, 0989
   Dugong, 1021
   Fatima, 1156
   Habid al-Nadjdjar, 1336
   Hadith, 1341
   Hafaza, 1343
   Harut and Marut, 1376
   Hatim, 1380
   Hegira, 1400
   Houri, 1470
   Hud, 1481
   Iblis, 1512
   Ifrits, 1521
   Israfel, 1570
   Kaaba, 1666
   Khadijah, 1712
   Koran,, 1749
   Lokman, 1885
   Malec, 1958
   Muhammad, 2104
   Munkar and Nakir, 2115
   Rabi'a al-'Adawiya, 2468
   Ramadan, 2484
   Ruh, 2560
   Sakatimuna, 2575
   Sakhar, 2576
   Saleh, 2583
   Salman al-Parisi, 2584
   Sang Gala Raja, 2606
   Shaitans, 2656
   Zamzam, 3204
Italian
   Bertoldo, 0553
   Hecatommithi, 1397
   Sancus, 2603
   Ugolino, Count, 2950

J

Japanese
   Abe no Seimei, 0009
   Abe no Yasuna, 0010
   Adachigahara, 0043
   Akubo, 0134
   Akuma, 0135
   Ama-no-hashidate, 0199
   Ama-no-Kawa, 0200
   Ama-no-Minaka-Nushi, 0201
   Amario, 0204
   Amaterasu Omikami, 0205
   Ama-tsu-kami and Kuni-tsu-
      kami, 0206
   Atago-Gongen, 0376
   Bakemono, 0459
   Benkei, 0542
   Benten, 0543
   Bimbo, 0580
   Daikoku, 0898
   Dosojin, 1004
   Ebisu, 1047
   Endo Morito, 1087
   Fuji Hime, 1216
   Fushi Ikazuchi, 1219
   Gama Sennin, 1229
   Hannya, 1354
   Heiki-Monogatari, 1402
   Hidari Jingoro, 1433
   Hiru Ko no Kikoto, 1445
   Hitomaru, 1446
   Hohodemi and Umi Sachi Hiko,
      1454
   Ho-no-Ikazuchi, 1461
   Horai, 1463
   Hotai, 1467
   Hotaru Hime, 1468
   Ichimokuren, 1514
   Ikazuchi, 1525
   Ikiryo, 1526
   Inari, 1540
   Izanagi and Izanami, 1581
   Jimmu Tenno, 1611
   Jingo Kogo, 1613
   Jo and Uba, 1618
   Joro Kumo, 1638
   Kakurezator, 1673
   Kami, 1684
   Kappa, 1688
   Karasu Tengu, 1690
   Ken-ro-ji-jin, 1702
   Kimon (demon gate), 1724
   Kishimojin, 1730
   Kitsune, 1735
   Kiyohime, 1736
   Kojiki, 1741
   Kojin, 1742
   Kompira, 1744
   Konsei dai-myojin, 1745
   Koshin, 1753
   Momotaro, 2083
   Nihongi, 2199
   Nijuhachi Bushu, 2200

No, 2216
No-no-Kami, 2218
Nure Onna, 2228
O-Ikazuchi, 2250
O Kiku, 2251
Oni, 2266
Otoroshi, 2290
Raiden, 2474
Saku-Ikazuchi, 2579
Sambiki Saru, 2591
Sansenjin, 2610
Shichi Fukujin, 2669
Susano, 2759
Tanuki Bozu, 2799
Tengu, 2827
Ujigami, 2953
Waki-Ikazuchi, 3079
Yama-otoko, 3159
Yama-uba, 3160
Yedo Go Nin Otoko, 3171
Yuki Onna, 3187
Jewish (including Old
   Testament and Apocrypha)
   Aaron, 0002
   Abdiel, 0006
   Abel, 0007
   Abezi-thibod, 0012
   Abigail, 0015
   Abraham, 0020
   Abraxas, 0021
   Absalom, 0022
   Adam and Eve, 0044
   Af and Hemah, 0087
   Agrat bat Mahalath., 0104
   Amnon of Mainz, 0216
   Anael, 0228
   Anakims, 0230
   Ancient of Days, 0236
   Angel, 0248
   Ariel, 0324
   Arioch, 0327
   Ark of the Covenant or
      Testimony, 0331
   Armilus, 0334
   Asmodeus, 0358
   Athaliah, 0385
   Azariel, 0429
   Azazel, 0430
   Azrael, 0433
   Babel, Tower of, 0437
   Balaam, 0460
   Belshazzar, 0536
   Benjamin, 0541
   Cain and Abel, 0689
   Chabriel, 0763
   Chamuel, 0771
   Chelm Goat, The, 0784
   Cherubim, 0793
   Daniel, 0917
   David, 0925
   Deborah, 0930
   Delilah, 0938
   Dumah, 1022
   Dybbuk, 1035

Elijah, 1073
Elisha, 1074
Enoch, 1092
Ephraim ben Sancho and the
  Parable of the Two Gems,
  1094
Esau, 1114
Esther, 1118
Eve, 1137
Exodus, 1140
Ezekiel, 1142
Ezra, 1143
Flaming Angel, 1177
Gabriel, 1222
Gideon, 1256
God and the Rising Waters,
  1270
Golem, 1283
Goliath, 1284
Hanukkah, 1363
Head and the Tail, The, 1392
Isaac, 1560
Isaiah, 1561
Ishmael, 1563
Israel, 1569
Jacob, 1585
Jephthah, 1603
Jeremiah, 1604
Jezebel, 1607
Job, 1620
Jonah, 1632
Jonathan, 1633
Jorkemo, 1637
Joseph, 1639
Joshua, 1642
Judith, 1651
Kezef, 1709
Lahash, 1800
Lamech, 1806
Leah, 1830
Lilith, 1863
Magen David, 1931
Manasseh, 1967
Melchizedek, 2024
Menorah, 2030
Mephistopheles, 2032
Metatron, 2042
Methuselah, 2043
Mezuzah, 2047
Michael, 2049
Midrash, 2054
Miriam, 2068
Moses, 2095
Nebuchadnezzar, 2165
Noah, 2217
Passover, 2340
Pope Elhanan, 2414
Purah, 2448
Rabbi Eliezer, 2467
Raphael, 2489
Raziel, 2504
Rebekah, 2506
Rival Schools of Thought, 2529

Rosebush and the Apple Tree,
  The, 2547
Rosh Ha-Shanah, 2551
Ruth, 2567
Salome, 2586
Samiasa, 2593
Sammael, 2594
Samson, 2597
Samuel, 2598
Sandalphon, 2604
Sarah, 2614
Saul, 2622
Seraphim, 2644
Sheol, 2667
Sodom and Gomorrah, 2718
Solomon, 2722
Sukkoth, 2748
Talmud, 2783
Tamar, 2786
Uriel, 2979
Urim and Thummin, 2980
Vretil, 3072
Wisdom to Fools, 3120
Witch of Endor, 3121
Yahweh, 3155
Yesod, 3175
Za'afiel, 3192
Zacharias, 3194
Zadkiel, 3196
Zadok, 3197
Zagzagel, 3199
Zohar, The, 3222
Zophiel, 3224
John the Evangelist

L
Lapland
  Aijeke, 0121
  Cacce-jielle and Cacce-jienne,
    0679
  Kied Kie Jubmel, 1721
  Leib-olmai, 1838

M
Malayan
  Badi, 0450
  Bajang, 0457
  Batara Guru, 0501
  Batu Herem, 0504
  Bisan, 0583
  Che Puteh Jambai, 0789
  Hantu, 1356
  Hantu Ayer and Hantu Laut,
    1357
  Hantu B'rok, 1358
  Hantu Denej, 1359
  Hantu Kubor, 1360
  Hantu Pemburu, 1361

Hantu Songkei, 1362
Harimau Kramat, 1368
Kuda Sembrani, 1770
Langsuyar, 1810
Pawang, 2347
Pawang Pukat, 2348
Penanngga Lan, 2362
Polong, 2407
Sumangat, 2751
Mayan
  Ab Kin Xoc, 0016
  Ah Puch, 0112
  Ah Raxá Lac, 0113
  Ah Raxa Tzel, 0114
  Ahtoltecat, 0116
  Ahulane, 0117
  Bacabs, 0441
  Balam-Quitzé, 0461
  Cabauil, 0675
  Cahá-Paluna, 0687
  Camazotz, 0702
  Chac, 0764
  Chay, 0783
  Ek Chauah, 1061
  Gagavitz, 1225
  Gucumatz, 1320
  Hacavitz, 1337
  Hex Chun Chan, 1431
  Homshuk, 1460
  Hunab Ku, 1489
  Hunahpú and Xbalanqúe, 1490
  Hurakán, 1493
  Itzamná, 1572
  Ixchel, 1576
  Ix-huyne, 1577
  Ixtab, 1579
  Popol Vuh, 2416
  Vacub-Caquix, 2993
  Votan, 3070
  Xaman Ek, 3143
  Xpiyacoc and Xmucané, 3151
  Yalahau, 3157
  Zakigoxol, 3202
Medieval
  Abracadabra, 0019
  Ahasuerus, 0108
  Alains le Gros, 0141
  Beatrix, 0514
  Bestiary, 0555
  Chanticleer, 0778
  Dance of Death, 0915
  Earthly Paradise, The, 1044
  Flying Dutchman, The, 1182
  Havelok the Dane, 1386
  Heinrich von Aue, 1404
  Holy Grail, 1457
  Iron Crown of Lombardy, 1557
  Pope Joan, 2415
  Prester John, 2431
  Reynard the Fox, 2514
  Tamburlaine the Great, 2788
  Tancred, 2792
  Troilus and Cressida, 2914
  Wandering Jew, 3086

Tahumers, 2774
Tishtrya, 2878
Verethraghna, 3023
Vis and Ramin, 3051
Vourukasha, 3071
Yazatas, 3170
Yima, 3178
Zahhak, 3200
Zal, 3203
Zarathustra, 3206
Zaremaya, 3207
Zurvan, 3228

Peruvian
Ekkekko, 1062
Mama Allpa, 1960
Pachacamac, 2299

Philippine
Indarapatra, 1541
Kadaklan, 1670

Phrygian
Attis, 0400

Plant
Acanthus, 0027
Almond, 0182
Apple, 0295
Apricot, 0298
Ash, 0348
Aspen, 0361
Bamboo, 0471
Bean, 0510
Birch, 0581
Cabbage, 0676
Carnation, 0727
Cedar, 0755
Cherry, 0792
Clover, 0834
Coffee, 0842
Corn, 0853
Daisy, 0900
Fig, 1172
Garlic, 1240
Ginseng, 1263
Grape, 1303
Hazel, 1391
Heliotrope, 1411
Hyacinth, 1496
Juniper, 1656
Laurel, 1824
Leek, 1835
Lentil, 1845
Lettuce, 1852
Lily, 1864
Lotus, 1894
Mandrake, 1970
Mistletoe, 2071
Mulberry, 2108
Mushroom, 2119
Myrrh, 2127
Myrtle, 2128
Nut, 2230
Oak, 2234
Onion, 2267
Orange, 2271
Palm, 2317

Parsley, 2334
Peach, 2351
Pine, 2396
Pomegranate, 2412
Potato, 2420
Radish, 2471
Rice, 2520
Rose, 2545
Rosemary, 2548
Rowan, 2555
Rue, 2558
Sage, 2573
Star of Bethlehem, 2733
Strawberry, 2740
Thistle, 2852
Tomato, 2892
Violet, 3045
Wheat, 3105
Willow, 3116
Yarrow, 3166
Yew, 3176

Polish
Bartek and Pies, 0494
Dziwozony, 1039

Polynesian
Ahoeitu, 0111
Atea and Papa, 0383
Haumea, 1385
Hikuleo, 1435
Iwa, 1575
Kae, 1671
Kana, 1685
Kumu-honua and Lalo-honua, 1779
Maui, 2011
Oro, 2278
Pahuanuiapitasitera'i, 2303
Pele, 2358
Pikoi, 2393
Tane, 2793
Tangaloa, 2794
Tiki, 2867
Tinirau, 2872
Tu, 2923

Portuguese
Inéz de Castro, Doña, 1545
Sebastian, Don, 2630

R

Roman
Acca Larentia, 0030
Acestes, 0032
Achates, 0033
Acidalia, 0038
Aeneas, 0075
Aeneid, The, 0076
Aequalitas, 0079
Amburbium, 0211
Amor, 0218
Ancile, 0237
Anna Perenna, 0258

Antinous, 0274
Arae, 0304
Ascanius, 0343
Astraea, 0371
Augures, 0404
Augustus, 0407
Aurora, 0409
Auster, 0411
Bacchants, 0444
Belisarius, 0530
Bellona, 0534
Berenice, 0546
Bidental, 0570
Bona Dea, 0607
Brutus, Lucius Junius, 0648
Brutus, Marcus Junius, 0649
Bulla, 0658
Caca, 0678
Cacus (bad), 0681
Caeculus, 0684
Camilla, 0705
Camillus, 0706
Camillus, Marcus Furius, 0707
Campus Martius, 0708
Canens, 0713
Capitol, 0716
Cardea, 0722
Carmenta, 0725
Carna, 0726
Cato the Younger, Marcus Porcius, 0746
Cincinnatus, Lucius Quinctius, 0825
Corydon, 0855
Curtius, Marcus, 0877
Decius Mus, 0931
Diana, 0969
Dido, 0971
Egeria, 1054
Elysium, 1082
Enceladus, 1084
Epona, 1096
Erulus, 1109
Etna, 1125
Evander, 1134
Fama, 1149
Fasces, 1155
Faunus, 1157
Februa, 1162
Feronia, 1168
Fides, 1170
Flamen Dialis, 1176
Flora, 1179
Fornax, 1187
Fortuna, 1189
Fraus, 1202
Fulgora, 1217
Furina, 1218
Genius, 1248
Germanicus Caesar, 1251
Girdle of Venus, 1264
Golden Age, 1274
Golden Bough, 1276
Gordian Knot, 1292

General Index

A

Aa, 0001
Aaron, 0002, 2293
Aaron's rod, 0182
Aba, 0003
Abaris, 0004
Abassi, 0377
Abbas Stultorum, 1889
Abbate, Niccolo dell' (1512–1571);
  Aristaeus, 0328
Abbot of Misrule, 1889
Abdallah and Amina, 2104
Abd Al Muttalib, 2104
Abderus, 0005
Abdhi-nagari, 1762
Abdiel, 0006
Abdu'llah (The Servant of Allah),
  1606
Abduction of Daniel Boone's
  Daughter, The, 0612
Abednego, 0917
Abel, 0007, 0689
Abe Lincoln in Illinois, 1865
Abenalmao, Moorish Infante, 0008
Abenamar and King Don Juan, 0008
Abe no Seimei, 0009, 0010
Abe no Yasuna, 0010
Abere, 0011
Abezi-thibod, 0012
Abgar, 0013
Abhaya mudra, 2103
Abhidhamma Pitaka, 2874
Abhinandana, 2877
Abhinna, 0014
Abhra-pisacha, 2473
Abiathar, 3197
Abigail, 0015
Abiram, 0002
Ab Kin Xoc, 0016
Abomination of desolation, 0017
aboon demon, 1358
Abore, 0018
Abracadabra, 0019, 0021
Abraham, 0020, 1666
Abraham Being Blessed by Melchizedek,
  0020
Abraham Lincoln, 1865
Abraxas, 0021
Absalom, 0022
Absalom, Absalom!, 0022
Absalom and Achitopel, 0022
Absyrtus, 0023, 2022
Abu-Bakr, 0424
Abuk and Garang, 0024
abundance; Chinese symbol of,
  1304; Near Eastern gods of, 0505

Abu Talib, 2104
Abyrga, 1890
Acacallis, 0289
Acamas, 0025, 1410, 1815, 2387
Acantha, 0026
acanthus, 0027
Acarnan and Amphoterus, 0028
Acarnania, 0028
Acastus, 0029
Acca Larentia, 0030
accidents, 1115; Islamic demon of,
  1512
Accolon of Gaul, 0031
Account of the Antiquities of Peru, 1477
Acesis, 0344
Acestes, 0032
Achaeans, 0317, 0910
Achaius, 0240
Achates, 0033
Achatius, 1191
Acheflour, 0034
Achelous, 0035, 0197
Achemorus, 2334
Acheron, 0036
Achillea, 0037
Achille et Polyxène, 0037
Achilles, 0037; Agamemnon and,
  0090; Ajax and, 0127; anger of,
  1531; Antilochus and, 0273;
  armor of, 1531; charioteer of,
  0413; Deidamia and, 0934;
  Hector and, 1531; horse of,
  3144; killed Hector, 2343; killed
  Penthesilea, 0207, 2365; killed
  Thersites, 2365, 2845; mourning
  Patroclus, 1531; Myrimidons
  and, 2126; Odysseus and, 2242;
  Polyxena and, 2411; steals cattle
  of Aeneas, 0075; Troilus and,
  2914
Achilles at the Court of Scyros, 0037
Achilles auf Skyros, 0037
Achilles Kills Hector, 0037
Achyuta, 3053
Acidalia, 0038
Acis, 1228, 2410
Acis and Galatea, 1228, 2410
Aclima, 0689
Acontius of Cea, 0039
acorn, 2234
Acosta, José de, 1968
Acrisius, 0040, 0911, 2371
Acrostic Dialogue on Theodicy, 1620
Actaeus, 0041
Acta Sanctorum, 3211
Actis, 0042

Actium, 0076
actors, 3058; Chinese god of, 1816
Acts of Andrew and Matthias, 0240
Acts of John, *The,* 2337
Acts of St. Paul, 2345
Acts of the Apostles, 0568, 2374
Adachigahara, 0043
Adad, 2523
Adam, 0044, 0450, 0868, 1666; first
  wife of, 1863
Adam, Adolphe Charles
  (1803–1856); *vila,* 3036
Adam and Eve, 2892
Adamanthaea, 0045
Adam Bell, 0046
Adam of Bremen; Odin, 2241
Adapa, 0047, 1175
Adaro, 0048
Addanc of the Lake, 0049
adder, 0050
Addin, Sheikh Muslih, 2570
Addison, Joseph (1672–1719; Cato
  the Younger, 0746
Ades, 1340
Adharma, 0051
Adi, 0052
Adi-Buddha, 0053, 2999
Adikavi, 0623
Adiri, 0054, 2681
Aditi, 0055
Adityas, 3014
Admetus, 0056, 0699
admiration; Victorian symbol of,
  0727
Adno-artina, 0057, 1985
Adonai, 3155
Adonis, 1175, 2127; Aphrodite and,
  0283
Ad Patream, 2276
Adrammelech, 0058
Adrasteia, 0059
Adrastus, 0060
Adrian, St., 0061
adulterer, 0871
Adu Ogyinae, 0062
Advent, 0063
Adventures of Uncle Sam, The,
  2966
Aeacus, 0064
Aeaea, 0065
Aeantis, 0389
Aëdon, 0066, 0221
Aeetes, 0023, 1597
Aegeus, 0067, 1597, 2022
Aegialeia, 0068
Aegichus, 3215

Ammon of Mayence, 2551
Amnon, 2786
Amnon of Mainz, 0216
Amoghasiddhi, 0217
Amor, 0218
Amores, 2295
Amoretti, 2280
Amos, 0568
Amphiaraus, 0060, 0219
Amphilochus, 0220
Amphion and Zethus, 0221, 0275
amphisbaena, 0222
Amphisusus, 1017
Amphitrite, 0223, 2580
Amphitryon, 0224, 1417
Amrita, 0225, 0772, 0821, 0961,
    1242, 1543, 2196, 2473
amulets; *bulla,* 0658
Amulius, 2541
Amun, 0226
Amunet, 0226
Amun-Ra, 0226, 2061, 2466, 2716;
    symbols of, 1289
Amycus, 0227
Anael, 0228
Anahit, 0229
Anahita, 0229
Anakims, 0230
Anala, 3014
Analects, 0846
Ananda, 0231
Ananse Kokroko, 2268
Anansi, 0232
Ananta, 2668, 3053
Anantanatha, 2877
Anatapindaka, 0233
Anath, 0234, 0300
Anatomy of Melancholy, *The,* 0248
Ancaeus, 0378, 0699
ancestor spirits; Australian, 0820
ancestral figure, 1801
Anchesmius, 3215
Anchin, 1736
Anchises, 0076, 0235, 0283; Aeneas
    and, 0075
Ancient Calendar, The, 0286, 1027
Ancient of Days, 0236
Ancient Spider, 2152
ancile, 0237
Ancrene Riwle, 2968
Andersen, Hans Christian
    (1805–1875), 0238; nightingale,
    2198; *Panchatantra, The,* 2322
Andhaka, 0239
Andhaka-ripu, 0239
Andhrimnir, 2572, 3006
Andrade, Mario de, 1926
Andreas, 0240
Andrew, St., 0240
Androcles and the Lion, 0241, 1868
Androgeos, 0067, 0242
Andromaca, 0243
Andromache, 0243, 1398, 1531,
    2275, 2359

Andromache Mourning Hector, 0243
Andromaque, 0243
Andromeda, 0244, 0737, 2371
Andromeda e Perseo, 0244
Androphonos, 0283
Andros, Sir Edmund, 0781
androygne, 0311
Andvaranaut, 0246
Andvari, 0165, 0246
Anemotis, Athena, 0389
Angantyr, Yarl, 1209
Angarad of the Golden Hand, 0247
angel, 0248, 0793, 2482, 2644
*Angel Gabriel Appearing to Muhammed,
    The,* 0248
Angelica, 0249
Angelico, Fra (1400–1455); St.
    Albertus Magnus, 0145
angel of death, 0292
Angel of Hadley, 0250
angels, 0248; Islamic, 1343, 1570,
    1958, 2115, 2560
anger, 2864; Persian spirit of, 0082
Angle, Thorbiorn, 1310
Angry Acrobat, The, 0251
Angurboda, 0252
Angurvadel, 1209
Anhanga, 0253
Anila, 3014
*Animadversions Upon the Remonstrant's
    Defence,* 0035
animal husbandry, 1806
animal protector; Persian, 0213
animals; Babylonian patron of,
    1089; Christian patron of, 1198;
    Roman goddess of, 2563
Animisha, 0254
Anius, 0255
Anjali mudra, 2103
Anjana, 1883
ankh, 0226, 0256, 2229, 2824, 2858,
    3101
Ankhesenamen, 2936
Anna, 0257
Annals, 0598
Annals of Cuauhtitlan, 2464
Annals of the Cakchiquels, The, 0783,
    1225, 3202
Anna Perenna, 0258
Annie Christmas, 0259
Annie get Your Gun, 2235
Annie Oakley, 2235
Annunciation, 0044, 1006, 1606,
    3047
anointing oil, 0210
Anokye, 1280
Anouilh, Jean (1910–); Joan of
    Arc, 1619; Medea, 2022;
    Orpheus, 2280; St. Thomas à
    Becket, 2853
Anpetu wi and Hanhepi wi, 0260
Ansar, 1090
Anshar, 0261, 1982
ant, 0262

Antaea, 0532
Antaeus, 0263
Antaka, 3158
Ant and Grasshopper, 0264, 1304
Antar, 0265
Antar-loka, 2908
antelope, 0266, 0554, 2649
Antenor, 0267
Anteros, 0268, 0283
Antero Vipunen, 0269, 0269
Anthony and Cleopatra, 2035, 2180
Anthony of Padua, St., 0270
Anthony the Abbot, St., 0256,
    0271
Antichrist, 0496, 0761, 1847
Antigone, 0272, 0316
Antigono, 0272
Antilochus, 0273
Antiope, 0275, 2846
Antiquities of the Jews, 0058
ants, 0003, 2126
Anu, 0047, 0058, 0276, 0277, 0525,
    0918, 1982
Anuanaitu, 1925
Anubis, 0266, 0278, 2941
Anunnaki, 0279
Anuruddha, 0280
Anus, 0277
Anush, 2865
Anything Goes, 1222
Aoi-no-ue, 2216
Aoyama, 2251
Ap, 3014
Apaosha, 2878
Aparimita-Dharani, 0653
Apauk-kyit Lok, 0281
Apava, 0623
ape, 0282
Apep, 0293
Apesantius, 3215
Aphaea, 0639
Aphareus, 0739
Aphesius, 3215
Aphneius, 0312
Aphrodisia, 0093
aphrodisiac; tomato as, 2892
Aphrodite, 0283, 2128; Acidalia,
    0038; Aeneas and, 0075, 1531;
    Anchises and, 0235; Anteros
    and, 0268; apple of discord and,
    0296; as Venus, 3020; Atalanta
    and, 0378; Atargatis and, 0380;
    Butes and, 0667; doves sacrificed
    to, 1006; Dryope and, 1017;
    Erymanthus and, 1111; fish
    sacred to, 1175; frog associated
    with, 1211; girdle of, 1264;
    Glaucus and, 1267; golden apple
    and, 0295; Jason aided by, 1597;
    Judgment of Paris and, 1650,
    2332; married to Hephaestus,
    1415; Paris and, 1236; partridge
    sacred to, 2337; Phaon and,
    2378; Psyche and, 2442; sides

Arne, 0336
Arnold, Edwin (1832–1904);
    Savitri, 2623
Arnold, Matthew (1822–88);
    Athena, 0389; Baldur, 0465;
    Bergelmir, 0547; Breidalblick,
    0627; Cadmus, 0682; Dionysus,
    0979; Erato, 1097; Hel, 1405;
    Hermod, 1422; Homer, 1459;
    Lok, 1884; Marsyas, 1991;
    Midgard, 2052; Nanna, 2148;
    Prose Edda, 2439; Sohrab and
    Rustum, 2719; St. Brendan,
    0628; Tristram and Iseult, 2912;
    Valhalla, 3006; Venus, 3020
Aroteh and Tovapod, 0337
Aroundight, 0338
arrowsmiths, 2631
Ars amatoria, 2295, 2364
Ars Amoris, 0607
Arsinoe, 0289
Artegal, 1072
Artegal and Elidure, 1072
Artemis, 0339, 0639, 0697, 0741,
    0969, 1088, 1908; Agamemnon
    and, 0090; Amphion and, 0221;
    Arethusa and, 0313; bear sacred
    to, 0512; bees and, 0519; birth
    of, 1851; birthplace of, 0368;
    Britomartis and, 0639; Callisto
    and, 0697; Calydon and, 0698;
    Carya and, 0730; Caryatis, 0731;
    Coronis and, 0344; Hippolytus
    and, 1442; identified with cat,
    0741; Iphigenia and, 1553;
    Judgment of Paris and, 2332;
    lion associated with, 1868;
    Niobe and, 2208; Orion and,
    2276; Otus and, 0183; protected
    Atalanta, 0378; punished
    Actaeon, 2730; sent Calydonian
    Boar, 0699
Artemisium at Ephesus, 0339
Artemis Lygodesma, 3116
Arthur, 0340, 2036, 2501, 2554,
    2989; mother of, 1524; sword of,
    1139
artisans, 2443; Aztec patrons of,
    3148; Chinese god of, 1912
Art of Poetry, 2098
Aruru, 0341
Arusha, 2758
Arval Brothers, 0030
Arzend, 2566
A Samantabhadra, 2444
Asanga, 0342
Asar, 2287
Ascanius, 0076, 0343; carried away
    to Idalia, 0076
Ascension of Muhammad, 1393, 2104
Aschenbrödel, 0826
Asch, Sholem (1880–1957); St.
    Paul, 2345
Asclepius, 0344, 0683, 0839

Asgard, 0345, 2203
Asgardreia, 0346
Asgaya Gigagei, 0347
asgopa, 2742
ash, 0348
Asha, 0213
Ashab al-Kahf, 2652
Ashakku, 2991
Asha-Vahista, 0213
Ashdod, 0894
Asherah, 0349
Ashkenaz, 1015
Ashonnutli, 1121
Ashta-mangala, 0350
Ashtavakra, 0351
Ashur, 0352
Ashura, 2748
Ashva-medha, 0353
Ash Wednesday, 0354, 2317
Ashwins, 0355
Asita, 0356
Asita-danshtra, 1956
Asiyah, 1156
Ask and Embla, 0357, 1453
Aslauga, 2190
Asmodeus, 0082, 0358, 2489
Asoka, 0359
Asopus, 0360
aspen, 0361
Asphodel Fields, 0362
Asruvindumati, 3169
ass, 0363, 0460, 1186, 2649
As-Sam (the hearer), 0175
Assassinio nella Catterdrale, 2853
Assemblies of Aesopic Tales, 0084
Ass in the Lion's Skin, The, 0364
Ass in the Tiger Skin, The, 2322
Ass's Brains, 0365
Assumption of BVM, 3047
Ast, 1568
Astad, 2492
Astaroth, 0367
Astarotte, 0366
Astarte, 0367, 0367, 1006, 1116
Astarte Syriaca, 0367
Asteria, 0283, 0368
Asterie, 0312
Asterius, 2066
Asterope, 0081, 0312
Astolat, 0369
Astolpho, 0150, 0370, 2308
Astolpho's Book, 0370
Astraea, 0371
Astraea Redux, 0371
Astraeus, 0372
astrology, 0393
Astyanax, 0243, 0373
Astydameia, 0029
Astynome, 0312
Astyoche, 0312, 1815
Asuras, 0374, 0821
Aswins, 0887, 3014
As You Like It, 1238
Ataensic, 0375, 0375, 1551

Atagatis, 2726
Atago-Gongen, 0376
Atai, 0377
Atalanta, 0378, 0699, 2769
Atalanta in Calydon, 0378, 0699,
    0979, 2025
Atar, 0379
Atargatis, 0380
Atchet, 0381
Ate, 0382
Atea and Papa, 0383
Atef crown, 2858
At Eleusis, 1069
Aten, 0130, 0384
Athaliah, 0385
Athamas, 0386, 1854
Athanasian Creed, 0387
Athanasius, St., 0387
Atharva-Veda, 2428, 3017
Atheh, 0380, 0388
Athelstane, 0240
Athena, 0389, 2064, 2146, 2169;
    Actis and, 0042; aegis and, 0071;
    Ajax and, 0127; apple of discord
    and, 0296; Arachne and, 0303; as
    virgin goddess, 2336; born fully
    armed from Zeus's head, 2044;
    Cadmus and, 0682; Cecrops and,
    0753; Daedalus and, 0890;
    Diomedes and, 0978;
    Erichthonius and, 1102; gave
    Harmonia robe, 1371; gave wood
    for *Argo*, 0318; invented olive
    tree, 2419; inventor of flute,
    1991; Jason aided by, 1597;
    Judgment of Paris and, 1650;
    Odysseus and, 2242; owl sacred
    to, 2296; Parthenos, 2336;
    Penelope and, 2364; Poseidon
    and, 2419; sides with Greeks,
    1531
Athenogenes, St., 2995
Athens, 0753
Athtar, 0194
Atla, 3093
Atlacamanc, 0390
Atlanta, 0312
Atlantes, 0391, 2559
Atlantiades, 0393, 1419
Atlantis, 0392
Atlantius, 1419
Atlas, 0393, 1427, 2371, 2674;
    Amphitrite and, 0223
Atlatonan, 0394
Atlaua, 0395
Atli, 0399, 1126, 1209, 3066
Atman, 0396, 0624
Atnatu, 0397
Atninous, 0274
Atotarho, 1432
Atreus, 0072, 0398
Attabira, 1549
Attar, Farid Al-Din; Simurgh, 2694
Attica, 0067, 0753

Burkhan, 0662
Burkhan-Baksh, 1105
Burland, C. A., 2264, 2888, 2890
Burne-Jones, Sir Edward
    (1833–1898); Cophetua, 0851;
    Frey, 1206; Merlin, 2036;
    Psyche, 2442; Uriel, 2979
Burnside, General, 0485
Burton, Robert (1577–1640);
    angels, 0248; Lamia, 1807
Bury St. Edmund's, 1051
Busiris, 0663
Busoni, Ferruccio (1866–1924);
    Faust, 1158; Mephistopheles,
    2032
Bussumarus, 0664
Bustan-Namah, 2655
Bustan, The, 0665, 2570
Butch Cassidy, 0666
Butch Cassidy and the Sundance Kid,
    0666
butchers, 0495, 2374
Butes, 0667
Buthrotum, 0076
Butler, Samuel (1835–1902);
    Nausicaa, 2162
Buto, 0668, 2721
Buttadeus, Johannes, 3086
butterfly, 0669, 2546
Buurt-kuuruk, 0670
buzzards, 2256
Byams-pa, 1953
Byelobog, 0671
Byggvir, 0672
Byleipt, 0673
byliny, 0674
Byrgir, 0576
Byron, George Gordon; Astarte,
    0367; Cain, 0689; Calypso, 0700;
    Cassandra, 0736; *Eagle and the
    Arrow, The,* 1043; Erato, 1097;
    Ivan Mazeppa, 2020; Minerva,
    2064; Nemesis, 2172; Niobe,
    2208; Pleiades, 2400; Pythia,
    2461; Roger Bacon, 0447;
    Samiasa, 2593; Sennacherib,
    2642; Zarathustra, 3206

C

Cabauil, 0675
cabbage, 0676
cab drivers, 1169
Cabeiri, 0677
Cabell, James Branch (1879–1958);
    Blunderbore, 0840; Kostchei,
    1755
Cabraca, 2993
Caca, 0678
cacao, 1061, 2678
Cacce-jielle, 0679
Cacce-jienne, 0679
Cachimana, 0680

Cacus, 0681
Cadmus, 0682
caduceus, 0683, 2035, 2716
Caeculus, 0684
Caedmon, 0568
Caeneus, 0685
Cagn, 0686
Cahá-Paluna, 0687
Caicas, 0688
Cain, 0007, 0689
Cain, A Mystery, 0689
cakra, 0416
calabash, 2678
Calaeno, 0289
Calais, 0690
calamity; Islamic demon of, 1512
Calamity Jane, 0691
Calchas, 0037, 0090, 0692, 3215
Calderón, Pedro (1600–1681); St.
    Patrick, 2342
caldron, 2240, 2761
Caldwell, Erskine (1903–1987);
    Clootie, 0832
Caledwlch, 1139
Calef, Robert (1648–1719); Giles
    Corey, 0852
calendar, 3225
Calends, 1657
Caleuche, 0693
Caliburn, 1139
Callicrates and Ictinus, 2336
Callidice, 0694
Callimachus, 0027
Calliope, 0289, 0695
Callipolis, 0148
Callirrhoë, 0153, 0696
Calliste, 0339
Callisto, 0697
calvary, 1993
Calydon, 0698
Calydonian boar hunt, 0056, 0148,
    0219, 0378, 0699; Acastus, 0029
Calypso, 0700
Camahueto, 0701
Camazotz, 0702, 1490
Cambria, 0143
Cambrian Annals, 0340
camel, 0703, 3023
Camel of Seleh, 0703
Camelot, 0340, 0704
Camilla, 0705
Camillus, 0706
Camillus and the Schoolmaster of Falerii,
    0707
Camillus, Marcus Furius, 0707
Camoes, Luiz de; Doña Inéz de
    Castro, 1545
Camolundunum, 0709
Campbell, Thomas (1777–1884);
    St. Columba, 0845
Campus Martius, 0708, 1990
Camrosh, 2694
Camulos, 0709
Camus, Marcel; Orpheus, 2280

Canace, 0710
Canary, Martha Jane, 0691
Canby, William, 2553
Cancer, 0711, 3221
Candide, 1065
Candlemas Day, 0712
candlestick, 2030
Canens, 0713
Canis, 2033
cannibalism, 0043, 0574, 0756,
    1671, 1680, 1785, 1916, 2227,
    3117, 3153, 3154
canon lawyers, 2503
Canopy, 0350
Canova, Antonio (1757–1822);
    Perseus, 2371
Canterbury Tales, The, 0037, 0513,
    0569, 0752, 0778, 0856, 0933,
    1080, 1231, 2035, 2853, 2950
Caoine, 0478
Capaneus, 0714
Cape Cicero, 0065
Capella, 0197
Caphaurus, 0715
Capitol, 0716
Capotas, 3215
Capricorn, 0717, 3221
Caprotina, 1657
Captain from Castile, 2464
Captain John Smith, His Life and Legend,
    2403
Captain Kidd, 0718
captives, 1846, 2192
Capys, 0719
Caractacus, 0720
Carausius, 0721
Caravaggio Michelangelo
    (1573–1609); Bacchus, 0445;
    David, 0925; St. John the
    Baptist, 1628; St. Matthew,
    2009; St. Peter, 2374; St.
    Sebastian, 2631
carbuncles, 0646
Cardea, 0722
Carlisle, Helen, 2731
Carloman, 0779
Carlos, Don, 0723
Carlyle, Thomas (1803–1855);
    Koran, 1749
Carme, 0724
Carmelites, 2830
Carmen Deo Nostro, 1997
Carmen Nuptialis, 2230
Carmenta, 0725
Carmentalia, 0725
Carmina, 0400
Carmina burana, 1189
Carna, 0726
Carnarvon, Lord, 2936
carnation, 0727
Carolsfeld, Julius Schnoor von; St.
    Roch, 2534

Venus, 3020; Vulcan, 3074;
  Zephyrus, 3213; Zodiac, 3221
Chausson, Ernest (1855–1899);
  Merlin, 2036; Viviane, 3060
Chávez, Carlos (1899–); Antigone,
  0272
Chay, 0783
Chelidonis, 0066, 0066
Chelm Goat, The, 0784
Chemosh, 0785
Cheng San-Kung, 0786
Ch'en Nan, 0787
Chenuke, 0788
Che Puteh Jambai, 0789
Cheremiss Kozla-ia, 2224
Chernobog, 0671
Cheron, St., 0790
Cherruve, 0791
cherry, 0792
cherubim, 0248, 0793
Chesnutt, Charles W., 2418
chest wounds; daisy as cure for,
  0900
cheval, 1878
Chhaya, 2758
Chia, 0801
Chia-Lan, 0794
Chiang Ko, 1101
Chiang Shih, 1101
Chia-yeh, 1693
Chibcachum, 0795
Chibcha Indians, 2726
Chibcho, 1486
Chicago Fire, 2101
Chicomecoatl, 2894
Chicomexochit, 2894
Chiconquiahuitl, 0796
Ch'ih Ching-tzu (fire), 0797, 3138
Chih Nu, 0798
Ch'i Ku=tzu, 0799
childbirth death during, 0554,
  0828; Armenian guardians of,
  1599; Chinese patron god of,
  0774; Egyptian gods of, 1444;
  Egyptian patron of, 2171; easing
  with boiling onions, 2267; Greek
  goddess of, 0339, 0402, 1227;
  Japanese gods of, 1730; Roman
  goddess of; 0725, 0969, 2007,
  0828
Childe Harold, 0700, 1097, 2461
Childe Harold's Pilgrimage, 0289, 2208,
  3206
Childermass, 1458
Child, F. J., 0467
children, 2192, 2502; Buddhist
  patron of, 1768
Children in the Wood, 0438
child-swallowing, 1425
Chilion, 2567
Chimaera, 0800
Chimalmat, 2993
Chimalmatl, 2074
Chimera, 0532, 2355

Chiminigagua, 0801
Chimizapagua, 2173
chimney sweeps, 1180
Chin, 0802
Chinese Thought, 1101
Ching Tu, 0803
Ch'in-kuang wang, 0804, 2885
Chinnan, 0787
Chinta-mani, 0772
Chinvat, 0805
Chione, 0289
Chipiripa, 0806
Chiron, 0037, 0344, 0759, 1597
Chitra-gupta, 3158
Chitrangada, 1937
Chiu-t'ien Lei Kung, 0807
Chiuyu, 1101
Chloris, 1179
Choephoroe, 0090, 2275
Chokaro, 0775
cholera; ginseng as remedy for,
  1263
Chonchon, 0808
Choral Hymns, 2522
Chorio, 0818
Chors, 0929
chörten, 2742
Chosroes, King of Persia, 0868
Chrétien de Troyes (d. c. 1183);
  King Arthur, 0340; Perceval,
  2368
Chretien, Felix; Aaron, 0002
Christ; called Lamb of God, 1805;
  cedar as symbol for, 0755;
  changed girl into owl, 2296;
  cross of, 1557; crucifixion of,
  0868; dove descends to, 1006;
  Grail and, 1457; Passion of,
  1281; pelican identified with,
  2360; Peter's denial of, 0839;
  robin at birth of, 2532; scourged
  with birtch switchesSecond
  Coming of, 0063, 0581; symbols
  of, 1042, 1175, 1281, 1868, 1917
Christ Child, 0810, 0811, 1763
Christian heresies, 1606
Christian Science, 3016
Christians, persecution of the, 1630
Christie, Agatha (1890?–1976);
  Akhenaton, 0130
Christina the Astonishing, St.,
  0809
Christ in the House of Martha and
  Mary, 1992
Christmas, 0810, 1889, 2192;
  Knecht Ruprecht and, 1738
Christmas carol, 0810
Christmas tree, 0810
Christ of Edessa, 1516
Christopher, St., 0811, 1191, 2574
Christs Victorie and Triumph, 0949
Chronicle of Nestor, 3061
Chronicle of Ssangang Ssetsen, The,
  1018

Chronicles, 0568, 0882, 1832
Chrosröes, King, 1138
chrysalis, 0669
Chryse, 0312
Chryseis, 0090, 1531
Chryses, 0090, 1531
Chrysippus, 0398
Chrysorthe, 0289
Chrysothemis, 1553
Chthonian gods, 0812
Chthonius, 3215
Chuai, 1613
Chuang Chou, 0813
Chuang Tzu, 0813
Ch'uan Hou, 2863
Chuan-lun wang, 2885
Chu Jung, 0814
Chu-ko Liang, 0815
Ch'u-kuang wang, 2885
Chu-lin Chi-i-Hsien, 0816
Chunda, 0817
Chung-li Chüan, 0818
Chung Yu, 1101
Chun T'i, 0819
Churchill, Winston (1874–1965);
  John Paul Jones, 1635
Churinga, 0820
churning of the ocean, 0821, 0961,
  1543, 2196, 2473, 3053
Chu Shou-ch'ang, 1101
Chyavana, 0822
cicada, 0583
Cicero, Marcus Tullius (106–43
  B.C.E.); Bona Dea, 0607; Scipio,
  2626
Cid, El, 0823
Cigouaves, 0824
Cilix, 0682
Cincinnatus, Lucius Quinctius,
  0825
Cinderella, 0826, 1793, 1845
cinnamon, 1824
cintamani, 0416
Cinthio, Giambattista Giraldi, 1397
Cinyras, 2127
Circe, 2243, 2388, 3116
circle, 0186
circumcision, 0451
Circumcision of Jesus, 1186
Cissaea, 0389
Cithaeron lion, 0148
Cities of the Plain, 2718
Citipati, 0827
Citlallicue, 2894
Citlaltonac, 2894
City of God, The, 0406, 2352
Ciuateteo, 0828
civilization; Greek symbol of,
  Lapiths, 1819
Civil War, 0335
Clare, St., 0829
Clarius, 3215
Clashing Rocks, 2280
Claudia Procla, 2394

Dinakara, 2758
Dinclinsin, 1928
Dino, 1299
Diocletian, Emperor, 0144, 2631, 3058
Diomede, 2914
Diomedes, 0978, 1267, 1531; Achilles and, 0037
Dionysius, 0909, 0946
Dionysius the Areopagite, 0248
Dionysus, 0363, 0444, 0445, 0979, 1269, 1868, 2638; Aphrodites and, 0283; Ariadne and, 0322; Butes and, 0667; Carya and, 0730; Erigone and, 1103; grape associated with, 1303; pine tree associated with, 2396; Rhoecus and, 2518
Dioscuri, 0739
Dipankara Buddha, 0653, 0980
Dirce, 0221, 0275
diroe, 0404
Dirona, 0981
Dirty Little Billy, 0579
Dis, 1340
discord, 1113; Greek goddess of, 0296, 0382
Discordia, 0382
Discourse on the Trinity, 0406
Discovery of Wine, 0979
Discovery, Settlement and Present State of Kentucke, 0612
discussion; Buddhist symbol of, 2103
disdain; English symbol of, 2558
dishonesty; Roman goddess of, 1825
Dismas, 0982
Disney, Walt (1901–1966); Br'er Rabbit, 0630; Cinderella, 0826; Ichabod Crane, 1513; mouse, 2494; Sleeping Beauty, 2714; Uncle Remus, 2965
Dis Pater, 1015, 2273
Dithyrambus, 0979
Diti, 0983
Divali, 0984
Divas-pati, 1543
Diva-ta-Zena, 1039
diver bird, 0081
Dives, 0985
divination, 1144, 1837, 2281; yarrow used for, 3166
Divine Comedy; Acheron, 0036; Achilles, 0037; Aeneas, 0075; Alcmaeon, 0153; Alecto, 0158; Brutus, 0649; Cato the Younger, 0746; demons, 0956; Dido, 0971; Diomedes, 0978; eagle, 1042; fox, 1192; Francesca da Rimini, 1196; Ganelon, 1231; Geryon, 1253; griffin, 1311; Helen, 1407; hell, 1393; Homer, 1459; Ixion, 1578; Joshua, 1642; Judas

Iscariot, 1648; leopard, 1847; Mars, 1990; Marsyas, 1991; Minos, 2065; Nessus, 2180; Niobe, 2208; Odysseus, 2242; Ovid, 2295; Phlegethon, 2383; Plutus, 2402; Rachel, 2470; Ripheus, 2527; Sinon, 2698; St. Bede, 0517; St. Gregory, 1308; St. James the Greater, 1589; St. Veronica, 3025; Ugolino, 2950; Ulysses, 2961; William of Orange, 3111
divinity; Chinese term for, 2665
Divji Moz, 0986
Diw-bund, 2774
Djahannam, 1393, 1958
Djanbun, 0987
Djanggawul, 0988
Djanna, 1393
Djaris, 0265
djinn, 0450, 0956
Djokhrane, 0989
dMu, 3189
Dobrizhoffer, Martin, 0107
dockalfar, 0165, 0990
Doctor of the Church, 0145, 0209, 0270, 0406, 0517, 0991, 1308, 1529, 1566
Doctor, The, 1282
doctrine; Buddhist term for, 0962
Dodona, 0992, 2234
Dörje Dölö, Guru, 2301
dog, 0112, 0993, 1480, 1985, 2306, 2900, 3058
Dog and His Shadow, The, 0994
Dogedoi, 2721
Dokko, 2778
Doktor Faust, 2032
Dolores, 2434
dolphin, 0223, 0289, 0995
Domenichino (1581–1641); Parnassus, 2333
domestic animals, 0209, 1846, 1993, 2502, 3058
domestic discord; Islamic demon of, 1512
Domiduea, Juno, 1657
Domitian, 0716, 1630
Domitilla, Nereus, and Achilleus, SS., 0996
Domitilla, Roman catacombs of, 0294
Domnu, 0997
Domovoi, 0998
domus aurea, 2178
Don, 0918
Donato of Arezzo, St., 0999
Don Carlos, 0723
Don Giovanni, 1000
Don Juan Tenorio, 0447, 0736, 1000
donkey, 1605, 2434
Donne, John (1573– 1631); Virgin Mary, 3047
Don Quixote, 2026, 2536

Don Sebastian, King of Portugal, 2630
Donskoy, Dmitri, 1828
Doodang, 1001
door pivots; Roman goddess of, 0722
doorways; Italian god of, 1594
Doris, 1002
Doritis, 0283
Dorothy, St., 1003, 1191
Dosojin, 1004
Dotis, 0312
Douban, 1005
Douglas, Archibald, 2048
Douglas, Gavin (c. 1474–1522), 0076
dove, 0283, 0380, 1006, 1040, 1564
drac, 1007
Dracula, 1008
dragon, 1009, 1249, 1847, 1910, 2195, 2294, 2540; Chinese, 0787, 1427; Fafnir, 1146, 3066; Ladon, 1794; oak as home of, 2234
dragon-serpent, 0682
Dragon's Throne, 1009
dragon teeth, 0682
drapers, 2983
Draupadi, 0330, 1010
Draupnir, 2241, 2697
Drayton, Michael (1563–1631); Endymion, 1088
Drayton, Samuel; Bevis of Hampton, 0557
Dream of Constantine, 0849
Dream of Fair Women, 1603
Dream of Four Women, 1650
dreams; Greek god of, 2093; Greek interpreter of, 0081
Dreamtime, 1011
drenching, 1045
Dreyer, Carl (1889– 1968); Joan of Arc, 1619
Dr. Faustus, 1158, 1407
Dr. Heidigger's Experiment, 3092
drink of the gods, 0772, 2166
Drithelm, St., 1012
Dromond, Thorstein, 1310
Drona, 1013
drought; Hindu demon of, 3073; Persian demons of, 2878
drowning, 2540
Drugaskan, 1014
Drughana, 0623
Druids, 1015
drum, 2671
drunkenness, 1993, 2217; Chibcha gods of, 1486
dryads, 1016, 1131, 2232
Dryden, John (1631–1700); Absalom, 0022; Aeneid, 0076; Alexander, 0162; Astraea, 0371; Curtana, 0876; Don Sebastian, 2630; St. Cecilia, 0752; Uriel, 2979
Dryope, 0289, 1017

Ix-huyne, 1577
Ixion, 1578
Ixtab, 1579
Ixtlilton, 1580
Izanagi, 1581
Izanagi and Izanami, 0199
Izanami, 1581
Izquitecatl, 1582
Iztaccihuatl, 1583
Iztac Mixcoatl, 2074
Izumo, 0205

J

Jabbor, 1747
Jaburu, 2678
jackal, 0278, 1447, 2226
Jack and the Beanstalk, 1584
Jack Frost, 1784
jack-o'-lanterns, 0181
Jackson, Stonewall, 0485
Jack the Giant Killer, 0596
Jacob, 1114, 1560, 1569, 1585,
    1830, 1845, 2470, 2737
Jacobs, Joseph, 1195
Jacob's ladder, 3216
jade; Chinese symbol of, 3186
Jaganmata, 0957
Jago, St., 1589
jaguar, 1060, 1705
Jaguarari, 3164
Jahannam, 1393
Jahi, 1586
Jaik-Khan, 2141
Jaladhija, 1804
Jala-murti, 2671
Jala-rupa, 1956
Jalut, 1284
Jamadagni, 3053
Jambavat, 1587
James I of England, 2852
James, Jesse, 1588
James the Greater or Major, St.,
    1589
James, William, 2574
Janácek, Leos (1854–1938); fox,
    1192; Sarka, 2615
Janaka, 1591
Janarddana, 3053
Jani gemini portoe, 1594
Janisais, 0344
jann, 0956
Jan-Teng Fo, 1592
Januarius, St., 1593
January, 1594
Janus, 1594
Jaras, 1652, 2590
Jara-sandha, 1595
Jarnvid, 1596
Jarnvidjur, 1596
Jason, 0318, 0699, 1278, 1597, 2022
Jata-dhara, 2671
Jataka, 1068, 1598, 2587, 2753

*Jatakas, or Birth-Stories of the Former
    Lives of the Buddha*, 0364, 1290,
    3126
Javerzaharses, 1599
Jayadratha, 0330
Jay and the Peacock, The, 1600
Jayanti, 1601
jaybird, 0989
jealousy, 1113
Jeffers, Robinson (1887–1962);
    Cassandra, 0736; Jason, 1597;
    Medea, 2022; Tamar, 2786
Jemshid, 1602, 2655, 2774, 3178
Jephtah Judge of Israel, 1603
Jephthah, 1603
Jerada, 2576
Jeremiah, 0568, 1604
Jericho, 1642
Jerome, St., 1605, 2360
Jeru, 1607
Jerusalem, 0324, 0850, 1015, 1604
Jerusalem Delivered, 0333, 0426, 2559,
    2581, 2791
Jesse, 2906
Jesuits, 1522
Jesus Christ, 0110, 1606;
    Crucifixion of, 0020, 0946;
    disciples of, 0294, 1630; John the
    Baptist and, 1628; Joseph of
    Arimathea and, 1640; Judas
    Iscariot and, 1648; Magi and,
    1932; Moses and Elijah appear at
    Transfiguration of, 1073;
    Nicodemus and, 2193; O.T.
    prefigurations of, 0044; Passion
    of, 0354; Pilate and, 2394;
    prefigurations of, 0460, 0925,
    1632, 2024; Resurrection of,
    1045; St. Joseph and, 1641; St.
    Mark and, 1989; St. Mary and,
    3047; St. Peter and, 2374; St.
    Philip and, 2380; St. Thomas
    and, 2856; Transfiguration of,
    1589; wine use of, 1303
Jethro, 2293
jewelers, 0093
jewels; Great Carbuncle, 1305
jewels of Harmonia, 0028, 0153
Jew of Malta, The, 3176
Jezebel, 0367, 1607
Jiburili, 1222, 1570
Jigoku, 1608
Ji-Kojin, 1742
Jim Bludso, 1609
Jim Bridger, 1610
Jimmu Tenno, 0205, 1611
Jina, 1612
jindai, 1611
Jingo Kogo, 1613
Jingu-ji, 1614
Jishu, 0330
Jiten, 1615
Jiu No O, 1616
Jizo, 2882

Jizo Bosatsu, 1617
Joachim, 0257
Jo and Uba, 1618
*Joan of Arc at the Coronation of Charles
    VII*, 1619
Joan of Arc, St., 1619
Joan the Woman, 1619
Job, 0568, 0956, 1620
Job, a Masque for Dancing, 1620
Jocasta, 1621, 2244
Joe Baldwin, 1622
Joe Magarac, 1623
Joel, 0568
John Barleycorn, 1624
John Brown of Osawatomie, 0644
John Chrysostom, St., 0519, 1625
John Henry, 1626
*John Henry: Tracking Down a Negro
    Legend*, 1626
Johnny Appleseed, 1627
John of Gaunt, 2048
John the Baptist, St., 0481, 0703,
    1391, 1628, 2586
John the Bear, 1629
John the Deacon, 1308
John the Evangelist, St., 1042,
    1308, 1630
John XV, Pope, 2574
Johul, 1644
Joinville, Jean (1225–1317); St.
    Louis, 1896
Jok, 1631
Jonah, 0568, 1632
Jonathan, 0925, 1633
Jonathan Moulton, 1634
Jonda Ebn Amru, 2583
Jones, John Luther, 0733
Jones, John Paul, 1635
Jonson, Ben (1572?–1637); Clem
    of the Clouth, 0831; Neptune,
    2175; Pocahontas, 2403
Jord, 0083, 1636
Jordan, Wilhelm
Jorkemo, 1637
Jorojin, 2669
Joro Kumo, 1638
Joseph, 1639
Joseph of Arimathea, 0340, 1266,
    1457, 1640
Joseph, St., 1006, 1641, 1864
Josephus, 0141, 1336
Joshua, 0568, 1642, 2204; Al-
    Khadir and, 0174
Jotham, 1885
Jotunheim, 1520, 2203
Joukahainen, 0122, 1645, 1676,
    2996
Jove, 1042, 1646, 3215
joy; Chinese god of, 1475
Joyce, James (1882–1941); Aengus,
    0077; Balor, 0469; Banba, 0474;
    Druids, 1015; *Fox and the Grapes,
    The*, 1194; Lir, 1872; Mananaan,
    1966; Odysseus, 2242; *Odyssey*,

Kunewarra, 2446
Kuninwa-wattalo, 1781
Kuni-Toko-Tachi-No-Mikoto, 0201
Kuni-tsu-kami, 0206
Kunmanggur, 2476
Kunthunatha, 2877
Kunti, 1010
Kuo Chu, 1101
Kuo Tzu-i, 1782
Kupalo, 1783
Kur-Ga, 2523
Kurgarru, 1564
Kurma, 0821, 3053
Kurma Purana, 2449
Kuro-Ikazuchi, 1525
Kurra, 1784
Kurriwilban, 1785, 3154
Kuru, 1937
Kururumany, 1786
Kusma-yudha, 1682
Kuurook, 2446
Kuvera, 0963
Kuyuta, 1393
Kuzunoha, 0010
Kvasir, 0083, 1787, 1884, 2240
Kwaku Ananse, 0232
Kwannon, 1768, 1788
Kwaten, 1789
Kwoiam, 1790
Kyllikki, 1676, 1842, 2305
Kytice, 2405

L

Laban, 2470
Labartu, 2991
La Belle au bois dormant, 2714
Labiche, Emmeline, 1135
labyrinth, 0890
Lacedamon, 1791
lacemakers, 2830
La cenerentola, 0826
Lachesis, 1792
La Cigale et la Fourmi, 0264
ladder to the sky, 1856
Lado and Lada, 1793
Ladon, 1236, 1275, 1427, 1794
Lady of Shalott, The, 0369, 1064, 1795
Lady of the Lake, 0340, 1139, 1796, 1809, 2036, 3060
Laerath, 1401
Laeretes, 1797
Laertes, 2242
Laestrygones, 1798
La Fontaine, Jean de, 1799
Lagerkvist, Par; Barabbas, 0482
Lahash, 1800
lai, 2608
Laindjung, 1801
Laius, 1802, 2244
lake, 0421, 1954
Lakhamu, 1982

Lakmé, 1804
Lakshamana, 1803, 2485
Lakshmi, 1804, 3053
Lakshmipati, 3053
Lalia Rookh, 3206
L'Allegro, 1394, 2280
L'Alouette, 1619
La Mandragola, 1970
Lamarr, Hedy, 1619
lamb, 1045, 1805, 3126
Lamba-karna, 1232
Lambodara, 1232
Lame Devil, The, 0358
Lamech, 1806
lameness, 3127
Lamentations, 0568, 1604
Lament for Beowulf, 0545
Lamia, 1807
Lammas, 1808
La Motte-Fouqué], Heinrich Karl; *Nibelungenlied,* 2190
Lamp Bearing Buddha, 1592
lance, 1990
Lancelot, 0338, 0340, 1064, 1796, 1809, 2809
Lancelot and Elaine, 0369
Land of Cockayne, *The,* 0840
Landor, W. S. (1775–1864); Eurydice, 1131; Midas, 2051; Paris, 2332; Penelope, 2364; Polyxena, 2411
Lang, Andrew (1844–1912); Elysium, 1082; Helen, 1407
Langoureth, Queen, 1703
langsuyar, 1810
Langton, Stephen, 3106
language, 0437, 2226
Lan Ts'ai-ho, 1811
Lan-yein and A-mong, 1812
Laocoön, 0076, 1813, 3131
Laodameia, 1814
Laodice, 1066, 1815
Lao Lai-tsu, 1101
Lao Lang, 1816
Laomedon, 1817, 2419
Lao Tzu, 1818
Lapiths, 1819
Lapponia, 0121
La Purcelle, 1619
Lara, 1821
Lares, 1821
lares compitales, 1821
Lares proestites, 1821
Lar familiaris, 1821
Largos, 1269
Larisaea, 0389
Lark, The, 1619
Lars Porsenna, 2624
Larunda, 0030, 1821
Larvae, 1821
La Sirène, 0106
Las Mocedades del Cid, 0823
Last Judgment, 0495, 0508, 1847, 2190

Last of the Mohicans, *The,* 2161, 2161
Last Oracle, The, 0289
Last Supper, 0020, 2374
Last Tournament, The, 0895
Lasya, 0904
Latimikaik, 1822
Latin Mass, 2002
Latinus, 0076, 1823
Latona, 1851
Laughead, W. B., 2344
Laughing Buddha, 2069, 2454
laurel, 0289, 0919, 1824
Laurin, 0165, 0165
Laus Veneris, 3020
Laverna, 1825
La Vestale, 3029
Lavinia, 1826
Lavinium, 0343
law; Buddhist term fora, 0962
Lawrence, D. H. (1885–1930); Priapus, 2434
Lawrence, St., 1443, 1827
Lawrence, D. H. 1885 – 1930); Huitzilopochtli, 1487
lawyers, 3191
Laxdala Saga, 1322
Lay of Frithiof, 1209
Lay of Grimnir, 2572
Lay of Hyndla, The, 3093
Lay of Igor's Army, The, 1828
Lays of Ancient Rome, 0739, 1465, 2541
lazar-houses, 3041
Lazarus, 1829, 1997
lead founders, 1169, 2631
Leah, 1830, 1970
Leanhaun Shee, 1831
Leaning Tower of Pisa, 2653
Learchus, 0386
Lear, King, 1832
Leather-Stocking Tales, 2161
leather workers, 0495
Lebe, 1833
Le Bestiaire Divin, 0555
Le Bestiaire Divin de Guillaume Clerc de Normandie, 2968
Le Brun, Charles (1619–1690); Apollo, 0289
Lecheates, 3215
Le coq d'or, 1277
Leda, 0739, 1407, 1834, 2768
Leda and the Swan, 1407, 1834
Le Damnation de Faust, 1158
Le Diable Boiteux, 0358
leek, 1835
Le-eyo, 1836
Legba, 1837, 2907
Legend of Good Women; Alcestis, 0149; Argonauts, 0319; Ariadne, 0322; Danaidae, 0912; Demophon, 0943; Dido, 0971; Hypsipyle, 1509; Jason, 1597; Lucretia, 1900; Medea, 2022; Philomela, 2382;

Sawoye, 1996
Saxony, 3058
sa'y, 0190
Scaevola, Gaius Mucius, 2624
Scamander, 0243
Scamander River, 3144
Scamandrius, 0373
scapegoat, 0430, 1269
scarab, 0520, 1714
Scarecrow, The, 1160
Sceiron, 2846
Scenes from Goethe's Faust, 1158
scepter, 0226, 2824, 2858, 3101
Scheffer, John, 0121
Schellhas, Paul, 0764, 2018, 3143
Scherzer, Carl, 2416
Schildburg, 2625
Schiller, Johann (1759–1805);
    Cassandra, 0736; Don Carlos,
    0723; Elysium, 1082; Joan of
    Arc, 1619; Pegasus, 2355; St.
    Elizabeth of Portugal, 1076;
    William Tell, 3114
Schmidt, I. J., 1254
Schneewittchen, 1282
Schoenberg, Arnold (1874–1951);
    Aaron, 0002; Moses, 2095
scholars, 1308, 1605, 2854
schoolboys, 1827
Schoolcraft, H. R., 1432
schoolgirls, 3042
Schopenhauer, Artur (1788–1860),
    2974
Schubert, Franz (1797–1828); Erl-
    King, 1106
Schumann, Robert; Faust, 1158
Schuman, William (1910–); Casey
    at the Bat, 0732
science; Greek god of, 0289; Hindu
    gods of, 2663
Scipio Africanus Major, Publius
    Cornelius, 2626
Scorpio, 3221
scorpion, 1568, 2627
Scotland, 0143, 0240
Scottish Thistle, 2852
Scott, Sir Walter (1771–1832);
    Alfheim, 0167; Allan-a-Dale,
    0177; Angel of Hadley, 0250;
    Erl-King, 1106; Richard the
    Lion-Hearted, 2521; Saladin,
    2581; Wayland the Smith, 3094
Scratch, Mr., 3096
screech owls, 2006
Scriabin, Alexander (1872–1915);
    Prometheus, 2438
scribe of the supreme god, 2884
scribes, 1902
Scylla and Charybdis, 2628
sea; Greek, Glaucus, 1267; Greek
    goddess of, 0223; Italian goddess
    of, 2004
sea cow, 1021
seafarers, 0628, 0878

sea giants, 2212
sea gods; Aegir, 0070; African,
    2259; Celtic, 0323, 1036, 1904,
    2222; Chinese, 2863; Eskimo,
    2633; Greek, 0639, 0739, 1854,
    2419, 2440, 2850; Haitian, 0106;
    Japanese, 1613; Malayan, 0501;
    Micronesian, 0193; Near Eastern,
    0349; Norse, 0070, 2704;
    Polynesian, 2303, 2872; Roman,
    2175
seamen; Celtic protector of, 1966
sea monster, 0701, 2628
seasickness; lettuce as remedy for,
    1852
seasons; Greek goddess of, 0728;
    Orinoco Indian gods of, 0680
sea spirits; Sjoran, 2704
sea travel; Roman goddess of, 2004
sea-witches, 1209
Sebald, St., 2629
Sebastian, Don, 2630
Sebastian, St., 2574, 2631
Sebau, 0293
Sebek, 0867, 2632
Seberg, Jean, 1619
Second Old Man's Story, The,
    0956
Seder, 2340
Sedit, 2256
Sedna, 2633
seeds of all life, 2678
seer, 0220
Segesta, 0032
Seiobo, 1476
Seker, 2287, 2634
Sekhet, 3101
Sekhet-Aaru, 2635
Sekhmet, 0499, 1868
Sela, 2124
Selene, 0969, 1088, 2636
self-conceit, 1212
self-created god, 0397
Selloi, 0992
Semaleus, 3215
Semargl, 2637
Semele, 2638
Semiramis, 0302, 2639
Semktet, 2466
Semo Sancus, 2603
Senakerim, King, 0926
Seneca, 1432, 2178; Aegisthus,
    0072; Agamemnon, 0090;
    Atlantis, 0392; Heracles, 1417;
    Hippolytus, 1442; Phaedra, 2376
Seng-don-ma, 2641
Seng-ge da dok, Guru, 2301
Senlis, France, 2508
Sennacherib, 2642
Sennadius, Dream of, 2643
sensuality; Ixion symbolic of, 1578
sensual love; Greek goddess of,
    0283
Seraphic Doctor, 0608

seraphim, 0248, 2644
Serapion the Sinonite, St., 2645
Serapis, 0285, 0344, 1635, 2646
serpent, 0222, 0293, 0554, 0607,
    0682, 0736, 0753, 0821, 0942,
    1371, 1564, 1678, 1751, 1813,
    2023, 2027, 2133, 2294, 2575,
    2606, 2668, 2829, 2963; Midgard,
    2053, 3132
Serpent and the File, The, 2647; Hydra,
    1499
serpent god, 0884, 0914
serpent spirit, 2654
Serqet, 2648
Serra, Juaquin; Doña Inéz de
    Castro, 1545
servant girls, 1902
Sessions, Roger; Montezuma, 2087
Sessrumnir, 1207
Set, 0266, 0363, 0867, 1444, 1466,
    1852, 2627, 2649
Seth, 0868, 1091
Seti I, 2466
Seven against Thebes, 0060, 0219,
    0220, 1123, 1371
Seven Are They, 2991
Seven Heads, *The,* 1820
Seven Immortals, 0816
Seven Sages of Greece, 2651
Seven Sleepers of Ephesus, 2652
Seventh Seal, The, 0915
Seven Wonders of the World,
    0339, 2653
Seville, 1662
sex; Aztec gods of, 2888, 3148,
    2949
sex stimulant, 0298, 1263
Sextus, 1900
sexual intercourse; associated with
    rice production in Java, 2520
sexual love; yarrow associated
    with, 3166
sexual potency; increased by
    pomegranate, 2412; restored by
    potato, 2420
Shadrach, 0917
Shahapet, 2654
Shahar, 0194
Shah Namah, 2655; Azadhak, 2865;
    Azhi Dahaka, 0432; Bahram
    Gur, 0454; Faridun, 1154;
    Gayomart, 1245; Husheng, 1495;
    Jemshid, 1602; Kavah, 1698;
    Minuchihr, 2067; Rustum, 2566;
    Sohrab, 2719; Tahumers, 2774;
    Yama, 3178; Zahhak, 3200; Zal,
    3203
Shahrevar, 0213
Shahriyar, 2859
shaitan, 0956, 2656
Shakespeare, William (1564–1616);
    Absyrtus, 0023; Acheron, 0036;
    Achilles, 0037; Aeneas, 0075;
    Albania, 0143; Alecto, 0158;

Ukuhi, 2955
Ulappala, 2932
ulcers, 1993; daisy as cure for, 0900
Ulfius, 2956
Ulfrun, 3093
Ulgen, 1105, 1948
Ulgn, 2957
Uli, 1685
Uli-tarra, 2958
Ull, 2959
Ulrich, St., 0106, 2960
ultimate reality, 0624
Ulysses, 0077, 0469, 0474, 1015, 1872, 1966, 2242, 2243, 2288, 2961
Ulysses Deriding Polyphemus, 2410
Uma, 2962
Umai-hulhlya-wit, 2963
Umbrella, 0350
Umi Sachi Hiko, 1454
Umm al-kitab, 1749
Unas, 2964
unborn babies; Roman protector of, 1054
Uncle Remus, 2965
Uncle Remus: His Songs and His Sayings, 0630, 2965
Uncle Sam, 2966
Uncle Tom's Cabin, 1375
underworld, 0036, 0421, 1393, 2811; African gods of, 0137; Armenian gods of, 2611, 2884; Aztec, 2050; Buddhist god of, 2882; Celtic gods of, 1334; Chinese, 2885; Egyptian, 1019; Eskimo gods of, 2633; fruit of, 0942; Greek god of, 0812, 1340, 1396, 2370, 2917; Greek gods of, 0812; Greek judge of, 2515; Hindu, 2341; Islamic angel in charge of, 1958; Mayan, 1490; Melanesian, 0054, 2681; Micronesian, 2138; Near Eastern, 0279, 0305, 1100, 1537, 2177; Norse, 1241; Polynesian gods of, 1435; pomegranate associated with, 2412; Siberian, 2113; Tupi Indian, 2298
undine, 2967
Undry, 0893
unicorn, 1164, 2968
Union flag, 0485
United States; personification of, 2966
universe; Egyptian symbol of, 1835; Hindu divisions of, 2908
Unixia, Juno, 1657
Unktomi, 2969
Unkulunkulu, 2970
unmarried girls; Greek patroness of, 0339
Unnefer, 2287
unrighteousness, 0051

unselfishness, 0262
Unsinkable Molly Brown, 2972
Untsaiyi, 2973
Upanishads, 0559, 2974
upasampada, 2607
Upatissa, 0604
Up Eel River, 2898
Upirikutsu, 2975
Urania, 0283, 2976, 3020
Uranian Venus, 3020
Uranus, 1224, 2977, 3215
Urban IV, Pope, 0854
Urd, 2219, 2978
Urdar-fount, 3177
Uriah the Hittite, 0925
Uriel, 0058, 1177, 2979
Urim and Thummin, 2980
Urna, 2981
Urre, 2982
Ursúa, Don Pedro de, 1065
Ursula, St., 2574, 2983
Urvasi, 2984
Usapu, 3046
Use and the Need of the Life of Carry A. Nation, The, 2158
Ushnisha, 2985
Utachet, 0668
Utchat, 2986
Utgard, 1643, 2987
Utgard-Loki, 2987
Uther Ben, 0625, 2988
Uther Pendragon, 0340, 1524, 2036, 2554, 2989
Utnapishtim, 0974, 1260, 2990
Utopia, 2855
Utset, 1510
Uttara-Kanda, 2485
Utu, 0974
utukku, 2991, 2991
Uwolowu, 2992

V

Vach, 2663
Vacub-Caquix, 2993
Vacuna, 2994
Vafthruthnismol, 2404
vagina, 1866
Vahagn, 2055, 2995
Vahni, 0101
Vaikuntha-natha, 3053
Vainamoinen, 0122, 1676, 2931, 2934, 2954, 2996; builds boat, 0269; Joukahainen and, 1645; killed the pike, 2595; promised Maiden of Pohjola, 1947; stole sampo, 1895
Vairocana, 0965, 2997
vairocana-mudra, 2997
Vairochi, 0472
Vaiśrávana, 0584
Vaivaswata, 1978
vajra, 1543

Vajra-Dhara, 2999
Vajrapani, 0964, 0965, 1543, 3000
Vajravarahi, 3001
Vaks-oza, 3002
Valaskjalf, 0345, 1450, 2241
Valásquez, Ruy, 1820
Valedjád, 3003
Valencia, 3042
Valens, Emperor, 0497
Valentine and Orson, 3004
Valentine, St., 3005
Valerius, 2501
Valgrind, 3006
Valhalla, 0345, 2241, 3006
Vali, 0083, 3007
Valkyries; Buynhild, 0650
Valla, Lorenzo, 0849
Valmiki, 2485
Vamana, 3053
Vamana Purana, 2449
vampire, 0431, 0808; Malayan, 2362
vampire-bat god, 0702, 1490
Vana, 1883
Vanadis, 0083
Vanaheim, 2203
Van Dyck, Anthony (1599–1641); Armida, 0333
Van Dyke; Endymion, 1088
Vanir deities, 0083, 1285, 3009; Freyja, 1207; Gollveig, 1285; Njord, 2215; Vanaheim, home of, 2203
vanity, 2352; Christian symbol of, 1935
Van-xuong, 3010
Var, 3011
Vara, 1208
Varaha, 3053
Varaha Purana, 2449
Vara mudra, 2103
Vardhamana, 1942
Varieties of Religious Experience, The, 2574
Varpulis, 2741
Varshavarti, 1980
Varuna, 1883, 2747, 3012
Varuni, 0821, 1929
Vasavadatta, 3013
Vase, 0350
Vashishtha, 1680
Vasupujya, 2877
Vasus, 3014
Vatapi, 0092
Vathek, an Arabian Tale, 1512
Vaugh'en, 2298
Vaughn Williams, Ralph (1872–1958); Job, 1620; Satan, 2618
Vayu, 1883, 3015
Vayubala, 1995
Vayucakra, 1995
Vayuha, 1995
Vayujvala, 1995